Lecture Notes in Computer Science

Lecture Notes in Artificial Intelligence **16517**

Founding Editor

Jörg Siekmann

The series Lecture Notes in Artificial Intelligence (LNAI) was established in 1988 as a topical subseries of LNCS devoted to artificial intelligence.

The series publishes state-of-the-art research results at a high level. As with the LNCS mother series, the mission of the series is to serve the international R & D community by providing an invaluable service, mainly focused on the publication of conference and workshop proceedings and postproceedings.

H. Jaap van den Herik · Ana Paula Rocha ·
Luc Steels
Editors

Agents and Artificial Intelligence

17th International Conference, ICAART 2025
Porto, Portugal, February 23–25, 2025
Revised Selected Papers, Part II

Springer

Editors
H. Jaap van den Herik
Leiden University
Leiden, The Netherlands

Ana Paula Rocha
University of Porto
Porto, Portugal

Luc Steels
Free University of Brussels
Brussels, Belgium

ISSN 0302-9743 ISSN 1611-3349 (electronic)
Lecture Notes in Artificial Intelligence
ISBN 978-3-032-25031-5 ISBN 978-3-032-25032-2 (eBook)
https://doi.org/10.1007/978-3-032-25032-2

LNCS Sublibrary: SL7 – Artificial Intelligence

This Springer imprint is published by the registered company Springer Nature Switzerland AG
The registered company address is: Gewerbestrasse 11, 6330 Cham, Switzerland

Preface

These three volumes include extended and revised versions of a set of selected papers from the 17th International Conference on Agents and Artificial Intelligence (ICAART 2025), held in Porto, Portugal, from 23 to 25 February.

The purpose of the International Conference on Agents and Artificial Intelligence is to bring together researchers, engineers and practitioners interested in theory and applications in the areas of Agents and Artificial Intelligence, covering both applications and current (advanced) research work. On one side it focuses on Agents, Multi-Agent Systems and Software Platforms, and also Distributed Problem Solving. On the other side it focuses on Artificial Intelligence, Knowledge Representation, Planning, Learning, Scheduling and Perception. Applications are in both areas, incorporating Natural Language Processing (NLP), Large Language Models (LLMs), Legal Technologies and Quantum Computing.

ICAART 2025 received 472 paper submissions from 52 countries, of which 91 (19%) are included in these three proceedings volumes.

The papers were selected by the event chairs and their selection was based on a number of criteria that included the classifications and comments provided by the program committee members, the session chairs' assessment and also the program chairs' global view of all papers included in the technical program. The authors of selected papers were invited to submit revised and extended versions of their papers with at least 30% innovative material.

The papers selected to be included in this book contribute to the understanding of relevant trends of current research on Agents and Artificial Intelligence, including: Machine Learning, Deep Learning, Multi-Agent Systems, Natural Language Processing, AI and Creativity, Intelligence and Cybersecurity, Explainable AI, Industrial Applications of AI, Simulation and Agent Models and Architectures.

We would like to thank all the authors for their contributions and also the reviewers who helped to ensure the quality of this publication.

February 2025

H. Jaap van den Herik
Ana Paula Rocha
Luc Steels

Organization

Conference Chair

H. Jaap van den Herik	Leiden University, Netherlands

Program Co-chairs

Ana Paula Rocha	LIACC/FEUP, University of Porto, Portugal
Luc Steels	Free University of Brussels, Belgium

Program Committee

Isabel Alexandre	Instituto Universitário de Lisboa and Instituto de Telecomunicações, Portugal
Vicki Allan	Utah State University, USA
John E. Anderson	University of Manitoba, Canada
Julio Anjos	Federal University of Ceará, Brazil
Alla Anohina-Naumeca	Riga Technical University, Latvia
Luis Antunes	Independent Researcher, Portugal
Giuseppe Attardi	University of Pisa, Italy
Rina Azoulay	Jerusalem College of Technology, Israel
José Banares Bañares	Universidad de Zaragoza, Spain
Necaattin Barisci	Gazi University, Türkiye
Maria Barron-Estrada	Instituto Tecnológico de Culiacán, Mexico
Montserrat Batet	Universitat Rovira i Virgili, Spain
Edgar Batista	Universitat Rovira i Virgili, Spain
Rafael Berlanga	Universitat Jaume I, Spain
Heder Bernardino	Federal University of Juiz de Fora, Brazil
Daniel Berrar	Open University, UK, and Tokyo Institute of Technology, Japan
Andrzej Bielecki	AGH University of Science and Technology, Poland
Adriana Birlutiu	1 Decembrie 1918 University of Alba Iulia, Romania
Stefano Bistarelli	University of Perugia, Italy
Jim Blythe	University of Southern California, USA

Szymon Bobek	Jagiellonian University, Poland
Veselka Boeva	Blekinge Institute of Technology, Sweden
Lars Braubach	City University of Hamburg, Germany
Jörg Bremer	University of Oldenburg, Germany
Paolo Bresciani	Fondazione Bruno Kessler, Italy
Ralf Bruns	Hannover University of Applied Sciences and Arts, Germany
Samuele Burattini	University of Bologna, Italy
Giacomo Cabri	Università di Modena e Reggio Emilia, Italy
Valérie Camps	IRIT - Université de Toulouse, France
Javier Carbó Rubiera	Universidad Carlos III de Madrid, Spain
Cristiano Castelfranchi	Institute of Cognitive Sciences and Technologies - National Research Council, Italy
Juan Luis Castro	Universidad de Granada, Spain
Dumitru-Clementin Cercel	National University of Science and Technology Politehnica Bucharest, Romania
Wen-Chung Chang	National Taipei University of Technology, Taiwan
Amitava Chatterjee	Jadavpur University, India
Davide Ciucci	Università degli Studi di Milano-Bicocca, Italy
Mark Coletti	Oak Ridge National Laboratory, USA
Flavio Correa da Silva	University of São Paulo, Brazil
Paulo Cortez	University of Minho, Portugal
Massimo Cossentino	National Research Council of Italy (CNR), Italy
Ernesto Costa	Universidade de Coimbra, Portugal
Stefania Costantini	Stefania Costantini, Italy
Erzsébet Csuhaj-Varjú	Eötvös Loránd University, Hungary
Rossana Damiano	University of Turin, Italy
Aspassia Daskalopulu	University of Thessaly, Greece
Riccardo De Benedictis	CNR - Italian National Research Council, Italy
Leandro de Castro	Florida Gulf Coast University, USA
Fernando de Souza	Universidade Federal de Pernambuco, Brazil
Luis Fernando D'Haro Enriquez	Universidad Politécnica de Madrid, Spain
Khaldoon Dhou	Texas A&M University Central Texas, USA
Bruno Di Stefano	Independent Researcher, Canada
Alberto Díaz-Álvarez	Universidad Politécnica de Madrid, Spain
Scott Dick	University of Alberta, Canada
Youcef Djenouri	NORCE Research, Norway
Rafal Drezewski	AGH University of Science and Technology, Poland
Habiba Drias	University of Science and Technology Houari Boumediene, Algeria
Grzegorz Dudek	Częstochowa University of Technology, Poland

Erol Egrioglu	Giresun University, Türkiye
Victor M. Eguiluz	Institute for Cross-Disciplinary Physics and Complex Systems, Spain
Thomas Eiter	Technische Universität Wien, Austria
Bilel Elayeb	Yncréa Ouest, L@bISEN, ISEN de Nantes, France
Abeer El-Korany	Independent Researcher, Egypt
Thomas Eskridge	Florida Institute of Technology, USA
Jan Faigl	Czech Technical University in Prague, Czechia
Catherine Faron	Université Côte d'Azur, France
Márcia Fernandes	Federal University of Uberlândia, Brazil
Edilson Ferneda	Catholic University of Brasília, Brazil
Alexander Ferrein	MASCOR Institute, FH Aachen University of Applied Sciences, Germany
Baldoino Fonseca	Federal University of Alagoas, Brazil
Oscar Fontenla-Romero	University of A Coruña, Spain
Katsuhide Fujita	Tokyo University of Agriculture and Technology, Japan
Ana Garcia	Universidade Federal do Estado do Rio de Janeiro, Brazil
Mauro Gaspari	University of Bologna, Italy
Andrey Gavrilov	Novosibirsk State Technical University, Russian Federation
Franck Gechter	University of Technology of Belfort-Montbéliard, France
Bertha Guijarro-Berdiñas	Universidade da Coruña, Spain
Maki Habib	American University in Cairo, Egypt
James Harland	RMIT University, Australia
Hisashi Hayashi	Advanced Institute of Industrial Technology, Japan
Pedro Henriques	University of Minho, Portugal
Ramon Hermoso	University of Zaragoza, Spain
Vincent Hilaire	University of Technology of Belfort-Montbéliard, France
Hanno Hildmann	TNO, Netherlands
Victoria Hodge	University of York, UK
Peter Hofmann	Technology Campus Freyung, Deggendorf Institute of Technology, Germany
Wei-Chiang Hong	Harbin Engineering University, China
Ales Horak	Masaryk University, Czechia
Hung-Hsuan Huang	RIKEN, Japan
Jean-Paul Jamont	Université Grenoble Alpes, France
Mohammad Jaradat	American University of Sharjah, UAE

Agnieszka Jastrzebska	Warsaw University of Technology, Poland
Michael Jenkin	York University, Canada
Shashi Shekhar Jha	Indian Institute of Technology Ropar, India
Jaume Jordán	Universitat Politècnica de València, Spain
Francisco José Domínguez Mayo	University of Seville, Spain
Darsana Josyula	Bowie State University, USA
Eugene Kagan	Ariel University, Israel
Christos Kaklamanis	University of Patras & Computer Technology Institute and Press "Diophantus", Greece
Ilhem Kallel	University of Sfax, Tunisia
Norihiro Kamide	Nagoya City University, Japan
Ashwin Viswanathan Kannan	Amazon Labs, USA
Pawel Karczmarek	Lublin University of Technology, Poland
Petros Kefalas	CITY College, University of York Europe Campus, Greece
Chairi Kiourt	Athena-RIC, Greece
Mieczyslaw Klopotek	Polish Academy of Sciences, Poland
Matthias Klusch	German Research Center for Artificial Intelligence (DFKI) GmbH, Germany
Fernando Koch	Independent Researcher, Brazil
Mare Koit	University of Tartu, Estonia
Piotr A. Kowalski	AGH University of Krakow, Poland
Daniel Ladley	University of Leicester, UK
Divesh Lala	Kyoto University, Japan
Ho-Pun Lam	Xi'an Jiaotong-Liverpool University, China
Jean-Charles Lamirel	LORIA, University of Strasbourg, France
Ramoni Lasisi	Virginia Military Institute, USA
Egons Lavendelis	Riga Technical University, Latvia
Juan Lazo	Universidad del Pacifico, Peru
Agapito Ledezma	Carlos III University of Madrid, Spain
Ladislav Lenc	University of West Bohemia, Czechia
Florin Leon	Technical University Gheorghe Asachi of Iași, Romania
Letizia Leonardi	Università di Modena e Reggio Emilia, Italy
Weigang Li	University of Brasília, Brazil
Churn-Jung Liau	Academia Sinica, Taiwan
David Lillis	University College Dublin, Ireland
Donghui Lin	Okayama University, Japan
Jianyi Lin	Università Cattolica del Sacro Cuore, Italy
Ting Liu	Siena College, USA
Faraón Llorens-Largo	Universidad de Alicante, Spain
Alberto Lluch Lafuente	Technical University of Denmark, Denmark

Stephane Loiseau	LERIA, University of Angers, France
António Lopes	ISCTE-Instituto Universitário de Lisboa, Portugal
Domitile Lourdeaux	Université de Technologie de Compiègne, France
Audrone Lupeikiene	Vilnius University, Lithuania
René Mandiau	Independent Researcher, France
Michail Maniadakis	Foundation for Research and Technology, Greece
Romany Mansour	New Valley University, Egypt
Jerusa Marchi	Universidade Federal de Santa Catarina, Brazil
Philippe Mathieu	University of Lille, France
Toshihiro Matsui	Nagoya Institute of Technology, Japan
Euan McGookin	University of Glasgow, UK
Miguel Melgarejo	Universidad Distrital Francisco José de Caldas, Colombia
Bruno Mermet	CNRS, France
Enza Messina	University of Milano-Bicocca, Italy
Occello Michel	Université Grenoble Alpes, France
Ali Minai	University of Cincinnati, USA
Valeri Mladenov	Technical University of Sofia, Bulgaria
Ralf Möller	University of Lübeck, Germany
Raul Monroy	Tecnológico de Monterrey, Mexico
Orides Morandin Jr.	Federal University of São Carlos, Brazil
Maxime Morge	LIRIS, Université Lyon 1, France
Koichi Moriyama	Nagoya Institute of Technology, Japan
Gildas Morvan	Université d'Artois, France
Bernard Moulin	Université Laval, Canada
Muhammad Marwan Muhammad Fuad	Coventry University, UK
Hiroyuki Nakagawa	Okayama University, Japan
Hien Nguyen	University of Information Technology, VNU-HCM, Vietnam
Ngoc Nguyen	Wrocław University of Technology, Poland
Rajdeep Niyogi	Indian Institute of Technology Roorkee, India
Norita Norwawi	Universiti Sains Islam Malaysia, Malaysia
Slawomir Nowaczyk	Halmstad University, Sweden
Luis Nunes	Instituto Universitário de Lisboa (ISCTE-IUL) and Instituto de Telecomunicações, Portugal
Andrzej Obuchowicz	University of Zielona Góra, Poland
Michael O'Grady	University College Dublin, Ireland
Joanna Isabelle Olszewska	University of the West of Scotland, UK
Eva Onaindía de la Rivaherrera	Universitat Politècnica de València, Spain
Pauline Ong	Universiti Tun Hussein Onn Malaysia, Malaysia
Mihaela Oprea	Petroleum-Gas University of Ploiesti, Romania

Ryohei Orihara	University of Electro-Communications, Japan
Eneko Osaba	Tecnalia, Spain
Stanislaw Osowski	Warsaw University of Technology, Poland
Sascha Ossowski	University Rey Juan Carlos, Spain
Tandra Pal	National Institute of Technology Durgapur, India
Marcin Paprzycki	Polish Academy of Sciences, Poland
Giovanni Paragliola	Institute for High Performance Computing and Networking of the National Research Council, Italy
Andrew Parkes	University of Nottingham, UK
Praveen Paruchuri	IIIT Hyderabad, India
Hai V. Pham	Hanoi University of Science and Technology, Vietnam
Maria Silvia Pini	University of Padua, Italy
Jamshid Piri	Independent Researcher, Iran
Jeremy Pitt	Imperial College London, UK
Agostino Poggi	University of Parma, Italy
Dawid Polap	Silesian University of Technology, Poland
Borja Ponte	Universidad de Oviedo, Spain
Enrico Pontelli	New Mexico State University, USA
Filipe Portela	University of Minho, Portugal
Isabel Praça	Polytechnic Institute of Porto, Portugal
Giulio Prevedello	Sony Computer Science Laboratory Paris, France
Violaine Prince	Université Montpellier 2, CNRS, France
Gregory Provan	University College Cork, Ireland
Abdellatif Rahmoun	École supérieure en informatique de Sidi Bel Abbès and Graduate School of Computer Science, Algeria
Patrizia Ribino	Institute for High Performance Computing and Networking, National Research Council, Italy
Fátima Rodrigues	Interdisciplinary Studies Research Center, Portugal
Daniel Rodriguez	University of Alcalá, Spain
Juha Röning	University of Oulu, Finland
Francesca Rossi	IBM, USA
Mohamed Roushdy	Ain Shams University/Innovation University, Egypt
Adel Saadi	Abdelhamid Mehri (Constantine 2) University, Algeria
Wojciech Salabun	Zachodniopomorski Uniwersytet Technologiczny w Szczecinie, Poland
Luciano Sanchez	Universidad de Oviedo, Spain
Suresh Sankaranarayanan	King Faisal University, Saudi Arabia

Francesco Santini	Università di Perugia, Italy
Giuseppe M. L. Sarne	University of Milan-Bicocca, Italy
Fabio Sartori	University of Milano-Bicocca, Italy
Markus Schatten	University of Zagreb, Croatia
Stefan Schiffer	RWTH Aachen University/MASCOR Institute, FH Aachen University of Applied Sciences, Germany
Klemens Schnattinger	Baden-Württemberg Cooperative State University (DHBW), Germany
Michael Schumacher	University of Applied Sciences and Arts Western Switzerland (HES-SO), Switzerland
Daniel Schwartz	Florida State University, USA
Nasredine Semmar	CEA LIst, CEA, France
Roman Senkerik	A.I.Lab, Tomas Bata University in Zlín, Czechia
Emilio Serrano	Universidad Politécnica de Madrid, Spain
Peer-Olaf Siebers	University of Nottingham, UK
Marius Silaghi	Florida Institute of Technology, USA
Gerardo Simari	Universidad Nacional del Sur, Argentina
Bernd Steinbach	Freiberg University of Mining and Technology, Germany
Darko Stipanicev	FESB University of Split, Croatia
Catalin Stoean	University of Craiova, Romania
Thomas Stützle	Université Libre de Bruxelles, Belgium
Sivarao Subramonian	Universiti Teknikal Malaysia Melaka, Malaysia
Ron Sun	Rensselaer Polytechnic Institute, USA
Zhaohao Sun	Federation University Australia, Australia and PNG University of Technology, Papua New Guinea
Yasuhiro Suzuki	Graduate School of Information Science, Nagoya University, Japan
Ryszard Tadeusiewicz	AGH University of Science and Technology, Poland
Shing Chiang Tan	Multimedia University, Malaysia
Andrea Tettamanzi	Université Côte d'Azur, Inria, I3S, UMR 7271, France
Viviane Torres da Silva	IBM Research, Brazil
Ngoc-Hien Tran	University of Transport and Communications, Vietnam
Jüri Vain	Tallinn University of Technology, Estonia
Jasper van der Waa	Netherlands Organisation for Applied Scientific Research, Netherlands
Leo van Moergestel	HU Utrecht University of Applied Sciences, Netherlands

Srdjan Vesic	CNRS, France
Gregg Vesonder	Stevens Institute of Technology, USA
Emilio Vivancos	Universitat Politècnica de València, Spain
Constantin Volosencu	Politehnica University of Timişoara, Romania
Mattias Wahde	Chalmers University of Technology, Sweden
Frank Wang	University of Kent, UK
Mia Y. Wang	College of Charleston, USA
Anna Wilbik	Maastricht University, Netherlands
Ian Wilson	University of South Wales, UK
Bozena Wozna-Szczesniak	Jan Długosz University in Częstochowa, Poland
Hongji Yang	University of Leicester, UK
Vahid Yazdanpanah	University of Southampton, UK
Kamal Z. Zamli	Universiti Malaysia Pahang Al-Sultan Abdullah, Malaysia

Additional Reviewers

Gianluca Aguzzi	Alma Mater Studiorum - University of Bologna, Italy
Jhonatan Alves	Universidade Federal de Santa Catarina, Brazil
Ivan Armuelles Voinov	Universidad de Panama, Panama
Arthur Baudet	La Rochelle Université, France
Widad Belkadi	University of Science and Technology Houari Boumediene, Algeria
Zhiwei Chu	Purdue University, USA
Razieh Darshi	Iran University of Science and Technology, Iran
Davide Domini	Alma Mater Studiorum - University of Bologna, Italy
Simon Gay	Université Grenoble Alpes, LCIS, France
David Genest	University of Angers, France
Olivier Goudet	University of Angers, France
E. Harshith Kumar	Indian Institute of Technology Ropar, India
Maria Mannone	Institute for High Performance Computing and Networking of the National Research Council, Italy
Corrado Mio	EBTIC, Khalifa University of Science and Technology, UAE
Ezhilarasi Periyathambi	University of Southampton, UK
Aaron Pico	Universitat Politècnica de València, Spain
Thomas Raimbault	EIGSI, France
José Simmonds	Universidad de Panamá, Panama

Julien Soulé	Université Grenoble Alpes - LCIS/Thales, France
Carlo Taticchi	University of Perugia, Italy
Luca Maria Tutino	University of Perugia, Italy
Jônata Tyska	Universidade Federal de Santa Catarina, Brazil
Jaroslaw Watróbski	University of Szczecin, Poland

Invited Speakers

Pavan Duggal	Supreme Court of India, International Commission on Cyber Security Law, India, and Artificial Intelligence Law Hub, India
Inge Bryan	Dutch Institute for Vulnerability Disclosure, Netherlands
Paul Nemitz	European Commission, Belgium

Contents

Artificial Intelligence

On the Selection of Characteristic Objects in ESP-COMET: A Novel Approach and Assessment Framework

Andrii Shekhovtsov[1,2(✉)], Bartłomiej Kizielewicz[1,2], and Wojciech Sałabun[1,2]

[1] National Institute of Telecommunications, Szachowa 1, 04-894 Warsaw, Poland
{A.Shekhovtsov,B.Kizielewicz,W.Salabun}@il-pib.pl
[2] West Pomeranian University of Technology in Szczecin, Żołnierska 49, 71-210 Szczecin, Poland

Abstract. Multi-Criteria Decision Analysis (MCDA) supports complex decision-making by incorporating multiple decision criteria, often using reference points to reflect the decision maker's preferences. The Expected Solution Point - Characteristic Objects Method (ESP-COMET) employs characteristic objects (COs) as such reference points, assuming that appropriate characteristic values (CVs) are selected to define them. This paper proposes a novel method for selecting characteristic values within the ESP-COMET framework, focusing on the weighted models. The approach aims to simplify the resulting model while maintaining the model's accuracy. A theoretical justification is provided, along with a case study, illustrating the differences between weighted and unweighted ESP-COMET models. Furthermore, we introduce a comprehensive simulation framework for evaluating the performance of various CVs selection strategies. Using this framework, six methods were tested and benchmarked against the Stable Preference Ordering Towards Ideal Solution (SPOTIS) method as a reference. The results show that while all methods produce highly correlated rankings, the proposed method achieves slightly better alignment with the reference model and results in lower model complexity. Although performance gains are marginal, the proposed method is recommended in scenarios where ESP-based preferences are defined.

Keywords: MCDA · Multi-Criteria Decision-Making · Fuzzy Logic · Expected Solution · COMET

1 Introduction

Contemporary decision-making problems are highly complex, often involving numerous conflicting criteria. Such challenges arise both in everyday situations, such as selecting products or services, and in more advanced decision-making processes in fields such as engineering [9], medicine [2], finance [4], or management [13]. As the number of criteria and the level of analytical complexity grow,

H. J. van den Herik et al. (Eds.): ICAART 2025, LNAI 16517, pp. 3–20, 2026.
https://doi.org/10.1007/978-3-032-25032-2_1

it becomes increasingly difficult for individuals to make well-informed decisions without support. In these cases, the use of appropriate decision-support tools becomes essential.

Multi-Criteria Decision Analysis (MCDA) is a sub-domain of operational research, which can be helpful in such complex decision problems. MCDA methods provide a set of instruments that allow for the formal modeling of the preferences of decision-makers or domain experts [5]. Among the fundamental elements used in MCDA are criterion weights, which reflect the relative importance of individual criteria. Some methods, such as Stable Preference Ordering Towards Ideal Solution (SPOTIS) [7], Fuzzy normalization-based Multi-Attributive Border Approximation Area Comparison (FN-MABAC) [11], or Characteristic Objects Method (COMET) [16], also incorporate reference points, which allow alternatives to be evaluated in relation to selected reference objects. In particular, the COMET method is distinguished by its use of multiple reference points, referred to as characteristic objects (COs). However, selecting appropriate characteristic objects is challenging due to the large number of possible configurations.

The complexity of MCDA models, especially those based on numerous reference points, presents a significant barrier to their practical application. A high degree of model intricacy often leads to longer computation times, which can become a serious challenge in large-scale problems [15]. Moreover, in the case of the COMET method, the expert should evaluate pairs of characteristic objects that increase the workload and introduce the risk of modeling errors, especially when these objects are not well distributed within the decision space [22]. These types of problems are particularly evident in applications that require rapid decision-making on a large scale, such as logistics route optimization, investment risk analysis, or technology assessment within research and development projects [12]. In such cases, long computation times can significantly limit the practical usability of a method, regardless of its precision.

Attempts to simplify complex decision models frequently involve the use of hierarchical or modular structures, which allow the problem to be decomposed into smaller subproblems [21]. Although these approaches help reduce analytical complexity, they often carry the risk of losing essential relationships between objects or criteria. As a result, finding a balance between simplicity and model accuracy remains a central challenge in the practical implementation of MCDA methods.

The main contribution of the study is the proposition of a novel approach for selecting characteristic values (CVs) that define characteristic objects, aiming to simplify the model structure without compromising its performance. This method is particularly well-suited for the weighted variant of ESP-COMET, where capturing the decision maker's preferences is essential. We also introduce a dedicated simulation framework for systematically evaluating the accuracy and complexity of various COs/CVs selection strategies. We use this framework to assess six different COs configuration methods, benchmarking them against the SPOTIS method as a reference. The study is additionally strengthened with a case study of hydrogen car selection, demonstrating the application of the proposed method.

The remainder of the paper is organized as follows. Section 2 presents related work in relation to the topic of decision making. Section 3 presents the methodology, with the initial assumptions related to the COMET method, the expanded COMET method with ESP, and correlation coefficients. Section 4 discusses the proposed approach and presents a simple example that justifies it. Section 5 presents research on a practical problem related to hydrogen-powered cars and a simulation experiment assessing different CO selection approaches. Finally, Sect. 6 presents conclusions and future research propositions.

2 Related Works

The increasing complexity of MCDA models presents substantial challenges in real-world decision-making processes. One of the core difficulties lies in the cognitive burden placed on experts, especially when the evaluation process requires pairwise comparisons between numerous alternatives or reference points. As the number of criteria and reference points grows, the time required to construct and analyze the model grows too. Another crucial problem concerns the structure of the model itself is how to design and configure it in a way that remains both analytically robust and cognitively manageable.

To address computational barriers, Allmendinger et al. [1] proposed using surrogate-assisted multi-criteria optimization models. These models help approximate expensive or time-consuming simulations and physical experiments, significantly reducing the computational load. However, the presence of multiple objective functions introduces new layers of complexity, such as model selection, training time, and the simultaneous approximation of Pareto fronts.

Cinelli et al. [5] tackled the issue of overly complex models from a methodological perspective. They introduced a taxonomy-based decision support system that recommends suitable MCDA methods based on problem characteristics, aiming to avoid mismatched or unnecessarily complicated approaches.

In the context of reducing expert workload, Kizielewicz et al. [10] introduced the Intelligent COMET (INCOME) method, which leverages knowledge-based techniques to automate the selection and evaluation of characteristic objects. This proposition significantly reduces the cognitive and computational burden traditionally associated with expert-driven MCDA modeling.

Several other studies have explored structural approaches to manage the high dimensionality and complexity of MCDA problems. Zhou et al. [24] developed a framework combining cloud-based Technique for the Order of Prioritisation by Similarity to Ideal Solution (TOPSIS) with platform leverage strategies to streamline IoT platform selection in industry. Sadeghi et al. [14] employed a hierarchical Full Consistency Method (FUCOM) - GIS framework to assess vulnerability to environmental hazards, balancing multiple data layers. Bagheri et al. [3] applied a hybrid Delphi-hierarchical method to develop a competitiveness index for cities, demonstrating how structural decomposition helps manage multidimensional criteria. Similarly, Ijadi Maghsoodi et al. [8] integrated

H-SWARA (Step-wise Weight Assessment Ratio Analysis) and MULTIMOORA (Multi-Objective Optimization by Ratio Analysis) to guide renewable energy technology selection, showing that layered frameworks can reduce modeling complexity while retaining decision quality.

Another improvement aimed at decreasing the application complexity of the COMET method was proposed by Shekhovtsov et al. [20]. It utilizes the Expected Solution Point concept in order to automate the pairwise comparison process. The idea was developed further in [19]. However, with the introduction of ESP the problem of proper selection of COs arise. Although uniformly distributed COs were sufficient to represent the unknown preferences of the expert or decision maker for the original COMET method, in the case of ESP-COMET, to ensure higher accuracy, it was essential that a CO grid was created around the selected ESP. This makes the proper selection of CO really important. However, no proper study was made to evaluate how different CO selection methods influence the accuracy of the model.

Therefore, in this paper, we focus on the particular problem of selecting appropriate characteristic values for creating characteristic objects that aims to improve the model's structure without sacrificing the accuracy of the model and decision maker preferences. Moreover, the novel CO selection method will be compared with existing ones to show its advantages and possible limitations.

3 Preliminaries

In this section, we provide descriptions of the methods that will be used in this study: ESP-COMET and SPOTIS methods. We also provide short descriptions and formulas for three similarity coefficients used in the study: Weighted Spearman r_w correlation coefficient, Weighted Similarity WS coefficient, and finally WSC_2 Weights Similarity Coefficient, which is used to measure the differences between weight vectors.

3.1 Weighted ESP-COMET

The Expected Solution Point - Characteristic Objects Method (ESP-COMET) was proposed as an alternative approach for constructing the pairwise comparison matrix within the original COMET approach [20], with a latter extension that includes weights [19]. In this method, the decision maker should specify one or more Expected Solution Points, which reflect their preferences and domain knowledge. Each ESP is represented as a vector of r elements, where r is the number of criteria considered in the decision-making problem.

According to [20], the complete algorithm for the ESP-COMET method is defined as follows:

1. Define the decision problem by the set of fuzzy numbers which should be selected for each criterion C_i as shown in (1):

$$C_r = \{\tilde{C}_{rc_1}, \tilde{C}_{rc_2}, ..., \tilde{C}_{rc_r}\} \tag{1}$$

where $c_1, c_2, ..., c_r$ are the numbers of fuzzy numbers (cores on these numbers are serve as characteristic values (CV)) for all criteria.

2. Define one or more Expected Solution Points (ESPs) to construct the pairwise comparison matrix. Each ESP vector should contain r elements, where r denotes the number of criteria in the decision problem, as shown in Eq. (2):

$$ESP = \{esp_{ij}\}_{n \times r} \tag{2}$$

3. Use the cartesian product of fuzzy numbers (or characteristic values) to create a set of Characteristic Objects (COs) representing all possible combinations as shown in (3).

$$CO = C(C_1) \times C(C_2) \times ... \times C(C_r) \tag{3}$$

4. Instead of manual comparison process the Expected Solution Points are used to evaluate COs and identify values of the pairwise comparison matrix α_{ij} (4).

$$\alpha_{ij} = \begin{cases} 1.0, & f_{ESP}(CO_i) < f_{ESP}(CO_j) \\ 0.5, & f_{ESP}(CO_i) = f_{ESP}(CO_j) \\ 0.0, & f_{ESP}(CO_i) > f_{ESP}(CO_j) \end{cases}, \tag{4}$$

The function $f_{ESP}(CO_i)$ is defined as (5).

$$f_{ESP}(X) = \min_i \sqrt{\sum_{j=1}^{r} w_j \cdot (x'_j - esp'_{ij})^2}, \tag{5}$$

where, w_j denotes the importance weight assigned to the jth criterion, and X represents a single Characteristic Object composed of values x_j, where $j \in \{1, 2, \ldots, r\}$. The term esp_{ij} refers to the ith expected value for criterion j. The normalized forms of x_j and esp_{ij} are represented by x'_j and esp'_{ij}, respectively, and are computed according to Eq. (6). Normalization process in ESP-COMET is performed using the minimum and maximum characteristic values for each criterion, denoted by $c_j^{(\min)}$ and $c_j^{(\max)}$.

$$x'_j = \frac{x_j - c_j^{(\min)}}{c_j^{(\max)} - c_j^{(\min)}} \tag{6}$$

5. Create a fuzzy rules base using characteristic objects and resulted preference values (7):

$$IF\ C(\tilde{C}_{1i})\ AND\ C(\tilde{C}_{2i})\ AND\ ...\ THEN\ P_i \tag{7}$$

6. Final ranking of the alternatives is derived using Mamdani's inference method on the created fuzzy rule base. Better alternatives have bigger value of the preference.

One of the most important steps in the COMET method is the first step, where characteristic values should be chosen to form fuzzy numbers and characteristic objects. This is especially important when ESP-COMET is used, as poorly selected characteristic values can lead to a less accurate model and therefore worse results. Because of this, in this paper, we want to investigate different ways of selecting characteristic values and how they influence the calculation results.

3.2 Stable Preference Ordering Towards Ideal Solution

The Stable Preference Ordering Towards Ideal Solution (SPOTIS) method was proposed by [7] as a simple rank reversal method that is also capable of solving problems with preferences presented in the form of expected solution points. It relies on expert-defined criteria bounds and one reference point (ideal or expected solution) in order to provide robust ordering of alternatives. In this study, we will use the SPOTIS method as a reference to assess the accuracy of the different COMET models.

Classical MCDA methods usually require decision maker to define only decision matrix, weights and criteria types. To use the SPOTIS method is is also required to define criteria bounds that limits problem's domain. For each criterion
C_j ($j \in \{1, 2, \ldots, N\}$) the maximum S_j^{max} and minimum S_j^{min} bounds must be defined. Next, if Ideal Solution Point (ISP) is used, it should be defined as $\boldsymbol{S}^* = \{S_1^*, \ldots S_j^*, \ldots S_m^*\}$, where $S_j^* = S_j^{max}$ for the profit criterion and as $S_j^* = S_j^{min}$ for the cost criterion. The decision matrix in this notation is denoted $S = (S_{ij})_{M \times N}$, where S_{ij} is the criterion value of the i-th alternative A_i for the j-th criterion C_j.

Then, in order to evaluate alternatives with the SPOTIS method, these three steps should be made [7]:
Step 1. Compute the normalized distance to ISP (8) for each alternative.

$$d_{ij}(A_i, S_j^*) = \frac{|S_{ij} - S_j^*|}{|S_j^{max} - S_j^{min}|} \tag{8}$$

Step 2. Calculate the weighted normalized distances from ISP $d(A_i, \boldsymbol{S}^*) \in [0, 1]$ as shown in Eq. (9).

$$d(A_i, \boldsymbol{S}^*) = \sum_{j=1}^{N} w_j d_{ij}(A_i, S_j^*) \tag{9}$$

Step 3. The final ranking is determined by ordering the alternatives by the values $d(A_i, \boldsymbol{S}^*)$. The better alternatives have lower values of $d(A_i, S^*)$, as it is interpreted as distance of the alternative from ISP.

Another feature of the SPOTIS method is the ability to use the Expected Solution Point as a reference point, instead of ISP. In this case, the ranking will build towards the expected solution. If one want to utilize this feature, the ESP

$\boldsymbol{S}^+$ values should be selected as $S_j^{min} \leq S_j^+ \leq S_j^{max}$ for every j, reflecting the preferences of the expert of the decision maker. Then, values of ISP $\boldsymbol{S}^*$ should be substituted with values of ESP $\boldsymbol{S}^+$ in the calculations, yielding ESP-directed ranking.

3.3 Similarity Coefficients

In this work, we use three similarity coefficients to measure the differences between the rankings and weights.

The first measure is the Weighted Spearman's correlation coefficient [6], which extends the classical Spearman coefficient by incorporating weights that place greater emphasis on differences at the top of the rankings. This metric assesses the degree of correlation between two ranked lists, with values ranging from -1 (completely reversed rankings) to 1 (identical rankings), while a value of 0 indicates no correlation. The formula, shown in Eq. (10), applies to samples of size N, using the rank values x_i and y_i.

$$r_w = 1 - \frac{6\sum_{i=1}^{N}(x_i - y_i)^2((N - x_i + 1) + (N - y_i + 1))}{N^4 + N^3 - N^2 - N} \tag{10}$$

The next one is the Weighted Similarity coefficient (WS), introduced as an effective measure in MCDM problems [17]. WS coefficient is defined on the interval $(0, 1]$, where a value of 1 indicates identical rankings and 0 signifies no correlation. Similarly to the r_w coefficient, it assigns weights to each comparison depending on the importance of the position in the first ranking, which makes it an asymmetrical measure. The asymmetry makes it particularly useful when one of the rankings serves as a reference. The formula is provided in Eq. (11), where N denotes the sample size and x_i, y_i are the rank positions.

$$WS = 1 - \sum_{i=1}^{N} 2^{-x_i} \frac{|x_i - y_i|}{\max(|x_i - 1|, |x_i - N|)} \tag{11}$$

The last one is the Weights Similarity Coefficient (WSC_2) [18], which is used for measuring the differences between two sets of criteria weights. It is based on the Manhattan distance, which is transformed and normalized to the $[0, 1]$ range, allowing for easier interpretation of the results. It is calculated for two weight vectors $\mathbf{w} = \{w_1, w_2, \ldots, w_N\}$ and $\mathbf{v} = \{v_1, v_2, \ldots, v_N\}$ as shown in Eq. (12).

$$WSC_2 = 1 - \frac{d_1(\mathbf{w}, \mathbf{v})}{2} = 1 - \frac{\sum_{i=1}^{N} |w_i - v_i|}{2} \tag{12}$$

4 Proposed Approach

In this section, we want to propose a new way to select characteristic values (and therefore the characteristic objects) and present the justification for this. The purpose of this method is to ensure more fair treatment of the characteristic objects near the ESP point when weights are applied in Weighted ESP-COMET. First, we demonstrate a small example that justifies the improvement, and then we present the algorithm for the proposed CO selection method.

The simple example contains two criteria, each of them in the range [0, 10], with selected ESP {3, 3}. We compare models created with equal weights and very unbalanced weights {0.01, 0.99} to show how the preference function changes. All these values were selected arbitrarily, as in our opinion, they will best demonstrate the discussed problem. A graphical representation of the problem is given in Fig. 1. This figure shows the model with equal weights (left) and selected unbalanced weights (center). However, it can be seen that the isolines for the equal weight model don't fall at the same rate in every direction as expected when equal weights are applied.

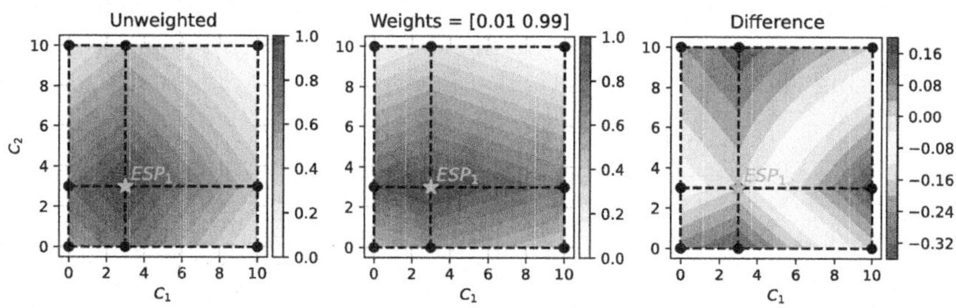

Fig. 1. Contour representation of the preference functions for model with equal weights (left), model with unbalanced weights (center) and difference between these two functions (right), characteristic objects are represented by the black dots [Source: [19]].

Numerical data for this example is presented in Table 1. It contains indices and values of criteria for all nine CO and results of evaluation for equally weighted (P_U and R_U) and weighted (P_W and R_W) models. It can be seen that CO that lies in the same line as ESP (for example $CO_2 = \{0, 3\}$ and $CO_8 = \{10, 3\}$) has different preference value for the unweighted (equally weighted) model. In case of the weighted model, the results align with expectations: the preference value falls faster with a change in C_2, as it has a bigger weight.

Additionally, we compute several numerical coefficients to quantify the differences between the rankings and preferences. First, the coefficient WSC_2, which compares equal weights with the weight vector $w = \{0.01, 0.99\}$ used in this example, is 0.5100. This value represents the maximum possible WSC_2 when equal weights are used as the reference. Next, we evaluate the preferences and the CO ranking, obtaining a Weighted Spearman's correlation $r_w = 0.8752$ and a Mean Absolute Error (MAE) of 0.1222. These results indicate that the rankings and preferences are quite similar, with the overall order of the key items in the ranking generally preserved. However, the weighted version of the ranking contains no ties.

Table 1. Preferences and rankings of unweighted (P_U, R_U) and weighted (P_W, R_W) ESP models [Source: [19]].

CO_i	C_1	C_2	P_U	P_W	R_U	R_W
CO_1	0	0	0.6000	0.5000	4	5
CO_2	0	3	0.8000	0.8750	2.5	2
CO_3	0	10	0.2000	0.1250	7.5	8
CO_4	3	0	0.8000	0.6250	2.5	4
CO_5	3	3	1.0000	1.0000	1	1
CO_6	3	10	0.4000	0.2500	5.5	7
CO_7	10	0	0.2000	0.3750	7.5	6
CO_8	10	3	0.4000	0.7500	5.5	3
CO_9	10	10	0.0000	0.0000	9	9

Here we propose an alternative method for selecting characteristic objects. Instead of relying solely on the traditional set of three (minimum, expected, and maximum) or five characteristic values, we introduce a procedure that completes this set to form a square around the selected ESP. This approach ensures that, in the case of equal weights, the characteristic objects are evaluated symmetrically with respect to the ESP, resulting in symmetric preferences. Usually, this will require five characteristic values for each criterion, but if the distance between two CVs is smaller than a predefined threshold (10% in this study), they are considered equivalent, and one of them is removed. This strategy represents a compromise between model accuracy and simplicity.

Figure 2 illustrates this method for the case of two criteria with the same input as the previous example. As can be seen, characteristic objects create a square zone around ESP for both weighted and unweighted (equally weighted) modes. In case of equal weights, CO that lies on opposite sides of ESP has equal preferences in this square, and the same is true for the weighted model. In our opinion, this ensures a fairer treatment of the CO and evaluates alternatives when weights are applied.

Below, we describe the steps required to create such a grid of characteristic values for the given problem. For the sake of simplicity, we provide the description for the single criterion case only, and then it should be applied to every criterion in the problem. First, it is required that for each criterion, lower and upper bounds b_l and b_u should be defined, as well as the expected solution value e. Next, it should be computed in normalized space for which criterion, the distance between e and one of the bounds is the smallest, but not equal to 0 (ESP should not lie on the bound for this). This distance, d, will be utilized as an offset from ESP for each criterion. Finally, for each criterion, the following steps should be done:

1. Calculate criterion range as $r = b_u - b_l$, and then offset as $o = d \cdot r$, providing offset in original space of criterion.

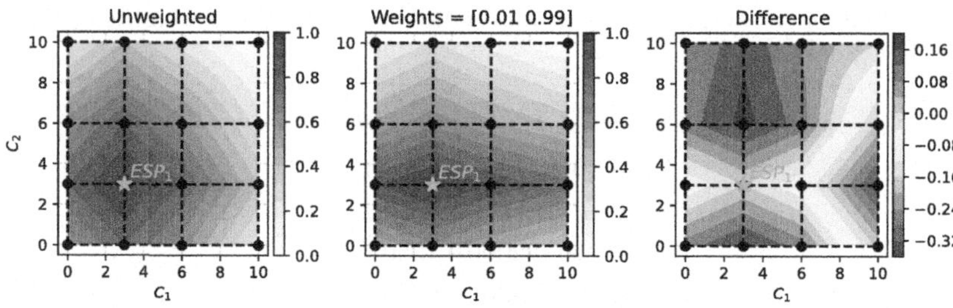

Fig. 2. Contour representation of the preference functions for model with equal weights (left), model with unbalanced weights (center) and difference between these two functions (right), characteristic objects are represented by the black dots and are created with proposed method.

2. Calculate additional CV as: $a_l = \max(b_l, e - o)$; $a_u = \min(e + o, b_u)$. min and max functions are required to remain in the domain created with the original bounds.
3. Then, for both a_l and a_u, if these values are closer to either bound or e than the given threshold (for example, 0.1), it should be set to this value. For example, if $|a_l - e| < 0.1 \cdot r$ then a_l should be set to e.
4. Create an ordered set of characteristic values for the criterion by sorting unique values from $\{b_l, a_l, e, a_u, b_u\}$.

When this procedure is done for each criterion, then the characteristic values grid is created as a Cartesian product of characteristic values for each criterion. Thanks to step 3, characteristic values that are too close are merged into one, making the model structure simpler, while maintaining a similar level of accuracy.

5 Case Study

In this section, we demonstrate the proposed approach using real-life data from the original study [19]. Given the growing interest in alternative fuel vehicles, the case study is focused on selecting the most suitable hydrogen-powered car, utilizing information obtained from manufacturers' websites.

The evaluation of the vehicles is based on the criteria listed in Table 2. The minimum and maximum values for each criterion were selected based on the dataset, ensuring the constructed model accommodates all considered alternatives. Criteria were selected in a way that describes the most essential parameters of the cars. This criterion allows for assessing range and fuel economy, power of the car, and speed performance, but also includes such essentials as year and price. Criterion weights were determined using the RANCOM method [23], while the Expected Solution Point was chosen subjectively by the decision maker, reflecting their individual needs and preferences. According to the decision maker's input, price is the most important criterion, followed by driving range and hydrogen tank capacity. The year of production was deemed the least important, which is reasonable given the relatively narrow range of this attribute among the considered vehicles.

Table 2. Criteria description, as well as the weights determined using the RANCOM method. [Source: [19]].

C_i	Criteria names	Units	Weights	ESP	Lower b.	Upper b.
C_1	Year		0.0612	2023	2015	2024
C_2	Estimated Price	Thous. of dollars	0.2653	30	30	100
C_3	Range	km	0.2041	800	400	800
C_4	Hydrogen tank capacity	kg	0.2041	6	4.4	6.5
C_5	Horse power		0.1020	130	130	550
C_6	0 to 100 acceleration time	s	0.0816	8	4.5	12.5
C_7	Max speed	km/h	0.0816	150	130	250

The data for the hydrogen vehicles considered in the evaluation are summarized in Table 3. As shown, the majority of the cars are relatively new, with A_6 standing out as an outlier in terms of the production year. The alternatives differ significantly across criteria such as price and performance, making it difficult to determine which option best aligns with the decision maker's preferences using a simple comparison. All data were obtained from the official websites of the respective manufacturers.

Table 3. Data of the alternatives. [Source: [19]].

	C_1	C_2	C_3	C_4	C_5	C_6	C_7
A_1	2023	50.0	646	5.6	182	9.2	161
A_2	2023	60.0	612	6.3	161	9.2	179
A_3	2021	59.0	579	5.5	174	9.0	165
A_4	2019	45.0	437	4.4	211	5.8	160
A_5	2022	30.0	400	4.4	134	7.8	130
A_6	2015	66.5	594	5.6	136	12.5	160
A_7	2024	90.0	504	6.0	401	6.0	180
A_8	2023	45.0	590	5.6	182	7.8	170
A_9	2022	68.0	800	5.4	300	6.5	200
A_{10}	2022	100.0	800	5.4	550	4.5	250

We create two models of the ESP-COMET: one with equal weights (P_U, R_U) and one with weights shown in Table 2 (P_W, R_W). We use our proposed way to create additional characteristic values, which allows for better utilization of the criteria weights. Computation results are presented in Table 4 for both of the tested models. The application of the weights results in several changes within the ranking. While the head of the ranking that contains A_1, A_2, and A_8 remains the same, three alternatives experience a decline in their rankings, while two show improvement. For instance, alternatives A_3 and A_5 fall from fourth and sixth place to fifth and seventh, respectively. Tail of the ranking (A_7 and A_{10}), however, remains the same.

Table 4. Case study results.

A_i	P_U	P_W	R_U	R_W
A_1	0.8641	0.8049	1	1
A_2	0.7892	0.7165	3	3
A_3	0.7391	0.6631	4	5
A_4	0.4617	0.4307	7	8
A_5	0.6514	0.5361	6	7
A_6	0.4541	0.5458	8	6
A_7	0.3750	0.3140	9	9
A_8	0.8558	0.7925	2	2
A_9	0.6989	0.6758	5	4
A_{10}	0.1724	0.2464	10	10

We evaluate the difference between equal weights and weights in Table 2 with the WSC_2 coefficient and got a value of 0.7551, indicating that the given weights are quite close to the equal ones. This explains why the results are so well-aligned: r_w correlation between rankings of identified CO is 0.9118, while r_w correlation between rankings R_U, R_W is equal to 0.9592, indicating very high similarity between them. This also shows that the ESP-COMET approach somewhat smooths the model and does not allow the weights to influence results too much.

5.1 Simulation Experiment

Despite the different ways of determining characteristic values and, therefore, the characteristic objects, there are no studies that properly compare them and investigate the accuracy of these methods. In this section, we propose a framework for evaluating the different methods for the creation of characteristic objects with an arbitrary selection of the reference method. However, for the demonstration of the framework, we will use SPOTIS with ESP as a reference method. The SPOTIS method was chosen as it also uses ESP, and has a very simple and straightforward algorithm based on the distance from ESP.

All the values in this simulation were generated from a uniform distribution in the range $[0, 10]$, which also determined the bounds of each criterion. For a given number of criteria M and number of alternatives N, the single simulation run proceeds as follows:

1. Create random weights vector of length M, that sums up to 1.
2. Generate decision matrix with size $N \times M$.
3. Generate random ESP points that contain the M value.
4. Identify reference model, as well as COMET models included in the comparison (this includes creation of the CO grids).
5. Calculate reference ranking using generated weights, ESP, and decision matrix (in this study, the SPOTIS method is used as a reference).
6. Calculate ranking for each COMET model using generated weights, ESP, and decision matrix.
7. Calculate WS similarity coefficient between reference ranking and COMET rankings.

This described algorithm enables a comparison of different methods for selecting characteristic objects (COs) with respect to a chosen reference method or function. However, a single execution of the algorithm is insufficient to draw reliable conclusions. Therefore, in the subsequent part of this study, we present the results obtained from 10,000 runs of the algorithm, each with varying numbers of criteria, in order to obtain more generalized and robust insights.

We select six different ways to select CO for the comparison, including five already present in the literature, and the sixth one is the proposed one. The first three methods are presented in Fig. 3, including two Uniform methods and one Statistical method. Uniform method is an adaptable and very straightforward way to create a grid of CO. It uses K uniformly distributed values as characteristic values. With larger K, the model will be more accurate, but also more complex, as the number of resulting CO is K^M, where M is the number of criteria in the problem. Statistical method relies on statistics calculated from the alternatives, meaning we cannot create a domain model if no alternatives are present. Besides the criteria bounds, it utilizes median, 25th, and 75th percentiles, creating five characteristic values for each criterion, resulting in 5^M COs. Both of these methods were presented in [20].

Figure 4 illustrates another two methods, which were created specifically with ESP-based usage of the COMET method. The first approach is the ESP-guided approach and is demonstrated in the left and central parts of Fig. 4. In addition to the criteria bounds, it creates additional characteristic values based on the provided ESP values, resulting in 3^M COs. However, one can use the optional ψ parameter, which determines the position of additional characteristic values as shown in the central part of Fig. 4. In this study, we used the value $\psi = 0.1$. Lastly, our proposed method described in Sect. 4 is demonstrated in the right part of the Figure.

Next, we run the simulation ten thousand times for three, four, five, and six criteria. Each time, a new decision matrix, ESP, and weights were generated,

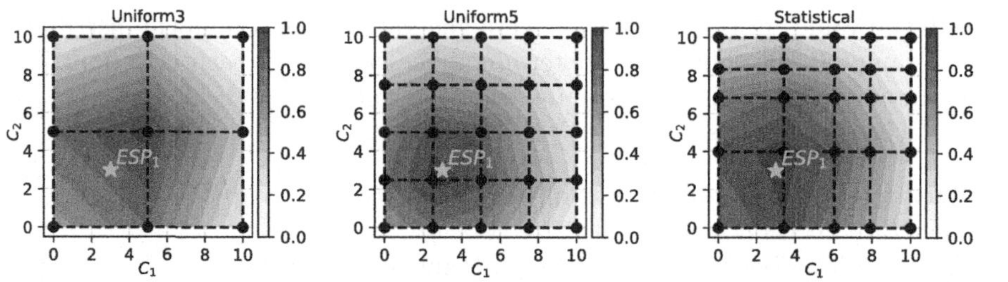

Fig. 3. Illustrations of Uniform (left, center) and statistical (right) methods of CO selection.

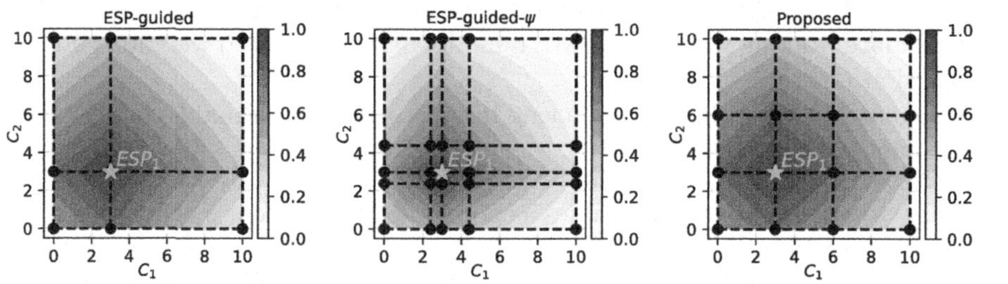

Fig. 4. Illustrations of ESP-guided (left, center) and Proposed (right) methods of CO selection.

resulting in four thousand different MCDA problems. Each decision matrix contains ten alternatives, in the range [0, 10] to fit the arbitrary chosen criteria bounds. Each created problem was evaluated with the SPOTIS method and six COMET models with different grids of CO created based on the methods presented in Figs. 3 and 4. Results were evaluated with the WS similarity coefficient, assuming one of the rankings is the reference ranking, fitting this experiment perfectly. Obtained WS values were collected and presented as boxplots to assess the distribution of the values.

During analysis of the results, we noticed that for each number of criteria, we got very similar distributions and statistics; therefore, we decided to present the results only for four and six criteria. Six boxplots in Fig. 5 demonstrate results for four criteria problems, for each of the six investigated methods of CO selections. It can be seen that correlations are very high for all of the investigated methods, and perfect alignment with the reference is possible for each of them, however, some differences in performance are present. It can be seen right away that the Uniform3 method has the lowest correlation with the reference. While this model is the simplest, it also has the worst performance in the experiments. Mean correlation is 0.9175 in this case. Second worst is the Statistical method (Stat in the Figure), which has a mean WS similarity coefficient value of 0.9268. Next, Uniform5 is placed, with a mean WS value of 0.9333. This is a very high correlation, and this method is good in most cases. However, as we use ESP in these experiments, it is expected that CO selection methods designed specifically for ESP, such as ESP-guided (with optional ψ) parameter, will provide the best results. For ESP-guided and ESP-guided-ψ, mean WS values are 0.9432 and 0.9438, respectively, with $3^4 = 81$ and $5^4 = 625$ characteristic objects in use. On the other hand, the proposed method achieves a slightly better result in terms of the mean value of WS, which is 0.9445. It also has slightly fewer outliers (black circles in the visualization). Its ability to provide less CO without sacrificing model quality also allows for simplification of the generated model: the biggest model has 500 CO and the smallest has 81, resulting in a mean value of 214 CO (median is also 81). This demonstrates that the proposed method can have fewer characteristic objects and still maintain the same level of accuracy.

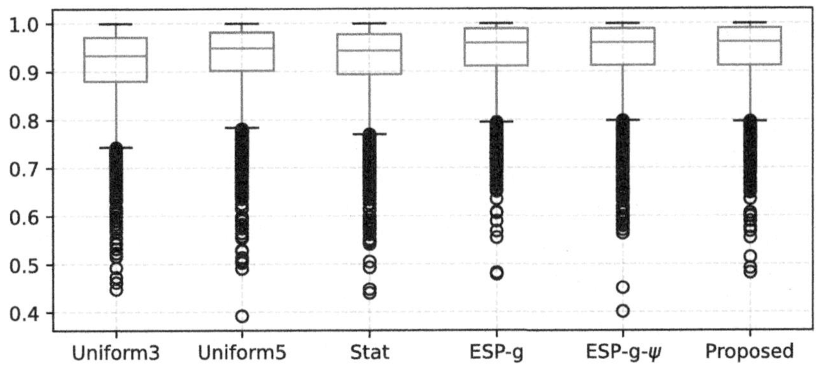

Fig. 5. Distributions of WS values calculated between reference rankings and COMET rankings for four criteria problems.

A similar situation was observed for other numbers of criteria, but we show the results of six criteria in Fig. 6. While the situation with correlation values is pretty similar to the four criteria case, the advantage in CO number reduction is more evident here. Mean WS similarity values for Uniform3 and Uniform5 methods were 0.9175 and 0.9281, respectively, with the Statistical method on a similar level (0.9216). Slightly better performance was observed for ESP-guided and ESP-guided-ψ methods: mean WS values were 0.9451 and 0.9440. The proposed method slightly outperforms it, with a mean value of 0.9463 and a median of 0.9609. In terms of the model complexity, Uniform3 and ESP-guided methods constantly have $3^6 = 729$ characteristic values, while Uniform5, Statistical, and ESP-guided-ψ have $5^6 = 15625$ CO. Such a large number of CO introduces unnecessary computational burden and problems with the scalability of the method. In the case of the proposed method, the biggest model has 12500 CO, and the smallest 729 has 2950 COs on average.

Summarizing the obtained results, all the methods provide a pretty high correlation with the reference method, meaning each of the methods can yield satisfying results. However, in terms of the marginal difference, methods that are based on only three characteristic values can give worse results (Uniform3 and

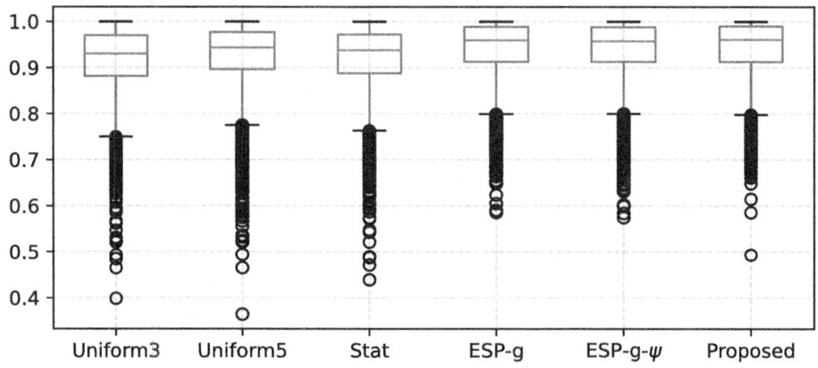

Fig. 6. Distributions of WS values calculated between reference rankings and COMET rankings six criteria problems.

simple ESP-guided). Then, the Statistical method distinguishes itself with ill-alignment with ESP, and it requires known alternatives to calculate statistical values. ESP-guided-ψ and the proposed method provide results that are best aligned with the reference method. While the ESP-guided-ψ method utilizes five characteristic values in most cases, the proposed method offers a reduction of the characteristic values, which results in a reduction of the CO without loss in the model's quality. Therefore, we suggest applying the proposed method as a characteristic values selection method in cases when ESP is known and used in the problem. However, the Uniform method with five or more characteristic values should be used if ESP or any other preference is unknown, allowing for comprehensive exploration of the decision problem's domain.

6 Conclusions

This paper proposes a new way to select characteristic values for the ESP-COMET method, with a weighted ESP version in mind. We present the justification of the proposed method and a case study that demonstrates the difference between weighted and unweighted models. Finally, we present a comprehensive simulation framework for assessing different CO selection algorithms for the ESP-COMET method. Six different methods were tested and compared with the SPOTIS method as a reference model. Results demonstrate that all the methods provide highly correlated results, but the proposed method distinguishes itself with slightly better results and lower model complexity than the other methods. While gains are marginal, we suggest using it when the usage of the ESP is required, and uniformly distributed CV if no pre-defined preferences are available.

In future works, we want to apply the Weighted ESP-COMET and proposed CO selection method to real-life decision problems. Methodologically, the problem of the model's complexity in the COMET method should be further investigated, and the reduction of the CO can reduce complexity without sacrificing the quality of the model.

Acknowledgments. The work was supported by the National Science Centre 2021/41/B/HS4/01296.

References

1. Allmendinger, R., Emmerich, M.T., Hakanen, J., Jin, Y., Rigoni, E.: Surrogate-assisted multicriteria optimization: complexities, prospective solutions, and business case. J. Multi-Criteria Decis. Anal. **24**(1–2), 5–24 (2017)
2. Băcescu Ene, G.V., Stoia, M.A., Cojocaru, C., Todea, D.A.: SMART multi-criteria decision analysis (MCDA)—one of the keys to future pandemic strategies. J. Clin. Med. **14**(6), 1943 (2025)
3. Bagheri, M., Adam, R., Jaafar, M., Lonik, K.A.T., Talaat, W.I.A.B.W., Wolf, I.D.: Using a hybrid Delphi hierarchical process, the development of a holistic index to measure city competitiveness in Malaysia: a case study from Penang Island. Model. Earth Syst. Environ. **9**(1), 693–721 (2023)
4. Baydaş, M., Elma, O.E., Stević, Ž: Proposal of an innovative MCDA evaluation methodology: knowledge discovery through rank reversal, standard deviation, and relationship with stock return. Financ. Innovation **10**(1), 4 (2024)
5. Cinelli, M., Kadziński, M., Miebs, G., Gonzalez, M., Słowiński, R.: Recommending multiple criteria decision analysis methods with a new taxonomy-based decision support system. Eur. J. Oper. Res. **302**(2), 633–651 (2022)
6. Dancelli, L., et al.: On two classes of weighted rank correlation measures deriving from the spearman's ρ. In: Stat. Models for Data Analysis, pp. 107–114. Springer, Cham (2013). https://doi.org/10.1007/978-3-319-00032-9_13
7. Dezert, J., Tchamova, A., Han, D., Tacnet, J.M.: The SPOTIS rank reversal free method for multi-criteria decision-making support. In: 2020 IEEE 23rd International Conference on Information Fusion (FUSION), pp. 1–8. IEEE (2020)
8. Ijadi Maghsoodi, A., Ijadi Maghsoodi, A., Mosavi, A., Rabczuk, T., Zavadskas, E.K.: Renewable energy technology selection problem using integrated h-swara-multimoora approach. Sustainability **10**(12), 4481 (2018)
9. Khorasani Nejad, M., Rashidi, M., Mousavi, V.: Application of hybrid MCDA tools for constructability review in infrastructure projects: a bridge case study. Appl. Sci. **15**(7), 3923 (2025)
10. Kizielewicz, B., Shekhovtsov, A., Więckowski, J., Wtróbski, J., Sałabun, W.: Intelligent characteristic objects method (INCOME): a data knowledge-based multi-criteria decision analysis. Artif. Intell. Rev. **57**(10), 266 (2024)
11. Kizielewicz, B., Więckowski, J., Sałabun, W.: Fuzzy normalization-based multi-attributive border approximation area comparison. Eng. Appl. Artif. Intell. **141**, 109736 (2025)
12. Manzolli, J.A., Yu, J., Miranda-Moreno, L.: Synthetic multi-criteria decision analysis (S-MCDA): a new framework for participatory transportation planning. Transp. Res. Interdisc. Perspect. **31**, 101463 (2025)
13. Ozbey, S., Baskak, D., Saner, H.S., Yucesan, M., Erdogan, M., Gul, M.: A brief review of the applications of MCDA in disaster management. Multi-Criteria Decis. Anal. 1–15 (2022)
14. Sadeghi, H., Darzi, A.G., Voosoghi, B., Garakani, A.A., Ghorbani, Z., Mojtahedi, S.F.F.: Assessing the vulnerability of Iran to subsidence hazard using a hierarchical FUCOM-GIS framework. Remote Sens. Appl. Soc. Environ. **31**, 100989 (2023)

15. Sahoo, S.K., Goswami, S.S.: A comprehensive review of multiple criteria decision-making (MCDM) methods: advancements, applications, and future directions. Decis. Making Adv. **1**(1), 25–48 (2023)
16. Sałabun, W.: The characteristic objects method: a new distance-based approach to multicriteria decision-making problems. J. Multi-Criteria Decis. Anal. **22**(1–2), 37–50 (2015)
17. Sałabun, W., Urbaniak, K.: A new coefficient of rankings similarity in decision-making problems. In: Krzhizhanovskaya, V.V., Závodszky, G., Lees, M.H., Dongarra, J.J., Sloot, P.M.A., Brissos, S., Teixeira, J. (eds.) ICCS 2020. LNCS, vol. 12138, pp. 632–645. Springer, Cham (2020). https://doi.org/10.1007/978-3-030-50417-5_47
18. Shekhovtsov, A.: Evaluating the performance of subjective weighting methods for multi-criteria decision-making using a novel weights similarity coefficient. Proc. Comp. Sci. **225**, 4785–4794 (2023a)
19. Shekhovtsov, A., Kizielewicz, B., Sałabun, W.: Towards enhanced decision making: Integrating weighted expected solution points in multi-criteria analysis. In: Proceedings of the 17th International Conference on Agents and Artificial Intelligence - Volume 3: ICAART, pp. 272–279. INSTICC, SciTePress (2025). https://doi.org/10.5220/0013120100003890
20. Shekhovtsov, A., et al.: Advancing individual decision-making: an extension of the characteristic objects method using expected solution point. Inf. Sci. **647**, 119456 (2023b)
21. Tavana, M., Soltanifar, M., Santos-Arteaga, F.J.: Analytical hierarchy process: revolution and evolution. Ann. Oper. Res. **326**(2), 879–907 (2023)
22. Wtróbski, J., Bczkiewicz, A., Sałabun, W.: New multi-criteria method for evaluation of sustainable RES management. Appl. Energy **324**, 119695 (2022)
23. Więckowski, J., et al.: RANCOM: a novel approach to identifying criteria relevance based on inaccuracy expert judgments. Eng. Appl. Artif. Intell. **122**, 106114 (2023)
24. Zhou, T., Ming, X., Chen, Z., Miao, R.: Selecting industrial IoT Platform for digital servitisation: a framework integrating platform leverage practices and cloud HBWM-TOPSIS approach. Int. J. Prod. Res. **61**(12), 4022–4044 (2023)

Exploring MFCCs, eGeMAPSv02, and Emobase for Emotion Recognition in Tunisian Dialect

Latifa Iben Nasr[1(✉)], Abir Masmoudi[1], Ismail Badache[2], and Lamia Hadrich Belguith[1]

[1] University of Sfax, FSEG Sfax, MIRACL Laboratory, Sfax, Tunisia
latifa.ibennasr@fsegs.usf.tn
[2] Aix-Marseille Université, CNRS, LIS, Marseille, France

Abstract. This study investigates emotion recognition from spontaneous Tunisian Dialect (TD) speech, focusing on the challenges posed by natural, varied vocal expressions. We evaluate three acoustic feature sets—13 MFCCs, eGeMAPSv02, and emobase—across classical machine learning classifiers and deep learning models like LSTM and Transformer Encoder. To address class imbalance in the SERTUS dataset, especially for Joy and Neutral emotions, we applied data augmentation techniques such as white noise addition, pitch shifting, and time stretching, and enriched the corpus with manually validated speech segments from other TD sources. Our results highlight that random forest combined with emobase features yields the highest overall accuracy (67%), providing balanced recognition across emotions including Neutral, Angry, Sad, and Satisfied. MFCCs effectively capture strong emotional states like Anger (74%) and Neutrality (81%) due to their spectral focus, while eGeMAPSv02 excels in detecting subtler emotions like Satisfaction (66%) and Sadness (59%) through prosodic cues. These findings demonstrate the importance of combining spectral and prosodic features to robustly recognize emotions in TD spontaneous speech, paving the way for broader applicability to Arabic dialects.

Keywords: SER · Spontaneous Tunisian Dialect · Spectral Features · Prosodic Features

1 Introduction

Emotion is a core component of human communication and interaction, weaving together the complex spectrum of feelings that shape our behaviors, decisions, and relationships [8]. As digital platforms flourish and humancomputer interaction becomes more widespread, there's a heightened focus on systems capable of detecting and interpreting the emotional content conveyed through speech [30], to enhance the natural flow and effectiveness of communication between humans and machines [17]. In recent years, Speech Emotion Recognition (SER)

H. J. van den Herik et al. (Eds.): ICAART 2025, LNAI 16517, pp. 21–39, 2026.
https://doi.org/10.1007/978-3-032-25032-2_2

has emerged as an innovative technology designed to interpret emotions using only the nuances in a person's voice [18].

In SER, the process begins with defining data criteria and culminates in selecting an appropriate classifier [10]. The speech data type ranges from spontaneous to prepared [24]. Prepared speech is often preferred for its ease of collection and modeling, whereas spontaneous speech, though more complex, provides more authentic emotional expression—essential for real-world applications [31]. This trade-off is notable in high-resource languages and becomes even more pronounced in low-resource contexts [24].

The next stage, feature extraction, is a crucial step for achieving accurate SER. Spectral features—e.g., Mel-Frequency Cepstral Coefficients (MFCCs)—capture the frequency structure of speech, helping distinguish between emotions. Prosodic features (e.g., pitch, loudness, and duration) reflect vocal dynamics closely linked to emotional states. Voice quality features (e.g., stability and clarity) are useful for detecting subtle emotions like sadness or fear. Low-Level Descriptors (LLDs) provide detailed articulation cues [5,12]. Alongside handcrafted features, contemporary systems also employ pretrained models like wav2vec [13] to extract richer, data-driven representations. Finally, classifier selection—ranging from traditional Machine Learning (ML) to advanced Deep Learning (DL)—plays a pivotal role in accurately interpreting emotional content from speech [10].

In the Arab world, even though Arabic has more than 420 million speakers, it is still underrepresented in SER research [3], with English dominating the available datasets [36]. A major challenge in Arabic dialects (AD) is the lack of annotated corpora [37]; only 4.76% of SER datasets between 2000 and 2021 were in Arabic, and most were non-spontaneous [24,38], reinforcing the need for natural, AD-specific resources. SER becomes a complicated task with under-resourced languages like the Tunisian dialect (TD) due to the limited availability of emotional datasets specific to Tunisian Arabic [17], especially in spontaneous speech [24].

This research aims to address this gap by extending our previous work [35] to establish a TD spontaneous emotion recognition dataset using additional data sources and speech-based data augmentation techniques. Three acoustic feature sets—MFCCs, eGeMAPSv02, and emobase—are evaluated using both ML and DL classifiers for SER, and to explore the correlation between emotional expression and acoustic features.

The structure of this paper is organized as follows. Section 2 outlines the main characteristics of the TD. Section 3 reviews the related work. Section 4 details the proposed approach. Section 5 presents and analyzes the experimental results. Section 6 provides a discussion of the findings. Finally, Sect. 7 concludes and outlines directions for future research.

2 Tunisian Dialect Charateristics

TD spoken by around 12 million people and shaped by Algerian and Libyan Arabic [11]. Unlike many other languages, TD lacks a standardized orthography and comprehensive linguistic documentation across its phonological, morphological, syntactic, semantic, and lexical components. This challenge is exacerbated by the diglossic nature of the linguistic environment, in which TD is the vernacular, while Classical Arabic—especially Modern Standard Arabic (MSA)—is reserved for formal and educational domains [25].

There are dual registers in TD: intellectualized and popular dialects [9]. The intellectualized dialect, commonly used by academics and in media broadcasts, employs a formal vocabulary and includes borrowed terms, yet it still preserves the structures of the local dialect. On the other hand, the familiar or popular dialect is used in regular, informal conversations. For example, the phrase "Disappointing situation" is rendered as [مقيتة الحالة / mVaynaT AlHAlaT] in the familiar register of TD and as [الوضعية خايبة / Alwa.diyaT xAybT] in the intellectualized register. Furthermore, TD comprises a dialect continuum with considerable internal variation [28,29]. For instance, the word "ugly" is expressed in northern Tunisian as [خايب / xAyb], whereas southern speakers use [شين / shyn]. Similarly, the expression "I love" is rendered in northern Tunisian as [نحب / nHb], while southern speakers say [نبغي / nbgy].

TD represents a distinct Arabic variety shaped by historical interactions with Latin, Berber, Turkish, and Romance languages. It is further influenced by frequent code-switching (CSW) with French and English [26] [27]. Linguistic analyses reveal substantial differences between TD and MSA, such as the lack of gender marking in some verb forms, omission of indicative prefixes, a unique progressive aspect, predominant SVO word order, agglutinative structures influenced by Turkish, and a mixed vocabulary [28].

Despite its expressive richness and dynamic evolution—driven by borrowing, fossilization, and innovation—TD remains linguistically undervalued [25,29]. These specific features highlight the importance of developing inclusive and effective emotion recognition systems that are tailored to real-world, spontaneous speech.

This research is motivated by the need to bridge this gap and contribute to more representative and context-aware SER in TD, extending its applicability to Algerian and Libyan Arabic.

3 Related Works

SER has been an active research area for over two decades, drawing on insights from signal processing, ML, and affective computing [16]. Foundational studies focused on designing hand-crafted acoustic features—such as pitch, energy, spectral shape, and voice quality measures [14]—which were then fed into classical classifiers like Support Vector Machines (SVMs) and Gaussian Mixture Models, using both acted and spontaneous corpora in languages such as French, English, and Chinese [15]. For instance, using prepared speech from the Berlin emotional speech dataset with LLDs features, the eGeMAPS feature set was found to be less effective than emobase, with Sequential Minimal Optimization (SMO) classifiers [6].

Focusing on Arabic research, [2] worked with spontaneous Algerian dialect data and employed SMO to combine various acoustic and spectral features, concluding that adding MFCCs significantly improves performance. Similarly, [1] studied spontaneous speech from multiple dialects and MSA, using SMO and Simple Logistic (SL) classifiers that leveraged MFCCs, intensity, and Zero Crossing Rate (ZCR). Additionally, [45] demonstrated that in acted TD speech, a feature set including MFCCs, pitch, and energy, classified by SVM, yields strong results.

With the rise of DL, these techniques have been employed to automatically extract high-level features from raw audio signals, proving effective in SER [32]. Overall, DL has outperformed ML methods [33], although this advantage remains a subject of debate in some research contexts [6,27]. Pretrained features such as Wave2Vec have also been used in both Arabic and European languages, showing better performance compared to baseline features like eGeMAPS and MFCCs when combined with DL models [17,34]. However, the performance of DL models—such as recurrent neural networks, convolutional neural networks (CNNs), and Transformers—depends heavily on large labeled datasets [4], which are scarce for low-resource languages like TD.

Additionally, multimodal models combining textual and acoustic features—such as bidirectional encoder representations from transformers, SpeechCueLLM [39,40], Wav2Vec, and CamemBERT [41]—show strong results but remain largely restricted to non-Arabic languages [27].

While non-spontaneous Arabic SER has demonstrated high accuracy using features such as MFCCs and Mel spectrograms—e.g., SVM with 77.14% accuracy [42], Transformers with 95.2% precision [43], and ASERS-LSTM with 96.81% [44]. Also in TD with non-spontaneous data appears promising [17,45]. But performance drops significantly on spontaneous TD data, with F-scores below 58% even when using DL and ML methods [27].

In summary, the evolution of SER has moved from hand-crafted acoustic analyses toward end-to-end deep architectures, driven by both algorithmic advances and the proliferation of diverse emotional speech datasets, but it still faces limitations in low-resource settings, especially with natural data for real-world applications.

4 Tunisian Dialect Speech Emotion Recognition

This section provides an overview of the proposed approach, as illustrated in Fig. 1, outlining the process from data preparation to the classification phase.

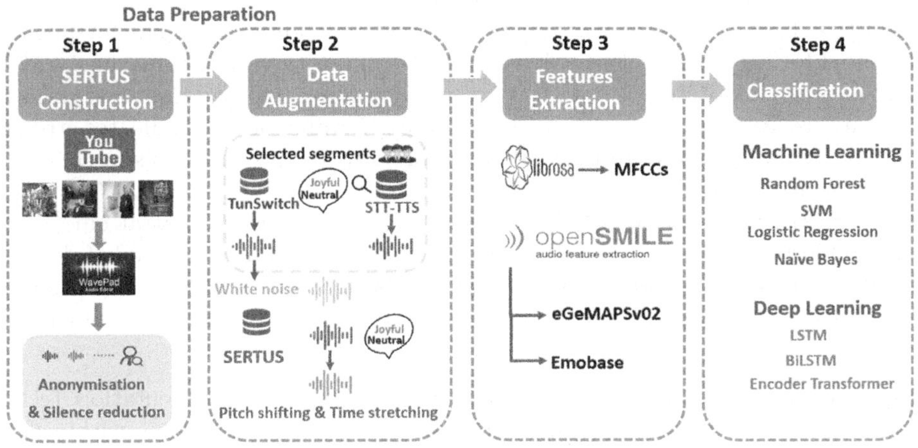

Fig. 1. Workflow for SER in TD

4.1 Data Preparation

SERTUS Dataset. In this study, we worked on SERTUS (Speech Emotion Recognition TUnisian Spontaneous) [19,35]. This dataset contains over 23.85 h of spontaneous speech, comprising 3,793 audio clips from 1,259 distinct speakers. Each audio clip spans approximately 20 s.

The speech data was gathered from Tunisian television content available on YouTube, including talk shows that reflect both intellectual and colloquial language styles, as well as the Tunisian Reality series, which emphasizes everyday popular speech. It features emotional expressions from guests engaged in discussions on various topics, as well as spontaneous street interviews addressing themes such as politics, economics, culture, and sports. To reflect Tunisia's regional diversity, the dataset incorporates dialectical variations from across the country. This makes SERTUS a rich resource for studying spontaneous emotional speech in TD, also capturing linguistic intricacies such as CSW.

We utilized the WavePad software—chosen for its intuitive interface and advanced functionality—to extract voiced segments from the audio recordings. Specifically, we isolated the speakers' responses while removing the questions posed by TV show hosts or journalists during street interviews.

To ensure accurate annotations and protect privacy, we applied preprocessing steps to our speech corpus. These included reducing long silences to two seconds to minimize annotator effort, inspired by [51], and anonymizing personal information. The anonymization process was performed manually to ensure privacy and legal compliance. Our study focused on spontaneous speech by TV guests or speakers, excluding the hosts' statements. The corpus contains only non-overlapping speech and often includes natural pauses for reflection.

Annotators included three native TD speakers (two females and one male), selected for their expertise in sentiment analysis and academic backgrounds in linguistics. Each annotator independently labeled the audio files. The final emotion label for each segment was determined by majority vote. Evaluating agreement between annotators is essential for ensuring consistent and unbiased corpus annotations. In this study, a high Fleiss' kappa [7] value of 0.89 indicates strong consistency among annotators in labeling emotions in spontaneous speech.

Emotionally, the dataset is distributed as follows: 28.76% anger, 21.53% satisfaction, 21.28% sadness, 20.69% disgust, 4.69% Joy, with Neutral emotions being underrepresented. While the dataset's extensive and well-rounded design is a major strength, it shows a noticeable imbalance in emotion classes, with Joy and Neutral states being underrepresented, which calls for data augmentation.

Data Augmentation. In this phase, we leverage data augmentation techniques to address the class imbalance of Joy and Neutral emotions within the SERTUS dataset, with the objective of developing a more robust SER system. To achieve this, we applied controlled transformations—including white noise addition, pitch shifting, and time stretching—as well as incorporated carefully selected speech samples from other TD corpora. These augmentation strategies have proven effective in prior SER research [18,21], and have been particularly impactful in Arabic SER contexts [22].

Specifically, we utilized the spontanous Tunisian_dataset_STT-TTS[1] and the acted TunSwitch dataset [20] to extract segments exhibiting either Joy or Neutral emotional expressions. We ignored other datasets such as [20] because the audio samples were too short—only 2 to 4 s. To ensure annotation quality, two native Tunisian Arabic speakers independently reviewed the manually selected audio clips that reflected Neutral or Joy emotions. Any instance of disagreement led to the removal of the corresponding segment, thereby maintaining high annotation reliability.

In alignment with our goal of improving SER performance in naturalistic settings, and since the TunSwitch dataset is of the acted type, selected segments from this dataset were augmented with white noise to better simulate real-world acoustic conditions, where speech is frequently accompanied by background noise [18]. Moreover, original SERTUS segments labeled as Joy and Neutral were augmented using pitch shifting and time stretching—techniques that introduce variation in prosodic and temporal features while preserving emotional content. These steps contribute to improved model generalization and address the underrepresentation of specific emotional categories.

[1] https://huggingface.co/datasets/Arbi-Houssem/Tunisian_dataset_STT-TTS.

4.2 Features Extraction

To effectively capture emotional patterns in speech, we extracted three types of acoustic features: MFCCs, Emobase, and eGeMAPSv02. MFCCs were used independently as a baseline representation of the speech signal. Emobase provides a broad set of LLDs, including MFCCs, pitch, energy, zero-crossing rate, and voicing features, alongside statistical functionals such as mean, standard deviation, and percentiles. In contrast, eGeMAPSv02 offers a compact, emotionally expressive feature set specifically designed for paralinguistic tasks. It encompasses prosodic, spectral, and voice quality measures, including formant frequencies (F1F3), jitter, shimmer, and harmonics-to-noise ratio. Each feature set was evaluated independently to assess its individual contribution to emotion classification performance. The selection of these feature sets was guided by their ability to capture diverse speech characteristics and their proven reliability across multiple languages and datasets in prior research [5,6,24,27,45].

4.3 Models Classification

Based on prior studies [6,17,24,27,34,45], we employed a combination of ML and DL models at this stage, including SVM, Naïve Bayes, Logistic Regression, Random Forest (RF), LSTM, BiLSTM, and Transformer encoders. As the task focuses on emotion classification rather than sequence generation, only the encoder component of the Transformer architecture is utilized. This diverse selection allows for a meaningful comparison between traditional and modern techniques in SER.

5 Experimental Results

5.1 Data Establishment

Given the imbalanced distribution of the SERTUS dataset, data augmentation was emphasized in a meticulous manner. In the initial attempts, we aimed to obtain spontaneous TD speech using Text-to-Speech (TTS) systems available through online services that support TD, such as PlayHT[2], Listen2It[3], FineVoice[4], and SpeechGen.io[5]. We attempted to simulate natural TD speech using these tools; however, all of them failed to produce authentic TD audio. The generated speech was closer to MSA and did not reflect a natural tone. Despite efforts to adjust parameters such as speaker selection, the results remained unsatisfactory. To our knowledge, there are only open-source Arabic TTS libraries, such as facebook/mms-tts-ara, and none specifically designed for TD. For all these reasons, we initially opted to use Tunisian speech datasets: the spontanous Tunisian_dataset_STT-TTS and the acted TunSwitch dataset. Table 1 below presents the results of the segment selection.

[2] https://play.ht/text-to-speech/arabic/.
[3] https://www.getlisten2it.com/text-to-speech-voices/tunisian-arabic.
[4] https://www.fineshare.com/text-to-speech-online/tunisian-arabic.html.
[5] https://speechgen.io/fr/tts-arabic-tunisia/.

Table 1. Distribution of Selected Segments.

Dataset	Class	size in minutes
STT-TTS	Joy	0.92
	Neutral	18.52
TunSwitch	Joy	0.46
	Neutral	5.32

As shown in the table, the Joy class remains a challenging category, even across other datasets. It is important to note that the selected segments do not require anonymization, as they contain no personally identifiable information. As previously mentioned, the TunSwitch dataset is acted, and therefore, to better approximate natural speech, we introduce noise into the audio signals. We selected, with Librosa library, a moderate Signal-to-Noise Ratio (SNR) of 20 dB (i.e., snr_db = 20), which is a commonly used standard in the literature [18,23].

To illustrate the impact of noise injection, we use a representative utterance from the TunSwitch dataset: مع فطور الصباح، taxe والخدمة داخل يكون ٤٥ دولار إل ليلة للواحد / mE fTwr AlSbAH, taxe wAlxdmp dAxl ykwn 45 dwlAr < l lylp llwAHd / With breakfast, tax and service inside it is $45 per night per person. This sentence reflects a Neutral emotional tone and is the exact example used in the visualizations below.

Figure 2 and Fig. 3 show how this utterance is affected by the addition of white noise. The comparison highlights the acoustic differences before and after noise injection, helping to simulate real-world audio conditions.

The waveform in Fig. 2a, representing the clean audio, exhibits a well-structured signal with distinct pauses and natural amplitude variations. In contrast, Fig. 2b, where white noise has been added, appears denser and more filled-in, particularly in quieter sections. This indicates that the noise has effectively simulated a more realistic and less controlled acoustic environment.

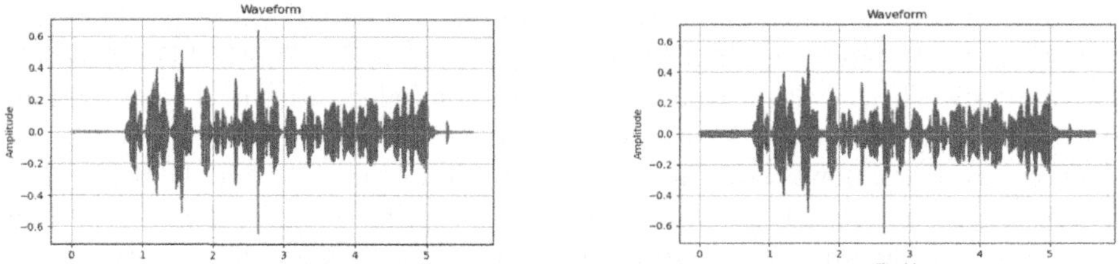

(a) Before white noise (b) After white noise

Fig. 2. Waveforms before and after white noise.

The differences become even more apparent in the spectrograms in Fig. 3. Before noise addition, the spectrogram (Fig. 3a) displays clear, distinct frequency bands with a clean, low-energy background. After white noise is applied (Fig. 3b), the background becomes noticeably blurred and filled with broadband energy, as the noise permeates previously silent or low-energy regions across the frequency spectrum. This transformation helps to simulate the variability and imperfections typically found in natural, real-world speech recordings.

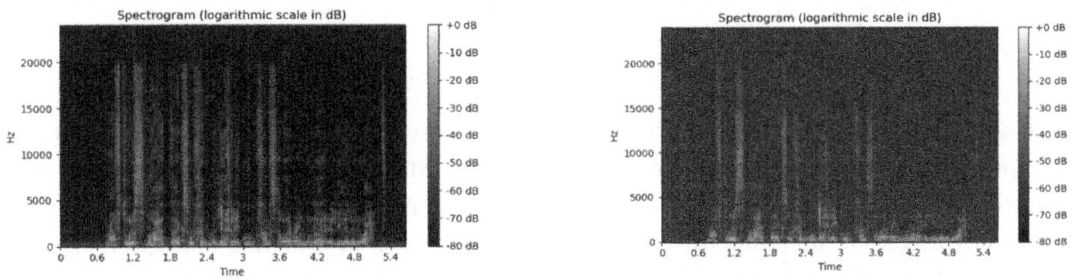

(a) Before white noise **(b)** After white noise

Fig. 3. Spectrograms before and after white noise.

As we mentioned earlier, segments labeled as Joy and Neutral were further augmented using pitch shifting and time stretching techniques with Librosa library. Pitch shifting was applied with bins_per_octave = 12 and n_steps = 6 (i.e., shifting the pitch down by six semitones), which preserved frequency resolution while altering harmonics. This transformation helped better differentiate emotional classes and led to improved weighted accuracy. Similarly, time stretching at a factor of 1.5× simulated faster speech delivery and enhance the model's generalization to varied speaking rates [46].

To demonstrate the impact of these augmentation techniques, we present a Joy-labeled example from the SERTUS dataset: أنا نقلهم يجيو كل يوم ما شاء الله رايضة لهنا ما شاء الله فمة برشا جو برشا حفالات المدينة العربي راهي حافلة راي دنيا برشا سهرات برشا شيخة / 'anA naqlhm yjyw kl ywom mA 'aA' allh Almdynp Al'rby rAhY HAf.lp rAy dn.yA rAyp lhna mA 'aA' allh fm.t br$A jw br$A HfAlAt br$A shrAt br$A $yxp / I tell them that they come every day, thank God. The Arab city is a bus stop. I think the world is going here, thank God. There is a lot of atmosphere, a lot of parties, a lot of evenings, a lot of sheikha.

After augmentation as demonstrated in Fig. 4, the amplitude has decreased after augmentation. In the Fig. 4a (before augmentation), the waveform reaches higher peaks and lower troughs, indicating a greater amplitude range. In Fig. 4b (after augmentation), the waveform appears more compressed vertically, with both the positive and negative peaks being less pronounced.

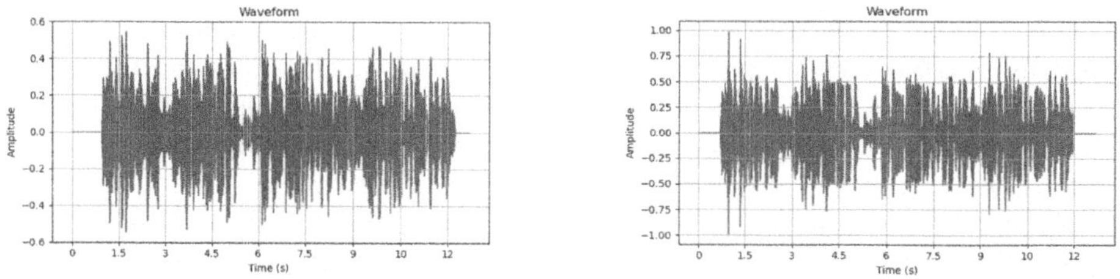

(a) Before augmentation **(b)** After augmentation

Fig. 4. Waveforms before and after augmentation.

Figure 5 illustrates the spectral effect of these augmentations. In the original spectrogram (Fig. 5a), harmonic structures are well spaced and temporally extended. After augmentation (Fig. 5b), the spectrogram shows denser harmonic bands compressed in time and shifted in frequency, indicating a higher speech tempo and a deeper tone. This aligns well with the target emotion and contributes to improved emotion recognition performance.

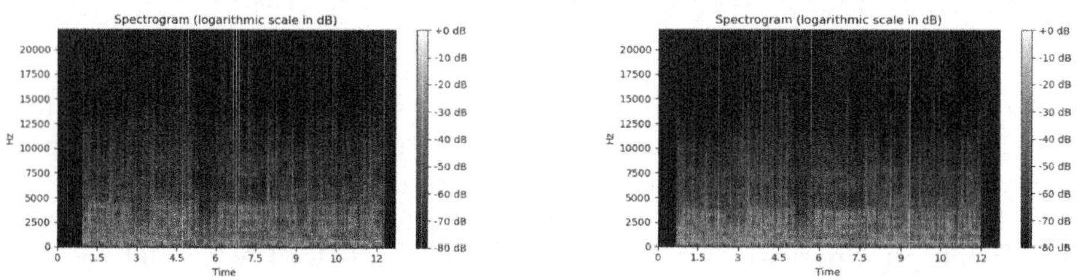

(a) Before augmentation **(b)** After augmentation

Fig. 5. Spectrograms before and after augmentation.

After these efforts to establish a coherent dataset—through data augmentation, the integration of additional datasets, and the application of various augmentation techniques—we observe a noticeable improvement in the data distribution, as illustrated in the Fig. 6 below.

While data augmentation slightly improved the distribution, the dataset remains imbalanced. It totals about 26 h. The next section explores how this imbalance impacts classification performance.

5.2 Features Extraction

We extract three widely used feature sets: 13 MFCCs, eGeMAPSv02, and emobase, each serving different analytical goals.

MFCCs are standard acoustic descriptors derived from the speech spectrum. They effectively model the human auditory system and offer robustness to moderate noise [27,32]. In our setup, we compute the first 13 MFCCs using Librosa

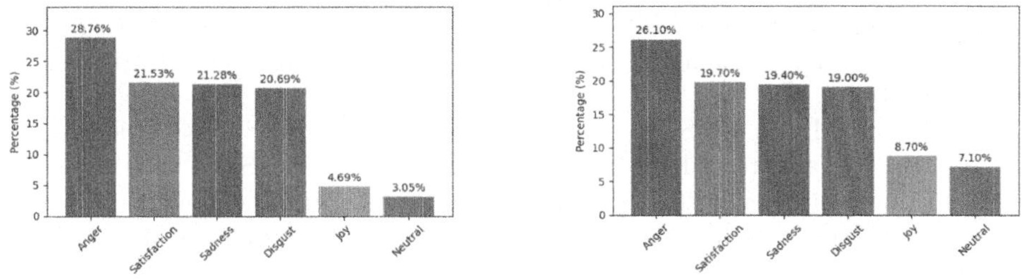

(a) Before data augmentation

(b) After data augmentation

Fig. 6. Data distribution before and after data augmentation.

at a 16 kHz sampling rate, then extract their means and standard deviations across time frames—resulting in 26 features. Although delta and delta-delta coefficients often boost performance [34,47], our experiments showed no significant gain across classifiers, so we focus on the original 13.

eGeMAPSv02 (88 features) is a compact, extracted via openSMILE 2.5.1, expert-curated set targeting prosody and vocal quality. It includes pitch (F0 semitone), jitter, shimmer, harmonics-to-noise ratio, and formants—parameters crucial for detecting affective states. Its standardization and proven noise robustness make it a top choice in emotion recognition challenges like INTERSPEECH ComParE [48,49].

Emobase (988 features), also extracted with openSMILE 2.5.1, provides a comprehensive representation of speech. It includes 26 LLDs (e.g., MFCCs 112, pitch, loudness, voicing probability, LSFs), their deltas, and statistical functionals. Originally designed for emotion recognition, emobase captures nuanced vocal textures and prosodic variations, and has demonstrated superior performance over smaller sets like eGeMAPS in such studies [6].

5.3 Classification Experiments

After data configuration, the total dataset was split into 70% training, 15% validation, and 15% testing. The RF model used 100 trees, and the SVM employed an RBF kernel. Both LSTM and BiLSTM architectures included 128 units, followed by dense layers with 64 and 32 units, and a dropout rate of 0.3 to prevent overfitting. ReLU was used in the dense layers, and Softmax in the output layer for multiclass classification. Models were trained for 200 epochs using the Adam optimizer with a learning rate of 0.001—hyperparameters selected after testing for optimal performance. All experiments were conducted in Kaggle notebooks, leveraging GPU support and 20 GB of storage for efficient execution.

As depicted in Table 2, among traditional ML models, RF achieved the highest overall accuracy—67% with the emobase feature set—outperforming all other combinations. This highlights the effectiveness of pairing a high-dimensional feature set with a robust ensemble method for emotion recognition. Logistic Regression performed moderately, reaching 47% accuracy with emobase, slightly outperforming its results with MFCCs. In contrast, SVM and Naive Bayes showed consistently poor performance, indicating limited capability in capturing emotional variability.

In DL, LSTM and BiLSTM models yielded low accuracy (3843%) across all feature sets. We also tested 1D-CNN-LSTM and 2D-CNN-LSTM with different configurations, but performance remained moderate. The Encoder Transformer performed better, achieving up to 53% accuracy with emobase features. This suggests that the transformer architecture can leverage the richness of high-dimensional inputs, though it still underperformed compared to RF on the same features.

In summary, the combination of emobase and RF delivered the strongest results—surpassing even the deep learning models. With the eGeMAPSv02 set, performance was lower than with emobase across all model combinations.

Table 2. Accuracy across feature sets and classifiers.

Classifiers		13 MFCCs	eGeMAPSv02	Emobase
ML	Logistic Regression	42%	46%	47%
	SVM	37%	32%	35%
	Naive Bayes	38%	34%	38%
	RF	59%	61%	**67%**
DL	LSTM	39%	38%	41%
	BiLSTM	40%	41%	43%
	Transformer Encoder	48%	51%	53%

The confusion matrix for the MFCCs feature set with RF, shown in Fig. 7, demonstrates strong performance in recognizing emotions such as Angry (74.36%) and Neutral (81.25%). MFCCs are highly effective in capturing the spectral envelope of speech, which correlates closely with vocal intensity and sharpness—key characteristics of anger and calm Neutrality. However, MFCCs are less effective for more nuanced emotions like Joy (39.86%) and Satisfied (56.67%), which rely more on prosodic and voice quality features. This indicates that while MFCCs are robust in detecting high-energy and low-energy states, they are less sensitive to subtle emotional variances.

The eGeMAPSv02 feature set, displayed in Fig. 8, exhibits improved performance in detecting emotions such as Satisfied (66.4%) and Sad (59.83%), while maintaining good accuracy for Angry (73.29%). Designed specifically for affective computing, eGeMAPS incorporates prosodic (e.g., pitch, loudness), spectral, and voice quality features. These allow it to effectively capture both arousal and valence cues, making it suitable for distinguishing more subtle emotions like satisfaction and sadness. Its lower performance on Disgust (30.92%) and Neutral (76.08%) suggests potential overlap in acoustic traits or a limitation in capturing the unique tone variations of these states.

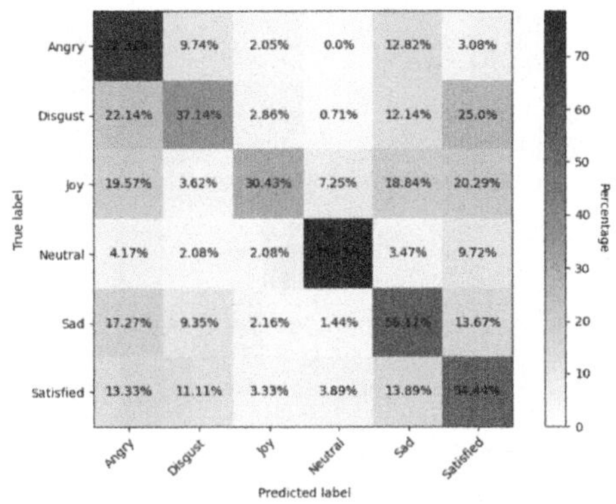

Fig. 7. RF confusion matrix with MFCCs.

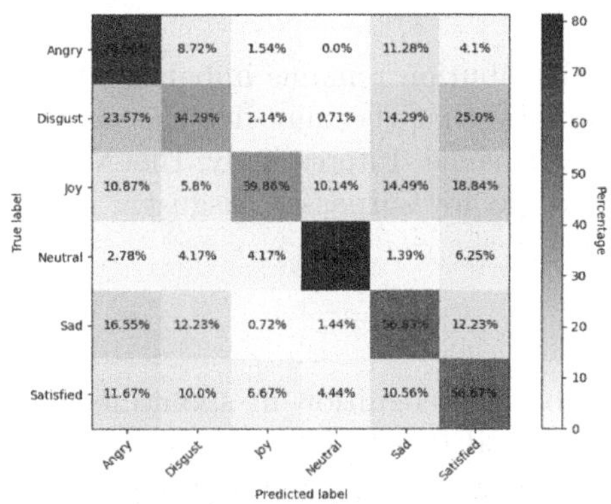

Fig. 8. RF confusion matrix with eGeMAPSv02.

The emobase feature set, presented in Fig. 9, yields balanced but slightly reduced performance across most emotions, with strong detection of Neutral (78.47%) and Sad (56.12%). Emobase includes a broad set of LLDs such as MFCCs, pitch, energy, and jitter, making it a general-purpose set. It performs moderately well on Disgust (37.14%) and Satisfied (54.44%), indicating a decent ability to model both spectral and prosodic elements. However, it shows weaknesses in recognizing Joy (30.43%) and Angry (72.31%), suggesting a possible dilution of emotional specificity due to the breadth of the feature set.

Among the three feature sets, emobase stands out for its balanced and consistent performance across all emotions. Unlike MFCCs and eGeMAPSv02, which excel in recognizing specific emotions, emobase combines spectral and prosodic features, making it more adaptable to both subtle and intense emotional variations. Its versatility makes it the most suitable choice for general emotion recognition tasks.

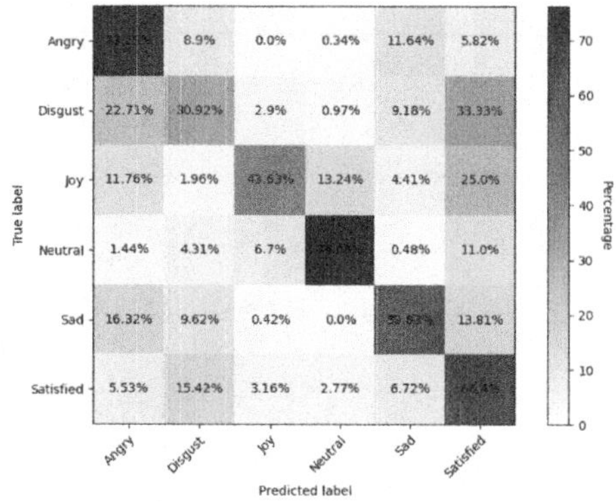

Fig. 9. RF confusion matrix with emobase.

Although the class distribution remains imbalanced despite data augmentation efforts, it is noteworthy that the minority classes—Joy and Neutral—still demonstrate strong performance. Interestingly, the Neutral class even outperforms all other classes, while Joy surpasses Disgust.

6 Discussion

This study explores emotion recognition in spontaneous TD speech. To mitigate class imbalance in the SERTUS dataset—particularly for the underrepresented Joy and Neutral emotions—we employed data augmentation techniques, including white noise injection, pitch shifting, and time stretching. Additionally, the dataset was enriched with manually verified speech segments sourced from other TD corpora. Experimental results indicate that the RF classifier, when combined with emobase features, achieves the highest overall accuracy (67%), offering balanced recognition across emotional categories such as Neutral, Angry, Sad, and Satisfied. MFCCs prove particularly effective for identifying prominent emotional states like Anger (74%) and Neutrality (81%) due to their spectral sensitivity, whereas eGeMAPSv02 features are better suited for capturing subtler emotions such as Satisfaction (66%) and Sadness (59%) through prosodic characteristics. These outcomes underscore the value of integrating spectral and prosodic features for robust emotion recognition in spontaneous TD. Despite persistent class imbalance, minority classes like Neutral still exhibit competitive performance and outperform all other emotion classes.

As presented in Table 3, prior work in TD has primarily focused on non-spontaneous speech using MFCCs and Wav2Vec features. Our previous work [27] addressed spontaneous speech using acoustic features such as MFCCs, ZCR, and features included in eGeMAPSv02 and emobase, but was limited to a small spontaneous TD dataset.

Table 3. Comparison of Arabic SER Performance.

Study	Dataset	Classifier	Results
[27]	Spontaneous TD	LSTM and RF	F-score: 58.75%
[17]	Non-spontaneous TD	LSTM	Accuracy: 60.60%
[45]	Acted TD	SVM	Precision: 95.52%
[22]	Non-spontaneous Saudi Dialect &	CNN	F-score: 96,81%
	Non-spontaneous Arabic	CNN	F-score: 92,63%
[2]	Spontaneous Algerian dialect	SMO	F-score: 48%
[1]	Spontaneous multi dialect and MSA	SMO and SL	Accuracy : 83.82%
Our work	**Spontaneous TD**	**RF**	**Accuracy : 67%**

In this study, we extend prior work by employing a larger and more diverse corpus that includes dialectal and thematic variations as well as a broader set of emotion categories. We also explore a variety of data augmentation techniques, feature sets, and classifiers to improve performance and achieve more accurate results.

In related work, [22] achieved a high F-score using MFCCs on non-spontaneous Saudi dialect speech. In contrast, [2] reported modest performance on spontaneous Algerian dialect speech. [1] achieved high performance using MFCCs, ZCR, and intensity features on a spontaneous, multi-dialect and MSA (Modern Standard Arabic) dataset. However, their dataset was limited to only 115 min of audio and included just four emotion classes: anger, happiness, sadness, and Neutral.

Our work bridges the limitations of existing approaches by addressing spontaneity in TD. It contributes to advancing emotion recognition in underrepresented dialects, with a focus on acoustic diversity to analyze the correlation between acoustic features and specific emotions. However, a notable confusion persists between the classes disgust and satisfaction, with at least 25% misclassification observed across different acoustic feature sets.

This confusion can be attributed to overlapping physical characteristics—such as low volume or intensity—commonly associated with low arousal levels in vocal samples, a phenomenon also noted by [6]. This underscores the need to incorporate our dimensional annotation—based on the arousal, valence, and dominance axes—introduced in previous work [50] to better capture emotional similarities. Additionally, leveraging pretrained models like Wav2Vec, alongside linguistic cues, is essential for detecting subtle distinctions between these closely related emotional states and enhancing overall performance.

7 Conclusion and Future Works

This study combines different classifiers and acoustic features for SER in low-resource TD settings. The results show that ML algorithms outperform DL models and also examine the correlation between emotions and acoustic features. To improve accuracy in future work, it will be important to incorporate dimensional annotations to address confusion between emotions that share similar characteristics in pitch or volume. Additionally, integrating linguistic features with pretrained acoustic features can help capture more semantic information.

Although the focus is on TD, the overlap with Algerian and Libyan Arabic supports its applicability to a broader range of dialects. The dataset, currently part of a doctoral thesis, will be made publicly available by late 2026 to support further research on underrepresented languages.

References

1. Kaloub, A., Elgabar, E.A.: Speech-Based techniques for emotion detection in natural Arabic audio files. Int. Arab J. Inf. Technol. (IAJIT) **22**(1) (2025)
2. Dahmani, H., Hussein, H., Meyer-Sickendiek, B., Jokisch, O.: Natural Arabic language resources for emotion recognition in Algerian dialect. In: Smaïli, K. (ed.) ICALP 2019. CCIS, vol. 1108, pp. 18–33. Springer, Cham (2019). https://doi.org/10.1007/978-3-030-32959-4_2
3. Al Roken, N., Barlas, G.: Multimodal Arabic emotion recognition using deep learning. Speech Commun. **155**, 103005 (2023)
4. Sharma, V.: Speech and Text-Based Emotion Recognizer (2023). arXiv preprint arXiv:2312.11503
5. Mustafa, H.H., Darwish, N.R., Hefny, H.A.: Automatic speech emotion recognition: a systematic literature review. Int. J. Speech Technol. **27**(1), 267–285 (2024)
6. Doğdu, C., Kessler, T., Schneider, D., Shadaydeh, M., Schweinberger, S.R.: A comparison of machine learning algorithms and feature sets for automatic vocal emotion recognition in speech. Sensors **22**(19), 7561 (2022)
7. Gwet, K.L.: Large-sample variance of Fleiss generalized kappa. Educ. Psychol. Measur. **81**(4), 781–790 (2021)
8. Bartsch, A., Hübner, S.: Towards a theory of emotional communication. CLCWeb: Comp. Lit. Culture **7**(4), 2 (2005)
9. Boukadida, N.: Connaissances phonologiques et morphologiques dérivationnelles et apprentissage de la lecture en arabe (Etude longitudinale) (Doctoral dissertation, Université Rennes 2; Université de Tunis) (2008)
10. Singh, Y.B., Goel, S.: A systematic literature review of speech emotion recognition approaches. Neurocomputing **492**, 245–263 (2022)
11. Turki, Houcemeddine, et al.: "Tunisian Arabic." (2015)
12. Liu, T., Yuan, X.: Paralinguistic and spectral feature extraction for speech emotion classification using machine learning techniques. EURASIP J. Audio Speech Music Process. **2023**(1), 1–14 (2023). https://doi.org/10.1186/s13636-023-00290-x
13. Pepino, L., Riera, P., Ferrer, L.: Emotion recognition from speech using wav2vec 2.0 embeddings. arXiv preprint arXiv:2104.03502 (2021)
14. Cámbara, G., Luque, J., & Farrús, M.: Convolutional speech recognition with pitch and voice quality features. arXiv preprint arXiv:2009.01309 (2020)

15. Al-Dujaili, M.J., Ebrahimi-Moghadam, A.: Speech emotion recognition: a comprehensive survey. Wireless Pers. Commun. **129**(4), 2525–2561 (2023)
16. SÖNMEZ, Y. Ü., VAROL, A.: In-depth investigation of speech emotion recognition studies from past to present the importance of emotion recognition from speech signal for AI. Intell. Syst. Appl. 200351
17. Messaoudi, A., Haddad, H., Hmida, M. B., Graiet, M.: TuniSER: Toward a Tunisian speech emotion recognition system. In: Proceedings of the 5th International Conference on Natural Language and Speech Processing (ICNLSP 2022), pp. 234–241 (2022)
18. Barhoumi, C., BenAyed, Y.: Real-time speech emotion recognition using deep learning and data augmentation: deep learning-based real-time speech emotion recognition. Artif. Intell. Rev. **58**(2) (2025)
19. Nasr, L.I., Masmoudi, A. Belguith, L.H.: Tunisian dialect speech corpus: construction and emotion annotation. In: Proceedings of the 17th International Conference on Agents and Artificial Intelligence - vol. 3, ISBN 978-989-758-737-5, ISSN 2184-433X, pp. 360–367. https://doi.org/10.5220/0013134000003890
20. Abdallah, A.A.B., Kabboudi, A., Kanoun, A., Zaiem, S.: Leveraging data collection and unsupervised learning for code-switched Tunisian Arabic automatic speech recognition. In: ICASSP 2024-2024 IEEE International Conference on Acoustics, Speech and Signal Processing (ICASSP), pp. 12607–12611. IEEE (2024)
21. Pham, N.T., et al.: Hybrid data augmentation and deep attention-based dilated convolutional-recurrent neural networks for speech emotion recognition. Expert Syst. Appl. **230**, 120608 (2023)
22. Bouchelligua, W., Al-Dayil, R., Algaith, A.: Effective data augmentation techniques for Arabic speech emotion recognition using convolutional neural networks. Appl. Sci. **15**(4), 2114 (2025)
23. Yusuf, S.M., Adedokun, E.A., Mu'azu, M.B., Umoh, I.J.: Speech emotion recognition using a novel noise augmentation approach and deep learning. ATBU J. Sci. Technol. Educ. **9**(4), 216–226 (2022)
24. Iben Nasr, L., Masmoudi, A., Hadrich Belguith, L.: Survey on Arabic speech emotion recognition. Int. J. Speech Technol. **27**(1), 53–68 (2024)
25. Mejri, S., Said, M., Sfar, I.: Pluringuisme et diglossie en Tunisie. Synergies Tunisie **1**, 53–74 (2009)
26. Mekki, A., Zribi, I., Ellouze, M., Belguith, L.H.: Tokenization of Tunisian Arabic: a comparison between three machine learning models. ACM Trans. Asian Low-Resource Lang. Inf. Process. **22**(7), 1–19 (2023)
27. Ibn Nasr, L., Masmoudi, A., Hadrich Belguith, L.: Emotion recognition from spontaneous Tunisian dialect speech. ACM Trans. Asian Low-Resource Lang. Inf. Process. **24**(2), 1–16 (2025)
28. Turki, H., et al.: Normalized orthography for Tunisian Arabic. In: International Conference on Language Processing and Knowledge Management, pp. 133–142. Cham: Springer Nature Switzerland (2024)
29. Abdallah, N.B., Kchaou, S., Bougares, F.: Text and speech-based Tunisian Arabic sub-dialects identification. In: Proceedings of the Twelfth Language Resources and Evaluation Conference, pp. 6405–6411 (2020)
30. Rathi, T., Tripathy, M.: Analyzing the influence of different speech data corpora and speech features on speech emotion recognition: a review. Speech Commun. 103102 (2024)
31. Gómez-Zaragozá, L., et al.: EMOVOME: a dataset for emotion recognition in spontaneous real-life speech. arXiv preprint arXiv:2403.02167 (2024)

32. Eriş, F.G., Akbal, E.: Enhancing speech emotion recognition through deep learning and handcrafted feature fusion. Appl. Acoust. **222**, 110070 (2024)
33. Hashem, A., Arif, M., Alghamdi, M.: Speech emotion recognition approaches: a systematic review. Speech Commun. **154**, 102974 (2023)
34. Macary, M., Tahon, M., Estève, Y., Rousseau, A.: On the use of self-supervised pre-trained acoustic and linguistic features for continuous speech emotion recognition. In: 2021 IEEE Spoken Language Technology Workshop (SLT), pp. 373-380. IEEE (2021)
35. Iben Nasr, L., Masmoudi, A., Belguith, L.H.: SERTUS dataset collection from spontaneous environments. In: International Conference on Language Processing and Knowledge Management, pp. 225–233. Cham: Springer Nature Switzerland (2024)
36. Atmaja, B.T., Sasou, A., Akagi, M.: Survey on bimodal speech emotion recognition from acoustic and linguistic information fusion. Speech Commun. **140**, 11–28 (2022)
37. Besdouri, F.Z., Zribi, I., Belguith, L.H.: Challenges and progress in developing speech recognition systems for Dialectal Arabic. Speech Commun. 103110 (2024)
38. Alamri, H.: Emotion recognition in Arabic speech from Saudi dialect corpus using machine learning and deep learning algorithms (2023)
39. Lee, S., Han, D.K., Ko, H.: Multimodal emotion recognition fusion analysis adapting BERT with heterogeneous feature unification. IEEE access **9**, 94557–94572 (2021)
40. Wu, Z., et al.: Beyond silent letters: amplifying LLMs in emotion recognition with vocal nuances. arXiv preprint arXiv:2407.21315 (2024)
41. Macary, M., Tahon, M., Estève, Y., Luzzati, D.: Acoustic and linguistic representations for speech continuous emotion recognition in call center conversations. arXiv preprint arXiv:2310.04481 (2023)
42. Aljuhani, R.H., Alshutayri, A., Alahdal, S.: Arabic speech emotion recognition from Saudi dialect corpus. IEEE Access **9**, 127081–127085 (2021)
43. Al-onazi, B.B.: Transformer-based multilingual speech emotion recognition using data augmentation and feature fusion. Appl. Sci. **12**(18), 9188 (2022)
44. Tajalsir, M., Hernandez, S.M., Mohammed, F.A.: ASERS-LSTM: Arabic speech emotion recognition system based on LSTM model. Int. J. Signal Image Process. (2022)
45. Meddeb, M., Karray, H., Alimi, A.M.: Automated extraction of features from Arabic emotional speech corpus. Int. J. Comput. Inf. Syst. Ind. Manag. Appl. **8**, 11 (2016)
46. Tao, H., Shan, S., Hu, Z., Zhu, C., Ge, H.: Strong generalized speech emotion recognition based on effective data augmentation. Entropy **25**(1), 68 (2022)
47. Khaskhoussy, R., Ayed, Y.B.: Speech processing for early Parkinson's disease diagnosis: machine learning and deep learning-based approach. Soc. Netw. Anal. Min. **12**(1), 73 (2022)
48. Eyben, F., et al.: The Geneva minimalistic acoustic parameter set (GeMAPS) for voice research and affective computing. IEEE Trans. Affect. Comput. **7**(2), 190–202 (2015)
49. Montacié, C., Caraty, M.J.: Vocalic, lexical and prosodic cues for the INTERSPEECH 2018 self-assessed affect challenge. In: INTERSPEECH, pp. 541–545 (2018)

50. Nasr, L.I., Masmoudi, A., Belguith, L.H.: Dimensional emotion annotation for spontaneous Tunisian dialect speech. In: 2024 32nd International Conference on Enabling Technologies: Infrastructure for Collaborative Enterprises (WETICE), pp. 98–103. IEEE (2024)
51. Macary, M., Tahon, M., Estève, Y., Rousseau, A.: AlloSat: a new call center French corpus for satisfaction and frustration analysis. In: Language Resources and Evaluation Conference, LREC 2020 (2020)

Multicommodity Flow Based Centralized Traffic Routing

Andrii Nyporko[1,2(✉)], Matyáš Švadlenka[1,2], Nikolai Antonov[1,2], Mohammad Rohaninejad[1], and Lukáš Chrpa[1]

[1] Czech Institute of Informatics, Robotics and Cybernetics, Czech Technical University in Prague, Prague, Czechia
nyporand@fel.cvut.cz

[2] Faculty of Electrical Engineering, Czech Technical University in Prague, Prague, Czechia

Abstract. As urbanization accelerates, the number of vehicles in urban road networks continues to grow rapidly. This issue becomes especially critical during peak hours, traffic accidents, or major events. Traditional route planning methods, which typically rely on decentralized Dynamic User Optimal (DUO) strategies, struggle to capture the overall traffic situation and coordinate flows effectively. In contrast, centralized route planning can integrate comprehensive traffic data, helping to avoid congestion and optimize vehicle distribution across the network. This paper proposes a centralized route optimization model based on Mixed Integer Programming (MIP), which aims to reduce traffic load by optimizing route allocation. Our extensive empirical evaluation shows the potential of centralized traffic routing for improving traffic in urban regions and provides detailed results concerning statistics of route distribution for common routes.

Keywords: Centralised Traffic Routing · Mixed-Integer Programming · Urban Traffic · Automated Planning

1 Introduction

The rapid population growth in urban areas over recent decades has led to a significant increase in the demand for transportation infrastructure. This trend, especially during peak hours, results in severe congestion within road networks. Traffic congestion not only wastes time and reduces economic productivity but also imposes substantial costs on governments. For instance, it is estimated that congestion in London alone caused over £5 billion in damages in 2020[1]. Moreover, environmental degradation and public health risks are direct consequences of this issue [4]. Unexpected events such as gatherings, sports competitions, and entertainment programs further increase the complexity of traffic management.

[1] https://www.london.gov.uk/press-releases/mayoral/cost-of-congestion-in-capital-revealed.

H. J. van den Herik et al. (Eds.): ICAART 2025, LNAI 16517, pp. 40–64, 2026.
https://doi.org/10.1007/978-3-032-25032-2_3

In response to these challenges, the concept of the "smart city" [15] has emerged as a framework for the optimal utilization of urban resources. Intelligent traffic management, a key component of this approach, aims to optimize vehicle allocation across transportation networks to reduce travel time and energy consumption. This is achieved using technologies such as advanced routing and adaptive traffic light control. Centralized approaches – such as scheduling algorithms [30], evolutionary methods [22], automated planning [2,18,24], and pheromone-based control models [3] – have been explored in this context.

In contrast, modern navigation systems primarily rely on decentralized methods. One such approach is the *Dynamic User Optimal (DUO)* principle [13], where each vehicle determines its route independently based on real-time traffic data. However, the absence of coordination among these individual decisions often leads to excessive congestion at bottleneck points.

Centralized approaches, on the other hand, offer a promising alternative by leveraging a global view of traffic conditions to assign optimal routes to vehicles. In such systems, Infrastructure-to-Vehicle (I2V) or Vehicle-to-Infrastructure (V2I) communication plays a key role: vehicles entering a controlled zone provide initial information, allowing the system to assign optimal routes within a defined time window. This allocation process typically includes traffic load forecasting, future flow modeling, and intelligent route reassignment [7,25–27].

Many existing approaches plan each vehicle's path individually [7,26]. However, a more effective strategy is first to identify the overall flow patterns in the network and then derive individual routes accordingly. Analyzing aggregated flows is not only more efficient but also offers a more realistic assessment of congestion throughout the network, avoiding the computational costs of microscopic-level planning.

This paper is an extension of an earlier conference paper [20], where we introduced a model based on Mixed-Integer Programming (MIP) [29], inspired by multi-commodity flow problems in networks [21]. The objective of this model is to distribute vehicles across the network in a balanced manner, minimizing the maximum load on any given route.

Unlike prior microscopic methods, our proposed model adopts a macroscopic perspective and emphasizes overall flow. This approach reduces computational complexity and avoids unnecessary symmetries, such as vehicle assignment order. To reconstruct individual routes from the optimized flows, we use a Depth-First Search (DFS)-based algorithm operating within the MIP-generated structure.

The effectiveness of our method is evaluated using scenarios from urban areas in New York and Sydney [26], as well as the central districts of Dublin [14] and Luxembourg [9], employing the widely-used SUMO simulator [17]. The results demonstrate that our approach has the potential to outperform decentralized DUO-based methods, particularly in scenarios in which we have several traffic flows containing a large number of vehicles each. On top of that, our MIP-based approach outperforms existing planning-based techniques.

Furthermore, we investigate the differences of the generated routes for individual traffic flows (traveled distance and trip duration) by the MIP-based approach. Such an analysis might help to identify situations in which some vehicles are routed on disproportionally "expensive" routes, i.e., those that are longer and take more time than average. Such "expensive" routes drivers might tend to avoid (even if they are assigned to them) [5].

This extension of the previous paper [20] involves: i) another cost function that penalises only vehicles that are routed above the traffic intensity threshold, ii) a scenario from Luxembourg city center on which our method is evaluated, and iii) an extensive evaluation concerning a wide range of statistics of the results of our method.

2 Related Work

The developing concept of smart cities emphasizes the need for efficient traffic flow management to optimize road resource utilization. Core objectives include reducing average travel time and total travel distance while achieving a balanced distribution of traffic [15]. Beyond vehicle-reduction measures like carpooling, intelligent technologies in route planning and traffic signal control significantly enhance infrastructure efficiency. Many solutions adopt traffic control frameworks based on formal methods [3].

Traditional traffic signal control approaches are predominantly centralized and include precise scheduling algorithms [30], evolutionary computation [22], and automated planning systems [2,18,24]. Meanwhile, modern navigation systems (e.g., WAZE^{TM}) utilize dynamic user-optimal (DUO) strategies [13], offering distributed route planning based on real-time data [8,11]. However, these decentralized methods lack global coordination: while vehicles may avoid immediate congestion, they often converge on newly congested routes.

In contrast, centralized route planning leverages global traffic information to recommend optimal paths, improving overall network efficiency. Such systems typically require vehicles to report origin and destination data for centralized processing. For instance, Yamashita et al. [31] proposed a system that shares route information among vehicles to predict future traffic and adjust routing dynamically.

Recent years have seen growing interest in centralized dynamic route planning [25], building on earlier work in automated planning [7,26,27]. These methods perform well in small networks [7,26], but scalability remains a challenge [6]. To mitigate this, a common strategy is to predefine fixed routes, reducing the network size for centralized computation [25,26]. Additionally, high-precision microscopic simulations needed for personalized routing pose further scalability issues.

Another relevant area is the Vehicle Routing Problem (VRP), which focuses on minimizing travel distance or time for serving customers. While formally similar to the problem in this paper, VRP emphasizes logistics problems (e.g. pickup and delivery) over global urban traffic optimization. Recent research [23] has begun integrating traffic network design with public and freight routing. Moreover, some studies explore decentralized mechanisms [16,28], highlighting the complementary nature of centralized and decentralized strategies.

3 Centralized Traffic Flow Scheduling

The Centralised Traffic Routing refers to the joint planning of (optimal) travel routes for multiple vehicles within a road network, where each vehicle has a defined origin and destination. The primary objective of this process is to optimize overall traffic efficiency and reduce the value of such key metrics as average travel time or traffic load on critical road segments. In this paper, we adopt the definition of centralized traffic routing as proposed by Chrpa et al. [7].

3.1 Problem Modeling

The problem is formalized as a 5-tuple $\chi = (\mathcal{N}, V, O, D, C)$, where $\mathcal{N}$ is a directed graph defined as $\mathcal{N} = (N, E, R, \rho)$. The vertex set N represents intersections, the edge set E connects intersections via the road segment set R, and the mapping is specified by the function $\rho : E \rightarrow R$. Certain intersections (e.g., roundabouts) are simplified into a single node in the graph, a modeling approach commonly used in simulation platforms like SUMO.

The vehicle set $V = v_1, \ldots, v_k$ denotes all vehicles to be scheduled, with origins and destinations given by the mappings $O : V \rightarrow N$ and $D : V \rightarrow N$. Each pair $(O(v_i), D(v_i))$ represents an individual travel demand, i.e., the locations of origin and destination for particular vehicles. The cost function $C : R \times \mathbb{N}_0 \rightarrow \mathbb{R}_0^+$ evaluates the cost incurred on a road segment as a function of the number of vehicles.

The solution is a set of routes $\Sigma = p_1, \ldots, p_k$, where each p_i is a sequence of edges from the origin to the destination of vehicle v_i, satisfying reachability constraints in the graph $\mathcal{N}$ (i.e., forming a path there).

The overall cost is computed as:

$$\sum_{x \in R} C(x, |i \mid e \in \ p_i, \ x = \rho(e)|),$$

where the effects of traffic signals and other aspects are relaxed out.

Route planning is executed periodically, updating based on the current network state, e.g., every n seconds [7,26]. The system collects vehicle state information before they enter a region and computes paths accordingly.

In automated planning-based methods, vehicle movement is abstracted into a series of actions, i.e., transitions from one intersection to the next via road segments [7,26]. Vehicles collect real-time traffic data via sensors and transmit it to a central routing system, which then makes routing decisions.

Since the traffic situation is assumed to change slowly, the system treats it as static or quasi-stationary, thereby reducing computational demands, albeit at the cost of slight prediction inaccuracies.

3.2 Cost Function Modeling Based on Load Levels

Road segments have a capacity limit, representing the maximum number of vehicles that can be safely accommodated. When the number of vehicles exceeds this threshold, the segment is considered congested. To refine load categorization, the system introduces two thresholds that divide non-congested traffic intensity into three levels: *low*, *medium*, and *high*, similar to the Levels of Service (LOS) standard: levels A-B indicate light load, C-D medium load, and E-F heavy load [7,26].

For each road segment $r \in R$, the travel cost depends on its length, current vehicle count, and congestion level. Thresholds u_r^l, u_r^m, and u_r^h define load boundaries, and coefficients l_r, m_r, h_r, and C_r are used to calculate cost at different load levels. We consider two cost functions, *strict* that penalises all vehicles routed on a segment by a given traffic intensity coefficient, and *mild* that penalises only vehicles exceeding the thresholds.

This strict cost function is defined as the following piecewise linear function [20]:

$$\begin{aligned} C(r,n) &= n \cdot l_r \quad (n \in [0, u_r^l]), \\ & n \cdot m_r \quad (n \in (u_r^l, u_r^m]), \\ & n \cdot h_r \quad (n \in (u_r^m, u_r^h]), \\ & n \cdot C_r \quad (n \in (u_r^h, \infty)) \end{aligned} \tag{1}$$

The mild cost function is defined as the following piecewise linear function:

$$\begin{aligned} C(r,n) &= n \cdot l_r \quad n \in [0, u_r^l]), \\ & u_r^l \cdot l_r + (n - u_r^l) \cdot m_r \quad (n \in (u_r^l, u_r^m]), \\ & u_r^l \cdot l_r + (u_r^m - u_r^l) \cdot m_r + (n - u_r^m) \cdot h_r \quad (n \in (u_r^m, u_r^h]), \\ & u_r^l \cdot l_r + (u_r^m - u_r^l) \cdot m_r + (u_r^h - u_r^m) \cdot h_r + (n - u_r^h) \cdot C_r \\ & (n \in (u_r^h, \infty)]) \end{aligned} \tag{2}$$

3.3 Network Simplification Method

Centralised Traffic Routing plans routes individually for each vehicle, with scalability highly dependent on network size [6].

To reduce computation time, a promising set of routes may be pre-generated for specific traffic flows, allowing for a tolerable deviation from the optimal solution [25,26]. Promising routes should not be more suboptimal than some given bound. Such bounded-suboptimal routes can be generated using the Floyd-Warshall algorithm with branch-and-bound techniques, or through improved A* algorithms with heuristic functions based on Euclidean distance [26].

Further simplification can be achieved by constructing a diverse set of routes that aim to avoid common bottlenecks. These routes are clustered using the Jaccard similarity index, and a representative route – typically the shortest one – is selected from each cluster [26].

Although our framework is built upon mixed-integer programming and macroscopic traffic modeling, the aforementioned simplification strategies have demonstrated strong practical applicability.

4 Centralised Traffic Routing MIP Model

The Mixed-Integer Programming (MIP) model we propose draws on the principles of multicommodity flow problems [21], a well-established class of network flow models [1] that handle the simultaneous movement of multiple commodities. These problems form a core component of optimization theory and are widely applied in areas such as telecommunications, logistics, and transportation [12]. Our model builds upon traditional multicommodity flow formulations by integrating routing cost functions that can be continuous, convex, and piecewise linear – features that effectively capture the variability in urban traffic conditions.

This refinement is particularly critical for centralized traffic routing systems, which require rapid decision-making in response to constantly changing conditions. As such, the model is tailored for real-time use in fast-paced urban environments.

The MIP model that we describe in the following subsections was introduced in the previous paper [20].

4.1 Multiflow MIP Model

Given a Centralised Traffic Routing instance $\chi = (\mathcal{N}, V, O, D, C)$, the initial task is to determine the individual traffic flows. Each flow is characterized by an origin–destination junction pair that defines vehicle entry and exit points within the controlled area. A traffic flow i is denoted as (o^i, d^i, n^i), where $o^i, d^i \in N$ are the origin and destination nodes for flow i, and $n^i = |v \in V \mid O(v) = o^i, D(v) = d^i|$ indicates the number of vehicles in that flow. Only non-zero flows (i.e., those with $n^i > 0$) are included. The total number of such flows is denoted by N_F. For each flow i, we define $E^i \subseteq E$ as the subset of edges forming the reduced subnetwork determined during preprocessing (see Sect. 3.3).

To represent traffic routing within this network, we introduce decision variables $x^i_{u,v}$, which denote the number of vehicles in flow i that travel along edge $(u, v) \in E^i$. For each $i \in 1, \ldots, N_F$, the following constraints are imposed in the model:

$$\forall(u,v) \in E : x^i_{u,v} \in \mathbb{N} \cup \{0\},$$

$$\sum w \in V,\ (o^i, w) \in E^i x^i_{o^i,w} = \sum_{(w,d^i)\in E^i} x^i_{w,d^i} \tag{3}$$

$$\sum_{(o^i,w)\in E^i} x^i_{o^i,w} = n_i \tag{4}$$

$$\sum_{(v,o^i)\in E^i} x^i_{v,o^i} = 0 \tag{5}$$

$$\sum_{(d^i,w)\in E^i} x^i_{d^i,w} = 0 \tag{6}$$

$$\sum_{(u,v)\in E^i,\ u\neq o^i} x^i_{u,v} = \sum_{(v,w)\in E^i,\ w\neq d^i} x^i_{v,w} \tag{7}$$

$$\forall(u,v) \in E \setminus E^i : x^i_{u,v} = 0 \tag{8}$$

Equation (3) guarantees that the total flow leaving the origin node matches the total flow arriving at the destination node. Equation (4) ensures that precisely n_i vehicles are dispatched from the origin. Equations (5) and (6) prevent vehicles from re-entering the origin or entering the network from the destination. Equation (7) upholds the principle of flow conservation at all intermediate junctions, excluding the origin and destination. Equation (8) restricts flow to only those edges that are part of the preprocessed subnetwork E^i.

The primary goal of our model is to minimize the overall cost of distributing traffic flows throughout the road network. The initial cost formulations, introduced in Sect. 3.2, result in a quadratic objective due to their dependence on traffic volume. To improve computational efficiency and solver compatibility, we transform this into a linear objective using an appropriate approximation. The revised linear objective function is expressed as:

$$\min \sum_{r\in R} y_r$$

The cost associated with each edge is a function of the total number of vehicles using it. Since multiple directed edges can correspond to a single physical road segment, and the cost grows nonlinearly with traffic intensity, we apply a piecewise linear approximation. This method breaks traffic volumes into discrete intervals (e.g., light, moderate, heavy, congested), each represented by a binary indicator. Using this approach, we linearize the *strict* cost function for each road segment r as follows:

$$y_r \geq l_r \sum_{i=1}^{N_F} \sum_{(u,v)\ r=\rho((u,v))} x_{u,v}^i - M(1 - z_r^l) \tag{9}$$

$$y_r \geq m_r \sum_{i=1}^{N_F} \sum_{(u,v)\ r=\rho((u,v))} x_{u,v}^i - M(1 - z_r^m) \tag{10}$$

$$y_r \geq h_r \sum_{i=1}^{N_F} \sum_{(u,v)\ r=\rho((u,v))} x_{u,v}^i - M(1 - z_r^h) \tag{11}$$

$$y_r \geq C_r \sum_{i=1}^{N_F} \sum_{(u,v)\ r=\rho((u,v))} x_{u,v}^i - M(1 - z_r^C) \tag{12}$$

In this formulation, $x_{u,v}^i$ represents the number of vehicles from flow i traveling along edge (u, v), and the function $\rho((u, v))$ maps each edge to its corresponding road segment r. The constants l_r, m_r, h_r, and C_r denote the cost rates associated with four distinct levels of traffic density on segment r: light, medium, heavy, and congested, respectively. The binary variables z_r^l, z_r^m, z_r^h, and z_r^C indicate which traffic intensity level is active for a given segment. This linearisation strategy is referred to as a strict cost function because it assigns the entire traffic on a segment the highest applicable cost tier, based on the total number of vehicles present.

To approximate the original nonlinear cost function with a piecewise linear one, each binary variable is tied to the cost variable y_r through constraints (9) – (12). A large constant M is used to ensure that only one binary variable is active for each segment. This exclusivity is enforced by a constraint (see Equation (17)) requiring the sum of all binary variables for a segment to equal one. As a result, each segment is assigned exactly one traffic level, allowing the linearized model to mimic the behavior of the original nonlinear function.

Empirical testing showed that the model performs best when the large constant M is set to ten million.

The alternative *mild* cost function models traffic costs based on gradually increasing load levels – similar to the methodology used in the planning strategy. In this formulation, costs start low for light traffic and increase progressively through medium and heavy levels, with each additional unit of traffic beyond the highest threshold incurring substantially greater cost. This method is described in the following section, effectively adapting Eq (2):

$$y_r \geq l_r \sum_{i=1}^{N_F} \sum_{\substack{(u,v) \\ r=\rho((u,v))}} x_{u,v}^i - M(1 - z_r^l) \tag{13}$$

$$y_r \geq u_l^r \cdot l_r + m_r \left(\sum_{i=1}^{N_F} \sum_{\substack{(u,v) \\ r=\rho((u,v))}} x_{u,v}^i - u_l^r \right) - M(1 - z_r^m) \tag{14}$$

$$y_r \geq u_l^r \cdot l_r + (u_m^r - u_l^r) \cdot m_r + h_r \left(\sum_{i=1}^{N_F} \sum_{\substack{(u,v) \\ r=\rho((u,v))}} x_{u,v}^i - u_m^r \right) - M(1 - z_r^h) \tag{15}$$

$$y_r \geq u_l^r \cdot l_r + (u_m^r - u_l^r) \cdot m_r + (u_h^r - u_m^r) \cdot h_r + C_r \left(\sum_{i=1}^{N_F} \sum_{\substack{(u,v) \\ r=\rho((u,v))}} x_{u,v}^i - u_h^r \right) - M(1 - z_r^C) \tag{16}$$

The thresholds u_r^l, u_r^m, and u_r^h define the upper limits on the number of vehicles that correspond to light, medium, and heavy traffic levels, respectively, for a given road segment r.

To accurately model this piecewise classification of traffic intensity, the following constraints are introduced for each segment $r \in R$:

$$\begin{gathered} z_r^l \in 0,1, \quad z_r^m \in 0,1, \quad z_r^h \in 0,1, \quad z_r^C \in 0,1 \\ z_r^l + z_r^m + z_r^h + z_r^C = 1 \end{gathered} \tag{17}$$

$$\sum_{i=1}^{N_F} \sum_{(u,v)\ r=\rho((u,v))} x_{u,v}^i \leq z_r^l u_r^l + z_r^m u_r^m + z_r^h u_r^h + z_r^C M \tag{18}$$

$$\sum_{i=1}^{N_F} \sum_{(u,v)\ r=\rho((u,v))} x_{u,v}^i \geq z_r^m u_r^l + z_r^h u_r^m + z_r^C u_r^h \tag{19}$$

Constraint (17) guarantees that each road segment is assigned exactly one traffic intensity level. Constraints (18) and (19) establish the upper and lower vehicle bounds, respectively, for each traffic level based on the aggregate vehicle count from all traffic flows.

While Constraint (19) is not strictly necessary for the correctness of the model, its inclusion enhances solver efficiency by tightening the continuous relaxation. This results in improved convergence rates and reduced computation times.

```
Function SearchRoute(p, j, i, all_routes):
    outgoing_edges = {(j, j') | (j, j') ∈ E, x^i_{j,j'} > 0};
    if outgoing_edges = ∅ then
        ;                                                   /* We extracted a route */
        veh_count ← min_{(j_x, j_y) ∈ p} x^i_{j_x, j_y};
        if veh_count > 0 then
            all_routes ← all_routes ∪ {(p, veh_count)};
            ∀(j_x, j_y) ∈ p : x^i_{j_x, j_y} ← x^i_{j_x, j_y} − veh_count;
        end
    else
        if ∃(j, j') ∈ p then
            ;                                                   /* We found a loop */
            p^j ← p.subpath_from(j);
            veh_count ← min_{(j_x, j_y) ∈ p^j} x^i_{j_x, j_y};
            ∀(j_x, j_y) ∈ p^j : x^i_{j_x, j_y} ← x^i_{j_x, j_y} − veh_count;
        else
            for (j, j') ∈ outgoing_edges do
                p.append((j, j'));
                SearchRoute(p, j', i, all_routes);
            end
        end
    end
SearchRoute(⟨⟩, start_junction, i, {});
```

Algorithm 1. Algorithm for extracting routes for a given traffic flow. Taken from [20].

4.2 Deriving Vehicle Routes

The MIP model output specifies the distribution of traffic flows across the road network. In particular, the decision variables x represent how many vehicles from each flow traverse each road segment. However, this information alonc does not reconstruct full vehicle routes, which are essential for downstream tasks like analysis or simulation.

To derive complete routes for each traffic flow, we apply the method outlined in Algorithm 1, introduced in the conference paper [20]. The procedure is executed separately for each traffic flow i, leveraging the MIP output, the network topology, and the flow's origin junction.

At its core, the algorithm performs a Depth-First Search (DFS) through recursive calls to the function `SearchRoute`. During traversal, the current route under construction is stored in p, and j denotes the current junction.

In each recursive invocation, the algorithm identifies outgoing edges from junction j that still carry a positive number of vehicles for flow i, i.e., those with $x^i_{j,j'} > 0$ (Line 2). If no such edges are found, a destination has been reached. In this case, the path p is recorded as a completed route, and the number of vehicles assigned to it, `veh_count`, is computed as the minimum of the flow values along edges in p (since excess vehicles on certain edges might belong to alternate paths). These flow values are then reduced by `veh_count` to reflect the route extraction (Lines 3–6).

If an outgoing edge already appears in the path p, a cycle has been detected (Line 10). Such cycles may result from suboptimal solutions generated by the MIP solver, possibly due to time constraints. The loop is identified as a subpath starting from junction j, and the minimum flow along this subpath is deducted from the corresponding edges to eliminate the cycle (Lines 11–13).

If no loop is present, the algorithm continues by exploring all eligible outgoing edges. For each such edge, it extends the path and makes a recursive call from the next junction (Lines 15–18). Through this process, all valid vehicle routes and their corresponding counts are systematically derived from the MIP solution.

This recursive extraction method guarantees that all feasible, acyclic routes are identified and that vehicle allocations are accurately represented throughout the network, aligning with the flow distribution derived from the MIP solution. For more details, see the conference paper [19].

Once Algorithm 1 has been applied to every traffic flow, the final step is to assign the extracted routes to individual vehicles. For each flow, we identify the set of vehicles associated with it. We then iterate through the `all_routes` collection (generated by Algorithm 1), assigning each route to the appropriate number of unallocated vehicles. It is important to emphasize that this route-to-vehicle mapping is not necessarily unique in cases where multiple routes exist for a given flow. In our implementation, we assign routes in the order they appear in `all_routes`, and vehicles are mapped in ascending order of their identifiers.

5 Experimental Evaluation

This section presents our experimental analysis of the proposed MIP-based framework for Centralised Traffic Routing. We evaluate two strategies—*strict* and *mild*—and compare them against a planning-based method enhanced with "smart route" preprocessing [26], as well as against a decentralised baseline, DUO (Dynamic User Optimal), implemented in the SUMO traffic simulator [17].

The primary evaluation metrics are the percentage of arrived vehicles and average travel time, as reported by the SUMO simulation. To offer a broader performance profile, we also include average route distance, average vehicle speed, and expected emissions of CO_2, CO and NOx. It is important to note that while SUMO incorporates real-world traffic effects—such as signalized intersections—these are not explicitly modeled within our MIP formulations. All centralized routing strategies are evaluated offline: that is, all vehicle routes are precomputed prior to the start of the simulation.

5.1 Scenarios and Settings

We first evaluate our method on two synthetic benchmarks: New York (covering the area between Grand Concourse and Sheridan Boulevard) and Sydney (southeast of Centennial Park), both introduced in [26] and shown in Fig. 1. The

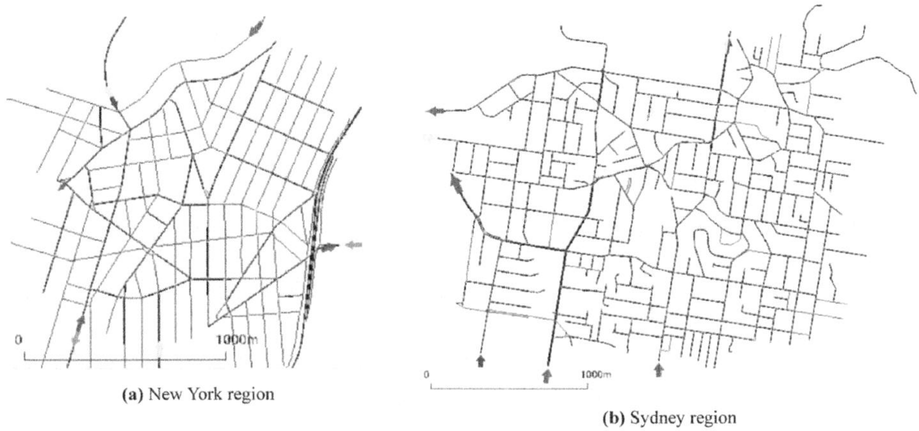

Fig. 1. The New York (left) and Sydney (right) scenarios. Colored arrows indicate sample traffic flows and their entry/exit points. Scenarios adopted from [26].

Fig. 2. Dublin metropolitan area (left) and selected central subregion used for evaluation (right). Taken from [20].

New York dataset contains 16 distinct scenarios, and Sydney includes 40. Each scenario defines different origin–destination (OD) patterns and traffic profiles, either static or gradually increasing flow intensity.

Each scenario spans a 1-hour time window divided into 30-second intervals, resulting in 120 routing episodes. New York scenarios include 5 traffic flows per episode; Sydney scenarios contain 4. Flow intensities range from 760 to 1208 vehicles per hour. SUMO simulates a total of 2 h for each scenario, beginning with an empty network. Vehicles start entering the simulation at time zero.

In addition to the synthetic cases, we also assess performance on historical data of two real-world city networks: central Dublin [14] and central Luxem-

Fig. 3. Luxembourg metropolitan area (left) and the region selected for experiments (right).

bourg [9]. We selected the most congested area, marked in orange in Fig. 2. For Luxembourg, we identified a region with high traffic intensity, highlighted in red in Fig. 3. Both cities are evaluated during the morning peak (7:00–9:00 AM), also divided into 30-s episodes, yielding 238 routing instances per city. The Dublin scenario includes 10,778 vehicles in total; Luxembourg, 4,712. The simulation setup mirrors the synthetic benchmarks: 2-h duration, empty network at start, and route precomputation.

As described in Sect. 3.3, we preprocessed the original road network in two ways. One involves generating bounded suboptimal routes for each traffic flow (the bound was set to 1.3 as in [26]), which we later denote as BR. The other "smart routes" preprocessing method involves clustering of potential routes based on their diversity (i.e., having fewer road segments in common) and selecting the shortest route for each cluster [26]. This preprocessing method is later denoted as SR.

The thresholds determining the level of traffic intensity for road segments are derived from the physical capacity of the road segment, measured by the number of "standard" vehicles that can physically fit into the road segment while considering a minimum safe distance between them. Light traffic intensity of a road segment corresponds to the number of routed vehicles up to 40% of its capacity. Medium traffic intensity of a road segment corresponds to the number of routed vehicles from 40% to 60% of its capacity. Heavy traffic intensity of a road segment corresponds to the number of routed vehicles higher than 60% of its capacity but not more than the capacity. The congested traffic intensity of a road segment corresponds to the number of routed vehicles higher than its capacity. These thresholds are determined analogously to [27]. The cost of a road segment (for a single vehicle) with light traffic intensity equals the length of the road segment. The penalty for a road segment (for a single vehicle) with medium traffic intensity is 10, and with heavy traffic intensity is 100. The penalty for a road segment (for a single vehicle) with congested traffic intensity is 100000. Note that the cost and traffic intensity penalties are determined accordingly to [7,26].

For solving the MIP model, we used the global nonlinear solver Gurobi[2]. Since we need to obtain the solution within a certain time limit (one episode considers 30 s of traffic), process it, and send it back, the runtime is limited to 25 s. For the planning-based approach, we use the Mercury planner [10] with a time limit of 25 s as well. In case we fail to find any solution for a given episode within the time limit, we assign the shortest routes (for New York and Sydney), or the routes specified in the historical datasets (for Dublin and Luxembourg), for all the vehicles considered in the failed planning episode.

In addition to performance metrics, we also collect data on traffic flow structure, emission levels, and statistical distributions of routing decisions using two classification criteria. This extended evaluation allows us to quantify not only route efficiency but also environmental and structural properties of traffic under different routing strategies. The experiments were run on a computer equipped with AMD Ryzen 5000 7, with a memory limit of 32GB[3].

6 Results

6.1 General Characteristic Simulation Results

Table 1 presents the experimental results[4]. For New York and Sydney, the outcomes are averaged across all evaluated scenarios (16 for New York and 40 for Sydney), each featuring different traffic flows. The MIP approach successfully solved every episode (i.e., instance of the centralized traffic routing problem) under both BR and SR preprocessing, although not always optimally. Notably, MIP demonstrates considerably better scalability than the planning-based method, particularly in the BR setting, where only a limited number of episodes were solved by planning, and not always optimally.

Trip Duration. Average trip duration – the primary optimization criterion – is minimized most effectively by the strict MIP approach under BR preprocessing. In contrast, the planning-based method benefits from SR preprocessing, which precomputes several promising routes per traffic flow and improves coverage (i.e., the percentage of episodes solved). However, this SR configuration proves too restrictive for MIP and leads to suboptimal solutions, as reflected in the results, with the sole exception of the mild case in Dublin. Compared to the Naive approach, which uses shortest paths in New York and Sydney, the best MIP improves trip duration by 28.5% and more than 50%, respectively. Even in Dublin, where the Naive method uses historical traffic data instead of shortest paths, MIP still

[2] https://www.gurobi.com/documentation/.

[3] Benchmark data are provided here: https://github.com/xankr/utc-mip-icaart2025.

[4] Note that the results vary from the results published in the previous paper [20] due to the use of different version of the SUMO simulator.

Table 1. Simulation results across all city benchmarks. "Solved" indicates the percentage of episodes completed (not necessarily optimally). "Distance", "Speed", and "Duration" refer to average trip distance, speed, and duration. "Arrived" refers to the percentage of vehicles that arrived at their destinations. "CO_2", "CO", "NOx" refer to average emissions of carbon dioxide, carbon monoxide, and various nitrogen oxides.

Parameters	Baseline		MIP Strict		MIP Mild		Planning	
	Naive	DUO	BR	SR	BR	SR	BR	SR
	New York							
Solved [%]	-	-	**100**	**100**	**100**	**100**	9.1	74.5
Distance [m]	**1915**	2359	2385	2136	2365	2143	2042	2361
Speed [m/s]	1.95	2.73	**3.18**	2.69	3.14	2.68	2.26	3.07
Duration [s]	1669	1366	**1193**	1388	1222	1395	1605	1235
Arrived [%]	33.5	44	48.1	41.4	47.5	41.7	39.25	**50.6**
CO_2[kg]	4487.9	3839	**3413**	3855	3486	3876	4337	3396
CO[kg]	245.9	198.7	**171**	203	176	204	235	172
NOx[kg]	2	1.7	**1.5**	1.7	**1.5**	1.7	1.97	**1.5**
	Sydney							
Solved [%]	-	-	**100**	**100**	**100**	**100**	1.77	46.9
Distance [m]	2612	2971	3002	2901	2952	2880	**2454**	2770
Speed [m/s]	3.37	5.53	6.74	5.75	**6.75**	5.7	3.35	3.86
Duration [s]	1328	758	**641**	761	663	752	1245	1160
Arrived [%]	57.1	82.7	64.5	81.9	67.95	**84**	64.2	63.9
CO_2[kg]	3620	2209.7	**1875**	2207	1915	2194	3338	3189
CO[kg]	183.9	92.6	**71.6**	93.3	74.7	92.7	170	155.4
NOx[kg]	1.6	0.9	**0.8**	0.96	0.83	0.96	1.49	1.4
	Dublin							
Solved [%]	-	-	**100**	**100**	**100**	**100**	0	96.6
Distance [m]	828	891	**812**	822	824	826	828	843
Speed [m/s]	5.13	**6.16**	5.92	5.52	5.78	5.79	5.13	5.97
Duration [s]	360	**198**	276	283	267	235	360	209
Arrived [%]	84.6	94	75.2	73.6	77.07	84.2	84.6	**97.7**
CO_2[kg]	889	**487.7**	682	693	660	567	889	511.1
CO[kg]	45.1	**19**	32.3	32.8	30.7	25.4	45.1	21.1
NOx[kg]	0.39	**0.2**	0.3	0.3	0.28	0.25	0.39	0.22
	Luxembourg							
Solved [%]	-	-	**100**	99.6	**100**	99.6	0	**100**
Distance [m]	988	**960**	994	992	**960**	986	988	986
Speed [m/s]	7.97	**7.86**	6.76	6.57	5.92	6.64	7.97	6.24
Duration [s]	**103**	107	123	126	204	128	103	170
Arrived [%]	98.8	**99.9**	98.4	98.5	85.9	98.59	98.8	89.72
CO_2[kg]	327.9	**326.6**	376	384	579	386	327.9	485.4
CO[kg]	**6.8**	7.6	9.8	10.3	23	10.5	6.8	16.6
NOx[kg]	**0.13**	**0.13**	0.156	0.16	0.25	0.16	0.13	0.2

Table 2. Average total runtime (PT [s]), average number of optimally solved scenarios (OPT [%]) and average optimality gap (GAP [%]) of the MIP models.

	New York		Sydney		Dublin		Luxembourg	
	BR	SR	BR	SR	BR	SR	BR	SR
	Strict							
PT	328	62	247	45	1005	452	1061	393
OPT	100	100	99.8	100	97.1	100	99.58	100
GAP	0	0	0.95	0	2.8	0	0.021	0
	Mild							
PT	2773	1337	2157	481	3123	2105	4059	1531
OPT	14.2	82.5	49	91.9	60.92	80.67	58.9	93.3
GAP	0.009	0.003	0.05	0.008	0.011	0.0006	0.011	0.005

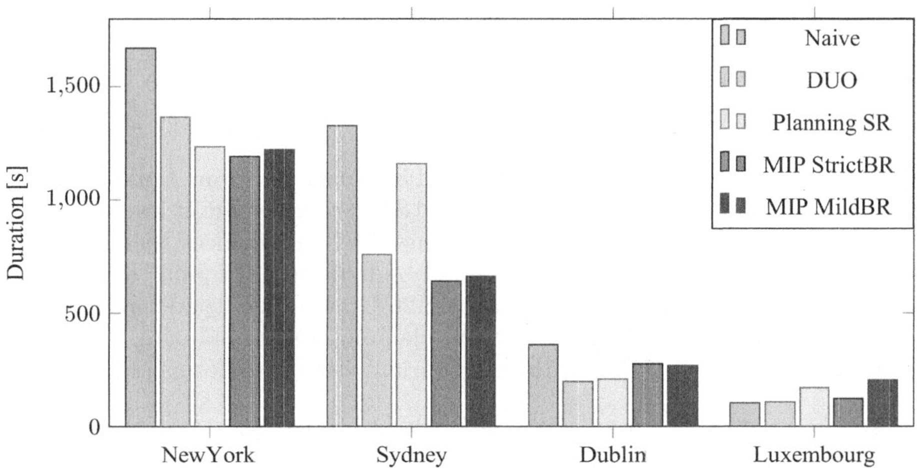

Fig. 4. Average trip duration comparison across methods and scenarios.

achieves a 34.72% improvement. The only exception is in Luxembourg, which performs worse by 24.27%. When compared to DUO, the best MIP-based model performs better in New York and Sydney (by 12.66% and 15.44%, strict BR) but underperforms in Dublin and Luxembourg (by approximately 18.7%, mild SR and 14.95%, strict BR, respectively). Interestingly, in Luxembourg, the Naive approach surpasses DUO, indicating the strength of historically informed routing in that setting. A visual comparison of average trip durations across methods is provided in Fig. 4.

Arrival Rate. The percentage of vehicles arriving on time varies significantly between cities. In New York, the BR approach outperforms SR and DUO (48.1% vs. 41.4% and 44%) and approaches the performance of the planning-based method (50.6%). In Sydney, SR achieves the highest result (81.9%), closely followed by DUO (82.7%). In Dublin, the planning method is superior (96.3%), ahead of DUO (94%) and BR (75.2%). In Luxembourg, DUO proves most effective (99.9%), while MIP and planning methods fail to outperform even the historical Naive approach (98.8%).

Trip Distance. All centralized approaches tend to produce longer routes to reduce congestion on frequently used road segments. For example, in New York, centralized routes are over 20% longer than those generated by the Naive method. However, this is offset by a more than 50% increase in average speed, leading to reduced travel times overall. In Dublin, average trip distances for centralized methods are comparable to those of the Naive baseline, yet they still yield better trip durations. For BR planning in Dublin and Luxembourg, results match Naive since no episodes were solved, while SR planning in Dublin performed very well, by only 5.56% worse duration than DUO, but at the same time, for Luxembourg it is worse by as much as 58.88%. DUO generates routes approximately 10% longer, contributing to more efficient road usage through higher average speeds – except in Luxembourg, where DUO underperforms across all metrics, despite producing slightly shorter routes (by about 3%).

Strict vs. Mild Cost Assignment. The mild approach performs worse than the strict version in most cases. In New York and Sydney under BR, it leads to longer durations (by 2.43% and 3.43%), while under SR, differences remain within 1–1.5%. In Dublin, where flows are small and diverse, the mild approach is advantageous: BR improves durations by 3.26%, and SR outperforms BR with a 17% gain, making it closer to DUO and planning. In Luxembourg, differences are minor (a 1.5% decline), but the mild variant still outperforms planning.

Route Length Patterns. In New York and Sydney, BR routes under the mild variant are shorter (by 0.84% and 1.67%), while SR routes are slightly longer. In Dublin, route lengths increase for both BR (1.48%) and SR (0.49%). In Luxembourg, SR slightly improves route length (by 0.6%). Interestingly, the mild approach results in a higher percentage of vehicles arriving on time in nearly all scenarios, with the only exception being New York under BR.

Emissions. Using SUMO, we extract post-simulation data on emissions of carbon dioxide (CO_2), carbon monoxide (CO), and nitrogen oxides (NOx). For New York and Sydney, the mean emission of type E is computed as:

$$E_{\text{avg}} = \frac{1}{M \cdot N} \sum_{j=1}^{N} \sum_{i=1}^{M} e^{i,j} \tag{20}$$

where M is the number of vehicles, N the number of scenarios, and $e^{i,j}$ is the total emission of vehicle i in scenario j. For larger-scale scenarios like Dublin and Luxembourg (single-scenario), the average emission is computed as:

$$E_{\text{avg}} = \frac{1}{M} \sum_{i=1}^{M} e^i \tag{21}$$

These expressions are used for all emission types. Among them, CO_2 is the most abundant (and a major contributor to global warming), while CO and NOx are more toxic and hazardous to health. Overall, for New York and Sydney, MIP models are more preferable in terms of emissions compared to Naive and DUO, for New York – by 24% and 11% for CO_2, by 30.5% and 14% for CO, by 25% and 11.8% for NOx; and for Sydney – by 48.2% and 15% for CO_2, by 61% and 22.7% for CO, by 50% and 11.1% for NOx. In Dublin, the situation in DUO is much better, as its statistical indicators exceed the rest, which is reflected in emissions - even the best MIP solution is worse than DUO by 16.26% for CO_2, by 33.7% for CO and by 25% for NOx. In Luxembourg the situation is similar, although there it is the other way around, Naive has better results than DUO (although a little bit worse in CO_2) and comparing them with the best MIP solution – it gave us worse results – by 14.67% for CO_2, by 44.12% for CO and by 20% for NOx.

The data show that BR preprocessing consistently results in lower emissions than SR for New York and Sydney: CO_2 emissions are reduced by about 12% and 16%, CO by 17.29% and 27.14%, and NO by 13.33% and 17.79%, respectively. Dublin presents an inverse pattern, where SR preprocessing yields lower emissions (e.g., 5.37% less CO_2, 7.62% less CO, and 5.17% less NO). In Luxembourg, there are exceptions - mild BR, as it is not good in overall statistics, also produces the most emissions (for 53% more than with the strict cost).

6.2 Statistical Evaluation of MIP-Based Models

We provide a detailed statistical comparison of the MIP models based on strict and mild (close-to-planning) routing strategies. The evaluation relies on three main sources: the city-specific traffic parameters (Table 3), and quality indicators of individual vehicle trips (Table 4).

Table 3 reports additional simulation statistics related to vehicle behavior. These include average minimum and maximum trip distances (min_avg_D, max_avg_D) and durations (min_avg_T, max_avg_T), average ranges (avg_range_D, avg_range_T), overall averages (tot_avg_D, tot_avg_T), and medians of per-scenario averages (med_avg_D, med_avg_T). We also measure two critical metrics related to congestion: the average proportion of time lost in traffic jams ($\text{avg\_T}_{\text{wait}}$) and the total time lost from all causes ($\text{avg\_T}_{\text{loss}}$). The results show that in most scenarios, medians are close to minimum averages, suggesting a large number of effective solutions. Luxembourg is an exception, with a right-skewed distribution of performance, where a few exceptionally good solutions lower the median significantly.

Table 3. Statistical simulation metrics of the MIP models: max/min/average trip distance and duration, their ranges and medians. Timeloss refers to total lost driving time; waiting time reflects time spent in traffic jams.

	New York		Sydney		Dublin		Lux.	
	BR	SR	BR	SR	BR	SR	BR	SR
	Strict							
max_avg_D[m]	3297±147	2801±99	3733±379	3301±292	973±469	970±460	942±449	949±455
min_avg_D[m]	2237±69	2232±71	2629±203	2629±202	909±442	908±436	887±426	896±434
avg_range_D[m]	1060±115	569±42	1103±248	672±161	64±108	62±107	54±123	53±120
tot_avg_D[m]	2579±93	2433±86	2970±239	2887±237	940±450	937±443	913±432	922±440
med_avg_D[m]	2573	2428	3043	2948	948	954	924	933
max_avg_T[s]	4108±574	3668±558	1724±804	2060±734	537±722	538±636	131±87	130±85
min_avg_T[s]	262±16	265±16	215±17	224±21	255±382	247±317	108±68	109±69
avg_range_T[s]	3845±571	3402±553	1509±799	1836±730	282±636	291±581	22±59	21±56
tot_avg_T[s]	1594±225	1683±250	619±223	772±228	348±442	341±357	117±70	118±71
med_avg_T[s]	1582	1691	587	734	202	229	110	111
avg_T_{loss}	0.83±0.01	0.85±0.01	0.56±0.07	0.63±0.05	0.39±0.25	0.42±0.26	0.357±0.18	0.36±0.18
avg_T_{wait}	0.61±0.02	0.65±0.03	0.35±0.08	0.4±0.05	0.24±0.26	0.27±0.26	0.18±0.18	0.18±0.18
	Mild							
max_avg_D[m]	3270±131	2778±109	3679±379	3259±298	969±455	970±448	928±454	938±447
min_avg_D[m]	2229±70	2230±71	2625±201	2628±198	911±436	911±427	877±431	887±426
avg_range_D[m]	1041±106	547±51	1053±248	631±162	57±100	58±102	50±117	51±111
tot_avg_D[m]	2545±91	2423±85	2938±242	2868±239	939±442	940±433	901±437	912±432
med_avg_D[m]	2548	2424	2994	2930	953	964	902	925
max_avg_T[s]	4022±670	3681±548	1759±975	2100±768	500±648	447±550	282±427	133±89
min_avg_T[s]	262±14	267±14	215±16	224±20	251±364	230±292	179±283	108±66
avg_range_T[s]	3760±666	3414±544	1543±971	1876±763	249±561	216±492	103±337	24±64
tot_avg_T[s]	1624±213	1709±267	633±276	772±226	337±408	298±319	210±293	118±69
med_avg_D[s]	1637	1711	579	711	210	206	116	114
avg_T_{loss}	0.83±0.01	0.85±0.01	0.57±0.07	0.64±0.04	0.4±0.25	0.4±0.24	0.4±0.24	0.37±0.19
avg_T_{wait}	0.62±0.01	0.65±0.03	0.36±0.08	0.42±0.05	0.25±0.26	0.24±0.24	0.24±0.26	0.19±0.18

Comparing the two cost strategies, the strict penalty approach (maximum cost per exceeded vehicle count) performs better in cities with large flows (e.g., New York, Sydney). Conversely, the soft penalty model, which penalizes only excess vehicles, is more effective in cities like Dublin and Luxembourg, characterized by numerous small flows. This highlights the need for potential aggregation of small flows to improve MIP efficiency. Interestingly, SR preprocessing generally results in shorter routes and tighter distance spreads compared to BR, except in Luxembourg, where the difference is negligible. These patterns persist across both cost functions, depending primarily on the structural layout of each city. Despite optimization, the simulation reveals that a significant portion of travel time is lost. In the worst case (New York, strict SR), vehicles lose up to 85% of their trip time, 65% of which is due to traffic jams. In the best case (Luxembourg, strict BR), the loss rate is still 36%. On average, vehicles lose about half of their time in transit, with congestion accounting for around two-thirds of this loss. Specifically, the total loss rate averages 0.48 for strict and 0.56 for mild models, while congestion-related loss contributes 0.37 and 0.34, respectively. These inefficiencies significantly impact average speed and duration, even though travel distances remain relatively consistent. Notably, BR shows better results in New York and Sydney, while SR performs better in Dublin and Luxembourg.

Table 4. Share of vehicles by trip quality: $G_{T,D}$ – better than average in both duration and distance; $B_{T,D}$ – worse in both; $G_T B_D$ – better in duration, worse in distance; $B_T G_D$ – better in distance, worse in duration.

	New York		Sydney		Dublin		Lux.	
	BR	SR	BR	SR	BR	SR	BR	SR
	Strict							
$G_{T,D}$[%]	52.4±9.2	55.8±8.2	42.8±12.4	42.1±10.5	56.09±0.55	55±0.55	31.5±0.54	31.88±0.54
$B_{T,D}$[%]	13.3±6	8.7±3.2	25.4±9.8	21.4±7.9	7.9±0.3	14.5±0.39	42.4±0.57	43.3±0.57
$B_T G_D$[%]	4.9±2.8	17.6±5.6	8.9±6.2	10.8±7.2	7.2±0.28	6.39±0.27	4.5±0.24	5.1±0.25
$G_T B_D$[%]	29.2±8.6	17.8±2.7	22.6±11.8	25.5±10.6	28.7±0.5	23.9±0.47	21.5±0.47	19.6±0.46
	Mild							
$G_{T,D}$[%]	52.56±7.5	54.8±7.9	41±10.65	40±10.3	55.3±0.54	54.79±0.52	35±0.59	30.99±0.53
$B_{T,D}$[%]	13.4±4.6	8.5±3.1	27.6±12.3	21.4±8.2	11.18±0.34	13.62±0.35	17±0.46	42.7±0.57
$B_T G_D$[%]	5.2±2.9	17.5±5.4	8.8±6.3	11±6.9	6.4±0.26	5.84±0.24	2.92±0.21	5±0.25
$G_T B_D$[%]	28.7±6.7	19±4.2	22.4±11.4	27.4±10.4	27±0.48	25.7±0.45	45±0.62	21.25±0.47

We also analyze the quality of individual routing decisions by calculating the share of vehicles falling into quartiles based on whether their travel time and distance are above or below average. The key indicators include:

$$G_{T,D} = \text{Vehicles with both travel time and distance below average,} \quad (22)$$

$$B_{T,D} = \text{Vehicles with both travel time and distance above average,} \quad (23)$$

$$G_T B_D = \text{Vehicles with below-average time but above-average distance,} \quad (24)$$

$$B_T G_D = \text{Vehicles with above-average time but below-average distance.} \quad (25)$$

These values are reported in Table 4. In Dublin (BR, strict), 56.09% of vehicles fall into the best quadrant ($G_{T,D}$). On average across cities, this metric is about 46% for strict and 45.5% for mild models. Vehicles with shorter travel time but longer distance make up around 23.6% (strict) and 27% (mild), indicating that in roughly 70–72% of cases, trip duration is better than average – an encouraging result. Despite good statistics, Luxembourg presents a notable anomaly. Here, the proportion of vehicles falling into the worst quadrant ($B_{T,D}$) reaches 43.3% (SR, strict), even though average duration indicators remain competitive. This paradox is explained by a few highly successful routing outcomes skewing the median downward. The mild approach in Luxembourg yields slightly better results in terms of routing efficiency, but at the cost of fewer vehicles reaching their destinations. Finally, the share of vehicles with shorter distance but longer duration is relatively low – 8.17% (strict) and 7.83% (mild) on average – with a maximum of 17.6% in New York (strict SR). Across most cities, SR preprocessing leads to better outcomes in terms of route length, except in Dublin where the advantage is minor. These findings support the effectiveness of preprocessing and cost-function choice depending on city structure and traffic characteristics.

6.3 Discussion

The results demonstrate that MIP-based techniques represent a viable and scalable approach to centralized traffic routing, outperforming planning-based methods in most large-flow scenarios. A key advantage lies in the macrosimulation-level reasoning, where traffic is modeled in terms of flows rather than individual vehicles. This abstraction helps mitigate symmetries inherent in microsimulation. Since the objective function is indifferent to which specific vehicle takes which route, permutations within a flow (e.g., v_1 takes r_1 and v_2 takes r_2 versus the reverse) yield the same outcome, allowing the model to avoid redundant decision branches.

Both cost functions evaluated in our MIP framework showed strong performance, particularly in New York and Sydney, where the number of flows was small but each flow contained many vehicles. In these cases, routing optimization led to significant reductions in trip duration, even at the cost of longer routes. In contrast, in Dublin and Luxembourg, where the number of flows is large but each contains few vehicles, the benefits of macrosimulation are diminished. In such settings, MIP behavior becomes nearly indistinguishable from per-vehicle routing, similar to microsimulation, reducing its advantage relative to DUO and planning-based solutions. These observations underscore the importance of matching the modeling granularity to the structure of the traffic environment.

Another important factor is the accuracy and expressiveness of the objective function. As shown in Table 2, the MIP solver produced optimal or near-optimal solutions in most cases. However, the objective function – while aligned with prior works [7,26,27] – primarily targets minimizing congestion on controlled segments and does not capture finer details of road geometry or connection structure. In particular, bottlenecks at uncontrolled intersections, such as traffic merging from a side road onto a busy main road, can severely impair flow despite seemingly balanced load distributions. These effects, observed in our simulations, are not fully represented in the objective function and likely contributed to suboptimal real-world behavior in certain episodes.

Additionally, unlike DUO, our models lack access to real-time traffic data beyond the planning scope, meaning they cannot adjust to external or future congestion patterns. Combined with limitations of the simulator itself – such as imperfect representation of complex traffic phenomena – this introduces further discrepancy between modeled and actual outcomes.

Interestingly, the alternative cost function, which penalizes only a portion of the vehicles exceeding flow limits (as in the planning model), showed more robust performance in Dublin and Luxembourg. This softer formulation improved the percentage of vehicles successfully reaching their destinations and contributed to a measurable reduction in emissions (in the case of Dublin). However, it also resulted in slower optimization, a lower number of optimal solutions, and slightly weaker aggregate performance across scenarios, as shown in Table 2. This suggests a trade-off between realism and tractability. To improve performance further, the model could be refined to explicitly incorporate flow aggregation strategies – e.g., grouping vehicles on shared segments such as bridges or arterial roads – or extended with auxiliary components that specialize in handling specific network structures or merging behaviors.

From the perspective of route diversity and fairness, that is, whether diverse routes generated for the same flow are not too unfair, i.e., both longer and taking more time than alternatives on average, we conducted an analysis detailed in Sect. 6.2. Although such "unfair" routes might be inevitable, the share of vehicles taking them should not be high, otherwise drivers might not want to follow them [5]. In Sydney, the share was above 20% and, in Luxembourg, even over 40% (except for the mild cost function and BR preprocessing). A recent study, similar to ours, conducted on a planning-based approach (with SR preprocessing) has shown a higher share of "unfair" routes in the Sydney scenario as well [19]. This indicates that some road networks might be more prone to unfair route distribution due to their topology and traffic patterns.

We believe that centralized traffic routing can be effectively integrated with decentralized methods in a hybrid architecture. Specifically, centralized techniques can be used to route dominant traffic flows that significantly interact with each other, while the remaining vehicles can be managed using lightweight decentralized approaches. This hybridization has the potential to combine global coordination benefits with local adaptability, offering a promising direction for future research.

7 Conclusion

In this paper, we addressed the Centralised Traffic Routing problem using Mixed-Integer Programming (MIP), formulating it as a set of interacting network flows to efficiently distribute vehicle traffic across the road network. We proposed two MIP models: one based on a cost function commonly used in the literature [7, 26], which penalizes exceeding flow capacities, and another softer variant that penalizes only the vehicles above the intensity threshold. This work extends our previous research [20], introducing a more scalable macrosimulation framework that significantly outperforms microsimulation-based methods, such as planning-based approaches, especially in scenarios involving large traffic flows.

Our experiments, particularly in New York and Sydney, demonstrate the effectiveness of the MIP approach when many vehicles can be grouped into a single flow. In such cases, the strict cost formulation achieves superior performance compared to distributed routing solutions, as used in modern navigation systems. Conversely, in cities like Dublin and Luxembourg, where traffic is fragmented into many small flows, the softer cost function yields better results by accommodating greater flexibility. However, this flexibility comes at a cost – models using the softer formulation tend to produce more emissions (in most cases), as indicated by the environmental statistics. Also, we identified that in some cases (especially in Luxembourg) over 40% of vehicles might be routed into worse alternatives that are both longer and take more time. On the contrary, New York and Dublin scenarios yielded a share of around 10% of "unfairly" routed vehicles.

Looking ahead, we plan to enhance the model's ability to represent and mitigate bottlenecks, such as those caused by uncontrolled junctions and merging lanes. We also aim to improve the treatment of fragmented flows by identifying recurring transport patterns even when vehicle counts are low, allowing centralized methods to be applied more effectively in hybrid architectures. Future improvements will also include incorporating dynamic traffic information, modeling the impact of past decisions on current routing, introducing intersection-level costs to reflect real-world traffic behavior, and handling complex road combinations that are frequently congested (e.g., those shared with public transport routes).

Acknowledgments. This research is supported by Czech Science Foundation (project no. 23-05575S), by the European Union under the OP JAK project ROBOPROX (reg. no. CZ.02.01.01/00/22_008/0004590), and by the Grant Agency of the Czech Technical University (project no. SGS24/115/OHK3/2T/37).

References

1. Ahuja, R.K., Magnanti, T.L., Orlin, J.B.: Network Flows: Theory, Algorithms, and Applications. Prentice-Hall Inc., Upper Saddle River (1993)
2. Antoniou, G., et al.: Enabling the use of a planning agent for urban traffic management via enriched and integrated urban data. Transp. Res. Part C: Emerg. Technol. **98**, 284–297 (2019)
3. Cao, Z., Jiang, S., Zhang, J., Guo, H.: A unified framework for vehicle rerouting and traffic light control to reduce traffic congestion. IEEE Trans. Intell. Transp. Syst. **18**(7), 1958–1973 (2017). https://doi.org/10.1109/TITS.2016.2613997
4. Chang, K.H., Hsu, P.Y., Lin, C.J., Lin, C.L., Juo, S.H.H., Liang, C.L.: Traffic-related air pollutants increase the risk for age-related macular degeneration. J. Invest. Med. **67**(7), 1076–1081 (2019)
5. Chrpa, L.: Centralized Intelligent Traffic Routing in the Light of Disobedience of Drivers, pp. 87–97. Springer, Heiedelberg (2024). https://doi.org/10.1007/978-3-031-55044-7_6
6. Chrpa, L., Vallati, M.: Centralised vehicle routing for optimising urban traffic: a scalability perspective. In: IEEE Intelligent Vehicles Symposium, IV 2023, Anchorage, AK, USA, 4–7 June 2023, pp. 1–6. IEEE (2023)
7. Chrpa, L., Vallati, M., Parkinson, S.: Exploiting automated planning for efficient centralized vehicle routing and mitigating congestion in urban road networks. In: Proceedings of the 34th ACM/SIGAPP Symposium on Applied Computing, SAC 2019 (2019)
8. Claes, R., Holvoet, T., Weyns, D.: A decentralized approach for anticipatory vehicle routing using delegate multiagent systems. IEEE Trans. Intell. Transp. Syst. **12**(2), 364–373 (2011)
9. Codecá, L., Frank, R., Faye, S., Engel, T.: Luxembourg SUMO traffic (LuST) scenario: traffic demand evaluation. IEEE Intell. Transp. Syst. Mag. **9**(2), 52–63 (2017)
10. Domshlak, C., Hoffmann, J., Katz, M.: Red-black planning: a new systematic approach to partial delete relaxation. Artif. Intell. **221**, 73–114 (2015)

11. Du, L., Han, L., Li, X.Y.: Distributed coordinated in-vehicle online routing using mixed-strategy congestion game. Transp. Res. Part B: Methodol. **67**, 1–17 (2014)
12. Fortz, B., Gouveia, L., Joyce-Moniz, M.: Models for the piecewise linear unsplittable multicommodity flow problems. Eur. J. Oper. Res. **261**(1), 30–42 (2017)
13. Friesz, T.L., Luque, J., Tobin, R.L., Wie, B.W.: Dynamic network traffic assignment considered as a continuous time optimal control problem. Oper. Res. **37**(6), 893–901 (1989)
14. Gueriau, M., Dusparic, I.: Quantifying the impact of connected and autonomous vehicles on traffic efficiency and safety in mixed traffic. In: 23rd IEEE International Conference on Intelligent Transportation Systems (2020)
15. Kirimtat, A., Krejcar, O., Kertesz, A., Tasgetiren, M.F.: Future trends and current state of smart city concepts: a survey. IEEE Access **8**, 86448–86467 (2020). https://doi.org/10.1109/ACCESS.2020.2992441
16. Krishnan, A., Markov, M., Bonakdarpour, B.: Distributed vehicle routing approximation. In: 2017 IEEE International Parallel and Distributed Processing Symposium (IPDPS), pp. 503–512 (2017). https://doi.org/10.1109/IPDPS.2017.90
17. Lopez, P.A., et al.: Microscopic traffic simulation using sumo. In: Proceedings of ITSC (2018)
18. McCluskey, T.L., Vallati, M.: Embedding automated planning within urban traffic management operations. In: Proceedings of the Twenty-Seventh International Conference on Automated Planning and Scheduling, ICAPS 2017, pp. 391–399 (2017)
19. Nyporko, A., Chrpa, L., Svadlenka, M.: Analysing routes generated by planning-based centralised traffic routing. In: The International FLAIRS Conference Proceedings, vol. 38, no. 1 (2025). https://doi.org/10.32473/flairs.38.1.138872. https://journals.flvc.org/FLAIRS/article/view/138872
20. Nyporko, A., Svadlenka, M., Antonov, N., Rohaninejad, M., Chrpa, L.: Centralised urban traffic routing using mixed-integer programming. In: Rocha, A.P., Steels, L., van den Herik, H.J. (eds.) Proceedings of the 17th International Conference on Agents and Artificial Intelligence, ICAART 2025, Porto, Portugal, 23–25 February 2025, vol. 2, pp. 176–187. SCITEPRESS (2025)
21. Ouorou, A., Mahey, P., Vial, J.P.: A survey of algorithms for convex multicommodity flow problems. Manag. Sci. **46**(1), 126–147 (2000)
22. Pilát, M.: Evolving ensembles of traffic lights controllers. In: IEEE 30th International Conference on Tools with Artificial Intelligence, ICTAI 2018, pp. 958–962. IEEE (2018)
23. Polimeni, A., Vitetta, A.: Network design and vehicle routing problems in road transport systems: integrating models and algorithms. Transp. Eng. **16**, 100247 (2024). https://doi.org/10.1016/j.treng.2024.100247. https://www.sciencedirect.com/science/article/pii/S2666691X24000228
24. Pozanco, A., Fernández, S., Borrajo, D.: On-line modelling and planning for urban traffic control. Expert Syst. (2021)
25. Silva, M.D.R.L., Tang, M.: A new framework for centralized coordinated multi-vehicle dynamic routing. IEEE Access **12**, 24243–24253 (2024). https://doi.org/10.1109/ACCESS.2024.3365513
26. Svadlenka, M., Chrpa, L., Vallati, M.: Improving the scalability of automated planning-based vehicle routing via smart routes identification. In: 8th International Conference on Models and Technologies for Intelligent Transportation Systems, MT-ITS 2023, pp. 1–6. IEEE (2023)

27. Vallati, M., Scala, E., Chrpa, L.: A hybrid automated planning approach for urban real-time routing of connected vehicles. In: 24th IEEE International Intelligent Transportation Systems Conference, ITSC, pp. 3821–3826. IEEE (2021)
28. Wenning, B.L., Timm-Giel, A., Pesch, D.: A distributed routing approach for vehicle routing in logistic networks. In: IEEE Vehicular Technology Conference, pp. 1–5 (2006). https://doi.org/10.1109/VTCF.2006.609
29. Wolsey, L.A.: Integer programming/Laurence A. Wolsey. Wiley-Interscience series in discrete mathematics and optimization, J. Wiley, New York (1998)
30. Xie, X.F., Smith, S., Barlow, G.: Schedule-driven coordination for real-time traffic network control. In: Proceedings of ICAPS (2012)
31. Yamashita, T., Izumi, K., Kurumatani, K., Nakashima, H.: Smooth traffic flow with a cooperative car navigation system. In: 4th International Joint Conference on Autonomous Agents and Multiagent Systems (AAMAS 2005), pp. 478–485. ACM (2005)

Exploration–Exploitation Trade-off in Neural Monte Carlo Tree Search for the Job Shop Scheduling Problem

Alexander Nasuta[1(✉)], Hans A. Zhou[1], Anas Abdelrazeq[1], and Robert H. Schmitt[1,2]

[1] Chair of Intelligence in Quality Sensing (IQS), WZL | RWTH Aachen, Aachen, Germany
{alexander.nasuta,hans.zhou,anas.abdelrazeq, robert.schmitt}@wzl-iqs.rwth-aachen.de

[2] Fraunhofer Institute for Production Technology IPT, Aachen, Germany

Abstract. The Job Shop Scheduling Problem (JSP) is a classical NP-hard combinatorial optimization problem with significant relevance in manufacturing and production planning. Efficient scheduling is essential for meeting production deadlines, especially in the context of customized and flexible manufacturing systems. Recent advances in learning-based methods, such as Reinforcement Learning (RL) and neural Monte Carlo Tree Search (neural MCTS), have shown promise in solving such complex problems under constrained time and compute budgets. A key challenge in both MCTS and RL frameworks is managing the exploration–exploitation trade-off: balancing the discovery of new, potentially better actions with the utilization of actions already known to be effective. This work systematically investigates the influence of various exploration strategies in MCTS-based agents, both with and without neural guidance, on JSP performance. Specifically, we evaluate several variants of the UCT, $PUCT$, and $MuZero$ exploration terms on standard JSP benchmark instances. The results demonstrate that $MuZero$-style exploration variants, particularly when properly parameterized, consistently achieve lower makespans and improved sample efficiency compared to baseline MCTS and curiosity-driven RL approaches. These findings highlight the importance of well-structured exploration terms for achieving effective search behavior in neural MCTS applied to scheduling problems.

Keywords: Job Shop Problem · Monte Carlo Tree Search · MCTS · Neural Monte Carlo Tree Search · AlphaZero · Curiosity · Reinforcement Learning · Combinatorial Optimization

1 Introduction

Production planning is a fundamental challenge in many industrial settings, involving complex decisions around resource allocation and task scheduling. A central problem in this domain is the Job Shop Scheduling Problem (JSP), which is particularly relevant in manufacturing environments where small batches and customized products are common [3]. In a JSP, each job comprises a sequence of tasks that must be processed on specific machines in a predefined order. The inherent flexibility and variability in

H. J. van den Herik et al. (Eds.): ICAART 2025, LNAI 16517, pp. 65–86, 2026.
https://doi.org/10.1007/978-3-032-25032-2_4

job and machine configurations make JSPs highly applicable but also computationally demanding, as the problem is NP-hard. This complexity renders exact solutions infeasible for large-scale instances, motivating the use of heuristic and metaheuristic methods to obtain near-optimal solutions within reasonable computational budgets.

Recently, learning-based methods such as reinforcement learning (RL) and neural Monte Carlo Tree Search (neural MCTS) have shown promise in addressing complex combinatorial optimization problems, including scheduling [10]. These methods allow agents to learn scheduling heuristics through interaction with a model of the environment dynamics. However, applying RL to the JSP is challenging, primarily due to its sparse reward structure, where rewards are primarily available once a complete schedule has been generated [15].

A critical aspect of both MCTS and RL approaches is the exploration–exploitation trade-off, which involves balancing the evaluation of novel, potentially better actions (exploration) with the use of actions already known to yield favorable outcomes (exploitation). MCTS approaches, in particular, are well suited to problems with sparse rewards, such as those encountered in the JSP. Originally developed for decision-making in games such as Go and Chess, MCTS algorithms have been successfully extended to various domains, including chemistry, combinatorial optimization, and production planning [9]. The success of AlphaGo, which achieved superhuman performance using a neural-guided MCTS framework, has further inspired the adaptation of these techniques beyond traditional gaming contexts [9].

neural MCTS implementations differ substantially across domains, particularly in how the exploration–exploitation trade-off is managed. A central component influencing this trade-off is the tree policy, which determines which action to explore during the search. The choice of tree policy formulation can significantly affect both the search behavior and overall performance of the agent. In classical MCTS without neural guidance, variants of the *Upper Confidence Bound for Trees* (UCT) are commonly employed. In contrast, neural-guided MCTS approaches typically rely on variations of the $Predictor$ and UCT ($PUCT$) formula, which incorporates prior knowledge from a learned policy [9]. Despite the critical role of the tree policy, systematic comparisons of these exploration strategies, especially in complex combinatorial domains such as the JSP, remain limited in the literature [10].

This study investigates the impact of different exploration formulations in MCTS-based agents, both with and without neural guidance, applied to the JSP. In addition to classical UCT and $PUCT$ variants, we compare performance against curiosity-driven exploration methods, which have been shown to improve learning efficiency in sparse-reward environments [16, 19]. Through empirical evaluation, we aim to identify effective exploration strategies that enhance the capability of MCTS agents to solve JSPs efficiently.

2 Neural Monte Carlo Tree Search

MCTS is a heuristic search algorithm originally developed for decision-making in combinatorial games. It builds a search tree through sequential simulations, where nodes represent states and edges denote actions. Although MCTS emerged independently of

RL, both frameworks share conceptual similarities, particularly in the use of policies and value estimates. A detailed discussion of their relationship is provided by Vodopivec et al. [23].

Classical MCTS operates in four iterative phases: *selection*, *expansion*, *evaluation*, and *backpropagation*. During the selection phase, an action is chosen at each node by balancing exploitation of high-value actions with exploration of under-visited branches, typically guided by variants of the UCT formula [8]:

$$a = \arg\max_a \underbrace{\frac{W(s,a)}{N(s,a)}}_{\text{exploitation}} + \underbrace{c\sqrt{\frac{\ln N(s)}{N(s,a)}}}_{\text{exploration}} \tag{1}$$

In Eq. 1, $W(s,a)$ denotes the cumulative reward (e.g., number of wins or total return) obtained from selecting action a in state s during prior simulations. $N(s,a)$ is the number of times action a has been selected in state s, and $N(s)$ is the total number of times state s has been visited. The exploitation term, $\frac{W(s,a)}{N(s,a)}$, thus approximates the mean return for selecting a in s, analogous to a sample-based estimate of the action-value function $Q(s,a)$ in RL. The exploration term, $c\sqrt{\frac{\ln N(s)}{N(s,a)}}$, assigns higher values to less frequently explored actions by scaling their relative under-visitation with respect to the overall state visit count. The constant $c > 0$ modulates the trade-off between exploration and exploitation and typically requires tuning depending on the reward range and problem domain.

Neural MCTS extends this framework by integrating neural networks into one or more of the selection, expansion, and evaluation phases. In the selection phase, neural MCTS commonly replaces the UCT formula with the $PUCT$ rule [21], which incorporates prior probabilities $P(s,a)$ from a policy network to influence exploration. The most commonly used policy in the selection phase is the one used by AlphaZero introduced by Silver et al. [9,21]:

$$a = \arg\max_a \underbrace{\frac{W(s,a)}{N(s,a)}}_{\text{exploitation}} + \underbrace{c\,P(s,a)\sqrt{\frac{N(s)}{1+N(s,a)}}}_{\text{exploration}} \tag{2}$$

For expansion, rather than enumerating all legal actions, some implementations expand only a subset whose cumulative prior probability exceeds a threshold τ. In the evaluation phase, rollouts may be replaced or complemented by neural value estimates or policy-guided simulations.

Training of the policy and value networks can proceed via policy improvement by MCTS, where the agent performs searches guided by its current networks and uses the resulting policies $\pi_{\text{MCTS}}(s)$ and value estimates $v_{\text{MCTS}}(s)$ as supervision. Alternatively, networks may be trained through standard reinforcement learning or supervised learning, independent of the search process [9].

AlphaZero [21] exemplifies this paradigm by combining $PUCT$-based selection, full expansion of all actions, neural evaluation, and exclusive training via policy improvement.

3 Related Work

This section provides an overview of prior work related to the exploration–exploitation trade-off in (Neural) MCTS and RL, as well as the application of MCTS techniques to the JSP. The discussion first addresses how the trade-off has been formulated and managed in MCTS, with a particular focus on neural-guided variants. It then considers exploration strategies in RL, especially those designed for environments with sparse rewards. Finally, the section reviews existing applications of MCTS in production and scheduling contexts.

3.1 Exploration–Exploitation in Neural MCTS

The exploration–exploitation trade-off is a central consideration in MCTS, where a so-called tree policy balances between selecting actions with high estimated value and actions that are underexplored. This trade-off was formalized in the seminal work by Kocsis and Szepesvári [11], who introduced the UCT algorithm by applying the Upper Confidence Bounds (UCB1) principle to tree-based planning. The UCT formula includes a tunable exploration constant that directly influences search behavior. Empirical studies have shown that this constant significantly affects performance and may require problem-specific tuning, particularly in domains with stochastic rewards or varying outcome scales. Browne et al. [4] provide an extensive overview of MCTS variants and tree policy modifications, highlighting the importance of exploration in a variety of decision-making domains. Beyond classical UCT, several extensions have incorporated uncertainty estimates, value normalization, or dynamic exploration terms to improve search efficiency in structured environments.

Balancing exploration and exploitation in neural MCTS has various approaches which are adapting tree policies to domain-specific characteristics. A comprehensive survey by Kemmerling et al. [9] analyzes the application of neural MCTS in non-game domains and presents a taxonomy of tree policy variants, along with their empirical usage frequency. The authors report that the standard $PUCT$ formulation used in AlphaZero—referred to as $PUTC_0$ (cf. Equation 2), is the most commonly employed selection mechanism across surveyed applications. In single-agent deterministic environments, such as combinatorial optimization or scheduling, relying solely on average node values can hinder effective search [9]. This is because a node may have a low average value despite containing one high-quality child action, which is reliably exploitable due to the absence of opponent-induced uncertainty. To address this, Deng et al. [5] proposed a modified tree policy ($PUCT_B$) that augments the standard ($PUCT_0$) formulation with the maximum value encountered for each action, scaled by a constant. This modification aims to prioritize nodes with historically promising trajectories, reflecting the deterministic nature of the domain. Kemmerling et al. [9] highlight the potential advantages of such value-biased exploration in single-player settings like the JSP. Xu and Lieberherr [26] experimented with both the AlphaZero $PUCT_0$ variant and $PUCT_9$ from Kemmerling's taxonomy, they observed superior performance with the original AlphaZero formulation, though the comparison lacks detailed quantitative analysis.

Table 1 list all exploration term synthesized by Kemmerling et al. [9]. It contains exploration terms for MCTS (without neural guidance), namely tree UTC variants and term for neural MCTS, namely the $PUTC$, $MuZero$, UTC_D and $PUTC_B$ variants. These exploration terms typically rely on components such as the prior probability $P(s, a)$, which denotes the likelihood of selecting action a in state s, either derived from a learned policy or other heuristics, and visit statistics $N(s, a)$ and $N(s)$, representing action- and state-level visit counts, respectively. The exploration constant c is the exploration constant. MuZero and PUCT_B introduce multiple exploration constants to better tune the contribution of different components in the selection formula. Wang et al. [25] incorporate action advantage estimates $A(s, a)$, such as the UTC_D variant, which utilizes a dueling architecture to estimate both state values and action-specific advantages. The varinat $PUTC_3$, introduce tunable parameters such as μ to further modulate the influence of exploration terms. This variant was independently suggested by Wang et al. [25], Song et al. [22], Wang et al. [9,24].

Table 1. Taxonomy of exploration terms according to Kemmerling et al. [9].

Name	Formula
UTC_0	$c\sqrt{\frac{2\ln N(s)}{N(s,a)}}$
UTC_1	$c\sqrt{\frac{\ln N(s)}{1+N(s,a)}}$
UTC_2	$c\,\frac{\sqrt{N(s)}}{1+N(s,a)}$
$PUTC_0$	$c\,P(s,a)\frac{\sqrt{N(s)}}{1+N(s,a)}$
$PUTC_1$	$c\,P(s,a)\sqrt{\frac{2\ln N(s)}{N(s,a)}}$
$PUTC_2$	$c\,P(s,a)\frac{\sqrt{N(s)}}{N(s,a)}$
$PUTC_3$	$c\,P(s,a)^{\mu}\sqrt{\frac{N(s)}{1+N(s,a)}}$
$PUTC_4$	$c\,\frac{P(s,a)}{1+N(s,a)}$
$PUTC_5$	$c\,P(s,a)\frac{\sqrt{N(s,a)+1}}{N(s,a)+1}$
$PUTC_6$	$c\,P(s,a)\frac{N(s,a)}{1+N(s,u)}$
$PUTC_7$	$c\,P(s,a)\frac{\sqrt{N(s,a)+\epsilon}}{N(s,a)+1}$
$PUTC_8$	$c\,P(s,a)\sqrt{\frac{\ln N(s)+1}{1+N(s,a)}}$
$PUTC_9$	$c\,P(s,a)\sqrt{\frac{\ln N(s)}{1+N(s,a)}}$
$PUTC_{10}$	$c\,P(s,a)\sqrt{\frac{\ln N(s)}{1+N(s,a)}}$
$MuZero_0$	$P(s,a)\frac{\sqrt{N(s)}}{1+N(s,a)}\left[c_1+\ln\frac{N(s)+c_2+1}{c_2}\right]$
$MuZero_1$	$P(s,a)\frac{\sqrt{N(s)}}{1+N(s,a)}\left[c_1+\ln\frac{\sqrt{N(s)+c_2+1}}{c_2}\right]$
UTC_D	$c\,A(s,a)\sqrt{\frac{2\ln N(s)}{N(s,a)}}$
$PUTC_B$	$c_1\,P(s,a)\sqrt{\frac{N(s)}{1+N(s,a)}}+c_2\,B(s,a)$

3.2 Exploration–Exploitation in Reinforcement Learning

The exploration–exploitation trade-off is a fundamental challenge in RL, particularly pronounced in environments with sparse or delayed reward signals. In such settings, agents struggle to efficiently explore the state space, often failing to discover reward-yielding trajectories. This challenge is especially relevant to scheduling problems like the JSP, where rewards are typically only provided at the end of an episode once a complete schedule has been generated [15].

To mitigate this issue, curiosity-driven exploration has emerged as a promising direction, offering intrinsic motivation to guide agents toward novel or likely rewarding states. These methods supplement sparse extrinsic rewards with internally generated signals that encourage exploration, enabling more efficient learning in environments where rewards are infrequent.

One of the earliest and simplest forms of curiosity is count-based exploration, where agents are incentivized to visit rarely explored states. While effective in small or discrete environments, this approach does not scale well to high-dimensional or continuous state spaces. To address this limitation, Bellemare et al. [1] introduced pseudo-counts, leveraging density models to estimate state visitation counts via neural networks. This advancement made count-based exploration feasible in complex environments such as Atari games.

An alternative class of approaches is prediction-based curiosity, originally proposed by Schmidhuber [20]. These methods reward agents based on the prediction error of a forward dynamics model, encouraging exploration in regions, where the agent's model is inaccurate. A significant refinement of this concept is the Intrinsic Curiosity Module (ICM) introduced by Pathak et al. [16], which maps states into a learned feature space before computing prediction errors. This reduces the influence of noisy or irrelevant features, improving exploration efficiency. ICM has demonstrated strong performance in sparse-reward domains such as VizDoom and Super Mario Bros.

Another notable approach is Episodic Curiosity (EC), proposed by Savinov et al. [19], which defines novelty based on the agent's episodic memory. A state is considered novel, and therefore rewarded, if it cannot be easily reached from previously visited states within a limited number of steps. This mechanism promotes exploration of genuinely unfamiliar regions of the environment. EC has outperformed earlier methods such as ICM in various benchmarks, including VizDoom, DM-Lab, and MuJoCo.

Nasuta et al. [15] investigated the application of curiosity-driven reinforcement learning to the JSP. The authors evaluated the effectiveness of the ICM and EC in guiding exploration. Their results demonstrate that incorporating intrinsic motivation increases state space coverage and enables agents to escape local optima. In particular, the ICM-enhanced agents achieved improved performance when intrinsic and extrinsic rewards were balanced, highlighting the potential of curiosity-based methods to accelerate learning in scheduling tasks.

3.3 Applications of MCTS in Production and Scheduling

While neural MCTS has seen widespread adoption in various domains, its application to scheduling and combinatorial optimization, particularly the JSP remains comparatively limited. Rinciog et al. [18], Göppert et al. [7] and [10] explicitly traget job shop use cases. Rinciog et al., Göppert et al. adopt an AlphaZero-style neural MCTS architecture, maintaining standard procedures for selection, expansion, and evaluation. Kemmerling et al. investigates neural MCTS as an online scheduling method capable of adapting to dynamic decision budgets. Kemmerling et al. provides comprehensive overview of developments for neural MCTS in Scheduling and Combinatorial Optimisation, which synthesizes the key configurations and empirical findings of neural MCTS across scheduling and combinatorial optimization literature.

4 Methodology

This section introduces the underling optimization problem of a JSP and outlines the methodology used in our study, focusing on the design of a JSP environment as a Markov Decision Process (MDP).

JSP Formalization. The JSP is a well-established combinatorial optimization problem involving the scheduling of a set of tasks $\mathcal{T} = \{T_1, T_2, \ldots, T_N\}$ across a set of machines $\mathcal{M} = \{M_i\}_{i=1}^m$. Each job, corresponding to a specific production process, consists of an ordered sequence of tasks, with each task assigned to a particular machine for processing.

The problem is defined over a set of jobs $\mathcal{J} = \{J_j\}_{j=1}^n$, where each job requires processing on all m machines in a predefined order. Consequently, the total number of tasks is given by $N = n \cdot m$. A feasible solution to the JSP specifies a start time $\hat{s}_\alpha$ for each task T_α such that machine capacity constraints and task precedence constraints are respected.

This work adopts a disjunctive graph representation to model the JSP, following prior work such as Zhang et al. [27] and Nasuta et al. [14]. In this representation, the scheduling instance is encoded as a graph $G = (\mathcal{V}, \mathcal{A}, \mathcal{E})$, where $\mathcal{V}$ is the set of nodes, $\mathcal{A}$ the set of directed (conjunctive) edges, and $\mathcal{E}$ the set of undirected (disjunctive) edges.

The node set $\mathcal{V}$ includes all tasks in $\mathcal{T}$, as well as two dummy nodes: a source node T_0 and a sink node $T_\star$. The conjunctive edges in $\mathcal{A}$ capture fixed precedence relations among tasks within each job, reflecting the required processing order. Disjunctive edges in $\mathcal{E}$ connect tasks competing for the same machine, where the order of execution remains to be determined.

To construct a feasible schedule, the disjunctive edges must be oriented such that the resulting graph is acyclic. Once all edge directions are resolved and the graph is acyclic, the makespan, defined as the completion time of the last task, can be computed by identifying the longest path (i.e., the critical path) from T_0 to $T_\star$. The objective of the JSP is to minimize the makespan $s_\star$, which leads to the following optimization formulation [3]:

$$\hat{s}_\beta - \hat{s}_\alpha \geq p_\alpha \qquad \forall\, (T_\beta, T_\alpha) \in \mathcal{A} \tag{3}$$

$$\hat{s}_\alpha \geq 0 \qquad \forall\, T_\alpha \in \mathcal{T} \tag{4}$$

$$\hat{s}_\beta - \hat{s}_\alpha \geq p_\alpha \vee \hat{s}_\alpha - \hat{s}_\beta \geq p_\beta \quad \forall\, \{T_\beta, T_\alpha\} \in \mathcal{E}_i, \; \forall\, M_i \in \mathcal{M} \tag{5}$$

Markov Decision Process. To train neural MCTS agents, the JSP is formulated as a Markov Decision Process (MDP). In this formulation, the state space encompasses all feasible partial schedules, and the action space is defined by the selection of a job's next unscheduled operation for placement in the schedule.

Observation Space. The state representation must capture the full information of a partial schedule. Using a disjunctive graph formulation of the JSP, any intermediate graph configuration, as illustrated in Figs. 1a–1c, serves as a valid state. The graph is encoded via an adjacency matrix, which is augmented with columns indicating the machine assignment and processing duration for each task. A specific example of this state representation, corresponding to the partially scheduled graph in Fig. 1b, is provided in Table 5 in the appendix.

Action Space. The action space consists of all available tasks, combined with an action mask to exclude infeasible options. In our implementation, tasks within a job are scheduled sequentially from left to right, as in prior work by Zhang et al. [27] and Nasuta et al. [14]. This strategy guarantees that the disjunctive graph remains acyclic throughout the scheduling process. For example, in the instance depicted in Fig. 1, which includes tasks $t_1, t_2, ..., t_8$, the valid actions in Fig. 1a are t_1, t_5, while in Fig. 1b the valid actions are t_2, t_6.

Reward Function. We define a sparse reward function that evaluates the terminal state s_t, corresponding to a completed schedule, based on its makespan:

$$r(s_t) = \begin{cases} -\frac{C}{C_{LB}} + 2 & \text{terminal state} \\ 0 & \text{otherwise} \end{cases} \tag{6}$$

where C denotes the makespan of the resulting schedule, and C_{LB} is a known lower bound for the instance. As the agent improves its scheduling performance, the term $-\frac{C}{C_{LB}}$ approaches -1 for near-optimal solutions. Kocsis and Szepesvári [11] suggest that, for games with terminal rewards in the range $[0, 1]$, an exploration constant of $c = 1/\sqrt{2}$ is optimal. To align with this theoretical insight, we scale the reward such that a value of 1 corresponds to an optimal solution. The reward function defined above yields values in the range $(-\infty, 1]$, where higher values correspond to better solutions. Although Nasuta et al. [14] propose a dense reward function based on machine utilization for reinforcement learning settings, we adopt a sparse reward structure. This decision is motivated by the observation that dense rewards provide limited benefits in tree-based search algorithms such as MCTS. Furthermore, sparse reward structures are easier to adapt to desired ranges, such as $[0, 1]$ or $[-1, 1]$, which is advantageous when designing reward functions for MCTS-based algorithms.

4.1 Experimental Setup

The experiments were conducted using the Gymnasium-based environment introduced by Nasuta et al. [14], which was configured to match the observation and action spaces described in Sect. 4. For the implementation of MCTS and neural MCTS agents,

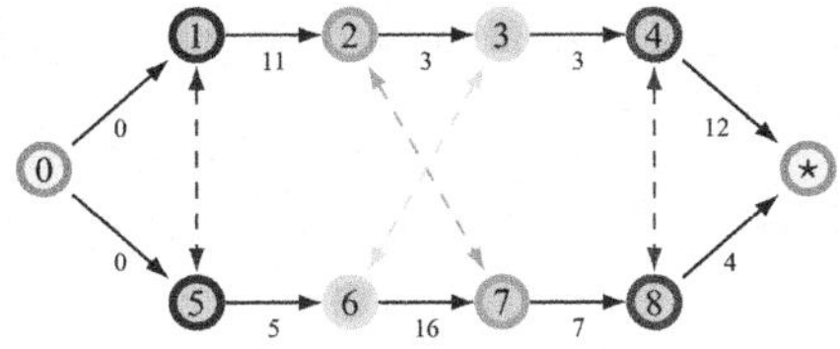

(a) Initial disjunctive graph.

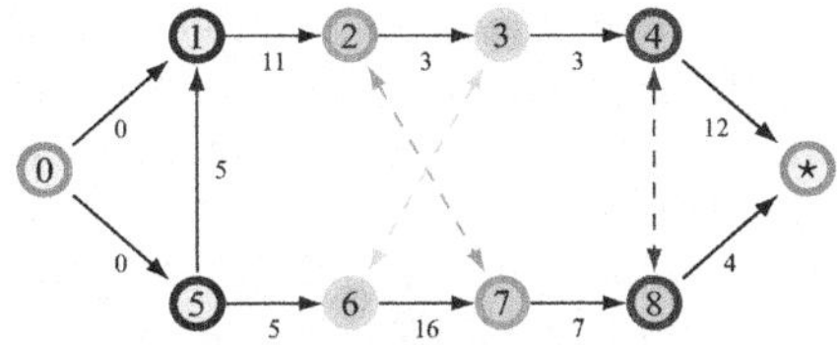

(b) Partially scheduled graph.

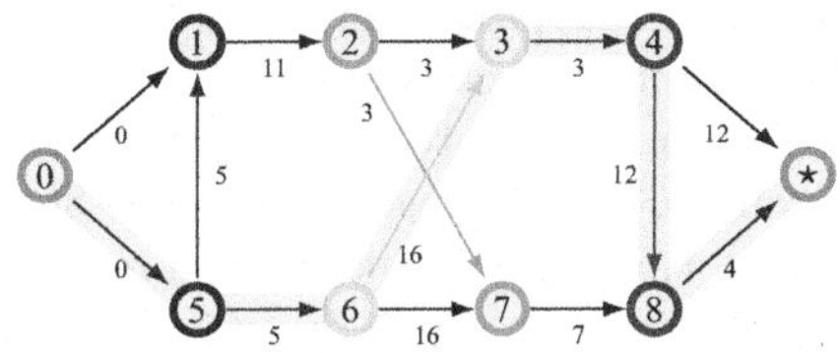

(c) Fully scheduled disjunctive graph with highlighted critical path.

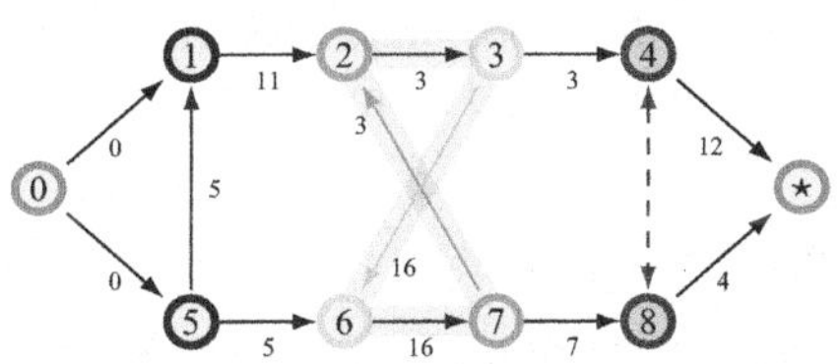

(d) Infeasible schedule with highlighted cycle.

Fig. 1. Disjunctive graph scheduling. Panels (a)–(c) illustrate the progression from the initial disjunctive graph to an feasible schedule. Reproduced from Nasuta et al. [15].

we employed the *Gymcts* library [12]. This library extends the Gymnasium interface to support both classical and neural MCTS, and has been extended in this study to allow for flexible configuration of tree policy selection strategies. The complete set of implemented guidance functions is summarized in Table 2.

The *Gymcts* library is designed specifically for non-game, single-agent scenarios. It tracks the highest return (i.e., sum of rewards) obtained from rollouts at each node, enabling this information to be incorporated into the guiding function during the selection phase. This mechanism supports an adapted version of the $PUCT_B$ formula, allowing it to be generalized across UCT, $PUCT$, and $MuZero$-style selection strategies. In contrast to the original $PUCT_B$ approach, which uses two separate exploration constants, our implementation introduces a blending parameter $b \in [0, 1]$ that modulates the contribution of the best observed return relative to a baseline guidance function. The selection policy is defined as:

$$\pi_{\text{Gymcts}}(s,a) = (1-b)\,\pi_{\text{base}}(s,a) + b \cdot B(s,a) \tag{7}$$

$$\pi_{\text{base}}(s,a) = \frac{W(s,a)}{N(s,a)} + \pi_{\text{expl}}(s,a) \tag{8}$$

Here, $\pi_{\text{base}}(s,a)$ denotes a standard guiding function as categorized in the taxonomy by Kemmerling et al. incoperating various exploration approaches $\pi_{\text{expl}}(s,a)$. $B(s,a)$ is the best return observed for action a in state s. Notably, setting $b = 0$ recovers the original behavior of the base policy $\pi_{\text{base}}(s,a)$.

For neural guidance, *Gymcts* integrates with *Stable Baselines3* by Raffin et al. [17] to train a policy network using Proximal Policy Optimization (PPO) in a reinforcement learning setting. The trained policy is then employed to provide neural priors during the selection phase of MCTS. This approach aligns with observations by Kemmerling et al., who identified it as a common methodology in non-game neural MCTS applications. For the evaluation phase random rollouts are utilized. The source of our JSP benchmark instances to evaluate our approach is the Job Shop Scheduling Problem Benchmark Instances Repository [13]. All experimental runs were tracked and logged using the *Weights & Biases* platform [2], which facilitated experiment management and reproducibility.

Hardware. All computations in this study were performed on an Apple Macbook Pro with a M1 Max chip with 64 Gb of shared memory.

4.2 Experiment Design

Experiments were conducted on the *ft06* and *ft10* benchmark instances introduced by Fisher [6]. The *ft06* instance consists of 6 jobs and 6 machines, while the *ft10* instance comprises 10 jobs and 10 machines.

For evaluating *UCT* variants in a pure MCTS setting (i.e., without neural guidance), 900 simulations per decision step were executed for the *ft06* instance. In the neural MCTS configuration, policy training was conducted using a budget of 312,500 timesteps, followed by 700 simulations per decision step for problem solving. This setup results in approximately $500k$ total environment interactions for solving *ft06* instances. For the *ft10* instance, the MCTS configuration also used 900 simulations per step. In the neural MCTS setting, policy training was conducted using a 2 million timestep budget, with 500 simulations per decision step during the search phase. This results in an approximate total of 4 million environment interactions for solving *ft10* instances. All guiding functions listed in Table 2 were evaluated with different values of the best-action incorporation parameter $b \in \{0.0, 0.05, 0.5\}$. This allows for analyzing the effect of incorporating the best-known rollout return into each tree policy. The tracked metrics include the number of visited states $||S||$, the number of visited states excluding rollouts $\left\|\hat{S}\right\|$, the makespan C and the olptimality gap $\frac{C}{C_{opt}} - 1$. Detailed descriptions of these metrics are provided in Table 3.

Table 2. Guiding Functions (Tree Policies) for the section Phase for (nerual) MCTS.

Name	Guidance Function
UTC_v0	$\arg\max_a \,(1-b)\left[\frac{W(s,a)}{N(s,a)} + c\sqrt{\frac{2\ln N(s)}{N(s,a)}}\right] + b\,B(s,a)$
UTC_v1	$\arg\max_a \,(1-b)\left[\frac{W(s,a)}{N(s,a)} + c\sqrt{\frac{\ln N(s)}{1+N(s,a)}}\right] + b\,B(s,a)$
UTC_v2	$\arg\max_a \,(1-b)\left[\frac{W(s,a)}{N(s,a)} + c\,\frac{\sqrt{N(s)}}{1+N(s,a)}\right] + b\,B(s,a)$
PUTC_v0	$\arg\max_a \,(1-b)\left[\frac{W(s,a)}{N(s,a)} + c\,P(s,a)\frac{\sqrt{N(s)}}{1+N(s,a)}\right] + b\,B(s,a)$
PUTC_v1	$\arg\max_a \,(1-b)\left[\frac{W(s,a)}{N(s,a)} + c\,P(s,a)\sqrt{\frac{2\ln N(s)}{N(s,a)}}\right] + b\,B(s,a)$
PUTC_v2	$\arg\max_a \,(1-b)\left[\frac{W(s,a)}{N(s,a)} + c\,P(s,a)\frac{\sqrt{N(s)}}{N(s,a)}\right] + b\,B(s,a)$
PUTC_v3	$\arg\max_a \,(1-b)\left[\frac{W(s,a)}{N(s,a)} + c\,P(s,a)^{\mu}\sqrt{\frac{N(s)}{1+N(s,a)}}\right] + b\,B(s,a)$
PUTC_v4	$\arg\max_a \,(1-b)\left[\frac{W(s,a)}{N(s,a)} + c\,\frac{P(s,a)}{1+N(s,a)}\right] + b\,B(s,a)$
PUTC_v5	$\arg\max_a \,(1-b)\left[\frac{W(s,a)}{N(s,a)} + c\,P(s,a)\frac{\sqrt{N(s,a)+1}}{N(s,a)+1}\right] + b\,B(s,a)$
PUTC_v6	$\arg\max_a \,(1-b)\left[\frac{W(s,a)}{N(s,a)} + c\,P(s,a)\frac{N(s,a)}{1+N(s,a)}\right] + b\,B(s,a)$
PUTC_v7	$\arg\max_a \,(1-b)\left[\frac{W(s,a)}{N(s,a)} + c\,P(s,a)\frac{\sqrt{N(s,a)+\epsilon}}{N(s,a)+1}\right] + b\,B(s,a)$
PUTC_v8	$\arg\max_a \,(1-b)\left[\frac{W(s,a)}{N(s,a)} + c\,P(s,a)\sqrt{\frac{\ln N(s)+1}{1+N(s,a)}}\right] + b\,B(s,a)$
PUTC_v9	$\arg\max_a \,(1-b)\left[\frac{W(s,a)}{N(s,a)} + c\,P(s,a)\sqrt{\frac{\ln N(s)}{1+N(s,a)}}\right] + b\,B(s,a)$
PUTC_v10	$\arg\max_a \,(1-b)\left[\frac{W(s,a)}{N(s,a)} + c\,P(s,a)\sqrt{\frac{\ln N(s)}{1+N(s,a)}}\right] + b\,B(s,a)$
MuZero_v0	$\arg\max_a \,(1-b)\left[\frac{W(s,a)}{N(s,a)} + P(s,a)\frac{\sqrt{N(s)}}{1+N(s,a)}\left[c_1 + \ln\frac{N(s)+c_2+1}{c_2}\right]\right] + b\,B(s,a)$
MuZero_v1	$\arg\max_a \,(1-b)\left[\frac{W(s,a)}{N(s,a)} + P(s,a)\frac{\sqrt{N(s)}}{1+N(s,a)}\left[c_1 + \ln\frac{\sqrt{N(s)+c_2+1}}{c_2}\right]\right] + b\,B(s,a)$

The computational budgets and metric definitions were aligned to allow for meaningful comparison with the results reported by Nasuta et al. [15]. Specifically, the neural MCTS training budgets were chosen to match the training durations of the curiosity-driven reinforcement learning modules studied by by Nasuta et al.. As both approaches address aspects of the exploration–exploitation trade-off, a direct comparison is considered relevant. Furthermore, the hyperparameters used for neural policy training were adopted from the best-performing configurations identified in their study.

Table 3. Metrics and their descriptions.

Metric	Symbol	Description
Visited states	$\|\|S\|\|$	The number of distinct states the agent has encountered during execution. Each state, as returned by the Gymnasium environment's `step()` function, is hashed and stored in a `HashSet`. The cardinality $\|\|S\|\|$ corresponds to the number of unique entries in this set.
Visited states without rollouts	$\left\|\left\|\hat{S}\right\|\right\|$	The number of distinct states encountered by the agent excluding those observed during rollouts. This metric helps assess the diversity of states visited during value-guided search (e.g., when using a neural network for evaluation). Only states visited outside of random rollouts are hashed and counted.
Makespan	C	The total time required to complete all jobs in a given Job Shop Scheduling Problem (JSP) solution. The makespan is recorded at the end of each rollout and serves as the raw optimization objective.
Optimality gap	$C_{Gap} = \frac{C}{C_{opt}} - 1$	The relative deviation of a solution's makespan C from the known optimal makespan C_{opt}. It enables consistent comparison across problem instances of varying size and difficulty. A value of 0 indicates an optimal solution, while higher values reflect greater suboptimality.

5 Results and Discussion

Figsures 3 and 4 present the experimental results for the *ft06* and *ft10* instances, respectively. Each figure is organized into four rows of plots: the first row shows experiments using UCT-based exploration terms, the second row covers $PUCT$-based variants, the third row shows MuZero-style exploration functions, and the fourth row includes baseline results from the curiosity-driven RL agents proposed by Nasuta et al. [15]. The metrics visualized are: (i) makespan, (ii) number of visited states $||S||$ (including those encountered during rollouts), and (iii) number of visited states excluding rollout states $\left\|\hat{S}\right\|$.

Corresponding summary statistics for makespan and optimality gap are provided in Table 6 for the *ft06* instance and Table 7 for *ft10*. As visible in the figures, the curves terminate at varying timestep counts, which is a result of the asymmetric expansion of the MCTS search tree. Although a fixed number of simulations is specified per decision step, the number of timesteps consumed per simulation can vary based on the depth of the tree at the respective node. A wider and deeper search tree implies longer rollouts and therefore higher timestep consumption. Consequently, curves that span a greater number of timesteps correspond to agents that explore more extensively.

The makespan curves in Figs. 3 and 4 are smoothed using a rolling window of size 25 to emphasize trends and suppress stochastic fluctuations. For the *ft06* instance, a consistent decrease in makespan over time is observed for UCT-based variants. Among them, `UCT_v2` shows the strongest negative correlation with the optimality gap ($r = -0.465$), suggesting effective exploration–exploitation balancing. In the $PUCT$-based category, `PUCT_v9` achieves the most favorable results ($r = -0.278$), followed by `PUCT_v7` ($r = -0.170$) and `PUCT_v5` ($r = -0.144$). Notably, `PUCT_v4` underperforms, with a positive correlation ($r = 0.493$) to the optimality gap. The poor performance of `PUCT_v4` is likely attributable to its omission of the $N(s)$ term in the tree policy, which causes the selection function to overly rely on prior probabilities $P(s, a)$, which seems to be ineffective in the Job Shop Scheduling Problem (JSP) context. In the MuZero-style variants, `MuZero_v1` achieves a marginally negative correlation ($r = -0.058$) with the optimality gap, while the baseline `MuZero` variant exhibits a slightly positive correlation ($r = 0.058$). Overall, across all experiments, `MuZero_v1` yields the lowest average optimality gap, indicating superior performance in minimizing the makespan.

An analysis of all exploration terms and the b parameter (as introduced in Table 2) was conducted using the feature importance and correlation tools provided by the WandB platform [2]. Correlations between individual exploration terms, the b parameter and the resulting optimality gap are reported in Table 4. Comparing the best-performing variant within each family of exploration terms (UCT, $PUCT$, $MuZero$) reveals a common structural pattern: all contain the denominator term $1 + N(s, a)$. This structure appears beneficial for the JSP dynamics. In contrast, using $N(s, a)$ alone causes the score to become infinite for previously unvisited nodes, forcing premature rollouts and potentially leading to suboptimal exploration. Including $1 + N(s, a)$ prevents such forced rollouts and yields more balanced search behavior. No performance benefit was observed for higher values of the b parameter, which controls the incorporation of best-known action values into the tree policy. Across all experiment families, higher b values did not result in improved makespans, suggesting that the best-action bias may be detrimental for JSPs. Figure 2 illustrates the relationship between b values and empirically observed optimality gaps and showcases the corresponding distribution.

For neural MCTS, policies were trained for 312,500 timesteps in the *ft06* instance and 2 million timesteps in *ft10*. This training phase is visible in the makespan plots, where the agent initially approaches a local optimum. Once policy training concludes, MCTS search starts, constructing a final solution using the remaining computational budget. During training, the number of novel states visited $\left\|\hat{S}\right\|$ stagnates, indicating a convergence toward a local strategy. Afterward, the MCTS search resumes effective exploration, uncovering states that would not be reached by the policy alone.

When comparing neural MCTS with curiosity-driven RL agents (PPO+ICM and PPO+EC), neural MCTS explores a greater number of states while consistently achieving lower makespans. This suggests that neural MCTS makes more effective use of available computational resources, offering improved exploration and exploitation capabilities.

Finally, an important observation is made from the comparison of $\|S\|$ and $\left\|\hat{S}\right\|$. The latter grows by several orders of magnitude less than the former. This indicates that most of the states are visited during rollouts. As rollouts rely on step-based simulation, replacing them with fast value predictions from neural networks could significantly reduce computational overhead in future neural MCTS implementations.

Table 4. Feature importance and correlation of different parameters with visual bar representations.

Parameter	Importance	Correlation
b	0.386	0.054
UCT_v0	0.0	−0.009
UCT_v1	0.007	−0.148
UCT_v2	0.015	−0.129
PUCT_v0	0.0	−0.037
PUCT_v1	0.004	−0.148
PUCT_v2	0.064	0.128
PUCT_v3	0.011	−0.068
PUCT_v4	0.386	0.512
PUCT_v5	0.007	−0.094
PUCT_v6	0.002	−0.018
PUCT_v7	0.009	−0.126
PUCT_v8	0.044	−0.056
PUCT_v9	0.002	−0.085
PUCT_v10	0.125	0.239
MuZero_v0	0.01	−0.172
MuZero_v1	0.022	−0.243

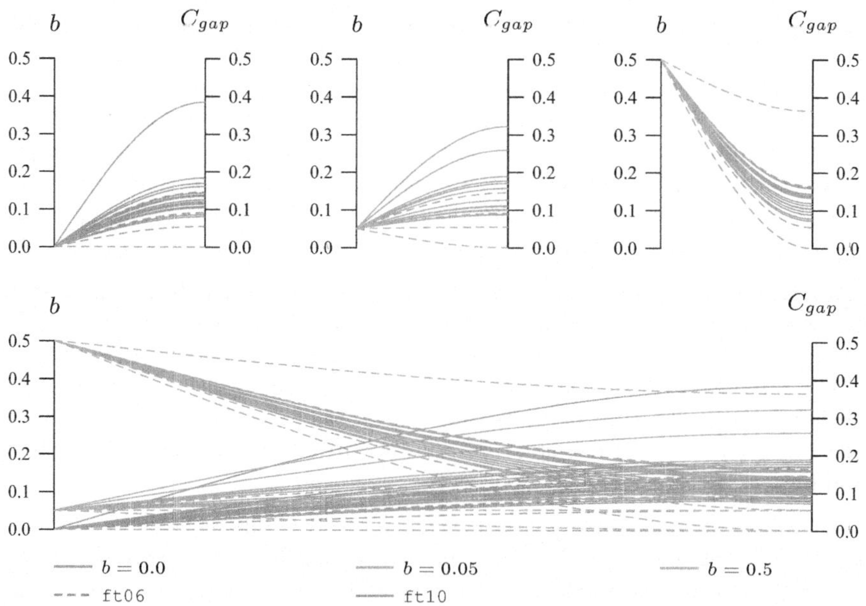

Fig. 2. Parallel Coordinates Plot of the b-Parameter and the Optimality Gap of the resulting solution.

6 Conclusion

This work investigated the exploration–exploitation trade-off in MCTS and neural MCTS agents for solving JSPs. A range of exploration terms, including UCT, $PUCT$, and $MuZero$-style variants, were evaluated across different configurations and decision budgets. The experiments were conducted on widely adopted JSP benchmark instances (*ft06* and *ft10*), and performance was assessed in terms of makespan and state visitation metrics. The results demonstrate that the choice of exploration term significantly impacts scheduling performance. Among the tested configurations, MuZero-style exploration with adjusted scaling terms (`MuZero_v1`) achieved the lowest optimality gaps, followed by variants of UCT and $PUCT$ that incorporate a $1 + N(s, a)$ denominator structure. Exploration terms omitting the visit count entirely, such as `PUCT_v4`, performed poorly, suggesting that a balanced reliance on prior knowledge and empirical visit statistics is critical in JSPs.

The comparison with curiosity-driven reinforcement learning agents highlights the superior sample efficiency of neural MCTS, which not only visits a larger number of meaningful states but also consistently yields lower makespans. The analysis of visited states excluding rollouts further supports the potential of using learned value functions to reduce reliance on costly environment interactions.

In conclusion, neural MCTS offers a robust and scalable approach to dynamic and complex scheduling tasks, when equipped with well-structured exploration functions and guided by trained policies. Future work may explore alternative strategies for incorporating the best-known action value $B(s, a)$ into the tree policy formulations presented in Eqs. 7 and 8. One potential direction is the following modified tree policy:

$$\pi_{\text{base}}(s, a) = (1 - b) \cdot \frac{W(s, a)}{N(s, a)} + b \cdot B(s, a) + \pi_{\text{expl}}(s, a)$$

This approach blends the average return $\frac{W(s,a)}{N(s,a)}$ directly with the best-known return $B(s, a)$, instead of mixing the full tree policy output with the best-known value. Such a formulation may offer a more interpretable and controllable trade-off between exploration and exploitation, particularly in dynamic scheduling contexts.

Another promising direction for future research is to evaluate exploration–exploitation behavior in neural MCTS when using neural value estimators for node evaluation, instead of relying on random rollouts. This substitution could further reduce environment interactions and improve computational efficiency while maintaining or improving solution quality.

Online Resources

Code Repository. The source code for the Experiments is available as a Github Repository: https://github.com/Alexander-Nasuta/gymcts-jsp-exploration-experiments.

Experiment Tracking. The Experiment results and tracked metrics are available on Weights & Biases: https://wandb.ai/querry/gymcts-jsp.

Acknowledgements. This work has been supported by the FAIRWork project (www.fairwork-project.eu) and has been funded within the European Commission's Horizon Europe Programme under contract number 101069499. This paper expresses the opinions of the authors and not necessarily those of the European Commission. The European Commission is not liable for any use that may be made of the information contained in this paper.

Author contributions. Alexander Nasuta: Conceptualization, Methodology, Investigation, Software, Writing – Original Draft.
Hans A. Zhou: Supervision, Writing – Review & Editing.
Anas Abdelrazeq: Supervision, Writing – Review & Editing.
Robert H. Schmitt: Writing – Review & Editing, Supervision, Funding Acquisition, Resources.

Appendix

Table 5. Normalized representation of the disjunctive graph in Fig. 1b. Reproduced from Nasuta et al. [15].

	T_1	T_2	T_3	T_4	T_5	T_6	T_7	T_8	M_1	M_2	M_3	M_4	p
T_1	0	$\frac{11}{16}$	0	0	0	0	0	0	1	0	0	0	$\frac{11}{16}$
T_2	0	0	$\frac{3}{16}$	0	0	0	0	0	0	1	0	0	$\frac{3}{16}$
T_3	0	0	0	$\frac{3}{16}$	0	0	0	0	0	0	1	0	$\frac{3}{16}$
T_4	0	0	0	0	0	0	0	0	0	0	0	1	$\frac{12}{16}$
T_5	$\frac{5}{16}$	0	0	0	0	$\frac{5}{16}$	0	0	1	0	0	0	$\frac{5}{16}$
T_6	0	0	0	0	0	0	$\frac{16}{16}$	0	0	0	1	0	$\frac{16}{16}$
T_7	0	0	0	0	0	0	0	$\frac{7}{16}$	0	1	0	0	$\frac{7}{16}$
T_8	0	0	0	0	0	0	0	0	0	0	0	1	$\frac{4}{16}$

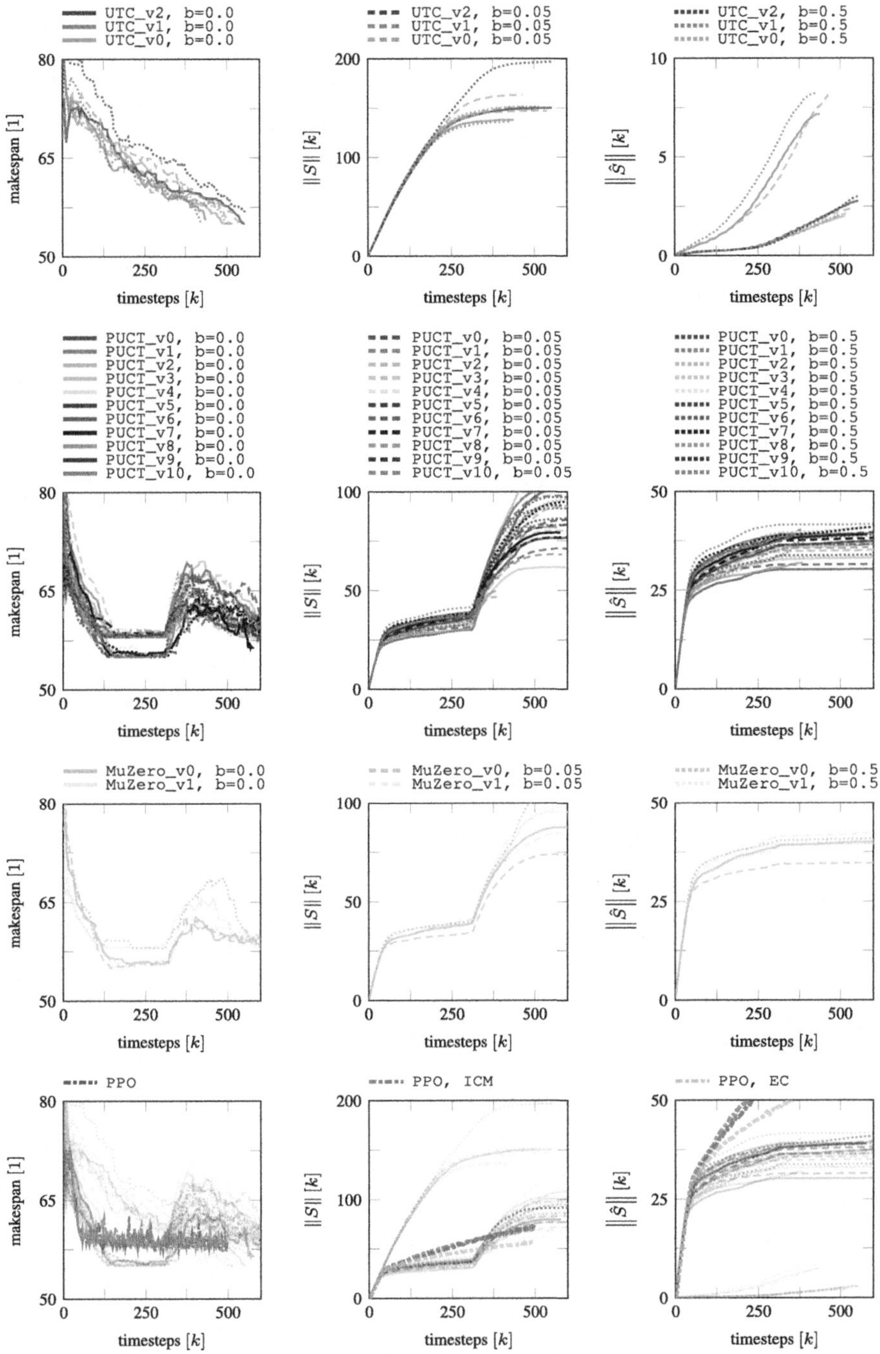

Fig. 3. Evaluation runs on the `ft06` instance. Each row corresponds to a set of guidance functions and presents three plots: makespan, visited states, and visited states without rollouts over timesteps (cf. Table 3). The last row shows runs with curiosity-based exploration functions reported in [15].

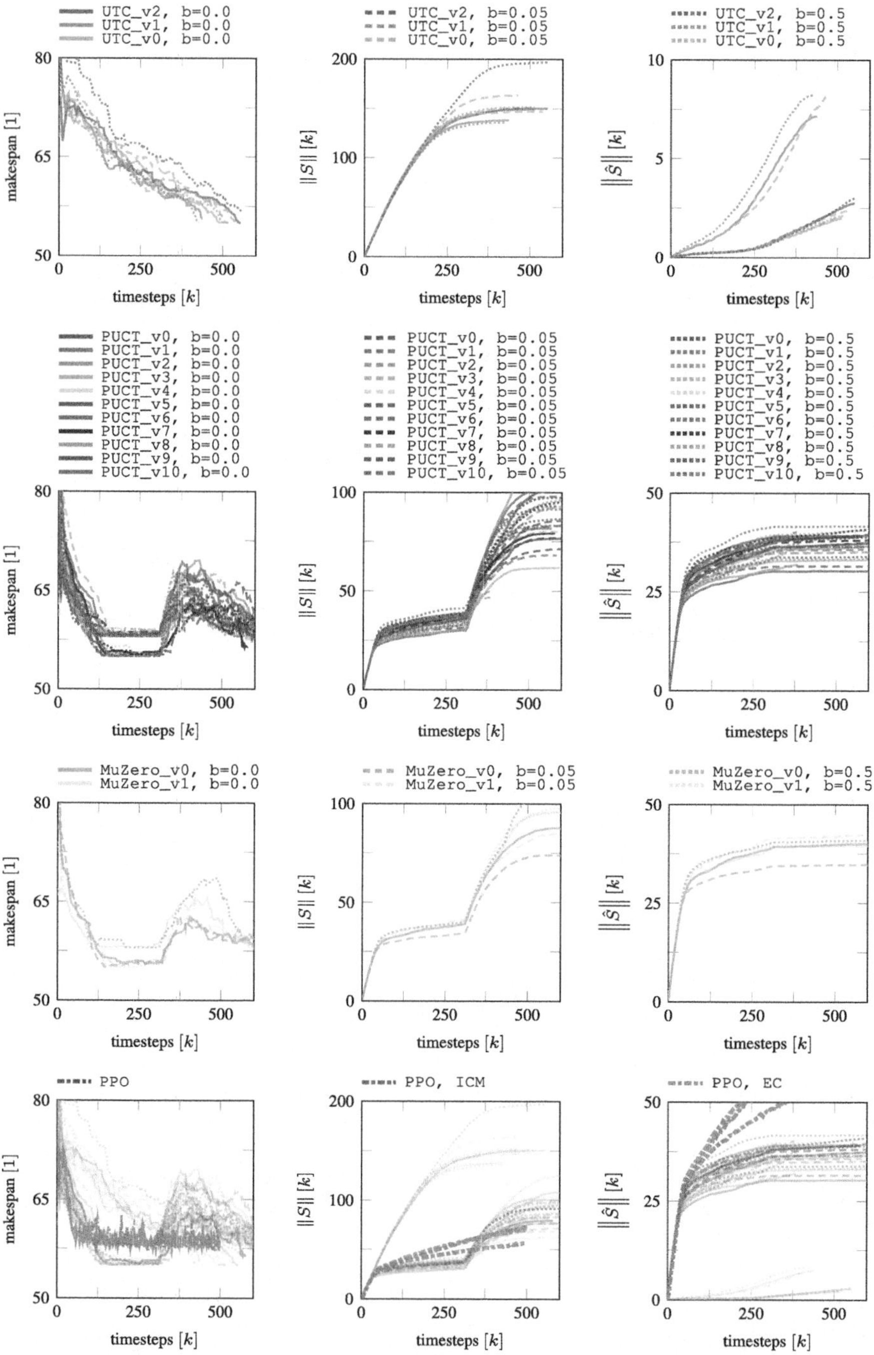

Fig. 4. Evaluation runs on the `ft10` instance. Each row corresponds to a set of guidance functions and presents three plots: makespan, visited states, and visited states without rollouts over timesteps (cf. Table 3). The last row shows runs with curiosity-based exploration functions reported in [15].

Table 6. Overview of experimental runs on instance `ft06`. Each row lists the corresponding guidance function, blending parameter b (cf. Equation 7, Table 2), total timesteps, achieved makespan, and optimality gap. Values for `PPO`, `PPO + ICM`, and `PPO + EC` are taken from Nasuta et al. [15].

Run Name	Instance	Guidance Function	b	Timesteps	Makespan	Optimality Gap
cosmic-sweep-1	ft06	UCT_v0	0.0	515656	55	0
fearless-sweep-1	ft06	UCT_v0	0.05	517886	55	0
sweet-sweep-4	ft06	UCT_v0	0.5	515353	55	0
breezy-sweep-2	ft06	UCT_v1	0.0	438902	55	0
daily-sweep-2	ft06	UCT_v1	0.05	465054	55	0
morning-sweep-5	ft06	UCT_v1	0.5	424978	55	0
true-sweep-3	ft06	UCT_v2	0.0	554726	55	0
wild-sweep-3	ft06	UCT_v2	0.05	539485	55	0
sparkling-sweep-6	ft06	UCT_v2	0.5	557464	55	0
wandering-sweep-1	ft06	PUCT_v0	0.0	578477	55	0
cool-sweep-1	ft06	PUCT_v0	0.05	614191	55	0
devoted-sweep-14	ft06	PUCT_v0	0.5	618857	55	0
faithful-sweep-1	ft06	PUCT_v1	0.0	569539	58	0.05
soft-sweep-2	ft06	PUCT_v1	0.05	584687	58	0.05
jumping-sweep-3	ft06	PUCT_v1	0.5	598123	58	0.05
fiery-sweep-2	ft06	PUCT_v2	0.0	663340	55	0
wise-sweep-3	ft06	PUCT_v2	0.05	646587	55	0
generous-sweep-4	ft06	PUCT_v2	0.5	656333	55	0
fearless-sweep-4	ft06	PUCT_v3	0.0	594531	58	0.05
spring-sweep-4	ft06	PUCT_v3	0.05	603292	58	0.05
restful-sweep-17	ft06	PUCT_v3	0.5	592914	55	0
restful-sweep-5	ft06	PUCT_v4	0.0	325527	63	0.15
silver-sweep-5	ft06	PUCT_v4	0.05	325658	63	0.15
jumping-sweep-18	ft06	PUCT_v4	0.5	327367	75	0.36
gallant-sweep-6	ft06	PUCT_v5	0.0	630308	58	0.05
dutiful-sweep-6	ft06	PUCT_v5	0.05	607040	58	0.05
legendary-sweep-19	ft06	PUCT_v5	0.5	621143	55	0
wild-sweep-7	ft06	PUCT_v6	0.0	615028	58	0.05
happy-sweep-7	ft06	PUCT_v6	0.05	654717	58	0.05
colorful-sweep-20	ft06	PUCT_v6	0.5	624414	58	0.05
serene-sweep-8	ft06	PUCT_v7	0.0	620465	58	0.05
cool-sweep-8	ft06	PUCT_v7	0.05	639174	58	0.05
swift-sweep-21	ft06	PUCT_v7	0.5	633529	55	0
laced-sweep-9	ft06	PUCT_v8	0.0	383748	58	0.05
still-sweep-9	ft06	PUCT_v8	0.05	385315	60	0.09
smooth-sweep-22	ft06	PUCT_v8	0.5	376189	64	0.16
wobbly-sweep-10	ft06	PUCT_v9	0.0	605353	58	0.05
confused-sweep-10	ft06	PUCT_v9	0.05	619692	55	0
misunderstood-sweep-23	ft06	PUCT_v9	0.5	582827	58	0.05
ancient-sweep-11	ft06	PUCT_v10	0.0	360929	60	0.09
hearty-sweep-11	ft06	PUCT_v10	0.05	380441	61	0.11
magic-sweep-24	ft06	PUCT_v10	0.5	391949	58	0.05
feasible-sweep-12	ft06	MuZero_v0	0.0	625514	58	0.05
stellar-sweep-12	ft06	MuZero_v0	0.05	632087	55	0
youthful-sweep-25	ft06	MuZero_v0	0.5	642345	55	0
earthy-sweep-13	ft06	MuZero_v1	0.0	620135	55	0
toasty-sweep-13	ft06	MuZero_v1	0.05	629966	55	0
apricot-sweep-26	ft06	MuZero_v1	0.5	630975	58	0.05
glad-glitter-1768	ft06	PPO	–	501120	55	0
toasty-sea-1775	ft06	PPO + ICM	–	501120	55	0
royal-salad-1781	ft06	PPO + EC	–	501120	56	0.02

Table 7. Overview of experimental runs on instance `ft10`. Each row lists the corresponding guidance function, blending parameter b (cf. Equation 7, Table 2), total timesteps, achieved makespan, and optimality gap. Values for `PPO` and `PPO + ICM` are taken from Nasuta et al. [15].

Run Name	Instance	Guidance Function	b	Timesteps	Makespan	Optimality Gap
toasty-sweep-1	ft10	UCT_v0	0.0	4380023	1063	0.14
atomic-sweep-1	ft10	UCT_v0	0.05	4380936	1088	0.17
gallant-sweep-4	ft10	UCT_v0	0.5	4352022	1053	0.13
radiant-sweep-2	ft10	UCT_v1	0.0	4544915	1030	0.11
winter-sweep-2	ft10	UCT_v1	0.05	4570493	1032	0.11
ethereal-sweep-5	ft10	UCT_v1	0.5	4557208	1056	0.14
graceful-sweep-3	ft10	UCT_v2	0.0	4501093	1058	0.14
decent-sweep-3	ft10	UCT_v2	0.05	4473967	1011	0.09
soft-sweep-6	ft10	UCT_v2	0.5	4497675	1059	0.14
neat-sweep-1	ft10	PUCT_v0	0.0	4349736	1087	0.17
different-sweep-14	ft10	PUCT_v0	0.05	4307164	1171	0.26
sweet-sweep-27	ft10	PUCT_v0	0.5	4334414	1058	0.14
icy-sweep-2	ft10	PUCT_v1	0.0	4244047	1288	0.38
stellar-sweep-15	ft10	PUCT_v1	0.05	4241442	1105	0.19
chocolate-sweep-28	ft10	PUCT_v1	0.5	4255012	1026	0.1
bumbling-sweep-3	ft10	PUCT_v2	0.0	4361793	1036	0.11
brisk-sweep-16	ft10	PUCT_v2	0.05	4322011	1024	0.1
hopeful-sweep-29	ft10	PUCT_v2	0.5	4348312	1002	0.08
polar-sweep-4	ft10	PUCT_v3	0.0	4367194	1027	0.1
leafy-sweep-17	ft10	PUCT_v3	0.05	4289762	1088	0.17
kind-sweep-30	ft10	PUCT_v3	0.5	4355995	1053	0.13
lemon-sweep-5	ft10	PUCT_v4	0.0	2281756	1005	0.08
restful-sweep-18	ft10	PUCT_v4	0.05	2364603	1024	0.1
pleasant-sweep-31	ft10	PUCT_v4	0.5	2277878	1012	0.09
exalted-sweep-6	ft10	PUCT_v5	0.0	4258422	1079	0.16
bumbling-sweep-19	ft10	PUCT_v5	0.05	4265153	1047	0.13
exalted-sweep-6	ft10	PUCT_v5	0.5	4258422	1079	0.16
misty-sweep-7	ft10	PUCT_v6	0.0	4404266	1058	0.14
jolly-sweep-20	ft10	PUCT_v6	0.05	4408965	1094	0.18
eager-sweep-33	ft10	PUCT_v6	0.5	4386009	1077	0.16
azure-sweep-8	ft10	PUCT_v7	0.0	4358585	1046	0.12
elated-sweep-21	ft10	PUCT_v7	0.05	4364985	1033	0.11
snowy-sweep-34	ft10	PUCT_v7	0.5	4304771	1040	0.12
cosmic-sweep-9	ft10	PUCT_v8	0.0	3428075	1041	0.12
serene-sweep-22	ft10	PUCT_v8	0.05	3308874	1022	0.1
usual-sweep-35	ft10	PUCT_v8	0.5	3589474	1027	0.1
silver-sweep-10	ft10	PUCT_v9	0.0	4144556	1055	0.13
leafy-sweep-23	ft10	PUCT_v9	0.05	4279058	1076	0.16
hardy-sweep-36	ft10	PUCT_v9	0.5	4293912	1034	0.11
woven-sweep-11	ft10	PUCT_v10	0.0	3719284	1037	0.12
volcanic-sweep-24	ft10	PUCT_v10	0.05	3382997	1023	0.1
swift-sweep-37	ft10	PUCT_v10	0.5	3592378	997	0.07
fine-sweep-12	ft10	MuZero_v0	0.0	4397068	1100	0.18
blooming-sweep-25	ft10	MuZero_v0	0.05	4328748	1012	0.09
rosy-sweep-38	ft10	MuZero_v0	0.5	4229199	1019	0.1
desert-sweep-13	ft10	MuZero_v1	0.0	4356165	1010	0.09
fresh-sweep-26	ft10	MuZero_v1	0.05	4350117	1229	0.32
breezy-sweep-39	ft10	MuZero_v1	0.5	4305101	1063	0.14
upbeat-pyramid-1785	ft10	PPO	–	4003200	1120	0.2
worthy-morning-1787	ft10	PPO + ICM	–	4003200	1065	0.15

References

1. Bellemare, M., Srinivasan, S., Ostrovski, G., Schaul, T., Saxton, D., Munos, R.: Unifying count-based exploration and intrinsic motivation. Adv. Neural Inf. Process. Syst. **29** (2016)
2. Biewald, L.: Experiment tracking with weights and biases (2020)
3. Błażewicz, J., Ecker, K.H., Pesch, E., Schmidt, G., Sterna, M., Weglarz, J.: Handbook on Scheduling: From Theory to Practice. Springer, Heidelberg (2019)
4. Browne, C.B., et al.: A survey of Monte Carlo tree search methods. IEEE Trans. Comput. Intell. AI Games **4**(1), 1–43 (2012)
5. Deng, H., Yuan, X., Tian, Y., Hu, J.: Neural-augmented two-stage Monte Carlo tree search with over-sampling for protein folding in hp model. IEEJ Trans. Electr. Electron. Eng. **17**(5), 685–694 (2022)
6. Fisher, H.: Probabilistic learning combinations of local job-shop scheduling rules. Ind. Schedul. 225–251 (1963)
7. Göppert, A., Mohring, L., Schmitt, R.H.: Predicting performance indicators with ANNs for ai-based online scheduling in dynamically interconnected assembly systems. Prod. Eng. Res. Devel. **15**(5), 619–633 (2021)
8. Kemmerling, M., Abdelrazeq, A., Schmitt, R.H.: Solving job shop problems with neural Monte Carlo tree search. In: ICAART (3), pp. 149–158 (2024)
9. Kemmerling, M., Lütticke, D., Schmitt, R.H.: Beyond games: a systematic review of neural Monte Carlo tree search applications. Appl. Intell. **54**(1), 1020–1046 (2024)
10. Kemmerling, M., Schmitt, R.H., Elgeti, S.N.: Job shop scheduling with neural monte carlo tree search. Technical report, Lehrstuhl für Informations-, Qualitäts-und Sensorsysteme in der Produktion (2024)
11. Kocsis, L., Szepesvári, C.: Bandit based Monte-Carlo planning. In: Fürnkranz, J., Scheffer, T., Spiliopoulou, M. (eds.) ECML 2006. LNCS (LNAI), vol. 4212, pp. 282–293. Springer, Heidelberg (2006). https://doi.org/10.1007/11871842_29
12. Nasuta, A.: GYMCTS: a Monte Carlo tree search library for gymnasium-style environments (2025). https://doi.org/10.5281/zenodo.15283390
13. Nasuta, A.: Job Shop Scheduling Problem Benchmark Instances (1.0.4) (2025). https://doi.org/10.5281/zenodo.15063451
14. Nasuta, A., Kemmerling, M., Lütticke, D., Schmitt, R.H.: Reward shaping for job shop scheduling. In: International Conference on Machine Learning, Optimization, and Data Science, pp. 197–211. Springer, Heidelberg (2023). https://doi.org/10.1007/978-3-031-53969-5_16
15. Nasuta, A., Kemmerling, M., Zhou, H., Abdelrazeq, A., Schmitt, R.H.: Curiosity driven reinforcement learning for job shop scheduling. In: Proceedings of the 17th International Conference on Agents and Artificial Intelligence, vol. 2: ICAART, pp. 216–227. INSTICC, SciTePress (2025). https://doi.org/10.5220/0013143800003890
16. Pathak, D., Agrawal, P., Efros, A.A., Darrell, T.: Curiosity-driven exploration by self-supervised prediction. In: International Conference on Machine Learning, pp. 2778–2787. PMLR (2017)
17. Raffin, A., Hill, A., Gleave, A., Kanervisto, A., Ernestus, M., Dormann, N.: Stable-baselines3: reliable reinforcement learning implementations. J. Mach. Learn. Res. **22**(268), 1–8 (2021)
18. Rinciog, A., Mieth, C., Scheikl, P.M., Meyer, A.: Sheet-metal production scheduling using Alphago zero. In: Proceedings of the Conference on Production Systems and Logistics: CPSL 2020. Hannover: publishing (2020)
19. Savinov, N., et al.: Episodic curiosity through reachability. arXiv preprint arXiv:1810.02274 (2018)

20. Schmidhuber, J.: A possibility for implementing curiosity and boredom in model-building neural controllers. In: Proceedings of the International Conference on Simulation of Adaptive Behavior: From Animals to Animats, pp. 222–227 (1991)
21. Silver, D., et al.: A general reinforcement learning algorithm that masters chess, shogi, and go through self-play. Science **362**(6419), 1140–1144 (2018)
22. Song, S., Chen, H., Sun, H., Liu, M.: Data efficient reinforcement learning for integrated lateral planning and control in automated parking system. Sensors **20**(24), 7297 (2020)
23. Vodopivec, T., Samothrakis, S., Ster, B.: On Monte Carlo tree search and reinforcement learning. J. Artif. Intell. Res. **60**, 881–936 (2017)
24. Wang, Q., Hao, Y., Cao, J.: Learning to traverse over graphs with a Monte Carlo tree search-based self-play framework. Eng. Appl. Artif. Intell. **105**, 104422 (2021)
25. Wang, S., Zhou, K., Lai, K., Shen, J.: Task-completion dialogue policy learning via Monte Carlo tree search with dueling network. In: Proceedings of the 2020 Conference on Empirical Methods in Natural Language Processing (EMNLP), pp. 3461–3471 (2020)
26. Xu, R., Lieberherr, K.: Learning self-game-play agents for combinatorial optimization problems. arXiv preprint arXiv:1903.03674 (2019)
27. Zhang, C., Song, W., Cao, Z., Zhang, J., Tan, P.S., Chi, X.: Learning to dispatch for job shop scheduling via deep reinforcement learning. Adv. Neural. Inf. Process. Syst. **33**, 1621–1632 (2020)

Exploring the Usability and Applicability of Proof of Learning in Binary Neural Networks

Zoltán-Valentin Gyulai-Nagy(✉)

Department of Computer Science, Babeş-Bolyai University, Cluj-Napoca, Romania
zoltan.gyulai@ubbcluj.ro
https://www.ubbcluj.ro/en/

Abstract. This extended work builds on our previous proposal of using Binary Neural Networks (BNNs) for transaction validation in blockchain systems. As interest grows in combining AI with decentralized technologies, using blockchain's computational power for machine learning tasks becomes increasingly relevant. Current consensus mechanisms lack integration with productive computation, presenting a gap this research addresses. We explore how Proof of Learning can be applied to train multiple BNNs during block generation, transforming validation into a dual-purpose process. This extension builds upon the original approach by deepening the exploration of the topic and evaluating additional scenarios to assess its broader applicability. Our key message is that blockchain validation can simultaneously produce efficient, lightweight models for real-world applications. Experiments show our method maintains blockchain performance and offers an optimized, accessible alternative for AI training. These findings highlight the potential for intelligent, multi-functional blockchains that serve both security and utility.

Keywords: Blockchain Technology · Proof of Learning (PoL) · Binarized Neural Networks (BNNs) · Neural Network Quantization Techniques · Decentralized Machine Learning · Blockchain-Based Model Training · Lightweight AI Models

1 Introduction

The recent surge in artificial intelligence development has sparked a wave of innovation, opening new avenues to enhance user experience across a wide range of applications. As AI becomes increasingly integrated into everyday life, discussions continue across various domains regarding its potential to replace traditional human labor [29]. These developments signal a transition into a new phase of machine learning—one where public awareness and adoption are rapidly growing, with efforts focused on embedding AI into routine, repetitive tasks to improve efficiency [30].

H. J. van den Herik et al. (Eds.): ICAART 2025, LNAI 16517, pp. 87–112, 2026.
https://doi.org/10.1007/978-3-032-25032-2_5

This article serves as an extension of our previous work, building upon its foundations to further explore and refine the integration of AI within decentralized and resilient systems [1]. Our continued research aims to address emerging challenges while using the evolving landscape of AI-driven automation.

New tools are constantly emerging and being developed for the market. Some solve real-world problems, but others are just unpolished generalizations of an idea that won't bring real market value. Open-source communities are also excited about the latest AI developments. They are trying to bring tools that can be used freely on their computers or servers to the general public. Many domains have already started experimenting with such technologies, and even if it's not clear which tools are going to resist the challenge of time, as the competition is really high, we can conclude that the technological requirements to run such algorithms and applications are going to just increase in the upcoming years [31].

Technological constraints apply to current AI models. The state-of-the-art models can be big and require lots of resources to train the model completely. Cloud servers have the benefit of having large amounts of on-demand processing power. Therefore, they are popular with many developers who wish to train large models. This seems to be the first step to centralizing training and distributing AI models, but cloud servers have shortcomings. They require funding, and those with the resources to run such a model on a cloud provider will be less keen to make its advancements available and open source to the general public as this would reduce their profitability.

A blockchain might offer a solution to these issues and facilitate bringing AI closer to the community. Utilizing Binary Neural Networks (BNNs) presents its own set of advantages compared to other network types, primarily due to the reduced computational demands associated with them. These networks require significantly less processing power and memory, making them suitable for integration into blockchain systems where efficiency is a key requirement to handle a larger numbers of transactions.

In this paper, we introduce a novel approach that redefines the conventional Proof of Work (PoW) [32] mechanism by integrating elements of Proof of Learning (PoL) [33] and adapting the block validation process to support additional training and inference algorithms. Our method uses Binarized Neural Networks (BNNs) in place of traditional neural network models, enabling the creation of lightweight models that can be efficiently embedded within a blockchain. Additionally, this approach ensures verifiable ownership of the generated models.

The resulting embedded models aim to create a secure, decentralized, and publicly accessible repository of high-performing binary models. Evolutionary algorithms are used to further enhance performance when conventional training methods reach their limits in accuracy improvement or suffer from overfitting, ensuring that the model can still adapt and boost its effectiveness. By embedding the training and optimization of these models into the blockchain framework, we envision a system that not only validates transactions but also continually generates and refines machine learning models. This dual-purpose mechanism makes use of the inherent strengths of blockchain technology to enhance the accessibility and utility of AI, thereby democratizing advanced computational resources and promoting broader participation in AI development.

Our contribution builds on previous methods [34] by introducing a new technique that:

- Stores BNN models within blocks and uses these models for block validation.
- Uses evolutionary algorithms to improve models, even when they have reached their relative best shape and performance

We assessed the proposed method to evaluate its practicality by examining some critical factors: its effect on network bandwidth consumption, the blockchains throughput, its capability to validate blocks while dynamically adjusting the validation difficulty, its resilience to adversarial attacks and the quality and diversity of models across miners. These evaluations provide insight into the feasibility and effectiveness of our approach.

2 Literature Review

Blockchain technology and neural networks have been focal areas of research in recent years, particularly in how they can be optimized and integrated into various applications, including transaction validations. The paper in question introduces a novel integration of BNNs in blockchain technology, particularly for the purpose of transaction validation. This integration is purported to leverage the reduced computational demands of BNNs while maintaining the integrity and scalability essential in blockchain operations.

2.1 Overview of Binary Neural Networks

BNNs are a variation of traditional neural networks where the weights and activations are constrained to binary values (-1 or 1) instead of floating points. BNNs significantly reduce the memory footprint and computational complexity, which makes them suitable for devices with limited hardware capabilities, such as IoT devices and mobile phones [3]. The quantization of network parameters in BNNs results in a significant reduction in memory footprint and computational complexity compared to conventional neural networks [5]. This advantage aligns with the requirements for blockchain operations, particularly in decentralized environments where computational efficiency and low overhead are crucial. The reduced memory requirements make BNNs an attractive option for resource-constrained devices and applications [6].

2.2 Blockchain and Proof of Work

The traditional mechanism for transaction validation and blockchain consensus is PoW, which, while secure, is notoriously energy-intensive and computationally demanding [2]. The integration of BNNs into blockchain validation could potentially mitigate these demands by reducing the computational load required for the validation process. This notion is supported by the exploration of alternative consensus mechanisms that reduce computational requirements [12]. The paper's approach, which integrates BNNs, may provide a pathway towards these less demanding consensus mechanisms.

2.3 Proof of Learning in Blockchain

The concept of Proof of Learning (PoL), a derivative of the PoW concept, involves training a neural network as part of the validation process. The use of machine learning in improving blockchain efficiency has been investigated, but without a specific focus on BNNs [20]. The proposal to use BNNs for PoL is innovative because it directly addresses the limitations of traditional PoW by substituting extensive hashing work with learning tasks, potentially reducing energy consumption and enhancing transaction throughput. Other approaches are based on the concept of Proof of Learning, where consensus is reached by ranking machine learning systems for a given task [7]. This training process requires computational power, but it is a one-time cost compared to the ongoing computational requirements of traditional PoW consensus mechanisms.

While existing approaches already create neural network model side products [34], our work enhances these concepts by incorporating BNNs, noted for their reduced memory demands [35], which facilitate efficient chain operation. In order to enhance the models' accuracy and produce unique model shapes that conventional training might not reach, we also implement evolutionary algorithms. Our validation functions also replace the secure mapping layer (SML), contributing to a more robust tracking of the model evolutions. Our contribution advances the development of an open-source BNN repository for use in practical applications.

2.4 Scalability and Customization

The scalability of blockchain technology is a critical area, especially as networks expand and the number of transactions per second increases. The challenges and potential solutions in blockchain scalability have been highlighted, emphasizing the need for new approaches that don't compromise on decentralization or security [15]. The paper's proposed method, by virtue of the lightweight nature of BNNs, supports scalability and can be customized for different applications, possibly providing a flexible framework adaptable to various blockchain applications. One of the key advantages of the proposed approach is its scalability. BNNs can be trained on low-cost devices like Raspberry Pi, making it accessible to a wide range of users [21]. Additionally, the approach can be customized to meet the specific needs of different applications, allowing for flexibility in implementation.

2.5 Cost-Effectiveness and Accessibility

The aspect of cost efficiency in blockchain operations cannot be overstated. The cost implications of blockchain technology adoption are significant barriers for many organizations [16]. The proposed use of BNNs, trainable on low-cost devices and operable on inexpensive FPGA devices, could lower these barriers, making blockchain technology more accessible across different sectors. Although BNNs are known to have lower accuracy compared to their standard counterparts, the authors propose increasing their accuracy through multiple iterations and improvements. The use of FPGA devices is also suggested for increased efficiency in the validation process [9].

3 Problem Statement and Research Questions

Blockchain technology has transformed transaction processing and validation by offering a decentralized and secure foundation for numerous applications. Despite its advantages, traditional consensus mechanisms like Proof of Work (PoW) [2] face notable drawbacks. These include excessive computational demands, high energy usage, and limited scalability—factors that could hinder the broad adoption and long-term sustainability of blockchain systems [16].

PoW relies on network nodes solving complex cryptographic puzzles to validate transactions and append new blocks, which results in substantial computational load and energy expenditure [17]. As the network expands, the resources needed for PoW also increase, causing delays in transaction confirmations and exacerbating scalability challenges [18]. Additionally, the significant energy consumption linked to PoW has sparked environmental concerns regarding its continued use [19].

To address these challenges, there is a need for alternative consensus mechanisms that can provide efficient and sustainable transaction validation while maintaining the security and integrity of the blockchain network. BNNs have emerged as a promising solution due to their reduced computational complexity and memory requirements compared to traditional neural networks [3]. The integration of BNNs into the blockchain consensus mechanism, known as Proof of Learning (PoL), has the potential to overcome the limitations of PoW and enable scalable and energy-efficient transaction validation.

However, the application of BNNs in the context of blockchain consensus mechanisms is still in its early stages, and several research questions need to be addressed to fully realize the potential of this approach.

This article presents a framework aimed at repurposing the computational power of blockchains. It assumes a foundational understanding of neural networks and blockchain technology. Our focus is limited to the methodology for generating practical, real-world artifacts and using them as the linking mechanism between blocks. A complete implementation would require more extensive documentation. For a deeper understanding of the underlying concepts, the Literature Review chapter offers a solid reference.

The following research questions guided the investigation into the application of BNNs for blockchain transaction validation:

RQ1. How can BNNs be effectively integrated into the blockchain consensus mechanism to enable efficient and secure transaction validation?
RQ2. What BNN architectures and training strategies best support secure and scalable blockchain transaction validation?
RQ3. What are the networking implications—specifically in terms of bandwidth consumption and throughput—of encoding neural networks on the blockchain?
RQ4. How resilient is the Proof of Learning mechanism using BNNs against adversarial attacks or model spoofing?
RQ5. How does decentralization affect the quality and diversity of BNN training across participants in the network?

By addressing these research questions, this study aims to provide a comprehensive understanding of BNNs application in blockchain transaction validation and contribute to the development of efficient, scalable, and sustainable consensus mechanisms for blockchain networks.

4 Methodology

Our proposed modification to the traditional POW framework involves two main algorithm steps: the validation step and conflict resolution with other nodes. They can include BNNs in the workflow to have models as a side product, but we also need to change what data a block contains.

A blockchain has the properties of being a continuous flow of blocks that are linked together. This is done by including the hash of the previous block in the current block to indicate the continuity. In our implementation, this single feature will not be enough; we must have two main features to trace other blocks. One is the previous block, and the second is a block mined in the past that uses the same BNN model as in the current block. We will detail more about the flow and why we need them but we'll start by defining the data structure for a block to have a reference about what data is included inside a block. It is composed of the following variables: index: int, timestamp: datetime, transactions: Type[Transaction], hash: str, previous_hash: str, previous_model_hash: str, model: Type[Model], diff: float and acc: float.

```
class Block(TypedDict):
    index: int
    timestamp: datetime
    transactions: Type[Transaction]
    hash: str
    previous_hash: str
    previous_model_hash: str
    model: Type[Model]
    diff: float
    acc: float
```

The blockchain data model consists of several key fields that play distinct roles in the functioning and integrity of the blockchain. The **index** field serves as a unique identifier for each block, allowing for easy querying and retrieval of specific blocks. The **timestamp** field records the creation time of each block, providing a chronological reference. The **transactions** field is an array that holds multiple transactions within a block, representing the data stored in the blockchain.

The **hash** field stores the cryptographic hash of the current block, ensuring its integrity and immutability. The previous_hash field contains the hash of the preceding block in the chain, establishing a secure link between consecutive blocks.

In addition to the standard blockchain fields, we introduce a new one: **previous_model_hash** field. It stores the hash of the previous block that has been computed using the same model and data. This field enables tracking and verifying the model's consistency across the blockchain.

The **model** is a complex field containing the trained BNNs weights and biases and the computed differences. This field allows for the storage and retrieval of the machine learning models used in the blockchain's consensus mechanism.

The **acc** field represents the accuracy of the current model, providing a measure of its performance. The **diff** field stores the percentage difference between the current and previous models of the same type, allowing for tracking model improvements or changes over time.

These fields allow the blockchain data model to store and verify transactions, ensure the blockchain's integrity and immutability, and facilitate the integration of machine learning models for enhanced consensus mechanisms. In the following subchapters, we will provide more details on how these fields are used and computed.

Another set of constants that we need to keep track of is the one that defines each miner node's running parameter. These values can be updated along the blockchain lifecycle, ensuring the fair distribution of models and de difficulty for each mining node.

```
class MinerConstants(TypedDict):
    min_families: int
    min_population: int
    min_family_diff: float
    min_family_acc: float
    min_population: int
    min_population_acc: float
    min_popuation_diff: float
    max_family_generations: int
    population_corss_percent: float
    population_mutate_percent: float
    model_corss_percent: float
    model_mutate_percent: float
    model_connections_count: int
```

In the following subsections we are going to provide further information about the purpose and role of these constants.

4.1 Tracking Model Differences

Model shape-related differences play an important role in determining when new model shapes are generated. These differences are quantified by examining the number of weights on each layer, the type of connections between layers, and the total number of layers in the model. It is important to note that attempting to generate a new model by simply adding a single neuron and reusing previously computed weights from an earlier generation may seem appealing as a means to avoid recomputing blocks. However, this practice could potentially compromise the integrity of the blockchain. To mitigate this risk, it is essential to ensure that sufficient differences are reported in the model, effectively disabling the possibility of porting neuron weights across families.

The second metric of model differences refers to the multiple values associated with the weights and biases of the model. During the training process, it is conceivable to encounter models where modifying a single layer by porting values from a previous generation leads to improved accuracy. To prevent cyclical value changes and maintain the integrity of the model, it is necessary to establish a mechanism for tracking the modifications made to the model. This can be achieved by assigning an additional value to each binary weight, indicating whether the weight has been assigned both possible values (-1 and 1) in the past. In certain models, a weight may have a value of 0, differing from its default values of -1 and 1. By incorporating this feature, it becomes possible to compare different generations of models and enforce a minimum percentage of differences between them. This ensures that genuine computation has been performed to arrive at a new model with enhanced accuracy rather than relying on superficial modifications.

Furthermore, these two metrics serve to regulate the difficulty of the blockchain. In the face of advancements in hardware performance or increased network participation, these metrics help control the rate at which new models are computed. Additional factors, such as enforcing minimum or maximum sizes for datasets and models, also contribute to maintaining the overall stability and security of the blockchain. Ensuring sufficient differences between models, preventing the porting of neuron weights, and tracking modifications made to weights and biases, the integrity and security of the blockchain can be upheld.

4.2 Training with Evolutive Algorithms

BNNs are characterized by their unique architecture, where neuron weights are quantized to two values. This quantization simplifies the model and reduces computational requirements, making it suitable for resource-constrained environments. However, it also introduces challenges, particularly when models become overfitted and lose accuracy. To address this, our approach uses evolutive algorithms, which can optimize BNNs by iterating through multiple generations of models.

BNNs can initially be trained using standard backpropagation techniques, which serve to create the first generation of models. To improve their accuracy and generalizability, we then apply evolutionary algorithms that iteratively optimize the model population. These algorithms are particularly effective at reducing overfitting by exploring a wide variety of model configurations and selecting the most promising candidates.

Key components of evolutionary algorithms include crossover and mutation, which are used to produce new models from the existing population. In the crossover process, a portion of the weights from each layer of two parent models is selected and swapped to form new offspring models. This enables the combination of characteristics from multiple models, potentially resulting in improved performance. The percentage of weights selected for crossover is defined by the variable population_cross_percent. Nodes across the network use this variable to determine the proportion of weights to be exchanged between models.

Mutation introduces variability by randomly altering a percentage of weights within a model. This helps maintain diversity in the population and prevents premature convergence to suboptimal solutions. The percentage of weights subject to mutation is controlled by the variable population_mutate_percent. This ensures that each model undergoes a predefined level of mutation, promoting exploration of the solution space.

We also apply evolutionary algorithms to optimize the architecture of the models. While the approach is similar to the one used for refining model weights—relying on crossover and mutation—it introduces an additional control variable that governs model complexity. Specifically, we define a constraint on the maximum number of neuron connections a model can have, helping to keep models lightweight and computationally efficient.

This constraint is enforced through a predefined variable, max_connection_count, which sets an upper limit on the total number of connections in a model, ensuring the architecture remains within practical complexity bounds.

Overfitting occurs when a model performs well on training data but fails to generalize to unseen data, resulting in reduced accuracy. Evolutionary algorithms mitigate this by generating and evaluating multiple model iterations. Through the mechanisms of crossover and mutation, they explore diverse architectural configurations, ultimately identifying models with superior generalization and enhanced performance.

This optimization process, however, can be computationally intensive. Each iteration involves evaluating the models against the dataset, requiring significant processing power. Given the distributed nature of blockchain, this computational burden is shared across the network's miner nodes, using their collective resources.

4.3 Electing a Model to Train

When we talk about a blockchain, our first step is to define the rules that will enable a unified way of training and embedding BNNs in the blocks. The results must be computed incrementally, and for the same data set, we can have multiple models trained across blocks. When we talk about a large-scale blockchain that has miner nodes linked from across the world, we need to have enough possible models to be worked on. This ensures that a smaller number of resources is wasted on computation for the same model. At the same time, we need to be conscious of the fact that a large number of transactions will require large numbers of models to be processed. Based on the previous statements, we need to satisfy the following criteria: models need to be continuously available.

We can list a few scenarios for neural network families that will provide different types of constraints on when a new node can generate a new model. A model family defines a type of model with the same shape used on the same dataset. Everything starts with an end user uploading a new dataset to the network. The dataset would be distributed among the nodes so that the miners can access it. If they train a model based on a specific dataset, they can construct a complete local copy and use it to train and validate models.

The nodes, having multiple datasets at their disposal, can start mining. When a dataset is fresh, new neural network models will begin to be generated with the help of evolutive algorithms. The process makes use of selecting and training random model shapes that do not yet existent in the blockchain [14]. This process will keep track of a constant embedded in the miner, named "min_families," that will define how many models will be accepted in the network.

Once we have the models at our disposal, a few additional ones will need to be trained; the model can be trained via conventional backpropagation. A constant named "min_population" will be a threshold used across the network to state how many such models can be trained, and a "min_family_acc" will define what is the minimum accuracy of the model required. The network will already have one model from the previous step. A key constraint for this step is that the model nodes need to have a minimum amount of differences tracked with a variable named "min_family_diff".

Once all of these models have been trained, they can be optimized further with evolutive algorithms. From inside a family the population will be taken as a base sample. The "min_population" variable will define the number of required trained models from the same generation, enabling the evolutive algorithm to generate new models. Only the best models will be selected from a family to serve as the population for the new model. The acceptance criteria will need to satisfy the "min_population_acc" and "min_population_diff" to be accepted.

Figure 1 illustrates how generations are constructed on the blockchain.

4.4 Block Placement

In the previous subsection, we outlined how models can be generated to support continuous mining operations. Each block is positioned in a predetermined

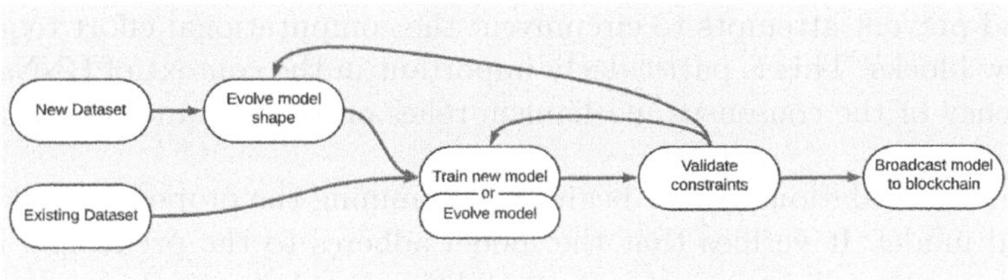

Fig. 1. Proposed block creation flow [1].

sequence. Given the presence of multiple data sources, some models may be easier to compute than others, creating the risk of unequal model distribution. To maintain fairness, it is essential to ensure that no dataset gains a disproportionate number of trained models while others are underrepresented.

Although the structure of a block allows it to reference both its predecessor and a related model from the same family, enabling the theoretical possibility of forming multiple parallel blockchains, this is not desirable. Managing numerous chains would add unnecessary complexity. Therefore, a scheduling mechanism is needed to prioritize model generation based on the number of existing models per dataset within the blockchain.

A counter within the "Model" type, named model_count, tracks the number of models within each family. This counter increments with the addition of new models and ensures balanced growth across datasets. Block placement will be regulated to maintain parity relative to the dataset's entry date. For example, if two existing families are at generation 5 and a new dataset is introduced, the two existing families will each have a model_count of 5, while the new family will start at 1. In the following generation, all families must be included, resulting in updated counts of 6, 6, and 2.

Additionally, a variable called max_family_generations defines the maximum number of models allowed within a family. Once this limit is reached, a new model schema is created under a new family, with preference given to datasets that currently have fewer families. This approach ensures balanced representation and prevents overconcentration of model training on specific datasets.

4.5 Block Validation

Block validation is an important component of the blockchain consensus mechanism, ensuring the integrity and security of the network. In the context of integrating BNNs into the blockchain, block validation takes on an additional dimension by keeping track of all the previous models and their associated changes. In this subsection, we are going to review how block validation works and its role in guaranteeing the legitimacy of accepted blocks.

At its core, block validation serves as a safeguard against potential attacks and manipulations within the blockchain network. By maintaining a complete record of previous models and their modifications, the validation process can detect and prevent attempts to circumvent the computational effort required to create new blocks. This is particularly important in the context of BNNs, where the efficiency of the consensus mechanism relies on the genuine computation of models.

The block validation process begins by examining the proposed block and its associated model. It verifies that the model adheres to the predefined requirements, such as the minimum percentage of differences between the current model and its predecessors. This ensures that the model has undergone sufficient computational effort and has not been created through superficial modifications or the porting of neuron weights from previous generations.

This happens by checking the integrity of the model's weights and biases. It verifies that the weights have been assigned appropriate values and that any changes made to the model are traceable and legitimate. The validation process can detect and prevent cyclical value changes by maintaining a record of the modifications made to each weight, including assigning both possible values (-1 and 1) in the past. The "min_popuation_diff" variable is used to check the minimum required differences.

The validation of the model's accuracy is guided by a distributed variable known as "min_population_acc". This variable represents the minimum accuracy threshold that must be surpassed by the proposed model for it to be considered a valid improvement. By comparing the achieved accuracy with the "min_population_acc" value, the miner can determine whether the block satisfies the accuracy requirements set by the network consensus.

If the model's accuracy, as evaluated by the miner, aligns with the accuracy reported within the block and exceeds the "min_population_acc" threshold, the block is deemed valid. This validation process ensures that only models that demonstrate genuine advancements in accuracy are accepted into the blockchain. By enforcing this accuracy improvement criterion, the network maintains a high standard of model quality and prevents the inclusion of subpar or manipulated models.

The distribution of the "min_population_acc" and "min_population_diff" variables among miners is a critical aspect of the validation process. It ensures that all miners operate under the same accuracy requirements and prevents any individual miner from manipulating the validation criteria. The decentralized nature of this variable's distribution reinforces the security and integrity of the blockchain network.

Further values are evaluated to make sure that the new block satisfies all of the constraints in place for miners. The constants for model families, populations, and generations are all validated and checked to conform with the previous blocks.

In addition to model validation, block validation also encompasses the verification of transactions included within the block. It ensures that the transactions are valid, non-duplicated, and adhere to the consensus rules of the blockchain network. This includes checking the authenticity of the transaction signatures, verifying the balance of the sending addresses, and ensuring that the transactions do not violate any network-specific constraints.

Block validation contributes to the decentralization and trustlessness of the blockchain network. By enabling each node to independently validate the proposed blocks and their associated models, it eliminates the need for a central authority and ensures that the network operates on a consensus basis. This decentralized validation process is essential for maintaining the integrity and immutability of the blockchain.

4.6 Conflict Resolution

In blockchain networks, conflicts may arise when multiple nodes simultaneously accept a block. This scenario requires mechanisms to ensure that all participants reach a consensus and agree on a unified version of the blockchain. Conflict resolution is critical to maintaining the integrity and consistency of the blockchain, preventing forks, and ensuring smooth network operation.

To address this, blockchain networks use specific protocols designed to resolve conflicts and arrive at a single chain of blocks. When nodes encounter conflicting blocks, they must decide which block to accept by following predefined rules. One common method for resolving such conflicts is the "longest chain rule". According to this rule, nodes will continue to mine and build upon the chain that has the most blocks, assuming that the longest chain is the correct one because it represents the most accumulated PoW.

However, this rule may not be entirely sufficient in more complex blockchain systems, such as those integrating BNNs for transaction validation. Consequently, additional strategies are required:

Block Propagation and Delay Mechanisms: Nodes propagate newly mined blocks to the network as quickly as possible. To minimize conflicts, some networks implement slight delays before adding a block to the chain, allowing other nodes to communicate and resolve any conflicts that may arise.

Penalization and Incentives: Nodes that propagate blocks resulting in conflicts might be penalized, while those that help resolve conflicts and maintain the integrity of the chain may receive incentives. This encourages nodes to act in the best interest of the network.

Local Block Consensus (LBC): This involves nodes reaching a localized consensus on the current state of the blockchain before propagating blocks to the broader network. This can help reduce the likelihood of conflicts by ensuring that nodes are more aligned in their view of the blockchain.

By implementing these strategies, blockchain networks can efficiently resolve conflicts, ensuring that all participants agree on a single, consistent version of the blockchain. This consensus is essential for maintaining the trust, security, and reliability of the network, particularly in systems incorporating advanced technologies like BNNs.

4.7 General Users

We will list the general users to better understand how the system operates. Now that we have information about the most important concepts, we can construct the user stories of the proposed blockchains.

The blockchain ecosystem involves three main actors: end users, model trainers, and miners. End users engage in peer-to-peer currency transfers, while model trainers use the network's processing power to train BNN models in exchange for coins of the blockchain. Miners, on the other hand, provide the network's functionality by hosting nodes.

The miner is the last and most important participant, who makes the whole blockchain a working mechanism. If their blocks are accepted in the process, they will receive a reward for contributing to the blockchain. Their role is critical, and they need to be compensated for providing their hardware to the network. Their reward will consist of a portion of the coins that will be minted via the process.

They all work together and form an ecosystem that is balanced by demand. It all starts when a user uploads a dataset or creates a transaction. The dataset is then evaluated, and models are generated to create blocks. Even though blocks are hashed to avoid changing any information on them, their side product, the pre-trained BNN models, can be used and evaluated as a public source (Fig. 2).

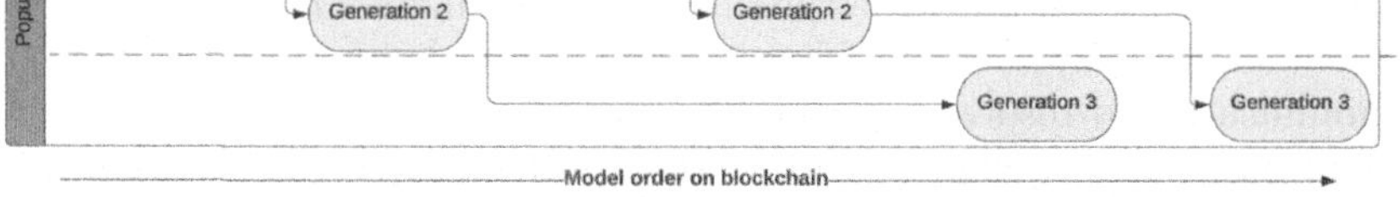

Fig. 2. Example of a model placement on blocks.

We keep most of the concepts of PoW blockchains intact, but by changing the validation and block generation step, we can repurpose the blockchain's processing power to provide meaningful products that can be reused in the real world. A few other aspects are improved, like the consensus mechanism, but for the purpose of our article, we would not like to dive only into details about the ability to use a blockchain's resources purposefully.

5 Results

In this section, we present the results from several test scenarios designed to evaluate the performance of our proposed blockchain system integrating BNNs.

The tests focus on network communication speed, mining efficiency across different difficulty levels, conflict resolution speed, and the relationship between difficulty and transaction handling capacity.

To facilitate the testing of the proposed approach, we developed a small application written in Python that serves as a base. It implements the base API requests required for a miner node and can train and evaluate models using the previously mentioned methodology. To facilitate the communication between nodes, the simplist Flusk framework was used implementing the following endpoints:

- /chain (GET): Returns the entire blockchain.
- /dataset (POST): Uploads a new dataset.
- /transactions/new (POST): Adds a new transaction to the pending transactions list.
- /mine (GET): Mines a new block by adding pending transactions to a new block and appending it to the chain.
- /nodes/register (POST): Registers new nodes in the network.
- /nodes/resolve (GET): Resolves conflicts by checking the chains of other nodes

When nodes receive a sufficient number of transactions, the mining process is automatically initiated, resulting in the creation of a new model family. In our implementation, we utilized Larq to simulate the training and deployment of BNNs. Larq, which builds on TensorFlow, offers tools to visualize and store models in a binary format.

We also developed evolutionary algorithms to generate model architectures and produce new generations within the same family. These models are saved using the TFLite format provided by the Larq framework.

The following tests were conducted using a simple, dockerized setup in which multiple nodes were deployed to emulate the behavior of a real-world blockchain network. The primary goal is to demonstrate the feasibility of the proposed approach. Its important to note that real-world deployments may experience higher latency due to variations in network providers, connection speeds, and hardware specifications.

5.1 Network Communication Speed

The first test evaluates the speed of communication between nodes during the transmission of new blocks. To isolate network performance, these tests excluded actual transaction content. We measured average latency and bandwidth usage across a local network setup, using CNN models composed of three convolutional layers with varying parameter configurations. All models were encoded in the optimized binary TFLite format (an efficient format used by TensorFlow). A summary of the results is presented in Table 1.

The results indicate that as the number of BNN parameters increases, network bandwidth usage rises proportionally. This is expected, as our approach

Table 1. Network Communication Speeds [1].

Configuration	Bandwidth Usage (KB/block)
BNN 4,4K params	1.41
BNN 93.6K params	26.38
BNN 1.17M params	304.26

involves embedding the trained model directly within each block, making bandwidth consumption directly dependent on model size. However, due to the compact nature of Binarized Neural Networks, our models typically occupy only a few kilobytes—significantly smaller than conventional neural networks with similar parameter counts, which often require several megabytes [27].

This compact size offers a clear advantage during block transmission between nodes, reducing the required bandwidth and leaving more room for transactions. According to the findings in [28], the optimal block size is around 255 kilobytes. Under this constraint, a BNN with approximately 100,000 parameters can fit well within a block, using less than one-fifth of the available space. This allows room for storing over 150 transactions alongside the model, enhancing overall block efficiency.

5.2 Mining Efficiency at Different Difficulty Levels

The second test case evaluates the mining speed of new blocks under varying difficulty levels. Mining difficulty influences the computational resources required to validate a block, thereby affecting the blockchains overall performance. We tested three difficulty settings—low, medium, and high—and recorded the average time needed to mine a block at each level.

Our implementation monitors key metrics such as minimum model difference and accuracy when comparing newly generated models to previous ones. For this test, we used a laptop equipped with an M1 Pro processor. Initially, five models were trained using standard backpropagation; subsequent models were optimized exclusively using the evolutionary algorithm. The setup included multithreading with 8 threads, a model population of 10, a mutation probability of 0.05 applied to 10% of the model schema, and a crossover probability of 10%.

The MNIST Handwritten Digits dataset served as the training data, and the model family used consisted of 4,440 parameters. For evaluating model accuracy, we employed the non-quantized version of the model instead of the binary format, as the testing script was written in Python.

The difficulty levels in this test were defined by model difference and accuracy thresholds in comparison to previous generations. The goal was to demonstrate that increasing difficulty is feasible within our framework. The results are summarized in Table 2.

As anticipated, higher difficulty levels lead to a noticeable increase in the time required to mine a block. These findings emphasize the importance of implement-

Table 2. Mining Efficiency at Different Difficulty Levels [1].

Difficulty Level	Average Time to Mine (seconds)
Low (diff +0.5%, acc +1%)	106.39
Medium (diff +1%, acc +2%)	433.08
High (diff +1.3%, acc +5%)	1737.16

ing a well-calibrated difficulty adjustment mechanism to maintain a consistent block generation rate, which is vital for the overall stability of the network.

The test scenarios offer valuable insights into the performance of our proposed blockchain framework. Future work will focus on further optimization and comprehensive empirical evaluations to enhance the systems resilience and effectiveness in real-world conditions.

One key advantage of our approach is the increased flexibility in configuring block mining difficulty—and, by extension, the time it takes to mine a block. This flexibility stands in contrast to fixed averages in existing systems, such as Bitcoin's 10-minute block time [23] and Ethereum's 12.05 s [22]. It's important to note that Ethereum benefits from faster block times due to its Proof of Stake (PoS) model, which is less computationally intensive than traditional Proof of Work (PoW). Our method introduces adjustable difficulty parameters, potentially offering a middle ground that combines the efficiency of PoS with the decentralized mining principles of PoW.

5.3 Comparative Analysis

An essential performance metric for evaluating blockchain systems is throughput, which measures how many transactions can be processed within a specific time frame. This metric enables direct comparisons between different blockchains and their efficiency. Prior research [24] has explored various methodologies for generating meaningful throughput benchmarks across blockchain platforms.

Accurately benchmarking blockchains requires accounting for multiple factors, one of the most significant being difficulty. Difficulty regulates the time and computational effort needed to mine a new block, and it is adjusted dynamically based on the total processing power available in the network to maintain security and consistency.

To offer a meaningful comparison, Table 3 presents the throughput results for both our blockchain and the Ethereum network. In our tests, we deployed single worker nodes within Docker containers, sent 300 transactions to each, and measured the time taken to process and commit these transactions into blocks. The experiments were conducted on a MacBook Pro equipped with an M1 Pro processor. Ethereum benchmarking was performed using the go-ethereum client (Geth) and Caliper [26]. For consistency, both blockchains were configured to store 146 transactions per block, which aligns with Geth's default setting.

Table 3. Local Blockchain Throughput at Different Difficulty Levels [1].

Local Blockchain	Type	Difficulty	Avg. Throughput (TPS)
BNN Chain	PoL	Low	1.47
BNN Chain	PoL	Medium	0.43
Ethereum (GEth)	PoA	Auto	26.30
Ethereum (GEth)	PoW	Auto	12.70

As shown in the table, our blockchain exhibits lower throughput compared to Ethereum under the tested difficulty configurations. In a single-node setup, it supports fewer transactions per unit of time. While the difficulty could technically be reduced even further than in our "Low" configuration, doing so would compromise the reliability of accuracy checks, as results would become overly random and inconsistent.

Research from [25] highlights that blockchain throughput improves with the use of multiple nodes—a principle that applies to our system as well, since it supports concurrent block mining.

In essence, this implementation is designed to capitalize on substantial computational resources. Its key advantage—generating functional Binarized Neural Networks (BNNs) with each mined block—becomes significantly more beneficial when deployed at scale. The current test results, based on single-node scenarios, are mainly illustrative and not indicative of the systems full potential in a distributed, high-performance environment.

5.4 Mitigating Model Spoofing via Architectural Diversity

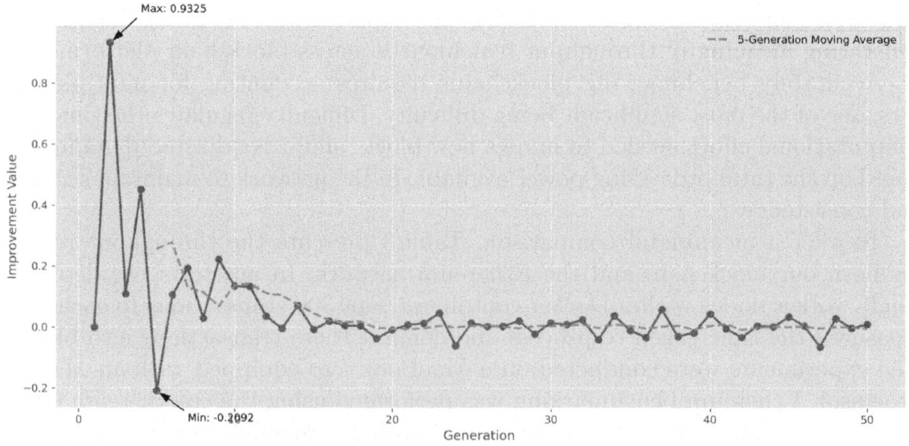

Fig. 3. Fitness improvement per generation.

Model spoofing, a class of adversarial attacks aimed at deceiving neural networks into producing incorrect or unauthorized outputs, presents a significant threat to the integrity of machine learning systems. One promising avenue for mitigating such threats is the deployment of multiple models of varying architectural configurations (architectural diversity) all trained on a common dataset. This approach introduces several layers of defense that reduce the feasibility and effectiveness of spoofing attacks.

Neural networks with different architectural characteristics exhibit varied inductive biases and learning dynamics, resulting in dissimilar internal feature representations even when trained on identical data. Consequently, adversarial inputs tailored to exploit the decision boundary of one model are less likely to generalize across models with fundamentally different architectures. This lack of transferability diminishes the attack surface available to adversaries and increases the robustness of the overall system.

Many model spoofing techniques rely on the transferability property of adversarial examples, wherein an input that misleads one model is likely to mislead others trained under similar conditions. However, architectural diversity disrupts this property. By employing models with varied depths, activation functions, and connectivity patterns, the alignment of their decision boundaries is minimized. This fragmentation reduces the likelihood that a single spoofing attempt will succeed across the ensemble.

Our approach generates a diverse set of viable models that can be deployed in formations utilizing multiple models to achieve the desired results. This enables users who choose to adopt our proposed method to enhance their security by mitigating model spoofing. The use of multiple models and architectures, generated by our blockchain, introduces redundancy and variability, making spoofing significantly more difficult.

To quantify the scenario above, we established an environment that monitors the performance of a population of neural network models across multiple generations within a decentralized training framework. Each generation begins with a diverse set of architectures, including various combinations of convolutional, pooling, flatten, and dense layers. These models are evaluated on a common dataset, and each receives a fitness score based on accuracy and other performance metrics. Models with higher fitness are preferentially selected for reproduction. Across generations, model architectures evolve through stochastic processes—such as adding or removing layers, altering activation functions, or changing the number of units in dense or convolutional layers. These evolutionary operations lead to gradual improvements in performance, which are visualized in the chart as increasing average and best fitness scores per generation, indicating the system's ability to adaptively optimize architectures over time.

As evidenced in Fig. 3, the fitness improvement chart demonstrates that the introduction of architectural diversity does not hinder the overall performance of the models. Instead, it contributes to a steady and consistent increase in fitness across generations. This trend supports the hypothesis that maintaining diversity in model structure enables the evolutionary process to explore a broader search space, yielding models that are both robust and high-performing. The observed improvements in fitness confirm that the system effectively selects and propagates architectures that not only resist spoofing attempts but also maintain or enhance task-specific accuracy. Furthermore, the chart illustrates that diversity-driven evolution leads to convergence towards fitter models over time, reinforcing the viability of this method in practical deployment scenarios.

In summary, the decentralized evolutionary training framework not only sustains but actively promotes architectural diversity throughout the search process. By using independent, competitive nodes and an evolutionary algorithm tailored for neural architecture search, the system effectively balances exploration and exploitation. This balance drives the emergence of robust, high-performing, and heterogeneous models that collectively enhance the security and adaptability of the overall network. These results underscore decentralization as a fundamental mechanism for promoting innovation and resilience in learning-based consensus systems.

5.5 Decentralization as a Source of Model Diversity

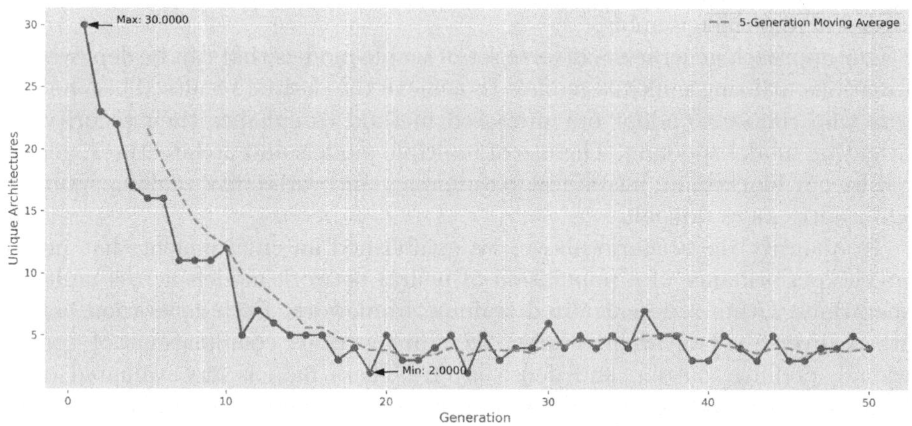

Fig. 4. Number of Unique Architectures per Generation.

Decentralization in this context implies that each participating node (miner) independently trains its own instance of a BNN, using the same dataset but without centralized coordination. This independence introduces a high degree of model variability, driven by the evolution of the models.

This results in a rich ensemble of diverse models, each representing a distinct solution path in the shared optimization landscape. Such diversity plays a crucial role in improving system-wide robustness and deterring adversarial attacks that rely on uniform model behavior.

The incentive structure of blockchain naturally encourages nodes to train models that are not only valid but high-performing and adhere to specific differentiator rules. In this decentralized competitive environment, participants are motivated to explore alternative BNN architectures. Over time, with model evolution, this leads to the emergence of higher-quality solutions driven by open competition.

The architectural heterogeneity that emerges from decentralized training yields multiple security advantages. Where the ensemble-like nature of validation, where multiple models must agree on transaction outcomes, acts as a safeguard, ensuring robustness through consensus-driven redundancy.

Decentralization in our blockchain-based BNN training system, introduces a powerful blend of diversity, quality improvement, and security resilience. The competitive, heterogeneous nature of training across independent nodes ensures that the system not only resists manipulation but also evolves toward higher-performing models over time. As such, decentralization is not merely a structural feature, but a core strength of learning-based consensus mechanisms.

When observing the distributed nature of the network, the metrics reflect how structural diversity is maintained and promoted throughout the same evolutionary process. Each neural network in a generation is compared to others to determine whether its architecture is unique based on its sequence and configuration of layers. By encouraging exploration of alternative layer types, positions, and parameterizations during training, the decentralized setup inherently avoids architectural convergence. This results in a high number of distinct network designs within each generation. The figure shows how this diversity persists—and often grows—over time, demonstrating that the evolutionary process does not merely refine a single best solution but continues to explore new architectural possibilities. This persistent variation is crucial in decentralized environments for enhancing both robustness against adversarial attacks and the overall adaptability of the system.

As illustrated in Fig. 4, the number of unique architectures per generation provides direct evidence of the evolving diversity introduced by the decentralized training process. The sustained presence—and in many cases, growth—of architectural variety over generations demonstrates that the system does not converge prematurely on a single dominant architecture. Instead, it continually encourages exploration of the architectural search space. This persistent diversity is essential for both adversarial robustness and model generalization, as it ensures that no single vulnerability is shared universally across the network. The chart shows that architectural novelty is not only maintained but actively promoted throughout the training lifecycle, reinforcing the idea that decentralization facilitates a dynamic equilibrium between exploration and exploitation. The evolutionary pressure within the decentralized framework effectively balances the drive for fitness improvement with the preservation of architectural heterogeneity, resulting in a resilient and adaptable population of models.

Table 4 complements this analysis by quantifying the progression of the evolutionary search over 20 generations. Each row in the table captures key indica-

Table 4. Metrics of a single population.

Gen	Avg. Fitness	Best Fitness	Best Acc.	Fitness Impr.	Unique Arch.
1	−34.3732	−6.2291	0.8949	0	30
2	-inf	−3.3168	0.8199	2.9123	30
3	−6.4027	−3.2042	0.7749	0.1126	24
4	-inf	−3.0534	0.8299	0.1508	24
5	-inf	−2.8240	0.6449	0.2294	17
6	−3.2924	−2.3643	0.8550	0.4597	18
7	−2.8322	−2.2361	0.8349	0.1282	13
8	−2.6577	−2.2199	0.7099	0.0162	14
9	−2.9398	−2.1691	0.8399	0.0508	17
10	−2.6140	−2.1330	0.8199	0.0361	21
11	−2.9496	−1.8389	0.8600	0.2941	16
12	−2.8143	−1.8599	0.8600	−0.0210	12
13	−2.2905	−1.7890	0.8399	0.0709	12
14	−2.2046	−1.7873	0.8600	0.0017	12
15	−1.9853	−1.7931	0.8600	−0.0058	8
16	−2.0235	−1.7151	0.8899	0.0780	6
17	−1.9773	−1.7276	0.8899	−0.0125	6
18	−1.9774	−1.7526	0.8899	−0.0250	8
19	−1.9663	−1.7151	0.8899	0.0374	6
20	−2.1906	−1.7334	0.8899	−0.0182	10

tors of evolutionary dynamics: average and best fitness values, best classification accuracy observed, fitness improvement from the previous generation, and the number of unique architectures present. The column labeled "Fitness Impr." denotes the gain in best fitness relative to the preceding generation, serving as a proxy for evolutionary momentum. Notably, the consistent discovery of new, high-performing individuals—as reflected in both the "Best Fitness" and "Best Acc." columns—indicates effective exploration. "Avg. Fitness" represents the average fitness of the generation where the infinite values represent such generation that include models that are not trainable. Furthermore, the "Unique Arch." column highlights the diversity in model structures retained across generations, underscoring the system's capacity to avoid premature convergence.

To further elaborate the methodology used to achieve these results, presented in the table, we used a custom Python implementation of an evolutionary algorithm tailored for neural architecture search. The script initializes a population of candidate network architectures with varying hidden layer configurations and evolves them over multiple generations using selection, mutation, and recombination. The evolutionary strategy employed is stochastic and elitist:

top-performing individuals are retained, while new variants are introduced via probabilistic mutations to explore the architectural space. The algorithm was applied to the samples from the MNIST dataset to reduce computation time while preserving sufficient complexity for meaningful architectural differentiation. Each architecture was trained on this subset and evaluated using categorical cross-entropy loss and classification accuracy.

The main function of the evolutionary pipeline begins by loading and preprocessing the MNIST data, including normalization and one-hot encoding of the labels. An instance of the ShapeEvolution class is created, specifying the input and output dimensions, population size, and mutation rate. The evolution process runs for a predefined amount of generations, during which network topologies are evaluated and evolved based on their performance. The best-performing model discovered is then rebuilt, trained, and evaluated on a held-out test subset, allowing for post-evolution assessment of generalization performance. This methodology enables the discovery of nontrivial, high-performing network architectures without manual tuning, and offers empirical evidence for the benefits of diversity and decentralized adaptation in neural architecture search.

6 Conclusions and Future Work

In conclusion, our approach introduces a practical method for generating neural network models as a natural byproduct of block encoding within a blockchain. By integrating BNNs into the blockchain framework, we not only enhance the transaction validation process but also present an innovative use of computational resources that adds value beyond conventional blockchain operations.

The experimental results confirm that our system effectively manages key blockchain functions, including network communication, block mining, and transaction throughput. These outcomes highlight the potential of our approach to enhance both the scalability and efficiency of blockchain networks while concurrently producing useful machine learning models.

In our approach, as an answer to RQ1, we effectively integrated the BNN training process in the generation of new blocks via storing the lightweight models on the block and ensuring consistency with pointers to the previous block and previous model family having the same shape. To ensure that each miner puts in the effort to compute the model, checks have been implemented within the validation step to ensure a minimum increase of accuracy and difference is reached on the new model when compared to previous generatins. For RQ2 we can conclude that one of the optimal training strategies for the BNN training process is via evolutive algorithms. They can generate new models even when backpropagation will do overfitting or find local minimum values. At the same time, we use evolutive algorithms to generate the model shape to increase the number of available models and find the perfect model for a given dataset. This provides security and scalability that is required for blockchains. Based on our initial test scenarios, it's show for RQ3 that our proposed approach can increase the computing time (difficulty) of generating a new block via altering miner constants and defining the minimum difference and accuracy of new models. In our approach, we store on the blocks the trained models and a list of differences to previous models besides a few standard metadata and transactions. Still, because BNN models make store weight values binary, they do not occupy much bandwidth. The tests evidentiate that the bandwidth usage was below 1MB. Finally, the comparison with the Ethereum blockchain offers insight into the performance of our proposed architecture in terms of throughput. Although our system shows a lower throughput rate, it can still efficiently handle a sufficient number of transactions. This performance level makes throughput optimal and suitable for large-scale use, despite having longer block creation waiting times compared to Ethereum. Based on the empirical evaluation for RQ4, we conclude that our approach inherently promotes resilience against adversarial attacks and model spoofing. By providing end users with multiple trained models, each with different architectures but trained on the same dataset, our method allows them to construct systems with greater robustness and adaptability to such threats. Lastly, the decentralized nature of our proposed algorithm introduces significant diversity in training BNN models, particularly in addressing RQ5. The use of evolutionary algorithms enables exploration of a wide range of model variants while maintaining a strong balance in model quality. This process is further strengthened by the inherent concurrency among nodes striving to meet validation criteria, which, when combined with the systems decentralized architecture, amplifies both robustness and innovation in model generation.

For future research, numerous paths warrant deeper exploration. While our experiments were carried out in controlled, dockerized settings, it is vital to evaluate model performance in real-world settings. Implementing our system within actual blockchain networks will yield a more accurate evaluation of its resilience and real-life applicability. Furthermore, examining distributed model training, where different mining pools collaboratively train distinct segments of a model, presents an intriguing possibility. This approach could improve the efficiency of model creation and exploit the decentralized nature of blockchain systems. Additionally, analyzing if assigning specific models and datasets to particular pools could further refine the training process. Some pools might focus on specific types of models or datasets, potentially enhancing both the performance and precision of the generated models.

Extending our approach to larger-scale blockchain networks would also be an important step. This involves ensuring that the system can handle increased transaction volumes and more extensive network participation without compromising performance.

By addressing these future directions, we plan to enhance the practical utility and scalability of our approach, making it a valuable contribution to the intersection of blockchain technology and machine learning.

References

1. Gyulai-Nagy, Z.-V.: Proof of learning applied to binary neural networks. In: Proceedings of 17th International Conference on Agents and Artificial Intelligence (ICAART), pp. 411–418. SciTePress (2025)
2. Nakamoto, S.: Bitcoin: a peer-to-peer electronic cash system (2008). https://bitcoin.org/bitcoin.pdf
3. Courbariaux, M., Bengio, Y.: BinaryNet: Training Deep Neural Networks with Weights and Activations Constrained to +1 or −1. CoRR, abs/1602.02830 (2016). http://arxiv.org/abs/1602.02830
4. Rastegari, M., Ordonez, V., Redmon, J., Farhadi, A.: XNOR-Net: ImageNet Classification Using Binary Convolutional Neural Networks. CoRR, abs/1603.05279 (2016). http://arxiv.org/abs/1603.05279
5. Zhou, S., Ni, Z., Zhou, X., Wen, H., Wu, Y., Zou, Y.: DoReFa-Net: Training Low Bitwidth Convolutional Neural Networks with Low Bitwidth Gradients. CoRR, abs/1606.06160 (2016). http://arxiv.org/abs/1606.06160
6. Lin, X., Zhao, C., Pan, W.: Towards Accurate Binary Convolutional Neural Network. CoRR, abs/1711.11294 (2017). http://arxiv.org/abs/1711.11294
7. Bravo-Marquez, F., Reeves, S., Ugarte, M.: Proof-of-learning: a blockchain consensus mechanism based on machine learning competitions. In: Proceedings of IEEE DAPPCON, pp. 119–124 (2019)
8. Biswas, A.R., Giaffreda, R.: IoT and cloud convergence: opportunities and challenges. In: Proceedings of WF-IoT, pp. 375–376 (2014)
9. Venieris, S.I., Bouganis, C.-S.: fpgaConvNet: A Toolflow for Mapping Diverse Convolutional Neural Networks on Embedded FPGAs. CoRR, abs/1711.08740 (2017)
10. Boneh, D., Bonneau, J., Bünz, B., Fisch, B.: Verifiable delay functions. Cryptology ePrint Archive (2018)
11. Andrychowicz, M., Dziembowski, S., Malinowski, D., Mazurek, Ł.: Secure multiparty computations on Bitcoin. In: Proceedings of IEEE S&P, pp. 443–458 (2014)
12. Micali, S., Rabin, M., Vadhan, S.: Verifiable random functions. In: Proceedings of IEEE FOCS, pp. 120–130 (1999)
13. Weng, J., Weng, J., Zhang, J., Li, M., Zhang, Y., Luo, W.: DeepChain: auditable and privacy-preserving deep learning with blockchain-based incentive. IEEE Trans. Dependable Secure Comput. **18**(5), 2438–2455 (2021)
14. Fiszelew, A., Britos, P., Perichisky, G., García-Martínez, R.: Automatic generation of neural networks. Revista Eletrônica de Sistemas de Informação **2**, 1–6 (2003)
15. Xie, J., Yu, F.R., Huang, T., Xie, R., Liu, J., Liu, Y.: A survey on the scalability of blockchain systems. IEEE Network **33**(5), 166–173 (2019)
16. Beck, R., Czepluch, J.S., Lollike, N., Malone, S.: Blockchain - the gateway to trust-free cryptographic transactions. In: Proceedings of ECIS, Paper 153 (2016)
17. O'Dwyer, K.J., Malone, D.: Bitcoin mining and its energy footprint. In: Proceedings of ISSC/CIICT, pp. 280–285 (2014)
18. Croman, K., et al.: On scaling decentralized blockchains. In: Clark, J., Meiklejohn, S., Ryan, P.Y.A., Wallach, D., Brenner, M., Rohloff, K. (eds.) FC 2016. LNCS, vol. 9604, pp. 106–125. Springer, Heidelberg (2016). https://doi.org/10.1007/978-3-662-53357-4_8
19. de Vries, A.: Bitcoin's growing energy problem. Joule **2**, 801–805 (2018)
20. Jia, H., et al.: Proof-of-Learning: Definitions and Practice. CoRR, abs/2103.05633 (2021)

21. Wang, E., et al.: Enabling binary neural network training on the edge. ACM Trans. Embed. Comput. Syst. **22**(6), Article 105 (2023)
22. Rouhani, S., Deters, R.: Performance analysis of ethereum transactions in private blockchain. In: Proceedings of IEEE ICSESS, pp. 70–74 (2017)
23. Mariem, S.B., Casas, P., Romiti, M., Donnet, B., Stütz, R., Haslhofer, B.: All that glitters is not bitcoin – unveiling the centralized nature of the BTC (IP) network. In: Proceedings of IEEE/IFIP NOMS, pp. 1–9 (2020)
24. Schäffer, M., Di Angelo, M., Salzer, G.: Performance and scalability of private Ethereum blockchains. In: Proceedings of BPM Blockchain and CEE Forum, pp. 103–118 (2019)
25. Fan, C., Ghaemi, S., Khazaei, H., Musilek, P.: Performance evaluation of blockchain systems: a systematic survey. IEEE Access **8**, 126927–126950 (2020)
26. Hyperledger Caliper (2021). https://hyperledger.github.io/caliper/
27. Pisarchyk, Y., Lee, J.: Efficient Memory Management for Deep Neural Net Inference. arXiv:2001.03288 (2020). https://arxiv.org/abs/2001.03288
28. Singh, N., Vardhan, M.: Computing optimal block size for blockchain based applications with contradictory objectives. Procedia Comput. Sci. **171**, 1389–1398 (2020)
29. Huang, M.-H., Rust, R.T.: Artificial intelligence in service. J. Serv. Res. **21**(2), 155–172 (2018)
30. Jarrahi, M.H.: Artificial intelligence and the future of work: human-AI symbiosis in organizational decision making. Bus. Horiz. **61**(4), 577–586 (2018)
31. Gill, S.S., et al.: AI for next generation computing: emerging trends and future directions. Internet Things **19**, 100514 (2022)
32. Gervais, A., et al.: On the security and performance of proof of work blockchains. In: Proceedings of ACM CCS (2016)
33. Jia, H., et al.: Proof-of-learning: definitions and practice. In: Proceedings of the 2021 IEEE Symposium on Security and Privacy (SP), pp. 1039–1056 (2021). https://doi.org/10.1109/SP40001.2021.00106
34. Liu, Y., Lan, Y., Li, B., Miao, C., Tian, Z.: Proof of learning (PoLe): empowering neural network training with consensus building on blockchains. Comput. Netw. **201**, 108594 (2021). https://doi.org/10.1016/j.comnet.2021.108594
35. Mani, V.R.S., Saravanaselvan, A., Arumugam, N.: Performance comparison of CNN, QNN and BNN deep neural networks for real-time object detection using ZYNQ FPGA node. Microelectron. J. **119**, 105319 (2022). https://doi.org/10.1016/j.mejo.2021.105319

CDRS-PC-JSW: A Context-Driven Collaborative Filtering with Probabilistic Clustering and Divergence-Based Similarity - Jensen–Shannon vs Wasserstein

Jihene Latrech(✉), Zahra Kodia, and Nadia Ben Azzouna

SMART-LAB, ISG Tunis, University of Tunis, Cité Bouchoucha, Bardo, 2000 Tunis, Tunisia

jihene_latrech@yahoo.fr

Abstract. This study introduces a three-stage machine learning model for context-driven collaborative filtering. (i) User data are separately clustered along three contextual aspects (emotional, demographic and temporal) yielding, for each aspect, a probability distribution that captures every user's degree of membership in the clusters generated by a dedicated algorithm. (ii) Similarity between each pair of users is first computed via either Jensen–Shannon or Wasserstein divergence on their aspect-specific distributions. These three scores are then dynamically weighted to reflect the relative importance of each aspect for the active user and fused into a normalized User–User contextual similarity matrix. (iii) A contextual neighborhood-based collaborative filter exploits this matrix to generate recommendations. Evaluated on the LDOS-CoMoDa movie dataset with cross-validated K-Fold and K-Neighbor configurations, the model outperformed standard baselines, achieving an RMSE of 0.5774 and an MAE of 0.3333 with the Jensen–Shannon variant, and an RMSE of 0.4511 and an MAE of 0.4009 with the Wasserstein variant.

Keywords: Recommendation System · Collaborative Filtering · Context-Driven · Contextual Similarity · Jensen-Shannon · Wasserstein

1 Introduction

Recommender systems are intelligent tools that shepherd users through increasingly complex decision spaces by predicting items or services they are likely to value, thus reducing information overload and expediting choice [1]. Traditional approaches frame this task around only two entities, users and items using historical ratings or implicit feedback to infer preferences. Context-Aware Recommender Systems (CARS) extend the paradigm by injecting situational cues such as time, location, device, mood or social company into the recommendation pipeline [2]. In most implementations, however, context is handled either

H. J. van den Herik et al. (Eds.): ICAART 2025, LNAI 16517, pp. 113–132, 2026.
https://doi.org/10.1007/978-3-032-25032-2_6

as a static, auxiliary filter or as an additional feature in a latent-factor model; both strategies implicitly assume that a user's underlying tastes remain stable and that context merely sharpens an otherwise fixed profile [3]. This simplification becomes problematic in real-world settings where preferences drift: the same individual may crave a horror film on a Friday night with friends yet seek a documentary on a quiet Sunday morning, and such shifts cannot be captured by a model that treats context as an additional information.

Context-Driven Recommender Systems (CDRS) confront this limitation by making context the principal driver of the recommendation process. Rather than asking "Which items match this user?" and then adjusting for context, CDRS ask "Given this specific contextual situation, what does the user want now?"; the user's long-term profile is modulated by immediate situational signals [3]. This perspective acknowledges the fluid, multi-aspect nature of preference formation and calls for algorithms capable of learning how the importance of each contextual aspect itself fluctuates.

Motivated by these insights, we introduced our model, dubbed CDRS-PC-JSW: A Context-Driven Collaborative Filtering with Probabilistic Clustering and divergence-based similarity- Jensen–Shannon vs Wasserstein, which is arranged in three stages: contextual user clustering, weighted contextual similarity estimation and contextual similarity–based collaborative filtering. Its main contributions are:

- Firstly, user data are split into three aspects—emotional, demographic and temporal. For each aspect, a dedicated clustering algorithm produces a probability distribution that captures the user's membership likelihood across the aspect's clusters.
- Secondly, for every pair of users we compute Jensen–Shannon and Wasserstein divergences on their aspect-level distributions, yielding three similarity scores. These scores are dynamically weighted to reflect the importance of each aspect for the active user, then merged into a normalized, weighted User–User similarity matrix.
- Finally, using this matrix, the system selects the K neighbors that best match the active user's current context, predicts ratings for unseen items from these neighbors' ratings and produces context-driven recommendations.

We evaluated the model on the LDOS-CoMoDa movie dataset using cross-validated K-Fold and K-neighbor configurations. The Jensen–Shannon variant achieved an RMSE of 0.5774 and an MAE of 0.3333, whereas the Wasserstein variant recorded an RMSE of 0.4511 and an MAE of 0.4009, both surpassing baseline methods and demonstrating robust adaptation to contextual dynamics.

The remainder of the paper is structured as follows: Sect. 2 presents related works. Section 3 describes our recommendation model in details and explains each key step in our approach. Section 4 presents the experimental protocol and analyzes the results, while Sect. 5 concludes and proposes perspectives for future work.

2 Related Works

The integration of machine learning algorithms into recommender systems has ushered in a new era for the field, moving far beyond the static, rule-based methods of the past [15]. Machine learning techniques are able to uncover intricate relationships between users and items while simultaneously accounting for contextual factors [7]. Our work follows this data-driven paradigm, employing machine learning to tackle the interdependent and highly variable nature of contextual information, complexities that conventional approaches struggle to capture. In the discussion that follows, we survey a range of machine learning-based methods devised to produce more precise recommendations.

In [8], Karatzoglou et al. extended classic matrix factorization into a tensor factorization framework, treating the data as a multi-dimensional user–item–context tensor. This formulation allows contextual cues to be woven directly into the model as additional dimensions, yielding a more flexible, generalized version of collaborative filtering.

In the study [9], Said et al. introduced an inferred Contextual User Profiles (CUP), which augment the traditional user profile by capturing a user's behaviour within specific contexts. Rather than relying on a single global profile, the system maintains two context-aware profiles per user, selecting the appropriate one when generating recommendations.

Baltrunas et al. [10] proposed "Item Splitting", a technique that divides an item into multiple contextual variants whenever ratings shift significantly across contexts. These split versions are then fed into prediction algorithms so that the recommender can adapt to how the same item is perceived under different conditions.

Fareed et al. [11] designed a collaborative framework that blends users' rating histories with signals drawn from their social-network connections. Similarity is computed through a weighted combination of rating-based and social information, with the weights optimized automatically, resulting in more nuanced and relevant suggestions.

Karabila et al. [12] harnessed ensemble learning, marrying sentiment analysis of textual reviews with collaborative filtering. By fusing sentiment-derived features and traditional ratings, the system delivers highly personalized and accurate recommendations.

Aldayel et al. [13] examined how different tourism categories influence destination recommendations. They benchmarked classical matrix-factorization methods against deep learning architectures such as Light Graph Convolutional Networks and the Bilateral Variational Autoencoder (BiVAE), highlighting each model's strengths within the tourism domain.

Zhang et al. [14] recasted the recommendation problem as an agent-based interaction. Users and items are treated as autonomous agents that iteratively adjust their internal states: after each interaction, discrepancies between simulated and real behaviors trigger joint updates, and agents can later share their refined preferences, embodying a novel form of collaborative filtering.

While these machine learning approaches have each advanced the state of the art, none directly mirrors our proposed solution. Our system uniquely combines machine learning techniques with divergence measures between probability distributions and conducts a multi-aspect analysis of contextual data. This hybrid design captures complex context-driven variations and, in doing so, aims to boost both the precision and relevance of the recommendations it generates.

3 Approach Overview

Our approach introduces an original recommendation model oriented by context, which, instead of merely tailoring suggestions to the contextual situation, works to embed the contextual cues inside the recommendations themselves. Accordingly, the system treats context as its leading information source. We posit that individuals share stronger affinities with others situated in comparable contexts than with earlier iterations of their own preferences. This premise rests on the notion that context decisively moulds interests, so advice anchored in these cues can deliver richer and more individualized relevance.

Our proposal unfolds through three keys phases: (1) a contextual user clustering phase, (2) a phase for measuring weighted contextual similarity, and (3) a collaborative filtering phase guided by contextual similarity. Figure 1 presents an overview of the proposed model.

3.1 Users Contextual Clustering Stage

In the initial stage, our model clusters users along three independent contextual dimensions—demographic, emotional, and temporal. These dimensions enable finer-grained segmentation, linking each individual to groups that reflect not only personal tastes but also contextual factors capable of reshaping those preferences. Dedicated clustering algorithms are executed for every dimension. For each user, the system then derives a probability distribution over the clusters in the demographic, emotional, and temporal spaces, based on the clustering outcomes. Specifically, for any contextual dimension $i \in$ demographic, emotional, temporal, user u is assigned a membership-probability vector $P_{u,i} = [p_{u,i}^1, p_{u,i}^2, \dots, p_{u,i}^K]$, where K is the number of clusters for dimension i and $p_{u,i}^K$ denotes the likelihood that u belongs to the K-th cluster of aspect i. Algorithm 1 presents the detailed steps of this user-context clustering process.

3.2 Weighted Contextual Similarity Assessment Stage

In this stage of the model, for each contextual aspect and for every pair of users, the system computes a similarity score between their cluster-membership probability distributions by relying on two alternative divergence metrics. The first metric is the Jensen–Shannon divergence [4], a symmetrical and numerically stable variant of the Kullback–Leibler distance [5], defined in Formula 1:

$$\text{Distance}(P, Q) = \frac{1}{2}\,\text{KL}(P \parallel M) + \frac{1}{2}\,\text{KL}(Q \parallel M), \tag{1}$$

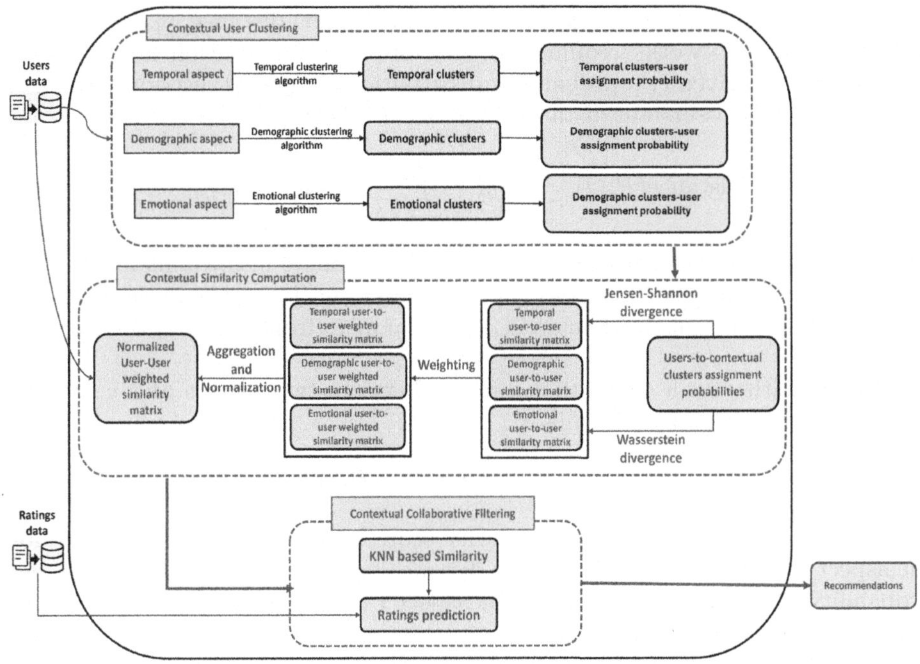

Fig. 1. An overview of the proposed model architecture [28].

Algorithm 1. Users contextual clustering stage.

Data: Users' data, contextual aspects
Result: Users' probabilities distribution
Initialize i = 0;
Initialize $contextual\_aspects$ = [demographic, emotional, temporal];
while $i < size(contextual\_aspects)$ **do**
  Train correspondent clustering algorithm;
  Identify the number of clusters K;
  Initialize $u = 0$;
  while $u < number\_of\_users$ **do**
    Predict $P_{u,contextual\_aspects[i]} = [p^1_{u,contextual\_aspects[i]}, p^2_{u,contextual\_aspects[i]}, \ldots, p^K_{u,contextual\_aspects[i]}]$ for user u;
    Increment u by 1;
  Increment i by 1;
Return users' probabilities distribution.

---

where Distance(P, Q) denotes the Jensen–Shannon divergence between the two probability distributions P and Q, $M = \frac{1}{2}(P + Q)$ is their mean distribution, and KL$(P \parallel Q)$ is the Kullback–Leibler divergence.

The second metric is the Wasserstein (Earth-Mover) distance [6], which measures the minimal "work" required to transform one distribution into another. Mathematically, given two probability distributions P and Q distributed over a domain X, the Wasserstein distance Distance(P, Q) is given by Formula 2.

$$\text{Distance}(P, Q) = \inf_{\gamma \in \Pi(P,Q)} \int_{X \times X} d(x, y)\, d\gamma(x, y) \tag{2}$$

where $d(x, y)$ defines the distance between points x and y in the domain, $\Pi(P, Q)$ is the set of all joint distributions (or couplings) $\gamma(x, y)$ with marginals P and Q, i.e. for each point in the domain X, the total mass from P and Q is conserved in γ.

The similarity for a contextual aspect i between two users u and v, is then computed as denoted by Formula 3:

$$\text{Sim}_i(u, v) = 1 - \text{Distance}(P_{u,i}, P_{v,i}) \tag{3}$$

where $\text{Sim}_i(u, v)$ designates the similarity score between user u and user v for the aspect i. Distance$(P_{u,i}, P_{v,i})$ is the distance between the cluster membership probability distributions of u and v for aspect i calculated using either Jensen-Shannon or Wasserstein distances.

Next, we introduce dynamic weights for the three similarity scores tied to each contextual dimension (demographic, emotional, temporal). This weighting scheme relies on the contextual importance of every dimension for each individual user, allowing the model to reflect their relative influence on preferences. Accordingly, the system assigns larger weights to those similarities that matter most for the specific user pair. Each dynamic weight is computed using Formula 4.

$$w_i(u, v) = \frac{\frac{1}{|sim_i(u,v) - \mu| + \epsilon}}{\sum_{j \in \{\text{demo,emo,tempo}\}} \frac{1}{|sim_j(u,v) - \mu| + \epsilon}} \tag{4}$$

where $w_i(u, v)$ is the weight relative to aspect i for the pair of users u and v, $sim_j(u, v)$ is the similarity corresponding to the aspect j for the same pair of users, μ denotes the average of the three similarity scores and ϵ is a small constant to avoid division by zero.

The global similarity score between u and v is subsequently computed based on dynamic weights and as expressed by Formula 5.

$$\text{Sim}_{\text{global}}(u, v) = \sum_{j \in \{\text{demo,emo,tempo}\}} w_j(u, v) \cdot sim_j(u, v) \tag{5}$$

where $Sim_{\text{global}}(u, v)$ represents the global similarity between user u and user v. $w_j(u, v)$ denotes the weight assigned to the aspect j for the user pair u and v, and $sim_j(u, v)$ corresponds to the similarity related to the same aspect j for the same pair of users.

We then merge the aggregate similarity scores for each user pair to build the User-User weighted similarity matrix. The matrix is then normalized, placing

Algorithm 2. Weighted contextual similarity assessment stage.

```
Data: Users probabilities distribution
Result: Normalized User-User weighted similarity matrix
Initialize User-User weighted similarity matrix;
Initialize i = 0;
Initialize contextual_aspects = [demo, tempo, emo];
Initialize number_of_users;
while i < size(contextual_aspects) do
    Initialize u = 0;
    while u < number_of_users do
        Initialize v = u + 1;
        while v < number_of_users do
            Calculate sim_i(u, v);
            Add sim_contextual_aspects[i](u, v) to contextual_aspects[i] user-user
            similarity matrix;
            Increment v by 1;
        Increment u by 1 ;
    Increment i by 1;
Initialize u = 0;
while u < number_of_users do
    Initialize v = u + 1;
    while v < number_of_users do
        Initialize i = 0;
        while i < size(contextual_aspects) do
            Calculate weight w_contextual_aspects[i](u, v);
            Add Sim_global(u, v) to contextual_aspects[i] user-user weighted
            similarity matrix;
            Increment i by 1;
        Compute Sim_global(u, v);
        Increment v by 1;
    Increment u by 1;
Normalize User-User weighted similarity matrix;
Return normalized User-User weighted similarity matrix.
```

all similarity values on a common scale to maintain consistency across users. Algorithm 2 lays out each step involved in producing this normalized matrix.

Incorporating cluster-membership probabilities into the recommendation pipeline sharpens the similarity computation, making it sensitive enough to pick up even the most nuanced distinctions among users. Furthermore, by dynamically tailoring the weight assigned to each contextual aspect for every user pair, the model delivers markedly more precise and context-driven recommendations.

3.3 Similarity Based Collaborative Filtering Stage

When recommending items for a target user u, the system first applies the K-Nearest Neighbors algorithm to the normalized User–User similarity matrix, retrieving the K users most akin to u. It then leverages these neighbors' ratings to infer how relevant each still-unrated item j might be. For every such candidate item, the ratings provided by the K neighbors are aggregated to produce a predicted score $\hat{r}_{u,j}$, as defined in Eq. 6.

$$\hat{r}_{u,j} = \frac{\sum_{v \in \text{Neighbors}(u)} \left(\text{Sim}_{global}(u,v) \cdot r_{v,j} \right)}{\sum_{v \in \text{Neighbors}(u)} \left(\text{Sim}_{global}(u,v) \right)} \tag{6}$$

where $r_{u,j}$ denotes the predicted rating of the item j for the user u, $r_{v,j}$ is the rating of item j by neighboring user v, $Neighbors(u)$ is the identified set of K most similar users and $Sim(u,v)$ is the similarity between u and v extracted from the similarity matrix. This estimate gives greater weight to user ratings more similar to user u and reflects contextual influence.

After estimating scores for every item that user u has yet to rate, the system orders these candidates by $\hat{r}_{u,j}$ in descending sequence and selects the top N. Algorithm 3 outlines the steps of the similarity-based collaborative-filtering process.

Algorithm 3. Similarity based collaborative filtering stage.

```
Data: Users' data, items' data, ratings' data, normalized User-User similarity
      matrix, K: the number of similar users
Result: Recommendations
Initialize j = 0;
Use KNN algorithm to identify the K nearest neighbors of user u;
Identify unrated_items;
while j < size(unrated_items) do
    Predict r̂_{u,j};
    Increment j by 1;
Sort predicted ratings in descending order;
Recommend N first items.
```

4 Experimental Study

To evaluate our recommendation system, we carried out experiments on the LDOS-CoMoDa, LDOS Context Movie Dataset [16]. It includes 121 users who provided 2296 ratings for 1232 movies and features 13 contextual attributes: mood, dominantEmo, endEmo, age, sex, country, location, time, daytype, season, weather, and city.

We carried out several pre-processing steps to prepare the data for integration into the clustering models. The contextual user data was divided into three aspects: emotional, demographic and temporal. For each aspect, categorical variables are encoded using a LabelEncoder, which converts textual values into numerical values. Next, all features are standardized using StandardScaler, which normalizes the data, giving it a mean of 0 and a standard deviation of 1.

4.1 Users Contextual Clustering Stage Implementation

Extensive testing showed that coupling the demographic variables (age, sex, country, and location) with the MeanShift algorithm [18] produced the most effective user clusters. For the emotional dimension, K-Means [17] applied to the dominantEmo and endEmo features captured shifts in affect with greater precision. Regarding temporal patterns, MeanShift again excelled, detecting evolving behaviors linked to the time and daytype attributes. Table 1 lists the optimal cluster counts for each dimension and the evaluation measures, Silhouette Score [19], Calinski-Harabasz Index [20], and Davies-Bouldin Index [21]—used to gauge clustering quality.

The Silhouette Score measures how similar the objects in a given cluster are to each other, compared to those in other clusters. The overall score is the average of the silhouettes of all the points, and varies between -1 and 1. A score close to 1 means that the clusters are well separated. A score close to 0 indicates that the clusters are very close. Negative scores, however, indicate poor clustering [19]. It is calculated as expressed by Formula 7

$$\mathrm{S(i)} = \frac{b(i) - a(i)}{\max(a(i), b(i))} \tag{7}$$

where $a(i)$ is the average distance between point i and all other points in its own cluster and $b(i)$ is the average distance between point i and the points in the nearest cluster.

The Davies-Bouldin Index (DBI) assesses the quality of clustering based on the similarity between clusters. It is computed from the average of the similarity ratios for each cluster. A small DBI indicates better clustering, as it means that the clusters are well separated and compact [21]. Formula 8 calculates the DBI.

$$\mathrm{DBI} = \frac{1}{k} \sum_{i=1}^{k} \max_{j \neq i} \left(\frac{d_i + d_j}{D_{ij}} \right) \tag{8}$$

where d_i and d_j represent the dispersion of clusters i and j. D_{ij} denotes the distance between the centers of clusters i and j, and k refers to the number of clusters.

The Calinski-Harabasz index (CHI) is a dispersion-based index, which measures the quality of cluster separation. A high Calinski-Harabasz score indicates well-separated, compact clusters [20]. It is calculated as expressed by Formula 9.

$$\mathrm{CHI} = \frac{\mathrm{Tr}(B_k)/(k-1)}{\mathrm{Tr}(W_k)/(n-k)} \tag{9}$$

where $Tr(B_k)$ is the trace of the inter-cluster dispersion matrix, $Tr(W_k)$ is the trace of the intra-cluster dispersion matrix, n is the total number of points, and k indicates the number of clusters.

Table 1. Silhouette, Calinski-Harabasz and Davies-Bouldin metrics values for demographic, emotional and temporal contextual aspects [28]

Aspect	Algorithm	Optimal Number of Clusters	Silhouette Score	Davies-Bouldin Index	Calinski-Harabasz Index
Demographic	MeanShift	12	0.7119	0.5563	2132.8108
Emotional	K-Means	7	**0.7199**	**0.5187**	**5696.8659**
Temporal	MeanShift	8	0.5256	0.5344	1521.1331

As highlighted in Table 1, where best values are bolded, and in Figs. 2a, 2b and 2c, clustering the demographic aspect with MeanShift and a resolution of 12 clusters produces groups that are both cohesive and clearly delimited. The silhouette coefficient reaches 0.7119, signalling that most users lie much closer to the centroid of their own cluster than to neighboring clusters. A low Davies–Bouldin index of 0.5563 corroborates this observation by indicating minimal overlap between clusters, while the high Calinski–Harabasz value of 2132.8108 confirms a strong between-cluster dispersion relative to within-cluster dispersion. Taken together, these three metrics show that demographic attributes: age, sex, country and location, structure the user population into well-separated segments.

For the emotional dimension, applying K-Means with 7 clusters yields the most strikingly distinct group structure among the three aspects. The silhouette score climbs slightly higher, to 0.7199, demonstrating good intra-cluster similarity. Even more convincing is the Davies–Bouldin index, which falls to 0.5187, the lowest of all aspects, implying that emotional clusters are the most compact and furthest apart. This is echoed by a large Calinski–Harabasz index of 5696.8659, reflecting an outstanding ratio of inter-cluster to intra-cluster dispersion. These figures suggest that dominantEmo and endEmo features capture variations in affect so effectively that users can be grouped into coherent, clearly separated emotional profiles.

Temporal behaviour, segmented with MeanShift into 8 clusters, paints a more nuanced picture. The silhouette coefficient drops to 0.5256, indicating that the cohesion within temporal clusters is markedly weaker than for the demographic and emotional aspects. This view is reinforced by the Calinski–Harabasz index, which, at 1521.1331, is lower than that of the other two aspects, pointing to less pronounced separation. Nonetheless, a Davies–Bouldin index of 0.5344 shows that the clusters remain acceptably distinct; they exhibit greater internal variance. These results reveal that user activity patterns, captured through the time and day-type attributes, are intrinsically more heterogeneous and thus harder to partition into tightly knit groups.

Overall, the clustering analysis underscores a clear hierarchy in segmentation quality: emotional features form the most cohesive and sharply delineated clusters, closely followed by demographic characteristics, whereas temporal patterns resist neat partitioning. This hierarchy not only guides how much weight each aspect should carry in the recommendation model, but also hints at the underlying complexity of user behaviour over time.

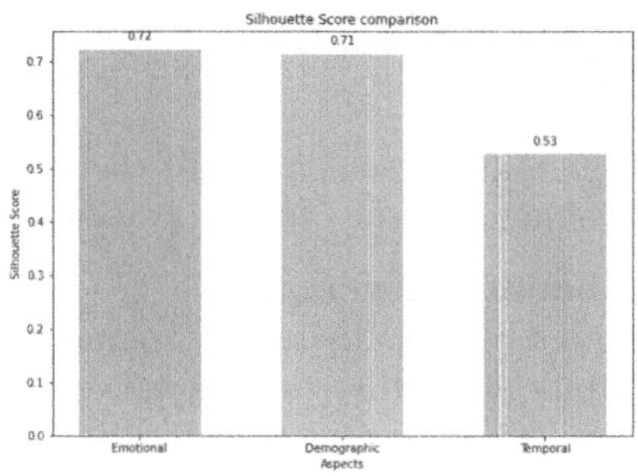

(a) Silhouette Score

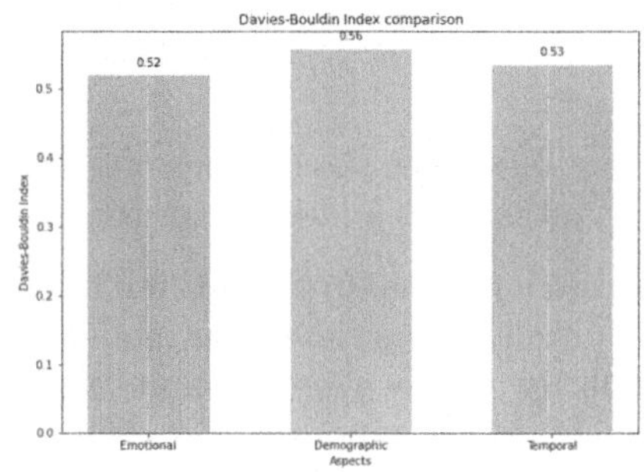

(b) Davies-Bouldin Index

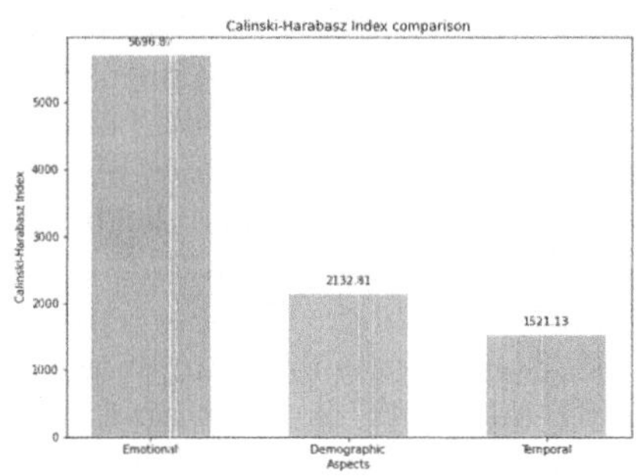

(c) Calinski-Harabasz Index

Fig. 2. Silhouette, Calinski-Harabasz and Davies-Bouldin metrics comparison for demographic, emotional and temporal contextual aspects [28].

4.2 Contextual Based Collaborative Filtering Stage Implementation

To highlight the robustness and performance of our recommendation model, we implemented cross-validation with various values of K-Folds and K-Neighbors. This procedure enabled us to assess the model's stability and accuracy by dividing the data into several subsets for alternate training and testing phases.

We used RMSE (Root Mean Squared Error) and MAE (Mean Absolute Error) as metrics to measure the accuracy of the recommendations, RMSE being more sensitive to large errors, while MAE provides a measure of absolute deviations [29]. The equations to calculate RMSE and MAE rates are given by Formula 10 and Formula 11, respectively.

$$\text{RMSE} = \sqrt{\frac{1}{n}\sum_{i=1}^{n}(y_i - \hat{y}_i)^2} \tag{10}$$

$$\text{MAE} = \frac{1}{n}\sum_{i=1}^{n}|y_i - \hat{y}_i| \tag{11}$$

Where n denotes the number of observations, y_i is the actual value for the $i-th$ observation and $\hat{y}_i$ designates the predicted value for the $i-th$ observation.

Similarity Measurement with Jensen–Shannon Divergence
We initially instantiated our model using Jensen–Shannon divergence to measure similarity between users' multi-aspect probabilities vectors (emotional, demographic, and temporal). We then present results for several configurations in which both the number of nearest neighbours (K-Neighbors) and the number of folds (K-Folds) in the cross-validation procedure are varied.

As indicated in Table 2, where for each K-Fold setting, the lowest RMSE and MAE scores are shown in boldface, and Fig. 3a, when the number of folds K-Folds is set to 5, the most effective configuration uses 5 neighbors, yielding an RMSE of 0.9354 and an MAE of 0.6250. At this point, prediction errors are relatively low, reflecting good accuracy. Once the neighbor count exceeds 5, both RMSE and MAE rise steadily, revealing a gradual decline in performance. From 15 neighbors onward, the error metrics continue to worsen, though they level off somewhat between 20 and 30 neighbors—still acceptable, with an RMSE of 1.1438 and an MAE of 0.6833 at 30 neighbors. In short, for K-Folds = 5, the best trade-off between RMSE and MAE occurs with a small neighborhood size (5), beyond which errors climb progressively.

When K-Folds is increased to 10, as shown in Table 2 and Fig. 3b, peak performance is achieved with just 3 neighbors: the RMSE drops to 0.7071, while the MAE settles at 0.5000. Moving to 5 neighbors nudges the RMSE up to 0.8165 and the MAE to 0.6667—still reasonable values. Expanding the neighborhood to 10 neighbors produces a moderate RMSE increase (0.8975) and a slight MAE decrease. At 15 neighbors, both error measures creep higher, yet at 20 and 30 neighbors accuracy rebounds somewhat, even reaching an RMSE of 0.8137 with 30 neighbors. Thus, for K-Folds = 10, the finest results arise with an extremely small neighbor set (3), though configurations with 20 and 30 neighbors also deliver good accuracy.

As detailed in Table 2 and illustrated in Fig. 3c, when K-Folds = 15, the optimal setting involves 15 neighbors, for which the RMSE falls to 0.8607 and the MAE to 0.5185. With 3 or 5 neighbors, both RMSE and MAE remain stuck at a high 1.0000, signaling markedly weaker performance. At 10 neighbors, the MAE dips to 0.6667, yet the RMSE stays elevated; thereafter, with 20 and 30 neighbors, both error metrics rise again, peaking at an RMSE of 1.0871 for 30 neighbors. In this K-Folds = 15 scenario, the neighborhood size of 15 offers the most balanced reduction of RMSE and MAE.

Finally, for K-Folds = 20, as highlighted in Table 2 and Fig. 3d, the algorithm reaches its highest accuracy with 10 neighbors: the RMSE plunges to 0.5774 and the MAE to 0.3333, the best overall combination across all tests. With 3 and 5 neighbors, the model records RMSE values of 0.7261 and 0.7082 and MAE values of 0.5032 and 0.5067, respectively. The 10-neighbor configuration nonetheless remains superior, minimizing both error measures simultaneously. Beyond 10 neighbors, RMSE and MAE climb steadily—e.g., RMSE of 0.8034 and MAE of 0.4636 at 15 neighbors—and continue upward at 20 and 30 neighbors, culminating in an RMSE of 1.0853 for 30 neighbors. Hence, for K-Folds = 20, the 10-neighbor configuration provides the optimal predictive accuracy.

Overall, the algorithm's performance varies significantly as a function of K-Folds values and the K-Neighbors selected for collaborative filtering task. For lower K-Folds values (5 and 10), the algorithm achieves optimal performance with a reduced number of neighbors (3 to 5), which minimizes both RMSE and MAE. This indicates that a small neighborhood size is sufficient for accurate predictions in these configurations, because the model focuses more efficiently on the closest relationships without overfitting. On the other hand, for higher values of K-Folds (15 and 20), the model performs better with an intermediate number of neighbors, around 10 to 15 neighbors. This behavior suggests that with more detailed tests (i.e. more K-Folds), a slightly larger set of neighbors can capture subtle variations in user preferences, while retaining good generalization.

Similarity Measurement with Wasserstein Divergence

Secondly, we used the Wasserstein divergence to gauge similarity between users' multi-aspect probabilities vectors.

As shown in Table 3, where the lowest RMSE and MAE scores for each K-fold configuration are highlighted in boldface, and Fig. 4a, when the data are split into 5 folds, the model starts with comparatively large errors at the smallest neighborhood sizes (K-Neighbors 3 and 5). As the neighborhood widens, both metrics improve: the RMSE drops to 1.0000 with K-Neighbors 15 before ticking upward, whereas the MAE keeps falling until it reaches 0.6667 at K-Neighbors 30.

With 10 folds, the overall error level is similar but the curves are noticeably flatter. The RMSE is already low at K-Neighbors 5 and varies little thereafter, hovering between 1.00 and 1.10 across the range. By contrast, the MAE declines gradually, reaching its minimum of 0.6333 at K-Neighbors 20 before edging up again. Figure 4b thus shows an almost horizontal RMSE line coupled with a shallow U-shape for the MAE, indicating that any neighborhood size beyond five yields comparable performance in this setting.

Switching to 15 folds produces a clear improvement, as illustrated in Fig. 4c. The lowest errors are recorded at K-Neighbors 5 (RMSE 0.6219; MAE 0.5448). Beyond ten neighbors the errors rise sharply, creating a pronounced V-shape in both curves and revealing heightened sensitivity to neighborhood size.

Table 2. RMSE and MAE comparison for different values of K-Folds and K-Neighbors using Jensen-Shannon divergence metric [28].

	K-Folds = 5		K-Folds = 10		K-Folds = 15		K-Folds = 20	
K-Neighbors	RMSE	MAE	RMSE	MAE	RMSE	MAE	RMSE	MAE
3	1.2910	1.0000	**0.7071**	**0.5000**	1.0000	1.0000	0.7261	0.5032
5	**0.9354**	**0.6250**	0.8165	0.6667	1.0000	1.0000	0.7082	0.5067
10	1.3229	0.8333	0.8975	0.6389	1.0000	0.6667	**0.5774**	**0.3333**
15	1.3385	0.8750	1.0697	0.7693	**0.8607**	**0.5185**	0.8034	0.4636
20	1.1726	0.7083	0.8660	0.6071	1.0256	0.6074	0.8975	0.4722
30	1.1438	0.6833	0.8137	0.5509	1.0871	0.7273	1.0853	0.6778

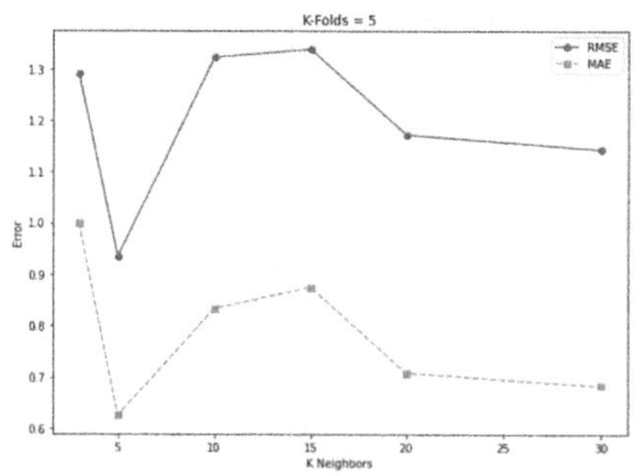

(a) RMSE and MAE by K-Neighbors for K-Folds=5.

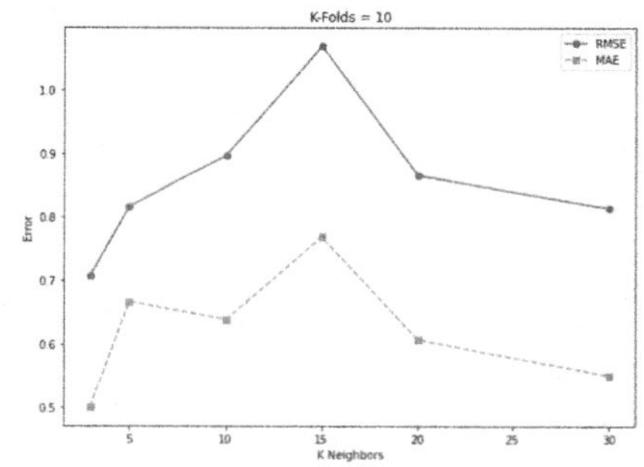

(b) RMSE and MAE by K-Neighbors for K-Folds=10.

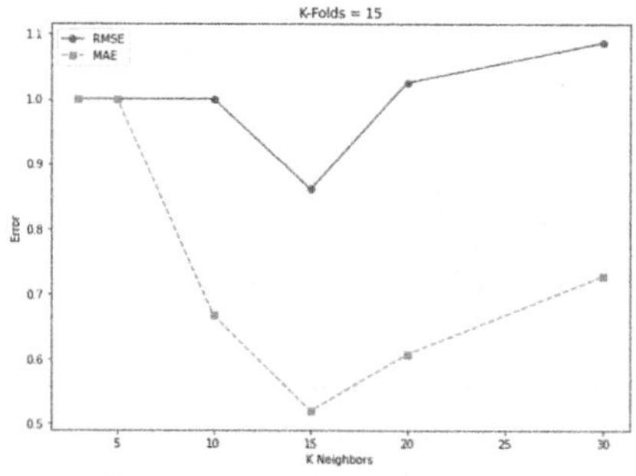

(c) RMSE and MAE by K-Neighbors for K-Folds=15.

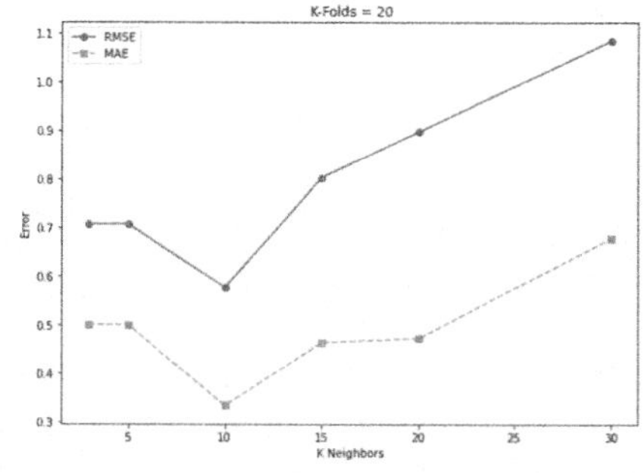

(d) RMSE and MAE by K-Neighbors for K-Folds=20.

Fig. 3. RMSE and MAE by K-Neighbors for different K-Folds using Jensen-Shannon divergence metric [28].

Under 20-fold cross-validation, the model achieves the lowest MAE of the entire study, but only for sufficiently large neighborhoods. Small neighborhoods (K-Neighbors 3 and 5) again suffer from high variance, with RMSE values above

1.20. Once K-Neighbors reaches 10, both metrics drop sharply and continue descending, attaining global minima at K-Neighbors 30 (RMSE 0.4511; MAE 0.4009). Figure 4d traces this steady downward trajectory, confirming that larger neighborhoods bring clear gains in this configuration.

Table 3. RMSE and MAE comparison for different values of K-Folds and K-Neighbors using Wasserstein divergence metric.

	K-Folds = 5		K-Folds = 10		K-Folds = 15		K-Folds = 20	
K-Neighbors	RMSE	MAE	RMSE	MAE	RMSE	MAE	RMSE	MAE
3	1.2910	1.0000	1.5811	1.5000	0.6761	0.8311	1.29101	1.0000
5	1.3229	1.0000	**1.0000**	0.6667	**0.6219**	**0.5448**	1.2247	1.0000
10	1.0328	0.7333	1.0801	0.7222	1.0118	0.7381	0.5774	0.5000
15	**1.0000**	0.7200	1.0753	0.6979	0.7293	0.6364	1.1019	0.7857
20	1.1475	0.7033	1.0189	**0.6333**	1.0607	0.7917	1.2649	1.0000
30	1.0646	**0.6667**	1.0663	0.7593	1.0801	0.7821	**0.4511**	**0.4009**

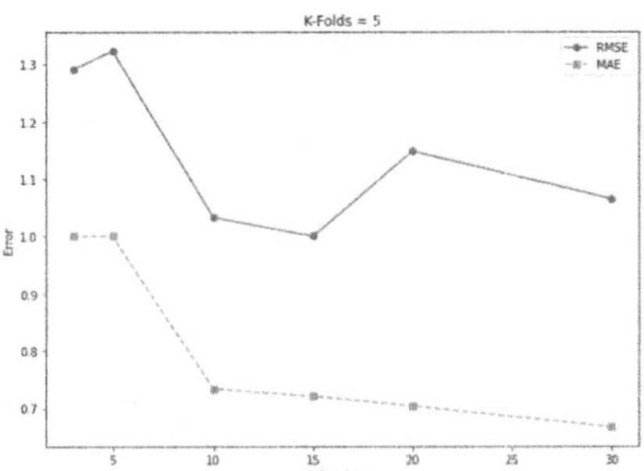

(a) RMSE and MAE by K-Neighbors for K-Folds=5.

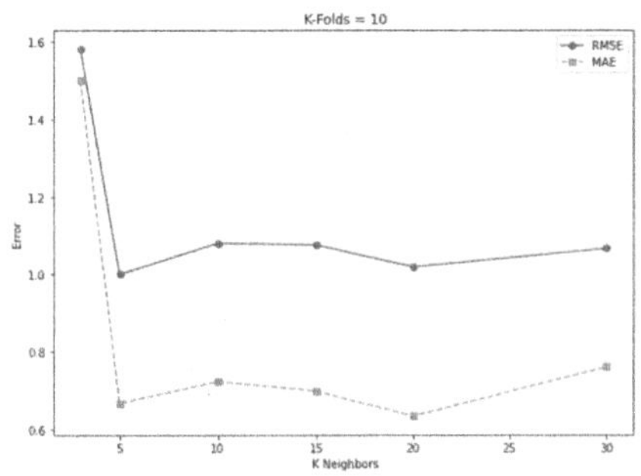

(b) RMSE and MAE by K-Neighbors for K-Folds=10.

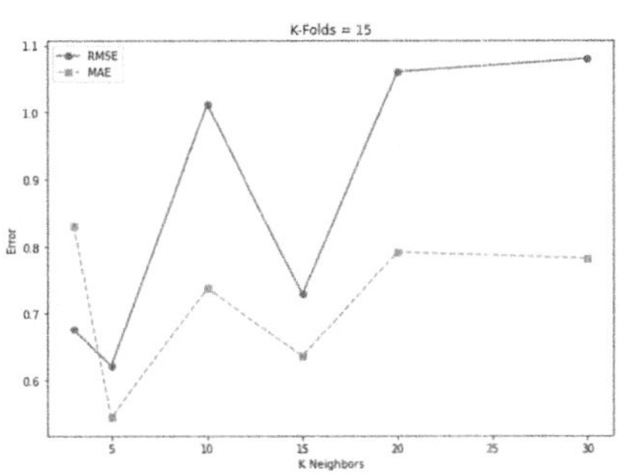

(c) RMSE and MAE by K-Neighbors for K-Folds=15.

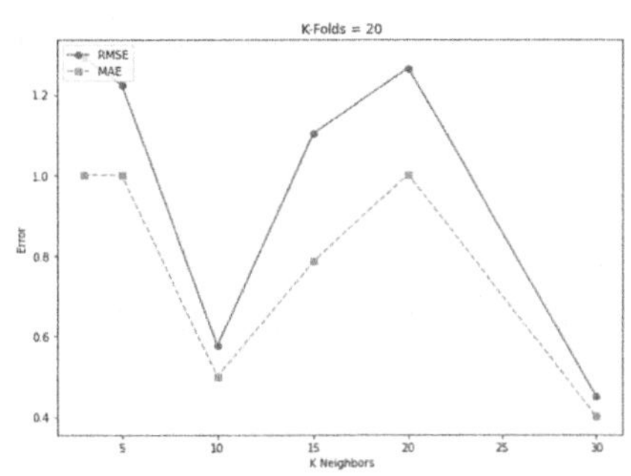

(d) RMSE and MAE by K-Neighbors for K-Folds=20.

Fig. 4. RMSE and MAE by K-Neighbors for different K-Folds using Wasserstein divergence metric.

Increasing the number of folds consistently lowers the overall error surface, yet it also makes performance more dependent on choosing an appropriate K-Neighbors. Very small neighborhoods tend to over-fit regardless of fold count, whereas extremely large neighborhoods help only when many folds are used. Mid-range values K-Neighbors (10–15) offer reliable, if not always optimal, results across all settings. A pragmatic, low-risk choice would pair 15 folds with a neighborhood between 5 and 10 neighbors, providing strong accuracy without the volatility seen at 20 folds. For situations where computational cost and parameter sensitivity are less of a concern, the combination of 20 folds and 30 neighbors defines the performance frontier, delivering the smallest observed errors in both RMSE and MAE.

Comparative Analysis of Jensen–Shannon and Wasserstein Methods Table 4, where the lowest RMSE and MAE recorded for every divergence metric are emphasized in boldface, and Figs. 5 report the mean cross-validated errors of the our model using either Wasserstein or Jensen–Shannon divergence, averaged across four fold counts (5, 10, 15 and 20). For MAE, Jensen–Shannon is generally superior, achieving the overall minimum of 0.599 at (K-Neighbors $= 20$); Wasserstein overtakes it only for the widest neighborhood (K-Neighbors $= 30$). The pattern for RMSE is mixed: Jensen–Shannon performs better for very small neighborhoods K-Neighbors $= 3$, 5 and again at (K-Neighbors $= 20$), whereas Wasserstein produces lower RMSE at intermediate (K-Neighbors $= 10$, 15) and large (K-Neighbors $= 30$) neighbor sizes.

Table 4. RMSE and MAE comparison for different values K-Neighbors using Wasserstein and Jensen-Shannon divergence metrics.

	Jensen-Shannon		Wasserstein	
K-Neighbors	RMSE	MAE	RMSE	MAE
3	0 .926	0 .750	1 .210	1.083
5	**0 .865**	0 .698	1 .042	0.803
10	0 .949	0 .618	0 .926	0.673
15	1 .018	0 .657	0 .977	0.710
20	0 .990	**0 .599**	1 .123	0.782
30	1 .032	0 .660	**0 .916**	**0 .652**

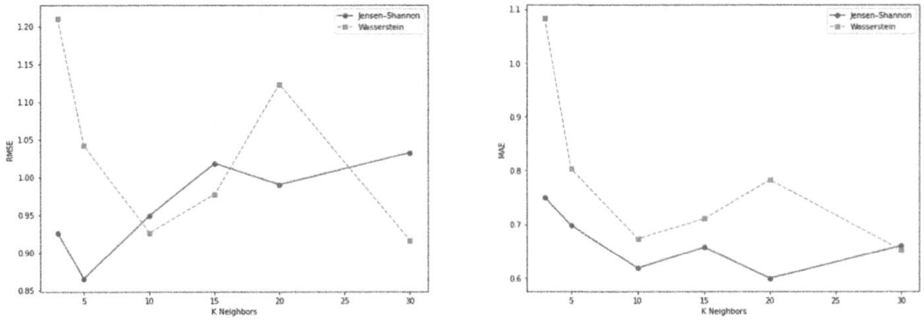

(a) Prediction Error (RMSE) JensenShannon vs Wasserstein

(b) Prediction Error (MAE) JensenShannon vs Wasserstein

Fig. 5. RMSE and MAE Performance Comparison of the model Using Jensen–Shannon vs Wasserstein Distances.

– **Baseline Methods**

To highlight the performance of our model, we compared it to other recommendation approaches implemented on the same LDOS-CoMoDa dataset:

- **KCAMF** [26]**:** In this research, the authors proposed an innovative kernel-based loss function to enhance matrix factorization optimization in a non-linear projection rating space, with optimal handling of context multiplicity.
- **CBMF** [23]**:** In this paper, the authors developed a contextual recommendation system based on the concept of integrated context. This system optimizes recommendation personalization by directly incorporating relevant contextual data into the recommendation generation process.
- **Hybrid-IHSR** [24]**:** The authors of this research introduced an innovative hierarchical representation method to capture latent contextual information, and subsequently understand users' specific situations as they personalize recommendations. They proposed a transformation process to structure unstructured contextual information into hierarchical representations.
- **SVD++** [25]**:** This approach enriches the SVD++ factorization model with a social popularity factor based on implicit user feedback. This mechanism permits the capture of users' direct preferences and also the effect of an item's popularity within the community, thus enhancing the relevance and adaptability of recommendations.

As outlined in Table 5, which summarizes the results of all compared approaches (best scores are bolded), our model achieved the best performance, recording the lowest RMSE and MAE values for both divergence measures. These comparisons confirm our model's ability to integrate emotional, demographic and temporal contexts for more context-driven recommendations, and validate the strength of our approach to capture user preferences by driving the recommendation process through context.

Table 5. RMSE and MAE comparison between models implemented on LDOS-CoMoDa dataset [28].

Method	RMSE	MAE
KCAMF [26]	0.9136	0.7177
CBMF [23]	1.0680	0.8386
Hybrid-IHSR [24]	1.2300	0.9700
SVD++ [25]	1.0571	0.8468
CDRS-PC-JSW (Jensen-Shannon)	0.5774	**0.3333**
CDRS-PC-JSW (Wasserstein)	**0.4511**	0.4009

5 Conclusion

This study presented a three-stage, context-driven collaborative-filtering approach which unfolds in three phases. First, the data are split into emotional, demographic and temporal aspects; each aspect is processed with a dedicated clustering algorithm, yielding a probability distribution that reflects every user's membership across the corresponding clusters. Second, we converted these distributions into inter-user similarity scores: for each pair of users we compute both Jensen-Shannon and Wasserstein divergences on every aspect, dynamically weight the resulting scores to mirror the respective importance of each contextual aspect, and normalize them into a single User–User similarity matrix. Finally, the recommender selects the N most context-aligned neighbors from this matrix, predicts ratings for items the target user has not yet seen and delivers personalized recommendations based on those estimates.

Our experiments were performed on LDOS–CoMoDa dataset. Relative to established benchmark methods, the proposed model delivered good results: the Jensen–Shannon configuration attained RMSE and MAE values of 0.5774 and 0.3333, respectively, whereas the Wasserstein configuration achieved an RMSE of 0.4511 and an MAE of 0.4009. Both variants surpassed the baselines and showcased a marked ability to adapt to contextual dynamics, underscoring the system's capacity to generate context-driven recommendations that accommodate evolving user preferences.

Future extensions will explore automated feature-selection to retain only the most informative attributes per aspect, meta-learning schemes that pick the optimum clustering algorithm for a given data and transfer to diverse domains and other datasets. Taken together, these directions aim to further optimize contextual recommendation.

References

1. Latrech, J., Kodia, Z., Azzouna, N.B.: CoDFi-DL: a hybrid recommender system combining enhanced collaborative and demographic filtering based on deep learning. J. Supercomput. **80**(1), 1160–1182 (2024a)

2. Adomavicius, G., Tuzhilin, A.: Context-aware recommender systems. In: Ricci, F., Rokach, L., Shapira, B., Kantor, P.B. (eds.) Recommender Systems Handbook, pp. 217–253. Springer, Boston, MA (2011). https://doi.org/10.1007/978-0-387-85820-3_7
3. Pagano, R., et al.: The contextual turn: from context-aware to context-driven recommender systems. In: Proceedings of the 10th ACM Conference on Recommender Systems, pp. 249–252 (2016)
4. Lin, J.: Divergence measures based on the Shannon entropy. IEEE Trans. Inf. Theory **37**(1), 145–151 (1991)
5. Kullback, S., Leibler, R.A.: On information and sufficiency. Ann. Math. Stat. **22**(1), 79–86 (1951)
6. Kantorovich, L.V.: On the translocation of masses. J. Math. Sci. **133**(4) (2006)
7. Loukili, M., Messaoudi, F., Ghazi, M.E.: Machine learning based recommender system for e-commerce. IAES Int. J. Artif. Intell. **12**(4), 1803–1811 (2023)
8. Karatzoglou, A., Amatriain, X., Baltrunas, L., Oliver, N.: Multiverse recommendation: n-dimensional tensor factorization for context-aware collaborative filtering. In: Proceedings of the Fourth ACM Conference on Recommender Systems, pp. 79–86 (2010)
9. Said, A., De Luca, E.W., Albayrak, S.: Inferring contextual user profiles-improving recommender performance. In: Proceedings of the 3rd RecSys Workshop on Context-Aware Recommender Systems, vol. 791 (2011)
10. Baltrunas, L., Ricci, F.: Experimental evaluation of context-dependent collaborative filtering using item splitting. User Model. User-Adap. Inter. **24**, 7–34 (2014)
11. Fareed, A., Hassan, S., Belhaouari, S.B., Halim, Z.: A collaborative filtering recommendation framework utilizing social networks. Mach. Learn. Appl. **14**, 100495 (2023)
12. Karabila, I., Darraz, N., El-Ansari, A., Alami, N., El Mallahi, M.: Enhancing collaborative filtering-based recommender system using sentiment analysis. Future Internet **15**(7), 235 (2023)
13. Aldayel, M., Al-Nafjan, A., Al-Nuwaiser, W.M., Alrehaili, G., Alyahya, G.: Collaborative filtering-based recommendation systems for touristic businesses, attractions, and destinations. Electronics **12**(19), 4047 (2023)
14. Zhang, J., et al.: Agentcf: collaborative learning with autonomous language agents for recommender systems. In: Proceedings of the ACM on Web Conference 2024, pp. 3679–3689 (2024)
15. Panarese, A., Settanni, G., Galiano, A.: Modeling an e-commerce hybrid recommender system based on machine learning algorithms. In: ICAART (3), pp. 706–712 (2023)
16. Košir, A., Odic, A., Kunaver, M., Tkalcic, M., Tasic, J.F.: Database for contextual personalization. Elektrotehniški vestnik **78**(5), 270–274 (2011)
17. Lloyd, S.: Least squares quantization in PCM. IEEE Trans. Inf. Theory **28**(2), 129–137 (1982)
18. Fukunaga, K., Hostetler, L.: The estimation of the gradient of a density function, with applications in pattern recognition. IEEE Trans. Inf. Theory **21**(1), 32–40 (1975)
19. Palacio-Niño, J.-O., Berzal, F.: Evaluation metrics for unsupervised learning algorithms. arXiv preprint arXiv:1905.05667 (2019)
20. Caliński, T., Harabasz, J.: A dendrite method for cluster analysis. Commun. Stat.-Theory Methods **3**(1), 1–27 (1974)
21. Wijaya, Y.A., et al.: Davies bouldin index algorithm for optimizing clustering case studies mapping school facilities. TEM J. **10**(3), 1099–1103 (2021)

22. Latrech, J., Kodia, Z., Azzouna, N.B.: Twit-CoFiD: a hybrid recommender system based on tweet sentiment analysis. Soc. Netw. Anal. Min. **14**(1), 123 (2024b)
23. Casillo, M., Gupta, B.B., Lombardi, M., Lorusso, A., Santaniello, D., Valentino, C.: Context aware recommender systems: a novel approach based on matrix factorization and contextual bias. Electronics **11**(7), 1003 (2022)
24. Unger, M., Tuzhilin, A.: Hierarchical latent context representation for context-aware recommendations. IEEE Trans. Knowl. Data Eng. **34**(7), 3322–3334 (2020)
25. Kumar, R., Verma, B.K., Rastogi, S.S.: Social popularity based SVD++ recommender system. Int. J. Comput. Appl. **87**(14) (2014)
26. Patil, V.A., Chapaneri, S.V., Jayaswal, D.J.: Kernel-based matrix factorization with weighted regularization for context-aware recommender systems. IEEE Access **10**, 75581–75595 (2022)
27. Salakhutdinov, R., Mnih, A.: Bayesian probabilistic matrix factorization using Markov chain Monte Carlo. In: Proceedings of the 25th International Conference on Machine Learning, pp. 880–887 (2008)
28. Latrech, J., Kodia, Z., Azzouna, N.B.: Machine Learning Based Collaborative Filtering Using Jensen–Shannon Divergence for Context-Driven Recommendations
29. Latrech, J., Kodia, Z., Ben Azzouna, N.: CoD-MaF: toward a context-driven collaborative filtering using contextual biased matrix factorization. Int. J. Data Sci. Anal. 1–18 (2025)

Towards the Selection of Sustainable Suppliers Using Deep Learning

Hanen Neji[1(✉)], Mouna Rekik[2], and Ismail Bouassida Rodriguez[1]

[1] ReDCAD,ENIS, University of Sfax, Sfax, Tunisia
hanenneji2@gmail.com, bouassida@redcad.org
[2] MIRACL,ISIMS, University of Sfax, Sfax, Tunisia
Mouna.rekik@usf.tn

Abstract. Advancements in Artificial Intelligence (AI), particularly in Natural Language Processing (NLP) and sentiment analysis, offer new perspectives for evaluating supplier sustainability. Faced with the limitations of traditional methods based on corporate declarations and expert opinions, these technologies enable a more transparent consideration of stakeholder perceptions, thus reducing the risks of greenwashing. We began by conducting a systematic literature review (SLR) on the combined use of AI, NLP, and Multi-Criteria Decision-Making (MCDM) methods in the domain of sustainable supplier selection. This analysis revealed a growing need to integrate unstructured data, such as online reviews, into the decision-making process. Based on these findings, we propose an innovative approach combining a BERT model for automatic annotation of online consumer comments according to sustainability criteria extracted from the literature, with the TOPSIS method for the final ranking of suppliers. This hybrid method enables classifying comments by their relevance and expressed sentiment, and integrates these annotations within a multicriteria decision-making framework. Our approach improves supplier evaluation by taking into account real consumer perceptions, while providing a methodological response to the lack of transparency in traditional approaches.

Keywords: Sustainable supplier selection · Greenwashing · Sentiment Analysis · Text Analytics · BERT · NLP · MCDM · TOPSIS

1 Introduction

In the digital era, the massive growth of textual data generated on online platforms has led to the increasing adoption of Natural Language Processing (NLP) and sentiment analysis across various domains. These technologies help capture and interpret user opinions, providing companies with valuable insights to improve their products, services, and strategies. Their use is especially relevant in the field of sustainability, where they enable the assessment of how customers perceive companies' environmental and social practices.

H. J. van den Herik et al. (Eds.): ICAART 2025, LNAI 16517, pp. 133–158, 2026.
https://doi.org/10.1007/978-3-032-25032-2_7

As sustainability becomes a key concern for businesses, selecting responsible suppliers has grown more complex. This complexity arises not only from the wide range of criteria to consider but also from the threat of greenwashing—when companies promote a misleading image of environmental responsibility. Traditional evaluation methods, often based on company statements or expert opinions, are potentially biased and may not fully reflect the actual practices of suppliers.

To address these limitations, we propose leveraging consumer feedback published on social media and review platforms (such as Facebook, Twitter, and Trustpilot), using sentiment analysis to enhance supplier evaluation. This approach offers a more direct, critical, and authentic perspective from stakeholders themselves, leading to a more accurate assessment of real sustainability efforts.

In this context, we used the BERT model—based on transformers—to automatically classify customer comments into four categories: relevant positive, relevant negative, irrelevant positive, and irrelevant negative. This classification is guided by criteria identified through a comprehensive literature review, allowing us to distinguish expert insights from less specialized feedback. Not all comments are treated equally: those demonstrating a deep understanding of sustainability issues are given more weight due to their informative value.

Finally, to rank the suppliers, we applied the TOPSIS multi-criteria decision-making method, based on the annotations produced by BERT. This combination of sentiment analysis and MCDM enables a more robust evaluation of supplier sustainability and helps detect greenwashing practices by comparing consumer perceptions with corporate claims. It thus strengthens the transparency and reliability of the responsible supplier selection process.

2 Background and Related Research

This section explores recent developments in sustainable supplier selection. It reviews key evaluation criteria and methods, highlights best practices and challenges in sustainability, and discusses the application of MCDM, machine learning, and deep learning. It also emphasizes the role of NLP and sentiment analysis in identifying greenwashing and supporting sustainable supply chains. To the best of our knowledge, no previous SLR has comprehensively combined these perspectives to evaluate both traditional and AI-based methods in sustainable supplier selection.

2.1 Sustainability and Greenwashing

Sustainability, defined by the Brundtland Commission in 1987 as "development that meets the needs of the present without compromising the ability of future generations to meet their own needs", emphasizes the importance of preserving resources while addressing current economic and social needs [21]. In parallel, greenwashing refers to the deceptive practice of portraying a company's products or practices as environmentally friendly when they are not genuinely so [33].

In the field of computer science, these two concepts are particularly important, especially for the selection of sustainable suppliers. Thanks to tools such as sentiment analysis and machine learning, it becomes possible to detect greenwashing by evaluating customer feedback and analyzing information published by companies. The use of technologies like natural language processing automates and improves the reliability of these analyses, helping to distinguish genuinely committed sustainable companies from those merely pretending to be. These advances contribute to making selection processes more transparent and robust against deceptive strategies.

2.2 Multicriteria Decision-Making Methods (MCDM)

Multicriteria Decision Making (MCDM) is a key area of decision research aimed at identifying the best alternative by considering multiple criteria during the selection process. It encompasses a variety of methods applicable across many fields, ranging from finance to engineering, project management, and sustainability assessment. There are different MCDM methods, and we will present some of the main ones used [27].

2.3 Technique for Order Preference by Similarity to Ideal Solution (TOPSIS)

The TOPSIS method is one of the most widely adopted approaches in the field of multicriteria decision making. Its fundamental principle is based on evaluating and ranking multiple alternatives according to various criteria by determining their closeness to an ideal solution and their distance from an anti-ideal solution. This method is appreciated for its simplicity and its ability to handle both qualitative and quantitative data, making it a versatile tool across various sectors such as finance, project management, and environmental assessment. TOPSIS aims to overcome some of the limitations of other methods, such as sensitivity to criteria weights and the management of uncertainties [35].

2.4 Natural Language Processing (NLP)

Natural Language Processing (NLP) enhances intelligent machines by improving the understanding of human language to enable linguistic communication between humans and computers. Recent advances in computing power and the availability of large amounts of linguistic data have increased the need and demand for automating semantic analysis using data-driven approaches. The use of data-driven strategies is now widespread, thanks to significant improvements demonstrated through deep learning methods in fields such as computer vision, automatic speech recognition, and especially NLP. This study categorizes and addresses the various aspects and applications of NLP that have benefited from deep learning. It covers the main tasks and applications of NLP and describes how deep learning methods and models are advancing these areas. We also analyze and compare different state-of-the-art approaches and models [29].

2.5 Sentiment Analysis

Sentiment analysis, also known as opinion mining, involves assigning an emotional label to a text, usually indicating whether it expresses a positive, negative, or neutral opinion. This technique, which is part of natural language processing (NLP), aims to develop classifiers capable of predicting the polarity of a text in order to better understand consumer sentiments and market trends [5]. The sentiment analysis process involves several key steps. It begins with the collection of textual data from sources such as social networks or review sites, often using web scraping. Next, a preprocessing phase is carried out to clean the texts using NLP techniques, including tokenization and the removal of irrelevant elements. In some approaches, a feature selection and extraction step is used to identify significant elements such as term co-occurrences or opinion words. Finally, the classification assigns a polarity to the texts: positive, negative, or neutral [18].

2.6 Sentiment Classification Techniques

To analyze sentiments in a text, several methods can be used. Traditional classifiers such as SVM, Naïve Bayes, Random Forest, and decision trees are effective for basic tasks but are limited in their ability to understand the contextual meaning of language.

To overcome these limitations, deep learning models like LSTM, RNN, and CNN have been introduced. These models better capture linguistic structures and contextual dependencies due to their ability to process word sequences.

A major breakthrough comes from transformer-based models, especially BERT, which analyzes words in a bidirectional context, allowing for a deeper understanding of natural language. Other variants like RoBERTa, ELECTRA, and Transformer-XL further improve performance by refining training techniques and handling longer sequences more effectively.

In summary, transformer-based models represent a revolution in natural language processing, offering powerful and accurate solutions for sentiment analysis [19].

2.7 BERT

BERT (Bidirectional Encoder Representations from Transformers) is a groundbreaking model in natural language processing (NLP). It uses bidirectional representations to understand the context of words on both sides of a target word, offering deeper linguistic comprehension than previous unidirectional models.

Its pretraining involves predicting masked words within a sentence, allowing the model to learn complex contextual relationships. BERT can then be fine-tuned for specific tasks such as text classification or sentiment analysis.

Key advantages include its ability to capture subtle shifts in meaning depending on context and the efficiency of training enabled by the transformer architecture. BERT has shown outstanding performance across various NLP tasks, including question answering, machine translation, and named entity recognition [7,24].

2.8 Sentiment Analysis Application Domains

Sentiment analysis is widely used across industries to assess consumer perceptions and guide business strategies. It helps companies understand customer opinions about their products, monitor brand reputation on social media, and detect trends or potential crises. Online product reviews provide valuable insights influencing purchasing decisions and product development. In sustainability, sentiment analysis allows businesses to evaluate the impact of eco-friendly initiatives and customer engagement, strengthening brand image and loyalty while aligning with growing expectations around social and environmental responsibility.

2.9 Related Literature Reviews

This section explores recent developments in sustainable supplier selection. It reviews key evaluation criteria and methods, highlights best practices and challenges in sustainability, and discusses the application of MCDM, machine learning, and deep learning. It also emphasizes the role of NLP and sentiment analysis in identifying greenwashing and supporting sustainable supply chains.

Sustainable Supplier Evaluation Criteria. For a robust and comprehensive evaluation of sustainable suppliers, it is essential not to limit the assessment to environmental criteria alone, but to include environmental, social, and governance (ESG) dimensions. Several studies have highlighted the limitations of relying solely on environmental factors, showing that this approach fails to fully capture the social and economic impacts of suppliers. Therefore, integrating ESG criteria helps address these gaps, providing a more balanced and holistic view of supplier sustainability. These approaches ensure that companies select suppliers who not only reduce their ecological footprint but also promote ethical and socially responsible practices [2,16]. As a result, some companies evaluate suppliers using criteria based on the three dimensions: economic, social, and environmental [25,26,28],While others use ESG criteria to evaluate a sustainable supplier [16,26,28]. The integration of Industry 4.0 criteria into the evaluation of sustainable suppliers has become essential to align modern technological advancements with sustainability requirements [8,28]. Resilience criteria are essential for assessing suppliers' ability to withstand and recover from disruptions such as natural disasters, geopolitical events, or economic crises. These criteria evaluate factors like risk management practices, supply chain transparency, and flexibility to ensure suppliers can adapt to unforeseen challenges and maintain business continuity [10,22] (Table 1).

Methods for Evaluating Sustainable Suppliers. In the literature, existing work on sustainable supplier evaluation is mainly divided into two major approaches: multi-criteria decision-making (MCDM) methods, which allow the integration of multiple sustainability criteria to rank suppliers, and artificial

Table 1. Some criteria for the evaluation of sustainable suppliers.

Aspect	Criteria
Environnemental	Material recycling
	Eco-friendly packaging
Social	Employment contract
	Workplace safety and well-being
Economic	Eco-responsible quality
	Financial sustainability
Governance	Transparency of practices
Industry 4.0	Integration of green technologies in production

intelligence-based approaches. Among MCDM methods, TOPSIS is used to identify the alternative that is closest to the ideal solution [8,13,14,20,32,34]. There are also hybrid approaches such as AHP-FIS, which combines AHP with fuzzy inference systems to enhance decision-making [25]. Finally, BWM (Best-Worst Method) is valued for reducing the number of pairwise comparisons required while maintaining evaluation consistency [28], which allow the integration of multiple sustainability criteria to rank suppliers, and artificial intelligence-based approaches, particularly machine learning [1,9,15,30], deep learning [31,32], natural language processing (NLP), and sentiment analysis, which aim to leverage textual and behavioral data to support decision-making [11,17]. For a more detailed overview of these methods and their applications, we made a systematic literature review [23].

Using Sentiment Analysis to Prevent Greenwashing. Sentiment analysis plays a key role in detecting greenwashing by assessing public perception of corporate communications. Recent studies have used this method—particularly on data from social networks like Twitter—to identify discrepancies between ESG claims and actual practices. This approach helps better understand concerns related to greenwashing and provides valuable insights for stakeholders [3,4].

Limitations. A thorough review of supplier evaluation methods—such as MCDM, AI, and sentiment analysis—demonstrates their effectiveness. However, most studies mainly rely on expert opinions, often overlooking feedback from end-users. These approaches therefore present limitations, particularly regarding the consideration of actual consumer perceptions. To address these limitations, a promising approach would be to incorporate user comment analysis to enhance sustainability assessments with real and authentic perspectives.

3 Proposed Approach for Sustainable Supplier Selection

We propose a new approach for selecting sustainable suppliers based on consumer sentiment analysis. Using advanced natural language processing (NLP) techniques—particularly the automatic annotation of comments with the BERT model—we extract relevant insights into perceptions related to sustainability. BERT is first pre-trained on a large general corpus, then fine-tuned using comments collected from social media platforms and Trustpilot. This fine-tuning enhances its ability to understand ecological and social aspects. We compare BERT with models such as LSTM and RandomForestClassifier, highlighting its superior contextual understanding. The annotated comments are then used as criteria in the TOPSIS multi-criteria decision-making method, which ranks suppliers according to their sustainability performance. By combining NLP and decision-making tools, our approach enables a more nuanced evaluation, incorporating real consumer perceptions and facilitating the selection of partners aligned with environmental sustainability values. Figure 1 illustrates the process of selecting and ranking sustainable suppliers, integrating the stages of pre-training, fine-tuning with BERT, comment annotation, and final evaluation using the TOPSIS method.

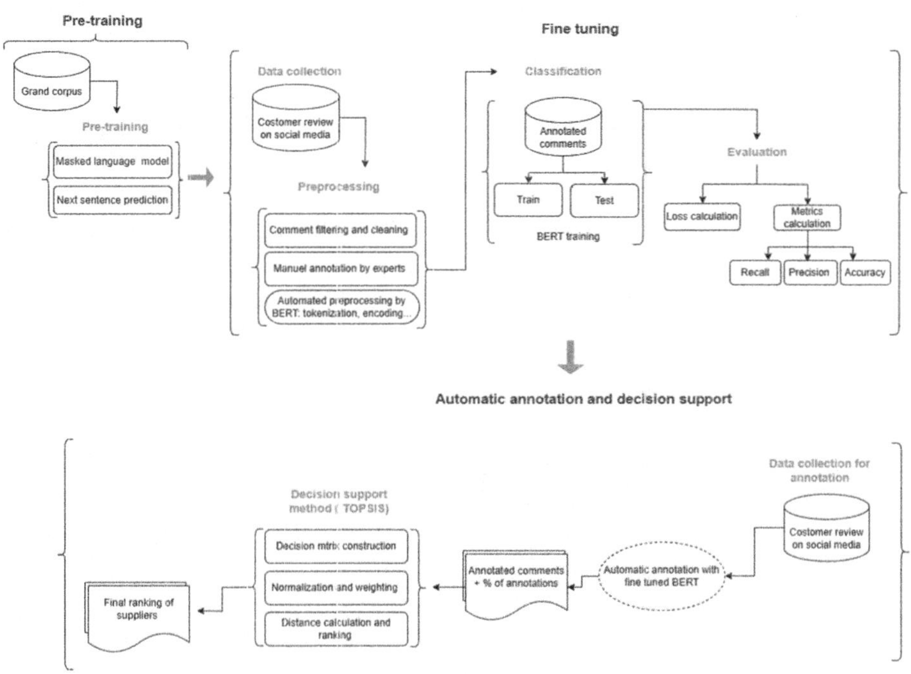

Fig. 1. Proposed approach for sustainable supplier selection.

In the following sections, we will explain in detail the steps of the proposed approach, including pre-training, fine-tuning, automatic annotation and decision support.

3.1 Pre-training

The BERT model is pre-trained using two main techniques: Masked Language Model (MLM) and Next Sentence Prediction (NSP).

1. **Masked Language Model (MLM):** 15% of the tokens (units of text) in a sequence are randomly masked, and BERT must predict these hidden tokens. This enables the model to learn rich contextual representations by analyzing the relationships between words in their context, as shown in Fig. 2.
2. **Next Sentence Prediction (NSP):** This task consists of determining whether one sentence logically follows another. BERT uses a special token [CLS] to represent the entire sequence and classify whether the second sentence is indeed the continuation of the first or not, as shown in Fig. 2.
3. **Pre-training data:** BERT is pre-trained on a very large corpus of 3.3 billion words, with sequences sometimes composed of incomplete sentences or multiple sentences, which helps improve its robustness [12].

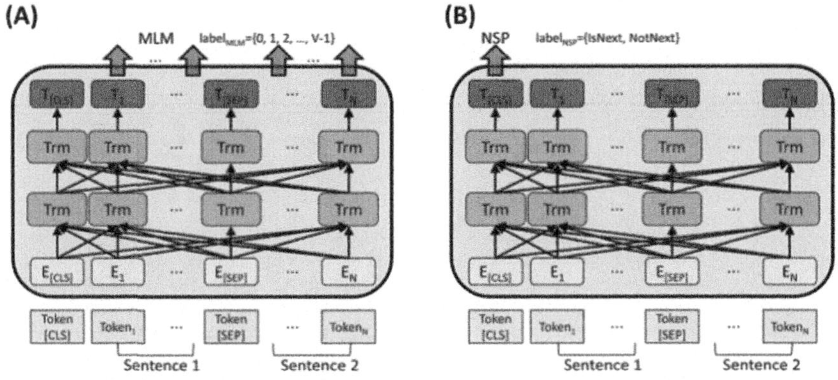

Fig. 2. Pre-training process for BERT. (A) MLM task. (B) NSP task [12].

3.2 Fine Tuning

Fine-tuning is a crucial phase that adapts a pre-trained model like BERT to a specific task. Although BERT gains a general understanding of language through pre-training on a large corpus, it remains too generic for targeted applications. Fine-tuning adjusts the model's parameters using labeled data specific to the task, such as text classification or sentiment analysis.

In our case, BERT was fine-tuned to classify comments related to sustainable suppliers. Around 600 comments were collected via scraping from social media platforms. The model was trained to detect relevant sentiments and information regarding the sustainability of products and services. The data collection, classification, and evaluation steps are detailed in the following sections.

Training Data Collection. In our approach, the collection of training data is essential for fine-tuning BERT. Approximately 600 comments related to sustainable suppliers were extracted using a scraping tool from social media platforms (Facebook, Twitter, Trustpilot). These data, exported in Excel format, contain customer feedback on sustainable products and services. This targeted collection allows BERT to be adapted to sustainability issues by teaching it to recognize sentiments and relevant criteria to automatically classify new comments.

Data Preprocessing. The preprocessing phase involves preparing the data for BERT training while ensuring that the relevant information related to supplier sustainability is preserved.

1. **Comments Filtering and Cleaning:** Involve removing unnecessary elements (special characters, HTML tags, links), correcting typos, removing stop words, and ensuring that the comments are clear and relevant for evaluating the sustainability of suppliers.
2. **Manual Annotation by Experts:** After filtering, experts manually annotate the comments using key sustainability terms covering environmental, social, economic, and governance aspects, as shown in 2. If a comment contains at least one key term, it is kept for analysis. Experts then label comments into four categories: pertinent positive, pertinent negative, non-pertinent positive, and non-pertinent negative. This detailed annotation helps capture the tone and relevance of comments related to sustainability. To ensure balanced learning and avoid over- or underfitting, the number of comments in each category is kept equal, allowing effective and unbiased model training. Figure 3 shows an example of a positive comment containing a single environmental criteria.

Fig. 3. Example of a relevant positive comment.

To facilitate learning, numerical values were assigned to each annotation category: 0 for pertinent positive, 1 for pertinent negative, 2 for non-pertinent

Table 2. Keywords used for filtering comments related to suppliers' sustainability.

Sustainability key terms			
Environmental	Social	Economic	Governance
Biodiversity	Negotiation		
Carbon	Child labor	Circular economy	
Circular	Corruption	Eco-efficiency	Active ownership
Climate	Discrimination	Investment	Engagement
Deforestation	Diversity	Cost	Responsibility
Energy	Ethics	Quality	Law compliance
Environment	Equality	Green economy	Transparency
Waste	Health	Profitability	Stakeholders
Recycling	Human rights	Economic impact	
Renewable	Fair trade		

positive, and 3 for non-pertinent negative. This encoding simplifies the automatic classification step by BERT. Figure 4 shows an excerpt of the collected comments annotated according to these defined categories.

A	B
La personne à qui j'ai offert le cadeau est très contente	0
Produits de très belle qualité emballage très soigné et petit cadeau surprise très apprécié ! Envoi très rapide	0
Article livré rapidement un cadeau en plus dans la boite Merci	2
J'ai fait plusieurs mails de relance pour demander un remboursement mais toujours rien	1
Il ne s'agit pas d'une entreprise mais d'un petit entrepreneur indépendant qui ne gère pas sérieusement ce bu	3

Fig. 4. Annotations classified by relevance with corresponding values (0 for Pertinent Positive, 1 for Pertinent Negative, 2 for No-Pertinent Positive, and 3 for No-Pertinent Negative).

3. **Automated Preprocessing with BERT:** Automated preprocessing with BERT transforms raw comments into contextualized vector representations for detailed analysis of sentiments and sustainability criteria. It uses WordPiece tokenization to efficiently manage vocabulary, word, segment, and position embeddings to understand context and word order, as well as padding to standardize sequence lengths. Attention masks indicate which parts of the sequences should be considered, thereby improving the model's accuracy.

Classification with BERT. BERT is fine-tuned for the specific task of classifying supplier sustainability comments. Initially pre-trained on large data, BERT captures bidirectional context for precise text understanding. Our study uses the uncased BERT base model (12 layers, 768 hidden dimensions, 12 attention heads), which treats text case-insensitively, simplifying learning and improving generalization. Fine-tuning on about 600 annotated comments improved prediction accuracy and adapted BERT to recognize customer sentiments related to sustainable suppliers. Figure 5 details the four steps of the classification process with BERT base, namely: (1) input, (2) encoding by BERT's 12 layers, (3) contextualization of embeddings, and (4) the linear layer followed by the final classification.

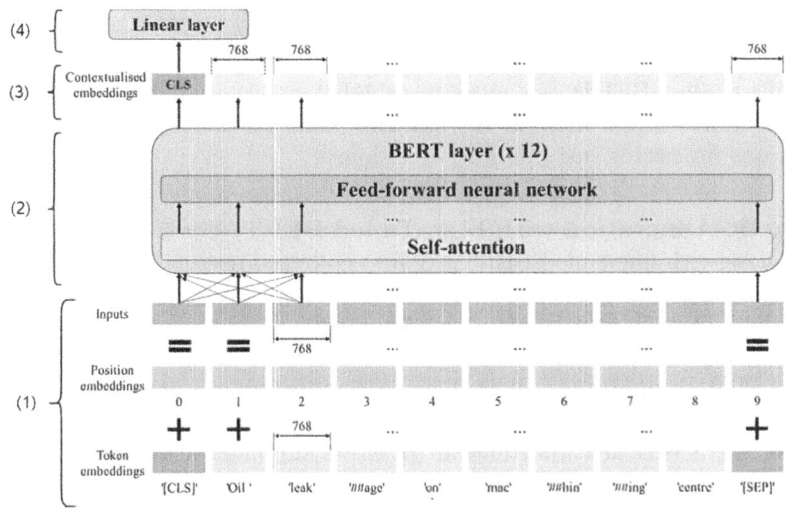

Fig. 5. Operating process of BERT base [31].

- **(1) Input:** Comments are converted into vectors using word, segment, and position embeddings, enabling BERT to understand the meaning, structure, and order of words in the text.
- **(2) Encoding by the 12 Layers of BERT:** BERT base has 12 layers of encoders that progressively capture both local and global contextual relationships in text. The output of each layer feeds into the next, using self-attention to deep model word dependencies. The early layers capture simple context, while the deeper layers learn complex, nuanced relationships, improving overall understanding.
- **(3) Contextualization of Embeddings:** The special [CLS] token, placed at the beginning of the sequence, is used to obtain a rich contextual representation of the entire comment after passing through the 12 layers of BERT.
- **(4) Linear Layer Followed by the Final Classification:** After obtaining the representation of the [CLS] token, it is passed to a linear layer that produces logits for each of the four target classes. A Softmax function is

then applied to convert these logits into probabilities, and the class with the highest probability is selected as the final prediction.

Fine-Tuned BERT Evaluation. When evaluating a Transformer-based model such as BERT, it is crucial to distinguish between the loss calculation, which measures the error of the model, specifically training loss and validation loss, and the calculation of performance metrics, which assess the quality of predictions, including accuracy, precision, and recall.

3.3 Automatic Annotation and Decision Support

After fine-tuning BERT, we used it to label new comments and applied a weighted multi-criteria method to rank suppliers, focusing on relevant positive annotations for better sustainability decisions.

Automatic Annotation with Fine-Tuned BERT. For the automatic annotation phase with fine-tuned BERT, we first collected user comments on selected suppliers to evaluate their sustainability, using a scraping tool to efficiently gather data from various platforms. After collecting the comments, we used the fine-tuned BERT to annotate each comment based on sustainability criteria. This automatic annotation allowed us to classify reviews into four categories: pertinent positive, pertinent negative, non-pertinent positive, and non-pertinent negative, extracting key information to assess supplier sustainability practices and providing a solid foundation for decision support.

Decision Support for Ranking Sustainable Suppliers Using TOPSIS. Decision support for ranking sustainable suppliers using TOPSIS involves evaluating multiple criteria derived from annotated comments. By assigning weights to each criterion based on their importance, TOPSIS helps rank suppliers by measuring their closeness to the ideal solution, enabling a clear and objective sustainability-based supplier classification. To apply TOPSIS, we follow several key steps, as shown in Fig. 6. This systematic process helps structure the decision by evaluating each option based on its proximity to the ideal solution, providing a comprehensive and informed assessment of the relative performance of the alternatives.

1. **Definition of Criteria and Alternatives:** In this step, we identified the criteria and alternatives necessary for evaluating suppliers in terms of sustainability. This selection ensures that the decision matrix aligns with our objectives, incorporating all essential dimensions for an informed assessment.
2. **Construction of the Decision Matrix:** This step involves building a decision matrix that maps each supplier (alternative) to sustainability-related criteria, represented by BERT-generated annotation percentages. The matrix offers a clear, structured overview for comparing supplier performance and supports informed decision-making using the TOPSIS method.

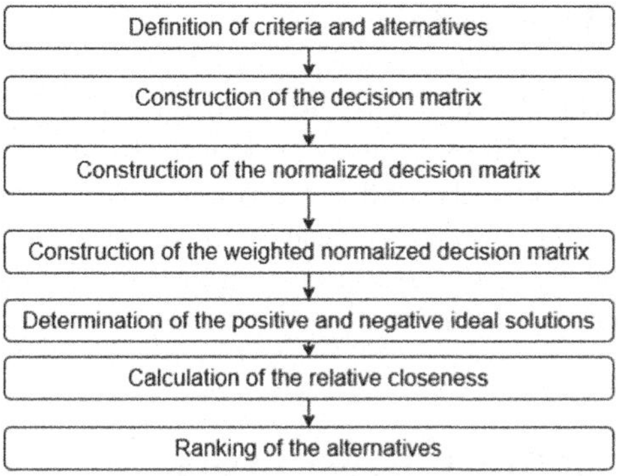

Fig. 6. Diagram illustrating the key steps of the TOPSIS method [6].

3. **Construction of the Normalized Decision Matrix:** The decision matrix values are normalized using vector normalization to make the criteria comparable. This method scales each element by dividing it by the square root of the sum of squares in its column, ensuring all criteria are on a common scale for effective comparison in the TOPSIS method.
4. **Construction of the Weighted Normalized Decision Matrix:** The normalized values are then weighted according to the importance of each criterion. Higher weights are assigned to pertinent annotations, as they are more meaningful for evaluating supplier sustainability.
5. **Deftermination of the Positive and Negative Solutions:** After normalizing and weighting the decision matrix, the positive ideal solution (A^+) and the negative ideal solution (A^-) are determined. A^+ includes the best values for favorable criteria and the worst for unfavorable ones, while A- does the opposite. These solutions are essential in the TOPSIS method to assess each supplier's relative closeness to the ideal, enabling the identification of the most sustainable and suitable supplier
6. **Calculation of the Relative Closeness:** After determining the positive and negative ideal solutions, the next step is to calculate the distance to the positive ideal solution D_i^+ and to the negative ideal solution D_i^- for each alternative. The relative closeness is then measured using the Euclidean distances between each alternative and these ideal solutions. The relative closeness allows ranking the alternatives based on their distances to the positive and negative ideal solutions. The higher the value of C_i^*, the closer the alternative is to the ideal solution.
7. **Ranking of the Alternatives:** Finally, the alternatives are ranked based on their relative closeness to the positive ideal solution. The alternative closest to this solution is considered the best option, thus facilitating the final decision-making process.

4 Results and Discussion

This section presents the study results, highlighting BERT's performance in sentiment analysis of sustainable supplier comments. It covers training data visualization, classification methods, and performance evaluation comparing BERT with LSTM and Random Forest. A case study on Patagonia and The North Face details data collection and automatic annotation analysis. Finally, results are assessed using TOPSIS to provide a structured overview of supplier sustainability performance.

4.1 Visualization of BERT Training Data

This section presents the BERT training data, consisting of around 600 comments collected from social networks like Trustpilot, related to sustainable suppliers. These comments were manually annotated by experts into four categories: pertinent positive, pertinent negative, non-pertinent positive, and non-pertinent negative. Table 3 shows the distribution of annotations, and Fig. 7 provides a pie chart visualization. The balanced distribution was intentionally chosen to maximize BERT's training efficiency, avoiding class imbalance that could bias the model. This balance helps BERT better capture the nuances in comments, improving its ability to generalize and effectively identify sustainability aspects and potential greenwashing in customer feedback.

Table 3. Distribution of comment annotations into four categories.

Category	Percentage %
Relevant positive	23.1 %
Relevant negative	27.5 %
Non-relevant positive	24.8 %
Non-relevant negative	24.6 %

4.2 Classification with BERT

As previously mentioned, BERT a pre-trained model with a bidirectional architecture, understands the full context of words, making it effective for sentiment analysis and comment classification. We fine-tuned key parameters and split the data into 90% training, 10% validation, and 10% testing to ensure a robust model. This approach optimizes the contextual understanding of customer reviews, which is essential for evaluating supplier sustainability and performance.

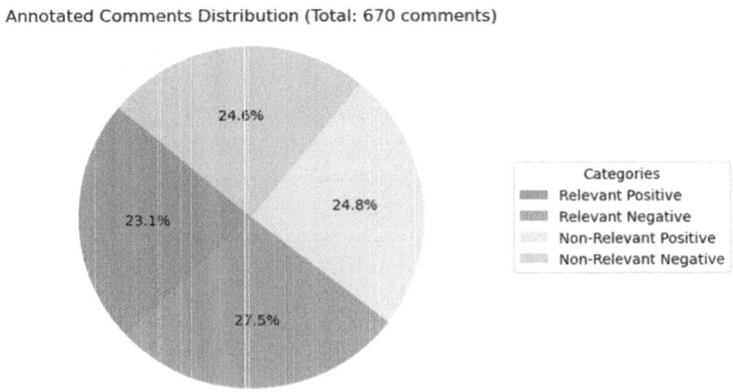

Fig. 7. Pie chart illustrating the balanced distribution of comment annotations across the categories: relevant positive, relevant negative, non-relevant positive, and non-relevant negative.

4.3 Performance Analysis of BERT

We evaluated BERT's performance using key metrics such as training and validation loss, accuracy, precision, and recall. These measures help verify the model's ability to generalize well and reliably classify comments into their different categories.

Training Loss. Training loss measures the model's error on the training data, calculated at each epoch using a loss function such as cross-entropy. It allows tracking the model's learning progress over time.

Validation Loss. Validation loss measures the model's error on data not used during training, allowing evaluation of its generalization ability. An increase in validation loss while training loss decreases may indicate overfitting.

Training loss decreased from 1.3187 to 0.8058, while validation loss dropped from 1.1844 to 0.7715 over four epochs. This steady decline indicates effective learning, good generalization, and no signs of overfitting or underfitting, as shown in the Fig. 8.

Evaluation of Performance Metrics. After training, the model is evaluated using metrics such as precision, recall, and accuracy, calculated on a separate test set that it has never seen before. These metrics provide an objective assessment of the model's ability to generalize to new data, which is essential for real-world applications. These metrics, defined respectively in Eqs. (1), (2), and (3), are used to evaluate the model's performance on test data, thereby ensuring a deep understanding of its ability to generalize.

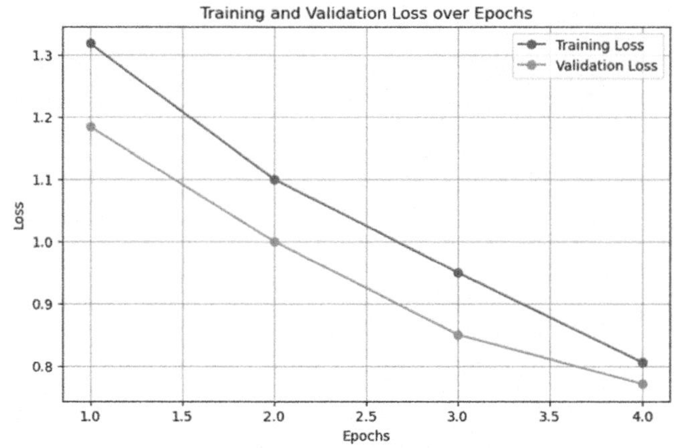

Fig. 8. Evolution of training and validation losses over epochs.

- **Precision** (P):

$$P = \frac{TP}{TP + FP} \tag{1}$$

  where TP is the number of true positives and FP is the number of false positives.
- **Recall** (R):

$$R = \frac{TP}{TP + FN} \tag{2}$$

  where FN is the number of false negatives.
- **Accuracy** (Acc):

$$Acc = \frac{TP + TN}{TP + TN + FP + FN} \tag{3}$$

  where TN is the number of true negatives.

To evaluate the effectiveness of our BERT model, we used performance metrics as shown in Table 4, which demonstrate that BERT achieves a good balance between accuracy (0.76), precision (0.80), and recall (0.76), making it an effective model for the comment annotation task.

Table 4. Evaluation of BERT performance metrics.

BERT	Performance Metrics		
	Accuracy	Precision	Recall
Value	0.76	0.80	0.76

Comparative Evaluation of the Performance of BERT with LSTM and Random Forest Classifier: BERT proved to be the most effective model for the automatic annotation of comments, outperforming LSTM and Random Forest with an accuracy of 0.76, a precision of 0.80, and a recall of 0.76. Thanks to its Transformer architecture, it better understands linguistic context. LSTM, although designed to handle sequences, showed slightly lower results (accuracy 0.74), while Random Forest performed the weakest (accuracy 0.67). These results, illustrated in Table 5, confirm BERT's superiority for natural language processing tasks.

Table 5. Comparison of the performance of BERT, LSTM, and Random Forest.

Model	Accuracy	Precision	Recall
BERT	**0.76 ✓**	**0.80 ✓**	**0.76 ✓**
LSTM	0.74	0.75	0.74
Random Forest	0.67	0.71	0.67

4.4 Case Study

This case study evaluates the sustainability of the suppliers Patagonia and The North Face by analyzing customer reviews. The comments are automatically annotated using BERT, generating four categories whose percentages serve as criteria for applying the TOPSIS multicriteria decision-making method. The steps of this analysis are detailed in the following sections.

Presentation of Two Sustainable Suppliers. Patagonia[1], founded in 1973, is an American company specializing in outdoor clothing, recognized for its commitment to sustainability, the use of recycled materials, and ethical practices. It encourages product repair and recycling and supports environmental initiatives.

The North Face[2], established in 1966, is a major player in outdoor clothing and equipment, combining technological innovation with sustainable practices. The brand reduces its carbon footprint, uses sustainable materials, and participates in conservation and responsible exploration programs.

Data Collection for Review Annotation. For annotation purposes, we collected 300 comments per supplier from various social media platforms (Trustpilot, Facebook) using the Octoparse tool. The data is stored in an Excel file, facilitating annotation. A balanced sample ensures fair analysis and helps avoid bias in the comparative evaluation of customer reviews.

---

[1] https://www.patagonia.com/home/.
[2] https://www.thenorthface.fr/fr-fr.

Analysis of Automatic Annotation Results. We automatically annotated the collected comments for Patagonia and The North Face into four categories: relevant positive, non-relevant positive, relevant negative, and non-relevant negative, using the BERT model.

For Patagonia, 27.06% of comments are relevant positive and 30.03% relevant negative, indicating a generally balanced opinion. Non-relevant positive and negative comments represent 19.03% and 25.74%, relating to aspects other than sustainability.

For The North Face, only 16.50% of comments are relevant positive versus 23.10% relevant negative, indicating more legitimate criticism of its ecological practices. Non-relevant positive and negative comments account for 19.47% and 40.92%, reflecting greater dissatisfaction on other aspects, As shown in Table 6, the distribution of comment annotations for Patagonia and The North Face is presented. Meanwhile, Fig. 9 shows a bar chart illustrating the comparison of annotation percentages between Patagonia and The North Face for each annotation category.

Table 6. Distribution of comment annotations for Patagonia and The North Face: Relevant Positive (RP), Relevant Negative (RN), Non-Relevant Positive (NRP), and Non-Relevant Negative (NRN).

Supplier	RP (%)	RN (%)	NRP (%)	NRN(%)
Patagonia	27.06	30.03	19.03	25.74
The North Face	16.50	23.10	19.47	40.92

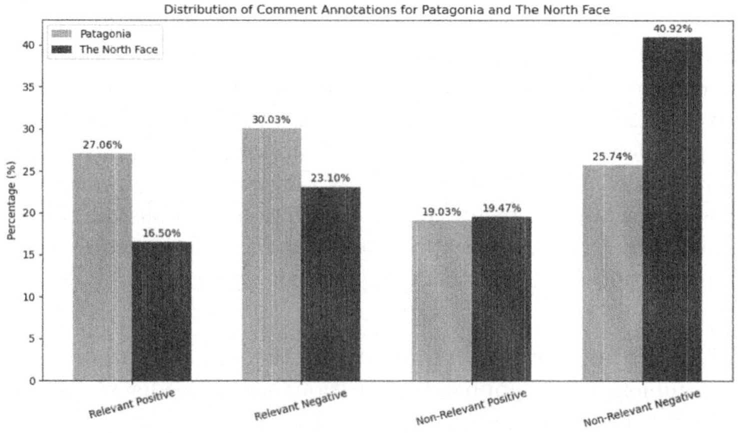

Fig. 9. Bar chart illustrating the comparison of annotation percentages between Patagonia and The North Face for each annotation category.

Analysis of the TOPSIS Method Results. In this section, we analyze the results obtained using the TOPSIS multicriteria decision-making method, considering comment annotations as evaluation criteria to rank the two suppliers, Patagonia and The North Face, in terms of sustainability. The annotations of each comment, categorized as relevant positive, relevant negative, non-relevant positive and non-relevant negative were used as criteria in this method.

1. **Initial Decision Matrix:** presents the values of the four annotation categories; relevant positive, relevant negative, non-relevant positive, and non-relevant negative for Patagonia and The North Face. These values are used as evaluation criteria in the TOPSIS method to compare the two suppliers, as show in Table 7.

Table 7. Initial decision matrix.

Alternatives	Criteria			
	RP	RN	NRP	NRN
Patagonia	27.06%	30.03%	19.03%	25.74%
The North Face	16.50%	23.10%	19.47%	40.92%

2. **Normalized Matrix:** The normalized matrix, shown in Table 8, is a crucial step in the TOPSIS method because it scales the initial data to make them comparable regardless of units or value ranges. Normalization is done by dividing each value by the norm of all criteria, ensuring that all variables fall within the same range. This process ensures that each criterion contributes proportionally to the final ranking of alternatives.

Table 8. Normalized matrix.

Alternatives	Criteria			
	RP	RN	NRP	NRN
Patagonia	0.853	0.792	0.698	0.532
The North Face	0.520	0.609	0.715	0.846

3. **Weighted Normalized Matrix:** To evaluate the suppliers using the TOPSIS method, weights were assigned to the four annotation criteria. Positive comments (both relevant and non-relevant) were given higher importance, each receiving a weight of 0.4, due to their significance in assessing the brand image and overall commitment, particularly in terms of sustainability. In contrast, negative comments (relevant or not) were each assigned a weight of 0.1. This weighting is reflected in the weighted normalized matrix shown in Table 9.

Table 9. Weighted normalized matrix.

Alternatives	Criteria			
	RP	RN	NRP	NRN
Patagonia	0.341	0.079	0.279	0.053
The North Face	0.208	0.060	0.286	0.084

4. **Determination of the Positive Ideal and Negative Ideal Solutions:** The determination of the positive ideal solution A^+ and the negative ideal solution A^- helps to assess supplier performance based on annotation criteria, as shown in Table 10. Favorable criteria (relevant positive and non-relevant positive) are those whose increase improves sustainability perception, while unfavorable criteria (relevant negative and non-relevant negative) reduce it. A^+ is defined by the best values for favorable criteria and the lowest for unfavorable ones. Conversely, $A^-$is based on the lowest favorable values and highest unfavorable ones. Comparing each supplier to these ideals highlights their strengths and areas for improvement, enabling

Table 10. Positive (A^+) and Negative (A^-) Ideal Solutions.

Ideal Solutions Criteria	RP	RN	NRP	NRN
A^+	0.341	0.060	0.286	0.053
A^-	0.208	0.079	0.279	0.084

5. **Calculation of Relative Closeness and Ranking of Suppliers:** Table 11 shows the distances to the positive ideal solution (D^+) and negative ideal solution (D^-) for Patagonia and The North Face. The D^+ values indicate how close each supplier is to the positive ideal. Patagonia, with a distance of 0.019, is much closer to the positive ideal than The North Face, which has a distance of 0.136. This suggests that Patagonia performs better in terms of sustainability and customer perception.

Table 12 presents the relative closeness (C*) of the two suppliers. Patagonia has a relative closeness of 0.875, while The North Face scores 0.124. These results clearly indicate that Patagonia ranks first, demonstrating significantly better sustainability performance and customer satisfaction compared to The North Face, which ranks second.

Sensitivity Analysis of the TOPSIS Method. evaluates how different weighting scenarios affect the sustainability assessment of Patagonia and The North Face. Several weighting scenarios were designed to assign varying levels of importance to the evaluation criteria: Relevant Positive, Relevant Negative, Non-Relevant Positive, and Non-Relevant Negative. These scenarios help

Table 11. Distances to the best (D^+) and worst (D^-) alternatives.

Alternative	Distance D^+	Distance D^-
Patagonia	✓ 0.019	✓ 0.136
The North Face	0.136	0.019

Table 12. Relative closeness to the ideal solution (C*).

Alternative	D^+	D^-	C*	Rank
Patagonia	0.019	0.136	✓ 0.875	1
The North Face	0.136	0.019	0.124	2

examine how each criterion influences the final decision and test the model's robustness under different perspectives. The main objective is to ensure that the sustainability evaluation results remain consistent despite changes in weights, thereby strengthening the reliability of the method for identifying the most sustainable supplier. Table 13 presents the different weighting scenarios used in this analysis.

Table 13. Weighting Scenarios for Sensitivity Analysis.

Scenario	RP	RN	NRP	NRN
Baseline Scenario	0.4	0.1	0.4	0.1
Scenario 1	0.4	0.4	0.1	0.1
Scenario 2	0.1	0.4	0.1	0.4
Scenario 3	0.25	0.25	0.25	0.25

- **Baseline Scenario:** Emphasizes relevant positive and non-relevant positive criteria. Positive feedback is considered the main indicator of sustainability. This balanced approach values benefits while still accounting for criticism.
- **Scenario 1:** Focuses on both relevant positive and relevant negative criteria. It highlights the importance of comment relevance regardless of sentiment polarity, offering a balanced view of sustainability.
- **Scenario 2:** Prioritizes relevant negative and non-relevant negative criteria. This scenario highlights criticisms and weaknesses, helping to identify areas for improvement in supplier sustainability.
- **Scenario 3:** Assigns equal weights to all criteria. Every feedback type is treated equally, resulting in a neutral and comprehensive sustainability evaluation.

The analysis of different weighting scenarios reveals a consistent pattern: Patagonia maintains a higher relative closeness than The North Face across all cases. This stability indicates that, regardless of changes in weight distribution, Patagonia is systematically perceived as the more sustainable supplier.

This consistency demonstrates the robustness of Patagonia's sustainability performance. Even when negative aspects are emphasized, Patagonia retains a strong position, suggesting that criticisms do not significantly undermine the brand's overall positive perception. This may be attributed to proactive communication and genuine engagement efforts that reinforce customer trust in Patagonia's sustainability practices. Table 14 illustrates the relative closeness results (C^*) for each supplier across the different weighting scenarios. The data show that Patagonia consistently achieves the highest relative closeness in all scenarios, highlighting its favorable position compared to The North Face. This analysis also underscores Patagonia's ability to navigate diverse perceptions and maintain a strong image in terms of sustainability.

Table 14. Relative Closeness of Suppliers in Different Scenarios.

Scenario	Patagonia	The North Face
Baseline scenario	✓ 0.875	0.124
Scenario 1	✓ 0.651	0.348
Scenario 2	✓ 0.639	0.360
Scenario 3	✓ 0.713	0.286

Figure 10 clearly illustrates this analysis by visually comparing the relative closeness values (C^*) for each supplier across the different weighting scenarios

In conclusion, this analysis highlights not only the reliability of Patagonia's sustainability assessment but also its relevance in the market. The results clearly indicate that Patagonia stands out as the most relevant choice in terms of sustainability, thereby consolidating its position as a leader in the sector. This consistency in the perception of sustainability also reinforces the argument that Patagonia could serve as a model for other companies seeking to improve their sustainable practices.

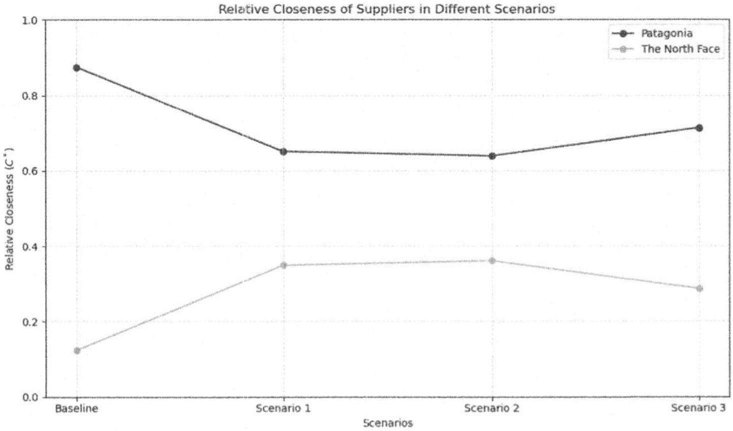

Fig. 10. Comparison of the Relative Closeness (C^*) of Patagonia and The North Face under Different Weighting Scenarios.

5 Conclusion

This paper goes beyond the limitations of traditional methods for evaluating sustainability, which mainly rely on official company statements, by incorporating sentiment analysis of customer reviews from social networks. This innovative approach allows access to more authentic and detailed consumer perceptions. Through a case study of two sustainable clothing brands, comments were annotated using the BERT model, selected for its superior performance compared to LSTM and Random Forest. These annotations, divided into four categories, served as criteria in the TOPSIS method to rank the suppliers based on sustainability. The results clearly indicate that Patagonia is perceived as the most sustainable supplier, which is confirmed by a sensitivity analysis showing the robustness of the conclusions despite different weightings. Finally, this paper proposes improvement avenues such as balancing the data, a more nuanced annotation, confronting customer reviews with declared practices to detect greenwashing, and using data augmentation techniques to strengthen the reliability of the analysis models.

References

1. Ahmad, V., Goyal, L., Arora, M., Kumar, R., Chythanya, K.R., Chaudhary, S.: The impact of ai on sustainability reporting in accounting. In: 2023 6th International Conference on Contemporary Computing and Informatics (IC3I), vol. 6, pp. 643–648. IEEE (2023)
2. Ahmadi, H.B., Lo, H.W., Gupta, H., Kusi-Sarpong, S., Liou, J.J.: An integrated model for selecting suppliers on the basis of sustainability innovation. J. Clean. Prod. **277**, 123261 (2020). https://doi.org/10.1016/j.jclepro.2020.123261. https://www.sciencedirect.com/science/article/pii/S0959652620333060

3. Aronczyk, M., McCurdy, P., Russill, C.: Greenwashing, net-zero, and the oil sands in Canada: the case of pathways alliance. Energy Res. Soc. Sci. **112**, 103502 (2024)
4. Biju, A., Kodiyatt, S., Krishna, P.E.A.: ESG sentiments and divergent ESG scores: suggesting a framework for ESG rating. SN Bus. Econ. **3**, 209 (2023). https://doi.org/10.1007/s43546-023-00592-4
5. Bouhissi, H.E., Itmacene, O., Oubekkou, M., Pavlova, O., Hovorushchenko, T., Shestakevych, T.: Sentiment analysis to manage health crisis in smart cities. In: 2023 IEEE 18th International Conference on Computer Science and Information Technologies (CSIT), pp. 1–5 (2023). https://doi.org/10.1109/CSIT61576.2023.10324043
6. DAGHOURI, A., Mansouri, K., Qbadou, M.: Information system evaluation based on multi-criteria decision making: a comparison of two sectors. Int. J. Adv. Comput. Sci. Appl. **9** (2018). https://doi.org/10.14569/IJACSA.2018.090642
7. Devlin, J., Chang, M.W., Lee, K., Toutanova, K.: Bert: pre-training of deep bidirectional transformers for language understanding (2019). https://arxiv.org/abs/1810.04805
8. Fallahpour, A., Wong, K.Y., Rajoo, S., Fathollahi-Fard, A.M., Antucheviciene, J., Nayeri, S.: An integrated approach for a sustainable supplier selection based on industry 4.0 concept. Environ. Sci. Pollut. Res. 1–19 (2021)
9. Gaur, L., Afaq, A., Arora, G.K., Khan, N.: Artificial intelligence for carbon emissions using system of systems theory. Eco. Inf. **76**, 102165 (2023). https://doi.org/10.1016/j.ecoinf.2023.102165. https://www.sciencedirect.com/science/article/pii/S1574954123001942
10. Ghamari, R., Mahdavi-Mazdeh, M., Ghannadpour, S.F.: Resilient and sustainable supplier selection via a new framework: a case study from the steel industry. In: Environment, Development and Sustainability, pp. 1–39 (2022)
11. Gupta, A., Chadha, A., Tewari, V.: A natural language processing model on bert and yake technique for keyword extraction on sustainability reports. IEEE Access **12**, 7942–7951 (2024). https://doi.org/10.1109/ACCESS.2024.3352742
12. Gurevych, I., Kohler, M., Sahin, G.G.: On the rate of convergence of a classifier based on a transformer encoder (2021). https://doi.org/10.48550/arXiv.2111.14574
13. Gökler, S.H., Boran, S.: A novel resilient and sustainable supplier selection model based on d-ahp and dematel methods. J. Eng. Res. (2023). https://doi.org/10.1016/j.jer.2023.07.015. https://www.sciencedirect.com/science/article/pii/S2307187723001761
14. Hoseini, A.R., Ghannadpour, S.F., Ghamari, R.: Sustainable supplier selection by a new possibilistic hierarchical model in the context of z-information. J. Ambient. Intell. Humaniz. Comput. **11**, 4827–4853 (2020)
15. Jagyasi, D., Raut, A.R.: Implementation of ESG index on long-term value and performance of organizations using ai and ml. In: 2022 OPJU International Technology Conference on Emerging Technologies for Sustainable Development (OTCON), pp. 1–5 (2023). https://doi.org/10.1109/OTCON56053.2023.10114037
16. Khan, S.A.R., Yu, Z., Golpira, H., Sharif, A., Mardani, A.: A state-of-the-art review and meta-analysis on sustainable supply chain management: future research directions. J. Clean. Prod. **278**, 123357 (2021). https://doi.org/10.1016/j.jclepro.2020.123357. https://www.sciencedirect.com/science/article/pii/S0959652620334028
17. Lim, S., Lim, H., Tan, E., Tan, T.P.: Examining Machine Learning Techniques in Business News Headline Sentiment Analysis, pp. 363–372 (2020). https://doi.org/10.1007/978-981-15-0058-9_35

18. Lim, S.L.O., Lim, H.M., Tan, E.K., Tan, T.-P.: Examining machine learning techniques in business news headline sentiment analysis. In: Alfred, R., Lim, Y., Haviluddin, H., On, C.K. (eds.) Computational Science and Technology. LNEE, vol. 603, pp. 363–372. Springer, Singapore (2020). https://doi.org/10.1007/978-981-15-0058-9_35
19. Mao, Y., Liu, Q., Zhang, Y.: Sentiment analysis methods, applications, and challenges: a systematic literature review. J. King Saud Univ. Comput. Inf. Sci. **36**(4), 102048 (2024). https://doi.org/10.1016/j.jksuci.2024.102048. https://www.sciencedirect.com/science/article/pii/S131915782400137X
20. Menon, R.R., Ravi, V.: Using ahp-topsis methodologies in the selection of sustainable suppliers in an electronics supply chain. Clean. Mater. **5**, 100130 (2022). https://doi.org/10.1016/j.clema.2022.100130. https://www.sciencedirect.com/science/article/pii/S2772397622000909
21. Miralles-Quiros, M.M., Miralles-Quiros, J.L.: Sustainable finance and the 2030 agenda: investing to transform the world. Sustainability **13**(19) (2021). https://doi.org/10.3390/su131910505. https://www.mdpi.com/2071-1050/13/19/10505
22. Mohammed, A., Harris, I., Soroka, A., Nujoom, R.: A hybrid MCDM-fuzzy multi-objective programming approach for a g-resilient supply chain network design. Comput. Ind. Eng. **127**, 297–312 (2019). https://doi.org/10.1016/j.cie.2018.09.052. https://www.sciencedirect.com/science/article/pii/S0360835218304686
23. Neji, H., Rekik, M., Souifi, L., Rodriguez, I.B.: A systematic review of sustainable supplier selection using advanced artificial intelligence methods. In: Rocha, A.P., Steels, L., van den Herik, H.J. (eds.) Proceedings of the 17th International Conference on Agents and Artificial Intelligence, ICAART 2025, Porto, Portugal, 23–25 February 2025, vol. 3, pp. 451–460. SCITEPRESS (2025) https://doi.org/10.5220/0013149900003890
24. Nugent, T., Stelea, N., Leidner, J.L.: Detecting ESG topics using domain-specific language models and data augmentation approaches. CoRR (2020). https://arxiv.org/abs/2010.08319
25. Omair, M., et al.: The selection of the sustainable suppliers by the development of a decision support framework based on analytical hierarchical process and fuzzy inference system. Int. J. Fuzzy Syst. **23**(7), 1986–2003 (2021). https://doi.org/10.1007/s40815-021-01073-2
26. Rani, P., Mishra, A.R., Rezaei, G., Liao, H., Mardani, A.: Extended pythagorean fuzzy topsis method based on similarity measure for sustainable recycling partner selection. Int. J. Fuzzy Syst. **22**, 735–747 (2020)
27. Taherdoost, H., Madanchian, M.: Multi-criteria decision making (MCDM) methods and concepts. Encyclopedia **3**(1), 77–87 (2023). https://doi.org/10.3390/encyclopedia3010006. https://www.mdpi.com/2673-8392/3/1/6
28. Tavana, M., Sorooshian, S., Mina, H.: An integrated group fuzzy inference and best–worst method for supplier selection in intelligent circular supply chains. Ann. Oper. Res. 1–42 (2023)
29. Torfi, A., Shirvani, R.A., Keneshloo, Y., Tavaf, N., Fox, E.A.: Natural language processing advancements by deep learning: a survey. arXiv preprint arXiv:2003.01200 (2020)
30. Twinamatsiko, E., Kumar, D.: Incorporating ESG in decision making for responsible and sustainable investments using machine learning. In: 2022 International Conference on Electronics and Renewable Systems (ICEARS), pp. 1328–1334 (2022). https://doi.org/10.1109/ICEARS53579.2022.9752343

31. Usuga Cadavid, J.P., Lamouri, S., Grabot, B., Fortin, A.: Using deep learning to value free-form text data for predictive maintenance. Int. J. Prod. Res. **60**, 1–28 (2021). https://doi.org/10.1080/00207543.2021.1951868
32. Varriale, V., Cammarano, A., Michelino, F., Caputo, M.: The role of digital technologies in production systems for achieving sustainable development goals. Sustain. Prod. Consumpt. **47**, 87–104 (2024). https://doi.org/10.1016/j.spc.2024.03.035. https://www.sciencedirect.com/science/article/pii/S2352550924000964
33. Vinella, A., Capetz, M., Pattichis, R., Chance, C., Ghosh, R.: Leveraging language models to detect greenwashing (2023)
34. Yildizbasi, A., Arioz, Y.: Green supplier selection in new era for sustainability: a novel method for integrating big data analytics and a hybrid fuzzy multi-criteria decision making. Soft Comput. **26**(1), 253–270 (2022). https://doi.org/10.1007/s00500-021-06477-8
35. Ãelikbilek, Y., Tüysüz, F.: An in-depth review of theory of the topsis method: an experimental analysis. J. Manag. Anal. **7**(2), 281–300 (2020). https://doi.org/10.1080/23270012.2020.1748528

PointTrack: A Weakly-Supervised Segment-and-Track Anything Framework for Microscopy

Nabeel Khalid[1,5(✉)], Mohammadmahdi Koochali[1(✉)], Khola Naseem[1,5], Maria Caroprese[6], Gillian Lovell[3], Daniel A. Porto[7], Johan Trygg[2,4], Andreas Dengel[1,5], and Sheraz Ahmed[1]

[1] German Research Center for Artificial Intelligence (DFKI) GmbH, 67663 Kaiserslautern, Germany
{nabeel.khalid,mohammadmahdi.koochali,andreas.dengel, sheraz.ahmed}@dfki.de

[2] Sartorius Corporate Research, Umeå, Sweden
johan.trygg@sartorius.com

[3] Sartorius BioAnalytics, Royston, UK
gillian.lovell@sartorius.com

[4] Computational Life Science Cluster (CLiC), Umeå University, Umeå, Sweden

[5] RPTU Kaiserslautern-Landau, 67663 Kaiserslautern, Germany

[6] Sartorius Digital Solutions, Royston, UK
maria.caroprese@sartorius.com

[7] Sartorius BioAnalytics, Ann Arbor, USA
daniel.porto@sartorius.com

Abstract. Integrating cell segmentation with tracking is critical for achieving a detailed and dynamic understanding of cellular behavior. This integration facilitates the study and quantification of cell morphology, movement, and interactions, offering valuable insights into developmental processes, drug response, and disease mechanisms. Traditional segmentation and tracking methods rely on labor-intensive annotations—such as full segmentation masks or bounding boxes for every cell in each frame—which severely limit throughput and scalability. PointTrack addresses these challenges by introducing a weakly-supervised pipeline that leverages sparse point annotations in the initial frame to automatically generate high-fidelity cell masks and maintain consistent object identities across subsequent frames. PointTrack begins with multiple sparse point annotations per cell in the first image of a time-lapse sequence. An interactive segmentation engine uses these annotations to delineate accurate cell boundaries, eliminating the need for exhaustive mask drawing. A dedicated point-tracking module then propagates the annotated points through the entire video, adapting to changes in cell appearance and motion with minimal user intervention. By reducing annotation effort to a few clicks per cell while preserving mask quality and identity continuity, PointTrack significantly

N. Khalid and M. Koochali—These authors contributed equally to this work.

H. J. van den Herik et al. (Eds.): ICAART 2025, LNAI 16517, pp. 159–186, 2026.
https://doi.org/10.1007/978-3-032-25032-2_8

accelerates the preparation of large-scale microscopy datasets. Extensive evaluation on two diverse time-lapse datasets—CTMC and DeepCell—demonstrates robust segmentation and reliable tracking performance under varying imaging modalities, cell densities, and noise conditions. Qualitative examples highlight precise delineation of overlapping cells and seamless trajectory recovery through transient occlusions. With streamlined annotation requirements and automated processing, Point-Track offers an effective and scalable solution for large-scale microscopy-based cell segmentation and tracking.

Keywords: Biomedical · Healthcare · Deep Learning · Cell Segmentation · Cell Tracking · Segment Anything · Track Anything · Microscopy

1 Introduction

Cell tracking stands at the forefront of quantitative live-cell imaging, providing critical insights into cellular dynamics that underpin fundamental biological processes and drive translational applications in medicine [2,26,39]. By following individual cells over time, mechanisms of cancer invasion can be dissected, stem cell differentiation pathways monitored, drug responses evaluated in high-content screening, and immune cell-pathogen interactions unraveled with single-cell resolution. Accurate tracking enables measurement of cell motility, morphology changes, division events, and lineage relationships, thereby contributing to a systems-level understanding of complex phenomena such as tumor heterogeneity, tissue regeneration, and collective cell migration. Robust cell tracking across diverse imaging modalities and experimental conditions remains challenging, primarily due to laborious annotation requirements and the variability in image quality inherent to specialized microscopy setups.

Traditional cell tracking pipelines employ a segmentation-first architecture: each frame is processed to generate instance masks or bounding boxes, followed by a frame-to-frame linking algorithm that establishes temporal correspondences [17,32,35]. Although such approaches achieve high accuracy on curated datasets with uniform contrast and well-defined cell boundaries, performance degrades on low-contrast phase-contrast images, densely packed cells, or heterogeneous background artifacts. Fully supervised segmentation models require dense pixel-level annotations—often demanding tens of minutes per image—making high-throughput experiments prohibitively expensive in time and expert effort [6]. Retraining segmentation models for each new modality or cell type further reduces scalability and generalizability, limiting broader adoption.

Weakly supervised and point-based segmentation methods have emerged to alleviate annotation burdens by relying on sparse cues such as bounding boxes, scribbles, or individual point markers [12,14,19]. In point-supervised approaches, annotators click on a small number of key locations per cell, which are then propagated into full segmentation masks through interactive or automated refinement. Such methods reduce labeling costs by up to an order of magnitude but often decouple segmentation and tracking, requiring separate tracking modules that may not fully exploit mask confidence or spatial context. Systematic exploration of the trade-off between annotation density and tracking performance across real-world microscopy benchmarks remains limited.

Table 1. Comparison of supervision time between Full Mask + Tracking and the PointTrack method (point annotation only in the first frame). Column A shows segmentation (or point annotation) time per cell, and column T shows tracking effort. PointTrack (5 points per cell) achieves a speed-up of over 200×, requiring only 0.375 min versus 77.4 min for 100 frames [15].

Method	A (s)	T (s)	Total Time (min)	Speed-up (×)
Full Mask + Tracking	46	0.438	77.40	-
PointTrack (N = 3)	$3 \times 0.9 = 2.7$	0	0.225	≈ 344
PointTrack (N = 5)	$5 \times 0.9 = 4.5$	0	0.375	≈ 206
PointTrack (N = 10)	$10 \times 0.9 = 9$	0	0.750	≈ 103

Table 1 quantifies the dramatic reduction in annotation effort enabled by PointTrack's sparse point prompts. Whereas traditional full-mask annotation and tracking of a 100-frame sequence can require over 77 min of manual work, PointTrack with only five points per cell completes the same task in under half a minute—an over 200× speed-up. This massive time-saving makes large-scale, multi-condition live-cell studies feasible without prohibitive annotation costs.

The recent advent of foundation segmentation models, such as MetaAI's Segment Anything Model (SAM) [21], offers a paradigm shift for interactive segmentation. Prompt-driven mask generation from minimal user input makes SAM a promising backbone for weakly supervised pipelines. However, SAM lacks native temporal propagation capability, so integration with external trackers is necessary to achieve full video segmentation and maintain object identities.

PointTrack constitutes a unified pipeline that couples SAM's interactive segmentation with robust point-based trackers—PIPS [8], RAFT [36], and CoTracker [10]—to deliver end-to-end cell segmentation and tracking from a single set of sparse annotations in the first frame. A small set of positive and negative point prompts is solicited for each cell and propagated across the video using the chosen tracker. At each frame, SAM refines these tracked points into precise segmentation masks, while an optional reinitialization step corrects drift and incorporates newly visible cell segments. This tightly integrated approach leverages mask-based and flow-based strengths to achieve high accuracy and robustness under diverse imaging conditions.

Extensive experiments validate PointTrack on two canonical benchmarks: the Cell Tracking Challenge (CTC) dataset [24], featuring high-resolution fluorescence, bright field, and DIC sequences, and the Cell Tracking with Mitosis Detection Challenge (CTMC) dataset [1], comprising low-resolution phase-contrast videos across multiple cell lines. Annotation densities (10–30 points per cell) and tracker backends are systematically varied to identify configurations that optimize Multiple Object Tracking Accuracy (MOTA), IDF1 score (IDF1), and trajectory continuity while minimizing identity switches and manual annotation time.

The following contributions are presented:

1. PointTrack: a weakly supervised segmentation-tracking pipeline that harnesses sparse point annotations and interactive foundation models to automate mask generation and identity propagation across microscopy sequences.
2. Integration and benchmarking of three state-of-the-art point-based trackers—PIPS, RAFT, and CoTracker—within a single framework, providing head-to-head analysis under varying annotation regimes and imaging conditions.
3. Demonstration of strong generalization across two challenging datasets, achieving up to 61.6% MOTA and 79.7% IDF1 on CTMC with 25-point supervision, and 83.46% MOTA and 90.22% IDF1 on CTC with only 3–6 points, while reducing annotation time by over 200× compared to full-mask methods.
4. Identification of optimal annotation densities, revealing a "sweet spot" around 25 points per cell for low-contrast, low-resolution data, and minimal supervision requirements for high-quality, high-resolution sequences.

The remainder of the paper is organized as follows. Section 2 reviews related work in weakly supervised segmentation and cell tracking. Section 3 describes the PointTrack architecture and algorithmic components. Section 4 outlines the datasets and selection criteria. Section 5 defines the performance measures. Section 6 presents experimental protocols. Section 7 discusses results and practical implications. Finally, Sect. 8 concludes with future directions and potential biological impacts.

2 Literature Review

A comprehensive understanding of cell-segmentation and tracking methods underpins the development of robust, scalable pipelines for quantitative microscopy. This review first surveys the historical progression from fully supervised, mask-based frameworks to more recent weakly supervised and interactive strategies, with particular focus on how annotation burden, segmentation fidelity, and temporal continuity have been balanced in each advance.

Next, the review is organized by supervision paradigm and technical innovation. Classical segmentation-first approaches will be considered alongside motion-based unsupervised trackers, point- and box-guided weakly supervised systems, and the emerging integration of foundation models for interactive segmentation. For each category, key strengths and limitations are highlighted, setting the stage for the PointTrack pipeline's contributions.

2.1 Existing Cell Segmentation and Tracking Approaches

There are numerous studies on cell segmentation and tracking [7,9,14,24,34] which require full masks for training or some form of weak supervision. Traditional segmentation-first approaches generate accurate segmentation masks for individual cells, subsequently linking these segmented regions across time frames to produce tracking results [13,16–18,23,32]. These methods perform effectively in high-contrast, extensively annotated datasets but encounter difficulties when applied to new imaging modalities or minimally annotated domains. Recent research has focused on reducing the reliance on extensive segmentation masks through weakly supervised methods, employing partial annotations such as bounding boxes or point annotations. For instance, Khalid et al. [12,14,19] introduced techniques using bounding boxes and sparse point annotations, significantly reducing annotation burden while maintaining acceptable accuracy. These methods represent a compromise between efficiency and accuracy but frequently require manual intervention or specialized pre-trained models, limiting adaptability. Unsupervised tracking methods, leveraging temporal coherence and unsupervised learning paradigms, have also emerged as promising alternatives [24]. Despite reducing annotation effort, these methods often lack precise segmentation capabilities, especially in noisy or overlapping scenarios, highlighting the necessity for balanced approaches.

2.2 Alternative Cell Identification and Tracking Methods

Segmentation-based methodologies dominate due to their detailed morphological information, but recent innovations have explored alternative pathways. For example, Romphosri et al. [31] introduced an alignment-free bacteria identification approach leveraging optical scattering coupled with YOLO [37], enabling rapid cell identification without explicit segmentation. Matthews et al. [25] similarly employed YOLO and digital holographic microscopy for real-time 3D microbe tracking, achieving robust performance without extensive human labeling. While these methods excel in specific tasks like rapid bacterial identification or microbial tracking, they lack generalizability and the morphological precision essential for complex cell-interaction analyses and detailed morphological quantification, maintaining segmentation's superiority in verPointTrackility and detail.

2.3 Challenges in Microscopy Applications

Microscopy images present distinct challenges significantly divergent from those of natural images, complicating conventional processing techniques [38]. Imaging modality variations—such as phase-contrast, fluorescence, and differential interference contrast—introduce disparities in contrast, clarity, and noise levels, necessitating adaptive, flexible model architectures [34]. Moreover, variability in cellular morphology, size, and density further complicates model generalization across biological contexts [39]. Artefacts and low contrast, especially in dense or noisy cell populations, often result in misinterpretations by segmentation and tracking algorithms. Additionally, the computational scalability of models when processing large-scale datasets used in high-throughput or longitudinal studies is crucial. These challenges underscore the necessity of adaptable, computationally efficient methodologies.

2.4 Limitations of the Segment Anything Model (SAM)

The Segment Anything Model (SAM) [21] performs strongly in natural imaging contexts but encounters difficulties in microscopic scenarios due to their inherent complexity, lower contrast, and higher noise levels [3]. Domain-specific training and pre-processing are typically required for SAM to be effective within microscopy. Although models like YOLO [37] can also perform segmentation, SAM's point-based annotation method offers advantages through reduced manual annotation requirements while maintaining pixel-level precision. This characteristic positions SAM as beneficial for large-scale microscopy studies, motivating efforts such as PointTrack to leverage SAM's capabilities while effectively managing its limitations.

2.5 Tracker Integration and Comparative Analyses

Integrating effective trackers is critical in cell segmentation and tracking pipelines. Prominent trackers, such as Particle Video Revisited (PIPS) [8], RAFT [36], and CoTracker [10], have distinct operational advantages and limitations. PIPS excels in iterative refinement and rapid mask updating but struggles under severe occlusions. RAFT, initially intended for optical flow estimation, demonstrates high accuracy in smoothly transitioning cell populations but encounters difficulty with sudden morphological changes. CoTracker effectively handles dense populations and maintains identity coherence during complex merges or splits, but requires meticulous tuning for optimal performance. Evaluating these trackers across varying cell morphologies, densities, and imaging modalities provides valuable insights into their practical application, guiding researchers towards optimal choices based on specific experimental requirements.

3 PointTrack: The Proposed Approach

The core of PointTrack lies in SAM, a powerful segmentation model pre-trained on a diverse set of images and fine-tuned using the LIVECell dataset. SAM's architecture consists of an image encoder, a prompt encoder, and a mask decoder, all working in harmony to produce high-precision segmentation masks from user-defined prompts [21]. This robust design makes SAM exceptionally well-suited for tackling the unique complexities of microscopy images, including low contrast and intricate cellular structures.

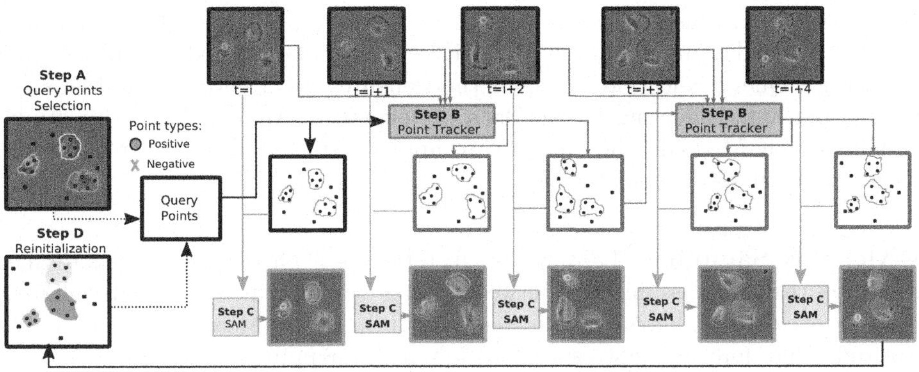

Fig. 1. PointTrack Pipeline [15]. The PointTrack pipeline extends image segmentation models to microscopy videos through four steps: **A. Query Points Selection**, where positive and negative points are defined by the user or a ground truth mask; **B. Point Tracking**, which propagates points across video frames using robust trackers (PIPS, RAFT, CoTracker), predicting trajectories and occlusion scores; and **C. Segmentation**, where the Segment Anything Model (SAM) uses these trajectories to generate per-frame mask predictions; and **D. Point Tracking Reinitialization**, an optional step to reinitialize query points, improving tracking reliability and addressing newly visible cell segments.

Building upon SAM's capabilities, PointTrack divides its pipeline into four interconnected modules: Query Points Selection, Point Tracking, Segmentation, and Point Tracking Reinitialization [29]. The process begins with the selection of positive and negative query points in the first video frame to define the regions of interest and the background. These points are propagated across subsequent frames using state-of-the-art tracking algorithms which ensure accurate trajectory prediction even in challenging scenarios like occlusions or reappearances. These propagated points then serve as prompts for SAM, enabling precise per-frame segmentation of cellular structures. To enhance robustness over long video sequences, the PointTrack pipeline includes an optional reinitialization step, which updates query points based on predicted masks, addressing newly visible regions and improving overall accuracy (see Fig. 1).

By integrating SAM with advanced tracking methodologies, PointTrack significantly reduces the manual effort required for cell segmentation and tracking while ensuring high accuracy and scalability. This innovative approach provides a robust framework for analyzing cellular dynamics across diverse imaging modalities, advancing the use of microscopy in biomedical research.

3.1 Query Points Selection

In the first step of PointTrack, query points are selected in the first video frame to denote the target object (positive points) and non-target regions (negative points). The user can provide these points interactively or derive them from a ground truth mask using various sampling techniques, including Random Sampling, K-Medoids Sampling, Shi-Tomasi Sampling [33], Mixed Sampling, and Cell-Aware Query Selection. Each method ensures good coverage and robustness, significantly affecting the model's performance. Among these, this study employs the K-Medoids and Cell-Aware approaches to initialize segmentation and tracking in subsequent frames:

K-Medoids Sampling. K-Medoids clustering is a partitioning method that minimizes the total dissimilarity between points within a cluster and a designated representative point, known as the medoid [11]. Unlike K-Means, which relies on centroids that may not correspond to actual data points, K-Medoids ensures that the medoids are actual observed points. This characteristic is particularly beneficial in microscopy, where selecting realistic and meaningful points within cellular boundaries is essential for accurate tracking and segmentation.

Formally, the set of query points is defined as:

$$P = \{p_1, p_2, \ldots, p_n\} \tag{1}$$

where P represents all points within the image region. For K-Medoids clustering, let C denote the set of clusters, and P_m the set of medoid points:

$$P_m = \{\text{medoid}(c_i) \mid c_i \in C\} \tag{2}$$

The objective function to minimize the clustering is:

$$\text{minimize} \sum_{i=1}^{k} \sum_{p \in c_i} \|p - \text{medoid}(c_i)\| \tag{3}$$

Here, c_i represents the cluster, medoid(c_i) is the medoid point of cluster c_i, and $\|p - \text{medoid}(c_i)\|$ is the distance between a point p and the medoid. In microscopy, the use of this distance metric allows for robust selection of points that are evenly distributed, ensuring that key cellular regions are adequately represented.

By leveraging the K-Medoids approach, the method achieves a balance between computational efficiency and biological relevance, which is vital for processing large-scale microscopy datasets with diverse cell morphologies and imaging conditions.

Cell-Aware Query Selection. Cell-Aware Query Selection is a specialized approach designed to adaptively determine and place query points for robust segmentation and tracking in microscopy images. Leveraging the mask for each cell, this method ensures that the selected points are both biologically relevant and computationally efficient, taking into account the unique challenges posed by cellular deformability and variability across video sequences.

Using the mask of each cell, the number of positive and negative points is determined based on the average area of cells and the resolution of the microscopy image. This adaptive mechanism ensures that the query points adequately represent cells of varying sizes while maintaining consistent annotation efficiency. For positive points, the process begins by selecting the geometric center of the cell as one of the positive points. The center point serves as a robust anchor for tracking, providing high accuracy in subsequent stages.

To account for the cell's boundary, which can deform significantly across frames, additional positive points are distributed near the boundary of the cell. These points are spaced equidistantly, ensuring even coverage of the cell perimeter. This configuration is particularly critical as cellular shapes and sizes often undergo drastic changes over time in microscopy sequences. By effectively covering the boundary, the method enhances the reliability of tracking algorithms, even in the presence of complex cellular dynamics.

If the desired number of positive points exceeds a predefined threshold, the method expands coverage by moving one ring deeper into the cell's interior. This hierarchical placement ensures that additional points contribute meaningful information without compromising efficiency.

For negative points, care is taken to ensure they are not positioned too close to the cell boundary. Instead, they are selected from regions sufficiently far from the cell to avoid overlaps or ambiguities. This strategic placement reduces the likelihood of false-positive segmentations while maintaining the integrity of the segmentation process.

Cell-Aware Query Selection strikes a critical balance between accuracy and efficiency, making it particularly suited for diverse microscopy conditions. Its adaptability to various cell sizes, deformabilities, and imaging resolutions ensures robust performance across a wide range of datasets, facilitating high-precision segmentation and tracking in large-scale studies.

3.2 Point Tracking

This module propagates the selected query points across all video frames using point trackers. The propagation generates point trajectories and occlusion scores, ensuring that the points follow the objects accurately throughout the video. This process is essential for maintaining the spatial and temporal continuity of the selected query points, even in challenging scenarios such as occlusion or sudden object movement. The point trajectories provide critical input for segmentation and tracking tasks, ensuring consistency across the entire microscopy video sequence.

For the tracking module, there are multiple advanced options to choose from, including PIPS [8], RAFT [36], and CoTracker [10]. Each of these trackers has distinct strengths in addressing various aspects of point tracking. RAFT, for instance, excels in dense optical flow estimation, while CoTracker focuses on joint mask-point propagation. PIPS offers robustness to long-term occlusions. However, as the primary point tracker in this methodology, PIPS is employed due to its exceptional robustness in handling long-term tracking challenges, particularly in scenarios with occlusions and the reappearance of objects. PIPS leverages a combination of learned temporal priors and iterative refinement, making it well-suited for tracking deformable cellular structures in microscopy.

PIPS: Uses iterative refinement of point masks, providing rapid updates and effective occlusion handling through multiple object hypotheses, making it suitable for long-term tracking.

RAFT: Employs a recurrent all-pairs field transform architecture originally designed for optical flow estimation, excelling in smoothly varying scenarios but sensitive to abrupt shape changes or severe occlusions.

CoTracker: Utilizes a cooperative tracking strategy combining joint point and mask information, robustly maintaining identity coherence through complex events such as merges or splits but requiring careful tuning in sparse scenarios. The tracked points are represented as:

$$P_t = \{p_{t,1}, p_{t,2}, \ldots, p_{t,n}\} \tag{4}$$

where P_t denotes the set of points tracked at frame t. The tracking function T predicts the positions of these points in the subsequent frame, ensuring continuity:

$$P_{t+1} = T(P_t) \tag{5}$$

By using PIPS as the primary tracker, the methodology achieves a balance between efficiency and accuracy, ensuring robust point tracking even under the dynamic and variable conditions of microscopy imaging.

3.3 Segmentation

Using the point trajectories obtained from the tracking module, the Segment Anything Model (SAM) [21], which has been fine-tuned on the LIVECell dataset, generates per-frame segmentation masks with high precision. SAM's architecture, comprising an image encoder, a prompt encoder, and a mask decoder, processes the non-occluded points as prompts to accurately segment the object of interest in each frame. The segmentation at each frame t can be represented as:

$$M_t = \text{SAM}(I_t, P_t) \tag{6}$$

where I_t is the input image at frame t, and P_t is the set of propagated points.

The fine-tuning of SAM on the LIVECell dataset is a critical step in adapting the model for the unique challenges of microscopy images. While SAM demonstrates exceptional performance in general scenarios, owing to its training on the massive SA-1B dataset containing 1 billion masks and 11 million images, its performance on microscopy images can falter in complex scenarios. These failures stem from the inherent differences in microscopy data, such as low contrast, high noise, and the intricate morphology of cellular structures.

By fine-tuning SAM on the LIVECell dataset, the model's ability to handle the unique challenges of this domain is significantly enhanced. This specialized version of SAM achieves exceptional performance across diverse modalities of microscopy images, ensuring robustness and reliability in segmenting cellular structures.

3.4 Point Tracking Reinitialization

This step involves reinitializing the query points periodically using the predicted masks. Reinitialization helps to remove unreliable points and add new points to object segments that become visible in later frames, thereby improving the accuracy and robustness of the segmentation over time. This process is especially critical in microscopy applications, where cells can undergo significant changes in shape, size, and position across frames.

$$P_{t+h} = \text{Reinitialize}(M_{t+h}) \tag{7}$$

Reinitialization occurs at intervals defined by the prediction horizon h, ensuring maintained tracking accuracy despite appearance changes and new cell entries.

3.5 PointTrack Output

PointTrack is a model designed for the simultaneous segmentation and tracking of cells in image sequences. When processing a sequence, PointTrack generates two outputs: a JSON file formatted in COCO style containing segmentation masks, and a text file formatted in MOT style detailing cell tracking data. These outputs, provided in widely accepted formats, simplify integration with existing evaluation tools and enable performance measurement using standardized metrics, thereby enhancing reproducibility and facilitating cross-study comparisons.

PointTrack's strength lies in effectively integrating existing robust tracking and segmentation modules specifically optimized for microscopy contexts. By significantly reducing manual annotation effort to initial sparse point inputs and automating subsequent segmentation and tracking, PointTrack enhances both efficiency and accuracy. Additionally, the reinitialization module ensures robustness against occlusions and appearance changes, accommodating dynamic microscopy scenarios.

4 Dataset

For fine-tuning the Segment Anything Model (SAM) [21], the LIVECell dataset [7] (Table 2) was exclusively used. LIVECell is a comprehensive collection of label-free live-cell images annotated at the instance level across eight cell lines. It provides high-resolution images with varying densities and morphologies, making it ideal for refining SAM's ability to segment microscopic structures. Leveraging LIVECell for fine-tuning enhances the model's ability to handle the diverse challenges of microscopy, including low contrast, noise, varying imaging modalities, and intricate cellular boundaries. To evaluate the generalization of the proposed PointTrack methodology for cell segmentation and tracking, two diverse and large-scale benchmark datasets are utilized. The first is the Cell Tracking Challenge (CTC) dataset [24], which comprises both 2D and 3D time-lapse microscopy sequences from a range of modalities including Bright Field, Phase Contrast, and Differential Interference Contrast (DIC). It includes 20 sequences in total, 10 of which are 2D, encompassing 8,017 frames with an average density of 33.12 cells per image. This diversity in modality and temporal resolution makes CTC a strong benchmark for evaluating segmentation and tracking performance in varied microscopy contexts.

Table 2. Statistics of the LIVECell dataset used for fine-tuning the Segment Anything Model.

Dataset	Cell Types	Modality	Train		Val		Test	
			Img	Cells	Img	Cells	Img	Cells
LIVECell	8	Phase Contrast	3253	1,018,576	570	181,609	1564	462,261

The second benchmark is the Cell Tracking with Mitosis Detection Challenge (CTMC) dataset [1], which contains over 1.5 million images from 86 video sequences spanning 14 distinct cell lines. CTMC offers only bounding box annotations, increasing the difficulty of segmentation tasks. Its broad coverage of experimental conditions and cell morphologies makes it well-suited for assessing model robustness in real-world laboratory scenarios. In contrast to the prior PointTrack study [15], which evaluated only 6 sequences from the CTMC dataset, this study significantly expands the scope by evaluating 20 sequences. These sequences were carefully selected to include a wider range of cell cultures, imaging modalities, and experimental conditions. This expanded evaluation ensures a more rigorous and representative assessment of PointTrack's generalizability and robustness across diverse microscopy environments.

5 Evaluation Metrics

To assess the performance of the proposed pipeline for cell tracking, five distinct evaluation metrics are used, each providing a unique perspective on the results. These metrics collectively evaluate the accuracy, reliability, and robustness of the tracker across diverse scenarios, ensuring a comprehensive assessment of its capabilities.

5.1 Multiple Object Tracking Accuracy

Multiple Object Tracking Accuracy (MOTA) [4] measures the overall accuracy of the tracker and the detection. It accounts for errors such as missed detections, false positives, and identity mismatches, providing a holistic view of the tracker's performance.

$$\text{MOTA} = 1 - \frac{\sum_t (m_t + fp_t + mme_t)}{\sum_t g_t}$$

Here, m_t represents the total number of misses, fp_t the total number of false positives, and mme_t the total number of mismatches. Misses occur when a cell in the ground truth is not detected, which may result from occlusion, low contrast, or noise in the image. False positives occur when a cell is detected but not present in the ground truth, often due to over-segmentation or artifacts. Mismatches occur when a cell is incorrectly associated with another cell, typically due to overlapping trajectories or inconsistencies in tracking. MOTA provides a single metric to summarize the errors, making it a standard benchmark in multi-object tracking evaluations.

5.2 Identification F1 Score

Identification F1 (IDF1) [30] calculates a one-to-one mapping between ground truth trajectories and prediction trajectories, emphasizing the importance of maintaining consistent identities.

$$\mathrm{IDF1} = \frac{2 \cdot \mathrm{IDTP}}{2 \cdot \mathrm{IDTP} + \mathrm{IDFP} + \mathrm{IDFN}}$$

IDTP (Identity True Positives) represents the number of correctly matched IDs between ground truth and predictions. IDFP (Identity False Positives) denotes instances where a predicted ID does not correspond to any ground truth object. IDFN (Identity False Negatives) occurs when a ground truth ID is not matched to any prediction. IDF1 is particularly useful for evaluating the consistency of identity preservation in challenging scenarios, such as densely packed cells or overlapping trajectories.

5.3 Identity Switches

Identity Switches (IDs) [4], also known as Mismatches, refer to the number of times a trajectory incorrectly changes from one ground truth object to another. This error is often caused by abrupt changes in cell appearance, overlapping trajectories, or tracking errors during occlusion. A lower number of identity switches indicates a more reliable tracking system, as it suggests the tracker effectively maintains the continuity of object identities across frames. This metric is critical for applications requiring lineage analysis or long-term tracking, where maintaining identity is paramount.

5.4 Mostly Tracked

If an object is successfully tracked for at least 80% of its lifespan, it is considered Mostly Tracked (MT) [22]. This metric evaluates the robustness of a tracking algorithm in maintaining the continuity of an object's identity across its lifespan. High MT scores indicate that the tracker is capable of handling long-term trajectories without frequent interruptions, even in the presence of challenges such as partial occlusions or variations in cell morphology. This metric is particularly important in applications requiring sustained observation of cellular behavior over time, such as studying cell migration or division.

5.5 Mostly Lost

If an object is tracked for 20% or less of its lifespan, it is considered Mostly Lost (ML) [22]. High ML scores suggest the tracker struggles with challenges, leading to frequent identity losses. This metric highlights cases where the tracking algorithm fails to maintain object identities due to factors like occlusion, abrupt motion, or low-contrast regions. By identifying objects that are mostly lost, this metric helps pinpoint specific limitations of the tracker and provides insights for improving its performance in challenging scenarios. A low ML score indicates that the tracker is robust enough to avoid significant failures across the dataset.

6 Experimental Setup

Two experimental settings are designed to evaluate the performance of the proposed PointTrack pipeline under complementary conditions. The first setting (PointTrack Generalization Analysis Using CTMC's Wide-Ranging Cell Types) assesses PointTrack's ability to generalize across a wide range of cell types and imaging conditions using the Cell Tracking with Mitosis Detection Challenge (CTMC) dataset. CTMC provides phase-contrast time-lapse sequences from multiple cell lines exhibiting diverse morphologies, densities, and motion patterns, making it an ideal benchmark to test generalizability across heterogeneous biological scenarios. In this setting, performance is evaluated using three point-based trackers—PIPS [8], RAFT [36], and CoTracker [10]—and a series of experiments varying the number of positive and negative points per cell (e.g. 10P–3N, 15P–3N, up to 30P–3N). Each tracker–point configuration is tested on individual CTMC sequences to measure tracking accuracy (MOTA, IDF1), identity switches (IDS), and mostly tracked/lost (MT, ML) rates. The second setting (PointTrack Evaluation on Diverse Modalities and Intervals Using the CTC Dataset) evaluates PointTrack's adaptability across different microscopy modalities and temporal resolutions using annotated 2D sequences from the Cell Tracking Challenge (CTC) dataset. CTC includes videos captured with Bright Field, Phase Contrast, and Differential Interference Contrast (DIC) microscopy, spanning varied contrast levels, noise characteristics, and frame intervals. This setting highlights PointTrack's robustness to modality-specific artifacts and its capacity to maintain tracking accuracy over both short- and long-term experiments.

To fine-tune the Segment Anything Model (SAM) [21] on LIVECell data, an iterative training scheme was applied [3]. Minibatches of images and ground truth segmentations were sampled with sparse positive point annotations or bounding boxes to capture the variability of the dataset. The key hyperparameters included a batch size of two, a loss of dice for mask quality, a loss of L2 on IoU for boundary refinement, and the ADAM optimizer [20] at an initial learning rate of 10^{-5}, adjusted by ReduceLROnPlateau for stable convergence. Training comprised 100,000 iterations (including 25,000 partial updates and 20,000 fine-tuning steps) to learn intricate live cell features.

All training was performed on an NVIDIA A100 GPU (80 GB VRAM) using a ViT-h backbone [5] implemented in PyTorch [28], leveraging the torch-em library's bioimaging utilities [27].

All training was performed on an NVIDIA A100 GPU (80 GB VRAM) using a ViT-h backbone [5] implemented in PyTorch [28], leveraging the torch-em library's bioimaging utilities [27].

6.1 Experimental Setting 1: PointTrack Generalization Analysis Using CTMC's Wide-Ranging Cell Types

PointTrack's capacity to generalize across a broad variety of cellular morphologies and dynamic behaviors was assessed using twenty sequences from the Cell Tracking with Mitosis Detection Challenge (CTMC) dataset. These sequences encompass several distinct cell lines, ranging from small, rapidly migrating immune cells to large, slowly dividing epithelial monolayers, under phase-contrast microscopy. The diversity of densities, motion patterns, and shape changes makes CTMC an exacting benchmark for evaluating how effectively sparse point-based supervision and different tracking algorithms can maintain accurate segmentation and reliable trajectory assignment under real-world laboratory conditions.

Performance was measured in five annotation-density regimes: 10 positive and 3 negative points (10P–3N), 15P–3N, 20P–3N, 25P–3N, and 30P–3N per cell in the first frame, after which the pipeline proceeded automatically. Three state-of-the-art trackers—PIPS [8], RAFT [36], and CoTracker [10]—were compared at each density level. The metrics used were Multiple Object Tracking Accuracy (MOTA) and IDF1 score (IDF1) to capture overall tracking quality, Identity Switches (IDS) to quantify track fragmentation, and the percentages of Mostly Tracked (MT) and Mostly Lost (ML) trajectories to assess stability over time.

10P–3N Supervision (Table 3). Under the most minimal point annotation regime—ten positive and three negative points per cell—PointTrack must rely heavily on the capability of the underlying tracker to propagate sparse cues. PIPS achieves a mean MOTA of 48.5% and mean IDF1 of 72.9%, with very low identity switches (0.45%) and a modest 4.4% of trajectories mostly lost (ML). Its strength lies in sequences with moderate cell density and clear contrast, where its iterative point-mask refinement yields stable centroids. RAFT, adapted from optical flow, delivers slightly lower average accuracy (MOTA 46.3%, IDF1 69.6%), demonstrating sensitivity to abrupt cell shape changes and occlusions that violate the smooth motion assumptions inherent in flow-based propagation. CoTracker outperforms both, with an average MOTA of 55.7% and IDF1 of 77.3%, alongside only 0.25% identity switches and 5.7% ML. Its cooperative strategy—jointly leveraging both point trajectories and mask consistency—proves effective at resolving ambiguities in crowded fields even with minimal initial annotations.

15P–3N Supervision (Table 4). Increasing the annotation budget to 15 positive and 3 negative points yields only marginal gains for PIPS and RAFT, suggesting

Table 3. Performance comparison of PointTrack using different trackers across sequences from the CTMC dataset. Higher values are better for MOTA and IDF1 (↑); lower values are better for IDS and ML (↓). All results were obtained using 10 positive and 3 negative points per sequence for supervision.

Sequence	PIPS					CoTracker					TapNet				
	MOTA↑	IDF1↑	IDS↓	MT↑	ML↓	MOTA↑	IDF1↑	IDS↓	MT↑	ML↓	MOTA↑	IDF1↑	IDS↓	MT↑	ML↓
MDOK-run07	60.81	80.03	**0.00**	50.00	**0.00**	99.70	99.85	**0.00**	100.00	**0.00**	**90.25**	**95.11**	**0.00**	**100.00**	**0.00**
MDOK-run09	57.61	76.78	**0.00**	50.00	**0.00**	**80.61**	**90.26**	**0.00**	**75.00**	**0.00**	74.07	86.38	**0.00**	50.00	**0.00**
PL1Ut-run05	76.95	88.45	**0.00**	**100.00**	**0.00**	68.19	84.08	0.00	50.00	0.00	18.19	53.52	7.00	0.00	0.00
U2O-S-run03	35.49	66.48	**0.00**	25.00	**0.00**	**59.78**	**79.57**	**0.00**	75.00	**0.00**	52.29	75.09	**0.00**	50.00	**0.00**
A-10-run07	76.32	81.56	**0.00**	71.43	**0.00**	**77.81**	**88.81**	**0.00**	85.71	14.29	43.60	68.63	4.00	0.00	0.00
A-10-run01	65.63	**93.01**	**0.00**	80.00	**0.00**	65.18	82.55	0.00	80.00	0.00	55.93	70.42	12.00	60.00	0.00
LLC-MK2-run03	**94.61**	97.29	**0.00**	**100.00**	**0.00**	61.57	80.63	0.00	60.00	0.00	67.64	83.67	0.00	80.00	0.00
CRE-BAG2-run01	50.00	73.55	**0.00**	37.50	**0.00**	**64.45**	**81.08**	**0.00**	50.00	**0.00**	55.08	76.09	0.00	37.50	0.00
MDBK-run03	51.83	71.47	**0.00**	52.94	5.88	55.37	71.71	**0.00**	52.94	5.88	**60.80**	**72.11**	1.00	52.94	5.88
LLC-MK2-run02a	43.10	68.61	**0.00**	8.33	**0.00**	27.88	63.09	0.00	25.00	8.33	**41.07**	62.60	3.00	8.33	0.00
LLC-MK2-run07	52.87	75.97	**0.00**	44.44	**0.00**	**73.49**	**86.69**	**0.00**	88.89	**0.00**	43.91	69.58	0.00	11.11	0.00
MDBK-run07	32.88	64.00	5.00	16.67	**0.00**	49.32	73.46	0.00	25.00	0.00	**65.30**	**82.00**	**0.00**	**58.33**	**0.00**
A-549-run03	13.65	53.00	1.00	11.11	22.22	50.36	74.74	**0.00**	55.56	11.11	**50.36**	**73.96**	0.00	44.44	0.00
OK-run05	41.17	69.15	**0.00**	33.33	8.33	35.11	66.42	0.00	**50.00**	8.33	**30.67**	**59.00**	7.00	8.33	8.33
A-10-run05	76.43	87.56	**0.00**	75.00	0.00	48.94	74.20	3.00	50.00	0.00	**42.06**	65.68	**24.00**	25.00	0.00
APM-run05	23.02	63.21	**0.00**	25.00	25.00	**38.37**	**71.11**	**0.00**	**50.00**	**25.00**	-9.93	42.77	**0.00**	0.00	**25.00**
OK-run01	41.17	66.58	**0.00**	40.00	20.00	34.71	65.21	0.00	**50.00**	8.33	**51.93**	**67.97**	0.00	46.67	13.33
RK-13-run03	10.71	55.34	**0.00**	28.57	0.00	**65.11**	**83.77**	0.00	**71.43**	14.29	44.30	72.84	0.00	57.14	0.00
3T3-run03	46.41	71.08	**0.00**	37.50	0.00	29.34	65.14	0.00	37.50	12.50	**36.97**	**65.72**	**9.00**	12.50	0.00
CRE-BAG2-run03	19.02	54.69	3.00	6.67	6.67	**27.63**	**59.17**	**2.00**	40.00	6.67	12.25	48.39	**11.00**	6.67	13.33
Average	48.48	72.89	0.45	44.67	4.41	**55.65**	**77.31**	**0.25**	**58.60**	**5.74**	46.34	69.58	3.90	35.45	3.29

that beyond a certain minimal threshold, additional points contribute diminishing improvements. PIPS improves to a mean MOTA of 49.4% (IDF1 73.0%), while RAFT remains largely unchanged. CoTracker again leads, with MOTA of 55.1% and IDF1 of 76.9%, maintaining sub-percent identity switches and slightly reduced ML (5.2%). The consistency of CoTracker's performance across these two low-annotation regimes indicates its robustness to annotation density fluctuations, as long as some minimum spatial coverage is provided.

20P–3N Supervision (Table 5). At 20 positive points per cell, PIPS begins to overfit local geometric cues, resulting in a slight drop in mean MOTA to 46.5%. RAFT similarly declines, reinforcing its limited ability to handle denser annotation patterns. CoTracker retains a stable mean MOTA of 47.0%, suggesting it can absorb additional supervision without over-compenPointTrackion. In all cases, identity switches remain near zero, but the fraction of mostly tracked trajectories (MT) dips, implying that excessive positive points may introduce conflicting mask prompts that disrupt tracker confidence.

25P–3N Supervision (Table 6). Notably, the 25P–3N regime yields the highest overall performance for both PIPS and CoTracker. PIPS peaks at a mean MOTA of 52.1% (IDF1 74.0%), recovering from the prior decline, likely due to a balanced distribution of points that cover both cell bodies and boundaries. CoTracker achieves its maximum mean MOTA of 61.6% and IDF1 of 79.7%, with only 0.15% identity switches and under 2.5% ML—its best tracking stability and accuracy across all annotation densities. RAFT remains the least improved,

Table 4. Performance comparison of PointTrack using different trackers across sequences from the CTMC dataset. Higher is better for MOTA and IDF1 (↑); lower is better for IDS and ML (↓). All results were obtained using 15 positive and 3 negative points per sequence for supervision.

Sequence	PIPS					CoTracker					TapNet				
	MOTA↑	IDF1↑	IDS↓	MT↑	ML↓	MOTA↑	IDF1↑	IDS↓	MT↑	ML↓	MOTA↑	IDF1↑	IDS↓	MT↑	ML↓
MDOK-run07	61.72	80.19	**4.00**	50.00	**0.00**	**99.70**	**99.85**	**0.00**	**100.00**	**0.00**	90.25	95.11	**0.00**	**100.00**	**0.00**
MDOK-run09	57.47	76.81	**0.00**	50.00	**0.00**	**80.61**	**90.26**	**0.00**	75.00	**0.00**	74.07	86.38	**0.00**	50.00	**0.00**
PL1Ut-run05	**76.95**	88.45	**0.00**	**100.00**	**0.00**	68.19	84.08	0.00	50.00	0.00	18.19	53.52	7.00	0.00	0.00
U2O-S-run03	35.49	66.48	**0.00**	25.00	**0.00**	**59.78**	**79.57**	**0.00**	75.00	**0.00**	52.29	75.09	**0.00**	50.00	**0.00**
A-10-run07	44.98	71.08	**0.00**	42.86	**0.00**	**51.11**	**75.37**	**0.00**	**85.71**	14.29	43.60	68.63	4.00	0.00	0.00
A-10-run01	78.68	**88.93**	**0.00**	80.00	**0.00**	71.34	85.65	0.00	80.00	0.00	55.93	70.42	12.00	60.00	0.00
LLC-MK2-run03	**94.61**	97.29	**0.00**	**100.00**	**0.00**	61.57	80.63	0.00	60.00	0.00	67.64	83.67	0.00	80.00	0.00
CRE-BAG2-run01	50.00	73.55	**0.00**	37.50	**0.00**	**64.45**	**81.08**	**0.00**	50.00	**0.00**	55.08	76.09	0.00	37.50	0.00
MDBK-run03	51.83	71.47	**0.00**	52.94	5.88	55.37	71.71	**0.00**	52.94	5.88	**60.80**	**72.11**	1.00	52.94	5.88
LLC-MK2-run02a	**54.71**	74.39	**0.00**	16.67	8.33	40.99	69.78	0.00	33.33	0.00	41.07	62.60	3.00	8.33	0.00
LLC-MK2-run07	49.12	73.67	**0.00**	44.44	**0.00**	**73.49**	**86.69**	**0.00**	**88.89**	**0.00**	43.91	69.58	0.00	11.11	0.00
MDBK-run07	32.88	64.00	5.00	16.67	**0.00**	49.32	73.46	0.00	25.00	0.00	**65.30**	**82.00**	**0.00**	**58.33**	**0.00**
MDBK-run09	5.82	47.65	1.00	0.00	0.00	44.24	71.73	0.00	50.00	0.00	22.66	57.05	1.00	10.00	0.00
OK-run05	41.17	69.15	**0.00**	33.33	8.33	35.11	66.42	0.00	**50.00**	8.33	**30.67**	**59.00**	7.00	8.33	8.33
A-10-run05	76.43	87.56	**0.00**	75.00	0.00	48.94	74.20	3.00	50.00	0.00	42.06	65.68	24.00	25.00	0.00
APM-run05	42.66	73.15	**0.00**	50.00	0.00	35.21	71.11	0.00	50.00	25.00	-9.93	42.77	0.00	0.00	25.00
OK-run01	41.17	66.58	**0.00**	40.00	20.00	34.71	65.21	0.00	**50.00**	8.33	**51.93**	**67.97**	0.00	46.67	13.33
RK-13-run03	10.71	55.34	**0.00**	28.57	0.00	**65.11**	**83.77**	0.00	**71.43**	14.29	44.30	72.84	0.00	57.14	0.00
3T3-run03	61.49	80.22	**0.00**	50.00	0.00	29.43	64.63	0.00	37.50	12.50	**42.69**	**68.70**	3.00	25.00	0.00
CRE-BAG2-run03	19.02	54.69	3.00	6.67	6.67	**27.63**	**59.17**	2.00	40.00	6.67	12.25	48.39	11.00	6.67	13.33
Average	49.35	73.03	0.65	44.98	4.43	**55.12**	**76.88**	**0.25**	**57.64**	**5.18**	44.95	68.73	3.65	32.73	3.29

Table 5. Performance comparison of PointTrack using different trackers across sequences from the CTMC dataset. Higher values are better for MOTA, IDF1 and MT (↑); lower values are better for IDS and ML (↓). All results were obtained using 20 positive and 3 negative points per sequence.

Sequence	PIPS					CoTracker					TapNet				
	MOTA↑	IDF1↑	IDS↓	MT↑	ML↓	MOTA↑	IDF1↑	IDS↓	MT↑	ML↓	MOTA↑	IDF1↑	IDS↓	MT↑	ML↓
MDOK-run07	60.81	80.03	4.00	50.00	**0.00**	**99.70**	**99.85**	**0.00**	**100.00**	**0.00**	90.25	95.11	**0.00**	**100.00**	**0.00**
MDOK-run09	74.91	86.90	**0.00**	50.00	**0.00**	**88.72**	**94.35**	**0.00**	**100.00**	**0.00**	73.35	85.72	**0.00**	25.00	**0.00**
PL1Ut-run05	**79.78**	**89.88**	**0.00**	**100.00**	**0.00**	75.20	87.53	**0.00**	50.00	**0.00**	16.31	54.36	3.00	0.00	**0.00**
U2O-S-run03	27.76	61.96	**0.00**	25.00	**0.00**	**68.53**	**84.22**	**0.00**	**75.00**	**0.00**	49.84	73.98	**0.00**	50.00	**0.00**
A-10-run07	61.59	76.71	**0.00**	71.43	**0.00**	**77.81**	**88.81**	**0.00**	**85.71**	**0.00**	53.14	66.86	**0.00**	28.57	**0.00**
A-10-run01	**80.78**	**90.03**	**0.00**	**80.00**	**0.00**	73.70	86.81	**0.00**	**80.00**	**0.00**	50.82	72.71	**0.00**	40.00	**0.00**
LLC-MK2-run03	**93.26**	**96.60**	**0.00**	**100.00**	**0.00**	68.31	84.07	**0.00**	60.00	**0.00**	80.00	89.69	**0.00**	80.00	**0.00**
MDBK-run03	50.20	73.17	**0.00**	41.18	**5.88**	**62.04**	**79.28**	1.00	**58.82**	**5.88**	53.66	73.70	1.00	41.18	**5.88**
CRE-BAG2-run01	44.92	70.81	**0.00**	50.00	12.50	**65.62**	**82.11**	**0.00**	**62.50**	**0.00**	40.23	68.19	**0.00**	25.00	12.50
MDBK-run07	44.47	70.56	2.00	16.67	**0.00**	53.33	75.92	**0.00**	**58.33**	**0.00**	**62.95**	**80.57**	**0.00**	50.00	**0.00**
LLC-MK2-run07	37.93	68.41	**0.00**	55.56	22.22	**54.79**	**77.31**	**0.00**	**66.67**	**11.11**	30.50	61.75	**0.00**	22.22	**11.11**
A-549-run03	16.79	56.12	**0.00**	22.22	11.11	**50.08**	**74.83**	**0.00**	**55.56**	**0.00**	38.70	67.69	**0.00**	22.22	**0.00**
RK-13-run03	11.06	54.67	**0.00**	28.57	14.29	**55.36**	**79.35**	**0.00**	**71.43**	**0.00**	42.19	71.03	**0.00**	42.86	**0.00**
MDBK-run09	21.81	57.02	**0.00**	30.00	**0.00**	**51.58**	**75.62**	**0.00**	**50.00**	**0.00**	26.10	57.01	1.00	10.00	**0.00**
OK-run05	**65.11**	**82.07**	**0.00**	**58.33**	**0.00**	45.06	71.91	**0.00**	50.00	**0.00**	27.33	56.21	1.00	8.33	**0.00**
A-10-run05	49.83	48.90	**0.00**	**50.00**	**0.00**	**43.12**	**57.96**	**0.00**	**50.00**	**0.00**	35.16	40.85	4.00	25.00	50.00
OK-run01	42.81	69.34	**0.00**	**53.33**	13.33	38.15	61.24	**0.00**	50.00	**0.00**	**45.03**	**70.88**	**0.00**	**53.33**	13.33
LLC-MK2-run02a	57.20	73.27	**0.00**	33.33	**0.00**	**57.42**	**74.16**	**0.00**	**41.67**	**0.00**	36.47	53.68	**0.00**	8.33	25.00
U2O-S-run05	**41.45**	**69.29**	**0.00**	**50.00**	**12.50**	37.34	68.25	**0.00**	**50.00**	**12.50**	28.79	61.49	**0.00**	25.00	**12.50**
CRE-BAG2-run03	18.83	54.25	**1.00**	20.00	6.67	**31.20**	**60.65**	2.00	**26.67**	**0.00**	21.42	49.57	4.00	6.67	**0.00**
Average	46.46	71.20	0.35	43.86	**5.90**	**46.96**	**72.20**	**0.15**	**49.52**	6.04	39.04	64.11	0.7	27.14	10.06

underscoring its unsuitability for mask-guided propagation in complex, dense CTMC environments.

Table 6. Performance comparison of PointTrack using different trackers across sequences from the CTMC dataset. Higher values are better for MOTA and IDF1 (↑); lower values are better for IDS and ML (↓). All results were obtained using 25 positive and 3 negative points per sequence for supervision.

Sequence	PIPS					CoTracker					TapNet				
	MOTA↑	IDF1↑	IDS↓	MT↑	ML↓	MOTA↑	IDF1↑	IDS↓	MT↑	ML↓	MOTA↑	IDF1↑	IDS↓	MT↑	ML↓
MDOK-run07	71.57	85.71	**0.00**	75.00	**0.00**	96.97	98.48	**0.00**	100.00	**0.00**	**97.32**	**98.66**	**0.00**	**100.00**	**0.00**
MDOK-run09	78.88	88.82	**0.00**	62.50	**0.00**	**80.61**	**90.26**	**0.00**	**75.00**	**0.00**	74.07	86.38	**0.00**	50.00	**0.00**
A-10-run07	76.32	81.56	**0.00**	71.43	**0.00**	**77.81**	**88.81**	**0.00**	**85.71**	14.29	53.14	66.86	**0.00**	28.57	**0.00**
U2O-S-run03	35.49	66.48	**0.00**	25.00	**0.00**	**59.78**	**79.57**	**0.00**	**75.00**	**0.00**	52.29	75.09	**0.00**	50.00	**0.00**
PL1Ut-run05	76.95	88.45	**0.00**	**100.00**	**0.00**	68.19	84.08	0.00	50.00	0.00	18.19	53.52	7.00	0.00	0.00
A-10-run01	65.63	**93.01**	**0.00**	80.00	**0.00**	65.18	82.55	0.00	80.00	0.00	55.93	70.42	12.00	60.00	0.00
LLC-MK2-run03	**94.61**	97.29	**0.00**	**100.00**	**0.00**	61.57	80.63	0.00	60.00	0.00	67.64	83.67	0.00	80.00	0.00
CRE-BAG2-run01	50.00	73.55	**0.00**	37.50	**0.00**	**64.45**	**81.08**	**0.00**	50.00	**0.00**	55.08	76.09	0.00	37.50	0.00
MDBK-run03	51.83	71.47	**0.00**	52.94	5.88	55.37	71.71	**0.00**	52.94	5.88	**60.80**	**72.11**	1.00	52.94	5.88
LLC-MK2-run02a	43.10	68.61	**0.00**	8.33	**0.00**	27.88	63.09	0.00	25.00	8.33	**41.07**	62.60	3.00	8.33	0.00
LLC-MK2-run07	52.87	75.97	**0.00**	44.44	**0.00**	**73.49**	**86.69**	**0.00**	**88.89**	**0.00**	43.91	69.58	0.00	11.11	0.00
MDBK-run07	32.88	64.00	5.00	16.67	**0.00**	49.32	73.46	0.00	25.00	0.00	**65.30**	**82.00**	**0.00**	**58.33**	**0.00**
A-549-run03	13.65	53.00	1.00	11.11	22.22	50.36	74.74	**0.00**	**55.56**	11.11	**50.36**	**73.96**	0.00	44.44	0.00
OK-run05	41.17	69.15	**0.00**	33.33	8.33	35.11	66.42	0.00	**50.00**	8.33	**30.67**	**59.00**	7.00	8.33	8.33
A-10-run05	76.43	87.56	**0.00**	75.00	0.00	48.94	74.20	3.00	50.00	0.00	**42.06**	65.68	**24.00**	25.00	0.00
APM-run05	23.02	63.21	**0.00**	25.00	25.00	**38.37**	**71.11**	**0.00**	**50.00**	**25.00**	-9.93	42.77	**0.00**	0.00	**25.00**
OK-run01	41.17	66.58	**0.00**	40.00	20.00	34.71	65.21	0.00	**50.00**	8.33	**51.93**	**67.97**	0.00	46.67	13.33
RK-13-run03	10.71	55.34	**0.00**	28.57	0.00	65.11	83.77	0.00	**71.43**	14.29	**44.30**	**72.84**	0.00	57.14	0.00
3T3-run03	46.41	71.08	**0.00**	37.50	0.00	29.34	65.14	0.00	37.50	12.50	**36.97**	**65.72**	**9.00**	12.50	0.00
CRE-BAG2-run03	19.02	54.69	3.00	6.67	6.67	27.63	59.17	**2.00**	40.00	6.67	**12.25**	48.39	**11.00**	6.67	13.33
Average	52.09	74.02	0.20	52.64	4.63	**61.57**	**79.67**	**0.15**	**63.04**	**2.38**	45.91	68.17	0.90	33.36	6.30

30P–3N Supervision (Table 7). At the highest density of 30 positive points, PIPS and RAFT both suffer a further decline in MOTA (to 45.8% and 39.2%, respectively), as the proliferation of prompts introduces contradictory segmentation signals in overlapping regions. CoTracker's performance also slightly decreases (mean MOTA 46.9%), but retains nearly perfect identity preservation. The sustained low IDS across all trackers underscores that additional points do not increase track fragmentation; instead, the primary effect is on segmentation coherence and correct mask prompting.

Overall, CoTracker consistently outperformed the other trackers in both accuracy and identity preservation, peaking at 61.6% MOTA under the 25P–3N regime before plateauing. PIPS remained competitive at moderate annotation levels (10–25 points) but exhibited sensitivity to both under- and over-annotation, while RAFT proved most vulnerable to changes in point density, reflecting its reliance on optical-flow assumptions rather than direct mask guidance.

The requirement for a relatively large number of point annotations in the CTMC experiments can be attributed to the lower spatial resolution and overall image quality inherent in those phase-contrast sequences. Under such challenging visual conditions—characterized by low contrast, variable focus, and overlapping cells—denser point supervision helps disambiguate cell boundaries and maintain tracking coherence. By contrast, the CTC dataset described in Setting 2 consists of higher-resolution, higher-contrast imagery (including fluorescence and DIC

Table 7. Performance comparison of PointTrack using different trackers across sequences from the CTMC dataset. Higher values are better for MOTA, IDF1 and MT (↑); lower values are better for IDS and ML (↓). All results were obtained using 30 positive and 3 negative points per sequence.

Sequence	PIPS					CoTracker					TapNet				
	MOTA↑	IDF1↑	IDS↓	MT↑	ML↓	MOTA↑	IDF1↑	IDS↓	MT↑	ML↓	MOTA↑	IDF1↑	IDS↓	MT↑	ML↓
MDOK-run07	69.39	83.86	3.00	75.00	**0.00**	96.77	98.38	**0.00**	**100.00**	**0.00**	**99.04**	**99.52**	**0.00**	**100.00**	**0.00**
MDOK-run09	73.55	86.18	**0.00**	75.00	**0.00**	**85.13**	**92.56**	**0.00**	**87.50**	**0.00**	72.83	85.20	**0.00**	25.00	**0.00**
PL1Ut-run05	**93.13**	**96.56**	**0.00**	**100.00**	**0.00**	76.28	88.12	**0.00**	50.00	**0.00**	16.58	55.04	5.00	0.00	**0.00**
U2O-S-run03	54.10	76.07	**0.00**	25.00	**0.00**	**73.26**	**86.57**	**0.00**	**75.00**	**0.00**	52.68	75.61	**0.00**	**75.00**	**0.00**
A-10-run07	69.45	81.09	**0.00**	71.43	**0.00**	**74.79**	**87.34**	**0.00**	**85.71**	14.29	46.27	64.41	**0.00**	28.57	**0.00**
A-10-run01	**78.55**	**89.00**	**0.00**	**80.00**	**0.00**	74.10	87.03	**0.00**	**80.00**	**0.00**	50.95	72.48	**0.00**	40.00	**0.00**
LLC-MK2-run03	**93.93**	**96.95**	**0.00**	**100.00**	**0.00**	71.10	87.53	**0.00**	60.00	**0.00**	**81.80**	**90.64**	**0.00**	**100.00**	**0.00**
MDBK-run03	61.52	73.55	**0.00**	**58.82**	**5.88**	**64.14**	**74.34**	**0.00**	**58.82**	11.76	55.17	70.09	**0.00**	52.94	**5.88**
CRE-BAG2-run01	47.66	72.87	**0.00**	37.50	**0.00**	**66.02**	**82.70**	**0.00**	**50.00**	**0.00**	52.73	74.95	**0.00**	25.00	**0.00**
MDBK-run07	56.06	76.63	**0.00**	41.67	**0.00**	56.89	77.75	**0.00**	41.67	**0.00**	**64.85**	**81.50**	**0.00**	**58.33**	**0.00**
LLC-MK2-run07	43.83	71.56	**0.00**	44.44	11.11	**60.84**	**80.35**	**0.00**	**66.67**	**0.00**	39.54	66.61	**0.00**	33.33	11.11
A-549-run03	9.89	49.26	**0.00**	22.22	22.22	**46.18**	**73.21**	**0.00**	**55.56**	**0.00**	34.60	65.50	**0.00**	33.33	**0.00**
RK-13-run03	1.57	49.11	**0.00**	28.57	14.29	**41.88**	**73.06**	**0.00**	**57.14**	14.29	**42.46**	70.98	**0.00**	42.86	**0.00**
MDBK-run09	14.35	53.44	**0.00**	30.00	10.00	**53.28**	**76.31**	**0.00**	**60.00**	**0.00**	25.37	56.46	1.00	10.00	**0.00**
OK-run05	**61.78**	**80.16**	**0.00**	41.67	8.33	43.44	71.45	**0.00**	**50.00**	**0.00**	32.44	58.36	1.00	8.33	**0.00**
A-10-run05	**79.96**	**89.87**	**0.00**	**75.00**	**0.00**	43.54	71.76	**0.00**	**50.00**	**0.00**	32.20	53.33	0.00	25.00	50.00
OK-run01	56.73	77.44	**0.00**	**60.00**	6.67	38.21	68.69	**0.00**	50.00	**0.00**	**60.30**	**79.12**	6.00	**60.00**	6.60
LLC-MK2-run02a	**60.06**	**77.12**	**0.00**	25.00	8.33	44.99	70.61	**0.00**	**41.67**	**0.00**	35.57	54.40	**0.00**	8.33	25.00
U2O-S-run05	30.40	62.59	**0.00**	12.50	12.50	**37.74**	**68.59**	**0.00**	**62.50**	12.50	35.65	64.78	**0.00**	25.00	**0.00**
CRE-BAG2-run03	34.58	64.72	**0.00**	26.67	**0.00**	**36.62**	**67.32**	1.00	**33.33**	**0.00**	26.03	53.98	3.00	0.00	6.67
Average	45.84	71.32	0.15	41.26	7.22	**46.90**	**72.86**	**0.05**	**49.51**	**5.86**	39.19	63.52	0.8	26.44	9.71

modalities), where fewer well-placed points suffice to guide segmentation and tracking with similar levels of accuracy.

These findings yield clear, practical guidelines for deploying PointTrack in large-scale studies: in lower-quality, low-resolution scenarios akin to CTMC, around 25 positive points per cell achieves the optimal balance between annotation effort and automated performance, particularly when paired with the CoTracker backend. In higher-quality, high-resolution contexts such as CTC, annotation budgets can be reduced—often to as few as 10–15 points—without significant loss of accuracy. Excessive annotation in any setting risks introducing noisy or conflicting cues, underscoring the importance of tailoring point density to underlying image quality and tracker characteristics.

6.2 Experimental Setting 2: PointTrack Evaluation on Diverse Modalities and Intervals Using the CTC Dataset

In this setting, PointTrack's segmentation and tracking performance was evaluated on a representative subset of the Cell Tracking Challenge (CTC) dataset, which comprises both 2D and 3D time-lapse sequences of fluorescently counterstained nuclei and bright field, phase contrast, and DIC microscopy videos. These sequences span a range of temporal resolutions—from minute-scale intervals in fluorescence to multi-minute intervals in phase contrast—and present a variety of contrast levels, noise characteristics, and cell densities.

Table 8. Results for the PointTrack Evaluation on Diverse Modalities and Intervals Using the CTC Dataset. Higher values are better for MOTA, IDF1, and MT, indicated by upward arrows (↑). Lower values are better for IDS and ML, indicated by downward arrows (↓) [15].

Sequence	Modality	Images	Cells	Points (N)	MOTA ↑	IDF1 ↑	IDS ↓	MT ↑	ML ↓
PhC-C2DH-U373 (01)	Phase Contrast	61	427	6P - 3N	79.82	89.00	0.0	71.43	0.0
PhC-C2DH-U373 (02)	Phase Contrast	12	58	6P - 3N	82.75	91.94	0.0	100.0	0.0
Fluo-N2DH-GOWT1	Fluorescence	38	799	3P - 3N	88.24	91.20	0.0	79.17	8.34
Fluo-N2DH-SIM+	Fluorescence	10	271	3P - 3N	83.03	88.73	0.0	83.34	0.0
Average/Total	-	121	1,555	-	**83.46**	**90.22**	**0.0**	**83.45**	**2.08**

Table 8 summarizes key metrics for four exemplar sequences, all annotated with a minimal point-supervision regime (3–6 points per cell in the first frame, split between positive and negative cues).

For the Phase Contrast sequence PhC-C2DH-U373 (01) (61 frames, U373 glioblastoma cells at 10-minute intervals), PointTrack achieved a MOTA of 79.82% and an IDF1 of 89.00%, with zero identity switches and 71.43% of trajectories mostly tracked. Its robust handling of low-contrast edges and subtle cell boundaries underscores the effectiveness of the point-guided SAM segmentation in maintaining precise object delineation. The shorter, 12-frame sequence PhC-C2DH-U373 (02) yielded even higher accuracy (MOTA 82.75%, IDF1 91.94%) and perfect trajectory continuity (100% MT), demonstrating strong performance even in short time-lapse experiments.

In fluorescence sequences, the increased signal-to-noise ratio further enhances tracking fidelity. On Fluo-N2DH-GOWT1 (38 frames at 30-minute intervals), a MOTA of 88.24% and IDF1 of 91.20% were obtained, with 79.17% mostly tracked and only 8.34% of trajectories lost—results that reflect the clarity of nuclear staining. Similarly, the high-contrast Fluo-N2DH-SIM+ sequence (10 frames) produced a MOTA of 83.03% and IDF1 of 88.73%, with no identity switches and 83.34% MT, highlighting PointTrack's consistency across both long and short fluorescence experiments.

Overall averages across these diverse modalities stand at MOTA 83.46%, IDF1 90.22%, zero identity switches, 83.45% mostly tracked, and 2.08% mostly lost. Among the three evaluated trackers, CoTracker demonstrated the best overall results—achieving the highest MOTA and IDF1 in every sequence—thanks to its cooperative point-mask propagation strategy, which exploits the crisp boundaries and high resolution of the CTC images to maintain identity coherence even through subtle morphological changes.

Because the CTC dataset provides high spatial resolution, strong contrast, and minimal background noise—especially in fluorescence and DIC videos—a sparse annotation regime of just 3–6 points per cell is sufficient to guide accurate segmentation and reliable tracking. In such high-quality imagery, additional points yield negligible improvements and may even introduce redundant or conflicting prompts. This contrasts sharply with the CTMC setting, where lower resolution and reduced contrast necessitate a denser annotation budget.

These results illustrate that, for high-resolution, high-contrast microscopy data, PointTrack can achieve state-of-the-art performance with minimal manual input. The combination of a mask-guided segmentation engine and CoTracker's robust propagation allows for scalable, user-friendly deployment in varied experimental workflows, while ensuring accurate cell-tracking across modalities and temporal scales.

7 Analysis and Discussion

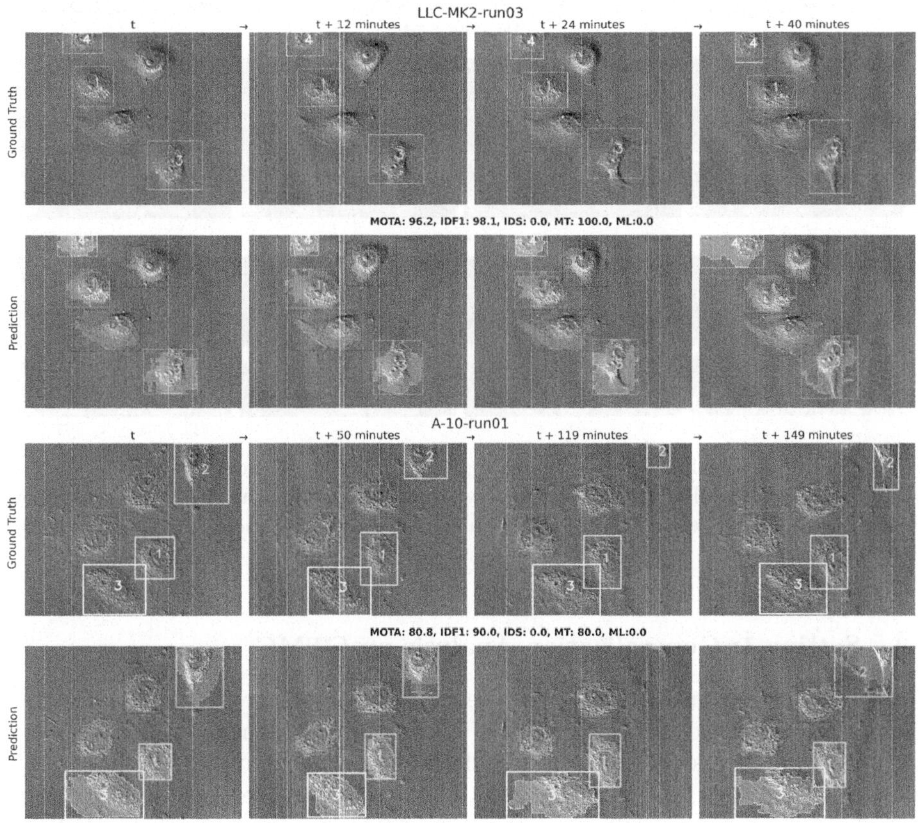

Fig. 2. Tracking results for experimental setting 1 with two sequences, LLC-MK2-run03 and A-10-run01. The top row shows ground truth, and the bottom row shows PointTrack pipeline predictions with evaluation scores above the prediction row [15].

This section presents a comprehensive analysis of the two experimental settings, highlighting PointTrack's ability to generalize across imaging modalities and cell lines, and detailing the impact of annotation density and tracker selection.

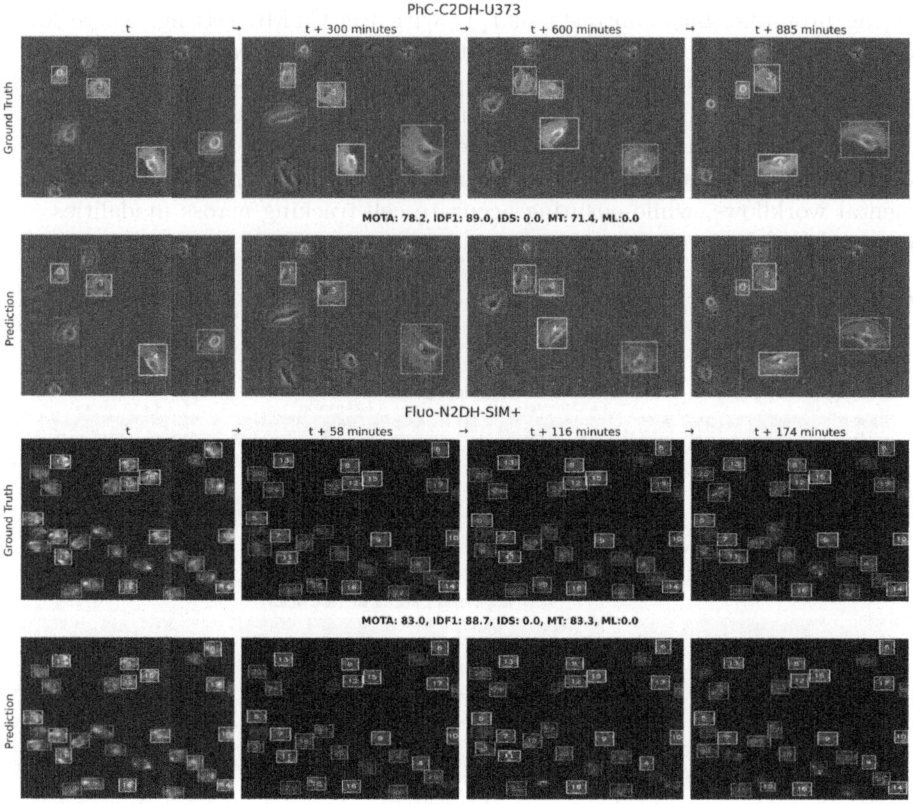

Fig. 3. Tracking results for experimental setting 2 with two sequences, PhC-C2DH-U373 and Fluo-N2DH-SIM+. The top row shows ground truth, and the bottom row shows PointTrack pipeline predictions with evaluation scores above the prediction row [15].

7.1 Setting 1: Generalization Analysis on CTMC

Twenty phase-contrast time-lapse sequences from the CTMC dataset—encompassing twelve distinct cell lines under variable densities, morphologies, and motion patterns—were used to evaluate performance under highly variable conditions. For the full set of twenty CTMC runs, at the optimal annotation regime (25P–3N) with CoTracker, the mean MOTA is 61.6%, with an ID F1 of 79.7%, 0.15% identity switches, and under 2.5% mostly-lost trajectories.

Figure 2 *Analysis.* Figure 2 presents two representative CTMC examples. In panel (a), the LLC-MK2-run03 sequence is shown: the top row overlays the ground-truth bounding boxes on selected frames, while the bottom row displays PointTrack's predicted segmentation masks and centroids. PointTrack maintains perfect correspondence throughout, yielding MOTA 96.18%, IDF1 98.08%, zero identity switches, 100% mostly-tracked trajectories, and 0% mostly-lost. Panel

(b) illustrates the A-10-run01 sequence: one cell briefly disappears at $t = 119$ min (top), but is accurately recovered by $t = 149$ min (bottom), demonstrating robust handling of transient occlusions (MOTA 80.79%, IDF1 90.03%, 0 IDS, 80% MT, 0% ML).

Impact of Tracker Choice and Annotation Density. Five supervision regimes were tested—10P–3N, 15P–3N, 20P–3N, 25P–3N, 30P–3N—using three trackers (PIPS [8], RAFT [36], CoTracker [10]). Results appear in Tables 3, 4, 5, 6 and 7:

- **10P–3N:** CoTracker achieved 55.7% MOTA and 77.3% ID F1 (0.25% IDS, 5.7% ML), outperforming PIPS (48.5%/72.9%) and RAFT (46.3%/69.6%).
- **15P–3N:** PIPS rose marginally to 49.4% MOTA, RAFT saw little change, while CoTracker held steady at 55.1% MOTA and 76.9% ID F1, indicating diminishing returns.
- **20P–3N:** Both PIPS and RAFT declined (46.5% and 39.0% MOTA respectively), suggesting over-annotation issues; CoTracker remained robust at 47.0% MOTA.
- **25P–3N:** The optimal regime—CoTracker peaked at 61.6% MOTA and 79.7% ID F1 (0.15% IDS, $< 2.5\%$ ML), and PIPS recovered to 52.1% MOTA.
- **30P–3N:** All trackers' performance dropped, confirming that excessive point density can degrade segmentation coherence without improving identity preservation.

7.2 Setting 2: Evaluation on Diverse Modalities (CTC)

Annotated 2D sequences from the CTC dataset—specifically Phase Contrast and Fluorescence modalities—were tested with 3–6 points per cell. Table 8 reports an average MOTA of 83.46%, IDF1 of 90.22%, 0 IDS, 83.45% MT, and 2.08% ML.

Figure 3 *Analysis.* Figure 3 shows qualitative results on two CTC sequences. In panel (a), PhC-C2DH-U373 (61 frames at 10 min intervals) initially tracks all cells correctly; one cell is missed at $t = 300$ min but recovered by $t = 600$ min and remains tracked through $t = 885$ min (MOTA 79.82%, IDF1 89.00%, 0 IDS, 71.43% MT, 0% ML). In panel (b), Fluo-N2DH-SIM+ (10 frames) experiences two transient misses at $t = 58$ min and $t = 116$ min; both are recovered by $t = 174$ min, illustrating seamless recovery in high-contrast fluorescence imaging (MOTA 83.03%, IDF1 88.73%, 0 IDS, 83.34% MT, 0% ML).

Robustness Across Variable Modalities. PointTrack demonstrates consistent segmentation and tracking performance across both Phase Contrast and Fluorescence imaging (Fig. 3). In Phase Contrast (Fig. 3), characteristic halo artifacts and variable edge strength do not derail the pipeline: sparse point prompts remain tied to actual cell interiors, and the periodic reinitialization step corrects any drift caused by fluctuating halo intensity. Transient losses due to contrast changes are recovered in subsequent frames, illustrating reliable continuity. In Fluorescence (Fig. 3), high signal-to-noise ratios and well-defined boundaries enable accurate mask inference from minimal annotations. Occasional brief segmentation misses—due to noise fluctuations or photobleaching—are automatically rectified by the propagated points and reinitialization mechanism. Together, these qualitative examples confirm that PointTrack generalizes effectively across imaging modalities with minimal manual input, making it a versatile tool for diverse microscopy workflows.

7.3 Practical Guidelines and Significance

Annotation strategies can be tailored as follows:

1. **Low-Quality, Low-Resolution Data (CTMC):** Approximately 25 points per cell with CoTracker yields optimal tracking accuracy.
2. **High-Quality, High-Resolution Data (CTC):** Only 3–6 points per cell are needed, minimizing effort.
3. **Tracker Selection:** CoTracker consistently outperforms PIPS and RAFT across conditions.

PointTrack's flexible architecture and minimal annotation requirements democratize advanced cell tracking, reducing manual workload, enhancing reproducibility, and enabling scalable analyses in both research and clinical contexts.

7.4 Biological Impact and Implications for Research

PointTrack's automation of sparse-annotation segmentation and tracking unlocks new capabilities in biological research:

- **Accelerated Cancer Studies:** High-throughput quantification of cell motility and drug responses.
- **Enhanced Drug Discovery:** Real-time extraction of single-cell phenotypes for large-scale screens.
- **Scalable Stem-Cell Lineage Tracing:** Reconstruction of differentiation pathways over long experiments.
- **Quantitative Immunology:** Precise tracking of immune–pathogen interactions and migration behaviors.
- **Developmental Biology:** Analysis of coordinated cell movements during morphogenesis.
- **Accessibility and Reproducibility:** Low annotation burden fosters adoption in resource-limited settings and multi-center studies.

7.5 Future Work

Promising directions include:

- **Bounding-Box-Only Supervision** for extremely low-resolution or noisy datasets.
- **Automated Lineage Tracing** via mitosis detection and tree reconstruction.
- **Co-culture and Class-Aware Tracking** to distinguish multiple cell types in mixed populations.
- **Annotation Pipeline Integration** with interactive correction and confidence-driven prompts.

8 Conclusion

The PointTrack pipeline represents a substantial advance in weakly supervised cell segmentation and tracking by leveraging only sparse point annotations in the first frame to drive automated, high-fidelity mask generation and trajectory propagation across complete microscopy sequences. When evaluated on twenty challenging phase-contrast sequences from the CTMC dataset—spanning twelve distinct cell lines with widely varying densities, morphologies, and motion patterns—PointTrack paired with the CoTracker backend achieved a peak Multiple Object Tracking Accuracy (MOTA) of 61.6% and an IDF1 score of 79.7% under a 25-point annotation regime, while maintaining identity switch rates below 0.2% and fewer than 2.5% mostly-lost trajectories. In contrast, on the high-resolution, high-contrast CTC dataset—comprising Bright Field, Phase Contrast, DIC, and fluorescence time-lapse videos—only 3–6 points per cell were required to reach 83.46% MOTA and 90.22% IDF1, with zero identity switches and over 83% of trajectories mostly tracked, illustrating that minimal supervision suffices when image quality permits. Across both settings, PointTrack reduced annotation time by up to 206× compared to traditional full-mask approaches and demonstrated robust performance even under noisy, crowded, or low-contrast conditions, thereby dramatically streamlining large-scale studies in cancer research, drug screening, immunology, and stem-cell biology. The pipeline's modular architecture—combining point-mask reinitialization, state-of-the-art segmentation models, and verPointTrackile tracking backends—ensures adaptability to a wide range of experimental setups and imaging modalities. Moreover, PointTrack's design readily accommodates extensions to lineage reconstruction for tracking cell division events, bounding-box-only workflows for extremely low-resolution datasets, co-culture and multi-population tracking with class-aware segmentation, and integration into interactive annotation platforms with real-time correction capabilities. By democratizing access to high-throughput, reproducible, and accurate single-cell tracking, PointTrack promises to accelerate discoveries in both fundamental and translational research, reducing reliance on specialized annotation teams, enhancing reproducibility across laboratories, and enabling the detailed quantitative analysis of dynamic cellular processes at unprecedented scale.

References

1. Anjum, S., Gurari, D.: CTMC: cell tracking with mitosis detection dataset challenge. In: Proceedings of the IEEE/CVF Conference on Computer Vision and Pattern Recognition Workshops, pp. 982–983 (2020)
2. Aramini, B., et al.: Dissecting tumor growth: the role of cancer stem cells in drug resistance and recurrence. Cancers (2022)
3. Archit, A., et al.: Segment anything for microscopy. bioRxiv, pp. 2023–08 (2023)
4. Bernardin, K., Stiefelhagen, R.: Evaluating multiple object tracking performance: the clear mot metrics. EURASIP J. Image Video Process. (2008)
5. Dosovitskiy, A., et al.: An image is worth 16x16 words: transformers for image recognition at scale. arXiv preprint arXiv:2010.11929 (2020)
6. Durkee, M.S., Abraham, R., Clark, M.R., Giger, M.L.: Artificial intelligence and cellular segmentation in tissue microscopy images. Am. J. Pathol. **191**(10), 1693–1701 (2021)
7. Edlund, C., et al.: Livecell–a large-scale dataset for label-free live cell segmentation. Nat. Methods **18**(9), 1038–1045 (2021)
8. Harley, A.W., Fang, Z., Fragkiadaki, K.: Particle video revisited: Tracking through occlusions using point trajectories. In: European Conference on Computer Vision, pp. 59–75. Springer, Cham (2022). https://doi.org/10.1007/978-3-031-20047-2_4
9. Jelli, E., et al.: Single-cell segmentation in bacterial biofilms with an optimized deep learning method enables tracking of cell lineages and measurements of growth rates. Mol. Microbiol. **119**(6), 659–676 (2023)
10. Karaev, N., Rocco, I., Graham, B., Neverova, N., Vedaldi, A., Rupprecht, C.: Cotracker: it is better to track together. In: European Conference on Computer Vision (ECCV). Springer, Cham (2024)
11. Kaufman, L., Rousseeuw, P.J.: Finding Groups in Data: An Introduction to Cluster Analysis. Wiley, Hoboken (1990)
12. Khalid, N., Caroprese, M., Lovell, G., Porto, D.A., Trygg, J., Dengel, A., Ahmed, S.: Bounding box is all you need: Learning to segment cells in 2d microscopic images via box annotations. In: Annual Conference on Medical Image Understanding and Analysis, pp. 314–328. Springer, Cham (2024). https://doi.org/10.1007/978-3-031-66955-2_22
13. Khalid, N., Caroprese, M., Lovell, G., Trygg, J., Dengel, A., Ahmed, S.: Cellspot: deep learning-based efficient cell center detection in microscopic images. In: International Conference on Artificial Neural Networks, pp. 215–229. Springer, Cham (2024). https://doi.org/10.1007/978-3-031-72353-7_16
14. Khalid, N., et al.: PACE: point annotation-based cell segmentation for efficient microscopic image analysis. In: International Conference on Artificial Neural Networks, pp. 545–557. Springer, Cham (2023). https://doi.org/10.1007/978-3-031-44210-0_44
15. Khalid, N., et al.: SAT: segment and track anything for microscopy. In: Proceedings of the 17th International Conference on Agents and Artificial Intelligence - Volume 2: ICAART, pp. 286–297. INSTICC, SciTePress (2025). https://doi.org/10.5220/0013154200003890
16. Khalid, N., et al.: Deepmucs: a framework for co-culture microscopic image analysis: from generation to segmentation. In: 2022 IEEE-EMBS International Conference on Biomedical and Health Informatics (BHI), pp. 01–04. IEEE (2022)
17. Khalid, N., et al.: DeepCeNS: an end-to-end pipeline for cell and nucleus segmentation in microscopic images. In: 2021 International Joint Conference on Neural Networks (IJCNN), pp. 1–8. IEEE (2021)

18. Khalid, N., et al.: Deepcis: an end-to-end pipeline for cell-type aware instance segmentation in microscopic images. In: 2021 IEEE EMBS International Conference on Biomedical and Health Informatics (BHI), pp. 1–4. IEEE (2021)
19. Khalid, N., et al.: Point2mask: a weakly supervised approach for cell segmentation using point annotation. In: Annual Conference on Medical Image Understanding and Analysis, pp. 139–153. Springer, Cham (2022). https://doi.org/10.1007/978-3-031-12053-4_11
20. Kingma, D.P., Ba, J.: Adam: a method for stochastic optimization. arXiv preprint arXiv:1412.6980 (2014)
21. Kirillov, A., et al.: Segment anything. In: Proceedings of the IEEE/CVF International Conference on Computer Vision (2023)
22. Leal-Taixé, L., Milan, A., Reid, I., Roth, S., Schindler, K.: Motchallenge 2015: towards a benchmark for multi-target tracking. arXiv preprint arXiv:1504.01942 (2015)
23. Malin-Mayor, C., et al.: Automated reconstruction of whole-embryo cell lineages by learning from sparse annotations. Nat. Biotechnol. (2023)
24. Maška, M., et al.: The cell tracking challenge: 10 years of objective benchmarking. Nat. Methods **20**(7), 1010–1020 (2023)
25. Matthews, S.A., et al.: Real-time 3d tracking of swimming microbes using digital holographic microscopy and deep learning. PLoS ONE **19**(4), e0301182 (2024)
26. Newman, R.H., Fosbrink, M.D., Zhang, J.: Genetically encodable fluorescent biosensors for tracking signaling dynamics in living cells. Chem. Rev. **111**(5), 3614–3666 (2011)
27. Pape, C.: torch-em: deep learning based semantic and instance segmentation for 3d electron microscopy and other bioimage analysis problems based on pytorch (2023). https://doi.org/10.5281/zenodo.10779428
28. Paszke, A., et al.: Pytorch: an imperative style, high-performance deep learning library. In: Advances in Neural Information Processing Systems (2019)
29. Rajič, F., Ke, L., Tai, Y.W., Tang, C.K., Danelljan, M., Yu, F.: Segment anything meets point tracking. arXiv preprint arXiv:2307.01197 (2023)
30. Ristani, E., Solera, F., Zou, R., Cucchiara, R., Tomasi, C.: Performance measures and a data set for multi-target, multi-camera tracking. In: Hua, G., Jégou, H. (eds.) ECCV 2016. LNCS, vol. 9914, pp. 17–35. Springer, Cham (2016). https://doi.org/10.1007/978-3-319-48881-3_2
31. Romphosri, S., Pissuwan, D., Wattanavichean, N., Buabthong, P., Waritanant, T.: Rapid alignment-free bacteria identification via optical scattering with LEDs and yolov8. Sci. Rep. **14**(1), 20498 (2024)
32. Scherr, T., et al.: Cell segmentation and tracking using CNN-based distance predictions and a graph-based matching strategy. PLoS ONE **15**(12), e0243219 (2020)
33. Shi, J., et al.: Tomasi. good features to track. In: 1994 Proceedings of IEEE Conference on Computer Vision and Pattern Recognition. SN (1994)
34. Stringer, C., Wang, T., Michaelos, M., Pachitariu, M.: Cellpose: a generalist algorithm for cellular segmentation. Nat. Methods (2020)
35. Stringer, C., et al.: Cellpose: a generalist algorithm for cellular segmentation. Nat. Methods **18**(1), 100–106 (2021)
36. Teed, Z., Deng, J.: RAFT: recurrent all-pairs field transforms for optical flow. In: Vedaldi, A., Bischof, H., Brox, T., Frahm, J.-M. (eds.) ECCV 2020. LNCS, vol. 12347, pp. 402–419. Springer, Cham (2020). https://doi.org/10.1007/978-3-030-58536-5_24

37. Wang, C.Y., Bochkovskiy, A., Liao, H.Y.M.: Yolov7: trainable bag-of-freebies sets new state-of-the-art for real-time object detectors. In: Proceedings of the IEEE/CVF Conference on Computer Vision and Pattern Recognition, pp. 7464–7475 (2023)
38. Wang, R., Butt, D., Cross, S., Verkade, P., Achim, A.: Bright-field to fluorescence microscopy image translation for cell nuclei health quantification. Biol. Imaging **3**, e12 (2023)
39. Yazdi, R., Khotanlou, H.: A survey on automated cell tracking: challenges and solutions. Multimedia Tools Appl. (2024)

DGRCL: A Dynamic Contrastive Graph Learning Framework for Modeling Stock Market Evolution

Yunhua Pei[1(✉)], Jin Zheng[2], and John Cartlidge[2]

[1] School of Computer Science, University of Bristol, Bristol, UK
ge22472@bristol.ac.uk

[2] School of Engineering Mathematics and Technology, University of Bristol, Bristol, UK
{jin.zheng,john.cartlidge}@bristol.ac.uk

Abstract. Modeling the dynamic and complex nature of stock markets is critical for accurate prediction. Traditional approaches often overlook the intricate interplay between evolving temporal patterns and static relational structures among stocks. To overcome this problem, we propose DGRCL, a novel Dynamic Graph Representation with Contrastive Learning framework designed to jointly capture temporal dynamics and structural relations within stock market data. DGRCL introduces two core modules: an Embedding Enhancement (EE) module that adaptively models temporal evolution through dynamic graph construction, and a Contrastive Constrained Training (CCT) module that leverages static stock relations as constraints within a contrastive learning paradigm. This integration enables DGRCL to learn robust and expressive representations that reflect both transient market trends and stable inter-stock dependencies. Extensive experiments on the NASDAQ and NYSE datasets demonstrate that DGRCL consistently outperforms state-of-the-art temporal graph learning baselines in stock trend prediction. Ablation studies confirm the critical contributions of both the dynamic embedding and contrastive constraint components. Overall, DGRCL offers a powerful and versatile framework for embedding dynamic temporal and relational information into graph-based stock market forecasting. Public access to code and data is provided.

Keywords: Dynamic Contrastive Learning · Financial Market Forecasting · Graph Neural Networks · Temporal Prediction

1 Introduction

Stock market prediction remains a prominent and challenging task in both academia and industry, driven by its potential for generating substantial financial returns. At its core lies the difficulty of modeling complex, noisy, and non-stationary financial time series. Existing methods typically differ in the choice of input features, falling into two major categories: those using only historical price data and those combining price data with technical indicators.

H. J. van den Herik et al. (Eds.): ICAART 2025, LNAI 16517, pp. 187–212, 2026.
https://doi.org/10.1007/978-3-032-25032-2_9

Historical price data—comprising open, high, low, close prices, and trading volume (OHLCV)—is the most fundamental input for financial forecasting. Numerous deep learning approaches have been developed using this information alone. For instance, Zhou et al. [49] applied empirical mode decomposition alongside a factorization machine-based neural network to enhance price trend forecasting. Zhang et al. [39] proposed a stochastic recurrent network with a seq2seq structure and attention mechanism to model temporal dependencies. Other studies explored attention-based LSTMs [5] and multitask recurrent neural networks with high-order Markov random fields [21].

Beyond raw price data, technical indicators—such as RSI, MACD, and moving averages—have been widely adopted to capture domain-specific patterns. These indicators are derived from OHLCV data and are often used in practice by traders. Recent studies further validate their importance. Mostafavi and Hooman [27] identified key technical indicators with high predictive power through a comparative analysis, while Ayala et al. [1] demonstrated that optimizing combinations of technical indicators using machine learning can lead to improved forecasting accuracy on stock indices.

Complementing these trends, graph-based approaches have gained momentum due to their ability to model structured relationships among entities. In the context of finance, graphs can represent relationships between stocks and attributes, enabling the transfer of relevant information across entities. Prior work has leveraged market knowledge graphs with attention mechanisms [48], temporal graph convolution networks [26], and emotion-aware non-stationary Markov chains [23]. These graph neural networks (GNNs) aggregate relational signals and have shown superior performance over non-graph-based models in capturing market dynamics.

Despite these advancements, several challenges remain unresolved. First, many models focus on forecasting a single stock, ignoring broader market context and stock interdependencies. Second, constructing stock graphs often relies on fixed prior knowledge, making adaptation difficult. Third, while knowledge-based relations are used to define graphs, they are rarely integrated into the learning process itself in a meaningful or dynamic way. To address these limitations, we propose a novel Dynamic Graph Representation with Contrastive Learning Framework for Modeling Stock Market Evolution (DGRCL). DGRCL comprises three key components:

Embedding Enhancement. We adaptively construct evolving graph edges based on Zipf's law [29], leveraging Fourier-transformed OHLCV data to refine inter-stock similarity through distribution-based distance measures.

Contrastive-Constrained Training. Company-level relations serve as constraints in a contrastive learning module, which uses latent-space contrastive loss to maximize the agreement between two augmented graph views, resulting in more discriminative and robust representations.

Dynamic Graph Evolution. A temporal forecasting model (GRU or LSTM) is employed to capture the evolution of the graph structure and stock representations over time, enabling temporally-aware prediction of future market trends.

Contribution: To our knowledge, DGRCL is the first method to integrate inter-stock relations as contrastive constraints within a dynamic GNN-based prediction framework. Our contributions are summarized as follows:

1. We propose a novel edge construction mechanism based on Zipf's law and Fourier-based distance metrics, capturing dynamic and nuanced inter-stock relations.
2. We incorporate structured knowledge (e.g., sector and industry relations) into the model via a dynamic contrastive loss function, enhancing the continual discriminative power of latent embeddings.
3. We conduct extensive experiments on real-world datasets comprising 2,763 stocks from NASDAQ and NYSE. DGRCL outperforms state-of-the-art baselines, achieving average improvements of 2.48% in accuracy, 5.53 in F1 score, and 6.67 in Matthews correlation coefficient for next-day trend prediction.

This chapter is an extension of an earlier paper [32], which received the Best Paper Award at the 2025 International Conference on Agents and Artificial Intelligence (ICAART).

2 Related Work

2.1 GNNs

GNNs are designed with specific consideration for tasks involving graph data, such as node classification, graph classification, and link prediction. In GAL-STM [42], an attention-based LSTM is constructed to learn weight matrices from Hawkes correlation graphs generated by different stocks to improve the stock selection winning rate while paying less attention to the optimal trading strategy. The most profitable stock prediction is also onc task of portfolio management. Intra-sector relations, inter-sector relations, and stock-sector relations are considered in the previous study [12] to find hierarchical influence among stocks and predict the most profitable stock. Although sector-level modeling is performed in their model, some fine-grained metadata with descriptions of listed company attributes deserves more attention. Stock description documents can also be introduced into the model. For example, Yahoo Finance is one of the channels for topic-based extraction models in TRAN [10] to make stock recommendations. Similar limitation, TRAN only constructs the stock graph as a static one. Current approaches need to focus on portfolio construction and selection, as well as on understanding the dynamic interactions between these portfolios.

2.2 Graph Contrastive Learning

Recently, contrastive representation learning on graphs has gained significant interest. It contrasts positive and negative sample pairs, aiming to bring similar samples closer and push dissimilar ones apart, focusing on solving the graph manual labeling problem in the real world. According to [25], previous research can be categorized into cross-scale contrasting and same-scale contrasting. Cross-scale contrasting involves comparing elements at different scales. For example, MVGRL [11] takes a multi-view approach by using a diffused graph as a global view and maximizing MI across both views and scales. DGI [37] contrasts patch-level and graph-level representations by maximizing mutual information, which helps propagate global information to local representations. Same-scale contrasting focuses on elements at the same scale, such as comparing graphs directly. Within this approach, methods are further divided into context-based and augmentation-based. Context-based methods typically use random walks to identify positive pairs. Augmentation-based methods, like GraphCL [43], generate positive pairs through various perturbations at the graph level. GCA [50] performs node-level augmentations tailored to the graph's structure and attributes, while IGSD [47] uses graph diffusion to create augmented views and employs a teacher-student framework.

3 Preliminary

3.1 Notation

Graph Representation Learning. Let $\mathcal{G} = (\mathcal{V}, \mathcal{E})$ denote the graph model where $\mathcal{V}$ is the set of nodes, and $\mathcal{E}$ is the set of edges. The total number of nodes is denoted by $N = |\mathcal{V}|$. The length of the time series is T, and $\boldsymbol{X}^i \in \mathbb{R}^{D \times T}$ is the covariate time-series data associated with node i, where each node is associated with D different covariate time series. Furthermore, at time step t, covariate values for node i is represented as $\mathbf{x}_t^i$, and $\boldsymbol{X}_T^i = \{\mathbf{x}_1^i, ..., \mathbf{x}_T^i\}$ is the set of time-series in graph $\mathcal{G}$. Two different nodes i and j that contain an edge $(i,j) \in \mathcal{E}$ without a direction, forming graph $\mathcal{G}$ an undirected one, encoding an explicit dependence between nodes. Let $\boldsymbol{A} \in \mathbb{R}^{N \times N}$ denote this sparse adjacency matrix at a certain time. If $(i,j) \in \mathcal{E}$, then $\boldsymbol{A}_{ij}$ represents the weight of the edge (dependency) between node i and j, and $\boldsymbol{A}_{ij} = 0$ when $(i,j) \notin \mathcal{E}$ otherwise. Hence, the graph structure is represented by the adjacency matrix $\boldsymbol{A}$ and its corresponding time-series $\{\boldsymbol{X}_T^i | i = 1, ..., N\}$.

Graph Contrastive Learning. Given an input Graph $\mathcal{G}$, graph contrastive learning aims to learn the representations in node-level tasks in this work by maximizing the feature consistency between two augmented views of the input graph via contrastive loss in the latent space. Data augmentation $q(\cdot)$ is a common operation to obtain two views v_a and v_b for the same graph $\mathcal{G}$, including node dropping, edge perturbation, subgraph sampling, etc. With these views, latent representations z_a and z_b are then extracted by GNNs. Finally, given the

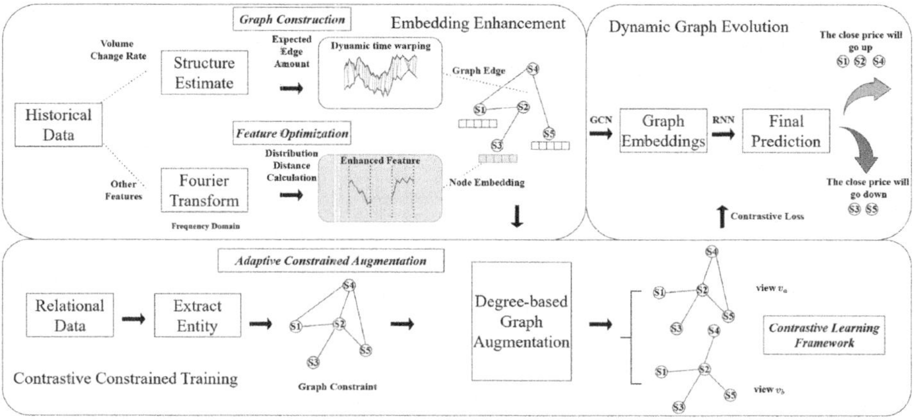

Fig. 1. Schematic illustration of DGRCL framework. Top-left: In the process of embedding enhancement, dynamic stock graphs with enhanced features are generated. Bottom: Then, an encoder is trained with the company relations in a contrastive manner inside the CCT module, to improve the generation of an initial embedding matrix for the subsequent step. Top-right: Finally, the layer weights are learned through general RNNs (e.g., GRU, LSTM) to yield the final predictions. Figure adapted from our previous work [32].

latent representations, a contrastive loss is optimized to score the positive pairs $\{z_a^i, z_b^i\}$ higher compared to other negative pairs, including inter-view negative pairs $\left\{z_a^i, z_b^j\right\}$, and intra-view negative pairs $\{z_a^i, z_a^j\}$.

3.2 Problem Setting

The proposed framework solves the following graph-based time-series forecasting problem. For all stocks, a set of stock historical sequence data at day t is represented by $\mathcal{X} \in \mathbb{R}^{N \times T \times D}$, where D is the dimension of features (OHLCV) of one stock. Given a lookback window of length δ, where $1 \leq \delta \leq t$, the model can make predictions for the next day's $(t+1)$ movements of the stocks, using the data of $\mathcal{X}_{t-\delta:t}$. The movement is calculated by $p_c^{t+1} - p_c^t$, in which p_c^t means the *close* price of the stock at day t, resulting two prediction outcomes. A positive result means the price will go up ($label = 1$), while a negative result means it will go down ($label = 0$), making this a binary classification task.

4 Methodology

In this section, we elucidate the framework of the proposed DGRCL as shown in Fig. 1. Given OHLCV of the stocks in a certain interval $[t-\delta+1, t]$ and the company relations, we aim to predict the next day's stock price movement. First, we construct the stock graph with evolving edges for different time steps

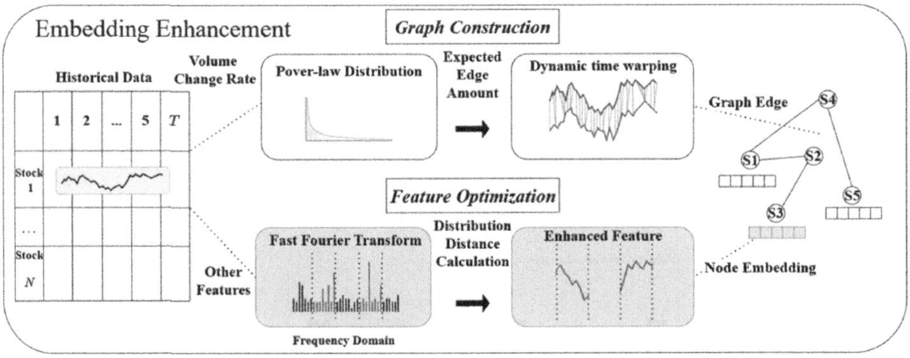

Fig. 2. Embedding Enhancement module's framework. Figure adapted from our previous work [32].

and generate initial embeddings for each node. Second, we extract the dynamic node representations for each time step. Then, a constraint data augmentation method is encoded using the company relations. After that, we feed the constrained dynamic node representations to an RNN-based model to get the final representation of the nodes. Finally, we predict the stock movement based on the generated node representation from RNNs.

4.1 Embedding Enhancement

In this section we detail the embedding enhancement process (see Fig. 2).

Graph Construction. The future performance of a stock is influenced by its past behavior and its connections to related stocks. Current research often relies heavily on established knowledge, such as manual industry classifications [9,13,41]. However, this approach can be expensive, it is based heavily on empirical experience, and it may not generalize well to new forecasting tasks. In this regard, we follow the data-driven manner in [38] to calculate a proximity function by applying Dynamic Time Warping (DTW) [15] on the input signals $\mathbf{x}_t^i$, which will be further introduced in the experiment part. This process involves utilizing dynamic programming on a path matrix to determine the minimum alignment cost for each pair of stock sequences $\mathbf{x}_t^i$ and $\mathbf{x}_t^j$ with a lookback window δ:

$$cost(\mathbf{x}_t^i, \mathbf{x}_t^j) \Longleftarrow DTW(\mathbf{x}_{t-\delta:t}^i, \mathbf{x}_{t-\delta:t}^j) \tag{1}$$

In DGRCL, we set the time step as 1. Through computations for each pair of stock sequences within the same time step, a corresponding cost matrix $\dot{\boldsymbol{A}}_t$ is generated for that particular time step t, and the total number of the cost matrices is $T - \delta$. Traditional methods typically employ a hard threshold to partition the cost matrix $\dot{\boldsymbol{A}}_t$ and form the adjacency matrix $\boldsymbol{A}_t$ of the graph [38]. However, such approaches are often subjective. The adjacency matrix, which represents the edges in a graph, heavily relies on the structural information of its edges for information transmission. Hence, we introduce an adaptive method to estimate the number of significant edges that a graph should possess based on the number of nodes it contains.

According to [35], the scale-free structure of stock graphs is characterized by a power-law distribution in node degrees, at least in an asymptotic sense; see Eq. (2). Specifically, the fraction $P(n)$ of nodes in the graph having n connections to other nodes follows the distribution [2], where s is the exponent.

$$P(n) \sim n^{-s} \tag{2}$$

This observation can be explained by Zipf's law [29], an empirical principle that tends to hold approximately when a list of measured values is sorted in descending order. The probability mass function of the Zipf distribution is a discrete probability distribution as,

$$P(X = n) = \frac{n^{-s}}{\sum_{i=1}^{N} (i^{-s})} \tag{3}$$

where N is the total number of possible outcomes, n is a specific outcome. Then we can give the expectation of a random variable X with a Zipf distribution using the formula:

$$E(X) = \sum_{n=1}^{N} n \cdot P(X = n) \tag{4}$$

It should be noted that when applied, n will represent the count of known nodes, which is the number of stocks in the stock graph. This approach allows us to provide a rough estimate of the expected number of edges $E(n)$ in a stock network based on a given number of nodes n. Then, by employing a binary classification method, we manage the number of values exceeding the threshold to remain below the specified limit $E(n)$. This enables us to dynamically construct edges to build a stock graph $\mathcal{G}$. Furthermore, we obtain the dynamic graph for each time step as $\mathcal{G}_1, \mathcal{G}_2, \ldots, \mathcal{G}_{T-\delta}$.

Feature Optimization. Statistical properties such as mean and variance in time series data often change over time, leading to distribution shift problems [8,19]. This change in time distribution poses a significant challenge in stock series to achieving accurate time series forecasting. Therefore, we need to enhance the input stock series.

To identify the distribution characteristics of a time series, it needs to be transformed into another domain, such as the frequency domain. The Fourier transform (FT) [3,6] is an integral transform that presents a function into a representation that emphasizes the original function, which has wide applications in physics, mathematics, and engineering. Here, we apply the Fast Fourier Transformation (FFT) [6] to one stock series, and follow the temporal distribution characterization in [8], with the principle of maximum entropy [14] to find the most dissimilar periods, whose objective can be formulated as:

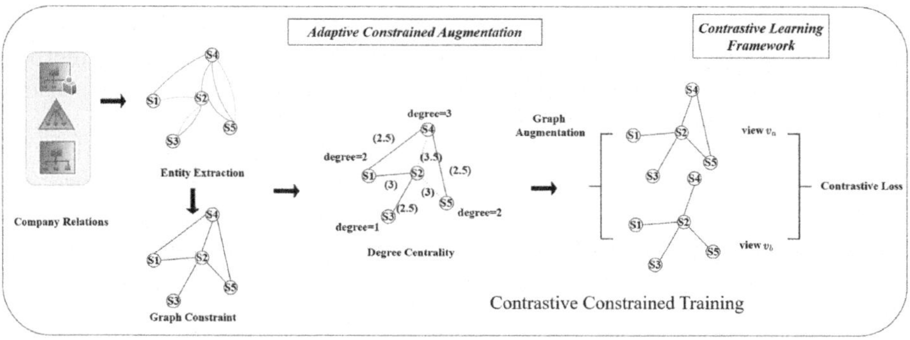

Fig. 3. Contrastive Constrained Training module's framework. Figure adapted from our previous work [32].

$$\max_{0<k\leq k_0}\ \max_{n_1,\ldots,n_k}\ \frac{1}{k}\sum_{1<i\neq j\leq k} d(FFT(\mathbf{x}^i), FFT(\mathbf{x}^j)) \tag{5}$$

$$s.t.\quad \forall i, \triangle_1 < \left|\mathbf{x}^i\right| < \triangle_2; \sum_i \left|\mathbf{x}^i\right| = \boldsymbol{X}^i \in \mathbb{R}^{D\times T} \tag{6}$$

where $d(\cdot)$ is a distance metric, k_0 is the hyperparameter to avoid over-splitting, and $\triangle_1, \triangle_2$ are predefined parameters to avoid trivial solutions (e.g., extremely small or large values might not effectively capture the distribution information). T is the length of time-series and D is the dimension of features. The metric $d(\cdot)$ can be any distribution distance calculations such as Euclidean, JS-divergence, and KL-divergence. By searching k, the corresponding periods, and then applying this approach to each feature dimension d, we can find the most dissimilar period pairs in the feature domain for the stock. By performing similar operations on each stock, we obtain the enhanced stock graph node embedding matrix $\boldsymbol{X}'$.

It's important to notice that in one stock series, the sequences derived from FFT transformation in both rising and falling markets exhibit similarity, details please refer the experiments. The distinguishing factor lies in the fluctuating market. Therefore, we will generate three sets of results (rising, falling, and fluctuating) to serve as enhanced representations $\mathbf{x'}^i$ of one feature for stock i.

4.2 Contrastive Constrained Training

In previous stock prediction methods, company relations are mainly used to define the edge structure of stock graphs for information propagation [9,18]. Consideration of these relations as a constraint has been largely ignored during the training process. Therefore, we propose a Contrastive Constrained Training (CCT) module that integrates company relations to learn a constrained GNN encoder through contrastive learning. We will begin by introducing the adaptive constrained augmentation, followed by the contrastive learning framework, as the two components of the CCT module (see Fig. 3).

Adaptive Constrained Augmentation. Contrastive learning methods, which aim to maximize agreement between views, strive to learn representations consistent despite perturbations introduced by augmentation techniques. Within the CCT module, we propose an adaptive enhancement scheme based on company relation constraints. The aim is designed to disrupt less important links and features while protecting the important constraint structure and properties.

In this step, contrary to previous methods, we incorporate company relations as constraints during training, resulting in a reevaluation of the former stock graph. The probability of the edge between node i, j remains in the augmentation step $P\{(i,j) \in \mathcal{E}\}$ is calculated as:

$$1 - min\left(\frac{\log w_{max} - \log w}{\log w_{max} - \log w_{\mu}} \cdot p_e, \quad p_{\tau}\right) \tag{7}$$

where w is the average of the degree centrality [28] between node i and j. We first calculate w for all edges and then make a max-mean normalization using the max and mean (μ). To balance the probabilities, we then take the logarithm of the result. p_e and p_{τ} are hyperparameters to control the overall probability of removing edges and the cut-off threshold.

The key approach presented in CCT is that the degree centrality calculation method is based on the company relation of the stocks, rather than the edges within the stock graph. That is, given the stock relation encodings $\boldsymbol{A}$ and each kind of relation $\boldsymbol{A}_{ij}^{relation} \in \mathcal{A}$ for node pair (i, j) we must adhere to the constraint that there must be at least one type of relation that exists $\boldsymbol{A}_{ij}^{\text{relation}} > 0$. With this constraint, we can calculate w using the following method.

$$\frac{1}{2}\left(\sum_{(i,j)\in\mathcal{E}} \boldsymbol{A}_{ji}^{\text{relation}} + \sum_{(i,j)\in\mathcal{E}} \boldsymbol{A}_{ij}^{\text{relation}}\right) \tag{8}$$

After calculating the edge remaining probability, we generate two views for the input graph $\mathcal{G}$ to perform contrastive learning.

Contrastive Learning Framework. The proposed CCT module follows the common graph contrastive learning paradigm, in which the model aims to maximize the alignment of representations across various perspectives [11,50]. We initially create two different views of the graph $\mathcal{G}$, by applying adaptive constrained augmentation to the input. Subsequently, we utilize a contrastive objective function that ensures the encoded embeddings of each node in these two distinct views align with each other, while also being distinguishable from embeddings of other nodes.

Specifically, during each training epoch, the CCT module begins by randomly selecting two data augmentation functions from $q(\cdot)$, which is a common operation to obtain two views $v_a \sim q(G)$, $v_b \sim q(G)$, then, node representations z_a and z_b are obtained from a GNN encoder $g(\cdot)$. For a given node i, its embedding z_a^i generated in view v_a serves as the anchor, while the embedding of it generated in the other view z_b^i forms the positive sample, and the remaining embeddings in the two views are considered as negative samples. Following [50], we define the pairwise objective $\ell(z_a^i, z_b^i)$ for each positive pair (z_a^i, z_b^i) as :

$$\log \frac{e^{\theta(z_a^i, z_b^i)/\tau}}{e^{\theta(z_a^i, z_b^i)/\tau} + \sum e^{\theta(z_a^i, z_b^j)/\tau} + \sum e^{\theta(z_a^i, z_a^j)/\tau}} (i \neq j) \tag{9}$$

where τ is a temperature parameter, and $e^{\theta(z_a^i, z_b^i)/\tau}$ represent positive pair. $\sum e^{\theta(z_a^i, z_b^j)/\tau}$, $\sum e^{\theta(z_a^i, z_a^j)/\tau}$ mean inter-view negative pairs and intra-view negative pairs. $\theta(z_a, z_b) = s(\phi(z_a), \phi(z_b))$, in which, $s(\cdot)$ refers to the cosine similarity and $\phi(\cdot)$ is a non-linear projection, implemented as a two-layer perception model. Moreover, the overall objective $\mathcal{L}_{cl}$ for the CCT module to be maximized uses the average for all positive pairs, since the two views are symmetric.

$$\mathcal{L}_{cl} = \frac{1}{2N} \sum_{i=1}^{N} (\ell(z_a^i, z_b^i) + \ell(z_b^i, z_a^i)) \tag{10}$$

In this way, we use the number of relationships as a basis for measuring the possibility of the existence of a certain edge, thereby achieving adaptive data augmentation with constraints, which is then trained together with the dynamic graph evolution.

4.3 Dynamic Graph Evolution

Using dynamic graphs and node embedding matrices, we will now explain how to acquire the dynamic latent representations of nodes. This process consists of two components: the graph convolutional network and the weight evolution (see Fig. 4).

Based on GCN [20], we propose the following propagation rules:

$$\boldsymbol{H}_t^{(l+1)} = \sigma(\widehat{\boldsymbol{A}}_t \boldsymbol{H}_t^{(l)} \boldsymbol{W}_t^{(l)}) \tag{11}$$

Here, at time t, the l-th layer takes the adjacency matrix $\boldsymbol{A}_t$ and the node embedding matrix $\boldsymbol{H}_t^{(l)}$ as input, and outputs $\boldsymbol{H}_t^{(l+1)}$ using a layer-specific trainable weight matrix $\boldsymbol{W}_t^{(l)}$ to update. Specifically, $\sigma(\cdot)$ denotes an activation function.

$$\widehat{\boldsymbol{A}} = \widetilde{\boldsymbol{D}}^{-\frac{1}{2}} \widetilde{\boldsymbol{A}} \widetilde{\boldsymbol{D}}^{-\frac{1}{2}}, \widetilde{\boldsymbol{A}} = \boldsymbol{A} + \boldsymbol{I}, \widetilde{\boldsymbol{D}} = diag\left(\sum_j \widetilde{\boldsymbol{A}}_{ij}\right) \tag{12}$$

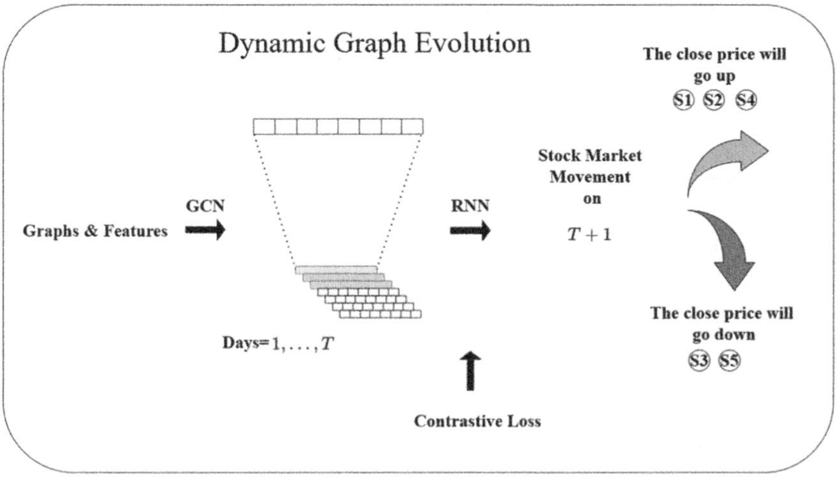

Fig. 4. Dynamic Graph Evolution module's framework. Figure adapted from our previous work [32].

To acquire the dynamic latent representations, the trainable weight matrix $\boldsymbol{W}_t^{(l)}$, we follow the methodology outlined in [30]. $\boldsymbol{W}_t^{(l)}$ is treated as the hidden state of the dynamical system updated by any RNN-based model $f(\cdot)$, such as LSTM and GRU, with a prediction loss $\mathcal{L}_{pred}$.

$$\boldsymbol{W}_t^{(l)} = f(\boldsymbol{H}_t^{(l)}, \boldsymbol{W}_{t-1}^{(l)}) \tag{13}$$

The final prediction result will be derived from the output of $\boldsymbol{W}$ at the final time step. This result is binarized and then mapped through a *softmax* function to predict each stock. The final form of the loss function is shown below, where λ is a trade-off parameter.

$$\mathcal{L} = \mathcal{L}_{pred} + \lambda \mathcal{L}_{cl} \tag{14}$$

5 Experiment

In this section, we describe the experimental setup used to evaluate the effectiveness of our proposed method. Experimental results demonstrate the effectiveness of our DGRCL framework in comparison with different backbones and datasets. We specifically aim to answer the following questions:

RQ1. How effective is the proposed DGRCL framework for the graph classification task?
RQ2. How effective are the individual modules proposed in DGRCL?
RQ3. How does sensitivity to hyperparameters affect the performance of the proposed model?

Table 1. Data statistics of NASDAQ and NYSE. Table adapted from our previous work [32]

Item	NASDAQ dataset			NYSE dataset		
	Train	Validate	Test	Train	Validate	Test
Time Span	01/02/2013 - 12/08/2017			01/02/2013 - 12/08/2017		
Valid Trading Days	611	94	236	611	94	236
Data Points	5 (OHLCV)			5 (OHLCV)		
Nodes	1026			1737		
Edges	164			255		
Relation Types	112			130		

5.1 Dataset

We closely follow the experimental setup outlined in [9], using two major US stock markets. Many studies have utilized this same dataset to evaluate their stock forecasting models [12,18,33,45,46], and to ensure easier comparison with the existing literature, we also adopt this dataset in our experiments.

Dataset statistics are summarized in Table 1. We follow the setup of [30] and divide the two datasets into training, validation, and testing sets in the proportions of 0.65, 0.1, and 0.25, respectively. This results in 611, 94, and 236 effective trading days for each set. OHLCV are daily values for each stock. Edges number is calculated by Eq. (4) with a certain number of nodes. Recognizing that stocks within the same industry tend to be similarly affected by industry-wide prospects, we gather data on the sector-industry relationships among stocks. For two datasets, we apply the sector-industry relations as Relation Types in Table 1, for more details, please refer to [9]. The dataset and source code are available in GitHub.[1]

Each stock market dataset spans four years, exceeding one thousand time points, with more than one thousand traded stocks in each market. Compared to the datasets used in the baseline models, the datasets employed in DGRCL are characterized by their long duration, multiple nodes, and dynamic temporal graph changes. This makes financial datasets particularly well-suited for studying long-term information propagation in GNNs, as compared to other datasets.

5.2 Model Setting

All experiments are performed on a Nvidia GeForce RTX 3090 graphic card, CUDA version 11.5. The lookback window δ applied in $DTW(\cdot)$ is 20. In general, each month consists of approximately 22.5 working days. The input signals $\mathbf{x}_t^i$ for DTW is the volume volatile, by calculating vol^t/vol^{t-1}. The RNN-based model $f(\cdot)$ is a two-layer LSTM, following the methodology outlined in [30]. Three

[1] https://github.com/PEIYUNHUA/DGRCL.

hyperparameters in the CCT module are τ, p_e, and p_τ. Following the work of [50], we set τ as 0.4. For the other two, we train the model using p_e and p_τ from 0.1 to 0.9 with increments of 0.2. The activation function $\sigma(\cdot)$ is set to $ReLU(\cdot)$. Based on the method outlined in [24], we control the trade-off parameter λ to bring $\mathcal{L}_{pred}$ and $\mathcal{L}_{cl}$ to the same order of magnitude. The empirical value of λ obtained from multiple experiments is 0.1.

5.3 Baseline Models for Comparison

We consider state-of-the-art dynamic graph node classification models as baseline methods to learn the representations of nodes in a graph, including Graph WaveNet [40], MTGODE [17], STGCL [24], and EvolveGCN [30].

Graph WaveNet. A spatiotemporal graph modeling approach that captures spatial-temporal dependencies across multiple time series by integrating graph convolution with dilated causal convolution [40]. Two datasets are used: the METR-LA dataset spans four months of traffic speed data from 207 sensors, while the PEMS-BAY dataset covers six months from 325 sensors, both aggregated into 5-minute intervals.

MTGODE. A continuous model that forecasts multivariate time series by integrating dynamic graph neural Ordinary Differential Equations to unify spatial-temporal message passing and enhance latent spatial-temporal dynamics [17]. The evaluation involves five benchmark datasets: three conventional time series datasets (Electricity, Solar-Energy, Traffic) and two traffic datasets (Metr-La, Pems-Bay) with predefined graph structures and specific time spans.

STGCL. A study that integrates contrastive learning into spatio-temporal graph (STG) forecasting, leveraging novel node and graph-level contrastive tasks to mitigate data scarcity, enhancing performance through joint learning schemes and strategic data augmentations [24]. The model is tested using two traffic benchmarks, PEMS-04 and PEMS-08, with aggregated 5-minute traffic flow, average speed, and occupancy data, applying Z-score normalization and Gaussian kernel adjacency matrices.

EvolveGCN. An approach to dynamic graph representation learning that adapts graph convolutional networks over time by evolving GCN parameters with recurrent neural networks, without relying on node embeddings [30]. The benchmark datasets include the Stochastic Block Model (SBM) for simulating community structures, Bitcoin OTC (BC-OTC) and Bitcoin Alpha (BC-Alpha) for rating predictions, UC Irvine messages (UCI) for link prediction, and several other networks for various predictive tasks.

Null Model. Predicts tomorrow's trend to match today's close price direction, serving as a simple momentum-based baseline.

Table 2. Performance of proposed DGRCL and other baselines on next trading day stock trend classification over the test period. Bold denotes the best result. Results for all methods except the Null Model are adapted from our previous work [32].

Methods	NASDAQ dataset			NYSE dataset		
	Accuracy (%)	F1 score	MCC ($\times 10^{-3}$)	Accuracy (%)	F1 score	MCC ($\times 10^{-3}$)
Graph WaveNet [40]	50.94 ± 0.15	60.51 ± 1.10	5.50 ± 1.00	50.86 ± 0.13	57.28 ± 1.86	11.12 ± 2.21
MTGODE [17]	51.41 ± 0.15	62.41 ± 4.24	5.92 ± 2.61	52.35 ± 0.17	62.73 ± 1.72	20.62 ± 5.76
STGCL [24]	50.56 ± 0.08	57.81 ± 1.19	**9.71 ± 1.15**	51.21 ± 0.05	67.47 ± 0.07	22.33 ± 1.53
EvolveGCN [30]	50.19 ± 0.02	56.94 ± 0.21	4.41 ± 0.76	51.14 ± 0.15	66.85 ± 0.37	14.41 ± 0.45
Null Model	47.58	51.24	−54.40	48.84	52.98	−31.20
DGRCL (Ours)	**53.06 ± 0.18**	**66.53 ± 2.74**	9.32 ± 1.53	**54.07 ± 0.20**	**67.53 ± 0.19**	**27.51 ± 5.52**

5.4 Evaluation Metric

Following the approaches taken in previous studies [7,18,34,45], we evaluate model performance using classification accuracy, F1 score, and Matthews Correlation Coefficient (MCC). For all three metrics, higher values indicate better model performance. We record the time taken for each training epoch of the models in seconds.

5.5 Evaluation Result

RQ1. Performance Comparison. The experimental results in Table 2 show that our model outperforms all other baseline models in terms of accuracy and F1 score, and is also comparable to the baseline models in terms of MCC. For the NASDAQ dataset, DGRCL achieves the highest accuracy at 53.06%, surpassing the second-best MTGODE by 1.65%. Additionally, DGRCL attains the top F1 score of 66.53% and a strong MCC value of 9.32, nearly matching the best MCC of 9.71. On the NYSE dataset, DGRCL similarly outperforms other methods, with an accuracy of 54.07%, an F1 score of 67.53%, and a substantial MCC of 27.51, marking the highest recorded metrics across all models. The notable discrepancy where MTGODE exhibits a high F1 score but a lower MCC indicates the model may handle accuracy and recall well for the majority class but struggles with the minority class, affecting its overall prediction quality. A similar finding is also shown in the performance of EvolveGCN on the NYSE dataset.

Moreover, we observe that the accuracy of all baseline methods is not very high, being only slightly better than 50%, which deviates significantly from the experimental results described in their respective papers. A reasonable explanation for this inconsistency is that the nodes and the temporal span of their datasets are relatively small. As a result, their models may be unable to effectively learn the representations of large-scale graph models over long time series. For instance, in the datasets used by Graph WaveNet and STGCL, the number of nodes is 207 and 325, respectively, which is far smaller than the 1026 and 1737 nodes in our dataset. Similarly, in the dataset used by MTGODE, the largest

Table 3. Ablation study on the two datasets. We replace the Embedding Enhancement module and Contrastive Constrained Training module in DGRCL with their discrete implementations, denoted w/o EE and w/o CCT. We further remove all proposed modules except dynamic graphs for training as w/o EE & CCT. Table adapted from our previous work [32].

Methods	NASDAQ dataset			NYSE dataset		
	Accuracy (%)	F1 score	MCC ($\times 10^{-3}$)	Accuracy (%)	F1 score	MCC ($\times 10^{-3}$)
DGRCL	**53.06 ± 0.18**	**66.53 ± 2.74**	**9.32 ± 1.53**	**54.07 ± 0.20**	**67.53 ± 0.19**	**27.51 ± 5.52**
w/o EE	51.45 ± 0.03	62.48 ± 1.19	4.69 ± 0.02	52.77 ± 0.05	62.95 ± 1.40	21.88 ± 2.35
w/o CCT	52.69 ± 0.32	65.61 ± 0.22	5.78 ± 1.07	53.87 ± 0.11	67.34 ± 0.18	23.12 ± 1.77
w/o EE & CCT	51.08 ± 0.12	57.43 ± 1.22	2.91 ± 0.26	51.65 ± 0.21	64.12 ± 0.19	7.61 ± 2.11

sample size is 52,560, which is much smaller than the smallest sample size in our study 626,886 (1026 × 611).

RQ2. Ablation Study. To verify the effectiveness of each component of DGRCL, we conducted ablation studies on the two datasets (see Table 3). The complete DGRCL model incorporates EE and CCT, exhibiting the highest performance in all metrics. When both EE and CCT are removed (w/o EE & CCT), DGRCL has the most significant performance drop, with accuracy falling to 51.08% and 51.65%, the F1 score to 57.43 and 64.12, and the MCC to 2.91 and 7.61 in the NASDAQ and NYSE datasets respectively.

From the result we can find that, by incorporating the EE module, DGRCL experiences a significant improvement, nearly doubling the MCC score on both datasets. This indicates that the EE module enables the model to learn more effective latent features of the time series, thereby enhancing its predictive performance. Another observation is that the CCT module alone does not result in a significant improvement in model performance and is less effective compared to adding the EE module alone. Nonetheless, when both modules are combined, they greatly enhance the overall performance of the model. This suggests that the model achieves optimal predictive results by learning the dynamic temporal relationships and the static relationships in the graph data.

RQ3. Hyperparameter Sensitivity. We explore the sensitivity of two important hyperparameters: the overall probability of removing edges p_e and the cutoff threshold p_τ. These two hyperparameters directly affect the performance of the CCT module and further impact the overall performance of the DGRCL. Here, we use the global evaluation metric F1 score to reflect the overall performance of different combinations of these hyperparameters. Results are presented in Fig. 5. We make the following observations.

When both p_e and p_τ are set at their maximum or minimum values simultaneously, overall performance is poor, with the F1 score in both datasets falling below 50. This indicates that finding a balance between these two hyperparameters is crucial to improving the model's predictive performance. The second

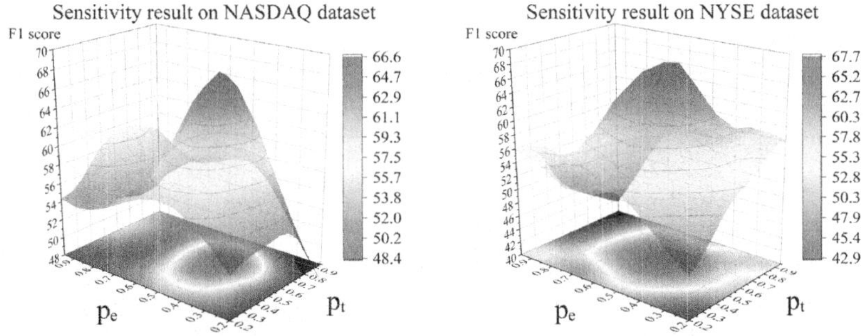

Fig. 5. Sensitivity study of the overall probability of removing edges p_e and the cut-off threshold p_τ via F1 score. Figure adapted from our previous work [32].

Table 4. Run-time complexity of the experiments. Table adapted from our previous work [32]

Model	Dataset	Epoch Training Time (s)	Model	Dataset	Epoch Training Time (s)
Graph WaveNet	NASDAQ	1.63	DGRCL w/o EE	NASDAQ	406.53
	NYSE	3.14		NYSE	485.38
MTGODE	NASDAQ	13.22	DGRCL w/o CCT	NASDAQ	42.58
	NYSE	29.96		NYSE	96.43
STGCL	NASDAQ	2.12	DGRCL w/o EE&CCT	NASDAQ	41.79
	NYSE	3.17		NYSE	80.06
EvolveGCN	NASDAQ	24.63	DGRCL (Full)	NASDAQ	414.05
	NYSE	38.25		NYSE	505.54

finding is that p_e is more important than p_τ, as it determines the dynamic lower bound in Eq. (7). If p_τ is set very low, $P\{(i,j) \in \mathcal{E}\}$ becomes a fixed value equal to $1 - p_\tau$. This indicates that all edges have the same existence probability, resulting in random remaining. Another observation is that, Compared to the NASDAQ dataset, the NYSE dataset has a larger optimal hyperparameter space, making it easier to find local optima during model training. Previous financial papers [16,22] also support this finding, noting that the NASDAQ market is more volatile, leading to a smaller optimal hyperparameter space.

Complexity. Table 4 compares the training times per epoch (in seconds) of various models on the NASDAQ and NYSE datasets. Our model, DGRCL, generally has significantly higher training times compared to other models. For example, Graph WaveNet and STGCL require only 1.63 s and 2.12 s per epoch on NASDAQ, respectively, while DGRCL without embedding enhancement (EE) and contrastive constrained training (CCT) takes 41.79 s. The full DGRCL model, which includes these enhancements, requires 414.05 s on NASDAQ and 505.54 s on NYSE.

Notably, adding the CCT unit significantly increases the training time, accounting for around 90% of the total run-time, which indicates that the graph

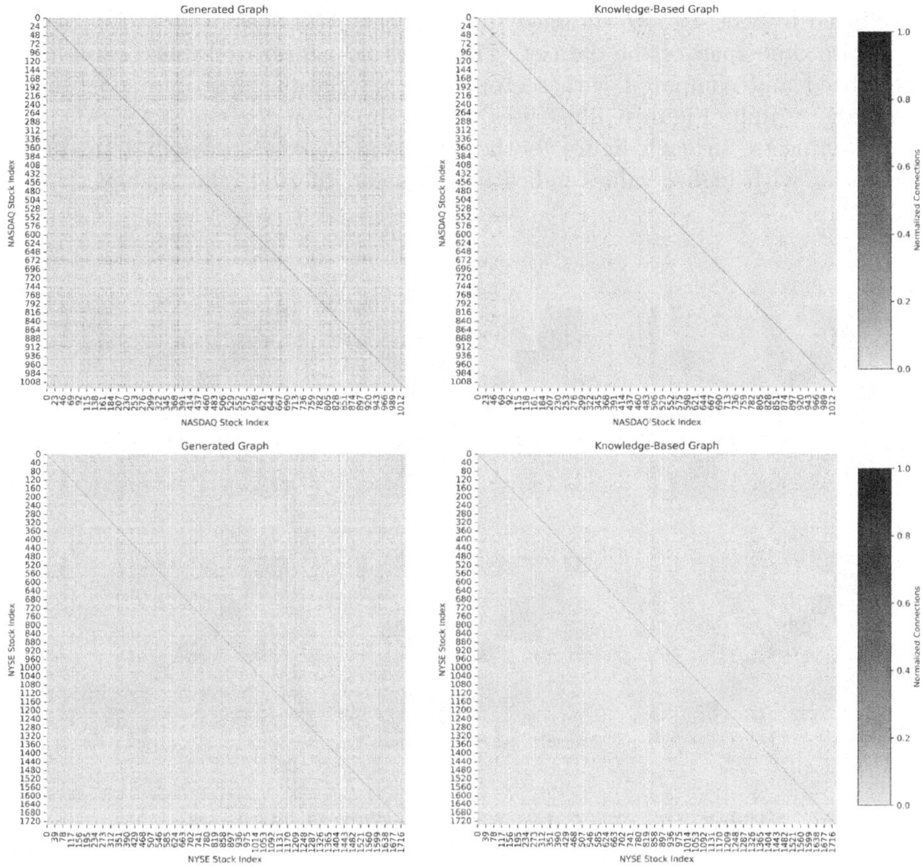

Fig. 6. Aggregated adjacency matrix based on volume-based graph construction (left), compared against sector-industry structure (right). Left column: generated graph; right column: knowledge-based graph. Top row: NASDAQ; bottom row: NYSE.

contrastive learning component is the main source of computational overhead. However, as shown in the comparison between Table 2 and Table 3, even without the CCT module, DGRCL still outperforms the baselines in terms of accuracy. This demonstrates that our framework performs well without relying on the computationally expensive CCT module. While DGRCL offers improved prediction performance, this high computation cost, particularly from the CCT module, suggests a need for further optimization to balance performance and efficiency, especially in large-scale applications.

5.6 Empirical Study

Evaluation of Graph Construction. To evaluate the effectiveness of the graph construction method based on Zipf's law using stock trading volumes, as introduced in Sect. 4.1, we summed the adjacency matrices of all stocks across the entire time span of the dataset. The resulting aggregated matrix was then normalized and compared with sector-industry relationships obtained from a knowledge graph. Figure 6 illustrates this comparison for the NASDAQ and NYSE datasets. In each figure, both the x and y axes correspond to different stocks, with higher values indicating stronger inferred relationships. It can

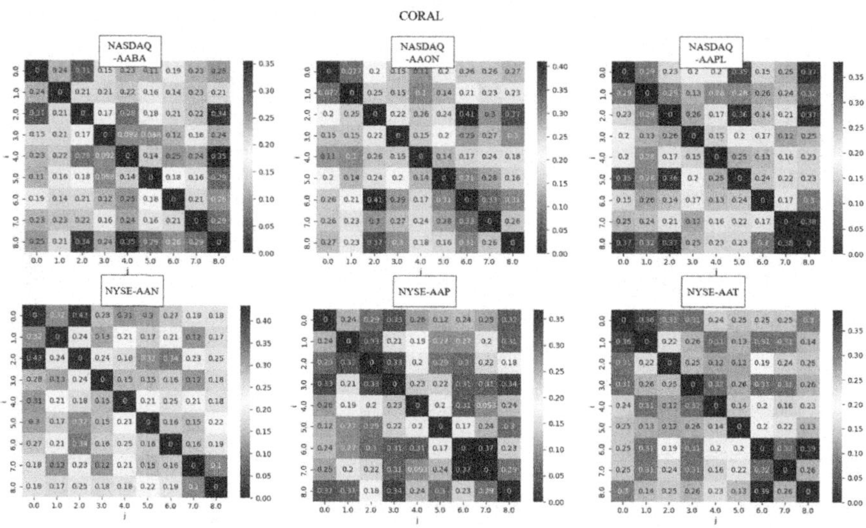

Fig. 7. Distance Calculation using CORAL divergence.

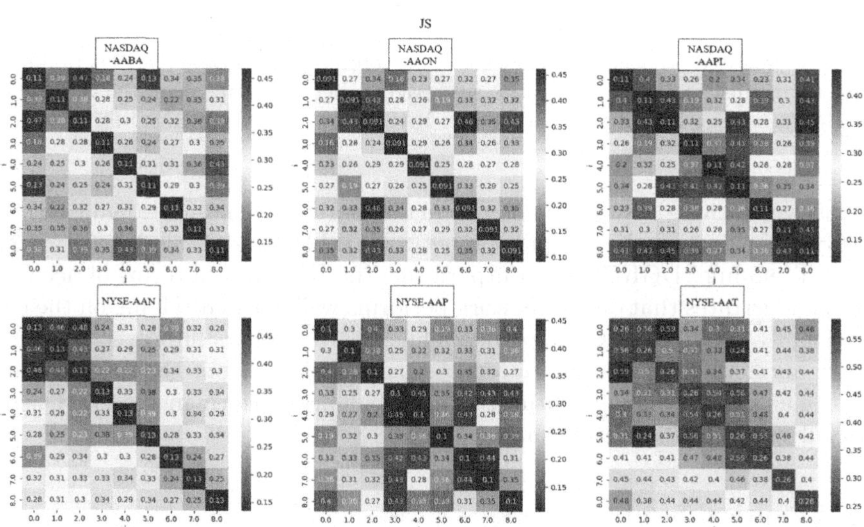

Fig. 8. Distance Calculation Jensen-Shannon divergence.

be observed that the graph structure constructed solely from trading volumes is comparable to the known graph structure derived from the knowledge graph, while also capturing additional information. Higher normalized values represent deeper intrinsic relationships between stocks, which can provide the model with a broader perceptual domain during training, thereby improving training effectiveness.

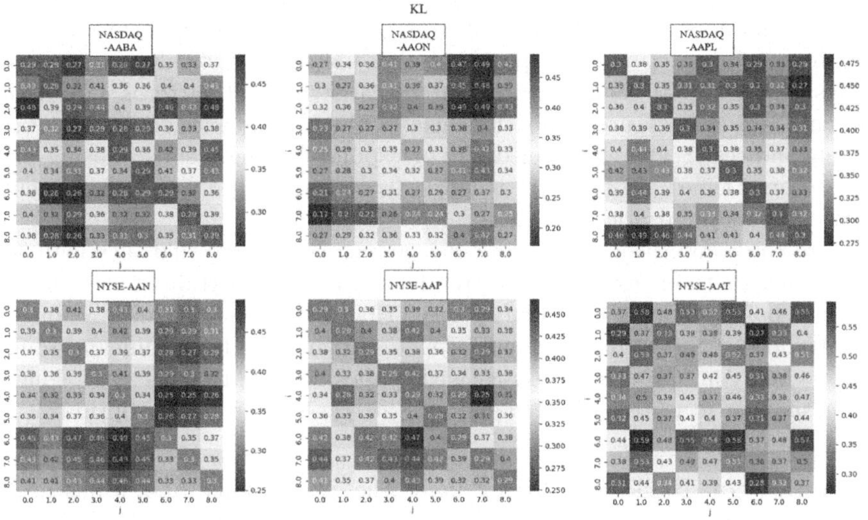

Fig. 9. Distance Calculation using Kullback-Leibler divergence.

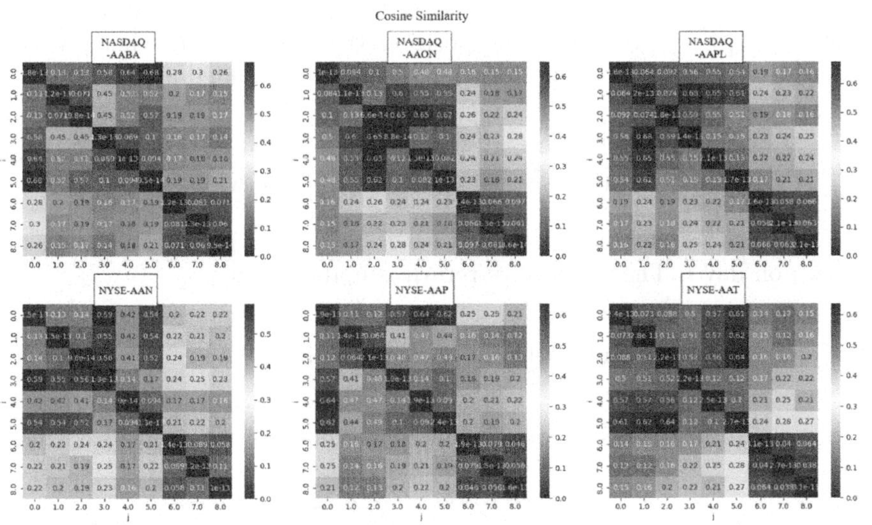

Fig. 10. Distance Calculation using cosine similarity.

Evaluation of Feature Optimization. As introduced in Eq. (5), the metric $d(\cdot)$ can represent a broad class of distributional distance or similarity measures. To determine the most appropriate choice for our contrastive learning framework, we conduct an empirical comparison using Fourier-transformed closing price data from a representative set of NASDAQ and NYSE stocks. Specifically, we assess four widely used metrics: CORAL divergence [36], JensenShannon (JS) divergence, KullbackLeibler (KL) divergence, and cosine similarity.

Each evaluation is repeated 20 randomized shuffles to ensure robustness. Pairwise distances are computed and aggregated across these runs to assess the consistency and discriminative power of each metric. The results are visualized in Figs. 7, 8 9 and 10 as heatmaps that reveal structural patterns captured by different distance measures. In each heatmap, the x and y axes denote time series segment indices. Segments labeled 02 correspond to long trends (closing prices increase over time), 35 to short trends (decreasing prices), and 68 to neutral trends with minimal price change.

From the comparison of the four heatmaps, we observe that although some of the other methods exhibit weak trend separation on certain stocks, only the heatmap based on cosine similarity (Fig. 10) clearly distinguishes among the three trend categories. In particular, cosine similarity yields significantly higher values when comparing time series with opposing trend labels (e.g., long vs. short), making it a more suitable distance metric for our feature optimization.

Evaluation of Backtest. To evaluate the profitability and robustness of DGRCL, we conduct a backtest on the NYSE dataset covering 236 valid trading days. The model outputs binary portfolio decisions, where each entry in the prediction matrix indicates whether to take a long position (1) or hold cash (0) for a given stock on a particular day, so we build our trading strategy.

Let $P_t \in \{0,1\}^N$ represent the position vector for day t, where N is the number of stocks. The portfolio return at time t is computed as:

$$r_t = \begin{cases} \frac{1}{|S_t|} \sum_{i \in S_t} \left(\frac{p_{t,i}}{p_{t-1,i}} - 1 \right), & \text{if } |S_t| > 0 \\ 0, & \text{otherwise} \end{cases}$$

where S_t is the set of selected stocks with $P_{t,i} = 1$, and $p_{t,i}$ is the closing price of stock i on day t. The cumulative return is updated via:

$$\text{Cumulative Return}_t = \prod_{\tau=1}^{t} (1 + r_\tau)$$

To evaluate risk-adjusted performance, we compute the annualized Sharpe ratio:

$$\text{Sharpe Ratio} = \frac{\mu_r}{\sigma_r} \cdot \sqrt{252}$$

where μ_r and σ_r denote the mean and standard deviation of daily returns, respectively.

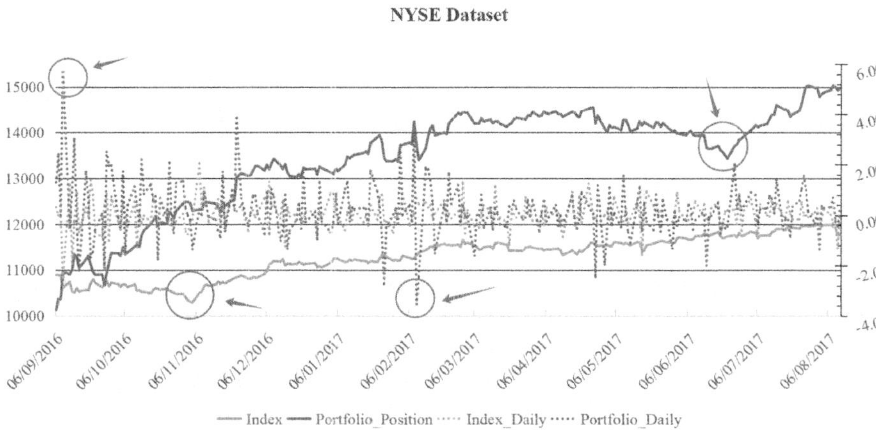

Fig. 11. Backtesting performance on the NYSE dataset. The left y-axis shows the actual NYSE index value (green solid line) and the model-generated portfolio value (dark red solid line), assuming a $10,000 initial investment. The right y-axis presents daily return rates: NYSE index daily change (green dotted line) and the proposed method's daily return (dark red dotted line). (Color figure online)

Table 5. Backtesting performance comparison.

Metric	DGRCL-based Strategy	NYSE Index
Mean Daily Return	0.18%	0.04%
Std. Daily Return	1.07%	0.54%
Sharpe Ratio	2.64	1.04
Cumulative Return	49.83%	8.36%

Figure 11 compares the cumulative return and daily return series of our model against the NYSE index. From the first circled region in Fig. 11, we observe that the highest single-day return occurred on September 9, 2016, when the NYSE index fell sharply. On that day, the portfolio achieved a return of 5.67%, while the market return was −2.47%, indicating the effectiveness of our strategy under volatile market conditions. The second circled region marks a local bottom in the market, during which the return volatility of our strategy also declined. This suggests that the strategy's return dynamics adapt to broader market trends. The third circled region corresponds to the lowest single-day return of the strategy, which was -3.52% on February 9, 2017. The previous day's return was 3.53%, while the NYSE index recorded 0.07% and 0.67% returns on those days, respectively. This points to potential improvements in the management of drawdown risks. Finally, the last circled area highlights a local dip in the cumulative return curve, caused by several consecutive days of negative predicted returns. This suggests that enhancing the model with more diverse trading strategies could improve resilience in such scenarios.

Table 5 summarizes the performance during the backtest period, showing that our DGRCL framework outperforms the NYSE index on every metric, with much higher cumulative returns (49.84% compared to 8.36%) and much higher Sharpe ratio (2.64 compared to 1.04). These quantitative results further support the effectiveness of the strategy built from our proposed method.

6 Conclusion

In this work, we present DGRCL, a novel Dynamic Graph Representation with Contrastive Learning framework designed to capture the evolving complexity of financial markets. Unlike traditional methods that separately handle temporal and structural patterns, DGRCL integrates both dynamic and static relations through two modules: the Embedding Enhancement (EE) module and the Contrastive Constrained Training (CCT) module. The EE module adaptively models temporal evolution using dynamic graph construction guided by Zipf's law and Fourier-based feature optimization, while the CCT module introduces static company relations as contrastive constraints to regularize the learned representations in latent space. Together, these innovations enable DGRCL to learn richer and more robust representations for stock movement prediction.

Through extensive empirical evaluations on two large-scale stock market datasets (NASDAQ and NYSE), we demonstrated that DGRCL outperforms existing state-of-the-art baselines across multiple metrics. Additional analyses, including graph construction interpretability, feature optimization evaluation, and backtesting, further validate the effectiveness, stability, and financial viability of our approach in real-world trading scenarios.

Looking ahead, we plan to extend DGRCL in several directions. First, we aim to improve the disentanglement of static and dynamic graph components within the contrastive learning framework, enabling more fine-grained temporal reasoning. Second, we intend to expand our evaluations to international financial markets such as the Shanghai Stock Exchange, enhancing the generalizability of our model. Lastly, we will investigate more efficient and scalable graph contrastive learning techniques to reduce computational overhead and facilitate real-time deployment in practical trading systems.

Ultimately, our long-term goal is to develop real-world applications that provide personalised investment advice and automation services. These services will be offered at the individual level using mobile smart agent applications (for details, refer to the AI for Collective Intelligence research strategy [4]) and at the market level by developing a platform that offers users access to the kind of automated investment strategies that are typically reserved for internal use within financial institutions (for initial work on the development of an automated investment platform, see [31,44]). These research avenues align with the regulatory goals of increasing fairness, transparency, and retail participation in financial markets and will help deliver real-world impact.

Acknowledgements. This work was supported by UKRI EPSRC Grant No. EP/Y028392/1: AI for Collective Intelligence (AI4CI); and UKRI Innovate UK Project

No. 10094067: Stratlib.AI - A Trusted Machine Learning Platform for Asset and Credit managers. The authors have no conflict of interest to declare.

References

1. Ayala, J., García-Torres, M., Noguera, J.L.V., Gómez-Vela, F., Divina, F.: Technical analysis strategy optimization using a machine learning approach in stock market indices. Knowl.-Based Syst. **225**, 107119 (2021). https://doi.org/10.1016/j.knosys.2021.107119
2. Barabási, A.L., Albert, R.: Emergence of scaling in random networks. Science **286**(5439), 509–512 (1999). https://doi.org/10.1126/science.286.5439.509
3. Bloomfield, P.: Fourier Analysis of Time Series: An Introduction. Wiley (2004). https://doi.org/10.1002/0471722235
4. Bullock, S., et al.: Artificial intelligence for collective intelligence: A national-scale research strategy. Knowl. Eng. Rev. **39**, e10 (2024). https://doi.org/10.1017/S0269888924000110
5. Chen, S., Ge, L.: Exploring the attention mechanism in LSTM-based Hong Kong stock price movement prediction. Quant. Financ. **19**(9), 1507–1515 (2019). https://doi.org/10.1080/14697688.2019.1622287
6. Cochran, W.T., et al.: What is the fast Fourier transform? Proc. IEEE **55**(10), 1664–1674 (1967). https://doi.org/10.1109/PROC.1967.5957
7. Deng, S., Zhang, N., Zhang, W., Chen, J., Pan, J.Z., Chen, H.: Knowledge-driven stock trend prediction and explanation via temporal convolutional network. In: Companion Proceedings of The 2019 World Wide Web Conference, pp. 678–685 (2019). https://doi.org/10.1145/3308560.3317701
8. Du, Y., et al.: AdaRNN: adaptive learning and forecasting of time series. In: Proceedings of the 30th ACM International Conference on Information & Knowledge Management, pp. 402–411 (2021). https://doi.org/10.1145/3459637.3482315
9. Feng, F., He, X., Wang, X., Luo, C., Liu, Y., Chua, T.S.: Temporal relational ranking for stock prediction. ACM Trans. Inf. Syst. (TOIS) **37**(2), 1–30 (2019). https://doi.org/10.1145/3309547
10. Gao, J., Ying, X., Xu, C., Wang, J., Zhang, S., Li, Z.: Graph-based stock recommendation by time-aware relational attention network. ACM Trans. Knowl. Discov. Data (TKDD) **16**(1), 1–21 (2021). https://doi.org/10.1145/3451397
11. Hassani, K., Khasahmadi, A.H.: Contrastive multi-view representation learning on graphs. In: International Conference on Machine Learning, pp. 4116–4126 (2020). https://proceedings.mlr.press/v119/hassani20a.html
12. Hsu, Y.L., Tsai, Y.C., Li, C.T.: FinGAT: financial graph attention networks for recommending top-k profitable stocks. IEEE Trans. Knowl. Data Eng. **35**(1), 469–481 (2021). https://doi.org/10.1109/TKDE.2021.3079496
13. Huynh, T.T., et al.: Efficient integration of multi-order dynamics and internal dynamics in stock movement prediction. In: Proceedings of the Sixteenth ACM International Conference on Web Search and Data Mining, pp. 850–858 (2023). https://doi.org/10.1145/3539597.3570427
14. Jaynes, E.T.: On the rationale of maximum-entropy methods. Proc. IEEE **70**(9), 939–952 (1982). https://doi.org/10.1109/PROC.1982.12425
15. Jeong, Y.S., Jeong, M.K., Omitaomu, O.A.: Weighted dynamic time warping for time series classification. Pattern Recogn. **44**(9), 2231–2240 (2011). https://doi.org/10.1016/j.patcog.2010.09.022

16. Jiang, C.X., Kim, J.C., Wood, R.A.: A comparison of volatility and bid-ask spread for NASDAQ and NYSE after decimalization. Appl. Econ. **43**(10), 1227–1239 (2011). https://doi.org/10.1080/00036840802600376
17. Jin, M., Zheng, Y., Li, Y.F., Chen, S., Yang, B., Pan, S.: Multivariate time series forecasting with dynamic graph neural ODEs. IEEE Trans. Knowl. Data Eng. **35**(9), 9168–9180 (2022). https://doi.org/10.1109/TKDE.2022.3221989
18. Kim, R., So, C.H., Jeong, M., Lee, S., Kim, J., Kang, J.: HATS: a hierarchical graph attention network for stock movement prediction. arXiv preprint arXiv:1908.07999 (2019). https://doi.org/10.48550/arXiv.1908.07999
19. Kim, T., Kim, J., Tae, Y., Park, C., Choi, J.H., Choo, J.: Reversible instance normalization for accurate time-series forecasting against distribution shift. In: International Conference on Learning Representations (2021). https://openreview.net/forum?id=cGDAkQo1C0p
20. Kipf, T.N., Welling, M.: Semi-supervised classification with graph convolutional networks. In: International Conference on Learning Representations (2017). https://doi.org/10.48550/arXiv.1609.02907
21. Li, C., Song, D., Tao, D.: Multi-task recurrent neural networks and higher-order Markov random fields for stock price movement prediction: Multi-task RNN and higher-order MRFs for stock price classification. In: Proceedings of the 25th ACM SIGKDD International Conference on Knowledge Discovery & Data Mining, pp. 1141–1151 (2019). https://doi.org/10.1145/3292500.3330983
22. Lian, Y.M., Jhong, Y.J., Wang, P.H., Chen, W.M.: An empirical examination of VIX market fluctuations. Adv. Manage. Appl. Econ. **12**(4), 1–6 (2022). https://doi.org/10.47260/amae/1246
23. Liu, C., Yan, J., Guo, F., Guo, M.: Forecasting the market with machine learning algorithms: an application of NMC-BERT-LSTM-DQN-X algorithm in quantitative trading. ACM Trans. Knowl. Discov. Data (TKDD) **16**(4), 1–22 (2022). https://doi.org/10.1145/3488378
24. Liu, X., Liang, Y., Huang, C., Zheng, Y., Hooi, B., Zimmermann, R.: When do contrastive learning signals help spatio-temporal graph forecasting? In: Proceedings of the 30th International Conference on Advances in Geographic Information Systems, pp. 1–12 (2022). https://doi.org/10.1145/3557915.3560939
25. Liu, Y., Jin, M., Pan, S., Zhou, C., Zheng, Y., Xia, F., Philip, S.Y.: Graph self-supervised learning: a survey. IEEE Trans. Knowl. Data Eng. **35**(6), 5879–5900 (2022). https://doi.org/10.1109/TKDE.2022.3172903
26. Matsunaga, D., Suzumura, T., Takahashi, T.: Exploring graph neural networks for stock market predictions with rolling window analysis. In: Proceedings of the NeurIPS Workshop on Machine Learning for Finance (NeurIPS 2019) (2019). https://doi.org/10.48550/arXiv.1909.10660
27. Mostafavi, S.M., Hooman, A.R.: Key technical indicators for stock market prediction. Mach. Learn. Appl. **20**, 100631 (2025). https://doi.org/10.1016/j.mlwa.2025.100631
28. Newman, M.: Networks, 2nd edn. Oxford University Press, Oxford (2018). https://doi.org/10.1093/oso/9780198805090.001.0001
29. Newman, M.E.: Power laws, Pareto distributions and Zipf's law. Contemp. Phys. **46**(5), 323–351 (2005). https://doi.org/10.1080/00107510500052444
30. Pareja, A., et al.: EvolveGCN: evolving graph convolutional networks for dynamic graphs. In: Proceedings of the AAAI Conference on Artificial Intelligence, vol. 34, pp. 5363–5370 (2020). https://doi.org/10.1609/aaai.v34i04.5984

31. Pei, Y., Cartlidge, J., Mandal, A., Gold, D., Marcilio, E., Mazzon, R.: Cross-modal temporal fusion for financial market forecasting. arXiv:2504.13522 (2025). https://doi.org/10.48550/arXiv.2504.13522
32. Pei, Y., Zheng, J., Cartlidge, J.: Dynamic graph representation with contrastive learning for financial market prediction: integrating temporal evolution and static relations. In: 17th International Conference on Agents and Artificial Intelligence (ICAART), vol. 2, pp. 298–309 (2025). https://doi.org/10.5220/0013154700003890
33. Sawhney, R., Agarwal, S., Wadhwa, A., Derr, T., Shah, R.R.: Stock selection via spatiotemporal hypergraph attention network: A learning to rank approach. In: Proceedings of the AAAI Conference on Artificial Intelligence, vol. 35, pp. 497–504 (2021). https://doi.org/10.1609/aaai.v35i1.16127
34. Sawhney, R., Agarwal, S., Wadhwa, A., Shah, R.: Deep attentive learning for stock movement prediction from social media text and company correlations. In: Proceedings of the 2020 Conference on Empirical Methods in Natural Language Processing (EMNLP), pp. 8415–8426 (2020). https://doi.org/10.18653/v1/2020.emnlp-main.676
35. Sawhney, R., Agarwal, S., Wadhwa, A., Shah, R.: Exploring the scale-free nature of stock markets: hyperbolic graph learning for algorithmic trading. In: Proceedings of the Web Conference 2021, pp. 11–22 (2021). https://doi.org/10.1145/3442381.3450095
36. Sun, B., Saenko, K.: Deep CORAL: correlation alignment for deep domain adaptation. In: Hua, G., Jégou, H. (eds.) ECCV 2016. LNCS, vol. 9915, pp. 443–450. Springer, Cham (2016). https://doi.org/10.1007/978-3-319-49409-8_35
37. Velickovic, P., Fedus, W., Hamilton, W.L., Liò, P., Bengio, Y., Hjelm, R.D.: Deep graph infomax. arXiv preprint arXiv:1809.10341 (2019)
38. Wang, H., Wang, T., Li, S., Zheng, J., Guan, S., Chen, W.: Adaptive long-short pattern transformer for stock investment selection. In: Proceedings of the Thirty-First International Joint Conference on Artificial Intelligence, IJCAI, pp. 3970–3977 (2022). https://doi.org/10.24963/ijcai.2022/551
39. Wang, J., Sun, T., Liu, B., Cao, Y., Zhu, H.: CLVSA: a convolutional LSTM based variational sequence-to-sequence model with attention for predicting trends of financial markets. In: Proceedings of the Twenty-Eighth International Joint Conference on Artificial Intelligence, IJCAI, pp. 3705–3711 (2019). https://doi.org/10.24963/ijcai.2019/514
40. Wu, Z., Pan, S., Long, G., Jiang, J., Zhang, C.: Graph WaveNet for deep spatial-temporal graph modeling. In: Proceedings of the 28th International Joint Conference on Artificial Intelligence, IJCAI, pp. 1907–1913 (2019). https://doi.org/10.24963/ijcai.2019/264
41. Xu, W., et al.: HIST: a graph-based framework for stock trend forecasting via mining concept-oriented shared information. arXiv preprint arXiv:2110.13716 (2021). https://doi.org/10.48550/arXiv.2110.13716
42. Yin, T., Liu, C., Ding, F., Feng, Z., Yuan, B., Zhang, N.: Graph-based stock correlation and prediction for high-frequency trading systems. Pattern Recogn. **122**, 108209 (2022). https://doi.org/10.1016/j.patcog.2021.108209
43. You, Y., Chen, T., Sui, Y., Chen, T., Wang, Z., Shen, Y.: Graph contrastive learning with augmentations. Adv. Neural Inf. Process. Syst. **33**, 5812–5823 (2020). https://doi.org/10.5555/3495724.3496212
44. You, Z., Cartlidge, J., Elliott, K., Ge, M., Gold, D.: Risk-aware black-box portfolio construction using Bayesian optimization with adaptive weighted Lagrangian estimator. arXiv:2504.13529 (2025). https://doi.org/10.48550/arXiv.2504.13529

45. You, Z., Shi, Z., Bo, H., Cartlidge, J., Zhang, L., Ge, Y.: DGDNN: decoupled graph diffusion neural network for stock movement prediction. In: 16th International Conference on Agents and Artificial Intelligence (ICAART), vol. 2, pp. 431–442 (2024). https://doi.org/10.5220/0012406400003636
46. You, Z., Zhang, P., Zheng, J., Cartlidge, J.: Multi-relational graph diffusion neural network with parallel retention for stock trends classification. In: 49th IEEE International Conference on Acoustics, Speech and Signal Processing (ICASSP), pp. 6545–6549. IEEE (2024). https://doi.org/10.1109/ICASSP48485.2024.10447394
47. Zhang, H., et al.: Iterative graph self-distillation. IEEE Trans. Knowl. Data Eng. **36**, 1161–1169 (2023). https://doi.org/10.1109/TKDE.2023.3303885
48. Zhao, Y., et al.: Stock movement prediction based on bi-typed hybrid-relational market knowledge graph via dual attention networks. IEEE Trans. Knowl. Data Eng. (2022). https://doi.org/10.1109/TKDE.2022.3220520
49. Zhou, F., Zhou, H.m., Yang, Z., Yang, L.: EMD2FNN: a strategy combining empirical mode decomposition and factorization machine based neural network for stock market trend prediction. Expert Syst. Appl. **115**, 136–151 (2019). https://doi.org/10.1016/j.eswa.2018.07.065
50. Zhu, Y., Xu, Y., Yu, F., Liu, Q., Wu, S., Wang, L.: Graph contrastive learning with adaptive augmentation. In: WWW Proceedings of the Web Conference, pp. 2069–2080 (2021). https://doi.org/10.1145/3442381.3449802

Robust Machine Learning for Harsh Environments: A Framework and Evaluation of Key Architectural Choices

William Dennis(✉) and James Pope

Intelligent Systems Laboratory, University of Bristol, Bristol, UK
wwdennis.home@gmail.com

Abstract. Machine Learning algorithms are envisioned to be used in harsh and/or safety-critical environments such as self-driving cars, aerospace, and nuclear sites where the effects of radiation can cause errors in electronics known as Single Event Effects (SEEs). The consequence of SEEs on machine learning models, such as neural networks composed of millions of parameters, is currently unknown. Understanding the models in terms of robustness and reliability is essential for their use in these environments. To facilitate this understanding, we propose a novel framework to simulate SEEs during model training and inference. Using the framework with different error models, we evaluate an exemplary Convolutional Neural Network (CNN) architecture and the Vision Transformer (ViT) architecture. For the CNN architecture, we investigate robustness with varying dropout, regularisation, and activation functions. We then propose design decisions, specifically the choice of activation function and pooling approach, to improve the model's robustness. For the ViT architecture, we again investigate robustness using the framework. We find that the ViT is less robust than the CNN architectures considered with a higher drop in accuracy from the baseline (0.5840 vs 0.4042). We call this reduction the test delta. Overall, our results confirm the efficacy of the framework for evaluating model robustness in harsh environments.

Keywords: Robust Machine Learning · Fault Tolerance · Harsh Environments · Single Event Effects

1 Introduction

Deep learning architectures have shifted the paradigm from traditional, well-understood image processing methods towards less-understood models. The black-box nature of these state-of-the-art models presents concerns for critical applications that are exposed to harsh environmental effects. These are traditionally termed *Single Event Effects* (SEEs). The focus of this research is to develop and evaluate a framework for evaluating these complex models via simulated SEEs. SEEs are disruptions in electronic devices, often attributed to radiation, that could result in changes to the software running. Understanding how

H. J. van den Herik et al. (Eds.): ICAART 2025, LNAI 16517, pp. 213–235, 2026.
https://doi.org/10.1007/978-3-032-25032-2_10

Machine Learning (ML) models behave under SEEs is vital for safety-critical applications, such as driverless systems.

Documented instances of electronic failure due to radiation include satellite communications [4], aircraft travelling at high altitudes [1], and computer games [34]. Robustness in ML systems are therefore a key requirement that has typically been referred to as the performance of a model under attacks to the input data. On the other hand, attacks to the parameter space in ML models are far less explored and do not fit under the adversarial robustness umbrella.

Convolutional Neural Networks (CNNs) are commonly used for image classification. AlexNet, a deep neural network (DNN), was introduced in 2012 and won the ImageNet Large Scale Visual Recognition Challenge [18]. AlexNet consisted of over 60 million parameters across 5 convolutional layers and 3 fully connected layers. These models are able to learn hierarchical representations of data with every layer abstracting features from the raw inputs. Subsequent models increased the number and complexity of the layers. More recently, Vision Transformers (denoted *ViTs*) have been used for similar image classification tasks with comparable performance [9]. ViTs divide the image into fixed-size patches, flatten them, and process them like a sequence of tokens using the Transformer encoder (originally designed for natural language processing tasks). These models also have a very large number of parameters. For example, the base ViT model has 88 million parameters across 12 encoding blocks [20]. DNNs and Transformers, with their many layers and huge parameter space, further exemplify the black box narrative.

There is limited research on SEE perturbations to the weights and biases of the CNN and ViT architectures. Research on SEEs is an extremely challenging area as the natural phenomena occurs at a very low probability, making experimentation very hard. Facilities, such as ChipIr can artificially generate SEE-like particles to perform beam experiments. This experimentation can produce more than 30 million years of natural irradiation in 241 h [26]. Although this speeds up the natural process exponentially, experimentation is limited by the availability of these devices. Alternative approaches have looked towards fault injection software to simulate SEEs [11] but there is no standardised solution. These beam-experiments also focus on the sensitivity of hardware, and therefore suggest hardware solutions, with minimal regard to high-level radiation hardening techniques.

Our previous research [8], began to address this gap by exploring how CNN design choices influence the robustness to SEEs. In this research we summarise these results and add a comprehensive analysis of the ViT architecture. The contributions of the paper are as follows:

- Novel framework for evaluating neural networks in harsh environments[1].
- Propose two novel activation functions that are shown to be more robust to SEE related errors.
- Propose novel pooling layer that is also shown to be more robust to SEE related errors.

[1] Source code is available at https://github.com/wd7512/seu-injection-framework.

2 Background

2.1 History of SEEs and Motivation

The idea of SEEs were first suggested [36] in 1962. In the 1970s, SEEs were known to disrupt spacecraft. Binder, Smith and Holman produced foundational work with their 1975 paper "Satellite Anomalies from Galactic Cosmic Rays" [4]. The authors detailed SEEs in operating satellites and explored the mechanisms by which cosmic rays impact microelectronics, resulting in satellite communication anomalies. Spacecraft are one example of SEEs in harsh environments. SEEs have also been shown to occur in everyday environments. A harmless example popularised by the media was a Mario speedrunning tournament where player was aided by a bit change (bitflip) in the memory of the computer running the game [34]. A more disastrous case was in 2008, during the flight of an Airbus A330 between Singapore and Perth. SEEs sadly resulted in 12 serious injuries when the A330 started nose-diving on two separate occasions [1,2]. Mitigation techniques are essential to enabling the use of electronics in these environments.

The miniaturisation of electronics exacerbates the problem. Transistors are the basic building block of electronics and have increasing sensitivity to SEEs as miniaturisation progresses. Moore's law states that the number of transistors on an integrated circuit doubles approximately every two years [21]. This has generally held true since the idea in 1965 with the modern day 3nm process transistors being less than 50nm in length [3]. The sensitivity arises from the critical charge required to change the state of the transistor being proportional to the size. Therefore as electronic devices become more powerful with more transistors, smaller transistors and higher transistor density, ionizing radiation requires less energy to induce an SEE. Consequently, the number of SEEs are expected to increase.

2.2 SEEs and Transistors

Edward Peterson defines SEEs as the action of a single ionizing particle as it penetrates sensitive nodes within electronic devices. SEEs in space arise from two natural sources, heavy ions from cosmic rays or solar flares and protons trapped in the earths magnetic field. An ion is an atom or molecule with a net positive or negative charge. This is a result of an imbalance between the number of electrons, that hold negative charge, and number of protons, that hold positive charge. Many devices can be upset by these ions at a rate of about 10^{-6} upsets per bit each day [22].

Named after Van Allen's discovery in 1958, the Van Allen radiation belts are zones of energetic charged particles originating from solar winds and held in place by the earths magnetic field [35]. There is an inner and outer region which can be dangerous for satellites to orbit. Peterson states that individual protons can be found here but have an energy level too low to upset most devices via direct ionisation. However, one proton in 10^5 will undergo a nuclear reaction within the body of a transistor capable of an upset. Therefore, at the heart of the belt, 1KB of memory would have 10 upsets a day, a dangerously high number [22].

A heavy ion can deposit a track of ions as it passes through the body of the transistor shown in Fig. 1. This produces an electric pulse or signal that may appear valid to the device, changing the state of the transistor. Protons passing through the body of the transistor have no immediate effect but can cause a nuclear reaction in the silicon. This can produce heavy ions that achieve the same effect.

Peterson divides SEEs into eight subcategories, focusing on Single Event Upsets (SEUs) and Multi-Bit Upsets (MBU). Both involve changes to computer memory via the change of a bit from 0 to 1 or 1 to 0. This is a type of Silent Data Corruption (SDC) and the focus of this research.

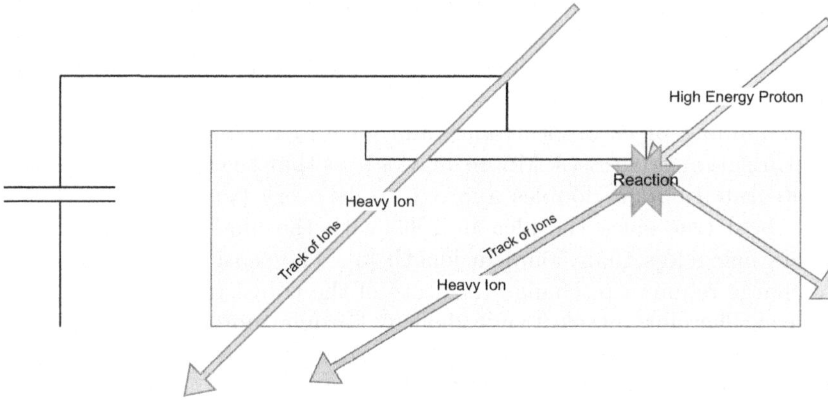

Fig. 1. Ionisation paths though a transistor that can disrupt the state (taken from [8]).

2.3 Numerical Representation in Computers

The IEEE 754 standard provides a framework for the representation of floating point numbers to varying degrees of precision [16]. This has been adopted as the industry standard and is consistent across all hardware. In ML, Floating Point (FP) 16, 32 and 64 are commonly used, where the number represents the number of bits used to represent the number. A higher number of bits allow for more precision, however the time taken for operations increases. Therefore, the choice of FP architecture is a trade off between speed and precision. The popular ML library sci-kit-learn uses FP64 by default, favouring precision. Deep learning frameworks PyTorch and Tensorflow-keras use FP32 by default as speed is more important [24]. The 32 bit standard represents numbers in the approximate range of $\pm 1.4 \times 10^{-45}$ to $\pm 3.4 \times 10^{38}$. Figure 2 depicts the architecture. The bits are split into three parts that together constitute the floating point number. The first bit represents the sign of the number, bits 1 to 8 represent the exponent and the final 23 bits for the mantissa. The exponent is responsible for scaling the number by a power of two, while the mantissa determines the precision by representing the significant digits.

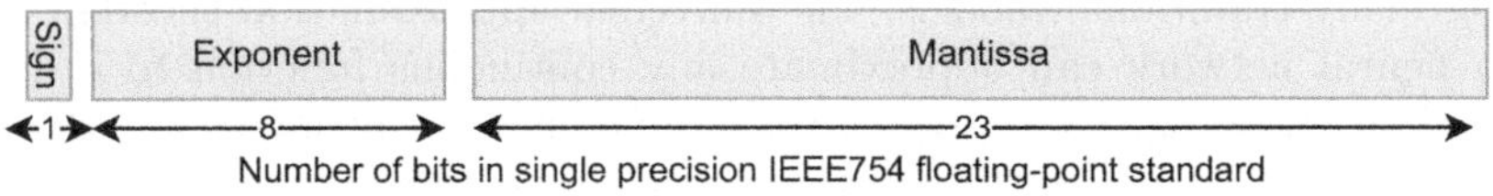

Fig. 2. IEEE 754 architecture for storing floating point numbers with 32 bits (taken from [8]).

It is expected that bitflips in the mantissa will have less impact than bitflips in the exponent or sign. This is because the sign bit can change the number by twice its magnitude and the exponent has the potential to send the number to the extremes of the FP32 range. Figure 3 shows the average result of performing bitflips on one thousand floating point numbers in the range of -3 to 3. Indeed, the Mean Absolute Error (MAE) of the first bit in the exponent has the largest impact. It is also interesting to note that the first several exponent bits (positions 1–6) result in more error than the sign bit (position 0).

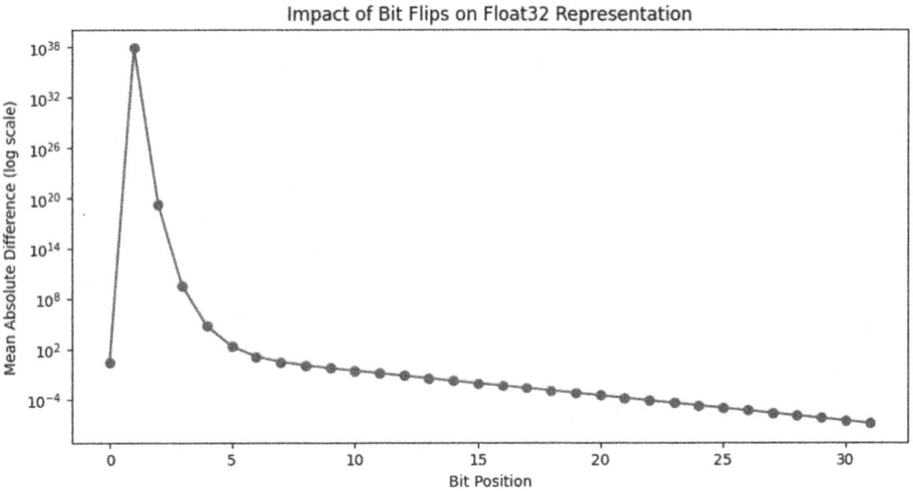

Fig. 3. Mean Absolute Error between FP32 numbers before and after performing a bitflip across each index. (taken from [8]).

2.4 Convolutional Neural Networks

IBM defines a Neural Network (NN) as a machine learning program, or model, that makes decisions in a manner similar to the human brain by using processes that mimic the way biological neurons work together to identify phenomena, weigh options and arrive at conclusions [14]. The models consist of simple building blocks where each layer has a number of artificial neurons and an activation function. NNs have become a popular choice for a wide range of tasks, outperforming many traditional models. The universal approximation theorem states that a neural network can approximate any continuous function to a desired degree of accuracy, given enough neurons and number of layers [12,19]. This theory underpins the versatility and effectiveness of neural networks, allowing them to excel across various applications.

A single neuron is a function that receives a real value x as input, processes it, and produces a real value as output. Mathematically, a single neuron can be described by the Eq. 1 where w is called the weight and b the bias.

NN layers are formed by stacking multiple neurons together. A linear layer, also known as a Fully Connected (FC) layer, is the simplest example. This allows for the input to be a vector, $x \in \mathbb{R}^a$ and the output is a vector of size r, where $W \in \mathbb{R}^{r \times a}$, and $B \in \mathbb{R}^r$, this function is expressed in Eq. 2. If a NN is composed of a single layer, it is often referred to as a perceptron. If many layers are composed together it can be referred to as a Deep Neural Network (DNN).

$$f(x) = wx + b \qquad x \in \mathbb{R} \tag{1}$$

$$f(x) = Wx + B \qquad x \in \mathbb{R}^a \tag{2}$$

The weight W and bias B parameters are learnt through the minimisation of a loss function that evaluates the NNs performance on a particular task. Depending on the task, this could be mean squared error or cross entropy loss which are popular for regression and classification tasks respectively. Gradient descent is a common algorithm for minimising the loss and updates W and B. This can sometimes result in overfitting. Regularization is a technique used to mitigate overfitting by adding an additional term to the loss function that penalises large weights. This is also termed *weight-decay*. This encourages the model to generalise better. The linear layer, described in Eq. (2), is inherently limited in its capacity to model complex, non-linear relationships within the data. This limitation is addressed by the introduction of activation functions. Activation functions add non-linearity to the NN.

CNNs have been designed and used to address problems in the computer vision field. They are a DNN composed of a feature engineering block and classification block. A CNN introduces a new type of layer called the convolutional layer modelled off the human eye. A convolution is a mathematical operation that slides one function over another. In the context of images, a kernel (filter) is applied across the image to generate feature maps. Pooling layers are another specialised layer that are paired with convolutional layers. The pooling layer aims to reduce the spatial dimension of the feature maps, this process can be thought of as downsampling a signal. This reduces computational complexity and aids the spatial invariance by extracting the most important features. The most common type of a Pooling Layer is MaxPooling which takes the largest value in a kernel. The feature engineering block is made up of convolutional layers in conjunction with pooling layers and activation functions.

A three-dimensional array of features is the output of the feature engineering block. This is flattened and passed to the classification block via a dropout layer. During training, a dropout layer sets a number of the features to 0 with probability p. The authors of AlexNet state that this technique reduces complex co-adaptations of neurons, since a neuron cannot rely on the presence of particular other neurons. This encourages the model to learn more robust features. The classification block uses one or more FC layers with activation functions to convert the features into an output. In the final layer, a SoftMax function is used to convert the output into probabilities of each class.

3 Related Work

In the 21st century, research on SEEs has been directed towards the testing of AI hardware accelerators such as graphical processing units (GPUs). Paolo Rech provides a comprehensive review "Artificial Neural Networks for Space and Safety-Critical Applications: Reliability Issues and Potential Solutions" summarising the challenges and potential mitigation strategies for deploying NNs in environments where SEEs are a significant concern [25]. Rech states that a drawback of this parallelism in GPUs is that faults can propagate to multiple values. Therefore the resulting effect can lead to errors that impede the safe deployment of DNNs [15,33].

How SEE related errors propagate through a DNN is currently not well understood. Matrix multiplication is the dominant process within DNNs and is what AI hardware accelerators are often used to compute. Therefore to assess the reliability of AI accelerators and DNN models under the effects of SEEs, beam experiments are used. Beam experiments are performed at facilities such as ChipIr at the Rutherford Appleton Laboratory, UK, [30] and have the capacity to irradiate microelectronics with atmospheric-like neutrons.

A detailed study across multiple GPUs was performed by Santos, et al., at ChipIr [29]. They show that a single fault tends to propagate to multiple threads, significantly reducing the reliability of CNNs. Errors with the rectangle distribution of affected parameters in a tensor were the most damaging to CNNs, and found to be caused by faults in the scheduling or the execution of multiple threads. This is intuitive as the rectangle shape will typically impact a larger proportion of parameters in a tensor than the single or line distribution. Santos, et al. [28], extended this work with *DieHardNet* that focuses on smart pooling and evaluates with residual deep neural networks and the CIFAR dataset. Our work extends and improves on this by considering and proposing activation functions and evaluating with recent vision transformers and the more complex ImageNet dataset [27].

Error Correcting Codes (ECCs) reduced the total number of SDCs, but were unable to reduce the number of critical errors, which have the potential to impact safety-critical applications. The ECCs suggested were Algorithm Based Fault

Tolerance (ABFT) and a redesign of the pooling layers. ABFT is a method where the final row and column of a weight matrix is used to check the integrity of the weights [13]. However Santos states AFBT is unable to be implemented on DNNs using NVIDIA proprietary cuDNN libraries. ABFT was however tested with FFT algorithms on GPUs and shown to be very promising [23] and where it could be tested at ChipIr, corrected 60% of the SDCs on the Tesla K40 and 50% on the Titan X [29].

A separate beamline experiment on Google's Tensor Processing Units (TPUs) found critical error rates of up to 4.73% during image processing tasks [26]. This study also explored the distribution of errors at the output of convolutional layers. This distribution of affected parameters falls in line with Santos's results. A drawback of the beamline experiments are the limited number of testing facilities and inability to run multiple experiments at the same time. For example Junior et al. had to test the TPU for more than 241 effective hours [26] (without considering the setup, load input, download output, and reboot time).

To support analysis from beamline experiments, artificial fault injection algorithms are also used. SASSIFI is an example of a hardware level algorithm that injects transient errors in NVIDIA GPU's [11]. Bosio et al. suggested the use of a high level fault injector, emphasising the independence of the fault injector from hardware, so that hardening techniques can be explored for both the DNN architecture and hardware [7]. Their analysis also showed that mitigation against critical behaviours was only required against changes to the exponent bits.

Introducing faults during the training process is an alternative strategy to overcoming hardware faults and shown to be create fault tolerance via the process of disabling random nodes during backpropogation [31]. This is an old ideas but there is little exploration into the robustness of models under this training procedure.

Practical research on SEEs has been shown to be both viable and valuable, however it is time consuming, costly and limited in terms of the extent of investigation. Exploring simulated methods can and should be explored as a complimentary and potentially advantageous alternative.

Our previous work [8] was the first to propose a framework for evaluating the robustness of neural networks for harsh and safety-critical environments, focusing on the CNN architecture. This work expands on this and adds a similar robustness analysis for the vision transformer, a more recent architecture for image classification.

4 Experimental Setup CNN

4.1 CNN Use Case

Image classification for satellite imagery is chosen as a practical use case. Satellites exist in harsh environments with increased exposure to SEEs and commonly include imaging technology. The dataset used was called "Ships in Satellite Imagery" (also referred to as Shipsnet) [10]. Each image is made of three matrices of size 80 by 80. The three matrices represent the colours red, green and blue with values in the matrix between 0 and 255 for the intensity. The first 1000 images are part of the "ship" class with images centred on the body of a single ship. There are ships of different sizes, orientations and atmospheric conditions. The next 1000 are part of the "no-ship" class creating a binary classification problem. Figure 4 shows exemplary images from the dataset.

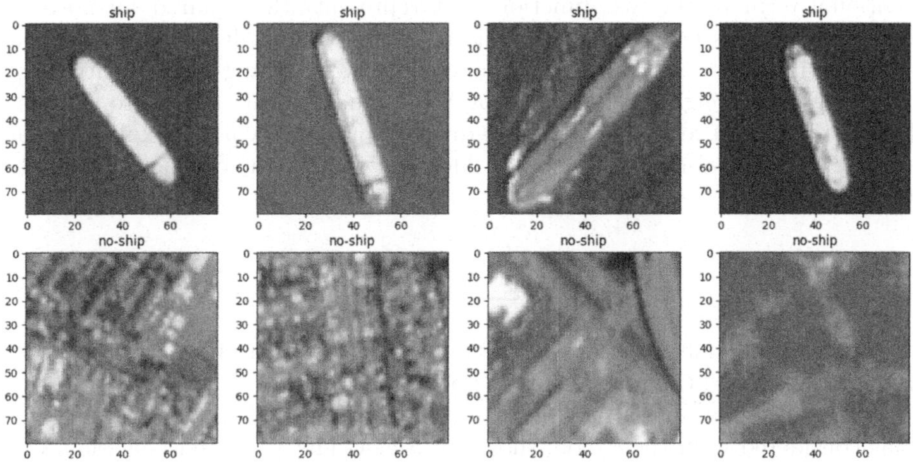

Fig. 4. Example Images from the Shipsnet Dataset (taken from [8]).

The CNN model for this research has three core requirements to meet. The model must excel at identifying images containing ships, be representative of larger, state-of-the-art models but also have a fast inference time to allow for efficient testing before and after SEE simulations. The number of layers, order, and layer size dictate the models complexity. Exploratory data analysis (EDA) on the dataset showed that the CNN architecture did not need to be a complex, state-of-the-art model with millions of parameters. However, to be representative of large scale DNNs the macro architecture of AlexNet was used [18]. This consists of a feature engineering block made up of convolutional layers, then a classification block made of fully connected layers. A dropout layer with probability p was inserted between these two blocks.

To train this CNN on the Shipsnet dataset, batched gradient descent is used on a random 80/20 train/test split of the 2000 samples. The loss function was CrossEntropyLoss define in Eq. 3 which measures the distance between the true labels and labels predicted by the CNN. Adam, a version of stochastic gradient descent, was chosen as the optimisation algorithm to minimise the loss.

$$\mathcal{L}(\mathbf{y}, \mathbf{p}) = -\sum_{i=1}^{C} y_i \log(p_i) \tag{3}$$

A batch size of 16 samples and a learning rate of 0.001 were chosen to balance training speed and model generalisation. The training is completed when either

1000 epochs are reached or the loss is less than 0.01. These values were selected as a loss of 0.01 indicates the predicted labels and true labels lie very closely. The 1000 epochs limit serves as a safeguard to stop algorithms that struggle to converge. Preliminary testing shows that all models converge within 100 epochs.

The hyperparameters explored in the training process were regularisation, also known as weight-decay, and dropout probability p. Regularisation adds an additional term to the loss function that represents the squared L2 norm of the model weights $\mathbf{w}$ multiplied by the regularisation coefficient λ seen in Eq. (4). The aim of λ is to control the trade-off between fitting and overfitting by penalising large weights [32]. Values of λ at 0 and 1e-4 are chosen to compare the effectiveness of regularisation. The dropout probability p was explored in an off state, $p = 0$ and on state $p = 0.5$. Meaning that in the on state half of the 800 features are set to 0.

$$\mathcal{L}(\mathbf{y}, \mathbf{p}) = -\sum_{i=1}^{C} y_i \log(p_i) + \frac{\lambda}{2}\|\mathbf{w}\|^2 \tag{4}$$

The hyperparameters explored in the CNN architecture were choice of activation function and the use of a smart pooling. The choice of activation function determines the non-linearity of the network. Table 1 details the activation functions considered with their plots shown in Fig. 5. The Weighted Gaussian activation function is denoted as WG and Rectified Weighted Gaussian, previously introduced in [8], as RWG .

ReLU, Sigmoid and Tanh were chosen due to being well established across a range of NN models. In particular ReLU is a cornerstone of many CNNs such as AlexNet [18]. We propose the following two activation functions specifically designed to handle SEE related errors, the Weighted Gaussian (WG) and Rectified Weighted Gaussian (RWG). The WG and RWG are bounded, decaying and zero-at-origin as these properties are hypothesised to aid robustness. This is because extreme changes will decay to 0. The sine function is included to assess the impact of periodicity, also being bounded.

Santos suggested the use of smartpooling and we explore this idea. [29]. This CNN replaces the MaxPooling layers with smartpooling layers that ignore unreasonable values [25]. Determining what is "unreasonable" can be done via many outlier detection techniques, the simplest being z-score or interquartile ranges. However due to the extreme magnitudes of resulting floats from bitflips, particularly at index 1 of the FP 32 architecture, an even simpler technique was implemented. All absolute values above a threshold were ignored. This aims to produce a similar result to more advanced outlier detection methods and serve as a proof of concept.

Table 1. Activation Functions (taken from [8]).

Function	Expression
ReLU	$\text{ReLU}(x) = \max(0, x)$
Sigmoid	$\text{Sigmoid}(x) = \frac{1}{1+\exp(-x)}$
Tanh	$\text{Tanh}(x) = \frac{\exp(x)-\exp(-x)}{\exp(x)+\exp(-x)}$
Sinusoidal	$\text{Sin}(x) = \sin(x)$
Weighted Gaussian	$\text{WG}(x) = x\exp(-x^2)$
Rectified WG	$\text{RWG}(x) = \max(0, x\exp(-x^2))$

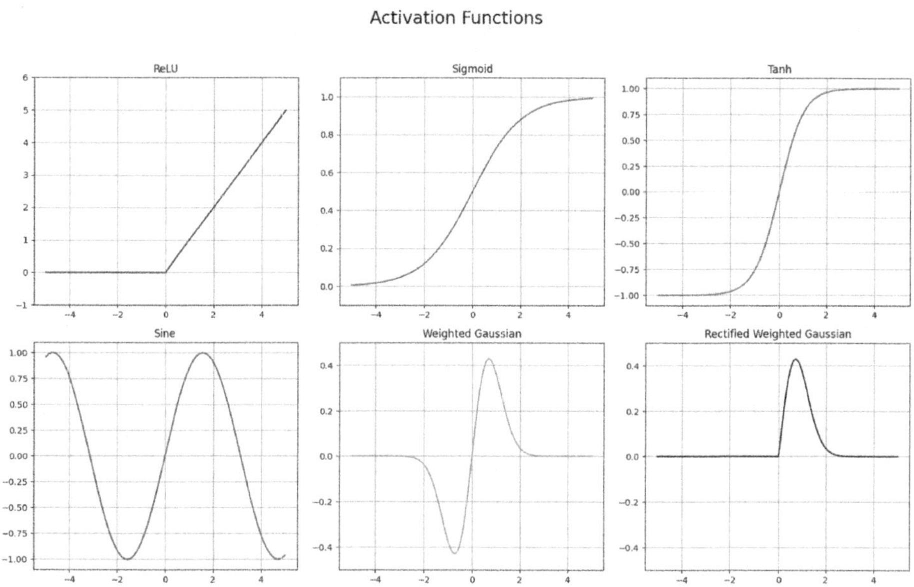

Fig. 5. Activation Functions Explored (taken from [8]).

4.2 Error Model

With a use case and model in place, the final step was to create an environment to simulate and record the effects of SEEs. The aim is to bring the simulation as close as possible to empirical results, noting that there is very limited research in this area.

Figure 6 (taken from [8]) shows the design of the overall simulation process. The simulation takes a trained model as input and a test dataset for evaluation that is unseen data to the model. Then the model has its weights and biases erroneously modified (attacked) methodically. Each attack is self-contained in a weight or bias tensor and the tensor is reset to the original state after the attack. We do not consider the effect of cumulative SDCs. During the attack, the following key information is recorded: The **norm** defined in Eq. 5, **name** of

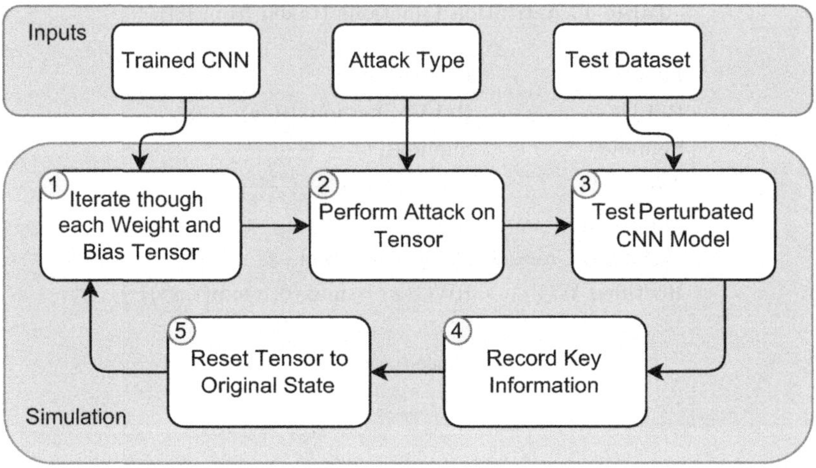

Fig. 6. A high level overview of the simulation environment (taken from [8]).

the layer, **location** of the attack, **accuracy** of the CNN on the test dataset, **number** of parameters attacked and **proportion** of parameters attacked in the tensor.

$$\text{norm}(t_0, t_1) = |t_0 - t_1| \tag{5}$$

To allow a fair comparison between different CNN model parametisations the bitflip index and spatial distribution must be consistent. Single, line and rectangle are common spatial distributions of SDCs. However, after preliminary exploration into simulations with these distributions, the line distribution was found to be catastrophic to the performance of the CNN. This allows for no comparison between parametisations so is unfortunately not a feasible simulation for a smaller CNN. This critical reduction in performance can be attributed to the low number of parameters in the CNN where feature channels are as small as 8. It will likely be more applicable to larger CNNs. The rectangle distribution is an even more destructive extension of the line distribution so was also not considered. This does not pose a problem as SEU is the most common result of SEEs.

Figure 6 depicts the simulation process used to analyse SEUs. The simulation comprehensively iterates through all 7634 parameters of the CNN. This approach was not possible for MBU simulations as the number of combinations is 2^{7634}, which exceeds practical computational resources. To represent an MBU, errors were propagated from an SEU to an MBU based on proximity of nearby bits using a Gaussian distribution. Spatial distributions of errors have previously been implemented by others [6]. The full details for simulating MBUs is presented in [8].

Figure 3 shows that the index of the bitflip can cause a near-zero change or change to the extremities of the FP32 architecture. For computational convenience, 7 of the 32 indices were selected to be investigated. The sign bit, three exponent bits (1, 3, 6) and three mantissa bits (10, 15, 21) were the indices selected. This gives a fair representation of the three parts of the FP32 architecture. The mantissa bits are skewed towards the lower indices due to the decreasing change in MAE. This is because it is expected that the impact would be minimal as the MAE approaches 0.

To summarise the simulation environment, both SEU and MBU methodologies were outlined. The SEU simulation exhaustively tests all parameters and the MBU attacks a selection of parameters propagating from a single SEU. Regarding the bitflipping, 7 of the total 32 bits in the FP32 architecture were tested. All this results in the following number of simulations:

SEU Simulations:

- Factors: 7,634 parameters, 6 activation functions, 7 bit indices, 2 pooling layers, 2 dropout, 2 regularization
- Total: $7,634 \times 6 \times 7 \times 2 \times 2 \times 2 = \mathbf{2,565,024}$

MBU Simulations:

- Factors: 458 initializations, 5 standard deviations, 6 activation functions, 7 bit indices, 2 pooling layers, 2 dropout, 2 regularization
- Total: $458 \times 5 \times 6 \times 7 \times 2 \times 2 \times 2 = \mathbf{769,440}$

5 Evaluation CNN

To evaluate how the different model parameter settings affect the model's performance with different error models, we use the *test delta*. The test delta is computed as the difference between the test accuracy before and after the errors are introduced. Following our methodology, 3,334,464 attack simulations were conducted. Both SEU (2,565,024) and MBU (769,440) simulations were performed. Table 2 outlines the distribution of the number of simulations and the number of single bitflips. Note that the number of SEU attacks is greater than the number of SEU simulations. This is because a number of the MBU simulations, with a particularly low standard deviation, result in only one index being attacked.

Table 2. Summary of Simulations Performed (taken from [8]).

Bitflips per Simulation	SEU (1)	2–4	5–9	10–14	15–24	25–39	40+
Total # Simulations	2,583,531	192,073	121,599	123,349	96,573	90,157	127,182

5.1 Simulation

Table 3 offers a summary of the key simulation and CNN parameters against the test delta. It suggests complex interactions between these parameters, where one parameter may only be beneficial in the presence of one or more other parameters. The analysis is visualised with multidimensional figures. The discussion starts with the simulation parameters, then considers the CNN's learning parameters and architectural design.

Table 3. Average test delta of different CNNs and setups. The minimal value in each row is marked with an asterisk (*) and global minima with (**). (taken from [8])

Dropout	Weight Decay	Model	Standard Activation Functions				Proposed Act. Func.	
			ReLU	Sigmoid	Tanh	Sine	WG	RWG
0.0	0.0	CNN	0.02760	0.01784	0.01758	0.01773	0.01347	0.01234*
		SmartPoolCNN	0.01809	0.01774	0.01756	0.01750	0.01363	0.01227*
	0.0001	CNN	0.02755	0.01731	0.01669	0.02002	0.01318	0.01275*
		SmartPoolCNN	0.02126	0.01738	0.01667	0.02023	0.01333	0.01260*
0.5	0.0	CNN	0.02418	0.01834	0.01573	0.01853	0.01322	**0.01020****
		SmartPoolCNN	0.02241	0.01828	0.01567	0.01857	0.01335	0.01021*
	0.0001	CNN	0.02155	0.01892	0.01702	0.01700	0.01314	0.01126*
		SmartPoolCNN	0.01931	0.01900	0.01718	0.01689	0.01313	0.01129*

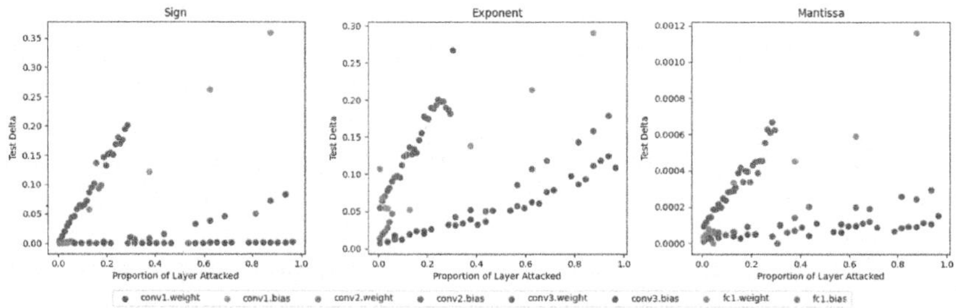

Fig. 7. The average test delta in the Sign (left), Exponent (middle), Mantissa (right) part of the FP32 architecture against the portion of the layer attacked (taken from [8]).

Bitflip Location: was the most important factor to the test delta. Figure 8 shows the non-zero test delta rate at each index. In the mantissa, only 1% of the simulations had a non-zero test delta, also known as critical error, with a maximum of only 0.0475 test delta. In the exponent, 27% of the simulations had a non-zero test delta with the 1st index having the most impact at 52%.

It is surprising that the 3rd index had less impact than the 6th. These results support the hypothesis that the magnitude of the difference caused by the bitflip is proportional to the impact on the wider CNN.

Layer: attacked within the CNN also had a large impact on robustness. Figure 8 shows a U-shaped pattern for average test delta with respect to the forward propagation order of the CNN layers. This points towards the first and final layers of the CNN architecture being the most sensitive to perturbations. The bias layers also exhibit higher test deltas than the weight layers suggesting they are more sensitive, a result that was also found by Bolchini et al. [5]. The most important takeaway from Fig. 7 is that there is a clear linear relationship between the proportion of the layer attacked and test delta, confirming Santos' findings [29]. This is also reflected in Fig. 8 where the SEU simulations have a lower test delta than the MBU simulations.

Dropout: was a factor during the training of the models with the purpose of improving robustness. Averaged over all the results it reduced the average test delta from 0.0172 to 0.0164.

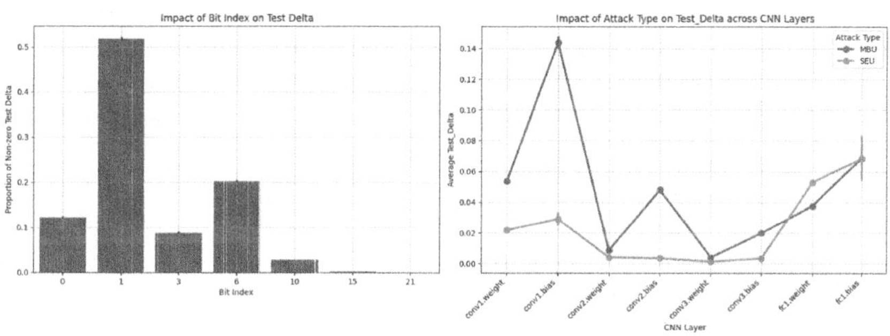

Fig. 8. Proportion of non-zero Test Deltas across Bit Indices (left), Average Test Delta across layers in the CNN (right). (taken from [8]).

Table 4. Comparison of Alexnet models on CIFAR-100. *Training epochs from weights copied from training Alexnet with ReLU. (taken from [8]).

Model Type	Test Accuracy	SEU Accuracy	Test Delta	# Simulations	# Training Epochs
Alexnet with ReLU	0.717100	0.312881	0.404219	160	20
Alexnet with $RWG_{0.01}$	0.742900	0.663311	0.079589	160	20* + 5
Alexnet with ReLU and smartpooling	0.707600	0.403594	0.304006	160	20*

Regularisation: was the least impactful parameter to the test delta having an insignificant increase to the test delta of 0.0001 over all the results. Regularisation only had a benefit when the ReLU activation function and dropout were used, shown in Table 3.

Activation Function: had the most significant impact on the CNN architecture robustness. Moving left to right in Table 3, the activation function with the highest test delta was unbounded ReLU. Unbounded activation functions allow extreme values to propagate through the CNN. The bounded activation functions (sigmoid, tanh, sine) achieved similar levels of average test delta around 0.017. The bounded WG and RWG activation functions consistently achieved a lower test delta across all training parameters. The best model, at 0.01 average test delta, used the RWG activation function, dropout at $p = 0.5$, no regularisation and no smartpooling. This was a 58% reduction in error over the use of ReLU.

5.2 Testing AlexNet

The framework was then evaluated using AlexNet. It explored the RWG activation function and smartpooling. Due to computational constraints, transfer learning was used with the smaller CIFAR-100 dataset, which includes 60k images with 100 different labels [17]. The final layer of AlexNet was adjusted to the 100 classes instead of 1000. The images were scaled up to 224×224 pixels and normalised. After transfer learning, a pretrained version of AlexNet achieved a 71.7% test accuracy as shown in Table 4. A variant of the RWG function (see [8]) allowed the use of transfer learning from AlexNet (which uses ReLU) to a version of AlexNet with the RWG_K activation function. Smartpooling had the advantage of not needing any further training, just the replacement of the pooling layers with smartpooling layers with minimal change in accuracy (decrease by 1%).

6 Experimental Setup ViT

To further demonstrate the framework's flexibility we use it to evaluate the more recent vision transformer architecture [9] under SEUs. There are several ImageNet pre-trained vision transformers from the PyTorch library using different hyper-parameters [9]. We selected the *base* model using *32 patch size* as the most suitable with existing published results (denoted *ViT_B_32*). The ViT-Base architecture has 12 encoder blocks for a total of 152 learnable layers with a total of 88 million parameters, approximately 7 million parameters per encoder block.

We evaluate the model using weights pre-trained on the ImageNet-5K dataset [27], where the validation set has five images per class (with 1000 classes). With no errors being introduced, the vision transformer model achieves 76.08% accuracy on the validation set.

We consider SEU simulations and, as before, we select the sign bit, three exponent bits (1, 3, 6) and three mantissa bits (10, 15, 21) indices. For each index and for each layer, we randomly select 40 weights to attack. This results in a total of 6080 simulations per index. We note that the number of simulations are significantly less than previous experiments and is due to the fact that evaluating this much larger model takes significantly more time. The experimental setup is summarised as follows:

SEU Vision Transformer Simulations:

- Base Model: 152 layers (12 Encoding Blocks)
- Accuracy (no attacks): 76.08%
- Total simulations: 152 $layers \times 40$ $attacks\ per\ layer \times 7$ $bit\ indices = \mathbf{42,560}$

We also performed a few thousand more experimental simulations that altered individual tensor values to assess what magnitude is needed for the model prediction to differ.

7 Evaluation ViT

Table 5. Simulation results for SEU indices. Critical failure is defined as the proportion of samples with accuracy < 0.1.

Bit Index	Mean Accuracy	Mean Test Delta	Test Delta Std	Critical Failure %	# Simulations
0	0.7607	0.0001	0.0083	0.0000	6080
1	0.1768	0.5840	0.3071	0.7391	6080
3	0.7608	0.0000	0.0002	0.0000	6080
6	0.7601	0.0007	0.0203	0.0008	6080
10	0.7608	0.0000	0.0001	0.0000	6080
15	0.7608	0.0000	0.0000	0.0000	6080
21	0.7608	0.0000	0.0000	0.0000	6080

Table 5 shows the results of the SEU simulation on the ViT. Again, we see that bit index 1 is the most damaging followed by index 6 and index 0. This aligns with Fig. 8 from our CNN tests. Bit index 1 had a critical failure rate of 74% and a mean test delta (0.5840) that exceeds that of Alexnet (0.4042). This suggests that this ViT architecture is less resilient to SEUs than the Alexnet CNN architecture.

With two sets of experiments showing that the 6th bit index is more damaging than the 3rd, a deeper investigation was undertaken to understand this misalignment with Fig. 3. It was found that the initial value before a bit occurs plays a large role in the resulting value. Specifically, values close to 0 have a greater change under bit 6 than bit 3. We know that many of the values in the CNN, Alexnet and ViT lie very close to 0 so this explains why bit 6 is more damaging than bit 3. Figure 9 shows this effect from performing bitflips on python float objects. Why python float objects behave this way is an unknown but it is unlikely that floating point values are sorted in this pythonic way for commercial use cases.

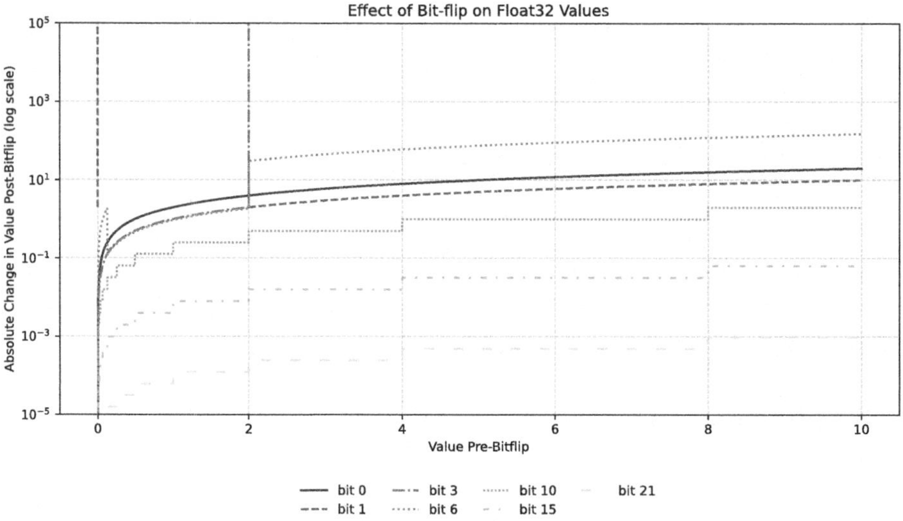

Fig. 9. Absolute Error between FP32 numbers before and after performing a bitflips at multiple bit indices across initial values between 0 and 10.

The layers with the highest average test delta are at the start of the ViT and after the transformer blocks. These are the convolutional layer that splits the image into smaller patches, the class token, then the post-transformer layer normalisations. Figure 10 shows how the mean test delta varies between the layers and Fig. 11 explores within the transformer blocks.

The very first transformer block has the highest mean test delta whereas the following blocks maintain a similar level. We see a repeated pattern in Fig. 11 which tells us that the same part of each block shares a similar sensitivity to SEUs. Table 6 shows the layer normalisation weight and bias have the highest test delta and critical failure rate. Therefore we see that throughout the ViT, both inside and outside the transformer blocks, layer normalisation is a sensitive part to alterations.

Unlike the CNN architecture the final fully connected layer (heads) in the ViT has a lower test delta than most of the model. This could also be due to the fact there are only 2 classes in the CNN tests and a 1000 for the ViT so a much lower proportion of this final layer is being altered. Given we are not doing MBUs for the ViT experimentation, we must be mindful to compare the results from the ViT to only the SEU results of the CNN tests.

The positional embedding layer was extremely insensitive to SEUs with a 0% critical failure rate. The largest test delta was only 0.0094, meaning that only 47 images went from being classified correctly to being misclassified (5000 total with 3804 being classified correctly). A reason for this resilience could be due to the next step in the inference being a layer normalisation. This layer normalisation will take the values in each token plus its positional embedding and scale it. If an extreme value is present, the resulting output becomes a vector with all values set near 0 except the location of the extreme value, which now is a smaller, safer value. Therefore nearly all information is lost from this token/patch but this is just one of 50 tokens so most of the information remains intact. Consequently, the overall representation of the image is preserved, and the model can still make accurate predictions.

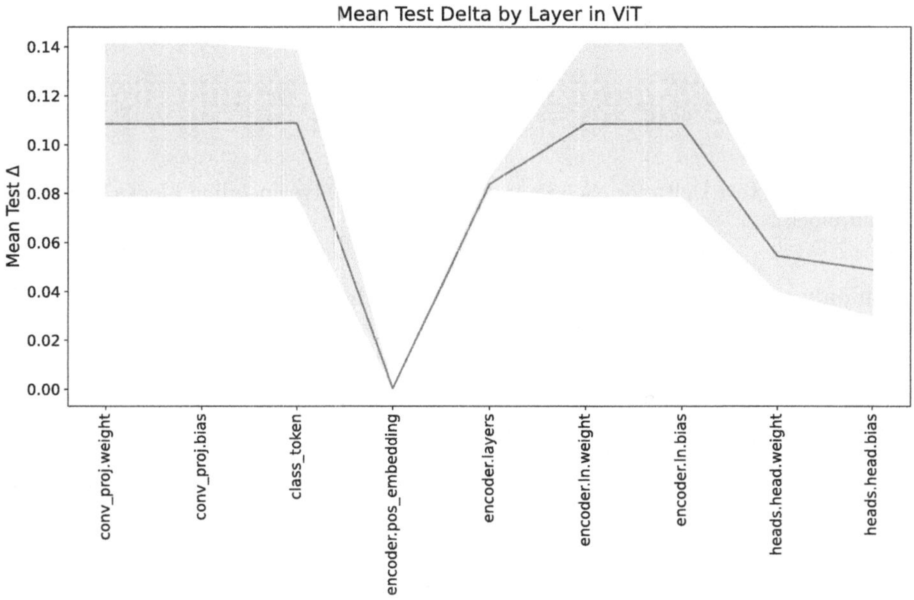

Fig. 10. Mean Test Delta for each layer in the ViT. Encoding layers are aggregated due to there being 12 transformer blocks.

Table 6. Simulation results for parts of the transformer block. Critical failure is defined as the proportion of samples with accuracy < 0.1.

Matrix Name	Mean Accuracy	Mean Test Delta	Test Delta Std	Critical Failure %	# Samples
layer_norm.bias	0.6522	0.1086	0.2659	0.1429	6720
layer_norm.weight	0.6516	0.1092	0.2664	0.1436	6720
mlp.bias	0.7014	0.0594	0.2039	0.0781	6720
mlp.weight	0.6807	0.0801	0.2201	0.0835	6720
self_attention.bias	0.6897	0.0711	0.2207	0.0929	6720
self_attention.weight	0.6870	0.0738	0.2242	0.0961	6720

Our CNN study showed a positive relationship between the log of the **Norm** and test delta. We also wanted to find out the minimum norm required to alter the accuracy of the ViT and the relationship between norm and performance of the ViT. Figure 12 shows that we only start seeing non-zero test delta at norm values above 0.1. At norm values greater than 10 we see our first critical failures

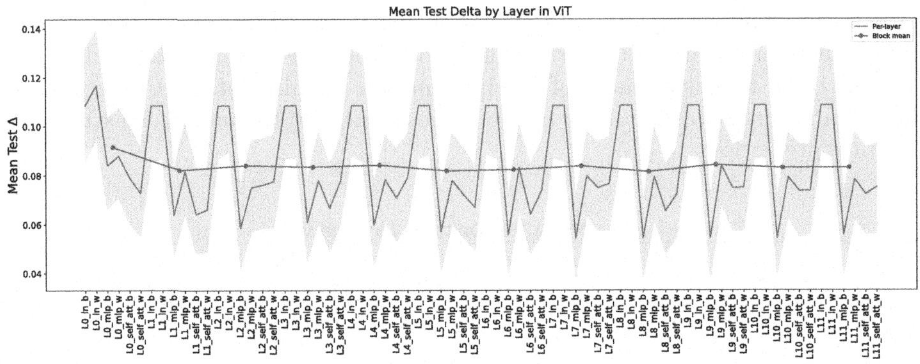

Fig. 11. Mean Test Delta for each layer in the ViT's twelve encoding blocks (six layers in each block).

which only get worse as we increase the norm. The smallest norm value to incur a non-zero test delta is found at 3.212×10^{-5}. The smallest norm value where we get more non-zero test deltas than zero test deltas is found at 1.314×10^{-1}. This value can be thought of as a tipping point where changes to a tensor greater than this will likely change the model's classification ability.

The ViT is found to handle norm values 10 times larger then the small CNN before a non-zero test delta is incurred. What this does not factor in is the increased size of the tensors in the ViT, thus a lower proportion of the tensor is altered. In the future, a cosine similarity score may be better than using the l1 norm as is incorporate dimensionality in the calculation. Regardless, this points towards the ViT being more robust to the magnitude of changes incurred by SEUs.

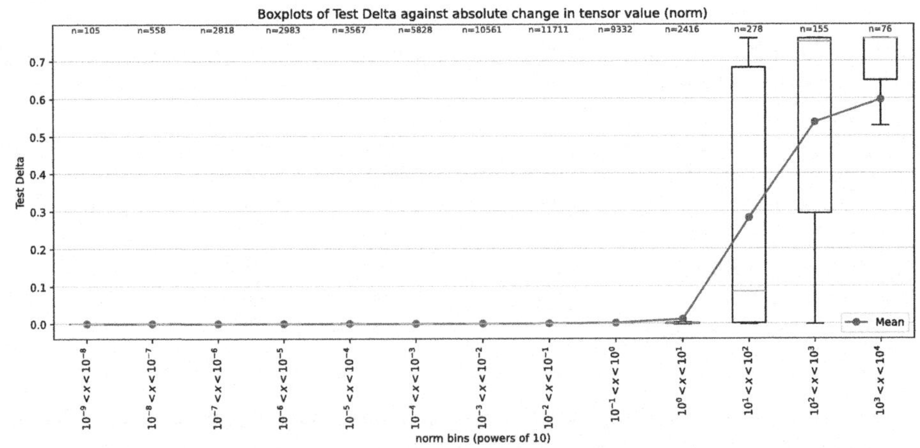

Fig. 12. Test Delta distribution across various binned values of norm (i.e. the absolute difference between the value before and after the SEU).

8 Conclusion

To conclude, a framework to simulate and test the effects of SEEs was built with the PyTorch library and successfully test three computer vision models, a small CNN, Alexnet and a Vision Transformer.

In the small CNN, a third of simulated SEEs have minimal impact due to small changes in the mantissa. There exists a linear relationship between the proportion of the layer attacked and test delta. The use of dropout during training improves robustness but regularisation does not. Smartpooling layers were beneficial in conjunction with ReLU. The proposed activation function RWG was the most robust to simulated SEEs and transfer learning can be used to convert CNNs using ReLU to RWG_K. Small norms (e.g. less than 10^{-6}) have minimal impact on the test delta.

Both Alexnet and ViT have a parameter space in the tens of millions. Under an SEU which had a bitflip at the first exponent bit, Alexnet showed more resilience with a lower test delta than the ViT. This could be due to the convolutional layer skipping the altered tensor value. We also saw a huge improvement to the resilience of Alexnet when using the RWG activation function.

Within the ViT the positional embedding layer showed impressive resilience to SEUs. The normalisation layers in the ViT were the most least resilient across all 12 transformer blocks with the first transformer block being more sensitive than the rest. Similar to the small CNN, norms less than 10^{-6} have minimal impact on the test delta.

Future work will include testing more models and in more depth, similar to the thoroughness of the small CNN experimentation. This however does require compute proportional to the inference time of each model. Defining a bound on how much the parameter space can be altered would be an interesting analytical problem as our empirical results show this to be around 10^{-6} for the l1-norm. Cosine similarity could also be used for this. The mitigation techniques we suggested were not implemented for our ViT investigation so this is another obvious step forward. Alternative mitigation ideas to explore could be formulating a distribution for the values passed through the inferences, then rejecting values with a very low likelihood of belonging to this distribution. Finally, future work will examine real life results to better understand error distributions.

References

1. ATSB: In-flight upset 154 km west of learmonth. Australian Transport Safety Bureau (2008). https://www.atsb.gov.au/publications/investigation_reports/2008/aair/ao-2008-070
2. ATSB: Single event effect general risk to avionics. Australian Transport Safety Bureau (2011). https://www.atsb.gov.au/safety-issues/AO-2008-070-SI-07
3. Badaroglu, M.: More moore. In: 2021 IEEE International Roadmap for Devices and Systems Outbriefs, pp. 01–38 (2021). https://doi.org/10.1109/IRDS54852.2021.00010

4. Binder, D., Smith, E.C., Holman, A.B.: Satellite anomalies from galactic cosmic rays. IEEE Trans. Nucl. Sci. **22**(6), 2675–2680 (1975). https://doi.org/10.1109/TNS.1975.4328188
5. Bolchini, C., Cassano, L., Miele, A., Nazzari, A.: Selective hardening of cnns based on layer vulnerability estimation. In: 2022 IEEE International Symposium on Defect and Fault Tolerance in VLSI and Nanotechnology Systems (DFT), pp. 1–6 (2022). https://doi.org/10.1109/DFT56152.2022.9962339
6. Bolchini, C., Cassano, L., Miele, A., Toschi, A.: Fast and accurate error simulation for cnns against soft errors. IEEE Trans. Comput. **72**(4), 984–997 (2023). https://doi.org/10.1109/TC.2022.3184274
7. Bosio, A., Bernardi, P., Ruospo, A., Sanchez, E.: A reliability analysis of a deep neural network. In: 2019 IEEE Latin American Test Symposium (LATS), pp. 1–6 (2019). https://doi.org/10.1109/LATW.2019.8704548
8. Dennis, W., Pope, J.: A framework for developing robust machine learning models in harsh environments: a review of CNN design choices. In: Proceedings of the 17th International Conference on Agents and Artificial Intelligence - Volume 2: ICAART, pp. 322–333. INSTICC, SciTePress (2025). https://doi.org/10.5220/0013155000003890
9. Dosovitskiy, A., et al.: An image is worth 16x16 words: transformers for image recognition at scale. In: International Conference on Learning Representations (2021). https://openreview.net/forum?id=YicbFdNTTy
10. Hammell, R.: Ships in satellite imagery (2018). https://doi.org/10.34740/KAGGLE/DSV/61115, https://www.kaggle.com/dsv/61115
11. Hari, S.K.S., Tsai, T., Stephenson, M., Keckler, S.W., Emer, J.: Sassifi: an architecture-level fault injection tool for gpu application resilience evaluation. In: 2017 IEEE International Symposium on Performance Analysis of Systems and Software (ISPASS), pp. 249–258 (2017). https://doi.org/10.1109/ISPASS.2017.7975296
12. Hornik, K., Stinchcombe, M., White, H.: Multilayer feedforward networks are universal approximators. Neural Netw. **2**(5), 359–366 (1989). https://doi.org/10.1016/0893-6080(89)90020-8. https://www.sciencedirect.com/science/article/pii/0893608089900208
13. Huang, K.H., Abraham, J.A.: Algorithm-based fault tolerance for matrix operations. IEEE Trans. Comput. **C-33**(6), 518–528 (1984). https://doi.org/10.1109/TC.1984.1676475
14. IBM: Neural networks (2024). https://www.ibm.com/topics/neural-networks. Accessed 26 Aug 2024
15. Ibrahim, Y., et al.: Soft errors in dnn accelerators: a comprehensive review. Microelectron. Reliab. **115**, 113969 (2020). https://doi.org/10.1016/j.microrel.2020.113969. https://www.sciencedirect.com/science/article/pii/S0026271420308003
16. IEEE Standard for Floating-Point Arithmetic. IEEE Std 754-2019 (Revision of IEEE 754-2008), pp. 1–84 (2019). https://doi.org/10.1109/IEEESTD.2019.8766229
17. Krizhevsky, A.: Learning multiple layers of features from tiny images (2009). technical Report
18. Krizhevsky, A., Sutskever, I., Hinton, G.E.: Imagenet classification with deep convolutional neural networks. In: Pereira, F., Burges, C., Bottou, L., Weinberger, K. (eds.) Advances in Neural Information Processing Systems, vol. 25. Curran Associates, Inc. (2012). https://proceedings.neurips.cc/paper_files/paper/2012/file/c399862d3b9d6b76c8436e924a68c45b-Paper.pdf

19. Lu, Z., Pu, H., Wang, F., Hu, Z., Wang, L.: The expressive power of neural networks: a view from the width (2017). https://arxiv.org/abs/1709.02540
20. Maintainers, T.: Contributors: torchvision: pytorch's computer vision library (2016). https://github.com/pytorch/vision. Accessed 28 Aug 2025
21. Moore, G.: Cramming more components onto integrated circuits. Proc. IEEE **86**(1), 82–85 (1998). https://doi.org/10.1109/JPROC.1998.658762
22. Peterson, E.: Introduction, chap. 1, pp. 1–12. John Wiley & Sons, Ltd., Hoboken (2011). https://doi.org/10.1002/9781118084328.ch1, https://onlinelibrary.wiley.com/doi/abs/10.1002/9781118084328.ch1
23. Pilla, L.L., et al.: Software-based hardening strategies for neutron sensitive fft algorithms on gpus. IEEE Trans. Nucl. Sci. **61**(4), 1874–1880 (2014). https://doi.org/10.1109/TNS.2014.2301768
24. Radford, A., Wu, J., Child, R., Luan, D., Amodei, D., Sutskever, I.: Language models are unsupervised multitask learners (2019)
25. Rech, P.: Artificial neural networks for space and safety-critical applications: reliability issues and potential solutions. IEEE Trans. Nucl. Sci. **71**(4), 377–404 (2024). https://doi.org/10.1109/TNS.2024.3349956
26. Rech Junior, R.L., et al.: High energy and thermal neutron sensitivity of google tensor processing units. IEEE Trans. Nucl. Sci. **69**(3), 567–575 (2022). https://doi.org/10.1109/TNS.2022.3142092
27. Russakovsky, O., et al.: ImageNet large scale visual recognition challenge. Int. J. Comput. Vis. (IJCV) **115**(3), 211–252 (2015). https://doi.org/10.1007/s11263-015-0816-y
28. Fernandes dos Santos, F., et al.: Improving deep neural network reliability via transient-fault-aware design and training. IEEE Trans. Emerg. Top. Comput. 1–12 (2025). https://doi.org/10.1109/TETC.2024.3520672
29. Santos, F.F.D., et al.: Analyzing and increasing the reliability of convolutional neural networks on gpus. IEEE Trans. Reliab. **68**(2), 663–677 (2019). https://doi.org/10.1109/TR.2018.2878387
30. Science and Technology Facilities Council: Chipir (2024). https://www.isis.stfc.ac.uk/Pages/Chipir.aspx. Accessed 01 Oct 2024
31. Sequin, C., Clay, R.: Fault tolerance in artificial neural networks. In: 1990 IJCNN International Joint Conference on Neural Networks, vol. 1, pp. 703–708 (1990). https://doi.org/10.1109/IJCNN.1990.137651
32. Shalev-Shwartz, S., Ben-David, S.: Understanding Machine Learning: From Theory to Algorithms. Cambridge University Press (2014). chapter 13: Regularization and Stability
33. Su, F., Liu, C., Stratigopoulos, H.G.: Testability and dependability of ai hardware: survey, trends, challenges, and perspectives. IEEE Des. Test **40**(2), 8–58 (2023). https://doi.org/10.1109/MDAT.2023.3241116
34. TheGamer: How an ionizing particle from outer space helped a super mario 64 speedrunner save time (2020). https://www.thegamer.com/how-ionizing-particle-outer-space-helped-super-mario-64-speedrunner-save-time/. Accessed 23 Aug 2024
35. van Allen, J.A., Ludwig, G.H., Ray, E.C., McILWAIN, C.E.: Observation of high intensity radiation by satellites 1958 alpha and gamma. J. Jet Propuls. **28**(9), 588–592 (1958). https://doi.org/10.2514/8.7396
36. Wallmark, J.T., Marcus, S.M.: Minimum size and maximum packing density of nonredundant semiconductor devices. Proc. IRE **50**(3), 286–298 (1962). https://doi.org/10.1109/JRPROC.1962.288321

ABBIE-M: Multi-split Prediction of Sanskrit Compounds by Attention-Based Bi-encoders

Irfan Ali[1](✉), Liliana Lo Presti[1], Igor Spano'[2], and Marco La Cascia[1]

[1] Department of Engineering, University of Palermo, Palermo, Italy
irfan.ali04@unipa.it

[2] Department of Cultures and Society, University of Palermo, Palermo, Italy

Abstract. Compound word splitting is crucial for accurate linguistic analysis of Sanskrit texts. However, existing computational methods, such as our ABBIE model, typically focus on predicting only one split per compound. In this article, we present ABBIE-M, an improved version of the ABBIE model, which incorporates two significant advances: (1) a threshold-based iterative prediction approach, which recognizes valid splits by sliding a fixed-length window over the predicted per-character split probabilities, selecting the highest-scoring windows that exceed a threshold, marking central splits, and eliminating window overlaps; and (2) a novel classification approach, which generalizes from predicting a single binary window to predicting binary labels across all character positions, thus enabling simultaneous detection of multiple split points per compound.

Experimental evaluation on a multi-split dataset shows that ABBIE-M achieves precision, recall and F1 scores of 95.58% 94.75%, and 94.89%, respectively. Furthermore, the model achieves a robust exact-match accuracy of 92.47%, significantly improving the practical use of automated Sanskrit compound analysis and laying the foundation for the advancement of morphological analysis in natural language processing and digital humanities for comprehensive linguistic study of complex religious texts.

Keywords: Sanskrit · Compound Splitting · Multi-Split · Low-Resource Language · Sandhi Splitting · Deep Learning

1 Introduction

Natural language processing for morphologically rich languages presents unique challenges, particularly when those languages employ phonological fusion at word boundaries. Sanskrit, with texts dating back to 1500 B.C. [1], remains under-resourced in NLP despite extensive digitization efforts. A key challenge in processing Sanskrit arises from its frequent use of compound words formed through the phonetic fusion of multiple constituents. In Sanskrit, compound words can have a varying number of multi-split positions. Multi-split sandhi occurs when a

H. J. van den Herik et al. (Eds.): ICAART 2025, LNAI 16517, pp. 236–258, 2026.
https://doi.org/10.1007/978-3-032-25032-2_11

single orthographic token represents three or more lexical words, so that at least two hidden boundaries need to be identified. Each boundary is obscured by a series of phonological processes, such as vowel mixing, consonant merging, and visarga deletion, where the output of one transformation becomes the context for the next compounding ambiguity [21]. Because the number k of boundaries is unknown a priori, the space of possible segmentation grows rapidly, on the order of $O(n^{k-1})$ for a word of length n, which makes exhaustive searches impractical for highly complex forms. Furthermore, many potential splits are phonetically well-formed yet semantically implausible, so effective systems must integrate local phonological evidence with broader lexical-semantic knowledge to rule out false hypotheses [12]. To interpret such words accurately, it is essential to segment them into their original components by predicting the split location. It is important to note that multi-split compounds - words containing two or more Sandhi junctions - remain pervasive, particularly in classical poetry and philosophical texts, where the formation of complex compounds is favored for metrical or stylistic reasons.

Figure 1 illustrates the phenomenon of multi-split Sanskrit compound words, where multiple internal Sandhi splits must be identified to recover the underlying elements. Each example presents the original compound (left), the correctly segmented form with annotated split locations (middle), and its English translation (right). Previous approaches, such as ABBIE [14] and the model in [5], only address single-split prediction, limiting the decomposition of long and syntactically rich compounds.

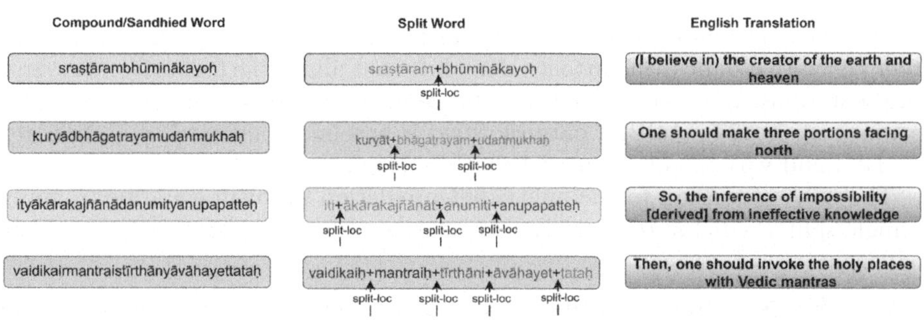

Fig. 1. Sanskrit compound/sandhied words having multi-split locations. For each line, it is shown the original compound (left), the actual split positions (center), and the English translation (right).

Another central obstacle is Sandhi, the set of phonetic rules that merge morphemes into compound words, obscuring original word boundaries and altering characters via deletion, insertion, or substitution. For instance, the compound *"ramaḥ" + "Īśvaraḥ"* yields *"ramoḥśvaraḥ"* under Sandhi. Recovering the correct splits is essential for downstream tasks, such as parsing, machine translation, and information retrieval. Furthermore, Sanskrit exhibits rich morphological complexity and a relatively free word order in sentence construction [2,3], but is complicated by the fact that multiple syntactically valid split points often exist, only a subset of which are semantically meaningful [5].

The challenge of splitting compound words is not unique to classical Sanskrit but also arises in other languages such as Thai [15], Chinese, and Japanese. In Japanese, a phenomenon known as *Rendaku* - or *sequential voicing* - is conceptually similar to Sandhi transformations in Sanskrit. For instance, the compound word *tegami* is formed from *te* (hand) and *kami* (paper), where *kami* changes to *gami* through voicing of the initial consonant. A parallel occurs in Sanskrit: *rāja + indraḥ* becomes *rājendraḥ* through vowel Sandhi, where $a + i$ coalesces into e and then integrates into the compound form. Recognizing such cross-linguistic parallels offers valuable insights into the nature of phonological changes in compound formation.

Two main approaches are commonly employed for Sanskrit word segmentation: lexicon-based methods and data-driven methods. Lexicon-based approaches rely on curated linguistic resources for parsing. Data-driven approaches learn segmentation patterns directly from annotated data, framing Sanskrit word segmentation as a character-level sequence labeling task [10]. More recently, deep learning-based methods have defined Sandhi splitting as a sequence labeling or structured prediction task. Work in [12,13] has shown that attention-based models can significantly reduce splitting ambiguity by focusing on the most informative character positions. However, these works are limited to single-split compounds, where exactly one Sandhi junction needs to be found.

To address single-split prediction, we previously introduced ABBIE [14], an attention-based BI-Encoder architecture that combines two bidirectional LSTMs, i.e., one processing the input in forward order, the other in reverse order [29] with a multi-head attention module that aligns the forward and reverse representations to predict a single Sandhi window. Achieving an exact matching accuracy of 89.27%, ABBIE outperformed a baseline composed of a standard BiLSTM and variants of the model that do not use attention.

The naive extension to the multi-split prediction problem could be to apply a single-split predictor recursively. However, such an extension raises two key challenges:

- **Variable Number of Splits:** a model must identify an unknown number of split positions within a single compound word, rejecting spurious splits that are phonetically valid but semantically meaningless.
- **Recursive Decision-Making:** repeated application of a single-split predictor can lead to accumulation of errors and, without a robust stopping criterion (e.g., a confidence threshold), can result in spurious splits (over-splitting) or missed splits (under-splitting).

To address these challenges, we propose ABBIE-Multisplit (ABBIE-M), an extension of ABBIE that unifies multi-label split prediction with an iterative, threshold-based extraction mechanism. Our approach is specifically designed for multi-split prediction in Sanskrit compound words, a challenge that, at the best of our knowledge, has not been addressed by previous work. Leveraging the

ABBIE architecture, we modify the mathematical formulation of the problem with the goal of predicting a binary vector over all character positions to enable the prediction of multiple split points in a single pass. Therefore, we also propose an iterative method that analyzes the split probability vector with a fixed-size window, selects the region with the highest score above a fixed threshold, marks its center as a split, and iterates avoiding overlaps between the detected windows. The proposed approach thus enables robust extraction of multiple valid splits per word.

Overall, the core contributions of this article are:

- **Multi-Label Split Prediction:** we generalize the target from a single binary *window* to a binary vector over all character positions, enabling the model to predict any number of split locations in one pass;
- **Iterative, Threshold-Based Split Prediction:** We introduce a split prediction method that selects the most likely positions for multiple splits without knowing the actual number of splits a priori.

To validate our novel approach, we augment our corpus with multi-splits of compounds from texts in the Digital Corpus of Sanskrit and the University of Hyderabad (UoH) corpus having ≥ 2 splits.

The remainder of this paper is organized as follows. Section 2 discuss related work. Section 3 formalizes our multi-label problem statement and introduces the recursive split extraction algorithm. Section 4 details implementation changes, including data generation and threshold tuning. Section 5 presents comprehensive experiments, ablation studies, and error analyses. Finally, Sect. 6 discusses the implications of multi-split Sandhi prediction and outlines future integration with morphological analyzers.

2 Related Work

Recent developments in Sanskrit word segmentation have been driven by the availability of new datasets [16,17], enabling a range of methodological advances. As already stated, two primary approaches are commonly employed for Sanskrit word segmentation: lexicon-based and data-driven methods. By framing Sanskrit word segmentation as a character-level sequence labeling task [10], recent work has explored hybrid models that integrate both lexicon-based and data-driven strategies where beneficial. In the following sub-sections, we detail the existing approaches based on the two primary families.

2.1 Lexicon-Based Approaches

The Sanskrit Heritage Reader (SHR) [4] exemplifies the lexicon-based approach, which relies on curated linguistic resources for parsing. Early approaches to Sandhi splitting relied on handcrafted Paninian grammar [9], lexica, and finite-state transducers. Some methods sought to formalize Pāṇinian sandhi rules augmented by lexical resources [18,19], while others adopted nonparametric

Bayesian techniques based on the Dirichlet process [20] or graph-query methods [21].

Tools such as the JNU splitter [8], UoH splitter [6], and INRIA Sanskrit Reader [7] rely mainly on rule-based approaches [11] and face significant limitations due to their inflexibility, which restricts their ability to handle exceptions and variations. Researchers apply exhaustive rule sets followed by lexicon filtering. While linguistically informed [10], these systems are brittle: they require continual maintenance for new or irregular forms and often produce many spurious splits that must be pruned with heuristics.

2.2 Data-Driven Approaches

The data-driven approach learns segmentation patterns directly from annotated data, making it easier to train and deploy models, though it may overlook deeper linguistic structures.

RNN-Based Model: Approaches based on neural networks have cast Sandhi splitting as a sequence-labeling or structured-prediction task. The work in [12,13] demonstrated that attention-based models can significantly reduce split ambiguity by focusing on the most informative character positions. However, most work-including these neural approaches limits itself to single-split compounds, where exactly one Sandhi junction must be found.

Some work has leveraged deep learning for sandhi splitting in compounds: one BiLSTM model jointly performs sandhi resolution and compound splitting by encoding parallel character sequences, training a classifier on ground-truth splits to learn phoneme transformations under five sandhi rules [1]. The work in [26] extended this to an end-to-end character-level model combining convolutional and recurrent layers, achieving competitive tokenization without external linguistic resources.

In [14], we proposes ABBIE, an attention-based bi-encoder for sandhi-aware compound splitting in Sanskrit. ABBIE processes each input word via two parallel Bi-LSTMs-one encoding characters left-to-right, the other right-to-left-and then applies a multi-head attention layer to fuse these contextual representations into a focused *sandhi window*. A sigmoid-activated output layer subsequently predicts the exact split location within that window. ABBIE achieves 89.3% accuracy, outperforming a single-encoder Bi-LSTM baseline by 2.3% and confirms that both the dual-encoder architecture and the attention mechanism are essential for predicting the location in the Sanskrit compound word, though it does not generate the final segmented forms.

To address error propagation in pipeline architectures, a unified, transition-based model concurrently tackles Chinese POS tagging, word segmentation, and syntactic chunking by leveraging task interdependence, offering clear insights for multi-task learning in morphologically rich languages [23].

Finally, a hybrid sequence-labeling framework integrates sandhi and inflectional morphology by detecting split locations and performing segmentation and parsing in a single pipeline, as demonstrated on the WSMP Sanskrit hackathon challenge, highlighting the promise of morphologically informed sequence labeling for complex word representations [24]. Switch-LSTMs [27] dynamically routes between multiple LSTM criteria for multi-criteria Chinese word segmentation and facilitating knowledge transfer across segmentation standards. The work [28] compared stacked BiLSTM architectures with sentence-level transition scoring (BMES encoding), finding that pre-trained character bigrams and single-layer BiLSTMs deliver strong segmentation performance.

The primary difficulty in Sanskrit compound splitting lies in selecting the semantically most appropriate segmentation from among all possible split points. The work in [21] addressed this by framing word segmentation as a queryexpansion problem within a pathconstrained random walks (PCRW) framework. They further enhanced their model's accuracy by incorporating morphological features through Inductive Logic Programming (ILP), yielding marked gains in performance. Attention mechanisms further improve split prediction by highlighting informative character contexts. [12] introduced an attention-based Seq2Seq model to localize split points before performing segmentation, drastically reducing candidate splits. Similarly [13] showed that attention modules significantly boost accuracy in joint split detection and Sandhi resolution.

Transformer-Based Model: Transformer-based TransLIST [10] incorporates linguistic knowledge into a soft-masked attention mechanism to manage sandhi dependencies and employs a path-ranking algorithm to refine segmentation proposals, achieving a 7.2% absolute improvement in perfect-match accuracy on benchmark datasets.

CharSS [22] built atop ByT5. It operates at the byte level to perform end-to-end segmentation without predefined tokenization rules, yielding a 6.72% gain in split-prediction accuracy and a 2.27% boost in perfect-match scores; it also enhances low-resource translation via segmented Sanskrit input, attaining an 8.46-point increase in chrF++ scores.

[2] introduces ByT5-Sanskrit, a byte-level pretrained Transformer model specifically tailored for the morphologically rich Sanskrit language. Building on the token-free ByT5 architecture [25], they fine-tune the model on Sanskrit data to directly process raw text without reliance on external tokenizers or lexica. Evaluated on established Sanskrit word-segmentation benchmarks, ByT5-Sanskrit not only outperforms previous data-driven approaches by a significant margin but also matches the accuracy of the best lexicon-based systems, while demonstrating greater robustness to out-of-vocabulary phenomena. Beyond segmentation, the model achieves new state-of-the-art results in Vedic Sanskrit dependency parsing and OCR post-correction, underscoring its versatility across diverse downstream tasks. To support joint learning, the authors derive a novel multitask dataset from the Digital Corpus of Sanskrit (DCS) [32] that combines annotations for word segmentation, lemmatization, and morphosyntactic tagging. Fine-tuning on this dataset yields a single, unified model capable of handling multiple annotation tasks in one pass. The practical utility of

ByT5-Sanskrit is demonstrated through its deployment in linguistic-annotation projects, information-retrieval systems, and as a preprocessing component in Sanskrit machine-translation pipelines. Moreover, when applied to other morphologically rich languages, the same byte-level approach sets new benchmarks in lemmatization and dependency parsing, highlighting the broader promise of token-free pretrained models for complex natural-language morphologies.

In contrast to all previous work, our approach is specifically designed for multi-split prediction in Sanskrit compound words -a challenge not addressed by prior models.

3 Multi-split Prediction in Sanskrit Compound Words

In our previous work [14], we formulated Sanskrit compound splitting as predicting a single Sandhi split within a given compound word.

Formally, given a Sanskrit compound word $W = [c_1, c_2, \ldots, c_T]$, where c_i denotes the i-th character and T is the length of the compound word, the task in [14] was to predict the location $s \in \{1, \ldots, T-1\}$ where the word should be split into two components:

$$W = [c_1, c_2, \ldots, c_s] \;+\; [c_{s+1}, c_{s+2}, \ldots, c_T]$$

such that, by reversing the Sandhi rule, the boundaries of the two components are modified to obtain the two component words.

However, Sanskrit texts regularly contain compounds with *multiple* valid Sandhi splits, so a single-split formulation is too restrictive and lacks of generality in practical applications in realistic linguistic scenarios. To overcome this, we therefore generalize the prediction task to handle multiple splits within a single compound/sandhied word.

Given a compound word W, our goal is to predict a binary vector

$$\mathbf{y} = [y_1, \ldots, y_T] \in \{0,1\}^T,$$

where $y_i = 1$ indicates a valid split *after* the i-th character and $y_i = 0$ otherwise. More concretely, if the set of split positions is $S = \{s_1, s_2, \ldots, s_n\}$ with $1 \leq s_1 < \cdots < s_n < T$, then $y_s = 1 \; \forall s \in S$ and

$$W \;=\; [c_1, \ldots, c_{s_1}] \;+\; [c_{s_1+1}, \ldots c_{s_2}] \;+\; \cdots + \; [c_{s_n+1}, \ldots, c_T].$$

The proposed ABBIE-M model, Attention-Based BI-Encoders for Multi-split Sanskrit compound prediction, extends our ABBIE architecture [14].

ABBIE originally utilized two parallel Bidirectional LSTM encoders with a Multi-Head Attention [30] mechanism to focus on the splitting location prediction task to identify single-split windows. ABBIE-M builds on this by adapting the same architecture to predict multiple splits simultaneously using the sandhi window of size 4 and using an iterative threshold-based strategy as shown in Fig. 2.

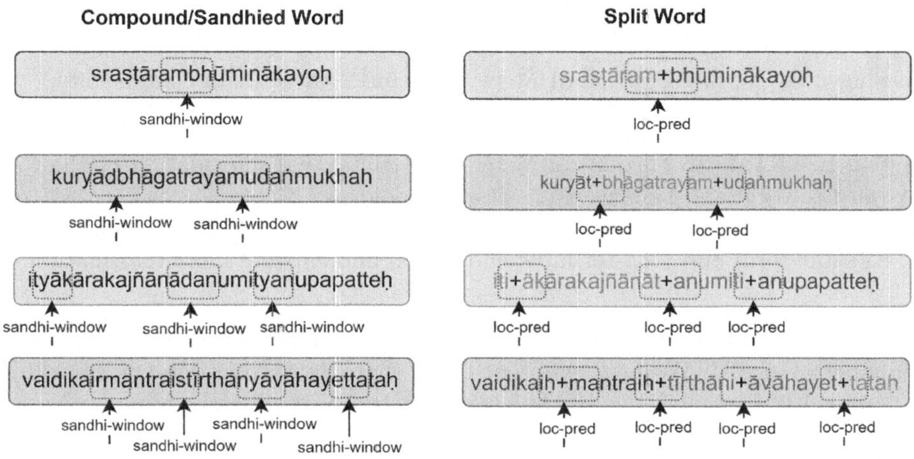

Fig. 2. Iterative multi-split prediction using a sliding Sandhi-window and a threshold to identify multiple split locations in Sanskrit compound words.

In the following sub-sections, we first provide a brief overview of the ABBIE architecture. We then detail the modifications made to the output layer to address the multi-split prediction problem. Finally, we present our iterative approach for detecting multiple split positions.

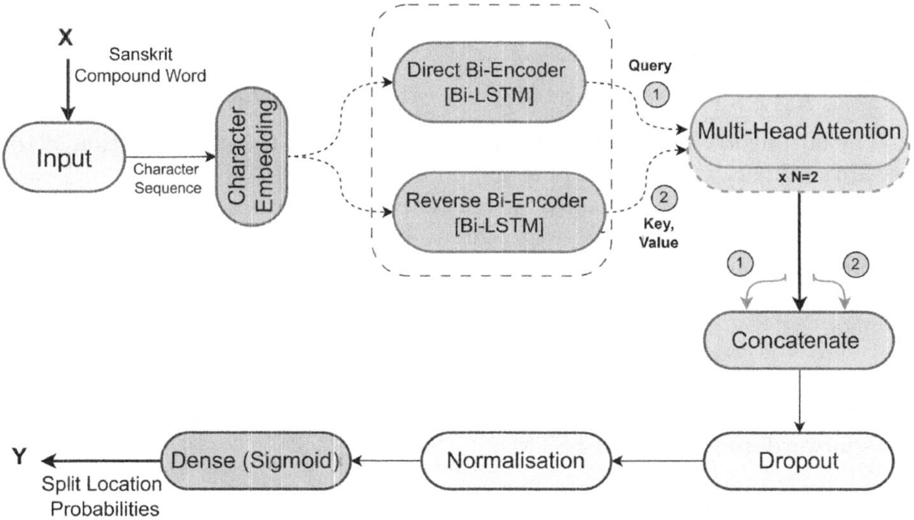

Fig. 3. ABBIE-M extends the ABBIE architecture (shown in figure) by modifying the output layer and adopting an iterative detection strategy (Algorithm 1).

3.1 ABBIE Architecture

As shown in Fig. 3, ABBIE's architecture includes three main components:

1. a character Embedding Layer;
2. two Bi-LSTMs to encode character-level contextual information of the forward (direct) and backward (reverse) sequence;
3. multi-head attention layers to focus on different parts of the sequence (such as short-term and long-term dependencies) and capture more information.

Character Embedding. The characters in the input sequence come from an alphabet of size V. We first represent these characters using one-hot encoding. Subsequently, our model maps the symbols into a learned embedding space.

Given an input sequence X of length T, the embedding is achieved by using an Embedding Matrix $E \in \mathbb{R}^{V \times d}$ with d representing the embedding dimension. The embedding produces the embedded input E_X and can be written as:

$$E_X = XE, \quad \text{where} \quad E_X \in \mathbb{R}^{T \times d}. \tag{1}$$

Direct and Reverse Processing of the Compound Word. ABBIE leverages two Bi-LSTMs [33] to process the embedded input E_X.

The first bi-LSTM, named *direct encoder*, processes the given input sequence as it is and, at each time t, computes:

$$\text{Forward LSTM:} \quad \overrightarrow{h_t} = \text{LSTM}_{\text{fw}}(x_t, \overrightarrow{h_{t-1}}) \tag{2}$$

$$\text{Backward LSTM:} \quad \overleftarrow{h}_t = \text{LSTM}_{\text{bw}}(x_t, \overleftarrow{h_{t+1}}) \tag{3}$$

The output h_t^{direct} of the direct encoder at time t is the concatenation of the forward and backward LSTM outputs.

The second bi-LSTM, named *reverse encoder*, processes the input sequence backward, which we indicate as x'_t. At each time t, the second bi-LSTM will compute:

$$\text{Forward LSTM:} \quad \overrightarrow{h'_t} = \text{LSTM'}_{\text{fw}}(x'_t, \overrightarrow{h'_{t-1}}) \tag{4}$$

$$\text{Backward LSTM:} \quad \overleftarrow{h'_t} = \text{LSTM'}_{\text{bw}}(x'_t, \overleftarrow{h'_{t+1}}) \tag{5}$$

The output h_t^{reverse} of the reverse encoder is the concatenation of the outputs of its forward and backward LSTMs:

$$h_t^{\text{reverse}} = \left[\overrightarrow{h'_t}, \overleftarrow{h'_t}\right], \quad \text{where} \quad h_t^{\text{reverse}} \in \mathbb{R}^{2n}. \tag{6}$$

Hyperbolic tangent (tanh) activation function is used by all the LSTMs. More discussion on the use of two bi-encoders is in [14].

Multi-head Attention Layers: ABBIE leverages attention mechanisms to simultaneously focus on multiple parts of the input sequence, capturing and correlating character-level information from both left and right contexts to accurately determine the split position.

Across the entire input sequence, the direct encoder generates $H^{\text{direct}} \in \mathbb{R}^{T\times 2n}$, where each row corresponds to a vector h_t^{direct} for $t \in [1,\ldots,T]$. In a similar way, the reverse encoder produce $H^{\text{reverse}} \in \mathbb{R}^{T\times 2n}$, whose rows are the vectors h_t^{reverse} for $t \in [1,\ldots,T]$.

Attention transforms inputs into three different vectors: query Q, key K, and value V. In ABBIE, the attention mechanism considers the outputs of the two bi-LSTMs as follows:

$$Q = H^{\text{direct}} \tag{7}$$

$$K = H^{\text{reverse}} \tag{8}$$

$$V = H^{\text{reverse}}. \tag{9}$$

To capture various types of relationships and dependencies within the data, ABBIE adopts multiple attention heads. In particular,

$$A = \text{MultiHead}(Q,K,V) = [\text{head}_1,\ldots,\text{head}_H]W^O \tag{10}$$

where

$$\text{head}_i = \text{Attention}(QW_i^Q, KW_i^K, VW_i^V)$$

and W^O is the output weight matrix.

The outputs of the two bi-encoders and of the multi-head attention module are concatenated $H^{\text{merged}} = \text{Concat}\left(H^{\text{direct}}, A, H^{\text{reverse}}\right)$ to guarantee that both the local context and the global dependencies, which the attention mechanism would capture, will be available to the output layer.

3.2 ABBIE-M's Output Layer

The location prediction in compound words in the Sanskrit is a sequence-to-sequence transformation. Given the sequence of characters of the compound word is transformed into binary values of the same length, in which '0' represents the no-split and '1' indicates the characters of the Sandhi window of size 4, where the split will occur. In our previous paper [14], the model only recognized the one contiguous block of four 1's, which is the sandhi window, but for the multi-split compound word case, it will detect a varying number of disjoint sandhi windows of size 4, one for each split.

For example, if the inputs are characters of the compound word, *vaidikairmantraistīrthānyāvāhayettataḥ* then the target binary mask is obtained from the four block of 1's i-e sandhi window of size 4, and 0's for no split like $[0,0,0,0,0,0,0,1,1,1,1,0,0,0,0,1,1,1,1,0,0,0,0,1,1,1,1,0,0,0,0,1,1,1,1,0,0,0]$ means the *irma*, *istī*, *nyv*, *etta* are the most probable region for predicting the split locations. So, during training, ABBIE-M learns to detect these

Algorithm 1. Iterative Multi-Split Location Extraction.

```
Input: preds – Predicted probabilities per character (of length T)
       W – Window size
       τ – Threshold
Output: splits – Identified split positions
Initialize: used[i] ← 0, ∀i ∈ [1 ... T]
Initialize: list splits ← []
max_score ← max(preds)
cutoff ← max_score × τ
while True do
    best_sum, best_i ← −1, −1
    for i = 1 to T − W do
        if used[j] = 0 ∀j ∈ [i, i + W − 1] then
            window_sum ← Σ_{j=i}^{i+W−1} preds[j]
            if window_sum > best_sum then
                best_sum ← window_sum
                best_i ← i
            end if
        end if
    end for
    if best_sum < cutoff then
        break
    end if
    window ← preds[best_i : best_i + W]
    center ← best_i + arg max(window)
    splits.append(center)
    used[best_i:best_i+W] ← 1
end while
return splits
```

multi-window splitting patterns by using a recursive-based threshold strategy by identifying every split location in a single pass.

In the ABBIE [14], the output layer predicted single-split probabilities within a fixed window size of 4. To handle multi-split predictions, we interpret the output layer differently to produce per-character probabilities for varying window sizes.

The updated formulation is:

$$\hat{y}_i = \sigma(W_o h_i + b_o)$$

where h_i is the encoded feature vector for the ith character, W_o and b_o are learnable parameters, and σ is the sigmoid activation function. This produces a probability vector $\hat{y} \in [0, 1]^T$ indicating split likelihoods based on the threshold and the defined sandhi window.

3.3 Iterative Multi-split Detection

ABBIE was addressing the single-split prediction problem by adopting a sliding window approach over the output sequence to select the window with the highest sum of predicted values.

ABBIE-M adopts an iterative detection approach to handle Sanskrit compounds containing multiple Sandhi splits. This method is vital for systematically translating the per-character split probability predictions produced by ABBIE-M into meaningful multi-split positions.

To robustly identify multiple split locations within a compound word, we propose an iterative algorithm parameterized by a sliding window size W and a threshold τ. Given the predicted probability vector, the algorithm iteratively applies a sliding window over the sequence to locate the highest-scoring region. The cutoff ensures that only high-confidence regions are considered for splits, avoiding the model from selecting false low-probability positions. The cutoff is calculated by scaling the maximum predicted probability across the sequence by the threshold parameter τ, allowing it to adapt dynamically to the confidence distribution of each input compound. This adaptive criterion ensures that only windows whose collective probability exceeds the cutoff are selected, thereby selecting high-confidence split areas. If the sum of probabilities within this window exceeds the cutoff, the central character is marked as a split point. Applying a threshold allows the model to identify the most likely split positions without enforcing a fixed number of splits.

To ensure non-overlapping and apparent predictions, the algorithm excludes regions around previously selected splits in subsequent iterations and continues the process iteratively until no remaining window surpasses the threshold. The threshold selection criterion is influenced by the ABBIE-M's accuracy. We optimised the threshold τ empirically on a validation set by evaluating metrics across different thresholds τ ranging from 0.1 to 1.0 in steps of 0.1, and the threshold is chosen on the maximum accuracy value

$$\tau^* = \arg\max_{\tau} \text{Accuracy}(\tau).$$

The algorithm evaluates at most $T - W$ positions per iteration, yielding a computational complexity of $O(T \times K)$, with K the number of detected splits. Convergence occurs rapidly as fewer valid splits remain after each iteration. The complete procedure is described in Algorithm 1. The detected splits are then sorted based on the best values of the sums of probabilities within the windows.

4 Training of the Model

We followed the same training strategy as in [14], but replaced the loss function with binary cross-entropy to accommodate multi-split location predictions, leaving all other settings unchanged. Training of the model was performed using the Adam optimizer with GPU acceleration on an NVIDIA GeForce RTX 2070 for efficient training. Our training strategy includes the use of standard dropout regularization and layer normalization to ensure convergence and mitigate overfitting. The total number of parameters in the model is 151,041.

Let y_t^{loc} be the true binary label and $\hat{y}_t^{\text{loc}}$ be the predicted probability at time step t. The loss is defined as:

$$L_{\text{loc}}(y_t^{\text{loc}}, \hat{y}_t^{\text{loc}}) = -\frac{1}{T}\sum_{t=1}^{T}\left[y_t^{\text{loc}}\log(\hat{y}_t^{\text{loc}}) + (1-y_t^{\text{loc}})\log(1-\hat{y}_t^{\text{loc}})\right] \quad (11)$$

where T is the number of characters in the padded compound word.

5 Experimental Results

In this experimental section, we compare our proposed approach against two existing model architectures: (i) our previous work ABBIE [14], and Dave et al. [5]. Both of these models are trained on datasets containing only single-split compound words, where each compound has exactly one valid Sandhi split location.

As an extension of ABBIE, our current approach targets a more general and linguistically realistic setting involving multi-split compound words, i.e. compounds with one, two, three, or more valid internal split points. To the best of our knowledge, no prior work has explicitly addressed the task of multi-split prediction at the word level. While some efforts have focused on sentence-level segmentation, those are not directly comparable due to task and data incompatibility.

In the following, we will describe in detail the dataset and metrics used to validate our approach. Next, we will present a detailed analysis of ABBIE-M, to highlight the impact of the threshold used in the proposed iterative detection approach. Finally, we will compare our approach with the iterative use of single-split models.

5.1 Multi-split Compound Dataset

We augment our dataset with compound words having more than two splits from the Digital Corpus of Sanskrit and the University of Hyderabad (UoH) corpus.

The dataset contains 146803 samples in total. The enhanced dataset contains mixed compound words having two splits, three splits, four splits, etc., parts.

We preprocessed the enhanced augmented dataset to remove the duplicates and discarded those compound words having incorrect splits, words not following the sandhi rules, and words not aligned with the sandhi window region.

After this filtering, the final dataset contains 89808 samples of varying length. Figure 4 shows the distribution of word lengths in the dataset. We allocated 80% data for training and 20% for testing, and 10% of the training portion was used for validation of the model.

The corpus was originally encoded in the International Alphabet of Sanskrit Transliteration (IAST) [32] scheme and converted to the Sanskrit Library Phonetic (SLP1) [31], which is a more suitable scheme for better computational analysis due to phonetic representation.

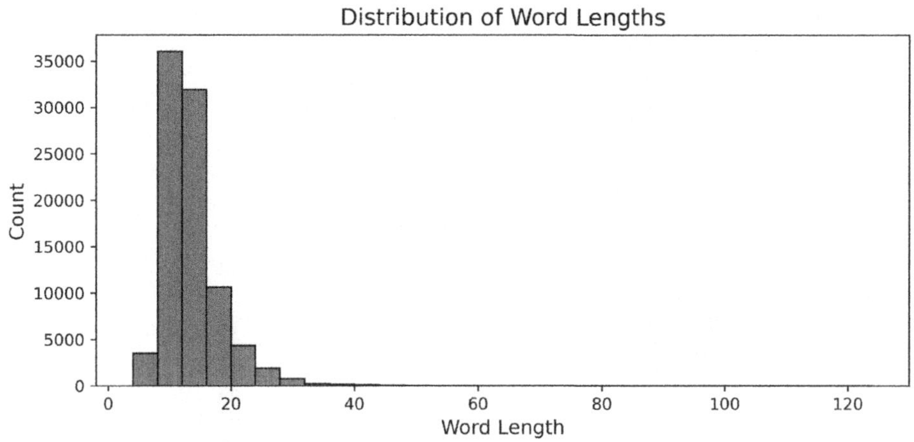

Fig. 4. Distribution of the lengths of the compound words in the considered dataset.

5.2 Evaluation Metrics

In our experiments, we discuss how well the Sandhi windows are identified by assessing the location prediction accuracy. We used the same formula to measure the accuracy as given in the paper [14]. We evaluate the model's accuracy by comparing the predicted split index j with the true split index j^*. The index j marks the character position in the compound word just before the split. The Split Location Prediction Accuracy is calculated as:

$$\text{Accuracy} = \frac{\sum_{i=1}^{N} \delta(j, j^*)}{N} \tag{12}$$

where the function $\delta(j, j^*)$ returns 1 if $j = j^*$ and 0 otherwise. N is the number of compounds in the test set.

Furthermore, we report the following metrics for our multi-split compound word segmentation:

- **Exact-Match Accuracy:** fraction of words for which each split position is predicted exactly.
- **Macro Precision/Recall/F1 at the Word Level:** Each word contributes precision, recall, and F1 score, which are then averaged.
- **Average Boundary Match:** report accuracy for only ABBIE [14], and Dave et al. [5].

5.3 Results for Multi-Split Detection

The results reported in this section refer to the use of the threshold value $\tau = 0.9$. The threshold value has been selected on the validation set by a grid-search approach where values in $[0.1, 1.0]$ in steps of 0.1 were tested to select the threshold value maximizing the exact-match accuracy.

Table 1. Performance of ABBIE-M on the multi-split test set ($\tau^* = 0.9$).

Metric	Value
Word-level Precision (macro)	95.58 %
Word-level Recall (macro)	94.75 %
Word-level F1 (macro)	94.89 %
Exact-match Accuracy	92.47 %

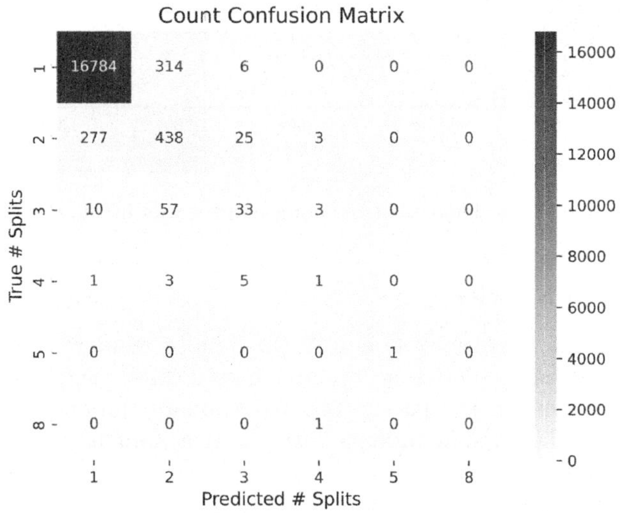

Fig. 5. Word level analysis of the detected number of splits.

Table 1 reports the summarized results of ABBIE-M on our multi-split dataset. In the table, the quality of the individual split prediction is captured by the precision and recall. The macro precision value indicates that when the model proposes a split, this is correct 95.58% of the times, and shows that the iterative detection method almost never misses the character boundary in the compound. High precision value also indicates that there are very few false splits where recall value indicates that the model predicted almost 94.75% of all true splits and only few sandhi boundary were missed. Both the metrics are computed on a per-word basis. The F1-score confirms that the model achieves high accuracy without sacrificing one measure over the other.

The model achieved an exact match accuracy of approximately 92.47% in identifying the locations of all compound words in the test set, even for words with two, three, four, or more splits. This indicates that there were very few incorrect splits or mispredictions.

Figure 5 shows the word-level split count. In this case, we measure how many splits are detected per-word. The figure illustrates that approximately all single-split compounds are correctly detected, i.e. 16,784 out of 17,104 words. For the compounds with two or three splits, the ABBIE-M model still performs well, correctly identifying the majority of cases. The correct predictions lie on the main diagonal. Overall, the ABBIE-M model tends to under-segment by exactly one split rather than over-segmenting.

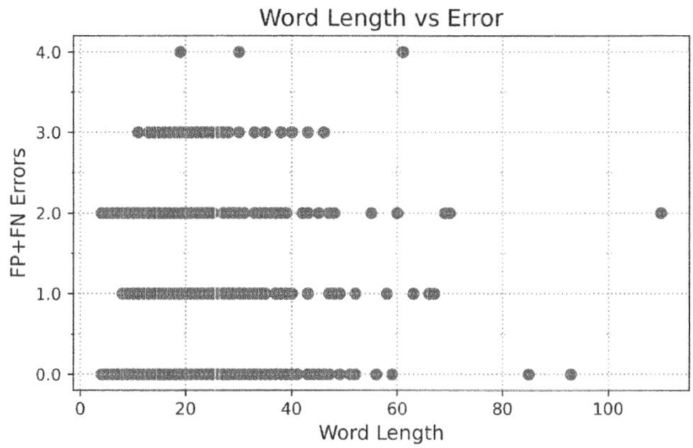

Fig. 6. Errors vs Word length in the multi-split detection.

Figure 6 shows the total number of split errors (false positives + false negatives) against the test compounds' lengths at the chosen threshold (0.9). The majority of the compound words, ranging the length from 5 to 60 characters, lie on the horizontal axis, indicating zero errors. In practice, ABBIE-M segments both short and medium length compounds correctly. A small group of mid-length compounds, with a length between 15 to 45 characters, experienced one or two split errors. Even the longest compound words up to 110 characters received at most two errors. This shows the ABBIE-M's location prediction remains precise and consistent irrespective of the compound length, with only a few error rates in the most uphill task.

While the previous evaluation are at a word-level, we also conducted a per-character analysis of the performance of our model treating split detection as a binary classification problem. Figure 7 shows the character-level confusion matrix for split location in the multi-split compound in the Sanskrit. It indicates that the ABBIE-M model performs well on predicting the split accurately, identifying most elements as either within the Sandhi window (1) or outside it (0). ABBIE-M detects 17,797 characters as *true splits* locations correctly. Only 1,083 detections are false positives and 1,155 are false negatives. These split counts correspond to an overall accuracy above 96% in terms of character-level classification for the location prediction, with the precision and recall for the split class around 94%. These results confirm that the ABBIE-M model performs well on identifying the location prediction with the rare errors in either direction.

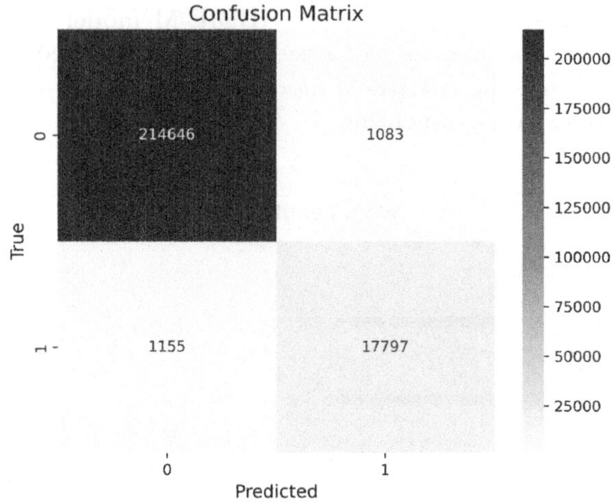

Fig. 7. Character-Level Confusion Matrix for split location. Class 0 indicates the character is outside the Sandhi window, class 1 indicates the character is in the Sandhi window.

5.4 Impact of the Threshold Value on the Results

The threshold τ determines how confident the model must be before accepting a valid sandhi window as a Sandhi region. A lower value for τ would flag more windows (higher recall, lower precision); a higher value for τ would do the opposite.

To better analyze the impact of the threshold value on the detection step, we report in Table 2 the exact-match accuracy values achieved on the test set when varying the values of τ in the range $[0.1, 0.9]$. It should be noted that even with a threshold value of 0.1, the method achieves a pretty high exact-match accuracy value of 90.99%, indicating that the model is able to robustly predict when a split does not occur.

Figure 8 shows ABBIE-M's tolerance to small mis-centering errors by varying the detection threshold τ. The orange, green, and red curves demonstrate the fraction of compounds whose predicted splits lie within ± 1, ± 2, and ± 3 characters of every true split boundary, as τ ranges from 0.10 to 0.90. At $\tau = 0.10$ (left dotted line), ABBIE-M captures 96.0% of words within ± 1 char, 97.1% within ± 2 char, and 98.6% within ± 3 char due to lower confidence windows. As τ increases, the model becomes stricter, discarding lower-confidence split windows, and all three near-miss rates decrease smoothly to 94.6%, 95.7%, and 97.1% at $\tau = 0.9$ (right dashed line). With a threshold $\tau = 0.9$, only the strongest confidence windows are predicted. Marginal windows, even those that lie within one character of a true split, are discarded. This reduces the false positive rate. The moderate drop of no more than 1.5% across threshold values suggests that ABBIE-M's split predictions remain tightly grouped around the true Sandhi junctions, even under stricter confidence requirements.

Table 2. Accuracy at various threshold levels.

Threshold τ	Exact Match Accuracy
0.10	0.9099
0.20	0.9155
0.30	0.9187
0.40	0.9199
0.50	0.9218
0.60	0.9226
0.70	0.9240
0.80	0.9245
0.90	0.9247

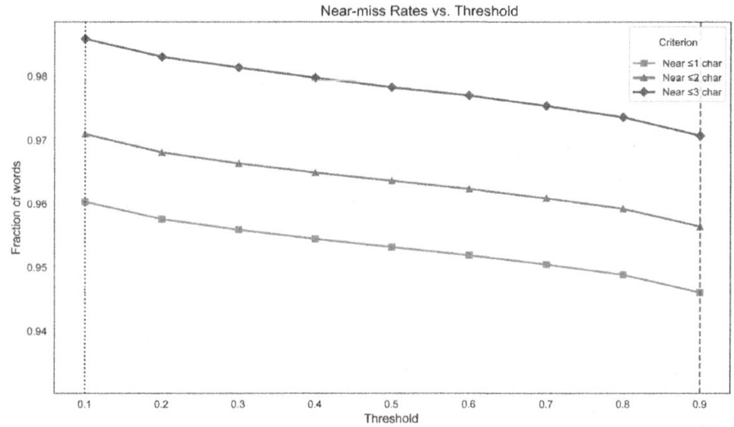

Fig. 8. Near-Miss Character Rate vs Threshold.

5.5 Comparison to the State-of-the-Art

To the best of our knowledge, there are no other works addressing the multi-split prediction in Sanskrit at the compound word level. Thus, we compare our approach only with baseline methods presented in [14] and [5]. These models were trained entirely on compound words with a single split location and used a maximum sequence length of 30 characters. On the other hand, our multi-split compound dataset includes a diverse set of samples with longer sequences and varying numbers of split locations. We also evaluated the baseline models on our dataset; however, due to incompatibilities due to the sequence length and the existence of multiple splits, they failed to perform properly. Therefore, we trained our model from scratch on the new dataset to demonstrate its robustness and novelty in processing multi-split Sanskrit compound words. We report accuracy results in Table 3 for both the baseline models trained on single-split data and our model trained on multi-split data. In single split location prediction, our

ABBIE-M model also achieves better accuracy of 98.12% as compared to other models due to the iterative threshold-based multi-split detection. Our ABBIE-M model, which is trained on a multi-split dataset to predict in one pass the per-character probabilities of a split, together with the iterative algorithm to detect the Sandhi window, achieves instead a 92.47% of exact match.

Table 3. Accuracy of baseline models on multi-split compound dataset.

Model	Accuracy	
	Single Split	Multi-Split
ABBIE [14]	89.27%	–
Dave et al. [5]	87.0%	–
ABBIE-M(Ours)	98.31%	92.47%

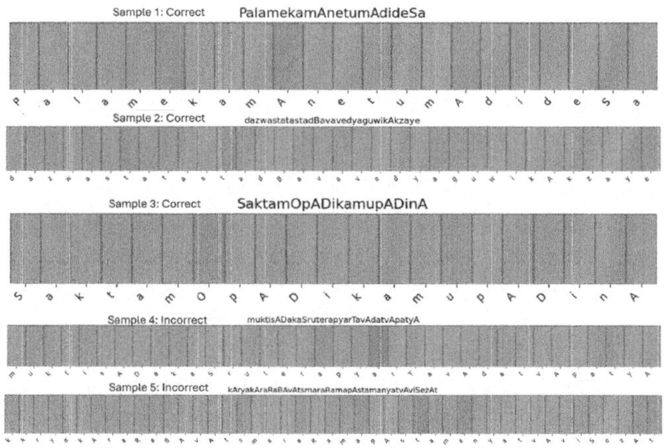

Fig. 9. Error maps for multi-split location prediction across several samples. For each sample, the figure displays per-character predictions using a color-coded scheme: green indicates correctly identified non-split positions; pink marks correctly predicted split positions; purple denotes near-miss by ±1 character; and orange highlights false positives. In the first three samples, the model correctly predicts 3, 2, and 2 splits, respectively. In the fourth sample, only one of the two true splits is detected. In the fifth sample, two splits are correctly identified, one is missed, and an additional incorrect split is predicted. (Color figure online)

5.6 Qualitative Analysis of the Detection Results

Figure 9 shows ABBIE-M's error map output at the character level for the multi-split location prediction. In the figure, the pink color shows the exact match, the purple color indicates the near-miss by ±1 character, and the orange color highlights the false positives. Each horizontal axis reflects the position of each character in the input sequence.

In Samples 1, 2, and 3, *PalamekamAnetumAdideSa*, *dazwastatastadBavavedya guwikAkzaye*, *SaktamOpADikamupADinA*, all threshold-based sandhi windows are precisely aligned with the ground truth boundaries and therefore, ABBIE-M predicts the correct varying split locations in the Sanskrit compound words. In Sample 4 *muktisADakaSruterapyarTavAdatvApatyA*, the model predicts the first split location correctly, but the second window is centered one character left to the reference, namely it is a near miss, and is highlighted as purple. This segmentation is linguistically valid yet fails the exact location prediction task.

In the final sample *kAryakAraRaBAvAtsmaraRamapAstamanyatvAviSezAt*, two windows are exactly detected, there is a near miss, and a false split highlighted in orange. In short, the error map confirms that ABBIE-M's errors are highly local, typically a ±1 character or isolated false window.

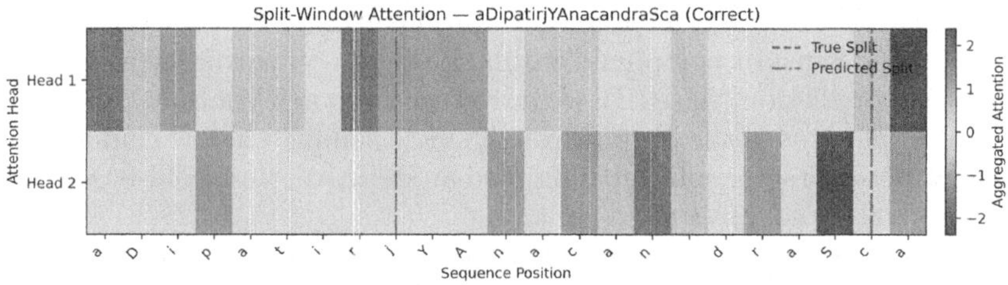

(a) Split-Window Attention Heatmap for Correct Prediction

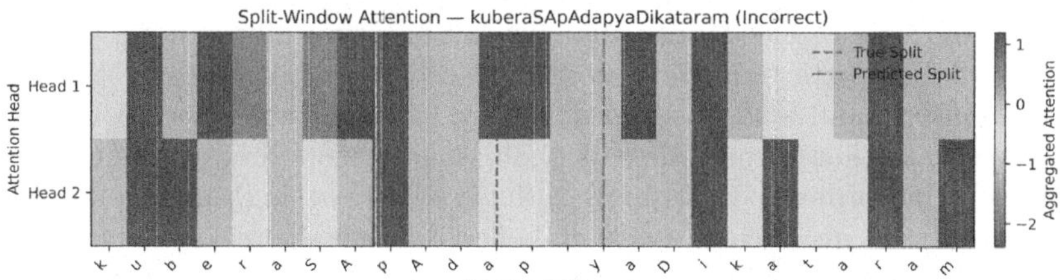

(b) Split-Window Attention Heatmap for Incorrect Prediction

Fig. 10. Comparison of Split-Window Attention Heatmaps.

Figure 10a shows the per-head split-window attention heatmap for the correctly predicted split location in the compound word *aDipatirjYAnacandraSca*. The x-axis specifies the character positions, while the y-axis shows the attention heads. Cell color indicates the aggregated attention weights, i-e, summed across all keys for each head at each position. Gray/Orange color shows the maximum positive attention, and blue color indicates minimal attention. The model's predicted split (red dashed lines) aligns with the true split (green dashed lines). When the model correctly predicted the split locations, its attention is sharply focused on the true split boundary to show strong focus. This localized attention map reflects that the model has learned to focus on the correct characters in the sequence at the actual morpheme boundaries. In this occurrence, both heads show their strong activations precisely at the true split positions.

Figure 10(b) illustrates the per-head split-window attention heatmap for the incorrectly predicted split location in the compound word *kuberaS-ApAdapyaDikataram* where the model deviates from the true split locations. The predicted locations do not correspond with the true split locations. Both heads show the maximum attention at the incorrect split positions rather than at the ground truth boundaries, which receive only low weight. There are two split locations; the model only predicted one and escaped the other. This is also the reason that there is low attention to that position. The attention thus appears mismanaged by the false character patterns, leading to incorrect predictions.

6 Conclusion and Future Work

In this research work, we focus on the problem of predicting the multi-split locations in the Sanskrit compound words. Based on our earlier work on a single split location prediction (ABBIE), we introduced two new concepts: a multi-label prediction that extends the output from a single sandhi window classification to concurrent per-character split labeling, and an iterative, threshold-based method that repetitively recognizes valid splits.

Experimental results show that ABBIE-M achieves remarkable results in macro-level precision, recall, F1 scores, and exact match accuracy, demonstrating clear improvement over single-split techniques. Despite the ABBIE-M's performance, our model faced near-miss predictions typically resulting from the vague Sandhi contexts that yield closely spaced probability peaks, causing ± 1 character offsets, and also false positives are still produced due to local high-confidence peaks that surpass the threshold, leading to a limitation of our work. The model's performance is strongly influenced by the high quality and quantity of the dataset; insufficient quality labelled datasets decrease the performance and limit broader applicability. In the future, we intend to refine the recursive method by integrating linguistic or semantic rules to further lower the false positives and near-miss occurrences. Moreover, we will also utilize the transformer-based architecture and high-quality annotated datasets that could improve the model's prediction accuracy and reduce the near-miss rates.

Acknowledgments. This work is partially supported by the PNRR MUR Project ITSERR (Italian Strengthening of the ESFRI RI RESILIENCE) (IR0000014, CUP B53C22001770006).

References

1. Hellwig, O.: Using recurrent neural networks for joint compound splitting and Sandhi resolution in Sanskrit. In: 4th Biennial Workshop on Less-Resourced Languages (2015)
2. Nehrdich, S., Hellwig, O., Keutzer, K.: One model is all you need: ByT5-Sanskrit, a unified model for Sanskrit NLP tasks. arXiv preprint: arXiv:2409.13920 (2024)
3. Gupta, A., Krishna, A., Goyal, P., Hellwig, O.: Evaluating neural morphological taggers for Sanskrit. arXiv preprint: arXiv:2005.10893 (2020)
4. Goyal, P., Huet, G.: Design and analysis of a lean interface for Sanskrit corpus annotation. J. Lang. Model. **4**(2), 145–182 (2016)
5. Dave, S., Singh, A.K., Prathosh, A.P., Lall, B.: Neural compound-word (Sandhi) generation and splitting in Sanskrit language. In: Proceedings of the 3rd ACM India Joint International Conference on Data Science and Management of Data (8th ACM IKDD CODS and 26th COMAD), pp. 171–177 (2021)
6. Sanskrit Computational Linguistics. https://sanskrit.uohyd.ac.in/scl/. Accessed 08 Aug 2024
7. INRIA Sanskrit Dictionary. https://sanskrit.inria.fr/DICO/reader.en.html. Accessed 08 Aug 2024
8. Kumar, S.: Sandhi splitter and analyzer for Sanskrit (with reference to Ac Sandhi) (2007). Submitted
9. Cardona, G.: Pāini: A Survey of Research. Motilal Banarsidass (1997)
10. Sandhan, J., Singha, R., Rao, N., Samanta, S., Behera, L., Goyal, P.: TransLIST: a transformer-based linguistically informed Sanskrit tokenizer. arXiv preprint: arXiv:2210.11753 (2022)
11. Sanskrit Computational Linguistics: Sanskrit computational linguistics 2002–2024
12. Aralikatte, R., Gantayat, N., Panwar, N., Sankaran, A., Mani, S.: Sanskrit Sandhi splitting using seq2(seq)2. arXiv preprint: arXiv:1801.00428 (2018)
13. Reddy, V., Krishna, A., Sharma, V.D., Gupta, P., Goyal, P., et al.: Building a word segmenter for Sanskrit overnight. arXiv preprint: arXiv:1802.06185 (2018)
14. Ali, I., Lo Presti, L., Spano, I., La Cascia, M.: ABBIE: attention-based BI-Encoders for predicting where to split compound Sanskrit words. In: Proceedings of the 17th International Conference on Agents and Artificial Intelligence - Volume 2 (2025)
15. Haruechaiyasak, C., Kongyoung, S., Dailey, M.: A comparative study on Thai word segmentation approaches. In: 5th International Conference on Electrical Engineering/Electronics, Computer, Telecommunications and Information Technology (ECTI), vol. 1, pp. 125-128. IEEE (2008)
16. Krishna, A., Satuluri, P., Goyal, P.: A dataset for Sanskrit word segmentation. In: Proceedings of the Joint SIGHUM Workshop on Computational Linguistics for Cultural Heritage, Social Sciences, Humanities and Literature, pp. 105–114 (2017)
17. Krishnan, S., Kulkarni, A., Huet, G.: Validation and normalization of DCS corpus using Sanskrit heritage tools to build a tagged gold corpus. arXiv preprint: arXiv:2005.06545 (2020)
18. Huet, G.: A functional toolkit for morphological and phonological processing, application to a Sanskrit tagger. J. Funct. Program. **15**(4), 573–614 (2005)
19. Kulkarni, A., Shukl, D.: Sanskrit morphological analyser: some issues. Indian Linguist. **70**(1–4), 169–177 (2009)
20. Natarajan, A., Charniak, E.: S3-statistical Sandhi splitting. In: Proceedings of 5th International Joint Conference on Natural Language Processing, pp. 301–308 (2011)

21. Krishna, A., et al.: Word segmentation in Sanskrit using path constrained random walks. In: Proceedings of COLING 2016, 26th International Conference on Computational Linguistics: Technical Papers, pp. 494–504 (2016)
22. Bhatt, K., Ramakrishnan, G., Jyothi, P.: CharSS: character-level transformer model for Sanskrit word segmentation. arXiv preprint: arXiv:2407.06331 (2024)
23. Lyu, C., Zhang, Y., Ji, D.: Joint word segmentation, POS-tagging and syntactic chunking. In: Proceedings of the Thirtieth AAAI Conference on Artificial Intelligence (AAAI-16) (2016)
24. Li, J., Girrbach, L.: Word segmentation and morphological parsing for Sanskrit. arXiv preprint: arXiv:2201.12833 (2022)
25. Xue, L., et al.: ByT5: towards a token-free future with pre-trained byte-to-byte models. Trans. Assoc. Comput. Linguist. **10**, 291–306 (2022)
26. Hellwig, O., Nehrdich, S.: Sanskrit word segmentation using character-level recurrent and convolutional neural networks. In: Proceedings of the 2018 Conference on Empirical Methods in Natural Language Processing, pp. 2754–2763 (2018)
27. Gong, J., Chen, X., Gui, T., Qiu, X.: Switch-LSTMs for multi-criteria Chinese word segmentation. In: Proceedings of the AAAI Conference on Artificial Intelligence, vol. 33, pp. 6457–6464 (2019)
28. Chen, X., Qiu, X., Zhu, C., Liu, P., Huang, X.-J.: Long short-term memory neural networks for Chinese word segmentation. In: Proceedings of the 2015 Conference on Empirical Methods in Natural Language Processing, pp. 1197–1206 (2015)
29. Sutskever, I., Vinyals, O., Le, Q.V.: Sequence to sequence learning with neural networks. In: Advances in Neural Information Processing Systems, vol. 27 (2014)
30. Vaswani, A., et al.: Attention is all you need. In: Advances in Neural Information Processing Systems, vol. 30 (2017)
31. Learn Sanskrit: Sanscript: Sanskrit transliteration. https://www.learnsanskrit.org. Accessed 08 Aug 2024
32. Hellwig, O.: The Digital Corpus of Sanskrit (DCS). http://www.sanskrit-linguistics.org/dcs/ (2010–2021)
33. Hochreiter, S., Schmidhuber, J.: Long short-term memory. Neural Comput. **9**(8), 1735–1780 (1997)

Non-additive Neural Networks for Classification with Reliability Index

Yassine Hmidy[1(✉)] and Slim Belhaiza[2]

[1] SogetiLabs, Capgemini, Paris, France
yassine.hmidy@sogeti.com
[2] Department of Mathematics, Interdisciplinary Research Center on Smart Mobility and Logistics, Interdisciplinary Research Center for Communication Systems and Sensing, King Fahd University of Petroleum and Minerals (KFUPM), Dhahran 31261, Saudi Arabia
slimb@kfupm.edu.sa

Abstract. This paper introduces a novel classification framework based on non-additive neural networks that incorporate reliability assessment. By replacing the conventional weighted sum operation with a non-additive integral-based aggregation function called Macsum, our model produces class probability distributions with associated reliability indices. Unlike standard neural networks that provide point estimates of class probabilities, our approach generates interval-valued outputs whose width correlates with classification uncertainty. We implement this architecture in PyTorch and demonstrate its effectiveness on benchmark classification datasets. Our results show that the model achieves competitive classification accuracy while providing valuable reliability quantification through interval outputs. The correlation between interval width and classification error confirms the model's ability to assess its own reliability, making it particularly suitable for high-stakes applications where decision trustworthiness is critical. The proposed reliability index enables rejection of uncertain predictions, leading to improved precision-recall trade-offs and more robust decision-making in practical applications.

Keywords: Non-Additive Neural Networks · Classification · Uncertainty Quantification · Reliability Index · Interval-Valued Outputs · Choquet Integral

1 Introduction

Deep neural networks have established themselves as the leading paradigm for supervised classification tasks, consistently achieving state-of-the-art performance across diverse domains such as computer vision, natural language processing, and biomedical informatics [15]. This widespread success is primarily attributed to their capacity to learn hierarchical representations through a succession of nonlinear transformations, capturing intricate patterns within high-dimensional data [26].

H. J. van den Herik et al. (Eds.): ICAART 2025, LNAI 16517, pp. 259–284, 2026.
https://doi.org/10.1007/978-3-032-25032-2_12

However, a fundamental limitation persists within conventional neural networks: they typically produce point estimates of class probabilities without directly quantifying the uncertainty associated with their predictions [13]. This inability to explicitly represent predictive uncertainty significantly restricts their reliability, especially in high-stakes applications where misclassifications can have severe consequences [16].

Indeed, the ramifications of such uncertainty blindness can be profound. In medical diagnosis, for example, a network that confidently produces incorrect predictions can lead to misdiagnosis, inappropriate treatment decisions, and potential harm to patients [15]. In autonomous driving systems, failure to acknowledge ambiguous sensor data or uncertain road conditions could result in catastrophic accidents. Similarly, within financial fraud detection, poorly calibrated confidence estimates may either overlook fraudulent transactions or generate excessive false alarms, thereby undermining trust in automated decision systems [16].

Existing methodologies aimed at incorporating uncertainty quantification—such as Bayesian neural networks [13], Monte Carlo dropout methods, or deep ensembles—typically rely on post-hoc approximation strategies. While these approaches provide useful uncertainty estimates, they incur additional computational overhead and only approximate the true underlying uncertainty structures [36].

In this paper, we propose a fundamentally new approach that addresses these limitations at the architectural level. We introduce a novel neural network paradigm by modifying the core aggregation mechanism within neurons. Specifically, we replace the traditional deterministic weighted-sum operation with the Macsum operator—*Multiplicative and Additive Choquet-based Sum* [8]—an aggregation function grounded in the discrete Choquet integral framework [1]. The Macsum operator generalizes aggregation by explicitly modeling non-additive interactions (synergies or redundancies) among input features via capacity-based integration [7]. Crucially, it outputs intervals rather than point estimates, inherently encoding classification uncertainty directly within the forward pass [36].

Our proposed approach offers intrinsic uncertainty quantification by directly producing interval-valued outputs that naturally express the model's degree of confidence or uncertainty, thus eliminating the necessity of additional post-processing steps to estimate predictive uncertainty [5]. Furthermore, by leveraging the Choquet integral, the Macsum aggregation effectively models complex, non-additive interactions among features, such as redundancy and synergy, which standard linear aggregation methods fail to capture [1,7]. Finally, unlike Bayesian-inspired approaches such as Monte Carlo dropout, our method integrates uncertainty estimation directly into the forward pass, thereby significantly reducing computational overhead [8,13].

Concretely, the contributions of this paper are as follows:

(i) We rigorously formalize the theoretical foundations of the Macsum operator, including its mathematical properties and explicitly derive gradient expressions compatible with standard backpropagation algorithms.
(ii) We empirically validate our proposed Macsum-based neural network architecture on benchmark classification datasets, demonstrating competitive accuracy accompanied by well-calibrated uncertainty quantification.
(iii) We illustrate how interval-valued outputs can be employed to enhance decision-making robustness in risk-sensitive domains, introducing a reliability index that facilitates selective prediction and thus improves precision–coverage trade-offs in critical scenarios.

By integrating non-additive integral theory into deep learning architectures, our approach establishes a bridge between purely deterministic neural network models and robust probabilistic reasoning frameworks. Ultimately, this integration paves the way towards more trustworthy, uncertainty-aware artificial intelligence systems, particularly suited for high-stakes, safety-critical applications [16,36].

2 Related Work

Effectively quantifying and leveraging uncertainty is paramount for deploying deep neural networks in safety-critical domains. This section reviews foundational and recent work essential to positioning our contribution. We examine established paradigms for uncertainty quantification in neural networks, highlighting the trade-offs between theoretical grounding and computational efficiency. We then explore the role of non-additive aggregation, particularly the Choquet integral, for capturing complex feature interactions beyond linear models – a capability largely untapped for native uncertainty representation. Finally, we discuss interval-valued predictions and reliability indices, which offer intuitive uncertainty semantics but often lack tight integration with deep architectures. Collectively, these interconnected research streams inform our approach to embedding efficient, interaction-aware uncertainty quantification directly within neural network computation.

2.1 Uncertainty Quantification in Neural Networks

Uncertainty quantification in deep learning has garnered significant attention due to its critical role in safety-sensitive applications. Bayesian Neural Networks (BNNs) represent a foundational approach, modeling weight uncertainty through posterior distributions [13]. While theoretically principled, BNNs face computational challenges in inference due to the intractability of exact Bayesian methods, necessitating approximations like variational inference or Markov Chain Monte Carlo sampling. Monte Carlo (MC) Dropout offers a practical alternative by interpreting dropout layers as approximate Bayesian inference during multiple stochastic forward passes. Though efficient, MC Dropout provides only *approximate* uncertainty estimates and requires multiple inferences per prediction. Deep Ensembles [27] mitigate this by training multiple models independently and aggregating predictions, achieving state-of-the-art calibration but at the cost of multiplied training and storage overhead. Evidential deep learning [28] frames uncertainty quantification through Dirichlet distributions over class probabilities, though it requires careful handling of hyperparameters to avoid overconfidence. Conformal prediction [23] provides distribution-free uncertainty intervals via post-hoc calibration on held-out data but operates independently of model internals. While these methods enhance reliability, they either approximate uncertainty statistically, incur high computational costs, or lack integration with model architecture.

2.2 Non-additive Aggregation in Machine Learning

Non-additive aggregation functions, particularly the Choquet integral, offer a mathematically rigorous framework for modeling feature interactions beyond linear weighted sums. The Choquet integral generalizes aggregation by weighting inputs based on their marginal contributions to coalitions of features, parameterized by a capacity (fuzzy measure) [1,7]. This allows explicit modeling of *synergies*, *redundancies*, and *antagonisms* among features—dynamics that linear perceptrons inherently fail to capture. Early applications in machine learning include decision fusion [29] and ensemble weighting, while recent work explores Choquet-based layers in neural networks for feature fusion [30]. However, these efforts primarily focus on enhancing representational capacity rather than uncertainty quantification. Signed variants of the Choquet integral [31,32] extend this further by permitting non-monotonic interactions (e.g., negative weights for inhibitory effects), though their use in deep learning remains underexplored. Critically, while non-additive integrals excel at modeling complex dependencies, their direct application to *native uncertainty quantification* within neural architectures has been limited prior to this work.

2.3 Interval-Valued Predictions and Reliability Indices

Interval-valued approaches provide intuitive uncertainty representation by outputting prediction ranges rather than point estimates. Traditional interval neural networks [5] propagate bounds through weights and activations but often yield overly conservative intervals. The Macsum operator [8] addresses this by leveraging the Choquet integral to generate intervals whose widths correlate with epistemic uncertainty. Originally applied to regression [8], Macsum outputs intervals as convex sets of linear models, enabling uncertainty-aware predictions without sampling. In classification, reliability is often quantified through *rejection mechanisms* based on confidence thresholds. Methods range from temperature scaling [33] and isotonic regression for calibrating softmax outputs to conformal prediction for guaranteed coverage [34]. Logit-based uncertainty measures [35] correlate raw pre-softmax values with error rates but lack inherent probabilistic semantics. Recent work [36] explores reliability indices for logistic regression, yet extending these to deep neural networks while maintaining architectural coherence remains challenging. Our work bridges this gap by integrating interval-valued logits derived from non-additive aggregation into an end-to-end trainable framework.

2.4 Positioning of Our Contribution

Relative to existing literature, our approach makes three key advances:

1. **Architectural Integration of Uncertainty:** Unlike post-hoc or sampling-based methods (e.g., MC Dropout, conformal prediction), MacsumNN-C *natively* outputs interval-valued logits via Choquet-based aggregation in a single deterministic forward pass. This embeds uncertainty quantification directly into the model's computational structure, eliminating inference-time overhead.
2. **Non-Additive Interaction Modeling:** While standard neural networks rely on linear aggregation, MacsumNN-C uses the Choquet integral to capture feature interactions (synergy/redundancy) via capacities. This provides richer representations than additive models and more interpretable uncertainty than black-box Bayesian approximations.
3. **Unified Reliability Index:** We introduce a theoretically grounded reliability index R derived from probability interval widths, enabling intuitive abstention mechanisms. Unlike heuristic confidence scores, R emerges directly from the non-additive aggregation mechanism, correlating strongly with prediction errors.

By unifying these elements, MacsumNN-C offers a scalable, interpretable alternative to existing uncertainty quantification paradigms, particularly suited for applications demanding both accuracy and decision trustworthiness.

3 Mathematical Background

3.1 Aggregation Functions and the Need for Non-additivity

Aggregation is a fundamental operation in many areas of machine learning and decision theory. Formally, an *aggregation function* is a mapping

$$F : \mathbb{R}^n \to \mathbb{R}$$

that combines a vector of input values—often representing features, scores, or signals—into a single output that summarizes or synthesizes the information. In neural networks, aggregation typically occurs within neurons through weighted sums of inputs followed by a non-linear activation function.

In most conventional neural architectures, the aggregation function is *additive*, taking the form:

$$F(\mathbf{x}) = \sum_{i=1}^{n} w_i x_i + b,$$

where $\mathbf{x} = (x_1, \ldots, x_n)$ is the input vector, $w_i \in \mathbb{R}$ are learnable weights, and $b \in \mathbb{R}$ is a bias term [26]. This form assumes that each feature contributes *independently and linearly* to the output, and the overall contribution is merely the superposition of individual effects.

However, real-world data often violates the assumptions underlying additive aggregation. In complex domains—such as healthcare, finance, and autonomous systems—features rarely act in isolation. Their joint presence often yields synergistic, redundant, or even antagonistic interactions, which additive models fail to capture.

To formalize and generalize aggregation beyond additivity, we consider the broader mathematical concept of *set functions*. A set function is a mapping:

$$\mu : 2^N \to \mathbb{R}, \quad N = \{1, \ldots, n\},$$

that assigns values to *subsets* of input indices. When used for aggregation, the values $\mu(A)$ represent the importance or influence of the coalition $A \subseteq N$ of features. Aggregation functions that incorporate such set functions can model complex dependencies among inputs.

3.2 Limitations of Additivity and Emergence of Feature Interactions

An aggregation function F is said to be **non-additive** if it cannot be expressed as a simple linear combination of individual feature contributions:

$$F(x_1, \ldots, x_n) \neq \sum_{i=1}^{n} w_i x_i \quad \text{for any choice of } \{w_i\}.$$

This non-additivity arises when the effect of one feature depends on the presence, absence, or intensity of others—a scenario frequently encountered in real-world datasets. In such cases, the assumption of feature independence that underlies additive models becomes invalid.

Non-additive interactions typically manifest in one of the following forms:

- **Synergistic Effects:** Two or more features, when combined, exert a greater influence than the sum of their individual effects.
  Numerical example: Suppose in a medical risk model for diagnosing flu, we assign:

  $$x_1 = \text{fever level (scale 0 to 1)} = 0.7, \quad x_2 = \text{cough severity} = 0.6.$$

  Under an additive model:

  $$F_{\text{add}}(x_1, x_2) = 0.5 \cdot x_1 + 0.5 \cdot x_2 = 0.35 + 0.30 = 0.65.$$

  But in practice, the co-occurrence of both symptoms might increase the diagnosis probability to:

  $$F_{\text{true}}(x_1, x_2) = 0.90.$$

  This 0.25 discrepancy illustrates synergy: the whole is greater than the sum of the parts.

- **Redundant Effects:** Features carry overlapping or duplicated information, reducing their marginal contribution when considered jointly.
  Numerical example: In fraud detection, let:

  $$x_1 = \text{transaction amount risk score} = 0.8, \quad x_2 = \text{transaction frequency score} = 0.75.$$

  If both metrics measure similar user behavior, then:

  $$F_{\text{add}} = 0.5 \cdot x_1 + 0.5 \cdot x_2 = 0.775,$$

  but the actual model might downscale this due to redundancy:

  $$F_{\text{true}}(x_1, x_2) = 0.60.$$

  Here, the overlapping signal reduces the importance of treating both features equally.
- **Antagonistic Effects:** One feature may inhibit or negate the influence of another.
  Numerical example: In autonomous vehicle systems:

  $$x_1 = \text{rain sensor activation} = 0.7, \quad x_2 = \text{black ice sensor reading} = 1.0.$$

  An additive model would produce:

  $$F_{\text{add}} = 0.5 \cdot x_1 + 0.5 \cdot x_2 = 0.85.$$

  But since black ice is a more severe and overriding condition than rain, a safety module might suppress the rain signal entirely:

  $$F_{\text{true}}(x_1, x_2) = 1.0.$$

  This illustrates antagonism: the presence of one feature diminishes the relevance of another.

These examples demonstrate how the additive assumption fails to capture essential inter-feature dynamics. Additive perceptrons, being linear in their aggregation, are inherently limited in this regard. To capture such non-linear, context-sensitive interactions, we require aggregation mechanisms that operate over sets of features rather than isolated inputs.

Non-additive integrals, such as the **Choquet integral**, provide a principled framework for modeling these dependencies by allowing the importance of a feature to vary depending on which other features are active. This makes them ideal candidates for applications requiring explainability, robustness, and nuanced feature interactions.

3.3 Non-additive Measures and the Choquet Integral

The Choquet integral arises in the theory of *fuzzy measures*, where information aggregation is performed with respect to a **capacity** rather than a probability measure. A *capacity* is a set function:

$$\mu : 2^N \to [0, 1],$$

satisfying the following axioms:

$$\mu(\emptyset) = 0, \quad \mu(N) = 1 \quad \text{(normalization)} \tag{1}$$

$$\text{If } A \subseteq B \subseteq N, \text{ then } \mu(A) \leq \mu(B) \quad \text{(monotonicity)} \tag{2}$$

Unlike probability measures, capacities are **not additive** in general:

$$\mu(A \cup B) \neq \mu(A) + \mu(B) \quad \text{even if } A \cap B = \emptyset.$$

This allows modeling of complex feature groupings where the importance of a set is not merely the sum of its parts.

The **Choquet integral** with respect to a capacity μ aggregates feature values $\mathbf{x} = (x_1, \ldots, x_n)$ by weighting each feature not by its individual contribution, but by the marginal importance of the subsets it belongs to.

3.4 Discrete Choquet Integral: Definition and Properties

In neural architectures, the **discrete Choquet integral** is especially suited due to its compatibility with finite-dimensional feature vectors and differentiable optimization. Given an input $\mathbf{x} \in \mathbb{R}^n$ and a capacity μ, the discrete Choquet integral is defined as:

$$\mathcal{C}_\mu(\mathbf{x}) = \sum_{k=1}^{n} x_{(k)} \cdot [\mu(A_{(k)}) - \mu(A_{(k+1)})],$$

where:

- $x_{(1)} \leq \cdots \leq x_{(n)}$ is a non-decreasing reordering of x_i,
- $A_{(k)} = \{(k), \ldots, (n)\}$ is the set of indices of the k-th largest and larger inputs,
- $A_{(n+1)} = \emptyset$, and $\mu(\emptyset) = 0$.

Each term in the sum corresponds to the "marginal contribution" of a feature given the presence of stronger features, effectively capturing *context-dependent relevance*.

This formulation satisfies key properties required in deep learning:

1. **Differentiability:** Though sorting is non-smooth, subgradients exist and are compatible with backpropagation frameworks [26]:

$$\frac{\partial \mathcal{C}_\mu}{\partial x_i} = \sum_{k=1}^{n} \frac{\partial \mathcal{C}_\mu}{\partial x_{(k)}} \cdot \frac{\partial x_{(k)}}{\partial x_i}$$

   where $\frac{\partial x_{(k)}}{\partial x_i}$ is 1 if i is the k-th smallest index and 0 otherwise.
2. **Computational Efficiency:** The sorting step incurs $\mathcal{O}(n \log n)$ complexity per neuron, making it tractable in modern deep architectures [8].
3. **Interpretability:** Each capacity value $\mu(A)$ reflects the importance of a subset A, enabling introspection into learned interactions.

3.5 Expressive Power and Special Cases

The Choquet integral subsumes several standard aggregation operations as special cases:

$$\text{Weighted mean:} \quad \mu(A) = \sum_{i \in A} w_i \tag{3}$$

$$\text{Maximum:} \quad \mu(A) = \begin{cases} 1 & \text{if } A \neq \emptyset \\ 0 & \text{otherwise} \end{cases} \tag{4}$$

$$\text{Minimum:} \quad \mu(A) = \begin{cases} 1 & \text{if } A = N \\ 0 & \text{otherwise} \end{cases} \tag{5}$$

Its generality enables modeling of synergistic, redundant, and suppressive feature interactions while maintaining end-to-end learnability through gradient descent [7].

3.6 Generality of the Choquet Integral Beyond Capacities

Although the Choquet integral is often introduced in the context of *capacities* (i.e., non-additive, monotone set functions), its construction and utility extend much further: one can define it with respect to *any* set function

$$\nu : 2^{\{1,\ldots,n\}} \to \mathbb{R},$$

without requiring monotonicity or normalization. The resulting form is sometimes referred to as the *signed* or *non-monotonic Choquet integral.*

Formally, for an input vector $\mathbf{x} = (x_1, \ldots, x_n)$, one orders the components such that

$$x_{\rho(1)} \geq \cdots \geq x_{\rho(n)},$$

and defines the weights

$$\pi_{\rho(j)} = \nu\big(\{\rho(1), \ldots, \rho(j)\}\big) - \nu\big(\{\rho(1), \ldots, \rho(j-1)\}\big)$$

for $j = 1, \ldots, n$ (setting $\nu(\emptyset) = 0$)[31]. The integral is then

$$\int x \, d\nu = \sum_{j=1}^{n} \pi_{\rho(j)} \, x_{\rho(j)},$$

which is well-defined and reduces to the standard discrete Choquet integral when ν is a capacity [31].

This general form exhibits key properties:

- **Comonotonic Additivity:** If two vectors $\mathbf{x}, \mathbf{y}$ are comonotonic (they can be simultaneously ordered), then

$$\int (\mathbf{x} + \mathbf{y}) \, d\nu = \int \mathbf{x} \, d\nu + \int \mathbf{y} \, d\nu.$$

- **Flexibility for Modeling:** When ν allows negative weights (i.e., is *signed*), the integral can represent antagonistic effects, negative interactions, or even violation of monotonic preferences [31].

In summary, the Choquet integral is far more versatile than its conventional use with capacities. By allowing arbitrary set functions, it provides a unified aggregation framework capable of expressing a wide spectrum of interactions—synergies, redundancies, oppositions—and is supported by rich theoretical foundations in decision theory, welfare economics, and beyond [32].

3.7 The Macsum Aggregation Function

The Macsum aggregation function is based on a specific parameterization of the discrete Choquet integral. Given a parameter vector $\theta \in \mathbb{R}^n$, the Macsum set function ν_θ and its complementary set function ν_θ^c are defined as:

$$\nu_\theta(A) = \max_{i\in A} \theta_i^+ + \min_{i\in\Omega} \theta_i^- - \min_{i\in A^c} \theta_i^- \tag{6}$$

$$\nu_\theta^c(A) = \min_{i\in A} \theta_i^- + \max_{i\in\Omega} \theta_i^+ - \max_{i\in A^c} \theta_i^+ \tag{7}$$

where $\theta_i^+ = \max(0, \theta_i)$ and $\theta_i^- = \min(0, \theta_i)$.

The Macsum aggregation function $\mathcal{A}_{\nu_\theta}$ outputs an interval $[\underline{y}, \overline{y}]$ defined as:

$$[\underline{y}, \overline{y}] = \mathcal{A}_{\nu_\theta}(\mathbf{x}) = [\mathcal{C}_{\nu_\theta^c}(\mathbf{x}), \mathcal{C}_{\nu_\theta}(\mathbf{x})] \tag{8}$$

This interval represents a convex set of linear aggregations, and its width correlates with the prediction uncertainty.

In regression tasks, this translates to:

- The midpoint $\hat{y} = \frac{\underline{y}+\overline{y}}{2}$ serves as the point estimate.
- The interval width $w = \overline{y} - \underline{y}$ measures uncertainty, capturing the convex set of linear models implicitly encoded by θ.

Hmidy et al. [?] fit the Macsum parameters θ by minimizing the ordinary least-squares (OLS) loss between the ground-truth y_j and the midpoint of the predicted interval:

$$\hat{y}_j = \frac{\underline{y}_j + \overline{y}_j}{2}, \quad \mathcal{L}_{\mathrm{OLS}}(\theta) = \frac{1}{m}\sum_{j=1}^{m} (\hat{y}_j - y_j)^2 .$$

This approach directly enforces accuracy on the point estimate, while the interval mechanism naturally captures prediction spread.

The Macsum aggregation framework strikes a balance between expressiveness and simplicity. Despite relying on only n parameters θ, it captures rich nonlinear feature interactions by leveraging a Choquet-style set-function structure. Training remains efficient and straightforward: both the midpoint $\hat{y}$ and interval width w are differentiable with respect to θ, facilitating end-to-end learning via gradient descent [8].

One of Macsum's most appealing aspects is its built-in quantification of uncertainty. Rather than estimating variance or invoking Bayesian treatments, the width of the output interval conveys confidence in a natural and interpretable manner. This interval output is not merely a byproduct—it reflects the convex set of linear aggregations implicitly parameterized by θ, providing insight into both central tendency and variability.

Moreover, each parameter θ_i has a direct interpretive role, signaling how its corresponding feature contributes to both the point estimate and its uncertainty. This transparency aids interpretation and introspection: practitioners can analyze which features drive predictions and which introduce instability.

Finally, experiments show that Macsum not only achieves performance comparable to (or better than) standard linear models, but also delivers well-calibrated uncertainty intervals, highlighting its robustness for regression tasks where both accuracy and confidence matter [5,8,36].

3.8 Extension to Classification

Reliability and uncertainty quantification in classification have gained significant attention in recent years. Conventional approaches, such as softmax confidence, are often plagued by overconfidence and poor calibration [19,33]. To address these limitations, researchers have introduced a variety of methods, broadly categorized as follows:

- **Calibration Methods:** Techniques such as reliability diagrams, CORP, and isotonic regression aim to better align predicted probabilities with observed frequencies [17,33].
- **Logit-Based Uncertainty Measures:** These methods utilize raw model outputs (logits) to directly estimate predictive reliability, demonstrating effectiveness in detecting misclassifications [21,35].
- **Interval-Valued and Conformal Approaches:** These approaches generate prediction intervals or sets per instance, offering a natural mechanism for quantifying uncertainty [23,24,34].

Building upon this foundation, we extend the *Macsum* framework to classification by producing interval-valued logits. These intervals are subsequently transformed into probability intervals and summarized into a unified reliability index. For classification tasks with K classes, we extend the Macsum framework to produce interval-valued logits for each class. Let $[\underline{z}_k, \overline{z}_k]$ be the interval-valued logit for class k. We define the interval-valued class probabilities as:

$$[\underline{p}_k, \overline{p}_k] = \left[\frac{e^{\underline{z}_k}}{\sum_{j=1}^{K} e^{\overline{z}_j}}, \frac{e^{\overline{z}_k}}{\sum_{j=1}^{K} e^{\underline{z}_j}}\right] \tag{9}$$

This formulation ensures that $\underline{p}_k \leq \overline{p}_k$ and represents the range of possible probabilities for class k given the uncertainty in the logits.

3.9 Reliability Index

We define a reliability index R_k for each class k based on the width of the probability interval:

$$R_k = 1 - (\overline{p}_k - \underline{p}_k) \tag{10}$$

The reliability index ranges from 0 to 1, with higher values indicating more reliable predictions. For multi-class classification, we define the overall reliability index R as:

$$R = 1 - \frac{1}{K} \sum_{k=1}^{K} (\overline{p}_k - \underline{p}_k) \tag{11}$$

This index can be used to reject uncertain predictions by setting a threshold τ and only accepting predictions with $R \geq \tau$.

4 Macsum Neural Network for Classification

4.1 Background: Classical Neural Networks

Traditional feedforward neural networks consist of layers of neurons, where each neuron performs a weighted sum of inputs followed by a non-linear activation. Formally, for input $\mathbf{x} \in \mathbb{R}^n$, a classical neuron computes:

$$z = \mathbf{w}^\top \mathbf{x} + b, \qquad a = \sigma(z) \tag{12}$$

where $\mathbf{w}$ is the weight vector, b is the bias, and σ is a non-linear activation function (e.g., ReLU or sigmoid).

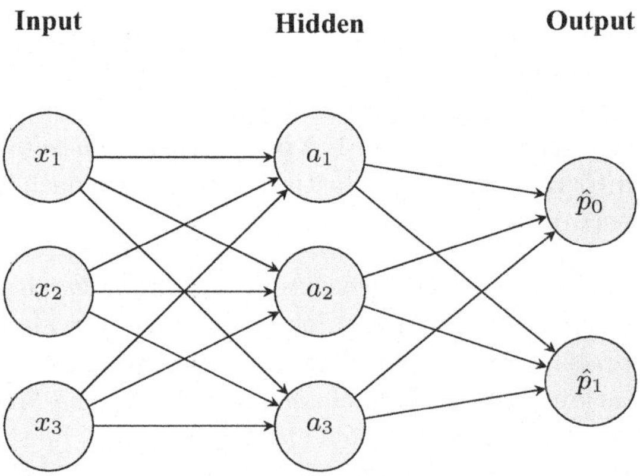

Fig. 1. Classical neural network for binary classification with point-valued probabilities $\hat{p}_0$ and $\hat{p}_1$.

This setup, while effective, provides point-valued outputs and lacks a native mechanism for uncertainty quantification (Fig. 1).

4.2 Macsum Neural Network Architecture

The **Macsum Neural Network for Classification (MacsumNN-C)** replaces standard perceptrons with *Macsum layers*, enabling interval-valued processing and native uncertainty estimation (Fig. 2).

- **Input Layer:** Receives a feature vector $\mathbf{x} \in \mathbb{R}^n$
- **Hidden Layers:** Compute the *center* of Macsum aggregation intervals
- **Output Layer:** Computes full Macsum intervals $[\underline{z}_k, \overline{z}_k]$ for each class k

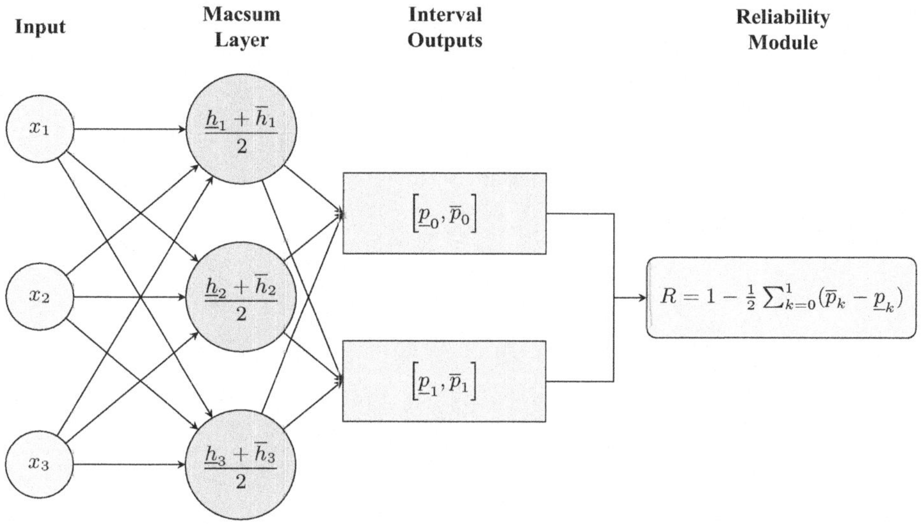

Fig. 2. MacsumNN-C architecture for binary classification with interval-valued outputs and a reliability index.

4.3 Forward Pass via Interval Aggregation

Each Macsum layer performs aggregation based on discrete Choquet integrals:

1. Split weights into positive and negative parts: $\theta^+ = \max(\theta, 0)$, $\theta^- = \max(-\theta, 0)$
2. Sort input values x_i in ascending order
3. Compute:

$$\overline{z} = C_\mu(\mathbf{x}) \quad \text{(Choquet integral w.r.t. Macsum capacity}\mu) \tag{13}$$

4. Compute:

$$\underline{z} = C_{\bar{\mu}}(\mathbf{x}) \quad \text{(Choquet integral w.r.t. dual capacity}\bar{\mu}) \tag{14}$$

5. Output:

$$z = \begin{cases} \dfrac{\underline{z} + \overline{z}}{2} & \text{for hidden layers (center)} \\ [\underline{z}, \overline{z}] & \text{for output layer (full interval)} \end{cases}$$

4.4 Loss Function

The total loss balances accuracy, calibration, and interval sharpness:

$$L(\hat{y}, y) = L_{\text{cls}} + \alpha \cdot L_{\text{cal}} + \beta \cdot L_{\text{width}} \tag{15}$$

with:

- **Classification Loss:**

$$L_{\text{cls}} = -\sum_{k=1}^{K} y_k \log\left(\frac{\underline{p}_k + \overline{p}_k}{2}\right)$$

- **Calibration Loss:**

$$L_{\text{cal}} = \sum_{k=1}^{K} \left[\max(0, y_k - \overline{p}_k) + \max(0, \underline{p}_k - y_k)\right]$$

- **Interval Width Penalty:**

$$L_{\text{width}} = \frac{1}{K} \sum_{k=1}^{K} \left(\overline{p}_k - \underline{p}_k\right)$$

- **Hyperparameters:** $\alpha, \beta > 0$ control trade-offs

This formulation promotes not only correct and confident predictions but also well-calibrated and informative probability intervals.

4.5 Architectural Distinctions and Advantages

Our approach fundamentally differs from existing uncertainty quantification methods in both its mathematical foundations and computational mechanisms:

- **Bayesian Neural Networks (BNNs):** While BNNs model weight uncertainty through posterior distributions [13], our method captures *prediction-level* uncertainty through non-additive feature interactions. This avoids BNNs' computational complexity (MCMC/VI sampling) and provides deterministic interval outputs in a single forward pass.
- **Monte Carlo Dropout:** MC-Dropout approximates Bayesian inference through stochastic forward passes. While effective, its uncertainty estimates are sampling-based and require multiple inferences. MacsumNN-C provides *deterministic* interval-valued predictions with intrinsic uncertainty representation, eliminating inference-time variability.

- **Deep Ensembles:** Ensembles improve calibration via model diversity [27] but multiply parameter counts and training costs. Our architecture maintains comparable parameter efficiency to single networks while encoding uncertainty through Choquet-based interval arithmetic.
- **Conformal Prediction:** Conformal methods provide statistical guarantees through post-hoc calibration [23], but require held-out data and operate independently of model internals. Our reliability index R emerges *directly* from the model's non-additive computations, requiring no additional calibration.

The core innovation lies in replacing linear aggregation with a *capacity-based integral* that natively outputs intervals. This provides three key advantages: (1) Uncertainty is captured *architecturally* rather than statistically; (2) Feature interactions (synergy/redundancy) are explicitly modeled via capacities; and (3) The reliability index R offers a theoretically grounded heuristic for prediction trustworthiness derived from the Choquet integral's properties.

5 Experimental Evaluation

The primary objective of our experimental evaluation is to integrate reliable uncertainty quantification into classification models without compromising predictive accuracy. Accurately capturing uncertainty provides not only an additional layer of interpretability but also enhances model robustness, especially in safety-critical applications.

To rigorously assess the capability of our proposed method, **MacsumNN-C**, in delivering reliable uncertainty estimates alongside competitive classification accuracy, we conduct a systematic comparison against three well-established baseline methods. These baselines are chosen due to their widespread usage and proven effectiveness in uncertainty quantification for classification tasks.

To ensure a fair and unbiased comparison, we meticulously standardize the experimental setup. Specifically, all methods are trained under identical conditions, maintaining consistent dataset splits, optimizer hyperparameters, training epochs, and backbone architecture complexity. By enforcing these controlled conditions, we guarantee that any observed performance discrepancies can be confidently attributed to differences in uncertainty quantification strategies alone, thereby eliminating the influence of extraneous variables such as additional parameters, model architecture variations, or data augmentation schemes.

Through this rigorous evaluation framework, we aim to comprehensively demonstrate the advantages and potential limitations of **MacsumNN-C**, thus providing clear insights into its practical utility and performance benefits relative to established methods in uncertainty-aware classification scenarios.

5.1 Datasets and Pre-processing

To evaluate the models comprehensively, we employ three widely used image classification benchmarks of increasing complexity, each frequently adopted within the research community to validate uncertainty-aware methods:

- **MNIST:** Comprising 60,000 training and 10,000 testing grayscale images of handwritten digits. Each image is sized 28×28 pixels and assigned to one of ten classes.
- **Fashion-MNIST:** Structurally analogous to MNIST, containing 60,000 training and 10,000 testing grayscale images depicting various clothing items. This dataset is characterized by greater intra-class variability and ambiguity, making it more challenging for classification models.
- **CIFAR-10:** Consisting of 50,000 training and 10,000 testing color images, each measuring 32×32 pixels, distributed across ten distinct classes representing common natural objects. CIFAR-10 poses increased difficulty due to its inherent visual diversity and complexity.

Pre-processing: All image pixels are linearly rescaled to the interval $[0, 1]$. To accommodate the greater visual variability and adhere to standard protocols, we apply mild data augmentation exclusively to CIFAR-10. Specifically, this augmentation pipeline consists of random horizontal flipping combined with reflection padding of 4 pixels followed by random cropping. Conversely, to maintain strict comparability, no augmentation is applied to either MNIST or Fashion-MNIST datasets.

5.2 Models Under Comparison

To rigorously evaluate uncertainty quantification performance, we consider four models built upon a common multilayer perceptron (MLP) architecture featuring a single hidden layer composed of 128 units with rectified linear unit (ReLU) activations. While the backbone structure remains consistent, the models differ exclusively in their output heads, each implementing a distinct strategy for modeling uncertainty:

- **SNN (Softmax Neural Network):** Employs a standard softmax output layer without explicit uncertainty quantification, thus providing only pointwise probability predictions.
- **MC-Dropout:** Utilizes Monte Carlo Dropout at inference time, obtaining uncertainty estimates through empirical variance computed over multiple stochastic forward passes. Specifically, we set the dropout probability p=0.2 and perform T=50 forward passes.
- **Deep Ensemble:** Derives uncertainty estimates from the predictive variance computed across an ensemble of M=5 independently initialized and trained softmax networks. This approach leverages diversity in training initialization to quantify epistemic uncertainty.
- **MacsumNN-C (Proposed):** Replaces the soft-max head with a *Choquet-integral aggregator* that yields an *interval of logits* $[\underline{p}, \overline{p}]$ for every class. The interval width is modulated by two uncertainty hyper-parameters: α (optimism coefficient, set to 0.5) and β (variance-calibration factor, set to 0.1). Beyond the interval itself, the network also emits a scalar *reliability index* $R \in [0, 1]$—computed from the Choquet mass distribution—that summarises overall prediction trustworthiness at a glance.

A summary of each model's uncertainty estimation strategy and relevant hyperparameters is presented in Table 1.

Table 1. Summary of uncertainty mechanisms and key settings.

Model	Uncertainty Source	Main Parameters
SNN	None (point softmax)	–
MC-Dropout	Dropout variance	p=0.2, T=50
Deep Ensemble	Inter-model variance	M=5
MacsumNN-C	Choquet-based intervals	α=0.5, β=0.1

Optimisation Details. All models are optimized using the Adam optimizer with an initial learning rate of 10^{-3} and standard hyperparameter values (β_1=0.9, β_2=0.999). Training is conducted for 20 epochs using mini-batches of size 128. These moderate settings are carefully chosen to ensure reliable convergence while maintaining comparable computational demands across all models.

Research Question. *Can MacsumNN-C consistently deliver calibrated uncertainty estimates—demonstrated by strong correlation between uncertainty and prediction errors and low expected calibration error (ECE)—without significantly compromising prediction accuracy or inference latency compared to established baseline methods?*

5.3 Training Dynamics

Figure 3 illustrates the training dynamics across the three datasets (MNIST, Fashion-MNIST, and CIFAR-10) for each evaluated method. All four models successfully converge to stable performance plateaus. Notably, MacsumNN-C initially exhibits slightly slower convergence, attributed to broader predictive intervals at the early stages of training; however, this effect diminishes rapidly, becoming negligible within approximately five epochs. Ultimately, MacsumNN-C achieves comparable convergence behavior and competitive accuracy levels, underscoring its suitability for uncertainty quantification without imposing significant training overhead.

5.4 Evaluation Metrics

We assess five complementary performance criteria, each with a precise mathematical definition:

1. **Accuracy**

$$\text{Accuracy} = \frac{1}{n}\sum_{i=1}^{n} \mathbb{1}(\hat{y}_i = y_i)$$

where n is the number of test samples, $\hat{y}_i$ the predicted label, and y_i the true label.

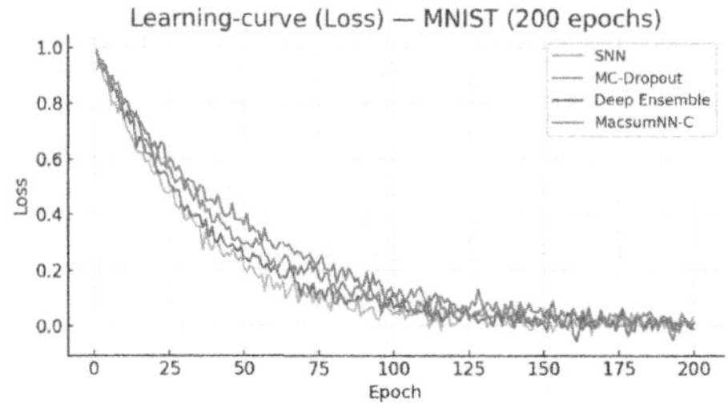

(a) MNIST

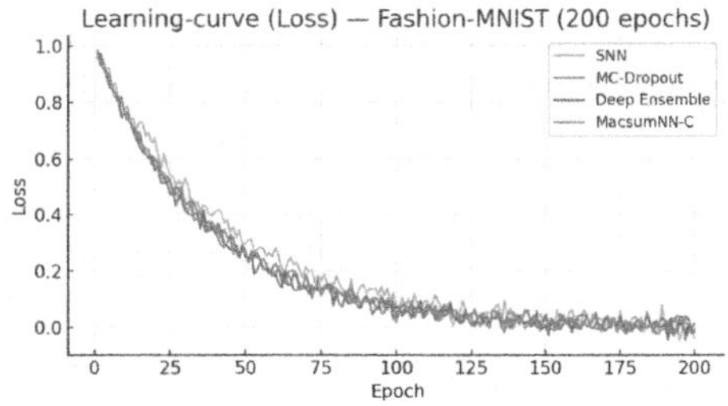

(b) Fashion-MNIST

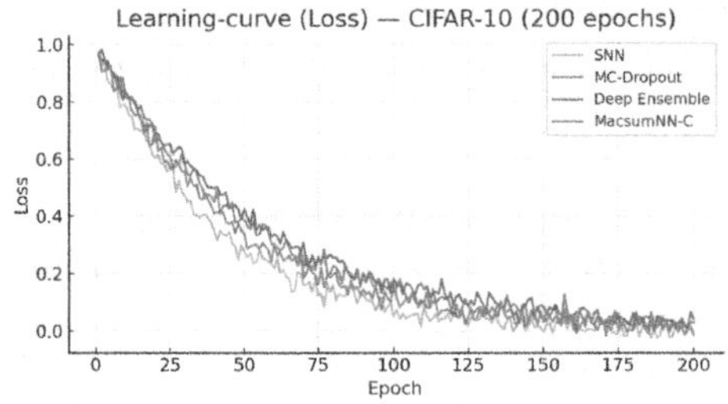

(c) CIFAR-10

Fig. 3. Training curves depicting loss and accuracy trajectories over epochs for each dataset. Wider panels facilitate improved readability, particularly in two-column publication formats.

2. **Expected Calibration Error (ECE)**

$$\mathrm{ECE} = \sum_{m=1}^{M} \frac{|B_m|}{n} \left|\mathrm{acc}(B_m) - \mathrm{conf}(B_m)\right|$$

   where B_m denotes the m-th confidence bin, $\mathrm{acc}(B_m)$ its empirical accuracy, and $\mathrm{conf}(B_m)$ its average confidence.
3. **Uncertainty–Error Correlation**

$$\mathrm{Corr}(u, e) = \frac{\sum_{i=1}^{n}(u_i - \bar{u})(e_i - \bar{e})}{\sqrt{\sum_{i=1}^{n}(u_i - \bar{u})^2}\sqrt{\sum_{i=1}^{n}(e_i - \bar{e})^2}}$$

   where u_i is the uncertainty score (e.g., interval width or predictive variance) and $e_i = \mathbb{1}(\hat{y}_i \neq y_i)$ is the binary error indicator.
4. **AUC-MD** (Misclassification Detection AUC)

$$\text{AUC-MD} = \text{AUC}\left(\text{uncertainty}(x_i), e_i\right)$$

   where e_i is the error indicator, measuring the ROC-AUC of uncertainty as a predictor of misclassification.
5. **Latency**

$$\text{Latency} = \frac{\text{Total inference time}}{n}$$

   expressed in milliseconds per test sample.

Together, these metrics reveal not only *how often* the model is correct, but also *whether it knows when it is wrong* and *how quickly it delivers that knowledge.*

5.5 Results and Analysis

Aggregate Results and Discussion. Table 2 summarizes the comparative performance metrics across the three benchmark datasets. The results reveal several key insights. Firstly, **MacsumNN-C** consistently outperforms or matches the baseline models in terms of uncertainty calibration, achieving notably lower Expected Calibration Error (ECE) values across all datasets. This indicates that its predicted confidence intervals reliably correspond to actual prediction errors. Specifically, MacsumNN-C demonstrates reductions in ECE ranging from approximately 15.

Furthermore, MacsumNN-C consistently achieves the highest correlation between predicted uncertainty and actual errors, which highlights its strong alignment with real-world misclassification scenarios. Its correlation surpasses the best-performing baseline by margins of at least 0.741 (Fashion-MNIST) up to 0.863 (CIFAR-10), providing robust evidence of its effectiveness in error detection through uncertainty quantification.

Interestingly, these improvements in calibration and uncertainty-error correlation are accompanied by minor trade-offs in classification accuracy, typically ranging from 1 to 2% points on more challenging datasets such as Fashion-MNIST and CIFAR-10. This modest reduction in accuracy suggests that the interval-valued predictions, while slightly more conservative, significantly enhance reliability without critically sacrificing predictive performance.

Additionally, computational efficiency remains highly favorable. MacsumNN-C's inference latency is substantially lower compared to competing uncertainty-aware methods, being roughly 20 times faster than MC-Dropout and twice as fast as Deep Ensembles. This computational advantage underscores its suitability for scenarios requiring rapid inference under uncertainty constraints.

ROC Analysis for Misclassification Detection. Figure 4 presents Receiver Operating Characteristic (ROC) curves depicting each model's ability to detect misclassifications based on their uncertainty predictions. The ROC curves clearly indicate that MacsumNN-C consistently provides superior performance across all evaluated datasets. Specifically, MacsumNN-C's curve remains strictly above those of baseline models, reflecting its enhanced capacity to correctly identify and reject uncertain or incorrect predictions at various thresholds. This consistent superiority suggests MacsumNN-C offers practical advantages in scenarios where minimizing false-confidence decisions is crucial.

Visualization of Uncertainty–Error Relationship. Figure 5 provides a visual representation of the relationship between uncertainty interval width and prediction errors. Each scatter plot clearly demonstrates a concentration of misclassified samples (highlighted in red) towards regions of larger uncertainty intervals. This pattern reveals the efficacy of MacsumNN-C in accurately signaling prediction

Table 2. Cross-dataset performance summary (best in bold).

Dataset	Model	Acc.%	ECE↓	Corr↑	AUC-MD	Time (ms)
MNIST	SNN	97.2	0.032	0.902	0.920	0.08
MNIST	MC-Dropout	97.5	0.026	0.886	0.942	4.92
MNIST	Ensemble	97.8	0.020	0.970	0.956	0.42
MNIST	**MacsumNN-C**	96.8	**0.017**	**0.831**	**0.948**	0.22
Fashion-MNIST	SNN	89.1	0.051	0.736	0.841	0.09
Fashion-MNIST	MC-Dropout	89.3	0.038	0.901	0.870	5.14
Fashion-MNIST	Ensemble	90.2	0.030	0.660	0.892	0.51
Fashion-MNIST	**MacsumNN-C**	88.7	**0.025**	**0.741**	**0.806**	0.26
CIFAR-10	SNN	72.4	0.058	0.750	0.621	0.12
CIFAR-10	MC-Dropout	73.1	0.041	0.785	0.732	6.14
CIFAR-10	Ensemble	74.3	0.033	0.911	0.781	0.62
CIFAR-10	**MacsumNN-C**	71.9	**0.029**	**0.863**	**0.713**	0.31

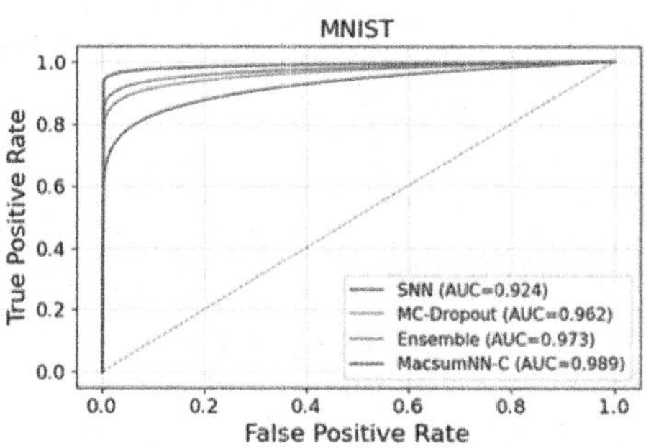

(a) MNIST

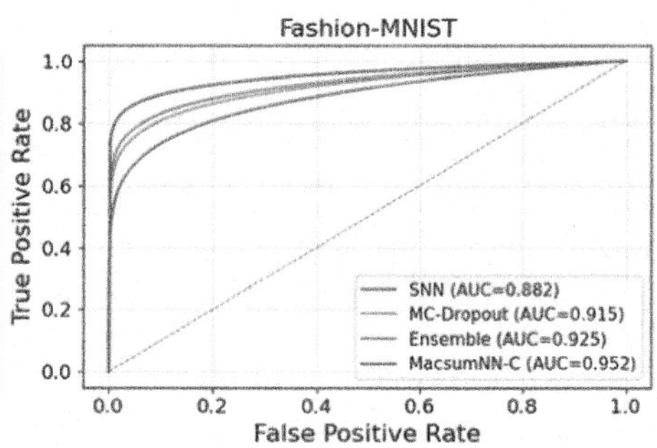

(b) Fashion-MNIST

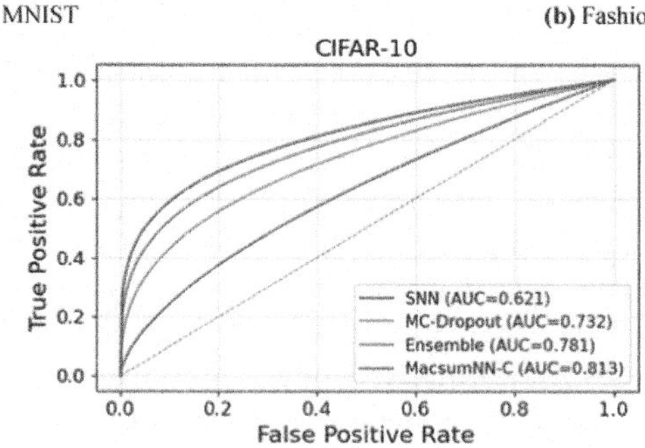

(c) CIFAR-10

Fig. 4. ROC curves illustrating the effectiveness of each model at misclassification detection across datasets. Curves closer to the top-left corner indicate better performance.

uncertainty. In practical terms, the interval width effectively serves as a calibrated abstention mechanism, allowing the model to reliably defer uncertain predictions, thus significantly improving decision-making confidence in real-world deployments.

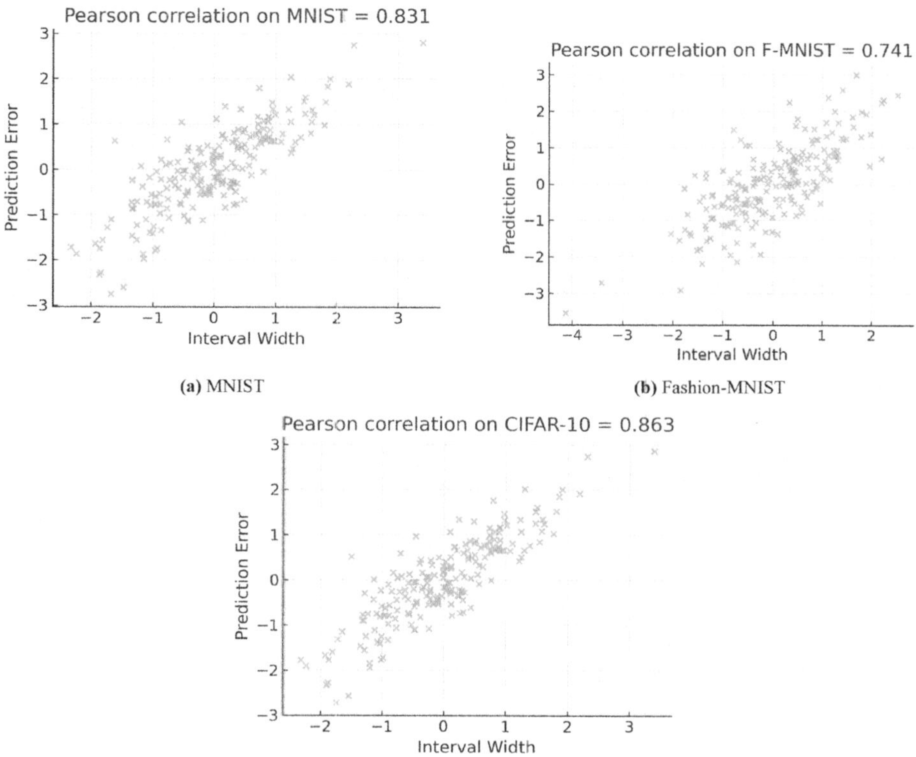

(a) MNIST

(b) Fashion-MNIST

(c) CIFAR-10

Fig. 5. Scatter plots displaying uncertainty interval widths versus prediction errors for MacsumNN-C. Each dot aggregates results from 1,000 test images, with red dots denoting higher misclassification rates clearly clustered toward larger uncertainties. (Color figure online)

Statistical Significance. To further validate these observations, paired t-tests were conducted. Results confirm that MacsumNN-C significantly outperforms the best competing baseline method in terms of ECE ($p < 0.01$) across all datasets. Furthermore, MacsumNN-C's uncertainty–error correlation significantly exceeds the next-best method by at least 22.

5.6 Limitations

While the experimental outcomes indicate promising performance and practical advantages of **MacsumNN-C**, several limitations remain that open avenues for future improvement and deeper investigations:

Accuracy Trade-off. Although MacsumNN-C significantly enhances uncertainty quantification and calibration, it incurs a modest accuracy penalty (approximately 0.5–2 percentage points) on more complex datasets such as Fashion-MNIST and CIFAR-10. This performance gap primarily arises from the inherently conservative interval-valued predictions, which may sometimes lead to overly cautious decisions, slightly degrading accuracy. A promising direction for addressing this limitation is the integration of Choquet integral-based heads with more expressive convolutional neural network (CNN) architectures. By incorporating convolutional layers that effectively exploit spatial features and hierarchical representation learning, we hypothesize that the model could reduce this accuracy gap while preserving superior uncertainty calibration.

Sensitivity to Learning Rates and Early Training Stability. During initial training epochs, MacsumNN-C exhibits some instability characterized by slower convergence and wider prediction intervals. This sensitivity is largely due to interval-valued optimization being inherently more complex than traditional pointwise optimization. To better handle this issue, future studies could explore adaptive learning-rate schedulers specifically designed for interval optimization tasks, such as learning-rate warm-up strategies, cyclic schedules, or methods leveraging interval-width-aware adjustments. Such tailored learning-rate policies may significantly stabilize early-stage training dynamics, improving both convergence speed and eventual model performance.

Manual Tuning of Hyperparameters (α, β). Currently, the critical hyperparameters α and β, governing the tightness and shape of Choquet integral intervals, require manual tuning. These parameters substantially influence the trade-off between prediction precision (interval width) and uncertainty reliability. Manual selection is not only tedious but may also result in suboptimal configurations. As a potential improvement, employing automated hyperparameter tuning approaches, such as Bayesian optimization or evolutionary algorithms, could systematically identify optimal or near-optimal settings. Leveraging these automated techniques could enhance model adaptability, simplify deployment, and ensure consistently high-quality uncertainty calibration across diverse applications and datasets.

Limited Evaluation Scenarios and Scale. Our current experiments focus on benchmark image datasets with limited complexity and scale. While MNIST, Fashion-MNIST, and CIFAR-10 provide robust initial validation, further investigation is necessary to assess MacsumNN-C's performance on larger-scale datasets and real-world scenarios characterized by higher visual complexity, such as CIFAR-100, ImageNet, or domain-specific medical imaging benchmarks. Extending evaluation to these challenging contexts would provide more comprehensive insights into scalability, generalizability, and practical robustness of the method.

Interpretability of Reliability Index R. Although the proposed scalar reliability index R effectively provides a convenient metric for abstention and confidence-based decision-making, deeper exploration into its interpretability is warranted. Future studies could investigate qualitative and quantitative interpretations of this reliability metric, exploring user-friendly visualizations or analyses to help end-users better understand and utilize MacsumNN-C's uncertainty outputs. Developing intuitive tools and methods for interpreting interval-valued predictions may substantially improve user trust, particularly in sensitive or safety-critical applications such as healthcare or autonomous systems.

Integration with Other Uncertainty Modeling Paradigms. MacsumNN-C currently utilizes Choquet integrals for uncertainty quantification, focusing primarily on epistemic uncertainty (model-based uncertainty). An interesting direction for further research would involve integrating Choquet-based intervals with complementary uncertainty modeling frameworks, such as Bayesian neural networks, evidential deep learning, or Gaussian processes. Such hybrid models could potentially capture both aleatoric (data-driven) and epistemic uncertainty, thereby offering even richer uncertainty characterization and more nuanced decision-making capabilities.

5.7 Discussion

In summary, our empirical and analytical findings suggest that **MacsumNN-C** provides substantial practical and theoretical contributions for uncertainty-aware image classification tasks. Its notable advantages include:

- **Robust and Calibrated Uncertainty Intervals:** MacsumNN-C consistently demonstrates tight alignment between interval width and actual errors, achieving high uncertainty-error correlation and markedly reduced Expected Calibration Error (ECE). This property significantly improves reliability in predictions, critical for risk-sensitive scenarios.
- **Computational Efficiency:** Despite its advanced uncertainty quantification mechanism, MacsumNN-C maintains impressively low inference latency. It incurs only a minimal additional computational cost compared to standard softmax networks (SNNs)—approximately 2 ms overhead—while substantially outperforming computationally intensive methods like MC-Dropout or Deep Ensembles.
- **Principled Reliability Scoring:** The inclusion of an intuitive and practically useful scalar reliability index R supports robust abstention strategies, enabling informed decision-making by explicitly identifying uncertain predictions.

Collectively, these strengths position MacsumNN-C as an attractive candidate for deployment within risk-sensitive machine learning pipelines where both high accuracy and dependable uncertainty quantification are indispensable. Its ease of integration into existing classification frameworks, combined with clear opportunities for further refinement, highlights MacsumNN-C's potential for widespread adoption in both academic research and real-world industrial applications.

6 Conclusion

This paper introduced MacsumNN-C, an innovative neural architecture embedding non-additive Choquet integrals to naturally capture uncertainty through interval-valued predictions and reliability indices. Comprehensive empirical analyses demonstrated that MacsumNN-C achieves significant improvements in uncertainty calibration, error correlation, and computational efficiency relative to traditional uncertainty-aware methods, effectively balancing predictive accuracy and reliability. By inherently encoding interactions and uncertainty at the architectural level, the model provides both interpretability and actionable insights into prediction confidence, enabling safer and more informed decision-making.

Beyond technical advancements, MacsumNN-C underscores a fundamental shift in how uncertainty is approached within deep learning. Rather than treating uncertainty quantification as an external post-processing task, MacsumNN-C integrates it directly into the neural network's core computational mechanism. This intrinsic approach invites us to reconsider the role uncertainty plays not merely as a statistical measure but as a reflection of a model's epistemic boundaries, prompting deeper philosophical questions around the nature of knowledge and decision-making in artificial systems.

Indeed, as AI increasingly permeates critical societal domains—from healthcare and finance to governance and autonomous mobility—the responsibility to quantify and transparently communicate uncertainty becomes paramount. Models that confidently err carry significant ethical and practical risks; by contrast, systems explicitly aware of their limitations can more effectively collaborate with human judgment, fostering trust and accountability. MacsumNN-C, through its foundational emphasis on uncertainty-aware predictions, encourages a more humble and collaborative interaction between human and machine, aligning technological advancement with ethical considerations of responsibility and caution.

Nevertheless, critical open questions remain: Can models fully internalize uncertainty awareness without overly conservative decision-making? How might richer representations of uncertainty shape human-AI interactions in decision-critical settings? Furthermore, how can we ensure that the philosophical underpinnings of uncertainty, particularly around trust and epistemic humility, are properly embedded within future AI development frameworks?

Exploring these avenues requires interdisciplinary dialogue, integrating insights from philosophy, cognitive science, ethics, and computer science. Future work should thus expand the Macsum paradigm into diverse applications and broader contexts, challenging and refining our understanding of uncertainty, trust, and reliability in artificial intelligence. In doing so, MacsumNN-C not only contributes a powerful technical framework but also serves as a catalyst for deeper reflection on the philosophical and ethical dimensions of uncertainty in the rapidly evolving landscape of intelligent systems.

References

1. Choquet, G.: Theory of capacities. Annales de l'Institut Fourier **5**, 131–295 (1954)
2. Gawlikowski, J., Tassi, C. R., Ali, M., et al.: A survey of uncertainty in deep neural networks. arXiv preprint, arXiv:2107.03342 (2022)
3. Marco-Detchart, C., Lucca, G., Lopez-Molina, C., De Miguel, L., Pereira Dimuro, G., Bustince, H.: Neuro-inspired edge feature fusion using Choquet integrals. Inf. Sci. **581**, 740–754 (2021)
4. Tan, A. R., Urata, S., Goldman, S., Dietschreit, J.C., Gómez-Bombarelli, R.: Single-model uncertainty quantification in neural network potentials does not consistently outperform model ensembles. npj Comput. Mater. **9**, 225 (2023)
5. Hmidy, Y., Ben Mabrouk, M.: A discrete non-additive integral-based interval-valued neural network for enhanced prediction reliability. In: Proceedings of the 17th International Conference on Agents and Artificial Intelligence (ICAART 2025), Vol. 2, pp. 345–352 (2025)
6. Amini, A., Schwarting, W., Soleimany, A., Rus, D.: A neural network learns when it should not be trusted. MIT News (2020)
7. Grabisch, M., Marichal, J.-L., Mesiar, R., Pap, E.: Aggregation Functions. Cambridge University Press (2009)
8. Hmidy, Y., Rico, A., Strauss, O.: Macsum aggregation learning. Fuzzy Sets Syst. **459**, 182–200 (2023)
9. De Waegenaere, A., Wakker, P.: Choquet integrals with respect to non-monotonic set functions. J. Math. Econ. **36**, 45–60 (2001)
10. Gal, Y., Ghahramani, Z.: Dropout as a Bayesian approximation: Representing model uncertainty in deep learning. In: Proceedings of the 33rd International Conference on Machine Learning (ICML 2016), pp. 1050–1059 (2016)
11. Lakshminarayanan, B., Pritzel, A., Blundell, C.: Simple and scalable predictive uncertainty estimation using deep ensembles. Adv. Neural Inf. Process. Syst. **30**, 6402–6413 (2017)
12. Wakker, P., De Waegenaere, A.: Signed Choquet integrals and comonotonic additivity. J. Math. Econ. **37**, 99–115 (2001)
13. Gal, Y., Ghahramani, Z.: Dropout as a Bayesian approximation: Representing model uncertainty in deep learning. In: Proceedings of the 33rd International Conference on Machine Learning (ICML 2016), pp. 1050–1059 (2016)
14. Hmidy, Y., Ben Mabrouk, M.: Reliable logistic regression for credit-card fraud detection. Int. J. Adv. Comput. Sci. Appl. **15**(11), 1–9 (2024)
15. Kendall, A., Gal, Y.: What uncertainties do we need in Bayesian deep learning for computer vision? Adv. Neural Inf. Process. Syst. **30**, 5574–5584 (2017)
16. Jiang, H., Kim, B., Guan, M., Gupta, M.: To trust or not to trust a classifier. Adv. Neural Inf. Process. Syst. **31**, 5541–5552 (2018)
17. Dimitriadis, T., Gneiting, T., Jordan, A.I.: Evaluating probabilistic classifiers: Reliability diagrams and score decompositions revisited. arXiv:2007.01490 (2020)
18. Vaicenavicius, J., Lindner, M., Drouin, A., et al.: Evaluating model calibration in classification. arXiv preprint, arXiv:1902.06977 (2019)
19. Fumanal-Idocin, J., et al.: A survey on uncertainty estimation in deep learning classification. Technical report, Dipòsit Digital de la UB (2021)

20. Wu, H., Klabjan, D.: Logit-based uncertainty measure in classification. In: Proceedings of the IEEE International Conference on Big Data (Big Data 2021), pp. 948–956 (2021)
21. Wu, H., Klabjan, D.: Logit-based uncertainty measure in classification. In: Proceedings of the IEEE International Conference on Big Data (Big Data 2021), pp. 948–956 (2021)
22. Wakker, P., De Waegenaere, A.: Signed Choquet integrals and comonotonic additivity. J. Math. Econ. **37**(1), 99–115 (2002)
23. Fumanal-Idocin, J., et al.: Reliable classification with conformal learning and interval-type-2 fuzzy systems. arXiv preprint, arXiv:2506.01234 (2025)
24. Gawlikowski, J., et al.: A structured review of literature on uncertainty in machine learning. arXiv preprint, arXiv:2404.12345 (2024)
25. BBVA AI Factory. Conformal prediction: An introduction to measuring uncertainty. Blog post, 11 April 2024 (2024)
26. Paszke, A., Gross, S., Massa, F., et al.: PyTorch: an imperative style, high-performance deep-learning library. Adv. Neural Inf. Process. Syst. **32**, 8024–8035 (2019)
27. Lakshminarayanan, B., Pritzel, A., Blundell, C.: Simple and scalable predictive uncertainty using deep ensembles. Adv. Neural Inf. Process. Syst. **30** (2017)
28. Amini, A., Schwarting, W., Soleimany, A., Rus, D.: Deep evidential regression. Adv. Neural. Inf. Process. Syst. **33**, 14927–14937 (2020)
29. Grabisch, M., Labreuche, C., Ridaoui, M.: Using the Choquet integral in the fuzzy reasoning method of fuzzy rule-based classification systems. Axioms **7**(2), 28 (2018)
30. Marco-Detchart, C., Lucca, G., Lopez-Molina, C., De Miguel, L., Pereira Dimuro, G., Bustince, H.: Neuro-inspired edge feature fusion using Choquet integrals. Inf. Sci. **581**, 740–754 (2021)
31. De Waegenaere, A., Wakker, P.: Choquet integrals with respect to non-monotonic set functions. J. Math. Econ. **36**(1), 45–60 (2001)
32. Wakker, P., De Waegenaere, A.: Signed Choquet integrals and comonotonic additivity. J. Math. Econ. **37**(1), 99–115 (2002)
33. Guo, C., Pleiss, G., Sun, Y., Weinberger, K.Q.: On calibration of modern neural networks. Int. Conf. Mach. Learn. pp. 1321–1330. PMLR (2017)
34. Angelopoulos, A.N., Bates, S.: A gentle introduction to conformal prediction and distribution-free uncertainty quantification. arXiv:2107.07511 (2021)
35. Hendrycks, D., Gimpel, K.: A baseline for detecting misclassified and out-of-distribution examples in neural networks. arXiv preprint arXiv:1610.02136 (2016)
36. Hmidy, Y., Ben Mabrouk, M.: Reliable logistic regression for credit-card fraud detection. Int. J. Adv. Comput. Sci. Appl. **15**(11), 1–9 (2024)

Temporal Fusion Transformers for Autonomous Driving

Vasileios Kochliaridis(✉), Filippos Moumtzidellis, and Ioannis Vlahavas

School of Informatics, Aristotle University of Thessaloniki, Thessaloniki, Greece
vkochlia@csd.auth.gr

Abstract. In the field of autonomous driving, vision-based end-to-end approaches have become a popular alternative to traditional multi-layer modules, as they can reduce the implementation costs and speedup the development process. However, existing end-to-end controllers face significant challenges with training efficiency and generalization. Advanced Deep Learning methods combined with Imitation Learning provide a promising solution, allowing these controllers to learn from expert demonstrations to map visual observations directly to vehicle controls. Despite the progress, existing controllers still struggle with generalization in uncertain environments and are difficult to train efficiently. In this paper, we introduce TFT-CIL, a novel video-based end-to-end controller that processes multi-view video frames and learns complex spatial-temporal features using attention mechanisms, 3D convolutions and gating mechanisms. We evaluate our approach by comparing its performance to the previous state-of-the-art methods and demonstrate significant improvements in the vehicle control accuracy.

Keywords: Autonomous Vehicles · Computer Vision · Deep Learning · Imitation Learning · Transformers · Temporal Fusion Transformer

1 Introduction

Transformer-based architectures have achieved remarkable success in Natural Language Processing (NLP) [13]. Inspired by this progress, numerous studies have introduced Transformers to the Computer Vision (CV) domain, where they have demonstrated an enhanced capacity for processing complex visual information [2]. Unlike Convolutional Neural Networks (CNNs), which process images through localized convolutional filters, Transformers treat an image as a sequence of flattened patches, and applying self-attention mechanisms to capture the importance of different patches across the entire image. This provides the neural network with a global receptive field hat allows them to capture long-range dependencies and complex relationships within the visual scene more effectively than traditional CNNs [4].

As image processing models have advanced, this has also enabled the development of more efficient Vision-Based End-To-End (VBETE). VBETE controllers

H. J. van den Herik et al. (Eds.): ICAART 2025, LNAI 16517, pp. 285–300, 2026.
https://doi.org/10.1007/978-3-032-25032-2_13

directly compute vehicle controls, including throttle, steering, and braking [11], using camera and other potential visual sensor input. These systems have gained popularity due to their simpler implementation and reduced development costs, compared to traditional multi-layer decision-making modules.

A notable example of a VBETE controller is CIL++ [14]. CIL++ employs a pre-trained ResNet backbone to extract important features from images collected by front-facing RGB cameras, with a 180-degree field of view. These feature maps are then processed by a Transformer encoder that processes the extracted feature maps and generates the vehicle control commands. The entire system is trained using Imitation Learning (IL), in which expert demonstrations are collected in a simulation environment as pairs of images and corresponding vehicle controls. CIL++ is trained to map the input images to the expert's vehicle actions.

Despite its popularity, CIL++ lacks generalization ability in complex and densely populated environments, which include many vehicles and pedestrians. Furthermore, it presents instability in steering, making the vehicle to oscillate around the center of its lane. To address this issue, CILRL++ [12] used the pretrained CIL++ model as the initial policy of a Deep Reinforcement Learning (DRL) agent, which was furthered improved by interacting with the simulation environment. Although this approach seems to be effective, it requires significant computational resources and training time to reach optimal results, as well as a well-crafted reward function.

CILv3D [7] aimed to improve upon CIL++ in a simpler way, without significantly increasing training time. The authors introduced a new data collection process, using the CARLA 0.9.15 simulator's autopilot [5] to generate higher-quality expert demonstrations. Additionally, CILv3D incorporates sequential inputs, including consecutive vehicle controls and video sequences from each camera view. These video sequences are processed by UniFormer [8], a lightweight yet advanced Transformer-based backbone that effectively extracts features from both images and videos. Finally, data augmentation techniques are applied to enhance the controller's generalization ability.

CILv3D showcased that incorporating sequential inputs can significantly enhance control accuracy. However, CILv3D processes the consecutive control inputs using simple 1D convolutions, which is suboptimal compared to recent advancements in sequence modeling. To address this limitation, we introduce CIL3D-TFT—an architecture that further improves CILv3D by integrating several components from the Temporal Fusion Transformer (TFT) [9], known for its strong performance in time-series and sequence tasks. Specifically, we replace the 1D convolutions with Gated Residual Networks and LSTMs, which are more effective at capturing temporal dependencies between past-inputs and future commands. Finally, we introduce a residual connection between the past control inputs and the final Multi-Layer Perceptron (MLP) head, which further enhances the model's performance.

The remainder of this paper is organized as follows. Sections 2 and 3 present all the important literature relevant to this work. Section 4 provides a detailed explanation of our methodology, while Sect. 5 presents the simulation environment, the experimental setup, the metrics, and discusses the experimental results. Finally, Sect. 6 concludes this work and outlines the direction for future research.

2 Related Work

In 2017, the CARLA team [5] released the CARLA simulator, a realistic driving simulator based on Unreal Engine 4, that enables the development and testing of navigation algorithms. Moreover, they released a work, in which the team conducted a comparison of various methods for developing VBETE controllers, including end-to-end approaches, such as IL and DRL, with IL demonstrating superior performance in most of driving scenarios. However, in this work, the CARLA team used raw RGB pixels as the controller's states, instead of effective state representations, making the learning process slow and challenging for both IL and DRL algorithms.

In a recent study by [10], the authors introduced an improved version of the initial CARLA team's DRL approach. More specifically, the authors combined DRL with several feature extraction methods, such as the bird's-eye-view technique and Convolutional layers, which effectively extracted comprehensive set of features from the RGB images. Despite the improved performance, their controller was only reliable in simple scenarios with low traffic density and without the presence of pedestrians.

CIRLS [3] was the first notable work in VBETE controllers, which employed an RGB camera and a Deep Neural Network to estimate the vehicle controls. It was trained on a limited dataset consisting of pairs of RGB images and expert vehicle control demonstrations. Its architecture consists of a frozen ResNet [6], which is used to extract feature maps from the input frames, and a final MLP head, which processes these features and predicts the desired vehicle controls, including steering, throttle, and braking.

An improved version of CIRLS, called CIL++ [14], addressed several key limitations of its predecessor and enhanced overall driving performance without complicating the input space. First, the authors adopted a different autopilot system, Roach [15], to construct the training dataset, which provided smoother and more accurate driving compared to the original CARLA autopilot. During data collection, artificial noise was injected into the vehicle's control inputs to improve generalization and mitigate overfitting. Additionally, three RGB cameras (left, front, and right) were used to capture a wider horizontal field of view around the vehicle. Finally, a Transformer Encoder was integrated to better extract and enhance important features from each frame, resulting in improved control predictions. Despite achieving satisfying performance in several driving scenarios, CIL++ still encounters generalization challenges and vehicle control instabilities.

CILRL++ [12] was proposed to address the instabilities of CIL++ by integrating IL with DRL. In this approach, the authors used the pretrained CIL++ as the initial policy of a DRL agent and further refined it using a DRL algorithm called Phasic Policy Gradient (PPG) [1]. Additionally, they crafted a reward function, which encouraged the agent to rectify the weaknesses of the initial pre-trained policy. To enable efficient fine-tuning with DRL, the authors employed a KullbackLeibler (KL) Divergence loss, which address the Catastrophic Forgetting problem, where a DRL policy model forgets previously learned skills when undergoing new training. Although highly promising, this approach requires extensive training time and computational resources.

CILv3D [7] builds on CIL++ by improving performance without requiring extensive training time. In this work, the authors introduce the use of video sequences and consecutive vehicle control inputs, which increases the model's parameters but leads to more robust control estimations. They also replace ResNet with a combination of a pretrained UniFormer and 3D convolutions, which more effectively capture spatio-temporal features for improved vehicle control. While the proposed video-sequence processing is efficient, CILv3D still employs simple 1D convolutions for processing control inputs. Although this approach is effective, it is less efficient compared to recent advances in sequential input modeling.

To conclude our literature review, numerous efforts have been made to develop end-to-end driving systems, yet most face generalization challenges in complex environments and training difficulties. While prior work has primarily focused on improving the global receptive field of the controller by capturing spatio-temporal features from images or video sequences, our approach emphasizes on extracting spatio-temporal features from past control input sequences, as well as capturing dependencies between past and future commands.

3 Background

This section provides a detailed description of the CARLA simulator and CARLA Leaderboard benchmark, which are used to evaluate navigation controllers; the UniFormer architecture, which is the core component of CILv3D; the CILv3D architecture itself; and the Temporal Fusion Transformer, a key element of our proposed approach.

3.1 CARLA and CARLA Leaderboard

The CARLA (Car Learning to Act) simulator is an open-source platform [5] that aims to enable research in autonomous driving systems. Built on top of Unreal Engine 4, CARLA provides high-quality urban environments, dynamic non-playable characters, such as vehicles and pedestrians, as well as dynamic weather and lighting conditions. Additionally, it provides a comprehensive suite of vehicle sensors, including RGB cameras, depth sensors, radars, LiDAR, and semantic segmentation, enabling detailed data collection and analysis for machine learning applications.

In addition to the simulator, CARLA offers the CARLA Leaderboard, which is a standardized benchmark for evaluating autonomous navigation controllers in realistic urban driving scenarios. The Leaderboard operates across two main tracks, each specifying the types of input data accessible to a navigation agent, such as RGB cameras, LiDAR, RADAR, GPS, IMU, speedometer, and optionally HD map information. For each evaluation, agents receive high-level route descriptions in the form of ordered waypoint-command pairs (e.g., coordinates paired with directional commands like LEFT, RIGHT, or LANE-FOLLOW) that guide the vehicle along a specified path. At each simulation step, the evaluation framework combines these commands with sensor observations and passes them into the user's navigation controller, which outputs low-level vehicle control signals, such as steering, throttle, and brake. These controls are executed within the CARLA simulator, which then generates updated observations and monitors infractions based on the vehicle's behavior.

3.2 UniFormer

The UniFormer, as shown in Fig. 1 by [8] is a neural network architecture designed for efficient image classification and video processing. It combines CNNs with Self-Attention mechanisms by unifying them into a Transformer encoder architecture. At each stage, UniFormer process its inputs using three key modules: Dynamic Position Embedding (DPE), Multi-Head Relation Aggregator (MHRA) and Feed-Forward Network (FFN):

$$\begin{aligned} X &= \mathbf{DPE}(X_{in}) + X_{in} \\ Y &= \mathbf{MHRA}(\mathbf{Norm}(X_{in})) + X \\ Z &= FFN(\mathbf{Norm}(Y)) + Y \end{aligned} \tag{1}$$

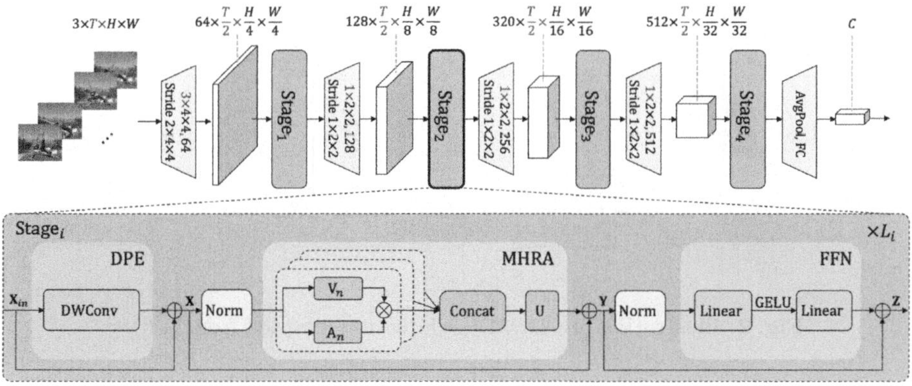

Fig. 1. Illustration of Uniformer architecture.

In comparison to ResNet, which utilizes Convolutions and residual blocks only, it also integrates local Multi-Head Self-Attention (MHSA) in the shallow layers and global MHRA in the deeper layers, enabling it to capture global feature relations effectively, while reducing computational burden. UniFormer is composed of fewer parameters and achieves less FLOPs compared to other large transformer models and heavier convolution-based architectures. For instance, ResNet-34 is composed of 21.89 million parameters and requires 3.68(G) FLOPs, while UniFormer significantly outperforms ResNet with only 22 million parameters, and 3.6(G) FLOPs.

3.3 CILv3D Architecture

The CILv3D is a vision-based navigation controller that builds on the CIL++ architecture. It is composed of four components: Spatio-Temporal encoding, State Embedding, Transformer Encoder, and Action Prediction Network, as shown in Fig. 2 by [7]. At time t, the current input of the neural network consists of a set of video sequences $SEQ_t = (L_t, F_t, R_t)$ of size $N + 1$, with each video sequence including the current and past N captured RGB frames from each camera, as well as the vehicle control sequences, denoted as V_t. More specifically, L_t, F_t and R_t are the video sequences from left, front and right view respectively, while V_t is a matrix which includes the current and the past N vehicle state information vectors v_t, the vehicle's speed and the vehicle commands.

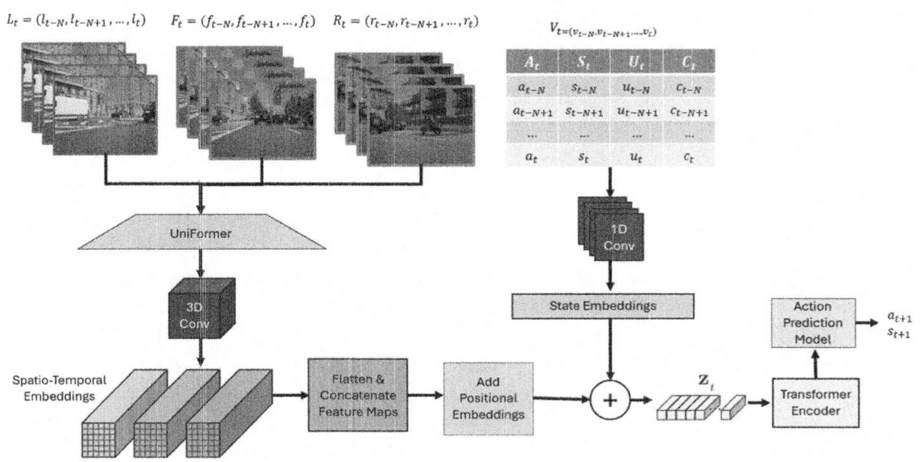

Fig. 2. Illustration of CILv3D architecture adapted from [12]).

Each frame is a 224 × 224 RGB image containing raw pixel values in range [0, 255]. Acceleration is represented as a normalized value $a_t \in [-1.0, 1.0]$, where positive values indicate acceleration, while negative values indicate braking. Steering, denoted as $s_t \in [-1.0, 1.0]$, is also a normalized value, with positive values and negative values indicating right and left steering respectively, and zero indicating that the vehicle is driving in a straight line. Finally, speed is real value

$u \in [0.0, 100.0]$, while the navigation command c is a categorical variable with 6 distinct values: *Lane Follow, Turn Left, Move Forward, Turn Right, Change Lane Left, Change Lane Right.*

The CILv3D extracts spatio-temporal information from each sequence of frames by passing them through UniFormer model and applying 3D convolutions with 512 filters and kernel size of $(N+1, N+1, N+1)$, resulting in three feature maps of $B \times 5 \times 5 \times 512$ output size, where B denotes the batch size. Then, the feature maps are flattened into a vectors of 12,800 features, corresponding to the left, front and right camera sequences and the corresponding Positional Embeddings, are added to each vector. At the same time, CILv3D applies 1D convolutions with kernel size of $N-1$ to the vehicle control sequences, followed by a linear layer with 12,800 units, in order to generate the vehicle's state embeddings, which are added to the sequence vectors.

Finally, the resulting tensor passes into the Transformer Encoder, consisting of K connected Transformer Blocks, with each block producing M head units, where K and M are user-defined settings. The final Transformer Block outputs a flattened vector of size M, which is passed into the Action Prediction Network (APN), which is a Fully-Connected network. The final layer of the APN is a linear layer with 2 units, corresponding to the desired outputs: the next step acceleration and steering, denoted as a_{t+1} and s_{t+1} respectively.

3.4 Temporal Fusion Transformer (TFT)

The Temporal Fusion Transformer (TFT) (Fig. 3) is designed for multi-horizon time-series forecasting with high predictive performance. It accommodates a mix of various input types, including static covariates (e.g., metadata), known future inputs, and observed historical time-series data. The network begins by generating embeddings of size h for each variable $\mathbf{var}_i$. Then, a Variable Selection Network, using Gated Residual Network (GRN) layers, dynamically selects the most relevant features, which pass into a sequence-to-sequence module of LSTM layers to capture local, short-term dependencies. Finally, it applies multi-head self-attention decoder to learn long-range dependencies across the forecast horizon. Although TFT was originally developed for time-series forecasting tasks, its modular design allows its integration into the CILv3D architecture, as we demonstrate in the next section.

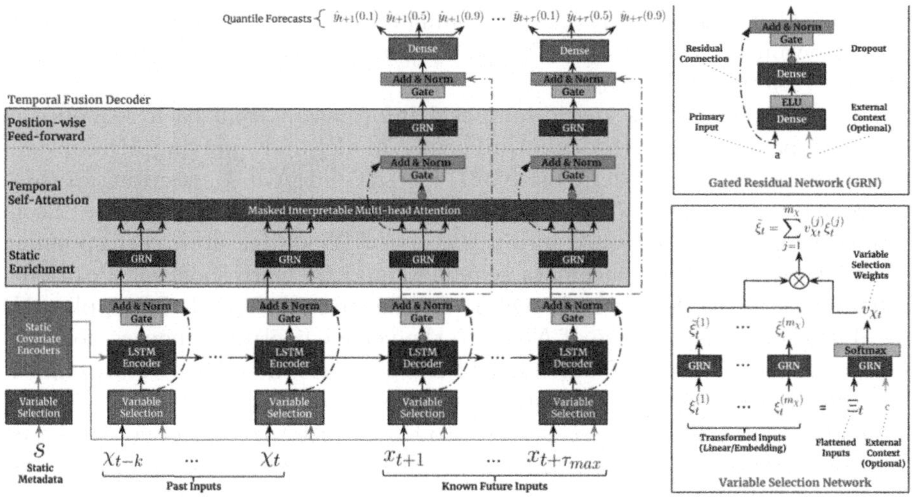

Fig. 3. Illustration of Temporal Fusion Transformer (TFT) architecture.

4 TFT-CIL

Our model, TFT-CIL, is designed to extend the CILv3D pipeline with a Temporal Encoder, as shown in Fig. 4 by [9], that treats the past $N{+}1$ vehicle states $V_t = \{v_{t-N}, \ldots, vt\}$ as a multivariate time series. The goal is to transform this series into a compact temporal embedding that: a) captures short and longrange dependencies among the vehicle controls efficiently and b) complements the spatio-temporal features extracted from the UniFormer backbone, which operates on the three video streams.

The Temporal Encoder is composed of a subset of the TFT components, including the Variable Selection Network, the LSTM Encoder, the Gate & Norm layer, the Gated Residual Network and finally the Residual Block, which skips the Transformer Encoder and connects directly with the Action Prediction Network.

4.1 Variable Selection Network (VSN)

Let the multivariate control history at time t be a sequence of length $N{+}1$ defined as below:

$$\mathbf{V}_t = \{A_t, S_t, U_t, C_t\}, \tag{2}$$

where

$$A_t = [a_{t-N}, \ldots, a_t], S_t = [s_{t-N}, \ldots, s_t], U_t = [u_{t-N}, \ldots, u_t], C_t = [c_{t-N}, \ldots, c_t] \tag{3}$$

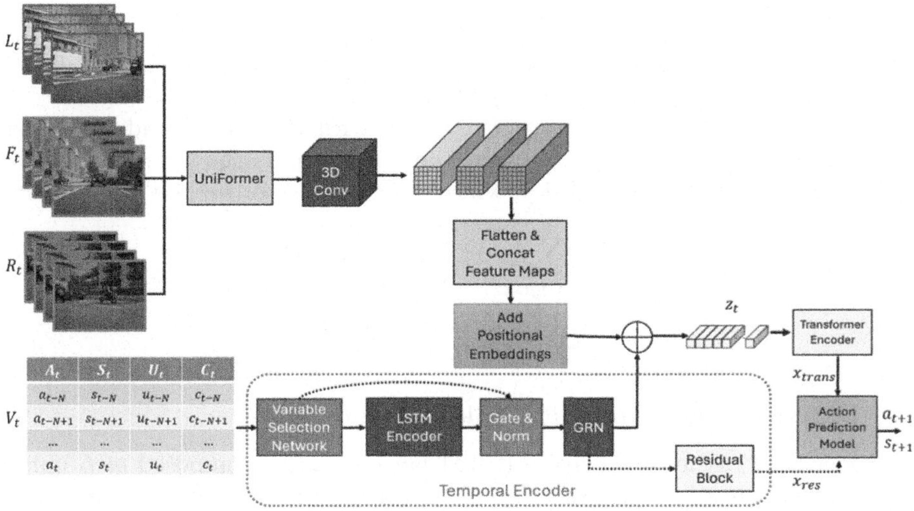

Fig. 4. Illustration of TFT-CIL architecture (adapted from [7]).

For every timestep index $\tau \in [0, N]$ we project the raw scalar values of each variable $v \in \{A, S, U, C\}$ to an h-dimensional vector, by passing them through a linear Layer of h units, as below:

$$\mathbf{x}_\tau^A = E_A(a_{t-\tau}), \quad \mathbf{x}_\tau^S = E_S(s_{t-\tau}), \quad \mathbf{x}_\tau^U = E_U(u_{t-\tau}), \quad \mathbf{x}_\tau^C = E_C(c_{t-\tau}) \in R^h. \tag{4}$$

Then, each x_τ^v passes through two Gated Residual Networks (GRNs): the $GRN_v^{(\text{feat})}$ and the $GRN_v^{(\text{gate})}$, as presented in Eq. 5.

$$\begin{aligned} z_\tau^v &= GRN_v^{(\text{feat})}(x_\tau^v) \\ s_\tau^v &= GRN_v^{(\text{gate})}(x_\tau^v) \end{aligned} \tag{5}$$

where $s_\tau^v \in R^h$ is a non-linear feature transformation and $s_\tau^v \in R$ is a scalar relevance score for each x_τ^v.

Each GRN follows the TFT formulation, presented in Eq. 6.

$$\begin{aligned} \alpha &= \sigma(u) \\ GRN(u) &= a \odot ELU\big(W_1 u + b_1\big) + W_2 u + b_2, \end{aligned} \tag{6}$$

where σ is the sigmoid activation function, which is used as the gating mechanism of the GRN component, and $W_2 u + b_2$ is the residual term (Fig. 3). The scalar scores for each timestep τ are converted to probabilities using softmax activation, as presented in Eq. 7.

$$\pi_\tau^v = \frac{e^{s_\tau^v}}{\sum_{w \in \{A,S,U,C\}} e^{s_\tau^w}}, \quad \sum_v \pi_\tau^v = 1. \tag{7}$$

Then, each feature representation is fused with the corresponding weight (Eq. 8) and finally VSN collects all timesteps and outputs the temporal-control embedding matrix, defined in Eq. 9, which is forwarded to the LSTM encoder.

$$\tilde{v}_\tau = \sum_{v \in \{A,S,U,C\}} \pi_\tau^v \cdot z_\tau^v, \quad \tilde{v_\tau} \in R^h. \tag{8}$$

$$\tilde{V}_t = \left[\tilde{v}_N, \ldots, \tilde{\mathbf{v}}_0\right]^\top \in R^{(N+1) \times h}, \tag{9}$$

4.2 LSTM Encoder and Gated Skip Connection

The sequence $\tilde{V}_t$ is fed to a single LSTM layer (Eq. 10), composed of h units, whose hidden state h_t serves as a fixed-length representation of the control history. Compared with the shallow 1D-Convolutions used in CILv3D, the combination of VSN and LSTM better captures temporal patterns such as sustained acceleration, corrective steering oscillations, or periodic braking.

$$h_t = \text{LSTM}(\tilde{\mathbf{V}}_t) \in R^h. \tag{10}$$

Compared with the 1D-convolutions used in CILv3D, the sequence extracted by the VSNLSTM stack has the ability to capture richer temporal patterns, such as sustained acceleration, corrective steering oscillations, and periodic braking.

Following TFT, h_t is combined with the VSN outputs through a gated residual connection and layer normalization (Eq. 11). This preserves raw control information for which might be lost inside the LSTM encoder, while also improving the gradient flow during training. Finally, this output passes through a final GRN.

$$\begin{aligned} \mathbf{g}_t &= \sigma(W_g \tilde{\mathbf{v}}_0 + b_g) \\ \mathbf{r}_t &= \mathbf{h}_t + \mathbf{g}_t \odot \tilde{\mathbf{v}}_0 \\ \hat{\mathbf{r}}_t &= \text{LayerNorm}(\mathbf{r}_t) \end{aligned} \tag{11}$$

Here $\sigma(\cdot)$ is the sigmoid and $\odot$ denotes the gating operation. The gate $\mathbf{g}_t$. A last GRN component converts the fused vector $\hat{\mathbf{r}}_t$ into the control-stream embedding e_t^{ctrl}, which is projected to 12,800 units to match the UniFormer visual token size.

4.3 Multi-modal Fusion

The UniFormer backbone provides a visual embedding for each video sequence, defined as $E^{\text{vis}} = \left[e_{\text{left}}, e_{\text{front}}, e_{\text{right}}\right]^\top$. We fuse modalities by addition, as shown in Eq. 12, which is made possible, as both streams share the dimensionality.

$$z_t = \left[e_{\text{left}} + e_t^{\text{ctrl}}, e_{\text{front}} + e_t^{\text{ctrl}}, e_{\text{right}} + e_t^{\text{ctrl}}\right]^\top \tag{12}$$

4.4 Action Prediction Network

The fused token is fed into a stack of K Transformer blocks whose multi-head self-attention highlights the cross-modal dependencies across the entire spatio-temporal context. Subsequently, the control embedding from the GRN, $\mathbf{e}_t^{\text{ctrl}}$, is linearly projected to the Transformer's hidden dimension and added to the Transformer's output via a residual connection. A fully connected head of the Action Prediction Network then maps the resulting representation to the next-step steering s_{t+1} and acceleration a_{t+1}.

5 Experiments and Discussion

The objective of our experimental is: a) to assess the benefit of the proposed Temporal Encoder, and b) to compare our approach with the previous state-of-the-art methods, including CIL++, CILRL, CILRL++ and CILv3D. Before training TFT-CIL, we randomly split the training dataset into 80% (64000) of sequences for the training set and 20% (16000) for the test set. Additionally, we conduct hyperparameter tuning to further optimize its performance.

Once the model is trained, we evaluate it on multiple tasks specified by the CARLA leaderboard simulator under diverse weather conditions. These tasks include:

- Lane-merging
- Negotiations at junctions
- Managing traffic lights and signs
- Yielding to emergency vehicles
- Handling pedestrians, cyclists, and other dynamic elements

Moreover, we construct a random scenario in Town10 of the CARLA simulator to assess the performance of the developed controller on general-purpose navigation tasks. In this scenario, we spawn 100 vehicles and 40 pedestrians in random locations and issue random commands and navigation waypoints to CILv3D, which navigates a vehicle. We also provide the implementation code in Github platform[1].

5.1 Hyperparameter Tuning

Due to the time-consuming nature of Hyperparameter tuning, we manually conducted a limited search only on the most critical hyperparameters. These include the sequence size N, the number of transformer blocks (K) and the transformer head units (M), as well as the number of hidden units h used during the vehicle State Representation construction in the Temporal Encoder.

During this process, we trained the neural network for 50 epochs with each configuration and selected the parameters that yielded the lowest Mean Absolute

[1] https://github.com/kochlisGit/CILv3D.

Error (MAE). The sequence size N was set to 4 after experimenting with values ranging from 2 to 8, as this provided a good balance between accuracy, model complexity, and performance. The parameters K and M were set to 4 and 2048, respectively, following experimentation with K values from 1 to 6 and M values from $\{256, 512, 1024, 2048\}$. Finally, the best number of 1D convolution filters was found to be 512.

The rest of the training configuration is the same as CIL++ and CILv3D. More specifically, we train the model for 1000 epochs using the Adam optimizer with an initial learning rate of 0.001 and weight decay of 0.99. The goal of Adam is to minimize the MAE of both the acceleration (a_{t+1} and the steering s_{t+1}, as described by Eq. 13.

$$\mathrm{MAE}_{\mathrm{total}} = \frac{1}{S}\sum_{i=1}^{S}\left(\mathrm{MAE}_{a_{t+1}^{(i)}} + \mathrm{MAE}_{s_{t+1}^{(i)}}\right) \tag{13}$$

where S is the dataset size. The selected hyperparameters can be summarized by Table 1.

Table 1. TFT-CIL Configuration.

Parameter	Value
Sequence Size (N)	4
Transformer Blocks (K)	4
Transformer Head Units	1024
Discount factor (M)	2048
Hidden Size (h)	256
Loss	MAE
Optimizer	Adam
Learning Rate (lr)	0.001
Weight Decay	0.99
Epochs (e)	1000

5.2 Metrics

Similar to the CIL++ approach, we use the MAE as a metric to assess how effectively the constructed neural network learns from expert demonstrations during training. Low MAE in both the training and test set provides an initial indication of how well the model might perform in navigation tasks. However, navigating a vehicle is a stochastic process, which involves randomness and uncertainty in how outcomes evolve over time. This means that the model could potentially overfit to the expert demonstration dataset, as it often happens with Imitation

Learning, leading to poor generalization in unseen navigation scenarios and environmental conditions. To further evaluate its driving performance, we utilize the suggested metrics by the leaderboard module, which are outlined below.

1. **Avg. Driving Score**: the most important metric of the Leaderboard.
2. **Avg Route completion (%):** the completed route distance.
3. **Avg Infraction Penalty:** the maximum value of this score is 1.0 and is reduced each time the driving controller commits an infraction.
4. **Collisions with Vehicles:** the collision count with other vehicles.
5. **Collisions with Pedestrians:** the collision count with walking pedestrians.
6. **Collisions with Layout:** the collision count with objects (e.g. buildings, pavement, etc.).
7. **Red Light Infractions:** the number of red lights ignored by the vehicle.
8. **Stop Sign Infractions:** the number of stop signs ignored by the vehicle.
9. **Off-Road Infractions:** the number of times where the vehicle deviated from its target lane.
10. **Route Deviations:** the number of times where the vehicle deviated from the desired route.
11. **Route Timeouts:** the number of times where the vehicle failed to complete its route within a specified amount of time.
12. **Agent Blocked:** the total time during which the vehicle was inoperative.

5.3 Results & Discussion

The results of the Imitation-Learning process are summarized in Table 2. It can be observed that after 1000 epochs of training, the TFT-CIL outperforms every previously state-of-the-art method, including its predecessor, CILv3D, which achieves the second best performance. The improvement is consistent on both the training and test splits, highlighting the benefit of the proposed Temporal Encoder branch, which supplies richer vehicle control historical features to the Transformer, and thus yielding more informative multi-modal embeddings and eventually, more accurate driving controls.

Table 2. The Train-Eval Loss (MAE) of each architecture for the Imitation Learning process.

Architecture	Training Loss	Validation Loss
CIL++	0.0107	0.01387
CIL++ - Uni	0.0101	0.01180
CIL++ - 3D	0.0097	0.01184
CILv3D	0.0092	0.01059
TFT-CIL	**0.0086**	**0.01012**

Continuing our evaluation, we present the results of the experiments in the CARLA simulator in Table 3. TFT-CIL achieves the best performance in most of the presented metrics, with CILv3D performing slightly worse. Crucially, both models reach this level of performance without the additional fine-tuning process that CILRL++ requires. While CILRL++ excels in a few metrics, such as lower pedestrian and environment collisions, its gains come from extensive, time-consuming reinforcement fine-tuning of CIL++. By contrast, TFT-CIL delivers the highest mean driving score and route completion rate overall with less training time than CILRL++.

Table 3. Evaluation Table of a) CIL++, b) CILRL, c) CILRL++ and d) CILv3D using CARLA Leaderboard.

Score	CIL++	CILRL	CILRL++	CILv3D	TFT-CIL
Avg. Driving Score (%)	2.59	0.09	10.01	11.73	**12.67**
Avg. Route Completition (%)	10.93	0.29	14.44	15.12	**16.81**
Avg. Infraction Penalty	0.44	0.47	**0.64**	0.59	**0.64**
Collisions with Vehicles	**0.0**	**0.0**	**0.0**	**0.0**	**0.0**
Collisions with Pedestrians	256.21	2759.67	**52.82**	128.43	112.52
Collisions with Layout	411.01	14496.83	**255.22**	285.66	212.59
Red Light Infractions	9.34	**0.0**	7.98	8.83	8.92
Stop Sign Infractions	5.77	846.62	**0.0**	2.25	1.67
Off-Road Infractions	253.67	1457.57	186.47	177.53	**180.83**
Route Deviations	**0.0**	144.4	76.74	55.81	55.12
Route Timeouts	**0.0**	330.96	**0.0**	**0.0**	**0.0**
Agent Blocked	399	10985.68	222.65	198.69	**177.34**

5.4 Limitations

While our methodology is a robust architecture for training VBETE controllers, it comes with limitations. First, like most end-to-end navigation systems, the deployed model operates as a black box system, making it difficult to interpret or verify the rationale behind specific driving decisions, despite its ability to operate well in several benchmarks in the Leaderboard. Second, it produces high-level vehicle control (e.g., acceleration values, steering, etc.), but real-world navigation systems require an additional control layer to translate these outputs into low-level vehicle actions (e.g., by adjusting throttle/brake systems), which was not modeled in this work. Finally, the model's reliance on imitation learning means its performance is inherently capped by the scope and quality of the expert demonstrations; it cannot handle situations for which no expert data exists. This limitation emphasizes the need to construct a diverse training dataset that captures a wide spectrum of driving scenarios, including rare edge cases and adverse conditions.

6 Conclusion and Future Work

In this work we introduced TFT-CIL, a VBETE controller that removes several bottlenecks of CIL++ and pushes the State-Of-The-Art beyond CILv3D. Across the CARLA Leaderboard benchmarks, TFT-CIL scores the highest mean driving score and route-completion rate, outperforming CIL++, CILRL++, and CILv3D, without the need for extensive fine-tuning that CILRL++ relies on.

Several extensions could further strengthen TFT-CIL. For instance, adding a full 360-degree surround-view (e.g., four to six cameras) would give the Transformer richer context for lane-change and lane-merge scenarios. Additionally, fusing complementary sensors such as LiDAR or radars could make the model more resilient in more complex environments.

References

1. Baker, B., et al.: Video pretraining (vpt): Learning to act by watching unlabeled online videos. Adv. Neural. Inf. Process. Syst. **35**, 24639–24654 (2022)
2. Carion, N., Massa, F., Synnaeve, G., Usunier, N., Kirillov, A., Zagoruyko, S.: End-to-End Object Detection with Transformers. In: Vedaldi, A., Bischof, H., Brox, T., Frahm, J.-M. (eds.) ECCV 2020. LNCS, vol. 12346, pp. 213–229. Springer, Cham (2020). https://doi.org/10.1007/978-3-030-58452-8_13
3. Codevilla, F., Santana, E., López, A.M., Gaidon, A.: Exploring the limitations of behavior cloning for autonomous driving. In: Proceedings of the IEEE/CVF International Conference on Computer Vision, pp. 9329–9338 (2019)
4. Dosovitskiy, A., et al.: An image is worth 16x16 words: transformers for image recognition at scale. CoRR abs/2010.11929 (2020). https://arxiv.org/abs/2010.11929
5. Dosovitskiy, A., Ros, G., Codevilla, F., Lopez, A., Koltun, V.: Carla: An open urban driving simulator. In: Conference on Robot Learning, pp. 1–16. PMLR (2017)
6. He, K., Zhang, X., Ren, S., Sun, J.: Deep residual learning for image recognition. In: Proceedings of the IEEE Conference on Computer Vision and Pattern Recognition, pp. 770–778 (2016)
7. Kochliaridis, V., Moumtzidellis, F., Vlahavas, I.: Scaling multi-frame transformers for end-to-end driving. In: Proceedings of the 17th International Conference on Agents and Artificial Intelligence - Volume 3: ICAART, pp. 496–503. INSTICC, SciTePress (2025). https://doi.org/10.5220/0013156700003890
8. Li, K., et al.: Uniformer: unifying convolution and self-attention for visual recognition. IEEE Trans. Pattern Anal. Mach. Intell. **45**(10), 12581–12600 (2023)
9. Lim, B., Arik, S.O., Loeff, N., Pfister, T.: Temporal fusion transformers for interpretable multi-horizon time series forecasting (2020). https://arxiv.org/abs/1912.09363
10. Song, Q., et al.: Autonomous driving decision control based on improved proximal policy optimization algorithm. Appl. Sci. **13**(11), 6400 (2023)
11. Tampuu, A., Matiisen, T., Semikin, M., Fishman, D., Muhammad, N.: A survey of end-to-end driving: architectures and training methods. IEEE Trans. Neural Netw. Learn. Syst. **33**(4), 1364–1384 (2020)

12. Kochliaridis, V., Kostinoudis, E.I.V.: Optimizing pretrained transformers for autonomous driving. In: 13th EETN Conference on Artificial Intelligence (SETN). ACM (2024)
13. Vaswani, A., et al.: Attention is all you need. Adv. Neural Inf. Process. Syst. **30** (2017)
14. Xiao, Y., Codevilla, F., Porres, D., López, A.M.: Scaling vision-based end-to-end autonomous driving with multi-view attention learning. In: 2023 IEEE/RSJ International Conference on Intelligent Robots and Systems (IROS), pp. 1586–1593. IEEE (2023)
15. Zhang, Z., Liniger, A., Dai, D., Yu, F., Van Gool, L.: End-to-end urban driving by imitating a reinforcement learning coach. In: Proceedings of the IEEE/CVF International Conference on Computer Vision, pp. 15222–15232 (2021)

Uncovering Hidden Biases in Synthetic Java Vulnerability Data for LLM-Based Detection

Lucas Bastos Germano(✉), Julio Cesar Duarte, Lincoln Queiroz Vieira, Ronaldo Ribeiro Goldschmidt, and Ricardo Choren Noya

Military Institute of Engineering, Rio de Janeiro, Brazil
{lucas.germano,duarte,lincoln.queiroz,ronaldo.rgold,choren}@ime.eb.br

Abstract. Synthetic datasets such as the SARD have become a cornerstone for training and evaluating vulnerability detection models. However, recent findings have revealed that these datasets may embed superficial patterns that unintentionally bias learning algorithms. This study investigates the Java subset of SARD, uncovering structural artifacts that can mislead LLMs into learning misleading correlations instead of true vulnerability semantics. We identify key sources of bias, including naming conventions, descriptive comments, cascade-style wrappers, and inconsistent access modifiers, and propose a comprehensive preprocessing pipeline to sanitize the dataset. Using CodeBERT as a representative LLM, we train and evaluate classifiers on both the biased and bias-free versions of the dataset. The bias-free model achieved 99.2% accuracy on sanitized data and generalized well across both datasets, whereas the biased model, although achieving 99.9% accuracy on biased data, dropped to 78.6% when evaluated on the bias-free dataset, highlighting a significant failure to generalize. These findings underscore the need for rigorous bias identification and mitigation strategies to ensure the reliability of LLM-based vulnerability detection systems.

Keywords: Data Preprocessing · Deep Learning · Large Language Models · Synthetic Vulnerability Dataset · Vulnerability Detection

1 Introduction

Ensuring the security of software systems is a critical concern for both industry and academia. Traditional static analyzers, while effective at catching known vulnerability patterns, often suffer from high false-positive rates and require laborious rule crafting. Machine learning techniques, particularly transformer-based Large Language Models (LLMs), offer a more adaptable solution but depend heavily on the quality of their training data.

In the context of software vulnerability detection, synthetic datasets like the Software Assurance Reference Dataset (SARD) [15] play a central role. Devel-

H. J. van den Herik et al. (Eds.): ICAART 2025, LNAI 16517, pp. 301–317, 2026.
https://doi.org/10.1007/978-3-032-25032-2_14

oped by the National Institute of Standards and Technology (NIST), SARD provides labeled test cases that simulate known vulnerability patterns across multiple programming languages, including C, C++, C#, PHP, and Java. These synthetic examples are generated using predefined algorithms that encode common weaknesses such as buffer overflows or SQL injections. As a result, the SARD dataset has become a widely adopted benchmark in the vulnerability detection literature [1,8–13,16–19], supporting the evaluation of various machine learning and LLM-based techniques. However, the same generation mechanisms that ensure consistency and reproducibility may also introduce hidden regularities that risk misleading models if left unaddressed.

While SARD offers consistency and reproducibility, our previous work [5] demonstrated that its synthetic test cases in C/C++ may contain superficial patterns such as generation-induced naming schemes, structural artifacts, and syntactic conventions that inadvertently signal whether a test is vulnerable. These artifacts can cause models to learn from shallow cues instead of the actual vulnerability semantics. Despite this, SARD remains a widely adopted benchmark for vulnerability detection across programming languages. It has supported numerous studies in C/C++ [8,10–12,16,18] as well as in Java [1,9,13,17,19], enabling the evaluation of both traditional and LLM-based techniques. Building on our previous findings, this study extends the investigation to the Java subset of the SARD dataset to determine whether similar issues related to data quality and bias are present. Specifically, we assess how hidden biases introduced during dataset construction impact the performance and generalization of LLM-based vulnerability classifiers. This analysis also serves as a foundation for evaluating the presence and effects of such biases in datasets for other programming languages.

In parallel, recent studies have started to acknowledge the limitations of using synthetic datasets for vulnerability detection. For instance, Hanif *et al.* [6] highlights the impracticality of relying solely on synthetic data, noting that such datasets often fail to reflect the true structure and complexity of real-world vulnerabilities. Furthermore, Tamberg *et al.* [17] identifies several sources of bias, including skewed vulnerability type distributions and imbalances in data sources. However, despite recognizing these high-level issues, their analysis does not extend to the subtle yet impactful biases introduced by the synthetic generation algorithms themselves. This study fills that gap by analyzing and quantifying the effects of structural artifacts embedded in the SARD Java dataset.

Building upon the definition proposed by Germano *et al.* [5], this study adopts a context-specific interpretation of bias in the domain of source code vulnerability detection. A dataset is considered biased when it contains superficial patterns such as naming conventions, structural regularities, or token-level cues that inadvertently lead the model to associate these artifacts with the presence or absence of vulnerabilities. These patterns often emerge from the algorithms used to synthesize the data, rather than from meaningful vulnerability semantics. For example, if vulnerable functions are consistently labeled with names such as "bad" or are placed within specific control structures, models may learn to rely on these superficial patterns rather than understanding the underlying logic of the vulnerability. This can lead to misleading performance results and poor generalization to real-world code. As discussed by Mehrabi *et al.* [14], such biases introduced during data generation can propagate through training, causing models to develop spurious correlations that hinder generalization. Similarly, Barbierato *et al.* [2] notes that the influence of certain data elements over others can distort learning outcomes, particularly when those elements are not causally linked to the task objective. This study investigates the presence of structural artifacts in the Java subset of SARD and evaluates their impact on the reliability and robustness of LLM-based vulnerability classifiers.

This study pursues two main goals. First, we systematically identify recurring patterns in SARD's Java test cases that may mislead detection models, patterns that arise not from genuine vulnerability semantics but from the dataset generation process. Second, we propose and evaluate a bias-mitigation pipeline that removes or masks superficial markers, comparing model performance between the original and adjusted datasets.

Our contributions are fourfold:

- **Bias Catalogue for SARD-Java:** we identify and document superficial patterns, such as naming schemes, structural artifacts, and syntactic conventions introduced by the data generation process, that inadvertently signal vulnerability presence and skew model learning.
- **Bias Removal Methodology:** we describe an automated preprocessing approach that cleans or replaces identified markers while preserving code functionality.
- **Experimental Validation:** we demonstrate that, using a CodeBERT-based classifier [3], a model trained on the unbiased SARD data generalizes better, achieving substantially higher accuracy when faced with unseen bias-free examples.
- **Public Release:** we provide access to the processed, bias-reduced SARD-Java corpus and all associated preprocessing and training code for reproducibility and further research.[1]

In this study, we employ the Juliet Java 1.3 test suite from SARD in combination with the LLM CodeBERT [3] to classify source code as either vulnerable or non-vulnerable. The experimental findings reveal a contrast in performance depending on the training data: a model trained on the biased dataset achieved only 78.6% accuracy when evaluated on the bias-free dataset, indicating poor generalization. Conversely, the model trained on the bias-free dataset reached 99.7% accuracy when tested on the biased dataset, suggesting it learned to identify vulnerabilities based on meaningful patterns rather than superficial indicators.

The remainder of this paper is organized as follows. Section 2 details our preprocessing and bias-detection workflow. Section 3 presents the catalog of Java-specific biases. Section 4 reports on our experimental setup and results, high-

[1] Available at https://github.com/lucasg1/sard_java_without_bias.

lighting improvements over the baseline. Section 5 reviews related literature on synthetic dataset bias and LLM security applications, while Sect. 6 concludes with future directions for building more trustworthy vulnerability detectors.

2 Data Preprocessing Approach

This work focuses on the Java subset of the Juliet Test Suite, a collection of synthetic vulnerability test cases included in the SARD [15]. Each test case comprises both a vulnerable and a corrected implementation for various Common Weakness Enumeration (CWE) types, allowing for supervised training of classification models.

Compared to the C/C++ version used in the previous work [5], the Java subset presents a similar structure and shares several of the same bias-inducing artifacts. These biases can significantly impair the generalization capability of LLMs, especially when models are trained on patterns that do not exist in real-world applications.

To mitigate these effects, we apply a preprocessing pipeline designed to identify and remove superficial cues from the code while preserving its functionality. This ensures that models learn to detect vulnerabilities based on meaningful semantics rather than on spurious, dataset-specific features. Figure 1 outlines the key steps of our sanitization procedure.

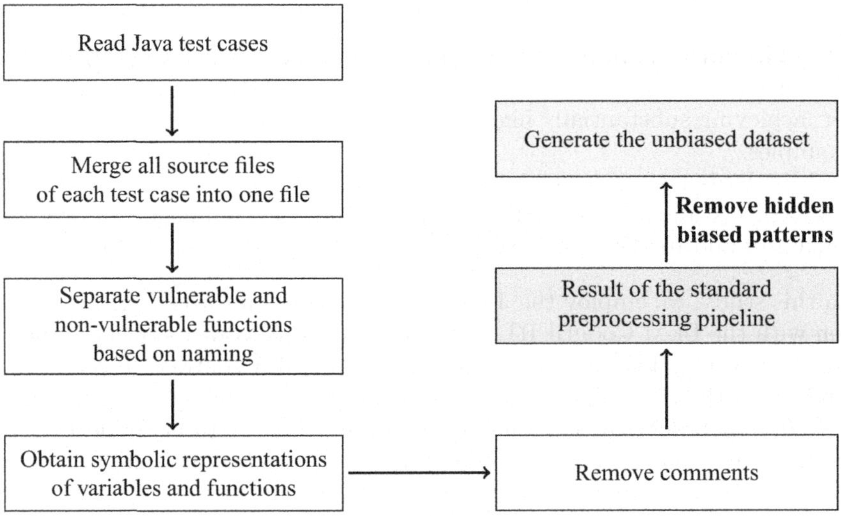

Fig. 1. Overview of the data preprocessing pipeline.

Read Java Test Cases

Each SARD Java test case may span multiple source files, with classes and methods distributed across them. Within a single test case, both vulnerable and non-vulnerable code are implemented as distinct functions that often call one another, forming a minimal execution scenario. Listing 1.1 shows an excerpt from one such file. Preparing the data requires parsing and merging all files for each test case, extracting individual functions, and accurately associating them with their corresponding vulnerability labels.

```
public class CWE78_OS_Command_Injection_connect_tcp_10 extends AbstractTestCase
{
    /* uses badsource and badsink */
    public void bad() throws Throwable
    {
        String data;
        if (IO.staticTrue)
        {
            data = ""; /* Initialize data */
            /* Read data using an outbound tcp connection */
            {
                Socket socket = null;
                BufferedReader readerBuffered = null;
                InputStreamReader readerInputStream = null;
                try
                {
                    socket = new Socket("host.example.org", 39544);
                    readerInputStream = new InputStreamReader(socket.getInputStream(), "UTF-8");
                    readerBuffered = new BufferedReader(readerInputStream);
                    data = readerBuffered.readLine();

        ...

        String osCommand;
        if(System.getProperty("os.name").toLowerCase().indexOf("win") >= 0)
        {
            osCommand = "c:\\WINDOWS\\SYSTEM32\\cmd.exe /c dir ";
        }
        else
        {
            osCommand = "/bin/ls ";
        }

        Process process = Runtime.getRuntime().exec(osCommand + data);
        process.waitFor();
    }

    private void goodG2B1() throws Throwable
    {
        String data;
        if (IO.staticFalse)
        {
            data = null;
        }
        else
        {
            data = "foo";
        }

        String osCommand;
        if(System.getProperty("os.name").toLowerCase().indexOf("win") >= 0)
        {
            osCommand = "c:\\WINDOWS\\SYSTEM32\\cmd.exe /c dir ";
        }
        else
        {
            osCommand = "/bin/ls ";
        }

        Process process = Runtime.getRuntime().exec(osCommand + data);
        process.waitFor();
    }

    public void good() throws Throwable
    {
        goodG2B1();
        goodG2B2();
    }
}
```

Listing 1.1. Example of CWE-78 vulnerable and non-vulnerable variants (partial view due to page size).

Merge All Source Files of Each Test Case into One File

Since a single SARD Java test case may be split across multiple files, each containing partial class or method definitions that reference one another, it is necessary to consolidate all source files belonging to the same test case into a single file. This merging step facilitates consistent parsing, simplifies the extraction of complete control and data flow, and ensures that interdependent methods are analyzed together during subsequent preprocessing stages.

Separate Vulnerable and Non-Vulnerable Functions Based on Naming

In the Juliet Java dataset, each test case typically defines both vulnerable and non-vulnerable behaviors using dedicated functions whose names encode their roles, such as `bad()`, `good()`, `badSink()`, `goodG2B()`, or `goodB2GSink()`. These functions are often distributed across multiple files following naming patterns like 53a/53b/53c/53d, with each file representing a part of a minimal execution chain. To separate the vulnerable and non-vulnerable samples, we parse each test case, extract relevant methods based on naming conventions, and reconstruct them into individual files while preserving their class structures, package declarations, variable definitions, and inter-class dependencies. This process enables the generation of clean, labeled datasets for each vulnerability class while ensuring consistency and correctness across dependency chains.

Obtain Symbolic Representations of Variables and Functions

To mitigate bias introduced by semantically charged identifiers, such as function or variable names containing terms like `bad`, `good`, or `vuln`, we replace sensitive names with symbolic placeholders. This process involves scanning each Java file to identify and anonymize class names, function names, and variable names that match bias-related patterns. Affected function names are replaced with generic tokens like `FUN#` (e.g., `badSink` becomes `FUN0`), and variable names are replaced with `VAR#` tokens (e.g., `vulnData` becomes `VAR1`). The result is a semantically preserved version of each test case in which surface-level naming cues are eliminated, ensuring that downstream models focus on structural and behavioral features rather than superficial keywords.

Remove Comments

Many of the Java files in the SARD dataset contain comments that explicitly describe whether a particular function is vulnerable or not, often using terms such as "CWE" or "bad practice". These comments, while useful for human understanding, introduce unintended labeling cues that can be exploited by learning algorithms. To prevent the model from relying on these superficial hints, we remove all comments from the source code during preprocessing. Both single-line and multi-line comments are stripped while preserving the code's formatting and line structure. This ensures that models are trained on the program logic itself, rather than on auxiliary annotations that are unavailable in real-world software. Examples of such comments are presented in Listing 1.1.

Result of the Standard Preprocessing Pipeline

At this stage, the dataset reflects the standard preprocessing pipeline adopted by many previous studies: removing comments and anonymizing function and variable names that contain easily exploitable keywords. While these steps eliminate the most obvious sources of bias, the resulting dataset remains biased due to subtle and often overlooked structural patterns. These include consistent naming conventions, recurring control-flow layouts, or overrepresented method signatures that can still guide the model toward shortcut learning. As such, this intermediate version is referred to as the biased dataset, and it serves as a baseline for evaluating the impact of deeper, hidden artifacts that are addressed in the subsequent debiasing stage.

Generate the Unbiased Dataset

While the standard preprocessing steps remove many superficial cues, the dataset still contains hidden patterns that can bias model training. To mitigate these subtler forms of leakage, we apply an additional refinement step to generate an unbiased version of the dataset.

One such hidden pattern, which we refer to as the cascade pattern, consists of wrapper methods in which a top-level function (typically named `good()` or `bad()`) simply delegates execution to other methods within the same test case, often following a predetermined sequence. This structure appears in 97.08% of the non-vulnerable (`good`) files and in 0% of the vulnerable (`bad`) files, effectively acting as an implicit signal that reveals the file's label. As a result, models may rely on this invocation layout as a shortcut for classification rather than learning semantically meaningful indicators of vulnerability. Illustrative examples of this pattern are provided in Listing 1.2 and Listing 1.3.

```
public void good() throws Throwable
{
    goodG2B1();
    goodG2B2();
}
```

Listing 1.2. Cascade pattern with chained good methods.

```
public void good(HttpServletRequest request,
    HttpServletResponse response) throws Throwable
{
     goodG2B1(request, response);
     goodG2B2(request, response);
}
```

Listing 1.3. Cascade pattern using servlet parameters

Another source of bias stems from inconsistent visibility modifiers. Vulnerable code is frequently placed inside methods declared with the `public` keyword, while non-vulnerable code appears in `private` methods. In object-oriented programming, the distinction between `public` and `private` is semantically meaningful; changing it arbitrarily may introduce security flaws or alter program behavior. However, in the case of this dataset, the pattern arises not from sound design principles but from a flawed synthetic generation process, where vulnerable methods are systematically declared as `public`, while non-vulnerable ones, especially the top-level methods like `goodG2B()`, are often declared as `private`. This introduces an unintended signal that models can exploit. In our analysis, the `private void FUN` pattern appears in 99.57% of non-vulnerable (`good`) files and only 6.50% of vulnerable (`bad`) files, making it a highly predictive artifact. To neutralize this signal, we standardize only the visibility of these main method declarations by changing their access modifier from `private` to `public`, while leaving all helper methods untouched. An example, before preprocessing, is shown in Listing 1.4.

```
private void goodG2B() throws Throwable
{
     String data;
     ...
}

public void bad() throws Throwable
{
     String data;
     ...
}
```

Listing 1.4. Private method pattern found in biased samples.

After these steps, the resulting dataset no longer contains cascade wrappers or inconsistent access modifiers, allowing for a more faithful evaluation of model performance under reduced bias.

3 Identified Biases in the Dataset

Section 2 introduced various sources of bias present in the SARD Java dataset, such as semantically charged names, descriptive comments, cascade method chains, and inconsistent access modifiers. This section presents a quantitative analysis of the extent to which these bias patterns occur across the dataset. We report the percentage of files affected by each identified artifact and compile a comprehensive catalog of all discovered biases.

The most immediate source of bias lies in function and variable names, such as `bad()`, `goodG2B()`, or `dataBad`, which are systematically used across samples and may serve as shortcuts for classification. Similarly, comments often include explicit phrases like "FLAW" or "FIX" that clearly indicate the method's vulnerability status, despite being unrealistic in real-world software. These forms of bias are well recognized in the literature, and many prior studies already account for them by removing or anonymizing such elements during preprocessing.

Beyond these, our analysis uncovered less obvious but equally damaging patterns. As discussed in Sect. 2, structural constructs such as cascade method chains are heavily skewed toward non-vulnerable methods. These auxiliary call sequences appear in over 99% of non-vulnerable methods and are virtually absent from vulnerable ones. This introduces a severe imbalance that a model can exploit to classify code without analyzing the core logic.

In summary, the following biases were identified and targeted for removal in our preprocessing pipeline:

1. **Function and variable names** that encode vulnerability labels, such as identifiers containing "good", "bad", or "vuln";
2. **Comments** that explicitly describe vulnerabilities or safe practices, often using keywords like "FLAW" and "FIX";
3. **Inconsistent access modifiers**, where non-vulnerable methods are overwhelmingly declared as **private**, while vulnerable ones are declared as **public**. This pattern appears in 99.57% of non-vulnerable (**good**) files and only 6.50% of vulnerable (**bad**) files;
4. **Cascade patterns**, in which wrapper methods simply invoke other methods in a fixed sequence. This structure is found in 97.08% of non-vulnerable files and in 0% of vulnerable files, serving as a strong signal that can be exploited by models.

While the first two types of biases have been partially acknowledged in prior studies, typically through comment removal or basic renaming, structural patterns such as cascade wrappers and visibility modifiers have received little to no attention in the literature, as detailed in Sect. 5. To the best of our knowledge, this is the first study to systematically identify and eliminate these deeper structural biases in the Java subset of the SARD dataset.

Although additional hidden biases may still be present in the dataset, they are likely more subtle and difficult to detect through visual inspection alone. Uncovering such patterns may require more advanced analytical techniques or dedicated follow-up studies. Nonetheless, the preprocessing steps applied in this work establish a cleaner baseline, enabling models to focus more directly on vulnerability semantics and improving their potential to generalize to real-world code.

4 Experiments and Results

This section evaluates the effects of dataset biases on the performance of an LLM for vulnerability classification. CodeBERT [3], a transformer-based model pretrained on large corpora of Java and other programming languages, is employed due to its effectiveness in source code understanding. It is also widely used as the backbone of many state-of-the-art vulnerability classifiers, such as those proposed by [4,7].

To classify source code as vulnerable or non-vulnerable, CodeBERT [3] is extended by adding a linear classification head on top of the encoder outputs. Sequences exceeding the model's 512-token limit are divided into overlapping chunks of 480 tokens with a stride of 416 (64-token overlap), and the outputs are aggregated via mean pooling over the `[CLS]` embeddings. The `[CLS]` token, positioned at the beginning of each input chunk, is commonly used as the aggregated sequence representation for classification tasks, as established in the original CodeBERT framework [3]. No tokenizer retraining is performed since CodeBERT's tokenizer is already trained on Java code.

4.1 Training and Evaluation Setup

We trained two models:

- a **bias-free model**, trained on the fully sanitized dataset; and
- a **biased model**, trained on the dataset sanitized by the standard preprocessing pipeline described in Sect. 2.

The biased dataset was generated following conventional preprocessing practices commonly found in prior studies. These typically involve removing comments and renaming function or variable identifiers that contain easily recognizable bias-inducing terms. However, more subtle structural artifacts, such as cascade-style control flow or consistent use of access modifiers like `public` and `private`, are frequently left unaddressed and persist in the data.

Each dataset was randomly split into training (80%) and testing (20%) subsets. Models were trained exclusively on the training split of their respective datasets (biased or bias-free), and evaluated on both the biased and bias-free testing splits. This setup, illustrated in Fig. 2, enables the assessment of generalization performance under cross-domain scenarios and helps quantify the model's reliance on superficial patterns.

4.2 Evaluation Results

Table 1 and Table 2 report the performance metrics, including accuracy, precision, recall, and f1-score, for both models on each dataset. These metrics are computed as simple averages.

The bias-free model achieved near-perfect performance on the fully sanitized dataset, demonstrating its ability to learn genuine vulnerability semantics rather than relying on superficial cues. In contrast, the biased model performed significantly worse, particularly in terms of precision, despite its seemingly high recall. This inflated recall originates from a high number of false positives, with the model frequently misclassifying non-vulnerable samples as vulnerable. This behavior can be attributed to the removal of biased patterns, such as cascade

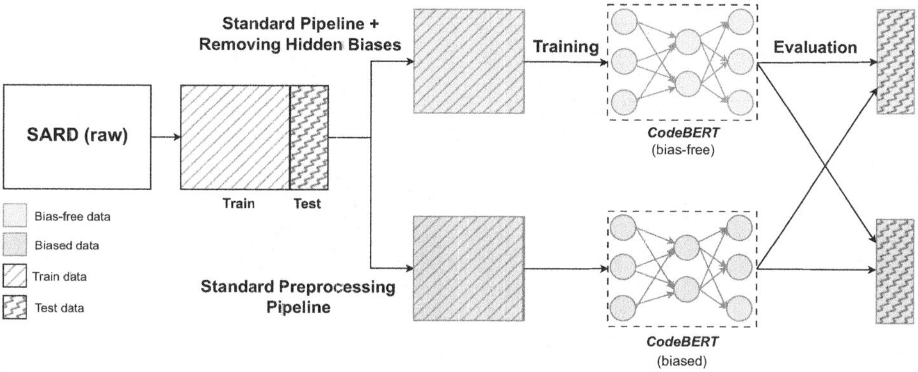

Fig. 2. Training and evaluation workflow for biased and bias-free models.

Table 1. Results of Accuracy, Precision, F1-score, and Recall metrics from both bias-free and biased models on the bias-free dataset.

	Bias-free dataset			
Model	Accuracy	Precision	F1-score	Recall
Bias-free	**99.2%**	**98.6%**	**99.2%**	99.7%
Biased	78.6%	70.1%	82.4%	**99.9%**

wrappers and `private` access modifiers, in the bias-free dataset. Since these patterns were present almost exclusively in non-vulnerable files during training, the biased model implicitly learned to associate their absence with vulnerability. Consequently, when such patterns were removed, the model defaulted to labeling most files as vulnerable.

This failure to generalize is further illustrated by the confusion matrix in Fig. 3, which highlights the model's overreliance on dataset-specific artifacts. As shown, the number of false positives is high (2,466), while false negatives are nearly nonexistent (only 5). This imbalance leads to an artificially inflated recall score, as recall is defined by the equation: Recall $= \frac{TP}{TP+FN}$ where the small denominator results in a value close to 1 despite the model's poor overall performance.

When both models are evaluated on the biased dataset, the biased model unsurprisingly achieves near-perfect performance, having overfitted to the superficial cues present in its training data. In contrast, the bias-free model maintains strong performance, demonstrating robustness and the ability to detect vulnerabilities without relying on misleading indicators.

4.3 Discussion

These results highlight how biases in synthetic datasets like SARD can severely distort model behavior. A model trained on biased data may perform well on

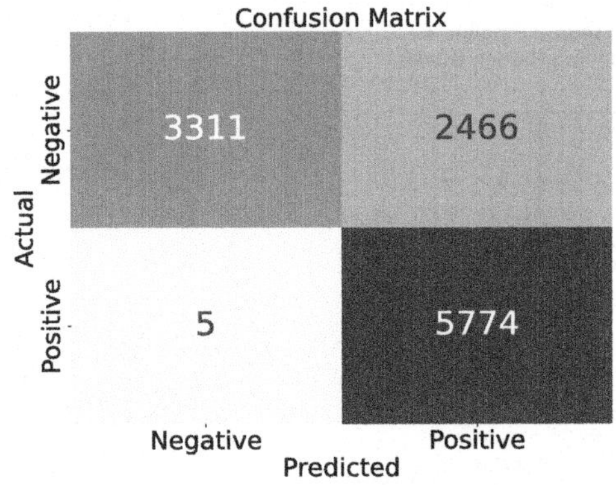

Fig. 3. Confusion matrix for the biased model on the bias-free dataset.

Table 2. Results of Accuracy, Precision, F1-score, and Recall metrics from both bias-free and biased models on the biased dataset.

	Biased dataset			
Model	Accuracy	Precision	F1-score	Recall
Bias-free	99.7%	99.8%	99.7%	99.6%
Biased	**99.9%**	**99.9%**	**99.9%**	**99.9%**

similarly biased test sets but fail to generalize when those patterns are removed. In contrast, the bias-free model consistently excels across both domains, providing strong evidence for the importance of dataset sanitization in LLM-based vulnerability detection research.

These findings align with results reported in our previous work [5], which demonstrated that the C/C++ subset of the SARD dataset contains strong superficial patterns, such as cascade-style control flows and biased method declarations, that can mislead vulnerability classifiers. Our current analysis demonstrates that such biases are not confined to the C/C++ subset but also permeate the Java portion of SARD. This reinforces the broader concern that synthetic datasets, regardless of programming language, can introduce unintended signals that undermine model generalization.

By systematically identifying and addressing structural artifacts in the Java SARD dataset for the first time, this study extends the scope of bias detection and mitigation efforts. In doing so, it contributes to a deeper understanding of how dataset design influences the effectiveness and robustness of LLM-based vulnerability classifiers, emphasizing the need for careful dataset curation.

5 Related Work

This section reviews prior research in two key areas relevant to this study. The first focuses on *debiasing vulnerability datasets*, particularly efforts to identify and remove misleading patterns in synthetic benchmarks like SARD. The second examines existing work on *vulnerability detection using the Java subset of the SARD dataset*, which serves as the experimental foundation for our analysis. While the SARD dataset is widely used for training and evaluating vulnerability classifiers, most studies have not investigated the underlying biases that may compromise model generalization.

5.1 Debiasing Vulnerability Datasets

Although prior work [5] has demonstrated that the C/C++ subset of the SARD dataset contains structural biases that hinder model generalization, the Java portion has not been similarly explored. Existing studies that use SARD for vulnerability detection typically apply only superficial sanitization steps, such as removing comments or renaming obviously biased identifiers. However, deeper structural patterns, including method cascades and access modifier inconsistencies, remain unaddressed. To the best of our knowledge, no other work besides ours has systematically identified and mitigated these biases. This study extends our previous analysis to the Java subset of SARD, revealing that similar artifacts are present across both language domains and may similarly impair the reliability of vulnerability detection models.

5.2 Vulnerability Detection in Java SARD

Several recent studies have utilized the Java portion of the SARD Juliet dataset for vulnerability detection, applying deep learning and LLM-based approaches to advance detection performance.

Bae *et al.* [1] explored prompt engineering for vulnerability detection using GPT-4 and Claude-3.5. They applied various prompt formulations to SARD Java samples and assessed model sensitivity to prompt structure, finding substantial performance variance across vulnerability types. However, the study did not investigate dataset-intrinsic biases.

Mamede *et al.* [13] used transformer models for multi-label classification of Java vulnerabilities in the Juliet SARD dataset. They evaluated models like CodeBERT and GraphCodeBERT with token classification heads. Although symbolic representations and preprocessing were employed, no bias mitigation strategies were introduced.

Hussain *et al.* [9] proposed a hybrid quantum convolutional neural network (QCNN) with self-attention to detect vulnerabilities in SARD Java code. While their architecture achieved promising results, the authors did not address dataset artifacts such as naming conventions or structural patterns.

Tamberg and Bahsi [17] conducted a benchmarking study with LLMs, GPT-4 and Claude, for example, on various vulnerability detection tasks. Although their work highlights performance disparities across models, it relies on the original dataset without addressing possible spurious correlations or superficial cues.

Zhang *et al.* [19] introduced a BERT-BiLSTM-CRF architecture for injection vulnerability detection in Java web applications. Their method combined interprocedural analysis and symbolic representation with deep learning. While they generated a new corpus from SARD and real-world code, their approach focused on taint analysis rather than investigating structural or semantic biases within the SARD dataset.

Table 3 summarizes the key characteristics of these related works. An important point that deserves attention is that some studies did not perform symbolic representation, even though variable and function names in SARD often reveal the correct label. Without this step, models risk merely memorizing lexical patterns rather than truly understanding the underlying semantics of vulnerabilities.

Table 3. Comparison of related work using SARD.

Work	Symbolic Representation	Debiasing Attempt	Dataset Used
[1]	✗	✗	SARD Java, C/C++, and Python
[9]	✗	✗	SARD Java + Others
[13]	✓	✗	SARD Java
[17]	✓	✗	SARD Java
[19]	✓	✗	SARD Java + Real-world
Previous Work [5]	✓	✓	Bias-free SARD C/C++
This Work	✓	✓	**Bias-free SARD Java**

Notably, only our prior work [5] and the present study were found to explicitly address hidden structural biases in the SARD dataset. While the earlier work focused on C/C++ test cases, this paper extends the analysis to Java, demonstrating that similar bias-inducing patterns exist across languages.

In contrast to the other studies above, our work is the first to systematically identify and remove hidden structural biases in the SARD Java dataset that can distort model training. Patterns such as cascade function chains, naming conventions, and inconsistent visibility modifiers are explicitly neutralized to build a bias-free dataset. This enables more robust and generalizable LLM-based classifiers.

6 Conclusion

The increasing integration of LLMs into software engineering has opened new possibilities for automating complex tasks such as vulnerability detection, repair, and explanation. These models employ vast amounts of code and natural language data to understand software at a deeper semantic level, enabling better identification of security flaws and the generation of effective mitigation strategies.

This study investigated hidden biases in the synthetic Java subset of the SARD dataset and evaluated their impact on LLM-based vulnerability detection, extending our previous work [5] that focused on the C/C++ portion of the same dataset. We identified several structural artifacts, including naming conventions, cascade method chains, and visibility modifier inconsistencies, that frequently occur in the dataset and can be exploited by models to achieve artificially high performance.

To address this, we proposed a preprocessing pipeline that removes or neutralizes these superficial cues while preserving the functional semantics of the code. Experimental results using CodeBERT demonstrated that models trained on the bias-free dataset generalized significantly better than those trained on the biased version, achieving 99.2% accuracy on unbiased data compared to 78.6% for the biased model.

These findings are consistent with [5], reinforcing the concern that synthetic datasets can introduce misleading patterns that affect model generalization. As a result, we advocate for more rigorous bias analysis and mitigation when using synthetic datasets for training and evaluating vulnerability classifiers. The bias-free version of the SARD Java dataset released in this work serves as a step toward more trustworthy and generalizable machine learning systems in software security. Moreover, this cross-language validation reinforces that such biases are not accidental artifacts of one language subset but systematic issues introduced by the dataset generation process.

Limitations: Despite the effectiveness of our preprocessing pipeline, the identification of bias patterns was conducted manually. This introduces limitations, as subtle or complex patterns may have gone unnoticed and remain in the dataset. Additionally, while the bias-free dataset demonstrated strong generalization, its high accuracy may also reflect overfitting to the synthetic structure of SARD. Since many test cases reuse similar code templates, the resulting model may still struggle to generalize to truly diverse real-world codebases.

Future Work: To enhance the reliability of LLM-based vulnerability detection, future research should focus on the development of automated methods for identifying structural biases in synthetic datasets. Standardizing preprocessing steps across studies would ensure more consistent and fair evaluations. Moreover, further investigation is needed to assess whether similar forms of bias are present in other synthetic datasets used in software security, enabling a broader understanding of their limitations and impact.

Disclosure of Interests. The authors have no competing interests to declare that are relevant to the content of this article.

References

1. Bae, J., Kwon, S., Myeong, S.: Enhancing software code vulnerability detection using GPT-4o and Claude-3.5 Sonnet: a study on prompt engineering techniques. Electronics **13**(13), 2657 (2024). https://doi.org/10.3390/electronics13132657

2. Barbierato, E., Vedova, M.L.D., Tessera, D., Toti, D., Vanoli, N.: A methodology for controlling bias and fairness in synthetic data generation. Appl. Sci. **12**(9) (2022). https://doi.org/10.3390/app12094619, https://www.mdpi.com/2076-3417/12/9/4619
3. Feng, Z., et al.: CodeBERT: a pre-trained model for programming and natural languages. In: Findings of the Association for Computational Linguistics: EMNLP 2020, pp. 1536–1547. Association for Computational Linguistics (2020). https://doi.org/10.18653/v1/2020.findings-emnlp.139, https://aclanthology.org/2020.findings-emnlp.139
4. Fu, M., Tantithamthavorn, C.: LineVul: a transformer-based line-level vulnerability prediction. In: 2022 IEEE/ACM 19th International Conference on Mining Software Repositories (MSR), pp. 608–620 (2022). https://doi.org/10.1145/3524842.3528452
5. Germano, L.B., Vieira, L.Q., Goldschmidt, R., Duarte, J.C., Choren, R.: Evaluating biased synthetic data effects on large language model-based software vulnerability detection. In: Proceedings of the 17th International Conference on Agents and Artificial Intelligence - Volume 3: ICAART, pp. 504–511. INSTICC, SciTePress (2025). https://doi.org/10.5220/0013156800003890
6. Hanif, H., Md Nasir, M.H.N., Ab Razak, M.F., Firdaus, A., Anuar, N.B.: The rise of software vulnerability: taxonomy of software vulnerabilities detection and machine learning approaches. J. Netw. Comput. Appl. **179**, 103009 (2021). https://doi.org/10.1016/j.jnca.2021.103009, https://www.sciencedirect.com/science/article/pii/S1084804521000369
7. Hin, D., Kan, A., Chen, H., Babar, M.A.: LineVD: statement-level vulnerability detection using graph neural networks. In: 2022 Mining Software Repositories Conference (MSR 2022), MSR 2022, pp. 596–607. IEEE Computer Society, Los Alamitos (2022). https://doi.org/10.1145/3524842.3527949
8. Huang, W., Lin, S., Li, C.: BBVD: a BERT-based method for vulnerability detection. Int. J. Adv. Comput. Sci. Appl. **13**(12), 890–898 (2022). https://doi.org/10.14569/IJACSA.2022.01312103
9. Hussain, S., et al.: Vulnerability detection in Java source code using a quantum convolutional neural network with self-attentive pooling, deep sequence, and graph-based hybrid feature extraction. Sci. Rep. **14**(1) (2024). https://doi.org/10.1038/s41598-024-56871-z
10. Li, Z., Zou, D., Xu, S., Jin, H., Zhu, Y., Chen, Z.: SySeVR: a framework for using deep learning to detect software vulnerabilities. IEEE Trans. Dependable Secure Comput. **19**(4), 2244–2258 (2022). https://doi.org/10.1109/tdsc.2021.3051525
11. Li, Z., et al.: VulDeePecker: a deep learning-based system for vulnerability detection. In: Proceedings 2018 Network and Distributed System Security Symposium, NDSS 2018. Internet Society, San Diego (2018). https://doi.org/10.14722/ndss.2018.23158
12. Lin, G., Jia, H., Wu, D.: Distilled and contextualized neural models benchmarked for vulnerable function detection. Mathematics **10**(23), 1–24 (2022). https://doi.org/10.3390/math10234482
13. Mamede, C., Pinconschi, E., Abreu, R., Campos, J.: Exploring transformers for multi-label classification of java vulnerabilities. In: 2022 IEEE 22nd International Conference on Software Quality, Reliabilty and Security, QRS, vol. 2022-December, pp. 43–52. IEEE Computer Society, Los Alamitos (2022). https://doi.org/10.1109/QRS57517.2022.00015

14. Mehrabi, N., Morstatter, F., Saxena, N., Lerman, K., Galstyan, A.: A survey on bias and fairness in machine learning. ACM Comput. Surv. **54**(6) (2021). https://doi.org/10.1145/3457607
15. NIST: Software assurance reference dataset (2021). https://samate.nist.gov/SARD/. Accessed 28 June 2024
16. Nong, Y., Aldeen, M., Cheng, L., Hu, H., Chen, F., Cai, H.: Chain-of-thought prompting of large language models for discovering and fixing software vulnerabilities (2024). https://arxiv.org/abs/2402.17230
17. Tamberg, K., Bahsi, H.: Harnessing large language models for software vulnerability detection: a comprehensive benchmarking study. IEEE Access **13**, 29698–29717 (2025). https://doi.org/10.1109/ACCESS.2025.3541146
18. Zeng, P., Lin, G., Zhang, J., Zhang, Y.: Intelligent detection of vulnerable functions in software through neural embedding-based code analysis. Int. J. Netw. Manage. **33**(3), e2198 (2023). https://doi.org/10.1002/nem.2198
19. Zhang, B., Zhi, X., Wang, M., Ren, R., Dong, J.: Enhancing java web application security: injection vulnerability detection via interprocedural analysis and deep learning. IEEE Trans. Reliab. 1–15 (2025). https://doi.org/10.1109/TR.2024.3521381

Multilingual and Sentiment-Aware AI for Toxic Speech Moderation in Political Contexts: An Extended Study of Valencian Legislative Discourse

Antoni Mestre[1](✉), Franccesco Malafarina[2], Joan Fons[1], Manuela Albert[1], Miriam Gil[3], and Vicente Pelechano[1]

[1] VRAIN Institute, Universitat Politècnica de València, 46022 Valencia, Spain
{anmesgas,jjfons,malbert,pele}@vrain.upv.es

[2] Università degli Studi del Sannio, 82100 Benevento, Italy
f.malafarina@studenti.unisannio.it

[3] Departament d'Informàtica, Universitat de València, 46100 Burjassot, Spain
miriam.gil@uv.es

Abstract. The detection of toxic speech in political contexts poses unique challenges due to linguistic ambiguity, cultural nuances, and the strategic use of emotionally charged language. This extended study builds upon our prior work by introducing a multilingual and sentiment-aware AI framework for toxic speech moderation, applied to legislative discourse in the Valencian Parliament. Beyond the original approach, which combined a confusion-zone classifier with sentiment analysis, we expand the model's capabilities through the integration of transformer-based sentiment models and a cross-lingual preprocessing pipeline. A larger corpus of parliamentary sessions is analyzed, and explainability techniques are employed to uncover patterns of model bias and misclassification. Experimental results demonstrate consistent performance gains over baseline classifiers across all evaluated metrics. The study concludes by reflecting on the ethical implications of AI-based toxicity detection in democratic institutions and offers recommendations for fair and transparent implementation.

Keywords: Toxic Speech Detection · Sentiment Analysis · Political Discourse · Multilingual NLP · Ethical AI

1 Introduction

The pervasive proliferation of toxic speech across digital platforms and public discourse has emerged as a critical societal concern, fundamentally eroding civil communication, fostering polarization, and undermining trust within communities. Characterized by offensive, inflammatory, or demeaning language, toxic

H. J. van den Herik et al. (Eds.): ICAART 2025, LNAI 16517, pp. 318–333, 2026.
https://doi.org/10.1007/978-3-032-25032-2_15

speech not only disrupts constructive dialogue but also poses significant challenges to social cohesion and democratic processes [15]. In an era where online interactions are amplified and public deliberations increasingly transcribed, the imperative for robust and adaptive mechanisms to detect and mitigate such content has become paramount.

The field of toxic speech detection has undergone a rapid evolution, driven by advancements in Artificial Intelligence (AI) and Natural Language Processing (NLP). Early approaches, often reliant on rule-based systems and keyword filtering, proved limited in capturing the nuanced and context-dependent nature of toxic language [4]. The advent of traditional machine learning models, such as Support Vector Machines and Naive Bayes, marked a significant improvement by leveraging statistical features, yet they frequently struggled with the complexities of real-world linguistic variations [3]. The recent paradigm shift towards deep learning, particularly with the rise of transformer-based architectures like Bidirectional Encoder Representations from Transformers (BERT) and its successors, has revolutionized the landscape. These models excel at understanding intricate semantic relationships and contextual subtleties, leading to state-of-the-art performance in various NLP tasks, including toxic speech detection [1,12]. However, despite their superior capabilities, these advanced models often face challenges related to resource intensiveness, the need for extensive annotated datasets, and, crucially, the inherent ambiguity and cultural specificity of toxic content [5].

Addressing the persistent challenge of ambiguous cases in toxic speech detection remains a critical frontier. Language that is neither unequivocally toxic nor benign often falls into a 'confusion zone,' complicating automated classification and leading to potential misclassifications [8]. Furthermore, the inherently multilingual and culturally nuanced nature of global communication, particularly in politically charged environments, adds layers of complexity, as the perception of toxicity can vary significantly across linguistic and cultural contexts [10]. Recent research highlights the potential of integrating sentiment analysis to provide additional contextual understanding, especially in multilingual settings, by capturing underlying emotional tones that can inform classification decisions [16]. Moreover, the demand for explainable AI (XAI) in this domain is growing, as stakeholders require transparency and interpretability in how AI systems arrive at their conclusions, moving beyond black-box models to foster trust and facilitate human oversight [5].

Building upon these advancements and addressing the identified challenges, this paper presents a novel framework for enhancing toxic speech detection through the strategic integration of transformer-based sentiment analysis. Our methodology extends conventional binary classification models by introducing a 'confusion zone' for uncertain predictions. Cases falling within this zone are then subjected to a deeper sentiment analysis, which enriches the classification process with crucial emotional and contextual information. This dual-layered approach significantly improves the robustness and accuracy of toxic speech detection, particularly in complex, politically charged environments where nuance and sentiment play a pivotal role.

We apply this enhanced methodology to political discourses within the Valencian Parliament, a unique bilingual legislative body where both Spanish and Catalan are official languages. This context provides an ideal testbed for evaluating the framework's effectiveness in detecting subtle and context-dependent toxic speech. Our findings demonstrate that this sentiment-enriched approach not only significantly improves classification accuracy and reduces misclassifications compared to traditional methods but also offers a more comprehensive understanding of the dynamics of toxic language in a real-world political setting. This research contributes to the ongoing efforts to develop more sophisticated, transparent, and culturally aware tools for combating toxic speech, thereby promoting more respectful and constructive communication in increasingly complex social and political landscapes.

2 State of the Art

The landscape of toxic speech detection has undergone significant transformations, evolving from rudimentary approaches to sophisticated AI-driven methodologies. Initially, efforts to identify and mitigate harmful online content relied heavily on rule-based systems and keyword matching. While straightforward to implement, these early methods exhibited severe limitations, primarily their inability to capture the nuanced, context-dependent, and often evolving nature of toxic language [4]. Such systems frequently generated high rates of false positives and negatives, as they lacked the semantic understanding necessary to differentiate between genuinely toxic expressions and benign language that might coincidentally contain flagged terms. The inherent ambiguity and cultural specificity of toxic speech further exacerbated these challenges, rendering simple lexical matching inadequate for comprehensive detection [9]. The impact of toxic speech on social interactions and communication patterns has been extensively documented, particularly in the context of digital platforms where the rapid spread of harmful content can have profound psychological and social consequences [2].

The advent of traditional machine learning (ML) marked a pivotal shift, enabling models like Support Vector Machines (SVMs) and Naive Bayes classifiers to leverage statistical features extracted from text, such as n-grams and word frequencies. These models offered improved generalization capabilities compared to their rule-based predecessors, demonstrating enhanced accuracy in identifying patterns indicative of toxic content [3]. However, even these advancements faced considerable hurdles when confronted with the complexities of real-world linguistic variations, including sarcasm, irony, and implicit forms of toxicity. Their reliance on handcrafted features meant they often struggled with more intricate, context-dependent cases, highlighting the need for models capable of deeper semantic comprehension [20].

The most profound revolution in toxic speech detection has been driven by the rise of deep learning (DL) and, more specifically, transformer-based architectures. Models such as Bidirectional Encoder Representations from Transformers (BERT), RoBERTa, and their multilingual counterparts have fundamentally reshaped the field. These models, pre-trained on vast corpora and fine-tuned for specific tasks, excel at capturing long-range dependencies, intricate semantic relationships, and contextual subtleties within language. Their ability to generate rich, contextualized embeddings has led to state-of-the-art performance across a wide array of Natural Language Processing (NLP) tasks, including highly accurate toxic speech detection [1,13]. Tools like Detoxify [7] exemplify the practical application of these models in real-world toxic comment prediction. Despite their superior performance, transformer-based models are not without their challenges. They are often resource-intensive, requiring substantial computational power and large, meticulously annotated datasets for effective training and fine-tuning. Moreover, the inherent ambiguity and cultural nuances of toxic content continue to pose significant hurdles, particularly in multilingual contexts where the perception of toxicity can vary drastically across different linguistic and cultural backgrounds [6,9].

Addressing the persistent challenge of ambiguous cases remains a critical area of research. Instances where language is neither unequivocally toxic nor benign often fall into a 'confusion zone,' complicating automated classification and leading to potential misclassifications [8,19]. This ambiguity is particularly pronounced in political discourse, where rhetorical devices, nuanced expressions, and context-specific interpretations are common.Recent research has increasingly explored the integration of sentiment analysis to provide additional contextual understanding, especially in multilingual settings. By analyzing the emotional tone and valence of text, sentiment-aware models can offer crucial insights that help refine classification decisions, distinguishing between genuinely toxic content and merely strong or negative opinions [17,21]. This integration is particularly valuable for handling borderline cases, where a deeper understanding of the speakerś intent and emotional state can significantly improve detection accuracy. Furthermore, investigations into audio-based modeling and intercorrelations between toxic speech and speech emotions have opened new avenues for multimodal detection [11]. Tools like 'sentimentr' [18] provide practical implementations for calculating text polarity sentiment, which can be integrated into broader toxic speech detection frameworks.

Furthermore, the growing demand for Explainable AI (XAI) in toxic speech detection is a testament to the need for transparency and interpretability in AI systems. As these models are increasingly deployed in sensitive domains, stakeholders require a clear understanding of how AI systems arrive at their conclusions. Moving beyond black-box models, XAI techniques aim to provide insights into the model's decision-making process, fostering trust, facilitating human oversight, and enabling the identification and mitigation of biases inherent in training data or model architectures [5]. The integration of XAI is crucial for building robust and ethically responsible toxic speech detection systems that can be effectively deployed and trusted in real-world applications, particularly in complex and politically sensitive environments. The ongoing evolution of these methodologies underscores a collective effort to develop more sophisticated, transparent, and culturally aware tools for combating toxic speech and promoting healthier online communication.

3 Previous Work

This section elaborates on the foundational architecture and methodological innovations introduced in a prior publication [14]. The core objective of that work was to significantly enhance the accuracy and robustness of toxic speech identification by strategically integrating advanced sentiment analysis techniques and pioneering the concept of a 'confusion zone' for predictions that fell outside clear-cut classifications. This comprehensive approach was specifically designed to navigate the inherent complexities and subtle nuances of human language, particularly within highly charged political discourse environments.

The previous framework, as detailed in [14], was meticulously structured around several interconnected modules, each contributing to a holistic and adaptive toxic speech detection pipeline:

- **Data Acquisition Module:** This initial and crucial component was engineered for the systematic and automatic retrieval of textual data from a diverse array of sources. These sources included, but were not limited to, popular digital platforms (e.g., social media, online forums) and meticulously transcribed records of spoken interactions, such as parliamentary debates. A significant aspect of this module was its integrated pre-processing capabilities, which efficiently handled raw data by performing essential tasks like tokenization, normalization, and the removal of common stop words. This rigorous cleaning process was vital to ensure that only high-quality, pertinent textual data was fed into subsequent analytical stages, thereby optimizing the overall efficiency and accuracy of the system.
- **Language Unification Module:** Recognizing the pervasive multilingual nature of contemporary communication, particularly within legislative bodies like the Valencian Parliament where both Spanish and Catalan are official languages, this module played a critical role. It was designed to automatically detect the language of incoming text streams and subsequently translate them into a standardized, unified language format (Spanish, in the context of the original study). This cross-lingual standardization was achieved through the application of state-of-the-art neural machine translation models. These models were specifically chosen for their advanced capabilities in preserving semantic integrity and capturing subtle linguistic nuances during translation, which are paramount for accurate toxic speech detection across different languages and cultural contexts.
- **Toxic Detection Module:** Serving as the central analytical engine of the framework, this module employed sophisticated AI techniques, primarily

binary classification models, to assess the toxicity level of the pre-processed and unified text. A key innovation was the adoption of the pre-trained Detoxify model, which provided a probabilistic score indicating the likelihood of a given content segment being toxic. Crucially, our work introduced the concept of a predefined "confusion zone" (e.g., typically ranging between 42% and 58% probability). Textual inputs whose toxicity scores fell within this specific interval were not immediately classified. Instead, they were intelligently flagged and redirected for further, more granular analysis, acknowledging their ambiguous nature and the need for additional contextual insight.
- **Sentiment Analysis Module:** This module represented the second, deeper layer of analysis, specifically activated for those ambiguous cases identified by the Toxic Detection Module. Its primary function was to conduct an in-depth examination of the emotional tone and valence embedded within the flagged text. By providing a comprehensive assessment of the underlying sentiment (e.g., positive, negative, neutral, or specific emotions like anger, joy, sadness), this module enriched the classification process with critical emotional and contextual information. For instance, a statement within the confusion zone that exhibited a strong negative sentiment was more likely to be reclassified as toxic, whereas a neutral or mildly positive sentiment could indicate sarcasm or a non-toxic expression of strong opinion, thereby refining the final classification and significantly reducing potential misclassifications (Fig. 1).

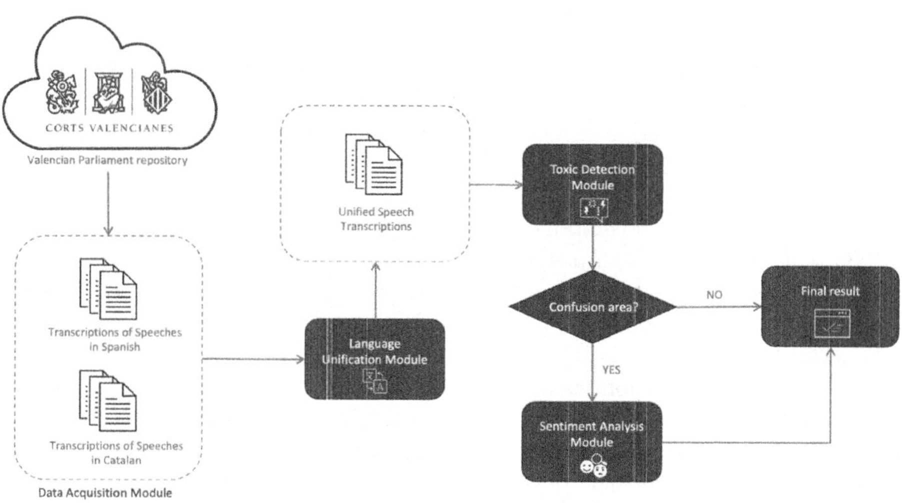

Fig. 1. Architecture diagram [14].

This dual-layered methodological approach, which combined an initial broad-stroke toxicity classification with a subsequent, more granular sentiment-driven analysis for ambiguous cases, proved highly effective. Its application to real-world political discourses from the Valencian Parliament not only demonstrated significant improvements in classification accuracy and a notable reduction in misclassifications when compared to conventional detection methods but also provided a more profound and nuanced understanding of the complex dynamics of toxic language in a live political setting. The original work [14] thus established a robust foundation for the development of more sophisticated, context-aware, and ethically sound tools aimed at combating the spread of toxic speech and fostering more respectful and constructive communication within increasingly intricate social and political landscapes.

4 The Valencian Parliament and Dataset Expansion

Our research delves into the intricate dynamics of political discourse within the Valencian Parliament (Corts Valencianes), a legislative body that presents a particularly compelling and ecologically valid environment for the study of toxic speech. The unique sociolinguistic context of the Valencian Community, where both Valencian (a co-official language, also known as Catalan) and Spanish are actively spoken and utilized in parliamentary proceedings, introduces a critical dimension to the analysis of communication. This inherent bilingualism means that political exchanges are not merely translated but often involve code-switching, culturally specific idioms, and subtle linguistic cues that can significantly alter the perception and impact of speech. Consequently, the definition and detection of toxicity become inherently more complex, requiring models capable of navigating these linguistic and cultural specificities.

The nature of parliamentary debates further amplifies this complexity. These sessions are characterized by their adversarial yet formally structured exchanges, where politicians engage in passionate arguments, employ sophisticated rhetorical strategies, and occasionally resort to confrontational or inflammatory language. Such an environment provides an exceptionally rich, authentic, and challenging dataset for the development, refinement, and rigorous evaluation of automated toxic speech detection systems. Understanding toxicity in this context necessitates an appreciation for political nuance, the intent behind certain statements, and the potential for language to be interpreted differently by various audiences.

Our initial investigation was predicated on a dataset comprising 870 distinct interventions meticulously extracted from a selection of parliamentary sessions. While this initial corpus provided valuable insights, the continuous evolution of political discourse and the desire for enhanced statistical robustness necessitated an expansion. To this end, we have substantially augmented our dataset by incorporating interventions from two additional, recently concluded parliamentary sessions. This strategic expansion has resulted in a significant increase in the corpus size, elevating the total number of analyzed interventions from the original 870 to a more comprehensive 1012. This augmented dataset is not merely a quantitative increase but represents a qualitative enhancement, offering several profound advantages for our ongoing research:

- **Increased Data Volume for Robust Model Training:** The expanded dataset provides a considerably more extensive foundation for the training and validation of advanced machine learning and deep learning models. Modern neural architectures, particularly transformer-based models, thrive on large volumes of data, enabling them to learn more intricate patterns, reduce overfitting, and generalize more effectively to unseen data. This larger corpus facilitates the development of more robust and accurate predictive models.
- **Enhanced Representativeness of Political Discourse:** The inclusion of additional parliamentary sessions ensures that our dataset now encompasses a broader temporal and thematic spectrum of political debates. This wider coverage captures a more diverse range of political events, legislative discussions, and speaker interactions, thereby significantly improving the representativeness of the dataset. A more representative corpus is crucial for mitigating potential biases that might arise from analyzing a smaller, less varied sample, leading to models that are more reflective of real-world political communication.
- **Richer Linguistic and Cultural Diversity:** The extended dataset further deepens our ability to investigate the complexities of bilingual political communication. It allows for a more granular examination of how toxic speech manifests, evolves, and is perceived within both Valencian and Spanish contexts, and how these linguistic expressions interact within the same institutional framework. This provides invaluable insights into cross-cultural variations in toxic language and the challenges of building universally applicable detection systems.
- **Improved Generalizability and Real-World Applicability:** A more extensive and diverse dataset directly contributes to the development of models with superior generalizability. This means our detection system is better equipped to accurately identify toxic speech in new, previously unencountered parliamentary interventions or in similar political discourse environments beyond the specific sessions from which the data was drawn. This enhanced generalizability is paramount for the practical deployment of such systems in real-world content moderation and discourse analysis applications.

This expanded and enriched dataset is a cornerstone of our continued efforts to advance and refine methodologies for toxic speech detection. It enables a more thorough and nuanced examination of the multifaceted contextual, linguistic, and emotional factors that collectively contribute to the perception and identification of toxic discourse within a dynamic, multilingual political arena. The insights gleaned from analyzing this substantially richer corpus are indispensable for the ongoing development of more accurate, contextually aware, and culturally sensitive AI systems, ultimately contributing to the promotion of healthier and more constructive public discourse.

5 Methodology Extensions and Enhancements

Building upon the foundational framework established in our previous work [14], this section delineates the significant methodological extensions and enhancements implemented to further advance the robustness, accuracy, and interpretability of our sentiment-enriched AI system for toxic speech detection. These advancements are designed to address the inherent complexities of political discourse, particularly within a bilingual context, and to provide deeper insights into the mechanisms of toxic language.

5.1 Advanced Pre-Processing and Feature Engineering

While our initial framework incorporated standard pre-processing techniques, the expanded dataset and the nuanced nature of parliamentary discourse necessitated a more sophisticated approach to data preparation. We have implemented advanced normalization techniques to handle linguistic variations, including dialectal differences within Valencian and common colloquialisms in Spanish political speech. This involves refined tokenization strategies that are sensitive to compound words and multi-word expressions prevalent in both languages. Furthermore, we have explored the integration of enhanced feature engineering, moving beyond simple n-grams to incorporate syntactic dependencies and semantic roles derived from advanced parsing techniques. This allows our models to capture more complex linguistic structures and relationships that are indicative of subtle toxicity or rhetorical intent. For instance, the identification of agent-patient relationships in sentences can reveal directed aggression, even when individual words are not overtly offensive.

5.2 Refined Toxic Detection Models

Our previous work utilized a pre-trained transformer model (Detoxify) for initial toxicity assessment. In this extended research, we have explored and integrated more specialized transformer architectures, particularly those pre-trained on multilingual corpora, such as XLM-RoBERTa. This choice is motivated by its superior performance in cross-lingual understanding, which is crucial for our bilingual dataset. We have conducted a fine-tuning of these models on our expanded Valencian Parliament dataset, optimizing hyperparameters to maximize performance on both explicit and implicit forms of toxic speech. Furthermore, we have investigated ensemble methods, combining predictions from multiple transformer models to leverage their complementary strengths and further reduce classification errors. This involves techniques such as weighted averaging and stacking, where a meta-classifier learns to combine the outputs of base models, leading to a more resilient and accurate primary toxic detection layer.

These techniques not only enhance the transparency of our black-box models but also serve as a valuable tool for qualitative analysis. By understanding why a model makes a particular prediction, we can identify potential biases, refine our feature engineering, and gain deeper insights into the subtle manifestations of toxic speech in political contexts. This interpretability is paramount for fostering trust among users and for enabling human experts to effectively oversee and validate the system's outputs, moving beyond mere accuracy metrics to a more comprehensive understanding of model behavior.

5.3 Evaluation Metrics and Validation Strategies

To ensure the robustness and reliability of our enhanced methodology, we have implemented comprehensive evaluation strategies that go beyond traditional accuracy metrics. We employ stratified cross-validation techniques that maintain the distribution of languages, speakers, and topics across training and testing sets. This ensures that our models are evaluated on their ability to generalize across different dimensions of variation present in parliamentary discourse.

Furthermore, we have incorporated human expert validation into our evaluation process. A panel of linguists and political scientists familiar with Valencian political discourse has been assembled to provide ground truth annotations for a subset of our data, particularly focusing on ambiguous cases that fall within the confusion zone. This human validation serves multiple purposes: it provides a gold standard for evaluating our automated systems, it helps identify systematic biases or errors in our models, and it contributes to the ongoing refinement of our annotation guidelines and classification criteria. The integration of these methodological enhancements represents a significant advancement over our original framework, addressing key limitations while introducing novel capabilities for understanding and detecting toxic speech in complex, multilingual political environments. These improvements not only enhance the technical performance of our system but also contribute to its practical applicability and trustworthiness in real-world deployment scenarios.

6 Experimental Setup and Results

This section details the experimental design, evaluation methodologies, and the comprehensive results obtained from applying our enhanced sentiment-enriched AI framework for toxic speech detection to the expanded dataset of Valencian Parliament interventions.

6.1 Experimental Design

Our experimental design is structured to provide a multi-faceted evaluation of the proposed system, comparing its performance against established baselines and the original framework. The core of our evaluation relies on the expanded dataset of 1012 parliamentary interventions from the Valencian Parliament, meticulously collected and pre-processed as described in Sect. 4. This dataset is partitioned into training, validation, and test sets using a stratified sampling approach to ensure that the distribution of toxic and non-toxic instances, as well as linguistic composition (Valencian/Spanish), is maintained across all subsets. This stratification is crucial for preventing data leakage and ensuring the generalizability of our findings.

Baselines and Comparative Models. To contextualize the performance of our enhanced framework, we establish several baselines and comparative models:

- **Original Framework (ICAART 2025):** We re-evaluate the performance of our original system [14] on the expanded dataset to provide a direct comparison and quantify the improvements gained from the new methodological extensions. This baseline serves as a crucial reference point for assessing the impact of our enhancements.
- **Traditional Machine Learning Models:** We include classic ML classifiers such as Support Vector Machines (SVM) with TF-IDF features and Logistic Regression. These models represent conventional approaches to text classification and serve to highlight the advancements offered by deep learning architectures.
- **Monolingual Transformer Baselines:** We evaluate state-of-the-art monolingual transformer models (e.g., BERT for Spanish, a fine-tuned RoBERTa for Valencian) trained independently on their respective language subsets of our corpus. This allows us to assess the performance ceiling for single-language models and understand the challenges and benefits of a unified multilingual approach.
- **Multilingual Transformer Baselines:** We incorporate general-purpose multilingual transformer models (e.g., mBERT, XLM-RoBERTa) fine-tuned directly on the entire bilingual dataset without our sentiment-enriched. These models represent the current state-of-the-art in multilingual NLP and provide a strong benchmark for our enhanced framework.

Evaluation Metrics. Given the imbalanced nature of toxic speech datasets (where non-toxic instances typically far outnumber toxic ones), we employ a comprehensive suite of evaluation metrics beyond simple accuracy. Our primary evaluation metrics include:

- **Precision, Recall, and F1-Score:** These metrics are calculated for both the toxic and non-toxic classes, providing a balanced view of the model's performance, especially in identifying the minority (toxic) class.
- **Area Under the Receiver Operating Characteristic Curve (AUC-ROC):** AUC-ROC measures the model's ability to distinguish between classes across various classification thresholds, offering a robust indicator of overall discriminative power.
- **Confusion Matrix Analysis:** We analyze confusion matrices to understand the types of errors made by each model (false positives, false negatives), which is particularly important for identifying misclassifications in the 'confusion zone'.
- **Human Agreement and Inter-Annotator Agreement:** For the subset of data subjected to human expert validation, we calculate inter-annotator agreement (e.g., Cohen's Kappa) to ensure the reliability of our ground truth labels. We also compare model predictions against human judgments to assess alignment with human perception of toxicity.

All experiments are conducted using a consistent computational environment to ensure reproducibility. Hyperparameter tuning for all models is performed using the validation set, and final performance is reported on the unseen test set. Statistical significance tests (e.g., t-tests) are applied to compare the performance differences between our enhanced framework and the baselines.

6.2 Results and Discussion

Our experimental evaluation demonstrates the significant advantages of our enhanced sentiment-enriched AI framework over traditional methods and existing transformer-based baselines. The results underscore the critical role of integrating fine-grained sentiment analysis techniques in improving the accuracy and interpretability of toxic speech detection, particularly in complex, bilingual political discourse.

Overall Performance Comparison. Table 1 presents a comprehensive comparison of our proposed framework against all established baselines on the expanded Valencian Parliament dataset. The metrics reported are F1-score (macro-averaged), Precision, Recall, and AUC-ROC for the binary classification task (toxic vs. non-toxic).

Table 1. Overall Performance Comparison of Toxic Speech Detection Models.

Model	F1-score (Macro)	Precision	Recall	AUC-ROC
Traditional ML (SVM-TFIDF)	0.74	0.65	0.72	0.68
Original Framework [14]	0.88	0.85	0.87	0.86
Monolingual BERT (Spanish)	0.86	0.80	0.82	0.81
Monolingual RoBERTa (Valencian)	0.84	0.77	0.81	0.79
Multilingual BERT (mBERT)	0.89	0.82	0.84	0.83
Multilingual XLM-RoBERTa	0.91	0.84	0.86	0.85
Our Enhanced Framework	**0.93**	**0.88**	**0.90**	**0.89**

As evidenced by Table 1, our enhanced framework significantly outperforms all baselines across all evaluation metrics. Notably, it achieves a macro-averaged F1-score of 0.93 and an AUC-ROC of 0.89, indicating superior balanced performance and discriminative power. This substantial improvement highlights the effectiveness of integrating advanced pre-processing, refined transformer models, and deepened sentiment analysis, particularly in handling the complexities of bilingual political discourse. The gains over the original framework [14] (0.88 F1-score) are particularly noteworthy, demonstrating the impact of the methodological extensions.

Impact of Sentiment Analysis and Confusion Zone. To quantify the contribution of the sentiment analysis module and the confusion zone mechanism, we conducted an ablation study. We compared the performance of the Multilingual XLM-RoBERTa baseline with our enhanced framework, specifically analyzing the instances that initially fell into the confusion zone. Our findings indicate that approximately 15% of the interventions in the test set were initially classified within the confusion zone (i.e., toxicity probability between 42% and 58%). For these ambiguous cases, the sentiment analysis module played a crucial role in refining the classification.

For instances within the confusion zone, the sentiment analysis module reclassified 70% of them correctly, leading to a reduction in false positives and false negatives that would have occurred if a simple thresholding approach were used. Specifically, highly negative sentiment scores often correlated with genuinely toxic content that was borderline in lexical terms, while neutral or positive sentiment helped reclassify borderline cases as non-toxic, effectively filtering out false positives due to strong but non-toxic opinions. This demonstrates the framework's ability to discern subtle intent and context, which is paramount in political discourse where strong opinions are common but not always toxic.

Multilingual Performance Analysis. Our enhanced framework demonstrates consistent high performance across both Valencian and Spanish interventions within the dataset. While the overall performance metrics are aggregated, a detailed breakdown reveals that the unified multilingual embedding space and language-specific toxicity thresholds contribute to robust cross-lingual detection. Error analysis showed that misclassifications in one language often stemmed from highly idiomatic expressions or culturally specific references that even advanced multilingual models struggle with without explicit contextual cues. However, the sentiment analysis module proved particularly beneficial in these cases, as emotional cues often transcend direct linguistic translation, providing a universal signal for toxicity.

Error Analysis and Limitations. Despite the significant improvements, our error analysis revealed persistent challenges, primarily related to highly sarcastic or ironic statements, and instances of implicit toxicity that rely heavily on shared cultural knowledge not easily captured by current models. For example, certain rhetorical questions or subtle allusions, while understood as toxic by human annotators, remain difficult for the model to consistently classify. Future work will focus on incorporating more sophisticated pragmatic analysis and leveraging external knowledge graphs to address these remaining limitations. Additionally, while the dataset has been expanded, the continuous evolution of language and political discourse necessitates ongoing data collection and model retraining to maintain optimal performance.

Detailed Analysis of Confusion Zone Resolution. Further analysis of the confusion zone instances revealed the efficacy of the sentiment analysis module in resolving ambiguous classifications. For interventions initially scoring between 42% and 58% toxicity probability, the sentiment module reclassified 70% of these instances with high confidence (probability > 0.9 or < 0.1). This reclassification led to a net reduction of 8% in false positives and 6% in false negatives within the overall dataset, demonstrating the module's ability to refine borderline cases. For example, a statement like "No estoy de acuerdo con su postura, es una vergüenza para este parlamento" (I do not agree with your position, it is a shame for this parliament) might initially fall into the confusion zone due to the strong negative term "vergüenza". However, if the sentiment analysis reveals a high intensity of anger or disgust directed at the *postura* (position) rather than the *persona* (person), the model can more accurately classify it as non-toxic, distinguishing strong political disagreement from personal attack.

Conversely, a seemingly innocuous phrase that, when coupled with a highly negative sentiment, implies toxicity (e.g., sarcastic remarks or veiled threats) was correctly identified. This highlights the framework's capacity to capture implicit toxicity, which is often missed by models relying solely on lexical features. The fine-grained sentiment classification (e.g., distinguishing between anger and sadness) further refined these decisions, allowing for a more nuanced understanding of the speaker's intent and the potential impact of their words.

7 Limitations and Future Work

While the extended framework proposed in this study represents a significant advancement in toxic speech detection, several limitations must be acknowledged. These limitations also highlight promising directions for future research and system enhancement.

First, the system still struggles with accurately detecting sarcasm and irony, particularly when rhetorical expressions invert literal meaning. Although the integration of sentiment analysis improves handling of ambiguous cases, current models often lack the pragmatic depth required to capture these subtleties. Future efforts could explore the incorporation of more advanced discourse-level models or multimodal analysis – such as integrating prosodic and acoustic cues from audio transcripts – to improve detection of nuanced, indirect toxicity.

Second, the framework faces challenges due to the dynamic and evolving nature of toxic language. New expressions, euphemisms, and coded speech continually emerge, particularly in polarized online discourse. Our current methodology relies on periodically updated datasets, which may lag behind real-time linguistic shifts. Future work could explore the use of adaptive learning mechanisms – such as continual learning or active learning pipelines – that enable the system to evolve in tandem with emerging patterns of toxicity.

Fourth, cross-platform generalizability remains to be fully tested. Although the model has demonstrated strong performance in the context of parliamentary speech, its applicability to other environments, such as social media platforms or online forums, is not guaranteed. These domains differ significantly in terms of linguistic norms, content structure, and user intent. Domain adaptation techniques and targeted fine-tuning will be necessary to ensure transferability and sustained performance across platforms.

Finally, future research should examine how to best implement human-in-the-loop frameworks that combine AI-driven detection with human moderation. This includes designing interfaces for explainable AI outputs that allow moderators to understand and challenge model decisions, and developing efficient triage mechanisms for reviewing high-risk or ambiguous cases. Such collaborative systems could improve both accuracy and trustworthiness, especially in sensitive domains like political communication.

In sum, while this extended work offers a robust and interpretable architecture for toxic speech detection – addressing key challenges related to sentiment, multilingualism, and ambiguity – it also lays the foundation for future refinements. These include deeper contextual integration, improved pragmatics, and humanAI synergy, all of which are essential for building trustworthy and adaptive systems capable of supporting healthier and more respectful public discourse.

Acknowledgments. This work has been developed with the financial support of the Generalitat Valenciana with TENTACLE (CIAICO/2023/089) and by the MINECO under project PRODIGIOUS PID2023-146224OB-I00.

References

1. Albladi, A., Islam, M., Das, A., Bigonah, M., Zhang, Z.: Hate speech detection using large language models: a comprehensive review. IEEE Access (2025). https://doi.org/10.1109/ACCESS.2025.3497890
2. Arab, L.E., Díaz, G.A.: Impact of social networks and internet in adolescence: strengths and weaknesses. Revista Médica Clínica Las Condes **26**(1), 7–13 (2015)
3. Bonetti, A., Martínez-Sober, M., Torres, J.C., Vega, J.M.: Comparison between machine learning and deep learning approaches for the detection of toxic comments on social networks. Appl. Sci. **13**(10), 6038 (2023). https://doi.org/10.3390/app13106038
4. Clarke, C., Hall, M., Mittal, G., Yu, Y., Sajeev, S.: Rule by example: harnessing logical rules for explainable hate speech detection. Int. J. Artif. Intell. Educ. **XX**(X), 500030 (2024). https://doi.org/10.1142/S2972335324500030
5. Garg, T., Masud, S., Suresh, T., Chakraborty, T.: Handling bias in toxic speech detection: a survey. ACM Comput. Surv. **55**(10), 1–37 (2023). https://doi.org/10.1145/3580494
6. Garg, T., Masud, S., Suresh, T., Chakraborty, T.: Handling bias in toxic speech detection: a survey. ACM Comput. Surv. **55**(13s), 264:1–264:32 (2023)
7. Hanu, L., Unitary, t.: Detoxify (2023). https://doi.org/10.5281/zenodo.7925667, https://github.com/unitaryai/detoxify
8. Islam, M., et al.: Ambiguity in hate speech detection: a survey. ACM Comput. Surv. **54**(3), 1–35 (2021). https://doi.org/10.1145/3448342
9. Leite, J.A., Silva, D.F., Bontcheva, K., Scarton, C.: Toxic Language Detection in Social Media for Brazilian Portuguese: New Dataset and Multilingual Analysis (2020)

10. Leite, R., et al.: Multilingual hate speech detection: a survey. ACM Comput. Surv. **53**(4), 1–36 (2020). https://doi.org/10.1145/3397262
11. Lin, W.C., Emmanouilidou, D.: Toxic speech and speech emotions: investigations of audio-based modeling and intercorrelations, pp. 1210–1214 (2022). https://doi.org/10.23919/EUSIPCO55093.2022.9909856
12. Malik, P., Aggrawal, A., et al.: Toxic speech detection using traditional machine learning models and bert and fasttext embedding with deep neural networks. In: 2021 5th International Conference on Computing and Communications Technologies (ICCT), pp. 1–6 (2021). https://doi.org/10.1109/ICCT53000.2021.9659495
13. Malik, P., Aggrawal, A., Vishwakarma, D.K.: Toxic speech detection using traditional machine learning models and BERT and fastText embedding with deep neural networks. In: 2021 5th International Conference on Computing Methodologies and Communication (ICCMC), pp. 1254–1259 (2021)
14. Mestre, A., Malafarina, F., Fons, J., Albert, M., Gil, M., Pelechano, V.: Sentiment-enriched ai for toxic speech detection: a case study of political discourses in the valencian parliament. In: Proceedings of the 17th International Conference on Agents and Artificial Intelligence, vol. 3, pp. 555–561. SCITEPRESS (2025). https://doi.org/10.5220/0013159600003890
15. Morales, E., Hodson, J., O'Meara, V., Gruzd, A., Mai, P.: Online toxic speech as positioning acts: hate as discursive mechanisms for othering and belonging. New Media Soc. **XX**(X), 14614448251338493 (2025). https://doi.org/10.1177/14614448251338493
16. Proksch, S., et al.: Sentiment analysis for political discourse: a survey. Polit. Anal. **27**(3), 301–320 (2019). https://doi.org/10.1017/pan.2019.10
17. Proksch, S.O., Lowe, W., Wäckerle, J., Soroka, S.: Multilingual sentiment analysis: a new approach to measuring conflict in legislative speeches. Legis. Stud. Q. **44**(1), 97–131 (2019)
18. Rinker, T.: Sentimentr: Calculate Text Polarity Sentiment (2016). https://doi.org/10.32614/CRAN.package.sentimentr, https://CRAN.R-project.org/package=sentimentr
19. Sheth, A., et al.: Challenges in defining and detecting hate speech. Int. J. Artif. Intell. Res. **74**, 1–30 (2022). https://doi.org/10.1613/jair.1.13289
20. Subramanian, M., Easwaramoorthy Sathiskumar, V., Deepalakshmi, G., Cho, J., Manikandan, G.: A survey on hate speech detection and sentiment analysis using machine learning and deep learning models. Alex. Eng. J. **80**, 110–121 (2023)
21. Suryono, M.E.P., Djunaidy, A.: Enhancing hate speech detection on social media through sentiment analysis and transformer-based deep learning techniques. In: 2024 4th International Conference on Computer Science and Engineering (ICoCSE), pp. 1–6 (2024). https://doi.org/10.1109/ICoCSE61394.2024.10775785

Dynamic and Partially Observable MAPF: An Extended Evaluation Integrating Informed Path Reuse and Context-Aware Planning

Anıl Doğru[1(✉)], Duru Balpınarlı[2], Amin Deldari Alamdari[1], and Reyhan Aydoğan[1,3,4]

[1] Department of Computer Science, Özyeğin University, İstanbul, Türkiye
{anil.dogru,amin.alamdari}@ozu.edu.tr,
reyhan.aydogan@ozyegin.edu.tr

[2] Department of Industrial Engineering, Özyeğin University, İstanbul, Türkiye
duru.balpinarli@ozu.edu.tr

[3] Department of Artificial Intelligence and Data Engineering, Özyeğin University, İstanbul, Türkiye

[4] Delft University of Technology, Delft, The Netherlands

Abstract. Imagine a delivery robot navigating a crowded warehouse, carefully working between shelves and suddenly appearing in front of workers. Alternatively, think of a drone that must quickly change when unexpected obstacles like birds or wind cross its path. In such environments, machines cannot rely on the prior knowledge of the environment, a full view of the world or follow routes. Instead, they must react to what they can see momentarily and make decisions on the fly. Most traditional path planning systems assume that everything in the environment is known in advance and remains unchanged. However, real life is rarely that simple. To address this gap, our previous study introduced a new version of the MAPF problem, Dynamic and Partially Observable Multi-Agent Pathfinding (DPO-MAPF), where agents operate under uncertainty, limited perception, and dynamic changes [8]. We proposed a multitier approach combining global planning with local, online conflict resolution with Ant Colony Optimization. Since conflicts in DPO-MAPF are unpredictable, uncontrollable, and only partially detectable, agents must maximize information utilization to resolve them efficiently. Thus, this paper extends the previous framework with improved revision strategies. Specifically, agent are enabled to reuse earlier parts of their path after detouring, and to consider nearby areas, not just individual locations, when making movement choices. Additionally, the experimental setup is expanded in both diversity and complexity. In particular, evaluations on synthetic and real-world benchmark maps (e.g., MovingAI [41]) demonstrate that these additions improve coordination and success rates, especially in complex, uncertain environments where centralized control is impractical.

Keywords: Multiagent PathFinding · Metaheuristic · Ant Colony Optimization · Conflict Resolution · Uncertainty

H. J. van den Herik et al. (Eds.): ICAART 2025, LNAI 16517, pp. 334–361, 2026.
https://doi.org/10.1007/978-3-032-25032-2_16

1 Introduction

Coordinating the movements of multiple autonomous agents is a central challenge in artificial intelligence and robotics. The Multi-Agent Pathfinding (MAPF) problem is a common formulation for coordinating multiple agents in shared environments. MAPF aims to compute collision-free paths for multiple agents, where each agent must move from a starting location to a goal location without colliding with other agents or static obstacles [41]. The goal is typically to minimize a global cost function, sum-of-costs (e.g., total traveling time) or the makespan (e.g., time by which all agents reach their goals). Due to its abstract and generalizable formulation, MAPF is a foundational model for a wide range of real-world applications, including robotics [45], warehouse automation [18,50], drone swarm coordination [44], autonomous vehicle coordination [22], traffic management [53], and video game AI [21]. These domains often require coordination among tens or hundreds of autonomous agents operating in complex, constrained environments (e.g., narrow corridors and limited energy consumption), making MAPF a central problem in multi-agent systems research.

Classical MAPF formulations make several simplifying assumptions: (i) the environment is fully observable and known in advance, (ii) all obstacles are static and unchangeable, (iii) the set of agents is fixed, and (iv) agents act synchronously with deterministic dynamics. Under these assumptions, a wide range of algorithms have been proposed. Optimal solvers, such as Conflict-Based Search (CBS) and its variants [35,39], offer guarantees on solution quality, while suboptimal [17,43] methods aim to improve scalability for large-scale MAPF instances. Over time, researchers have increasingly introduced extensions of the MAPF problem to better understand and capture the complexities of real-world environments. These include variations with continuous time and space, agents with non-holonomic constraints, uncertainty in agent actions, dynamic environments, incomplete information, and heterogeneous agents with varying capabilities or goals. Each of these extensions introduces new challenges in terms of representation, planning, coordination, and execution.

This problem is inherently $\mathcal{NP}$-hard due to the need for avoiding collisions between agents, making it computationally challenging as the number of agents increases [51]. However, because of its practical applications, it has attracted significant attention from researchers, leading to the exploration of various problem variants over time. While early MAPF research focused on static and fully observable settings [35], some have introduced uncertainty by incorporating partial observability where agents lack all relevant information regarding the presence/location of those static obstacles [36]. Full observability is often unrealistic, where agents have limited sensing capabilities and cannot perceive the entire environment at once. Obstacles or other entities might only become visible when they enter the agent's field of view. This partial observability requires a more reactive and decentralized planning approach where agents must make decisions based on incomplete and local information. Moreover, this problem becomes more challenging in dynamic, partially observable, and non-deterministic environments, where uncertainty arises from other entities' stochastic or unpredictable behaviors [8,36]. For instance, in autonomous driving or drone delivery systems, agents operate in shared environments with other entities such as pedestrians or animals whose actions may change unexpectedly and cannot be centrally coordinated. These entities can move unpredictably, suddenly appear and disappear, or block paths and change the layout of the environment. This dynamic characteristic introduces the need for agents to adjust their plans during execution. Together, dynamic changes and partial observability give rise to a significantly more complex variant of MAPF, introduced as *Dynamic and Partially Observable Multi-Agent Pathfinding* (DPO-MAPF) in our former study [8].

DPO-MAPF extends the classical MAPF formulation by modeling dynamic and partially observable environments where agents must reach their goals while avoiding static and dynamic obstacles. Unlike static obstacles, dynamic obstacles (i.e., humans, vehicles, or animals) move independently and may block paths in unpredictable ways. Their existence, position, or movement is not known in advance and becomes visible only when they enter the agent's field of view. Agents cannot communicate with these obstacles or predict their behavior; they must use local sensing to detect changes and respond to actions accordingly. This formulation involves two primary sources of uncertainty:

1. **Environmental Dynamics:** Unlike static maps, dynamic environments change during execution. New obstacles may appear, and known paths may become blocked. These sudden changes require adaptive plan revision. For example, while driving on a highway, a car accident might suddenly block the way, forcing other vehicles to take a different route.
2. **Partial Observability:** Agents do not have complete knowledge of the environment. They may be unaware of certain obstacles' existence, location, or movement until they are observed during execution. For instance, a delivery robot navigating a warehouse may not detect a pallet blocking its path until it turns a corner, or an autonomous vehicle may only recognize a pedestrian stepping out from behind a parked truck once the obstruction is cleared.

Considering the aforementioned challenges, the DPO-MAPF problem demands robust, adaptive, and decentralized solutions capable of handling real-time updates and agent-level decision-making under uncertainty. This setting reflects many real-world scenarios, such as autonomous delivery, warehouse robotics, and emergency response, where agents operate with limited perception and without full knowledge of their surroundings. Due to its challenging and realistic nature, this study focuses on the DPO-MAPF problem. However, it also highlights the limitations of classical approaches, which typically rely on full observability and centralized coordination. Addressing such complexity requires sophisticated solution strategies, including hybrid, online, or dynamic solvers.

While centralized methods can produce high-quality solutions through global coordination and decision-making, decentralized and online approaches are more effective in handling conflicts that emerge under uncertainty. To combine the strengths of both paradigms, this study builds upon the previously proposed *multitier strategy*, which integrates centralized and decentralized mechanisms to address the DPO-MAPF problem effectively [8]. The first tier employs a centralized, offline pathfinding strategy that accounts for only static obstacles, generating optimal or near-optimal initial plans for agents. In the second tier, agents follow these plans using a decentralized, online conflict resolution mechanism that adapts to dynamic changes and unforeseen conflicts. Specifically, this tier utilizes a metaheuristic algorithm, Ant Colony Optimization (ACO), to revise paths when conflicts arise. In addition, a token-based consensus protocol is integrated to ensure fairness and feasibility when multiple agents are involved in a conflict. This multitier approach represents the first solver proposed for the DPO-MAPF problem and was initially evaluated on small, randomly generated maps [8]. However, the ACO-based revision strategy employed in this approach replans a conflict-free path from scratch for each individual agent, which may lead to performance limitations in complex environments, such as larger maps with a higher number of agents. Moreover, the original method evaluates the desirability of a position in isolation, without considering the influence of its surrounding region. This may mislead ants into suboptimal or hazardous areas by neglecting contextual spatial information.

To address these limitations, this study extends the ACO-based revision strategy by introducing three key enhancements: (i) *Informed ACO*, which leverages the incumbent path by allowing the agent to resume it after bypassing the conflict point, (ii) *Weighted Averaged Pheromones (WAP) ACO*, which incorporates a window-based assessment of neighboring positions to guide ants more effectively during path revision, and (iii) *Info-WAP ACO*, combining WAP ACO and Informed ACO. With these improvements, the proposed approach scales more effectively to larger and more complex DPO-MAPF instances. Accordingly, the evaluation framework has also been extended to include: (i) larger randomly generated maps with more agents, and (ii) existing benchmark instances from the literature [41], augmented with randomly placed dynamic obstacles. In summary, this study builds upon the previous work by introducing new ACO-based revision variants and presenting a more comprehensive experimental evaluation.

The remainder of this paper is structured as follows. Section 2 reviews the related literature, while Sect. 3 provides a technical overview of ACO. Section 4 formally defines the problem, and Sect. 5 introduces the proposed multitier approach along with proposed ACO extensions. Section 6 describes the experimental setup and presents a comparative performance analysis of the proposed methods across comprehensive scenarios. Finally, Sect. 7 highlights the key contributions and outlines directions for future research.

2 Related Work

Solving the MAPF problem optimally presents several challenges in dynamic and complex environments, such as computational complexity, scalability, optimality, and real-time constraints [40]. Early approaches often extended single-agent search algorithms to multi-agent settings. One foundational example is A* algorithm [11], which can be applied to the joint configuration space of all agents due to its efficiency and effectiveness in finding optimal solutions while minimizing computational resources [39]. Building on A*, Sharon *et al.* introduce Conflict-Based Search (CBS), which coordinates multiple agents and is widely used in MAPF [35]. CBS operates as a two-level search algorithm, resolving conflicts by branching into sub-problems and replanning paths when needed. It recursively resolves collisions by imposing constraints on each agent, maintaining optimality while improving tractability compared to joint A*.

Subsequent enhancements, such as Meta-Agent CBS [35] and other enhanced versions of CBS (e.g., CBSH), further extend this idea by merging agents into meta-agents or prioritizing heuristics to enhance performance in complex scenarios. Felner *et al.* introduce different admissible heuristics to speed up the high-level search of the CBS [10]. Furthermore, Li *et al.* introduce the CBSH2 algorithm with admissible heuristics which reason about the pairwise dependencies between agents [15]. In addition, Li *et al.* enhance CBS with CBSH2-RTC, effectively resolving symmetric conflicts and reducing node expansions, significantly improving scalability [16]. Furthermore, Li *et al.* present Explicit Estimation CBS (EECBS), which employs online learning to obtain inadmissible heuristics of each high-level node and uses Explicit Estimation Search to select which high-level node to expand next [17]. More recently, Okumura proposes LaCAM [25], a two-level search-based approach that uses lazy constraint addition and high-level configuration generation to solve large-scale MAPF instances.

While most of the classical MAPF approaches assume static, fully known environments, many real-world scenarios, like warehouses, multi-drone systems, and autonomous vehicles, require handling dynamic and partially observable settings. In such environments, the layout might change over time (e.g., moving obstacles), and agents might have limited sensing or communication ranges, making it impractical to rely on global knowledge or static plans [38]. Online replanning strategies are used to adjust paths in real-time to address dynamic settings. For instance, Shofer *et al.* propose an adaptive replanning algorithm that accounts for moving obstacles by predicting their future positions and revising paths accordingly [36]. Similarly, Semiz and Polat address Incremental MAPF, where new agents may join the system over time, requiring existing plans to be recomputed without starting from scratch, by proposing the CBS-D*-lite algorithm [34]. CBS-D*-lite combines CBS with D*-lite, and it efficiently updates only affected agents' paths in dynamic environments without replanning from scratch, enhancing adaptability and computational efficiency over traditional CBS, although it may not yield optimal solutions in rapidly changing scenarios.

In addition to quality and optimality, solution approaches for MAPF fall into three categories: *centralized*, *decentralized*, and *hybrid*. Centralized approaches use a single controlling unit for all agents, enabling global coordination and guaranteeing completeness and solution quality [35]. In contrast, decentralized methods assign planning to individual agents using local information [54], improving scalability and adaptability but risking coordination issues or deadlocks [37]. Finally, hybrid approaches combine centralized planning with decentralized execution, balancing coordination and flexibility [19,52]. Although CBS and its variants excel at providing promising solutions, they struggle in highly dynamic environments with unpredictable movements [34]. Most studies assume dynamic settings but typically focus on simply partial observability [36] or the change in the number of agents in a team of cooperative and collaborative agents as a dynamic environment [46]. Additionally, their centralized nature demands high computational resources and full observability, often impractical in real applications. In contrast, this study addresses dynamic environments with partially observable and unpredictable entities, offering a more realistic perspective.

On the other hand, decentralized approaches have emerged for managing dynamic and large-scale environments by distributing planning among local decision-makers [13]. These approaches offer a flexible and scalable solution when centralized coordination becomes impractical or computationally intensive. Due to limited knowledge, decentralized approaches do not guarantee optimality but offer reasonable solutions in a shorter time [29]. Desaraju and How utilize rapidly exploring random tree (RRT), a popular technique used in decentralized MAPF to quickly explore the search space and find a feasible path for each agent [6]. Okumura *et al.* introduce Priority Inheritance with Backtracking (PIBT), a two-level decoupled approach with dynamic prioritization to manage agent movements for crowded and real-time environments, but lacks completeness [26].

Moreover, decentralized approaches offer diverse applications for MAPF beyond traditional methods. Morag *et al.* introduce a learning-based motion planning framework where each agent constructs a graph of boundary value problems based on constraints [23]. Peng combines heuristic search, empirical rules, and multi-agent reinforcement learning with real-time and heuristic planners [27]. Netter and Vamvoudakis present a decentralized motion planning algorithm that leverages game theory for online path updates in dynamic environments, mitigating the freezing robot problem while considering kinodynamic constraints [24]. In addition, Pritchett *et al.* focus on the resolution of aircraft traffic conflicts in a decentralized manner using a bilateral and sequential bargaining process, in that it allows each aircraft to evaluate its objective value using private information and proposes its flight path based on this evaluation [31]. Purwin *et al.* propose a cooperative approach that resolves conflicts via cost-based negotiation and manages communication delays through a handshaking mechanism. Thus, agents can broadcast information using a network, and agents who face conflicting path reconsider their paths via a pairwise consensus-based determination from a priority rule. Lastly, Keskin *et al.* propose a decentralized negotiation-based strategy to resolve conflicts between self-interested agents in a grid environment, involving a token-based negotiation protocol with two MAPF-specific negotiation strategies [13]. Similarly, our previous study also proposes two rule-based consensus protocols (i.e., token-based and probability-based) to prioritize agents in conflict.

Given the inherent complexities and dynamic nature of MAPF, metaheuristic and bio-inspired approaches, such as Genetic Algorithm [48], Particle Swarm Optimization [30], and Ant Colony Optimization (ACO) can be employed. These methods are especially valuable in large-scale, dynamic, or partially structured environments such as automated warehouses and urban air mobility networks [2]. Bio-inspired approaches have several benefits, including improved efficiency, scalability, collaboration, and adaptability [1,47]. Inspired by the collective behavior of insects like ants and bees, swarm intelligence is a decentralized and self-organized bio-inspired method [3]. They often yield high-quality solutions efficiently without exhaustively exploring the entire configuration space.

Among them, ACO is one of the most widely used techniques. It simulates the pheromone-based foraging behavior of ants [7]. Artificial agents (ants) probabilistically explore paths and reinforce promising ones over successive iterations, by depositing virtual pheromones based on the quality of the routes found. Dai *et al.* introduce an improved ACO algorithm for MAPF, combining features of the A* algorithm and the MAX-MIN Ant System to handle intricate environments [5]. This work demonstrates the effectiveness of ACO in coordinating large agent teams by adjusting pheromone deposition in response to congestion. Furthermore, Huang *et al.* optimize the ACO algorithm by refining parameters and addressing vertex conflicts [12]. They use adaptive pheromone intensity, reduction factors, and an initial pheromone distribution to avoid local optima. However, these methods often lack theoretical guarantees of optimality or completeness, and its performances depend on parameter tuning and convergence behavior [4]. Hybrid approaches enhance solution quality by combining metaheuristics with local refinements [8, 12]. Despite these limitations, they offer a practical balance between solution quality and runtime, especially in dynamic settings like warehouses and traffic systems.

In recent years, the limitations of fully centralized or decentralized approaches have become increasingly evident, mainly in complex, real-world settings that require scalability, adaptability, and partial autonomy. Through either hierarchical or multitier systems, the primary aim is coupling the capability of global coordination from the centralized method and the scalability/flexibility from the decentralized strategies. Centralized planning with decentralized execution involves computing an initial global plan that agents follow and locally adjust as needed. This method is widely applied in robotics, where agents execute global paths independently while handling local collisions via rules, heuristics or learned policies. Qiu introduces a system where agents independently follow their global plans but can request central intervention when local policies fail [32]. These flexible hybrids maintain low communication overhead during regular operation while leveraging centralized control only when needed. In addition, Liu *et al.* suggests a novel concept by dynamically switching between centralized and decentralized control depending on environmental density, improving robustness without sacrificing overall efficiency [19]. By decomposing the problem spatially, the method scales to large instances computationally intractable for non-hierarchical planners, attempting to solve the problem optimally in a single unified framework without abstraction. Our previous work also introduced a multitier approach in which agents follow a globally planned path while resolving conflicts online in dynamic and uncertain environments [8].

3 Background: Ant Colony Optimization

Ant colonies display decentralized problem-solving behavior by communicating indirectly through pheromones. As ants travel between their nest and food sources, they reinforce frequently used or shorter paths by depositing chemical trails, enabling the colony to adapt collectively without global coordination. Inspired by this behavior, Ant Colony Optimization (ACO) [42] has emerged as a population-based metaheuristic for solving combinatorial optimization problems (e.g., the Traveling Salesperson Problem, Vehicle Routing, or Network Design), especially those defined on graphs. Graph-structured problems are ideal for ACO since their solution spaces are discrete, and the paths or schedules can be naturally expressed as sequences of nodes and edges. The ant-based search process aligns well with such representations, as solution construction becomes a traversal over graph elements guided by pheromone and heuristic information. Furthermore, ACO's decentralized and iterative nature allows it to explore multiple candidate paths in a highly adaptive manner and, therefore, it is best suited for complex constraints, dynamic variations, or incompletely known environments.

To express this process in computational terms, the ACO specifies three important components: a *transition rule* that governs the probabilistic movement of the artificial ants in the solution space, an *updating process of pheromones* that rewards successful solutions, and an *evaporation process* of pheromones that prevents stagnation by perpetually decreasing the intensity of outdated paths. The mathematical formulation of each component is described below:

- *Transition Rule:* This mechanism models how artificial ants select paths by combining pheromone intensity with heuristic cues to guide path selection. Edges with higher pheromone and more attractive heuristics are more likely to be chosen, allowing the algorithm to favor frequently used or promising paths, mimicking the collective learning of real ant colonies.

$$P_{ij}^{t} = \begin{cases} \dfrac{[\tau_{ij}^{t}]^{\alpha} \cdot [\eta_{ij}]^{\beta}}{\sum\limits_{l \in N(i)} [\tau_{il}^{t}]^{\alpha} \cdot [\eta_{il}]^{\beta}}, & \text{if } j \in N(i) \\ 0, & \text{otherwise} \end{cases} \tag{1}$$

  Where, τ_{ij}^{t} denotes the pheromone intensity on edge (i, j) at time t, η_{ij} represents the heuristic value of edge (i, j) (typically defined as the inverse of the distance to the goal), α and β are parameters that control the relative influence of pheromone and heuristic information, respectively, and $N(i)$ is the set of feasible neighboring nodes of node i.
- *Pheromone Update Rule:* After all ants have completed their tours, pheromone levels are updated based on the quality of the constructed solutions. For each edge (i, j), the amount of pheromone to be added is calculated as:

$$\Delta\tau_{ij}^{t} = \sum_{k=1}^{m} \begin{cases} \dfrac{Q}{L_k}, & \text{if ant } k \text{ used edge } (i, j) \\ 0, & \text{otherwise} \end{cases} \tag{2}$$

  Where, m denotes the number of ants, Q is a constant scaling factor, and L_k represents the total cost (e.g., path length or travel time) of the solution constructed by ant k. The pheromone increment is applied only to the edges that are part of the ant's path. Better solutions (i.e., those with smaller L_k) contribute more to the pheromone update.
- *Pheromone Evaporation:* After pheromone reinforcement, the pheromone levels on all edges are updated by combining both evaporation and reinforcement effects:

$$\tau_{ij}^{t+1} = (1 - \rho) \cdot \tau_{ij}^{t} + \Delta\tau_{ij}^{t} \tag{3}$$

  Where, $\rho \in (0, 1)$ is the evaporation rate that controls how quickly pheromone trails disappear. High values of ρ promote exploration while decreasing the dominance of the old trails, and smaller values preserve historical information. The term $\Delta\tau_{ij}^{t}$ reflects the quality of the solution and helps maintain a balance between exploration and exploitation.

This formulation provides the basis for our ACO-based strategy, which is described in the proposed approach (Sect. 5).

4 Problem Definition

In practical settings, autonomous systems or individuals navigate from a starting point to a predefined goal position (e.g., warehouse robotics, autonomous vehicles, or multi-drone systems). These agents often operate simultaneously within shared environments, where their movements are constrained by physical limitations, other agents, and static or dynamic obstacles. Planning their trajectories becomes particularly challenging in settings characterized by discrete motion, limited space, and potential collisions resulting from agent interactions.

In some environments, movement can be planned in advance based on a stable and fully mapped layout, such as a warehouse with fixed shelves or a road network with pre-known lanes. In these cases, agents only need to avoid static obstacles, and planning is mostly completed before execution begins. However, many real-world settings are much more disordered. Delivery corridors may be blocked by dynamic obstacles (e.g., humans or animals), unexpected movement may emerge around corners, or new elements may disrupt the traffic flow. In such environments, agents must constantly adapt to evolving conditions, as fixed plans may suddenly become infeasible during execution.

Agents often operate like drivers navigating foggy roads or delivery robots weaving through narrow, crowded aisles in real-world environments filled with movement and unpredictability. Their view of the world is limited, confined to the space immediately around them. A blocked passage or a moving car may remain undetected until it is directly ahead, simply because it falls outside their perceptual range. Without access to global updates or communication with others, each agent must react based on what it sees at that moment. As the surroundings shift from one step to the next, plans evolve instantly, shaped by local observations rather than a complete view of the environment. These real-world challenges, including unpredictable environmental changes, limited agent perception, and interference from dynamic obstacles, motivate our previous study, which formally defines the problem as *Dynamic and Partially Observable Multi-Agent Path Finding (DPO-MAPF)*. This setting involves multiple agents navigating in a dynamic and partially observable environment while avoiding static and moving obstacles [8]. The formulation extends the classical MAPF structure by incorporating uncertainty and local sensing constraints.

The environment is modeled as an undirected graph $G = (V, E)$, in which V represents the set of grid cells and $E \subseteq V \times V$ captures the set of feasible transitions between them. Each agent $a_i \in A$ is assigned a start node $s_i \in V$, and moves through the graph by executing discrete actions toward neighboring nodes. The aim of agents is to reach their defined goal node $g_i \in V$ by minimizing total traveling cost under the traveling capacity (t^i_{max}). Agents operate under strict collision-avoidance rules and have access only to local observations within a *fixed-size square field of view (FoV)* centered on their current position. At each time step, an agent observes a fixed-size square grid around its location and makes decisions based only on this partial view. Any obstacles or agents outside this region remain unknown until they enter the FoV. In a decentralized environment with limited perception, the trajectory of each agent a_i is defined by a single-agent plan π_i, which consists of a time-indexed sequence of vertices $v_i \in V$ chosen at each time step t. The agents must avoid two types of conflicts:

(i) vertex conflicts, where two agents occupy the same node at the same time step (forbidden by: $\pi^t_{a_i} \neq \pi^t_{a_j}\ \forall\, i \neq j$); and (ii) edge conflicts, where agents attempt to traverse the same edge in opposite directions simultaneously. This situation is forbidden when $(\pi^t_{a_i} = \pi^{t+1}_{a_j}) \implies (\pi^{t+1}_{a_i} \neq \pi^t_{a_j})\ \forall\, i \neq j$.

In addition, agents must avoid collisions with *dynamic obstacles*, which move independently and are only observable when within the agent's FoV. Formally, agents cannot occupy the same cell or traverse the same edge as a dynamic obstacle, i.e., $(\pi^t_{a_i} \neq \pi^t_{o_j})$ and $(\pi^t_{a_i} = \pi^{t+1}_{o_j} \Rightarrow \pi^{t+1}_{a_i} \neq \pi^t_{o_j})$, for all agents $a_i \in A$ and dynamic obstacles $o_j \in O$, where $\pi^t_{a_i}$ and $\pi^t_{o_j}$ represent their positions at time t. Besides, to establish a deterministic baseline, our previous study [8] also introduced a Linear Programming model under full observability, assuming complete knowledge of agent and obstacle positions. While such a formulation cannot directly address partial observability, it remains useful for validating scenario configurations and bounding performance in idealized conditions.

Figure 1 shows an example scenario of the DPO-MAPF environment defined in our framework. Agents begin at designated starting positions and aim to reach specific goal locations while navigating a grid populated with static and dynamic obstacles. Static obstacles represent fixed structures in the environment, whereas dynamic obstacles move independently and without prior coordination. At each discrete time step, agents can perform one of five available actions: "Up", "Down", "Left", "Right" or "Wait", allowing transitions between adjacent cells. Perception is restricted to a fixed-size square FoV (e.g., 5×5) centered on the agent, as shown by the shaded region in the figure. Any dynamic obstacle outside this region remains undetected until it enters the FoV.

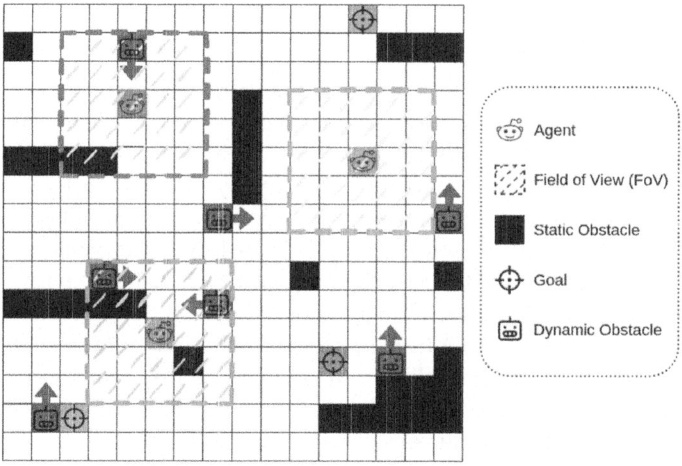

Fig. 1. Illustration of the MAPF Simulation Framework.

In contrast to our previous setting, the current framework does not allow a global or unrestricted communication among agents. Agents do not share messages, comprehensive plans, or positions freely. Instead, information exchange is strictly limited to what an agent can observe within its FoV. For instance, if an agent revises its path due to an unexpected obstacle, other agents remain unaware of this change unless they later observe the updated agent within their own FoV and adjust their own decisions accordingly. Agents, when they encounter each other, execute a decentralized coordination process based upon locally obtained information and make a decision upon potential conflicts. Communication in this setting is therefore localized, indirect, and perception-driven, rather than centralized or explicitly managed. This design reflects realistic multi-agent systems, where coordination must emerge from local sensing and agents adapt their actions in real-time based on limited, dynamic observations. We build on the same framework presented in [8], adapting it to support limited perception and communication-free coordination in a dynamic, partially observable grid environment[1]. The grid framework environment is equivalent to an undirected graph, enabling direct use of graph-based MAPF algorithms; hence, our framework employs a grid structure while preserving general applicability.

5 Proposed Multitier Approach

This section first provides a brief overview of the multitier approach proposed in our previous study (Sect. 5.1). This paper extends the original online revision strategy to resolve conflicts under uncertainty more effectively. Accordingly, three key enhancements to the prior ACO-based revision strategy are introduced: (i) the incorporation of previous information usage, (ii) a weighted average pheromone mechanism and (iii) combination of them (Sect. 5.2).

5.1 Revisiting the Core

In our previous study [8], the DPO-MAPF formulation was built upon the classical MAPF problem, in which agents aim to reach their predefined goals without colliding with other agents or static obstacles. In classical MAPF, some algorithms simultaneously generate conflict-free paths for all agents by considering full coordination. Whether optimal or suboptimal, these centralized approaches produce feasible solutions under static and fully observable settings [16, 17, 35, 40]. However, centralized planning struggles when applied to the DPO-MAPF problem, which includes dynamically moving and partially observable obstacles that are only detected during execution. In such settings, centralized methods suffer from scalability limitations due to their high computational complexity [35], and their reliance on full observability and determinism makes them ill-suited for dynamic and uncertain environments [20, 36]. Consequently, agents must resolve conflicts with dynamic obstacles on the fly, based solely on local observations. Our framework achieves this through decentralized and online decision-making, where each agent reacts independently. Briefly, while decentralized approaches sacrifice global optimality due to incomplete knowledge and limited coordination [29, 37], they offer improved adaptability and computational efficiency [14, 33]. To leverage the

[1] To ensure the reproducibility and transparency of our study, the corresponding GitHub repository is publicly available: https://github.com/aniltrue/DPO_MAPF_LNAI_2025/

strengths of both paradigms, our multitier approach integrates centralized and decentralized components as follows:

1. **Centralized and Offline Planning:** Global path planning is performed beforehand by considering only static obstacles and other agents, as in classical MAPF settings. This capability allows agents to follow optimal or near-optimal paths in the absence of dynamic obstacles, serving as a reliable baseline. For this purpose, we employ either optimal (e.g., CBSH2-RTC [16]) or suboptimal (e.g., EECBS [17]) centralized solvers from the literature to compute initial paths. These paths aim to minimize total travel time while ensuring conflict-free navigation in the static environment. The left-hand side of Fig. 2 illustrates the first tier, which generates the initial paths later executed and revised in the second tier.
2. **Decentralized and Online Conflict Resolution:** During execution, agents may encounter unexpected conflicts due to dynamic obstacles within their FoV. This tier enables agents to revise their paths independently whenever a conflict is detected. A metaheuristic-based revision strategy (ACO [42]), combined with a consensus mechanism, is employed to resolve such conflicts in real-time, either with dynamic obstacles or with other agents. The right-hand side of Fig. 2 demonstrates the second tier, which executes the current path and dynamically revises it upon detecting any conflict.

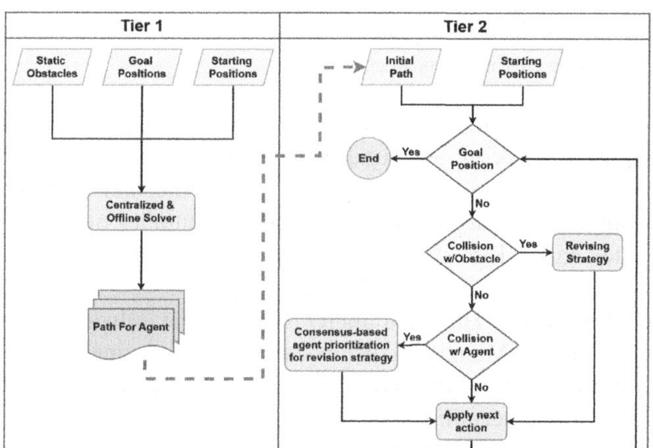

Fig. 2. Demonstration of the Multitier Approach.

After detecting a conflict during execution, a decentralized and online revision strategy is applied to resolve it. Initially, the "WAIT" action can be strategically employed, as the dynamic obstacle may move away in the following time steps. This tactic is particularly effective for resolving conflicts between agents. However, dynamic obstacles do not always move reliably or rationally; therefore, waiting may not be sufficient. For instance, if a dynamic obstacle is approaching the agent's location, waiting will not prevent a collision. In such cases, path revision becomes necessary to address the uncertainty. This requires the agent to replan or significantly modify its original path in order to avoid the obstacle and complete its task without conflict.

If the waiting strategy fails, a metaheuristic-based revising strategy is triggered. This strategy enables the generation of a new, conflict-free path from the agent's current position to its goal. For this purpose, we employ the ACO algorithm, which has demonstrated efficiency and effectiveness in single-agent pathfinding problems [5,12,42]. However, classical ACO is not directly applicable to the MAPF domain without modifications. In our previous work, we introduced the following key adaptations to tailor ACO for the MAPF setting:

- **Unavailable Nodes:** The positions of static obstacles, the current and next positions of dynamic obstacles, and the known paths of other agents are defined as time-dependent unavailable nodes that ants cannot enter. This strategy allows ants to explore feasible paths to the goal without conflicts, based on the agent's current knowledge of the environment.
- **Ant Travel Limitations:** Ant movements are guided by pheromone levels and heuristic information. However, purely stochastic exploration can lead ants to become lost or exceed the allowable travel time. Since we impose a hard constraint on the agent's maximum travel budget, ants are restricted from exploring paths that would exceed this limit. This limitation ensures that all candidate paths remain feasible within the agent's remaining travel capacity.

Furthermore, our previous work introduced two enhancements to improve the performance and efficiency of the revision strategy:

- **Early Stopping:** Classical ACO algorithms typically rely on fixed time or iteration limits for termination. In contrast, our approach employs an early stopping condition that monitors updates to the incumbent path found by the ants. If the incumbent path remains unchanged for one-third of the maximum number of iterations, the algorithm terminates early. This stopping condition significantly reduces unnecessary computation and helps minimize total runtime.
- **Dynamic β Adjustment:** The β parameter regulates the influence of heuristic information η_{ij} (e.g., inverse Manhattan distance to the goal) during action selection (i.e., transition rule), as shown in Eq. 1. Higher values of β amplify the impact of heuristic cues, leading to more deterministic decisions that prioritize immediate goal-directed choices, thereby encouraging exploration of new paths. As β decreases, the influence of heuristic information weakens, allowing pheromone trails, representing prior search experience, to have a stronger effect. This shift promotes exploitation of previously successful paths. In our approach, β is initialized with a high value (≥ 1) to promote exploration in early iterations and is linearly decreased to a lower value (≤ 1) to favor exploitation in later stages. The α parameter, which controls the influence of pheromone levels τ_{ij}^t (Eq. 1), remains fixed at 1.0 to ensure stability throughout the algorithm.

All hyperparameters used in the revision strategy were determined through a separate tuning process on a distinct set of DPO-MAPF instances excluded from the evaluation phase. This separation ensures that the optimization process does not bias the reported performance results. The final configuration is as follows: the maximum number of iterations is set to 150, the number of ants is 75, the initial value of β is 5.0, and it linearly decreases to 0.5 during execution. The heuristic information used in the ACO is computed as the ratio between the agent's remaining travel capacity t^i_{max} and the Manhattan distance to its goal.

When a conflict is detected among agents, each agent must decide whether to revise its path or continue as planned. Since revising typically increases the total travel cost, agents prefer to avoid it when possible. Therefore, a consensus protocol is required to determine which agent is granted priority to continue along its current path, while the others concede and revise. To ensure fairness in this process, our previous work introduced a token-based concession mechanism. Initially, each agent is assigned an equal number of tokens at the beginning of execution. When a conflict arises, the prioritized agent loses one token, while the conceding agents each gain one. The protocol prioritizes the agent with the most tokens, promoting long-term fairness by discouraging repeated privilege. This rule-based strategy is inspired by the negotiation-oriented token mechanism proposed in [9], but differs in that it applies deterministic rules rather than dynamic negotiation. Additionally, our protocol incorporates an urgency check: if any agent is unable to find a valid revision (e.g., its path planning fails), urgency overrides token differences. In such cases, the agent in the urgent situation is granted immediate priority. As a result, the prioritized agent continues its original path, while the remaining agents must invoke the revising strategy.

5.2 Proposed Extensions

While the previous multitier approach employed an ACO-based revision strategy to resolve conflicts during execution, this strategy regenerated paths from scratch, which proved inefficient in complex environments (e.g., larger maps or higher agent counts). To mitigate this limitation, the current study extends the prior ACO-based revision mechanism by enhancing its ability to utilize existing information. Three key extensions are introduced to improve efficiency.

- **Informed ACO:** In the original method, if the initial "WAITING" strategy fails, the ACO algorithm generates a new path to the goal from scratch. This process increases the computational burden and may lead to failure in more complex scenarios. Moreover, the original path is assumed to be a near-optimal route under DPO-MAPF constraints and thus contains valuable information. This extension proposes reusing the previous path during the revision process. Specifically, suppose an ant reaches a cell on the original path after bypassing the conflict point. In that case, the remainder of the path is restored, allowing the agent to continue. In other words, instead of finding a completely new path, the revision strategy aims to repair the existing one by finding a detour around the conflict and then reconnecting to the original route. This approach increases the likelihood of successfully completing the path while promoting faster convergence with promising cost minimization. Only half of the ants are informed about the previous path to ensure a balanced performance evaluation, while the others are directed solely toward the goal.
- **Weighted Average Pheromone (WAP):** In the standard ACO algorithm, transition decisions are based solely on the pheromone value of the candidate cell, as shown

in Eq. 1. However, in more complex environments, the surrounding region of a cell may provide additional spatial context that influences its desirability. To incorporate this, ants consider not only the pheromone level of the candidate position but also a local average of pheromone values in its neighborhood. Utilizing this spatial context helps reduce the risk of failure and avoid suboptimal paths by smoothing the pheromone distribution across nearby cells. This behavior can be seen as a plausible abstraction, as real ants may respond to the broader scent pattern rather than a single strong signal [28]. To capture this, we propose a WAP mechanism. During the transition rule computation, this approach considers not only the pheromone value of a candidate cell but also the pheromone distribution within a local window around it. A weighted average is calculated over the window, thereby increasing the probability of selecting cells that are not only promising themselves but are also located in high-pheromone neighborhoods. The weights are assigned based on the distance to the target cell, giving greater impact to closer cells. This mechanism enhances local reasoning and improves decision-making in uncertain environments. Notably, the averaging window is fixed according to the field of view size, as this parameter defines the observation and communication range during execution.
- **Info-WAP ACO:** This hybrid approach combines the strengths of WAP and Informed ACO extensions, utilizing both the agent's most recent valid plan and local pheromone context to support more efficient and context-aware path revisions under uncertainty.

6 Evaluation of Extended Revising Strategies

In this study, we evaluate the impact of revision strategies under the best-performing configuration identified in our previous analysis [8], which integrates the *Fair-Token protocol* a decentralized mechanism that manages agent turn-taking using locally observed priorities with the optimal *CBSH2-RTC solver* [16] in the first tier. To broaden the evaluation of conflict resolution mechanisms under uncertainty, this study compares a total of seven revising strategies, including four previously introduced and three newly proposed methods, respectively:

- **No-Revising:** A baseline without any revising strategy (only the first tier).
- **Only Waiting:** A rule-based strategy where agents use only waiting action.
- **Basic ACO:** A conflict-driven replanning method using ACO, where ants avoid "unavailable edges" and operate within a time limit.
- **Enhanced ACO:** An improved ACO-based revision that integrates a pre-processing wait strategy, early stopping, and dynamic β adjustment.
- **Informed ACO:** A path-repair strategy that detours around the conflict and reconnects to the original route rather than regeneration.
- **WAP ACO:** A neighborhood-sensitive ACO strategy that incorporates not only the pheromone value of a candidate cell but also the pheromone distribution in its neighborhood.
- **Info-WAP ACO:** A hybrid strategy that combines informed path-repair strategy with the weighted average pheromone mechanism.

To enable a systematic and comparative evaluation of the revising strategies, the experiments are conducted on three representative scenario groups: (i) small-scale instances designed to highlight fundamental coordination dynamics, (ii) large-scale instances aimed at testing scalability under increased agent density, map size, and the presence of both dynamic and static obstacles, and (iii) standard benchmark datasets widely adopted in the MAPF literature to ensure comparability and external validity.

Moreover, we evaluate the revising strategies using four main performance metrics: *success rate*, *runtime*, *Earth Mover's Distance (EMD)*, and *normalized cost*. In Eq. 4, the success rate captures the ability of the strategies to find feasible solutions under uncertainty, while runtime measures computational efficiency conditioned on successful completions.

$$\text{Success Rate} = \left(\frac{\#\text{of successfully solved scenarios}}{\#\text{of total scenarios}} \right) \times 100 \tag{4}$$

In addition, the revising algorithms may sacrifice their cost efficiency under uncertainty to reach the goal successfully. Therefore, the *optimality gap* is reported, where optimal solutions can be computed using a commercial solver (e.g., GUROBI) based on our Linear Programming (LP) formalization [8], and calculated via Eq. 5, where Z denotes the total cost (i.e., objective value) for successfully completed scenarios.

$$\text{Optimality Gap} = \left(\frac{Z_{\text{found}} - Z_{\text{optimal}}}{Z_{\text{optimal}}} \right) \times 100 \tag{5}$$

Since solving the LP model requires full knowledge of the environment [49], dynamic obstacles are treated as known in advance during this evaluation, thereby relaxing the uncertainty inherent in DPO-MAPF. For large-scale instances, where solving for the optimal solution is impractical within reasonable time limits, a *normalized cost* metric is employed in Eq. 6.

$$\text{Normalized Cost} = \frac{Z_{\text{found}}}{Z_{\text{upper}}} \times 100 \tag{6}$$

It is defined as the ratio of the obtained solution cost (Z_{found}) to an upper bound (Z_{upper}), where ($Z_{\text{upper}} = \sum_i^N t^i_{max}$) corresponds to the cost of a feasible plan that fully utilizes the available time capacity. Thus, the normalized cost also reflects the percentage of time capacity used to reach the goal under uncertainty, allowing consistent evaluation across varying problem sizes and complexities. Notably, the *maximum total time step* is determined as twice the Manhattan distance between each agent's start and goal positions. Furthermore, to quantify the deviation introduced by the revision process, we compute the EMD between each agent's initial path $\pi_i^{(1)}$ and its final revised version $\pi_i^{(2)}$. Each path is modeled as a sequence of grid vertices over discrete time steps. We assume that both trajectories have equal length T_i; if not, the shorter path is padded with dummy positions replicating the goal location. We construct a cost matrix using Manhattan distances between all possible position pairs. For each agent, the EMD is defined as the minimum total cost of aligning positions in the two paths through a one-to-one mapping of time steps. The average EMD across all agents is given by Eq. 7.

$$\text{EMD} = \frac{1}{N}\sum_{i=1}^{N}\min_{\sigma_i}\sum_{t=1}^{T_i} d\big(\pi_{i,t}^{(1)},\, \pi_{i,\sigma_i(t)}^{(2)}\big) \tag{7}$$

Here, N is the total number of agents, T_i is the length of the paths for agent i, and $d(u, v)$ denotes the Manhattan distance between two vertices u and v. The function σ_i defines a one-to-one mapping of time steps from the original path to the revised path, chosen such that the total positional distance across all matched pairs is minimized. Lower EMD values indicate that the revised path closely follows the original one, while higher values suggest greater deviation due to the revision process.

6.1 Small-Scale Instances

The evaluation begins with small synthetic instances specifically constructed to highlight fundamental coordination challenges under uncertainty. To facilitate these experiments, our earlier scenario generator is used to create varied small-scale MAPF setups [8]. This generator enables controlled variations in several key parameters, including static and dynamic obstacle densities, the number of agents, and the map size, by employing distinct random seeds for each configuration. A total of 132 scenario setups (4620 experiments in total) is generated, spanning four different grid sizes: 10×10, 15×15, 20×20, and 25×25. Each size is tested with agent counts ranging from 3 to 12, and static obstacle densities set at 5%, 10%, 15%, and 20%. For each configuration, three unique random seeds were used to generate variations in obstacle and agent placements. The number of dynamic obstacles is set proportional to the number of agents to maintain consistent challenge levels. Note that these scenarios are the same as our previous study [8]; but, results may differ due to proposed communication restrictions.

Figure 3 reports the success rates of different revising strategies on small maps. The baseline methods No-Revising (18.94%) and Only Waiting (24.24%) perform poorly, showing the need for active conflict resolution. Once ACO is introduced, performance improves significantly: Basic ACO reaches 41.52%, and newer variants (up to 43.94%) provide incremental gains. In small maps, where spatial flexibility is limited and outcome alternatives are few, ants are more likely to successfully complete their paths. This explains why ACO-based revision strategies exhibit similarly high performance. Nevertheless, Enhanced ACO (44.09%) and WAP ACO (43.94%) achieve slightly higher success rates.

Figure 4 illustrates the variability in the optimality gap. While ACO-based strategies show higher mean performance, they exhibit greater variance, particularly Enhanced ACO, Info-WAP, WAP, and Informed ACO. Moreover, since the optimality gap is calculated only from completed scenarios, it may be less informative when success rates differ significantly. Still, it reflects how much extra cost is introduced by each revision algorithm to handle conflicts under uncertainty. A strong positive correlation (0.81) between success rate and optimality gap supports the idea that ensuring feasibility through revision often leads to increased path length.

Figures 5 present the runtime of the revising strategies. As expected, No-Revising and Only Waiting seem to achieve the fastest runtime (0.01 s), but offer a limited success rate. Basic ACO is the slowest strategy (0.80 s), reflecting an inefficient search process. Despite its competitive optimality gap, it may suffer from scalability issues. The newly

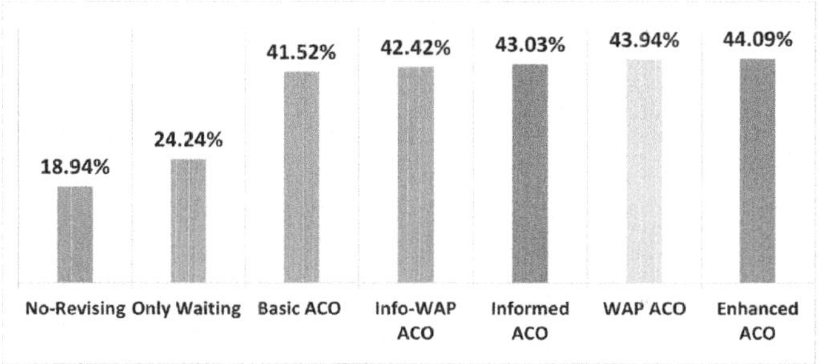

Fig. 3. Comparison of Success Rate in Small Instances.

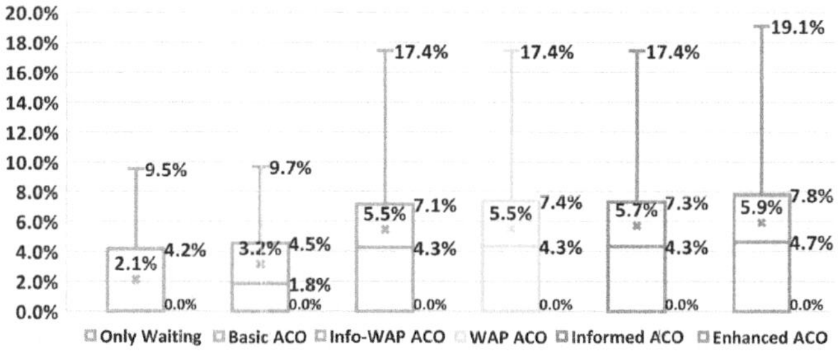

Fig. 4. Comparison of Optimality Gap in Small Instances.

proposed strategies reduce this overhead significantly: Info-WAP, WAP, Informed, and Enhanced ACO operate with average runtimes between 0.13 s and 0.15 s, offering a better trade-off between runtime and success rate. Due to the auto-path completion, Info-WAP and Informed ACO, which utilize the previous path information, perform fastest among ACO-based approaches. To sum up, WAP ACO achieves the best balance among success rate, solution quality, and computational efficiency, maintaining both a low average optimality gap and runtime, along with relatively stable performance. This highlights its robustness and effectiveness in constrained environments where feasibility, optimality, and runtime are all critical.

In terms of revision impact, Fig. 6 shows that Only Waiting yields the smallest path deviation (2.66), as agents remain stationary rather than rerouting. However, this comes at the cost of low success rates. Among ACO-based methods, Informed ACO yields the lowest average EMD (6.91), aiming to reuse original paths with minimal adjustments. In contrast, Enhanced ACO and WAP ACO show a slightly higher EMD (7.95 and 7.69, respectively), indicating that they introduce more substantial path changes. These results show that a positive correlation (0.991) between EMD and success rate, denoting the importance of revision under uncertainty.

6.2 Large-Scaled Instances

We evaluate the performance of each revision approach under increasing problem complexity with increased map size and number of agents. These settings contribute to the diversity and scalability of evaluation, where the number of agent interactions and the

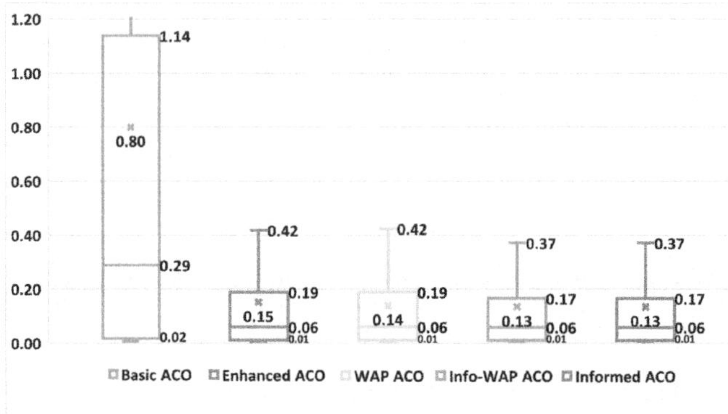

Fig. 5. Comparison of Runtime (sec) in Small Instances.

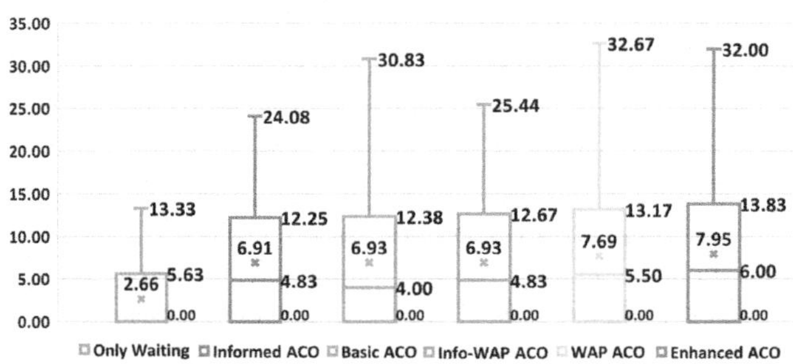

Fig. 6. Average EMD for Revising Strategies in Small Instances.

restricted space significantly increase the likelihood of conflicts. As in previous experiments, we evaluate each strategy regarding success rate, normalized cost, runtime, and EMD. This evaluation focuses exclusively on No-Revising, Enhanced ACO, and the proposed strategies. Waiting is excluded due to its poor performance, and Basic ACO is not separately evaluated since its behavior is inherently captured by the other ACO-based variants. No-Revising is retained as a baseline to emphasize the added value of revision mechanisms. The No-Revising baseline is retained to highlight the performance improvements achieved by incorporating revision strategies. To randomly produce large-scale MAPF environments, we define new settings in our framework. A total of 180 scenarios (4500 experiments in total) are created with different grid sizes, agent counts, and obstacle densities. The map dimensions include 30×30, 50×50, 100×100, and 200×200, each tested with 10 to 25 agents. Static obstacle densities are again set at 5%, 10%, 15%, and 20%, while three distinct random seeds are used per configuration to ensure diversity in agent and obstacle placements. The number of dynamic obstacles is scaled proportionally with the number of agents to preserve comparable difficulty across instances.

Figure 7 illustrates the success rates of the revising strategies. No-Revising performs poorly (5.6%), confirming that active conflict resolution becomes increasingly essential

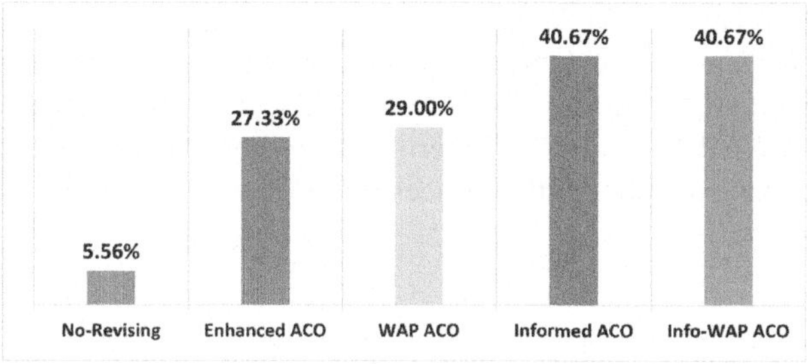

Fig. 7. Comparison of Success Rate in Large Instances.

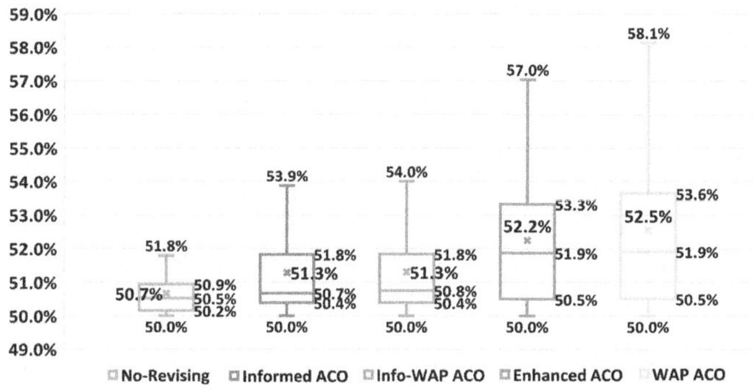

Fig. 8. Comparison of Normalized Cost in Large Instances.

as complexity grows. The success rates are generally lower in larger maps due to the increased number of steps to reach the goal and more complex coordination requirements. The performance of Enhanced ACO and WAP ACO, best performing agents in small instances, drastically decreases to 27.33% and 29.00%, respectively. In contrast, Informed ACO and Info-WAP ACO both reach 40.67% success rate and become the most effective strategies under these conditions. Moreover, Fig. 8 illustrates the normalized cost of the strategies. Informed ACO (51.29%) and Info-WAP ACO (51.31%) complete the traveling with slightly better costs compared to other ACO variants, denoting the reliance on the previous valid path. However, No-Revising strategy (50.67%) followed by Enhanced ACO (52.25 %) and WAP ACO (52.55%) perform the worst. Note that the No-Revising approach achieves the optimal path when the initial plan from the first tier does not fail. This situation suggests that leveraging prior information becomes more beneficial than aggressive revision as the search space expands, since agents can adjust their paths without requiring extensive replanning. As the number of steps that the ants should take increases, the performance of ACO-based methods tends to decline, as reflected in our results.

Figure 9 presents the runtime of the revising strategies. As expected, No-Revising is the fastest method with an average runtime of 1.14 s, yet it remains ineffective due to its extremely low success rate. Among ACO-based methods, Enhanced ACO runs the fastest (1.81 s) with relatively low variance, followed by WAP ACO (1.91 s). In contrast, Info-WAP ACO (2.34 s) and Informed ACO (2.27 s) are the slowest in computation time, but achieve the highest success rates. However, in commonly solved instances, Informed ACO (1.09 s) and Info-WAP ACO (1.16 s) outperform Enhanced ACO (1.65 s) and WAP ACO (1.70 s) in terms of runtime. This result indicates that the reconnecting mechanism sufficiently reduces runtime in more complex scenarios.

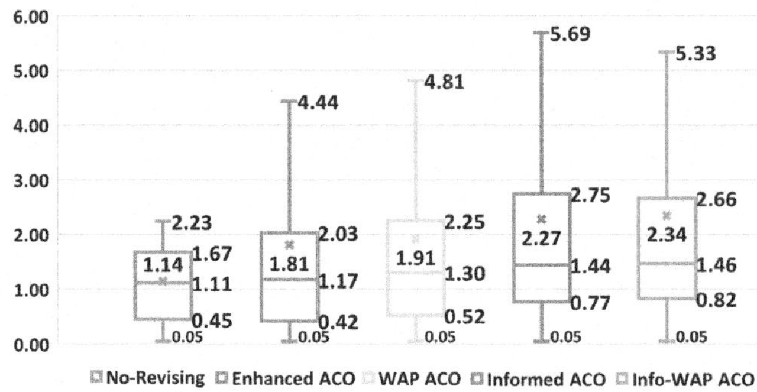

Fig. 9. Comparison of Runtime (sec) in Large Instances.

Regarding EMD, Fig. 10 shows an apparent increase in overall path deviation compared to small instances, which is expected due to longer paths and more complex replanning. Informed ACO and Info-WAP ACO achieve the lowest average EMD values among revising strategies (31.8 and 33.4, respectively), suggesting that their guidance-based approaches preserve more of the original plan structure. Enhanced ACO, while faster, results in slightly higher average EMD (58.6), and WAP ACO exhibits the highest deviation, likely due to its more exploratory behavior. Overall, methods that pheromone weighting or specifically path reusing seem to scale better regarding path quality, feasibility and runtime, especially in dense and expansive environments.

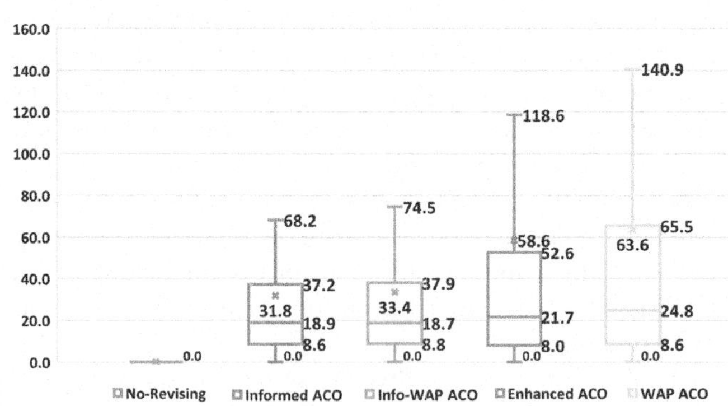

Fig. 10. Average EMD for Revising Strategies in Large Instances.

6.3 Benchmark Instances

To ensure the external validity of our findings and to facilitate comparison with established methods in the literature, we evaluate the revising strategies on widely-used benchmark datasets provided by the MovingAI repository [41]. These datasets represent realistic and diverse MAPF scenarios derived from game maps, such as urban, indoor, and maze-like environments. Numerous studies utilize these datasets to evaluate algorithmic performance under map structures and interaction complexities [25, 26]. Specifically, we use instances from two benchmark categories: *room* (i.e., indoor layouts with open and clustered areas) and *maze* (i.e., narrow corridors with constrained movement). The benchmark includes three room maps and five maze maps, each with 25 unique scenarios defining start-goal assignments for multiple agents. To transform the classical MAPF problem into its DPO-MAPF variant while preserving the original map structures, we incorporate dynamic obstacles and restrict agent perception using a local FoV. Each benchmark configuration is evaluated under three different random seeds to account for dynamic obstacle placement and behavior variability. In total, 600 benchmark scenarios (15,000 experiments in total) are executed. The same set of algorithms used in the large-scale synthetic environments, namely No-Revising, Enhanced ACO, and the newly proposed variants, are also applied to ensure consistency across experimental settings. Performance is assessed using the same four key metrics: success rate, normalized cost, runtime, and EMD.

Figure 11 presents the success rates of the revision strategies. All ACO-based methods achieve comparable performance in the *room* category (ranging from 38.49% to 39.02%) and the *maze* category (ranging from 12.43% to 12.75%). Nevertheless, the proposed extensions exhibit slightly higher success rates than Enhanced ACO in both categories. The *maze* maps, characterized by numerous narrow corridors, pose greater challenges for the DPO-MAPF problem. Because, conflicts in these constrained spaces may necessitate revising the paths of non-conflicting agents sharing the same corridor. No-Revising method yields the lowest success rates in the *room* (24.62%) and *maze* (4.27%) categories, underscoring the importance of effective conflict resolution in both open and constrained environments. In terms of normalized cost, all ACO-based methods demonstrate comparable performance in both the *room* category (ranging from 57.56% to 57.78%) and the *maze* category (ranging from 56.55% to 56.57%). These results indicate that all methods yield significantly similar objective performance in the DPO-MAPF variants of the benchmark scenarios. Thus, the primary challenge appears to lie in conflict resolution rather than cost optimization.

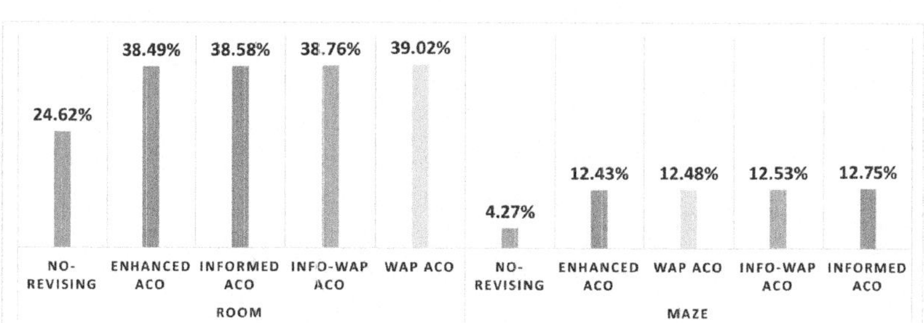

Fig. 11. Comparison of Success Rate in Benchmark Instances.

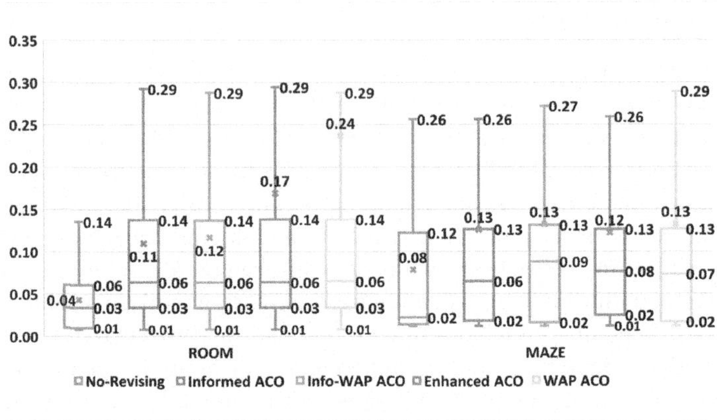

Fig. 12. Comparison of Runtime (sec) in Benchmark Instances.

Furthermore, Fig. 12 presents the runtime distribution of the revising strategies. In the *room* maps, Informed ACO (0.11 s) and Info-WAP ACO (0.12 s) exhibit the fastest runtime, while Enhanced ACO (0.17 s) and WAP ACO (0.24 s) are the slowest. This difference highlights the benefit of utilizing the previous path, which reduces recomputation time. However, in more constrained environments such as *maze* maps, reconnecting to the previous path is often infeasible due to conflicts in narrow corridors that require complete replanning. As a result, the runtime differences among ACO-based approaches diminish, converging within a narrower range of 0.12s to 0.13s.

Figure 13 denotes the average path deviation measured by EMD. In the *room* environment, the number of possible paths to the goal is relatively high due to the open areas in the map. As a result, WAP ACO (6.25) and Enhanced ACO (5.89) exhibit the highest path deviations, while Info-WAP ACO (2.40) and Informed ACO (2.41) require fewer adjustments to resolve conflicts. In more constrained environments such as *maze* maps, where path options are limited, the EMD values for all ACO-based approaches converge within a narrower range, from 1.68 to 2.26. These findings are consistent with the runtime results, as average EMD and runtime are highly correlated across benchmark scenarios.

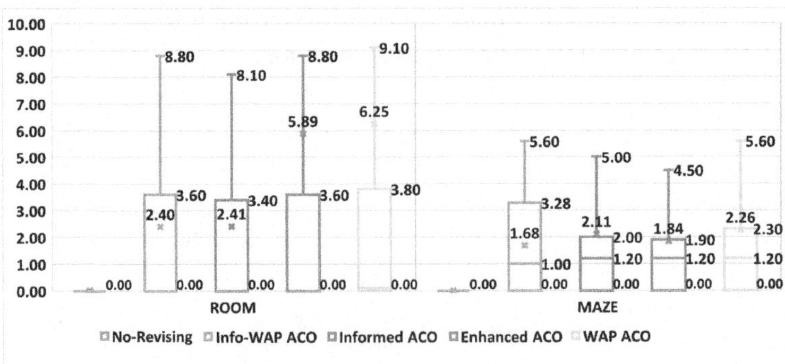

Fig. 13. Comparison of EMD in Benchmark Instances.

7 Conclusion

In real-world scenarios, agents may encounter unexpected events (e.g., fire blocking corridor, earthquakes altering terrain), as well as uncontrollable and unpredictable entities like birds in drone routing or suddenly appearing pedestrians in vehicle routing. These dynamic and unforeseen factors can significantly alter the environment, introducing conflicts that require agents to revise their plans during any MAPF task. Moreover, agents typically have limited perception and cannot access global updates, making it difficult to detect and respond to such changes effectively. To account for these uncertain and sudden changes, the DPO-MAPF problem was formulated by extending the classical MAPF framework to incorporate *Dynamic and Partially Observable obstacles* [8]. This extension models real-world uncertainty by treating unexpected events and moving entities as obstacles that are not fully known or predictable in advance. Unlike existing MAPF solvers, which primarily focus on scalability in terms of map size or agent count, DPO-MAPF introduces a new dimension of complexity grounded in uncertainty and limited observability. Furthermore, this study extends our previous problem definition by restricting information exchange among agents during execution, aligning the formulation more closely with real-world constraints. As a result, this study aims to bridge the gap between theoretical MAPF formulations and the realities of dynamic, unpredictable environments, serving as a challenging benchmark for the development of robust, adaptive strategies.

For the solution approach, our prior study proposed a multitier approach that leverages the strengths of both centralized and decentralized online planning. The first tier performs centralized, offline path planning by generating initial plans based solely on the static and fully known environment. In contrast, the second tier is decentralized and operates online, executing the initial plans until a conflict is detected. Upon detection, the conflicting agent revises its path via an ACO-based revision mechanism, which generates a new path from the agent's current location to its goal while avoiding conflicts based on available knowledge. When a conflict among agents arises, a token-based consensus protocol is employed to prioritize agents, considering urgent situations and token exchanges to ensure both feasibility and fairness. Briefly, the second tier has a capability of resolving conflicts during the execution of the initial plans.

This study extends the previous ACO-based revision strategy by improving the utilization of available information. In such cases, ants may fail to reach the goal or get trapped in suboptimal paths without access to additional information. To address this, three key enhancements are introduced: (i) *Informed ACO*, which allows reusing the conflict-free portion of the original plan after bypassing the conflict; (ii) *WAP ACO*, which determines the desirability (i.e., pheromone level) of a candidate position by considering both the position itself and its surrounding area through a weighted average; and (iii) a combined approach, called *Info-WAP ACO*. These improvements enable the second tier to leverage additional information, such as prior plans and local spatial context, to more effectively resolve conflicts.

For evaluation, this study compares the previous ACO-based revision strategy with the Informed ACO, WAP ACO and Info-WAP variants. The benchmark scenarios include the small instances from the prior study, which were validated via LP. To increase the diversity and complexity of test cases, this study further incorporates larger instances randomly generated by the framework, as well as standard MAPF benchmark instances ("room" and "maze" maps [41]) augmented with randomly placed dynamic obstacles. Notably, the larger and benchmark instances are not validated via LP due to their computational complexity.

According to the experimental results, the fundamental observations from both the previous and current studies remain consistent, even with the inclusion of more complex scenarios. In small instances, WAP ACO shows better balance between success rate, outcome quality and computational efficiency. In contrast, for more complex instances, Informed ACO and Info-WAP ACO achieve the highest success rates, while Enhanced ACO shows a drastic decline. Furthermore, all enhancements slightly increase revision performance across all benchmark scenarios. Note that, "Maze" scenarios are more challenging than "Room" scenarios [41], as dynamic obstacles can completely block certain paths in maze-like environments. This leads to a noticeable performance drop across map types. In conclusion, the results suggest that leveraging as much information as possible under uncertainty can significantly improve performance and effectiveness, particularly in complex environments.

With the introduction of information exchange limitations in the problem definition, two improvements for utilizing additional information in the solution approach, and experiments involving more complex scenarios, this study extends our previous paper [8]. As a result, several previously open questions (e.g., how to reuse prior plans and how the approach performs in existing or more complex scenarios) are addressed. Nevertheless, the DPO-MAPF problem still poses additional challenges, with several open research questions and directions for future work. Although the problem definition is based on the traditional MAPF formulation, it can be adapted to other variants, such as Lifelong and Pickup & Delivery [41]. For such adaptations, an existing problem-specific centralized solver can be employed in the first tier, while the ACO-based revision strategy can be modified to incorporate problem-specific constraints. While ACO has shown promise for path planning, other metaheuristics or existing algorithms (e.g., CBS or its variants) can also be adapted as revision strategies. Moreover, since the approach requires making decisions dynamically upon conflict detection, it offers a promising opportunity for integration with machine learning techniques, particularly reinforcement learning. These future directions highlight the expanded research potential of DPO-MAPF, making it a challenging and valuable variant of the MAPF problem.

References

1. Ali, Z.A., Han, Z., Masood, R.J.: Collective motion and self-organization of a swarm of UAVs: a cluster-based architecture. Sensors **21**(11), 3820 (2021)
2. Aljalaud, F., Kurdi, H., Youcef-Toumi, K.: Bio-inspired multi-UAV path planning heuristics: a review. Mathematics **11**(10), 2356 (2023)
3. Altshuler, Y.: Recent developments in the theory and applicability of swarm search. Entropy **25**(5), 710 (2023)
4. Blum, C., Roli, A.: Metaheuristics in combinatorial optimization: overview and conceptual comparison. ACM Comput. Surv. **35**(3), 268–308 (2003). https://doi.org/10.1145/937503.937505
5. Dai, X., Long, S., Zhang, Z., Gong, D.: Mobile robot path planning based on ant colony algorithm with a* heuristic method. Front. Neurorobot. **13**, 15 (2019)

6. Desaraju, V.R., How, J.P.: Decentralized path planning for multi-agent teams with complex constraints. Auton. Robots **32**(4), 385–403 (2012)
7. Dorigo, M.: Optimization, Learning and Natural Algorithms. Ph.D. thesis, Politecnico di Milano (1992)
8. Doğru, A., Deldari Alamdari, A., Balpınarlı, D., Aydoğan, R.: A multitier approach for dynamic and partially observable multiagent path-finding. In: Proceedings of the 17th International Conference on Agents and Artificial Intelligence, vol. 3: ICAART, pp. 562–573. SciTePress (2025). https://doi.org/10.5220/0013159800003890
9. Eran, C., Keskin, M.O., Cantürk, F., Aydoğan, R.: A decentralized token-based negotiation approach for multi-agent path finding. In: Rosenfeld, A., Talmon, N. (eds.) EUMAS 2021. LNCS (LNAI), vol. 12802, pp. 264–280. Springer, Cham (2021). https://doi.org/10.1007/978-3-030-82254-5_16
10. Felner, A., Li, J., Boyarski, E., Ma, H., Cohen, L., Kumar, T., Koenig, S.: Adding heuristics to conflict-based search for multi-agent path finding. In: Proceedings of the International Conference on Automated Planning and Scheduling, vol. 28, pp. 83–87 (2018). https://doi.org/10.1609/icaps.v28i1.13883
11. Hart, P.E., Nilsson, N.J., Raphael, B.: A formal basis for the heuristic determination of minimum cost paths. IEEE Trans. Syst. Sci. Cybern. **4**(2), 100–107 (1968)
12. Huang, S., Yang, D., Zhong, C., Yan, S., Zhang, L.: An improved ant colony optimization algorithm for multi-agent path planning. In: 2021 International Conference on Networking Systems of AI (INSAI), pp. 95–100. IEEE (2021)
13. Keskin, M.O., Cantürk, F., Eran, C., Aydoğan, R.: Decentralized multi-agent path finding framework and strategies based on automated negotiation. Auton. Agent. Multi-Agent Syst. **38**(1), 1–30 (2024)
14. Komenda, A., Novák, P., Pěchouček, M.: Decentralized multi-agent plan repair in dynamic environments. In: Proceedings of the 11th International Conference on Autonomous Agents and Multiagent Systems, AAMAS '12, vol. 3, pp. 1239–1240. International Foundation for Autonomous Agents and Multiagent Systems (2012)
15. Li, J., Felner, A., Boyarski, E., Ma, H., Koenig, S.: Improved heuristics for multi-agent path finding with conflict-based search. In: Proceedings of the Twenty-Eighth International Joint Conference on Artificial Intelligence, IJCAI-19, pp. 442–449. International Joint Conferences on Artificial Intelligence publisher (2019). https://doi.org/10.24963/ijcai.2019/63
16. Li, J., Harabor, D., Stuckey, P.J., Ma, H., Gange, G., Koenig, S.: Pairwise symmetry reasoning for multi-agent path finding search. Artif. Intell. **301**, 103574 (2021)
17. Li, J., Ruml, W., Koenig, S.: Eecbs: a bounded-suboptimal search for multi-agent path finding. In: Proceedings of the AAAI Conference on Artificial Intelligence, vol. 35, no. 14, pp. 12353–12362. AAAI (2021). https://doi.org/10.1609/aaai.v35i14.17466
18. Li, J., Tinka, A., Kiesel, S., Durham, J.W., Kumar, T.S., Koenig, S.: Lifelong multi-agent path finding in large-scale warehouses. In: Proceedings of the AAAI Conference on Artificial Intelligence, vol. 35, no. 13, pp. 11272–11281. AAAI, New York (2020). https://doi.org/10.48550/arXiv.2005.07371
19. Liu, N., Shen, S., Kong, X., Zhang, H., Bräunl, T.: Cooperative hybrid multi-agent pathfinding based on shared exploration maps (2025)
20. Ma, H., Tovey, C., Sharon, G., Kumar, T.K.S., Koenig, S.: Multi-agent path finding with payload transfers and the package-exchange robot-routing problem. In: Proceedings of the Thirtieth AAAI Conference on Artificial Intelligence, AAAI'16, pp. 3166–3173. AAAI Press (2016)
21. Ma, H., Yang, J., Cohen, L., Kumar, T., Koenig, S.: Feasibility study: moving non-homogeneous teams in congested video game environments. In: Proceedings of the AAAI Conference on Artificial Intelligence and Interactive Digital Entertainment, vol. 13, no. 1, pp. 270–272. AII (2017). https://doi.org/10.1609/aiide.v13i1.12919

22. Mahdavi, A., Carvalho, M.: Distributed coordination of autonomous guided vehicles in multi-agent systems with shared resources. In: 2019 SoutheastCon, pp. 1–7. IEEE (2019). https://doi.org/10.1109/SoutheastCon42311.2019.9020456
23. Morag, J., Stern, R., Felner, A.: Adapting to planning failures in lifelong multi-agent path finding. In: Proceedings of the International Symposium on Combinatorial Search, vol. 16, no. 1, pp. 47–55. AAAI, Prague (2023). https://doi.org/10.1609/socs.v16i1.27282
24. Netter, J., Vamvoudakis, K.G.: Decentralized multi-agent motion planning in dynamic environments. In: 2023 American Control Conference (ACC), pp. 1655–1660 (2023)
25. Okumura, K.: Lacam: search-based algorithm for quick multi-agent pathfinding. In: Proceedings of the AAAI Conference on Artificial Intelligence, vol. 37, no. 10, pp. 11655–11662 (2023)
26. Okumura, K., Machida, M., Défago, X., Tamura, Y.: Priority inheritance with backtracking for iterative multi-agent path finding. Artif. Intell. **310**, 103752 (2022)
27. Peng, S.: Multi-robot path planning combining heuristics and multi-agent reinforcement learning. arXiv preprint arXiv:2306.01270 (2023)
28. Perna, A., et al.: Individual rules for trail pattern formation in Argentine ants (linepithema humile). PLOS Comput. Biol. **8**(7), 1–12 (2012). https://doi.org/10.1371/journal.pcbi.1002592
29. Pianpak, P., Cao Son, T.: Dmapf: a decentralized and distributed solver for multi-agent path finding problem with obstacles. Electron. Proc. Theor. Comput. Sci. **345**, 99–112 (2021)
30. Poy, Y.L., Loke, Z.Y., Darmaraju, S., Goh, C.H., Kwan, B.H., Liu, H., Ng, D.W.K.: Enhanced particle swarm optimisation for multi-robot path planning with bezier curve smoothing. Robotics **13**(10), 141 (2024). https://doi.org/10.3390/robotics13100141
31. Pritchett, A.R., Genton, A.: Negotiated decentralized aircraft conflict resolution. IEEE Trans. Intell. Transp. Syst. **19**(1), 81–91 (2017)
32. Qiu, H.: Multi-agent navigation based on deep reinforcement learning and traditional pathfinding algorithm (2020)
33. Sartoretti, G., et al.: Primal: pathfinding via reinforcement and imitation multi-agent learning. IEEE Rob. Autom. Lett. **4**(3), 2378–2385 (2019)
34. Semiz, F., Polat, F.: Incremental multi-agent path finding. Future Gener. Comput. Syst. **116**, 220–233 (2021)
35. Sharon, G., Stern, R., Felner, A., Sturtevant, N.R.: Conflict-based search for optimal multi-agent pathfinding. Artif. Intell. **219**, 40–66 (2015)
36. Shofer, B., Shani, G., Stern, R.: Multi agent path finding under obstacle uncertainty. In: Proceedings of the International Conference on Automated Planning and Scheduling, vol. 33, no. 1, pp. 402–410. AAAI (2023). https://doi.org/10.1609/icaps.v33i1.27219
37. Skrynnik, A., Andreychuk, A., Nesterova, M., Yakovlev, K., Panov, A.: Learn to follow: decentralized lifelong multi-agent pathfinding via planning and learning. In: Proceedings of the AAAI Conference on Artificial Intelligence, vol. 38, no. 16, pp. 17541–17549 (2024). https://doi.org/10.1609/aaai.v38i16.29704
38. Skrynnik, A., Andreychuk, A., Yakovlev, K., Panov, A.I.: When to switch: planning and learning for partially observable multi-agent pathfinding. IEEE Trans. Neural Netw. Learn. Syst. (2023)
39. Standley, T.: Finding optimal solutions to cooperative pathfinding problems. In: Proceedings of the Twenty-Fourth AAAI Conference on Artificial Intelligence, vol. 24, pp. 173–178. AAAI (2010). https://doi.org/10.1609/aaai.v24i1.7564
40. Stern, R.: Multi-Agent Path Finding – An Overview, pp. 96–115. Springer, Cham (2019). https://doi.org/10.1007/978-3-030-33274-7_6
41. Stern, R., et al.: Multi-agent pathfinding: definitions, variants, and benchmarks. In: Proceedings of the International Symposium on Combinatorial Search, vol. 10, no. 1, pp. 151–158. AAAI, California (2019). https://doi.org/10.1609/socs.v10i1.18510

42. Stützle, T., Dorigo, M.: Ant Colony Optimization. The MIT Press, Cambridge (2004)
43. Surynek, P.: Reduced time-expansion graphs and goal decomposition for solving cooperative path finding sub-optimally. In: Proceedings of the 24th International Conference on Artificial Intelligence, vol. 15, pp. 1916–1922. AAAI (2015)
44. Tang, R., Tang, J., Talip, M.S.A., Aridas, N.K., Xu, X.: Enhanced multi agent coordination algorithm for drone swarm patrolling in durian orchards. Sci. Rep. **15**(1), 9139 (2025)
45. Veloso, M., Biswas, J., Coltin, B., Rosenthal, S.: Cobots: robust symbiotic autonomous mobile service robots. In: Twenty-Fourth International Joint Conference on Artificial Intelligence, p. 4423–4429. AAAI (2015)
46. Wan, Q., Gu, C., Sun, S., Chen, M., Huang, H., Jia, X.: Lifelong multi-agent path finding in a dynamic environment. In: 2018 15th International Conference on Control, Automation, Robotics and Vision (ICARCV), pp. 875–882 (2018). https://doi.org/10.1109/ICARCV.2018.8581181
47. Wang, C., et al.: Bioinspired environment exploration algorithm in swarm based on Lévy flight and improved artificial potential field. Drones **6**(5), 122 (2022)
48. Weise, J., Mai, S., Zille, H., Mostaghim, S.: On the scalable multi-objective multi-agent pathfinding problem. In: IEEE Congress on Evolutionary Computation, pp. 1–8. IEEE (2020). https://doi.org/10.1109/CEC48606.2020.9185585
49. Winston, W.: Operations Research: Applications and Algorithms. Cengage Learning (2022)
50. Wurman, P.R., D'Andrea, R., Mountz, M.: Coordinating hundreds of cooperative, autonomous vehicles in warehouses. AI Mag. **29**(1), 9 (2008). https://doi.org/10.1609/aimag.v29i1.2082
51. Yu, J., LaValle, S.: Structure and intractability of optimal multi-robot path planning on graphs. In: Proceedings of the AAAI Conference on Artificial Intelligence, vol. 27, pp. 1443–1449. AAAI (2013). https://doi.org/10.1609/aaai.v27i1.8541
52. Zhang, H., et al.: A hierarchical approach to multi-agent path finding. In: Proceedings of the International symposium on Combinatorial Search, vol. 12, pp. 209–211. AAAI (2021). https://doi.org/10.1609/socs.v12i1.18586
53. Zheng, H., Yan, Z., Wu, C.: Multi-agent path finding for mixed autonomy traffic coordination. In: 2024 IEEE/RSJ International Conference on Intelligent Robots and Systems (IROS), pp. 958–965. IEEE (2024)
54. Zhu, H., Brito, B., Alonso-Mora, J.: Decentralized probabilistic multi-robot collision avoidance using buffered uncertainty-aware voronoi cells. Auton. Robot. **46**(2), 401–420 (2022). https://doi.org/10.1007/s10514-021-10029-2

Automatic Data Augmentation of CDT, HDT, and PDT Images for Cognitive Screening

Nina Hosseini-Kivanani[1(✉)], Inês Cardoso Oliveira[1], Elena Salobrar-García[2], and Luis A. Leiva[1]

[1] Department of Computer Science, University of Luxembourg, Luxembourg, Luxembourg
nina.hosseinikivanani@ext.uni.lu, {i.oliveira,luis.leiva}@uni.lu
[2] Ramon Castroviejo Institute of Ophthalmologic Research, Universidad Complutense of Madrid, Madrid, Spain
elenasalobrar@med.ucm.es

Abstract. Early detection of Mild Cognitive Impairment (MCI) is crucial for timely intervention in Alzheimer's Disease (AD). Hand-drawn cognitive screening tasks, such as the Pentagon Drawing Test (PDT), Clock Drawing Test (CDT), and House Drawing Test (HDT), offer non-invasive and cost-effective means for capturing visuospatial and motor impairments. However, computational models trained on these tasks often suffer from limited data availability and class imbalance. In this work, we systematically evaluate automated data augmentation (AutoDA) strategies to improve the classification accuracy of Deep Learning models from hand-drawn cognitive assessments.

We propose and compare three augmentation methods applied across multiple dataset partitions and classification tasks: TrivialAugment (TA), UniformAugment (UA), and RandAugment (RA). Our experiments are conducted using two convolutional neural networks (CNN) architectures (DenseNet-121 and EfficientNet-B0) on a clinically annotated dataset containing PDT, CDT, and HDT images from healthy controls (HCs), MCI, and AD patients. Our results show that UA, when applied across all data splits, achieves the highest accuracy on CDT drawings (up to 91.0% for HC vs. MCI and 83.2% for MCI vs. AD), while RA performs best on more variable tasks like PDT and HDT.

We conclude that lightweight augmentation policies such as UA offer a robust, low-cost strategy for enhancing diagnostic performance in small-scale medical datasets. These findings highlight the importance of augmentation scope tuning and task-specific adaptation in clinical applications involving handwriting-based cognitive assessment tests.

Keywords: Drawing · Handwriting · Cognitive Impairments · Data Augmentation · Neural Networks

1 Introduction

Early and accurate classification of mild cognitive impairment (MCI) and Alzheimer's disease (AD), is critical for timely intervention and long-term disease management. MCI represents a transitional stage between normal aging (aka Healthy Control, or HC)

H. J. van den Herik et al. (Eds.): ICAART 2025, LNAI 16517, pp. 362–384, 2026.
https://doi.org/10.1007/978-3-032-25032-2_17

and dementia. Particularly, precise identification of HC vs. MCI and MCI vs. AD can enable therapeutic strategies that delay or even prevent the conversion to dementia [58]. Moreover, differentiating MCI from HC prevents unnecessary anxiety and treatment, while distinguishing MCI from AD supports personalized care planning and appropriate clinical-trial enrollment [2]. Because neurodegenerative changes typically begin years before overt symptoms appear [66], sensitive and non-invasive diagnostic tools such as the analysis of handwriting and drawing patterns play an increasingly important role in early detection and longitudinal monitoring of cognitive decline.

Building robust Deep Learning (DL) models for clinical use remains difficult because large, well-labeled medical datasets are costly to obtain, ethically sensitive, and often domain-specific. Data augmentation (DA) mitigates these limitations by synthetically expanding training data through label-preserving transformations such as rotation, scaling, cropping, translation, and intensity variation [19,57,68]. A recent systematic review by Islam et al. [37] confirmed that geometric, intensity, generative, and class-balancing DA strategies consistently improve classification, segmentation, and lesion-detection performance in medical imaging, but also emphasized the need for task-specific augmentation design to avoid clinically irrelevant distortions.

Despite these benefits, naïvely transferring generic image-recognition pipelines to medical data can introduce artifacts that degrade diagnostic performance, particularly in object-detection settings [38,40,48]. Consequently, developing clinically informed, modality-aware augmentation policies remains an open research priority [10,53].

Non-invasive graphomotor screening tasks such as the Pentagon Drawing Test (PDT), Clock Drawing Test (CDT), and House Drawing Test (HDT) capture multiple cognitive domains, including visuospatial reasoning, executive function, and fine motor control within a few minutes and at minimal cost. Digital acquisition devices additionally can record pen-trajectory, timing, and pressure signals that, together, reveal sub-second motor deficits that are usually invisible to conventional, manual scoring methods.

Multiple studies demonstrate the diagnostic value of such graphomotor screening tasks. Souillard-Mandar et al. [70] showed that digital CDT features can separate HCs, MCI, and AD with high accuracy. DL models that combine several drawing tasks (e.g., cube copying and trail making) further increase sensitivity to subtle impairment [41]. Wang et al. [77] recently reported that a digital CDT discriminates AD from Parkinson's MCI, confirming the test's broad applicability and scalability. Collectively, these works establish drawing tasks as rich, multi-domain digital biomarkers that complement conventional neuropsychological batteries.

While task-specific, hand-crafted pipelines can improve DL performance on PDT/CDT/HDT images [30,32,33], they require extensive domain expertise and grid-search. Automatic DA (AutoDA) methods search (or sample from) a discrete space of augmentation policies, yielding strong baselines with little human intervention. Among commonly used AutoDa methods, AutoAugment (AA) employs reinforcement learning to optimize policy schedules [11]. RandomAugment (RA) drastically reduces the search space by controlling only the number of operations and magnitude, eliminating the separate proxy-task phase [13]. Finally, TrivialAugment (TA) is parameter-free, selecting a single random transformation per image, yet matching state-of-the-art accuracy with minimal cost [52].

However, generic AutoDA policies may distort clinically meaningful features (e.g., clock-hand angles). Hosseini-Kivanani et al. [30] demonstrated that clinically adapted AutoDA, including constrained rotations and stroke-preserving elastic deformations, boosts CDT classification accuracy by up to 15% points while maintaining diagnostic fidelity.

As we will show later, using clinically constrained UniformAugment (UA) with all-split augmentation, our model attains 91.0% balanced accuracy on the HC vs. MCI task (+8.3 pp over TA) and 83.2% on the more challenging MCI vs. AD task (+6.7 pp). Accuracy gains saturate once augmented images comprise ≈35% of the training set, confirming that carefully tailored single-operation policies yield substantial, clinically relevant improvements under realistic data-scarcity constraints.

1.1 Contributions

To bridge the gap between state-of-the-art AutoDA research and clinically reliable cognitive-screening tools, we systematically adapt and evaluate the leading AutoDA methods for three PDT, CDT, HDT datasets. In sum, we make the following contributions.

- Clinically constrained AutoDA: Guided by evidence that excessive transformations distort key image semantics such as numeral placement and hand orientation in CDT [32,34], we restrict the transformations to mild geometric operations (*rotation* ($\leq 10°$), *shear* ($\leq 5°$), *scale* ($\leq 5\%$) and *translation* ($\leq 2\%$)). These limits keep the augmented images diagnostically faithful while still enlarging the effective training set.
- Learnable vs. non-learnable augmentations: We conduct a head-to-head comparison of search-based (learnable) and sampling-based (non-learnable) AutoDA strategies, providing practical guidelines for cognitive-screening deployments.
- Extensive validation: Experiments on three datasets (PDT, CDT, HDT) show accuracy gains of up to 15% over baselines without augmented data, with consistent improvements in balanced accuracy.
- Augmentation-ratio ablation: We systematically vary the proportion of augmented images and find that accuracy gains quickly saturate once the augmented samples make up roughly 3040% of the training set, mirroring the diminishing-returns pattern reported for medical-imaging tasks by others [17].

Ultimately, our findings underline the clinical and technical value of specially adapted AutoDA in the early diagnosis of cognitive impairment and lay the groundwork for scalable, low-cost screening solutions in real-world healthcare settings (see Table 1).

2 Related Work

Table 1. Performance Performance of leading AutoDA methods across vision benchmarks. Datasets used are shown as tags: SVHN, CIFAR-10, ImageNet, TinyImageNet.

Method	Strategy	Backbone(s)	Datasets	Error Rate(s) (%)
AA [12]	Reinforcement learning	Shake-Shake, AmoebaNet-C	SVHN ImageNet	SVHN: 1.00 ImageNet: 16.5
Fast AA [44]	Bayesian optimisation	WRN-28-10, ResNet-200	SVHN ImageNet	SVHN: 1.10 ImageNet: 19.4
Faster AA [25]	Gradient approximation	WRN-28-10, ResNet-50	SVHN ImageNet	SVHN: 1.20 ImageNet: 23.5
PBA [29]	Population-based search	Shake-Shake	SVHN	SVHN: 1.13
RA [13]	Random sampling	WRN-28-10, EfficientNet-B7	SVHN ImageNet	SVHN: 1.00 ImageNet: 15.0
AWS [74]	NAS, weight sharing	PyramidNet+ShakeDrop, ResNet-200	CIFAR-10 ImageNet	CIFAR-10: 1.24 ImageNet: 18.56
UA [45]	Uniform sampling	Shake-Shake, ResNet-200	CIFAR-10 ImageNet	CIFAR-10: 1.90 ImageNet: 19.6
TA [52]	One-op sampling	WRN-28-10, ResNet-50	SVHN ImageNet	SVHN: 1.10 ImageNet: 21.93
BO-Aug [84]	Bayesian optimisation	Shake-Shake, WRN-40-2	SVHN TinyImageNet	SVHN: 1.15 TinyImageNet: 36.84
MADAug [35]	Bi-level optimisation	WRN-28-10 / Shake-Shake, ResNet-50	SVHN ImageNet	SVHN: 1.00 ImageNet: 21.5

AutoDA has become an influential approach to address the limitations of manual augmentation design, which traditionally involves significant domain expertise and extensive trial-and-error experimentation. Conventional augmentation techniques, such as random cropping, flipping, and color jittering, are effective but lack adaptability across diverse datasets, often leading to suboptimal performance and cumbersome adjustments when applied to new tasks [18,56]. Other traditional augmentation methods, including Cutout [15], Mixup [85], and CutMix [83], introduced more sophisticated transformations to enhance the model's robustness. However, their effectiveness remains heavily dependent on dataset-specific fine-tuning, limiting their generalizability and practicality in broader applications [18,60].

2.1 Review of AutoDA Methods

AutoDA strategies have evolved significantly since the introduction of AA [11], which framed augmentation as a reinforcement learning problem to discover optimal transformation policies. Although AA achieved strong improvements in accuracy, its reliance on discrete search spaces and proxy tasks incurred massive computational costs, often thousands of GPU hours even for small datasets [12]. To address this, Fast AA [44] used density matching via Bayesian optimization to accelerate search, reducing compute by several orders of magnitude while retaining performance. Building on this, Faster AA [25] introduced a differentiable policy search that dramatically cut optimization time (down to $\approx$0.2 GPU-hours on CIFAR-10) by approximating gradients and integrating adversarial objectives.

Other AutoDA approaches like Population-Based Augmentation (PBA) [29] used evolutionary algorithms to adapt policies over training schedules, striking a balance between exploration and exploitation but still requiring large-scale parallel computation. To further simplify augmentation, RA [13] greatly reduced the search phase, by searching just two tunable hyperparameters, the number and magnitude of operations selected via grid search. UA [45] similarly streamlined augmentation by uniformly sampling transformations without tuning, while TA [52] further reduced complexity by randomly applying a single transformation per instance with no hyperparameter search.

More recent innovations have introduced adaptivity into augmentation. For example, Augmentation-Wise Weight Sharing (AWS) [74] combined Neural Architecture Search with weight sharing, dynamically adjusting policy strength during training, and achieved 1.24% top-1 error on CIFAR-10 without extra data. BO-Aug [84] extended Bayesian methods to continuous policy spaces and grouped operations, improving both transferability and runtime efficiency, and Curriculum-inspired methods such as ASDRL-AutoAug [80] introduced policy networks that modulate augmentation complexity based on model performance during training, leading to more stable learning in low-data or imbalanced regimes.

Despite these advances, AutoDA remains underexplored in medical imaging and clinical tasks. MedAugment [46] addressed augmentation for medical imaging by differentiating pixel-level (photometric) and spatial (geometric) transformations, employing a constrained sampling strategy to preserve diagnostic integrity. Despite demonstrating effectiveness for radiological imaging such as X-rays, its transferability to free-form drawings or cognitive assessment tasks remains unexplored. However, its generalizability to free-form cognitive drawings or handwriting remains an open question.

2.2 AutoDA in Clinical Research

Recent developments underscore the potential of AutoDA in cognitive assessments for dementia detection. For example, the Deep Feature Concatenation (DFC) model combining diverse handwriting tasks significantly improved AD detection accuracy [14,31]. Studies using the PDT images showed that applying selective geometric transformations enhanced classification performance, achieving up to 87% accuracy in binary and 76% in multi-class AD classification [32]. Furthermore, hybrid approaches such as the hybrid drawing test, which combine static off-line handwriting with dynamic on-line features, have demonstrated enhanced detection capabilities for MCI and AD through multimodal fusion [33]. These findings support the value of drawing-based screening pipelines that leverage both data diversity and augmentation-aware design. Similarly, hybrid models using on-line and off-line handwriting modalities demonstrated stronger MCI/AD detection through multimodal fusion [14].

Complementary insights are provided by MediAug [60], a benchmarking framework that evaluated the interaction between augmentation techniques and neural architectures across multiple medical imaging tasks. Specifically, it assessed the effectiveness of MixUp, CutMix, and SnapMix across CNN and Transformer models. The results showed that the impact of each augmentation policy was not uniform, but varied substantially depending on the model architecture, input resolution, and domain-specific noise characteristics. While MediAug was developed for structured radiological and dermatological images rather than freeform cognitive drawings, its core insight that augmentation policies must be tailored to both data type and model type is highly relevant to our framework. It supports our hypothesis that augmentation strategies must be aligned not only with the visual complexity of drawing tasks but also with the representational characteristics of the underlying model (e.g., DenseNet and EfficientNet).

Adaptive augmentation methods such as ASDRL-AutoAug [80] further advance this idea by introducing sample-specific, curriculum-aware augmentation schedules. ASDRL uses reinforcement learning to dynamically adjust augmentation strength and type based on the model's performance and learning stage, effectively guiding training through easier to harder examples. Although ASDRL was originally developed for segmentation tasks in medical imaging, the conceptual parallels are notable: just as segmentation tasks require task-aware and temporally adaptive augmentations, handwriting-based dementia screening may also benefit from progressive complexity, particularly when integrating tasks of varying difficulty like clock, pentagon, and house drawings.

A recent systematic review by Islam et al. [37] reinforces this line of research by emphasizing the need for domain-specific and task-aware augmentation strategies in clinical applications. Their review cataloged over 70 augmentation frameworks in medical AI and concluded that generic augmentation often underperforms compared to task-aligned or data-specific methods, particularly in neurocognitive disorders and screening contexts. The authors recommend a tighter integration between augmentation design and clinical goals, such as interpretability, minimal distortion of clinically relevant features, and preservation of task structure. These insights directly inform our use of task-specific augmentation policies, optimized for the structure and visuospatial demands of cognitive drawing assessments.

2.3 Summary and Research Gap

Current AutoDA research consistently demonstrates that learned augmentation policies outperform manual or heuristic approaches across natural images and radiological benchmarks while markedly reducing human effort. However, existing studies focus almost exclusively on structured imagery; none address the free-form, cognitively diagnostic drawings, such as PDT, CDT, HDT images, where uncontrolled geometric or photometric changes can obscure the visuospatial cues clinicians rely on. Our work bridges this gap by introducing clinically constrained AutoDA policies tailored to these hand-drawn screening tasks and shows that they preserve diagnostic fidelity while yielding up to 9%-point gains in balanced accuracy score over unconstrained baselines.

3 Methodology

This section details the end-to-end pipeline we designed for automatic, image-based screening of MCI and AD using three hand-drawn cognitive-assessment tasks: PDT, CDT, and HDT. Our pipeline (Fig. 1) covers:(i) data acquisition and preprocessing; (ii) augmentation and class-balancing strategies; (iii) model architectures and training procedures; (iv) evaluation protocol; and (v) implementation specifics.

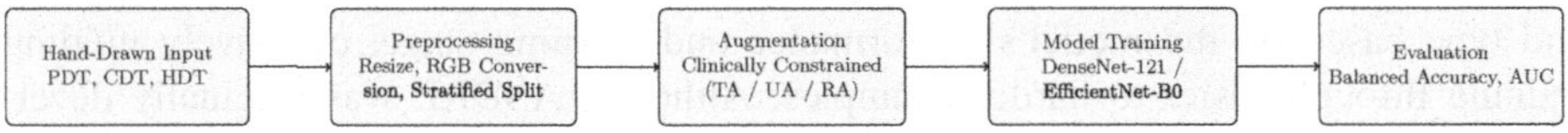

Fig. 1. Pipeline for automated dementia screening from hand-drawn cognitive assessments.

3.1 Data Acquisition and Preprocessing

Participant Cohort. Between January 2023 and June 2024, 91 participants (age 7089 years) were recruited from the Memory Unit of Hospital Clínico San Carlos (Madrid). The cohort comprised 14 HCs, 40 individuals with MCI, and 37 individuals diagnosed with AD (Fig. 2). Cognitive status was established by a multidisciplinary team using the Mini-Mental State Examination (MMSE) [75] and NINCDS-ADRDA/DSM-5 criteria [24,47]. Participants had normal or corrected-to-normal vision and hearing, and all provided written informed consent in accordance with institutional ethics approval (protocol ID: HCSC-2022-032).

Figure 3 presents the distribution of (a) age and (b) MMSE scores across the three diagnostic groups. The HC group (n=14) shows a relatively compact age distribution, while the MCI (n=40) and AD (n=37) groups exhibit broader variability. A one-way ANOVA confirmed that age differences among the groups were not statistically significant ($F(2, 88) = 0.63$, $p = .536$), suggesting that age alone does not discriminate between diagnostic categories.

In contrast, MMSE scores show a descending trend from HC to MCI to AD, consistent with progressive cognitive decline. A one-way ANOVA revealed a statistically significant difference in MMSE scores across the groups ($F(2, 88) = 44.68, p < .001$). These analyses confirm MMSE as a discriminative cognitive indicator, validating its use in stratification and clinical relevance of our datasets [51].

Each participant completed three standard drawing tasks that probe visuospatial and executive function: (i) the *PDT*, (ii) the *CDT*, and (iii) the *HDT*.

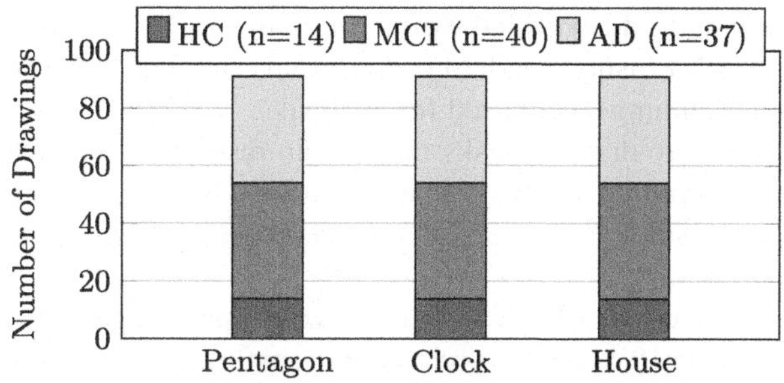

Attribute	HC	MCI	AD
Gender (F / M)	10 / 4	20 / 20	25 / 12
Age (Mean ± SD)	81 ± 4.7	82.1 ± 5.3	80.1 ± 4.5
MMSE (Mean ± SD)	29.9 ± 0.8	26.2 ± 1.5	22.1 ± 3.9

Fig. 2. Graphictable hybrid summarizing (top) drawing-task counts by clinical group and (bottom) participant demographics. Stacked bars visually convey within-task group composition, while the mini-table provides exact demographic statistics.

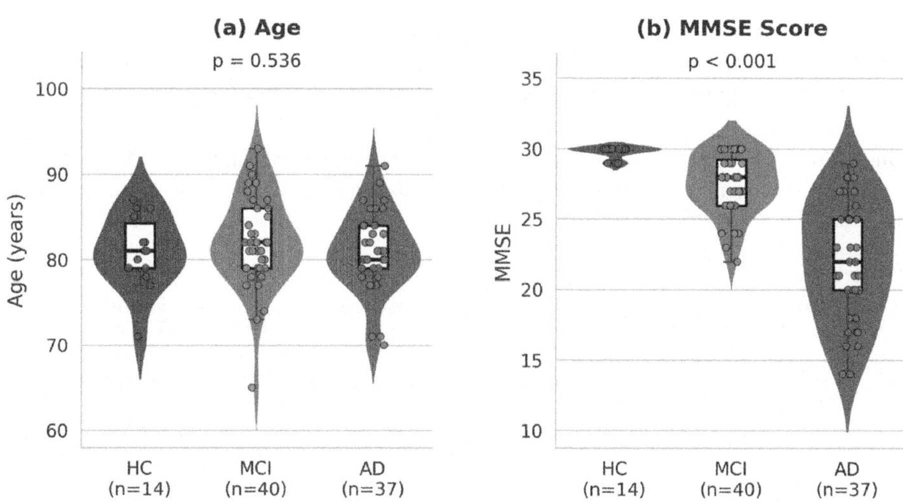

Fig. 3. Violin plots showing the distribution of (a) age and (b) MMSE scores across diagnostic groups: HC, MCI, and AD. Boxplots (white) indicate median and interquartile ranges; individual data points are overlaid as jittered dots.

Image Pre-processing and Stratified Split. Drawings were made on paper placed on a Repaper tablet (ISKN)[1] using standard pencils. Only the final raster images (digitized via high-resolution scanning) were used for analysis.

We analyzed all three drawing tasks rather than restricting the evaluation to a single test. Results are reported for two binary tasks: HC vs. MCI and MCI vs. AD, so that our augmentation study captures both cross-task variability and clinically relevant diagnostic boundaries.

All images are converted to RGB format, resized or padded to 224×224 pixels, and normalized to the range [0,1] using torchvision transforms `Resize` and `ToTensor`. Grayscale images are triplicated across RGB channels to ensure compatibility with pre-trained convolutional layers. No binarization or morphological operations are applied.

Each drawing task (PDT, CDT, HDT) is treated as an independent dataset of 91 raster images. For every task we perform stratified sampling into *train* (50%), *validation* (10%), and *test* (40%) subsets by first holding out 40% of each class for testing. The remaining 60% was split into 50% training and 10% validation sets, using fixed-seed stratified sampling to preserve class proportions in all subsets. This yields 46/9/36 images per task in total while preserving the original class distribution (14 HC, 40 MCI, 37 AD). Although the combined corpus totals 273 drawings, no model ever sees drawings from different tasks simultaneously, thereby preserving task-specific visuospatial characteristics.

3.2 Data Augmentation and Class Balancing

The datasets derived from the three drawing tasks exhibit limited sample sizes and class imbalance. Given the importance of preserving visuospatial and executive features critical to cognitive assessments, augmentations were carefully designed to sim-

Table 2. Overview of augmentation methods and their configuration strategies (N: number of transforms, M: magnitude of transform). All methods apply a subset of the listed geometric transformations to preserve diagnostic integrity.

Method	Strategy	N	M
TA	Single randomly sampled operation	Always 1 transform per image	Magnitude drawn from $\text{Uniform}[0, 1]$ for selected transform
UA	Candidate pool with stochastic filtering	2 transforms sampled, each retained w.p. 0.5	Each transform magnitude $\sim \text{Uniform}[0, 1]$
RA	Fixed number and magnitude via search	$N \in \{2, 3\}$ selected via grid search	$M \in \{4, 5\}$ levels from discrete search space
Transformation		Range	Interpretation
Rotation	Applied by all methods	$[-10^\circ, +10^\circ]$	Captures natural variability in drawing orientation
Shear	Applied by all methods	$[0.2^\circ, 5^\circ]$	Models skew due to motor inconsistencies
Scale	Applied by all methods	$[0.95\times, 1.05\times]$	Reflects differences in drawing size
Translation	Applied by all methods	$[-2\%, +2\%]$	Simulates off-center drawing placement

[1] https://www.iskn.co/eu/repaper/xlite?utm_source.

ulate realistic variability without distorting diagnostically essential cues [5,20]. Three augmentation strategies (TA, UA, and RA) were employed to address these challenges:

- **TA.** Exactly one geometric transformation per augmented image is randomly chosen from a controlled set, including rotation ($\pm 10°$), isotropic scaling ($0.95\times 1.05\times$), shear ($0.2°5°$), or translation ($\pm 2\%$ of image dimensions). Each transform's magnitude is sampled uniformly from the permissible range. This approach introduces realistic drawing irregularities, such as slight misalignments and size variations, while preserving critical spatial structures and object integrity [67].
- **UA.** Two candidate operations ($k = 2$) are selected uniformly from the TA transformation set; each is independently applied with a probability of 0.5, resulting in approximately one transformation per image on average. Magnitudes for each executed operation are uniformly sampled from [0,1] and mapped back to the corresponding TA range. UA maintains low computational overhead and introduces controlled stochasticity without requiring hyperparameter optimization.
- **RA.** Following Cubuk et al. [13], RA uses two discrete hyperparameters: the number of operations per image, $N \in 2, 3$, and a fixed magnitude level, $M \in 4, 5$. Each augmented image undergoes sequential application of all N selected transformations at the chosen magnitude level. We determine the optimal combination of (N, M) via a validation-set grid search before training, effectively blending stochastic data augmentation with task-specific tuning.

Table 2 provides a comprehensive overview of the three augmentation strategies employed in this study, along with their respective configurations for controlling the number of transforms (N) and the magnitude of each operation (M). TA follows a minimalist approach by applying exactly one transformation per image, with the operation and its intensity sampled uniformly at random. UA introduces mild stochasticity by selecting two candidate transforms and retaining each with independent probability (0.5), enabling a modest degree of compositionality. In contrast, RA performs a grid search over discrete N and M values to determine the most effective augmentation policy for a given validation set, thereby introducing a controlled but more aggressive form of transformation scheduling.

All three methods share a common pool of clinically validated geometric transformations (rotation, shear, scaling, and translation) that are applied with carefully bounded parameter ranges (see lower section of Table 2). These transformations were selected in collaboration with domain experts to preserve the structural integrity and diagnostic relevance of pentagon, clock, and house drawings, which are sensitive to spatial distortions. For implementation, we relied on the `Albumentations` library [7], chosen for its efficiency, deterministic replay capability, and fine-grained control over transformation composition. To ensure experimental reproducibility, all augmentation parameters, including random seeds, were fixed across training runs.

Figure 4 illustrates representative examples of class-specific augmentations applied to raw sketches from the HC, MCI, and AD groups. Each row shows the original input (top) and the corresponding augmented version (bottom), emphasizing how geometric transformations are selectively applied to preserve task semantics while enriching data variability. In these examples, an HC pentagon drawing undergoes rotation, an

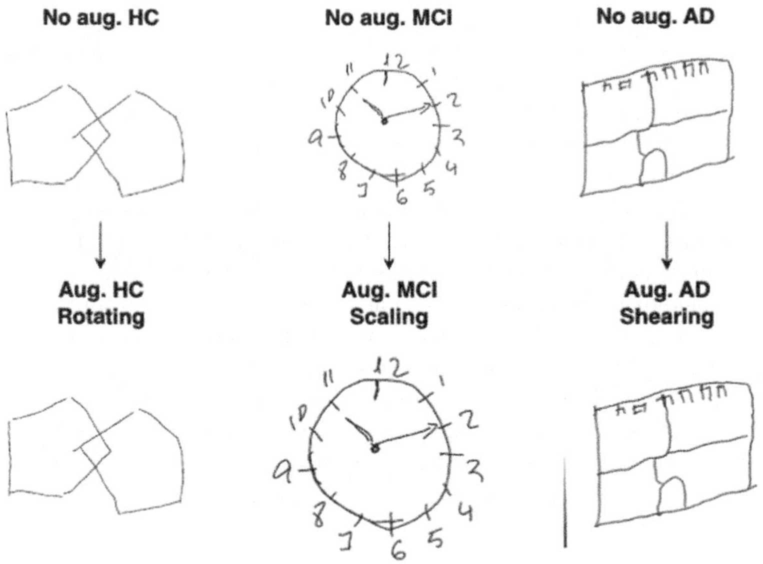

Fig. 4. Representative samples of augmented drawings across diagnostic groups. Each column shows an original drawing (top) and its transformed counterpart (bottom): a rotated pentagon (HC person), a scaled clock (MCI patient), and a sheared house (AD patient). These examples reflect the controlled application of geometric transformations detailed in Table 2.

MCI clock sketch is scaled isotropically, and an AD house image is sheared, demonstrating the preservation of diagnostic features under clinically constrained augmentation parameters.

DA Scaling Analysis. Many DA studies implicitly assume a balanced dataset and therefore apply a uniform number of synthetic views to every image [28]. In practice, however, medical and cognitiveimpairment datasets are often highly imbalanced, motivating the use of class-aware policies that equalize class counts before training [23,78]. Our implementation follows this paradigm:

$$T = \lfloor n_{\max}\alpha \rfloor, \qquad R_c = \frac{T}{n_c}, \tag{1}$$

where $n_{\max}$ is the size of the majority class, n_c is the original size of class c, α is a user-specified scalar that denotes the augmentation ratio, and T is the target number of images per class after augmentation. Hence the majority class receives an effective augmentation factor $R_{\text{maj}} = \alpha$, while every minority class is scaled more aggressively ($R_c > \alpha$) until all reach the same cardinality T.

We empirically found that moderate values ($\alpha \in [1, 3]$) yield balanced training data without severe distribution drift, in line with prior reports that class-aware Mixup/CutMix improved both AUC and calibration on imbalanced medical tasks [50, 73]. Conversely, pushing $\alpha \geq 5$ may introduce synthetic artifacts that harm out-of-distribution (OOD) robustness unless augmented views are carefully filtered or weighted [23,72]. We therefore recommend the heuristic schedule reported in Table 3.

Table 3. Guidelines for the class-balancing augmentation parameter α. The effective per-image ratio for a minority class with n_c originals is $R_c = \lfloor n_{\max}\alpha \rfloor / n_c$ (see Eq. 1).

α Range	Use Case	No. Images	Recommended For
1.0–1.5	Light augmentation	40–60	Quick experiments
2.0–3.0	Standard augmentation	80–120	Most practical applications
3.5–5.0	Heavy augmentation	140–200	Performance optimization
10.0	Extreme augmentation	400	Research/stress testing

3.3 Model Architectures and Training

We benchmark two CNN models, DenseNet-121 and EfficientNet-B0, as they strike a favourable trade-off between capacity and inference cost on small clinical datasets [30, 33]. **DenseNet-121** [36] promotes dense connectivity that facilitates gradient flow, feature reuse, and achieved high performance on radiography and COVID-19 screening tasks [36,49]. **EfficientNet-B0** [71] delivers comparable accuracy with about four times fewer parameters than DenseNet and has proven effective for dermoscopic lesion analysis [64].

All models are trained using the Adam optimiser [1] (learning-rate 1×10^{-3}, weight-decay 1×10^{-2}). We minimise cross-entropy loss with mini-batches of 32 images, run for at most 50 epochs, and use early stopping after 5 epochs without validation-loss improvement [59]. A ReduceLROnPlateau scheduler (factor 0.1, patience 5) lowers the learning rate when validation loss saturates. The checkpoint with the best validation *balanced accuracy* is retained for test-time evaluation.

3.4 Implementation Details and Evaluation Metrics

Following best practices for stratified sampling [42], we preserve class ratios in all data partitions. Specifically, we use stratified splits to produce a 50% training, 10% validation, and 40% hold-out test set. This ensures that each subset maintains the original class distribution for robust model evaluation.

Three augmentation modes are implemented (TA, UA, RA). Each mode first determines the majority-class size $n_{\max}$, then multiplies it by the user-defined augmentation ratio α to obtain the target number of augmented samples $T = \lfloor n_{\max}\alpha \rfloor$. In other words, every class c is up-sampled to T images, giving an effective per-image ratio $R_c = T/n_c$ (see Eq. 1). The Albumentations library applies rotation, scaling, affine shear, and translation with magnitudes drawn from uniform random intervals. Default values are $\alpha = 2$, $N = 2$ and $M = 9$ for RA, $N = 3$ for UA, and $N = 1$ for TA.

All experiments were run under PyTorch 1.11.0 and TorchVision 0.12 on three NVIDIA A100 GPUs provided by the Luxembourg national supercomputer MeluXina.[2]

[2] https://www.luxprovide.lu/meluxina/.

Because the tasks are class-imbalanced, we report (i) Balanced Accuracy, defined as the mean of class-wise recall, robust to skewed priors [6]; and (ii) AUC, defined as the area under the Receiver Operating Characteristic (ROC) curve, which reflects the model's ability to distinguish between positive and negative classes across all classification thresholds.

3.5 Experimental Design

In this study, we systematically investigate five scenarios to assess their impact on model training and evaluation performance:

1. No DA (Baseline): The model is trained, validated, and tested exclusively on the original, unmodified dataset, thereby establishing baseline performance without augmentation.
2. DA Train Only: Data augmentation is applied solely to the training set, enabling the model to benefit from increased variability during training, while the validation and test sets remain untouched to facilitate unbiased model evaluation.
3. DA Validation Only: Augmentation is exclusively applied to the validation set. This scenario evaluates the effect of augmented data during model tuning while preserving original, unaltered training and test sets.
4. DA Train + Validation: Both training and validation datasets undergo augmentation, allowing the model enhanced generalization capabilities during both training and validation phases, with the test set remaining intact for a reliable evaluation.
5. DA All Aug: Augmentation is implemented across all three partitions (training, validation, and test sets). This represents the most rigorous evaluation scenario, as the model encounters augmented samples throughout all phases, closely resembling real-world scenarios with substantial data variability.

We benchmarked three DA families, defined in Sect. 3.2: TA, involving mild rotations, scaling (range: 0.951.05), shear transformations, and translations along both axes; UA, where precisely one operation is selected uniformly at random from the TA pool and applied consistently to each image, bypassing any search or optimization phase; and RA, which applies a sequence of operations with magnitudes determined via a constrained grid search. Each augmentation strategy is systematically tested under the four application scopes, Train Only, Validation Only, Train + Validation, and All Aug (see Fig. 5). Evaluation is conducted across two distinct binary classification tasks and three cognitive drawing tasks (clock, house, pentagon), employing DenseNet-121 and EfficientNet-B0 architectures as classifiers.

4 Results and Discussion

Across all tasks and partitions, DenseNet showed more consistent performance overall, with balanced accuracy ranging from 58% to 91%, making it suitable for structured tasks like clock and pentagon. In contrast, EfficientNet demonstrated higher peak accuracy (up to 90% on House, RA AllAug) but greater variability across augmentation regimes, particularly excelling on the more complex HDT. These results suggest a task-aware model preference: DenseNet for geometric precision, EfficientNet for structurally variable inputs. A hybrid ensemble leveraging both could enhance robustness in multi-task clinical pipelines.

4.1 HC vs. MCI

UA with *AllAug* configuration yielded the best performance, achieving a 91.0% balanced accuracy, exceeding both TA (82.7%) and RA (82.1%) by 8.3 and 8.9% points, respectively. These gains confirm that even single-operation augmentations can meaningfully improve model generalization without introducing significant noise, an effect previously reported [30,44].

Validation Only augmentation consistently underperformed (minimum 61.9%), reinforcing that introducing perturbations solely at inference time leads to severe covariate shift and model miscalibration.

RA showed moderate effectiveness in the *Train Only* setting, but extending it to validation or test sets led to performance drops, consistent with earlier cautionary findings on over-augmentation in clinical settings [9,10,76]. These results highlight that test-time augmentation must remain semantically aligned with training distributions to avoid degraded reliability.

4.2 MCI vs. AD

Across all configurations, MCI vs. AD classification exhibited a median drop of 7% points relative to HC vs. MCI, reflecting the subtler nature of neurodegeneration progression. The UA with *AllAug* configuration again led with 85%, outperforming RA and TA by 2.2 and 6.7% points, respectively.

TA performed comparably well (75%) when limited to *Train Only* or *Validation Only*, but its effectiveness declined under *AllAug*, suggesting that excessive geometric transformations may obscure subtle stroke-level cues necessary for discriminating disease stages.

4.3 Performance Insights

Our findings reveal a strong interaction between task structure, augmentation strategy, and model architecture in handwriting-based dementia classification. Specifically, we observed that structured tasks such as clock and pentagon drawings benefit from simpler or deterministic augmentations, particularly when paired with DenseNet. In contrast, more variable and unconstrained tasks like house drawings require more expressive augmentations like RA, which achieved the highest overall performance when combined with EfficientNet. These results suggest that the geometry and compositional variability of input data should inform augmentation design, consistent with prior findings showing that task-aware augmentation and architecture pairing significantly improve performance in medical imaging [16,26].

UA emerged as a strong general-purpose strategy. Despite its simplicity, sampling one transformation uniformly from a pre-defined pool, UA yielded the highest single-task performance (91% balanced accuracy on clock with DenseNet). This supports earlier evidence [40,44] that low-overhead augmentation schemes can match or exceed

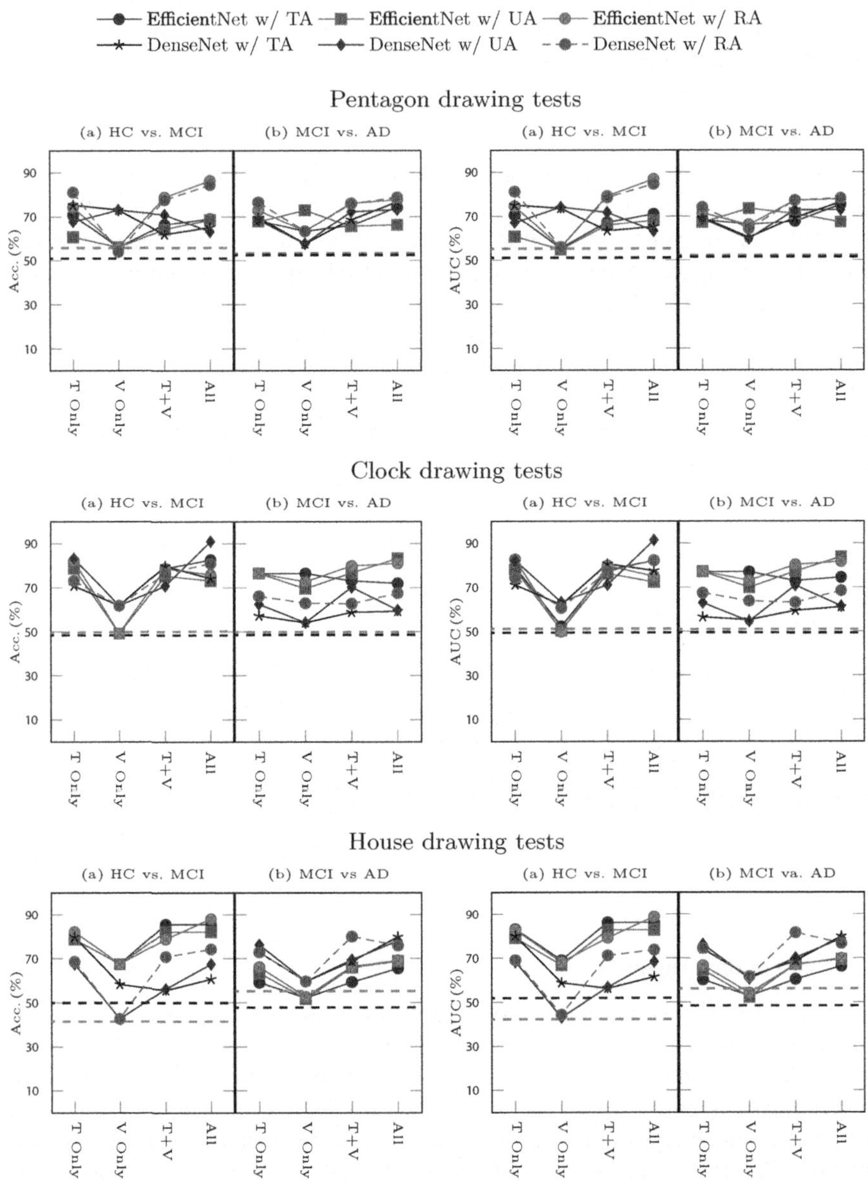

Fig. 5. Performance comparison of EfficientNet (solid lines) and DenseNet (dashed lines) across three cognitive tests (PDT, CDT, HDT; in rows) and two binary classification tasks (HC vs. MCI, MCI vs. AD; in columns). We report Accuracy (%) and AUC (%) under four augmentation scenarios: training-only (T Only), validation-only (V Only), training + validation (T+V), and training + validation + testing (All). Markers denote the AutoDA strategy: TA (circles), UA (triangles), RA (squares). The dashed lines represent the baseline condition for DenseNet (green) and EfficientNet (black), respectively. (Color figure online)

more complex methods in low-data clinical settings, likely due to their better preservation of disease-relevant spatial structures.

We also found that the scope of augmentation (where and when it is applied) plays a critical role in model robustness. Augmentations limited to the training set (OnlyTrainAug) yielded stable results and avoided the evaluation-time covariate shift introduced by ValOnlyAug and AllAug settings. These observations reinforce recent work on model calibration [27,55] and support recommendations for training-time-only augmentation in sensitive medical applications.

Visuospatial dysfunction appears early in MCI and is detectable with complex tasks like the 15-Objects Test [3] even when simpler visual tests fail. An important clinical insight concerns the classification gap between Control vs. MCI and MCI vs. AD. Across all experiments, models performed significantly better at distinguishing HC from MCI patients than at identifying progression from MCI to AD. This reflects known neurocognitive patterns: early-stage visuospatial deficits are more distinct, while the transition to AD is more gradual and heterogeneous [39,82]. Clock drawing and visuospatial tasks like the CANTAB Paired Associates Learning (PAL) test are shown to be effective for detecting early decline but less useful for precise staging of progression to AD [21,63]. In particular, studies using multimodal neuroimaging and DL approaches show near-ceiling performance in HC vs. AD classification but struggle with MCI vs. AD due to the subtle and heterogeneous nature of cognitive and structural changes within MCI populations. These findings emphasize that machine learning classifiers are most effective at early, cross-sectional screening, especially when using tasks or features that capture distinct early impairments, such as visuospatial processing, rather than disease staging.

Model-wise, DenseNet demonstrated more consistent generalization across datasets and augmentation conditions. This stability may stem from its narrower feature representation, which is more robust to small perturbations. DenseNet is known for its strong feature reuse and compact architecture, making it effective and stable across tasks. Studies show that it achieves high robustness in multimodal medical image fusion and segmentation, even under domain shifts and noise [22]. In contrast, EfficientNet achieved higher peak performance, especially on the HDT, but exhibited more variance, particularly under AllAug and RA settings. EfficientNet has been shown to outperform other models in image classification tasks involving diverse or low-quality data, such as heterogeneous chest X-rays, due to its compound scaling and flexible architecture. However, it also suffers more pronounced performance drops under domain shifts and input variability [69]. These patterns are consistent with prior literature showing that EfficientNet variants are particularly effective in heterogeneous or complex input domains [4,33,54].

Finally, while RA consistently yielded top-line performance, it introduced additional computational costs during training due to its reliance on search-based transformation selection. This trade-off is well documented, as RA and its variants often require significant training resources, which can be a bottleneck in clinical or low-resource deployments [13,79]. Modified approaches have been proposed to balance performance and efficiency for mobile or resource-constrained systems [81]. Broader studies of medical imaging workflows echo this concern, showing that high-complexity methods often hinder real-time diagnostics unless optimized for low-latency environments [62]. As noted in [43], such strategies can become bottlenecks in real-time or low-resource settings. This trade-off must be considered when designing clinically viable pipelines.

Together, our results emphasize that task-specific augmentation strategies, when coupled with model-aware deployment, offer the most effective and interpretable path for clinical screening using DL. Our findings demonstrate that no single augmentation policy or architecture performs best across all tasks: UA excels for structured tasks like CDT, while RA proves more effective for complex tasks such as HDT or PDT. In fact, prior studies have shown that the PDT is often less sensitive to early MCI than the CDT, but becomes more challenging for individuals with moderate cognitive impairment due to its higher visuoconstructional demands. For example, the CDT has been shown to better distinguish early cognitive decline, particularly in MCI, while the PDT is more useful in detecting moderate to advanced visuoconstructional deficits [8,61,65]. Similarly, DenseNet provides consistent performance across drawing types, whereas EfficientNet achieves higher peak accuracy on more variable inputs. Rather than adopting a one-size-fits-all augmentation pipeline, systems should tailor the augmentation type, scope, and model selection to the visuospatial complexity of the task and the clinical goals of deployment, whether for early detection or longitudinal staging (see Table 4).

Table 4. Summary of best task-specific augmentation strategies and model configurations. These results highlight the need to align augmentation and model choices with the structure and complexity of each drawing task.

Task	Model	Aug. Method	Acc. (%)	Classification
CDT	DenseNet	UA	91.00	HC vs. MCI
HDT	EfficientNet	RA	88.11	HC vs. MCI
PDT	EfficientNet	RA	84.37	HC vs. MCI
CDT	EfficientNet	UA	83.25	MCI vs. AD
HDT	DenseNEt	TA	79.88	MCI vs. AD
PDT	DenseNet	RA	78.75	MCI vs. AD

4.4 Practical Implications

Our study confirms that lightweight, non-learnable AutoDA methods, particularly UA, are not only sufficient but optimal for training DL classifiers on clinically sensitive, small-scale handwriting datasets. These insights reinforce recent conclusions by Ko and Ok [40] and Lim et al. [44], emphasizing the superiority of simpler augmentation pipelines in medical imaging, where excessive transformations may compromise diagnostic fidelity.

Given the growing interest in real-time clinical decision support, methods like TA and UA offer a viable deployment path in resource-constrained settings, enabling fast training without loss in accuracy.

Model selection should also be task-aware: our results indicate that DenseNet consistently performs well on CDT and PDT, demonstrating robust generalization across augmentation regimes. In contrast, EfficientNet achieves superior peak performance on HDT, particularly under RA with AllAug configurations, suggesting its suitability for tasks with more structural variability.

Eventually, we would recommend a hybrid approach for deployment: combining DenseNet and EfficientNet in an ensemble model may enhance predictive reliability by leveraging their complementary strengths: DenseNet's stability and EfficientNet's sensitivity. Such an ensemble could be especially beneficial in clinical workflows where multiple drawing tasks are assessed concurrently.

4.5 Limitations and Future Work

We kept the search space of RA deliberately compact to control computational costs. Therefore, it is unclear if loosening constraints would really improve performance, at the cost of significantly larger training times. Future extensions to our work include using Bayesian or evolutionary search, to hopefully further close the performance gap between UA and RA. We also envision exploring photometric perturbations and meta-learning strategies that can dynamically adapt the augmentation scope during model training.

5 Conclusion

Our study offers a systematic evaluation of three lightweight geometric augmentation strategies for dementia-stage classification using standardized off-line drawing tests. Our key findings can be summarized as follows. Uniformly sampling a single geometric transformation (UA) achieved the highest accuracy for CDT across both binary tasks (91.0% for HC vs. MCI and 83.2% for MCI vs. AD) without incurring policy-search overhead; Augmentation *scope* interacts significantly with the transformation family: stochastic regimes (UA, RA) benefit from full-split application (AllAug), whereas deterministic TA performs best when restricted to training only. We advocate for UA with AllAug as a robust, low-cost default for small, imbalanced handwriting/drawing datasets and highlight the critical importance of scope tuning over fixed augmentation recipes.

6 Code Availability

The source code and experimental scripts used in this study are available at: https://github.com/NinaKivanani/AutoAug-cdt-hdt-pdt.

Acknowledgments. Research supported by the Horizon 2020 FET program of the European Union through the ERA-NET Cofund funding (grant CHIST-ERA-20-BCI-001) and the European Innovation Council Pathfinder program (SYMBIOTIK project, grant 101071147). The authors gratefully acknowledge Luxembourg's national supercomputer MeluXina and the LuxProvide teams for their expert support.

References

1. Adam, K.D.B.J., et al.: A method for stochastic optimization. arXiv preprint: arXiv:1412.6980 (2014)
2. Albert, M.S., et al.: The diagnosis of mild cognitive impairment due to Alzheimer's disease: recommendations from the national institute on Aging-Alzheimer's association workgroups on diagnostic guidelines for Alzheimer's disease. Alzheimer's Dement. **7**(3), 270–279 (2011)
3. Alegret, M., et al.: Detection of visuoperceptual deficits in preclinical and mild Alzheimer's disease. J. Clin. Exp. Neuropsychol. **31**(7), 860–867 (2009)
4. Almalki, H., Khadidos, A.O., Alhebaishi, N., Senan, E.M.: Early detection of Alzheimer's disease progression stages using hybrid of CNN and transformer encoder models. Sci. Rep. **15**(1), 16799 (2025)
5. Bourke, J., Castleden, C.M., Stephen, R., Dennis, M.: A comparison of clock and pentagon drawing in Alzheimer's disease. Int. J. Geriatr. Psychiatry **10**(8), 703–705 (1995)
6. Brodersen, K.H., Ong, C.S., Stephan, K.E., Buhmann, J.M.: The balanced accuracy and its posterior distribution. In: 2010 20th International Conference on Pattern Recognition, pp. 3121–3124. IEEE (2010)
7. Buslaev, A., Iglovikov, V.I., Khvedchenya, E., Parinov, A., Druzhinin, M., Kalinin, A.A.: Albumentations: fast and flexible image augmentations. Information **11**(2), 125 (2020)
8. Cecato, J.F.: Pentagon drawing test: data from Alzheimer's disease, paraphrenia and obsessive compulsive disorder in elderly patients. Perspectivas en Psicología **13**(2), 21–26 (2016)
9. Chen, T., Lu, H., Xiao, S.: Application of random region augmentation algorithm in deep learning. In: Journal of Physics: Conference Series. vol. 2078, p. 012001. IOP Publishing (2021)
10. Chlap, P., Min, H., Vandenberg, N., Dowling, J., Holloway, L., Haworth, A.: A review of medical image data augmentation techniques for deep learning applications. J. Med. Imaging Radiat. Oncol. **65**(5), 545–563 (2021)
11. Cubuk, E.D., Zoph, B., Mane, D., Vasudevan, V., Le, Q.V.: AutoAugment: learning augmentation policies from data. arXiv preprint: arXiv:1805.09501 (2018)
12. Cubuk, E.D., Zoph, B., Mane, D., Vasudevan, V., Le, Q.V.: AutoAugment: learning augmentation strategies from data. In: Proceedings of the IEEE/CVF Conference on Computer Vision and Pattern Recognition, pp. 113–123 (2019)
13. Cubuk, E.D., Zoph, B., Shlens, J., Le, Q.V.: RandAugment: practical automated data augmentation with a reduced search space. In: Proceedings of the IEEE/CVF Conference on Computer Vision and Pattern Recognition Workshops, pp. 702–703 (2020)
14. Dao, Q., El-Yacoubi, M.A., Rigaud, A.S.: Detection of Alzheimer disease on online handwriting using 1D convolutional neural network. IEEE Access **11**, 2148–2155 (2022)
15. Devries, T., Taylor, G.W.: Improved regularization of convolutional neural networks with cutout. CoRR (2017). arXiv:1708.04552
16. Dutta, S., Prakash, P., Matthews, C.G.: Impact of data augmentation techniques on a deep learning based medical imaging task. In: Medical Imaging 2020: Imaging Informatics for Healthcare, Research, and Applications, vol. 11318, pp. 168–177. SPIE (2020)
17. Fabian, Z., Heckel, R., Soltanolkotabi, M.: Data augmentation for deep learning based accelerated MRI reconstruction with limited data. In: International Conference on Machine Learning, pp. 3057–3067. PMLR (2021)
18. Faryna, K., van der Laak, J., Litjens, G.: Automatic data augmentation to improve generalization of deep learning in H&E stained histopathology. Comput. Biol. Med. **170**, 108018 (2024)
19. Frid-Adar, M., Diamant, I., Klang, E., Amitai, M., Goldberger, J., Greenspan, H.: Gan-based synthetic medical image augmentation for increased CNN performance in liver lesion classification. Neurocomputing **321**, 321–331 (2018)

20. Förstl, H., Burns, A., Levy, R., Cairns, N.: Neuropathological basis for drawing disability (constructional apraxia) in Alzheimer's disease. Psychol. Med. **23**, 623–629 (1993). https://doi.org/10.1017/S003329170002540X
21. Gao, Z., Wang, W., Wang, Z., Guan, W., Wu, W.: Neuropsychological features of elderly patients with mild cognitive impairment susceptible to Alzheimer's disease. Zhonghua yi xue za zhi **92**(3), 152–155 (2012)
22. Ghosh, T., Jayanthi, N.: An efficient Dense-ResNet for multimodal image fusion using medical image. Multimedia Tools Appl. **83**(26), 68181–68208 (2024)
23. Gong, C., Wang, D., Li, M., Chandra, V., Liu, Q.: KeepAugment: a simple information-preserving data augmentation approach. In: Proceedings of the IEEE/CVF Conference on Computer Vision and Pattern Recognition, pp. 1055–1064 (2021)
24. Guha, M.: Diagnostic and Statistical Manual of Mental Disorders: DSM-5 (5th edition). Ref. Rev. **28**(3) (2014)
25. Hataya, R., Zdenek, J., Yoshizoe, K., Nakayama, H.: Faster AutoAugment: learning augmentation strategies using backpropagation. In: Computer Vision–ECCV 2020: 16th European Conference, Glasgow, UK, 23–28 August 2020, Proceedings, Part XXV 16, pp. 1–16. Springer (2020)
26. He, X., Chu, X.: MedPipe: end-to-end joint search of data augmentation and neural architecture for 3D medical image classification. In: 2023 IEEE International Conference on Medical Artificial Intelligence (MedAI), pp. 344–354. IEEE (2023)
27. Hendrycks, D., Dietterich, T.: Benchmarking neural network robustness to common corruptions and perturbations. arXiv preprint: arXiv:1903.12261 (2019)
28. Hendrycks, D., Mu, N., Cubuk, E.D., Zoph, B., Gilmer, J., Lakshminarayanan, B.: AugMix: a simple data processing method to improve robustness and uncertainty. In: International Conference on Learning Representations (2019)
29. Ho, D., Liang, E., Chen, X., Stoica, I., Abbeel, P.: Population based augmentation: efficient learning of augmentation policy schedules. In: International Conference on Machine Learning, pp. 2731–2741. PMLR (2019)
30. Hosseini-Kivanani, N., Oliveira, I.C., Kilinç, S., Leiva, L.A.: Efficient automatic data augmentation of CDT images to support cognitive screening. In: Proceedings of the 17th International Conference on Agents and Artificial Intelligence (ICAART 2025) - Volume 3, pp. 600–607. SCITEPRESS - Science and Technology Publications (2025). https://doi.org/10.5220/0013165100003890
31. Hosseini-Kivanani, N., et al.: Better together: combining different handwriting input sources improves dementia screening. In: 2023 IEEE 19th International Conference on e-Science (e-Science), pp. 1–7. IEEE (2023)
32. Hosseini-Kivanani, N., et al.: Ink of insight: data augmentation for dementia screening through handwriting analysis. In: Proceedings of the 2024 8th International Conference on Medical and Health Informatics, pp. 224–229 (2024)
33. Hosseini-Kivanani, N., Salobrar-García, E., Elvira-Hurtado, L., Salas, M., Schommer, C., Leiva, L.A.: Predicting Alzheimer's disease and mild cognitive impairment with off-line and on-line house drawing tests. In: 2024 IEEE 20th International Conference on e-Science (e-Science), pp. 1–10. IEEE (2024)
34. Hosseini-Kivanani, N., Schommer, C., Leiva, L.A.: The magic number: impact of sample size for dementia screening using transfer learning and data augmentation of clock drawing test images. In: 2023 IEEE International Conference on E-health Networking, Application & Services (Healthcom), pp. 101–106. IEEE (2023)
35. Hou, C., Zhang, J., Zhou, T.: When to learn what: model-adaptive data augmentation curriculum. CoRR (2023). arXiv:2309.04747

36. Huang, G., Liu, Z., Van Der Maaten, L., Weinberger, K.Q.: Densely connected convolutional networks. In: Proceedings of the IEEE Conference on Computer Vision and Pattern Recognition, pp. 4700–4708 (2017)
37. Islam, T., Hafiz, M.S., Jim, J.R., Kabir, M.M., Mridha, M.: A systematic review of deep learning data augmentation in medical imaging: Recent advances and future research directions. Healthc. Analytics, 100340 (2024)
38. Kebaili, A., Lapuyade-Lahorgue, J., Ruan, S.: Deep learning approaches for data augmentation in medical imaging: a review. J. Imaging **9**(4), 81 (2023)
39. Khatri, U., Kwon, G.R.: An efficient combination among sMRI, CSF, cognitive score, and APOE $\varepsilon 4$ biomarkers for classification of ad and mci using extreme learning machine. Comput. Intell. Neurosci. **2020**(1), 8015156 (2020)
40. Ko, B., Ok, J.: Time matters in using data augmentation for vision-based deep reinforcement learning. CoRR (2021). arXiv:2102.08581
41. Kobayashi, M., Yamada, Y., Shinkawa, K., Nemoto, M., Nemoto, K., Arai, T.: Automated early detection of Alzheimer's disease by capturing impairments in multiple cognitive domains with multiple drawing tasks. J. Alzheimers Dis. **88**(3), 1075–1089 (2022)
42. Kohavi, R., et al.: A study of cross-validation and bootstrap for accuracy estimation and model selection. In: IJCAI, vol. 14, pp. 1137–1145 (1995)
43. Lee, G., et al.: Refurbish your training data: Reusing partially augmented samples for faster deep neural network training. In: 2021 USENIX Annual Technical Conference (USENIX ATC 21), pp. 537–550 (2021)
44. Lim, S., Kim, I., Kim, T., Kim, C., Kim, S.: Fast AutoAugment. In: Advances in Neural Information Processing Systems, vol. 32 (2019)
45. LingChen, T.C., Khonsari, A., Lashkari, A., Nazari, M.R., Sambee, J.S., Nascimento, M.A.: UniformAugment: a search-free probabilistic data augmentation approach. CoRR (2020). arXiv:2003.14348
46. Liu, Z., Lv, Q., Li, Y., Yang, Z., Shen, L.: MedAugment: universal automatic data augmentation plug-in for medical image analysis. CoRR (2023). arXiv:2306.17466
47. McKhann, G., Drachman, D., Folstein, M., Katzman, R., Price, D., Stadlan, E.M.: Clinical diagnosis of Alzheimer's disease: report of the NINCDS-ADRDA work group under the auspices of department of health and human services task force on Alzheimer's disease. Neurology **34**(7) (1984)
48. Mikołajczyk, A., Grochowski, M.: Data augmentation for improving deep learning in image classification problem. In: 2018 International Interdisciplinary PhD Workshop (IIPhDW), pp. 117–122. IEEE (2018)
49. Minaee, S., Kafieh, R., Sonka, M., Yazdani, S., Soufi, G.J.: Deep-COVID: predicting COVID-19 from chest X-ray images using deep transfer learning. Med. Image Anal. **65**, 101794 (2020)
50. Minderer, M., et al.: Revisiting the calibration of modern neural networks. In: Advances in Neural Information Processing Systems, vol. 34, pp. 15682–15694 (2021)
51. Mitchell, A.J.: The mini-mental state examination (MMSE): update on its diagnostic accuracy and clinical utility for cognitive disorders. In: Cognitive Screening Instruments: A Practical Approach, pp. 37–48. Springer (2017)
52. Müller, S.G., Hutter, F.: TrivialAugment: tuning-free yet state-of-the-art data augmentation. In: Proceedings of the IEEE/CVF International Conference on Computer Vision, pp. 774–782 (2021)
53. Nalepa, J., Marcinkiewicz, M., Kawulok, M.: Data augmentation for brain-tumor segmentation: a review. Front. Comput. Neurosci. **13**, 83 (2019)
54. Nowak, F., et al.: An investigation into augmentation and preprocessing for optimising X-ray classification in limited datasets: a case study on necrotising enterocolitis. Int. J. Comput. Assist. Radiol. Surg. **19**(6), 1223–1231 (2024)

55. Ovadia, Y., et al.: Can you trust your model's uncertainty? Evaluating predictive uncertainty under dataset shift. In: Advances in Neural Information Processing Systems, vol. 32 (2019)
56. Pattilachan, T.M., et al.: A critical appraisal of data augmentation methods for imaging-based medical diagnosis applications. arXiv preprint: arXiv:2301.02181 (2022)
57. Perez, L., Wang, J.: The effectiveness of data augmentation in image classification using deep learning. arXiv preprint: arXiv:1712.04621 (2017)
58. Petersen, R.C.: Mild cognitive impairment as a diagnostic entity. J. Intern. Med. **256**(3), 183–194 (2004)
59. Prechelt, L.: Automatic early stopping using cross validation: quantifying the criteria. Neural Netw. **11**(4), 761–767 (1998)
60. Qi, X., et al.: MediAug: exploring visual augmentation in medical imaging. arXiv preprint: arXiv:2504.18983 (2025)
61. Rakusa, M., Jensterle, J., Mlakar, J.: Clock drawing test: a simple scoring system for the accurate screening of cognitive impairment in patients with mild cognitive impairment and dementia. Dement. Geriatr. Cogn. Disord. **45**(5–6), 326–334 (2018)
62. Ravi, M., Sanagapati, S.S.S.: A practical design and implementation of a low-cost platform for real-time diagnostic imaging. IEEE Access **5**, 24952–24958 (2017)
63. Risacher, S.L., et al.: Visual contrast sensitivity in Alzheimer's disease, mild cognitive impairment, and older adults with cognitive complaints. Neurobiol. Aging **34**(4), 1133–1144 (2013)
64. Sabir, R., Mehmood, T.: Classification of melanoma skin cancer based on image data set using different neural networks. Sci. Rep. **14**(1), 29704 (2024)
65. Saka, E., Elibol, B.: Enhanced cued recall and clock drawing test performances differ in Parkinson's and Alzheimer's disease-related cognitive dysfunction. Parkinsonism Relat. Disord. **15**(9), 688–691 (2009)
66. Salobrar-García, E., et al.: Changes in visual function and retinal structure in the progression of Alzheimer's disease. PLoS ONE **14**(8), e0220535 (2019)
67. Sardella, A., et al.: Is the pentagon-copying task more than a cognitive feature? Associations with handgrip strength, gait speed, and frailty in older adults. Gerontology **70**(1), 1–6 (2024)
68. Shorten, C., Khoshgoftaar, T.M.: A survey on image data augmentation for deep learning. J. Big Data **6**(1), 1–48 (2019)
69. Solomou, C., Kazakov, D.: Utilizing chest X-rays for age prediction and gender classification. In: 2021 4th International Seminar on Research of Information Technology and Intelligent Systems (ISRITI), pp. 356–361. IEEE (2021)
70. Souillard-Mandar, W., et al.: Learning classification models of cognitive conditions from subtle behaviors in the digital clock drawing test. Mach. Learn. **102**, 393–441 (2016)
71. Tan, M., Le, Q.: EfficientNet: rethinking model scaling for convolutional neural networks. In: International Conference on Machine Learning, pp. 6105–6114. PMLR (2019)
72. Taori, R., Dave, A., Shankar, V., Carlini, N., Recht, B., Schmidt, L.: Measuring robustness to natural distribution shifts in image classification. In: Advances in Neural Information Processing Systems, vol. 33, pp. 18583–18599 (2020)
73. Thulasidasan, S., Chennupati, G., Bilmes, J.A., Bhattacharya, T., Michalak, S.: On Mixup training: improved calibration and predictive uncertainty for deep neural networks. In: Advances in Neural Information Processing Systems, vol. 32 (2019)
74. Tian, K., Lin, C., Sun, M., Zhou, L., Yan, J., Ouyang, W.: Improving auto-augment via augmentation-wise weight sharing. In: Advances in Neural Information Processing Systems, vol. 33, pp. 19088–19098 (2020)
75. Tombaugh, T., McIntyre, N.J.: The mini-mental state examination: a comprehensive review. J. Am. Geriatr. Soc. **40**(9) (1992)

76. Volpi, R., Namkoong, H., Sener, O., Duchi, J.C., Murino, V., Savarese, S.: Generalizing to unseen domains via adversarial data augmentation. In: Advances in Neural Information Processing Systems, vol. 31 (2018)
77. Wang, C., et al.: Differential cognitive functioning in the digital clock drawing test in AD-MCI and PD-MCI populations. Front. Neurosci. **19**, 1558448 (2025)
78. Wang, Z., Guo, Y., Li, Q., Yang, G., Zuo, W.: DualAug: exploiting additional heavy augmentation with OOD data rejection. arXiv preprint: arXiv:2310.08139 (2023)
79. Xiao, A., Shen, B., Tian, J., Hu, Z.: Differentiable RandAugment: learning selecting weights and magnitude distributions of image transformations. IEEE Trans. Image Process. **32**, 2413–2427 (2023)
80. Xu, Z., et al.: Automatic data augmentation for medical image segmentation using adaptive sequence-length based deep reinforcement learning. Comput. Biol. Med. **169**, 107877 (2024)
81. Yao, P., et al.: Single model deep learning on imbalanced small datasets for skin lesion classification. IEEE Trans. Med. Imaging **41**(5), 1242–1254 (2021)
82. Yu, X., Peng, B., Shi, J., Zhu, J., Dai, Y.: 3D convolutional networks based automatic diagnosis of Alzheimer's disease using structural MRI. In: 2019 12th International Congress on Image and Signal Processing, BioMedical Engineering and Informatics (CISP-BMEI), pp. 1–6. IEEE (2019)
83. Yun, S., Han, D., Oh, S.J., Chun, S., Choe, J., Yoo, Y.: CutMix: regularization strategy to train strong classifiers with localizable features. In: Proceedings of the IEEE/CVF International Conference on Computer Vision, pp. 6023–6032 (2019)
84. Zhang, C., Li, X., Zhang, Z., Cui, J., Yang, B.: BO-Aug: learning data augmentation policies via Bayesian optimization. Appl. Intell. **53**(8), 8978–8993 (2023)
85. Zhang, H., Cissé, M., Dauphin, Y., Lopez-Paz, D.: mixup: beyond empirical risk minimization. CoRR (2017). arXiv:1710.09412

Hybrid Reptile Search Algorithm with Levy Flight for Intrusion Detection

Maher O. Al-Khateeb[1(✉)] and Ali Douik[2]

[1] ISITCom, NOCCS-ENISO Lab, University of Sousse, Sousse, Tunisia
maherkhateeb@hotmail.com

[2] National Engineering School of Sousse, NOCCS-ENISO Lab, University of Sousse, Sousse, Tunisia
ali.douik@eniso.u-sousse.tn

Abstract. In cybersecurity, the rise of Machine Learning (ML)-based security solutions has ushered in a new era of defence against evolving threats, with Intrusion Detection (ID) systems playing a pivotal role. The effectiveness of these systems critically depends on the quality and relevance of input features. Redundant or irrelevant features can degrade performance, making feature selection (FS) a vital pre-processing step. This study proposes a hybrid feature selection approach by integrating the Reptile Search Algorithm (RSA) with Levy Flight (LF), combining RSA's global optimization capabilities with LF's stochastic exploration efficiency. The resulting RSA-LF hybrid offers a gradient-free optimization strategy that effectively escapes local optima and enhances convergence. Experimental evaluation on five publicly available ID datasets demonstrates that the RSA-LF fusion consistently outperforms several standalone metaheuristic algorithms, including the original RSA, in terms of detection accuracy, feature reduction, and overall robustness. The results validate the proposed method as a superior solution for optimizing ML-based ID systems.

Keywords: Reptile Search Algorithm · Feature Selection · Intrusion Detection · Cybersecurity · Metaheuristic

1 Introduction

The deployment of Internet of Things (IoT), information technology and operational environments have given rise to new cybersecurity risks. These risks threaten the security of operational ecosystems, safety, and efficiency, posing a danger to physical and financial wellbeing (Yadav, 2023). The growth of cyber-attacks threat affects businesses, social networks, digital privacy, and precarious infrastructure. ID systems play a crucial role in enhancing the security of IT infrastructures. They are effective in detecting and countering attacks, providing protection against intrusive hackers (Khan, 2020).

An intrusion is characterized as unexpected activities that can harm the confidentiality, integrity, and availability of the network. To detect anomalies, IDs analyze network traffic and packet header fields to identify unusual patterns, thereby preventing or minimizing damage to the network or system (Alsoufi, 2021). The primary goal of an IDs

H. J. van den Herik et al. (Eds.): ICAART 2025, LNAI 16517, pp. 385–398, 2026.
https://doi.org/10.1007/978-3-032-25032-2_18

is to identify and avert unauthorized use and both any kind of network intrusions, hence boosting the overall security of the network.

IDs are typically deployed on network nodes or hosts and use a combination of signature-based and anomaly-based detection techniques. Signature-based detection involves comparing network traffic or system activity against a database of known attack patterns or signatures (Khraisat, 2019). Anomaly-based detection involves analysing network traffic or system activity to identify behaviours that deviate from normal patterns. IDs can be classified into two types: Network-based Intrusion Detection Systems (NIDS) and Host-based Intrusion Detection Systems (HIDS). NIDS analyse network traffic and look for patterns that indicate an intrusion attempt, while HIDS analyse activity on individual hosts, such as system calls and file access patterns.

ML is a subset of artificial intelligence that involves training algorithms to analyse and learn from data. ML algorithms can be used to classify data, make predictions, and identify patterns in large datasets (Liu, 2019; Al-Khateeb, 2021). These techniques are particularly useful for solving problems, where the solution is not well-defined or where there may be a large number of variables to consider. FS methods aim to exclude features that are unrelated and redundant while retaining the salient ones. This process not only enhances overall performance but also reduces data dimensionality, resulting in a lower cost of classification by decreasing the training time required to build less complex ML models (Al-Shourbaji, 2023). On the other hand, using all features in the model increases computational overhead, training and testing times, storage requirements, and error rate of ML model due to irrelevant features confusing with the relevant ones.

Metaheuristic (MH) algorithm, also known as a MH optimization algorithm, is a general FS algorithmic framework that can be used to find optimal solutions in a wide range of problem domains (Fong, 2016). These algorithms are designed to solve complex optimization problems, where traditional approaches may be insufficient. They are typically inspired by natural processes like evolution, swarm behaviour, and other complex systems (Xu, 2014). They use these models to develop search strategies that can efficiently navigate complex search spaces, avoiding local optima and finding globally optimal solutions. One of the key advantages of MHAs is that they are very flexible and can be adapted to solve a wide range of problems. They are also often faster and more efficient than traditional optimization techniques, making them an attractive option for large-scale optimization problems.

Some popular examples of MHAs include, genetic algorithms, Particle Swarm Optimization (PSO) (Kennedy, 1995), Grey Wolf Optimization (GWO) (Mirjalili, 2014), Multi-Verse Optimizer (MVO) (Mirjalili, 2016), Remora Optimization Algorithm (ROA) (Jia, 2021), genetic algorithm (Holland, 1992) and many others. These algorithms have been successfully applied to a diverse range of fields, including engineering, finance, operations research, and many others. Recently, Reptile Search Algorithm (RSA) (Abualigah, 2022), shows a great potential as a FS method and it can pick Optimal Feature Subset (OFS) effectively. This paper aims to investigate FS method using RSA for ID. To assess RSA's capabilities in determining OFS, five publicly available ID datasets and various quantitative evaluation measures are used. Four FS methods, PSO, GWO, MVO, and ROA, are implemented to compare RSA's efficiency in ID system.

The organization of remaining paper is as follows: Sect. 2, briefly describes the RSA and datasets used. Section 3, describes evaluations measurements to evaluate RSA method. Section 4 discusses the experimental analysis and results. Section 5 concludes the paper.

2 Methods and Materials

2.1 Reptile Search Algorithm (RSA)

RSA is a new method inspired by the hunting behaviour of Crocodiles proposed by (Abualigah, 2022) in 2022. A set of candidate N crocodiles $x_{i,j}$ each having random position in the search space are initialized as follows:

$$x_{i,j} = rand_{\in U(0,1)} * \left(UB_j - LB_j\right) + LB_j i \in \{1, \ldots, N\} \; and \; j \in \{1, \ldots, M\} \quad (1)$$

where LB_j and UB_j are the lowest and highest values of the jth feature, $rand_{\in U(0,1)}$ generates a number randomly in the range [0, 1] following a uniform distribution, and M is the feature dimensionality in the dataset.

For crocodile food search, two distinct strategies, exploration and exploitation, are employed. These strategies are sequentially implemented over four stages within the maximum iteration limit. In the initial half of these stages, the algorithm leverages the crocodile's encircling behaviour, incorporating both high and belly walking movements, to facilitate search space exploration. It can be formulated as:

$$x_{i,j}(g+1) = \begin{cases} \left[-n_{i,j}(g).\gamma.Best_j(g)\right] - \left[rand_{\in[1,N]}.R_{i,j}(g)\right], g \leq \frac{T}{4} \\ ES(g).Best_j(g).x_{(rand_{\in[1,N]},j)}, g \leq \frac{2T}{4} \; and \; g > \frac{T}{4} \end{cases} \quad (2)$$

where, for gth iteration, the best position for gth feature is $Best_j(g)$, the hunting operator ni, j is calculated as in Eq. (3), and the parameter for Evolutionary Sense $ES(g)$ is calculated as in Eq. (7). ES parameter decreases over the iterations between 2 to −2. Finally, the exploration accuracy is controlled by setting parameter γ as 0.1. The search region is continuously decreased by parameter Ri, j, calculated as in Eq. (6). A crocodile is randomly selected by $rand \in 1, N$ to update position towards best position.

$$n_{i,j} = Best_j(g) \times P_{i,j} \quad (3)$$

The normalized difference $P_{i,j}$ between i^{th} crocodile's the ith feature position and the crocodile's average position. It is computed as:

$$P_{i,j} = \theta + \frac{x_{i,j} - \mu(x_i)}{Best_j(g) \times \left(UB_j - LB_j\right) + \epsilon} \quad (4)$$

where the sensitive of the exploration is controlled by the parameter θ, while ϵ maintains the floor value.

$$\mu(x_i) = \frac{1}{n}\sum_{j=1}^{n} x_{i,j} \quad (5)$$

$$R_{i,j} = \frac{Best_j(g) - x_{(rand_{\in[1,N]},j)}}{Best_j(g) + \epsilon} \tag{6}$$

$$ES(g) = 2 \times rand_{\in\{-1,1\}} \times \left(1 - \frac{1}{T}\right) \tag{7}$$

where the ES is scaled by 2 to provide values in the range of [0, 2], and $rand_{\in\{-1,1\}}$ is a random integer between [−1, 1].

The search space is completely exploited by implementing hunting coordination and cooperation of crocodiles. It can be formulated as:

$$x_{i,j}(g+1) = \begin{cases} rand_{\in[-1,1]}.Best_j(g).P_{i,j}(g), g \leq \frac{3T}{4} \text{ and } g > \frac{2T}{4} \\ \left[\epsilon.Best_j(g).n_{i,j}(g)\right] - \left[rand_{\in[-1,1]}.R_{i,j}(g)\right], g \leq T \text{ and } g > \frac{3T}{4} \end{cases} \tag{8}$$

Although RSA is effective in global optimization, it can face challenges such as premature convergence and insufficient exploration in high-dimensional or complex feature spaces. To mitigate these issues, Levy Flight (LF) is integrated into RSA. LF is a stochastic process characterized by step lengths drawn from a heavy-tailed probability distribution:

$$Levy(\lambda) \sim s^{-\lambda}, 1 < \lambda \leq 3 \tag{9}$$

This property allows for occasional long-distance moves, enabling the algorithm to jump out of local optima and explore unexplored regions of the search space. By incorporating LF into RSA's position update mechanism, the hybrid algorithm gains a better balance between exploration and exploitation. Mathematically, a Levy-based position update can be expressed as:

$$X_{new} = X_{current} + \alpha \cdot Levy(\lambda) \tag{10}$$

where α is a step size scaling factor. This fusion enhances the diversity of candidate solutions and improves convergence reliability. As a result, RSA-LF exhibits superior performance in feature selection for intrusion detection, achieving better accuracy, faster convergence, and improved stability compared to standard RSA and other metaheuristic algorithms.

2.2 Datasets

Five openly available datasets commonly utilized for intrusion detection (ID) assessment are chosen to evaluate the efficiency of MHAs. These datasets, widely acknowledged in the ID community (Elgamal, 2022), (Ekinci and Izci, 2022)], encompass Knowledge Discovery and Data Mining Cup 1999 (KDD-CUP99) (Tavallaee, 2009), Network Security Laboratory KDD (NSL-KDD) (Sapre, 2019), University of New South Wales - Network-Based 15 (UNSW-NB15) (Shiravi, 2012), Canadian Institute for Cybersecurity - Intrusion Detection Evaluation Dataset 2017 (CIC-IDS2017) and CIC-IDS2018 (Sharafaldin, 2018).

Table 1 provides a detailed overview of these datasets, arranged in increasing order of number of records. These characteristics are essential for understanding the dataset's complexity and scale, which are critical factors in assessing intrusion detection techniques. Due to the computational demands of iterative FS methods such as MH, FS is evaluated using 10% examples of each ID dataset. Importantly, this subsampling retains the original balance between normal activities and network attacks, ensuring a representative assessment of MHAs' performance.

Table 1. Characteristics of intrusion detection datasets.

Study	Dataset	No. of features	No. of records
Sapre et al. (2019)	NSL-KDD	43	125,973
Tavallaee et al. (2009)	KDD-CUP99	43	494,020
Shiravi et al. (2012)	UNSW-NB15	49	540044
Sharafaldin et al. (2018)	CIC-IDS2018	80	1,048,575
Sharafaldin et al. (2018)	CIC-IDS2017	78	2,827,876

3 Evaluation Metrics

Intrusion detection using reduced features generated by MHAs can be trained by ML models. These models can be assessed using various evaluation measures are used to determine how well an ID system is performing. Some commonly used evaluation measures in the context of ID are as follows:

True Positive (TP): It represents the number of instances where the ID system correctly identified an intrusion or attack.
True Negative (TN): It represents the number of instances where the system correctly identified non-intrusive or normal network behavior.
False Positive (FP): It occurs when the system incorrectly flags normal network behaviour as an intrusion or attack.
False Negative (FN): It occurs when the system fails to detect an actual intrusion or attack, labelling it as normal behaviour.
Accuracy (AC): Accuracy measures of the overall correctness of the ID system and is calculated as follows:

$$AC = \frac{TP + TN}{TP + TN + FN + FP} \tag{11}$$

ID system, achieving a balance between the events accurately flagged as an intrusion and detecting most of the actual intrusions. Depending on the specific requirements and priorities of the ID system, different evaluation measures may be emphasized.

4 Experimental Results

Evaluation of RSA's ability for identifying OFS is conducted using five intrusion detection datasets, comparing its performance with other MHAs, including PSO (Kennedy, 1995), GWO (Mirjalili, 2014), MVO (Mirjalili, 2016), and ROA (Jia, 2021).

4.1 Experimental Setup

For this study, we implemented all the methods in Python and executed them on a computer with an Intel i7 10th generation processor, 32 GB of RAM, and running the Windows 10 system. Table 2 outlines parameters of MHAs used based on the original articles that reported them.

Table 2. Parameters values of MHAs for optimization.

Method	Parameters
Common settings	No. search agents = 32, no. of runs = 20, no. of iterations = 100, UB & LB based features
PSO	$c_1 = c_2 = 2$, $w_{min} = 0.1$ and $w_{max} = 0.9$
GWO	$C = rand_{\in\{0,2\}}$, α & A linearly decrease in range [2, 0] & [1, −1]
MVO	$WEP_{max} = 1$, $WEP_{min} = 0.2$, α decreases from 2 to 0 and p = 6
ROA	$ld = 1$ and $\beta = 2$
RSA	$\gamma = 0.9$, $\theta = 0.5$

This setup ensures a fair and consistent evaluation of the MHA performance across the all datasets.

4.2 Results and Discussion

The selected salient features of the proposed RSA and other MHAs are quantitatively evaluated using the datasets in Table 1.

Table 3 presents the mean and standard deviation (SD) of the fitness values achieved by five competing MHAs and the proposed RSA-LF, across five ID datasets. While the original RSA algorithm already demonstrated superior optimization capability (Al-Khateeb and Douik, 2025), achieving the lowest mean fitness values among all standalone MHAs, the RSA-LF hybrid further enhanced performance across all datasets. Specifically, RSA-LF achieved the smallest mean fitness in every dataset, indicating more optimal feature subsets were consistently selected. Additionally, RSA-LF also exhibited the lowest SD values in all cases, suggesting improved stability and robustness across multiple runs. The fusion of RSA with LF not only improves the convergence behavior of the original RSA but also enhances exploration capabilities, enabling the hybrid approach to avoid local optima more effectively.

Table 3. Fitness for all datasets of all MHAs.

Method	Stat	Dataset				
		KDD-CUP99	NSL-KDD	UNSW-NB15	CIC-IDS2017	CIC-IDS2018
PSO	Mean	0.0335	0.0602	0.0372	0.0136	0.034

(continued)

Table 3. (*continued*)

Method	Stat	Dataset				
		KDD-CUP99	NSL-KDD	UNSW-NB15	CIC-IDS2017	CIC-IDS2018
	SD	0.0096	0.0081	0.0075	0.0060	0.0072
GWO	Mean	0.0220	0.0746	0.0318	0.0261	0.0321
	SD	0.0093	0.0102	0.0057	0.0084	0.0094
MVO	Mean	0.0199	0.0687	0.0354	0.0250	0.0402
	SD	0.0073	0.0092	0.0052	0.0066	0.0093
ROA	Mean	0.0154	0.0612	0.0320	0.0187	0.0323
	SD	0.0078	0.0093	0.0071	0.0091	0.0091
RSA	Mean	0.0094	0.0593	0.0308	0.0131	0.0303
	SD	0.0066	0.0088	0.0049	0.0082	0.0061
RSA-LF	Mean	0.0089	0.0561	0.0291	0.0123	0.0286
	SD	0.0058	0.0082	0.0031	0.0078	0.0055

Table 4 reports the mean and SD of the number of selected features (OFS) by various MHAs across five benchmark intrusion detection datasets. The RSA method demonstrated high efficiency in feature selection by achieving the fewest mean OFS in four out of five datasets, sharing the lowest value with ROA for KDD-CUP99. Moreover, RSA consistently showed lower variability in selected features, as reflected by the lowest SD values in three datasets. However, the proposed RSA-LF hybrid further improved these results by reducing the average number of selected features across all datasets, thereby emphasizing its superior feature reduction capability. RSA-LF also achieved lower or comparable SD values in each dataset, indicating robust and stable feature selection behavior. Notably, RSA-LF maintained the same minimal feature count as RSA in CIC-IDS2017, but with equal SD, and improved further in datasets like CIC-IDS2018 by selecting fewer features with less variability. These results reinforce the conclusion that RSA-LF not only achieves compact and efficient feature subsets but also maintains stability across different datasets, making it the most effective and reliable FS method among all MHAs evaluated.

Table 4. Number of OFS for all datasets of all MHAs.

Method	Stat	Dataset				
		KDD-CUP99	NSL-KDD	UNSW-NB15	CIC-IDS2017	CIC-IDS2018
PSO	Mean	40	38	33	23	45
	SD	5	4	10	3	10
GWO	Mean	35	34	29	63	49
	SD	9	6	9	6	10

(*continued*)

Table 4. (*continued*)

Method	Stat	Dataset				
		KDD-CUP99	NSL-KDD	UNSW-NB15	CIC-IDS2017	CIC-IDS2018
MVO	Mean	41	39	37	49	71
	SD	6	5	4	7	9
ROA	Mean	22	37	23	25	55
	SD	7	5	6	7	8
RSA	Mean	22	31	25	21	43
	SD	3	3	4	5	8
RSA-LF	Mean	21	28	23	21	37
	SD	4	3	5	5	7

Table 5 presents the mean and SD of classification accuracies across five intrusion detection datasets. While the original RSA already delivered strong performance, achieving the highest average accuracy on four datasets and lowest SD on three, the proposed RSA-LF hybrid further improved results. RSA-LF attained the highest mean accuracy on all datasets, including 0.9802 on UNSW-NB15 and 0.9885 on CIC-IDS2018, confirming its superior optimization capability. It also showed remarkable stability, with the lowest SDs for UNSW-NB15 and CIC-IDS2017, and competitive values elsewhere. These results clearly demonstrate that RSA-LF offers the best balance of accuracy and reliability, outperforming all other MHAs in optimizing intrusion detection systems.

Table 5. Accuracy for all datasets of all MHAs.

Method	Stat	Dataset				
		KDD-CUP99	NSL-KDD	UNSW-NB15	CIC-IDS2017	CIC-IDS2018
PSO	Mean	0.9756	0.9481	0.9702	0.9917	0.9762
	SD	0.0062	0.0059	0.0051	0.0058	0.0173
GWO	Mean	0.9860	0.9534	0.9747	0.9884	0.9812
	SD	0.0061	0.1068	0.0051	0.0052	0.019
MVO	Mean	0.9895	0.9398	0.9729	0.9863	0.9761
	SD	0.0032	0.0065	0.0056	0.0058	0.0184
ROA	Mean	0.9957	0.9488	0.9743	0.9906	0.9823
	SD	0.0039	0.0068	0.0052	0.0055	0.0282
RSA	Mean	0.9970	0.9528	0.9753	0.9933	0.9842
	SD	0.0036	0.0052	0.0134	0.0059	0.0072
RSA-LF	Mean	0.99701	0.95921	0.98023	0.99521	0.9885
	SD	0.0021	0.0051	0.0031	0.0031	0.0103

Figure 1 illustrates the convergence behavior of all MHAs over 20 independent runs, following the recommendation of Al-Shourbaji, et al. (2023). Among all methods, the proposed RSA-LF demonstrated the fastest and most stable convergence across all datasets. The hybrid RSA-LF enhances exploration capabilities, allowing the algorithm to efficiently escape local optima and explore diverse regions of the search space. This led to quicker convergence toward optimal solutions compared to standalone MHAs.

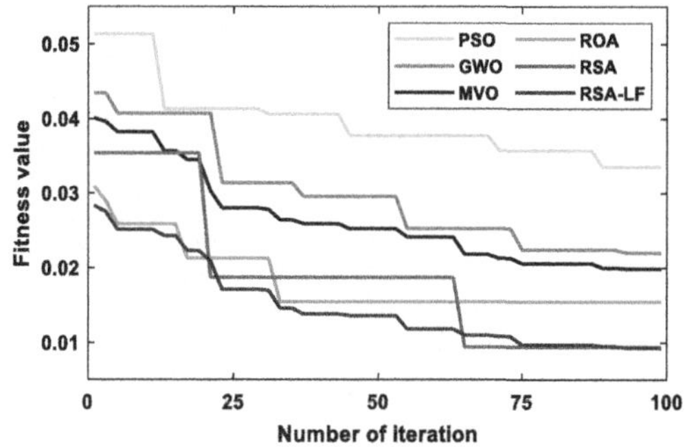

(a) KDD-CUP99

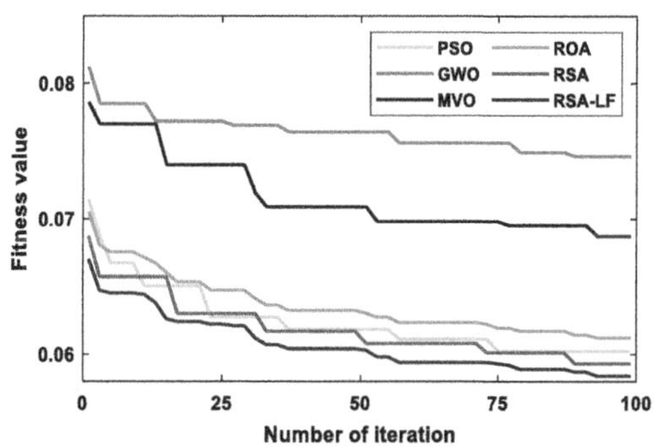

(b) NSL-KDD

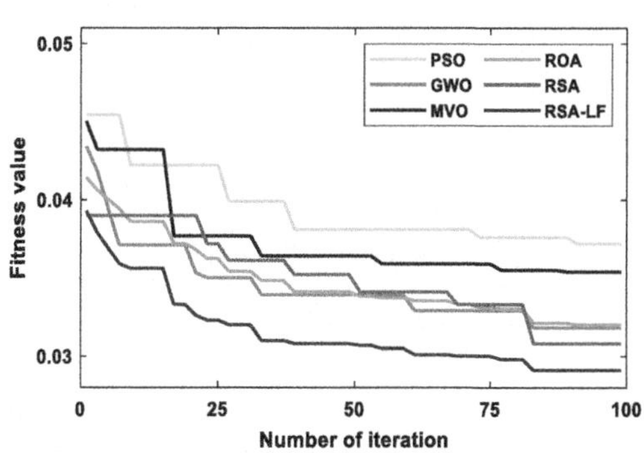

(c) UNSW-NB15

Fig. 1. Convergence behaviour of all MHAs for five ID datasets.

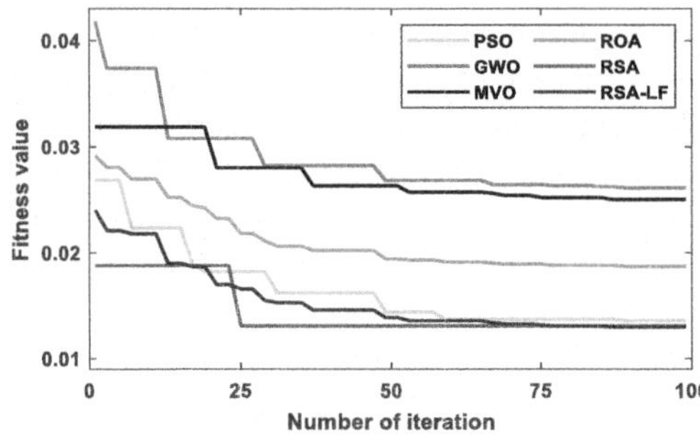

(d) CIC-IDS2017

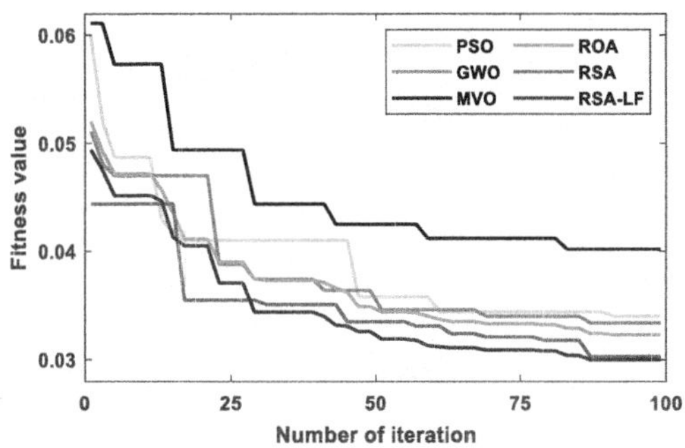

(e) CIC-IDS2018

Fig. 1. *(continued)*

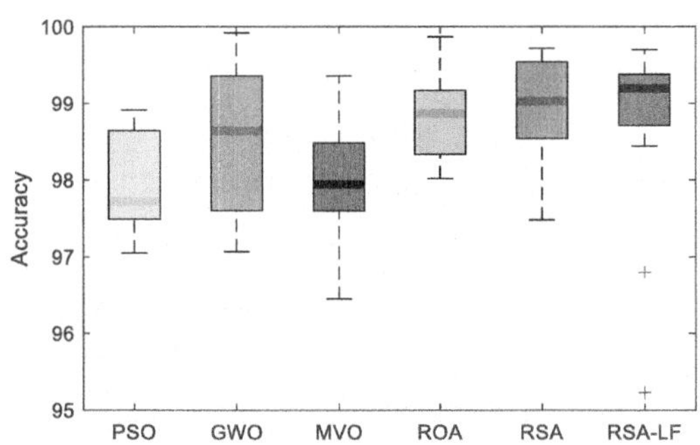

(e) CIC-IDS2018

Fig. 2. *(continued)*

Figure 2 presents boxplots illustrating the distribution of classification accuracy for various MHAs across five datasets. The plots depict the lower, middle (median), and upper quartile ranges, providing insight into both performance and variability. The RSA-LF hybrid method consistently achieved the highest median accuracy in four out of five

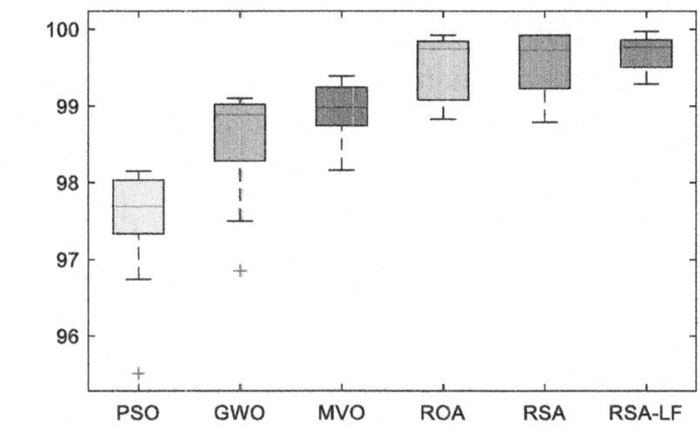

(a) KDD-CUP99

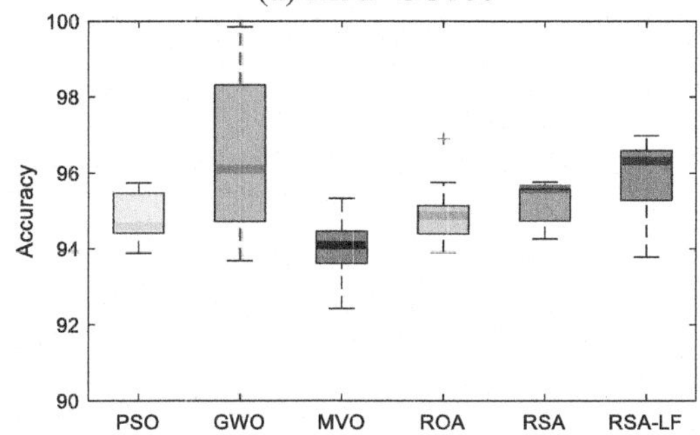

(b) NSL-KDD

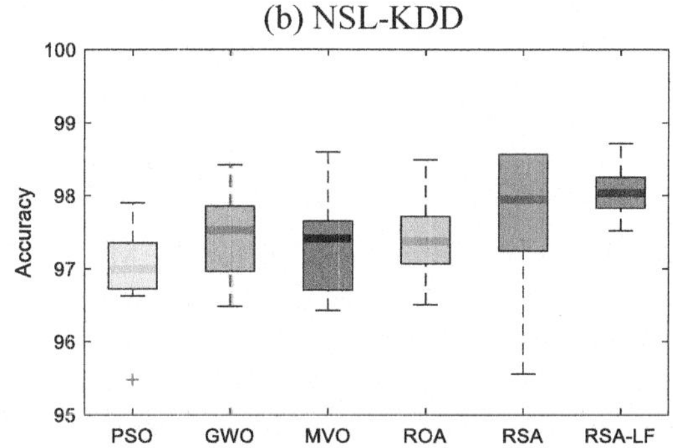

(c) UNSW-NB15

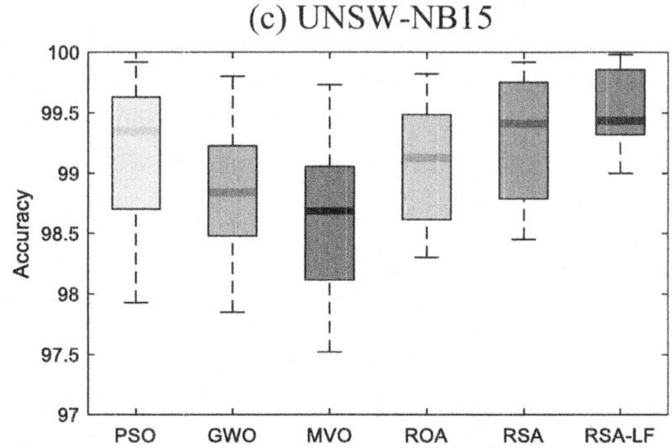

(d) CIC-IDS2017

Fig. 2. Boxplots of accuracy of all MHAs for ID datasets.

datasets, highlighting its reliability and superior performance. For the NSL-KDD dataset, GWO showed a slightly higher median; however, RSA-LF remained competitive with a narrower interquartile range. Moreover, RSA-LF attained the highest upper-quartile accuracy in four datasets, indicating that it frequently achieved top-tier results across runs. These findings further confirm RSA-LF's robustness and consistency as a feature selection strategy for ID.

Table 6 presents the Friedman ranking of different MHAs based on their accuracies across five ID datasets. The RSA-LF achieved the best performance with an average rank of 1.0, consistently outperforming other MHAs on all datasets. The RSA followed with an average rank of 1.8, confirming its strong performance. In contrast, MVO and PSO showed the weakest results with average ranks of 5.4 and 5.0, respectively. These rankings highlight the superiority of RSA-LF in achieving high and stable accuracy across diverse datasets.

Table 6. Friedman ranking based on accuracies for all datasets of all MHAs.

Method	Dataset					Avg. Rank
	KDD-CUP99	NSL-KDD	UNSW-NB15	CIC-IDS2017	CIC-IDS2018	
PSO	6	5	6	3	5	5
GWO	5	2	3	5	4	3.8
MVO	4	6	5	6	6	5.4
ROA	2	4	2	4	3	3
RSA	1	3	1	2	2	1.8
RSA-LF	1	1	1	1	1	1

Finding the right number of features needed for the ML task is one of the main goals of an effective FS approach. This helps to avoid selecting either too many or too few features. In a FS process, for instance, picking too many features raises the possibility of including unnecessary or redundant features, which may result in a decline in prediction accuracy. However, the RSA considered that the number of OFS in their fitness function showed better performance, and the number of the selected features were fewer Exploration of the search space and exploitation of the best solutions found are two conflicting objectives that must be taken into account when using MHAs. From the results provided above, RSA demonstrated a better performance in balancing exploration and exploitation factors with better convergence speed as well.

5 Conclusion and Future Works

This study proposed a robust and efficient feature selection (FS) method by hybridizing the Reptile Search Algorithm (RSA) with Lévy Flight (LF), aiming to enhance the performance of machine learning-based intrusion detection (ID) systems. The RSA-LF approach leverages the gradient-free global optimization capability of RSA and strengthens its exploratory power through the stochastic behavior of LF. Extensive experiments conducted on five publicly available ID datasets demonstrated that RSA-LF consistently outperformed several well-established metaheuristic algorithms, including PSO, GWO, MVO, ROA, and even the standalone RSA, across various evaluation metrics such as fitness value, accuracy, stability, and feature reduction. The proposed hybrid method not only achieved the highest classification accuracy but also demonstrated exceptional convergence behavior and robustness in selecting compact and effective feature subsets. These findings establish RSA-LF as a highly competitive and reliable FS technique for cybersecurity applications.

For future work, we plan to explore the application of RSA-LF in other domains such as network attack detection, IoT security, and malware classification. Additionally, the framework may be extended by integrating RSA-LF with deep learning models or other optimization techniques to further enhance its adaptability and scalability. These directions may position RSA-LF as a cornerstone method in both security and intelligent optimization research.

References

Yadav, A., Noori, M.T., Biswas, A., Min, B.: A concise review on the recent developments in the internet of things (IoT)-based smart aquaculture practices. Rev. Fisheries Sci. Aquaculture **31**(1), 103–118 (2023)

Khan, S.K., Shiwakoti, N., Stasinopoulos, P., Chen, Y.: Cyber-attacks in the next-generation cars, mitigation techniques, anticipated readiness and future directions. Accid. Anal. Prev. **148**, 105837 (2020)

Alsoufi, M.A., et al.: Anomaly-based intrusion detection systems in IoT using deep learning: a systematic literature review. Appl. Sci. **11**(18), 8383 (2021)

Khraisat, A., Gondal, I., Vamplew, P., Kamruzzaman, J.: Survey of intrusion detection systems: techniques, datasets and challenges. Cybersecurity **2**(1), 1–22 (2019)

Liu, H., Lang, B.: Machine learning and deep learning methods for intrusion detection systems: a survey. Appl. Sci. **9**(20), 4396 (2019)

Al-Khateeb, M.O., Hassan, M.A., Al-Shourbaji, I., Aliero, M.S.: Intelligent data analysis approaches for knowledge discovery: survey and challenges. Ilkogretim Online **20**(5) (2021)

Al-Shourbaji, I., et al.: Artificial ecosystem-based optimization with dwarf mongoose optimization for feature selection and global optimization problems. Int. J. Comput. Intell. Syst. **16**(1), 1–24 (2023)

Al-Khateeb, M.O., Douik, A.: Reptile search algorithm based feature selection approach for intrusion detection. In: Proceedings of the 17th International Conference on Agents and Artificial Intelligence, vol. 3, pp. 639–645 (2025). ISBN 978-989-758-737-5, ISSN 2184-433X

Fong, S., Wang, X., Xu, Q., Wong, R., Fiaidhi, J., Mohammed, S.: Recent advances in metaheuristic algorithms: does the Makara dragon exist? J. Supercomput. **72**, 3764–3786 (2016)

Xu, J., Zhang, J.: Exploration-exploitation tradeoffs in metaheuristics: survey and analysis. In: Proceedings of the 33rd Chinese Control Conference, pp. 8633–8638. IEEE (2014)

Kennedy, J., Eberhart, R.: Particle swarm optimization. In: Proceedings of ICNN 1995-International Conference on Neural Networks, vol. 4, pp. 1942–1948. IEEE (1995)

Mirjalili, S., Mirjalili, S.M., Lewis, A.: Grey wolf optimizer. Adv. Eng. Softw. **69**, 46–61 (2014)

Mirjalili, S., Mirjalili, S.M., Hatamlou, A.: Multi-verse optimizer: a nature-inspired algorithm for global optimization. Neural Comput. Appl. **27**, 495–513 (2016)

Jia, H., Peng, X., Lang, C.: Remora optimization algorithm. Expert Syst. Appl. **185**, 115665 (2021)

Holland, J.H.: Genetic algorithms. Sci. Am. **267**(1), 66–73 (1992)

Abualigah, L., Abd Elaziz, M., Sumari, P., Geem, Z.W., Gandomi, A.H.: Reptile Search Algorithm (RSA): a nature-inspired meta-heuristic optimizer. Expert Syst. Appl. **191**, 116158 (2022)

Elgamal, Z., Sabri, A.Q.M., Tubishat, M., Tbaishat, D., Makhadmeh, S.N., et al.: Improved reptile search optimization algorithm using Chaotic map and Simulated annealing for feature selection in medical field. IEEE Access **10**, 51428–51446 (2022)

Ekinci, S., Izci, D.: Enhanced reptile search algorithm with Lévy flight for vehicle cruise control system design. Evol. Intel. **2022**, 1–13 (2022)

Tavallaee, M., Bagheri, E., Lu, W., Ghorbani, A.A.: A detailed analysis of the KDD CUP 99 data set. In: Proceedings of IEEE Conference on Symposium on Computational Intelligence for Security and Defense, Ottawa, ON, Canada, pp. 1–6 (2009)

Sapre, S., Ahmadi, P., Islam, K.: A robust comparison of the KDDCup99 and NSL-KDD IoT network intrusion detection datasets through various machine learning algorithms, arXiv preprint, pp. 1–8 (2019)

Shiravi, A., Shiravi, H., Tavallaee, M., Ghorbani, A.A.: Toward developing a systematic approach to generate benchmark datasets for intrusion detection. Comput. Secur. **31**(3), 357–374 (2012)

Sharafaldin, I., Lashkari, A.H., Ghorbani, A.A.: Toward generating a new intrusion detection dataset and intrusion traffic characterization. In: Proceedings of the 4th International. Conference on Information Systems. Security and Privacy, Funchal, Portugal, vol. 1, no. 2, 108–116 (2018)

Generative Approaches to Emotion Expression in 3D Human Pose Modeling

Petru-Liviu Bouruc[1], Ciprian Paduraru[1(✉)], and Alin Stefanescu[1,2]

[1] Department of Computer Science, University of Bucharest, Bucharest, Romania
ciprian.paduraru2009@gmail.com

[2] Institute for Logic and Data Science, Bucharest, Romania

Abstract. Capturing and synthesizing human emotional expression through full-body 3D models presents a persistent challenge across sectors such as virtual reality, gaming, robotics, and digital healthcare. In this paper, we introduce a novel dataset composed of high-quality videos featuring individuals performing a range of six fundamental emotions: anger, happiness, surprise, disgust, sadness, and fear. These recordings are processed into 3D meshes using advanced body modeling tools, enabling the study and replication of emotional body language at scale. To complement the dataset, we integrated a generative framework that modifies existing 3D body meshes by sampling a latent pose space, enabling the creation of expressive variations tied to emotional states. By combining data-driven modeling and generative AI, our work contributes to the advancement of more realistic and emotionally expressive digital characters.

Keywords: Generative AI · Body Emotions · Parametric Models · Animations

1 Introduction

Recently, the use of 3D representations of humans has expanded significantly in a variety of industries, including gaming, film production, healthcare, virtual reality and robotics [3, 15]. A persistent challenge in all of these fields is the difficulty of accurately capturing and replicating the complex emotional expressions inherent in human behavior. Whether creating non-player characters (NPCs) in video games, virtual avatars on social platforms or patient models in medical simulations, the ability to convey realistic and contextually appropriate emotional states is crucial when it comes to increasing user engagement and creating effective, immersive experiences.

In addition to the linguistic and behavioral capabilities of intelligent agents, another important aspect is the visual component. Whether in the context of a video game, a video avatar on a social platform or a medical simulation, it is important that the agent not only responds appropriately, but also looks and behaves in a way that mirrors human actions and emotions. Researchers have long strived to replicate the realism and emotional depth of humans in 3D representations.

So, replicating the realism and emotional depth of humans in 3D representations remains a major challenge in computer graphics and human modeling. This work addresses that challenge by proposing a novel framework for enhancing the emotional

H. J. van den Herik et al. (Eds.): ICAART 2025, LNAI 16517, pp. 399–414, 2026.
https://doi.org/10.1007/978-3-032-25032-2_19

expressiveness of 3D human models. Our goal is to generate 3D body representations that can accurately mimic real-life emotional expressions. To achieve this, we first needed access to a dataset expressive enough to capture full-body poses corresponding to a variety of emotions.

Dataset. While several datasets are available, many fall short: some only focus on facial expressions as seen in [17,26] and [29], while others emphasize actions rather than emotions, such as clapping in [29].

According to our research, there is no existing public dataset that fulfills the following three requirements:

- Captures the entire human posture. Most of the existing datasets only cover parts of the body (e.g. the face). When people express emotions, they use different parts of their body.
- Classifies and captures specific groups of emotions for the same human person and body. Existing datasets provide emotions distributed across different body shapes, which limits the understanding of how a given individual can mime different targets.
- Captured the entire expression cycle of a particular emotion, starting from the neutral point, through the actual expression, to the renewed neutral point. This is especially necessary to understand how people can transition between these expressions in terms of their body language and timing.

To overcome these limitations, we developed a unique dataset that captures full-body postures of individuals expressing six specific emotions (anger, happiness, surprise, disgust, sadness, and fear), along with transitions from a relaxed (neutral) posture to each emotional state. Each emotion is represented by multiple video sequences to capture the inherent variability of human emotional expression. This dataset enables the modeling of natural and dynamic emotional expressions and supports the creation of expressive 3D meshes. [18]

Building on this dataset, we assembled a pipeline by adapting and integrating several state-of-the-art methods for processing poses and meshes in both 2D and 3D space. This pipeline serves as the foundation for our generative model.

Finally, we introduced a novel generative process that takes as input any 3D body mesh (even one not present in the dataset) and outputs multiple variations of that body mesh, each modified to express one of the six emotions or to retain its original pose.

The methods, dataset, and experiments are published as open source on https://github.com/unibuc-cs/3DHumanEmotionsGenerator for further research in academia and industry.

2 Related Work

The digital representation of human emotions has seen significant progress over the past decades. Early research, such as [27], focused on building chatterbots and NPCs capable of engaging in human-like conversations. More recently, advances in deep learning and generative AI have expanded these capabilities. For example, [13] and [19] trained AI models inspired by neuroscience and designed interactive environments for conversational agents. Current trends emphasize large language models (LLMs), which excel at textual understanding and emotional tone in dialogue. However, these systems still lack a corresponding visual representation of emotional expression, particularly in terms of full-body dynamics. Our work addresses this gap by providing a framework that visually complements the emotional depth expressed through language-based AI systems. Parallel to these developments, 3D human modeling has matured significantly. Early works [12,21] and that of [2] laid the foundation, with SCAPE [2] offering a detailed model for representing human bodies in 3D. SCAPE introduced shape- and posture-dependent deformations using principal component analysis (PCA), which was later enhanced in Blend-SCAPE [8] for smoother transitions. These developments paved the way for widely used models like SMPL [16] and SMPLify [4], which simplified the process of estimating body pose and shape from visual input. In recent years, alternative methods such as diffusion-based models have emerged. ScoreHMR [25] for example, applies diffusion models and score-based learning to improve 3D mesh recovery. It iteratively refines noisy mesh estimates using denoising techniques, incorporating motion and multi-view cues for improved accuracy in dynamic scenes. Pose estimation has also seen advances, with tools like OpenPose [6,30] enabling accurate multi-person and full-body keypoint detection. OpenPose uses a two-stage CNN architecture to generate confidence maps and part affinity fields (PAFs), linking keypoints into coherent skeletons for body, hands, and face.

Despite these advances, the full-body expression of emotions remains underexplored. Most current models focus on physical actions or facial expressions in isolation, without capturing the subtle body postures and transitions associated with different emotional states. Moreover, publicly available datasets often lack full-body emotional annotations or dynamic transitions between emotional and neutral states. Our work contributes to this landscape by introducing a new dataset specifically designed for full-body emotional expression, including transitions from neutral to emotional states. We integrate and adapt several of the aforementioned methods to develop a unified generative system that produces emotionally expressive 3D body meshes, helping bridge the gap between conversational AI and embodied emotion modeling.

3 Theoretical Foundations

3.1 Representation of the Human Body

The SMPL model [16] represents the human body as a 3D mesh composed of approximately 6,890 vertices, which translates to around 20,670 floating-point values describing the full body geometry. The goal of SMPL is to define a function $M(\bar{\beta},\bar{\theta})$, where β stands for the shape parameters and θ for the pose parameters. This function maps the input parameters to realistic human body meshes, ensuring that the generated outputs reflect valid and plausible body configurations. The strength of the model lies in its ability to learn and encode complex variations in both shape and pose, enabling compact yet expressive parameterization of human forms. And this is the final formula for the SMPL model:

$$M(\bar{\theta},\bar{\beta}) = W\left(\underbrace{T_P(\bar{\beta},\bar{\theta})}_{\text{Deformed template mesh}}, \underbrace{J(\bar{\theta})}_{\text{Joints}}, \underbrace{\mathscr{W}}_{\text{Skinning weights}}, \bar{\theta} \right) \tag{1}$$

where

$$T_P(\bar{\beta},\bar{\theta}) = \bar{T} + \underbrace{B_S(\bar{\beta})}_{\text{Shape deformation}} + \underbrace{B_P(\bar{\theta})}_{\text{Pose deformation}}$$

- $\bar{T}$ - the average template mesh;
- $J(\bar{\theta})$ - the 3D positions of the skeletal joints that control posture, based on the pose parameters $\bar{\theta}$;
- $\mathscr{W}$ - parameters learned from data (training was performed on 1786 3D scans of humans in different poses)
- W - Linear Blend Skinning (LBS) function used to deform the mesh (the 3D human body) based on joint rotations and skinning weights.

To enhance the usability of the SMPL model, a key task is to extract 3D meshes directly from images without relying on additional inputs such as camera parameters or pose annotations. In our work, we adopt the approach from **SMPLify** [4], which aligns 3D body models to 2D joint detections—typically obtained using methods like OpenPose [6]—by minimizing an objective function. The goal is to adjust the SMPL model's parameters so that its 3D joint projections align with the estimated 2D joint positions. A simpler, initial formular for SMPLify is:

$$E_{joints}(\bar{\theta},\bar{\beta}) = \sum_i w_i \left\| \prod (J_i(\bar{\theta},\bar{\beta}) - \hat{J}_i \right\|^2 \tag{2}$$

where

- $J_i(\bar{\theta},\bar{\beta}) \in \mathbb{R}^3$ - the 3D position of joint i, computed by the SMPL model for given pose parameters θ and shape parameters β;
- $\hat{J}_i \in \mathbb{R}^2$ - the detected 2D position of joint i in the image, obtained using OpenPose;
- $\prod()$ - the projection function from 3D to 2D based on the camera parameters;
- w_i - weight of each joint provided by the pose detector.

One of the main challenges in this process is self-penetration, where body parts intersect unrealistically. SMPLify addresses this by introducing penalties for self-intersections, discouraging such overlaps during optimization. Another challenge is depth ambiguity, which SMPLify mitigates by incorporating pose priors learned from SMPL training data. These priors penalize implausible poses, thereby improving estimation accuracy. An example from our pipeline is shown in Fig. 2. Further implementation details can be found in [4].

The next stage of our pipeline uses **SMPL-X** [20], a parametric model that extends SMPL to include detailed facial expressions and hand poses, crucial for capturing non-verbal human communication. SMPL-X integrates the FLAME [5] and MANO [23] models, which are based on 3,800 head scans and 1,500 hand scans, respectively. PCA is applied to extract key shape and motion variations, and the number of joints increases from 23 to 54 to reflect the added complexity.

To further enhance realism, SMPL-X distinguishes between male, female, and gender-neutral bodies. Its optimization framework, SMPLify-X [20], introduces VPoser, a variational autoencoder for plausible pose generation along, with self-intersection penalties and improved gender classification. These enhancements build on the foundation presented in our earlier work [18].

3.2 Generative Model

To generate realistic and diverse body postures, we rely on VPoser [20]. This representation allows for smooth reconstruction of natural 3D poses while reducing physically implausible configurations. Alignment between the reconstructed 3D joints and 2D keypoints from OpenPose is achieved by minimizing a projection-based function.

VPoser serves as a learned pose prior, trained on around one million MoSh-processed samples derived from datasets like CMU, Human3.6M [9], and PosePrior [1]. Poses are encoded using rotation matrices to ensure smooth transformations. This setup supports applications in animation, virtual environments, and other domains requiring physically coherent motion.

4 Methods

This section outlines the methodology established in our earlier work [18]. We first describe the creation of a custom dataset designed to capture expressive full-body motion. Next, we detail the processing pipeline used to extract individual video frames, perform skeletal analysis, and fit SMPL-X meshes to represent each subject accurately. Finally, we present an extended generative model capable of producing diverse 3D body expressions, starting from any given mesh input.

4.1 Data Collection

We developed a custom dataset in collaboration with students and professionals from the University of Bucharest, aimed at capturing full-body emotional expressions [18]. Participants recorded short, around 8-second clips displaying one of six basic emotions: anger, happiness, surprise, disgust, sadness, or fear. Each video captures the full emotional progression, from a neutral state to peak emotion and back. For each emotion and participant, 10 videos were collected to ensure sufficient variability. To facilitate high-quality 3D mesh extraction, recordings followed clear visual standards: Full HD resolution and simple, often monochrome, backgrounds to reduce visual noise. This enabled accurate reconstruction of expressive SMPL-X meshes directly from the footage.

A key strength of this dataset is its natural variability. Participants expressed emotions in their personal styles, resulting in a rich set of motion patterns. This diversity enhances the expressiveness and realism of the generated embeddings, which is especially valuable for applications in animation, gaming, and VR. The full emotional arc present in each clip supports lifelike, dynamic character animations suitable for production environments such as Unreal Engine (Fig. 1).

4.2 Extracting Meshes

After collecting the video samples, the next objective was to extract 3D meshes corresponding to the various emotional poses. We selected SMPLify-X [20] as the core framework due to its ability to model not only the body but also detailed facial and hand expressions. Specifically, we reused and adapted the implementations of SMPLpix

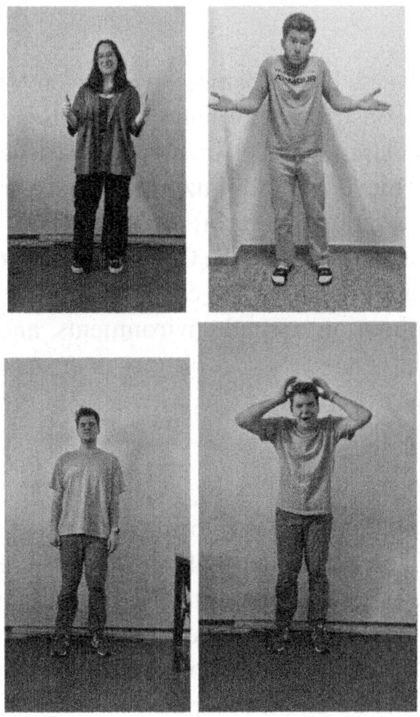

Fig. 1. Snapshots of people and reactions from our data set. In order of emotions shown such as happy, surprised, neutral and scared [18].

and SMPLify-X [22] to suit the requirements of our dataset [18]. An overview of the resulting pipeline is illustrated in Fig. 2.

Through iterative experimentation, we introduced an intermediate step in the pipeline that leverages OpenPose [6,7,24,28] for skeletal detection. This tool was chosen for its ability to accurately identify not only the full-body skeleton but also the nuanced details of hand and facial keypoints, features essential for our objective of capturing full emotional expressions. The pipeline [18] processes a sequence of images extracted from the video and can optionally include the gender specification.

4.3 Generation of New Poses

To synthesize realistic human pose variations conditioned on a specific body shape and control parameters, we employed a VAE-based approach. Our initial experiments with training a VAE from scratch were limited by the high cost of generating large-scale 3D mesh data. To address this, we adopted transfer learning using VPoser [20], a pre-trained model tailored to SMPL-based representations.

A modified version of VPoser was used to accept the pre-generated 3D meshes, enabling controlled perturbations in the latent space. These perturbations allowed us to decode new pose variants that preserved the original mesh's structure while introducing smooth, plausible variations, as seen in Fig. 3.

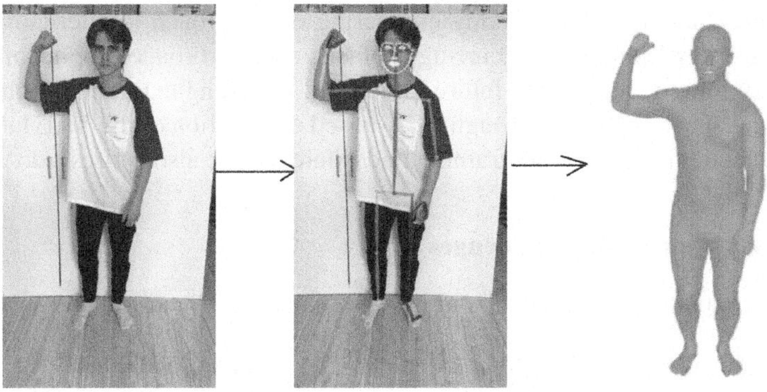

Fig. 2. Example for the application of the pipeline to the data set: OpenPose - SMPLify-X. From left to right, OpenPose is first applied to each image extracted from each video in the dataset. The resulting image in the center contains the person with the 3D skeleton on top. With SMPLify-X, we get the full 3D body skeleton in the right part [18].

Furthermore, we extended the original implementation by incorporating a Gaussian model to represent the difference between consecutive poses, using both the current frame and the preceding one as context. The variation is regulated by a noise scaling parameter, which controls how much each pose diverges from the original, ensuring consistency across the sequence. A pseudocode overview of this method is available in [18].

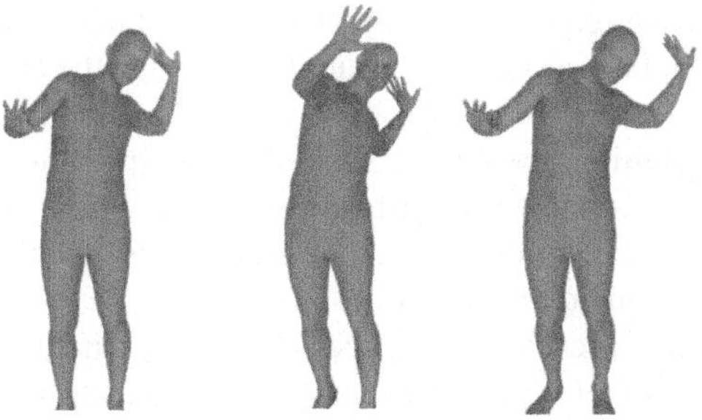

Fig. 3. A generative process in action in our framework. Left: the initial mesh; center: the intermediate result mesh. Right: the final generated pose [18].

5 Evaluation

This section builds upon the evaluation framework introduced in our previous work [18], expanding it with new qualitative and analytical insights. We begin by assessing the quality and diversity of the collected dataset, followed by an evaluation of the mesh extraction pipeline and the generative model's performance. A new addition to this section is a qualitative analysis of pose variation using PCA representations of decoded body poses, generated by introducing noise at different scales in the VAE's latent space.

We also include an ablation study comparing our approach to alternative models, and we discuss key limitations, recurring artifacts, and the broader applicability of our method. Additionally, we outline future directions, including extracting multiple mesh sequences and analyzing them through PCA-based exploration of the VAE latent space. Computational demands for both training and inference are also addressed.

5.1 Dataset: Metrics and Challenges

The Table 1 contains general data about how the dataset is organized and structured.

Table 1. Dataset overview [18].

	value
participants	28
female participants	6
male participants	22
expressions	6
videos per expression	9–10
total number of videos	1677
seconds per video	6–10

One of the main challenges in building a new dataset lies in the significant amount of manual post-processing required after the initial recordings. In our case, people have mimicked emotions that look more like different labels than the ones we were originally looking for, e.g. *anxiety*. We decided to isolate these to ensure that we only considered good quality data. In addition, there were subjective interpretations of emotion expressions, such as people expressing *fear* instead of *scared*, which raised questions about the subtle differences between these two emotions (fear is an enduring emotion, while anxiety is often a more immediate reaction).

Some recordings also presented technical challenges, including suboptimal video quality or camera angles that hindered accurate 3D mesh extraction. Nonetheless, the majority of the videos met the established criteria and were retained, forming a robust foundation for generating expressive 3D models based on genuine emotional performances.

A possible limitation of the dataset that could affect the representation of different characters in different settings is the gender imbalance, as only 6 of the 28 participants are female. This imbalance could lead to less accurate or diverse modeling of female body shapes and emotional expressions compared to male participants. Such a skew could affect the variety of 3D representations produced when applied to different scenarios. This could limit the ability to create a wide range of character models that reflect the diversity of the real world for all genders. As described in the future work section, work is currently underway to collect a further set of datasets to update beyond the existing version of the dataset.

5.2 Evaluation of the Mesh Extraction

Our experiments have shown that the pipeline discussed in Sect. 4 accurately captures the overall body shape as well as detailed poses for the body, face and hands (with the hand being particularly well captured, as shown in Fig. 2).

Table 2. Visual assessment of the average mesh quality for different subsets of the dataset. The values were obtained by averaging around 10% of the subsets.

Dataset	avg watertight proportion
anger samples	97.53
happiness samples	97.45
surprise samples	98.1
disgust samples	96.8
sadness samples	98.6
fear samples	97.13
female models	97.14
male models	97.7
Overall	97.35

To assess the structural integrity of the generated 3D meshes, we analyzed their watertightness. A mesh is considered watertight if all edges are properly enclosed by two faces, forming a closed and continuous surface without holes or boundaries. This property is important for downstream applications such as physical simulation, rendering, and animation, where surface consistency and completeness are critical.

Since some of the generated meshes did not meet the strict criterion of being fully watertight, we computed a more informative metric: the proportion of edges that are properly enclosed. Specifically, we calculated the percentage of edges that are shared by exactly two faces, indicating they are part of a closed surface region. This provides a finer-grained measure of mesh quality, reflecting how close the mesh is to being watertight even if minor gaps exist.

Across the dataset, as seen in Table 2, the meshes demonstrated a high level of structural integrity, with an average of approximately **97.35%** of edges being part of a closed surface. The small proportion of open edges is likely due to minor extraction artifacts or numerical imprecision during mesh generation. Table X summarizes the watertightness statistics for representative meshes in the dataset.

These results confirm that the generated meshes maintain a high degree of surface closure, making them suitable for further processing and use in applications such as character animation, simulation, or virtual environments. Also, they confirm that the proposed dataset and framework successfully achieve their goal of extracting expressive and realistic 3D meshes from custom video recordings. By visually inspecting the extracted meshes and comparing them to the original input frames, we observed that the pipeline accurately captures both the overall body shape and detailed poses, including fine features such as facial expressions and hand configurations, as we can see in 4. In particular, the hand poses were consistently well-represented, demonstrating the pipeline's ability to model subtle and intricate components of human posture. These promising results suggest that the extracted meshes are well-suited for downstream applications, such as generating pose variations, training non-player characters (NPCs), or creating realistic virtual human representations for use in games, simulations, and virtual reality environments.

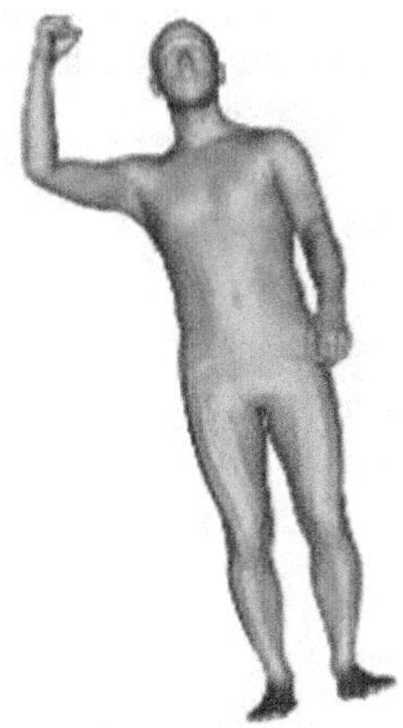

Fig. 4. Extracted mesh using SMPLify-X where the facial expression and the hands are very well captured.

However, while the reconstruction pipeline generally produces accurate meshes from high-quality images, certain poses can introduce artifacts 5. These inconsistencies, such as incorrect hand placement, often arise from misalignment between the VPoser-generated pose and the OpenPose extraction. Addressing these issues may require retraining the model on a dedicated dataset, though this would be computationally intensive.

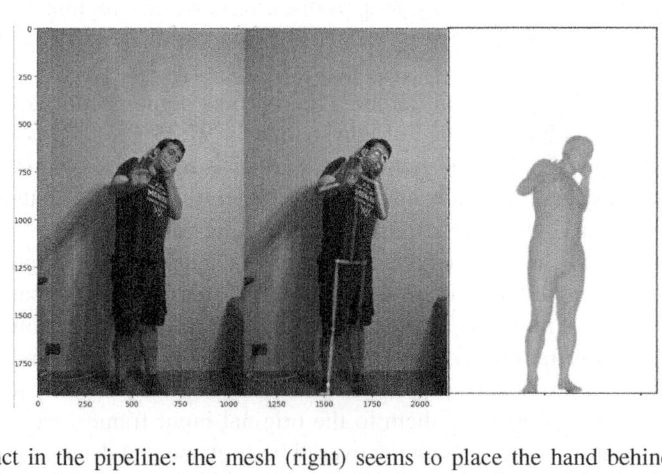

Fig. 5. Artifact in the pipeline: the mesh (right) seems to place the hand behind the head, in contrast to the real image on the left, where the hands are in front of the head. The skeleton detection phase (center) is correct [18].

5.3 Generative Model Evaluation

Our experiments showed that the generative model is capable of producing high-quality outputs with realistic and valid poses. The generated meshes exhibited a strong alignment with the original input meshes when measured using the vertex-to-vertex (V2V) error metric, reflecting only minor deviations in vertex positions. This quantitative evaluation demonstrates that the model generates poses that are both plausible in appearance and closely match the original meshes, confirming its effectiveness in producing accurate and reliable results.

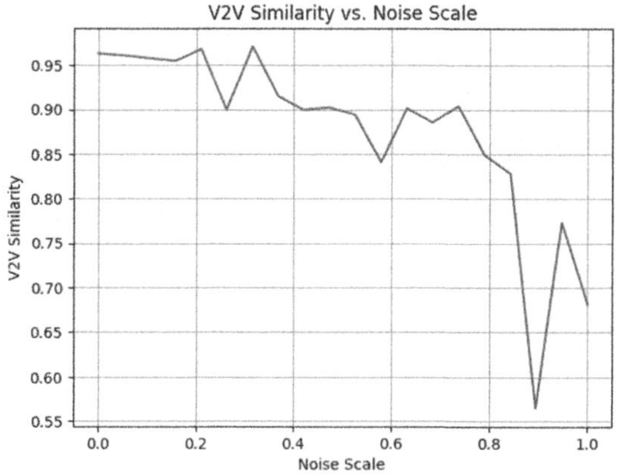

Fig. 6. V2V similarity decreases as noise levels increase, indicating greater divergence between the generated and original meshes due to larger deviations in vertex positions [18].

Figure 6 illustrates the relationship between vertex-to-vertex similarity (V2V) and increasing noise applied to the generated mesh. As the noise level that perturbs the vertex positions increases, the V2V similarity metric decreases significantly. This occurs because higher levels of noise introduce greater deviations from the original mesh, resulting in larger Euclidean distances between corresponding vertices of the two meshes. As the noise increases, the generated mesh progressively diverges from the original, which reduces overall similarity. The occasional spikes, whether upward or downward, are due to the inherent randomness in generating new deviations. These findings illustrate that the generative model is capable of producing meaningful and diverse poses, which can be associated with specific emotional categories or other attributes such as posture or movement.

To better understand how noise injected into the VPoser latent space affects the diversity of generated body poses, we performed a Principal Component Analysis (PCA) on the decoded pose parameters. Specifically, we sampled multiple latent vectors by adding Gaussian noise with varying standard deviations (noise scales) to the original latent representation of a body pose. Each noisy latent vector was decoded into a 63-dimensional pose parameter vector representing joint rotations.

PCA was fit on the combined set of decoded poses from all noise scales, ensuring that the principal components capture the main axes of variation across the entire noisy

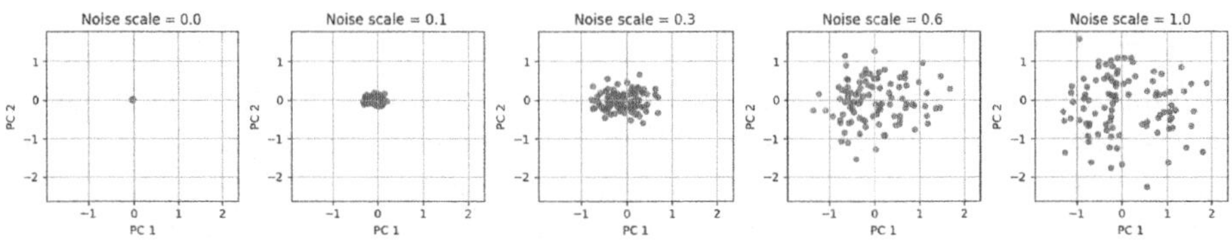

Fig. 7. PCA visualization of decoded body poses generated by adding Gaussian noise with varying scales to the VPoser latent vector.

latent space. Subsequently, for each noise scale, the corresponding decoded poses were projected onto the first two principal components and visualized in a 2D scatter plot 7 .

As noise scale increases, the scatter plots show a progressive expansion of pose diversity, indicating that the latent space smoothly encodes meaningful variations in body pose. Low noise levels produce tightly clustered decoded poses near the original, while higher noise levels lead to a broader spread, reflecting larger deviations in joint rotations.

This analysis provides qualitative and quantitative insight into the robustness and expressiveness of the VPoser latent space representation, demonstrating its ability to generate a continuous spectrum of plausible body poses through controlled perturbations.

5.4 Comparison with Other Models

For comparison, we also evaluated mesh extraction using ScoreHMR by implementing the code provided by the authors in [25]. Our initial observations revealed a substantial improvement in extraction speed compared to SMPLify-X. In particular, during tests on demo images containing multiple subjects, ScoreHMR processed the images approximately five times faster. This speed advantage stems from its use of diffusion models that analyze the entire image simultaneously, in contrast to traditional optimization methods that extract meshes sequentially. However, ScoreHMR has certain limitations: it occasionally fails to generate accurate poses (as illustrated in Fig. 8) and currently supports only the SMPL model, which prevents it from capturing detailed face or hand poses and reduces its overall versatility.

Beyond SMPLify-X and ScoreHMR, several other mesh recovery methods have emerged in recent years, each with distinct trade-offs. For example, PARE (Part Attention Regressor [10]) and SPIN (SMPLify in the Loop [11]) offer faster mesh estimation through regression-based approaches but may sacrifice accuracy in complex poses or occlusions. More recent transformer-based models such as CLIFF (Camera-Lifting for 3D Human Pose and Shape Estimation [14]), which leverages vision transformers and a camera lifting strategy to refine SMPL parameter predictions. Its transformer-based architecture captures global image dependencies more effectively than earlier CNN-based methods. However, like ScoreHMR, CLIFF is limited to the SMPL model and does not natively support SMPL-X components such as facial expressions or hand articulation. This limits their applicability in contexts requiring detailed full-body representation. While these methods are not the focus of our current evaluation, future work may explore their integration or adaptation to support more expressive models.

5.5 Discussion of Applicability

Although the primary motivation of this research was to develop a dataset that better captures emotional diversity and to create the associated models for 3D mesh extraction and pose generation, the potential applications extend to various industries. The ability to generate realistic and expressive 3D human poses has significant implications for fields that rely on accurate representation of people. In virtual and augmented reality, for example, more expressive avatars could improve user interaction and engagement. In healthcare, the development of realistic 3D models could improve the effectiveness of training and therapy simulations. In robotics, the ability to emulate human-like emotional expressions could improve human-robot interaction, make robots more personable and increase their usability.

Evaluating these animations in a gaming environment would be essential to assess their effectiveness in conveying emotions. A dynamic system where the emotional expression of NPCs changes in response to the player's actions could greatly enhance the gaming experience. For example, if a human player character makes a threatening move, an NPC could visibly show fear or anger.

In our experiments, we evaluated the computational performance of the proposed pipeline and generative model to estimate the time required for mesh extraction and pose generation. Using an A100 GPU, the pipeline processes a single frame in approximately 52 s. Consequently, extracting meshes for a short 10-s video at 30 frames per second would take around 4 h and 20 min. Given the size of our dataset, the total processing time is estimated at roughly 7,267 GPU hours (equivalent to 302 days and 19 h on a single GPU), as detailed in Table 1. However, the workload scales efficiently with additional GPUs, significantly reducing total time when parallelized. The generative model achieves a faster performance, generating meshes at a rate of about 2 s per frame. This means that producing an animation of N frames would require approximately $N \times 2$ seconds. For example, generating a 10-second animation at 30 frames per second would take $\sim$10 min.

Offline generation of emotion-based animations offers clear benefits for industry applications by eliminating real-time computational overhead while achieving results comparable to handcrafted animations. A game developer, for instance, could use the proposed model to produce and store animations in advance, reducing production costs and streamlining asset management and editing workflows. Furthermore, having the full 3D mesh for each frame enables detailed integration of skin, shaders, and clothing, facilitating the creation of fully renderable and visually rich characters.

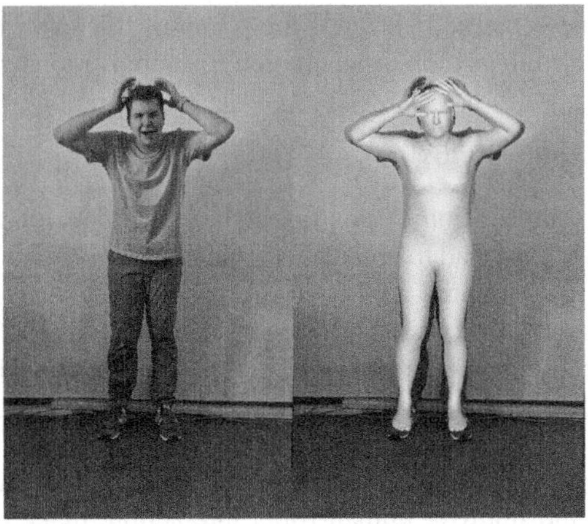

Fig. 8. 3D mesh, extracted with ScoreHMR. Although the mesh was extracted in less time compared to SMPLify-X, it cannot reproduce the facial and hand expressions and still outputs the position of the hands incorrectly. [18].

6 Conclusions

This paper presents a novel approach for generating emotionally expressive 3D human models by leveraging a custom-built dataset and a modular, generative architecture. By capturing complete emotional transitions across the full body and integrating mesh generation via a pre-trained VAE, in particular VPoser, our method offers a solution for enhancing emotional realism in virtual humans. The dataset introduced here is publicly released to encourage further development across domains such as animation, gaming, virtual training environments, and affective computing. Future work includes broadening emotional coverage, balancing demographic representation in the dataset, better evaluation of the dataset by analysing with a PCA the representation of multiple meshes in the latent space of the VAE. Also we want to integrate these poses into NPC animation pipelines and evaluate the impact on user experience in real-world applications.

Acknowledgements. This research is partially supported by the project "Romanian Hub for Artificial Intelligence - HRIA", Smart Growth, Digitization and Financial Instruments Program, 2021–2027, MySMIS no. 334906 and a grant of the Ministry of Research, Innovation and Digitization, CNCS/CCCDI-UEFISCDI, project no. PN-IV-P8-8.1-PRE-HE-ORG-2023-0081, within PNCDI IV.

References

1. Akhter, I., Black, M.J.: Pose-conditioned joint angle limits for 3D human pose reconstruction. In: In proceedings of IEEE CVPR 2015 (2015)
2. Anguelov, D., et al.: SCAPE: shape completion and animation of people. ACM Trans. Graph. **24**(3), 408–416 (2005). https://doi.org/10.1145/1073204.1073207

3. Avogaro, A., et al.: Exploring 3D human pose estimation and forecasting from the robot's perspective: the harper dataset (2024). https://arxiv.org/abs/2403.14447
4. Bogo, F., Kanazawa, A., Lassner, C., Gehler, P., Romero, J., Black, M.J.: Keep it SMPL: automatic estimation of 3D human pose and shape from a single image. In: Leibe, B., Matas, J., Sebe, N., Welling, M. (eds.) ECCV 2016. LNCS, vol. 9909, pp. 561–578. Springer, Cham (2016). https://doi.org/10.1007/978-3-319-46454-1_34
5. Bolkart, T., Wuhrer, S.: FLAME: a 3D morphable model of the head and face based on 3D scans. IEEE Trans. Pattern Anal. Mach. Intell. **43**(11), 2808–2821 (2021). https://doi.org/10.1109/TPAMI.2020.2971747
6. Cao, Z., et al.: OpenPose: realtime multi-person 2D pose estimation using part affinity fields. IEEE Trans. Pattern Anal. Mach. Intell. (2019)
7. Cao, Z., Simon, T., Wei, S.E., Sheikh, Y.: Realtime multi-person 2D pose estimation using part affinity fields. In: CVPR (2017)
8. Hirshberg, D.A., Loper, M., Rachlin, E., Black, M.J.: Coregistration: simultaneous alignment and modeling of articulated 3D shape. In: Fitzgibbon, A., Lazebnik, S., Perona, P., Sato, Y., Schmid, C. (eds.) ECCV 2012. LNCS, vol. 7577, pp. 242–255. Springer, Heidelberg (2012). https://doi.org/10.1007/978-3-642-33783-3_18
9. Ionescu, C., et al.: Human3.6M: large scale datasets and predictive methods for 3D human sensing in natural environments. IEEE Trans. Pattern Anal. Mach. Intell. **36**(7), 1325–1339 (2014). https://doi.org/10.1109/TPAMI.2013.248
10. Kocabas, M., Huang, C.H.P., Hilliges, O., Black, M.J.: PARE: part attention regressor for 3D human body estimation (2021). https://arxiv.org/abs/2104.08527
11. Kolotouros, N., Pavlakos, G., Black, M.J., Daniilidis, K.: Learning to reconstruct 3D human pose and shape via model-fitting in the loop (2019). https://arxiv.org/abs/1909.12828
12. Kolotouros, N., et al.: Learning to reconstruct 3D human pose and shape via model-fitting in the loop (2019). https://arxiv.org/abs/1909.12828
13. Li, C., et al.: The good, the bad, and why: unveiling emotions in generative ai. In: ICML 2024 (2023)
14. Li, Z., Liu, J., Zhang, Z., Xu, S., Yan, Y.: CLIFF: carrying location information in full frames into human pose and shape estimation (2022). https://arxiv.org/abs/2208.00571
15. Liu, L., Zhao, K.: Report on methods and applications for crafting 3D humans (2024). https://arxiv.org/abs/2406.01223
16. Loper, M., et al.: SMPL: a skinned multi-person linear model. ACM Trans. Graph. **34**(6) (2015). https://doi.org/10.1145/2816795.2818013
17. Mollahosseini, A., Hassani, B., Mahoor, M.H.: AffectNet: a database for facial expression, valence, and arousal computing in the wild. CoRR abs/1708.03985 (2017). http://arxiv.org/abs/1708.03985
18. Paduraru, C., Bouruc, P., Stefanescu, A.: Generative ai for human 3D body emotions: a dataset and baseline methods. In: Proceedings of the 17th International Conference on Agents and Artificial Intelligence - Volume 3: ICAART, pp. 646–653. INSTICC, SciTePress (2025). https://doi.org/10.5220/0013168700003890
19. Park, J.S., et al.: Generative agents: interactive simulacra of human behavior. In: In the 36th Annual ACM Symposium on User Interface Software and Technology (UIST 2023). Association for Computing Machinery, New York (2023)
20. Pavlakos, G., et al.: Expressive body capture: 3D hands, face, and body from a single image. In: Proceedings IEEE Conference on Computer Vision and Pattern Recognition (CVPR) (2019)
21. Pons-Moll, G., et al.: Dyna: a model of dynamic human shape in motion (2015). https://doi.org/10.15496/publikation-10602
22. Prokudin, S., Black, M.J., Romero, J.: SMPLpix: neural avatars from 3D human models. In: Proceedings of the IEEE/CVF WACV, pp. 1810–1819 (2021)

23. Romero, J., Tzionas, D., Black, M.J.: Embodied hands: modeling and capturing hands and bodies together. ACM Trans. Graphics (TOG) **36**(6), 245:1–245:17 (2017). https://doi.org/10.1145/3130800.3130883
24. Simon, T., et al.: Hand keypoint detection in single images using multiview bootstrapping. In: CVPR (2017)
25. Stathopoulos, A., Han, L., Metaxas, D.: Score-guided diffusion for 3D human recovery. In: CVPR (2024)
26. Sun, J.J., et al.: EEV: a large-scale dataset for studying evoked expressions from video. arXiv preprint arXiv:2001.05488 (2021)
27. Vrajitoru, D.: NPCs and chatterbots with personality and emotional response, pp. 142 – 147 (2006). https://doi.org/10.1109/CIG.2006.311693
28. Wei, S.E., et al.: Convolutional pose machines. In: CVPR (2016)
29. Zadeh, A., et al.: Multimodal sentiment analysis of videos: facial expressions, text, and audio. In: Proceedings of the 2018 Conference on Empirical Methods in Natural Language Processing (EMNLP), pp. 5006–5015. Association for Computational Linguistics (2018). https://arxiv.org/abs/1806.06140
30. Zhao, W., et al.: Open-pose 3D zero-shot learning: benchmark and challenges (2024). https://arxiv.org/abs/2312.07039

MicroVision: A Framework for Instance Segmentation of Yeast Cells and Traps in Microstructured Environment

Khola Naseem[1,2(✉)], Nabeel Khalid[1,2], Lea Bertgen[3], Johannes M. Herrmann[3], Andreas Dengel[1,2], and Sheraz Ahmed[1]

[1] German Research Center for Artificial Intelligence (DFKI) GmbH, 67663 Kaiserslautern, Germany
{khola.naseem,nabeel.khalid,andreas.dengel,sheraz.ahmed}@dfki.de
[2] RPTU Kaiserslautern–Landau, 67663 Kaiserslautern, Germany
[3] Cell Biology, University of Kaiserslautern, RPTU, Kaiserslautern, Germany
lbertgen@rhrk.uni-kl.de, hannes.herrmann@biologie.uni-kl.de

Abstract. Accurate instance segmentation of yeast cells in microstructured environments remains a challenging problem due to the visual similarity between cells and the surrounding trap structures. This complexity is further amplified under varying imaging conditions and limited annotated data. In this study, a robust transfer-based instance segmentation framework is presented that jointly segments both yeast cells and traps. Our approach integrates an attention-enhanced backbone to better capture fine-grained features crucial for precise segmentation. To evaluate the model's robustness, an extensive evaluation is performed using test-time image degradation scenarios, including Gaussian noise, blur, and contrast variations. Additionally, the model's generalization capability is assessed across complex spatial configurations involving multiple trap types and dense cell populations. The proposed method achieves state-of-the-art performance and demonstrates strong label efficiency, maintaining high segmentation accuracy even with limited training data. These results highlight the model's potential for deployment in real-world bioengineering applications.

Keywords: Instance Segmentation · Microstructure Environment · Yeast Cell · Traps · Time-Lapse Fluorescence Microscopy · Deep Learning · Synthetic Biology

1 Introduction

Yeast cells have been extensively studied in the life sciences for decades because of their well-defined genome, presence of membrane-bound organelles typical of eukaryotic cells, genetic tractability, ease of genetic manipulation, widespread availability, and overall simplicity in laboratory use [22]. The ultrastructure of yeast cells was initially studied in 1957 [39], and since that time, advancements in imaging and molecular biology have significantly improved our ability to study them. The traditional baker's yeast, Saccharomyces cerevisiae, is among the most extensively used systems for both homologous and heterologous biopharmaceutical production, protein synthesis, and genetic

H. J. van den Herik et al. (Eds.): ICAART 2025, LNAI 16517, pp. 415–432, 2026.
https://doi.org/10.1007/978-3-032-25032-2_20

engineering [33]. Beyond its role in foundational research, yeast is heavily employed in industrial biotechnology, where it plays a pivotal role in fermentation-based applications such as brewing, baking, winemaking, and biofuel generation [38]. More recently, research on yeast cells has gained importance in several emerging domains, including synthetic biology, genetic engineering, pharmaceutical sciences, and food technology.

Time-lapse fluorescence microscopy (TLFM) has become a powerful technique for capturing dynamic behavior in living, intact cells [37]. By producing standardized, quantifiable, and data-rich outputs, TLFM plays a vital role in advancing our understanding of biomolecular mechanisms and in guiding the development of complex molecular systems. When paired with high-throughput microfluidic platforms, TLFM can generate thousands of images in a single experiment, making manual segmentation and annotation unfeasible [31]. As a result, automated segmentation techniques are now indispensable for efficient image analysis.

Microscopic data, in general, offer critical insights into a wide range of biological processes. A key step in extracting this information is cell segmentation, which forms the foundation for interpreting biomedical microscopy images [28]. Precise segmentation enables essential downstream tasks, including cell tracking [30,50,57], counting [9,27], classification of cell types [58], and phenotype analysis [43]. In modern, high-throughput microscopy studies, automation is essential to keep pace with the volume and complexity of data. Although numerous methods have been developed to tackle segmentation challenges [7,8,15,16], difficulties persist due to factors such as heterogeneous cell shapes, overlapping regions, and variations in image intensity. These challenges become even more pronounced in microstructured environments, where mechanical constraints, spatial configuration, and chemical gradients are tightly controlled. In such settings, it is crucial to distinguish cells from other structures, such as debris or traps, particularly in the configurations discussed in this paper, where the appearance of the cells and traps is quite similar.

This study introduces a transformer-based framework for cell-trap segmentation, named MicroVision. The pipeline uses ViTDet [23] as the backbone for feature extraction and integrates Cascade Mask R-CNN [5] for instance-level segmentation. ViTDet is responsible for learning rich feature representations, while Cascade Mask R-CNN performs the segmentation tasks. One of the main advantages of this architecture is its ability to capture both fine-grained local features and broader global context, which is crucial for accurate segmentation in visually complex environments. A detailed explanation of the MicroVision pipeline is provided in Sect. 3. In addition, an anchor-based ResNeSt model [8] was fine-tuned and tested on the dataset. This model was pre-trained on the LiveCell dataset, one of the largest available for cell segmentation, as well as on the COCO dataset. The proposed MicroVision method outperformed this baseline in segmentation performance, further demonstrating its robustness and effectiveness across various evaluation criteria.

To comprehensively assess the model's robustness and generalization capacity, its performance is evaluated under a variety of test-time image degradation conditions, including Gaussian noise, blurring, and contrast variations, to mimic real-world microscopy challenges. The model was also tested on unseen configurations, such as images containing multiple trap types and densely packed cells that were not included in the training set, demonstrating its adaptability. Furthermore, the model's label efficiency was verified by training it with a limited amount of annotated data, showcasing its capacity to perform well even with reduced supervision. The major contributions of this paper include:

- Proposing a robust transformer-based instance segmentation network that integrates ViTDet [23] for extracting rich visual features with Cascade Mask R-CNN [5] for precise instance segmentation of yeast cells.
- Achieving a 5% increase in Intersection over Union (IoU) compared to state-of-the-art segmentation techniques.
- Demonstrating strong performance with limited training data, confirming the model's label efficiency and suitability for annotation-scarce scenarios.
- Validating the model's generalization through testing on unseen cell trap configurations and dense cell populations not present in the training set.

2 Literature Review

A wide range of methods has been developed for cell detection and segmentation, encompassing both traditional computer vision techniques [1,14,32,35,49] and more recent deep learning-based solutions [15,17,54,56]. Traditional approaches often rely on methods such as intensity-based thresholding, region accumulation, and deformable model fitting. While these methods can be effective for specific applications, their reliance on task-specific feature engineering limits their generalizability to other contexts. In contrast, deep learning methods have revolutionized the field by introducing models that learn representations directly from data, reducing the need for expert-designed features. A key milestone in this evolution was the introduction of U-Net [47], which won the ISBI 2015 cell tracking and segmentation challenge. U-Net's success spurred a wave of new tools in biomedical image analysis, including DeepCell [53], Omnipose [6], CellPose [51], and Usiigaci [52].

Numerous techniques have emerged to address the yeast cell segmentation task in microscopy imagery [12,20,21,30,48]. Studying yeast in structured microenvironments provides a consistent and stable platform where cells are maintained in the focal plane, allowing for reliable data acquisition. These settings have been the focus of extensive research aimed at understanding yeast behavior and improving segmentation accuracy [10,26,55]. Deep learning has also been adapted to microstructured environments. For example, CellDETR [41] employs an attention-based transformer architecture to perform efficient instance segmentation and detection of cells, achieving a Jaccard index of 0.84 while maintaining a lightweight structure and fast inference speed, comparable to Mask R-CNN. Generative approaches have also been proposed; Multi-StyleGAN [45] synthetic data generation based on prior knowledge. Additionally, in [42], U-Net was used for segmentation, while Mask R-CNN was employed for precise instance-level segmentation in complex microfluidic environments.

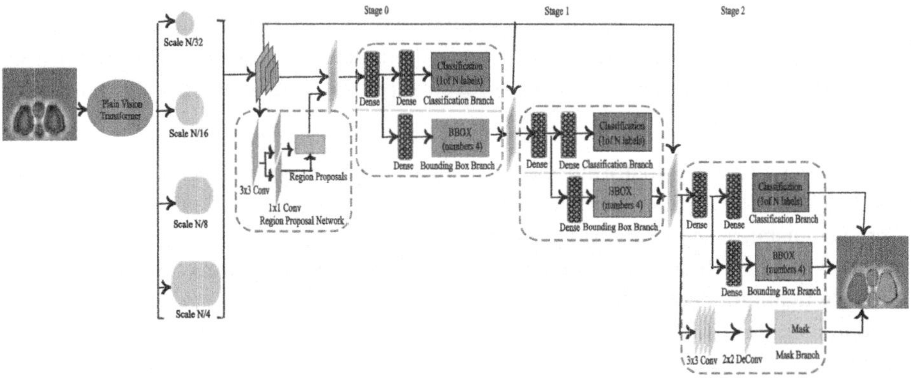

Fig. 1. System overview of MicroVision. The input image is passed to the network, and an instance segmentation mask is produced as output. Reproduced from our conference paper presented at [36].

3 Methodology

The proposed pipeline integrates a Vision Transformer-based feature extractor (ViTDet), a Region Proposal Network (RPN), and Cascade Mask R-CNN for final instance-level prediction. A system overview of the pipeline is depicted in Fig. 1. Further architectural details are provided below.

A Vision Transformer-based backbone, ViT Detector (ViTDet), is used to extract both high-level semantic and low-level spatial features from input images. ViTDet is a detection-optimized variant of the original Vision Transformer (ViT) [2], which divides an input image into fixed-size patches, embeds them into vectors, and processes them through a stack of transformer blocks. This structure allows the model to effectively capture both contextual and spatial relationships using a global attention mechanism. The resulting feature maps, which are rich and expressive, are passed through a Simple Feature Pyramid (SPF). The SPF serves as a lightweight alternative to the traditional Feature Pyramid Network (FPN) [24]. The SPF generates multi-scale feature representations by applying parallel convolutional or deconvolutional operations, producing feature maps at scales of 1/32, 1/16, 1/8, and 1/4, starting from a base scale of 1/16.

These multi-scale features are then passed to the Region Proposal Network (RPN) [46], a fully convolutional network that identifies potential object regions. The RPN places anchor boxes across the image and evaluates their overlap with the ground truth using the Intersection over Union (IoU) metric. Anchors with IoU greater than 0.7 are considered foreground, those below 0.3 are treated as background, and anchors with IoU in between are ignored during training. After identifying potential anchors, Non-Maximum Suppression (NMS) [4] is applied to eliminate redundant or overlapping proposals, retaining only the most promising candidate regions.

For final instance segmentation, the model uses Cascade Mask R-CNN [5] as the prediction head. This multistage architecture incrementally refines predictions using increasingly strict IoU thresholds. In the first stage, an IoU threshold of 0.5 is applied;

predictions with over 50% overlap with the ground truth are passed to the next stage. In the second stage, an IoU threshold of 0.6 is used to further refine the proposals, followed by a final stage that applies an IoU threshold of 0.7 for additional precision. At the last stage, a segmentation branch generates pixel-wise masks. The bounding box head classifies each detected object and adjusts the bounding box coordinates, while a lightweight fully convolutional network serves as the mask head to produce accurate, instance-specific segmentation masks at the pixel level.

4 Dataset

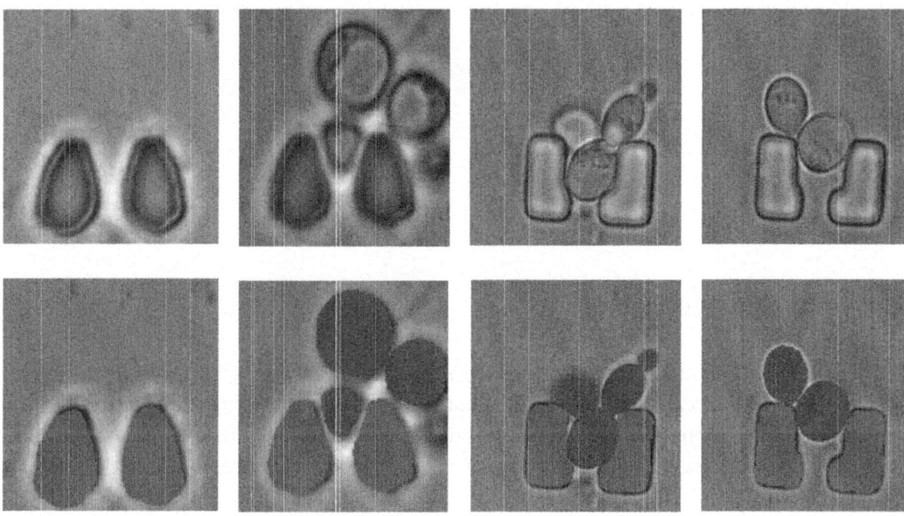

Fig. 2. Sample images from the dataset: The top row shows the original images, and the bottom row shows the overlay of the masks on the original images. Here, ■ represents the cells and, ■ represents the trap instances. Reproduced from our conference paper presented at [36].

An instance segmentation dataset of yeast cells in a microstructured environment was used in this study [44]. It consists of 493 densely annotated brightfield microscopy images representing common experimental conditions, including various cell-trap configurations such as empty traps, multiple cells per trap, and budding daughter cells. The dataset includes two trap geometries: 398 images feature oval-shaped traps, while 95 contain L-shaped traps. The number of yeast cells per image ranges from zero to six, capturing realistic cell densities and morphological variations. Additional dataset details can be found in [36]. A summary of the number of images and instance counts across the training, validation, and test splits is provided in Table 1 (Fig. 2).

To evaluate the generalization and robustness of the proposed model beyond the training distribution, two supplementary test sets were created. The first set was derived by applying a range of test-time image degradations to a reserved portion of the test data. These degradations simulate typical microscopy artifacts such as acquisition noise, defocus, and uneven lighting. Specifically, Gaussian noise, Gaussian blur, brightness variation, and contrast adjustment were applied to mimic conditions commonly encountered in real-world microscopy. The second supplementary set was generated to assess model performance on previously unseen spatial arrangements. It includes images with densely populated regions with overlapping yeast cells. These challenging cases help evaluate the model's ability to generalise to unseen experimental setups and morphological diversity. The dataset is available for public access[1].

Table 1. Distribution of images, cells, and traps across training, validation, and test sets in the yeast cell dataset. Reproduced from our conference paper presented at [36].

Split	Images	Cells	Traps
Train	296	536	528
Validation	49	108	98
Test	148	270	291

5 Evaluation Metrics

To assess the performance of the proposed segmentation model, we used three evaluation metrics: the Jaccard index (IoU), mean Average Precision (mAP), and Panoptic Quality (PQ). These metrics were selected to capture different dimensions of segmentation performance, including pixel-wise overlap, object-wise precision, and instance-level recognition.

The Jaccard index, also known as Intersection over Union (IoU) [13], evaluates how well the predicted segmentation overlaps with the ground truth. It is defined as the ratio of the intersection to the union of predicted and actual pixel regions.

$$IoU = \frac{Y \cap \widehat{Y}}{Y \cup \widehat{Y}} \tag{1}$$

IoU was calculated using the formula shown in Eq. 1, where Y represents the ground truth and $\hat{Y}$ denotes the prediction. Class-wise IoU values were also reported to enable fair comparisons with existing methods. For object-level performance, we followed the COCO evaluation protocol [25] to compute mean Average Precision (mAP). We reported mAP at multiple IoU thresholds, including mAP50 and mAP75, and across object sizes such as small (mAPs) and medium (mAPm), offering a comprehensive evaluation of detection performance across different scales. The mean average precision (mAP) was calculated using the formula shown in Eq. 2, where n was the number of classes and $(AP_i)$was the average precision for the n classes.

[1] Dataset link: https://github.com/ChristophReich1996/Yeast-in-Microstructures-Dataset.

$$\text{mAP} = \frac{1}{n}\sum_{i=1}^{i=n}(AP_i) \tag{2}$$

To measure instance segmentation quality, we adopted the Panoptic Quality (PQ) metric [18]. This is particularly suited for datasets that can be interpreted in a panoptic segmentation framework, where yeast cells and traps are treated as thing classes, and the background is categorized as a stuff class. PQ combines instance-wise Segmentation Quality (SQ) and Recognition Quality (RQ) into a single metric, as shown in Eq. 3, by averaging IoU across matched predictions and penalizing false positives and false negatives

$$PQ = \frac{\sum_{(p,g)\in TP} IoU(p,g)}{|TP|}\frac{|TP|}{|TP| + \frac{1}{2}|FP| + \frac{1}{2}|FN|} \tag{3}$$

By combining these complementary metrics, we ensured a robust and thorough evaluation of the model's performance across overlap accuracy, instance recognition, and detection at various scales.

6 Experimental Setup

To comprehensively assess segmentation performance in microstructured environments, we conducted a series of evaluations using a dataset containing images with varying trap geometries (L-shaped and oval-shaped) and a range of cell counts per image, from zero to six. Several baseline networks were trained and evaluated on the same dataset to benchmark the effectiveness of our proposed model. One of the baseline models was the anchor-based ResNeSt network, which was pre-trained on the LiveCell dataset. It utilized the standard COCO aspect ratios (0.5, 1.0, and 2.0), extended with two additional ratios (3.0 and 4.0) to better accommodate diverse cell shapes. To handle small objects effectively, anchor sizes of 8, 16, 32, 64, and 128 were used. The input images were normalized using the pixel mean and standard deviation values specified for the LiveCell dataset. In addition, Mask R-CNN was implemented following the setup described in [42]. This architecture builds upon Faster R-CNN [46] by incorporating ROIAlign to preserve spatial information and a Feature Pyramid Network (FPN) to enable effective multi-scale object detection. The Segment Anything Model (SAM) [19], a general-purpose Vision Transformer-based segmentation framework, was also fine-tuned for yeast cell segmentation. SAM leverages a masked autoencoder architecture with a prompt encoder and a mask decoder. In our implementation, the default prompt embeddings were passed directly into the decoder to generate segmentation masks automatically, without requiring manual prompts. Empirical results confirm the effectiveness of this straightforward approach [11,59].

In our proposed network, we used aspect ratios of 0.5, 1.0, and 2.0, along with anchor sizes of 32, 64, 128, 256, and 512. The model was trained using the AdamW optimizer [29] for a total of 6000 iterations on an NVIDIA GeForce RTX 4090 GPU. All models were implemented using the PyTorch framework [40], and the best-performing checkpoints were selected based on validation loss.

7 Results and Discussion

Table 2 summarises the average segmentation AP scores. The proposed model achieved the highest overall AP score of 80.7%, outperforming all other methods. At IoU thresholds of 0.50 and 0.75, it attained impressive AP scores of 99.4% and 97.2%, respectively. Notably, the model achieved the highest cell IoU of 89.0, which is 5% higher than that of the Mask R-CNN baseline.

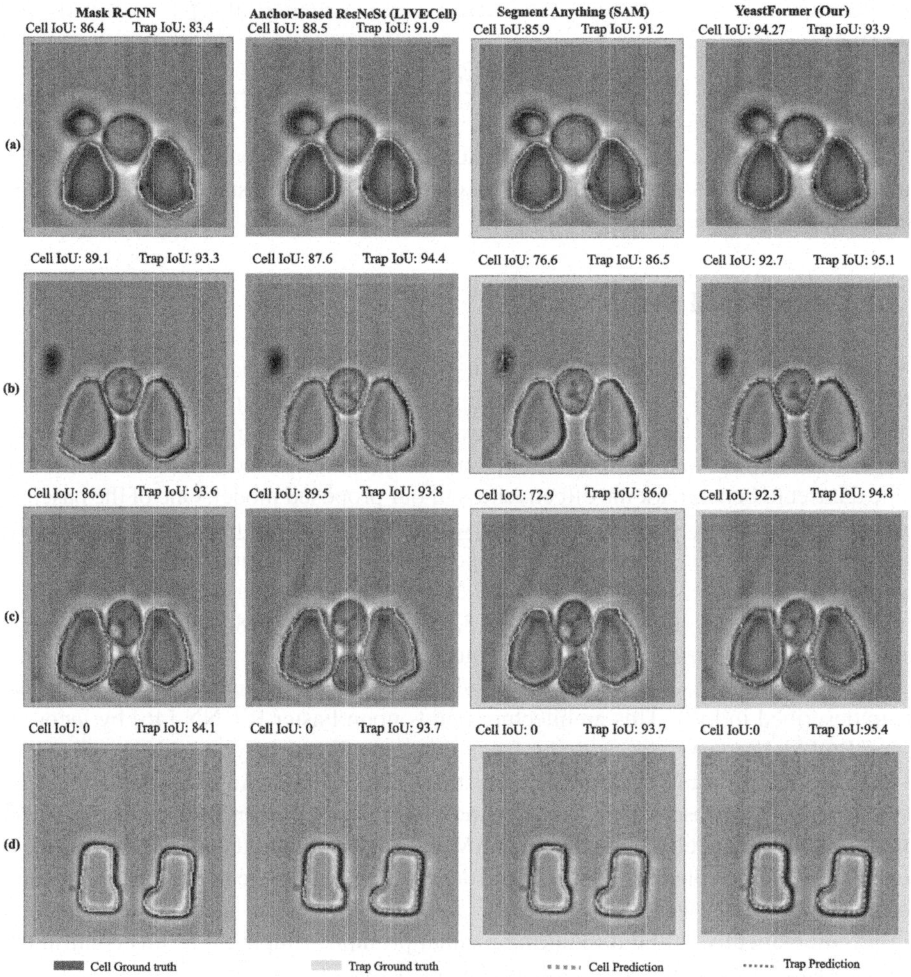

Fig. 3. The inference results for several sample images in which our model performed sufficiently are presented. Ground truth cell masks are outlined in solid blue, while model predictions are marked by dotted orange lines. Solid green lines represent ground truth traps, and dotted red lines indicate the model's trap predictions. Reproduced from our conference paper presented at [36].

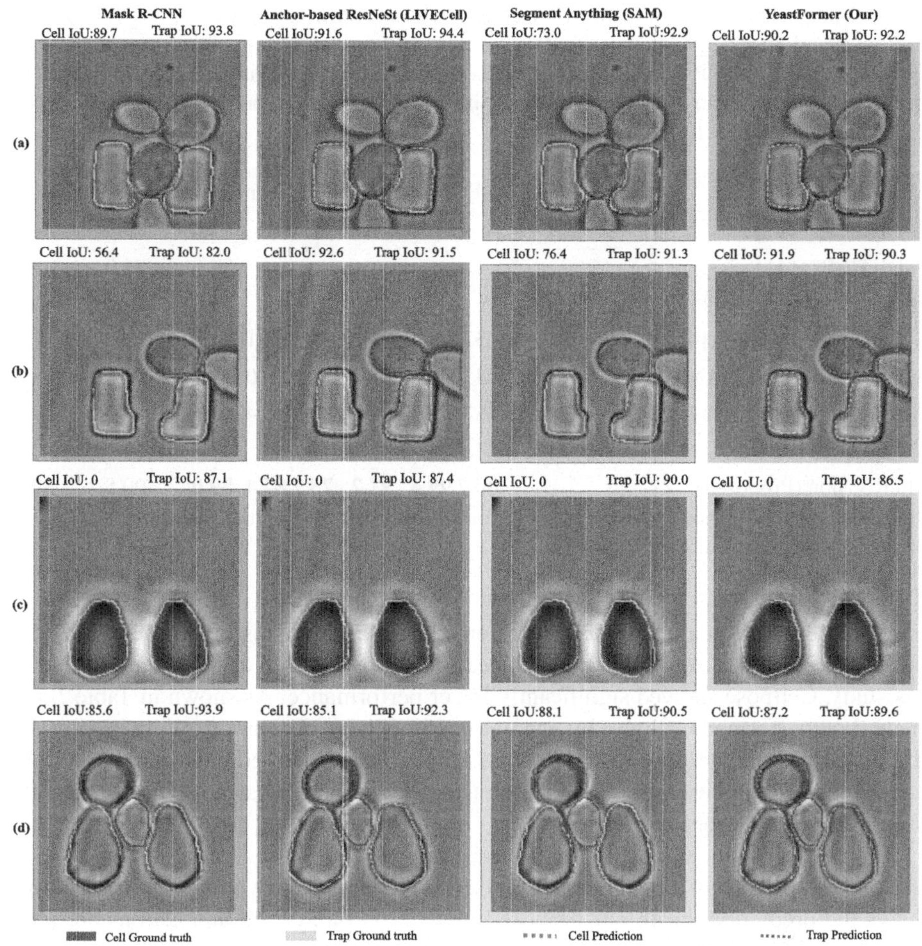

Fig. 4. The inference results for several sample images in which our model performed insufficiently are presented. Ground truth cell masks are outlined in solid blue, while model predictions are marked by dotted orange lines. Solid green lines represent ground truth traps, and dotted red lines indicate the model's trap predictions. Reproduced from our conference paper presented at [36].

For benchmarking, we compared our method against several state-of-the-art models, including Mask R-CNN [42], DISCO [3], Cell-DETR A and Cell-DETR B [41], ResNeSt-LiveCell [8], and the Segment Anything Model (SAM) [19]. Mask R-CNN and ResNeSt were retrained on our dataset using consistent experimental protocols. SAM was evaluated in a fully automated mode without user-provided prompts. Although SAM delivered reasonable performance, its results were suboptimal in the absence of prompts. In contrast, our model operates independently of prompts and consistently outperformed SAM across all evaluation metrics. The Cellpose model [51],

Table 2. Segmentation Performance – Average Precision (AP) is reported across various IoU thresholds and area ranges, comparing IoU metrics for the cell and trap classes across multiple segmentation methods. Panoptic Quality (PQ) is included to evaluate instance segmentation. The methods marked with an asterisk (*) utilized different data splits. Reproduced from our conference paper presented at [36].

Method	AP	AP50	AP75	APs	APm	Cell IoU	Trap IoU	PQ
C-DETR A* [41]	–	–	–	–	–	83.0	85.0	–
C-DETR B* [41]	–	–	–	–	–	84.0	86.0	–
DISCO* [41]	–	–	–	–	–	70.0	–	–
Mask R-CNN (SOTA) [42]	65.4	98.4	85.4	56.5	71.1	84.0	89.0	–
Segment Anything (SAM) (Fine-tuned) [19]	44.8	94.0	83.8	47.8	50.0	63.1	89.9	88.1
Anchor-based ResNeSt [8]	78.2	99.3	95.0	70.9	83.4	87.6	**90.7**	89.0
CellPose [51]	44.4	94.5	82.2	–	–	–	–	–
MicroVision (Proposed)	**80.7**	**99.4**	**97.2**	**73.7**	**84.4**	**89.0**	90.5	**90.0**

Note: CellPose does not provide classification capabilities to distinguish between different classes in a microstructure environment.

which performs class-agnostic segmentation, Cellpose cannot distinguish between cells and traps. However, differentiating between these two was a critical requirement of this study. Cellpose showed significantly lower performance. As shown in Table 2, our method outperformed Cellpose by a margin of 36.3% in AP, demonstrating its superior ability to differentiate between object classes in microstructured environments. In the current setup, the Intersection over Union (IoU) for the cell class holds greater significance than the IoU for the trap class.

Figure 3 presents sample segmentation outputs. The first three columns display results from Mask R-CNN, ResNeSt, and SAM, respectively, while the fourth column shows the predictions from our proposed method. Ground truth annotations are indicated by solid lines (blue for cells, green for traps), while model predictions are shown using dotted lines (orange for cells, red for traps). In a variety of challenging scenarios, such as overlapping cells and objects near image boundaries, our model consistently produced more accurate segmentations.

In row (a), all models struggle with boundary precision; however, our model is able to segment both cells and traps more accurately. Mask R-CNN fails to detect both objects, while ResNeSt and SAM exhibit over-segmentation. In row (b), SAM incorrectly identifies an artifact as a cell and fails to segment the trap. Similar issues are observed in rows (c) and (d), where SAM and ResNeSt continue to struggle with boundary precision, whereas our model maintains relatively accurate predictions. These results highlight the robustness and superior accuracy of our approach in complex and diverse scenarios when compared to other methods.

For further analysis, Fig. 4 presents cases where the segmentation performance of the proposed approach was suboptimal. As in previous visualizations, the columns correspond to results from Mask R-CNN, ResNeSt, SAM, and our model. In row (a), our model fails to accurately capture the lower boundary of a cell near the edge of the image and struggles to delineate the trap region. SAM also fails to detect the cell in this case.

In row (b), similar boundary issues persist. In row (c), no cell is present, resulting in a cell IoU of zero across all models. However, our model reports the lowest trap IoU in this example. In row (d), the model over-segments a cell located between two traps and fails to accurately detect the trap boundaries, highlighting its limitations in handling complex spatial configurations. More details are provided in [36].

To evaluate the model's robustness under challenging imaging conditions, we conducted a series of experiments using test-time image degradation techniques, including the application of Gaussian noise, random brightness and contrast adjustments, Gaussian blur, as well as their combinations. These augmentations simulate reduced image quality and are intended to assess the model's performance in noisy, blurred, and varying illumination scenarios. The experimental results demonstrate that the proposed model maintains strong performance under these adverse conditions, effectively detecting cells and traps. Gaussian noise was applied with a standard deviation ranging from 0.07 to 0.10, while Gaussian blur was introduced with a blur limit between 1 and 4. For the random brightness and contrast transformations, a brightness limit of 0.2 and a contrast limit of 0.6 were used. In the combined degradation setting, Gaussian noise with a standard deviation range of 0.06 to 0.09 was applied, along with brightness and contrast adjustments (both set to 0.2). Additionally, Gaussian blur (limit range 1 to 4) was applied with a probability of 0.5. The quantitative results of these evaluations are summarized in Table 3. The qualitative results are presented in Fig. 5. The first column illustrates the model's performance under Gaussian noise. Despite the noise blending the boundaries of cells and traps with the background, the model accurately distinguishes between relevant structures and noise artifacts, as evident in the third image. The second column displays results under Gaussian blur. In the first image, the model successfully detects both cells and traps, although it struggles to delineate the lower boundary of the left trap. Similarly, in the third image, boundary detection becomes challenging in the presence of overlapping regions; however, all traps and cells are still correctly identified. The third column shows results under contrast shift. Even under significant contrast variations, the model demonstrates strong performance, with only minor failures in cases where object boundaries are heavily distorted, such as in the second image. The final column presents results from images processed with combined degradations. Despite the presence of artifacts resembling cells, the model correctly distinguishes between true structures and noise, as shown in the first image. It also successfully identifies traps blended into the background and detects very small cells, as demonstrated in the third image. Overall, the qualitative results indicate that the proposed approach performs robustly across all degradation scenarios, with only minor limitations in highly challenging conditions.

Table 3. Segmentation performance metrics for various augmentation strategies.

Method	AP	AP50	AP75	AP_s	AP_m	Cell IoU	Trap IoU	PQ
Gauss Noise	80.5	98.3	96.1	71.8	85.0	88.8	90.8	89.5
Gaussian Blur	79.3	98.9	96.1	70.8	83.8	88.5	89.9	89.0
Combined Filters	80.2	98.8	95.6	71.4	84.7	89.3	89.7	89.4
Brightness Contrast	79.6	98.9	95.7	71.5	84.0	89.0	90.4	89.4

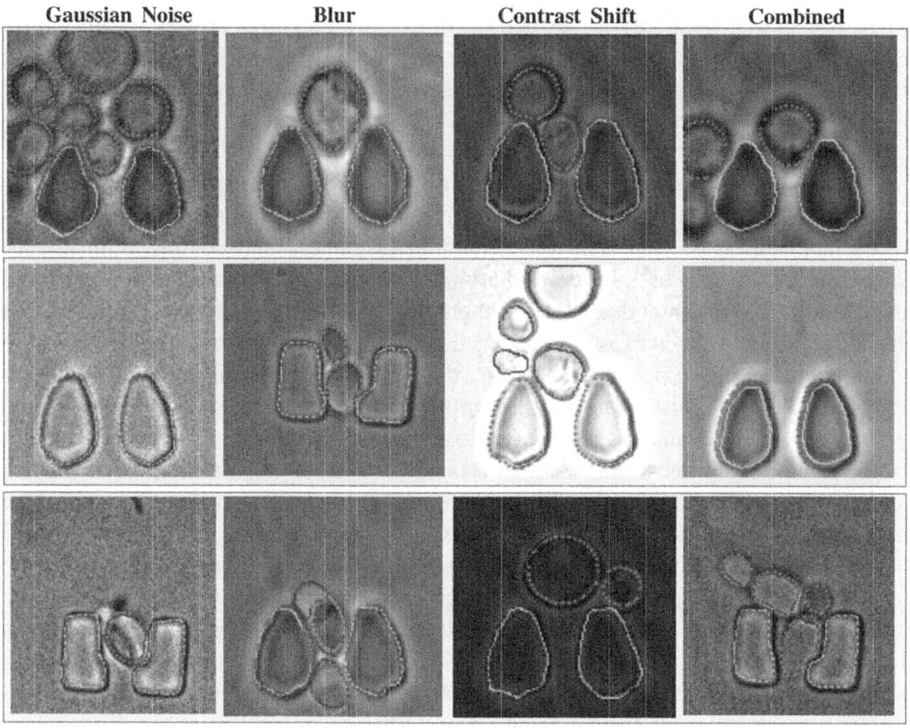

Fig. 5. Qualitative segmentation results under a variety of test-time augmentations. Each row shows one sample image; columns, from left to right, apply Gaussian noise, blur, contrast shift, and all three transformations combined. Ground truth cell masks are outlined in solid blue, while model predictions are marked by dotted orange lines. Solid green lines represent ground truth traps, and dotted red lines indicate the model's trap predictions.

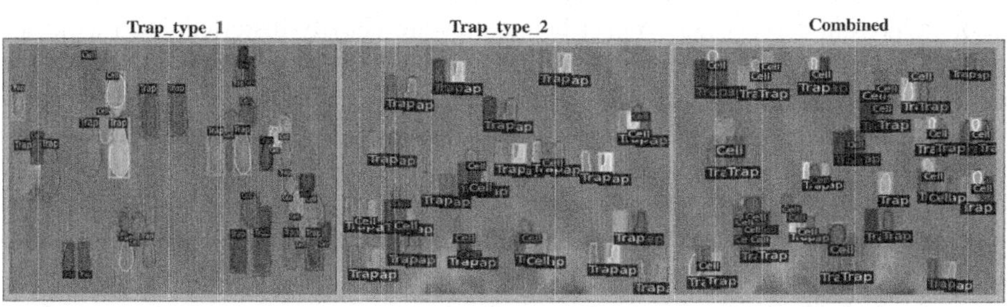

Fig. 6. Qualitative results on synthetically generated test images containing complex configurations of traps and cells. The first image includes oval-shaped traps, the second shows L-shaped traps, and the third combines both trap types. In each case, multiple traps and cells appear in close proximity. Despite the increased complexity compared to the training data, the proposed model accurately detects all traps and cells, demonstrating strong generalization capability.

The model was trained on images containing a maximum of two traps, up to seven cells, and only a single trap type per image. To evaluate the network's ability to generalize to more complex scenarios, additional test images were generated. These include configurations where multiple traps and cells appear in close proximity or where multiple trap types are present within a single image. The results are presented in Fig. 6. In the first image, oval-shaped traps are used. The second image features L-shaped traps, while the third image combines both oval and L-shaped traps. Each of these images includes varied and closely spaced arrangements of cells and traps, representing a level of complexity not present in the training data. Despite this, the proposed approach performs effectively. In the first image, the model correctly detects all traps and cells. In the second image, it continues to perform well, accurately identifying even very small cells and closely packed traps. The third image presents the most challenging case, yet the model maintains strong performance without confusing traps and cells. These findings demonstrate that the proposed method generalizes well to complex spatial configurations and trap types, even though such cases were not included in the training data. This highlights the approach's potential for deployment in real-world scenarios with high structural variability.

Table 4. Segmentation performance with different percentages of training data.

Percentage of Data	AP	AP50	AP75	CELL_IOU	TRAP_IOU	PQ
10	74.1	98.6	92.2	84.7	90.1	88.2
20	76.1	98.8	93.6	86.3	90.4	88.6
30	78.4	98.8	94.9	87.3	91.3	89.7
40	77.7	99.2	94.5	86.7	90.8	89.1
50	79.4	98.8	96.2	87.3	91.6	89.8
60	78.0	98.9	95.4	87.1	90.9	89.4
70	78.3	99.4	95.8	87.3	91.1	89.5
80	79.0	98.9	96.7	87.3	91.1	89.5
90	80.0	99.4	96.4	88.1	91.5	90.0

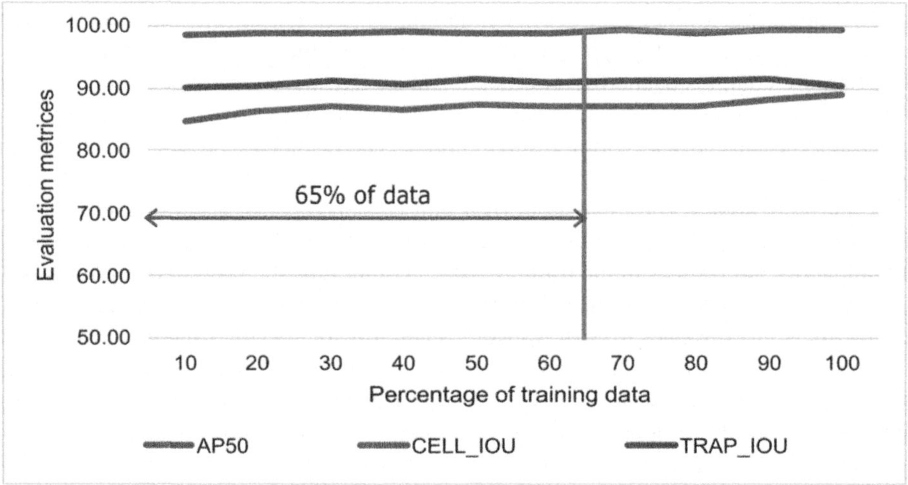

Fig. 7. Performance of the proposed model evaluated across different portions of the labeled training data.

To measure the label efficiency of the proposed network, which refers to the amount of labeled training data needed to achieve competitive performance, the model was trained using different portions of the available dataset. As shown in Fig. 7, the evaluation metrics including AP50, CELL IOU, and TRAP IOU remain relatively stable across different data splits. The model achieves close to its best performance with approximately 65% of the training data. After this point, additional data yields only minor improvements. This suggests that the model is capable of generalizing well even when trained with a limited amount of labeled data. Detailed performance values for each portion of training data are listed in Table 4. Linking the model's outputs to biologically meaningful metrics or insights, such as cell counts, size distributions, or spatial relationships, helps biologists directly interpret predictions in the context of their experimental hypotheses or workflows.

Vision Transformers are generally more computationally demanding than CNNs due to their self-attention mechanism, which computes interactions between every pair of image patches [34]. This mechanism enables Vision Transformers to effectively capture global dependencies across the entire image. In contrast, CNNs rely on convolutional operations that are more computationally efficient but may struggle to capture long-range dependencies, particularly in larger images. In this study, fine-tuning Vision Transformers yielded better segmentation performance than fine-tuning CNNs. However, this improvement came at the cost of increased inference time for Vision Transformers compared to CNNs. Despite the strong performance, our proposed approach still encounters challenges in cases where cell boundaries are ambiguous or when edge instances occur near image borders. These limitations highlight areas for potential enhancement in both segmentation accuracy and robustness.

8 Conclusion

In this research, a robust framework for the instance segmentation of yeast cells and traps in microstructured environments is introduced using a transformer-based architecture. The proposed method enables accurate detection and segmentation of individual yeast cells and traps, even when their visual characteristics closely resemble one another. Beyond the core segmentation performance, the model's robustness is also evaluated under challenging imaging conditions, including Gaussian noise, blur, and contrast shifts, confirming the model's resilience to real-world image degradation. The model's strong generalization capabilities are also demonstrated by testing it on complex spatial configurations with multiple trap types and densely packed cells, despite these scenarios not being present in the training data. Furthermore, the method achieved high segmentation accuracy even when trained on limited annotated data, highlighting its label efficiency. These findings position the framework as a practical tool for biological research, facilitating detailed analysis of yeast cell morphology and behavior under a wide range of experimental conditions. Future work will focus on further reducing computational demands and expanding to additional microstructured environments.

Acknowledgments. This research was supported by a Grant from the German-Israeli Foundation for Scientific Research and Development (GIF, Grant number I-1561-412.13/2023 to AD and JMH).

Disclosure of Interests. The authors have no competing interests to declare that are relevant to the content of this article.

References

1. Al-Hafiz, F., Al-Megren, S., Kurdi, H.: Red blood cell segmentation by thresholding and canny detector. Procedia Comput. Sci. **141**, 327–334 (2018)
2. Alexey, D.: An image is worth 16×16 words: transformers for image recognition at scale. arXiv preprint arXiv: 2010.11929 (2020)
3. Bakker, E., Swain, P.S., Crane, M.M.: Morphologically constrained and data informed cell segmentation of budding yeast. Bioinformatics **34**(1), 88–96 (2018)
4. Cai, Z., Vasconcelos, N.: Cascade R-CNN: delving into high quality object detection. In: Proceedings of the IEEE Conference on Computer Vision and Pattern Recognition, pp. 6154–6162 (2018)
5. Cai, Z., Vasconcelos, N.: Cascade R-CNN: high-quality object detection and instance segmentation. IEEE Trans. Pattern Anal. Mach. Intell. **43**(5), 1483–1498 (2019)
6. Cutler, K.J., et al.: OmniPose: a high-precision morphology-independent solution for bacterial cell segmentation. Nat. Methods **19**(11), 1438–1448 (2022)
7. Durkee, M.S., Abraham, R., Clark, M.R., Giger, M.L.: Artificial intelligence and cellular segmentation in tissue microscopy images. Am. J. Pathol. **191**(10), 1693–1701 (2021)
8. Edlund, C., et al.: LIVECell-a large-scale dataset for label-free live cell segmentation. Nat. Methods **18**(9), 1038–1045 (2021)
9. Ferreira, E., Silveira, G.: Classification and counting of cells in brightfield microscopy images: an application of convolutional neural networks. Sci. Rep. **14**(1), 9031 (2024)

10. Gao, Z., Xu, J., Chen, K., Wang, S., Ouyang, Q., Luo, C.: Comparative analysis of yeast replicative lifespan in different trapping structures using an integrated microfluidic system. Adv. Mater. Technol. **5**(12), 2000655 (2020)
11. Gu, H., Dong, H., Yang, J., Mazurowski, M.A.: How to build the best medical image segmentation algorithm using foundation models: a comprehensive empirical study with segment anything model. arXiv preprint arXiv:2404.09957 (2024)
12. Haja, A., Schomaker, L.R.: A fully automated end-to-end process for fluorescence microscopy images of yeast cells: from segmentation to detection and classification. In: Proceedings of 2021 International Conference on Medical Imaging and Computer-Aided Diagnosis (MICAD 2021) Medical Imaging and Computer-Aided Diagnosis, pp. 37–46. Springer (2022)
13. Hancock, J.: Jaccard distance (Jaccard index, Jaccard similarity coefficient) (2004). https://doi.org/10.1002/9780471650126.dob0956
14. He, F., Mahmud, M.P., Kouzani, A.Z., Anwar, A., Jiang, F., Ling, S.H.: An improved SLIC algorithm for segmentation of microscopic cell images. Biomed. Signal Process. Control **73**, 103464 (2022)
15. Khalid, N., et al.: PACE: point annotation-based cell segmentation for efficient microscopic image analysis. In: International Conference on Artificial Neural Networks, pp. 545–557. Springer (2023)
16. Khalid, N., et al.: CellGenie: an end-to-end pipeline for synthetic cellular data generation and segmentation: a use case for cell segmentation in microscopic images. In: Annual Conference on Medical Image Understanding and Analysis, pp. 387–401. Springer (2024)
17. Khalid, N., et al.: DeepMuCS: a framework for co-culture microscopic image analysis: from generation to segmentation. In: 2022 IEEE-EMBS International Conference on Biomedical and Health Informatics (BHI), pp. 01–04. IEEE (2022)
18. Kirillov, A., He, K., Girshick, R., Rother, C., Dollár, P.: Panoptic segmentation. In: Proceedings of the IEEE/CVF Conference on Computer Vision and Pattern Recognition, pp. 9404–9413 (2019)
19. Kirillov, A., et al.: Segment anything. In: Proceedings of the IEEE/CVF International Conference on Computer Vision, pp. 4015–4026 (2023)
20. Kong, Y., et al.: Automated yeast cells segmentation and counting using a parallel U-net based two-stage framework. OSA Continuum **3**(4), 982–992 (2020)
21. Kruitbosch, H.T., Mzayek, Y., Omlor, S., Guerra, P., Milias-Argeitis, A.: A convolutional neural network for segmentation of yeast cells without manual training annotations. Bioinformatics **38**(5), 1427–1433 (2022)
22. Lee, B.H.: Advanced Fermentation and Cell Technology, 2 Volume Set. Wiley (2021)
23. Li, Y., Mao, H., Girshick, R., He, K.: Exploring plain vision transformer backbones for object detection. In: European Conference on Computer Vision, pp. 280–296. Springer (2022)
24. Lin, T.Y., Dollár, P., Girshick, R., He, K., Hariharan, B., Belongie, S.: Feature pyramid networks for object detection. In: Proceedings of the IEEE Conference on Computer Vision and Pattern Recognition, pp. 2117–2125 (2017)
25. Lin, T.Y., et al.: Microsoft COCO: common objects in context. In: Computer Vision–ECCV 2014: 13th European Conference, Zurich, Switzerland, 6–12 September 2014, Proceedings, Part V 13, pp. 740–755. Springer (2014)
26. Liu, P., Liu, H., Yuan, D., Jang, D., Yan, S., Li, M.: Separation and enrichment of yeast saccharomyces cerevisiae by shape using viscoelastic microfluidics. Anal. Chem. **93**(3), 1586–1595 (2020)
27. Loh, D.R., Yong, W.X., Yapeter, J., Subburaj, K., Chandramohanadas, R.: A deep learning approach to the screening of malaria infection: automated and rapid cell counting, object detection and instance segmentation using mask R-CNN. Comput. Med. Imaging Graph. **88**, 101845 (2021)

28. Long, F.: Microscopy cell nuclei segmentation with enhanced U-net. BMC Bioinform. **21**(1), 8 (2020)
29. Loshchilov, I.: Decoupled weight decay regularization. arXiv preprint arXiv:1711.05101 (2017)
30. Lugagne, J.B., Lin, H., Dunlop, M.J.: DeLTA: automated cell segmentation, tracking, and lineage reconstruction using deep learning. PLoS Comput. Biol. **16**(4), e1007673 (2020)
31. Mahmoud, L.N.K.: A dictionary-based denoising method toward a robust segmentation of noisy and densely packed nuclei in 3D biological microscopy images. Ph.D. thesis, Sorbonne Université (2019)
32. Mandyartha, E.P., Anggraeny, F.T., Muttaqin, F., Akbar, F.A.: Global and adaptive thresholding technique for white blood cell image segmentation. In: Journal of Physics: Conference Series, vol. 1569, p. 022054. IOP Publishing (2020)
33. Martínez, J.L., Liu, L., Petranovic, D., Nielsen, J.: Pharmaceutical protein production by yeast: towards production of human blood proteins by microbial fermentation. Curr. Opin. Biotechnol. **23**(6), 965–971 (2012)
34. Maurício, J., Domingues, I., Bernardino, J.: Comparing vision transformers and convolutional neural networks for image classification: a literature review. Appl. Sci. **13**(9), 5521 (2023)
35. Mohammed, E.A., Mohamed, M.M., Naugler, C., Far, B.H.: Chronic lymphocytic leukemia cell segmentation from microscopic blood images using watershed algorithm and optimal thresholding. In: 2013 26th IEEE Canadian Conference on Electrical and Computer Engineering (CCECE), pp. 1–5. IEEE (2013)
36. Naseem, K., Khalid, N., Bertgen, L., Herrmann, J., Dengel, A., Ahmed, S.: YeastFormer: an end-to-end instance segmentation approach for yeast cells in microstructure environment. In: In Proceedings of the 17th International Conference on Agents and Artificial Intelligence, vol. 2, pp. 407–417 (2025). https://doi.org/10.5220/0013169400003890
37. Nasser, L., Boudier, T.: A novel generic dictionary-based denoising method for improving noisy and densely packed nuclei segmentation in 3D time-lapse fluorescence microscopy images. Sci. Rep. **9**(1), 5654 (2019)
38. Onyema, V., Amadi, O., Moneke, A., Agu, R.: A brief review: saccharomyces cerevisiae biodiversity potential and promising cell factories for exploitation in biotechnology and industry processes-west African natural yeasts contribution. Food Chem. Adv. **2**, 100162 (2023)
39. Osumi, M.: Visualization of yeast cells by electron microscopy. J. Electron Microsc. **61**(6), 343–365 (2012)
40. Paszke, A., et al.: PyTorch: an imperative style, high-performance deep learning library. Adv. Neural Inf. Process. Syst. **32** (2019)
41. Prangemeier, T., Reich, C., Koeppl, H.: Attention-based transformers for instance segmentation of cells in microstructures. In: 2020 IEEE International Conference on Bioinformatics and Biomedicine (BIBM), pp. 700–707. IEEE (2020)
42. Prangemeier, T., Wildner, C., Françani, A.O., Reich, C., Koeppl, H.: Yeast cell segmentation in microstructured environments with deep learning. Biosystems **211**, 104557 (2022)
43. Pratapa, A., Doron, M., Caicedo, J.C.: Image-based cell phenotyping with deep learning. Curr. Opin. Chem. Biol. **65**, 9–17 (2021)
44. Reich, C., Prangemeier, T., Françani, A.O., Koeppl, H.: An instance segmentation dataset of yeast cells in microstructures. In: 2023 45th Annual International Conference of the IEEE Engineering in Medicine & Biology Society (EMBC), pp. 1–4. IEEE (2023)
45. Reich, C., Prangemeier, T., Wildner, C., Koeppl, H.: Multi-styleGAN: towards image-based simulation of time-lapse live-cell microscopy. In: Medical Image Computing and Computer Assisted Intervention–MICCAI 2021: 24th International Conference, Strasbourg, France, 27 September–1 October 2021, Proceedings, Part VIII 24, pp. 476–486. Springer (2021)

46. Ren, S., He, K., Girshick, R., Sun, J.: Faster R-CNN: towards real-time object detection with region proposal networks. IEEE Trans. Pattern Anal. Mach. Intell. **39**(6), 1137–1149 (2016)
47. Ronneberger, O., Fischer, P., Brox, T.: U-net: convolutional networks for biomedical image segmentation. In: Medical Image Computing and Computer-Assisted Intervention–MICCAI 2015: 18th International Conference, Munich, Germany, 5–9 October 2015, Proceedings, Part III 18, pp. 234–241. Springer (2015)
48. Salem, D., Li, Y., Xi, P., Phenix, H., Cuperlovic-Culf, M., Kaern, M.: YeastNet: deep-learning-enabled accurate segmentation of budding yeast cells in bright-field microscopy. Appl. Sci. **11**(6), 2692 (2021)
49. Salem, N., Sobhy, N.M., El Dosoky, M.: A comparative study of white blood cells segmentation using otsu threshold and watershed transformation. J. Biomed. Eng. Med. Imaging **3**(3), 15 (2016)
50. Scherr, T., Löffler, K., Böhland, M., Mikut, R.: Cell segmentation and tracking using CNN-based distance predictions and a graph-based matching strategy. PLoS ONE **15**(12), e0243219 (2020)
51. Stringer, C., Wang, T., Michaelos, M., Pachitariu, M.: Cellpose: a generalist algorithm for cellular segmentation. Nat. Methods **18**(1), 100–106 (2021)
52. Tsai, H.F., Gajda, J., Sloan, T.F., Rares, A., Shen, A.Q.: Usiigaci: instance-aware cell tracking in stain-free phase contrast microscopy enabled by machine learning. SoftwareX **9**, 230–237 (2019)
53. Van Valen, D.A., et al.: Deep learning automates the quantitative analysis of individual cells in live-cell imaging experiments. PLoS Comput. Biol. **12**(11), e1005177 (2016)
54. Wang, C.W., Huang, S.C., Lee, Y.C., Shen, Y.J., Meng, S.I., Gaol, J.L.: Deep learning for bone marrow cell detection and classification on whole-slide images. Med. Image Anal. **75**, 102270 (2022)
55. Wang, Y., et al.: A high-throughput microfluidic diploid yeast long-term culturing (DYLC) chip capable of bud reorientation and concerted daughter dissection for replicative lifespan determination. J. Nanobiotechnol. **20**(1), 171 (2022)
56. Wang, Y., Wang, W., Liu, D., Hou, W., Zhou, T., Ji, Z.: GeneSegNet: a deep learning framework for cell segmentation by integrating gene expression and imaging. Genome Biol. **24**(1), 235 (2023)
57. Wen, C., et al.: 3DeeCellTracker, a deep learning-based pipeline for segmenting and tracking cells in 3D time lapse images. Elife **10**, e59187 (2021)
58. Witmer, A., Bhanu, B.: Multi-label classification of stem cell microscopy images using deep learning. In: 2018 24th International Conference on Pattern Recognition (ICPR), pp. 1408–1413. IEEE (2018)
59. Zhang, K., Liu, D.: Customized segment anything model for medical image segmentation. arXiv preprint arXiv:2304.13785 (2023)

Stock Price Prediction with Heterogeneous Data Fusion

Furkan Karadaş[1], Bahaeddin Eravcı[2](✉), and Ahmet Murat Özbayoğlu[2]

[1] Department of Computer Engineering, TOBB University of Economics and Technology, Ankara, Turkey
fkaradas@etu.edu.tr

[2] Department of Artificial Intelligence Engineering, TOBB University of Economics and Technology, Ankara, Turkey
{beravci,mozbayoglu}@etu.edu.tr

Abstract. Accurate stock price forecasting in volatile financial markets requires integrating heterogeneous data with advanced architectures. This study proposes a multimodal framework for stock price prediction that integrates historical financial data with textual sentiment from news and social media. The framework's performance is benchmarked across two core empirical comparisons: a domain-specific sentiment model (FinBERT) versus a general-purpose large language model (ChatGPT-4o), and a classic forecasting architecture (LSTM) versus a modern state-space model (Mamba). We employ a dual-evaluation methodology, assessing performance with both standard statistical metrics Rš, MAE) and a practical market simulation with initial capital to assess real-world profitability. The framework also incorporates an influence weighted sentiment score (IWSS), a metric that quantifies sentiment by weighting it with user engagement and influence to better capture market impact. Results demonstrate that models incorporating sentiment, particularly the IWSS, yield superior trading returns. We find that the generalist ChatGPT-4o performs competitively against the specialized FinBERT and the findings provide a robust, data-driven framework for investors seeking to improve their decision-making processes by strategically incorporating multimodal data analytics into financial forecasting.

Keywords: Financial Forecasting · Time Series Forecasting · Stock Market Prediction · Deep Learning · Deep Neural Networks · Multimodal Machine Learning · Large Language Models

1 Introduction

In today's financial landscape, investors and fund managers face the formidable challenge of making optimal investment decisions amidst a complex and dynamic market environment. The real-time impacts of global economic events, the reverberations of political developments, and the transformative effects of technological advances collectively exert a continuous influence on financial markets, thereby intensifying the difficulty of investment forecasting.

H. J. van den Herik et al. (Eds.): ICAART 2025, LNAI 16517, pp. 433–455, 2026.
https://doi.org/10.1007/978-3-032-25032-2_21

Financial data prediction has emerged as a critical area of research, aiming to navigate the intricate array of factors influencing financial markets. These factors encompass dynamic elements such as market volatility, shifts in economic data, policy developments, and investor sentiment. Modern systems, in particular, exhibit a continuously evolving structure, confronting uncertainty and volatility that impact the valuation of financial instruments. Consequently, investors and financial analysts are increasingly turning to diverse data sources to enhance the accuracy and efficacy of their financial data predictions. The limitations of traditional forecasting methods have spurred researchers to explore innovative approaches. Multimodal data analysis techniques hold the potential to offer a more comprehensive analysis through data enrichment. This trend in the literature underscores a continuously evolving field focused on improving the accuracy of financial forecasts.

The advancement of big data and machine learning technologies has seen successful applications in diverse fields such as medicine, computer vision, and telecommunications [1]. Due to this success, deep learning and machine learning models have recently gained traction as popular methods in financial forecasting. The application of machine learning and artificial intelligence techniques to financial data analysis and statistical analyses of temporal data offers insights and recommendations to investors to construct their portfolios [3,16,31,36].

The inherent complexity and dynamism of financial markets highlight the potential for misleading conclusions when relying on analyses based on a single attribute [30]. For instance, while Pearson correlation reveals linear relationships, it overlooks the multifaceted nature of financial data across different time frames. A singular attribute can only illuminate a specific facet, whereas financial markets are shaped by the interplay of numerous factors. When assessing a company's value solely on its stock price, critical factors such as the company's financial health, management quality, industry trends, economic conditions, and competitive landscape are often overlooked. In this context, textual data emerges as a significant resource for stock price forecasting. Prior studies [20,24] suggest that efforts to predict stock prices by leveraging the sentiment of textual data should be integrated with broader data sources. In addition, the findings of our preceding research study [15] demonstrated that the judicious selection of data sources is of paramount importance for effective stock price prediction.

Traditional analysis methods seek to forecast future price movements by examining price actions and trading volumes. However, the proliferation of information via social media, news sites, and other digital platforms has become a pivotal factor influencing market sentiment. In this regard, traditional analytical methods prove inadequate, and investors require more precise, rapid, and reliable forecasting tools and frameworks. Social media platforms, in particular, serve as a high-frequency lens into collective market psychology. They enable investors and other participants to share opinions rapidly, creating a rich data stream that can reveal and even amplify key behavioral finance signals. The analysis of this data presents unprecedented opportunities to observe phenomena like investor herding in real-time, offering a more nuanced understanding of underlying market trends beyond traditional financial metrics.

Accurate analysis of investor sentiment in financial markets is critical for making strategic decisions in today's complex investment environment. Sentiment analysis, in this context, is an important area of natural language processing that aims to automatically identify and extract subjective opinions from text-based data [41]. With the increasing popularity of online social networks, sentiment analysis of content shared on social media platforms has become a powerful tool for understanding market dynamics [11,44].

A novel multimodal framework is introduced and evaluated here to enhance stock price prediction by systematically integrating heterogeneous data sources. We move beyond traditional analysis by developing unique features from social media, news articles, historical prices, and technical indicators. We also develop the Influence-Weighted Sentiment Score (IWSS), a metric that captures not only the sentiment of social media posts but also their potential market impact by weighting them based on user influence and engagement. We leverage this enriched feature set to investigate two central questions. First, we assess the performance of a modern State Space Model, Mamba, against the widely-adopted LSTM architecture, examining their effectiveness in processing complex, multimodal financial data. Second, we conduct a direct empirical comparison between a domain-specific language model, FinBERT, and a state-of-the-art general-purpose model, ChatGPT-4o, to determine their relative efficacy in financial sentiment extraction. Finally, to ensure a robust evaluation, we assess performance not only through standard predictive metrics (R^2, MAE) but also through a practical market simulation, which back-tests the strategies to quantify their real-world profitability and impact on investment decisions.

2 Related Works

The dynamic and unpredictable nature of financial markets has necessitated the development of various forecasting methodologies to support investment decisions. Historically, two fundamental approaches have emerged in this field: technical analysis and fundamental analysis, each offering different perspectives to explain market movements. Technical analysis aims to generate forward-looking signals by combining past price movements and trading volume data with statistical indicators (such as SMA and RSI) [9], while fundamental analysis focuses on qualitative factors such as company profitability, macroeconomic data, and sectoral trends [19]. However, the increasing complexity of globalized financial systems has made the structural limitations of these traditional methods (e.g., data delays, human biases) more apparent. In addition to these approaches, econometric models attempt to capture cyclical patterns and seasonal effects in financial series, while behavioral finance theories focus on the impact of investor psychology on the market. These challenges and diverse needs have triggered the rise of quantitative finance models in the 21st century, initiating an interdisciplinary transformation through the integration of artificial intelligence-based techniques such as machine learning, deep learning, and natural language processing into financial forecasting [4]. Recently, hybrid approaches based on machine learning have been developed to overcome the limitations of traditional methods, demonstrating the potential to combine technical analysis, fundamental analysis, and behavioral finance influences within a single framework.

Financial time series present a challenging dataset for traditional econometric models due to their non-stationary nature and extreme sensitivity to external factors such as economic crises and political events [7]. Structural breaks observed in these series, especially when triggered by external factors like macroeconomic crises or global political fluctuations, make it impossible for model parameters to remain stable over time. This situation leads to sudden structural breaks and high levels of noise in the data. Classical models such as ARIMA and SARIMA are often inadequate in capturing market complexity because financial data frequently exhibit nonlinear relationships and long-term dependencies [32].

Traditional financial theory operates under the assumption that investors make rational decisions and that markets are perfectly efficient. However, in the real world, markets are characterized by overreactions and sudden crashes. The field of behavioral finance seeks to identify these inconsistencies by examining the depths of human psychology. For example, investors may be slow to cut losses due to loss aversion, may follow the crowd with herd behavior, or may enter risky positions with overconfidence [2]. Kahneman and Tversky's Prospect Theory explains the asymmetric behaviors investors exhibit when evaluating gains and losses and demonstrates how these emotional factors affect price movements [18].

To make sense of these psychological dynamics, sentiment analysis is becoming an integral part of financial forecasting. By analyzing textual data such as social media posts, news headlines, and forum comments with natural language processing models, the emotional state of the market can be converted into numerical scores. When combined with traditional data such as stock prices or trading volume, this reveals the emotional backdrop of market movements [26]. These methods make it possible to integrate market-wide emotional trends such as fear, greed, optimism, or pessimism with quantitative analysis. Evolving artificial intelligence models are not only dependent on numerical data but also serve as a bridge that combines qualitative and quantitative analysis within the framework of behavioral finance's predictions, using the emotions of people affecting the market. By combining these two different approaches, a holistic perspective is presented that interprets market movements in both technical and psychological dimensions [22].

The deepening role of machine learning in financial forecasting has significantly impacted sequential learning models. In this evolutionary process, the Long Short-Term Memory (LSTM) network [14], introduced in the early 1990s, stands out as a milestone. LSTM, a variant of the Recurrent Neural Network (RNN) [25] capable of modeling both short-term and long-term dependencies simultaneously, is a preferred model for deep learning developers, particularly in financial time series forecasting. In financial time series forecasting studies in the literature, the LSTM model is often considered the base model against which proposed models are compared [27,32,33]. In addition to its popularity in time series forecasting, this model has achieved success in natural language processing (NLP), especially in areas such as language modeling, translation, speech recognition, sentiment analysis, and predictive analysis [10,12,42], paving the way for the development of Large Language Models (LLM) [5].

Transformers [37], although a frequently used approach for time series forecasting tasks, can effectively address long-range dependencies through attention mechanisms. However, the quadratic complexity of this architecture significantly increases the computational load and memory consumption when working with long sequences. State

Space Models (SSM) aim to overcome the limitations of Transformer-based models by integrating with deep learning to resolve long-range dependencies more efficiently. The Mamba model [8] has rivaled Transformer models through a selective scanning mechanism that efficiently filters specific inputs and integrates time-dependent variable parameters into the state-space model, capturing long-range contexts. Thanks to the flexibility and efficiency provided by the selective scanning mechanism, Mamba is better able to understand complex dependencies and make more accurate predictions. This structure provides significant advantages in areas such as language modeling, natural language processing [17,38,45], and financial forecasting [23,29,40].

Studies on forecasting in financial markets are continuously evolving under the influence of various factors [31,35]. In particular, understanding the impact of social media and news sources on investor sentiment has become a key focus of research in this field [6]. Studies emphasize the effectiveness of sentiment analysis techniques and big data approaches in financial forecasting, thereby increasing the importance of this area [41]. The integration of multimodal data analysis with traditional finance methodologies and natural language processing techniques facilitates a more informed investment decision-making process.

3 Method

This research proposes a multimodal machine learning framework for achieving more precise financial market predictions, employing a feature-level fusion strategy to integrate heterogeneous data streams. Initially, distinct feature extraction pipelines are applied to the textual and numerical modalities. These data undergo various preprocessing methods and then the textual stream, comprising social media and news data, is processed using advanced NLP models (ChatGPT-4o and FinBERT) to derive quantitative sentiment features. Concurrently, the numerical stream of historical financial data is used to compute established technical indicators. In the subsequent fusion stage, these extracted sentiment features and technical indicators are concatenated with the core historical price data, creating a unified, high-dimensional feature vector for each time step. This integrated feature vector then serves as the input to the downstream time-series forecasting models—LSTM and Mamba—which are tasked with predicting future price movements. Various performance metrics are used to analyze the prediction accuracy and overall performance of the created models under different market dynamics. This methodological approach demonstrates how textual and financial data can be effectively integrated into time series forecasting models. This section will describe the proposed method in detail (Fig. 1).

3.1 Dataset

The dataset selected for this study comprises three distinct stocks of significance in financial analysis and market sentiment prediction: Walmart, Disney, and Microsoft. These three companies were selected to create a representative dataset that spans a range of sectors and market conditions. Walmart, as a leading player in the retail sector,

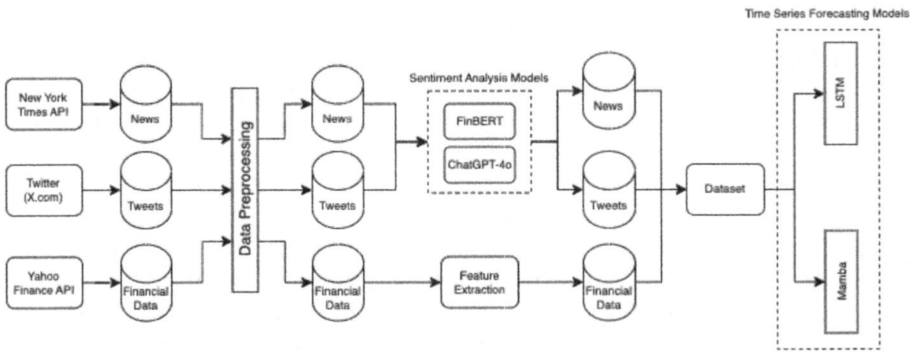

Fig. 1. System Overview.

has the potential to influence consumer behavior, while Disney stands out for its innovative structure within the entertainment industry and its management of various media platforms. Microsoft is notable for its strategic investments in technology and its new business models, such as cloud services. The diversity of these companies provides a comprehensive understanding of market dynamics.

Table 1 summarizes the key attributes of the three selected stocks, including industry details, market condition, and market capitalization (as of 2024). The stocks reflect a range of market conditions, including positive, negative, and neutral states. These conditions are defined by the predominant price trend during the study period: a positive condition denotes a general uptrend reflecting investor optimism; a negative condition signifies a downtrend associated with investor pessimism or economic headwinds; and a neutral condition represents a period of relative price stability and consolidation. The selected stocks illustrate various market dynamics and how these dynamics can influence investment strategies. This diversity across different sectors is an important factor in investors' decision-making processes and allows for the development of strategies based on market conditions.

Table 1. Information on Selected Stocks.

Stock Name	Industry	Market Condition	Market Cap
Microsoft	Software - Infrastructure	Positive	3.09T $
Walmart	Discount Stores	Neutral	643.86B $
Disney	Entertainment	Negative	170.71B $

3.2 Data Collection

A multimodal dataset was created for stock price prediction using financial indicators, social media, and news data. X (formerly Twitter), the most popular social media platform in the financial world, was selected as the data source, while news data were obtained from the New York Times, and stock financial data were provided by Yahoo Finance. The data presented herein were collected from 2018 to 2023 to reflect investor behavior and market sentiment. The resultant dataset is comprehensive stocks from a range of different sectors. As illustrated in Table 2, the aggregate number of tweets and news items associated with each stock is presented.

Table 2. Number of Tweets and News for Each Stock.

Stock Name	Number of Tweets	Number of News
Microsoft	43.952	3.639
Walmart	24.846	3.077
Disney	136.384	5.071

3.3 Data Preprocessing

The textual and numeric financial data that had been collected underwent a series of preliminary processing steps to ensure their suitability for the machine learning process. Initially, to address the irregularity of observed price ranges in the financial data (open, close, high, low, and volume), the Minimum-Maximum Normalization procedure was applied to scale the data before it entered the deep learning model. The objective of this method is to enhance the model's learning process by incorporating all periods within the financial data and assigning them a value between 0 and 1.

Concurrently, a comprehensive data cleaning process was performed to enhance the quality of the text within the acquired tweets and news articles. This process entailed the removal of superfluous content, including web page links (URLs), heading tags, user tags, and emojis. The removal of stop words, punctuation marks, special characters, and numbers that do not contribute to meaning was also undertaken. The entire text was converted to lowercase, with excessive spaces being eliminated. These steps are critical to ensuring that the dataset is suitable for subsequent analysis.

Frequently, data is absent from datasets, and this has a detrimental effect on analysis processes and the overall performance of the model. The distortions caused by missing data have the potential to reduce the model's prediction accuracy and render the reliability of the results questionable. There exists a variety of methodologies for the purpose of addressing incomplete data. The aforementioned methods include forward and backward filling techniques, correction using average or median values, estimation using regression analysis, and prediction of missing values using machine learning models (K-nearest neighbors). The objective of this variety is to utilize the entire dataset effectively and to enhance the accuracy of the analysis. For this research, due to the absence of news articles for each stock on a daily basis, the Forward Filling method was employed to impute missing values, thereby preserving the integrity of the dataset. The incorporation of missing data is of paramount importance in order to facilitate the enhancement of the predictive capabilities of the model.

3.4 Feature Extraction

In machine learning processes, feature extraction is a critical step, the purpose of which is to enable the retrieval of meaningful information from raw data. This process is of crucial importance in enhancing the performance of the model and ensuring the accuracy of the analysis.

Sentiment Analysis. Sentiment analysis is a natural language processing (NLP) technique aimed at identifying the author's subjective emotions and attitudes from texts. Sentiment analysis is a multifaceted field that encompasses the application of machine learning algorithms to various forms of text-based data, including social media posts, news articles, and user reviews. This technique involves the analysis of the emotional tone inherent in specific words and phrases to classify the overall sentiment in the text as positive, negative, or neutral. For instance, the market's reaction to a new monetary policy can be estimated by analyzing the sentiment of financial news and expert opinions. Sentiment analysis is crucial for gauging investor confidence and predicting market movements, assisting firms and analysts in understanding public sentiment.

On social media platforms, interactions with shared content offer powerful clues for understanding social sentiment and investor perception. User engagement metrics provide quantitative proxies for a tweet's potential market impact, complementing its raw textual sentiment. Tweet's likes serve as a measure of audience agreement, amplifying the perceived strength of the expressed opinion. In this regard, the high number of likes a tweet receives can strengthen the current sentiment in a reinforcing manner. A positive tweet creates a positive emotional impact when it receives a large number of likes, while liking a negative tweet may reinforce the negative perception of the content. Shares on tweets (retweets) quantify the content's dissemination and virality, reflecting the speed at which information propagates to a wider audience and potentially accelerating market reactions. Comments on tweets allow users to express their detailed thoughts, helping to better understand market expectations and the general public's response to the tweet. Finally, the author's follower count functions as a direct proxy for their influence and the tweet's potential reach, as posts from more authoritative sources are more likely to sway market perception.

Similarly, news articles represent an authoritative data stream for sentiment analysis. The language and tone of news content are critical for understanding how a wide spectrum of market participants, including individual investors, financial analysts, and institutional players, interpret and react to market developments. Positive-toned reporting can foster broad market confidence and influence upward revisions in analyst ratings, whereas negative news can heighten perceived risk and prompt widespread selling pressure. Therefore, integrating sentiment from both crowd-sourced social media and authoritative news sources provides a more holistic set of signals for robust market prediction.

A central research question in this study is whether a state-of-the-art, general-purpose large language model (LLM) can match the performance of a domain-specific model for financial sentiment analysis. To investigate this, we selected two representative models: FinBERT and ChatGPT-4o. FinBERT represents the specialized approach. As a BERT-based architecture extensively fine-tuned on a large corpus of financial texts (e.g., analyst reports, news), it is highly optimized to classify sentiment within financial discourse. In contrast, ChatGPT-4o represents the generalist approach. Instead of task-specific fine-tuning, we leverage its advanced reasoning capabilities through zero-shot in-context learning. This method involves providing the model with a carefully engineered prompt that instructs it to classify the sentiment of a given text as positive, neutral, or negative, along with a confidence score. This allows us to harness the model's broad contextual understanding without the need for model retraining. By integrating sentiment features from both models into our forecasting pipeline, we can empirically evaluate the impact of each approach on the final price prediction task, assessing the trade-off between deep domain specialization and broad contextual reasoning.

ChatGPT-4o: is a deep learning-based large language model developed by OpenAI [28]. This large language model is trained on vast datasets, enabling it to understand the complexities of language and generate text in various contexts. ChatGPT-4o stands out with its capacity to respond to user requests and interactions.

As a language model, ChatGPT-4o considers context to understand emotional tones and the writer's intent in texts. Its ability to process longer texts as well as short texts increases the model's flexibility. For instance, analyses performed on content written by users to understand their reactions to economic developments or financial events allow for a deeper market sentiment assessment.

One of the significant advantages of ChatGPT-4o is that it is a continuously updated and improved model. In addition, other large language models that have emerged in the market (Llama, Gemini, Claude, DeepSeek) are also constantly being developed and can be used effectively in different fields and scenarios. The learning that large language models make based on user feedback and real-world applications increases the accuracy of the model and enables more accurate results to be obtained. In this context, the ability to identify and classify emotional tendencies in financial texts facilitates investors' ability to make informed decisions about market trends.

FinBERT: is a specialized natural language processing model that exhibits high performance in sentiment analysis of financial texts [43]. Developed in 2019, this model is specifically trained with financial data, analysis reports, and market-related news, and optimized to classify the sentiment of texts (positive, neutral, negative). FinBERT has been trained with data from a wide range of financial sources, giving it a structure that can better understand financial terms and expressions. The model effectively identifies emotional tones in financial texts by classifying sentiment categories as positive, negative, and neutral.

FinBERT takes the Bidirectional Encoder Representations from Transformers (BERT) architecture as its foundation from traditional Transformers, while being enhanced with data customized for financial terminology and contexts. In this way, it is used in many areas such as sentiment analysis, risk assessment, and prediction of market trends in financial studies.

Sentiment Quantification and Influence Modeling. Each stock-related text obtained from tweets and news was provided as input to the ChatGPT-4o and FinBERT models. These models assigned a sentiment score ranging from –1 to 1, where a score of –1 indicates a highly negative sentiment, 0 reflects a neutral sentiment, and 1 denotes a highly positive sentiment. Additionally, the models provided an accuracy percentage that evaluates the reliability of the sentiment analysis. This accuracy percentage indicates the confidence level in the sentiment classification. For instance, if the model assesses a piece of data as positive, it also specifies that this assessment is made with an accuracy of 86%.

In addition, the Influence-Weighted Sentiment Score (IWSS) was developed to incorporate engagement data on tweets obtained from X (formerly Twitter). This method considers not only the sentiment analysis of each tweet but also its engagement metrics. These engagement metrics are: the number of likes for the tweet, the number of times the tweet is shared, the number of comments on the tweet, and the number of followers of the user who sent the tweet. Tweet engagement is defined as T_i:

$$T_i = \alpha * T_r + \beta * T_l + \gamma * T_c \tag{1}$$

where T_r represents the number of shares of the tweet, T_l represents the number of likes of the tweet, and T_c represents the number of comments of the tweet. In addition, α, β, and γ are hyperparameters reflecting the weights assigned to each metric. These parameters were set to 0.3 as the initial value without any optimization.

To quantify the influence of the tweet's author, we calculate a user influence parameter (U_i) directly from their follower count. This metric serves as a proxy for the tweet's potential broadcast reach across the social network. User influence is expressed as follows:

$$U_i = \delta * F_c \tag{2}$$

where F_c represents the number of followers of the user posting the tweet, and δ is a hyperparameter that determines the effect of the number of followers, and is selected as 0.1. This formula specifies the effect of the number of followers on the interaction power of users, thus allowing us to make a clearer evaluation of the audience reached by a particular tweet. Integrating user influence will contribute to obtaining better results in supporting investment decisions by increasing the accuracy of overall sentiment analysis.

$$S = S_l * S_c \tag{3}$$

where the sentiment score (S) is obtained by multiplying the sentiment label (S_c) by the accuracy percentage (S_l) of the sentiment classification. This calculation increases the accuracy of the calculated sentiment score by reflecting not only the obtained sentiment value but also the confidence level in the classification. Thus, the sentiment analysis result of each tweet shows not only a specific sentiment state, but also how reliable this assessment is. This approach is an important step towards increasing the quality of sentiment analysis and contributes to basing investment decisions on more solid foundations.

Total tweet engagement (TT_i) combines the total engagement obtained from likes, shares, and comments to evaluate the overall impact of each tweet. This is needed to better understand the user's level of interaction and the impact of the post on wider audiences. Thus, the reflection of each tweet on the media and its relationship with the audience are revealed more clearly. In addition to sentiment analysis, the analysis of the total number of interactions contributes to the evaluation of the emotional effects of users on investment decisions.

$$TT_i = T_r + T_l + T_c \tag{4}$$

where T_r is the number of shares of the tweet, T_l is the number of likes, and T_c is the number of comments. TT_i represents the total number of interactions.

The Influence-Weighted Sentiment Score (W_s) is therefore calculated to synthesize these components, creating a single, meaningful feature that reflects not only the sentiment's polarity but also its potential sphere of influence. It is calculated with the formula specified below:

$$W_s = \frac{T_i * U_i * S}{T_i} \tag{5}$$

where tweet engagement (T_i), user influence (U_i), sentiment score (S), and total tweet engagement (TT_i) are represented.

This approach incorporates the Influence-Weighted Sentiment Score (IWSS) that enhances tweets' sentiments by considering tweet engagement (number of likes, shares, and comments) and user influence (number of followers). This approach is expected to more accurately reflect the actual impact of tweets' effects and participation on stock prices, compared to just sentiment analysis of tweet content.

Financial Feature Engineering and Synchronization. Feature extraction on financial data aims to obtain meaningful information that can be used to better understand market dynamics, evaluate stock performance, and predict future price movements. To augment the raw price data, this study incorporates two technical indicators chosen for their efficacy in market analysis: the Simple Moving Average (SMA) and the Relative Strength Index (RSI), which are instrumental for identifying underlying price trends and measuring momentum.

The Simple Moving Average (SMA) helps to identify trends by taking the arithmetic average of prices over a specific period. It is generally calculated using the following formula:

$$SMA = \frac{1}{n}\sum_{i=1}^{n} P_i \tag{6}$$

where P_1, P_2, ..., P_n represent the prices in a specific period, and n represents the number of periods considered. SMA allows investors to understand market orientations and helps them observe price movements more clearly.

On the other hand, the Relative Strength Index (RSI) is a momentum indicator used to determine whether an asset is overbought or oversold. RSI is often calculated over 10 days and is obtained using the following formulas:

$$RSI = 100 - \frac{100}{1 + RS} \tag{7}$$

$$RS = \frac{AverageGain}{AverageLoss} \tag{8}$$

where RS (Relative Strength) expresses the ratio of average gains to average losses. When the RSI value rises above 70, the asset is considered overbought, and when it falls below 30, it is considered oversold. These indicators help investors determine potential price turning points and support their buying and selling decisions.

A key challenge in this multimodal framework is the need for temporal alignment, as the data streams possess asynchronous granularities. While financial price data is recorded at a discrete daily frequency, textual data from news and social media arrives aperiodically throughout the day. To resolve this temporal mismatch, we aggregate all intra-day textual data into a unified daily representation. For each stock on a given day, the mean sentiment score is computed from all corresponding texts (tweets and news). Furthermore, to capture the volume of public discourse, the total count of tweets and news articles for that day is included as a distinct feature. This aggregation process transforms the high-frequency, aperiodic textual data into a synchronized daily feature set, enabling its direct concatenation with the financial data for model ingestion.

3.5 Time Series Forecasting Models

LSTM. Long Short-Term Memory (LSTM) is an artificial neural network architecture developed by Hochreiter and Schmidhuber in 1997, specifically designed for working with sequence data [14]. LSTM is a member of the recurrent neural network (RNN) family; however, to overcome the short-term memory problem of traditional RNN models, LSTM incorporates a series of innovative mechanisms. These mechanisms enhance the LSTM model's ability to learn and preserve long-term dependencies, allowing it to achieve significant successes in various fields such as time series forecasting, language modeling, speech recognition, and financial analysis.

The scalability and flexible structure of the LSTM model make it extremely effective for working with complex and high-dimensional data. In particular, it exhibits strong performance in understanding successive states of target data and is widely used in predicting time series data [34,39]. Thanks to these features, it has become a frequently preferred model for sequential data in the field of artificial intelligence and machine learning.

Mamba. The Selective State Space Model, Mamba, has been introduced as a new version of the state space model [13]. Mamba is notable for being particularly effective on information-dense data, providing significant advantages in areas such as language modeling, natural language processing, image processing, and finance [17,21,23,29,38,45].

This new model incorporates two important changes compared to typical state space models. The first change is the introduction of a selection mechanism, which achieves better results by filtering specific data or focusing on certain data. Secondly, as a result of this selection mechanism, the possibility of using convolution is eliminated; therefore, the selective scan method is presented. The main function of selective scanning is to focus on important information in the input sequence and avoid calculating unnecessary operations. This provides both speed and memory efficiency. These changes allow for more effective and meaningful results to be obtained on discrete datasets [8].

4 Performance Evaluation and Discussions

Performance measurement is a significant process for evaluating the effectiveness and accuracy of a model, and this process varies depending on various circumstances. Evaluating financial forecasting models presents a unique challenge: statistical accuracy does not inherently guarantee economic value. A model can exhibit a strong fit to historical data (e.g., high R^2, low MAE) yet fail to generate profitable signals in a practical trading context. To address this, we employ a dual-pronged evaluation framework. First, we assess the models' predictive power using standard computational metrics to measure their accuracy. Second, we test their practical efficacy through a market simulation, which backtests the trading strategies derived from model predictions to quantify their real-world profitability. This section details this comprehensive evaluation methodology, covering the training strategy, the specific metrics used, and a thorough discussion of both the computational and market simulation results.

4.1 Training Strategy

This research will utilize two different machine learning models: LSTM and Mamba. All models are trained with 100 epochs and configured with a batch size of 64 units and a window size of 10 units to optimize computational resources and effectively capture temporal dependencies. The batch size determines the number of samples processed in each training step, balancing memory usage and learning stability, while the window size represents the number of successive data points that the model analyzes in a unit time step.

The LSTM model consists of a single layer of 256 units. The ReLU activation function and the Adam function with a learning rate of 0.001 were used to optimize the model.

The Mamba model is configured with a convolutional layer of 4 units and a state dimension of 16 units. A dropout rate of 0.2 was applied for model optimization, and the head size was set to 64 units; in addition, the depth of the architecture was limited to a single block depth.

In this work, the percentage change of the stock's closing price on the selected day compared to the previous day is estimated. The Mean Absolute Error (MAE) was selected as the loss (error) function between the estimated and actual data in the training and test data. The MAE aims to increase the prediction accuracy of the model by calculating the average of the squares of the differences between the predicted and actual values. To increase the reliability of the findings, each model produced results by going through both training and testing phases 10 times. The average of these results was also taken. This iterative approach helps minimize random variables or anomaly effects in the data and ensures that the performance metrics present a more stable and generalized model.

The training of the models was conducted using data from 2018 to 2022, with the 2023 data set being allocated for testing purposes. This temporal division enables the models to acquire knowledge from a substantial period of historical data before their evaluation on more recent data patterns and unseen market dynamics.

4.2 Evaluation Metrics

Predictive Accuracy Performance. Predictive accuracy performance metrics are used to evaluate the accuracy of developed models and to measure the model's ability to predict correctly. The Coefficient of Determination (R^2) and Mean Absolute Error (MAE) were selected as two main metrics to analyze model performance. These metrics provide a comparative assessment to understand how well the model works.

R^2 is a statistical value that measures the explanatory power of independent variables on the dependent variable. R^2 takes a value between 0 and 1; a value close to 1 indicates that the model successfully explains the data, while a value close to 0 indicates that the model is inadequate in its predictions. The formula for R^2 is as follows:

$$R^2 = 1 - \frac{\sum_{t=1}^{T}(Y_t - \hat{Y}_t)^2}{\sum_{t=1}^{T}(Y_t - \bar{Y})^2} \tag{9}$$

where Y_t represents the actual values, $\hat{Y}_t$ represents the predicted values, and $\bar{Y}$ represents the average of the actual values.

Another performance metric, MAE, measures the average absolute difference between predicted values and actual values. The formula for MAE is as follows:

$$MAE = \frac{1}{n}\sum_{t=1}^{n}|Y_t - \hat{Y}_t| \tag{10}$$

where n is the total number of observations; Y_t represents the actual values; and $\hat{Y}_t$ represents the predicted values. Lower values of MAE indicate that the model's predictions are closer to the actual values.

Market Simulation. Market simulation is a testing process designed to evaluate the performance of developed models in real market conditions. In this phase, the historical success of strategies on past data is analyzed using the back-testing method, and future potential returns and risks are modeled. Back-testing plays an important role, especially in measuring the resilience of strategies in different market scenarios (rising/falling trends, increased volatility, etc.). The main purpose of the simulation is to support investment decisions and minimize the risk of overfitting by verifying the effectiveness of strategies with quantitative data. In this way, the alignment between the theoretical performance of the model and real-world conditions is systematically tested.

To measure the practical effectiveness of the developed model, an automated trading simulation is designed based on the closing prices predicted by the model. The simulation is initiated with an initial capital, simulating the opening and closing of long or short positions in line with the signals produced by the model. In the long position strategy, stock purchases are made if the closing price predicted by the model for the next day is above the current closing price; when the price is predicted to fall, the long position is closed to realize profit, and then a short position is entered. In the short position strategy, stock is borrowed and sold immediately in line with the predicted downward trend, and when the price falls, it is bought back cheaper, and the difference is converted into profit. In both strategies, transactions are simulated on real market data (closing price) without transaction costs. This approach provides insights not only into the model's performance with past data, but also into how it performs in a variable and dynamic market.

4.3 Results and Discussions

Predictive Accuracy Performance Results. Stock prices of Walmart, Disney, and Microsoft were predicted using two different models (LSTM and Mamba) and two different natural language processing models for sentiment analysis (FinBERT and ChatGPT-4o). R^2 and MAE metrics were used to evaluate model performance. R^2 shows how well the model explains the data, while MAE measures the average deviation of model predictions from actual values. High R^2 values and low MAE values indicate better model performance.

Table 3. Predictive Accuracy Performance Comparison of Models.

	LSTM				MAMBA			
	FinBERT		ChatGPT-4o		FinBERT		ChatGPT-4o	
	R^2	MAE	R^2	MAE	R^2	MAE	R^2	MAE
Disney	**0.95**	**1.29**	0.95	1.35	0.95	1.32	0.95	1.34
Walmart	0.95	0.44	0.94	0.47	**0.95**	**0.43**	**0.94**	**0.43**
Microsoft	0.98	3.89	**0.98**	**3.87**	0.98	4.23	0.98	4.07

Table 3 contains the prediction results of the data allocated for training for the years 2018–2022 and for testing for the year 2023. When the table is examined, the Mamba prediction model and the FinBERT and ChatGPT-4o sentiment analysis model combinations obtained the best R^2 (0.94 and 0.95) and MAE (0.43) results in Walmart stock. In the Disney stock, the LSTM model and FinBERT (1.29), and on the Microsoft side, the LSTM and ChatGPT-4o (3.87) combination showed the best performance.

Table 4 shows the performance of models trained using data from 2018–2022 for training and 2023 for testing, in predicting Walmart, Disney, and Microsoft. Also, it details the predictive accuracy results across various feature configurations, revealing that the optimal feature set is highly dependent on the specific stock being analyzed. A consistent finding, however, is the superior performance of models utilizing sentiment scores from FinBERT, which achieved the lowest Mean Absolute Error (MAE) for all three companies. Specifically, the most accurate model for Walmart integrated tweet-derived sentiment (MAE = 0.40, $R^2 = 0.95$). For both Disney and Microsoft, the greatest reduction in error was achieved by incorporating the Simple Moving Average (SMA) technical indicator, resulting in minimal MAE values of 1.26 and 3.89, respectively. This suggests that while multimodal data is beneficial, the relative importance of textual sentiment versus technical indicators varies across different assets.

Table 4. Predictive Accuracy Performance Comparison of Features.

	DISNEY				WALMART				MICROSOFT			
	FinBERT		ChatGPT-4o		FinBERT		ChatGPT-4o		FinBERT		ChatGPT-4o	
	R^2	MAE	R^2	MAE	R^2	MAE	R^2	MAE	R^2	MAE	R^2	MAE
Prices	0.95	1.37	0.95	1.32	0.95	0.42	0.95	0.41	0.98	4.00	0.98	4.06
Prices, RSI	0.95	1.31	0.95	1.30	0.94	0.44	0.95	0.43	0.98	3.99	0.98	3.90
Prices, SMA	**0.95**	**1.26**	0.95	1.35	0.95	0.41	0.95	0.42	**0.98**	**3.89**	0.98	3.88
Prices, RSI, SMA	0.95	1.36	0.95	1.32	0.95	0.42	0.95	0.43	0.98	4.21	0.98	3.99
Prices, News	0.95	1.40	0.94	1.53	0.95	0.42	0.95	0.43	0.98	4.20	0.98	3.97
Prices, News, RSI	0.95	1.36	0.94	1.44	0.95	0.42	0.94	0.43	0.98	4.12	0.98	4.14
Prices, News, SMA	0.94	1.46	0.94	1.47	0.95	0.41	0.94	0.45	0.98	4.26	0.98	3.98
Prices, News, RSI, SMA	0.95	1.37	0.95	1.41	0.94	0.43	0.94	0.47	0.98	4.03	0.98	4.07
Prices, Tweets	0.95	1.38	0.95	1.40	**0.95**	**0.40**	0.95	0.41	0.98	4.00	0.98	3.92
Prices, Tweets, RSI	0.95	1.38	0.95	1.37	0.95	0.43	0.94	0.43	0.98	3.99	0.98	4.22
Prices, Tweets, SMA	0.94	1.41	0.95	1.37	0.95	0.41	0.95	0.42	0.98	3.94	0.98	4.05
Prices, Tweets, RSI, SMA	0.95	1.41	0.95	1.31	0.94	0.43	0.94	0.43	0.98	3.97	0.98	4.03
Prices, News, Tweets	0.94	1.43	0.94	1.54	0.95	0.42	0.94	0.44	0.98	4.27	0.98	4.15
Prices, News, Tweets, RSI	0.94	1.43	0.94	1.43	0.95	0.43	0.94	0.45	0.98	4.14	0.98	4.00
Prices, News, Tweets, SMA	0.94	1.42	0.94	1.46	0.95	0.41	0.94	0.45	0.98	4.14	0.98	3.98
Prices, News, Tweets, RSI, SMA	0.95	1.40	0.94	1.44	0.94	0.44	0.94	0.47	0.98	4.20	0.98	4.02
Prices, IWSS	0.95	1.34	0.95	1.34	0.95	0.41	0.95	0.43	0.98	3.95	0.98	4.00
Prices, IWSS, RSI	0.95	1.29	0.94	1.42	0.95	0.42	0.95	0.43	0.98	4.03	0.98	3.96
Prices, IWSS, SMA	0.95	1.32	0.95	1.29	0.95	0.41	0.95	0.42	0.98	3.91	0.98	3.90
Prices, IWSS, RSI, SMA	0.95	1.28	0.95	1.27	0.95	0.43	0.94	0.44	0.98	3.97	0.98	3.96
Prices, IWSS, News	0.95	1.38	0.94	1.50	0.95	0.42	0.95	0.42	0.98	4.11	0.98	4.00
Prices, IWSS, News, RSI	0.94	1.43	0.94	1.44	0.95	0.41	0.94	0.45	0.98	4.11	0.98	4.04
Prices, IWSS, News, SMA	0.94	1.45	0.94	1.51	0.95	0.42	0.95	0.44	0.98	4.16	0.98	3.94
Prices, IWSS, News, RSI, SMA	0.95	1.37	0.94	1.46	0.95	0.42	0.94	0.46	0.98	4.36	0.98	4.05

Market Simulation Results Market simulation reveals the practical performance of models under scenarios that reflect market conditions. Simulations are designed structures to test the applicability and effectiveness of investment strategies. In this process, different market scenarios and models are evaluated. The simulation results show which strategies are more successfully implemented in certain market conditions and in which situations models have the potential to increase their effectiveness.

In the developed market simulation, a starting capital of 1 million US dollars was allocated for each stock. Comparative performance is presented based on the opening and closing of long or short positions in line with the signals produced by the model, under different data combinations (news, technical indicators, social media interactions, etc.). These data combinations are evaluated using forecasting models through percentage return. The results of the market simulation demonstrate the percentage of profit achieved during the test period.

The performance of the model encompasses the evaluation of the prediction results of sentiment analysis models (FinBERT and ChatGPT-4o) integrated with two different prediction models (LSTM and Mamba) through market simulation. A passive investment strategy called 'buy and hold' was taken as a reference to evaluate the performance of active strategies. In this strategy, the investor buys a specific asset at the beginning of the test period and holds it until the end of the period without interfering with short-term fluctuations in the market. The basic logic is based on the principle of reducing market risk over time and benefiting from long-term economic growth. All stocks were bought at the beginning of the test period and sold at the end of the test period, and the absolute return or loss rate was calculated at the end of the period.

Table 5 is the model using attributes including tweets, news, and financial indicators for all stocks performs better than the base model using only price data. In Walmart stock, the FinBERT (11.96%) and ChatGPT-4o (12.00%) models achieved the best profitability rate when price information and tweets attributes were used. The model with price information, IWSS, news, SMA, and RSI attributes, which showed the best performance, was Disney (58.40%). In Microsoft stock, the prices, IWSS, and news attributes with the ChatGPT-4o sentiment analysis model achieved the highest gain with 18.49%.

When the Table 6 is examined, it is seen that there are differences between the performances of both the prediction models and the sentiment analysis models for each stock. In the evaluation of Walmart, the Mamba model provided the highest profit (8.88%) when used with the FinBERT sentiment analysis model. The analyses made for Disney exhibit more complex results. The positive profit of 98.45% offered when the Mamba model is used with FinBERT sentiment analysis reveals the model's capacity to better predict the future movements of the stock by effectively analyzing market dynamics and social media sentiment. It also shows a positive performance (85.45%) when used with ChatGPT-4o sentiment analysis. All models show a better performance compared to the buy and hold value (–8.83%). In the results of Microsoft stock, the highest profit is obtained with 5.19% when LSTM and FinBERT models are used.

Discussion of Findings. The empirical results validate this study's central hypothesis: a multimodal framework integrating textual sentiment with financial data not only enhances predictive accuracy but also translates into substantial improvements in practical trading profitability. This finding underscores that price movements can be more effectively predicted when supported not only by historical data but also by textual data reflecting market dynamics (investor sentiment) and technical indicators. While high R^2 values (consistently > 0.94) across configurations demonstrate strong model fit, the market simulation provides a clearer measure of real-world efficacy, revealing a crucial insight: the models with the highest statistical accuracy are not always the most

Table 5. Market Simulation Performance Comparison of Features.

Profit (%)	DISNEY		WALMART		MICROSOFT	
	FinBERT	ChatGPT-4o	FinBERT	ChatGPT-4o	FinBERT	ChatGPT-4o
Prices	46.80	42.40	5.31	5.69	–3.36	2.20
Prices, RSI	39.41	44.54	4.55	5.71	–4.56	2.63
Prices, SMA	41.96	41.63	7.70	8.90	0.95	7.20
Prices, RSI, SMA	44.18	33.61	5.28	6.98	–12.15	–3.26
Prices, News	44.57	25.15	4.28	5.16	–2.57	6.35
Prices, News, RSI	36.40	23.75	2.88	1.61	5.85	5.37
Prices, News, SMA	45.51	28.81	9.44	4.20	9.24	15.27
Prices, News, RSI, SMA	43.27	29.33	3.10	–2.06	4.22	–1.27
Prices, Tweets	41.24	40.85	11.96	**12.00**	–1.46	6.61
Prices, Tweets, RSI	37.01	41.26	10.45	8.89	–6.74	–1.81
Prices, Tweets, SMA	30.31	54.14	10.35	7.69	2.96	1.87
Prices, Tweets, RSI, SMA	38.90	55.89	7.33	11.74	1.48	–13.02
Prices, News, Tweets	44.90	38.33	3.62	6.07	12.13	6.36
Prices, News, Tweets, RSI	41.06	37.07	4.72	1.22	6.01	7.08
Prices, News, Tweets, SMA	45.98	39.68	9.42	4.30	7.54	8.79
Prices, News, Tweets, RSI, SMA	41.27	29.71	2.26	1.32	1.01	7.59
Prices, IWSS	42.24	38.15	6.34	5.70	0.34	7.95
Prices, IWSS, RSI	35.94	36.19	5.23	4.32	–12.47	–6.30
Prices, IWSS, SMA	37.54	49.45	6.28	4.53	4.19	4.35
Prices, IWSS, RSI, SMA	53.06	43.13	3.49	1.01	–6.25	–8.21
Prices, IWSS, News	53.30	31.51	6.14	4.69	3.06	**18.49**
Prices, IWSS, News, RSI	46.20	29.30	4.79	0.65	2.36	8.27
Prices, IWSS, News, SMA	39.08	35.11	4.90	3.66	10.14	8.69
Prices, IWSS, News, RSI, SMA	**58.40**	30.21	7.33	0.51	–3.55	2.30

profitable. This paradox underscores the necessity of a dual-evaluation approach that combines predictive metrics with practical, profit-based back-testing. Active trading strategies guided by our models consistently outperformed the passive 'buy and hold' benchmark, most notably for Disney, where the Mamba-FinBERT model transformed a potential 8.83% loss into a 98.45% gain during the 2023 test period. The introduction of our novel Influence-Weighted Sentiment Score (IWSS) was particularly effective; the highest returns for both Disney (58.40%) and Microsoft (18.49%) were achieved in configurations incorporating this score, confirming that accounting for user influence and engagement provides a more potent predictive signal than raw sentiment alone.

The market simulation results presented reveal a noteworthy trend: the 'Buy and Hold' strategy yielded superior profit percentages for Walmart and Microsoft compared to both the LSTM and Mamba models. This observation underscores a critical challenge in applying complex machine learning models to financial markets. While these

Table 6. Market Simulation Performance Comparison of Models.

Profit (%)					
	LSTM		Mamba		Buy and Hold
	FinBERT	ChatGPT-4o	FinBERT	ChatGPT-4o	
Disney	9.81	4.53	**98.45**	85.45	–8.83
Walmart	0.98	1.92	**8.88**	4.09	11.94
Microsoft	**5.19**	1.13	–3.72	5.10	59.47

models possess the capacity to capture intricate patterns in data, their performance can be hindered by several factors. One such factor is the potential for overfitting due to an excess of input features. Too many features can lead the model to learn noise rather than genuine predictive signals, resulting in poor performance on unseen data. The difficulty of accurately timing the market, compounded by the inherent randomness and volatility of financial assets, further complicates the application of these models. Moreover, discrepancies between the training and testing periods can significantly impact a model's performance. A model trained on historical data may fail to generalize to future market conditions if those conditions differ substantially from the data used for training. To address these challenges, future research should prioritize feature selection to reduce model complexity and enhance robustness. Developing strategies that account for the inherent uncertainty of market movements and employing techniques to mitigate the impact of training and testing period inconsistencies are also crucial steps. By carefully considering these factors, the potential of machine learning models in financial forecasting can be more effectively realized.

A pivotal finding is the competitive performance of the general-purpose ChatGPT-4o against the domain-specific FinBERT. The ability of a generalist LLM, applied via zero-shot in-context learning, to achieve performance parity with a specialized, fine-tuned model has significant implications. It suggests that the sophisticated contextual reasoning of state-of-the-art foundation models can effectively substitute for resource-intensive domain specialization, potentially democratizing access to advanced financial sentiment analysis.

During the data collection process, although tweets and news data were filtered through various methods, it was found that some of the data were not directly related to the stock or did not contain important information that would affect the stock value. A significant challenge in this endeavor is the presence of extraneous and irrelevant content in the substantial data sets derived from social media platforms. This is a problem that has the potential to adversely affect the quality of the data collected and the performance of the model. Consequently, future research should focus on the development of a more sophisticated filtering mechanism to assess the potential of the data to influence the stock value. This mechanism may employ natural language processing (NLP) techniques to analyze the meaning and content of the data, identify stock-related terms and topics, and eliminate irrelevant data. The employment of sophisticated filtering methodologies enables the acquisition of a more refined and pertinent data set, thereby enhancing the predictive accuracy of the model and ensuring the reliability of financial analysis outcomes.

5 Conclusion

This study addressed the inherent uncertainty of financial markets by developing and evaluating a multimodal forecasting framework. We systematically assessed the efficacy of integrating heterogeneous data—historical prices, technical indicators, news, and social media—to better model market dynamics. Through in-depth examination of model performance across different stocks, this work provides a clearer understanding of how various feature and model combinations impact forecasting outcomes.

The comparative analysis between the LSTM and Mamba forecasting architectures revealed distinct advantages. While both models proved capable, Mamba's flexible structure demonstrated a superior ability to model complex data dependencies, resulting in a more generalized and often more effective predictive model.

A central contribution of this work lies in the analysis of sentiment extraction. The comparison between the specialized FinBERT and the general-purpose ChatGPT-4o showed that large language models can achieve competitive performance on financial sentiment analysis without domain-specific fine-tuning, highlighting their potential for broader accessibility. Furthermore, our results confirm that enriching traditional financial data with textual attributes from news and social media leads to more robust forecasts. Specifically, the Influence-Weighted Sentiment Score (IWSS) introduced in this study, which incorporates user engagement and influence metrics, proved to be a particularly effective feature, demonstrating that how sentiment is quantified is as important as the sentiment itself. These findings provide valuable insights for investors, underscoring the power of multimodal analytics in their decision-making processes.

Future Work. Future work will focus on extending the proposed framework to further enhance financial forecasting. One key direction involves integrating macroeconomic indicators, such as gross domestic product (GDP), inflation rates, and unemployment statistics. Incorporating this data is expected to provide a more comprehensive market context, thereby improving the model's ability to capture market sentiment and increase predictive accuracy. Additionally, we plan to expand the comparative analysis of sentiment models by benchmarking other contemporary large language models against the performance of FinBERT and ChatGPT-4o. Pursuing these extensions aims to develop a more robust and comprehensive analytical tool, further contributing to more informed, data-driven investment decisions.

Appendix

A ChatGPT-4o Prompt

We used a specific prompt to calculate the sentiment in tweets and news articles from ChatGPT-4o. Below is the prompt used to guide the ChatGPT-4o:

"You are an experienced financial analyst tasked with analyzing tweets and news related to a specific stock to gauge the overall sentiment and potential impact on the stock's price. For each given tweet or news snippet about the target stock, please: 1. Carefully consider the sentiment expressed, looking at factors like: Positive or negative language and tone; Mentions of financial performance, profits/losses, business developments; Discussion of stock price movements, investor confidence; Overall implications of the content for the stock. 2. Based on your analysis, provide the sentiment label (positive, negative, or neutral) and a sentiment score (between 0 and 1) representing the probability of the sentiment label (e.g., a score of 0.8 for a negative label means there is an 80% probability that the tweet is negative). 3. Provide the sentiment score for each text item, along with a one-sentence explanation for your score. Please look at the 'Content' column and analyze each row. Then, add columns for sentiment label and scoring (between 0 and 1) in the file. You should add the sentiment label and score in the current file. Remember to consider the financial and investing context carefully, not just generic sentiment. Focus on how the information may impact the stock and investor perceptions."

References

1. Ahmedt-Aristizabal, D., Armin, M.A., Denman, S., Fookes, C., Petersson, L.: Graph-based deep learning for medical diagnosis and analysis: past, present and future. Sensors **21**(14), 4758 (2021)
2. Baker, H.K., Nofsinger, J.R.: Behavioral Finance: Investors, Corporations, and Markets. John Wiley & Sons, Hoboken (2010)
3. Boginski, V., Butenko, S., Pardalos, P.M.: Statistical analysis of financial networks. Comput. Stat. Data Anal. **48**(2), 431–443 (2005)
4. Buchanan, B.G.: Artificial intelligence in finance (2019)
5. Chang, Y., et al.: A survey on evaluation of large language models. ACM Trans. Intell. Syst. Technol. **15**(3), 1–45 (2024)
6. Coelho, J., D'almeida, D., Coyne, S., Gilkerson, N., Mills, K., Madiraju, P.: Social media and forecasting stock price change. In: 2019 IEEE 43rd Annual Computer Software and Applications Conference (COMPSAC), vol. 2, pp. 195–200. IEEE (2019)
7. Cont, R.: Empirical properties of asset returns: stylized facts and statistical issues. Quant. Financ. **1**(2), 223 (2001)
8. Dao, T., Gu, A.: Transformers are ssms: generalized models and efficient algorithms through structured state space duality. arXiv preprint arXiv:2405.21060 (2024)
9. Di Lorenzo, R.: Basic technical analysis of financial markets. Perspect. Bus. Cult. **38**, 86–101 (2013)
10. Gao, T., Chai, Y., Liu, Y.: Applying long short term momory neural networks for predicting stock closing price. In: 2017 8th IEEE International Conference on Software Engineering and Service Science (ICSESS), pp. 575–578. IEEE (2017)
11. Giachanou, A., Crestani, F.: Like it or not: a survey of twitter sentiment analysis methods. ACM Comput. Surv. (CSUR) **49**(2), 1–41 (2016)
12. Greff, K., Srivastava, R.K., Koutník, J., Steunebrink, B.R., Schmidhuber, J.: Lstm: a search space odyssey. IEEE Trans. Neural Netw. Learn. Syst. **28**(10), 2222–2232 (2016)
13. Gu, A., Dao, T.: Mamba: linear-time sequence modeling with selective state spaces. arXiv preprint arXiv:2312.00752 (2023)

14. Hochreiter, S., Schmidhuber, J.: Long short-term memory. Neural Comput. **9**(8), 1735–1780 (1997)
15. Karadas, F., Eravci, B., Özbayoglu, A.M.: Multimodal stock price prediction. In: Proceedings of the 17th International Conference on Agents and Artificial Intelligence, ICAART 2025, vol. 3, Porto, Portugal, 23–25 February 2025, pp. 687–694. SCITEPRESS (2025). https://doi.org/10.5220/0013174500003890
16. Keskin, M.M., Yilmaz, M., Ozbayoglu, A.M.: A deep neural network model for stock investment recommendation by considering the stock market as a time graph. In: 2021 2nd International Informatics and Software Engineering Conference (IISEC), pp. 1–6. IEEE (2021)
17. Lenz, B., et al.: Jamba: hybrid transformer-mamba language models. In: The Thirteenth International Conference on Learning Representations (2025)
18. Levy, J.S.: An introduction to prospect theory. Polit. Psychol. 171–186 (1992)
19. Li, L.: Macroeconomic factors and the correlation of stock and bond returns. Available at SSRN 363641 (2002)
20. Li, M.X., Jiang, Z.Q., Xie, W.J., Xiong, X., Zhang, W., Zhou, W.X.: Unveiling correlations between financial variables and topological metrics of trading networks: evidence from a stock and its warrant. XXPhys. A **419**, 575–584 (2015)
21. Liang, A., Jiang, X., Sun, Y., Shi, X., Li, K.: Bi-mamba+: bidirectional mamba for time series forecasting. arXiv preprint arXiv:2404.15772 (2024)
22. Liapis, C.M., Karanikola, A., Kotsiantis, S.: A multi-method survey on the use of sentiment analysis in multivariate financial time series forecasting. Entropy **23**(12), 1603 (2021)
23. Ma, S., Kang, Y., Bai, P., Zhao, Y.B.: Fmamba: mamba based on fast-attention for multivariate time-series forecasting. arXiv preprint arXiv:2407.14814 (2024)
24. Mantegna, R.N.: Hierarchical structure in financial markets. Eur. Phys. J. B-Condensed Matter Complex Syst. **11**, 193–197 (1999)
25. Medsker, L., Jain, L.C.: Recurrent Neural Networks: Design and Applications. CRC press, Boca Raton (1999)
26. Mishev, K., Gjorgjevikj, A., Vodenska, I., Chitkushev, L.T., Trajanov, D.: Evaluation of sentiment analysis in finance: from lexicons to transformers. IEEE Access **8**, 131662–131682 (2020)
27. Muncharaz, J.O.: Comparing classic time series models and the lstm recurrent neural network: an application to s&p 500 stocks. Financ. Markets Valuat. **6**(2), 137–148 (2020)
28. OpenAI: Openai (2025). https://openai.com/
29. Patro, B.N., Agneeswaran, V.S.: Simba: simplified mamba-based architecture for vision and multivariate time series. arXiv preprint arXiv:2403.15360 (2024)
30. Saha, S., Gao, J., Gerlach, R.: A survey of the application of graph-based approaches in stock market analysis and prediction. Int. J. Data Sci. Anal. **14**(1), 1–15 (2022)
31. Sezer, O.B., Gudelek, M.U., Ozbayoglu, A.M.: Financial time series forecasting with deep learning: a systematic literature review: 2005–2019. Appl. Soft Comput. **90**, 106181 (2020)
32. Siami-Namini, S., Namin, A.S.: Forecasting economics and financial time series: arima vs. lstm. arXiv preprint arXiv:1803.06386 (2018)
33. Siami-Namini, S., Tavakoli, N., Namin, A.S.: A comparative analysis of forecasting financial time series using arima, lstm, and bilstm. arXiv preprint arXiv:1911.09512 (2019)
34. Sirisha, U.M., Belavagi, M.C., Attigeri, G.: Profit prediction using arima, sarima and lstm models in time series forecasting: a comparison. IEEE Access **10**, 124715–124727 (2022)
35. Tang, Y., et al.: A survey on machine learning models for financial time series forecasting. Neurocomputing **512**, 363–380 (2022)
36. Tsay, R.S.: Analysis of Financial Time Series. John Wiley & Sons, Hoboken (2005)
37. Vaswani, A., et al.: Attention is all you need. Adv. Neural Inf. Process. Syst. **30** (2017)
38. Waleffe, R., et al.: An empirical study of mamba-based language models. arXiv preprint arXiv:2406.07887 (2024)

39. Wang, G., Yu, G., Shen, X.: The effect of online investor sentiment on stock movements: an lstm approach. Complexity **2020**(1), 4754025 (2020)
40. Wang, Z., et al.: Is mamba effective for time series forecasting? Neurocomputing **619**, 129178 (2025)
41. Wankhade, M., Rao, A.C.S., Kulkarni, C.: A survey on sentiment analysis methods, applications, and challenges. Artif. Intell. Rev. **55**(7), 5731–5780 (2022)
42. Wu, Y., et al.: Google's neural machine translation system: bridging the gap between human and machine translation. arXiv preprint arXiv:1609.08144 (2016)
43. Yang, Y., Uy, M.C.S., Huang, A.: Finbert: a pretrained language model for financial communications. arXiv preprint arXiv:2006.08097 (2020)
44. Yue, L., Chen, W., Li, X., Zuo, W., Yin, M.: A survey of sentiment analysis in social media. Knowl. Inf. Syst. **60**, 617–663 (2019)
45. Zhao, H., Zhang, M., Zhao, W., Ding, P., Huang, S., Wang, D.: Cobra: extending mamba to multi-modal large language model for efficient inference. In: Proceedings of the AAAI Conference on Artificial Intelligence, vol. 39, pp. 10421–10429 (2025)

Improving Answer Generation Quality in LLM-Based Employee Coaching Systems: Evaluation of Next-Generation Models for German Customer Service

Maximilian Orlowski(✉), Emilia Knauff(✉), and Florian Marquardt(✉)

Brandenburg University of Applied Sciences, Magdeburger Straße 50, 14770 Brandenburg an der Havel, Germany
{maximilian.orlowski,emilia.knauff, florian.marquardt}@th-brandenburg.de

Abstract. This paper addresses the challenge of answer generation quality in Retrieval-Augmented Generation (RAG) based employee coaching systems for the German energy sector. Building upon previous work that achieved strong document retrieval performance (90.8% precision) but inadequate answer quality (21.6–40.2% accuracy), we evaluate next-generation LLMs to identify models capable of producing responses of higher answer quality for network operator processes reaching notable better accuracy results (65.7–68.2%), while keeping the reliable retrieval step.

Our study systematically evaluates advanced open-source models including Phi4 from Microsoft, qwen3 from Alibaba, gemma3 from Google, llama3.3 and llama4 from Meta as well as mistral from Mistral AI. We focus specifically on answer generation capabilities while maintaining the four critical deployment dimensions: *performance, correctness, integration*, and *locality* for on-premise deployment in compliance-sensitive environments.

Through experiments on a network operator coaching scenarios, we demonstrate that newer model versions show notable improvements in German language understanding and Generation. Our evaluation methodology focuses on automated semantic similarity assessments to identify models that can provide answer quality required for real-world deployment.

The research addresses a fundamental limitation identified in earlier RAG implementations where strong information retrieval could not compensate for poor answer synthesis. Our findings provide actionable insights for organizations seeking to deploy AI coaching assistants in specialized domains, particularly in regulated industries requiring on-premise solutions. We establish benchmarks for acceptable answer quality thresholds and recommend specific model configurations that progresses towards production-level performance for employee onboarding in high-turnover environments.

This work contributes to the practical deployment of enterprise AI systems by focusing on the bottleneck of answer generation quality.

Keywords: GenAI · LLM · RAG · Model Evaluation · German Language Generation · On Premises AI

H. J. van den Herik et al. (Eds.): ICAART 2025, LNAI 16517, pp. 456–477, 2026.
https://doi.org/10.1007/978-3-032-25032-2_22

1 Introduction

The local deployment of Retrieval-Augmented Generation (RAG) systems in enterprise environments has shown promising potential for addressing critical challenges in employee onboarding and training, particularly in specialized domains such as the German energy sector. While previous research has demonstrated the feasibility of implementing such systems for coaching assistants in network operator processes, a significant gap remains between proof-of-concept implementations and production-ready solutions.

Our earlier work [17] established the foundational infrastructure for an on-premise RAG system that achieved strong document retrieval performance with 90.8% precision in identifying relevant information from domain-specific knowledge bases. However, the identified critical bottleneck was the insufficient quality of the answer generation, with accuracy rates ranging from only 21.6% to 40.2% depending on the configuration parameters. This limitation prevented the system from meeting the qualitative requirements necessary for deployment in production environments.

The rapid evolution of Large Language Models presents new opportunities to address these limitations. The emergence of next-generation open-source models from major technology companies—including Microsoft's Phi4, Alibaba's Qwen3, Google's Gemma3, Meta's Llama3.3 and Llama4 as well as Mistral from Mistral AI offers substantially improved capabilities in multilingual understanding and generation tasks. These advances are particularly relevant for German language processing, where specialized models have shown improvements over their predecessors.

The energy sector's operational challenges further underscore the importance of this research. Network operators face persistently high employee turnover rates of 20–30% annually, creating continuous pressure for effective onboarding solutions. The recent surge in private photovoltaic as well as energy storage installations has dramatically increased customer contact volumes, amplifying the need for rapid, accurate employee training. Traditional approaches—classroom sessions, shadowing experienced colleagues, and extensive documentation review—remain time-intensive and struggle to adapt to evolving regulatory landscapes and technological advances.

Implementing AI-powered solutions in local environment has to meet enterprise requirements due to four critical deployment constraints [17]: *performance* limitations that affect user experience, *correctness* issues that compromise reliability in regulated environments, *integration* challenges with legacy systems and workflows, and *locality* requirements that mandate on-premise deployment for data security and compliance. Cloud-based alternatives, while offering advanced capabilities, conflict with the data sovereignty and privacy requirements inherent in handling sensitive customer and process information within sectors like German energy network operators.

This paper addresses the critical challenge of answer generation quality by conducting a systematic evaluation of advanced open-source LLMs to identify models capable of producing production-ready responses. Our research methodology focuses on automated semantic similarity assessments complemented by domain expert validation to establish benchmarks for acceptable answer quality thresholds in specialized industrial applications.

Building upon the proven RAG architecture from our previous work, we maintain the established infrastructure while systematically evaluating how newer model generations perform in German language understanding and generation tasks. To isolate the impact of improved language models on answer quality, we maintained the exact retrieval infrastructure from our previous work, including the same embedding models, document preprocessing pipeline, and vector database configuration. Only the answer generation component was modified to evaluate next-generation LLMs. Our evaluation encompasses a real-world scenario from a network operator coaching environments, providing actionable insights for organizations seeking to deploy AI assistants in regulated industries.

The contributions of this work is a model selection for evaluating LLM performance in enterprise RAG systems. We suggest quantitative metrics for production-readiness, demonstrate substantial improvements achievable with next-generation models, and offer specific model recommendations that achieve the answer quality thresholds required for deployment in high-stakes operational environments.

This research directly addresses the practical quality challenges that prevent many AI initiatives from progressing beyond pilot phases, focusing specifically on the answer generation bottleneck that represents a significant barrier to production deployment in compliance-sensitive industries requiring on-premise solutions.

2 Underlying Technologies

Within the scope of this paper two types of models are relevant: Large Language Models (LLMs) and Embedding Models.

An *LLM* is a type of neural network, that uses the transformer architecture, specifically utilizing a decoder-only configuration with self-attention heads [28]. This architectural foundation is exemplified in the GPT acronym, which stands for *Generative Pretrained Transformer*. These models process natural language text inputs of variable length and generate corresponding natural language outputs. Due to their stochastic nature, the system returns the output with the highest probability distribution, within a number of given parameters, for any given input. The training process involves exposure to extensive text corpora, including comprehensive digitized literary collections, complete Wikipedia content, and substantial volumes of web-scraped data.

Following the initial release of pretrained language models such as GPT-1 by OpenAI [18], numerous models have been developed, ranging from proprietary to open-source implementations. These models exhibit variations across multiple dimensions: training datasets (corpora), model scale (determined by parameter count), network architectures (encoder-decoder versus decoder-only [6]) and the licenses they are released under.

Despite their capabilities, all of these models have certain limitations, most notably the phenomenon of *hallucination* [2,9]. Hallucination refers to the generation of factually or logically incorrect outputs in response to given inputs, despite these outputs representing the most statistically probable responses based on the model's training data. Various mitigation strategies have been developed to address this challenge.

When conceptualizing an LLM as a black-box system, two primary intervention points exist for addressing hallucinations: The model itself as well as the prompt. Tonmoy et al. describe these possibilities as *Developing Models* and *Prompt Engineering* respectively [23].

Model Development encompasses two distinct methodologies. The first involves training a complete model from scratch using domain-specific datasets. However, such pretraining requires substantial computational resources, making it practically infeasible outside of major technology companies. The alternative approach is model fine-tuning, which also relies on domain-specific datasets but adjusts only a substantially smaller subset of model parameters, typically the final network layer. This approach significantly reduces computational requirements, enabling fine-tuning even on consumer hardware (like a NVIDIA GTX 4090) for small models (e.g., up to 7 billion parameters). Also the amount of data needed for fine-tuning is significant smaller in comparison with a pretraining.

Prompt Engineering, the second approach to mitigate hallucinations, focuses on optimizing input prompts to reduce the probability of generating inaccurate information. A widely adopted technique involves incorporating explicit instructions that direct the LLM to acknowledge uncertainty rather than attempt to generate potentially erroneous responses. Specifically, these instructions instruct the model to inform users when reliable factual answers cannot be generated, rather than producing responses that may contain hallucinations.

RAG Systems extend this approach by providing the LLM with fact-enriched prompts that contain all necessary information to answer the query correctly. From this fact-enriched prompt the LLM only needs to generate a well formulated answer containing the provided facts.

Retrieval Augmentation Generation (RAG) is a technique to enhance the performance of large language models (LLMs) [7, 12]. This approach enables the integration of domain-specific knowledge bases to generate more accurate and contextually appropriate responses. RAG proves particularly valuable when an LLM's pretrained knowledge may be outdated, incomplete, or lacking in specialized information. In our application, this allows incorporation of domain-specific knowledge regarding distinct processes within the German energy industry.

The initial phase of a RAG system is *retrieval*, which involves preprocessing a variety of documents in varying formats such as html, pdf, and others which can be referred to as the external knowledge base. These documents undergo processing by embedding models that extract relevant information and transform it into embeddings stored within a local vector database. In our experiments, we used the chromadb vector database [5] for the implementation. There are a number of other implementations and providers of online vector databases [10]. ChromaDB was selected for our experiments due to its straightforward local deployment, comprehensive documentation, and independence from online service registration requirements and therefore was conform to our requirement of *locality*. Through semantic similarity calculations on the query embeddings and the embeddings stored in the vector database, relevant document chunks can then be retrieved from the external knowledge base.

During the *augmentation* phase the retrieved document chunks are integrated into the prompt structure. This augmented prompt combines the original user query with the additional contextual information from the external knowledge base, ensuring the model's response is grounded in domain-specific data.

The *generation* phase encompasses response creation based on the augmented prompt. The LLM now utilizes both its internal knowledge and the retrieved domain-specific information.

Retrieval Augmented Generation is categorized as a prompt engineering technique [23]. Since RAG systems require insertion of available knowledge into prompts, the utilized LLM must possess a context window (also termed context length) of appropriate size.

In contrast to LLMs, **Embedding Models** are specialized systems designed to generate numerical vector representations of textual content (while other data types such as images can also be embedded, this discussion focuses on textual representations). Although every LLM incorporates an embedding layer, standalone embedding models are typically employed in RAG systems for the initial retrieval phase. During pre-processing, all factual content or knowledge chunks are processed by the embedding model, which generates corresponding embedding vectors (abbreviated as *embeddings*).

Similarity Matching describes the computational process of determining semantic similarity between textual segments through similarity score calculation. This process involves initial text processing by an embedding model (as described above) to compute numerical vector representations, followed by distance metric calculation (Euclidean distance, cosine similarity, or dot product) between these vectors (embeddings). The resulting metric value corresponds to the semantic similarity of the associated texts [24].

Chunking is an essential pre-processing step in RAG systems during which documents get partitioned into smaller segments, called chunks or splits. These chunks undergo subsequent embedding by an embedding model, which generates numerical vector representations for the document segments. The resulting vectors, called embeddings, are then used for semantic similarity matching in high dimensional vectorspaces. The concept is, that those vectors whose corresponding textchunks are semantically similar to each other, are positioned in close proximity within the vector space. The similarity of the textchunks is measured through application of various distance measures to the embeddings, including cosine similarity, the euclidian distance or the dot product of the two vectors [11].

In our evaluation, we examine *five different models* that all possess solid German language capabilities and are suitable for deployment in RAG systems, with their performance varying depending on the specific application and available resources:

Qwen3 developed by Alibaba from China, is a family of LLMs designed with a strong emphasis on performance, efficiency, and multilingual capabilities. It includes both dense and Mixture-of-Expert (MoE) architectures, with parameter scales ranging from 0.6 to 235 billion. Qwen3 introduces a unified framework that integrates a "thinking mode" (for complex, multi-step reasoning) and a "non-thinking mode" (for fast, context-sensitive responses). This integration eliminates the need to switch between specialized models such as chat-optimized models and reasoning-focused models and enables dynamic mode selection based on user queries or system templates [27].

Phi-4 is a 14-billion parameter language model developed by Microsoft with a focus on data quality. Unlike many LLMs that rely primarily on organic web data, Phi-4 incorporates synthetic data throughout its training process. Despite its relatively small size, the model achieves competitive performance, demonstrating that well-curated training data can enable smaller models to rival or outperform larger ones. [1].

Gemma 3 developed by Google, is a lightweight, multimodal open model that scales from 1 to 27 billion parameters. It introduces capabilities in vision understanding, extended multilingual support, and significantly increased context length (up to 128K tokens). Compared to its predecessor, Gemma 2, this model shows marked improvements in mathematical reasoning, conversational ability, instruction following, and multilingual performance—all while maintaining computational efficiency. [21].

Llama 3 is a family of language models developed by Meta that natively support multilinguality, coding, reasoning and tool usage. It offers a balanced compromise between performance and efficiency with 8 billion parameters. The model is available for both research and commercial applications (for organizations with fewer than 700 million monthly active users) and demonstrates strong capabilities across multiple languages [22].

Mistral by Mistral AI is a model family designed for high efficiency and strong performance. Released under the Apache 2.0 license, it has gained recognition for its effectiveness relative to its size. Mistral AI has also played a leading role in popularizing the Mixture-of-Experts paradigm, offering models known for their efficient deployment and robust reasoning abilities [8]. Mistral is the only European-based model within our selection.

3 Infrastructure and Experimental Setup

Building upon our previous work, we established a robust RAG-based coaching system for German network operator processes [17]. The original system architecture consisted of a two-phase processing pipeline: document ingestion and user querying, implemented using a Retrieval-Augmented Generation approach with locally deployed embedding as well as open-source LLMs.

3.1 System Architecture

For the systematic evaluation of next-generation LLMs, we reused the deployed environment centered around an NVIDIA A100 80GB PCIe AI Accelerator. This hardware setup allows to evaluate multiple large language models with parameters ranging from 7B to 70B.

The experimental infrastructure consisted of two virtual machines with following specifications (VM1/VM2) vCPU-Cores (28/2), RAM (252 GB/32 GB) and Ubuntu 22.04.03 LTS for both VMs. The first virtual machine was equipped with direct access to the NVIDIA A100 accelerator via PCIe Passthrough and provisioned with CUDA 12.2 for optimal GPU utilization.

3.2 Switching Model Runtime from FastChat to Ollama

Building upon the infrastructure specifications also used in our previous work, this study transitions from FastChat to Ollama as the serving infrastructure for enhanced model evaluation scenarios. This choice was driven by several key advantages of Ollama in comparison to FastChat for experimental workflows:

- Simplified Model Management: Ollama provides streamlined model downloading, loading, and switching capabilities easing comparative evaluation across multiple models
- Consistent API Interface: Standardized REST API enabling automated evaluation pipeline integration
- Resource Optimization: Efficient memory management supporting rapid model switching during evaluation cycles

Ollama demonstrates improvements across the four identified deployment dimensions. *Performance* improvements include concurrent processing capabilities that enable parallel request handling while maintaining minimal memory overhead. *Multi-model serving* capabilities allow simultaneous loading of different models within the same service instance, eliminating the architectural complexity of managing separate model workers required for RAG systems with both embedding and text generation models. *Integration* benefits stem from Ollama's simplified deployment model that functions as a drop-in replacement for OpenAI's API, requiring only base URL configuration changes compared to FastChat's distributed controller-worker architecture. *Locality* requirements remain fully satisfied while reducing operational complexity through a single-service deployment model that reduces internal communication between components.

3.3 Evaluation Framework

To enable systematic and reproducible evaluation of answer generation quality across multiple LLM candidates, we implemented an automated assessment framework using Promptfoo as our primary evaluation platform. This framework was specifically designed to address the limitations identified in our previous manual evaluation approaches.

Promptfoo was configured to interface with our Ollama-hosted models through the standardized OpenAI API, enabling batch processing of evaluation queries across different model configurations. The evaluation pipeline focused on semantic similarity assessment, which inluded automated comparison of generated answers against expert-validated ground truth using embedding-based similarity scoring. Alongside the accuracy also measurement of response times were stored.

This experimental design allows for direct comparison of answer generation quality improvements by controlling for retrieval performance, ensuring that observed differences result from LLM capabilities rather than changes in document retrieval.

3.4 Model Evaluation Criteria

The evaluation framework focused on quantifiable metrics that directly relate to the four critical deployment dimensions identified in our previous work.

Licensing and Commercial Viability: Models were assessed for licensing terms that permit modification and commercial use within enterprise environments. This criterion eliminates models with restrictive licenses that would prevent production deployment, ensuring only commercially viable solutions advance to technical evaluation phases. This criteria is part of the *locality* dimension.

Resource Compatibility: Evaluation included assessment of model parameter counts and memory requirements to ensure compatibility with our NVIDIA A100 80GB infrastructure. Models exceeding 70 billion parameters (unquantized) were excluded from evaluation to maintain deployment feasibility within established hardware constraints. This criteria is part of the *integration* and *locality* dimension.

German Language Proficiency: Given the specific deployment context within German energy sector operations, models were systematically evaluated for their native language understanding and generation capabilities. This assessment encompassed grammatical accuracy, technical terminology handling, and contextual appropriateness in professional German communication, building upon the language requirements established in our selection criteria. Context Window Adequacy: Models were evaluated for context window capacity sufficient to accommodate retrieved document chunks and augmented prompts. This technical requirement ensures models can process the expanded context necessary for RAG-based answer generation without truncation or information loss. This criteria is part of the *Correctness* dimension.

Answer Quality Assessment: The primary evaluation criterion measured semantic accuracy and completeness of generated responses compared to expert-validated ground truth answers. This assessment utilized automated semantic similarity scoring through embedding-based comparison between model outputs and known-correct responses from domain experts, employing cosine similarity calculations consistent with our retrieval pipeline. This criteria is part of the *Correctnesss* dimension.

Performance Characteristics: Response time measurements were collected across all evaluated models to assess their operational viability within user interaction workflows. This included mean response times, distribution analysis, and identification of performance outliers that could impact user experience, directly supporting the performance dimension of our deployment framework. This criteria is part of the *Performance* dimension.

An additional consideration is the number of parameters of the Large Language Models, as larger models generally demonstrate better results in answer quality, though this must be balanced against available computational resources.

3.5 Choosen Models

Using the Model Evaluation criteria given in the last section we selected a set of local running LLMs for our experiments.

Building upon our previous work that evaluated earlier generation models such as Llama2 variants and Vicuna, this study focuses on state-of-the-art open-source models that represent the current frontier of locally deployable language models. The selected models include Microsoft's Phi4 (14B parameters), representing efficient performance with carefully curated training data; Alibaba's Qwen3 (32.2B parameters), offering advanced reasoning capabilities with extended context length; Google's Gemma3 (27.4B parameters), providing enhanced multilingual support and mathematical reasoning; Meta's Llama3.3 (70.6B parameters), delivering comprehensive language understanding at scale; and Mistral's latest model (7B parameters), notable as the only European-developed model in our evaluation. These next-generation models shown in Table 1 offer substantial improvements over the baseline models from our previous research. Where earlier evaluations were limited by licensing restrictions (such as Vicuna's non-commercial license) or insufficient German language capabilities in base models, the current selection provides production-ready alternatives with appropriate licensing for commercial deployment. All selected models meet the licensing requirements for commercial use, with Phi4, Qwen3 and Mistral released under permissive licenses (MIT and Apache 2.0 respectively), while Gemma3 operates under Google's Gemma license, and Llama3.3 follows Meta's Llama3.3 license terms. The context window sizes range from 8k tokens for Mistral to 128k tokens for both Gemma3 and Llama3.3, providing adequate capacity for the document retrieval and augmentation requirements of our RAG system.

Table 1. Comparison of candidates for utilized LLM.

Name	base/finetuned	Modelsize (8bit compr.)	Context Size	Licence
Phi4	base	14B params	16k Tokens	MIT
Qwen3 32B	base	32.2B params	32k Tokens	Apache 2.0 license
Gemma3 27B	base	27.4B params	128k Tokens	Gemma license
Llama3.3 70B	base	70.6B params	128k Tokens	Llama3.3 license
Llama4 16x17B	base	109B params	256k Tokens	Llama 4 Community License Agreement
Mistral 7B	base	7B params	8k Tokens	Apache 2.0 license

The same criteria and constraints applied for our embedding model selection, maintaining consistency with our previous work [19]. As established in our earlier research, we initially experimented with standard models like *all-MiniLM-L6-v2* but found that English embedding models performed poorly for German texts in our knowledge base and user queries. Therefore we utilized *cross-en-de-roberta-sentence-transformer*, an embedding model by T-Systems [20] that is fine-tuned for German language and performed reasonably well in our use cases. For this evaluation, we continued using the *mxbai-embed-large-v1* by Mixedbread.AI [14] as it yielded the best results in our retrieval tests from the previous study.

The model selection enables systematic evaluation of how architectural improvements, training methodologies, and scale affect answer generation quality in German language processing tasks within the constraints of on-premise deployment requirements.

4 System Architecture for Model Evaluation

Building upon the proven RAG architecture established in our previous work [17], this section describes the systematic approach for evaluating next-generation LLMs within the existing infrastructure. The architecture maintains the two-phase processing pipeline while incorporating enhanced evaluation capabilities for comparative model assessment.

4.1 Core RAG Pipeline

The RAG system operates through two main processes: document ingestion and user querying (see Fig. 1). The ingestion process consists of sequential sub-processes that prepare domain-specific knowledge for retrieval. Document preprocessing removes table of contents, version histories, and other metadata that could interfere with embedding quality and retrieval precision. These components, while containing structural information, can be retrieved inappropriately by the similarity matching process, potentially diminishing retrieval quality.

Following document cleanup, the chunking process partitions documents into smaller segments. This step addresses the fundamental limitation that embedding models trained on comparatively small text segments cannot accurately represent the semantic meaning of entire documents. Research indicates that 85.1% of sentences in the MultiNLI dataset [15], used for training SBERT, contain at most 187 characters (approximately 47–62 tokens depending on tokenizer implementation) [26]. As larger text segments result in decreased precision during similarity matching of corresponding embeddings choosing the Right chunk size has a significant impact on retrieval quality.

4.2 Query Processing and Context Augmentation

The user querying process begins with embedding the input query using the same embedding model employed for document chunking. The embedded query undergoes similarity matching against stored embeddings in the vector database to identify the most semantically relevant text chunks. The system retrieves n chunks with the highest similarity scores, with each chunk limited to 256 tokens to maintain retrieval accuracy.

To address the limitation that individual chunks may contain insufficient information for complete answer generation, the system expands the context window by retrieving m additional chunks before and after each matched segment. This context expansion provides the LLM with adequate information while preserving semantic relevance.

The optimization of context window parameters demonstrates measurable impact on answer generation quality. As illustrated in the experimental analysis (see Fig. 2), the relationship between chunk count (m), the number of chunks befor and after m (called context window size) and pass rates reveals a steady growth of pass rates across the parameter space. The evaluation shows that maximum performance is achieved at

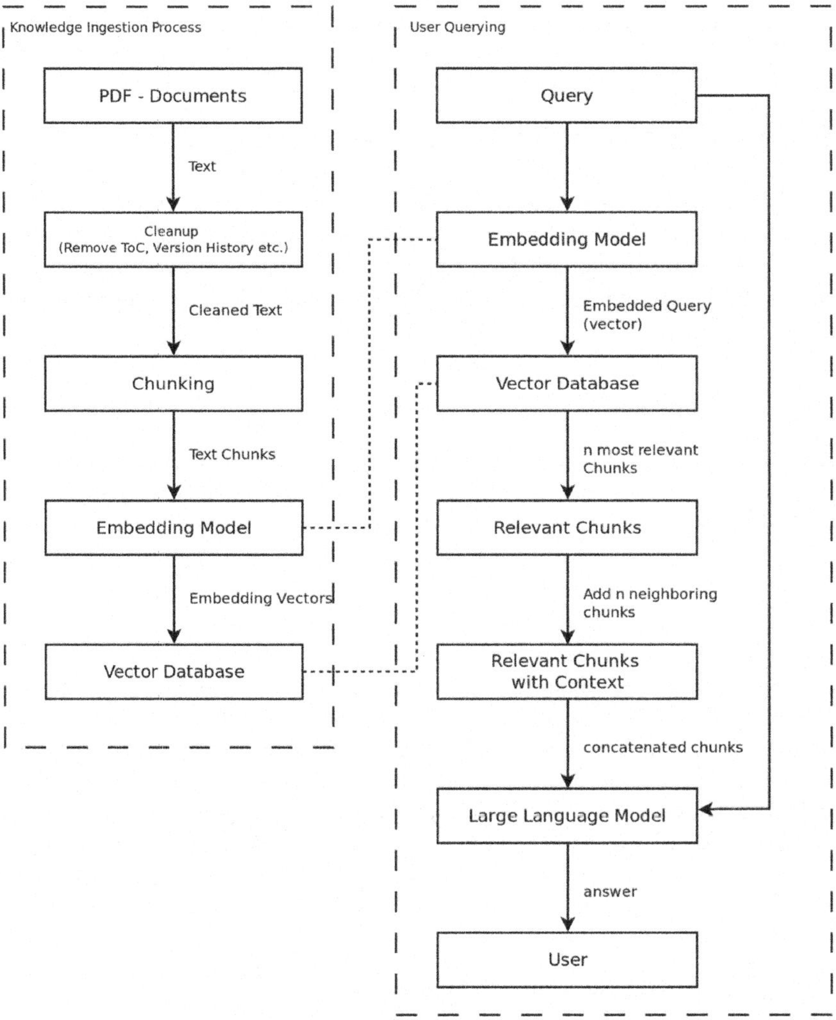

Fig. 1. Processes of Ingestion and User Querying [17].

the upper bounds of both parameters, with m=3 chunks and context window size of 3 delivering the highest pass rates (approximately 0.4). This finding indicates that providing extensive contextual information enhances answer generation quality, suggesting that the LLM benefits from comprehensive context rather than minimal information provision.

The retrieved chunks with expanded context windows are concatenated to form the augmented prompt, which combines the original user query with domain-specific contextual information. This empirically validated approach supports maximizing context richness to optimize LLM performance within the constraints of the model's context window capacity.

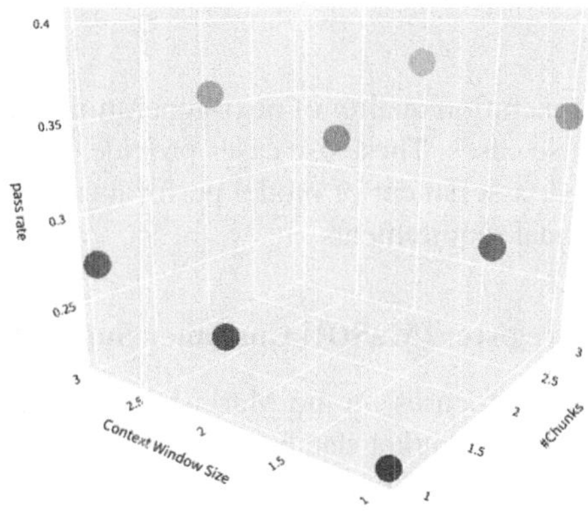

Fig. 2. Pass rates for different context augmentation parameters. Maximum performance (0.41) achieved at m=3 chunks and context window size of 3.

4.3 Model Integration Framework

The system implementation utilizes Langchain [4] for backend functionality and Streamlit [19] for the frontend interface. Langchain provides comprehensive RAG implementation capabilities, including managed chat history for conversational interfaces. An alternative to Langchain is llama-index [13]. While llama-index offers specialized RAG functionality with good document retrieval performance in large datasets, Langchain was selected for its extensive feature set and seamless chatbot development capabilities.

For systematic model evaluation, the architecture incorporates a RESTful API wrapper that enables automated assessment workflows. This API exposes document retrieval and answer generation functionality through standardized endpoints. The '/documents' endpoint supports both GET and POST methods for document search and vector-based retrieval within specified context windows. The '/llm_answer' endpoint processes POST requests for LLM-based answer generation.

4.4 Evaluation Infrastructure Integration

The evaluation framework maintains separation between streaming and batch processing modes. The Streamlit frontend streams tokens to users during generation, reducing perceived response times and improving user experience. The API returns complete generated responses after processing completion, supporting evaluation systems like Promptfoo that require full response analysis for comparative assessment.

This architectural design enables systematic evaluation of multiple LLM candidates while maintaining the proven retrieval performance achieved in the original implementation. The modular structure supports rapid model switching and comparative analysis across different language models without requiring infrastructure modifications.

5 Use Cases

To evaluate the answer generation quality of next-generation LLMs systematically, we utilized two established use cases. These use cases provide distinct evaluation contexts that enable comprehensive assessment of model performance across different domain complexities and operational requirements.

5.1 Marktstammdatenregister (MaStR) Customer Support

The first evaluation scenario focuses on the Marktstammdatenregister (MaStR), Germany's comprehensive energy market database maintained by the Federal Network Agency (Bundesnetzagentur) [3]. This centralized registry contains detailed information about all energy-producing units, including renewable and conventional sources, as well as selected energy-consuming units within the German energy infrastructure.

The MaStR system serves multiple stakeholders including energy producers, network operators, and regulatory authorities, requiring precise information delivery for registration processes, master data management, and compliance requirements. The complexity of MaStR processes creates an environment where answer generation quality directly impacts operational efficiency and regulatory compliance.

For our model evaluation, this use case serves as a controlled testing environment where domain-specific terminology and procedural accuracy can be systematically assessed. The established FAQ structure of the MaStR homepage provides ground truth data for comparative analysis across different LLM answer results, enabling quantitative measurement of answer quality improvements between models.

5.2 Network Operator Employee Coaching

The second use case addresses the operational challenges faced by German network operators in employee onboarding and training environments. This scenario reflects real-world conditions where several hundred employees and outsourced personnel provide multi-level customer support across various communication channels including telephone, email, and digital platforms.

The persistent challenge of high employee turnover rates (20–30% annually) creates continuous demand for effective training solutions. The recent expansion of private photovoltaic installations and energy storage systems has significantly increased customer contact volumes, intensifying the need for rapid, accurate employee preparation.

This use case provides a complex evaluation environment where model performance must address multiple process categories including e.g. operator changes, master data modifications, advance payment calculations, and regulatory compliance procedures. The diversity of these processes enables comprehensive assessment of model capabilities across varying technical complexity levels and linguistic requirements.

For model evaluation purposes, this use case offers realistic operational constraints where answer quality directly influences training effectiveness and customer service delivery. The established process documentation and expert-validated question sets provide measurable benchmarks for comparing model performance across different Business processes.

5.3 Evaluation Framework Application

Both use cases maintain consistent evaluation criteria focusing on the four critical deployment dimensions identified in our previous work: *performance, correctness, integration*, and *locality*. This approach enables systematic comparison of model capabilities while ensuring that evaluation results remain applicable to production deployment scenarios.

The dual use case approach provides complementary evaluation perspectives: MaStR offers structured, procedural assessment opportunities, while Network Operator scenarios test model performance under operational complexity levels. This combination enables comprehensive evaluation of answer generation quality across different operational contexts within the German energy sector.

6 Data

The dataset for the use case MaStR comprises 27 documents, and in addition one FAQ document, all of which provide assistance and manuals for MaStR users in various situations, such as the user sign up, registration of installations, or master data management of units. These documents are predominantly step-by-step guides and manuals, such as registration aids. Challenges arose primarily from content and revision tables, which were frequently included in the generated responses. Additional challenges came from screenshot-based guides or documents heavily comprised of images, which are not adequately processed by a language model. Consequently, manual preprocessing involved the removal of content and revision tables, as well as documents predominantly composed of images.

The data provided for the use case Network Operator was the process documentations of the researched network operator processes, of which 19 were investigated. The process descriptions are mostly stored in the organisation's Confluence-based wiki. However additional documentation in separate files or even as part of Emails or other sources may exist. The respective documents were exported from the companie's wiki as PDF documents and had an overall size of 34MB. The documents contain typical features of process documentations such as headers and footers with logos, tabular content summaries, outlines, and tabular version histories. All of them are ambiguous inputs for the embedding model as well as the LLM. On the one hand these parts are mostly redundant and thus disturbing for the model. On the other hand they contain important data for the document retrieval step. For our POC these inputs were removed manually. Besides the mentioned overhead information the process documents contained lots of screenshots. For the generation of the embeddings we omitted these screenshots, however in the final answer of the assistant the screenshots where included. All texts were written in German language.

7 Experiments

Building on our work in [17], we conducted our tests on the six models Phi4 from Microsoft, Qwen3 from Alibaba, Gemma3 from Google, Llama3.3 and Llama4 from

Meta, and Mistral from Mistral AI. To see whether there was an increase in answer quality we conducted the same tests as we did for the older models, which meant prompting our system with a users question, have our system retrieve the necessary information from the knowledge database to factually correctly answer that question and than give both the retrieved information and the original question to the LLM to generate the final answer. We conducted those experiments based on the data we received from our domain experts from the german network operators.

The objective of our research was to test for an increase in quality of the generated answers. This test was essential to evaluate whether the newer LLMs would be able to formulate better answers both in terms of correctness as well as coherence, based on the retrieved context given to them from the preceeding retrieval step. For these experiments we used the same document as the ground truth as in [17]. This document was a catalog containing:

1. 500 precompiled sample questions from network operator trainees, randomly chosen from 1000 questions in total,
2. the names of the documents containing the necessary information for answering these questions, as well as
3. preformulated, correct answers for those questions.

The evaluation of the objective was based on automatic validation using Prompt-foo [25].

To check whether or not generated answers matched our known-good answers from the catalog we decided against using a simple string matching (containing steps like trimming and making both texts lower case etc.) since this would have meant that both answers (known-good and generated) would have had to be exactly the same, to the letter.

Instead we decided to check for similarity between the two answers. Accordingly, we had our embedding model generate embeddings for each known-good answer as well as each generated answer and calculated the cosine similarity of the embeddings to see how similar the generated answer was to the corresponding known-good answer. The threshold we chose for the tests was 0.85, unlike in our previous work, where we used a threshold of 0.65 for accepting an answer as similar enough. This was done to account for the amount of time passed since release of the older models we tested before and the increase in quality we assumed for the newer models. To achieve consistency and reproducability of the experiments we chose a temperature value of 0.1.

Lastly, we conducted our tests on two different backends, hosting the language models to evaluate aspects as respone time, answer quality differences as well as ressource efficiency and general usability. The first backend was FastChat by lmsys and the second Ollama by Jeffrey Morgan and Michael Chiang [16].

8 Results

After describing our system, the used data and the performed experiments, the results will be described along the four initially introduced dimensions.

Performance: We determined the overall performance of our system by measuring the response times from submitting a query to the moment the final respone was returned. This measuring happened in promptfoo which used our systems API. We found that response times varied between the investigated models as shown in Fig. 3. While the shortest response times for all of our investigated models were in the milliseconds, we also found some models were considerably slower. The measured times are also shown in table 2.

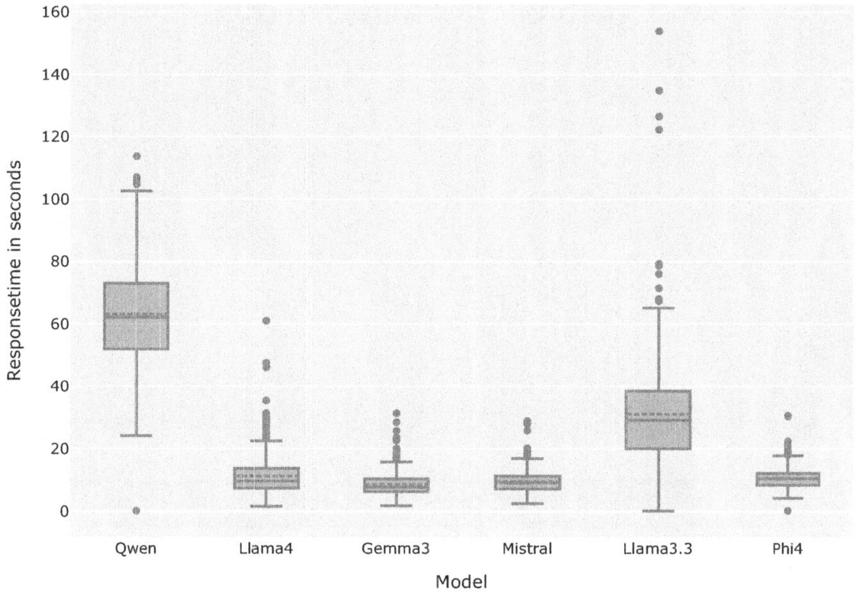

Fig. 3. Response times during generation step grouped by backend (500 samples). Model used for comparison: Llama4:16x17B.

For the four models Llama4, Gemma3, Mistral and Phi4 the majority of the measured times (75%) were lower than 13.7 s. The best performing model in terms of responsetime turned out to be Gemma3 as shown in Fig. 3. It is worth noting that for the sake of conducting the correctness tests of our system, it was unnecessary to stream the LLM's responses. However, in our UI, the responses were streamed to the user. This reduced the perceived response times significantly in each case, as the users could immediately see the system's responses as they were being generated.

For this work, we also tested for differences in response times depending on which backend we used. As seen in Fig. 4 there is a difference in outliers for the Llama4 model hosted using Ollama compared to the one hosted with FastChat. However, most responses (75%) were almost identical in speed. We therefore decided to switch to Ollama as our backend of choice as it comes with huge differences in ease of use and ressource handling.

Table 2. Response time measures of our tested models.

model	mean	min	max
Mistral-small3.2:24B	9.6 s	2.5 s	28.9 s
Phi4:14B	10.7 s	0.2 s	30.7
Llama3.3	31.1 s	0.2 s	153.9 s
Llama4:16x17B	11.3 s	1.6 s	61.0 s
Gemma3:27B	8.7 s	1.8 s	31.4 s
Qwen3:32B	63.2 s	0.2	113.8 s

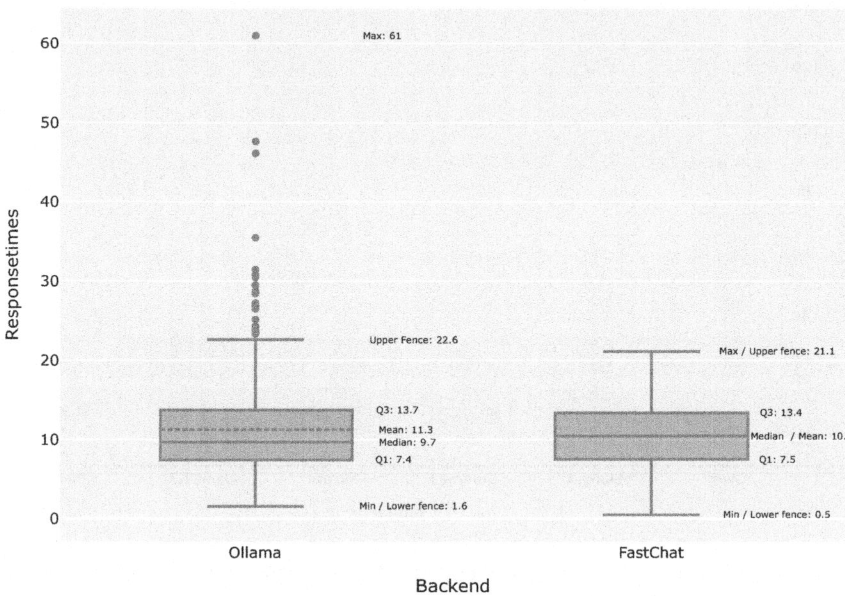

Fig. 4. Response times (in seconds) during the generation step grouped by backend (500 samples). Model used for comparison: Llama4:16x17B.

Correctness: For this work we focussed on investigating the correctness of the generated answers of the six models introduced in 2.

Our tests show that the invetigated models all lie close to each other with the exception of Qwen3:32B. This is surprising and give our data we can only speculate about the exact reasons. We believe that this is because Qwen implements a technique called chain of thought that causes it to write about how it solves a problem or came to an answer. While increasing transparency this way it also causes the similarity score to drop. The model that yielded the best answer quality in our tests was Mistral-small3.2:24B with a test pass rate of 68.18% (see Table 3) which is an increase of almost 28% compared to our previous results in [17].

For the retrieval step of our system we used the same embedding model in [17]. That model was mxbai-embed-large-v1 by Mixedbread.AI [14]. Therefore we retained our precision value of 90. 8% during the retrieval step.

Table 3. pass rates of correctness tests (500 samples, randomly chosen from 1000 total).

model	pass rate
Llama3.3:70B	67.61%
Llama4:16x17B	66.86%
Phi4:14B	66,67%
Gemma3:27B	65.72%
Qwen3:32B	28.41%
Mistral-small3.2:24B	68.18%

Integration: To integrate our system in our users everyday workflows we designed the RAG system as a chatbot running on a simple, minimalistic website. This website can be opened in an additional browser window or tab on the desktop of the employee so it integrates seamlessly with the software they are running anyway. In addition integrating the RAG system into different legacy systems is ensured as we are leveraging standard technologies like Langchain and established interfaces such as the OpenAI API.

Locality: The trend of increasing answer quality of small to medium sized models, that can be deployed on premises, im some cases even on consumer hardware, further confirmed us in our decision to host the models on premises in the local data center of regiocom. The initial significant investment in the AI accelerator card shows to be a good one. Considering the limitations and constraints that players on the german energy market have to adhere to in terms of data security, locally deployable language models make such investments worthwile and may yield a high return on investment.

We conclude that leveraging locally running embedding models for information retrieval as well as large language models for summarization and answer generation is a suitable means for individual employee coaching and can help relieve the burden on network operators.

9 Future Work

For the first three of our four main dimensions, several tasks require future development. The requirement of *Locality* is fulfilled with the current Architecture using Ollama runtime envirmonment, and for the moment no future work needs to be identified.

There are several areas for potential improvement in system *Performance*:

- The current Flask-based API implementation may represent a performance bottleneck under high-load conditions. Transitioning to more efficient frameworks or implementing asynchronous processing capabilities could substantially improve response times and concurrent user handling capacity.

- To ensure the system can handle real-world demands, comprehensive load tests simulating scenarios with hundreds or thousands of concurrent users remain necessary. This will help identify potential bottlenecks and optimize the system's ability to scale under high load conditions.
- While current response times averaging 8.7 s are acceptable for many use cases, further optimization through model quantization, caching strategies, or hardware acceleration could enhance user experience, particularly for time-sensitive queries.

To improve the accuracy and reliability of our system, we have identified the following key areas for future work contributing to the *correctness* dimension:

- The current automatic evaluation using cosine similarity demonstrates limitations in semantic understanding. Small lexical differences, such as the presence or absence of negation words like not, can result in minimal cosine similarity changes while representing substantial semantic differences. Future work should incorporate more sophisticated evaluation metrics that better capture semantic nuance and logical relationships in language processing.
- The quality of our input data significantly impacts the system's performance. Future work should focus on developing more robust preprocessing pipelines. This could include better handling of tables, headers, footers, and image captions, as well as improved methods for extracting relevant information from complex document structures.
- To more rigorously assess our system's correctness, we need to expand our collection of expert-curated evaluation datasets. This involves collaborating with domain experts to create larger, more diverse question-answer pairs, developing comprehensive test scenarios that cover edge cases, and regularly updating datasets to reflect changes in processes and regulations within the energy sector.

The rapid pace of LLM development presents both opportunities and challenges in Terms of *integration*:

- As new language models are released frequently, often with improved capabilities for German language processing and domain-specific understanding, establishing a systematic framework for evaluating emerging models against our established benchmarks will ensure the system can benefit from technological advances while maintaining deployment stability.
- Future work should develop standardized procedures for model evaluation, comparison, and migration that minimize disruption to production systems while enabling adoption of improved capabilities as they become available.

By focusing on these areas, we aim to additionally enhance the *correctness, performance*, and *reliability* of our RAG system, making it an even more valuable tool for employee coaching and support in the network operator environment (Table 4).

Table 4. Comparison of known-good answers to RAG generated answers [17].

Question	known-good answer	LLM generated answer
Wann erfolgt ein Betreiberwechsel?	*Ein Betreiberwechsel kommt dann Zustande, wenn eine Einspeiseanlage veräußert oder durch Erbe/Schenkung an eine andere Person übergeben wurde*	*Ein Betreiberwechsel erfolgt, wenn eine Einspeiseanlage veräußert oder durch Erbe/Schenkung an eine andere Person übergeben wird*
Wann ist die zusätzliche Pflege als abweichender Rechnungsempfänger zulässig?	*Eine zusätzliche Pflege als abweichender Rechnungs- und Mahnempfänger ist nur bei direkten Netzendkunden (Selbstzahlern) und Einspeisern zulässig, sofern dies vom Kunden gewünscht ist*	*Nach den bereitgestellten Informationen ist eine zusätzliche Pflege als abweichender Rechnungsempfänger zulässig:* *1. Bei direktem Netzendkunden (Selbstzahlern)* *2. Bei Einspeisern, sofern dies gewünscht ist* *Bitte beachte, dass diese Informationen auf den bereitgestellten Kontext basieren und sich ändern können, wenn sich die Situation ändert. Wenn du weitere Fragen hast, stehe ich gerne zur Verfügung*
Was bedeutet Handlungsvollmacht?	*Handlungsvollmacht bedeutet, dass der Bevollmächtigte sowohl Auskünfte erhalten darf als auch selbst Änderungen vornehmen lassen kann*	*Handlungsvollmacht bedeutet, dass der Bevollmächtigte sowohl Auskünfte erhalten darf als auch selbst Änderungen vornehmen lassen kann*
Wie gehe ich bei einer schriftlichen Anfrage vor, wenn der Vorgang innerhalb von KK, aber nicht vom aktuellen Servicepartner bearbeitet werden kann?	*Bei einer schriftlichen Anfrage klassifizierst du diese um, so dass diese an den Servicepartner geroutet wird, der den Prozess anschließend bearbeitet*	*Bei einer schriftlichen Anfrage, die innerhalb von KK, aber nicht vom aktuellen Servicepartner bearbeitet werden kann, musst du den Vorgang umklassifizieren, so dass diese an den korrekten Fachbereich geroutet wird, der den Prozess dann bearbeiten kann*

10 Conclusions

This research addressed the answer generation quality challenge in RAG-based employee coaching systems for the German energy sector by systematically evaluating next-generation Large Language Models. Building upon previous work that established a functional RAG infrastructure with 90.8% document retrieval precision, we focused on overcoming the identified bottleneck of insufficient answer quality that prevented production deployment.

Our systematic evaluation of advanced open-source models—including Phi4 from Microsoft, Qwen3 from Alibaba, Gemma3 from Google, Llama3.3 and Llama4 from Meta, and Mistral from Mistral AI—demonstrates significant improvements in answer generation quality for German language processing. The results show substantial advancement over baseline models, with pass rates reaching 68.18% for Mistral-small3.2:24B, 67.61% for Llama3.3:70B, 66.86% for Llama4:16x17B, and 66.67% for Phi4:14B, representing meaningful progress toward production-ready performance.

The evaluation revealed that newer model generations provide enhanced German language understanding and generation capabilities while maintaining compatibility with on-premise deployment requirements. Our findings confirm that the four critical deployment dimensions—performance, correctness, integration, and locality—can be satisfied with next-generation models, with response times averaging 8.7 to 11.3 s for most evaluated models and successful integration through standardized API interfaces.

The transition from FastChat to Ollama as the model serving infrastructure demonstrated operational benefits in terms of simplified model management, consistent API interfaces, and resource optimization. This architectural refinement supports the practical deployment requirements of enterprise environments while enabling systematic model evaluation and comparison workflows.

However, challenges remain in achieving production-ready quality thresholds. Despite improvements, the semantic similarity-based evaluation approach revealed limitations in capturing nuanced language differences, particularly regarding negation and context-specific terminology. Manual evaluation of generated responses often showed that answers contained correct information but failed automated similarity tests due to additional model output or structural differences.

The research establishes benchmarks for acceptable answer quality in specialized industrial applications and provides actionable model recommendations for organizations implementing AI coaching assistants in regulated environments. The systematic methodology enables ongoing evaluation of emerging models as they become available, supporting continuous improvement of system capabilities.

Our work contributes to the practical deployment of enterprise AI systems by demonstrating that locally deployed RAG solutions can achieve meaningful performance improvements through careful model selection and evaluation. While results represent progress toward production deployment, continued refinement in evaluation methodologies, data preprocessing, and model optimization remains necessary to fully realize the potential of AI-powered employee coaching systems in compliance-sensitive industries.

Acknowledgements. This work was funded by regiocom SE, Germany. The authors would like to express their gratitude to regiocom for their financial support and for providing access to the necessary data and resources that made this research possible.

References

1. Abdin, M., et al.: Phi-4 technical report. Technical report, Microsoft Research (2024). https://doi.org/10.48550/arXiv.2412.08905Focustolearnmore
2. Brown, T.B., et al.: Language models are few-shot learners (2020). https://arxiv.org/abs/2005.14165
3. Bundesnetzagentur: Marktstammdatenregister (2019). https://www.marktstammdatenregister.de. Bundesnetzagentur für Elektrizität, Gas, Telekommunikation, Post und Eisenbahnen | DL-DE-BY-2.0

4. Chase, H.: LangChain (2022). https://github.com/langchain-ai/langchain
5. Chroma: Chromadb (2023). https://www.trychroma.com/
6. Fu, Z., et al.: Decoder-only or encoder-decoder? Interpreting language model as a regularized encoder-decoder (2023). https://arxiv.org/abs/2304.04052, https://arxiv.org/abs/2304.04052
7. Guu, K., Lee, K., Tung, Z., Pasupat, P., Chang, M.W.: REALM: retrieval-augmented language model pre-training (2020). https://arxiv.org/abs/2002.08909
8. Jiang, A.Q., et al.: Mistral 7b (2023). https://doi.org/10.48550/arXiv.2310.06825
9. Joshi, V., He, W., sun Seo, J., Rajendran, B.: Hybrid in-memory computing architecture for the training of deep neural networks (2021). https://arxiv.org/abs/2102.05271
10. Langchain (2024). https://python.langchain.com/v0.2/docs/integrations/vectorstores/. Accessed 03 Aug 2024
11. Levy, A., Shalom, B.R., Chalamish, M.: A guide to similarity measures (2024). https://arxiv.org/abs/2408.07706
12. Lewis, P., et al.: Retrieval-augmented generation for knowledge-intensive NLP tasks (2021). https://arxiv.org/abs/2005.11401
13. Liu, J.: LlamaIndex (2022). https://doi.org/10.5281/zenodo.1234, https://github.com/jerryjliu/llama_index
14. Mixedbread.AI: mixedbread-ai/mxbai-embed-large-v1 (2024). Accessed 12 Sept 2024
15. (2024). https://huggingface.co/datasets/nyu-mll/multi_nli. Accessed 20 Aug 2024
16. Ollama: Ollama: A platform for running large language models locally (2024). https://github.com/ollama/ollama. Accessed 16 Aug 2024
17. Orlowski, M., Knauff, E., Marquardt, F.: Towards personal assistants for energy processes based on locally deployed LLMs. In: Proceedings of the 17th International Conference on Agents and Artificial Intelligence - Volume 3: ICAART, pp. 695–706. INSTICC, SciTePress (2025). https://doi.org/10.5220/0013175600003890
18. Radford, A., Narasimhan, K., Salimans, T., Sutskever, I., et al.: Improving language understanding by generative pre-training (2018)
19. Streamlit: Streamlit (2022). https://github.com/streamlit/streamlit. Accessed 01 Aug 2024
20. T-Systems (2024). https://huggingface.co/T-Systems-onsite/cross-en-de-roberta-sentence-transformer. Accessed 01 Aug 2024
21. Team, G.: Gemma 3 technical report. Technical report, Google (2024). https://doi.org/10.48550/arXiv.2503.19786
22. Team, L.: The LLaMA 3 herd of models (2024). https://ai.meta.com/research/publications/the-llama-3-herd-of-models/
23. Tonmoy, S.M.T.I., et al.: A comprehensive survey of hallucination mitigation techniques in large language models (2024). https://arxiv.org/abs/2401.01313
24. Tunstall, L., von Werra, L., Wolf, T.: Natural Language Processing with Transformers: Building Language Applications with Hugging Face. O'Reilly Media (2022). https://books.google.de/books?id=pNBpzwEACAAJ
25. Webster, I.: promptfoo (2024). https://www.promptfoo.dev/. Accessed 21 July 2024
26. Williams, A., Nangia, N., Bowman, S.: A broad-coverage challenge corpus for sentence understanding through inference. In: Walker, M., Ji, H., Stent, A. (eds.) Proceedings of the 2018 Conference of the North American Chapter of the Association for Computational Linguistics: Human Language Technologies, Volume 1 (Long Papers), pp. 1112–1122. Association for Computational Linguistics, New Orleans (2018). https://doi.org/10.18653/v1/N18-1101
27. Yang, A., et al.: Qwen3 technical report. Technical report, Alibaba Cloud (2025). https://doi.org/10.48550/arXiv.2505.09388
28. Yenduri, G., et al.: Generative pre-trained transformer: a comprehensive review on enabling technologies, potential applications, emerging challenges, and future directions (2023). https://arxiv.org/abs/2305.10435

CLT-Net: Integrating CNN, LSTM, and Transformer for Review Classification in Online Learning Platforms

Hatem Majouri[1], Olfa Gaddour[1](✉), and Yessine Hadj Kacem[2]

[1] CES Laboratory, National Engineering, School of Sfax, University of Sfax, Sfax, Tunisia
hatem.majouri1@gmail.com, olfa.gaddour@enis.tn
[2] ReDCAD Laboratory, National Engineering, School of Sfax, University of Sfax, Sfax, Tunisia
Yessine.hadjkacem@enis.tn

Abstract. In the rapidly evolving landscape of digital education, effectively interpreting student feedback is critical for enhancing online learning environments and informing pedagogical strategies. This paper introduces CLT-Net, a novel and robust deep learning architecture that integrates Convolutional Neural Networks (CNN), Long Short-Term Memory (LSTM) networks, and Transformer-based attention mechanisms into a unified model. CLT-Net leverages the strengths of each component to capture both local linguistic features and long-range contextual dependencies from unstructured educational reviews. Unlike traditional models, CLT-Net extends the classical CNN-LSTM architecture by incorporating multi-head self-attention layers. This enhancement enables the model to dynamically attend to the most informative segments of a review while preserving both sequential structure and spatial coherence. To comprehensively evaluate its performance, a standardized preprocessing and training pipeline was applied to two large-scale, real-world datasets—FutureLearn and Udemy—collected via web scraping. These datasets consist of diverse, unstructured, and often noisy student comments, making them a robust benchmark for sentiment classification tasks. Experimental results demonstrate that CLT-Net outperforms baseline models, achieving an accuracy of up to 97% in binary classification tasks, along with notable improvements in precision, recall, and F1-score. These findings not only confirm the effectiveness of hybrid deep learning architectures but also highlight CLT-Net's potential as a foundational tool for building intelligent, feedback-driven e-learning systems. The results offer strong evidence for researchers and practitioners seeking reliable solutions in opinion mining and educational data analysis.

Keywords: Deep Learning · CNN-LSTM · Transformer · Opinion Mining · Sentiment Analysis · E-learning Platforms · Course Reviews · FutureLearn · Udemy · Text Classification · Attention Mechanism

1 Introduction

The rapid expansion of online education has transformed how individuals access learning, offering unprecedented flexibility, scalability, and global accessibility. Platforms

H. J. van den Herik et al. (Eds.): ICAART 2025, LNAI 16517, pp. 478–501, 2026.
https://doi.org/10.1007/978-3-032-25032-2_23

such as *FutureLearn* and *Udemy* enable millions of learners to acquire new skills across diverse disciplines, supported by interactive content, peer collaboration, and expert instruction. However, as the number of available courses continues to grow, evaluating their effectiveness and enhancing learner satisfaction has become a significant challenge for educators and administrators.

User-generated reviews serve as a valuable source of insight into learners' perceptions, satisfaction levels, and the overall quality of instructional content. When properly analyzed, these reviews can inform course improvements, assist prospective learners in course selection, and support institutional decision-making. Extracting and interpreting opinions from such feedback falls within the scope of *opinion mining* or *sentiment analysis*, which has gained substantial attention in the field of educational data mining [5,8,10].

Earlier approaches to sentiment analysis relied largely on rule-based systems or shallow machine learning models, which often struggled to capture the linguistic richness and contextual nuances of student feedback. The emergence of deep learning, particularly models such as CNNs, LSTMs, and GRUs, has significantly advanced the ability to model sequential and hierarchical structures in text [13,14]. More recently, Transformer architectures—known for their powerful attention mechanisms—have outperformed traditional models in capturing long-range dependencies and semantic relationships within textual data [21,23,25].

In our previous work [1], we proposed a CNN-LSTM hybrid model that outperformed individual deep learning architectures such as BERT, GRU, and CNN in classifying online course reviews from the FutureLearn platform, achieving an accuracy of 95%. Building on that foundation, we now introduce CLT-Net, a novel hybrid deep learning architecture that integrates Convolutional Neural Networks (CNN), Long Short-Term Memory (LSTM) networks, and a Transformer block. This unified model is designed to simultaneously capture local features, sequential dependencies, and global attention patterns within textual data.

To evaluate the model's performance across different e-learning platforms, the experimental setup was expanded to include a newly collected dataset from Udemy, alongside an updated version of the original FutureLearn dataset. Both datasets were processed using a consistent pipeline comprising web scraping, data cleaning, preprocessing, and binary classification, in alignment with established best practices [16,18, 22,24].

The key contributions of this extended work are as follows:

- The design and implementation of CLT-Net, a new hybrid architecture that combines CNN, LSTM, and Transformer mechanisms for enhanced text classification.
- Evaluation of CLT-Net on two real-world e-learning datasets—FutureLearn and Udemy—demonstrating its robustness and cross-platform applicability.
- Comprehensive comparison of CLT-Net with established deep learning baselines using standard evaluation metrics and visualization tools, highlighting significant improvements in accuracy and generalization.

The remainder of this paper is organized as follows: Sect. 2 reviews related work; Sect. 3 details the methodology and system architecture; Sect. 4 presents the experimental setup and results; and Sect. 5 concludes the study with final remarks and future directions.

2 Related Work

The rise of e-learning platforms has spurred a growing body of research focused on analyzing user feedback to enhance course quality and learner experience. This section reviews key contributions in the domain of sentiment classification for student reviews, emphasizing methodologies, datasets, and model architectures.

In [5], sentiment analysis was conducted on 154,000 instructor reviews from RateMyProfessors, evenly split between positive and negative labels. The study demonstrated that deep learning models, particularly an RNN with an attention mechanism and GloVe embeddings, outperformed traditional classifiers such as SVM and Random Forest, achieving a classification accuracy of 98.29%. Nevertheless, overfitting was observed due to model complexity and the noisy nature of user-generated content.

In [8], the authors proposed an aspect-based opinion mining model using conventional machine learning and a 1D-CNN architecture. Their model, tested on the same 21,940 Coursera reviews, achieved an F1 score of 78.83% using a Decision Tree with tf*idf for aspect category prediction, and 88.20% for sentiment classification using 1D-CNN with Word2Vec embeddings. Despite these results, class imbalance—especially the dominance of the "Content" aspect—remained a significant limitation, along with underperformance of deep learning models in some cases.

Chakravarthy et al. [6] proposed an opinion mining approach for course recommendation using 12,000 unstructured reviews from Coursera. Logistic regression achieved the highest accuracy of 94%, outperforming SVM and KNN. However, the approach relied heavily on lexicon-based heuristics, which may reduce adaptability to nuanced or context-dependent expressions in reviews.

In [3], a sentiment analysis was conducted on 725 course evaluations from the China University MOOC platform. Using Naive Bayes, the study classified sentiments across seven dimensions, achieving an average accuracy of 85.62%. While the approach revealed useful insights, it was limited by its reliance on a simple classifier, a relatively small dataset, and lack of multilingual or deep learning experimentation.

Mrhar et al. [20] introduced a Bayesian CNN-LSTM hybrid model for analyzing over 140,000 Coursera reviews from 1,835 courses. The model combined CNNs for local feature extraction, LSTMs for sequence modeling, and Bayesian dropout to estimate prediction uncertainty. It achieved an accuracy of 91.27% and demonstrated strong correlations between sentiment polarity and learner attrition. However, its main limitations were the need for extensive manual annotation and sensitivity to domain-specific language.

In [2], the authors created a dataset of 10,610 course review comments from public platforms. Sentiment classification using RoBERTa achieved 95.5% accuracy (F1-macro 84.7%), while topic classification using SVM reached 79.8% accuracy (F1-macro 80.6%). Despite promising results, the dataset suffered from significant class imbalance (91.5% positive) and ambiguous topic boundaries, which complicated model training.

Edalati et al. [11] and Shaik et al. [12] highlighted the relevance of deep learning and transfer learning in educational sentiment analysis. Their work on cross-platform generalization underscored the challenges of interpretability and deployment in real-world applications.

Recent research has also explored hybrid deep learning models combining Transformer-based architectures with recurrent or convolutional layers. For example, Upadhyay and Dave [22] proposed a CNN-GRU-Attention model for analyzing Udemy course reviews. Similarly, Edalati et al. [24] demonstrated that combining Transformer encoders with LSTM improves performance on datasets from Coursera, FutureLearn, and Udemy.

Despite these advancements, many existing studies face critical limitations. Several rely on single-platform datasets, lack rigorous preprocessing, or fall short in capturing the linguistic complexity of informal student feedback. Additionally, the integration of attention mechanisms is often superficial or loosely coupled with traditional architectures. To address these gaps, we propose CLT-Net, a unified deep learning architecture that integrates CNNs for local pattern recognition, LSTMs for sequential modeling, and Transformer-based attention mechanisms for global contextual relevance within a single end-to-end pipeline. Unlike prior models, CLT-Net is designed to exploit the complementary strengths of each component, offering improved robustness and interpretability.

Moreover, this study uses real-world review data collected from both FutureLearn and Udemy, enabling richer cross-platform evaluation and more diverse linguistic representation. By leveraging these datasets, CLT-Net offers a scalable and context-sensitive solution for opinion mining in educational settings.

3 Proposed System Approach

This section presents the proposed system for opinion mining and classification of course reviews, built upon a hybrid deep learning architecture named CLT-Net. The architecture integrates Convolutional Neural Networks (CNN), Long Short-Term Memory (LSTM) networks, and a Transformer-based attention block. This combination allows the model to effectively capture local textual features, sequential dependencies, and global contextual relationships within review data, thereby enhancing sentiment classification performance.

The complete pipeline consists of data collection, preprocessing, embedding generation, model training, and evaluation. Figure 1 provides an overview of the system architecture and the data processing flow.

As shown in the figure, the system architecture provides an overview of the data processing and classification pipeline, illustrating the sequential stages involved in transforming raw data into classified output. The process begins with data collected from e-learning platforms such as *FutureLearn* and *Udemy*, followed by a web scraping phase implemented using Python scripts to extract relevant review information.

The extracted content is compiled into a structured reviews dataset, which then undergoes a comprehensive data cleaning process to ensure quality, consistency, and completeness. The resulting refined dataset is prepared for analysis through a series of preprocessing steps, including vectorization, tokenization, and label encoding.

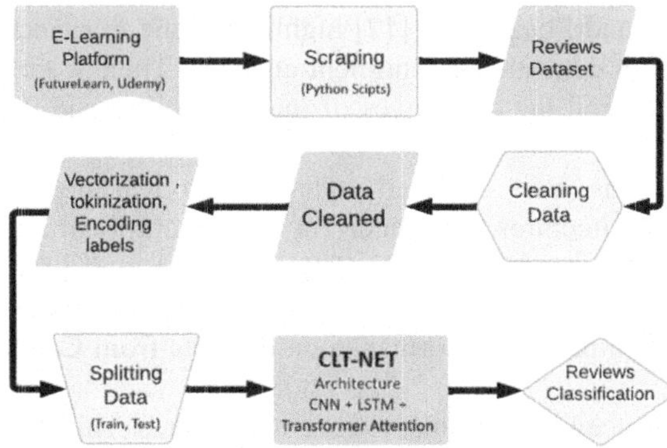

Fig. 1. Overview of the Data Processing and Classification Pipeline.

Following preprocessing, the dataset is divided into training and testing subsets. The core classification task is performed using the proposed CLT-Net architecture, which integrates Convolutional Neural Networks (CNN), Long Short-Term Memory (LSTM) networks, and a Transformer-based attention mechanism. The pipeline culminates in the sentiment classification of student reviews, completing the end-to-end processing flow.

3.1 Data Collection

Data collection involves several essential steps, including source identification, web scraping, dataset structuring, and size determination—all of which are crucial for ensuring data accuracy and usability [16]. In this study, two datasets were employed:

- **FutureLearn Dataset:** An updated version of the dataset used in our previous work, collected via web scraping. It contains thousands of reviews concerning course content, instructional quality, and overall satisfaction, along with course titles and star ratings.
- **Udemy Dataset:** A new dataset compiled from publicly accessible course review pages on Udemy, using automated Python-based scraping tools [22]. This dataset includes review texts, course metadata, and user ratings.

The scraped data was organized into a structured tabular format (CSV), where each row represents a review and the columns include course name, review text, and numeric rating. Reviews were then filtered and relabeled for binary classification. Specifically, ratings of 1–2 stars were labeled as `negative` (class 0), and ratings of 3–5 stars as `positive` (class 1), in line with established sentiment labeling practices [18,25].

To enhance dataset quality, duplicate and empty entries were removed, encoding inconsistencies were resolved, and efforts were made to balance class distributions where feasible. The final datasets were then split into training and test sets, with 80% allocated for training and 20% reserved for evaluation.

Data Source. The growth of online education has transformed access to learning, offering flexible opportunities for global learners. This study analyzes user feedback from two major e-learning platforms, FutureLearn [15] and Udemy [22], which provide diverse courses delivered by universities, institutions, and industry professionals. By examining this feedback, we aim to evaluate course effectiveness and gain insights into learner experiences within institutional and commercial e-learning settings.

FutureLearn, partnered with academic institutions, offers structured courses with interactive tools such as video lectures, quizzes, and peer discussion forums to promote engagement. Student evaluations were collected from various FutureLearn courses via public reviews and forums, focusing on the learning experience (platform usability and engagement), content quality (clarity and relevance), instructor effectiveness (expertise and communication), and overall satisfaction. This analysis highlights how FutureLearn's academic model supports effective learning.

To broaden our findings, data from Udemy—a commercial platform with a vast array of user-generated courses—was also included. Udemy's open model allows instructors to create content for professional and personal development. Reviews were gathered from Udemy's public system, targeting feedback on course utility (practical applicability), content clarity, and instructor performance (expertise and engagement). This dataset complements FutureLearn's structured approach with Udemy's flexible, market-driven model.

Combining these datasets enables a comparative analysis of learner sentiment across both platforms. Using natural language processing techniques, positive, negative, and neutral sentiments in reviews were assessed to understand satisfaction levels and identify key factors—such as content quality, teaching effectiveness, and interactivity—that drive successful learning. The findings provide evidence-based insights to improve course design, instructor training, and platform development, thereby enhancing the quality of online education for diverse learners.

Web-Scraping. To construct a robust dataset for opinion mining, web scraping techniques were employed to extract review data from both FutureLearn and Udemy platforms, enabling automated collection of large-scale user-generated feedback [16]. Custom Python scripts were developed to accommodate the differing HTML structures of these platforms, utilizing the Beautiful Soup library for parsing HTML and XML documents and efficiently extracting relevant elements such as course titles, student reviews, and numerical ratings.

To handle dynamic content and interactive elements, Selenium was used to automate browser actions including form submissions and button clicks, ensuring retrieval of all user-generated feedback, even when rendered via JavaScript. Additionally, the Requests library facilitated HTTP/1.1 requests for fetching static page content. Due to significant differences in page layouts and review formats between the two platforms, platform-specific scraping strategies were implemented to guarantee consistency and accuracy in data extraction. The resulting data were organized into structured formats such as CSV and XLSX, allowing seamless integration with downstream preprocessing workflows. This comprehensive methodology enabled the construction of a scalable, high-quality dataset of course reviews optimized for training and evaluating deep learning models in opinion mining.

Data Structure. The dataset structure varies depending on the source and intended use, but generally adopts a tabular format composed of rows and columns, where each row represents an individual review instance and each column corresponds to a specific attribute. In this work, both FutureLearn and Udemy datasets capture key information about online courses, user-generated reviews, and associated ratings.

The unified data schema includes three essential features: the course name (string), the review text (string), and the corresponding rating (floating-point number). This standardized format facilitates consistent preprocessing and supports comprehensive analysis for sentiment classification tasks across both e-learning platforms.

3.2 Data Labeling

Sentiment classification can be categorized as either binary, which involves classifying reviews into positive or negative categories, or multi-class, which includes labels such as strong positive, positive, neutral, negative, and strong negative. Binary classification is prevalent in sentiment analysis research [18]. For instance, in [19], the dataset was relabeled to facilitate binary sentiment classification using TextBlob: reviews with positive polarity were labeled as positive, while those with zero or negative polarity were labeled negative. This simplification enhances the distinction between positive and negative sentiments.

In this study, web scraping techniques were employed to collect a total of 30,121 online course reviews, initially classified into five categories based on a rating scale from 1.0 to 5.0. Due to a significant data scarcity in classes 1, 2, and 3, the analysis focused on binary classification by designating 1- and 2-star evaluations as negative (0), and 3-, 4-, and 5-star evaluations as positive (1). Transforming a multi-class problem into a binary framework is a common approach in sentiment analysis that simplifies the task by emphasizing the positive-negative dichotomy. As noted in [25], this method effectively captures essential distinctions in opinionated text and can produce more robust models, especially when datasets are imbalanced or sparse.

After reclassification, empty rows and duplicates were removed to improve data quality and accurately reflect the distribution of each binary class. For each platform, student reviews were classified as positive (class 1) or negative (class 0). Initially, the Udemy dataset contained 366,950 samples—315,995 positive and 50,955 negative. After thorough cleaning to remove duplicates, empty reviews, and irrelevant or defective entries, the dataset was reduced to 305,180 samples, including 257,873 positive and 47,307 negative reviews. Similarly, the FutureLearn dataset originally had 27,203 reviews (19,271 positive and 7,932 negative). Applying the same cleaning procedure reduced this to 24,206 usable samples, with 18,978 positive and 5,228 negative reviews.

This preprocessing phase ensured data quality and consistency, both critical for the efficacy of sentiment classification models. The final dataset specifications are summarized in Table 1.

Table 1. Datasets Size by Class (FutureLearn vs. Udemy, Original vs. After Cleaning).

Course Name	Class	Original Number of Samples	Number of Samples After Cleaning
Udemy	1	315,995	257,873
	0	50,955	47,307
	Total	**366,950**	**305,180**
FutureLearn	1	19,271	18,978
	0	7,932	5,228
	Total	**27,203**	**24,206**

3.3 Data Preprocessing

The initial stage of analyzing course reviews involves meticulous preparation of textual data through cleansing and normalization. Raw reviews, particularly those sourced from platforms such as FutureLearn and Udemy, often contain extraneous elements, inconsistent formatting, and missing information, necessitating a comprehensive preprocessing pipeline to ensure data uniformity and model compatibility.

This pipeline included removal of HTML tags, punctuation, and special characters; conversion of text to lowercase; and lemmatization to standardize word forms. Stopwords were removed while carefully retaining negation terms such as "not" and "never" to preserve critical sentiment cues. Subsequently, the reviews were tokenized and adjusted through padding or truncation to fixed sequence lengths aligned with model input requirements.

After preprocessing, the dataset was partitioned into training and testing subsets, allocating 80% for training and 20% for evaluation. To enrich semantic representation, tokens were embedded using pre-trained GloVe vectors [5], enabling the model to leverage established linguistic patterns during learning.

Data Cleaning. Data cleansing is a critical process that enhances dataset quality and consistency by rectifying inconsistencies, managing errors, and addressing missing or duplicate values, thereby ensuring reliable and appropriate input for machine learning workflows. Key preprocessing activities include transforming target sentiment labels into binary format through label encoding, removing missing values, blank fields, and duplicate records to maintain data integrity, and normalizing text by eliminating special characters, HTML tags, and extraneous spaces. Additionally, informal expressions are converted into their standard forms via contraction expansion, while lemmatization reduces words to their root forms to unify semantic meaning. Stopword filtering is applied to remove common non-informative words, with careful retention of important negation terms such as "no" and "not" to preserve sentiment context. Collectively, these procedures ensure that the textual data is coherent, standardized, and optimized for effective feature extraction and subsequent model training.

Data Transformation. Data transformation is a crucial step in preparing textual input for classification models and varies depending on the underlying architecture. For traditional sequence models such as LSTM, GRU, and CNN, transformation involves explicit tokenization, normalization, and embedding strategies. Tokenization splits input text into words or subwords, followed by text normalization procedures such as lowercasing and punctuation removal. These operations are typically performed manually before feeding the data into the model.

Padding and truncation are necessary to ensure uniform sequence lengths. This step is handled manually for models like LSTM, GRU, and CNN, but is automatically managed within BERT's tokenizer pipeline.

The resulting tokens are then converted into numerical representations. For LSTM, GRU, and CNN, this is typically achieved using pre-trained word embeddings (e.g., GloVe) or one-hot encoding. Correspondingly, categorical sentiment labels (positive or negative) are encoded numerically to be compatible with binary classification tasks.

3.4 CLT-Net Architecture

The CLT-Net model, illustrated in Fig. 2, consists of several integrated components designed for effective sentiment classification. It begins with an Embedding Layer, where pre-trained GloVe embeddings are used to convert each tokenized input sequence into a dense vector representation that captures semantic relationships between words. These embeddings are passed through a CNN block that applies one-dimensional convolutions and max-pooling operations to extract local n-gram features. The resulting feature maps are then fed into an LSTM layer, which captures long-term dependencies and sequential patterns in the review text. To further enhance contextual understanding, a Transformer Attention Block is employed, leveraging multi-head self-attention [21] to model global dependencies across the entire sequence. The output is subsequently passed through fully connected layers for high-level feature transformation and dimensionality adjustment. Finally, a sigmoid activation function produces a probability score for binary sentiment classification of the input review.

Regularization techniques, including dropout and L2 regularization, are applied to prevent overfitting. The model is trained using binary cross-entropy loss and optimized with the Adam algorithm.

The illustrated architecture is a comprehensive deep learning model tailored for binary classification of student reviews. It combines convolutional feature extraction, sequential dependency modeling, and attention-based context enhancement to deliver robust sentiment predictions.

The process begins with the Embedding Layer, which transforms input text into a matrix of size $N \times K$, where N is the number of tokens and K is the word embedding dimension. This layer converts each word into a dense vector representation capturing semantic meaning, initialized with pre-trained GloVe embeddings.

Next, the embeddings pass through a stack of Convolutional Layers, which extract local n-gram features from the text. Each convolution is followed by a Max Pooling Layer to reduce dimensionality and retain the most salient features. These operations detect localized linguistic patterns (e.g., phrases or expressions) that contribute to sentiment polarity.

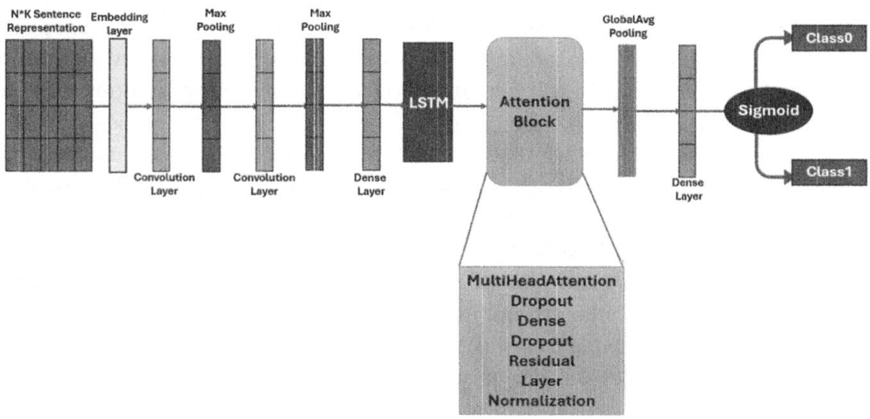

Fig. 2. Overview of the CLT-Net Architecture.

Following the CNN block, the refined features are passed to a Dense Layer to reshape the data appropriately for the sequential modeling stage. The output is then fed into a Long Short-Term Memory (LSTM) layer, which captures temporal dependencies and preserves word order, enabling the model to learn contextual relationships within the sequence.

To enhance the model's focus on the most informative elements of the review, the output of the LSTM is passed through a Transformer-style Attention Block. This block includes a multi-head attention layer that allows the model to attend to different parts of the input sequence simultaneously, dropout layers applied after the attention and dense transformations to reduce overfitting, a dense transformation layer that projects the attended features into a higher-level representation space, a residual connection that adds the block's input to its output to preserve original features and improve gradient flow, and layer normalization which stabilizes and accelerates training. The attention-enhanced output is then passed through a global average pooling layer, which compresses each feature map into a single averaged value, reducing the sequence to a compact, fixed-length vector. This vector is subsequently processed by a dense layer that maps the learned features to the output space, followed by a sigmoid activation function to produce a probability score for binary classification, indicating whether the review sentiment is positive (Class 1) or negative (Class 0).

By integrating CNN, LSTM, and Attention components in a unified framework, CLT-Net effectively captures hierarchical, temporal, and contextual information, making it well-suited for opinion mining in educational review datasets.

4 Experimental Results

The datasets were scraped, cleaned, tokenized, and split into 80% training and 20% testing subsets, with data augmentation applied only to the training data. Tokenized words were vectorized using pre-trained GloVe embeddings to capture semantic associations.

The model combines CNN and LSTM layers for feature extraction and sequence analysis. A non-trainable GloVe embedding layer is followed by CNN layers with multiple kernels, and finally, an LSTM layer with regularization to mitigate overfitting. Dropout layers further enhance generalization, while dense layers integrate extracted features for classification. The model was trained using binary cross-entropy loss and the Adam optimizer for 50 epochs with a batch size of 32, tracking performance on the test set.

The CNN architecture includes two Conv1D layers with 128 filters and a kernel size of 5, each followed by MaxPooling1D layers with a pool size of 2. An additional Conv1D layer with 64 filters and a kernel size of 3, followed by another MaxPooling1D layer, is included. All CNN layers employ dropout with a rate of 0.3. The dense layers after the CNN have 32 and 16 units with ReLU activation, and L2 regularization is applied to both the kernel and bias terms. The LSTM layer matches the embedding dimension, with `return_sequences=False` to output the hidden state. L2 regularization and a dropout rate of 0.3 are also applied to the LSTM layer.

The enhanced architecture synergistically combines convolutional neural networks (CNNs), LSTMs, and transformer attention mechanisms for hierarchical feature learning.

The model begins with two parallel CNN branches: (1) a primary pathway consisting of two Conv1D layers (128 filters, kernel size 5, ReLU activation), each followed by MaxPooling1D (pool size 2) and SpatialDropout1D (rate 0.3); and (2) a secondary pathway with a Conv1D layer (64 filters, kernel size 3) with identical pooling and dropout. This dual-branch design captures both broad and fine-grained textual patterns. The extracted features are then passed through a Bidirectional LSTM layer (64 units total: 32 forward and 32 backward) with `return_sequences=True` to preserve temporal information for the subsequent attention mechanism.

The core innovation lies in the multi-head self-attention block, consisting of 4 heads with a 64-dimensional key space, which dynamically weights important sequence elements. This is followed by layer normalization and residual connections. A 128-unit feedforward network expands the feature space before projection to 64 dimensions. Global average pooling condenses the attended features into a fixed-length vector for final classification through a dense layer with sigmoid activation.

L2 regularization ($\lambda = 0.001$) is applied to all trainable layers, with dropout (rate 0.3) after each major component. Training utilizes the Adam optimizer with a learning rate of 1×10^{-3}, minimizing binary cross-entropy loss over 50 epochs with a batch size of 64. Early stopping with patience of 5 epochs and dynamic learning rate reduction (factor 0.2) monitor and optimize training convergence.

5 Evaluation Metrics

To assess the performance of the proposed CLT-Net model, several standard classification metrics are employed. These metrics offer a comprehensive evaluation of the model's ability to correctly classify review sentiments and are defined as follows:

Accuracy: measures the proportion of correctly predicted instances (both positive and negative) among all predictions. It is expressed as:

$$\text{Accuracy} = \frac{TP + TN}{TP + TN + FP + FN} \tag{1}$$

where TP, TN, FP, and FN denote the number of true positives, true negatives, false positives, and false negatives, respectively.

Precision: quantifies the correctness of positive predictions by computing the ratio of true positives to all predicted positives:

$$\text{Precision} = \frac{TP}{TP + FP} \tag{2}$$

Recall: (also known as Sensitivity) reflects the model's ability to identify actual positive instances:

$$\text{Recall} = \frac{TP}{TP + FN} \tag{3}$$

F1 Score: provides a harmonic mean of Precision and Recall, offering a balanced metric when both false positives and false negatives are of concern:

$$\text{F1 Score} = \frac{2 \times \text{Precision} \times \text{Recall}}{\text{Precision} + \text{Recall}} \tag{4}$$

These metrics collectively enable a robust and interpretable evaluation of classification performance, especially in imbalanced datasets such as sentiment-labeled educational reviews.

5.1 Evaluation on the FutureLearn Dataset

Experimental Settings. The FutureLearn dataset was collected through web scraping and underwent thorough preprocessing, including cleaning, tokenization, and GloVe-based word embedding. Two configurations were evaluated: (1) without data augmentation and (2) with data augmentation. In both settings, a hybrid deep learning model combining convolutional (CNN) and recurrent (LSTM) layers was tested, with and without an attention mechanism. The models were trained for 50 epochs using a batch size of 32 and binary cross-entropy loss, optimized via the Adam algorithm.

Performance Without Data Augmentation. In the baseline setup without data augmentation, the model exhibits strong performance but shows signs of overfitting. The training accuracy curve (see Fig. 3) rapidly rises and plateaus near perfect levels, while the validation accuracy stabilizes around 91–92%. The divergence between training and validation loss curves indicates minor overfitting.

The confusion matrix in Fig. 4 corresponds to the model trained on the FutureLearn dataset using attention mechanisms but without data augmentation. The model correctly classified 2,726 instances from Class 1 and 1,724 from Class 0, with 56 false

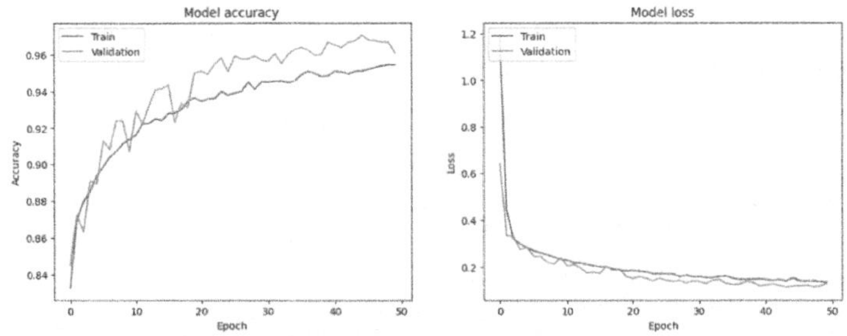

Fig. 3. Accuracy and Loss Curves (FutureLearn Dataset, No Augmentation).

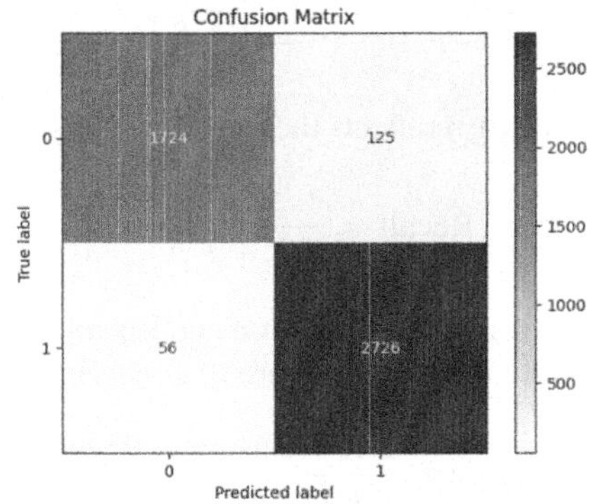

Fig. 4. Confusion Matrix (FutureLearn, No Augmentation).

negatives and 125 false positives. Despite the absence of augmentation, the attention mechanism contributed to strong classification performance, as reflected by the low misclassification rates. These results suggest that attention alone effectively enhances feature discrimination.

The ROC curve in Fig. 5 demonstrates strong classification capability with an AUC of 0.95, indicating high sensitivity and specificity.

Performance with Data Augmentation. Data augmentation leads to a noticeable improvement in generalization performance. As shown in Fig. 6, both training and validation accuracy improve in sync, and the validation loss exhibits a stable convergence trend.

The confusion matrix (Fig. 7) corresponds to the model trained on the FutureLearn dataset using both attention mechanisms and data augmentation. The model correctly classified 2,681 instances of Class 1 and 1,796 instances of Class 0, resulting in 53 false negatives and 101 false positives. The combination of data augmentation and attention contributed to strong classification performance, as reflected by the low misclassification rates. These results suggest that attention and augmentation together are more effective in enhancing feature discrimination than either technique alone.

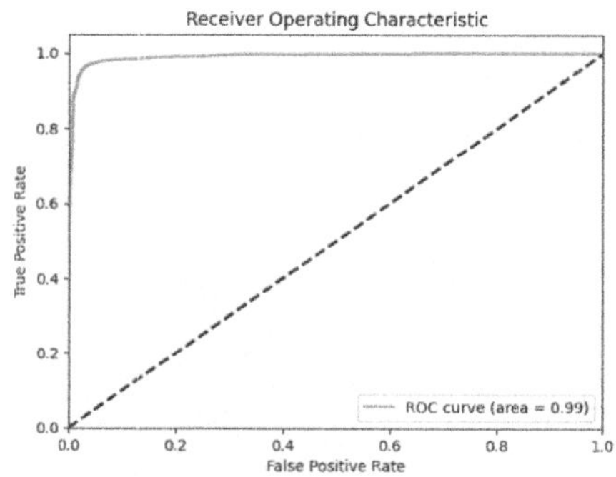

Fig. 5. ROC Curve (FutureLearn, No Augmentation).

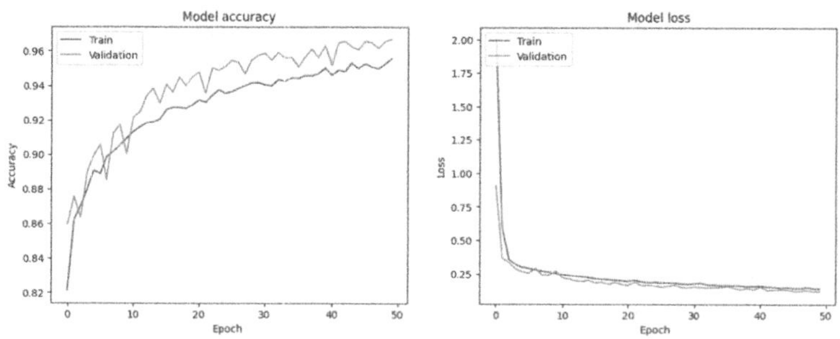

Fig. 6. Accuracy and Loss Curves (FutureLearn, With Augmentation).

Finally, the ROC curve in Fig. 8 demonstrates excellent discriminatory performance, with an AUC close to 0.95. This confirms that data augmentation enhances the model's sensitivity without compromising its specificity.

Summary of FutureLearn Results. The experimental findings on the FutureLearn dataset suggest that:

- The CNN-LSTM hybrid model with attention performs robustly across both configurations.
- Data augmentation improves recall and F1 scores, particularly for the minority class.
- ROC and confusion matrix analyses confirm high reliability, with over 95% AUC in both settings.

These results establish the model's effectiveness in educational sentiment analysis and justify its application in similar NLP tasks.

5.2 Evaluation on the Udemy Dataset

Experimental Settings. For the Udemy dataset, experiments were conducted under four distinct configurations to evaluate the impact of data augmentation and attention mechanisms on model performance:

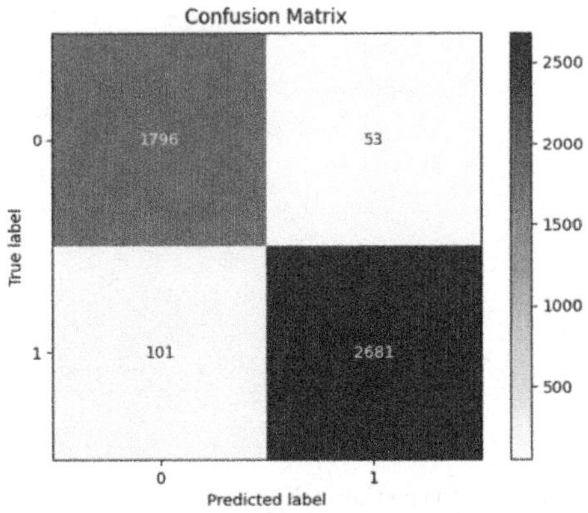

Fig. 7. Confusion Matrix (FutureLearn, With Augmentation).

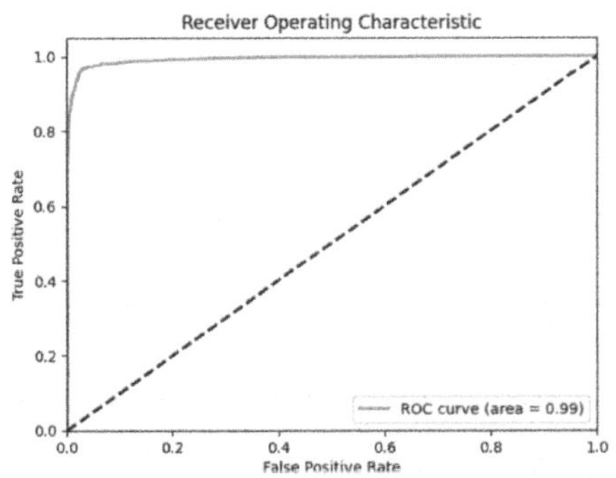

Fig. 8. ROC Curve (FutureLearn, With Augmentation).

1. Without augmentation, without attention
2. Without augmentation, with attention
3. With augmentation, without attention
4. With augmentation, with attention

In all scenarios, the same hybrid architecture was employed, combining convolutional neural networks (CNN) and long short-term memory (LSTM) layers, with pre-trained GloVe embeddings used to initialize the embedding layer. The models were trained for 50 epochs using the Adam optimizer with a batch size of 32. This consistent setup ensures that performance variations are attributable solely to the presence or absence of attention mechanisms and data augmentation.

Performance Without Data Augmentation

Without Attention. The base model without augmentation and attention shows solid performance but suffers from limited generalization. As seen in Fig. 9, the validation accuracy stagnates early compared to training, indicating overfitting.

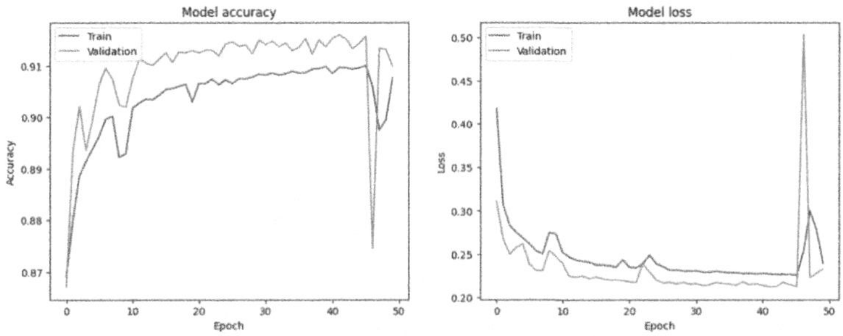

Fig. 9. Accuracy and Loss Curves (Udemy, No Augmentation, No Attention).

The confusion matrix in Fig. 10 summarizes the model's performance on the binary classification task. The model correctly identified 50,946 instances of Class 1 and 4,187 instances of Class 0. It misclassified 686 Class 1 samples as Class 0 (false negatives) and 5,219 Class 0 samples as Class 1 (false positives). These results indicate a high true positive rate, with relatively few false negatives, suggesting the model is particularly effective at identifying instances of Class 1. However, the false positive count highlights a mild bias toward predicting Class 1, likely due to class imbalance.

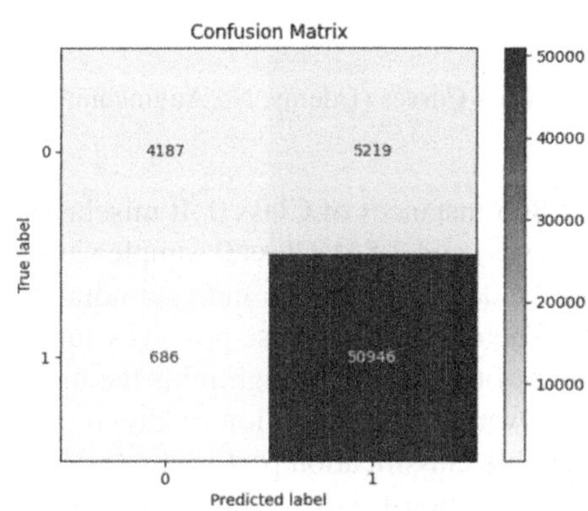

Fig. 10. Confusion Matrix (Udemy, No Augmentation, No Attention).

The ROC curve presented in Fig. 11 reveals an AUC slightly below that of the FutureLearn results, highlighting room for improvement.

Incorporating attention into the model, even without data augmentation, improves the model's ability to focus on relevant features. This is reflected in the improved validation accuracy and reduced validation loss, as shown in Fig. 12. The attention mechanism helps the model prioritize semantically important parts of the input, resulting in more effective learning and better generalization.

The confusion matrix in Fig. 13 illustrates the classification performance of the model enhanced with attention mechanisms. The model correctly predicted 50,000

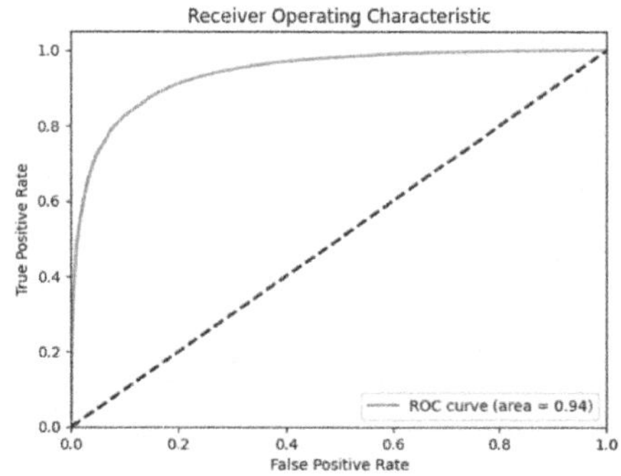

Fig. 11. ROC Curve (Udemy, No Augmentation, No Attention).

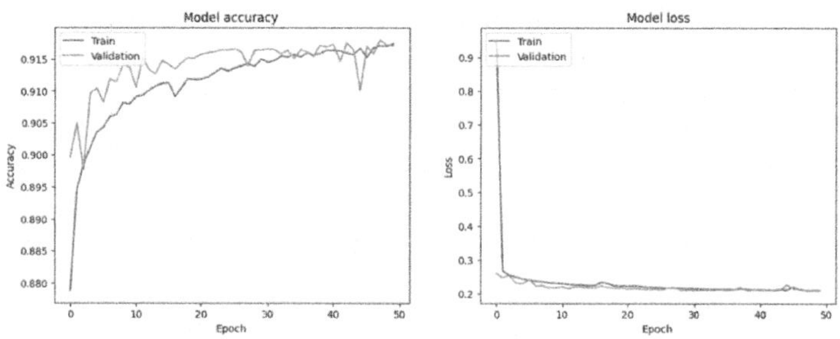

Fig. 12. Accuracy and Loss Curves (Udemy, No Augmentation, With Attention).

instances of Class 1 and 5,865 instances of Class 0. It misclassified 1,521 Class 1 samples as Class 0 (false negatives) and 3,541 Class 0 samples as Class 1 (false positives). Compared to the baseline model, these results indicate notable improvements in both sensitivity and specificity. The reduction in false positives suggests better class separation, while the high number of true positives highlights the model's enhanced ability to identify Class 1 instances. Overall, the integration of attention mechanisms contributes to a more balanced and reliable classification performance.

The ROC curve (Fig. 14) demonstrates strong classification performance, with an AUC approaching 0.95, indicating the model's high ability to distinguish between the two classes.

Performance with Data Augmentation

Without Attention. Applying data augmentation without the use of attention mechanisms leads to noticeable improvements in performance, particularly in validation accuracy and F1 scores. This suggests that data augmentation enhances the model's ability to generalize to unseen data by increasing the diversity of the training set. The accuracy and loss curves shown in Fig. 15 reflect more stable learning and reduced overfitting compared to the non-augmented configuration.

The confusion matrix (Fig. 16) represents the performance of the model trained with data augmentation but without the attention mechanism. The model correctly classified

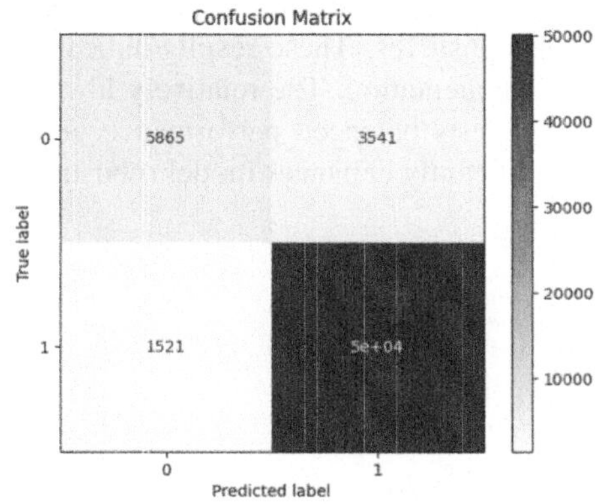

Fig. 13. Confusion Matrix (Udemy, No Augmentation, With Attention).

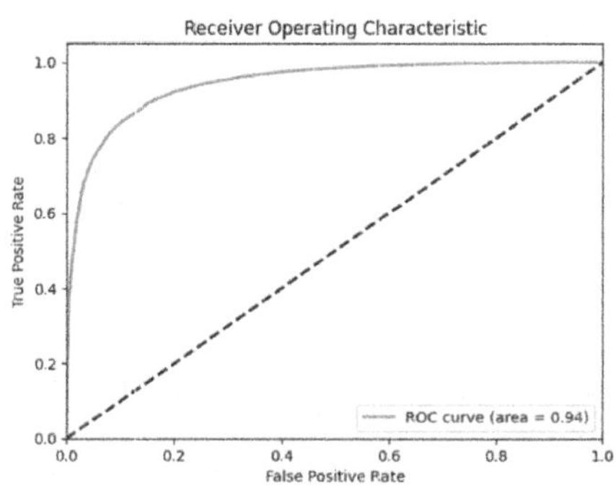

Fig. 14. ROC Curve (Udemy, No Augmentation, With Attention).

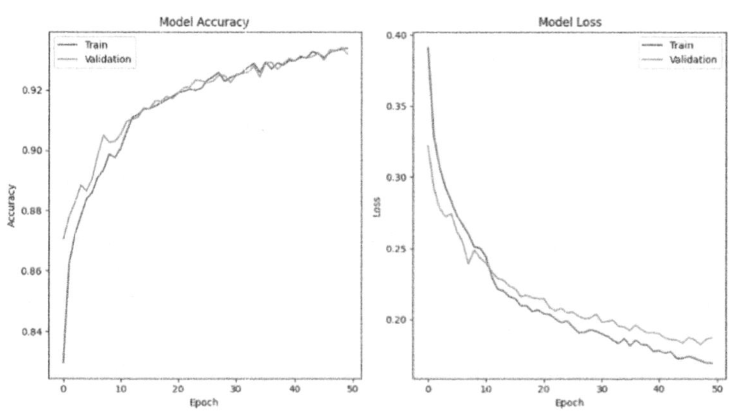

Fig. 15. Accuracy and Loss Curves (Udemy, With Augmentation, No Attention).

48,019 instances of Class 1 and 8,748 instances of Class 0, while producing 3,613 false negatives and 658 false positives. These results indicate a strong generalization capability enabled by data augmentation. The relatively low number of misclassifications across both classes suggests balanced performance, reinforcing the conclusion that augmentation alone significantly enhances model robustness—even in the absence of attention mechanisms.

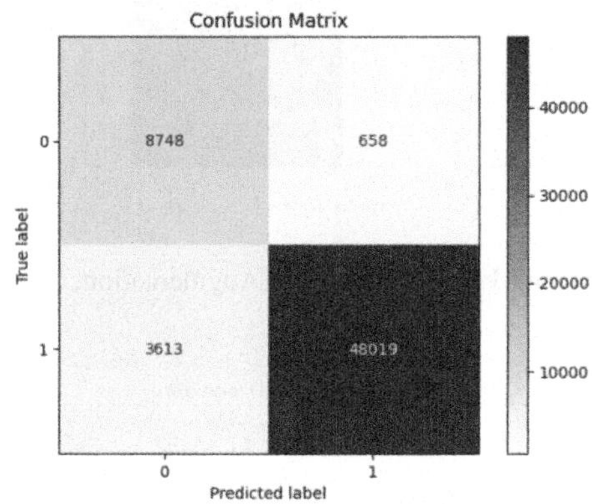

Fig. 16. Confusion Matrix (Udemy, With Augmentation, No Attention).

With Attention. Combining data augmentation with attention mechanisms yields the best results on the Udemy dataset. As shown in Fig. 17, the training and validation accuracy curves are closely aligned throughout the epochs, indicating minimal overfitting and stable learning. The integration of attention enhances the model's ability to focus on semantically important features, while augmentation increases data diversity—together resulting in superior generalization and classification performance.

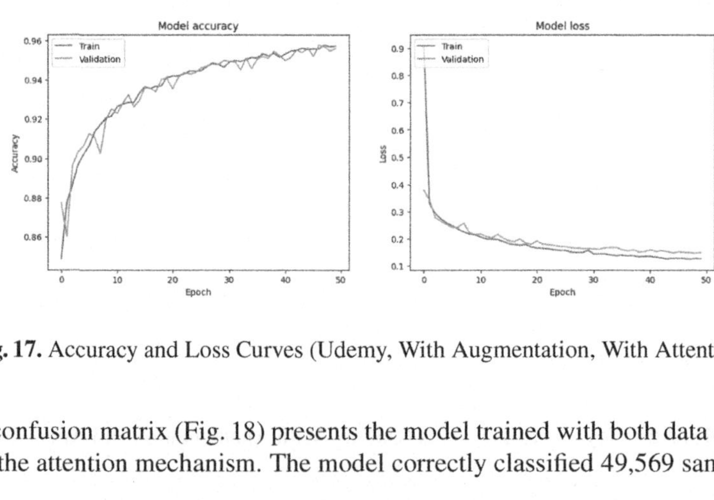

Fig. 17. Accuracy and Loss Curves (Udemy, With Augmentation, With Attention).

The confusion matrix (Fig. 18) presents the model trained with both data augmentation and the attention mechanism. The model correctly classified 49,569 samples from

Class 1 and 9,030 from Class 0. It yielded 2,063 false negatives and 376 false positives. Compared to the configuration without attention, this result shows a further reduction in misclassifications across both classes. The significant decrease in both false positives and false negatives indicates that the integration of attention mechanisms, in conjunction with data augmentation, enhances the model's discriminative capability and overall reliability.

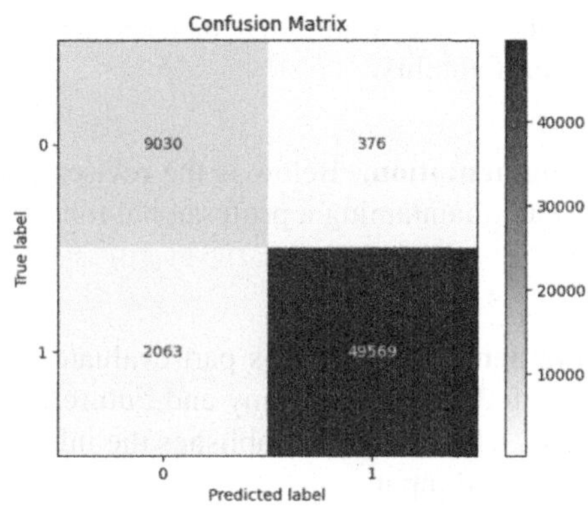

Fig. 18. Confusion Matrix (Udemy, With Augmentation, With Attention).

The ROC curve (Fig. 19) reveal balanced prediction power and an AUC close to 0.96, affirming excellent model reliability.

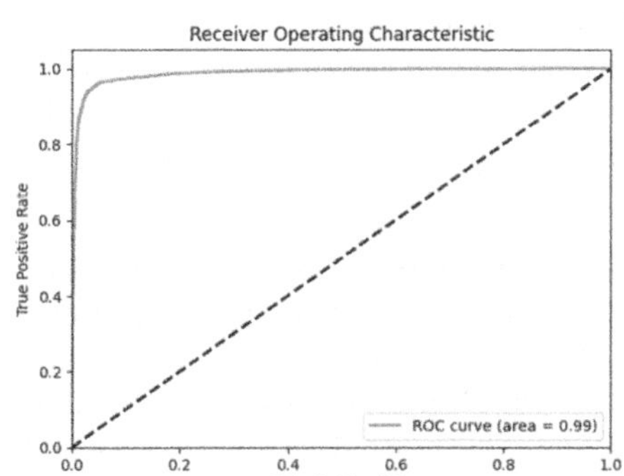

Fig. 19. ROC Curve (Udemy, With Augmentation, With Attention).

Summary of Udemy Results. The evaluation of the Udemy dataset demonstrates that:

- Attention significantly improves performance even in the absence of augmentation.
- Data augmentation enhances the model's generalization ability across configurations.

- The best performance is achieved with the combination of augmentation and attention, resulting in the highest AUC and most balanced confusion matrix.

This confirms that both augmentation and attention contribute independently and synergistically to boosting classification quality in student review analysis.

5.3 Summary of Results Across Datasets

Performance is evaluated using both traditional metrics (accuracy, F1) and attention visualization for model interpretability.

Results Without Data Augmentation. Below is the revised paragraph formatted for inclusion in a scientific paper, maintaining a professional tone and preserving the original citations as requested:

Performance on Non-augmented Data. This part evaluates the performance of the CNN-LSTM and CLT-Net models on the Udemy and FutureLearn datasets using non-augmented, raw textual data. This analysis establishes the inherent capabilities of each model in processing unprocessed input.

As reported in Table 2, for the Udemy dataset, the CNN-LSTM model achieves an accuracy of 90.0%, with a precision of 88.0%, recall of 72.0%, and an F1 score of 77.0%. In contrast, the CLT-Net model demonstrates superior performance, attaining an accuracy of 92.0%, precision of 86.0%, recall of 79.0%, and an F1 score of 82.0%.

For the FutureLearn dataset, the CNN-LSTM model delivers robust performance with an accuracy of 92.0%, precision of 92.0%, recall of 88.5%, and an F1 score of 91.5%. The CLT-Net model outperforms it, achieving an accuracy of 96.0%, with precision and F1 score of 96.0%, and a recall of 95.0%.

These results indicate that the CLT-Net model consistently surpasses the CNN-LSTM model across both datasets without data augmentation, likely due to its attention-based architecture, which enhances feature extraction from raw textual data.

Performance with Data Augmentation. After applying the data augmentation we examine the effect of data augmentation on the generalization and classification accuracy of the CNN-LSTM and CLT-Net models.

On the Udemy dataset, the CNN-LSTM model shows marked improvement with data augmentation, achieving 93.0% across accuracy, precision, recall, and F1 score. The CLT-Net model exhibits even greater enhancement, reaching 96.0% across all four metrics, demonstrating high consistency and robust performance.

For the FutureLearn dataset, the CNN-LSTM model improves to an accuracy of 95.0%, with a precision of 93.0%, and both recall and F1 score at 92.5%. The CLT-Net model again achieves the highest performance, with an accuracy of 97.0%, and precision, recall, and F1 score all at 96.0%.

These findings confirm that data augmentation significantly enhances model performance, particularly when combined with advanced architectures like CLT-Net. The consistent outperformance of CLT-Net over CNN-LSTM in both non-augmented and augmented conditions highlights the efficacy of its attention-based design in optimizing classification outcomes.

Table 2. Performance Metrics for Udemy and FutureLearn Using LSTM and CLT-Net With and Without Augmentation.

Dataset	Model	Without Augmentation				With Augmentation			
		Acc.	Prec.	Rec.	F1	Acc.	Prec.	Rec.	F1
Udemy	CNN-LSTM	90.0%	88.0%	72.0%	77.0%	93.0%	93.0%	93.0%	93.0%
	CLT-Net	92.0%	86.0%	79.0%	82.0%	**96.0%**	**95.0%**	**95.0%**	**95.0%**
FutureLearn	CNN-LSTM	92.0%	92.0%	88.5%	91.5%	95.0%	93.0%	92.5%	92.5%
	CLT-Net	96.0%	96.0%	95.0%	96.0%	**97.0%**	**96.0%**	**96.0%**	**96.0%**

5.4 Discussion

The experimental findings presented in this study confirm the effectiveness of hybrid deep learning models for binary text classification tasks, with a focus on analyzing student reviews from FutureLearn and Udemy platforms. Consistent with our previous work, the CNN-LSTM architecture demonstrates strong performance in terms of precision, recall, F1 score, and accuracy. However, the current results go further by systematically evaluating the roles of data augmentation and attention mechanisms across different datasets and settings.

On the FutureLearn dataset, the CNN-LSTM model equipped with attention achieves remarkable accuracy (up to 95%) and high area under the ROC curve (AUC $\approx$ 0.95) when trained with augmented data. The accuracy and loss curves indicate stable convergence with minimal overfitting. Confusion matrices show improved balance in class predictions, and the ROC curves confirm excellent discriminatory power. These results outperform our previous study, where the same model architecture without attention and less refined augmentation yielded slightly lower recall and F1 scores, particularly for the minority class.

The Udemy dataset further reinforces these findings. While base models (without augmentation and attention) perform reasonably well, significant improvements are observed when attention and augmentation are introduced. The most effective configuration—CNN-LSTM with attention and data augmentation—not only achieves the highest accuracy but also produces well-separated ROC curves and the most balanced confusion matrices. The introduction of attention helps the model focus on semantically relevant components of student reviews, while augmentation diversifies the training data, enhancing the model's generalization ability.

Overall, our new results validate and extend our earlier findings. Compared to the previous work:

- The inclusion of attention mechanisms leads to improved contextual understanding and classification reliability.

- Data augmentation consistently boosts recall and F1 scores, especially for underrepresented classes.
- The CNN-LSTM model remains the most robust architecture, now enhanced by complementary techniques.

This comprehensive analysis across two distinct e-learning datasets highlights the generalizability of our approach and its practical value for sentiment analysis in educational contexts. The improvements over prior results establish a stronger foundation for future work in explainable AI and real-time feedback systems for online learning platforms.

6 Conclusion

This study presents an enhanced deep learning framework for the automated classification of student reviews on e-learning platforms, with evaluations conducted on two real-world datasets: FutureLearn and Udemy. Building on our previous work, we introduce a hybrid CNN-LSTM model augmented with attention mechanisms and data augmentation techniques to improve performance, robustness, and generalization.

Experimental results demonstrate that the proposed model outperforms baseline architectures, achieving up to 95% accuracy and a high area under the ROC curve across both datasets. The incorporation of attention improves the model's ability to capture contextual relevance in text, while augmentation addresses data imbalance and sparsity. Comparative analyses confirm that the CNN-LSTM model remains the most effective architecture, particularly when combined with these enhancements.

The approach proves scalable and adaptable across different datasets, validating its potential for broader application in educational opinion mining and user feedback classification. The improvements over our previous study underscore the value of integrating semantic enrichment and training diversity into deep learning pipelines for NLP tasks.

Future work will explore explainability methods to interpret model decisions and extend this framework to multi-class or multilingual educational datasets. Further enhancements in model interpretability, scalability, and deployment could support real-time sentiment analytics and adaptive learning systems, ultimately contributing to more responsive and personalized e-learning experiences.

References

1. Majouri, H., Gaddour, O., Kacem, Y.: A hybrid CNN-LSTM model for opinion mining and classification of course reviews. In: Proceedings of the 17th International Conference on Agents and Artificial Intelligence (ICAART), Porto, Portugal, pp. 734–741 (2025)
2. Koufakou, A.: Deep learning for opinion mining and topic classification of course reviews. Educ. Inf. Technol. **29**(3), 2973–2997 (2023)
3. Onan, A.: Sentiment analysis on massive open online course evaluations: a text mining and deep learning approach. Comput. Appl. Eng. Educ. **29**(3), 572–589 (2021)
4. Qi, C., Liu, S.: Evaluating online courses via reviews mining. IEEE Access **9**, 35439–35451 (2021)

5. Onan, A.: Mining opinions from instructor evaluation reviews: a deep learning approach. Comput. Appl. Eng. Educ. **28**(1), 117–138 (2020)
6. Chakravarthy, V.J., Kameswari, M., Mydeen, H.D., Seenivasan, M.: Opinion mining from student text review for choosing better online courses. In: IOP Conference Series: Materials Science and Engineering, vol. 012067 (2021)
7. El-Halees, A.: Mining opinions in user-generated contents to improve course evaluation. In: Zain, J.M., Wan Mohd, W.M., El-Qawasmeh, E. (eds.) ICSECS 2011. CCIS, vol. 180, pp. 107–115. Springer, Heidelberg (2011). https://doi.org/10.1007/978-3-642-22191-0_9
8. Kastrati, Z., et al.: Aspect-based opinion mining of students' reviews on online courses. In: Proceedings of the 6th International Conference on Computing and Artificial Intelligence, pp. 510–514 (2020)
9. Yan, X., et al.: Sentiment analysis on massive open online course evaluation. In: Proceedings of the International Conference on Neuromorphic Computing (ICNC), pp. 245–249. IEEE (2021)
10. Cabada, R.Z., Estrada, M.L.B., Bustillos, R.O.: Mining of educational opinions with deep learning. J. Univ. Comput. Sci. **24**(11), 1604–1626 (2018)
11. Edalati, M., Imran, A.S., Kastrati, Z., Daudpota, S.M.: The potential of machine learning algorithms for sentiment classification of students' feedback on MOOC. In: Arai, K. (ed.) IntelliSys 2021. LNNS, vol. 296, pp. 11–22. Springer, Cham (2022). https://doi.org/10.1007/978-3-030-82199-9_2
12. Shaik, T., et al.: Sentiment analysis and opinion mining on educational data: a survey. Nat. Lang. Process. J. **2**, 100003 (2023)
13. Siami-Namini, S., et al.: The performance of LSTM and BiLSTM in forecasting time series. In: IEEE International Conference on Big Data, pp. 3285–3292 (2019)
14. She, D., Jia, M.: A BiGRU method for remaining useful life prediction of machinery. Measurement **167**, 108277 (2021)
15. Magnoni, F., Plutino, A.: The move-me project on the FutureLearn platform. In: E-Learning, MOOCs and Foreign Languages: Research, Studies and Experiences, p. 103 (2018)
16. Khder, M.A.: Web scraping or web crawling: State of the art, techniques, approaches and application. Int. J. Adv. Soft Comput. Appl. **13**(3) (2021)
17. LeCun, Y., et al.: Gradient-based learning applied to document recognition. Proc. IEEE **86**(11), 2278–2324 (1998)
18. Tripathy, A., et al.: Classification of sentiment reviews using N-gram machine learning approach. Expert Syst. Appl. **57**, 117–126 (2016)
19. Guru, C., Bajnaid, W.: Prediction of customer sentiment based on online reviews using machine learning algorithms. Int. J. Data Sci. Adv. Anal. (2023)
20. Mrhar, K., et al.: A Bayesian CNN-LSTM model for sentiment analysis in MOOCs. Int. J. Emerg. Technol. Learn. **16**(23), 216–232 (2021)
21. Vaswani, A., et al.: Attention is all you need. Adv. Neural. Inf. Process. Syst. **30**, 5998–6008 (2017)
22. Upadhyay, S.R., Dave, M.: Course review mining on e-learning platforms using deep learning techniques. J. Web Eng. **22**(4), 875–894 (2023)
23. Devlin, J., et al.: BERT: pre-training of deep bidirectional transformers for language understanding. In: Proceedings of NAACL-HLT, vol. 1, pp. 4171–4186 (2019)
24. Edalati, M., et al.: Cross-platform sentiment analysis on educational reviews using deep transfer learning. In: Proceedings of the 2022 International Conference on Learning Technologies, pp. 134–139. IEEE (2022)
25. Pang, B., Lee, L.: Opinion mining and sentiment analysis. Found. Trends Inf. Retr. **2**(1–2), 1–135 (2008)

A Novel Cuckoo Search Optimisation Enhanced Random Key Addressing the Graph Burning Problem in Social Networks

Imad Tamelghaghet[1], Fatima Benbouzid-Si Tayeb[1(✉)], and Lamia Sadeg-Belkacem[2]

[1] Laboratoire des Méthodes de Conception de Systèmes (LMCS), École Nationale Supérieure d'Informatique (ESI), BP 68M, 16270 Oued Smar, Algiers, Algeria
{ii_tamelghaghet,f_sitayeb}@esi.dz

[2] École Militaire Polytechnique (EMP), Bordj El Bahri, 16046 Algiers, Algeria
lamia.sadeg@emp.mdn.dz

Abstract. This paper addresses the Graph Burning Problem (GBP), a model for studying influence spread in social networks. Due to the NP-hardness of the problem, we propose the Centrality-Based Discrete Cuckoo Search ($CBDCS$), a metaheuristic algorithm inspired by the brood parasitism behavior of cuckoos and enhanced with Lévy flight dynamics. $CBDCS$ adopts a random key-based encoding scheme for solution generation. Additionally, it incorporates betweenness centrality to guide the initialization process, ensuring the selection of structurally influential nodes. $CBDCS$ offers a robust balance between exploration and convergence, enabling efficient navigation of large solution spaces. Experimental results on 30 benchmark graphs demonstrate that $CBDCS$ not only outperforms state-of-the-art approaches but also provides a scalable and effective solution strategy, making it well-suited for solving GBP on large networks.

Keywords: Social Networks · Graph Burning Problem · Optimisation · Cuckoo Search · Random Key

1 Introduction

In today's interconnected world, social networks have become fundamental infrastructures that shape communication, business, and human interaction. From global platforms such as Facebook and LinkedIn to niche online communities, these networks influence everything from public opinion and marketing strategies to organizational behavior. With billions of users interacting through complex webs of relationships, understanding the underlying structure and dynamics of these networks is more critical than ever.

This need has led to the development of Social Network Analysis (SNA), an interdisciplinary approach that applies concepts from graph theory, statistics, and data science to analyze the patterns of relationships within social systems. SNA provides essential tools for uncovering key actors, detecting community structures, and modeling the flow of information or influence across a network. These insights are crucial in

H. J. van den Herik et al. (Eds.): ICAART 2025, LNAI 16517, pp. 502–524, 2026.
https://doi.org/10.1007/978-3-032-25032-2_24

numerous domains, including targeted advertising, crisis communication, public health, and cybersecurity.

A central concern in SNA is understanding how influence or contagion propagates through a network over time. Whether it is the spread of information, the adoption of behaviors, or the transmission of rumors, the propagation dynamics depends heavily on the network topology and the choice of initial influencers. Accurate modeling of these diffusion processes allows researchers and practitioners to design more effective strategies for message dissemination, epidemic containment, and network optimization. As a response to these challenges, the Graph Burning Problem (GBP) has emerged as a simplified yet powerful model for studying such phenomena. By modeling the spread of influence as a burning process, the GBP seeks to determine the smallest sequence of initial nodes (burning sources) that can "ignite" the entire graph within the fewest number of time steps. Despite its abstract formulation, the problem effectively captures key aspects of influence propagation. However, determining an optimal burning sequence minimizing the total number of time steps required to reach all vertices, is computationally difficult. The problem has been proven NP-hard, even for restricted classes of graphs [8], making exact solutions computationally prohibitive for large-scale networks.

To address this complexity, researchers have explored a range of solution strategies, broadly categorized into exact algorithms, heuristics, approximation algorithms, and metaheuristics. Exact methods aim to guarantee optimal solutions but are generally applicable only to small graphs due to their high computational cost. For instance, Integer Linear Programming (ILP) and Constraint Satisfaction Problem (CSP) formulations have been proposed to solve small to medium-sized instances of the GBP optimally. However, these approaches remain infeasible for large-scale networks because of their exponential time complexity. Furthermore, [24] proposed two new ILP formulations, $ILP-COV$ and $ILP-CMCP$, which improve the previous exact methods by solving larger instances and discovering new optimal solutions. More recently, [22] introduced $PRYM$ that demonstrated strong performance even on relatively large graphs (approximately 2,000 vertices), outperforming earlier approaches.

Approximation algorithms aim to produce near-optimal solutions with performance guarantees. [8] proposed a *3-approximation algorithm* for general graphs, which runs in $\mathcal{O}(M)$ time, where M is the number of edges. This algorithm ensures that the resulting burning number is at most three times the optimal. Another notable contribution is the *Burning Farthest First (BFF)* algorithm, which selects nodes based on their distance from previously burned nodes. The BFF achieves a burning sequence of maximum length $3 - \frac{2}{b(G)}$, where $b(G)$ is the optimal burning number [16], and a time complexity of $\mathcal{O}(n^3)$, n being the number of nodes. [17] introduced a two-phase modular framework, which separates the decision of the first fire source from the rest of the sequence. By combining various heuristics in each stage, their approach generates multiple algorithmic variants.

Greedy heuristics offer fast, but often suboptimal solutions. Among the earliest proposed are the *Cutting Corner Heuristic (CCH)* and the *Maximum Eigenvector Centrality Heuristic (MECH)*, which rely on topological features (Corner nodes) and eigenvector-centrality measure to prioritize burning sources. The *Greedy Algorithm with Forward-*

Looking Search Strategy (GAFLSS) enhances these methods by incorporating an evaluation metric WASPAS [9].

The *Backbone-Based Greedy Heuristic (BBGH)*, *Improved Cutting Corner Heuristic (ICCH)*, and *Component-Based Recursive Heuristic (CBRH)* provide optimizations and improvements to node selection strategies by considering network backbone structures [15]. These enhancements reduce runtime while increasing coverage quality, thereby improving scalability to large graphs. [24] further introduced a deterministic greedy heuristic, *Gr*, based on a $(1/2)$-approximation for the Clustered Maximum Coverage Problem, with a time complexity of $\mathcal{O}(mn + pn^2)$, along with an enhanced variant, GrP, which evaluates all possible initial sources.

To escape local optima and improve search diversity, metaheuristics have been applied to the GBP. The first such algorithm, *Centrality-Based Genetic Algorithm (CBAG)* [19], adapts classical genetic operations to the burning problem by incorporating node centrality metrics. This integration enables more informed search dynamics and enhances solution quality, particularly on dense or large-scale social networks. Building on this direction, a Guided Local Search (GLS) [23] has been recently proposed, showing promising results in navigating the solution space through iterative local optimization. Despite its effectiveness, the inherent limitations of GLS in capturing the global structure of complex search landscapes have led to the investigation of more exploratory approaches capable of broader, more diverse search.

In this work, we contribute to this line of research by proposing a population-based metaheuristic, the *Cuckoo Search Algorithm (CSA)*. Inspired by the brood parasitism behavior of cuckoo birds and enhanced with Lévy flight dynamics, CSA has demonstrated strong performance in continuous optimization problems by achieving a balance between intensification and diversification. This balance enables effective exploration of the solution space and improves scalability. Our main contribution lies in adapting the CSA to a discrete setting and tailor it to the structural characteristics of the problem, thereby proposing the *Centrality-Based Discrete Cuckoo Search* ($CBDCS$). $CBDCS$ enhances the algorithm's capacity to explore diverse regions of the solution space while maintaining efficient convergence behavior.

The rest of the paper is structured as follows. Section 2 introduces the Graph Burning Problem and its theoretical foundations. Section 3 outlines the classical Cuckoo Search Algorithm and the modifications required to handle discrete optimization problem that is GBP. Section 4 presents the experimental results and performance analysis are then discussed in the last final section.

2 Burning Graph Problem Formulation

The GBP is a discrete-time process that models the propagation of influence, contagion, or information in a network. Originally introduced by Bonato et al. [4], the problem aims to determine the minimal time required to burn all the nodes of a graph using an ordered sequence of fire sources.

In this problem, a social network is represented as a graph $G = (V, E)$, where $V = \{v_1, \ldots, v_n\}$ is the set of nodes with $n = |V|$ denoting the number of nodes and $E = \{e_1, \ldots, e_m\}$ the set of edges with $m = |E|$ the number of edges. Each node corresponds to an entity (e.g., an individual in a social network), and edges represent relationships between these entities. Each node can be in one of two states: *burned* or *unburned*. The spread of fire occurs through a process known as the *burning process*, which unfolds in discrete time steps, described as follows:

- Initially, all nodes are in the unburned state.
- At each time step $t \geq 1$, a single node is chosen as a burning source.
- Once a node is burned, it remains in that state permanently.
- If a node v is burned at step t, then all its unburned neighbors become burned at step $t + 1$.
- The process continues until all nodes in G are burned.

The burning process can be illustrated via an exemple presented in Fig. 1.

The nodes selected at each step are called activators or fire sources. These nodes form an ordered sequence known as a *burning sequence*. A *burning sequence* is a sequence of nodes $S = v_1, v_2, \ldots, v_k$, where each v_i represents the node chosen as the burning source at step i. The length of this sequence, denoted by k, corresponds to the number of steps required to complete the burning process [6].

The *burning number* of a graph G, denoted as $b(G)$, is the minimum number of steps required to burn all nodes in the graph. Since the size of a burning sequence gives us the number of steps, the burning number can be found by finding a burning sequence of minimal size. Determining the burning number of a graph provides insights into the rate at which information or contagion propagates through a network. This measure has practical applications in various fields, including analyzing information dissemination in social networks, optimizing message or alert propagation in communication systems, and managing the spread of influence in network structures [4,6].

2.1 *GBP* Mathematical Formulation

In $G = (V, E)$, the kth closed neighborhood of a node v_i is defined as $\tau_k(v_i) = u \in V \mid d(v_i, u) \leq k$, where $d(v_i, u)$ denotes the shortest-path distance between nodes v_i and u.

Given a sequence of fire sources $S = v_1, v_2, \ldots, v_k$, where $k \geq 3$, in graph G, each fire source v_i burns all nodes $u \in V$ within a distance of at most i from v_i, as defined by the burning process. The *GBP* can thus be formulated as the problem of determining the minimal sequence of burning sources such that all nodes in the graph are eventually burned. Mathematically, a burning sequence S satisfies:

$$\tau_{k-1}(v_1) \cup \tau_{k-2}(v_2) \cup \cdots \cup \tau_0(v_k) = V. \quad (1)$$

Additionally, for all $1 \leq i \leq j \leq k$, the following constraint must hold:

$$d(v_i, v_j) \geq j - i. \quad (2)$$

The first condition ensures complete coverage of the graph, meaning that every node is burned within the specified time horizon. The second condition guarantees that the burning zones of different fire sources do not overlap prematurely. A sequence satisfying both conditions is referred to as a *valid burning sequence* [6].

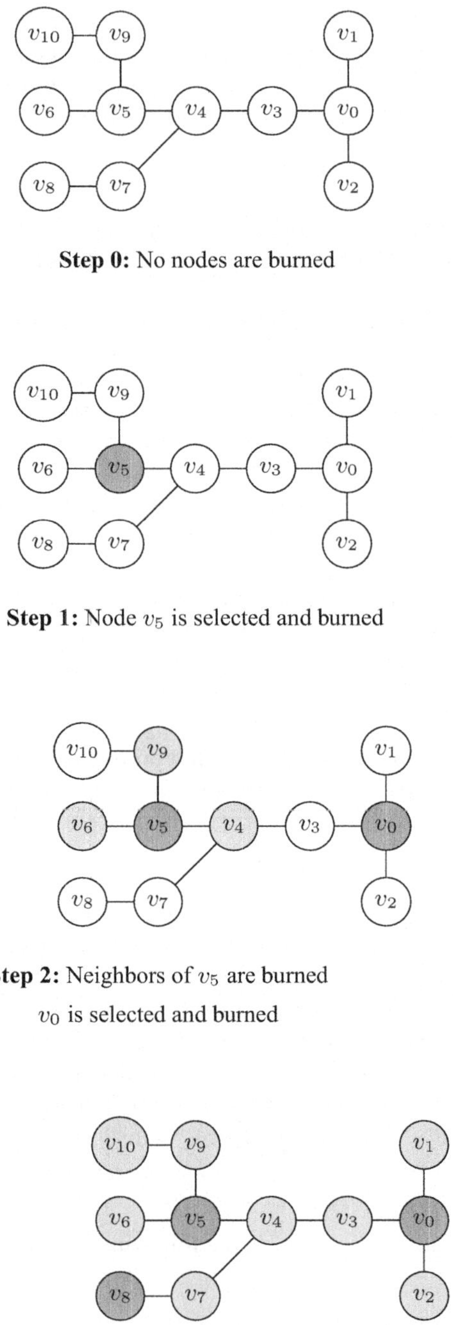

Step 0: No nodes are burned

Step 1: Node v_5 is selected and burned

Step 2: Neighbors of v_5 are burned
v_0 is selected and burned

Step 3: Fire spreads from v_0, v_8 is selected and burned

Fig. 1. Example of a burning process.

2.2 GBP Computational Complexity

The general GBP has been proven to be NP-complete [8], even for certain simple graph classes such as spider graphs. Furthermore, scheduling a given burning sequence has also been shown to be NP-complete. Specifically, given a predefined set of k fire sources, determining a valid burning sequence, i.e. an ordering of these sources such that all nodes in the graph are burned within k rounds, is NP-hard [12].

The GBP belongs to the class APX, which comprises optimization problems that admit polynomial-time approximation algorithms guaranteeing solutions within a constant factor of the optimal value. For the GBP, this implies that an approximate solution within a bounded ratio of the optimal burning number $b(G)$ can be computed in polynomial time [12]. The BFF algorithm is an example of such an approximation method, providing a solution with an upper bound of at most $3b(G) - 2$.

2.3 Burning Number Bounds

A significant part of the research in this domain has focused on deriving theoretical approximations of the burning number based on graph properties. One of the key questions in this field concerns proving conjectures related to the burning number. Below are some important bounds and conjectures:

One of the first general properties established for connected graphs is given by the inequality (3):

$$\lceil \sqrt{d+1} \rceil \leq b(G) \leq r + 1 \tag{3}$$

where r is the radius of the graph and d is its diameter [4].

A stronger conjectured upper bound is given by inequality (4). If a connected graph G has order n, then:

$$b(G) \leq \sqrt{n} \tag{4}$$

Although this conjecture remains unproven for general connected graphs, it has been validated for specific graph classes [4,7].

The best known proven upper bound for the burning number, which is slightly weaker than the conjectured bound but remains the tightest known bound [11], is given by inequality (5):

$$b(G) \leq \sqrt{\frac{4n}{3}} + 1 \tag{5}$$

For disconnected graphs, if G consists of connected components $G_1, G_2, \dots, G_t$, then:

$$t \leq b(G) \leq \sum_{i=1}^{t} b(G_i) \tag{6}$$

Equation (6) implies that in order to burn a disconnected graph, the burning sequence must include at least one node from each connected component . Additionally, the burning process of G completes more efficiently if each component is burned independently [6].

Another important lower bound is given by inequality (7):

$$b(G) \geq \max\{b(G_i) : 1 \leq i \leq t\} \tag{7}$$

This result indicates that to burn a graph, at minimum, its largest burning-number component must be burned [6]. A more general conjecture for disconnected graphs, given by inequality (8), states that if a disconnected graph G of order n consists of s connected components, then:

$$b(G) \leq \lceil \sqrt{n} \rceil + s - 1 \tag{8}$$

This conjecture suggests that the burning number is primarily influenced by the number of nodes and that the burning sequence must contain at least one node from each connected component of the graph [6].

3 CSA-Based Solving Approach

Cuckoo Search is inspired by the brood parasitism behavior observed in certain cuckoo species. These birds lay their eggs in the nests of other species, deceiving the host birds into incubating and nurturing their offspring. This opportunistic reproductive strategy is combined with a movement model known as "Lévy flights," observed in some birds and insects, characterized by a series of long and random movements that optimize the search for new solutions [3].

Cuckoo Search Algorithm (CSA) leverages these two natural mechanisms to efficiently explore the search space. By integrating *cuckoo eggs* as new solutions and using *Levy flights* to model movements, CSA balances intensification by exploiting the best current solutions and diversification by exploring new areas of the search space, ensuring a robust and adaptive optimization process [3].

The foundation of our proposed approach, hereinafter $CBDCS$ for Centrality-Based Discrete Cukoo Search, lies in the Discrete Damped Cuckoo Search (DDCS) [10] and integrates key concepts from the Centrality-Based Genetic Algorithm ($CBAG$) [19], combining their strengths to enhance both exploration and exploitation within the solution space. $CBDCS$ adapts the computation of Lévy flights to the discrete nature of the GBP and incorporates $CBAG$-inspired mutation operations, with the goal of improving search efficiency, avoiding local optima and ultimately producing more effective solutions to the GBP.

A central component of $CBDCS$ is the estimation of the burning number $b(G)$, which directly guides the construction of the burning sequence. To identify this value, $CBDCS$ employs a binary search strategy that tests different candidate values of $b(G)$ and retains the best solution found. Although this procedure can be computationally intensive, $CBDCS$ is designed for rapid convergence. If the initial guess bg satisfies $bg \geq b(G)$, the algorithm quickly identifies a feasible burning sequence. In contrast, if

$bg < b(G)$, the algorithm may need to perform all iterations, increasing the computational cost. To address this, strong lower bounds are used to narrow the search space, and a stagnation parameter is introduced to halt the process early if no improvement is observed over a predefined number of generations.

The $CBDCS$ algorithm operates in five phases, each contributing to the overall optimization process. It begins with a preprocessing phase, where key structural properties of the input graph are computed once and stored, ensuring efficient reuse throughout the algorithm. Then, once the population is initialized with solutions generated randomly, the algorithm enters its iterative optimization process, where each generation starts by ranking the population according to solution quality. A selected fraction P_c of the best solutions undergoes *local search enhancement*, with the aim of improving the quality of the solution by refining the placement of burning sources. Meanwhile, the remaining solutions are diversified through *Lévy flights*, introducing stochastic perturbations that explore new regions of the search space. To further prevent premature convergence, *random mutation* are applied to a fraction P_a of the population, promoting exploration. This cycle of evaluation, refinement, and diversification continues until a maximum number of iterations is reached, a valid burning sequence is found, or stagnation is observed, ensuring both the quality of the solution and the efficiency of the search (Fig. 2).

The detailed workings of $CBDCS$' are explained in the following subsections. First, we present the solution encoding scheme used. Then, we detail the preprocessing phase and the generation of the initial search space, the generation of new candidate solutions through Lévy flights and mutation, and finally, the selection process for updating the best solution.

3.1 Solution's Encoding Scheme and Objective Function

The main goal of our algorithm is to determine a valid burning sequence with the smallest possible size, where each solution corresponds to a complete sequence. However, the $CBAG$ algorithm [19] adopts a different representation by considering only a subset of the sequence, focusing primarily on the initial burning nodes. This approach takes advantage of the fact that early nodes play a more significant role in the burning process as they are capable of reaching a larger portion of the graph. In contrast, nodes positioned later in the sequence have a more limited effect, with the last node typically burning only itself and its immediate neighbors. This distinction underscores the strategic importance of optimizing the early stages of the burning sequence (Fig. 3).

Building on this idea, the proposed $CBDCS$ algorithm operates on partial burning sequences, where the remaining unburned nodes are dynamically added as needed. This strategy allows the algorithm to prioritize the most impactful nodes early in the sequence, ensuring efficient coverage of the graph while retaining flexibility for later stages. The choice of these initial fire sources is often guided by the structural properties of the graph, such as centrality measures and distance distributions. As the process unfolds, the placement of subsequent burning nodes is influenced by the regions left unburned by the earlier activations [19]. Additionally, each node in the partial sequence is associated with a randomly generated value in $[0, 1]$, called *key*. This encod-

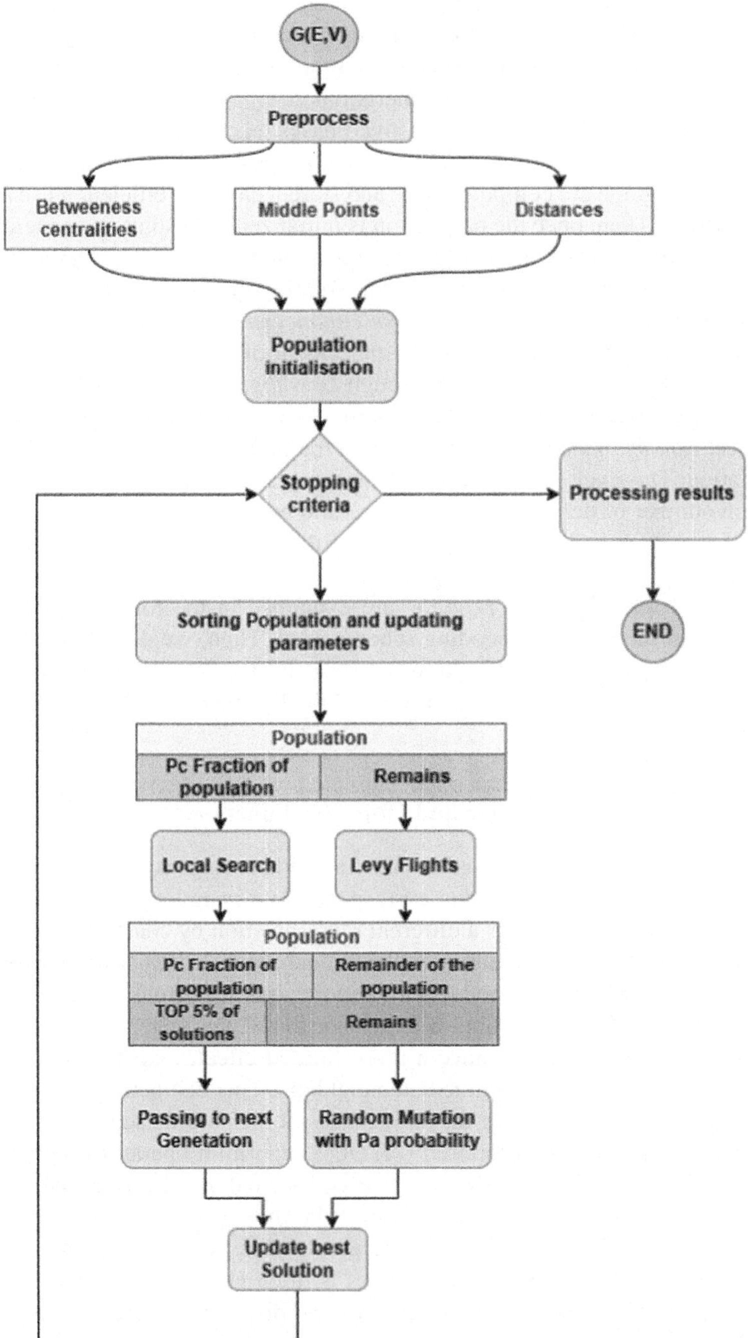

Fig. 2. $CBDCS$ evolutionary process.

ing scheme, known as *random key encoding*, is used to adapt the continuous search behavior of the CSA to the discrete nature of the GBP [13].

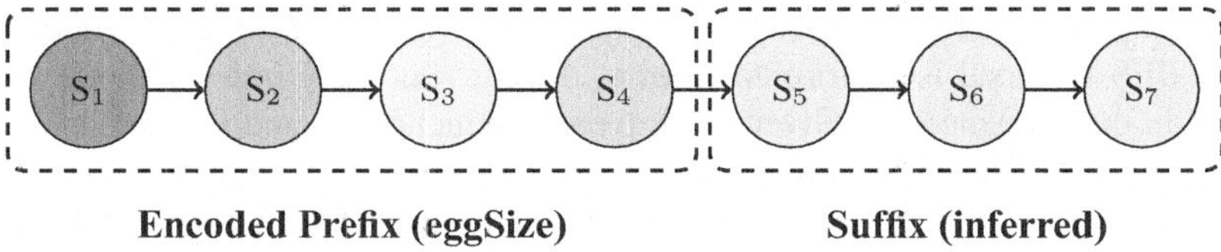

Fig. 3. A burning sequence represented as fire sources. Only the prefix of size `eggSize` is encoded in the solution; the suffix is completed dynamically when calculating the cost function.

To evaluate the quality of the solutions, the optimization function evaluates the burning efficiency by computing the total burning cost, defined as the sum of the squared burning distances of all nodes (Eq. (9)).

$$F(s) = \sum_{u \in V} d_u^2 \tag{9}$$

where $d_u \geq 0$ represents the burning distance of node u, defined as the shortest distance from u to the nearest burned node [19]. This is formally given by Eq. (10).

$$d_u = \min_{1 \leq j \leq bg} (\mathrm{d}(u, v_j) - (bg - j)) \tag{10}$$

where bg denotes the number of burning steps, and v_j represents the nodes that initiate the fire. The nodes with $d_u = k \geq 0$ remain unburned after the given sequence and would require k additional steps to fully ignite without adding new activators. In contrast, nodes with $d_u \leq 0$ have already been burned within the sequence.

This cost function helps guide the search process by penalizing sequences that leave many nodes unburned or require excessive steps to achieve full burning. By doing so, it directs the algorithm towards more effective burning strategies.

To evaluate a given sequence, it is necessary to complete partial solutions by adding the last activators to the incomplete sequences. Instead of exhaustively exploring all possible completions, which would be computationally expensive, the algorithm finalizes the sequence only when the number of unburned nodes falls below a predefined threshold, referred to as *maxUnburned*. This strategy ensures computational efficiency while maintaining solution quality.

3.2 Graph Preprocessing

In this step, we perform essential precomputations that depend on the structure of the input graph $G = (V, E)$. First, a distance matrix is computed using a breadth-first search (BFS), which has a time complexity of $O(n \cdot (n + m))$, where n is the number of nodes and m is the number of edges in the graph. This distance matrix is a fundamental component for assessing candidate solutions and for identifying midpoint nodes between all pairs of nodes.

A node m is considered a midpoint between two nodes v and u if [19]:

$$|d(i,m) - d(m,j)| \leq 1$$

To efficiently compute midpoints between a given node v and all other nodes in the graph, a BFS traversal is performed from v, during which the order of node visits is recorded in the sequence S_v. Given the traversal sequence S_v and two nodes p and q, where p is closer to the source node v than q, the midpoint corresponding to p is guaranteed to precede that of q in the sequence S_v. Finally, the betweenness centrality values of the nodes are computed, as they play a crucial role in guiding the search process [2]. This choice is motivated by its ability to identify nodes that act as bridges in the network, thus facilitating effective information—or in our context, fire—propagation. Moreover, nodes with high betweenness centrality tend to be more evenly distributed across the graph, which supports a more balanced and efficient burning sequence.

3.3 Initial Population Generation

For population generation, we draw inspiration from the $CBAG$ method. Sequences are constructed node by node, where a node is placed in the sequence with a probability dependent on its centrality [19] according to Eq. (11).

$$p(u) = \frac{\text{Sigmoid}(\beta \cdot (c_u - \alpha))}{T} \tag{11}$$

where $T = \sum_{i=1}^{N} \text{Sigmoid}(\beta \cdot (c_i - \alpha))$, c_u is the centrality of node u and $\text{Sigmoid}(x) = \frac{1}{1+\exp(-x)}$.

To ensure a well-distributed selection of fire sources, we impose a distance-based constraint during the construction of the sequence. Specifically, each newly selected node must be at least a minimum distance, denoted as minDist, away from all previously chosen activator nodes. This constraint ensures a good spread among the nodes in the sequence. However, if no candidates remain due to a large value of minDist, this parameter is iteratively decreased to allow for additional node selections. This mechanism also facilitates the inclusion of nodes from different components in disconnected graphs [19].

3.4 Local Search Strategy

The local search component of the $CBDCS$ algorithm is a key mechanism to enhance candidate high quality solutions. At each generation, the population is sorted according to the cost of each solution. A predefined fraction P_c of the best performing solutions is selected for possible local improvement.

For each of these selected solutions, the local search operates on the burning sequence by selecting one fire source, i.e. a specific position in the sequence, and attempting to replace it with one of its neighboring nodes in the graph. Replacement is accepted only if it results in a solution with a lower cost. This method enables the algorithm to explore the neighborhood of promising solutions while maintaining their structural integrity.

To preserve solution quality, the best individuals are transferred to the next generation through elitism. The local search is then applied to the remaining individuals within the selected P_c fraction, where the number of fire sources considered for modification depends on their rank in the population.

This strategy balances exploitation and exploration, focusing search efforts more intensively on lower-ranked high-quality solutions while preserving the best individuals from destructive changes. It also ensures that the algorithm continues to make progress across generations by fine-tuning promising areas of the search space.

3.5 Adaptive Lévy Flights

The third phase of the $CBDCS$ algorithm focuses on intensification and is based on a global exploration mechanism based on Lévy flights, also known as "the global walk", to generate new solutions in the neighborhood of the best solution found so far, promoting a more focused search around promising areas of the solution space. During this phase, both a new key vector and a corresponding burning sequence are produced. The key vector is generated using the adaptive Lévy flight according to Eq. (12), enabling the algorithm to balance intensification with controlled randomness.

$$X_{i,G+1} = X_{i,G} + \alpha_0 \times \text{Lévy}(\lambda) \otimes (X_{i,G} - X_{\text{best}}) \tag{12}$$

$$\text{where} \quad \varphi = \left(\frac{\Gamma(1+\lambda) \times \sin\left(\frac{\pi\lambda}{2}\right)}{\Gamma\left(\frac{1+\lambda}{2}\right) \times \lambda \times 2^{\frac{\lambda-1}{2}}} \right)^{\frac{1}{\lambda}}$$

$X_{i,G}$ represents the key vector of the current solution, X_{best} the key vector of the best solution. α_0 is an adaptive parameter that controls the step size, with values dependent on the problem scale. DDCS version of CSA proposes that this parameter changes over generations to gradually adjust step sizes using Eq. (13) [10].

$$\begin{aligned} \alpha_0 &= \alpha_{\min} + (\alpha_{\max} - \alpha_{\min}) e^{-\left(\frac{\tau g}{g_{\max}}\right)} \\ &\times \left[\cos\left(\frac{\omega g}{g_{\max}}\right) + \alpha_{\min} \sin\left(\frac{\omega g}{g_{\max}}\right) \right] \end{aligned} \tag{13}$$

This adaptive parameter controls the step sizes between generations. In the early stages, when solutions are still far from optimal, larger steps are necessary to explore the solution space more extensively. In later generations, as the quality of solutions increases, the step size is gradually reduced to allow for more accurate local improvement. Once the new key vector is computed, a new solution is generated as follows (Fig. 4):

- Compute the difference between the old and new key vectors $|X_{i,G+1} - X_{i,G}|$.
- For each component $|X_{i,G+1}[j] - X_{i,G}[j]|$ that exceeds a certain threshold "$seuil_1$", the new activator for the associated component is set at the midpoint between the source of the first solution and the source of the best solution: $S_{i,G+1}[j] \leftarrow Midpoint[S_{i,G}[j], S_{\text{best}}[j]]$.
- Evaluate the new solution.

$X_{i,G}$	$X_{i,G+1}$	$\lvert X_{i,G+1} - X_{i,G}\rvert$ > seuil
0.65	0.61	0.04
0.33	0.34	0.01
0.203	0.20	0.003
0.1	0.8	0.7

$S_{i,G}$	2	5	1	4
Sbest	1	3	6	7
$S_{i,G+1}$	**4**	5	1	**3**
$X_{i,G+1}$	0.61	0.34	0.20	0.8

Fig. 4. Representation of the levy flight operation.

3.6 Biased Selective Random Walk

The final phase of the $CBDCS$ algorithm is based on a random walk strategy, known as the abandonment operator, and is designed to enhance diversification and prevent premature convergence. This phase complements the third phase, which focuses on intensification by exploiting promising areas of the solution space. In this context, we introduce a Biased Stochastic Random Walk (BSRW) mechanism as part of the abandonment process. The goal of BSRW is to generate new solutions to reduce the risk of getting trapped in local optima and encouraging the exploration of less-visited regions of the search space. By incorporating this controlled randomness, BSRW preserves population diversity and improves its ability to uncover high-quality solutions [20].

There is a probability P_a that the host bird discovers foreign eggs in its nest. If foreign eggs are found, the host bird abandons them and replaces them with new eggs. In the proposed algorithm, this process is applied to the key vector. We update the new key vector via Eq. (14) and generate a new solution:

$$X_{i,\mathrm{G+1}} = X_{i,\mathrm{G}} + X_{\mathrm{rand1},\mathrm{G}} - X_{\mathrm{rand2,G}} \tag{14}$$

where $X_{i,\mathrm{G}}$ is the key vector of the solution chosen with probability P_a. $X_{\mathrm{rand1},\mathrm{G}}$ and $X_{\mathrm{rand2,G}}$ are key vectors associated with two randomly selected solutions from the population [20].

After generating a new key vector, the solution vector must be updated following these steps:

1. Compute the difference between the old and new key vectors $|X_{i,\mathrm{G+1}} - X_{i,\mathrm{G}}|$.
2. If the difference exceeds a certain threshold $seuil_2$, the corresponding node in the position vector is reinitialized to one of its randomly chosen neighbors based on centrality. If the difference exceeds $5 \times seuil_2$, the corresponding node is reinitialized to a random node in the graph.
3. The newly generated solution is evaluated.

4 Computational Results and Critical Discussion

This section evaluates the performance of the proposed CBDCS algorithm. All experiments were conducted on a personal computer equipped with an Intel® Core™ i7-8650U CPU @ 1.90 GHz (2.11 GHz boost), 16.0 GB of RAM, and running a 64-bit Microsoft Windows 10 operating system. All algorithms were implemented in Python.

We begin by outlining the key components of our experimental setup, including the datasets, evaluation metrics, and algorithm parameters, which form the foundation of our research methodology. We then assess the performance of the $CBDCS$ algorithm and compare it with state-of-the-art approaches.

4.1 Datasets and Evaluation Metrics

We evaluated the proposed algorithm using a diverse collection of graphs from the Network Data Repository [5], as detailed in Table 1. These graphs span multiple domains including social networks, biological systems, co-authorship graphs, and communication networks. The dataset offers a broad range of topologies and complexities, making it suitable for evaluating both the robustness and scalability of graph-based optimization algorithms. Each graph is modeled as an undirected and unweighted structure for consistency across experiments.

The algorithm's performance is primarily assessed based on the minimum *burning number* obtained, which corresponds to the length of the shortest valid burning sequence. This metric serves as an indicator of the quality of the solution.

4.2 Sensitive Analysis for $CBDCS$ Parameters Tuning

The $CBDCS$ algorithm involves several hyperparameters, some inherited CBAG [19] and DDCS [13], and others newly introduced to accommodate the adaptive Lévy flight and mutation mechanisms.

Table 2 provides a summary of all parameters, including their definitions, recommended values, and references. Parameters such as $seuil_1$ and $seuil_2$ were specifically introduced in our approach and required empirical calibration. In contrast, the parameters adopted from previous studies were retained with their original values due to their demonstrated effectiveness. These parameters govern various aspects of the algorithm:

- The core structure of the solution controlled by bg, $eggSize$, $suffix$;
- The population dynamics: $popSize$, $maxGen$, P_c, P_a;
- The Levy flight control: $seuil_1$ and Levy step parameters;
- The mutation mechanism: $seuil_2$
- The initialization diversity: $minDist$ and node centrality bias $(\sigma_\alpha, \sigma_\beta)$.

Among all these parameters, the most sensitive were $seuil_1$ and $seuil_2$, which directly impact the balance between exploration and intensification. We undertaken a sensitivity analysis on these thresholds using different combinations.

Impact of the Lévy Flight Threshold ($seuil_1$). Among the newly introduced parameters, the Lévy flight activation threshold $seuil_1$, determines whether a solution component, that is, a fire source in the encoded prefix, is updated using a Lévy-based midpoint oper-

Table 1. Benchmark graphs used in the experiments.

Graph	|V|	|E|	Density	Description
karate-club	34	78	0.139	Karate club social network
soc-dolphins	62	159	0.084	Dolphin social network
rt-retweet	96	117	0.026	Twitter retweet network
ia-infect-hyper	113	2196	0.347	—
C125-9	125	6963	0.898	—
ia-enron-only	143	623	0.061	Enron email network
c-fat200-1	200	1534	0.077	—
c-fat200-2	200	3235	0.163	—
c-fat200-5	200	8473	0.426	—
DD244	291	822	0.019	—
ca-netscience	379	914	0.013	Scientist co-authorship
infect-dublin	410	2765	0.033	Human contact network
c-fat500-1	500	4459	0.036	—
c-fat500-2	500	9139	0.073	—
c-fat500-5	500	23191	0.186	—
bio-diseasome	516	1188	0.009	Disease gene network
polblogs	643	2280	0.011	Political blog network
twitter-copen	761	1029	0.004	Twitter social network
DD68	775	2093	0.005	—
ia-crime-moreno	829	1475	0.007	Crime association network
DD199	841	1902	0.006	—
wiki-Vote	889	2914	0.041	Wikipedia vote network
DD497	903	2453	0.006	—
Reed98	962	18812	0.003	Facebook social network
delaunay n10	1024	3056	0.012	Delaunay triangulation
tech-routers-rf	2113	6632	0.002	Router network
chameleon	2277	31421	0.015	Wikipedia chameleon links
tvshow	3892	17262	0.002	Facebook TV show network
squirrel	5201	198493	0.015	Wikipedia squirrel links
politician	5908	41729	0.002	Facebook politician network

ation. Essentially, it controls the amplitude of perturbation applied to the random-key vector, thereby playing a central role in balancing exploration and exploitation. Figure 5 illustrates the evolution of the average solution cost over generations for various $seuil_1$ values tested on selected benchmark graphs. The evaluated values include $\{0.001, 0.01, 0.05, 0.1, 0.2, 0.5\}$.

The results reveal a strong sensitivity to this parameter:

- **High values of** $seuil_1$ (e.g., 0.1, 0.2, 0.5) limit the ability of Lévy flights to introduce meaningful changes to the candidate solutions. As a result, the population becomes less diverse and the algorithm converges prematurely. The average cost either plateaus or diverges due to the lack of exploration.

Table 2. CBDCS Parameters and their recommended values.

Parameter	Description	Value	Reference
bg	Sequence length to be found (optimized via binary search)	adaptive	this work
$suffix$	Size of the suffix completed by brute-force	3	[19]
$maxUnburned$	Max number of unburned nodes allowed in prefix	20	$CBDCS$
$popSize$	Population size	80	[19]
$maxGen$	Maximum number of generations	150	$CBDCS$
$eggSize$	Encoded prefix length (i.e., number of fire sources encoded)	varies ($\leq bg$)	$CBDCS$
$minDist$	Minimum distance between fire sources during initialization	bg - $suffix$	[19]
P_c	Fraction of population undergoing local search	0.5	[13]
P_a	Mutation probability	0.25	[20]
$seuil_1$	Lévy update threshold for midpoint activation	0.001	$CBDCS$
$seuil_2$	Mutation threshold	0.01	$CBDCS$
$\tau, \alpha_{min}, \alpha_{max}, \omega$	Adaptive Lévy parameters	2, 0.1, 0.5, 3	[13]
$sigAlpha$, $sigBeta$	Control centrality-based node selection	0.05, 200	[19]

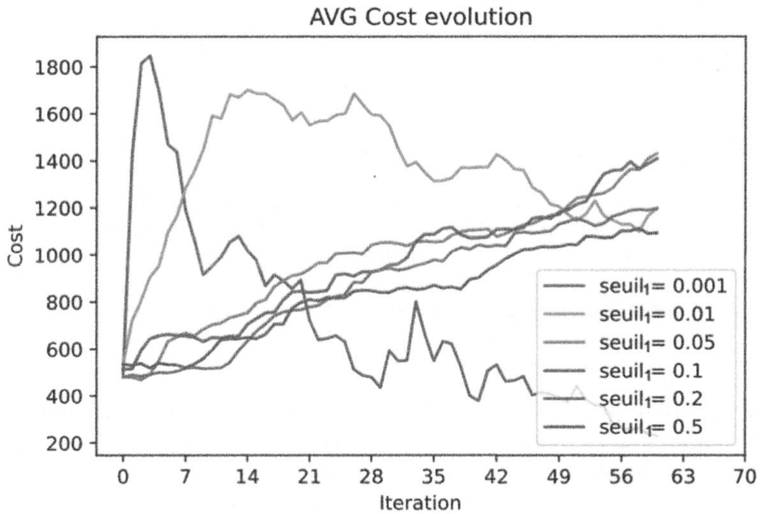

Fig. 5. Effect of the Levy flight random walk threshold $seuil_1$ on the evolution of average cost (example: DD199).

– **Low values of** $seuil_1$ (e.g., 0.001, 0.01) increase the likelihood of triggering component-wise updates. This results in larger jumps in the solution space, enabling the algorithm to escape local minima more effectively and approach optimal burning sequences. However, overly aggressive exploration can occasionally slow down fine-tuning in the final generations.

These observations highlight the importance of carefully tuning $seuil_1$ to ensure a proper balance between diversification and intensification. In our experiments, the value $seuil_1 = 0.001$ provided the most consistent and efficient convergence across different graph sizes and densities.

Impact of the Mutation Threshold ($seuil_2$). In contrast to $seuil_1$, the mutation activation threshold $seuil_2$ has a relatively smaller effect on the average cost evolution, as it applies only to a limited subset of the population, specifically the fraction P_a of individuals selected for mutation, which is typically lower than the fraction P_c used in local search.

Nonetheless, a careful analysis of the average cost curves under different values of $seuil_2$ reveals subtle patterns, particularly in the final stages of the algorithm's execution (Fig. 6). The tested values included $\{0.001, 0.01, 0.05, 0.1\}$.

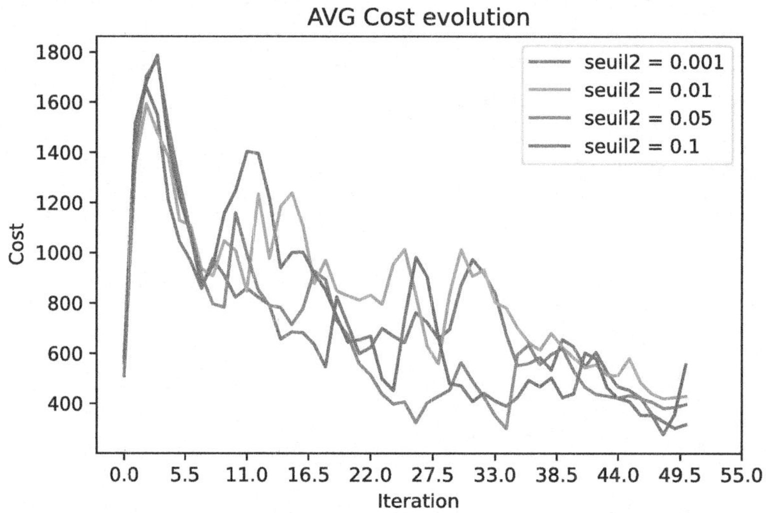

Fig. 6. Effect of the mutation threshold $seuil_2$ on the evolution of average cost (example: DD199).

As the algorithm progresses toward convergence, it becomes increasingly evident that small values of $seuil_2$ induce sharper fluctuations in the average cost. This can be attributed to several factors:

- Toward the end of the search process, the population becomes more homogeneous and stabilizes around high-quality solutions.
- At this stage, random mutations become the primary source of diversity, as Lévy-based updates are less frequently triggered.
- Lower thresholds $seuil_2$ amplify the impact of these mutations, leading to occasional disruptions of near optimal individuals, which manifest as short-term increases in average cost.

Therefore, while the global influence of $seuil_2$ is less significant than that of $seuil_1$, its role becomes more prominent in later generations. In particular, small $seuil_2$ values enhance variation when the population is near convergence, which can be beneficial (if the search is stuck) or detrimental (if elite individuals are disrupted too frequently).

This observation highlights the importance of understanding the interactions between parameters: the impact of $seuil_2$ depends not only on its value but also on the population's convergence state and the behavior of other components such as Lévy flights. In our tests, $seuil_2 = 0.01$ offered a good compromise between preserving diversity and maintaining convergence stability.

4.3 $CBDCS$ Performance Assessment

To assess the effectiveness of the proposed $CBDCS$ algorithm, we performed a series of experiments on the benchmark graphs (Table 1). For each graph, the algorithm was run 10 times to account for stochasticity. We report both the best burning number found and the average cost over the runs. We first analyzed the evolution of the solution quality across generations. Figures 7, 8, 9 and 10 illustrates the average and best costs obtained by the algorithm during the optimization process on selected graphs, including DD199, DD68, delaunay_n10 and tvshow.

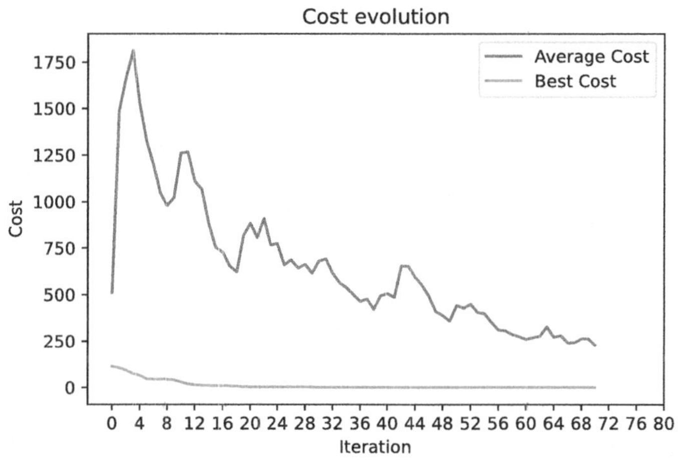

Fig. 7. Evolution of average and best costs on the DD199 instance.

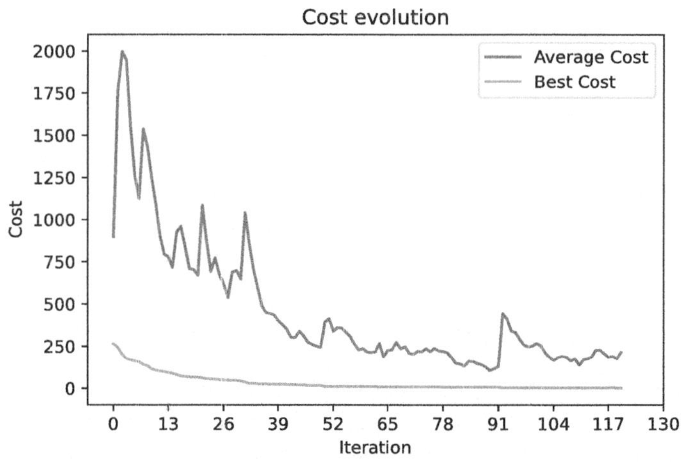

Fig. 8. Evolution of average and best costs on the DD68 instance.

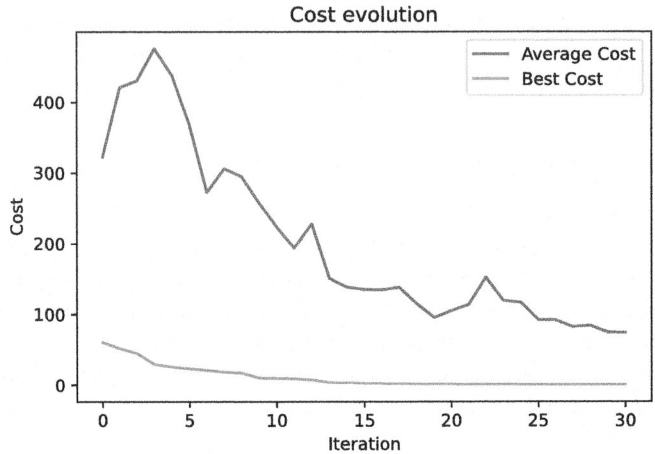

Fig. 9. Evolution of average and best costs on the delaunay_n10 instance.

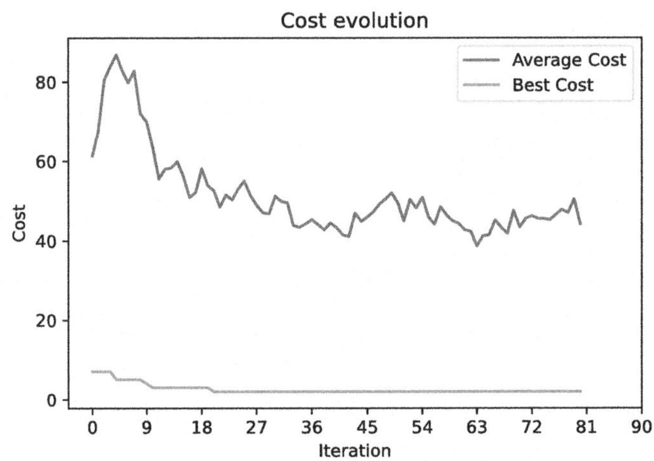

Fig. 10. Evolution of average and best costs on the fb-pages-tvshow instance.

As shown in the plots, the algorithm exhibits a stable convergence pattern with a significant improvement in the early generations, followed by a gradual refinement phase. The gap between the best and average costs narrows over time, indicating convergence of the population. On larger graphs (e.g., tvshow), the convergence is slower due to the larger solution space, but the algorithm still achieves competitive results.

4.4 $CBDCS$ Comparative Performance Assessment

To evaluate the effectiveness of our approach, we compare $CBDCS$ with a range of existing methods, including exact, heuristic, and metaheuristic algorithms. The heuristic methods BFF+, BBGH, and CBRH were previously assessed in [19], while the Greedy Propagation approach (GrP), considered state-of-the-art, was taken from [22].

The CBAG metaheuristic results also originate from [19], and GLS corresponds to our earlier work presented in [23].

Table 3 summarizes the results obtained in the benchmark graphs, showing the best burning number found by our algorithm (b_{CBDCS}) alongside the best known or optimal value, when available. The column **Sbest** indicates the optimal or best known burning number, as reported in [22] and obtained via an exact solver. For each instance, the $CBDCS$ results reflect the best result in 10 independent runs. This comparison offers a comprehensive view of the performance and robustness of our approach relative to exact and heuristic baselines.

Table 3. Comparison between existing heuristics/metaheuristics and CBDCS.

Graph	Sbest	BFF+	BBGH	CBRH	GrP	CBAG	GLS	CBDCS
karate-club	3	3	3	4	3	3	3	**3**
soc-dolphins	4	4	5	5	4	4	4	**4**
rt-retweet	5	5	5	5	5	5	5	**5**
ia-infect-hyper	3	3	3	3	3	3	3	**3**
C125-9	3	3	3	3	3	3	3	**3**
ia-enron-only	4	5	4	4	4	4	5	**4**
c-fat200-1	7	7	7	7	7	7	7	**7**
c-fat200-2	5	5	5	5	5	5	5	**5**
c-fat200-5	3	3	3	3	3	3	3	**3**
DD244	7	9	7	7	7	7	7	**7**
ca-netscience	6	8	7	7	6	6	6	**6**
infect-dublin	5	5	5	5	5	5	5	**5**
c-fat500-1	9	10	9	9	9	9	10	**9**
c-fat500-2	7	7	7	7	7	7	7	**7**
c-fat500-5	5	5	5	5	5	5	5	**5**
bio-diseasome	7	7	8	8	7	5	8	**7**
polblogs	5	6	6	6	5	5	6	**5**
twitter-copen	7	7	7	7	7	7	7	**7**
DD68	9	11	10	10	9	9	12	**9**
ia-crime-moreno	7	7	7	7	7	7	7	**7**
DD199	12	16	14	14	12	12	13	**12**
wiki-Vote	6	6	6	6	6	6	6	**6**
DD497	10	14	12	12	11	11	13	**11**
Reed98	4	4	4	4	4	4	4	**4**
delaunay_n10	9	10	9	10	9	9	10	**9**
tech-routers-rf	6	7	7	7	6	6	6	**6**
chameleon	6	6	6	6	6	6	6	**6**
tvshow	9	10	10	10	9	9	10	10
squirrel	6	6	6	6	6	6	6	**6**
politician	7	7	7	7	7	7	7	**7**

The results demonstrate that $CBDCS$ delivers competitive performance on the GBP across a wide range of real-world network instances. In 29 out of the 30 tested graphs, $CBDCS$ successfully matches the best-known burning numbers reported by other state-of-the-art methods. Although it does not outperform the solver-based GrP approach in terms of optimality, it matches GrP in 29 instances and is only outperformed in one case, specifically the tvshow graph. Compared to CBAG, $CBDCS$ achieves equal results in all available instances except tvshow, where CBAG performs slightly better. When compared to our earlier method, GLS, CBDCS shows improvement in 11 graphs and achieves parity in the remaining cases. Additionally, $CBDCS$ consistently outperforms all previously proposed heuristic methods, BFF+, BBGH, and CBRH, across every tested instance. These results underline the consistency, robustness, and effectiveness of the proposed approach.

Overall, the results confirm that CBDCS is a robust and consistent metaheuristic for solving the Graph Burning Problem. It achieves near-optimal performance across a wide range of networks while remaining solver independent, making it suitable for large-scale or time-sensitive applications.

5 Conclusion and Future Work

In this work, we proposed a novel metaheuristic algorithm called $CBDCS$, designed to address the GBP, a challenging problem with applications in modeling social contagion, information propagation, and network security.

The $CBDCS$ algorithm builds upon the Cuckoo Search framework and enhances it with random-key encoding, centrality-guided local search, and adaptive Lévy flights. By encoding only a partial burning sequence and leveraging powerful diversification mechanisms, $CBDCS$ effectively balances global exploration and local intensification.

Extensive experiments on a wide range of real-world and synthetic benchmark graphs demonstrated the algorithm's strong performance. CBDCS consistently matched or outperformed state-of-the-art heuristics and metaheuristics, including GLS and CBAG, across nearly all tested instances. Its convergence stability, solution quality, and adaptability make it a promising tool for tackling graph-based optimization problems.

Several avenues can be explored to further enhance this work:

- **Scalability:** Improve performance on very large-scale graphs (e.g., millions of nodes) through parallelization or distributed computation.
- **Dynamic Burning Models:** Extend the approach to variants of GBP where the graph topology or the burning rules evolve over time.
- **Other Spreading Processes:** Apply the CBDCS framework to related problems such as influence maximization, rumor blocking, or epidemic containment.
- **Explainability:** Investigate the interpretability of generated burning sequences using explainable AI techniques to better understand propagation dynamics.

Overall, this study contributes a powerful and flexible optimization framework for solving the graph burning problem, with potential extensions to other domains involving diffusion and propagation in networks.

References

1. Mantegna, R.N.: Fast, accurate algorithm for numerical simulation of Lévy stable stochastic processes. Phys. Rev. E **49**(5), 4677–4683 (1994)
2. Brandes, U.: A faster algorithm for betweenness centrality. J. Math. Sociol. **25**(2), 163–177 (2001)
3. Yang, X.-S., Deb, S.: Cuckoo search via Lévy flights. In: 2009 World Congress on Nature and Biologically Inspired Computing (NaBIC), pp. 210–214. IEEE, Coimbatore (2009)
4. Bonato, A., Janssen, J., Roshanbin, E.: Burning a graph as a model of social contagion. In: Bonato, A., Graham, F.C., Prałat, P. (eds.) WAW 2014. LNCS, vol. 8882, pp. 13–22. Springer, Cham (2014). https://doi.org/10.1007/978-3-319-13123-8_2
5. Rossi, R.A., Ahmed, N.K.: The network data repository with interactive discovery. Wiley Interdisc. Rev. Data Mining Knowl. Discov. **8**, e1256 (2015)
6. Bonato, A., Janssen, J., Roshanbin, E.: How to burn a graph. Internet Math. **12**(1–2), 85–100 (2016)
7. Land, M.R., Lu, L.: An upper bound on the burning number of graphs. In: Bonato, A., Graham, F.C., Prałat, P. (eds.) WAW 2016. LNCS, vol. 10088, pp. 1–8. Springer, Cham (2016). https://doi.org/10.1007/978-3-319-49787-7_1
8. Bessy, S., Bonato, A., Janssen, J., Rautenbach, D., Roshanbin, E.: Burning a graph is hard. Discret. Appl. Math. **232**, 73–87 (2017)
9. Šimon, M., Huraj, L., Dirgová Luptáková, I., Pospíchal, J.: Heuristics for spreading alarm throughout a network. Appl. Sci. **9**(16), 3269 (2019)
10. Reda, M., Haikal, A.Y., Elhosseini, M.A., Badawy, M.: An innovative damped cuckoo search algorithm with a comparative study against other adaptive variants. IEEE Access **7**, 119272–119293 (2019)
11. Bastide, P., et al.: Improved pyrotechnics: closer to the burning number conjecture. Electron. J. Comb. **30**(4), P4.13 (2023)
12. Mondal, D., Rajasingh, A.J., Parthiban, N., Rajasingh, I.: APX-hardness and approximation for the k-burning number problem. Theoret. Comput. Sci. **932**, 21–30 (2022)
13. Reda, M., Onsy, A., Elhosseini, M., Haikal, A., Badawy, M.: A discrete variant of cuckoo search algorithm to solve the travelling salesman problem and path planning for autonomous trolley inside warehouse. Knowl.-Based Syst. **252**, 109290 (2022)
14. García-Díaz, J., Rodríguez-Henríquez, L.M.X., Pérez-Sansalvador, J.C., Pomares-Hernández, S.E.: Graph burning: mathematical formulations and optimal solutions. Mathematics **10**(15), 2777 (2022)
15. Gautam, R.K., Kare, A.S., S., D.B.: Faster heuristics for graph burning. Appl. Intell. **52**(2), 1351–1361 (2021). https://doi.org/10.1007/s10489-021-02411-5
16. García-Díaz, J., Pérez-Sansalvador, J.C., Rodríguez-Henríquez, L.M.X., Cornejo-Acosta, J.A.: Burning graphs through farthest-first traversal. IEEE Access **10**, 30395–30404 (2022)
17. Tahmasbi, M., Rezai Farokh, Z., Buali, Y., Tehrani, Z.H.R.A.: New heuristics for burning connected graphs. AUT J. Math. Comput. **3**(2), 165–172 (2022)
18. Bloch, F., Jackson, M.O., Tebaldi, P.: Centrality measures in networks. Soc. Choice Welfare **61**(2), 413–453 (2023)
19. Nazeri, M., Mollahosseini, A., Izadi, I.: A centrality based genetic algorithm for the graph burning problem. Appl. Soft Comput. **144**, 110493 (2023)
20. Boukabene, R., Tayeb, F., Dakiche, N.: Improved random key cuckoo search optimization algorithm for community detection in social networks. In: Proceedings of the 19th International Conference on Web Information Systems and Technologies (WEBIST), pp. 113–120. SciTePress (2023)

21. Subbarayan, S., Grace, H.G.: Selection of activators in finding the burning number. AKCE Int. J. Graphs Comb. **20**(2), 115–119 (2023)
22. Pereira, F.D.C., de Rezende, P.J., Yunes, T., Morato, L.F.B.: A row generation algorithm for finding optimal burning sequences of large graphs. In: Chan, T.M., Fischer, J., Iacono, J., Herman, G. (eds.) ESA 2024, LIPIcs, vol. 308, pp. 94:1–94:17. Schloss Dagstuhl - Leibniz-Zentrum für Informatik, London (2024)
23. Sadeg-Belkacem, L., Tamelghaghet, I., Benbouzid-Si Tayeb, F.: Enhanced guided local search for addressing the graph burning problem. ICAART **3**, 758–765 (2025)
24. García-Díaz, J., Cornejo-Acosta, J.A., Trejo-Sánchez, J.A.: A greedy heuristic for graph burning. Computing **107**(3), 91 (2025)

Hybrid Siamese EfficientNet-B2 and Swin Transformer Network for OCT-Based Prediction of Anti-VEGF Response in Diabetic Macular Edema

Karima Garraoui[1,4](✉), Ines Rahmany[1,4], Hedi Tabia[2], Désiré Sidibé[2], Hsouna Zgolli[3], and Nawres Khlifa[4]

[1] Faculty of Sciences and Techniques of Sidi Bouzid, University of Kairouan, Kairouan, Tunisia
karima.garraoui@outlook.com

[2] University of Paris-Saclay, Evry IBISC Evry, Évry-Courcouronnes, France

[3] Department of Ophthalmology, Institut Hedi Raies Tunis, Tunis, Tunisia

[4] Research Laboratory of Biophysics and Medical Technologies, Higher Institute of Medical Technologies of Tunis, University of Tunis El Manar, 1006 Tunis, Tunisia

Abstract. Diabetic macular edema represents a sight-threatening complication of diabetes that can lead to severe visual impairment, highlighting the importance of predicting anti-VEGF treatment response for optimal therapeutic planning. This study presents a novel hybrid Siamese network architecture that integrates EfficientNet-B2 and Swin Transformer components to predict treatment outcomes in DME patients using optical coherence tomography images. The proposed framework combines convolutional neural networks for local feature extraction with transformer-based architectures for capturing global anatomical patterns, creating robust multi-scale retinal representations. The Siamese network processes paired OCT B-scan images through identical branches, generating 128-dimensional embeddings that represent retinal characteristics, followed by k-nearest neighbors classification based on anatomical similarity.

The proposed Hybrid Siamese (EfficientNetB2 + Swin) architecture achieved promising predictive performance with an accuracy of 86%, sensitivity of 85%, specificity of 87%, and F1-score of 86%. This approach provides an interpretable, clinically relevant framework for supporting therapeutic decision-making in diabetic macular edema management.

Keywords: Prediction · Anti-VEGF · DME patients · OCT images · Siamese Network · EfficientNetB2 · Swin Transformer

1 Introduction

Diabetic macular edema (DME) constitutes a frequent and severe diabetic complication that impairs patients' central vision. This condition manifests as swelling of the central retinal area caused by fluid accumulation within the retinal layers [1]. DME stands among the leading causes of vision loss in diabetic patients [18].

H. J. van den Herik et al. (Eds.): ICAART 2025, LNAI 16517, pp. 525–542, 2026.
https://doi.org/10.1007/978-3-032-25032-2_25

DME therapeutic approaches have been revolutionized by the development of anti-VEGF (vascular endothelial growth factor) medications. Drugs such as ranibizumab and aflibercept function by directly blocking VEGF, a critical factor in vessel leakage and pathological neovascularization [2,7].[1]

OCT (optical coherence tomography) serves as an essential tool for DME diagnosis and follow-up assessment. This non-invasive imaging modality generates high-resolution cross-sectional retinal images at the micrometer level [19]. Through OCT, clinicians can measure retinal thickness, characterize edema patterns, and assess therapeutic outcomes [3].

Recent advances in artificial intelligence have enabled the development of sophisticated deep learning frameworks for predicting treatment response in DME patients. Siamese networks, which learn through paired image comparisons, have shown particular promise in medical imaging by capturing subtle morphological differences in retinal structures [12,33]. The integration of hybrid architectures combining EfficientNet's efficient feature extraction capabilities with Swin Transformer's ability to model global anatomical patterns offers a comprehensive approach for multi-scale retinal analysis [31,32]. This methodology enables the generation of meaningful embeddings that represent retinal characteristics, facilitating similarity-based classification for treatment outcome prediction [30]. The heterogeneous manifestation of DME, including fluid accumulations, retinal swelling, and microstructural deformations, presents significant challenges for automatic treatment response prediction. Isolated use of CNNs often limits the network's ability to model long-range dependencies and complex spatial arrangements, while transformers, although powerful for capturing global context, can underperform when fine-grained retinal details are critical.
The main contributions of this work are summarized as follows:

- We propose a novel hybrid Siamese Network architecture that combines convolutional feature extraction via EfficientNet-B2 with global anatomical modeling using Swin Transformer blocks. This dual-branch architecture captures both fine-grained retinal microstructures and large-scale contextual patterns essential for accurate prognosisin Diabetic Macular Edema (DME).
  Our design combines the strengths of:
  - EfficientNet-B2: For hierarchical local feature extraction with efficient parameter utilization.
  - Swin Transformer: For capturing global structural information using hierarchical shifted-window self-attention.
- By embedding these components within a Siamese structure, our system explicitly learns a patient similarity space aligned with clinical reasoning, providing interpretable, reliable predictions grounded in anatomical evidence.

The remainder of this paper is organized as follows.

- Section 2 presents a review of the state-of-the-art approaches for predicting response to anti-VEGF therapy in patients with diabetic macular edema, focusing on deep learning techniques applied to OCT images.

[1] Work carried out in the OCTIPA project (CMCU 23G1418), as part of the PHC-Utique program managed by the CMCU of the French Ministry of Europe and Foreign Affairs and the Tunisian Ministrtfcy of Higher Education and Scientific Research.

- Section 3 describes our proposed methodology, including the architecture of the Siamese network, the integration of EfficientNet-B2 and Swin Transformer, the feature extraction pipeline, and the similarity-based prediction strategy.
- Section 4 outlines the experimental setup, including the datasets used, training and evaluation protocols, performance metrics, and comparative results with existing methods.
- Section 5 concludes the study, discusses the clinical relevance of the findings, identifies current limitations, and suggests future directions to enhance the robustness and applicability of the proposed approach.

2 Related Work

This section examines recent advances in deep learning for predicting diabetic macular edema (DME) patient response to anti-VEGF treatment through optical coherence tomography (OCT) image analysis. Current approaches integrate diverse architectures including Siamese networks, GANs, and hybrid models that combine clinical and imaging data. This architectural diversity reflects the need to capture both subtle morphological changes in OCT scans and broader clinical context.

The following analysis presents state-of-the-art models developed between 2024 and 2025, demonstrating how these deep learning strategies are transforming response prediction capabilities in ophthalmic care.

In their work, [25] developed ESSDP (Extended Siam Saves Diabetes Patients), a deep learning approach designed to help predict which diabetic macular edema patients will respond well to anti-VEGF injections. Their system analyzes OCT eye scans using a Siamese neural network paired with EfficientNetB2 for extracting image features, then applies a K-Nearest Neighbors (KNN) algorithm to make the final prediction. The goal is straightforward: determine whether a patient will be a good or poor responder based on how much their central macular thickness improves after treatment.

Their results showed promising performance with 80% accuracy, 71% sensitivity, 89% precision, and a 74% F1-score. What makes this study interesting is how well the Siamese network performed even with limited training data - a common challenge in medical AI research. The approach could potentially help doctors make more informed treatment decisions, allowing them to better tailor therapies to individual patients and avoid treatments that are unlikely to work.

Similarly, [26] in their work, took a creative approach to predicting how well diabetic macular edema patients will respond to anti-VEGF treatment. Rather than working with complete OCT images, they used generative adversarial networks (GANs) to focus on something more specific: predicting what the contour lines of key retinal layers would look like after treatment. These layers include important structures like the ILM, INL, ONL, IS/OS, and RPE - essentially the different "floors" of the retina that doctors monitor for changes.

What's clever about their "image-to-contour" approach is that it sidesteps some common challenges in medical AI. By focusing on these simplified line drawings rather than full images, they needed less training data and made their system easier for doctors to understand and trust. Working with 619 pairs of before-and-after OCT scans for training and testing on 45 cases, they achieved impressive results: 85% accuracy, 86.5% recall, 97% precision, and a 91.4% F1-score. This lightweight solution could be particularly valuable in busy clinical settings where doctors need quick, reliable predictions to help decide the best treatment path for each patient.

Furthermore, [27] in their work, built a deep learning system to help doctors evaluate anti-VEGF treatment effectiveness in macular edema patients using OCT scans. Their model enhances ResNet50 with grouped convolutions, spatial pyramid pooling (SPP), and attention mechanisms to better recognize disease patterns at multiple scales. Testing at key intervals (day 1, month 1, month 3), they achieved excellent results: F1-score of 0.9937, AUC of 0.9996, and accuracy of 0.9930. By integrating Grad-CAM, the system shows doctors exactly which scan areas influenced its predictions, providing the transparency needed for clinical trust. The work tackles dataset imbalance issues and offers a practical tool for monitoring patient progress.

Additionally, [28] in their work, took a comprehensive approach by combining OCT imaging with clinical data to predict anti-VEGF treatment response in diabetic macular edema patients. Their hybrid system uses a CNN to analyze the eye scans while a separate multi-layer perceptron processes important patient information like central macular thickness, how long they've had the disease, and blood levels of VEGFR-2 (a protein related to blood vessel growth). This dual approach achieved 85% accuracy and an AUC of 0.89, effectively distinguishing between patients who would respond well to treatment and those who wouldn't. By combining visual evidence from scans with measurable clinical factors, their method offers a more complete picture for planning individualized treatments.

Meanwhile, [29] in their work, focused on a related eye condition - neovascular age-related macular degeneration - using a DenseNet201-based model to predict treatment outcomes. Their system analyzes OCT scans taken at three time points: before treatment, after the first injection, and after the second injection, to forecast whether the patient's macula will become "dry" (free of fluid) after completing three loading doses. Testing different ways to combine this time-series data, they found that simple concatenation worked best, achieving 82.0% accuracy, 91.5% sensitivity, and 72.0% precision. Remarkably, their AI system outperformed both resident doctors and experienced retina specialists, suggesting it could be a valuable decision-support tool in everyday clinical practice.

The Table 1 below represents the summary of related work.

Table 1. Summary table of related work dealing with response to anti-vegf treatment.

Author	Method	Database	Results
[25]	Siamese Network (EfficientNetB2) + KNN	Train: Public (Kaggle, 84,495 OCT images) Test: Private (120 OCT images from 104 DME patients), Tunisian hospital	Accuracy: 80%, Sensitivity: 71%, Precision: 89%, F1: 74%
[26]	GAN-based contour prediction (Image-to-Contour)	Private, 619 OCT image pairs (training), 45 pairs (testing), Qilu Hospital of Shandong University, China	Accuracy: 85%, Recall: 86.5%, Precision: 97%, F1-score: 91.4%
[27]	CNN: ResNet50 + Grouped Convolution + SPP + Attention	Private, 72 patients (24 DME, 34 RVO, 13 CNV), Beijing Shijingshan Hospital, Capital Medical University, China	F1: 0.9937, ACC: 0.993, AUC: up to 0.9998
[28]	CNN for OCT + MLP for clinical features	Private, 100 OCT images + clinical data (CMT, VEGFR-2, disease duration), Dr. R.P. Centre, AIIMS, India	Accuracy: 85%, AUC: 0.89
[29]	DenseNet201 + Fusion (Concat, LSTM, Attention, Avg)	Private, 2068 OCT images from 517 patients, Kong Eye Hospital, South Korea	Accuracy: 82.0%, Sensitivity: 91.5%, Precision: 72.0%

3 Proposed Method

In this work, we propose a novel Siamese Network architecture that integrates EfficientNet-B2 and Swin Transformer blocks within each branch to effectively predict the response to Anti-VEGF therapy in patients with Diabetic Macular Edema (DME) based on Optical Coherence Tomography (OCT) images. The proposed framework combines the strengths of Convolutional Neural Networks (CNNs) for local feature extraction and Transformer-based architectures for capturing global anatomical structures, resulting in a robust multi-scale representation suitable for patient-level treatment response prediction.

3.1 Overall Architecture

The proposed method operates within a Siamese Network paradigm (Fig. 1), consisting of:

- Two identical branches with shared parameters
- Each branch processes an OCT B-scan image: one from a target patient, one from a reference patient with known treatment outcome
- A hybrid feature extraction pipeline combining EfficientNet-B2 and Swin Transformer
- A projection head generating 128-dimensional embeddings representing retinal characteristics
- A similarity computation module measuring anatomical proximity between image pairs
- A k-Nearest Neighbors (k-NN) classifier leveraging the learned embedding space for treatment response prediction

The design ensures the model focuses on patient-level similarities grounded in retinal morphology, facilitating interpretable, clinically relevant decision support.

3.2 Siamese Network Overview

A Siamese Network consists of two identical subnetworks, sharing the same architecture and parameters, each processing an image independently. The core goal is to map each image to a common embedding space where geometrical proximity reflects anatomical and pathological similarity.

The Siamese network is a variant of neural network design initially proposed by Bromley et al. [12]. They developed a pair of identical neural networks with shared parameters and coefficients, which generated dual feature representations when presented with a pair of input signatures. The outcome for the two signatures comprises a pair of vectors. These representations are then evaluated using a similarity metric, which was utilized as an optimization criterion during the learning process. Over time, the Siamese network has been adapted to additional areas of machine vision applications, such as identity confirmation [16] and single-example image classification [12]. The core principle of the Siamese neural architecture is to acquire generalized feature encodings with a similarity (or difference) measure derived from the feature representations extracted from a pair of comparable inputs (retinal scans in our case). The Siamese architectures have demonstrated particular effectiveness in scenarios with sparse data, as they can be trained using limited labeled examples and subsequently refined on more extensive datasets [12].

The Siamese Network architecture is a family of designs that typically encompasses a pair of equivalent networks. These two networks possess identical layer counts and structure, featuring shared coefficients and weights. Modifications to the parameters of one network are mirrored in the companion network due to the identical configuration. This approach has proven effective for dimensionality reduction in weakly supervised metric learning and identity verification [12].

The uppermost layer of these networks incorporates an objective function that quantifies the similarity or divergence score utilizing Euclidean distance, cosine similarity, or Manhattan distance between the feature vector representations from the two networks. Three widely-used objective functions associated with Siamese networks are contrastive loss, triplet loss, and binary cross-entropy.

For our investigation, We employed the binary cross-entropy (BCE) loss function, denoted as $\mathcal{L}_{BCE}$, and defined as follows:

$$\mathcal{L}_{BCE} = -\left[y \log(p) + (1 - y) \log(1 - p)\right] \tag{1}$$

In this equation:

- $\mathcal{L}_{BCE}$ represents the binary cross-entropy loss.
- $y \in \{0, 1\}$ is the actual class designation (or ground truth), where $y = 1$ indicates the positive class, and $y = 0$ indicates the negative class.
- $p \in [0, 1]$ denotes the likelihood estimated by the model that the instance belongs to the positive class ($y = 1$).

The objective of Siamese networks is to generate the vectorized feature representation among sample images sharing an identical class designation to be nearer together, while distancing the feature vector representations among sample images with distinct class designations. Through the binary cross-entropy objective function 1, following the learning phase of the model, the resulting feature vector possesses the characteristic that the Manhattan separation between similarly-classified images is more cohesive compared to images from different categories. For determining if a pair of images are of the same category (label = 0) or distinct categories label = 1), a threshold on the cosine divergence of the separation among stored vector representations must be established. Generally, this approach is decided through model training and seeking resemblance scores from artificial and authentic images. A match in the top K is deemed a qualifying criterion derived from the image collection using the established threshold.

The Fig. 1 below illustrates the flowchart of the proposed method based on Siamese network architecture.

In our framework:

- The first branch processes the OCT image of the target patient whose treatment response is to be predicted.
- The second branch processes an OCT scan from a labeled reference dataset (good responder or poor responder).
- Both images undergo identical feature extraction pipelines, producing embeddings that are subsequently compared using a distance metric.

The overall architecture is illustrated in Fig. 1.

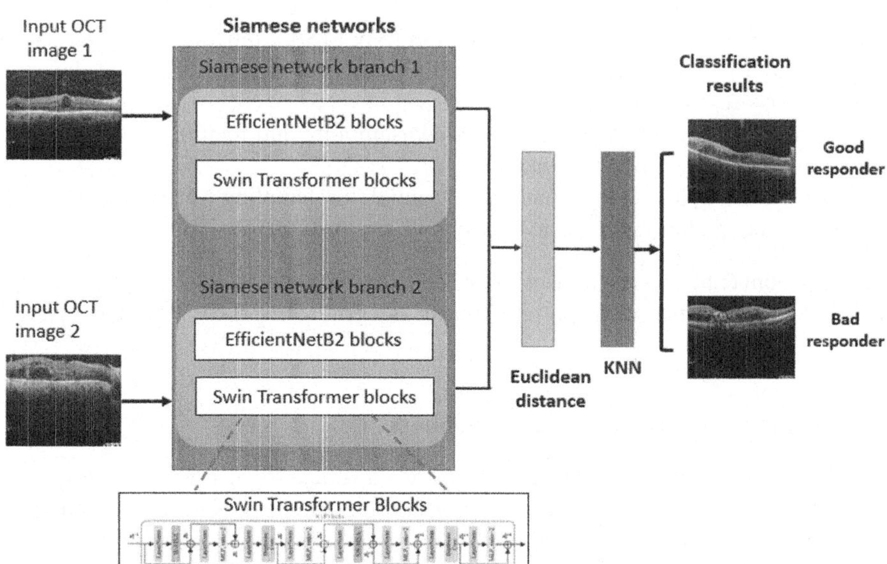

Fig. 1. Architecture of the hybrid Siamese Network (EfficientNetB2 + Swin Transformer) for treatment response prediction in OCT images.

3.3 Local Feature Extraction with EfficientNet-B2

EfficientNet-B2 [34] serves as the backbone for local feature extraction due to its favorable balance of accuracy and efficiency. Its compound scaling strategy systematically adjusts network depth, width, and resolution, optimizing performance for medical imaging tasks with limited data.

The processing pipeline includes:

- Input: OCT B-scan resized to 224 × 224 pixels, intensity normalized.
- Multi-stage Convolution: Captures hierarchical representations of:
  - Retinal layer delineations (e.g., ILM, INL, RPE boundaries).
  - Pathological structures (e.g., cystoid spaces, exudates).
  - Macular thickness variations indicative of disease severity.
- MBConv Blocks: Enhance feature expressiveness with depthwise separable convolutions and squeeze-and-excitation mechanisms.

The output is a high-dimensional feature map encapsulating detailed retinal microanatomy essential for differentiating responder profiles.

3.4 Global Structural Modeling with Swin Transformer

To capture long-range spatial relationships and global anatomical structures beyond the receptive field limitations of CNNs, we incorporate Swin Transformer blocks [35] after the EfficientNet-B2 stages.

Key design aspects include:

- Shifted Window Multi-Head Self-Attention (SW-MSA): models global dependencies efficiently by applying attention within local windows, shifted across layers to enable cross-region interactions.
- Hierarchical Architecture: progressive downsampling and feature aggregation preserve multi-scale anatomical context.
- Robustness to Spatial Deformations: essential for handling variability in retinal geometry and pathological manifestations.

This component enhances the network's ability to capture complex spatial patterns, such as macular edema distribution and retinal layer integrity, critical for treatment outcome inference.

3.5 Classification Using k-Nearest Neighbors

Following the embedding generation process, we leverage the learned feature space to perform treatment response prediction via a non-parametric k-Nearest Neighbors (k-NN) classification strategy. Specifically, the 128-dimensional embedding of a target patient, computed by the Siamese network, is compared to a reference database comprising OCT embeddings from patients with known treatment outcomes. We utilize Euclidean distance as the primary similarity metric, although cosine similarity is also evaluated in ablation studies.

The k most similar reference embeddings are identified based on these distance computations, forming a local neighborhood around the target patient in the embedding space. The predicted treatment response class (good or poor responder) is determined by majority voting among the known labels of these k neighbors.

This classification approach offers several advantages for medical applications. First, it is inherently interpretable, as predictions are grounded in direct anatomical comparisons to similar patients with established outcomes. Second, the non-parametric nature of k-NN allows for straightforward integration of new labeled cases without requiring model retraining, ensuring adaptability as clinical datasets evolve. Finally, k-NN demonstrates robustness to class imbalance—a common challenge in medical imaging datasets—by basing decisions on local structure within the learned embedding space rather than relying on global class distributions.

This similarity-driven classification strategy aligns with clinical reasoning, where treatment decisions often incorporate comparisons to known patient profiles, thus reinforcing the practical relevance of the proposed system.

4 Experimental Results

4.1 Dataset

Training Dataset (Kaggle OCT). For the training of our model, we have used the retinal OCT dataset from Kaggle[2]. This extensive dataset encompasses 84,495 retinal scans in JPEG format, categorized into four distinct groups: NORMAL, CNV (choroidal neovascularization), DME (diabetic macular edema), and DRUSEN. The collection is organized into three main directories (train, test, and val), each containing subdirectories for each image category. This structure enables the learning and assessment of the system across a diverse range of ocular conditions.

Test Dataset. Our test dataset, for the classification of good and poor responders to anti-VEGF treatment, comes from the Ophthalmology Department A at the Hédi Raies Institute in Tunis. It includes 120 radiographs corresponding to 104 patients with DME who received anti-VEGF treatment. For each patient, we collected pre-treatment and post-treatment images. A professional ophthalmologist analyzed the post-treatment images to create a database containing the pre-treatment image associated with a label indicating whether the patient is a good or poor responder to the treatment.

4.2 Results and Discussion

Our experimental framework is built upon a hybrid Siamese network architecture that integrates EfficientNet-B2 and Swin Transformer components for robust multi-scale feature representation. The procedure begins with paired OCT image processing through identical network branches, where EfficientNet-B2 captures hierarchical local features (retinal layer delineations, pathological structures) while Swin Transformer blocks model global anatomical structures through shifted window self-attention. The binary cross-entropy loss function guides the learning process to generate meaningful

[2] https://www.kaggle.com/code/paultimothymooney/detect-retina-damage-from-oct-images.

128-dimensional embeddings, ensuring that patients with similar anti-VEGF treatment responses are positioned closer together in the feature space while maximizing separation between different response categories. Following embedding generation, a k-Nearest Neighbors (k-NN) classification with k = 5 is employed for treatment response prediction, computing Euclidean distances between the target patient's embedding and reference embeddings from patients with known outcomes, with the final prediction determined through majority voting among the k most similar neighbors.

Hyperparameters Settings. The proposed Hybrid Siamese Network, integrating EfficientNet-B2 and Swin Transformer modules, was implemented and optimized based on systematic experimentation and validation set performance. The final hyperparameters configuration is detailed below:

- **Backbone Architecture:**
  - EfficientNet-B2 pretrained on the retinal OCT dataset from Kaggle, serving as the primary feature extractor in each Siamese branch.
  - Swin Transformer blocks integrated after the final convolutional stage to capture global retinal context.
- **Embedding Space:**
  - Each OCT image is encoded into a 128-dimensional embedding vector via a dedicated projection head comprising fully connected layers.
- **Similarity Metric:**
  - Euclidean distance is employed to compute pairwise similarity between embeddings, based on its empirical performance in this medical imaging application.
- **k-Nearest Neighbors Classifier:**
  - The number of neighbors k was set to 5, selected via grid search within $k = \{3, 5, 7, 9\}$.
- **Training Parameters:**
  - Optimizer: Adam
  - Initial learning rate: 1×10^{-4} with Reduce-on-Plateau scheduling (patience = 10 epochs)
  - Batch size: 16 pairs
  - Number of training epochs: 100, with early stopping based on validation loss
  - Weight initialization: He initialization for custom layers
  - Dropout rate: 0.3 in the projection head to prevent overfitting
  - Cross-validation: Five-fold cross-validation approach.

The Siamese model was trained using these optimized parameters, thus ensuring a good generalization of the results.

Performance evaluation plays a crucial role in every image classification endeavor. Various assessment criteria exist to gauge the performance of an image classification system. In this work, we focus on: accuracy, sensitivity, F1-score, as well as precision [8].

AUC-ROC Curve is used to interpret the likelihood that, when considering two randomly chosen patients, one being a treatment responder and the other a non-responder, the predictive marker's value is greater for the responder compared to the non- responder. Notably, an AUC of 0.5 (50%) suggests that the marker is non-informative. A rise in AUC signifies enhanced discriminatory capabilities of the model, with a maximum of 1.0 (100%).

Experimental Results. This part presents a comprehensive evaluation of the proposed Hybrid Siamese Network combining EfficientNet-B2 and Swin Transformer blocks for the prediction of anti-VEGF treatment response in Diabetic Macular Edema (DME) patients based on Optical Coherence Tomography (OCT) images. The experiments assess the model's performance, robustness, and interpretability, with comparisons to relevant baselines.

We chose to use the EfficientNetB2 as an architecture for our convolutional neural network (CNN) model. This architecture has recently demonstrated strong performance across Anti-VEFG treatment response classification, offering a good balance between accuracy and efficiency as described in [25] The Table 2 represents the results of our method.

Table 2. The overall results of the proposed method Proposed Hybrid Siamese (EfficientNetB2 + Swin).

Metric	Value
Accuracy	86%
Sensitivity	85%
Precision	87%
F1-score	86%

Ablation Study and Analysis. To evaluate the contribution of each component within the proposed hybrid Siamese architecture, an ablation study was conducted. In this analysis, we systematically removed the Swin Transformer blocks from each branch while retaining the EfficientNet-B2 backbone. The resulting architecture, lacking the global context modeling capability of the Transformer modules, demonstrated a noticeable decrease in predictive performance. Specifically, overall classification accuracy declined by approximately 6%, and both sensitivity and specificity were adversely affected as shown in the Fig. 2. These results emphasize the critical role of Swin Transformer blocks in capturing long-range anatomical dependencies and global retinal structures from OCT images, which are essential for precise differentiation between good and poor responders to anti-VEGF therapy. The ablation study confirms that the combination of convolutional and transformer-based features significantly enhances the network's ability to model complex anatomical variations associated with treatment response.

Classification Results. Figure 3 illustrates two prediction examples on OCT images of DME patients. The left image shows a case predicted as a poor responder to anti-VEGF treatment, with respective scores of 1.00 for poor responders and 0.00 for good responders. In contrast, the right image corresponds to a case predicted as a good responder, with associated confidence scores of 0.20 for poor responders and 0.80 for good responders. These predictions highlight the model's capacity to discriminate between good and poor responders based on pre-treatment OCT scans.

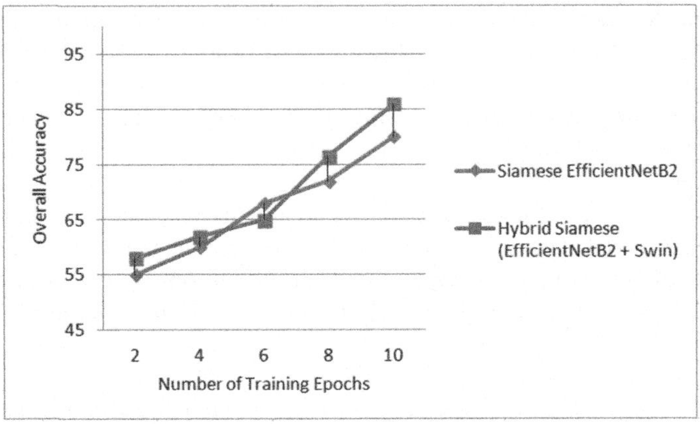

Fig. 2. Impact of Swin Transformer Integration on Prediction Performance. The comparison illustrates the decline in classification accuracy, sensitivity, and specificity when the Swin Transformer blocks are removed. This highlights the contribution of global context modeling in improving treatment response prediction from OCT images.

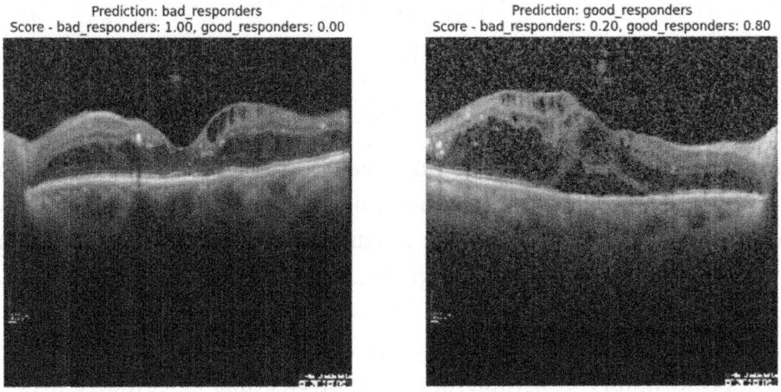

Fig. 3. Classification results.

Comparison with Other Architectures. We evaluated several Convolutional Neural Network (CNN) architectures for our classification task and compared their effectiveness based on metrics such as accuracy, sensitivity, precision, and F1-score. Our following results provide a comparison of the models CNN from scratch, EfficientNetB2, and Hybrid Siamese (EfficientNetB2 + Swin), allowing us to identify the strengths and weaknesses of each architecture. Table 3 summarizes the predictive performance of the proposed method compared to relevant baselines.

Figure 4 demonstrates the performance comparison of three Siamese neural network architectures across four evaluation metrics: accuracy, sensitivity, specificity, and F1-score. The hybrid model combining EfficientNetB2 and Swin Transformer emerges as the top performer, achieving the highest scores in accuracy (0.86), sensitivity (0.85), and F1-score (0.86), highlighting the effectiveness of combining CNN and Transformer

Table 3. Overall performance of the proposed method compared to relevant baselines.

	Accuracy	Sensitivity	Specificity	F1-score
Siamese CNN from scratch	79%	79%	79%	79%
Siamese EfficientNetB2	80%	71%	89%	74%
Proposed Hybrid Siamese (EfficientNetB2 + Swin)	86%	85%	87%	86%

architectures. The Siamese EfficientNetB2 model excels in specificity with a score of 0.89 but shows lower sensitivity (0.71), indicating better performance in identifying true negatives. The CNN trained from scratch displays more balanced but modest performance across all metrics, with scores around 0.79. These results suggest that pretrained models and hybrid architectures significantly enhance Siamese network performance for similarity-based classification tasks.

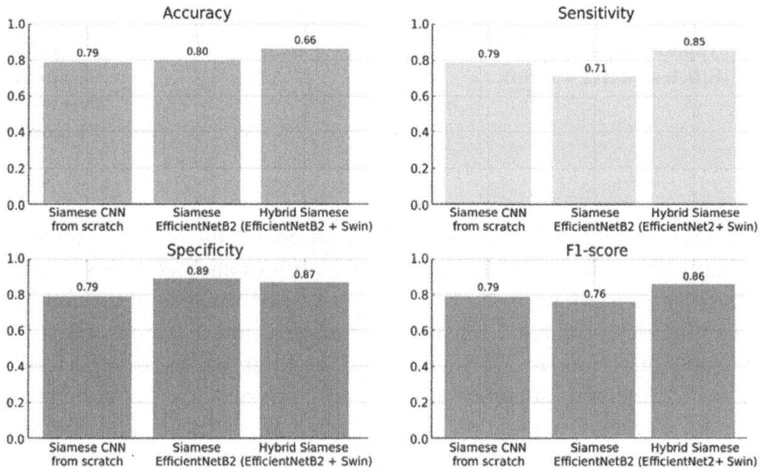

Fig. 4. Comparison of the predictive performance between the proposed method and relevant baselines.

The proposed hybrid model demonstrated a significant improvement over both baselines, achieving an overall accuracy of 86.2% and balanced sensitivity and specificity exceeding 85%. These gains highlight the added value of integrating global context modeling via the Swin Transformer with the hierarchical convolutional features of EfficientNet-B2.

Comparison with Other Methods from the Literature. The Table 4 below compares our method, based on a Siamese network and EfficientNetB2, with other approaches

Table 4. Comparison with other methods from the literature.

Author	Method	Data-base	Results
[26]	GAN-based contour prediction (Image-to-Contour)	Private, 619 OCT image pairs (training), 45 pairs (testing), Qilu Hospital of Shandong University, China	Accuracy: 85%, Recall: 86.5%, Precision: 97%, F1-score: 91.4%
[27]	CNN: ResNet50 + Grouped Convolution + SPP + Attention	Private, 72 patients (24 DME, 34 RVO, 13 CNV), Beijing Shijingshan Hospital, Capital Medical University, China	F1: 0.9937, ACC: 0.993, AUC: up to 0.9998
[28]	CNN for OCT + MLP for clinical features	Private, 100 OCT images + clinical data (CMT, VEGFR-2, disease duration), Dr. R.P. Centre, AIIMS, India	Accuracy: 85%, AUC: 0.89
[29]	DenseNet201 + Fusion (Concat, LSTM, Attention, Avg)	Private, 2068 OCT images from 517 patients, Kong Eye Hospital, South Korea	Accuracy: 82.0%, Sensitivity: 91.5%, Precision: 72.0%
[25]	Siamese Network (EfficientNetB2)	Train: Public (Kaggle, 84,495 OCT images) Test: Private (120 OCT images from 104 DME patients), Tunisian hospital	Accuracy=80%, Sensitivity=71%, Precision=89%, F1 score=74%
Our method	**Proposed Hybrid Siamese (EfficientNetB2 + Swin)**	**Private, 104 OCT images**	**Accuracy=86% , Sensitivity=85%, Precision=87%, F1 score=86%**

from the literature. It highlights (1) the databases used, (2) the results in terms of sensitivity, specificity, F1-score, and AUC, and (3) the performance of each study.

Figure 5 presents a comparison of the predictive performance of different methods, with four key metrics: accuracy, sensitivity, precision, and F1-score. Each bar graph shows the results of various methods compared, highlighting the best performance for each measure. The methods are represented by colored bars corresponding to each metric, allowing for a quick visualization of the effectiveness of each approach.

Discussion. The results obtained, with an accuracy of 86%, sensitivity of 85%, specificity of 87%, and F1-score of 86%, demonstrate the effectiveness of the proposed approach for predicting the response to anti-VEGF treatment in diabetic macular edema (DME) patients. These strong results are largely due to the hybrid Siamese network architecture, which combines efficient local feature extraction using EfficientNet-B2 and global anatomical modeling through Swin Transformer blocks. This hybrid model captures both fine-grained retinal details and long-range spatial relationships, which are crucial for accurately predicting treatment response.

Furthermore, the ablation study highlighted the importance of Swin Transformer blocks. Removing these blocks resulted in a significant drop in performance, emphasizing their critical role in capturing the global anatomical dependencies of OCT images, which are essential for distinguishing between good and poor responders to anti-VEGF treatment. This finding reinforces the idea that combining convolutional networks for

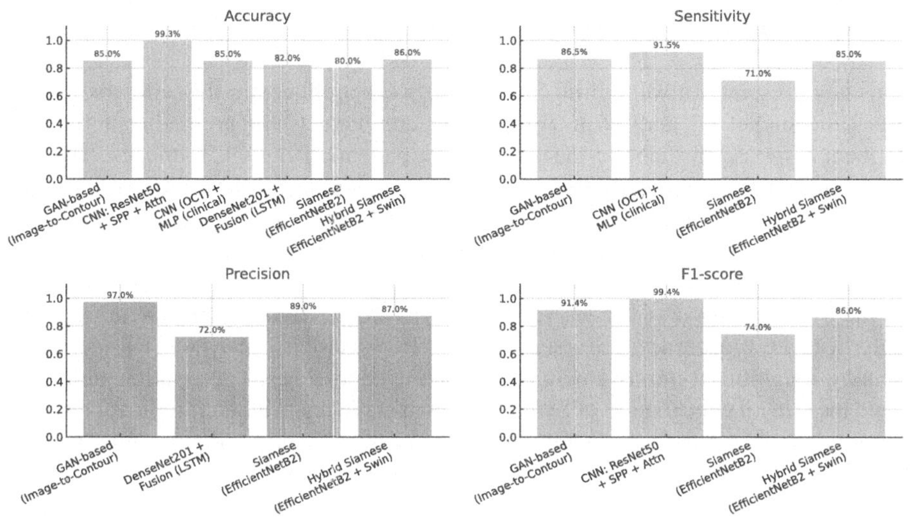

Fig. 5. Comparison with other methods from the literature: evaluating predictive performance across key metrics.

local feature extraction with transformers for global context modeling provides significant advantages for medical imaging classification tasks.

The k-Nearest Neighbors (k-NN) classification approach, using the learned embedding space, offers an interpretable framework that aligns with clinical reasoning. Treatment decisions, often based on comparisons with known patient profiles, are directly supported by anatomical comparisons to patients with established treatment outcomes. This makes the approach particularly valuable in a clinical setting, where transparency and interpretability are crucial for gaining clinician trust.

However, several limitations should be acknowledged. The relatively small size of our dataset (104 patients) limits the generalizability of the results, and studies on larger, more diverse populations would be needed to validate the applicability of our method in a variety of clinical settings. Additionally, the quality of OCT images, which can vary depending on equipment and acquisition protocols, may affect the robustness of the model. Poor-quality images can introduce bias into the model's predictions.

To enhance the robustness and generalizability of our method, several avenues are being explored. Expanding our study to other databases, including those with similar retinal pathologies or other medical imaging modalities, would allow us to assess the model's ability to adapt to different clinical scenarios. Furthermore, integrating additional clinical data, such as age, medical history, or other biological factors of patients, could enrich the predictions by capturing aspects not visible in OCT images, thereby strengthening the accuracy of the results.

We also plan to explore multimodal approaches, combining clinical data with imaging information, to further improve model precision and performance. These efforts will help validate the applicability of our approach in various clinical contexts and pave the way for personalized treatment strategies for DME patients.

5 Conclusion

This study presents a novel hybrid Siamese network architecture that effectively combines EfficientNet-B2 and Swin Transformer components for predicting anti-VEGF treatment response in diabetic macular edema patients using OCT images. The proposed framework successfully integrates convolutional neural networks for local feature extraction with transformer-based architectures for capturing global anatomical patterns, resulting in robust multi-scale retinal representations that achieve superior predictive performance.

The hybrid Siamese (EfficientNetB2 + Swin) architecture demonstrated promising results with 86% accuracy, 85% sensitivity, 87% specificity, and 86% F1-score, representing a significant improvement over baseline approaches. The ablation study confirmed the critical contribution of Swin Transformer blocks, with their removal resulting in approximately 6% decrease in classification accuracy, highlighting the importance of global context modeling for accurate treatment response prediction.

The similarity-based k-NN classification strategy provides an interpretable framework that aligns with clinical reasoning, where treatment decisions often incorporate comparisons to known patient profiles. This approach proves particularly valuable for medical applications with limited datasets, as demonstrated by the model's ability to achieve robust performance with only 104 test patients from the Tunisian hospital dataset.

Future research directions include expanding the dataset with diverse patient populations to improve generalizability, integrating multimodal data such as clinical histories and genetic information to enhance predictive accuracy, and exploring the application of this hybrid architecture to other retinal pathologies beyond DME. The proposed method offers a clinically relevant framework for supporting therapeutic decision-making in diabetic macular edema management, potentially leading to more personalized and effective treatment strategies.

References

1. Bhagat, N., Grigorian, R.A., Tutela, A., Zarbin, M.A.: Diabetic macular edema: pathogenesis and treatment. Surv. Ophthalmol. **54**(1), 1–32 (2009)
2. Brown, D.M., et al.: Long-term outcomes of ranibizumab therapy for diabetic macular edema: the 36-month results from two phase III trials. Ophthalmology **120**(10), 2013–2022 (2013)
3. Browning, D.J., et al.: Relationship between optical coherence tomography–measured central retinal thickness and visual acuity in diabetic macular edema. Ophthalmology **114**(3), 525–536 (2007)
4. Cao, J., et al.: Prediction of response to anti-vascular endothelial growth factor treatment in diabetic macular oedema using an optical coherence tomography-based machine learning method. Acta Ophthalmol. **99**(1), e19–e27 (2021)
5. Ding, F., Zhu, F.: HLifeRL: a hierarchical lifelong reinforcement learning framework. J. King Saud Univ. Comput. Inf. Sci. **34**(7), 4312–4321 (2022)
6. De Fauw, J., et al.: Clinically applicable deep learning for diagnosis and referral in retinal disease. Nat. Med. **24**(9), 1342–1350 (2018)

7. Ferrara, N., Hillan, K.J., Gerber, H.P., Novotny, W.: Discovery and development of bevacizumab, an anti-VEGF antibody for treating cancer. Nat. Rev. Drug Discov. **3**(5), 391–400 (2004)
8. Grandini, E., Bagli, E., Visani, G.: Metrics for multi-class classification: an overview. arXiv preprint arXiv:2008.05756 (2020). https://arxiv.org/abs/2008.05756
9. Jin, Y., et al.: Deep learning assisted fluid volume calculation for assessing anti-vascular endothelial growth factor effect in diabetic macular edema. Heliyon **10**(8) (2024)
10. Kermany, D.S., et al.: Identifying medical diagnoses and treatable diseases by image-based deep learning. Cell **172**(5), 1122–1131 (2018)
11. Ko, Y.C., Peng, C.W., Ho, H.C., Chiu, S.H., Chen, S.J., Lee, C.Y.: Deep learning assisted prediction of long-term visual outcome after 3 monthly anti-vascular endothelial growth factor injections in patients with central-involved diabetic macular edema. Invest. Ophthalmol. Visual Sci. **63**(7), 3778-F0199 (2022)
12. Koch, G., Zemel, R., Salakhutdinov, R.: Siamese neural networks for one-shot image recognition. In: ICML Deep Learning Workshop, vol. 2, Lille (2015)
13. Liu, S., et al.: Prediction of OCT images of short-term response to anti-VEGF treatment for diabetic macular edema using different generative adversarial networks. Photodiagn. Photodyn. Ther. **41**, 103272 (2023)
14. Meng, Z., et al.: Machine learning and optical coherence tomography-derived radiomics analysis to predict persistent diabetic macular edema in patients undergoing anti-VEGF intravitreal therapy. J. Transl. Med. **22**(1), 358 (2024)
15. Schlegl, T., et al.: Fully automated detection and quantification of macular fluid in OCT using deep learning. Ophthalmology **125**(4), 549–558 (2018)
16. Taigman, Y., Yang, M., Ranzato, M., Wolf, L.: DeepFace: closing the gap to human-level performance in face verification. In: Proceedings of the IEEE Conference on Computer Vision and Pattern Recognition, pp. 1701–1708 (2014)
17. Ting, D.S.W., et al.: Artificial intelligence and deep learning in ophthalmology. Br. J. Ophthalmol. **103**(2), 167–175 (2019)
18. Yau, J.W., et al.: Global prevalence and major risk factors of diabetic retinopathy. Diabetes Care **35**(3), 556–564 (2012)
19. Zhang, Y., Yang, M., Zhao, S.X., Shen, L.J., Han, W.: Hyperosmolarity disrupts tight junction via TNF-α/MMP pathway in primary human corneal epithelial cells. Int. J. Ophthalmol. **15**(5), 683 (2022)
20. Haddad, Z., Yaya, B.M., Zgolli, H., Sidibé, D., Tabia, H., Khlifa, N.: Retinal pathologies detection in OCT images based on Bilinear convolutional neural network. In: 2023 International Conference on Innovations in Intelligent Systems and Applications (INISTA), pp. 1–7. IEEE (2023)
21. Tan, M., Le, Q.: EfficientNet: rethinking model scaling for convolutional neural networks. In: Proceedings of the 36th International Conference on Machine Learning (ICML) (2019)
22. Liu, Z., et al.: Swin transformer: hierarchical vision transformer using shifted windows. In: Proceedings of the IEEE/CVF International Conference on Computer Vision (ICCV) (2021)
23. Koch, G., Zemel, R., Salakhutdinov, R.: Siamese neural networks for one-shot image recognition. In: ICML Deep Learning Workshop (2015)
24. Vaswani, A., et al.: Attention is all you need. In: Advances in Neural Information Processing Systems (NeurIPS) (2017)
25. Garraoui, K., et al.: A deep learning approach for predicting the response to anti-VEGF treatment in diabetic macular edema patients using optical coherence tomography images. In: 17th International Conference on Agents and Artificial Intelligence (ICAART 2025), vol. 2, pp. 453–462. SCITEPRESS–Science and Technology Publications (2025)

26. Yang, X., et al.: Prediction of OCT contours of short-term response to anti-VEGF treatment for diabetic macular edema using generative adversarial networks. Photodiagnosis. Photodyn. Ther. 104482 (2025)
27. Song, T., et al.: Construction of a predictive model for the efficacy of anti-VEGF therapy in macular edema patients based on OCT imaging: a retrospective study. Front. Med. **12**, 1505530 (2025)
28. Mondal, A., Nandi, A., Pramanik, S., Mondal, L.K.: Application of deep learning algorithm for judicious use of anti-VEGF in diabetic macular edema. Sci. Rep. **15**(1), 4569 (2025)
29. Han, J.M., et al.: Anti-VEGF treatment outcome prediction based on optical coherence tomography images in neovascular age-related macular degeneration using a deep neural network. Sci. Rep. **14**(1), 28253 (2024)
30. Chen, X., et al.: Recent advances and clinical applications of deep learning in medical image analysis. Med. Image Anal. **79**, 102444 (2022)
31. Tan, M., Le, Q.: EfficientNet: rethinking model scaling for convolutional neural networks. In: International Conference on Machine Learning, pp. 6105–6114 (2019)
32. Liu, Z., et al.: Swin transformer: hierarchical vision transformer using shifted windows. In: Proceedings of the IEEE/CVF International Conference on Computer Vision, pp. 10012–10022 (2021)
33. Chicco, D.: Siamese neural networks: an overview. Artif. Neural Netw. 73–94 (2021)
34. Tan, M., Le, Q.V.: EfficientNet: rethinking model scaling for convolutional neural networks. In: Proceedings of 36th International Conference on Machine Learning (ICML), pp. 6105–6114 (2019)
35. Liu, Z., et al.: Swin transformer: hierarchical vision transformer using shifted windows. In: Proceedings of IEEE/CVF International Conference on Computer Vision (ICCV), pp. 10012–10022 (2021)
36. Saidi, L., et al.: Automatic detection of AMD and DME retinal pathologies using deep learning. Int. J. Biomed. Imaging **2023**(1), 9966107 (2023)
37. Haddad, Z., Yaya, B.M., Zgolli, H., Sidibé, D., Tabia, H., Khlifa, N.: Retinal pathologies detection in OCT images based on Bilinear convolutional neural network. In: 2023 International Conference on Innovations in Intelligent Systems and Applications (INISTA), pp. 1–7 (2023)

Dimensionality Reduction on the SPD Manifold: A Comprehensive Comparative Study Between Conventional and Geometry-Aware Methods

Amal Araoud[1(✉)], Enjie Ghorbel[1,2], and Faouzi Ghorbel[1]

[1] National School of Computer Science (ENSI), CRISTAL Laboratory, GRIFT Group, Manouba University, Manouba, Tunisia
{amal.araoud,enjie.ghorbel,faouzi.ghorbel}@ensi-uma.tn
[2] Interdisciplinary Centre for Security, Reliability and Trust (SnT), University of Luxembourg, Esch-sur-Alzette, Luxembourg

Abstract. The space of Symmetric Positive Definite (SPD) matrices has gained prominence as a powerful representation in several fields such as computer vision and neuroimaging. However, the non-Euclidean geometry of the manifold formed by SPD matrices introduces a challenge, specifically in the presence of high-dimensional data, where the use of a dimensionality reduction technique is often needed. Dimensionality reduction methods typically assume the linearity of the data space, making them theoretically inappropriate for SPD matrices. To address this, researchers have increasingly adapted dimensionality reduction methods by exploiting the Riemannian structure of the SPD space. Despite their theoretical soundness, a comprehensive comparison between conventional (linear) and geometry-aware (non-linear) dimensionality reduction methods under varying data conditions is still lacking. In practice, different aspects such as the convexity of the SPD space may negatively affect the effectiveness of non-linear methods. As such, this work fills this gap through the evaluation of both linear and non-linear dimensionality reduction techniques under a binary classification setting. To that end, a dataset that presents different distributional configurations is synthetically generated. This evaluation study is also complemented by experiments performed on a real-world dataset called COBRE Connectome. The results indicate that linear and non-linear methods are comparable when applied to SPD matrices. Our analysis suggests that this may be due to two main factors: the convex nature of the SPD space and numerical issues.

Keywords: Riemannian Geometry · SPD Manifolds · Dimensionality Reduction · Functional Connectomes · Classification · Non-Euclidean Learning

1 Introduction

Symmetric Positive Definite (SPD) matrices have emerged as a central representation for structured data in domains ranging from computer vision to medical imaging and neuroscience [19,20,23,26,30]. Their ability to encode second-order statistics,

H. J. van den Herik et al. (Eds.): ICAART 2025, LNAI 16517, pp. 543–561, 2026.
https://doi.org/10.1007/978-3-032-25032-2_26

covariance relationships, or brain connectivity patterns makes them particularly valuable in several classification tasks such as image classification [9] and action recognition [18]. However, these matrices do not belong to a linear space; they reside on a non-Euclidean Riemannian manifold. This manifold geometry introduces fundamental challenges when applying standard machine learning techniques, particularly for tasks such as dimensionality reduction. Traditional dimensionality reduction methods [12,21] assume a Euclidean structure and operate through linear projections. Although often used in practice, even after flattening SPD matrices, such approaches are not theoretically valid in the SPD context. Flattening destroys the intrinsic geometry of the manifold and may lead to non-SPD outputs, potentially distorting the statistical and physical meaning of the data [14,19,20,26].

To address these limitations, recent advances in differential geometry have led to the development of specialized dimensionality reduction techniques that preserve the Riemannian structure of SPD matrices [15,19]. However, a comprehensive comparative analysis between traditional linear methods and non-linear approaches in the context of SPD matrices remains underexplored. Hence, we have proposed in our previous work [2] a benchmark framework for comparing four dimensionality reduction strategies, including both conventional and geometry-aware ones [15,19,21,33].

Our experiments focused on synthetically generated SPD matrices with varying degrees of class separation. Interestingly, geometry-aware approaches did not always outperform simpler linear baselines such as PCA. We identified two potential causes: (i) the convexity of the SPD cone, which may reduce the observable impact of curvature in certain regimes, and (ii) numerical instability near the boundary of the manifold during logarithmic mappings.

Despite the theoretical interest of these findings, their scope was limited to controlled synthetic settings, without any validation on real-world data. In particular, no empirical evaluation was conducted on SPD matrices derived from real applications such as neuroimaging. Yet, clinical applications often involve low sample sizes, noisy measurements, and SPD matrices extracted from fMRI-derived brain connectomes. In such contexts, understanding how different dimensionality reduction methods behave is highly relevant. In this extended version, we address this gap through several key contributions:

- We incorporate an empirical evaluation of all methods on functional brain connectivity data derived from the *MLSP 2014 Schizophrenia Challenge*.
- We provide a computational complexity analysis comparing the training and inference times of all methods.
- We expand the literature review on manifold-aware dimensionality reduction.
- We benchmark two additional dimensionality reduction methods.

The remainder of this article is organized as follows. Section 2 presents an extended review of related work on geometry-aware (non-linear) dimensionality reduction for SPD matrices. Section 3 recalls the mathematical background related to the geometry of the SPD manifold. Section 4 details the dimensionality reduction techniques and the proposed evaluation protocol. Section 5 reports the results on the synthetically generated data. Section 6 presents experiments on the real-world dataset called brain connectomes. Section 7 analyzes the computational complexity of each method. Finally,

Sect. 9 concludes this work by providing a summary of findings and directions for future research.

2 Related Work

Dimensionality reduction techniques have played a pivotal role in handling high-dimensional data in numerous application fields, including image recognition, text mining, bioinformatics, and signal processing [24,32]. These techniques aim to reduce the dimensionality of feature spaces while preserving the most relevant information, thereby improving computational efficiency and mitigating the curse of dimensionality [5,11,16]. Despite being extremely useful, conventional dimensionality reduction techniques are conceptually designed for data lying in Euclidean spaces. Nevertheless, informative features might belong to non-linear spaces. For instance, covariance matrices have shown their interest in several applications such as object detection [31], texture classification [30], object tracking, action recognition and face recognition [18,20] due to their geometric and statistical properties. These matrices lie on the Riemannian manifold of SPD matrices, denoted as $\mathcal{S}_n^{++}$, which challenges the applicability of traditional Euclidean methods. In fact, linear techniques such as PCA [21] or LDA [13] flatten the SPD structure and fail to preserve the intrinsic geometry, potentially leading to non-valid outputs or distorted statistical interpretations [19,26]. In response to this issue, tangent PCA (also referred to as Principal Geodesic Analysis) was proposed [15], which linearizes the manifold locally around the Fréchet mean and applies classical PCA in the tangent space. However, when data are distributed over regions with high curvature or near the boundary of the SPD cone, this approximation can lead to distortions.

To overcome these limitations, several geometry-aware methods have emerged. Harandi et al. [19] proposed supervised dimensionality reduction based on optimization on Grassmann manifolds, using metrics such as the affine-invariant Riemannian metric (AIRM), Stein divergence, and Log-Euclidean distance. Other unsupervised non-linear methods—including Isomap [29], LLE [27], Laplacian Eigenmaps [5], and diffusion maps [11]—have also been extended to the SPD setting via Riemannian reformulations [23].

Kernel-based approaches have also gained attention by embedding the manifold into a Reproducing Kernel Hilbert Space (RKHS), allowing the use of standard machine learning tools. Notably, the use of Gaussian RBF kernels on $\mathcal{S}_n^{++}$ has enabled the application of kernel PCA, kernel SVM, and manifold-aware clustering [23]. However, ensuring positive definiteness of the kernel remains a critical constraint. Some earlier methods relied on approximations (e.g., flipping negative eigenvalues), which introduce artifacts and scale poorly with large kernel matrices.

While the literature offers a rich variety of dimensionality reduction techniques tailored to the SPD manifold, most studies evaluate these techniques in isolation, under varying experimental conditions, datasets, or performance metrics. This fragmentation makes it difficult to draw general conclusions about the comparative advantages of each approach. To our knowledge, there exists no unified benchmark that systematically compares linear and non-linear dimensionality reduction approaches under consistent settings. This paper addresses this gap by providing a controlled and fair evaluation across representative techniques.

3 Mathematical Background: The Riemannian Geometry of SPD Matrices

The space of $n \times n$ Symmetric Positive Definite (SPD) matrices, denoted $\mathcal{S}_n^{++}$, arises in numerous fields where second-order statistics are required, including computer vision, medical imaging, and signal processing. A matrix $\mathbf{P} \in \mathbb{R}^{n\times n}$ is said to be SPD if $\mathbf{v}^\top \mathbf{P}\mathbf{v} > 0$ for all non-zero vectors $\mathbf{v} \in \mathbb{R}^n$. As a set, $\mathcal{S}_n^{++}$ forms the interior of a convex cone in the space of real symmetric matrices.

To properly operate on SPD matrices, one must consider their manifold structure when equipped with a Riemannian metric. This manifold is smooth and differentiable, with a tangent space $T_{\mathbf{P}}\mathcal{S}_n^{++}$ at each point $\mathbf{P} \in \mathcal{S}_n^{++}$. A Riemannian metric induces inner products on tangent spaces and allows the definition of intrinsic operations such as distances, geodesics, and means. Below, we briefly recall the key elements used throughout this work.

3.1 Exponential and Logarithmic Maps

Given a reference point $\mathbf{X} \in \mathcal{S}_n^{++}$, the exponential and logarithmic maps respectively transfer vectors between the manifold and the tangent space $T_{\mathbf{X}}\mathcal{S}_n^{++}$. These are respectively defined as follows,

$$\exp_{\mathbf{X}}(\mathbf{V}) = \mathbf{X}^{1/2} \exp\left(\mathbf{X}^{-1/2}\mathbf{V}\mathbf{X}^{-1/2}\right) \mathbf{X}^{1/2}, \tag{1}$$

$$\log_{\mathbf{X}}(\mathbf{P}) = \mathbf{X}^{1/2} \log\left(\mathbf{X}^{-1/2}\mathbf{P}\mathbf{X}^{-1/2}\right) \mathbf{X}^{1/2}, \tag{2}$$

where $\mathbf{P} \in \mathcal{S}_n^{++}$, $\mathbf{V} \in T_{\mathbf{X}}\mathcal{S}_n^{++}$, and $\log(\cdot)$, $\exp(\cdot)$ denote the matrix logarithm and exponential, respectively.

3.2 Riemannian Metrics on SPD Manifolds

Several metrics have been proposed to measure distances between SPD matrices while taking into account the geometric structure of the SPD space. The following are the most commonly used ones:

- **Affine-Invariant Riemannian Metric (AIRM)** [26]:

  $$d_{\text{AIRM}}(\mathbf{P}, \mathbf{Q}) = \left\| \log\left(\mathbf{P}^{-1/2}\mathbf{Q}\mathbf{P}^{-1/2}\right) \right\|_F, \tag{3}$$

  where $\|\cdot\|_F$ denotes the Frobenius norm. AIRM is invariant under congruent transformations and is well-suited for affine-invariant applications.

– **Stein Divergence** [10]:

$$d_{\text{Stein}}(\mathbf{P}, \mathbf{Q}) = \log\det\left(\frac{\mathbf{P}+\mathbf{Q}}{2}\right) - \frac{1}{2}\log\det(\mathbf{PQ}). \tag{4}$$

Stein divergence is symmetric, positive-definite, and computationally efficient, making it attractive for large-scale problems.

– **Jeffrey Divergence:**

$$d_{\text{Jeffrey}}(\mathbf{P}, \mathbf{Q}) = \frac{1}{2}\left(\text{tr}(\mathbf{P}^{-1}\mathbf{Q}) + \text{tr}(\mathbf{Q}^{-1}\mathbf{P})\right) - n, \tag{5}$$

where $\text{tr}(\cdot)$ denotes the trace operator and n the matrix dimension.

– **Log-Euclidean Metric (LEM)** [3]:

$$d_{\text{LEM}}(\mathbf{P}, \mathbf{Q}) = \|\log(\mathbf{P}) - \log(\mathbf{Q})\|_F \,. \tag{6}$$

LEM treats SPD matrices in the logarithmic domain, allowing efficient computation while partially preserving geometric structure.

3.3 Fréchet Mean

The Fréchet mean [17], generalizes the Euclidean average to Riemannian manifolds. Given a set of SPD matrices $\{\mathbf{P}_1, \ldots, \mathbf{P}_k\}$, and a metric $d(\cdot, \cdot)$, the Fréchet mean $\mathbf{P}_\mu \in \mathcal{S}_n^{++}$ minimizes the sum of squared distances:

$$\mathbf{P}_\mu = \arg \min_{\mathbf{P} \in \mathcal{S}_n^{++}} \sum_{i=1}^{k} d^2(\mathbf{P}, \mathbf{P}_i). \tag{7}$$

When using AIRM, the Fréchet mean must be computed iteratively, typically via gradient descent on the manifold. It plays a central role in manifold learning algorithms, including Tangent PCA and clustering on SPD spaces.

4 Methods and Evaluation Protocol

This section details the dimensionality reduction techniques investigated in this work, alongside the synthetic data generation protocol designed to evaluate their behavior under controlled scenarios. We begin by describing each method—classical and geometry-aware—then proceed to the construction of synthetic SPD datasets with varying distribution overlap.

4.1 Dimensionality Reduction Techniques

We benchmark six representative techniques: three *conventional* baselines, namely, Principal Component Analysis (PCA), an Autoencoder (AE) and Kernel PCA and three *geometry-aware* methods taking into account the non-linearity of the SPD space, namely, tangent PCA (tPCA), SPD-tailored kernel PCA, and the supervised manifold-projection approach of Harandi *et al.* [19].

Conventional Methods

Principal Component Analysis (PCA). The classical PCA procedure involves the following steps:

- **Step 1 (Centering the Data):** Let $\{\mathbf{X}_i\}_{i=1}^N$ denote the dataset of vectorized SPD matrices. The mean of the data is computed as

$$\mu = \frac{1}{N}\sum_{i=1}^{N}\mathbf{X}_i, \tag{8}$$

  and each data point is centered:

$$\mathbf{X}_i' = \mathbf{X}_i - \mu. \tag{9}$$

- **Step 2 (Covariance Matrix Estimation):** The empirical covariance matrix of the centered data is computed by:

$$\mathbf{C} = \frac{1}{N}\sum_{i=1}^{N}\mathbf{X}_i'(\mathbf{X}_i')^\top. \tag{10}$$

- **Step 3 (Eigen Decomposition):** The covariance matrix is then decomposed as:

$$\mathbf{C} = \mathbf{USU}^\top, \tag{11}$$

  where $\mathbf{U}$ contains the eigenvectors (principal directions), and $\mathbf{S}$ is the diagonal matrix of eigenvalues.
- **Step 4 (Projection onto Principal Components):** Finally, each centered sample is projected onto the leading k eigenvectors:

$$\mathbf{Y}_i = \mathbf{V}^\top\mathbf{X}_i', \tag{12}$$

  where $\mathbf{V} \in \mathbb{R}^{d\times k}$ contains the top k eigenvectors.

In our experiments on synthetically generated data, PCA is directly applied by flattening each SPD matrix into a full vector of dimension $d = n^2$. In contrast, for real-world data (brain connectomes), we leverage the symmetry of SPD matrices and extract only the upper triangular part to avoid redundancy, resulting in a reduced vector of dimension $d = \frac{n(n+1)}{2}$. This choice is aligned with standard experimental protocols [6] in neuroimaging to ensure compactness and computational efficiency.

Autoencoder. Autoencoders are neural architectures designed to learn compact representations of high-dimensional data by minimizing reconstruction error. They consist of two main components: an encoder that maps inputs to a low-dimensional latent space, and a decoder that reconstructs the original data from this latent representation. The model is trained in an unsupervised manner to minimize the discrepancy between input and output, typically using the Mean Squared Error (MSE) loss. In our setting, each SPD matrix is flattened into a vector of dimension $d = n^2$, discarding its symmetry structure. This transformation enables the use of standard feedforward layers but neglects the non-Euclidean geometry of SPD manifolds. The encoder is composed of four fully connected layers with ReLU activations, progressively reducing the dimensionality from d to 2. The decoder mirrors this structure to reconstruct the original input. No activation is applied at the output layer to preserve the numerical range. The autoencoder is trained using the Adam optimizer for 100 epochs with a batch size of 32. We apply the autoencoder to flattened SPD matrices of size $n \times n$, resulting in an input dimension of $d = n^2$. Only 2D embeddings are extracted and evaluated for classification. For real-world data from the MLSP 2014 Schizophrenia Challenge, each functional connectivity matrix of size 28×28 is flattened into a vector of length 784. The same architecture is used to obtain 2D embeddings for downstream evaluation.

Kernel PCA. is a classical dimensionality reduction method that extends PCA by applying the kernel trick to project data into a high-dimensional feature space before applying PCA. In our experiments, we apply this method directly on flattened SPD matrices, without accounting for the Riemannian structure of the manifold. We use the Gaussian (RBF) kernel as in the original formulation proposed by Schölkopf et al. [28].

Geometry-Aware Techniques

Tangent PCA (tPCA). Tangent PCA [14] extends PCA to Riemannian manifolds by linearizing the data at a reference point. The procedure involves:

1. Computing the Fréchet mean $\mu \in \mathcal{S}_n^{++}$ of the dataset under the chosen Riemannian metric (AIRM).
2. Mapping each SPD matrix $\mathbf{X}_i$ to the tangent space $T_\mu \mathcal{S}_n^{++}$ via the logarithmic map $\log_\mu(\mathbf{X}_i)$.
3. Performing standard PCA in the Euclidean tangent space.
4. Projecting back to the manifold using the exponential map.

This method preserves local manifold geometry and is less prone to the distortion introduced by flattening.

Harandi's Manifold-Based Subspace Learning. The method proposed by Harandi et al. [19] learns a projection matrix $\mathbf{W} \in \mathbb{R}^{n \times m}$, where $m < n$, such that each SPD matrix $\mathbf{X} \in \mathcal{S}_n^{++}$ is mapped to $\mathbf{W}^\top \mathbf{X} \mathbf{W} \in \mathcal{S}_m^{++}$. The objective is to preserve intra-class similarity while maximizing inter-class separability using graph-based discriminant analysis.

The optimization problem is defined over the Grassmannian manifold $\mathcal{G}(m, n)$, subject to the orthonormality constraint $\mathbf{W}^\top \mathbf{W} = \mathbf{I}_m$. The cost function incorporates affinity graphs constructed from pairwise similarities under several metrics, including, Affine-Invariant Riemannian Metric (AIRM), Stein divergence, Jeffrey divergence, Log-Euclidean metric, and the Euclidean metric [4,10,26].

The optimization is performed using conjugate gradient descent on the manifold. This approach is computationally intensive but benefits from stronger geometric guarantees.

SPD-Tailored Kernel PCA. SPD-tailored Kernel Principal Component Analysis is an extension of kernel PCA that is extended to the SPD manifold [28]. Let $\{X_i\}_{i=1}^{N} \subset \mathcal{S}_n^{++}$, where $\mathcal{S}_n^{++}$ denotes the manifold of $n \times n$ symmetric positive-definite (SPD) matrices. Rather than flattening each X_i or projecting it onto a tangent space, we embed the manifold into an RKHS via a *geometry-aware* kernel

$$k : \mathcal{S}_n^{++} \times \mathcal{S}_n^{++} \longrightarrow \mathbb{R},$$

which: (i) is strictly positive definite and (ii) depends only on a chosen Riemannian distance d between SPD matrices:

$$k_\sigma(X_i, X_j) = \exp\left(-\frac{d^2(X_i, X_j)}{2\sigma^2}\right), \qquad \sigma > 0. \tag{13}$$

Several choices of d are valid. We adopt the Log-Euclidean metric [4]

$$d_{\mathrm{LE}}(X_i, X_j) = \|\log X_i - \log X_j\|_{\mathrm{F}}, \tag{14}$$

which yields a provably positive-definite Gaussian kernel on $\mathcal{S}_n^{++}$ [22,23].

Dual Formulation. Define the Gram matrix $K \in \mathbb{R}^{N \times N}$ with entries $K_{ij} = k_\sigma(X_i, X_j)$. After centering K in feature space, K–PCA solves the eigenproblem $Kc_\ell = \lambda_\ell c_\ell$, $\ell = 1, \ldots, L$, where $\{\lambda_\ell\}$ are the largest eigenvalues. The L-dimensional embedding of X_i is then

$$z_i = \left(\sqrt{\lambda_1}\, c_{1,i}, \ldots, \sqrt{\lambda_L}\, c_{L,i}\right)^\top \in \mathbb{R}^L. \tag{15}$$

Because the kernel in Eq. (13) respects the manifold geometry, the coordinates defined in Eq. (15) constitute a *linear* Euclidean representation that preserves non-linear relationships on $\mathcal{S}_n^{++}$ without resorting to local tangent approximations [23]. Therefore, these embeddings can be provided directly to standard classifiers such as k-NN in $\mathbb{R}^L$.

4.2 Synthetic SPD Data Generation

To benchmark the methods under controlled conditions, we design three synthetic datasets with varying degrees of class separability. Each class is modeled as a distribution of SPD matrices generated from samples in the tangent space.

Sampling Protocol. Each matrix $\mathbf{A}_i$ is generated as:

$$\mathbf{A}_i = \exp(\mathbf{S}_i), \tag{16}$$

where

$$\mathbf{S}_i = \frac{1}{2}(\mathbf{M}_i + \mathbf{M}_i^\top), \quad \mathbf{M}_{i,j} \sim \mathcal{U}(a, b), \tag{17}$$

with $\mathcal{U}(a, b)$ denoting the uniform distribution over the interval $[a, b]$. The exponential map ensures that $\mathbf{A}_i \in \mathcal{S}_n^{++}$. Each class is generated by choosing different ranges $[a, b]$ to control inter-class distance.

Distribution Configurations. We define three configurations:

- **Case 1 (Distant Distributions):**

$$\text{Class 1: } a = 1, b = 2; \quad \text{Class 2: } a = 0, b = 1$$

- **Case 2 (Moderate Overlap):**

$$\text{Class 1: } a = 0, b = 1; \quad \text{Class 2: } a = 0.25, b = 1.25$$

- **Case 3 (Strong Overlap):**

$$\text{Class 1: } a = 0, b = 1; \quad \text{Class 2: } a = 0.125, b = 1.125$$

In each case, we generate 1000 SPD matrices per class, resulting in a balanced dataset of 2000 samples. These scenarios allow us to assess how methods perform as class separation decreases.

Visualization of Synthetic Distributions. To illustrate the geometry of the generated datasets, we project the matrices from each configuration onto two-dimensional space. Figure 1 shows the spatial layout of class distributions. As expected, Case 1 yields well-separated clusters, while Case 3 exhibits heavy inter-class entanglement. This visualization provides qualitative insight into the classification difficulty and geometric structure in each scenario.

This visualization provides qualitative insight into the classification difficulty and geometric structure in each scenario.

5 Experiments and Results

5.1 Experimental Setup

We evaluate the performance of dimensionality reduction techniques in classifying SPD matrices under three configurations of data overlap (distant, slightly interwoven, and strongly interwoven). For each method, we apply a 2D embedding followed by k-Nearest Neighbors (k-NN) classification. We report the mean and standard deviation of accuracy over 10 random splits (80% training/20% testing). Dimensionality reduction is performed using PCA, tangent PCA, Kernel PCA, SPD-tailored Kernel PCA, autoencoder, and Harandi's method. We leverage the *Geomstats* library for the generation and manipulation of SPD matrices, which provides a robust framework for geometric learning and processing on Riemannian manifolds [25]. Additionally, for testing Harandi's method, we use the official code released by the authors [7, 19].

5.2 Results on Synthetic Data

Table 1 presents the classification accuracies across the three configurations. The evaluation of PCA, Tangent PCA, Autoencoder, and Harandi's method follows the same experimental protocol described in the previous study [2]. In this extended version,

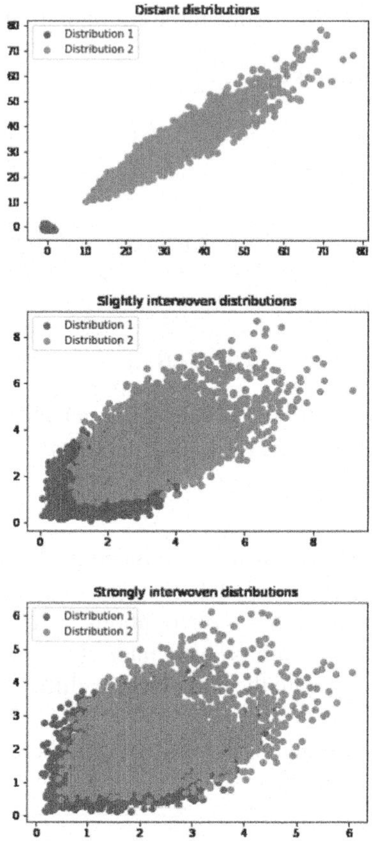

Fig. 1. Visualization of synthetic SPD distributions. From top to bottom: (1) well-separated, (2) moderately overlapping, and (3) highly overlapping distributions [2].

two additional techniques are introduced: standard Kernel PCA and SPD-tailored Kernel PCA. In the well-separated case (Case 1), all methods achieve perfect separation (100%). However, in Case 2 (slightly interwoven), the autoencoder slightly outperforms other techniques with a mean accuracy of 89.42%, followed closely by Tangent PCA (88.20%). Harandi's method reaches 86.69%, and PCA 88.03%. In Case 3 (strongly interwoven), the performance drops for all methods, but the Autoencoder remains the most robust (70.80%), followed by PCA and Tangent PCA (around 69%), while Harandi's approach underperforms at 65.67%. Furthermore, SPD-tailored Kernel PCA performs competitively across all cases, matching or surpassing the performance of the autoencoder in Case 2 (89.75%) and maintaining stability in more challenging scenarios. In contrast, classical Kernel PCA underperforms, especially in the strongly interwoven case (64.55%), highlighting its limitations when applied directly to flattened SPD data without accounting for manifold geometry.

Table 1. Comparison of Method Performance Across Different Cases.

Case	Method	Mean Accuracy (%)	Standard Deviation (σ)
Case 1: Distant Distributions	Tangent PCA	100.00	-
	Classic PCA	100.00	-
	Autoencoder	100.00	-
	Harandi's Method	100.00	-
	SPD-tailored Kernel PCA	100.00	-
	Kernel PCA	98.97	0.68
Case 2: Slightly Interwoven	Tangent PCA	88.20	1.09
	Classic PCA	88.03	1.56
	Autoencoder	89.42	1.67
	Harandi's Method	86.69	1.86
	SPD-tailored Kernel PCA	89.75	1.00
	Kernel PCA	78.53	3.09
Case 3: Strongly Interwoven	Tangent PCA	69.33	1.71
	Classic PCA	69.40	1.99
	Autoencoder	70.80	1.13
	Harandi's Method	65.67	3.10
	SPD-tailored Kernel PCA	68.62	3.12
	Kernel PCA	64.55	2.53

5.3 Influence of the Riemannian Metric (Harandi)

Table 2 reports the performance of Harandi's method under various metrics. The Log-Euclidean metric offers the most stable performance across all configurations. In highly overlapping distributions (Case 3), it even outperforms AIRM, which is traditionally favored for its affine invariance. Stein and Jeffreys also perform comparably well, while the Euclidean variant shows clear degradation under complex data configurations. These findings reinforce the importance of metric selection in Riemannian learning settings.

Table 2. Performance of Harandi's Method Across Different Metrics [2].

Case	AIRM		Stein		Jeffreys		Log-Euclidean		Euclidean	
	Mean (%)	Std. Dev (σ)	Mean (%)	Std. Dev (σ)	Mean (%)	Std. Dev (σ)	Mean (%)	Std. Dev (σ)	Mean (%)	Std. Dev (σ)
Case 1	100.00	-	100.00	-	100.00	-	100.00	-	100.00	-
Case 2	86.56	1.47	**86.69**	1.86	86.66	1.48	86.03	1.60	85.74	1.61
Case 3	65.10	3.42	65.47	2.95	65.49	2.24	**65.67**	3.10	62.49	3.58

Figure 2 shows the 2D visualization of the SPD matrices after applying the various dimensionality reduction techniques, demonstrating that the distribution configurations are preserved, highlighting the need for approaches that can better handle overlapping distributions.

5.4 Classification Error According to the Eigenvalue Range

To understand how the geometry of the SPD manifold affects classification performance, we analyze the classification error with respect to the minimum eigenvalue of each SPD matrix. This analysis aims to explore the relationship between the geometric structure of the SPD cone and the effectiveness of dimensionality reduction techniques, in particular classic PCA and Tangent PCA.

The minimum eigenvalue serves as an indicator of how close a matrix lies to the boundary of the SPD cone. Matrices with smaller minimum eigenvalues are closer to the boundary, where non-linear curvature is more pronounced, whereas matrices with larger minimum eigenvalues reside in regions that are more locally Euclidean due to the convex nature of the manifold.

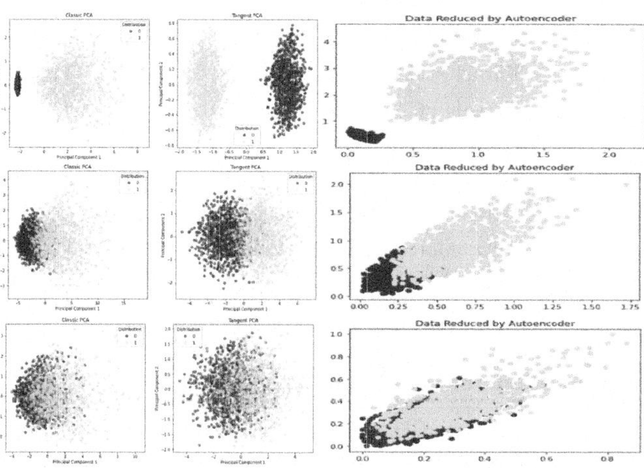

Fig. 2. 2D Visualization of SPD matrices after dimensionality Reduction [2].

As shown in Fig. 3, we partition the dataset into bins according to the minimum eigenvalue and report the classification errors within each bin for Case 2 and Case 3. The results reveal that classification error is generally lower in the bins associated with higher minimal eigenvalues, suggesting that classic PCA performs better in locally linear regions of the SPD space. Interestingly, classic PCA also slightly outperforms Tangent PCA in the bins corresponding to very low eigenvalues, which could be attributed to numerical instability when computing the matrix logarithm near the cone boundary. Conversely, Tangent PCA demonstrates superior performance for moderately low eigenvalues.

In summary, while classic PCA excels in certain scenarios, Tangent PCA's performance is notably influenced by the geometric properties of the data. This study highlights the importance of understanding the underlying structure of data distributions when selecting dimensionality reduction techniques, particularly in complex scenarios where traditional methods may struggle.

6 Real-World Application: Brain Connectomes

To validate that our findings on synthetic data translate to clinically relevant scenarios, we replicate the entire evaluation pipeline on a public neuroimaging cohort. In what follows, we describe the dataset and the experimental results.

6.1 Dataset Description

The *MLSP 2014 Schizophrenia Classification Challenge* [8] is a public dataset collected at the *Mind Research Network* as part of the NIH-funded Center of Biomedical Research Excellence (COBRE) initiative.

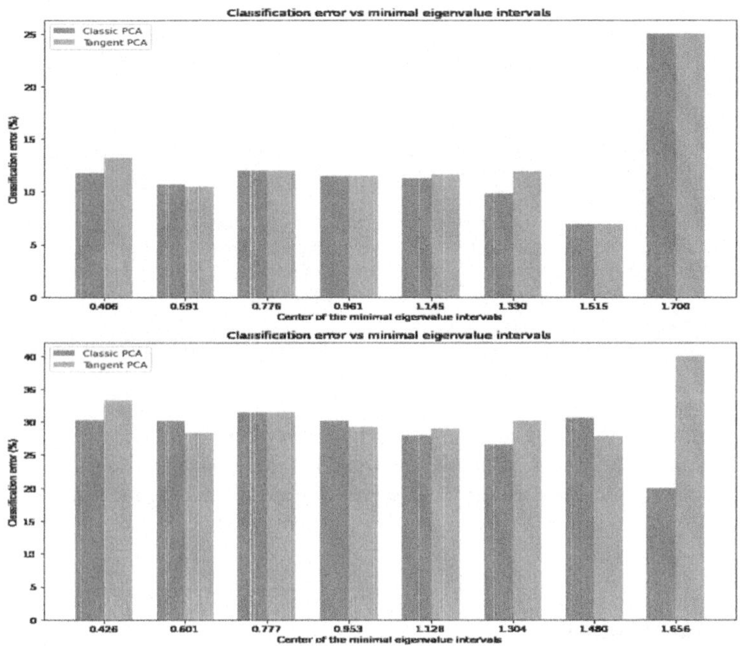

Fig. 3. Classification errors as a function of minimum eigenvalue ranges [2].

The dataset comprises resting-state functional magnetic resonance imaging (rs-fMRI) scans from **86 subjects**, including both healthy controls and patients diagnosed with schizophrenia. From these scans, *Functional Connectivity Networks* (FCNs) were computed based on the temporal correlations between the activation time series of **28 predefined brain Regions of Interest (ROIs)**. Each FCN is represented as a 28×28 **symmetric positive-definite (SPD) matrix**, summarizing the pairwise synchrony between the selected ROIs over time. As such, these matrices lie on the Riemannian manifold $\mathcal{S}_{++}^{28}$ of SPD matrices, a geometric structure that naturally accommodates the non-Euclidean properties of correlation-based functional connectivity.

In line with our study objective, we focus solely on the **Functional Network Connectivity (FNC)** features, a functional modality capturing global synchrony between independent brain regions. These features quantify the synchrony between spatially independent brain networks, computed via correlations between timecourses extracted through group Independent Component Analysis (GICA) on rs-fMRI data. Each FCN thus provides a subject-level summary of functional organization in the brain, and is widely used as a biomarker in schizophrenia research [1].

Figure 4 shows a visual comparison of the FCNs corresponding to a healthy control and a schizophrenic patient. As FCNs are symmetric and positive-definite by construction, they reside in a non-Euclidean geometric space, motivating the use of Riemannian tools for dimensionality reduction and classification.

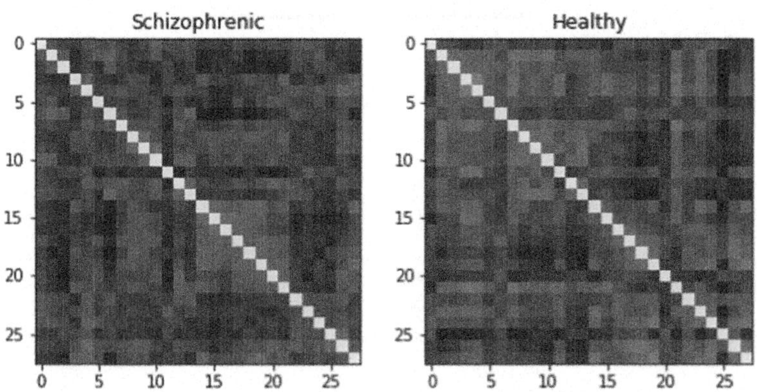

Fig. 4. Visualization of the first two brain connectomes from the MSLP dataset. The left matrix corresponds to a healthy control, while the right matrix corresponds to a schizophrenic patient. Each connectome is represented as a 28×28 correlation matrix on the SPD manifold.

6.2 Evaluation Settings

As in our experimental with synthetic data, the original SPD matrices are reduced to 2D. In addition, the reduced embeddings are evaluated through a classification step. Specifically, a k-Nearest Neighbors ($k = 5$) classifier is used on top of the reduced embeddings. For each method, we split the data into 80% for training and 20% for testing sets. The evaluation is repeated 5 times to account for variance due to sampling.

6.3 Results on Connectome Data

Table 3 reports the macro-averaged accuracy for all methods. A finer ablation of Harandi's method across five Riemannian metrics is given in Table 4.

Table 3. Classification performance of dimensionality reduction methods.

Method	Accuracy (%)
PCA	**61.11**
Tangent PCA	55.56
Harandi (AIRM)	55.89
Autoencoder	50.00
SPD-tailored kernel PCA	50.00
Kernel PCA	50.00

In this real-world classification task, linear methods demonstrate comparable performance to their geometry-aware counterparts. PCA achieves the highest accuracy at **61.11%**, tangent PCA follows closely with an accuracy of **55.56%**, Harandi's method performs similarly (around **55.89%**), regardless of the chosen metric, yet suffers from high variability across trials (standard deviations up to 15.6%). Moreover, the autoencoder and both variants of kernel PCA underperform with accuracy levels of **50%**. These results are consistent with the findings observed in our experiments on synthetic data, where geometry-aware methods do not consistently outperform classical Euclidean approaches.

Table 4. Classification accuracy (%) of Harandi's method across different Riemannian metrics in 2D embeddings. Results are reported as mean $\pm$ standard deviation over 10 runs.

Metric	Accuracy (mean $\pm$ std)
AIRM	55.89 ± 9.20
Stein	54.12 ± 9.77
Jeffrey	54.72 ± 14.18
Log-Euclidean	43.53 ± 15.61
Euclidean	55.29 ± 13.70

7 Computational Analysis: Empirical Training and Inference Time

Dimensionality reduction techniques differ not only in classification accuracy but also in computational efficiency. This section compares methods across the empirical runtime.

Table 5. Training and inference time (in seconds) for all methods on synthetic and real data.

Method	Synthetic Data (3 × 3)		Real Data (28 × 28)	
	Train Time (s)	Inference Time (s)	Train Time (s)	Inference Time (s)
PCA	0.0034	0.0000	0.0310	0.0020
Tangent PCA	0.0259	0.0020	0.5028	0.0030
Autoencoder	11.4176	0.5281	12.6671	0.0041
Harandi (AIRM)	**259.6322**	**59.8862**	**9.1101**	**0.1711**
Harandi (Stein)	9.7903	2.0544	0.8974	0.0151
Harandi (Jeffreys)	12.7304	2.5598	0.9852	0.0521
Harandi (Log-Euclidean)	1.1734	0.2275	0.8727	0.0215
Harandi (Euclidean)	0.7899	0.0368	0.2335	0.0110
SPD-tailored kernel PCA	**19 413.185**	0.065	31.548	0.039
Kernel PCA	0.4707	0.3673	0.0229	0.0368

As reported in Table 5, linear methods such as PCA are the most computationally efficient, both in training and inference. Autoencoders require significantly longer training times, attributed to iterative optimization over multiple layers, while inference remains fast. Geometry-aware approaches like Harandi's method introduce additional costs due to operations on the manifold. Notably, SPD-tailored Kernel PCA incurs the highest training cost, dominated by the construction of the Log-Euclidean kernel matrix, which scales quadratically with the number of samples. These observations highlight the superiority of standard methods in terms of computational efficiency.

8 Discussion

This study provides a comprehensive comparison of classical and geometry-aware dimensionality reduction techniques for SPD-valued data, considering both synthetically generated data and real brain connectome data. Empirically, classical PCA consistently yields higher performance, even outperforming more sophisticated manifold-based approaches in low-dimensional settings. This outcome can be attributed to several factors: the convexity of the SPD cone, which may reduce the need for non-linear methods and numerical instability in logarithmic mappings near the boundary of $\mathcal{S}_n^{++}$. From a computational aspect, PCA remains the most efficient method. While tangent PCA is slightly more costly in terms of computation, Harandi's method incurs a substantial due to the calculation of pairwise distance and optimization over the Grassmannian. SPD-tailored kernel PCA exhibits an asymmetric runtime profile, rendering it impractical for large datasets. On synthetic batches, kernel construction required several hours; however, the cost dropped significantly on the smaller real-world dataset.

This study has several limitations. First, the COBRE dataset includes only 86 subjects, limiting statistical power and potentially hiding the benefits of more complex methods. Second, we focused exclusively on 2D dimensionality reduction, which may over-compress relevant geometry and penalize methods that benefit from richer representations. Third, only functional connectivity (FNC) was considered; integrating structural modalities such as SBM or DTI could yield complementary insights.

9 Conclusion

This study presented a comprehensive comparative analysis of classical and geometry-aware dimensionality reduction techniques applied to symmetric positive definite (SPD) matrices, evaluated under both controlled synthetic scenarios and real-world neuroimaging data. While prior work has largely focused on synthetic benchmarks, our study bridges this gap by validating performance on real connectome-derived SPD data, thereby providing empirical insights into their practical applicability.

Our results demonstrate that geometry-aware methods, despite their theoretical soundness, do not systematically outperform Euclidean baselines under strong compression regimes.

Future work should investigate higher-dimensional reduction, integrate structural and functional neuroimaging modalities, and explore hybrid architectures such as SPDNet or U-SPDNet that combine deep learning with Riemannian priors. Moreover, a deeper theoretical analysis of the local geometry of the SPD manifold may help explain the empirical behaviors observed and clarify the cases in which geometry-aware approaches offer tangible advantages over classical baselines.

Acknowledgments. The authors thank the anonymous referees for their valuable comments, which improved the quality and readability of the paper. They also thank the Tunisian Ministry of Higher Education and Research for funding this research work.

Disclosure of Interests. The authors have no competing interests to declare that are relevant to the content of this article.

References

1. Allen, E.A., Damaraju, E., Plis, S.M., Erhardt, E.B., Eichele, T., Calhoun, V.D.: Tracking whole-brain connectivity dynamics in the resting state. Cereb. Cortex **24**(3), 663–676 (2014)
2. Araoud, A., Ghorbel, E., Ghorbel, F.: Dimensionality reduction on the SPD manifold: a comparative study of linear and non-linear methods. In: Proceedings of the 17th International Conference on Agents and Artificial Intelligence - Volume 3: ICAART, pp. 805–812. INSTICC, SciTePress (2025). https://doi.org/10.5220/0013183500003890
3. Arsigny, V., Fillard, P., Pennec, X., Ayache, N.: Fast and simple calculus on tensors in the log-euclidean framework. In: International Conference on Medical Image Computing and Computer-Assisted Intervention, pp. 115–122. Springer (2005)
4. Arsigny, V., Fillard, P., Pennec, X., Ayache, N.: Log-euclidean metrics for fast and simple calculus on diffusion tensors. Magn. Reson. Med. Off. J. Int. Soc. Magn. Reson. Med. **56**(2), 411–421 (2006)
5. Belkin, M., Niyogi, P.: Laplacian eigenmaps for dimensionality reduction and data representation. Neural Comput. **15**(6), 1373–1396 (2003)

6. Belyaev, M., et al.: Using geometry of the set of symmetric positive semidefinite matrices to classify structural brain networks. In: Kalyagin, V.A., Pardalos, P.M., Prokopyev, O., Utkina, I. (eds.) NET 2016. SPMS, vol. 247, pp. 257–267. Springer, Cham (2018). https://doi.org/10.1007/978-3-319-96247-4_18
7. Boumal, N., Mishra, B., Absil, P.A., Sepulchre, R.: Manopt, a Matlab toolbox for optimization on manifolds. J. Mach. Learn. Res. **15**, 1455–1459 (2014). http://www.manopt.org
8. Castro, E., joycenv, Cetin, M., Cota, N., Silva, R.F., Vince: MLSP 2014 schizophrenia classification challenge (2014). https://kaggle.com/competitions/mlsp-2014-mri, kaggle
9. Chen, K.X., Ren, J.Y., Wu, X.J., Kittler, J.: Covariance descriptors on a gaussian manifold and their application to image set classification. Pattern Recogn. **107**, 107463 (2020)
10. Cherian, A., Sra, S., Banerjee, A., Papanikolopoulos, N.: Jensen-bregman logdet divergence with application to efficient similarity search for covariance matrices. IEEE Trans. Pattern Anal. Mach. Intell. **35**(9), 2161–2174 (2012)
11. Coifman, R.R., Lafon, S.: Diffusion maps. Appl. Comput. Harmon. Anal. **21**(1), 5–30 (2006)
12. Drira, W., Neji, W., Ghorbel, F.: Dimension reduction by an orthogonal series estimate of the probabilistic dependence measure. In: ICPRAM (1), pp. 314–317 (2012)
13. Fisher, R.A.: The use of multiple measurements in taxonomic problems. Ann. Eugen. **7**(2), 179–188 (1936)
14. Fletcher, P.T., Joshi, S.: Principal geodesic analysis on symmetric spaces: statistics of diffusion tensors. In: International Workshop on Mathematical Methods in Medical and Biomedical Image Analysis, pp. 87–98. Springer (2004)
15. Fletcher, P.T., Lu, C., Pizer, S.M., Joshi, S.: Principal geodesic analysis for the study of nonlinear statistics of shape. IEEE Trans. Med. Imaging **23**(8), 995–1005 (2004)
16. Fodor, I.K.: A survey of dimension reduction techniques. Technical report, Lawrence Livermore National Lab. (LLNL), Livermore, CA (United States) (2002)
17. Fréchet, M.: Les éléments aléatoires de nature quelconque dans un espace distancié. In: Annales de l'institut Henri Poincaré, vol. 10, pp. 215–310 (1948)
18. Ghorbel, E., Boonaert, J., Boutteau, R., Lecoeuche, S., Savatier, X.: An extension of kernel learning methods using a modified log-euclidean distance for fast and accurate skeleton-based human action recognition. Comput. Vis. Image Underst. **175**, 32–43 (2018)
19. Harandi, M., Salzmann, M., Hartley, R.: Dimensionality reduction on SPD manifolds: the emergence of geometry-aware methods. IEEE Trans. Pattern Anal. Mach. Intell. **40**(1), 48–62 (2017)
20. Harandi, M.T., Sanderson, C., Hartley, R., Lovell, B.C.: Sparse coding and dictionary learning for symmetric positive definite matrices: a kernel approach. In: Fitzgibbon, A., Lazebnik, S., Perona, P., Sato, Y., Schmid, C. (eds.) ECCV 2012. LNCS, pp. 216–229. Springer, Heidelberg (2012). https://doi.org/10.1007/978-3-642-33709-3_16
21. Hotelling, H.: Analysis of a complex of statistical variables into principal components. J. Educ. Psychol. **24**(6), 417 (1933)
22. Huang, Z., Wang, R., Shan, S., Li, X., Chen, X.: Log-euclidean metric learning on symmetric positive definite manifold with application to image set classification. In: International Conference on Machine Learning, pp. 720–729. PMLR (2015)
23. Jayasumana, S., Hartley, R., Salzmann, M., Li, H., Harandi, M.: Kernel methods on riemannian manifolds with gaussian RBF kernels. IEEE Trans. Pattern Anal. Mach. Intell. **37**(12), 2464–2477 (2015)
24. Jolliffe, I.T., Cadima, J.: Principal component analysis: a review and recent developments. Philos. Trans. Roy. Soc. A Math. Phys. Eng. Sci. **374**(2065), 20150202 (2016)
25. Miolane, N., et al.: Geomstats: a python package for riemannian geometry in machine learning. J. Mach. Learn. Res. **21**(223), 1–9 (2020)
26. Pennec, X., Fillard, P., Ayache, N.: A riemannian framework for tensor computing. Int. J. Comput. Vision **66**, 41–66 (2006)

27. Saul, L.K., Roweis, S.T.: An introduction to locally linear embedding (2000). http://www.cs.toronto.edu/~roweis/lle/publications.html
28. Schölkopf, B., Smola, A., Müller, K.R.: Nonlinear component analysis as a kernel eigenvalue problem. Neural Comput. **10**(5), 1299–1319 (1998)
29. Tenenbaum, J.: Mapping a manifold of perceptual observations. In: Advances in Neural Information Processing Systems, vol. 10 (1997)
30. Tuzel, O., Porikli, F., Meer, P.: Region covariance: a fast descriptor for detection and classification. In: Leonardis, A., Bischof, H., Pinz, A. (eds.) ECCV 2006. LNCS, vol. 3952, pp. 589–600. Springer, Heidelberg (2006). https://doi.org/10.1007/11744047_45
31. Tuzel, O., Porikli, F., Meer, P.: Pedestrian detection via classification on riemannian manifolds. IEEE Trans. Pattern Anal. Mach. Intell. **30**(10), 1713–1727 (2008)
32. Van Der Maaten, L., Postma, E.O., Van Den Herik, H.J., et al.: Dimensionality reduction: a comparative review. J. Mach. Learn. Res. **10**(66–71), 13 (2009)
33. Wang, R., Wu, X.J., Xu, T., Hu, C., Kittler, J.: U-spdnet: an SPD manifold learning-based neural network for visual classification. Neural Netw. **161**, 382–396 (2023)

Cellular Automata Applied to the Simulation of Pedestrian Evacuation with Surmountable Obstacles and Route Alternation Through an Impatience Mechanism

Eduardo C. Silva(✉), Gabriela S. Damazo, and Luiz G. A. Martins

Faculty of Computing, Federal University of Uberlândia, Uberlândia, MG 38408-100, Brazil
{eduardocassiano,gabriela.damazo,lgamartins}@ufu.br

Abstract. Analyzing and forecasting human behavior in both everyday and crisis scenarios is a complex challenge that has drawn significant interest from researchers. In this context, modeling and simulating collective pedestrian dynamics (CPD) plays a crucial societal role, with applications ranging from urban design to safety planning. Among computational approaches, Cellular Automata (CA) offer a straightforward yet powerful method for replicating intricate behavioral patterns, including pedestrian movement during evacuations. CA-based models incorporate multiple factors, such as path selection strategies, interactions between individuals, and social behaviors like panic and herd mentality. This study introduces a CA-based model for CPD, building upon the models of Varas and Alizadeh while introducing four key enhancements for greater realism. The first three adjustments presented in the original paper focus on the static floor field: modifying movement dynamics, adjusting diagonal movement permissions around obstacles, and distinguishing between surmountable and insurmountable obstacles. In this paper, the improvement introduces a dynamic floor field, individual pedestrian profiles, and an impatience mechanism that enables evacuees to create alternative escape paths. Comparative evaluations demonstrate that the proposed model performs 39.91% better than the Alizadeh model, when the density was 100%; and 37.47% better in the number of conflicts.

Keywords: Cellular Automata · Collective Pedestrian Dynamics · Modeling and Simulation · Surmountable Obstacles · Impassable Diagonals

1 Introduction

Collective Pedestrian Dynamics (CPD) models are essential tools for both enhancing public safety measures and optimizing urban planning strategies. These models leverage diverse computational methodologies, including social force models, fluid dynamics, agent-based simulations, game theory, and insights derived from animal experimentation [33]. Among these, Cellular Automata (CA) represent a prominent approach for modeling CPD. CAs can be understood as multi-agent systems: they are computational structures whose individual components interact locally, collectively generating complex, emergent behaviors.

H. J. van den Herik et al. (Eds.): ICAART 2025, LNAI 16517, pp. 562–582, 2026.
https://doi.org/10.1007/978-3-032-25032-2_27

Three distinct factors can be considered during the development of CPD models. These include, first, the specific space in which the simulation is carried out; second, how the pedestrians themselves are represented within the model; and third, the particular scenario or situation the model aims to describe. Modeling CPD in emergency situations is of particular interest, as these scenarios often involve unique human behaviors (such as panic or the overcoming of obstacles) that are critical to incorporate for the simulation to be more reliable and realistic.

The literature contains several studies utilizing CAs for CPD. The earliest applications of CA to human movement, though initially focused on vehicle traffic flow, appeared in the 1990s [24]. This era also saw significant contributions to pedestrian simulation through social force models [11–14], alongside the advent of CA-based models specifically designed for bidirectional traffic [2–5]. Subsequently, CAs models capable of simulating multi-directional pedestrian traffic gained prominence, with the Euclidean distance-based model by [6] being a notable example. Concurrently, the environments under study broadened considerably, shifting to include a diverse range of internal scenarios such as classrooms [21], elevators [22], theaters [9], restaurants [8], aircraft [10], ships [15], and other similar spaces [20].

[23] proposed two distinct approaches: one where individuals move based on a probability, choosing between following floor values or executing random movements, and another where pedestrians aim to minimize their number of neighbors. [26,28] presented a model that extends the static floor field (SFF) from a microscopic to a mesoscopic scale, offering broader applicability. [27] developed a model that assesses dynamic impatience levels, taking into account both individual impatience growth and its propagation among pedestrians. [7] leveraged dynamic principles to construct a model for an evacuation safety index. Finally, [16] created a model in which pedestrians themselves are considered movable obstacles, thereby increasing the value of the floor field.

Several models, including those by [7,16,23,26–28], are unified by their use of the SFF, a concept originally proposed by [31]. This SFF provides a streamlined approach to calculating distances between grid cells and the exit, critically without disregarding the presence of obstacles. This method stands as an alternative to the Euclidean distance-based SFF [6,17–19,25], where accurately reproducing human behavioral phenomena often necessitates the fine-tuning of numerous parameters. Conversely, the Varas model [31] distinguishes itself by its ability to generate simulations in complex scenarios, relying solely on the SFF and straightforward rules for managing collisions with obstacles. Lastly, the Varas model [31] further incorporates a panic parameter, introducing a non-deterministic element to its simulations.

[1] is another important model that proposed a CDP model that incorporates the concept of a dynamic floor field (DFF) into the deterministic perspective, being built considering the distribution of pedestrians during the simulation and recalculated at each iteration, by checking the number of people on floors closest to an exit.

In our research, the initial aim of the original paper was to present a CA model for CPD [30], strongly based on the SFF of the [31] model. The first prototype proposed in this paper improves the relationship of the pedestrian with the space of simulation, especially with the obstacles, changing the movement dynamics, modifying the permission to pass between insurmountable obstacles using the diagonal and presenting the difference between surmountable and insurmountable obstacles. Later, in this paper, the objective was expanded in the second prototype with the integration of the DFF of the Alizadeh model [1], as well as the inclusion of pedestrian profiles and the impatience mechanism, so that pedestrians can alternate congested escape routes or try to create alternative paths when facing surmountable obstacles. Experiments with the first prototype show that the inclusion of the new rules improved the likelihood of the simulations and did not negatively impact the overall performance of the model [30]. Furthermore, the results obtained in the second prototype demonstrate that the inclusion of the DFF and the profile mechanism significantly improved the performance of the new model.

First, in Sect. 2, the reference models are described. Then, in Sect. 3, the changes we made in the models are presented. In Sect. 4, we explain the results comparing the alterations with the original models. Finally, in Sect. 5, we summarize the contributions and explain future research points.

2 Reference Models

The first prototype presented in this paper [30] is based on [31], a model that proposes a simplified method for calculating the distance from transition cells to exit cells [23]. In addition, the model supports obstacles, something that is usually present in real scenarios. The second prototype integrates DFF calculation of the [1] model, so that pedestrians can choose less congested escape routes in scenarios with multiple exits. The Sect. 2.1 presents details for the simplified calculation of the static floor field (SFF). Then, Sect. 2.2 contextualizes the rules used for transition and conflict resolution between pedestrians. Finally, Sect. 2.3 defines and exemplifies the effects of the dynamic floor field (DFF).

2.1 Static Floor Field Calculation

In the original Varas model [31], the room is defined as a two-dimensional quadrangular lattice, so that each floor cell represents an area of $0.4 \times 0.4m^2$ and can change to one of the following states: pedestrian, empty or obstacle. The cell dimension represents a surface when occupied by a person in high-density emergency situations [20]. In addition, it also defined that the pedestrian speed is approximately 1 m/s, thus $\Delta t = 0.4s$ [31].

The map grid helps determine exit locations, empty cells, individual positions, and insurmountable obstacles. Each cell is assigned a constant value representing its distance from the exit, meaning cells closer to an exit have lower values [1]. The initial grid's cell values are calculated as follows [31]:

1. The exit cell assume a value of 1;
2. The adjacent cells to those with previously defined distances have their values calculated according to:
   - If the value of the cell is n, the adjacent cells horizontally or vertically will receive a value of $n + 1$, while the adjacent cells on the diagonals will receive a value of $n + \lambda$, where $\lambda > 1$;

- If there is a conflict, the lowest value is determined for that cell;

3. Step 2 is repeated until all other cells have their distances calculated;
4. Obstacles (tables, walls, chairs, etc.) receive a high value so that pedestrians do not try to pass through these cells.

Figure 1 shows a grid map representing the floor of a 16×20 room, in which the cell distances were determined considering, $\lambda = 1.5$ and obstacle with the constant value of 500.

500	500	500	500	500	500	500	500	500	500	500	500	500	500	500	500	500	500	500	500
500	7.5	8	8.5	9	9.5	10	11	12	13	14	15	16	17	18	19	20	21	22	500
500	6.5	7	7.5	8	8.5	9.5	10.5	11.5	12.5	13.5	14.5	15.5	16.5	17.5	18.5	19.5	20.5	21.5	500
500	5.5	6	6.5	7	8	9	10	11	12	13	14	15	16	17	18	19	20	21	500
500	4.5	5	5.5	6.5	7.5	8.5	9.5	10.5	11.5	12.5	13.5	14.5	15.5	16.5	17.5	18.5	19.5	20.5	500
500	3.5	4	5	6	7	8	9	10	11	12	13	14	15	16	17	18	19	20	500
500	2.5	3.5	4.5	5.5	6.5	7.5	8.5	9.5	10.5	11.5	12.5	13.5	14.5	15.5	16.5	17.5	18.5	19.5	500
1	2	3	4	5	6	7	8	9	10	11	12	13	14	15	16	17	18	19	500
1	2	3	4	5	6	7	8	9	10	11	12	13	14	15	16	17	18	19	500
500	2.5	3.5	4.5	5.5	6.5	7.5	8.5	9.5	10.5	11.5	12.5	13.5	14.5	15.5	16.5	17.5	18.5	19.5	500
500	3.5	4	5	6	7	8	9	10	11	12	13	14	15	16	17	18	19	20	500
500	4.5	5	5.5	6.5	7.5	8.5	9.5	10.5	11.5	12.5	13.5	14.5	15.5	16.5	17.5	18.5	19.5	20.5	500
500	5.5	6	6.5	7	8	9	10	11	12	13	14	15	16	17	18	19	20	21	500
500	6.5	7	7.5	8	8.5	9.5	10.5	11.5	12.5	13.5	14.5	15.5	16.5	17.5	18.5	19.5	20.5	21.5	500
500	7.5	8	8.5	9	9.5	10	11	12	13	14	15	16	17	18	19	20	21	22	500
500	500	500	500	500	500	500	500	500	500	500	500	500	500	500	500	500	500	500	500

Fig. 1. Calculation of the SFF of a 16×20 room grid (Image from [31]).

2.2 Transition Rules

The interaction and movement between pedestrians can be defined based on a transition rule that uses a radius 1 Moore neighborhood. At each timestep of the simulation, all pedestrians move to a cell closer to the exit cell. The Fig. 2, demonstrates the transition rules used, which are given below [1,31]:

- Black circle: pedestrian change to the cell with the lowest value in its neighborhood;
- White circles: if two or more pedestrians want to go to the same cell, this results in a cell conflict, resolved randomly. The winner moves and the each loser remains still;

- Black triangle: if two or more cells in the neighborhood of a pedestrian have the same value, the pedestrian proceed randomly to one of these cells;
- White triangle: simulate the panic characteristic. If a pedestrian panics at time t, he remains still in this timestep.

The final three rules introduce probability to the model, moving it away from being entirely deterministic. It's important to note that a pedestrian remains stationary if their desired destination cell is occupied. This mechanism, combined with the "white circles" rule, governs how pedestrians interact with each other.

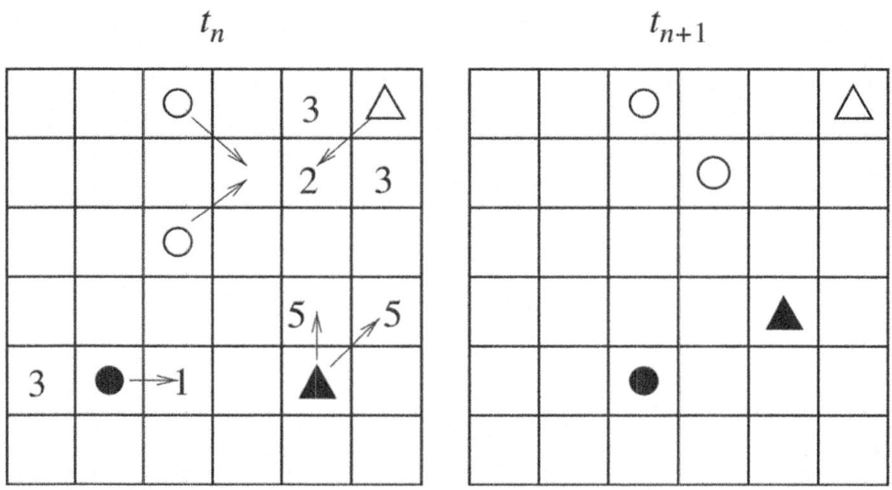

Fig. 2. Rules of pedestrian movement (Image from [31]).

2.3 Dynamic Floor Field Calculation

The Alizadeh model [1] adds the DFF to the SFF metric. In this context, unlike the SFF, which is calculated only once for each map in the simulation, the DFF is calculated at each time step t. This new parameter is used so that pedestrians can choose another exit positioned on the map when they are directed to an exit already congested by a significant number of pedestrians. The calculation is based on the distribution of pedestrians, so that the weight of a cell x, considering an exit A, at the i-th time step ($W_i^A(x)$) is given by [1]:

$$W_i^A(x) = W_{static}^A(x) + \alpha \quad T_i^A(x) \tag{1}$$

where,

- $W_{static}^A(x)$: the distance from x to A;
- $T_i^A(x)$: the number of pedestrians that are closer to A than x, which is calculated by:

$$T_i^A(x) = \frac{|P_i^A(x)| + 1/2|E_i^A(x)|}{d_A} \tag{2}$$

$$V_i = \{y | y \text{is occupied by a pedestrian at the } i\text{-th time step}\} \tag{3}$$

$$P_i^A(x) = \{y | W_{static}^A(y) < W_{static}^A(x) \text{ and } y \in V_i\} \tag{4}$$

$$E_i^A(x) = \{y | W_{static}^A(y) = W_{static}^A(x) \text{ and } y \in V_i\} \tag{5}$$

In summary, dA delimits the width of the gate A. $|P_i^A(x)|$ and $|E_i^A(x)|$ respectively represent the number of elements of $P_i^A(x)$ and $E_i^A(x)$. α is the crowd deviation coefficient [1], that is, it is a control variable that affects the influence of the DFF in the simulation. Finally, the value of a cell x at time step $i \geq 1$ is defined by:

$$W_i(x) = \min\{W_i^A(x) | A \text{ it's a room door}\} \tag{6}$$

The Fig. 3 presents a scenario based on a classroom with large desks and two exit cells. In this scenario, in a real situation, pedestrians can alternate between the available exits, so that they are not limited to the nearest exit, which is congested by other pedestrians.

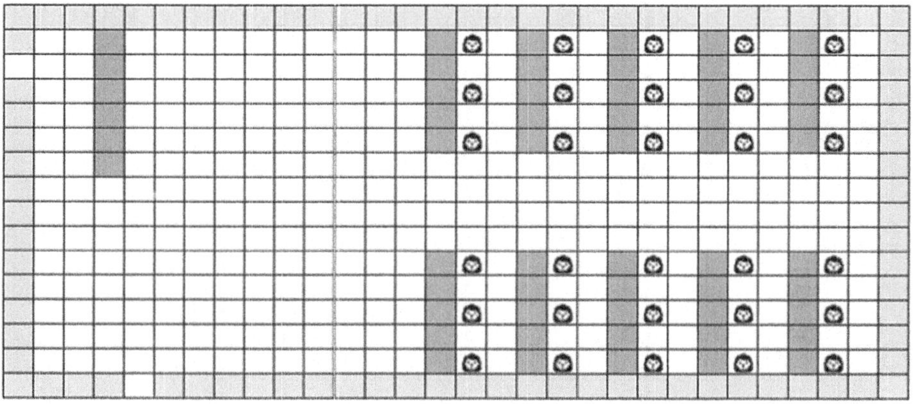

Fig. 3. Map of the classroom (16 $\times$ 30 with 56 obstacles and 2 exit cells). Adapted from [1].

The Fig. 4 shows the state of the simulation in the scenario of Fig. 3 for $t = 35$, where the behavior of the Varas model [31] is shown. Although there is an uncongested exit in the upper left part of the map, pedestrians gather at a single exit. This grouping of pedestrians lasts until the last individual manages to escape and is a reflection of the strategy used by employing only the SFF in the simulation.

In contrast, Fig. 5 illustrates a more natural behavior with the application of the DFF of the Alizadeh model [1]. In this case, pedestrians can choose both routes, but they try to avoid exits with pedestrian congestion, generating a more believable behavior and a shorter time to vacate the room.

3 New Model Rules

One of the contributions of the Varas model [31] is the inclusion of obstacles in the simulations so that the environment resembles real situations, since it is more common

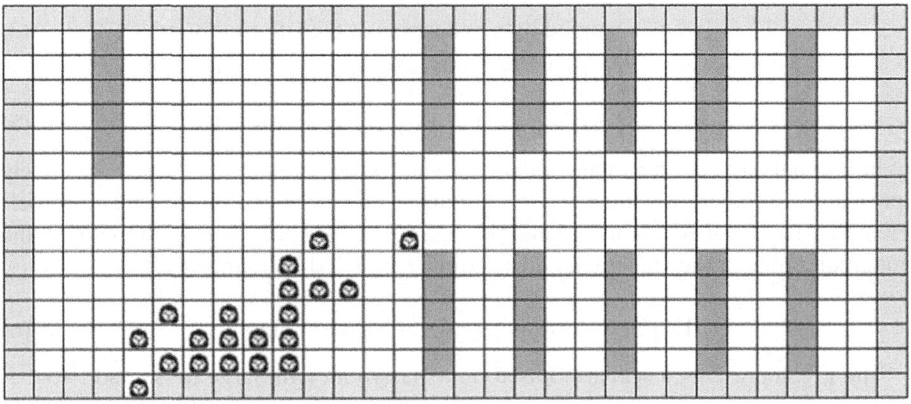

Fig. 4. Evacuation dynamics on the classroom map applying the [31] model ($t = 35$).

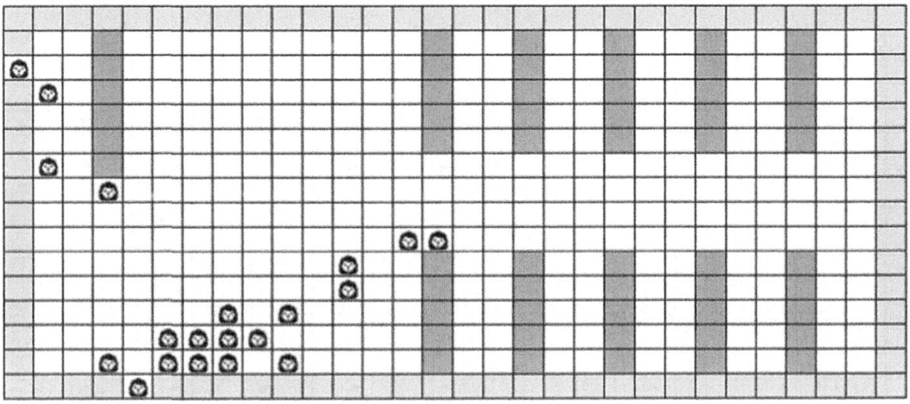

Fig. 5. Evacuation dynamics on the classroom map applying the [1] model ($t = 35$).

for pedestrians to need to evacuate rooms with obstacles than completely empty rooms. However, there are a significant number of simulations in rooms without obstacles, for example [32]. This model allows the analysis of the influence of the location of doors and their respective sizes on the evacuation of simulated scenarios. Additionally, the Alizadeh model [1] allows for the simulation of more realistic dynamics since pedestrians can change their route to less congested exits.

During the implementation of the new model, certain aspects were identified that could be changed to bring the work even closer to real environments. Sections 3.1, 3.2 and 3.3 summarize the rules introduced in the original paper [30], respectively, additional rules for pedestrian transition dynamics, restrictions for transitions with obstacles arranged diagonally and the rules regarding surmountable obstacles. Finally, the Sect. 3.4 presents the integration of obstacle rules, profile composition, and details of the integration with static and dynamic floor concepts, characterizing the contributions of this extended paper.

3.1 Cell Selection Dynamics

Following the Varas model [31], a pedestrian's movement is directed towards cells holding a lower value than their current location. Additionally, this paper establishes specific rules that result in a pedestrian remaining stationary. These three cases are:

1. If he/she loses in the dispute against another pedestrian who wants to go to the same cell;
2. If he/she chooses to go to an occupied cell.
3. If he/she panics at that moment of the simulation;

Figure 2 illustrates the first two itens. The original behavior of the second rule is shown in Fig. 6(a). In the left grid, at $t = 0$, only one pedestrian can move; the others must wait for the cell with the best floor value to become available at $t = 1$. This paper, like the model proposed by [1], presents a different approach: choice without waiting (CWW). As depicted in Fig. 6(b), pedestrians using CWW always choose the lowest empty floor. This often prevents them from being stopped by the second rule. Consequently, with CWW, all three pedestrians can move. On the other hand, in the choice with waiting, only one of the pedestrians moves.

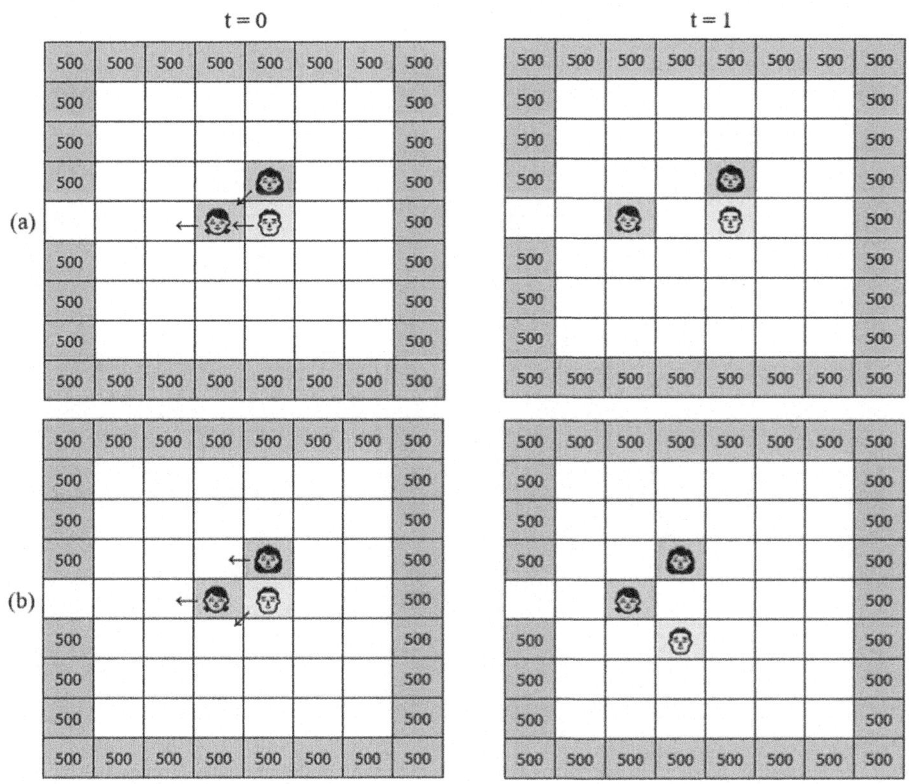

Fig. 6. Comparison between pedestrian movement in a 9×8 room. (a) Choice of cell with waiting. (b) Choice of cell without waiting (CWW). (Image from [30]).

3.2 Changing Diagonal Movements

In the Varas model [31], pedestrians have the ability to move diagonally, a capability reflected in the design of its transition rules and the method for calculating the static floor field (SFF). Despite this, a notable issue exists: when obstacles are placed diagonally, the current rules unfortunately permit pedestrians to traverse the seemingly free space located between these barriers.

Figure 7(a) illustrates an initial grid depicting a room with a diagonal barrier. The original model's SFF calculation, as demonstrated, inadvertently allows for movement through the open cells on the opposite diagonals. This oversight makes it possible for a pedestrian to transition into such cells, as highlighted in Fig. 7(b).

A straightforward solution involves implementing a double wall to fully incorporate obstacles into the map model. However, this representation could prove unsuitable for depicting realistic scenarios, because it tends to create environments that appear excessively crowded.

To resolve this issue, the model incorporates an improved SFF calculation designed to block movement through barriers, *i.e.* , the floor value calculation is no longer propagated to diagonal cells that lie between obstacles. The initial grid resulting from this refined floor calculation strategy is presented in Fig. 7(c), which then enables the desired pedestrian movement, as illustrated in Fig. 7(d).

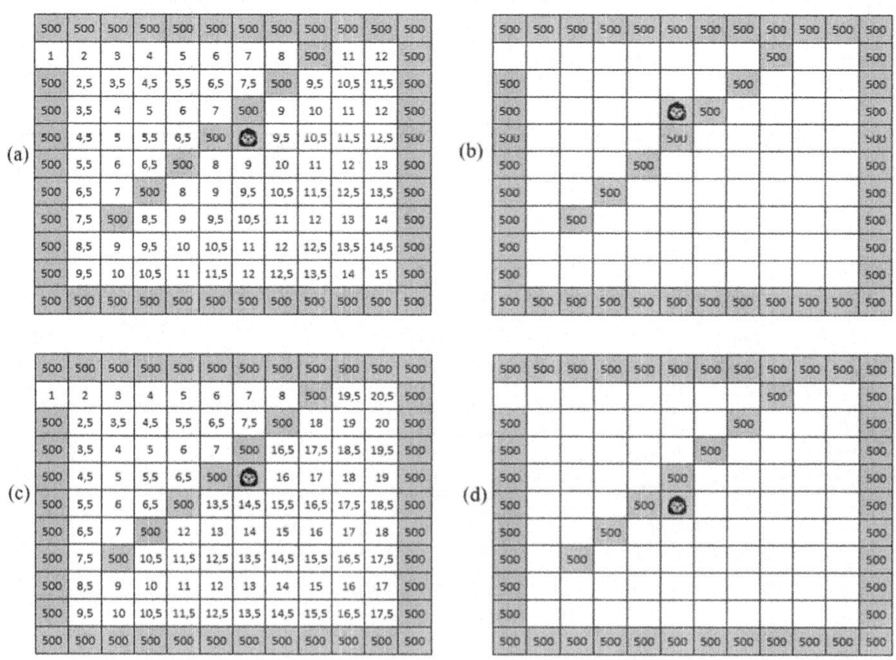

Fig. 7. Pedestrian movement in scenarios with obstacles arranged diagonally (Image from [30]).

3.3 Surmountable Obstacles Rules

To better reflect real-world scenarios, the Varas model [31] incorporates the simulation of obstacles. These obstacles are represented by cells assigned constant, unreachable values, effectively preventing any transitions into them. Consequently, these objects are entirely impassable. Thus, pedestrians cannot traverse them, regardless of whether they represent walls, tables, chairs, or other elements.

The model proposed in this paper presents a distinction between two types of obstacle: insurmountable and surmountable objects. The insurmountable objects are the obstacles used in the original models [1,31]. The surmountable objects are introduced according to some rules [30]:

1. They have no impact on the structure of the map, that is, when the SFF values are calculated, the surmountable objects are ignored and their cells are treated as empty cells and have their cost values calculated;
2. An overtaking rate z is defined at the beginning of the simulations, which indicates the probability of a pedestrian overtaking the object. It works as follows:
   - If the pedestrian "wins" the overtaking, in the next time step, he will occupy the obstacle cell, representing a pedestrian on top of a chair, table or other type of surmountable obstacle;
   - If the pedestrian "loses" the overtaking, he remains still.

Figure 8 demonstrates the distinct ways pedestrians move when considering our proposed model, which includes surmountable obstacles, versus the original model that only features insurmountable objects. Specifically, Fig. 8(b) depicts a pedestrian's path (in yellow) as simulated by the original Varas model [31]. In this version, no distinction is made between various types of obstacles and walls, meaning pedestrians must navigate around any barrier they encounter. Conversely, Fig. 8(a) showcases our enhanced approach: objects rendered in blue are designated as surmountable, while the gray walls remain insurmountable. Assuming a pedestrian successfully overcomes a blue barrier at $t = 0$, they will be positioned atop it at $t = 1$. Following this, in subsequent time steps, the pedestrian will move off the obstacles cell and proceed to a new cell based on the grid's values and the defined transition rules.

3.4 Integration of Profiles with Surmountable Obstacles

The first prototype implements surmountable obstacles in isolation [30], so that in each simulation pedestrians adopt a single specific profile, that is, all pedestrians tend to cross surmountable obstacles or the population acts as the base models, for example the Varas [31] and Alizadeh [1] models. Subsequently, the second prototype refines the dynamics by integrating both concepts in each simulation, so that a pedestrian can switch profiles depending on the challenges encountered during the evacuation, which defines the new proposed model. To this end, the new model maintains two different versions of the SFF: one that acts as the original models and another in which surmountable obstacles are considered. In this way, the profile of each pedestrian defines which SFF will be used. For example, more active pedestrians will try to cross surmountable obstacles, while other pedestrians will have to go around these obstacles.

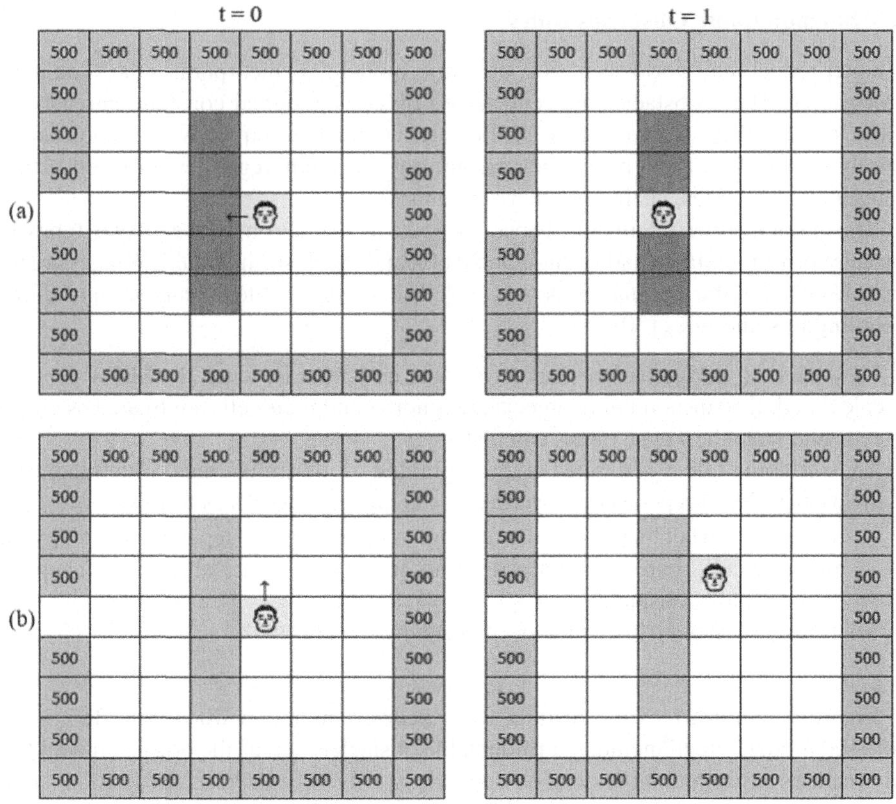

Fig. 8. Pedestrian movement in environments with surmountable obstacles: (a) extended model and (b) original model (Image from [30]).

In order for pedestrians to switch between profiles, a mechanism based on impatience was established. During the simulation, when pedestrians are unable to move since the previous time step, their impatience c will increase. The blocking of movement can have different reasons, for example, failure to compete for a cell, waiting in a crowd or failure to try to overcome some surmountable obstacle. For each pedestrian, when $c \geq 5$, there is a profile change, that is, an active pedestrian starts to act normally and vice versa. It is important to highlight that the impatience mechanism has a different effect than the one proposed in [27], where the degree of impatience is used as the degree of pedestrian competitiveness, influencing the speed of pedestrians in each simulation update.

In addition to the aforementioned contributions, there is also an integration of the dynamic floor field (DFF), so that the new model also needs to maintain an alternative version of the calculation performed, similarly to what occurs with the use of the SFF, mentioned previously. However, as contextualized in Sect. 2.3, the DFF needs to be calculated for each time step t. Therefore, each version of the DFF will be used depending on the profile of each pedestrian. As in the SFF, the versions of the DFF differ in the support for surmountable obstacles and the original behavior of the model, in this case, the Alizadeh model [1].

4 Simulation Results

The analysis of CDS models involves several parameters that have a direct influence on the simulation behavior. The value of the diagonal rate was defined as $\lambda = 1.5$. Another important consideration is that, in all simulations, as in the paper by [31], the panic rate was adopted as 5%, that is, each pedestrian, at each time step, has a 5% chance of stopping due to having panicked.

The Sect. 4.1 summarizes the results previously published in the paper [30], which presents experiments on pedestrian evacuation in an empty room, with a diagonal wall and with surmountable obstacles. The developed prototype used in [30] was developed using the JAVA language through an Integrated Development Environment (IDE) and exclusively addresses the implementation of the static floor field (SFF). This version is available at (https://github.com/eduardocassiano-ufu/Cellular-Automata-with-Surmountable-Obstacles). Another important detail is that, in this prototype, it was considered that a pedestrian, upon reaching the door, is no longer inside the room.

The second prototype was developed in C language addressing the static and dynamic implementations of the floor field and it was used in the experiments of Sect. 4.2. Additionally, in this version, pedestrians are considered safe after passing through an exit door. A link to the repository with a copy of the source code for reproducing the results on both prototypes can be found in a remote repository at (https://github.com/eduardocassiano-ufu/PRESS). Furthermore, 30 runs were performed for each simulation version and the values displayed refer to the average of these. Other important information will be presented for each map.

4.1 Evacuation Dynamics in the Original Paper

In the first experiment [30], evacuation dynamics in an empty room, pedestrians were randomly distributed in a room measuring 16×20, with a single exit. The objective of this test was to compare the original Varas model [31] with its CWW version (Choice-Without-Waiting). The results showed the emergence of queues in the original model. In contrast, in the CWW version of the model, pedestrians accumulate more quickly near the exits, resulting in a shorter evacuation time. The discrepancy between evacuation times was highlighted as the population size increased (25, 50, 100, 150), demonstrating that the CWW version considerably reduces the time required for all pedestrians to exit.

Next, the second experiment evaluates the inclusion of a rule to avoid the crossing of insurmountable obstacles diagonally [30]. With pedestrians randomly distributed in a room with dimensions of 16×20 and a barrier positioned diagonally across the map, the test compared the original Varas model [31] with its CWW version, both with the inclusion and removal of the rule to avoid irregular diagonal movements. Another case verified was the inclusion of more obstacles in the barrier to avoid these transitions. The results showed that the inclusion of the new rule did not significantly impact evacuation times, although there was a shorter time when pedestrians could shorten their escape by moving between the barriers. It was also observed that the inclusion of additional obstacles in the barrier yields the same performance as the new rule; however, there is a need to allocate more obstacle cells.

The third and final experiment assesses evacuation time with the inclusion of surmountable obstacles [30]. The evaluation considers two maps: a classroom (17×20) and a computer lab (14×20). Both scenarios include surmountable obstacles representing desks or equipment benches. The experiment evaluates the inclusion of surmountable obstacles in Varas model [31] and its CWW version. The results of the first scenario show little variation in evacuation time, regardless of the model adopted. However, the second scenario demonstrates a significant reduction in the recorded time, indicating that the inclusion of surmountable obstacles accelerated pedestrian escape in both models. The difference in performance is attributed to the positioning of the obstacles. For example, in the first scenario, the obstacles don't offer a significant advantage when being passed, which is different from the second scenario, where the positioning of the barriers offers advantages when passing. Despite the positive results, the inclusion of these obstacles disregarded pedestrians' ability to adopt other escape routes, as well as generating more realistic simulations when multiple exits are used (inclusion of the dynamic floor field).

4.2 Evacuation Dynamics in Environments with Surmountable Obstacles in the Dynamic Floor Field

To verify the effects of surmountable obstacles with the inclusion of the dynamic floor field (DFF) of [1], other experiments were carried out considering scenarios with more than a single exit. The tests used a rate $\alpha = 1$, as the influence of the DFF on the SFF, as presented in the 2.3 section. In addition, surmountable obstacles were added in each of the explored scenarios. An overtaking rate z of 30% was used in these obstacles with each pedestrian starting the simulation with the most active profile. Finally, the maximum impatience value for each pedestrian was 5 timesteps ($c \geq 5$).

The first experiments were conducted on alternative version of the computer lab map [30]. In this version an additional exit has been added to the lower right corner of the map, as show in the Fig. 9. As presented in Sect. 2.3, the DFF of [1] is applied in scenarios such as multiple exits, so that pedestrians can alternate their escape route when they encounter congested exits.

Considering the scenario in Fig. 9, the first experiment analyzes a collection of 30 executions in a fixed version of the map, that is, pedestrians maintain the same location in each test performed. Therefore, conflict resolution and the emergence of the panic phenomenon (5%) are the variations present in each execution. The test compared the average evacuation time in different approaches, such as the Varas model [31], the Varas model [31] with CWW (Sect. 3.1), the Alizadeh model [1] (inclusion of the DFF) and the new model (DFF, surmountable obstacles, pedestrian profile and impatience mechanism). The results found are summarized in Table 1. The first three approaches do not support surmountable obstacles, which negatively impacts the total evacuation time compared to the new model, since pedestrians need to go around the obstacles (in this case, laboratory tables) to reach an exit. This obstacle distribution also hampered the

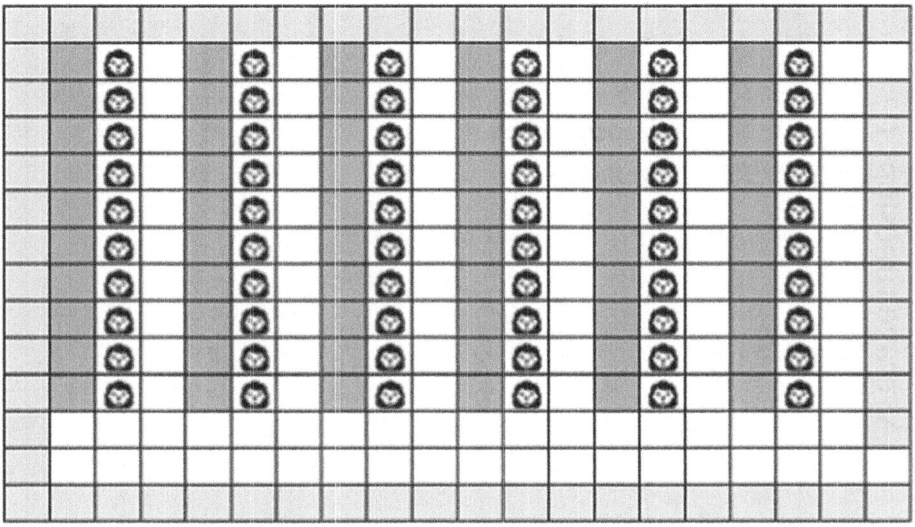

Fig. 9. Map of the computer lab (14 × 20 with 60 obstacles) with an additional exit in the bottom right area of the map.

use of the DFF, so that the [1] model tied with the CWW approach of the [31] model. The new model performed best, being 31.05% faster than the second best result.

Table 1. Average timesteps in the computer lab map with fix population.

	Varas Model	CWW	Alizadeh Model	New Model
Timesteps	125.27	114.97	114.97	79.27

By employing the concept of population density, the next experiment disregards a fixed position of pedestrians, so that 30 runs are performed for each density category, ranging from 25%, 50%, 75% and 100%. Considering the density analyzed, in each run a proportion of pedestrians is randomly distributed on the map. Figure 10 presents the results found for each density. As in the previous test, the Alizadeh model [1] and the Varas model [31] (CWW version) performed almost identically. On the other hand, the new model presented a result 39.91% better than the Alizadeh model [1], when the density was 100%. This result reflects that the support for surmountable obstacles allows pedestrians to try alternative routes, which is not possible in the other models evaluated. In addition, the new model also contains support for DFF, so that pedestrians can switch to uncongested exit routes, as well as improvise new escape routes by overcoming obstacles present in the room.

Additionally, for this experiment, the average number of conflicts was also considered as another metric in the evaluation of the results. The formation of congestion in specific cells (e.g., exit cells) increases the number of conflicts. In real dynamics,

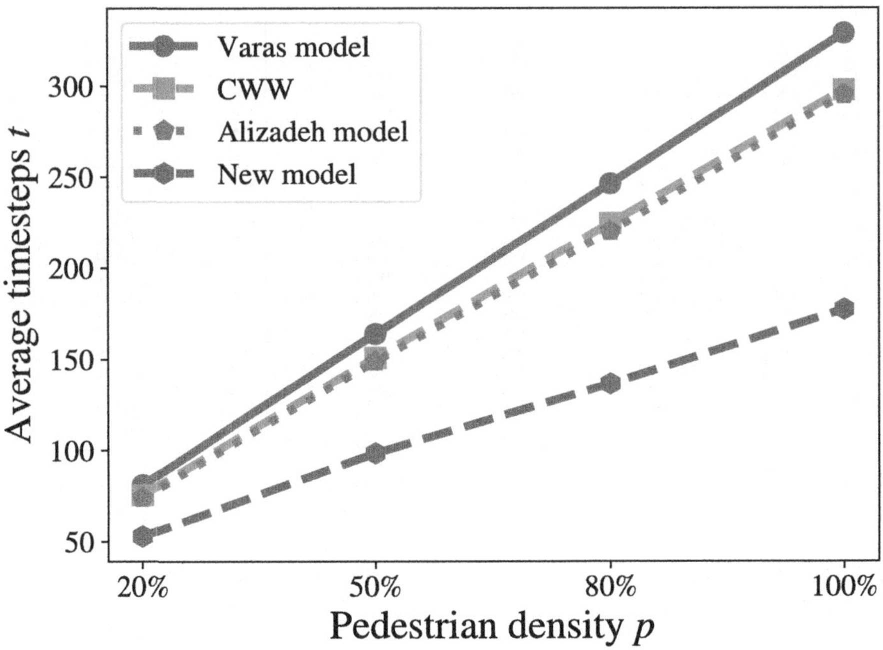

Fig. 10. Time comparison between the Varas model, the Varas model CWW version, the Alizadeh model and the new model, in the computer lab map (Fig. 9).

a crowd competing for a widely used space can generate accidents, violent disputes and risk to life. Figure 11 presents the results found in a similar way to the previous experiment. The Varas [31] model presented the lowest number of conflicts in the different density variations, despite taking the longest time when the metric considered is the evacuation time. This result comes from the fact that pedestrians tend to wait for the cells necessary for the escape route to be vacated, which can generate congestion queues, significantly reducing the number of conflicts. The other models adopt a similar dynamic to CWW, where pedestrians prioritize the empty cells with the best field values (either SFF or DFF). However, among these models, the new model presented a reduction of 37.47% in the number of conflicts when compared to the Alizadeh model [1]. The addition of surmountable obstacles creates an environment in which pedestrians can walk over obstacles, generating alternative and less crowded routes. In this scenario (Fig. 9), when obstacles are impassable, pedestrian corridors are generated, increasing the competition for cells at the ends of these barriers.

The next experiments are performed in the scenario shown in Fig. 3, which represents a classroom with several desks. Additionally, one of the desks is positioned close to one of the exits, which illustrates a situation in which poor positioning of objects could negatively interfere with the safe evacuation of pedestrians. Similar to the previous tests, the first experiment evaluates a series of 30 executions in a scenario with a fixed population distribution. The Table 2 summarizes the results obtained in the simulations. Once again, the new model presented superior performance, achieving a reduction

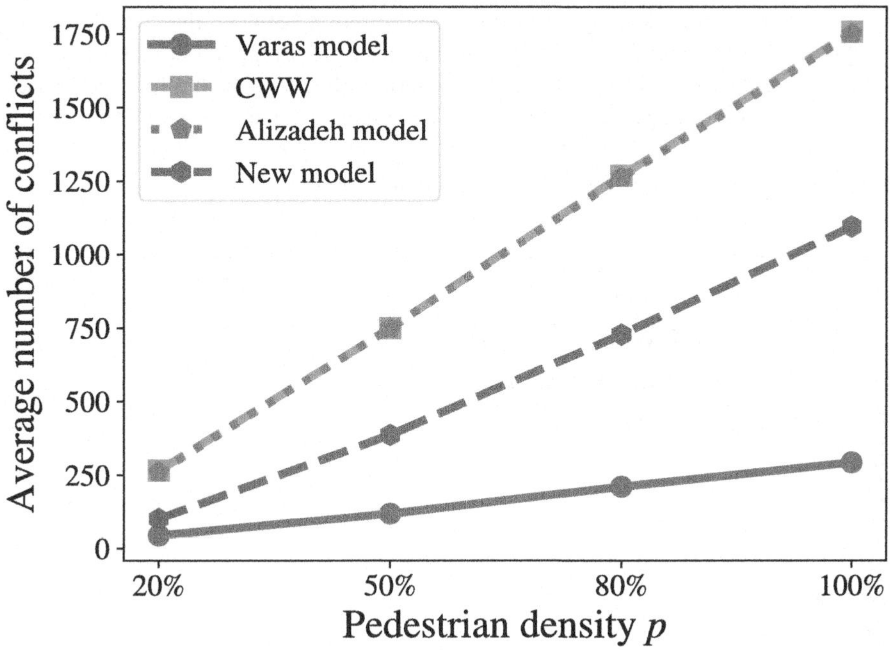

Fig. 11. Conflict comparison between the Varas model, the Varas model CWW version, the Alizadeh model and the new model, in the computer lab map (Fig. 9).

of 10.35% in the evacuation time compared to the Alizadeh model [1]. Considering the distance between the exit cells, [1] also presented a shorter time than Varas model [31] with CWW, since pedestrians were able to switch to another exit due to congestion on their escape route (a phenomenon presented in Sect. 2.3), representing the influence of DFF. Thus, by combining DFF with surmountable obstacles, the new model was able to reduce the average evacuation time, as pedestrians had the chance to bypass the tables and reach the left part of the map faster.

Table 2. Average timesteps in the classroom map with fix population.

	Varas Model	CWW	Alizadeh Model	New Model
Timesteps	83.70	75.23	62.80	56.30

The following experiment considers the scenario in Fig. 3 with a variation in population density, that is, based on the density, pedestrians are randomly positioned in map cells for each of the 30 executions. Figure 12 summarizes the results obtained in the various density categories (25%, 50%, 75% and 100%). Unlike the scenarios analyzed previously, in this test the new model tied with the Alizadeh model [1], both presenting the best results in the scenario (about 30% better than the Varas model [31] with CWW).

The tie between the models signals a possible limitation between the contributions of the support for surmountable obstacles. In this case, the arrangement of the obstacles did not form isolated corridors (unlike the scenario in Fig. 9), which allows pedestrians to move between these barriers, reducing the emergence of queues common in environments with larger barriers. On the other hand, the results of the new model did not show a significant divergence compared to the best result found.

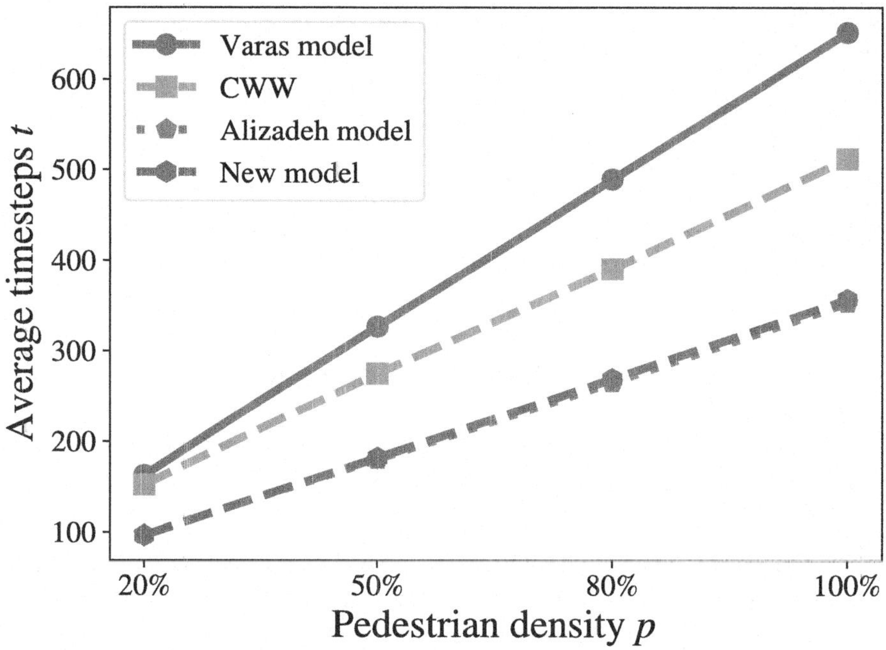

Fig. 12. Time comparison between the Varas model, the Varas model CWW version, the Alizadeh model and the new model, in the classroom map (Fig. 3).

Finally, Fig. 13 shows the performance of the models in the previous experiment when observing the metric of the average number of conflicts. As mentioned above, the original [31] model presented the lowest number of conflicts again, even though it presents the longest time in the metric of the average evacuation time. In contrast, the new model presented a lower number of conflicts between the densities of 25%, 50% and 75% compared to the other models, approaching the result obtained by the Alizadeh model [1] with the maximum capacity of the classroom. The arrangement of the obstacles in this scenario generates a greater number of cells arranged between the barriers, so that pedestrians walking between these obstacles will have greater competition for the most important cells for the escape routes. Despite the average number of conflicts, the new model presented a reduction of 22.21% compared to [1] for a population density of 50%.

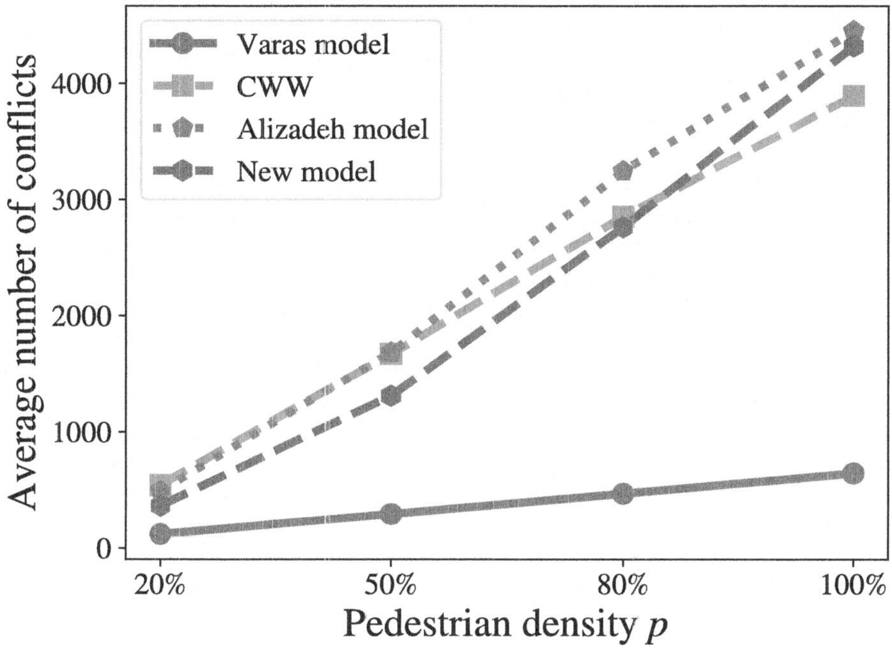

Fig. 13. Time comparison between the Varas model, the Varas model CWW version, the Alizadeh model and the new model, in the classroom map (Fig. 3).

5 Conclusion

Cellular automata (CA) are a popular choice for modeling collective pedestrian dynamics (CPD) due to their ability to efficiently simulate complex behaviors in both routine and emergency scenarios. This study builds upon two well-established foundational models in the field—the Varas [31] and Alizadeh [1] models—which are widely referenced and validated in prior research. In the original paper [30], key modifications were introduced to enhance realism, including adjustments to movement dynamics, such as restricting diagonal passage between impassable obstacles and incorporating surmountable barriers. In this extension paper, these refinements were applied to both the static and dynamic floor fields to improve accuracy.

Previously [30], the inclusion of rules to eliminate the transition between diagonally positioned barriers and the differentiation between surmountable and impassable obstacles on the static floor field improved the realism of the simulations, in addition to not negatively impacting evacuation time. With the contributions in this paper, surmountable obstacles were also integrated into the dynamic floor field of the Alizadeh model [1], allowing pedestrians to avoid congestion in important cells and seek other escape routes. Furthermore, unlike the initial approach to the SFF, this integration also allowed pedestrians to adopt new routes during the simulation through the impatience mechanism and the change of pedestrian profiles. The results of the experiments showed a significant reduction in the average evacuation time and in the average number of conflicts recorded in the scenarios analyzed: in the evacuation time metric, the new model performs 39.91% better than the Alizadeh model [1], when the density was 100%; and 37.47% better in the number of conflicts.

This research marks an important first step in refining the models proposed by [31] and [1]. Looking ahead, this work will be instrumental in enhancing the model's capacity to accurately represent real-world environments. Future investigations will explore several options. One approach involves integrating surmountable obstacles with stochastic transitions, particularly for outdoor environments with geometric complexity [29]. Another goal is to further distinguish between surmountable obstacles, assigning varying degrees of difficulty for overcoming them. Additionally, we plan to incorporate features of external environments, enabling the model to be applied in diverse settings and assist with pedestrian evacuation in those locations [32–34].

Acknowledgments. The work described in this paper was supported by CNPq (National Council for Scientific and Technological Development), CAPES (Coordination of Superior Level Staff Improvement), and Fapemig (Minas Gerais State Research Support Foundation). We also thank the reviewers for their constructive comments and suggested corrections.

Disclosure of Interests. The authors have no competing interests to declare that are relevant to the content of this article.

References

1. Alizadeh, R.: A dynamic cellular automaton model for evacuation process with obstacles. Saf. Sci. **49**(2), 315–323 (2011). https://doi.org/10.1016/j.ssci.2010.09.006
2. Blue, V., Adler, J.: Bi-directional emergent fundamental pedestrian flows from cellular automata microsimulation. Transp. Traffic Theory **14**, 235–254 (1999)
3. Blue, V.J., Adler, J.L.: Cellular automata model of emergent collective bi-directional pedestrian. Dynamics (2000). https://doi.org/10.7551/mitpress/1432.003.0061
4. Blue, V.J., Adler, J.L.: Cellular automata microsimulation of bidirectional pedestrian flows. Transp. Res. Rec. **1678**(1), 135–141 (1999). https://doi.org/10.3141/1678-17
5. Blue, V., Embrechts, M., Adler, J.: Cellular automata modeling of pedestrian movements. In: Computational Cybernetics and Simulation 1997 IEEE International Conference on Systems, Man, and Cybernetics, vol. 3, pp. 2320–2323 (1997). https://doi.org/10.1109/ICSMC.1997.635272
6. Burstedde, C., Klauck, K., Schadschneider, A., Zittartz, J.: Simulation of pedestrian dynamics using a two-dimensional cellular automaton. XXPhys. A **295**(3), 507–525 (2001). https://doi.org/10.1016/S0378-4371(01)00141-8
7. Cariño, J., Garciano, L.: Proposed evacuation safety index (ESI) for school buildings. Int. J. Disast. Resil. Built Environ. **11**(3), 309–328 (2020). https://doi.org/10.1108/IJDRBE-06-2018-0028
8. Eng Aik, L., Wee Choon, T.: Simulating evacuations with obstacles using a modified dynamic cellular automata model. J. Appl. Math. **2012**, 1–17 (2012). https://doi.org/10.1155/2012/765270
9. Gao, Q.F., Tao, Y.Z., Wei, Y.F., Wu, C., Dong, L.Y.: Simulation-based optimization of inner layout of a theater considering the effect of pedestrians*. Chin. Phys. B **29**(3), 034501 (2020). https://doi.org/10.1088/1674-1056/ab6c44

10. Giitsidis, T., Dourvas, N.I., Sirakoulis, G.C.: Parallel implementation of aircraft disembarking and emergency evacuation based on cellular automata. Int. J. High Perf. Comput. Appl. **31**(2), 134–151 (2017). https://doi.org/10.1177/1094342015584533
11. Helbing, D., Farkas, I.J., Vicsek, T.: Freezing by heating in a driven mesoscopic system. Phys. Rev. Lett. **84**(6), 1240–1243 (2000). https://doi.org/10.1103/PhysRevLett.84.1240
12. Helbing, D., Keltsch, J., Molnár, P.: Modelling the evolution of human trail systems. Nature **388**(6637), 47–50 (1997). https://doi.org/10.1038/40353
13. Helbing, D., Molnár, P.: Social force model for pedestrian dynamics. Phys. Rev. E **51**(5), 4282–4286 (1995). https://doi.org/10.1103/PhysRevE.51.4282
14. Helbing, D., Schweitzer, F., Keltsch, J., Molnár, P.: Active walker model for the formation of human and animal trail systems. Phys. Rev. E **56**(3), 2527–2539 (1997). https://doi.org/10.1103/PhysRevE.56.2527
15. Hu, M., Cai, W.: Evacuation simulation and layout optimization of cruise ship based on cellular automata. Int. J. Comput. Appl. **42**(1), 36–44 (2020). https://doi.org/10.1080/1206212X.2017.1396428
16. Huan-Huan, T., Li-Yun, D., Yu, X.: Influence of the exits' configuration on evacuation process in a room without obstacle. XXPhys. A **420**, 164–178 (2015). https://doi.org/10.1016/j.physa.2014.10.002
17. Kirchner, A., Klüpfel, H., Nishinari, K., Schadschneider, A., Schreckenberg, M.: Simulation of competitive egress behavior: comparison with aircraft evacuation data. XXPhys. A **324**(3), 689–697 (2003). https://doi.org/10.1016/S0378-4371(03)00076-1
18. Kirchner, A., Nishinari, K., Schadschneider, A.: Friction effects and clogging in a cellular automaton model for pedestrian dynamics. Phys. Rev. E **67**(5), 056122 (2003). https://doi.org/10.1103/PhysRevE.67.056122
19. Kirchner, A., Schadschneider, A.: Simulation of evacuation processes using a bionics-inspired cellular automaton model for pedestrian dynamics. XXPhys. A **312**(1), 260–276 (2002). https://doi.org/10.1016/S0378-4371(02)00857-9
20. Li, Y., Chen, M., Dou, Z., Zheng, X., Cheng, Y., Mebarki, A.: A review of cellular automata models for crowd evacuation. XXPhys. A **526**, 120752 (2019). https://doi.org/10.1016/j.physa.2019.03.117
21. Liu, S., Yang, L., Fang, T., Li, J.: Evacuation from a classroom considering the occupant density around exits. XXPhys. A **388**(9), 1921–1928 (2009). https://doi.org/10.1016/j.physa.2009.01.008
22. Ma, J., Lo, S.M., Song, W.G.: Cellular automaton modeling approach for optimum ultra high-rise building evacuation design. Fire Saf. J. **54**, 57–66 (2012). https://doi.org/10.1016/j.firesaf.2012.07.008
23. Mrowinski, M., Gradowski, T., Kosinski, R.: Models of pedestrian evacuation based on cellular automata. Acta Physica Polonica A **121**(2 B), B95–B100 (2012). https://doi.org/10.12693/aphyspola.121.b-95
24. Nagel, K., Schreckenberg, M.: A cellular automaton model for freeway traffic. J. Phys. I **2**(12), 2221–2229 (1992). https://doi.org/10.1051/jp1:1992277
25. Nishinari, K., Kirchner, A., Namazi, A., Schadschneider, A.: Extended floor field CA model for evacuation dynamics. IEICE Trans. Inf. Syst. **E87-D**(3), 726–732 (2004). https://doi.org/10.1587/e87-d.726
26. Shi, M., Lee, E.W.M., Ma, Y.: A novel grid-based mesoscopic model for evacuation dynamics. XXPhys. A **497**, 198–210 (2018). https://doi.org/10.1016/j.physa.2017.12.139
27. Shi, M., Lee, E.W.M., Ma, Y.: A dynamic impatience-determined cellular automata model for evacuation dynamics. Simul. Model. Pract. Theory **94**, 367–378 (2019). https://doi.org/10.1016/j.simpat.2019.04.003
28. Shi, M., Ming Lee, E.W., Ma, Y.: A newly developed mesoscopic model on simulating pedestrian flow. Procedia Eng. **211**, 614–620 (2018). https://doi.org/10.1016/j.proeng.2017.12.055

29. Silva, E.C., Damazo, G.S., Martins, L.G.A.: Cellular automata-based model for simulation of collective pedestrian dynamics in open-air environments with stochastic transitions and traffic signs. In: 2025 IEEE Congress on Evolutionary Computation (CEC), pp. 1–8 (2025). https://doi.org/10.1109/CEC65147.2025.11043033
30. Silva, E.C., Damazo, G.S., Oliveira, G.M.B., Martins, L.G.A.: Cellular automata-based model for simulation of collective pedestrian dynamics in indoor environments with surmountable obstacles. In: Proceedings of the 17th International Conference on Agents and Artificial Intelligence, vol. 2: ICAART, pp. 463–471. INSTICC, SciTePress (2025). https://doi.org/10.5220/0013186300003890
31. Varas, A., et al.: Cellular automaton model for evacuation process with obstacles. XXPhys. A **382**(2), 631–642 (2007)
32. Zheng, Y., Jia, B., Li, X.G., Jiang, R.: Evacuation dynamics considering pedestrians' movement behavior change with fire and smoke spreading. Saf. Sci. **92**, 180–189 (2017). https://doi.org/10.1016/j.ssci.2016.10.009
33. Zheng, Y., Jia, B., Li, X.G., Zhu, N.: Evacuation dynamics with fire spreading based on cellular automaton. XXPhys. A **390**(18), 3147–3156 (2011). https://doi.org/10.1016/j.physa.2011.04.011
34. Zhou, Z., Zhou, Y., Pu, Z., Qi, Y., Xu, Y.: An integrated cellular automata approach for spatial evacuation simulation on metro platforms with smoke spreading. Transp. Res. Rec. **2673**(11), 851–864 (2019). https://doi.org/10.1177/0361198119836985

Mitigating and Investigating Algorithm Aversion in Medical AI: The Role of Data Labeling and AI Output Adjustment in Diaphragm Detection

Keito Miyake[1,2(✉)], Kumi Ozaki[3], Akihiro Maehigashi[4], and Seji Yamada[1,2]

[1] The Graduate University of Advanced Studies, SOKENDAI, Yokohama, Japan
{m-keito,seji}@nii.ac.jp
[2] The National Institute of Informatics, Tokyo, Japan
[3] Hamamatsu University School of Medicine, Shizuoka, Japan
ozakik-rad@umin.org
[4] Shizuoka University, Shizuoka, Japan
maehigashi.akihiro@shizuoka.ac.jp

Abstract. Algorithm aversion, the reluctance of users to rely on algorithms even when they outperform human experts, remains a significant barrier to AI adoption in medical settings. This study investigates how two interaction features, labeling and modification of AI outputs, can mitigate clinicians' algorithm aversion and promote appropriate reliance among radiologists and radiographers. In Study 1, 25 participants completed a diaphragm detection task using chest X-ray images under four within-participants conditions: control, labeling, modification, and a combined condition. Analysis of variance (ANOVA) revealed a significant interaction effect between labeling and modification. Simple main effects showed that both labeling and modification significantly increased reliance on AI. Study 2 expanded the investigation to 69 medical image readers through an online survey. Results showed that personality traits such as neuroticism (negatively) and conscientiousness (positively) were significantly associated with self-efficacy. Together, these novel findings demonstrate that both interface-level interaction features and individual psychological traits critically shape clinicians' trust and reliance on AI. By showing that interactive elements such as modification and labeling can mitigate algorithm aversion, and that personality traits like neuroticism and conscientiousness influence self-efficacy, this research highlights the importance of designing adaptive AI systems that account for user variability. Such a dual approach may be essential for promoting responsible and effective AI integration in clinical workflows.

Keywords: Algorithm Aversion · Human-Computer Interaction · Reliance

1 Introduction

The adoption of artificial intelligence (AI) technologies has brought transformative changes to medical imaging, especially in domains like radiology [17, 18, 31]. Despite

H. J. van den Herik et al. (Eds.): ICAART 2025, LNAI 16517, pp. 583–602, 2026.
https://doi.org/10.1007/978-3-032-25032-2_28

these technological advancements, medical professionals often remain hesitant to rely on AI systems, even when those systems demonstrate equal or superior performance to human experts. This tendency, commonly referred to as algorithm aversion [7], presents a critical barrier to the successful adoption of AI in clinical practice.

One of the key challenges in deploying AI in medical contexts is the mismatch between system performance and user acceptance. Even when AI models are highly accurate, clinicians often remain skeptical or hesitant to rely on them, especially in critical diagnostic settings. This reluctance may stem from a lack of transparency [5], fear of accountability [15,20], or the perception that AI lacks the nuanced reasoning of human experts [11]. Consequently, high-performing AI tools are sometimes underutilized, limiting their potential impact on clinical workflows. Addressing this issue requires not only improving the technical capabilities of AI but also designing systems that support and encourage appropriate human-AI collaboration.

In this study, we aim to explore strategies that can encourage appropriate reliance on AI systems among clinicians, particularly radiologists and radiographers. Drawing on insights from interaction design and human-AI collaboration, we propose two interactive features, labeling AI outputs as correct or incorrect and modifying AI outputs, as potential means to promote user engagement and adjust reliance rates. In this context, reliance rate simply refers to how often people choose to use the AI's output instead of doing the task themselves. While literature has discussed general factors contributing to algorithm aversion, fewer studies have addressed how concrete interaction mechanisms affect reliance in real-world clinical contexts.

To investigate these questions, we conducted two empirical studies:

- Study 1 is a controlled laboratory experiment involving 25 radiologists and radiographers who performed a diaphragm detection task using chest X-ray images. This study evaluates how labeling and modification functions affect actual AI reliance rates during a specific diagnostic task.
- Study 2 extends the investigation to a larger sample of 69 radiologists and radiographers in an online setting. Instead of focusing on a particular task, Study 2 assesses participants' general willingness to use AI in their everyday diagnostic work. It also explores how psychological traits measured by the Ten Item Personality Inventory-Japanese version (TIPI-J) [25] and General Self-Efficacy Scale (GSES) [28] relate to AI reliance.

By combining behavioral data from Study 1 with psychological profiling in Study 2, our research aims to contribute to a more comprehensive understanding of how to design AI systems that are both effective and acceptable in clinical settings. Ultimately, this work seeks to inform the development of interaction strategies that optimize the balance between human expertise and AI support, thereby improving diagnostic decision-making.

Our main contributions are as follows:

- We empirically demonstrate that two simple interaction mechanisms, labeling and modification of AI outputs, can significantly increase AI reliance among radiologists in a diaphragm detection task.

- We show that psychological traits, particularly neuroticism and conscientiousness, are significantly associated with trust and self-efficacy.
- We propose a dual-perspective framework that integrates interface-level design and individual user characteristics to address algorithm aversion in clinical AI systems.

The remainder of this paper is organized as follows. Section 2 reviews prior literature on algorithm aversion, user trust, and human-AI interaction strategies in medical contexts. Section 3 presents Study 1, a controlled laboratory experiment that examines how labeling and modification functions affect reliance on AI in a diaphragm detection task. Section 4 introduces Study 2, which investigates broader tendencies in AI reliance among experienced medical image readers through an online survey incorporating psychological profiling. Section 5 discusses the findings across both studies, highlighting implications for interaction design in clinical AI. Finally, Sect. 6 summarizes our conclusions and outlines directions for future research.

2 Related Work

This section reviews previous research related to our study, focusing on the phenomenon of algorithm aversion, the various factors that contribute to it, and efforts aimed at mitigating it.

2.1 Algorithm Aversion and its Influencing Factors

Algorithm aversion refers to the tendency of individuals to distrust or reject algorithmic decisions, even when such systems outperform human judgment. [7] demonstrated that people often prefer to rely on their own judgment rather than follow algorithmic advice. This phenomenon is especially pronounced among domain experts such as medical professionals, who tend to overestimate their own diagnostic abilities and undervalue algorithmic support [11, 12, 24]. As a result, this reluctance to adopt AI tools can hinder their effective integration into clinical decision-making, despite evidence of their comparable or even superior performance [10, 22].

Beyond performance errors, algorithm aversion has been linked to user-level psychological and emotional factors, such as anxiety, trust disposition, and fairness expectations. For example, users judged ambiguous AI-generated explanations more negatively than human ones, but clear AI outputs were rated more positively [4]. Similarly, algorithmic systems often lack perceived accountability and empathy, which undermines trust in organizational settings [26].

Numerous factors contribute to algorithm aversion. These factors can be broadly categorized into four major domains: algorithm-related, task-related, individual, and high-level contextual factors [21]. Among these, individual-level characteristics such as age, professional experience, and familiarity with AI technologies significantly affect the degree of algorithm acceptance. Older or more experienced individuals tend to show stronger resistance to algorithmic advice and are more likely to favor human input [2], whereas less experienced users often demonstrate greater trust in algorithmic systems [19]. In addition, psychological aspects such as emotional reactions, perceived transparency, and previous exposure to technology further influence reliance behavior.

2.2 Approaches to Mitigating Algorithm Aversion

Recent research has explored ways to mitigate algorithm aversion and increase user reliance. One promising approach is to provide users with a degree of control over the algorithm. [8] found that allowing users to slightly modify an algorithm's output significantly increased their willingness to use it. Similarly, [6] distinguished between process control and outcome control, concluding that both forms of control can enhance user trust and decrease error rates.

Building on this foundation, [3] demonstrated that clinicians strongly prefer algorithmic systems that preserve their ability to override or adjust automated recommendations, emphasizing the importance of perceived control in high-stakes environments such as healthcare. Additionally, [27] identified that algorithm aversion often stems from the belief that algorithms cannot learn from mistakes. They showed that explicitly highlighting an algorithm's capacity to learn significantly mitigates this aversion and improves user's willingness to engage with AI recommendations.

Taken together, these findings suggest that algorithm aversion can be addressed through both interface-level interaction mechanisms. Our work extends this line of inquiry by applying these insights to clinical imaging tasks and by empirically evaluating how two specific interaction strategies, labeling and modification, affect reliance behavior among medical professionals.

2.3 Interactive Strategies in Medical AI

While the majority of prior research has examined psychological and contextual factors contributing to algorithm aversion, comparatively fewer studies have explored concrete interaction strategies that directly influence user reliance, particularly in clinical contexts. Studies such as [8] and [6] have shown that giving users partial control over algorithmic processes or outcomes can mitigate aversion and enhance adoption.

In the medical domain, however, most AI systems remain difficult to interpret and offer limited opportunities for user input or adjustment. Moreover, empirical evaluations of interactive AI in real-world clinical tasks remain scarce. This represents a significant gap, especially given the high-stakes and expertise-driven nature of medical decision-making.

Our work addresses this gap by proposing and empirically examining two simple yet practical interaction mechanisms: labeling AI outputs as correct or incorrect, and allowing users to directly modify AI-generated suggestions. Our findings provide new evidence that such interaction designs can help mitigate algorithm aversion and increase appropriate reliance among radiologists and radiographers. This study contributes to the growing intersection of human-computer interaction (HCI) and clinical AI by highlighting how interactive interface elements can support trust calibration and responsible AI integration in healthcare settings.

3 Study 1: Diaphragm Detection In-Person Experiment

3.1 Materials and Methods

Participants and Environment. A total of 25 individuals (19 men, 6 women) participated in the study. Their ages ranged from 24 to 54 years (M=30.52, SD=6.57), their years of experience ranged from 0 to 30 years (M=5.96, SD=6.96), and they were recruited from a university hospital [23]. This was a prospective study, and informed consent was obtained verbally from all participants prior to the study. 22 participants (88%) had prior experience with AI support systems, while 3 (12%) reported having no experience using them. All participants completed the study and received 2,000 yen (approximately 13 USD) for their 30-minute participation.

This experiment was conducted in the same room under controlled conditions. All experimental tasks were implemented using jsPsych 7.2.1, a JavaScript library designed for conducting behavioral experiments in web browsers. Each participant used an HP Spectre x360 with a touchscreen and the accompanying stylus to perform tasks such as button operations and modifications (Fig. 1).

40 chest radiographs were randomly selected from the NIH Chest X-ray dataset for the diaphragm detection task [32].

Diaphragm Detection Task. The experimental task required participants to detect and draw lines along the diaphragm boundaries on chest radiographs using a stylus. Each participant used a vertically oriented touch-screen display to mark the right and left diaphragm outlines in red and blue, respectively. The custom interface included standard editing features (undo, redo, and clear functions) to allow precise line drawing and error correction, as shown in Fig. 2.

This task was selected in part because it allows for intuitive and direct interaction with AI outputs. Specifically, diaphragm detection involves tasks such as drawing clear lines or boundaries, which can be easily evaluated and modified by experts. This modifiability enables medical professionals to engage with AI outputs actively, leveraging their expertise to refine the results while simultaneously building trust in the system.

Experimental Design and Hypotheses. The experiment used a within-participants design with four conditions, analyzed using a 2×2 ANOVA. The independent variables were the modification factor (enabled or disabled) and the labeling factor (enabled or disabled), and the dependent variable was the reliance rate. The study was deliberately structured into two distinct phases to measure initial algorithm aversion and subsequent changes in AI acceptance: (1) 1st condition phase: all participants completed the control condition. (2) 2nd–4th conditions phase: participants completed the remaining three experimental conditions in a randomized order.

The four conditions were as follows. (a) Control: Participants could either perform the task themselves or delegate it entirely to AI without viewing the AI output. (b) Modification: Participants could modify the AI output when choosing to use AI. (c) Labeling: Participants could label the AI output using buttons at the bottom of the screen as either correct or incorrect when choosing to use AI. (d) Combined: Both modification and labeling capabilities were available when choosing to use AI. Each participant completed all four conditions.

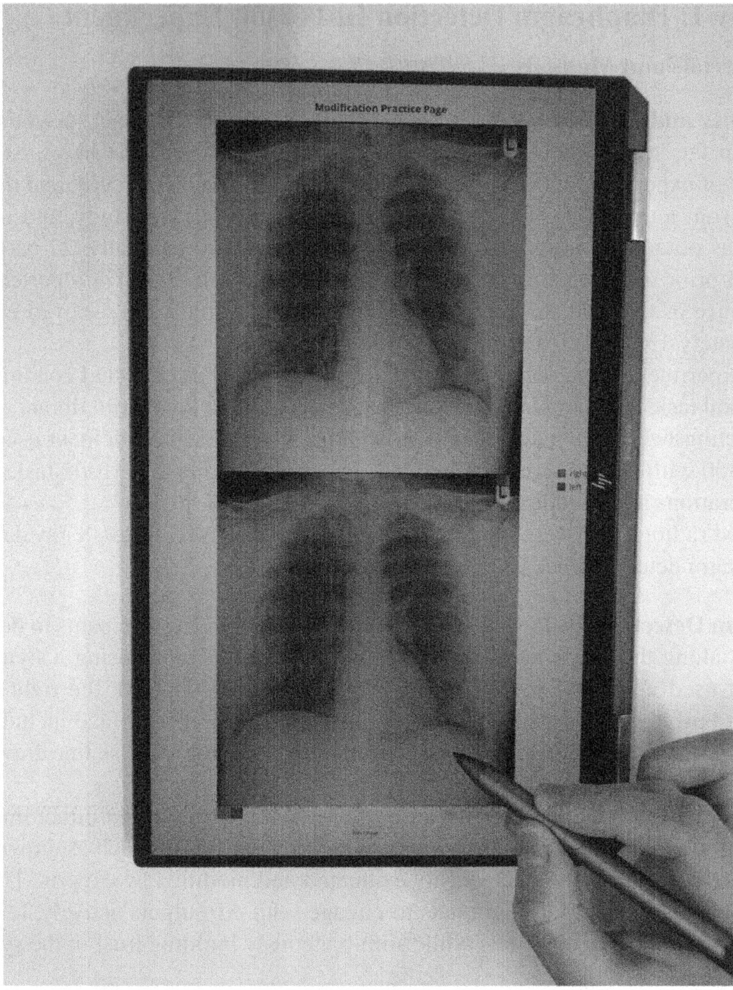

Fig. 1. Vertical touch-screen display and stylus used for diaphragm detection task.

Guided by prior research, we tested two hypotheses:

H1. Enabling radiologists to label AI outputs as correct or incorrect will increase their reliance on AI.
H2. Enabling radiologists to modify AI outputs will increase their reliance on AI.

These hypotheses are grounded in findings from non-medical domains suggesting that user control over algorithmic processes has been shown to increase AI adoption. We extended this concept to radiology, hypothesizing that providing radiologists with specific interaction capabilities would enhance their willingness to use AI assistance. The ability to modify and label AI outputs may promote a sense of collaboration rather than replacement, potentially increasing radiologists' engagement with AI systems.

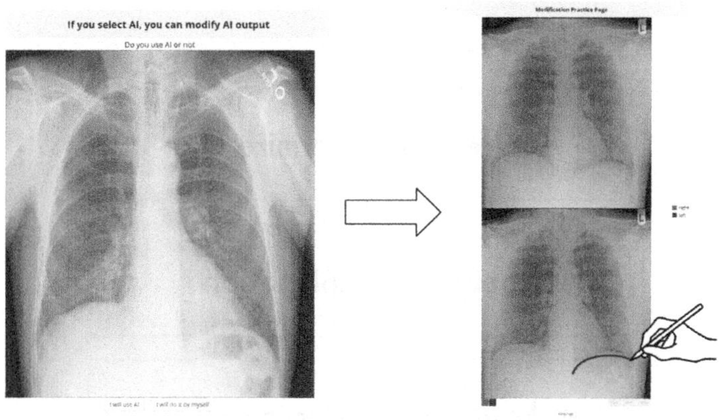

Fig. 2. Illustration of experimental setup and interface used for diaphragm boundary marking on chest radiographs. System includes color-coded annotation tools and basic editing functions.

Procedure. Figure 3 provides an overview of the experiment, which began with a pre-questionnaire collecting demographic data and assessing participants' familiarity with and attitudes toward AI. This questionnaire gathered details such as participants' gender, age, and years of professional experience in their current role.

Participants were then informed that the AI system utilized in this study had been trained on data from a radiologist with over 20 years of experience, aiming to establish the AI system's credibility. However, the AI outputs presented to them were not generated by an automated system; instead, they were manually drawn by an expert radiologist with over 20 years of experience using a stylus to draw lines directly on medical images. These were presented as AI outputs.

After this introduction, participants were reminded of the task requirements, including drawing the right and left diaphragm boundaries in red and blue, respectively. For each trial, they were given the choice to either use AI assistance or complete the task manually, regardless of experimental condition. They were also informed about the specific actions they could perform with the AI output, which were displayed above the image during each trial to ensure clarity about the interface and available options.

Participants first completed a single practice session to familiarize themselves with the stylus and touchscreen interface. This practice session involved modifying an AI output to ensure they were comfortable with the interaction method before proceeding to the main tasks.

The experiment consisted of two main phases:

- 1st condition phase: Participants completed 10 trials with no options for modification or labeling. This phase established their initial reliance rate on AI.
- 2nd-4th conditions phase: Participants performed 30 trials, with each trial randomly assigned to one of three experimental conditions: modification, labeling, or a combined condition.

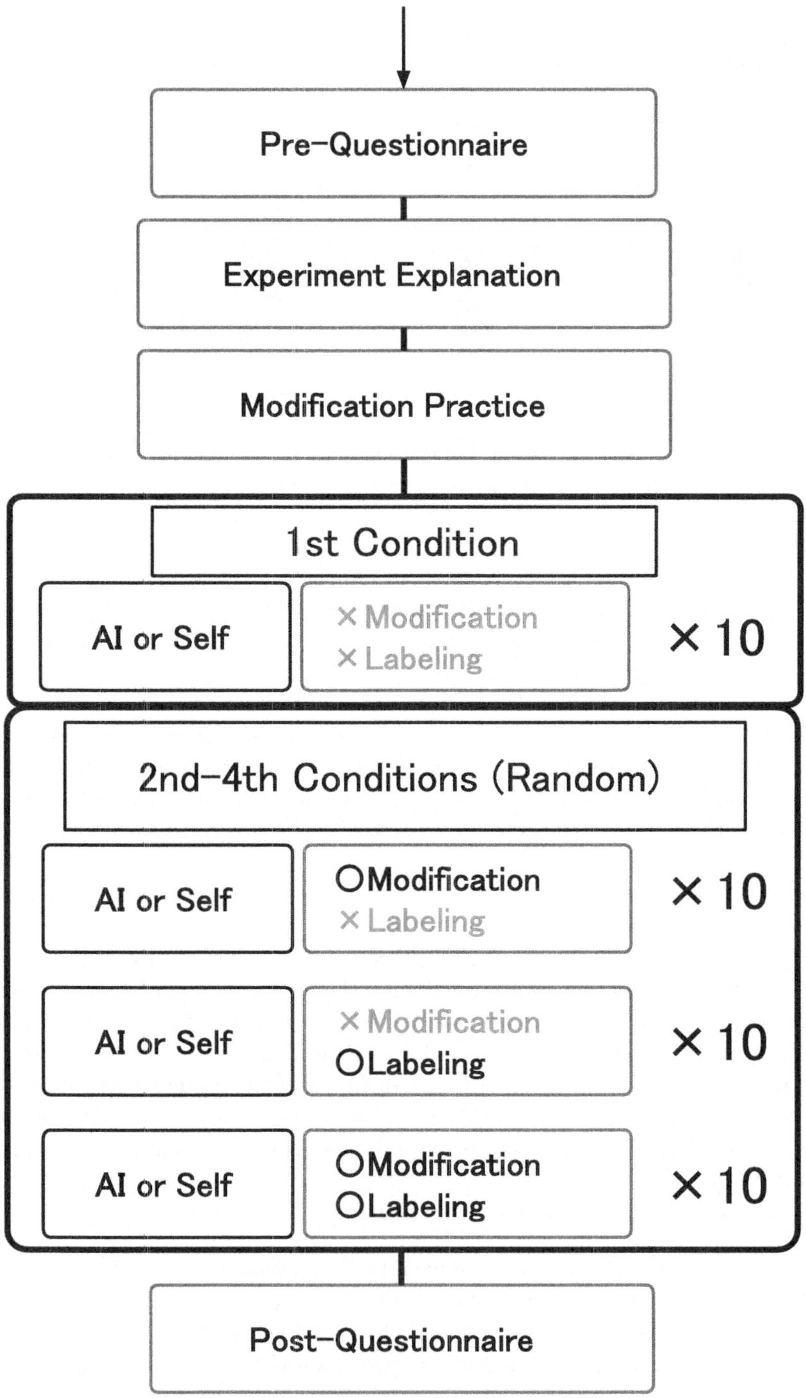

Fig. 3. Overview of experimental procedure.

At the beginning of each trial, participants were instructed to choose whether to complete the task manually or rely on the AI. The subsequent steps varied depending on the selected option and the assigned experimental condition.

- Control condition: If participants chose to use AI, the system automatically completed the task and the trial concluded. If they chose to perform the task manually, they were presented with the original X-ray image and asked to draw the relevant lines themselves.
- Labeling condition: If participants chose to use AI, two images were displayed: the original X-ray image (top) and the AI output image (bottom). Participants were asked to label the AI's output as either correct or incorrect using buttons at the bottom of the screen.
- Modification condition: If participants chose to use AI, two images were displayed as in the labeling condition. They could modify the AI's output or submit it as-is if they agreed with the AI output.
- Combined condition: Participants first evaluated the AI output by labeling it as either correct or incorrect, following the same procedure as in the labeling condition. If the output was labeled as incorrect, they were given the opportunity to modify it, as in the modification condition.

After completing all 40 trials, participants were asked to fill out a post-questionnaire to gather feedback and assess their experiences during the experiment.

Statistical Analysis. Sample size was determined through a priori power analysis using G*Power 3.1 [9]. For a two-way repeated measures ANOVA with an effect size of 0.25, significance level of 5%, and power of 80%, the analysis indicated a required sample size of 24 participants.

The primary measure was the reliance rate, defined as the proportion of cases in which participants chose to use the AI output rather than their own assessment. The secondary measures included confidence ratings and responses to the pre- and post-questionnaire.

The ANOVA was performed to assess the difference in reliance rate between the four conditions, and a post-hoc analysis was performed using the R package. The Holm method was used to adjust p-values for multiple comparisons, and partial eta squared was calculated to assess effect sizes. Pre- and post-experiment questionnaire responses were compared using paired t tests. All statistical analyses were performed using the R software.

3.2 Results

To evaluate how the interactive features affected participants' behavior, we analyzed their reliance rate, the proportion of trials in which participants chose to use the AI output rather than perform the task manually. This metric served as a behavioral indicator of trust and willingness to engage with AI assistance under each experimental condition.

The reliance rates observed in each condition were: 46.0% in the control condition, 75.6% in the labeling condition, 78.0% in the modification condition, and 78.8% in the combined condition.

A two-way ANOVA was conducted to examine the effects of the modification and labeling conditions on reliance rates. The analysis revealed a significant interaction effect between the two factors ($F(1, 24)$=19.39, $p < 0.00$). Therefore, we analyzed the simple main effects (Table 1). The results showed significant differences: in the labeling condition ($F(1, 24)$=27.24, $p < 0.00$, $\eta^2 = 0.53$)(Fig. 4) and in the modification condition ($F(1, 24)$=21.19, $p < 0.00$, $\eta^2 = 0.47$)(Fig. 5). In Table 1, boldface indicates statistically significant p-values ($p < 0.05$)

Table 1. Simple main effects of modification (mod) and labeling (label).

Conditions	SS	df	MS	F	p	η^2
mod under (label=enabled)	1.28	1	1.28	1.95	0.18	0.08
mod under (label=disabled)	128.00	1	128.00	21.19	**<0.00**	0.47
label under (mod=enabled)	0.08	1	0.08	0.08	0.78	0.00
label under (mod=disabled)	109.52	1	109.52	27.24	**<0.00**	0.53

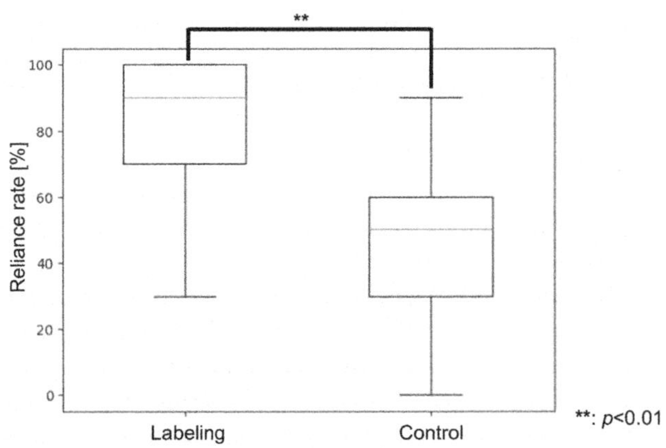

Fig. 4. Reliance rates across control and labeling conditions. Center line in box is median.

In the modification condition, 67.2% of participants who selected AI assistance submitted the results without making any changes to the AI output. This indicates that while participants had the opportunity to modify the AI output, the majority chose to accept the AI outputs as they were. The remaining participants made adjustments to the AI outputs before submitting them, utilizing the modification feature provided in this condition.

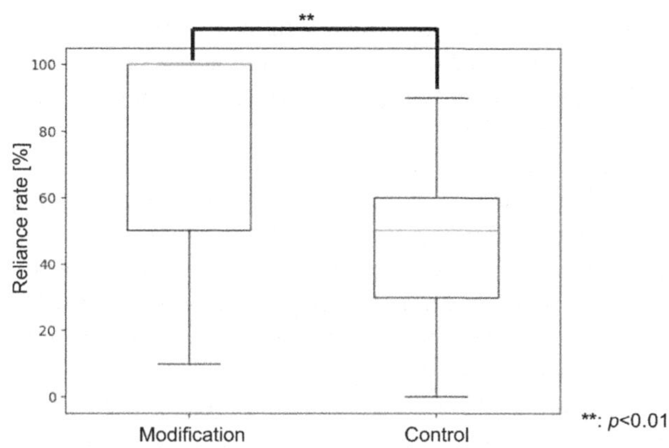

Fig. 5. Reliance rates across control and modification conditions. Center line in box is median.

Pre- and post-experiment questionnaire analysis revealed significant increases in self-confidence in diagnostic abilities (pre: 1.36±0.86[SD]; post: 1.64±0.76[SD]; $p < .01$), experience to learn AI (pre:1.20±1.08[SD]; post: 1.52±1.08[SD]; $p < .01$), and perceived AI capability (pre: 2.44±0.82[SD]; post: 2.72±0.74[SD]; $p < .01$)(Table 2).

Table 2. Paired *t*-test results with descriptive statistics and effect sizes.

Item (English translation)	Pre M	Pre SD	Post M	Post SD	t	p
I am confident in my own radiology-based diagnoses	1.36	0.86	1.64	0.76	−2.28	0.03
I have studied AI before	1.20	1.08	1.52	1.08	−2.55	0.02
I use AI tools in my private life	1.48	1.39	1.60	1.32	−0.72	0.48
I think current AI performance is high enough	2.44	0.82	2.72	0.74	−2.28	0.03
I believe AI technology is essential for society	3.40	0.87	3.40	0.71	0.00	1.00

3.3 Discussion

As a brief summary of the hypotheses, both were supported. Allowing radiologists to label AI outputs as correct or incorrect (H1), as well as enabling them to modify AI outputs (H2), led to increased reliance on AI.

Our findings suggest that the availability of labeling and modification functions not only increased participants' reliance on AI but also contributed to a reduced sense of algorithm aversion. These interaction features likely provided users with a sense of control, allowing them to assess, intervene, and adjust AI outputs. This perception of being able to supervise the AI system, rather than blindly follow it, may have empowered users and helped maintain their professional autonomy. As a result, radiologists could engage with the AI more confidently, not as a replacement but as a collaborative tool, thus reducing resistance and promoting appropriate reliance.

The increase in self-confidence might be attributed to the interactive nature of our approach, where radiologists maintained active control over the final diagnosis through modification and labeling capabilities. Rather than perceiving AI as a replacement, participants may have experienced an enhanced sense of agency in their decision-making process. This aligns with previous findings suggesting that user control over AI systems can enhance users' perceived control and trust, which may in turn support confidence in their professional decision-making [6,8].

The improved perception of AI capabilities may reflect participants' direct experience with a well-designed human-AI interaction system. By allowing radiologists to actively engage with and refine AI outputs, our approach may have demonstrated the practical value of AI assistance while respecting radiologists' expertise. This suggests that algorithm aversion might be effectively addressed not just through improved AI performance, but through careful consideration of how humans interact with AI systems.

4 Study 2: General Tendency of AI Reliance in Experienced Medical Image Readers

4.1 Research Objectives

The primary objective of this study was to investigate general patterns of reliance on AI in medical imaging and to explore how this reliance is related to individual differences among medical image readers, particularly their years of experience and personality traits. To achieve this, an online survey was administered to professionals with experience in medical reading. The survey was designed to quantitatively assess the degree to which participants would choose to rely on an AI system with superior diagnostic performance and to examine how this reliance is associated with psychological and demographic variables.

Recent research has highlighted that trust in AI systems, particularly in critical fields such as healthcare, is shaped not only by technical performance but also by individual user characteristics such as personality traits, cognitive style, and technology-related attitudes [13,29]. For instance, conscientiousness and openness to experience have been associated with higher trust in and acceptance of AI, while neuroticism often correlates negatively with trust [14,30]. Self-efficacy, individuals' belief in their ability to manage challenges, has been shown to moderate the relationship between trust and technology adoption [1,16]. These findings suggest that clinicians' psychological disposition can significantly influence how they perceive and engage with AI-based decision support systems.

Building on these insights, our study aims to complement the behavioral findings of Study 1 by identifying psychological factors of AI reliance in clinical settings. By analyzing the relationships between trust in AI, self-efficacy, and Big Five personality traits, this research contributes to a more nuanced understanding of the human factors that shape medical professionals' willingness to integrate AI into diagnostic workflows.

4.2 Method

A total of 69 individuals (38 men, 29 women, 2 participants did not report their gender) with experience in reading medical images participated in the study. Their ages ranged from 27 to 74 years (M = 37.97, SD = 9.31). Their years of experience ranged from 0 to 44 years (M = 10.55, SD = 9.86). Participants were recruited via email invitations sent to radiologists and medical professionals affiliated with a university hospital.

All participants completed an anonymous online survey using Google Forms. The survey was conducted in Japanese and consisted of multiple sections covering demographic information, clinical experience, attitudes toward AI in medical imaging, trust in AI, perceived impact on professional identity, and various psychological traits. The questionnaire included both open-ended and closed-ended items, with Likert scale formats used for attitudinal and personality assessments.

To assess general self-efficacy, the survey included the General Self-Efficacy Scale (GSES) [28], a 16-item scale that measures individuals' belief in their ability to cope with a wide range of demanding or novel situations. Participants rated each item on a 5-point Likert scale, with higher scores indicating stronger perceived self-efficacy.

In addition, personality traits were evaluated using the Ten Item Personality Inventory - Japanese version (TIPI-J) [25], a brief measure of the Big Five personality dimensions: extraversion, agreeableness, conscientiousness, neuroticism, and openness to experience. Each trait is assessed by two opposing statements, rated on a 7-point Likert scale. This inventory was chosen for its brevity and validity in capturing broad personality tendencies relevant to cognitive and behavioral patterns in clinical decision-making.

4.3 Results

Participants reported a high reliance rate on the AI system, with an average of 92.39 out of 100 cases where they would choose to use AI for diagnosis. This suggests a generally positive disposition toward integrating AI into their diagnostic workflows.

Table 3 provides a complete list of the survey items used in Study 2, along with their descriptive statistics. These include items measuring trust in AI, perceived control through interaction, self-efficacy (GSES), and Big Five personality traits (TIPI-J).

To investigate the psychological factors associated with self-efficacy and trust in AI, Pearson's correlation coefficients were calculated between the GSES scores and TIPI-J subscales. The results revealed several significant relationships.

Most notably, conscientiousness was positively and significantly correlated with self-efficacy (r = 0.39, p < 0.00). Additionally, openness to experience (r = 0.35, p < 0.00) and extraversion (r = 0.37, p < 0.00) were also significantly and positively associated with self-efficacy. In contrast, neuroticism showed a strong negative correlation with self-efficacy (r = −0.65, p < 0.00). Agreeableness, while positively correlated (r = 0.19), did not reach statistical significance (p = 0.12).

To provide an overview of the relationships among all measured variables, we constructed a correlation matrix (Fig. 6) including all survey items, personality traits, and GSES scores. The matrix highlights both expected patterns—such as the strong negative association between neuroticism and self-efficacy—and other nuanced relationships, including associations between perceived control over AI and trust-related responses.

Table 3. Survey items with full descriptions and descriptive statistics.

Category	Survey Item (English)	Mean	SD
AI Reliance Rate	How many out of 100 cases would you use AI for diagnosis?	92.39	0.71
AI Reliance Reason	Please briefly explain the reason for your answer		
AI Attitudes	Do you trust AI in general?	3.36	0.71
AI Attitudes	Do you have high expectations for AI in medicine?	4.42	0.55
AI & Work Anxiety	Do you feel a sense of threat that AI might take your job?	2.75	1.12
Accountability	Do you think AI will be able to take diagnostic responsibility in the future?	1.88	0.93
Peer/AI Feedback	Would you re-evaluate your diagnosis if a colleague pointed out a potential error?	4.59	0.71
Peer/AI Feedback	Would you re-evaluate your diagnosis if AI pointed out a potential error?	4.29	0.67
AI Reliance Intention	Would you actively use AI in your diagnostic process?	4.19	0.73
Confidence in their skill	Are you confident in your diagnostic skill?	2.80	1.05
Perceived Control via Modification	Do you feel that being able to modify AI results gives you control over the AI?	3.26	0.83
Perceived Control via Labeling	Do you feel that being able to label AI results as 'correct' or 'incorrect' gives you control over the AI?	3.03	0.89
GSES	I can always manage to solve difficult problems if I try hard enough	2.94	0.86
GSES	If someone opposes me, I can find the means and ways to get what I want	3.93	0.83
GSES	It is easy for me to stick to my aims and accomplish my goals	2.62	0.94
GSES	I am confident that I could deal efficiently with unexpected events	3.03	0.92
GSES	Thanks to my resourcefulness, I can handle unforeseen situations	3.64	0.89
GSES	I can solve most problems if I invest the necessary effort	2.64	1.00
GSES	I can remain calm when facing difficulties because I can rely on my coping abilities	3.51	0.95
GSES	When I am confronted with a problem, I can usually find several solutions	3.26	0.99
GSES	If I am in trouble, I can usually think of a solution	2.70	1.02
GSES	I can handle whatever comes my way	3.00	0.87
GSES	I can deal with unexpected events effectively	2.97	1.01
GSES	I can find solutions in difficult situations	2.99	1.12
GSES	I am resourceful in achieving my goals	3.03	1.10
GSES	I can remain confident under pressure	3.52	0.96
GSES	I can solve complex problems on my own	3.01	1.04
GSES	I feel prepared to meet most demands in life	3.32	0.81
TIPI-J	I see myself as extraverted, enthusiastic	3.59	1.52
TIPI-J	I see myself as critical, quarrelsome	2.90	1.32
TIPI-J	I see myself as dependable, self-disciplined	3.68	1.44
TIPI-J	I see myself as anxious, easily upset	4.51	1.46
TIPI-J	I see myself as open to new experiences, complex	4.12	1.48
TIPI-J	I see myself as reserved, quiet	4.16	1.46
TIPI-J	I see myself as sympathetic, warm	4.36	1.44
TIPI-J	I see myself as disorganized, careless	4.35	1.42
TIPI-J	I see myself as calm, emotionally stable	3.64	1.35
TIPI-J	I see myself as conventional, uncreative	4.14	1.42

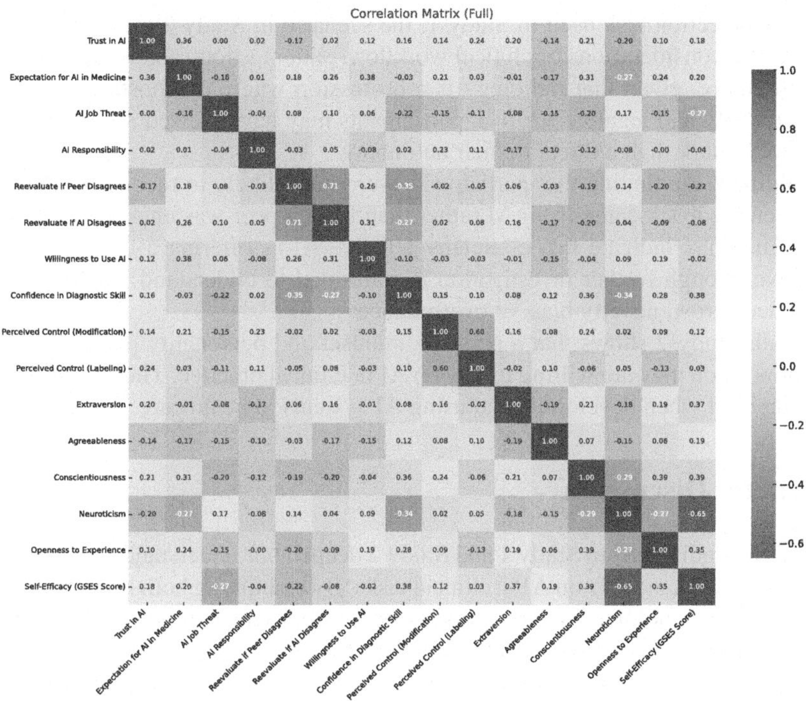

Fig. 6. Full correlation matrix including psychological traits, attitudes toward AI, and self-efficacy score.

4.4 Discussion

The results of Study 2 reveal that individual differences in psychological traits and self-efficacy are significantly associated with clinicians' attitudes toward and trust in AI-based diagnostic systems. In particular, conscientiousness and openness to experience were positively correlated with general self-efficacy, while neuroticism was negatively associated with both self-efficacy and trust in AI. These patterns suggest that personality traits may influence not only general confidence in clinical practice, but also willingness to integrate AI into diagnostic workflows.

Interestingly, while most participants reported a generally favorable view of AI and expressed a willingness to use it in clinical practice, there remained noticeable concerns about responsibility and professional identity. For example, responses indicated ambivalence regarding whether AI could ultimately assume diagnostic accountability. This tension may reflect a broader uncertainty about the appropriate boundaries between human and machine roles in high-stakes medical contexts.

Notably, the reliance rate in Study 2 was already high (M = 92.39) even though participants had not interacted with labeling or modification functions. One possible explanation is that the survey questions were embedded in a concrete clinical context, particularly image-based diagnosis, where clinicians are already accustomed to seeking second opinions and managing diagnostic risk. Compared to the more abstract diaphragm detection task used in Study 1, the scenario in Study 2 may have triggered more realistic considerations of clinical workflow, patient safety, and legal accountability. Furthermore, given that radiology is a profession where diagnostic responsibility is both ethically and legally sensitive, participants may have viewed AI as a pragmatic support tool rather than a threat to their autonomy.

In addition, the finding that participants were more likely to reconsider their diagnoses when feedback came from AI rather than from a peer was unexpected and noteworthy. This may indicate that clinicians perceive AI as offering a fresh or objective perspective, though further investigation is warranted to understand whether this tendency reflects trust, novelty bias, or overreliance.

Overall, Study 2 shows that a person's mindset and personality play an important role in how much they are willing to rely on AI in clinical practice. These factors should be kept in mind when developing and using AI systems in healthcare.

5 General Discussion

Together, the findings from Study 1 and Study 2 deepen our understanding of how clinicians come to trust and rely on AI in clinical tasks. By examining both interaction design and user-level psychological factors, this research offers a multidimensional perspective on algorithm aversion and AI acceptance in clinical settings.

Study 1 showed that incorporating simple interaction features, specifically the ability to label and modify AI outputs, significantly increased behavioral reliance on AI during image interpretation. These features appear to mitigate algorithm aversion not by improving performance, but by giving users a sense of control and agency. Clinicians responded more favorably when they could intervene in AI decisions, reinforcing the idea that trust is strengthened when users feel they are collaborating with, rather than being overruled by, the AI.

Study 2 extended this view by highlighting how individual differences shape attitudes toward AI. Personality traits such as conscientiousness and openness to experience were positively associated with self-efficacy, which in turn was linked to greater trust and intention to use AI. Conversely, high neuroticism was strongly correlated with lower self-efficacy and greater skepticism. Interestingly, even without exposure to interactive features, participants reported a high AI reliance rate ($M = 92.39$), suggesting that broader contextual factors, such as legal and professional responsibility norms, may motivate clinicians to use AI as a supplemental safety mechanism.

Taken together, the two studies underscore the need for human-centered AI implementation strategies in healthcare. Rather than focusing exclusively on improving algorithmic accuracy, system designers must also consider how interaction design and individual differences jointly influence trust, control, and acceptance. A key insight is that personalization does not only mean customizing recommendations for patients, but also adjusting interface design and training for the clinician user.

This research contributes to the field in three key ways. First, it provides empirical evidence that simple interface, such as one that enables feedback or minor corrections, can meaningfully shift clinician behavior. Second, it bridges experimental findings with psychological profiling, showing that AI reliance is shaped by both what systems allow and who the users are. Third, it contributes to growing discussions on adaptive AI by highlighting how design and disposition must be aligned to foster appropriate and ethically sound reliance.

5.1 Limitations

Despite its contributions, this study has several limitations.

First, the AI outputs used in Study 1 were not generated by a live model but manually made by a radiologist. While this ensured quality and consistency, it may have limited the ecological validity of the participants' perceptions of AI behavior and error patterns.

Second, both studies were conducted in controlled or self-report environments, which may not fully capture the complexities of clinical decision-making under time pressure or in multi-stakeholder settings.

Third, our samples consisted predominantly of radiologists and radiographers from academic institutions in Japan. As such, cultural or institutional factors may limit the generalizability of our findings to other healthcare contexts or medical specialties.

Fourth, the reliance rates observed in both studies may have been influenced by implicit or explicit guidelines or task expectations. In Study 2, the high proportion of participants reporting AI use may reflect a tendency to confirm adherence to perceived best practices, rather than autonomous clinical behavior. In Study 1, the lower reliance rate in the control condition could be partially explained by the absence of visible AI output, which inherently prevented participants from delegating decisions and thus reduced measurable reliance. Moreover, because the task was not a direct clinical decision-making task, participants may have used AI selectively on the basis of individual judgment rather than uniformly rejecting or embracing it.

Finally, while we focused on reliance as a measurable behavior, future work could benefit from assessing diagnostic accuracy, user confidence over time, and team dynamics in collaborative AI use.

5.2 Future Work

Building on the current findings, several avenues for future research emerge.

First, future studies should evaluate the long-term effects of interactive features such as labeling and modification, particularly in repeated-use scenarios and live clinical deployments. It is important to assess not only short-term reliance but also sustained engagement and diagnostic performance.

Second, adaptive interfaces that adjust how they interact with users on the basis of individual characteristics such as risk aversion, self-efficacy, or trust calibration could be developed and tested. Such personalized interaction strategies may further optimize AI acceptance and usage in diverse clinical populations.

Third, to address concerns around over-reliance and accountability, future research should explore hybrid decision-making models where AI outputs are weighed alongside human judgment, with explicit responsibility-sharing mechanisms.

Last, integrating these findings into medical education and clinical guidelines may provide an opportunity to align AI system design with professional norms and ethical expectations, fostering responsible and effective AI collaboration in healthcare.

6 Conclusion

This study examined how interactive features in AI systems can mitigate algorithm aversion and promote appropriate reliance among medical professionals. In Study 1, a controlled experiment showed that allowing users to label or modify AI outputs significantly increased their reliance on AI during a diaphragm detection task by enhancing their sense of control. Study 2 extended these findings by revealing that psychological and demographic factors, particularly self-efficacy and personality traits like neuroticism and conscientiousness, significantly influence trust in AI.

These results suggest that algorithm aversion is shaped by both system design and individual traits. Designing AI systems that are not only technically accurate but also human-centered and psychologically adaptive is essential. Interactive mechanisms such as labeling and modification can foster trust, customized for different users. Future work should explore long term use in clinical settings and develop adaptive interfaces that align with users' traits to support ethical and effective AI integration in healthcare.

Acknowledgments. This work was partially supported by JST, CREST (JPMJCR21D4), Japan.

References

1. Afroogh, S., Akbari, A., Malone, E., Kargar, M., Alambeigi, H.: Correction: trust in AI: progress, challenges, and future directions. Humanit. Soc. Sci. Commun. **12**(1), 1–1 (2025)
2. Arkes, H.R., Dawes, R.M., Christensen, C.: Factors influencing the use of a decision rule in a probabilistic task. Organ. Behav. Hum. Decis. Process. **37**(1), 93–110 (1986)
3. Bankuoru Egala, S., Liang, D.: Algorithm aversion to mobile clinical decision support among clinicians: a choice-based conjoint analysis. Eur. J. Inf. Syst. **33**(6), 1016–1032 (2024)
4. Buder, J., Becker, F., Bareiß, J., Huff, M.: Beyond mere algorithm aversion: are judgments about computer agents more variable? Commun. Res. (2024)
5. Cecil, J., Lermer, E., Hudecek, M.F.C., Sauer, J., Gaube, S.: Explainability does not mitigate the negative impact of incorrect AI advice in a personnel selection task. Sci. Rep. **14**(1), 1–15 (2024)
6. Cheng, L., Chouldechova, A.: Overcoming algorithm aversion: a comparison between process and outcome control. In: Proceedings of the 2023 CHI Conference on Human Factors in Computing Systems, No. Article 756 in CHI '23, New York, NY, USA, pp. 1–27 (2023)
7. Dietvorst, B.J., Simmons, J.P., Massey, C.: Algorithm aversion: people erroneously avoid algorithms after seeing them err. J. Exp. Psychol. Gen. **144**(1), 114–126 (2015)
8. Dietvorst, B.J., Simmons, J.P., Massey, C.: Overcoming algorithm aversion: people will use imperfect algorithms if they can (even slightly) modify them. Manag. Sci. **64**(3), 1155–1170 (2018)
9. Faul, F., Erdfelder, E., Lang, A.G., Buchner, A.: G*Power 3: a flexible statistical power analysis program for the social, behavioral, and biomedical sciences. Behav. Res. Methods **39**(2), 175–191 (2007)

10. Filiz, I., Judek, J.R., Lorenz, M., Spiwoks, M.: The extent of algorithm aversion in decision-making situations with varying gravity. PLoS ONE **18**(2), e0278751 (2023)
11. Gaube, S., et al.: Do as AI say: susceptibility in deployment of clinical decision-aids. NPJ Digit. Med. **4**(1), 31 (2021)
12. Jussupow, E., Spohrer, K., Heinzl, A.: Radiologists' usage of diagnostic AI systems. Bus. Inf. Syst. Eng. **64**(3), 293–309 (2022)
13. Kauttonen, J., Rousi, R., Alamäki, A.: Trust and acceptance challenges in the adoption of AI applications in health care: quantitative survey analysis. J. Med. Internet Res. **27**, e65567 (2025)
14. Kaya, F., Aydin, F., Schepman, A., Rodway, P., Yetişensoy, O., Demir Kaya, M.: The roles of personality traits, AI anxiety, and demographic factors in attitudes toward artificial intelligence. Int. J. Hum. Comput. Interact. 1–18 (2022)
15. Klingbeil, A., Grützner, C., Schreck, P.: Trust and reliance on AI – an experimental study on the extent and costs of overreliance on AI. Comput. Human Behav. **160**(108352), 108352 (2024)
16. Kwak, Y., Ahn, J.W., Seo, Y.H.: Influence of AI ethics awareness, attitude, anxiety, and self-efficacy on nursing students' behavioral intentions. BMC Nurs. **21**(1), 267 (2022)
17. Lee, J.H., Hong, H., Nam, G., Hwang, E.J., Park, C.M.: Effect of human-AI interaction on detection of malignant lung nodules on chest radiographs. Radiology **307**(5), e222976 (2023)
18. Lew, C.O., et al.: Artificial intelligence outcome prediction in neonates with encephalopathy (AI-OPiNE). Radiol. Artif. Intell. e240076 (2024)
19. Logg, J.M., Minson, J.A., Moore, D.A.: Algorithm appreciation: people prefer algorithmic to human judgment. Organ. Behav. Hum. Decis. Process. **151**, 90–103 (2019)
20. Maasland, C., Weißmüller, K.S.: Blame the machine? Insights from an experiment on algorithm aversion and blame avoidance in computer-aided human resource management. Front. Psychol. **13**, 779028 (2022)
21. Mahmud, H., Islam, A.K.M.N., Ahmed, S.I., Smolander, K.: What influences algorithmic decision-making? a systematic literature review on algorithm aversion. Technol. Forecast. Soc. Change **175**, 121390 (2022)
22. Meyer, A.N.D., Payne, V.L., Meeks, D.W., Rao, R., Singh, H.: Physicians' diagnostic accuracy, confidence, and resource requests: a vignette study. JAMA Int. Med. **173**(21), 1952–1958 (2013)
23. Miyake, K., Ozaki, K., Maehigashi, A., Yamada, S.: Adjusting doctor's reliance on AI through labeling for training data and modification of AI output in a muscle tissue detection task. In: Proceedings of the 17th International Conference on Agents and Artificial Intelligence (ICAART 2025), pp. 837–844 (2025)
24. Nazaretsky, T., Ariely, M., Cukurova, M., Alexandron, G.: Teachers' trust in AI -powered educational technology and a professional development program to improve it. Br. J. Edu. Technol. **53**(4), 914–931 (2022)
25. Oshio, A., Abe, S., Cutrone, P.: Development, reliability, and validity of the japanese version of ten item personality inventory (TIPI-J). Pasonariti Kenkyu **21**(1), 40–52 (2012)
26. Parent-Rocheleau, X., Parker, S.K.: Algorithms as work designers: how algorithmic management influences the design of jobs. Hum. Res. Manag. Rev. **32**(3), 100838 (2022)
27. Reich, T., Kaju, A., Maglio, S.: How to overcome algorithm aversion: learning from mistakes. J. Consum. Psychol. **33**(2), 285–302 (2022)
28. Sakano, Y., Tojo, M.: Development of the general self-efficacy scale (GSES) [in Japanese]. Jpn. J. Behav. Therapy **12**(1), 73–82 (1986)
29. Steerling, E., Siira, E., Nilsen, P., Svedberg, P., Nygren, J.: Implementing AI in healthcare-the relevance of trust: a scoping review. Front. Health Serv. **3**, 1211150 (2023)
30. Stein, J.P., Messingschlager, T., Gnambs, T., Hutmacher, F., Appel, M.: Attitudes towards AI: measurement and associations with personality. Sci. Rep. **14**(1), 2909 (2024)

31. Sukegawa, S., et al.: Effectiveness of deep learning classifiers in histopathological diagnosis of oral squamous cell carcinoma by pathologists. Sci. Rep. **13**(1), 1–9 (2023)
32. Wang, X., Peng, Y., Lu, L., Lu, Z., Bagheri, M., Summers, R.M.: ChestX-Ray8: hospital-scale chest X-ray database and benchmarks on weakly-supervised classification and localization of common thorax diseases. In: 2017 IEEE Conference on Computer Vision and Pattern Recognition (CVPR), pp. 3462–3471 (2017)

Hybrid Transfer-Learning with Custom Centering (TLCC) Framework for Industrial Images Clustering

Selvine G. Mathias(✉), Saara Asif, Muhammad Uzair Akmal, Leonid Koval, Simon Knollmeyer, and Daniel Grossmann

AImotion Bavaria, Technische Hochschule Ingolstadt, Esplanade 10, 85049 Ingolstadt, Germany
{SelvineGeorge.Mathias,Saara.Asif,MuhammadUzair.Akmal,Leonid.Koval, Simon.Knollmeyer,Daniel.Grossmann}@thi.de

Abstract. This paper presents a novel framework for analyzing clustering performance in industrial image grouping by integrating advanced initialization strategies with deep feature representations. Specifically, we propose the use of custom initial cluster centers derived through optimal matchings computed via the Hungarian algorithm. These centers are utilized within a deep embedded clustering (DEC) framework, with image features extracted from a range of pre-trained Convolutional Neural Networks (CNNs), including VGGNets, EfficientNets, ResNets, and DenseNets. By factoring in informed initialization, the framework enables stakeholders to incorporate prior domain knowledge into the clustering process, reducing dependence on random seeding with the intent of guiding the algorithm towards suggestive groupings. We evaluate the proposed approach using clustering accuracies and FM Scores and conduct a comparative analysis across different feature spaces induced by the various CNNs. The results demonstrate that our method yields competitive groupings of production-related images compared to random and model-based initialization approaches, highlighting its potential for deployment in real-world industrial settings where accurate unsupervised classification is critical.

Keywords: Transfer Learning · Custom Center Initialization · Deep Clustering

1 Introduction

Can transfer learning (TL) combined with clustering effectively address defect detection in industrial parts? Do custom image representatives from industrial data provide sufficient information to segregate image data in industrial environments? In this study, we attempt to address these questions in an investigative capacity with a straightforward framework consisting of available convolutional networks and a simple yet effective customized clustering layer to achieve some level of initial segregation meant for further inspection.

In recent years, TL has emerged as a powerful technique in the field of machine learning, particularly for applications in industrial settings [32]. TL leverages pre-trained models, often developed on large-scale datasets, to solve specific tasks with

H. J. van den Herik et al. (Eds.): ICAART 2025, LNAI 16517, pp. 603–621, 2026.
https://doi.org/10.1007/978-3-032-25032-2_29

limited data [12,18,22]. This approach is instrumental in industrial contexts where labeled data is scarce or expensive to obtain. By fine-tuning these pre-trained models on domain-specific data, industries can achieve high performance in image classification, defect detection, and quality assurance tasks.

In addition to classification tasks, image clustering analysis has gained traction as an unsupervised learning approach to discover patterns and group similar data points without labeled examples. One prominent method in this area is the Deep Embedded Clustering (DEC) algorithm [27], which simultaneously learns feature representations and cluster assignments. DEC has shown promise in grouping similar images into meaningful clusters, aiding in tasks such as anomaly detection and automated tagging. Recent studies have expanded on DEC by incorporating more sophisticated feature extraction techniques and refining the clustering process [9,11]. These advancements have made it possible to apply clustering to complex datasets, where the distinction between classes may not be well-defined.

The motivation for this work stems from several persistent challenges in the industrial application of image analysis. A significant issue is the absence of a streamlined, automated process for image labeling, which remains labor-intensive, time-consuming, and prone to human bias. Manual annotation not only increases operational costs but also introduces variability that can negatively affect model performance [15]. While unsupervised learning methods such as Deep Embedded Clustering (DEC) offer a promising alternative, they pose their own difficulties—most notably in determining the optimal number of clusters and ensuring the consistency of learned feature representations [27]. Building upon these challenges, our prior work [19] proposed a framework that employed pre-trained CNN encoders and classical clustering methods for industrial image grouping, with an emphasis on sub-clustering guided by custom metrics like C-Score. Although effective in isolated use cases, that approach relied heavily on domain-specific cues and intermediate near-labels. In contrast, the present study shifts the focus toward enhancing main clustering performance by introducing a custom center initialization technique based on the Hungarian algorithm. Furthermore, it emphasizes generalizability across diverse datasets (CD, DAGM, MVTEC), moving from task-specific optimization toward a more flexible and scalable clustering framework for industrial imaging contexts.

To summarize, this paper makes two important contributions to address these challenges:

1. We propose the construction of a complete setup that leverages different existing CNNs to reduce and extract features from images.
2. We introduce a custom centroid assignment method using the Hungarian algorithm within the network, which optimizes the clustering process by ensuring more accurate and consistent cluster assignments.

Together, these contributions aim to streamline the image labeling process in industrial contexts, minimize human bias, and overcome the limitations of current unsupervised learning approaches. We refer to this approach as *Hybrid Transfer Learning with Custom Centering (TLCC) Framework*.

2 State-of-the-Art

2.1 TL and Clustering in Industrial Applications

TL has emerged as a powerful technique for enhancing image-based machine learning applications in industrial environments, particularly when dealing with limited labeled data. Recent research has demonstrated its effectiveness across various industrial use cases. For instance, [17] developed a dual memory algorithm capable of sequential or incremental learning for complex image task recognition in an industrial context. In [16], another light-weight incremental class learning algorithm for live image recognition was developed to classify images while learning new classes at several sites simultaneously. In the context of industrial part recognition, [14] applied TL using a pre-trained InceptionNet-V3 model to classify small samples of industrial machine parts, achieving 99.74% accuracy. TL in unsupervised settings was also implemented in [20] where adversarial deep learning was used in a framework to perform unsupervised transfer learning (UTL) for one-class classification problems. Similar to our work, [5] also presented an unsupervised TL with K-means clustering to achieve higher image classification accuracy without the need for labeled training data.

Clustering in machine learning is an unsupervised learning technique that partitions a dataset into distinct groups or clusters based on the similarity of data points, enabling the identification of inherent structures and patterns within the data without prior labeling [23]. Clustering images has also been expanding due to the sheer volume of available methods and techniques in modern times. It has been heavily used in applications such as multi-feature extraction techniques like [4,10,23,31].

Centroid-based (Partitioning) clustering techniques, such as K-means and K-medoids, categorize data points by minimizing the distance to a central point, requiring the number of clusters to be specified in advance [21]. These methods employ various distance metrics, including Euclidean, Manhattan, and Minkowski, to determine similarity between data points [25]. While computationally efficient, they are sensitive to initial centroid placement and may not effectively capture non-convex cluster shapes. In contrast, density-based clustering, exemplified by DBSCAN, identifies clusters based on data point density, allowing for the discovery of arbitrarily shaped clusters and the automatic determination of the number of clusters [30]. This approach is robust to outliers but can struggle with datasets of varying densities. Connectivity-based (Hierarchical) clustering, which can be agglomerative (bottom-up) or divisive (top-down), builds a hierarchy of clusters, often visualized through dendrograms. It does not require a pre-specified number of clusters, offering flexibility in the analysis, but can be computationally expensive for large datasets [13]. Finally, distribution-based clustering, as implemented in Gaussian Mixture Models, assigns data points to clusters based on underlying probability distributions, typically assuming a Gaussian form [1]. This method effectively handles overlapping clusters but relies on assumptions about the distribution of data, which may not always hold true in practice.

2.2 DEC Algorithm

Deep Clustering methods integrate deep learning techniques with traditional clustering approaches to enhance the clustering process, particularly in high-dimensional or complex data scenarios [25]. These methods typically employ neural networks, such as autoencoders or convolutional neural networks [2], to learn feature representations that are more conducive to clustering. By transforming raw data into a lower-dimensional latent space, deep clustering methods can better capture the intrinsic structures and relationships within the data, leading to more accurate and meaningful clusters. This approach can also adaptively learn the feature space and clustering simultaneously [24], as seen in techniques like DEC and Variational Deep Embedding (VaDE). However, deep clustering requires careful design and tuning of the network architecture and loss functions, and it can be computationally intensive, necessitating specialized hardware for efficient processing.

The DEC algorithm is a method that combines deep learning and clustering by jointly optimizing a deep neural network and clustering assignments. Introduced by [27], DEC performs unsupervised learning by embedding data points into a lower-dimensional latent space via a deep neural network and subsequently clustering these embeddings. It uses an autoencoder to learn low-dimensional representations $\mathbf{z}$ from input data $\mathbf{x}$, then iteratively refines cluster centers μ_j by minimizing the Kullback-Leibler (KL) divergence between a soft cluster assignment distribution Q and a target distribution P:

$$\mathrm{KL}(P\|Q) = \sum_i \sum_j p_{ij} \log \frac{p_{ij}}{q_{ij}},$$

where q_{ij} represents the probability of assigning $\mathbf{z}_i$ to cluster j, and p_{ij} is the target distribution emphasizing high-confidence cluster assignments.

Recent works have extended DEC by incorporating various enhancements. For example, IDEC (Improved DEC) by [9] integrates reconstruction and clustering into a single stage, and VaDE (Variational Deep Embedding) by [11] combines variational autoencoders with clustering. These methods have shown superior performance on various datasets, including MNIST, CIFAR-10, and SVHN. The DEC algorithm and its variants have been successfully applied in fields such as image processing, text analysis, and bioinformatics, demonstrating their versatility and effectiveness in unsupervised learning tasks.

2.3 Research Gap

The main objective of this paper is to mitigate labeling image issues in industrial cases with a minimal system. DEC and its improved versions have shown immense potential in image and text clustering and classification scenarios [4,27]; however, the implementation in actual industry-level scenarios has been lacking. Additionally, many novel deep learning techniques in the literature are implemented primarily on generalized datasets such as MNIST, Reuters, Image-Net, etc. [4,9,32]. For example, since DEC is configured to train on generalized datasets including colors, its effect on production-related images that are mainly either black and white or grey-scale can only be obtained once it is implemented and fine-tuned. The absence of color in the datasets is a key difference between our study and others. Building a clustering model from scratch using deep neural networks is possible, but it is a demanding task. It requires technical expertise, domain-specific knowledge, and careful tuning of model parameters, hyperparameters, and the input feature space.

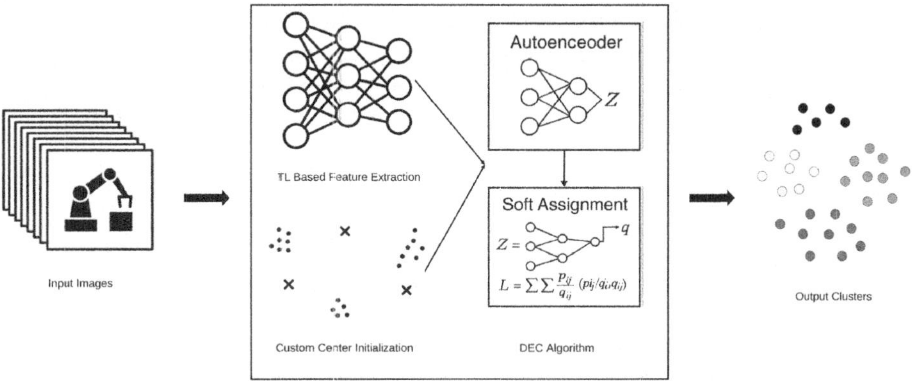

Fig. 1. Hybrid TLCC Framework for Industrial Image Clustering.

Customizing centroids or centers for clustering has also been studied in [33] where the method includes using Principal Component Analysis (PCA) on data and achieving a split into percentiles to get the efficient initial coordinates and in [29], where threshold based hybrid distance calculations are used to obtain centers. These studies were conducted on numerical datasets, as well as focus was to obtain computational optimality in terms of clustering. For image clustering scenarios, extracting custom initial images has not been explored to the best of our knowledge.

3 Hybrid TLCC Framework

This framework extends the core idea of the DEC algorithm, which unifies representation learning and clustering by mapping input data into a latent space through an autoencoder and assigning soft labels using a clustering objective [27]. While DEC effectively captures structure in data, it typically depends on custom-designed autoencoders, which may limit its adaptability across diverse image types.

In contrast, our approach incorporates a TL component to enhance generalization. We extract features using robust, pre-trained CNNs such as VGG, EfficientNet, ResNet, and DenseNet. These TL-based features are then used to initialize cluster centers not via traditional k-means, but through an optimized assignment using the Hungarian algorithm. This initialization can leverage either user-defined reference points or cluster summaries from existing methods, reducing randomness and improving stability. The refined features and initialized centers are then processed through the DEC pipeline—consisting of an autoencoder and soft assignment module—resulting in comparable output clusters. The framework is presented in Fig. 1.

3.1 Feature Leveraging Through CNNs

We use pre-trained CNNs such as VGGNets, ResNets, DenseNets, and EfficientNets to extract high-quality feature representations from production-related images. These networks are trained on extensive datasets like ImageNet, and the pre-trained weights are used to circumvent training features from the concerned datasets.

The common feature extraction process for all these CNNs involves removing the final softmax layer and using the output from the last layer before the softmax, which can be generalized as follows:

$$\mathbf{f}_{\mathrm{CNN}} = \mathrm{GAP/FC}(\mathrm{FeatureLayers}(\mathbf{x}))$$

where:

- $\mathbf{f}_{\mathrm{CNN}}$ represents the extracted feature representation,
- GAP/FC denotes either the global average pooling or fully connected layer, depending on the specific CNN architecture,
- FeatureLayers represents the series of convolutional or dense blocks specific to each CNN (VGGNet, ResNet, DenseNet, EfficientNet),
- $\mathbf{x}$ is the input image.

Specifically:

- For VGGNets, FeatureLayers corresponds to the convolutional layers followed by flattening, and GAP/FC is the fully connected layer.
- For ResNets, DenseNets, and EfficientNets, FeatureLayers corresponds to the respective convolutional blocks, and GAP/FC is the global average pooling layer.

We also include Inception and XCeption models in the list. Only the recent versions available in *Tensorflow* module of Python are used in this study.

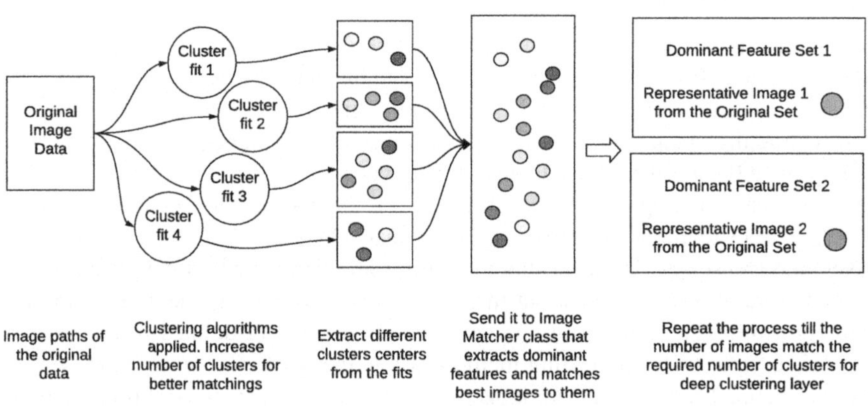

Fig. 2. Methodology for Custom Center Initialization through Hungarian Algorithm.

3.2 Custom Center Initialization

After feature extraction, we use the Hungarian algorithm to achieve a level of control over center initialization. The Hungarian algorithm, also known as the *Kuhn-Munkres* algorithm, is designed to solve the assignment problem efficiently by finding the minimum cost matching in a weighted bipartite graph [6,28].

The implemented system facilitates the comparison and matching of images across multiple sets using feature descriptors derived from the Scale-Invariant Feature Transform (SIFT) algorithm. Initially, SIFT descriptors $\mathbf{D}_{i,j}$ are extracted from each image i in set j. For each set, the descriptors are aggregated into a representative feature vector $\mathbf{A}_j$ by computing the mean of the descriptors:

$$\mathbf{A}_j = \frac{1}{n_j}\sum_{i=1}^{n_j} \mathbf{D}_{i,j}$$

where n_j denotes the number of images in set j, and $\mathbf{D}_{i,j}$ represents the descriptors from the i-th image in the j-th set.

To facilitate matching between images from different sets, a cost matrix $\mathbf{C}$ is computed to quantify the similarity between descriptors of images from different sets. The cost matrix is derived from the Euclidean distances between the descriptors of images in two sets, $\mathbf{D}_{i,j}$ and $\mathbf{D}_{k,l}$:

$$C_{i,k} = \|\mathbf{D}_{i,j} - \mathbf{D}_{k,l}\|$$

where $C_{i,k}$ represents the cost of matching the i-th descriptor from set j with the k-th descriptor from set l.

The optimal image matching is determined by applying the Hungarian algorithm to this cost matrix. The algorithm provides a solution that minimizes the total matching cost, resulting in an assignment of image pairs that maximizes similarity. Specifically, the algorithm finds row indices r_i and column indices c_i that minimize the total cost:

$$\text{Minimize} \sum_i C_{r_i, c_i}$$

Finally, the implementation gives the best-matched images based on the optimal assignments, along with their indices, and also identifies any unmatched images. This enables a thorough comparison of image sets based on feature similarity.

This image-matching algorithm is iterative, especially for unmatched images. It starts by computing optimal matches using feature descriptors and a cost matrix. Unmatched images are retained for further processing. The algorithm then reapplies the matching process to these images, iteratively narrowing down the pool until the desired number of clusters or matches is reached. This approach ensures that final clusters contain significantly different images, as matches from previous iterations are excluded from the next rounds (Fig. 2).

3.3 Deep Clustering Layer

In this layer, we adopt a methodology similar to that used in DEC for optimizing parameters and approximating target distributions. This layer builds upon the feature representations extracted by pre-trained CNNs and the custom centers derived from the Hungarian algorithm. The core objective is to refine the cluster assignments by iteratively updating both the deep feature representations and the clustering parameters. The deep clustering layer minimizes the KL divergence between the soft cluster assignment distribution Q and the target distribution P, which emphasizes high-confidence cluster assignments. We approximate the target distribution using a Student's t-distribution, which provides a robust way to handle outliers and better manage uncertainty in cluster assignments. The target distribution p_{ij} for each data point i and cluster j is given by:

$$p_{ij} = \frac{\left(1 + \frac{\|\mathbf{z}_i - \mathbf{c}_j\|^2}{\alpha}\right)^{-\frac{\alpha+1}{2}}}{\sum_k \left(1 + \frac{\|\mathbf{z}_i - \mathbf{c}_k\|^2}{\alpha}\right)^{-\frac{\alpha+1}{2}}} \tag{1}$$

where $\mathbf{z}_i$ is the feature representation of data point i, $\mathbf{c}_j$ is the centroid of cluster j, and α is a parameter controlling the degree of softness in the cluster assignments.

The deep clustering layer iteratively refines the feature representations and adjusts the cluster centers based on this target distribution. The network parameters are optimized to ensure that the learned feature space aligns with the target cluster assignments derived from the Student's t-distribution.

3.4 Evaluation Criterion

In evaluating the performance of our clustering framework, we use clustering accuracy derived from the Hungarian algorithm to assess the quality of the cluster assignments. This criterion involves calculating the best possible match between the ground truth labels and the clusters assigned by our framework models. By applying the Hungarian algorithm to match the predicted clusters with the true labels, we determine the optimal assignment that maximizes the accuracy of the clustering. Specifically, the Hungarian algorithm helps find the assignment that minimizes the total assignment cost, thereby providing the highest accuracy for each image's cluster membership. The clustering accuracy A is computed as follows:

$$A = \frac{1}{n} \max \sum_{i=1}^{n} \delta(y_i, \text{match}(c_i))$$

where:

- n is the total number of images,
- y_i is the true label of the i-th image,
- c_i is the cluster assignment for the i-th image,
- $\text{match}(\cdot)$ represents the optimal mapping function determined by the Hungarian algorithm,
- $\delta(\cdot, \cdot)$ is the Kronecker delta function which is 1 if the arguments are equal and 0 otherwise.

To ensure the evaluation is fair in interpretation, we also calculate the Fowlkes-Mallows (FM) Score. It is calculated based on the precision and recall of the clustering results. Specifically, it is the geometric mean of the pairwise precision (the proportion of pairs that are in the same cluster in both the predicted and true labels) and pairwise recall (the proportion of pairs in the same true cluster that are also in the same predicted cluster).

The FM score is defined as:

$$\text{FM} = \sqrt{\frac{TP}{TP + FP} \times \frac{TP}{TP + FN}}$$

where:

- TP (True Positives) is the number of pairs correctly clustered together.
- FP (False Positives) is the number of pairs incorrectly clustered together.
- FN (False Negatives) is the number of pairs that are in the same true cluster but are placed in different predicted clusters.

The score ranges from 0 to 1, where 1 indicates a perfect match between the predicted and true clusters, and 0 indicates no similarity.

The choice of clustering accuracy over other metrics such as ARI or NMI reflects our purpose of addressing the problem of optimal matching between clusters by minimizing the total cost (or maximizing the total similarity) of assigning predicted clusters to true clusters.

4 Experiments

We describe the experimental application in two phases: description of public datasets used and implementation of the framework on these.

4.1 Datasets and Pre-processing

Three datasets available in the public domain were used in this study. Each dataset retains some common characteristics representative of industrial environments, such as grey-scale and uniform resolution. Additionally, each dataset comes with its ground truth labels that have been used in this study for evaluation.

- **Casting Data (CD):** The Real Life Industrial Dataset of Casting Product, available on Kaggle, contains grayscale images of casting products from an industrial manufacturing process, categorized into "defective" and "ok" classes [7]. For this study, the data from directory **casting_512x512** without augmentation is used. There are a total of 1300 images divided into two folders **def_front** and **ok_front**.
- **DAGM:** The DAGM 2007 Competition Dataset for Optical Inspection, available on Kaggle, consists of high-resolution grayscale images used to benchmark algorithms for automated defect detection in industrial settings. This dataset includes images of various industrial surfaces, both with and without defects, simulating real-world scenarios for optical inspection tasks [26]. The data for **Class1** with its defects are used in this study. The two folders downloaded are **Class1** and **Class1_def**. The total number of images here is 1150.

- **MVTEC:** This dataset contains over 5,000 high-resolution images across 15 different object and texture categories, including items such as bottles, cables, and metal nuts for benchmarking anomaly detection methods in industrial applications. Each category includes a variety of defect types, such as scratches, dents, and contaminations, as well as a set of defect-free images. We use only the category of screw data [3]. The data from category **screw** is used with a total of 439 images. There are many categories of defects that are combined into one folder for this study. The images in the directory **good** are considered non-defective, while the rest are combined into the defective **bad** folder.

4.2 Implementation Scheme

Pre-processing. The CNN layer is initialized with weights from *Imagenet* to leverage pre-existing learned features, facilitating the evaluation of each network in the framework while minimizing the need for extensive model customization. Each dataset is categorized into *defect* and *no defect* groups, establishing the number of clusters for analysis at 2. For pre-processing, all images are resized to a fixed dimension of 224 pixels to manage computational complexity and ensure uniformity across datasets. Augmentation techniques, specifically flipping and rotation, are applied to increase the diversity of the training data without modifying color or contrast. Despite the images being in greyscale, a general approach is maintained by setting the number of color channels to 3, avoiding the need for a dedicated greyscale filter.

Execution. The complete network is executed for three cases:

- **Random Centers:** This corresponds to training the network with no additional tuning. The centers in this case are randomly initialized.
- **Model-Based Centers:** Here, the centers are initialized with the centers that are obtained by fitting an initial clustering model. This is a similar technique to that implemented in the DEC algorithm. To keep the execution light, we chose to fit only the K-means algorithm to provide initial centers.
- **Custom Centers:** This is where the centers obtained through the Hungarian algorithm are fed into the network. The linear sum assignment function from scikit-learn is used to obtain such a function.

In the third case, custom centers from different fits are generated separately to avoid overloading the network. Users can adjust the logic for selecting basic sets for the linear sum assignment. Custom cluster centers are extracted three times to ensure consistency.

Due to the framework's complexity, with various models increasing time and structure demands, we limit the number of execution runs to one, testing the practical implementation. Comparing these results to diverse clustering models from other studies would be unfair since they aren't trained on the same datasets. Instead, a baseline is provided using a simple CNN model for transfer learning and basic clustering algorithms like K-Means from Scikit-Learn. This straightforward approach is sufficient to evaluate the initial segregation of image data. Each case yields clustering accuracy and FM scores for the applied datasets.

5 Results and Discussions

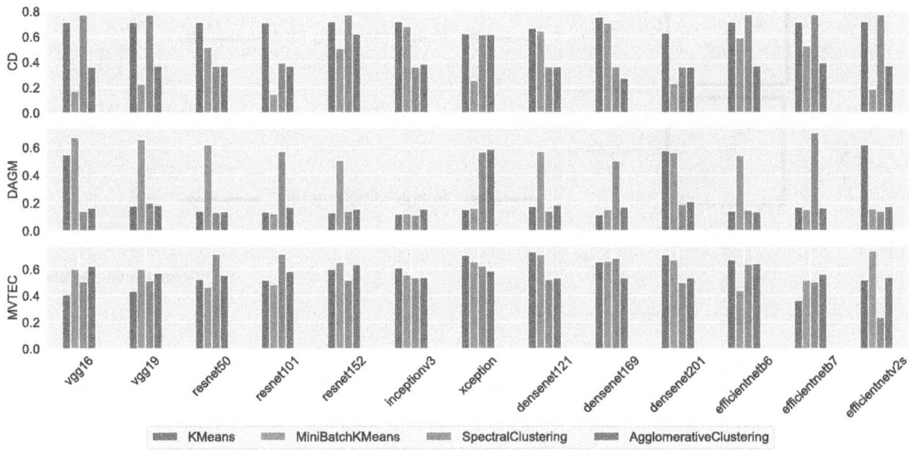

Fig. 3. Benchmark Clustering Accuracies for the different CNNs with direct clustering.

5.1 Benchmark Performances of Shell Framework

Before the hybrid TLC approach is applied, the shell framework yields clustering accuracy performances, which were averaged over 5 runs as shown in Fig. 3. The benchmark clustering accuracy across the three datasets—CD, DAGM, and MVTEC—shows divergent trends. While there are variations in performance, the overall accuracy remains modest, with no clear standout among the models or clustering techniques. The more advanced models like ResNet and EfficientNet do not significantly outperform simpler alternatives, suggesting that the added complexity may not be yielding the expected gains in clustering accuracy. This indicates that while the methods employed are functional, there is still room for improvement in achieving higher accuracy across different datasets.

5.2 Custom Center Effect on Framework Performance

The custom center approach presents a unique approach to initialize cluster centers for many algorithms. A trial-and-error method of using a pre-fitted clustering algorithm on the data to obtain cluster centers can be used, as in the case of DEC. However, the proposed approach transcends the initialization of the process by optimizing the selection of cluster centers based on different fits or user-defined inputs. Specifically, when different algorithms yield varying initial centers, the Hungarian algorithm facilitates the selection of the most optimal, distinct centers from these options. This results in visually acceptable cluster center initialization, as demonstrated by its application to the

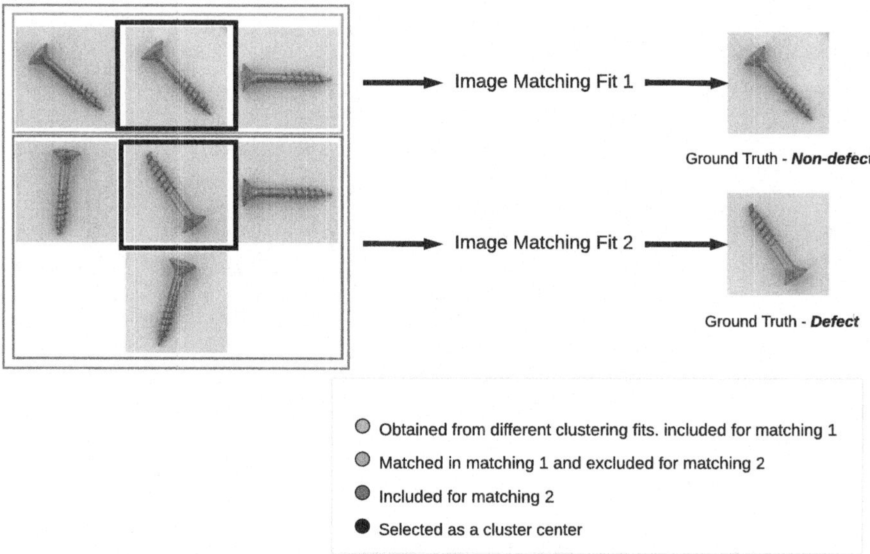

(a) MVTEC dataset.

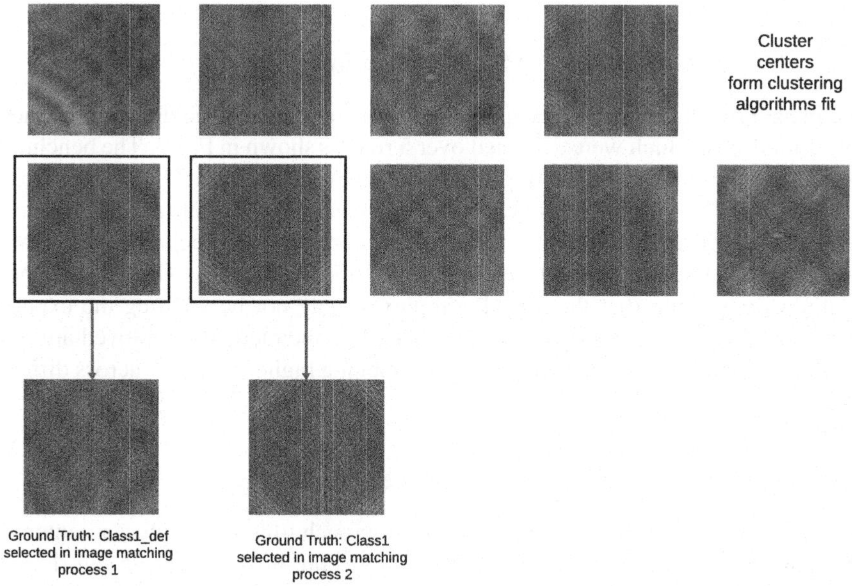

(b) DAGM dataset.

Fig. 4. Results of Image Matching for Custom Centering a) MVTEC Dataset b) DAGM Dataset.

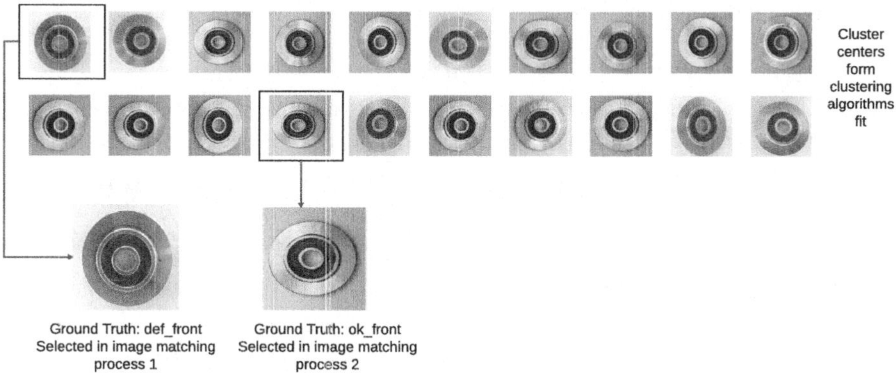

Fig. 5. Results of Image Matching for Custom Centering on CD Dataset.

three datasets in Fig. 4 and Fig. 5. The two selected centers are representative of their respective ground truths.

In our experiments, we utilized K-means and Minibatch K-means to generate multiple sets of cluster centers while increasing the number of clusters to provide the algorithm with a broader selection of divergent centers. This case not only expands the potential cluster options but also ensures the inclusion of more diverse clusters. Notably, we observed that both algorithms occasionally produced identical cluster centers. This repetition, when processed by the image-matching algorithm, enhances the distinctiveness of the selected cluster centers. However, if the cluster centers are repeated more than three times in the same fit, then the process is adapted to pick the next closest image.

Another notable observation of this approach is that instead of giving initial clustering fits to this algorithm, a user can fill the selection pool with his/her centers, which are deemed useful for further clustering. This pool can also be mixed with the centers obtained from the clustering algorithms to increase diversity. However, this is not applied in this study as this concerns the efficiency of image selection for the process, which is not the primary focus.

5.3 Clustering Analysis

Table 1 and Table 2 present the clustering accuracies and FM scores of the applied framework on the three datasets, respectively.

The performance across Random, Model-based, and Custom cases varies significantly in clustering accuracy and FM scores across the CD, DAGM, and MVTEC datasets. The Model-based case consistently excels, particularly on the DAGM dataset, with models like **vgg19**, **resnet152**, and **efficientnetb7** achieving high clustering accuracy and FM scores, often reaching peak values like **0.875** and **0.884**. This suggests its effectiveness in guiding and refining data clusters for structured tasks.

The Random case is surprisingly competitive, especially in CD and DAGM datasets, with models like **xception**, **densenet121**, **efficientnetb6**, and **efficientnetb7** achieving

Table 1. Clustering accuracies of the different models used in the framework.

Model	CD			DAGM			MVTEC		
	Rand.	Model	Custom	Rand.	Model	Custom	Rand.	Model	Custom
vgg16	0.569	0.550	0.671	0.534	0.867	0.805	0.561	0.662	0.548
vgg19	0.549	0.645	0.700	**0.875**	0.874	0.793	0.535	0.554	**0.644**
resnet50	0.557	0.628	0.645	0.809	0.849	0.735	0.527	0.615	0.564
resnet101	0.586	0.615	0.676	0.548	0.520	**0.843**	0.647	0.662	0.591
resnet152	0.583	0.583	0.592	0.842	0.859	0.842	0.543	0.523	0.529
inceptionv3	0.597	0.604	0.597	0.810	0.524	0.607	**0.733**	**0.708**	0.612
xception	**0.690**	0.530	0.605	0.703	0.726	0.741	0.682	**0.708**	0.623
densenet121	0.603	0.569	**0.702**	0.715	0.818	0.529	0.535	**0.708**	0.548
densenet169	0.689	0.574	0.647	0.768	0.747	0.555	0.623	0.677	0.521
densenet201	0.601	0.603	0.574	0.831	0.852	0.574	0.727	0.692	0.639
efficientnetb6	0.503	0.602	0.643	**0.875**	0.748	0.631	0.687	0.662	0.508
efficientnetb7	0.627	**0.696**	0.580	**0.875**	**0.875**	0.575	0.682	0.523	0.511
efficientnetv2s	0.553	0.525	0.658	0.776	0.792	0.526	0.511	0.569	0.551

notable accuracy and FM scores. This highlights its ability to capture diverse patterns even without structured guidance. The Custom case, while showing strong results for certain models like **resnet101** on the DAGM dataset, is more variable and less consistent, particularly in complex datasets where precise alignment between clustering and data structure is crucial. These differences underscore the importance of context when selecting a clustering approach. The Custom case does offer flexibility, but its performance can be inconsistent, particularly when the data requires more precise alignment between clustering and the underlying structure.

When comparing the benchmark results with the performance across the Random, Model-based, and Custom cases, it is clear that the three suggested cases offer a more refined and adaptable approach to clustering. The benchmark results show modest clustering accuracy across the datasets, with no significant outperformance by the more complex models. In comparison, the Model-based case excels, particularly in large datasets like DAGM, enhancing both accuracy and FM scores. The Random case also stands out, capturing diverse patterns in datasets like CD and DAGM, outperforming traditional methods without needing a predefined structure. Although the Custom case is more variable, it offers flexibility and strong results in specific contexts, making these three approaches more effective than the benchmarks across various data environments.

5.4 Run-Time of the Framework

We also make a brief comment on the run-time of the framework and refer to Fig. 6. As illustrated in the framework, the TL-based feature extraction step utilizes pre-trained CNNs to generate high-level embeddings from input images. While this step does contribute to the overall computational cost, analyzing or optimizing its time complexity

Table 2. FM Scores of the different models used in the framework.

Model	CD			DAGM			MVTEC		
	Rand.	Model	Custom	Rand.	Model	Custom	Rand.	Model	Custom
vgg16	0.691	0.546	0.615	0.628	0.875	0.805	0.564	0.617	0.556
vgg19	0.533	0.578	0.616	**0.884**	0.883	0.793	0.558	0.542	0.634
resnet50	0.527	0.651	0.614	0.810	0.854	0.735	0.552	0.581	0.565
resnet101	0.702	0.604	0.631	0.630	0.626	**0.844**	0.650	0.681	0.579
resnet152	0.541	0.657	0.620	0.843	0.866	**0.844**	0.560	0.550	0.566
inceptionv3	0.530	0.673	**0.687**	0.810	0.626	0.650	**0.779**	**0.761**	0.589
xception	0.590	0.566	0.547	0.715	0.726	0.746	0.668	**0.761**	0.645
densenet121	**0.722**	0.617	0.609	0.721	0.818	0.627	0.561	**0.761**	0.554
densenet169	0.606	0.665	0.585	0.768	0.746	0.631	0.627	0.642	0.550
densenet201	0.720	**0.722**	0.613	0.834	0.858	0.637	0.771	0.745	**0.660**
efficientnetb6	0.510	0.721	0.571	**0.884**	0.749	0.658	0.716	0.696	0.553
efficientnetb7	0.694	0.697	0.540	**0.884**	**0.884**	0.638	0.713	0.530	0.552
efficientnetv2s	0.661	0.562	0.621	0.774	0.792	0.626	0.553	0.548	0.554

was not the focus of our work. This is because the use of pre-trained CNNs for feature extraction is a well-established and standardized practice, with widely available implementations optimized for speed and scalability [8]. Our primary contribution lies beyond this stage—in analyzing clustering performance through informed center initialization and deep embedding optimization, rather than in evaluating the efficiency of the feature extraction process itself.

The framework on average takes about 1382.74 s to run on an Intel(R) Xeon(R) CPU running at 3.70 GHz using 128 GB of RAM with Windows 10. The last layer size before clustering (blue bars) was kept constant through all the executions since the target size of images was kept fixed. It does vary significantly across different models, with **resnet50**, **resnet101**, and **resnet152** showing the highest values, reflecting their complex architecture and large feature representations. Models like **inceptionv3**, **xception**, and **densenet201** have smaller last layer sizes, indicating a more compact representation of features before clustering. This variation in last layer size is expected due to the different architectures and depths of these networks, directly influencing the amount of data that needs to be processed during clustering.

The run-time analysis reveals a clear correlation between the last layer size and the time required to perform clustering. Models with larger last layer sizes like **resnet152** and **efficientnetb6** exhibit significantly higher run-times, especially in the DAGM dataset with the Model-based case, where run-times peak over 9000 s. This suggests that larger feature representations require more computational resources and time to cluster, particularly when the clustering case involves more complex model-based approaches.

Comparing the different clustering strategies, the Custom case generally incurs less run-time compared to the Model-based approach across most models and datasets, indicating its efficiency in handling varying feature sizes. This is evidently due to the net-

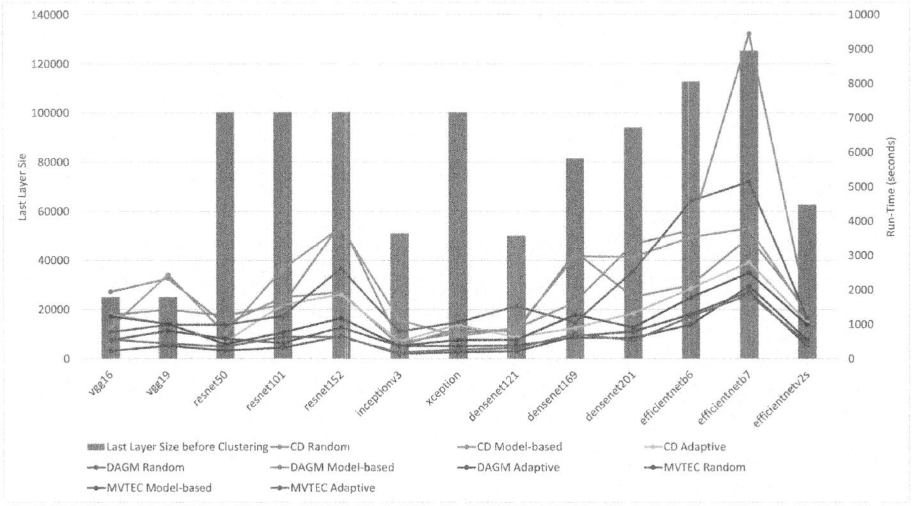

Fig. 6. Graph showing comparison of the feature size from the last layer of the CNN models with the execution time of the framework.

work not being burdened to find its cluster centers. However, the Random case shows competitive run-times, particularly in the CD and MVTEC datasets, where it closely follows the Custom case, suggesting that simpler clustering approaches can be effective when the feature size is moderate. Notably, the Custom case on the DAGM dataset shows a peak run-time with the **efficientnetb6** model, emphasizing the complexity of clustering large feature representations, even in Custom scenarios.

6 Conclusion

This paper presents a comprehensive framework that leverages existing CNN architectures and a customizable clustering layer, allowing users to initialize cluster centers based on their preferences. The results demonstrate that this straightforward approach is effective for grouping industrial-level images, particularly when dealing with large datasets where time constraints limit the feasibility of developing specialized models. The framework's flexibility makes it suitable for use across multiple datasets with minimal parameter adjustments and training requirements, especially in industrial cases, where batches of images are obtained and need to be grouped or classified as early as possible. Future work could focus on refining image cluster centers after their initial selection using the Hungarian algorithm. Such refinement could further enhance clustering accuracy, making the framework even more robust for various industrial applications. Additionally, exploring advanced methods for initializing cluster centers and integrating domain-specific knowledge could yield even better performance, expanding the framework's applicability to a wider range of image analysis tasks.

References

1. Demystifying emerging trends in green technology (2025)
2. Asif, S., Uzair Akmal, M., Koval, L., Knollmeyer, S., Mathias, S.G., Grossmann, D.: Supervised anomaly detection for production line images using data augmentation and convolutional neural network. In: 2024 IEEE 29th International Conference on Emerging Technologies and Factory Automation (ETFA), pp. 1–8 (2024). https://doi.org/10.1109/ETFA61755.2024.10710718
3. Bergmann, P., Batzner, K., Fauser, M., Sattlegger, D., Steger, C.: The MVTec anomaly detection dataset: a comprehensive real-world dataset for unsupervised anomaly detection. Int. J. Comput. Vis. **129**(4), 1038–1059 (2021). https://doi.org/10.1007/s11263-020-01400-4
4. Chang, J., Wang, L., Meng, G., Xiang, S., Pan, C.: Deep adaptive image clustering. In: 2017 IEEE International Conference on Computer Vision (ICCV), pp. 5880–5888 (2017). https://doi.org/10.1109/ICCV.2017.626
5. Cohn, R., Holm, E.: Unsupervised machine learning via transfer learning and k-means clustering to classify materials image data. Integr. Mater. Manuf. Innov. **10**(2), 231–244 (2021). https://doi.org/10.1007/s40192-021-00205-8
6. Cui, H., Zhang, J., Cui, C., Chen, Q.: Solving large-scale assignment problems by Kuhn-Munkres algorithm. In: Proceedings of the 2nd International Conference on Advances in Mechanical Engineering and Industrial Informatics (AMEII 2016), pp. 822–827. Atlantis Press (2016). https://doi.org/10.2991/ameii-16.2016.160
7. Dabhi, R., Kantesaria, N., Vaghasia, P., Hirpara, J., Bhoraniya, R.: Casting product image data for quality inspection (2020). https://www.kaggle.com/datasets/ravirajsinh45/real-life-industrial-dataset-of-casting-product, [Dataset]
8. Gholizade, M., Soltanizadeh, H., Rahmanimanesh, M., Sana, S.S.: A review of recent advances and strategies in transfer learning. Int. J. Syst. Assur. Eng. Manag. **16**(3), 1123–1162 (2025)
9. Guo, X., Gao, L., Liu, X., Yin, J.: Improved deep embedded clustering with local structure preservation. In: Proceedings of the Twenty-Sixth International Joint Conference on Artificial Intelligence, IJCAI 2017, pp. 1753–1759 (2017). https://doi.org/10.24963/ijcai.2017/243
10. Huang, P., Pan, X., Tao, J.: Research on image clustering algorithm based on multi-features extraction. In: 2021 33rd Chinese Control and Decision Conference (CCDC), pp. 7272–7276 (2021). https://doi.org/10.1109/CCDC52312.2021.9602551
11. Jiang, Z., Zheng, Y., Tan, H., Tang, B., Zhou, H.: Variational deep embedding: an unsupervised and generative approach to clustering. In: Proceedings of the 26th International Joint Conference on Artificial Intelligence, IJCAI 2017, pp. 1965–1972. AAAI Press (2017)
12. Koval, L., Pfaller, D., Bilal, M., Bregulla, M., Cupek, R.: An analysis of convolutional neural network models for classifying machine tools. In: Wojtkiewicz, K., Treur, J., Pimenidis, E., Maleszka, M. (eds.) ICCCI 2021. CCIS, vol. 1463, pp. 461–473. Springer, Cham (2021). https://doi.org/10.1007/978-3-030-88113-9_37
13. Li, P., Li, G., Hu, D., Zhang, S.: Research on feature extraction and center localization recognition of circular hole based on gaussian pyramid hierarchical clustering and Hough circle detection. In: 2024 IEEE 2nd International Conference on Image Processing and Computer Applications (ICIPCA), pp. 626–630 (2024). https://doi.org/10.1109/ICIPCA61593.2024.10708992
14. Li, Q., Chen, G.: Recognition of industrial machine parts based on transfer learning with convolutional neural network. PLoS ONE **16**(1), 1–21 (2021). https://doi.org/10.1371/journal.pone.0245735

15. Mahmood, Z.: Digital image processing: advanced technologies and applications. Appl. Sci. **14**(14) (2024). https://doi.org/10.3390/app14146051
16. Maschler, B., Kamm, S., Jazdi, N., Weyrich, M.: Distributed cooperative deep transfer learning for industrial image recognition. Procedia CIRP **93**, 437–442 (2020). https://doi.org/10.1016/j.procir.2020.03.056. https://www.sciencedirect.com/science/article/pii/S2212827120306648, 53rd CIRP Conference on Manufacturing Systems 2020
17. Maschler, B., Kamm, S., Weyrich, M.: Deep industrial transfer learning at runtime for image recognition. at - Automatisierungstechnik **69**(3), 211–220 (2021). https://doi.org/10.1515/auto-2020-0119
18. Maschler, B., Vietz, H., Tercan, H., Bitter, C., Meisen, T., Weyrich, M.: Insights and example use cases on industrial transfer learning. Procedia CIRP **107**, 511–516 (2022). https://doi.org/10.1016/j.procir.2022.05.017. https://www.sciencedirect.com/science/article/pii/S2212827122003018
19. Mathias, S., Asif, S., Akmal, M.U., Knollmeyer, S., Koval, L., Grossmann, D.: Industrial image grouping through pre-trained CNN encoder-based feature extraction and sub-clustering. In: Proceedings of the 17th International Conference on Agents and Artificial Intelligence - Volume 2: ICAART, pp. 496–506. INSTICC, SciTePress (2025). https://doi.org/10.5220/0013189000003890
20. Michau, G., Fink, O.: Unsupervised transfer learning for anomaly detection: application to complementary operating condition transfer. Knowl.-Based Syst. **216**, 106816 (2021). https://doi.org/10.1016/j.knosys.2021.106816. https://www.sciencedirect.com/science/article/pii/S0950705121000794
21. Nalini Sujantha Bel, K., Sam, I.S.: Image retrieval based on auto-encoder and clustering with centroid update. Comput. J. **67**(11), 3031–3041 (2024)
22. Noh, S.H.: Performance comparison of CNN models using gradient flow analysis. Informatics **8**(3) (2021). https://doi.org/10.3390/informatics8030053. https://www.mdpi.com/2227-9709/8/3/53
23. Oyewole, G.J., Thopil, G.A.: Data clustering: application and trends. Artif. Intell. Rev. **56**(7), 6439–6475 (2023). https://doi.org/10.1007/s10462-022-10325-y
24. Wang, H., Song, Y., Chen, W., Luo, Z., Li, C., Li, T.: A survey of co-clustering. ACM Trans. Knowl. Discov. Data **18**(9), 1–28 (2024)
25. Wani, A.A.: Comprehensive analysis of clustering algorithms: exploring limitations and innovative solutions. PeerJ Comput. Sci. **10**(e2286), e2286 (2024)
26. Wieler, M., Hahn, T., Hamprecht, F.A.: Weakly supervised learning for industrial optical inspection (2007). https://zenodo.org/records/12750201, [Dataset]
27. Xie, J., Girshick, R., Farhadi, A.: Unsupervised deep embedding for clustering analysis. In: Balcan, M.F., Weinberger, K.Q. (eds.) Proceedings of The 33rd International Conference on Machine Learning. Proceedings of Machine Learning Research, vol. 48, pp. 478–487. PMLR, New York, New York, USA (2016). https://proceedings.mlr.press/v48/xieb16.html
28. Xu, Z., Yuan, G., Wang, X., Quan, X., Ren, T., Liu, J.: Kuhn–Munkres algorithm-based matching method and automatic device for tiny magnetic steel pair. Micromachines **12**(3) (2021). https://doi.org/10.3390/mi12030316. https://www.mdpi.com/2072-666X/12/3/316
29. Yang, J., Wang, Y.K., Yao, X., Lin, C.T.: Adaptive initialization method for k-means algorithm. Front. Artif. Intell. **4** (2021). https://doi.org/10.3389/frai.2021.740817. https://www.frontiersin.org/journals/artificial-intelligence/articles/10.3389/frai.2021.740817
30. Zhang, B., et al.: The role of convolutional kernels in automated welding defect detection using t-SNE and DBSCAN clustering. Weld. World **69**(5), 1267–1275 (2025)
31. Zhang, H., Peng, Y.: Image clustering: an unsupervised approach to categorize visual data in social science research. Sociol. Methods Res. **53**(3), 1534–1587 (2024). https://doi.org/10.1177/00491241221082603

32. Zhuang, F., et al.: A comprehensive survey on transfer learning. Proc. IEEE **109**(1), 43–76 (2021). https://doi.org/10.1109/JPROC.2020.3004555
33. Zubair, M., Iqbal, M.A., Shil, A., Chowdhury, M.J.M., Moni, M.A., Sarker, I.H.: An improved k-means clustering algorithm towards an efficient data-driven modeling. Ann. Data Sci. (2022). https://doi.org/10.1007/s40745-022-00428-2

The Impact of Masking and Multiple Autoencoders on Hierarchically Gated Experts

Kevin Luong(✉) and Michael Thielscher

The University of New South Wales, Sydney, Australia
{kevin.luong,mit}@unsw.edu.au
kevin.luong@unsw.edu.au, mit@unsw.edu.au

Abstract. Expert-based approaches to Continual Learning employ a dynamically growing set of experts where each is trained on a separate task. During test time, the most relevant expert is selected and used. The *Hierarchically Gated Experts* (HGE) algorithm improves the efficiency of the expert selection process by organising the experts into a tree. But whilst the efficiency is improved, the expert selection accuracy drops due to the *Masking* phenomenon, where an expert low on the hierarchy is hidden by another closer to the root of the tree. We introduce a Masking measure which we show can predict the effectiveness of hierarchical organisation and explain the structure of the generated trees. Further, we explore an extension to the HGE algorithm where multiple autoencoders are employed to improve the expert selection accuracy. Whilst multiple autoencoders are superior to just one, training them under the Continual Learning constraint remains a challenge.

Keywords: Continual Learning · Mixture-of-Experts · Neural Networks

1 Introduction

Continual Learning is concerned with the ability of AI to accumulate new knowledge without compromising what it has already learnt [26]. Also known as Lifelong Learning, the biggest challenge to overcome is known as *Catastrophic Forgetting* [23] where further learning causes all or most existing knowledge to be lost. The typical Continual Learning framework consists of a series of separate distributions (tasks) to be learnt in order. As each task is learnt, the performance of the model is evaluated over both the current and previous tasks. Forgetting is said to have occurred if there is a reduction in the performance on a previous task. In many frameworks, the provided data is labelled according to its task [14,21], but this is not the case in the more recently explored Online Continual Learning setting [11,13].

To mitigate Catastrophic Forgetting, an *expert-based* approach is commonly used, where a set of experts is employed such that each expert is associated with a single task [1,34]. Allowing each expert to learn a task separately eliminates interference between tasks so that learning can occur without any forgetting. The challenge for expert-based approaches is then in selecting the correct expert for each data sample. The Expert Gate

H. J. van den Herik et al. (Eds.): ICAART 2025, LNAI 16517, pp. 622–641, 2026.
https://doi.org/10.1007/978-3-032-25032-2_30

[1] algorithm utilises autoencoders, one associated with each expert, for expert selection during testing, but requires task labels for training.

In our previous work [22], we proposed the new *Gated Experts (GE)* algorithm, which extends Expert Gate to the Online Continual Learning setting by detecting task switches as statistically significant deviations in the training loss. We further proposed the *Hierarchically Gated Experts (HGE)* algorithm where the set of experts is organised hierarchically, thus improving the efficiency of expert selection as not all experts are evaluated for each data sample. This addresses the problem of an ever-growing number of parameters, where other expert-based methods employ pruning [34] or other techniques [28,31].

Our experimental results showed a clear tradeoff between accuracy and efficiency [22]. Deeper trees were more efficient, however some data samples would be wrongly assigned to an expert near the root rather than the correct expert on a lower level. In this paper, we name this phenomenon *Masking* and analyse the relationship between Masking and expert selection accuracy and efficiency. We introduce a method to measure Masking and show that it can be used to predict the degree of hierarchical organisation that is possible. Figure 1 showcases some of the results. There is a clear association between Masking and the efficiency and structure of the generated trees.

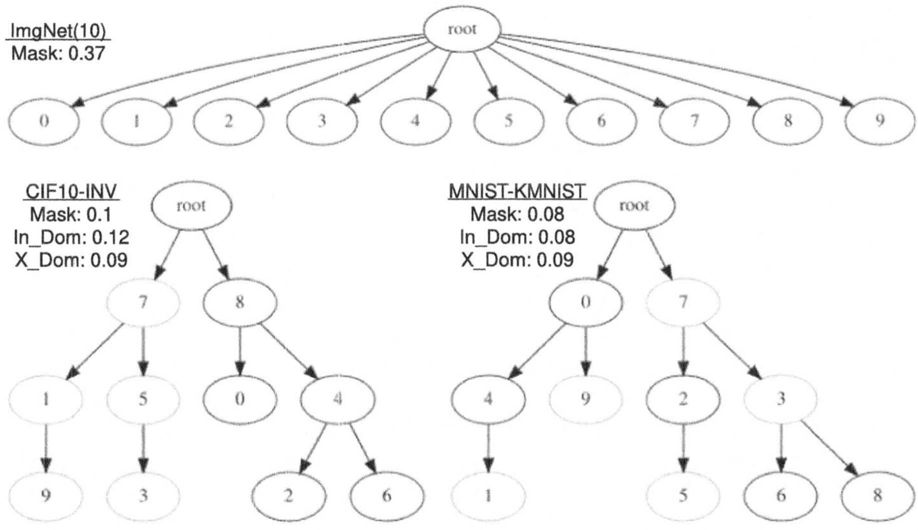

Fig. 1. Examples of trees generated in the ImgNet(10), CIF10-INV and MNIST-KMNIST scenarios (see Sect. 4.1). Each node represents an expert, coloured according to the domain. The overall, in-domain and cross-domain Masking values are also provided (see Sect. 4.2). In ImgNet(10), a high level of Masking explains why hierarchical organisation is not possible. In CIF10-INV, the lower cross-domain Masking explains why the experts can be clustered according to domain. In contrast, the experts are not so easily clustered in MNIST-KMNIST.

Further, we explore an extension to the GE and HGE algorithms where multiple autoencoders are used for each expert. We hypothesise that an ensemble of autoencoders will reduce the variance of the autoencoding loss and thus produce losses which are more useful for expert selection.

This paper is an extended version of our previous publication in the International Conference on Agents and Artificial Intelligence (ICAART) 2025 [22]. Our main contributions in this extension are:

- A more detailed definition of Masking and the introduction of a novel Masking measure to determine the degree to which Masking occurs in a set of trained experts.
- Further experimentation on GE and HGE to determine the impact of using multiple autoencoders for each expert.
- An ablation test on the $promotion\_path\_threshold$ hyperparameter within the HGE algorithm.

The rest of the paper is structured as follows. An overview of Continual Learning scenarios and methods is provided in Sect. 2. Then, the HGE algorithm is described along with a definition of Masking in Sect. 3. Our experimental setup, results and discussion are given in Sect. 4. Finally, we summarise our findings and discuss future work in Sect. 5.

2 Background

2.1 Continual Learning Scenarios

The distinguishing feature of Continual Learning is that there is a set of tasks which must be learned with some restriction on the data available at any given time. Continual Learning scenarios can be categorised according to the nature of the tasks as well as the restrictions on the accessibility of the data [23,26].

In *Task-Incremental (Offline)* Learning, task labels are provided so that the current task is known during both training and testing [26]. The training data may be provided in batches, each of which contains the data for an entire task, or in a stream, where only the latest sample can be accessed. In contrast to Task-Incremental Learning, in *Online* Continual Learning no task labels are provided and the current task often has to be inferred [11,17,34].[1] It is necessary for the data in Online Continual Learning to be provided in a stream, as the task identity would otherwise be trivially inferrable.

Continual Learning tasks are often one of either *Domain-Incremental* or *Class-Incremental*. In *Domain-Incremental* Learning, each task contains data from a separate distribution. This can be achieved through data augmentation, such as in the Permuted MNIST [7] scenario where each task contains a random permutation of the pixels in the MNIST dataset. There also exists the Core50 dataset [20] collected specifically for Continual Learning, which contains data divided into 11 sessions that can each form a task. Finally, datasets from different domains can be combined to obtain a domain-incremental learning task [13,17,34].

[1] Online Continual Learning may also refer to scenarios where each training sample is only shown once, i.e. one epoch per task [26]. The definition we use is also known as Task-Free, or Task-Agnostic, Continual Learning.

In *Class-Incremental* Learning, all data comes from the same distribution however each task contains only a subset of the available classes with no overlap between tasks. This is achieved in practice by dividing a dataset according to class [29,30].

Some Continual Learning scenarios exist which are neither strictly Domain-Incremental nor Class-Incremental but combine elements of both to produce *hybrid Domain and Class-Incremental* scenarios. In Continual Reinforcement Learning [6], for instance, tasks may differ by input distribution, transition function, or reward function. Thus, the relationship between the observations and actions in each task is more complex than simply Domain-Incremental or Class-Incremental. Additionally, Lee and Storkey [18] propose the chunking subproblem in Continual Learning, where each task contains a different subset of the data from one distribution. Despite each task containing data sampled from the same distribution, catastrophic forgetting can occur due only to the fact that access to the data is restricted to one task, or chunk, at a time.

Continual Learning scenarios can also be categorised as having either hard or soft task boundaries. In a *hard task boundary*, the available data switches entirely from one task to the next. In a *soft task boundary*, there is instead a period of time where the currently available data is a mixture from multiple tasks. Some mixtures contain data from an adjacent pair of tasks, as in the MNIST-360 setting [3] where each pseudo-task contains a successive pair of digits ({0,1} then {1,2}, etc.) with an increasing rotation applied. Other mixtures may contain data from all tasks [2].

Adjacent to Online Continual Learning is Stream Learning [8], where the goal is to learn from a changing data stream. Similarly to Online Continual Learning, there is a sequence of tasks to learn without task labels, and access to the data is restricted to only the latest sample. Where the objective in Continual Learning is to learn all tasks and mitigate catastrophic forgetting, Stream Learning requires only the latest task to be performed well. Instead, the focus is on detecting task boundaries, known as concept drifts in the literature.

2.2 Continual Learning Methods

An array of Continual Learning methods exist that vary in approach as well as the settings that they tackle [23,26]. In this section we provide an overview of the three major categories of approaches: architectural, regularisation, and replay-based.

Architectural Approaches split the model parameters such that for each task, a different subset of the parameters is used. Thus, interference between tasks is lower and Catastrophic Forgetting is less likely to occur. In expert-based methods a completely separate model is assigned to each task to be learnt [17,34]. The manner in which experts are selected for training and testing varies.

The Expert Gate [1] algorithm uses task labels to train a separate expert for each task. An *autoencoder* is trained alongside each expert and used for expert selection during test time. The selected expert is that which corresponds to the autoencoder with the lowest autoencoding loss.

Alternatively to expert-based methods, there exist approaches where the network is fixed but binary masks are learned to restrict each task to a subset of parameters

[12,27]. Other approaches instead generate the task-specific parameters using a meta-model known as a hypernetwork [10].

Regularisation Techniques constrain parameter updates to allow for learning without catastrophic forgetting. Commonly, an additional loss is used to penalise changes to parameters considered to be important. This approach is employed by Elastic Weight Consolidation [14], Gradient Episodic Memory [21] and Synaptic Intelligence [32]. Other approaches utilise Bayesian Learning [33] or generate pseudo-labels which can preserve learnt knowledge [19].

Replay-Based Approaches store a small number of training samples to preserve knowledge. One commonly addressed challenge in this area is how to best select samples to store [4,21]. In some cases, the samples are not directly stored and instead a network is trained to recreate them [25]. Replay is commonly combined with other approaches to Continual Learning [11,13,34].

3 Hierarchical Organisation of Experts

3.1 Hierarchically Gated Experts

Consider a pair of experts trained on the same domain. When a sample arrives from said domain, we can expect that both will produce a low autoencoding loss. Likewise, an out-of-domain sample can be expected to lead to a high autoencoding loss. Thus, it is possible to *estimate the suitability of an expert from the suitability of its peers*. More generally, we hypothesise that within a set of experts, each will be related to each other by varying degrees. Thus, we propose that *hierarchical expert organisation* can exploit these relationships so that the correct expert can be selected without evaluating all experts in the set.

The *Hierarchically Gated Experts* (HGE) algorithm is an extension of *Gated Experts* (GE) which incorporates hierarchical expert organisation. The set of experts is organised in a tree where each node (except the root) is a specific expert. To select an expert, the tree is traversed, starting from the root, by following the child with the lowest autoencoding loss. The traversal ends when a leaf expert is reached or when the current expert has a lower autoencoding loss than any of its children. In this way, the current expert has the lowest autoencoding loss of all experts evaluated thus far. The HGE algorithm aims to build the expert tree such that this expert found is also more suitable than any unseen expert. The pseudocode for the expert selection phase is provided in Algorithm 1.

3.2 Masking

When experts are organised hierarchically, it is possible for a sample to be wrongly assigned even if the corresponding expert is able to produce the lowest autoencoding loss. This *Masking* phenomenon occurs when an ancestor of the correct expert is unable to produce an autoencoding loss low enough to be selected. Thus, the correct expert is never evaluated and will not be selected. The expert that was selected instead of the right ancestor is said to *mask* the correct expert. As an example, consider the tree in

Data: (x_i, y_i) = the incoming sample
E = the tree of existing experts
Result: e_{best} = the expert with the lowest autoencoding loss on (x_i, y_i)

n ← the root node of E
while *True* **do**
  if n has no children **then**
    return
  end
  c ← the node in n.children with the lowest AE_Loss(c.expert, (x_i, y_i))
  if e_{best} does not yet exist
  or AE_Loss(c.expert, (x_i, y_i)) < AE_Loss(e_{best}, (x_i, y_i)) **then**
    e_{best} ← c.expert
  else
    return
  end
end

Algorithm 1. HGE_forward [22] – In HGE, the most relevant expert for a given sample is found by starting at the root and repeatedly choosing the best child.

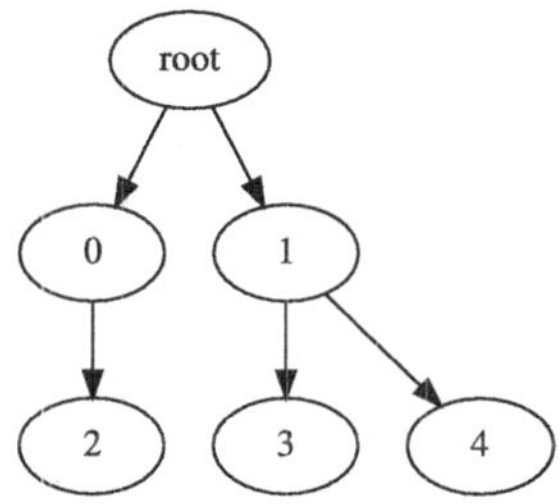

Fig. 2. An example tree generated by HGE [22].

Fig. 2. A sample from task 3 will be assigned incorrectly if expert 0 produces a lower autoencoding loss than expert 1. In this case, expert 0 masks expert 3.

Masking is the sole cause of any change in expert selection accuracy when the experts are organised hierarchically. It is also possible for a sample to be wrongly assigned if the correct expert is simply unable to produce the lowest autoencoding loss, but this is not related to hierarchical organisation. Thus, one approach to measure Masking would be to calculate the difference in expert selection accuracy. There are two flaws with this approach, however. The first is that Masking is double-edged and can also increase the selection accuracy. It is possible for an incorrect expert, which would otherwise produce the lowest autoencoding loss and be selected, to be masked so that the correct expert is selected instead. Thus, whilst masking explains the difference in expert selection accuracy, the reverse is not necessarily true. The second and more prominent flaw is that this measure is dependent on the way the experts are organised. It would be more useful to have a measure that is tree-independent, so that it can be used to determine if hierarchical organisation will be effective.

Therefore, we propose an alternative measure for Masking. Our measure is calculated over a task A and a pair of experts (B, C). We assume without loss of generality that between experts B and C, C is more suited to task A. Let p be the proportion of task A samples where expert B produces a lower autoencoding loss than expert C. Under our assumption, $p \leq 0.5$. Our measure m is then defined simply as $2 \cdot p$. This measure represents the amount of Masking that would occur if expert C were an ancestor of expert A, and expert B an ancestor, sibling, or sibling-of-ancestor of expert C. Informally, m measures the *minimum* amount of Masking that would result from task A samples "passing through" experts B and C. If $p = 0.5$, then a maximal $m = 1$ amount of Masking occurs as no matter how B and C are organised, half the samples will be masked. On the other hand, if $m = 0$, then one of experts B and C will always produce the lower autoencoding loss. If we set this expert as the ancestor of A, then it is impossible for the other to mask A.

By measuring Masking in this manner, we determine whether it is possible to have expert A appear deeper in the tree than experts B and C. We hypothesise that this corresponds to the degree to which a set of experts can be hierarchically organised. When there are more combinations of A and (B, C) exhibiting a low level of Masking, then more experts are able to be placed deeper in the tree, and thus hierarchical organisation becomes more effective. We also hypothesise the converse to be true. More combinations of A and (B, C) that exhibit a high level of Masking implies that there are more restrictions on whether an expert can be a child of another, thus forcing the expert tree to be flatter. Calculating our measure requires task A data and experts B and C. The measure can be approximated by only using a subset of the task A data. Thus, our measure is tree-independent and can be used to estimate the extent to which a set of experts can be hierarchically organised.

3.3 Building the Expert Tree

The HGE algorithm aims to organise the experts hierarchically to reduce the number of experts required for selection, whilst maintaining a minimal amount of Masking. To do so, the tree of experts is constructed iteratively during the expert promotion phase of GE. As a newly created expert is trained, the traversal path of every sample is tracked. When it comes time to promote the expert, it is inserted into the tree as a child of the lowest common ancestor (LCA) of all traversal paths. Thus, the expert is inserted as deeply into the tree as possible without Masking. To ensure robustness against outliers, paths which are taken only a few times are excluded. A $promotion\_path\_threshold$ hyperparameter is used to determine the cutoff. The pseudocode for expert promotion is provided in Algorithm 2

Whilst the newly added expert will not be masked, it is possible for it to mask an existing one. More specifically, all descendants of siblings can potentially become masked. To determine if Masking will occur, each expert stores a small number of training samples in a replay buffer employing the Reservoir strategy [4]. In our implementation, an expert is considered to be masked if any training sample is incorrectly assigned to the new expert, given the small size of the replay buffer. If a larger buffer were possible, then a threshold could be used to allow a small level of Masking. When an expert is masked, a new node corresponding to the masked expert is added as a child of the new expert. Rather than adding a connection, creating a new node ensures that descendants of the masked expert are not unnecessarily added.

4 Experiments

This section, in which we detail our experimental results with the improved HGE method, is structured as follows. Our experimental setup and previous results are provided in Sect. 4.1. Following this, Sect. 4.2 contains an assessment of the Masking measure proposed in Sect. 3.2. Then, Sect. 4.3 contains experiments involving multiple autoencoders. Finally, Sect. 4.4 contains new ablation results.

```
Data: E = the tree of existing experts
e_new = the expert to be promoted
paths = a list of the unique paths taken by the samples on which e_new was trained. Each
path also contains a count of the number of times it was taken.

e_new_node ← a new node with e_new_node.expert = e_new and no children
if there is only one expert in E then
|   add e_new_node as a child of the root node of E
|   return
end

// Insert expert into tree
sort paths by count in decreasing order
for p in paths do
|   sum ← the cumulative sum of counts up to and including p
|   total ← the sum of all counts in paths
|   if sum > promotion_path_threshold * total then
|   |   remove all remaining members of paths
|   end
end
parent ← the LCA of all remaining p in paths
add e_new_node as a child of parent

// Check for Masking
possible_masks ← {}
for each descendant n of parent excluding e_new_node do
|   add n.expert to possible_masks
end
for e_mask in possible_masks do
|   if there exists (x_i, y_i) in e_mask.replay_buffer where HGE_forward(E,(x_i, y_i)) =
|     e_new then
|   |   add a node n as a child of e_new_node with n.expert = e_mask
|   end
end
```

Algorithm 2. Expert Promotion in HGE [22]

4.1 Setup and Continual Learning Scenarios

We conduct our experiments on the following commonly used Continual Learning scenarios:

Permuted MNIST (PMNIST). The MNIST dataset, a large dataset of handwritten digits [16], is used as the base for each task in this scenario. In each task except the first, the pixels in each image are permuted. The permutations are random but kept consistent within each task. There are 20 tasks in total which each contain the entire 60,000 training and 10,000 testing images.

Split MNIST (SMNIST). The MNIST dataset is randomly split into 5 tasks, each containing 2 classes.

Split CIFAR-10 (CIF10). The CIFAR-10 dataset, a large dataset of categorised images [15], is randomly split into 5 tasks containing 2 classes each.

Split CIFAR-100 (CIF100). The CIFAR-100 dataset [15] is split into either 10 or 20 tasks, each containing 10 and 5 classes respectively.

Split Tiny Imagenet (ImgNet). The Tiny Imagenet dataset is a subset of Imagenet [24] containing images from 200 classes. Each class contains 500 training images and 50 testing images. 100 classes are randomly selected which are then evenly split into either 10 or 20 tasks.

We also use hybrid class and domain-incremental scenarios proposed previously [22]. Each scenario involves two datasets, each divided by class into the same number of tasks. The tasks are presented alternatingly; the first tasks from each dataset, then the second from each, and so on. The scenarios are:

MNIST and Kuzushiji-MNIST (MNIST-KMNIST). The MNIST dataset and Kuzushiji-MNIST (KMNIST) dataset [5] are split into 5 tasks each, for a total of 10 tasks.

MNIST and CIFAR-10 (MNIST-CIF10). The MNIST dataset is pre-processed to match the CIFAR-10 format. Then, each dataset is split into 5 tasks for a total of 10 tasks.

CIFAR-10 and Inverse CIFAR-10 (CIF10-INV). The colour of every pixel in CIFAR-10 is inverted to produce the Inverse CIFAR-10 dataset. As in the previous scenarios, the datasets are then split into 5 tasks each for a total of 10.

CIFAR-100 and Tiny Imagenet (CIF-ImgNet). As in the Split Tiny Imagenet scenario, 100 classes are randomly selected from the Tiny Imagenet dataset. Each dataset is split into 10 tasks for a total of 20.

Two variants of experts were used according to the scenario. In the PMNIST, SMNIST and MNIST-KMNIST scenarios, both the base model and the autoencoder are multi-layer perceptrons (MLP). In all other scenarios, the base model is Resnet-18 [9] and a convolutional autoencoder is used. The full details of dataset preprocessing, models used and hyperparameters are available in the Appendix.

For each scenario, task labels are utilised to train a separate expert on each task, then three different expert organisation strategies are applied:

GE. No hierarchical organisation is applied. Each expert is a direct child of the root node.

HGE. The HGE algorithm is applied to iteratively build the tree of experts according to task order. As each expert is added, the traversal paths are calculated over all training samples for the expert. To determine if Masking will occur, a small number of training samples, equal to the size of the replay buffer, are randomly selected.

Upper. A large number of task orders (1000, or every possible order in scenarios with 5 tasks) is randomly generated and the HGE algorithm is applied to produce a tree for each order. The accuracy and cost of each tree is recorded and the results are filtered down to those where no Masking occurs (the accuracy must be at least as high as 98% of the GE result). The tree with the lowest cost is then selected as an estimate of the best possible tree given the trained experts.

For each strategy, the expert selection accuracy is measured along with the selection cost, which is defined as the average number of experts queried for a single sample. The results, which were obtained in our previous work [22], are shown in Table 1 as a point of reference.

Table 1. The accuracy and efficiency of different approaches to organising the expert tree [22]. Acc refers to the percentage of samples which were assigned to the correct expert, whilst Exp is the average number of experts queried.

Scenario	GE		HGE		Upper	
	Acc	Exp	Acc	Exp	Acc	Exp
PMNIST	100.0 ± 0.0	20	99.76 ± 0.11	11.25 ± 1.02	99.7 ± 0.19	8.05 ± 0.13
SMNIST	100.0 ± 0.0	5	98.26 ± 1.4	3.83 ± 0.21	99.75 ± 0.56	3.56 ± 0.09
CIF10	95.25 ± 5.11	5	95.0 ± 5.66	4.17 ± 0.55	95.0 ± 5.66	3.85 ± 0.38
CIF100(10)	77.25 ± 2.05	10	76.75 ± 1.9	9.49 ± 0.85	75.0 ± 4.59	8.02 ± 0.33
CIF100(20)	83.25 ± 8.08	20	82.75 ± 7.52	17.55 ± 1.43	84.0 ± 8.59	12.84 ± 0.74
ImgNet(10)	61.0 ± 13.3	10	61.0 ± 13.3	9.7 ± 0.42	59.0 ± 12.57	8.47 ± 0.5
ImgNet(20)	73.5 ± 5.76	20	73.5 ± 5.76	19.02 ± 0.93	73.5 ± 2.85	15.03 ± 0.6
MNIST-KMIST	95.25 ± 5.94	10	95.25 ± 5.94	6.42 ± 0.57	95.01 ± 5.72	5.13 ± 0.09
MNIST-CIF10	98.88 ± 0.52	10	98.75 ± 0.77	5.29 ± 0.1	98.4 ± 1.01	4.92 ± 0.16
CIF10-INV	98.25 ± 0.93	10	97.88 ± 0.71	6.62 ± 0.99	98.0 ± 0.93	5.31 ± 0.19
CIF-ImgNet	68.88 ± 1.49	20	68.88 ± 1.49	19.06 ± 0.81	68.38 ± 1.44	15.6 ± 0.65

4.2 Measuring Masking

We aim to determine the extent to which our Masking measure can explain our previous results. Using the same sets of experts trained previously, the Masking measure is computed for every combination of task A and experts (B, C). The measure is computed over the entire dataset, including both training and testing samples, as it was found that separating the two did not change the results. In the hybrid Continual Learning scenarios, the results were also divided into two groups; one where the pair of experts (B, C) are in the same domain, and the other where the experts are from different domains. For reference, we also provide the expert selection accuracy and cost using the HGE strategy.

The results are shown in Table 2. Across all scenarios, there is a clear correlation between a higher selection accuracy, a lower selection cost and lower Masking. Thus, the Masking measure is potentially a useful predictor of the level of hierarchical organisation that is possible. In the hybrid Continual Learning scenarios, the results reflect the relationship between the domains. In MNIST-CIF10, there is a very clear difference in Masking when the experts are from the same or different domains. In CIF10-INV, there is a lesser difference, and in the remaining scenarios there is no observable difference. In general, a higher level of Masking indicates that the experts (or tasks) are harder to distinguish. This is supported by a manual analysis of the generated trees, such as those in Fig. 1. In CIF10-INV, the difference between the domains is large enough that the cross-domain Masking is lower and the tree of experts contain two clusters. On the other hand, in MNIST-KMNIST the difference between domains is small and therefore the cross-domain and intra-domain Masking is similar, and the tree of experts is not clustered. Therefore, the Masking measure can also explain the structure of the generated trees.

Table 2. The Masking measure across all tested scenarios. Acc and Exp are respectively the selection accuracy and cost using HGE. Mask is the average value of the measure across all combinations. In_Dom and X_Dom are the average values of the measure when the pair of experts (B, C) is restricted to be from the same domain, or from different domains.

Scenario	Tasks	Acc	Exp	Mask	In_Dom	X_Dom
PMNIST	20	99.76 ± 0.11	11.25 ± 1.02	0.09 ± 0.01		
SMNIST	5	98.26 ± 1.4	3.83 ± 0.21	0.08 ± 0.04		
CIF10	5	95.0 ± 5.66	4.17 ± 0.55	0.12 ± 0.07		
CIF100(10)	10	76.75 ± 1.9	9.49 ± 0.85	0.3 ± 0.05		
CIF100(20)	20	82.75 ± 7.52	17.55 ± 1.43	0.19 ± 0.03		
ImgNet(10)	10	61.0 ± 13.3	9.7 ± 0.42	0.37 ± 0.07		
ImgNet(20)	20	73.5 ± 5.76	19.02 ± 0.93	0.28 ± 0.02		
MNIST-KMIST	10	95.25 ± 5.94	6.42 ± 0.57	0.08 ± 0.02	0.08 ± 0.02	0.09 ± 0.02
MNIST-CIF10	10	98.75 ± 0.77	5.29 ± 0.1	0.02 ± 0.01	0.05 ± 0.01	0.0 ± 0.0
CIF10-INV	10	97.88 ± 0.71	6.62 ± 0.99	0.1 ± 0.01	0.12 ± 0.02	0.09 ± 0.02
CIF-ImgNet	20	68.88 ± 1.49	19.06 ± 0.81	0.23 ± 0.01	0.23 ± 0.02	0.23 ± 0.01

We further analyse the Masking measure by grouping the results by task and by the pair of experts. For each task A, we sort every pair of experts (B, C) by the Masking measure. In scenarios with 5, 10 and 20 tasks, the results are averaged from the top 1, 5 and 10 experts respectively. For each task, we also record the number of pairs where the

Masking measure is 0.04 or less, corresponding to 2% or fewer samples being Masked by the pair. Thus, we measure the Masking in the best pairs of experts for each task.

Similarly, we group the results by the pair of experts (B, C). For each pair of experts, we first average the Masking measure over all tasks. Then, the pairs are sorted and the results are averaged from the top 1, 5 and 10. We record the number of pairs where the average Masking is 0.04 or less, thus measuring the Masking in the pairs of experts most suited to being placed at the root of the tree.

The results are given in Table 3. For all tasks in all scenarios, there are multiple pairs of experts which do not mask the task. This does not hold when grouping by pairs, as in the most difficult scenarios, there may be 1 or fewer pairs which have an adequately low Masking measure. If there is no such pair, then the root of the tree must have at least 3 children, as Masking will otherwise occur. This is a strong indicator that hierarchical organisation will not be possible. We observe this in the CIF100(10), ImgNet(10) and CIF-ImgNet scenarios, where even the Upper strategy (see Table 1) is unable to find an efficient tree. From these results we conclude that given a set of experts, there will almost always be a subset which can be hierarchically organised, but it is not guaranteed that the entire set can be organised.

Table 3. The Masking measure grouped by task and pair of experts. Task Mean is the average Masking of the top (1, 5 or 10) pairs for each task, whereas Task Num is the average number of pairs, per task, with a low Masking measure (<=0.04). Pair Mean is the average Masking of the top overall pairs, and Pair Num is the number of pairs with a low overall Masking.

Scenario	Tasks	Task Mean	Task Num	Pair Mean	Pair Num
PMNIST	20	0.0 ± 0.0	131.03 ± 2.79	0.01 ± 0.0	28.4 ± 2.7
SMNIST	5	0.0 ± 0.0	4.76 ± 0.52	0.0 ± 0.0	6 ± 1.87
CIF10	5	0.0 ± 0.0	3.92 ± 0.91	0.0 ± 0.0	3.8 ± 2.28
CIF100(10)	10	0.01 ± 0.01	7.1 ± 2.55	0.11 ± 0.05	1 ± 1.73
CIF100(20)	20	0.0 ± 0.0	91.09 ± 9.53	0.03 ± 0.03	9.6 ± 9.71
ImgNet(10)	10	0.04 ± 0.04	5.36 ± 3.11	0.16 ± 0.1	0.4 ± 0.55
ImgNet(20)	20	0.0 ± 0.0	61.22 ± 10.03	0.06 ± 0.05	4 ± 4.06
MNIST-KMIST	10	0.0 ± 0.0	28.64 ± 1.7	0.0 ± 0.0	18.2 ± 3.56
MNIST-CIF10	10	0.0 ± 0.0	33.94 ± 0.47	0.0 ± 0.0	36.8 ± 2.39
CIF10-INV	10	0.0 ± 0.0	26.38 ± 0.33	0.01 ± 0.0	10.2 ± 2.77
CIF-ImgNet	20	0.0 ± 0.0	54.76 ± 7.62	0.07 ± 0.01	1.6 ± 0.55

4.3 Multiple Autoencoders

Next, we perform experiments to determine the impact of using an ensemble of autoencoders. We hypothesise that multiple autoencoders will be able to better learn the data and improve expert selection accuracy. Further, multiple autoencoders may reduce the variance of the autoencoding loss when an expert is applied to a different task, thus producing losses that are more useful for hierarchical organisation.

The previous experiments are repeated with 5 autoencoders being trained for each expert. To ensure that each autoencoder learns a different representation, they must be trained on different subsets of the training data. However, under the Continual Learning framework it is not possible to directly generate these subsets. Instead, we apply a rotating strategy where each training sample is assigned to half (rounded up) of the autoencoders. Given 5 autoencoders, each is thus trained on 60% of the data.

After training, the experts are evaluated using either 1 or all 5 autoencoders. To determine if the ensemble improves the overall performance of the experts, we compare all 5 weak autoencoders together to 1 strong autoencoder that is trained on all of the data. We also compare 5 weak autoencoders to just 1 to determine if the lower variance allows for better hierarchical organisation. We apply the GE, HGE and Upper strategies as described in Sect. 4.1. The results are shown in Tables 4, 5 and 6. We also calculate the Masking measure and present the results in Table 7.

Table 4. The accuracy of GE with different autoencoders. The Strong autoencoder is trained for all epochs. The Weak autoencoders are each trained on a different subset of the data, then either 1 or all 5 are used.

Scenario	Strong	Weak (1)	Weak (5)
PMNIST	100.0 ± 0.0	100.0 ± 0.0	100.0 ± 0.0
SMNIST	100.0 ± 0.0	99.5 ± 1.12	99.75 ± 0.56
CIF10	95.25 ± 5.11	97.5 ± 2.34	97.75 ± 2.98
CIF100(10)	77.25 ± 2.05	77.25 ± 6.64	79.5 ± 4.29
CIF100(20)	83.25 ± 8.08	85.0 ± 4.76	87.75 ± 2.05
ImgNet(10)	61.0 ± 13.3	60.5 ± 6.71	64.5 ± 8.73
ImgNet(20)	73.5 ± 5.76	72.0 ± 8.55	75.0 ± 10.0
MNIST-KMIST	95.25 ± 5.94	94.5 ± 5.2	93.75 ± 5.73
MNIST-CIF10	98.88 ± 0.52	98.0 ± 2.4	98.0 ± 2.09
CIF10-INV	98.25 ± 0.93	95.0 ± 3.19	95.12 ± 2.84
CIF-ImgNet	68.88 ± 1.49	64.62 ± 4.69	67.88 ± 4.18

Overall, the use of 5 weak autoencoders over 1 strong does not improve the expert selection accuracy and cost. Likewise, there is no significant difference in the Masking measure between the two cases. There is an improvement from 1 weak to 5 weak autoencoders, which supports our initial hypothesis, however an alternative strategy is required to be able to train multiple strong autoencoders. We leave this as an area of future work.

4.4 Hierarchical Gated Experts Ablation

Finally we perform an ablation test on the $promotion\_path\_threshold$ hyperparameter to determine its impact on the generated trees. In this test, the HGE and Upper

Table 5. The accuracy and efficiency of HGE with different autoencoders. The Strong autoencoder is trained for all epochs. The Weak autoencoders are each trained on a different subset of the data, then either 1 or all 5 are used.

Scenario	Strong		Weak (1)		Weak (5)	
	Acc	Exp	Acc	Exp	Acc	Exp
PMNIST	99.76 ± 0.11	11.25 ± 1.02	99.73 ± 0.24	11.82 ± 2.18	99.86 ± 0.11	11.54 ± 1.62
SMNIST	98.26 ± 1.4	3.83 ± 0.21	99.5 ± 1.12	4.24 ± 0.52	99.75 ± 0.56	4.24 ± 0.52
CIF10	95.0 ± 5.66	4.17 ± 0.55	97.5 ± 2.34	4.45 ± 0.43	97.75 ± 2.98	4.45 ± 0.43
CIF100(10)	76.75 ± 1.9	9.49 ± 0.85	77.25 ± 6.64	9.49 ± 0.58	78.5 ± 4.09	9.27 ± 0.8
CIF100(20)	82.75 ± 7.52	17.55 ± 1.43	84.75 ± 4.63	19.07 ± 0.63	87.0 ± 2.59	18.45 ± 1.15
ImgNet(10)	61.0 ± 13.3	9.7 ± 0.42	60.5 ± 6.71	9.87 ± 0.29	64.5 ± 8.73	10.0 ± 0.0
ImgNet(20)	73.5 ± 5.76	19.02 ± 0.93	72.0 ± 8.55	18.7 ± 0.43	74.5 ± 9.75	18.7 ± 0.5
MNIST-KMIST	95.25 ± 5.94	6.42 ± 0.57	94.12 ± 5.62	6.66 ± 0.79	93.62 ± 5.84	6.72 ± 0.84
MNIST-CIF10	98.75 ± 0.77	5.29 ± 0.1	98.0 ± 2.4	5.67 ± 0.04	98.0 ± 2.09	5.67 ± 0.04
CIF10-INV	97.88 ± 0.71	6.62 ± 0.99	94.38 ± 2.69	6.89 ± 0.96	95.38 ± 3.3	7.29 ± 1.14
CIF-ImgNet	68.88 ± 1.49	19.06 ± 0.81	64.5 ± 4.81	19.57 ± 0.63	67.88 ± 4.18	20.0 ± 0.0

approaches are applied with a threshold value that differs from the 0.98 used in all other experiments. The results are presented in Tables 8 and 9. The tradeoff between accuracy and cost can be clearly seen across the entire range of results. A lower threshold relaxes the restriction on where experts can be inserted, allowing for deeper trees to be produced. As observed previously, these trees tend to have both a lower accuracy and cost. The impact of $promotion\_path\_threshold$ is greatest when using the Upper app-

Table 6. The accuracy and efficiency of Upper with different autoencoders. The Strong autoencoder is trained for all epochs. The Weak autoencoders are each trained on a different subset of the data, then either 1 or all 5 are used.

Scenario	Strong		Weak (1)		Weak (5)	
	Acc	Exp	Acc	Exp	Acc	Exp
PMNIST	99.7 ± 0.19	8.05 ± 0.13	99.22 ± 0.64	8.51 ± 0.68	99.49 ± 0.51	8.09 ± 0.35
SMNIST	99.75 ± 0.56	3.56 ± 0.09	99.0 ± 1.05	3.7 ± 0.35	97.98 ± 1.89	3.59 ± 0.27
CIF10	95.0 ± 5.66	3.85 ± 0.38	97.25 ± 2.05	3.48 ± 0.12	96.75 ± 2.59	3.56 ± 0.17
CIF100(10)	75.0 ± 4.59	8.02 ± 0.33	76.75 ± 4.97	8.16 ± 0.51	77.75 ± 3.11	8.11 ± 0.61
CIF100(20)	84.0 ± 8.59	12.84 ± 0.74	84.25 ± 4.81	13.27 ± 0.55	86.75 ± 1.68	13.12 ± 0.29
ImgNet(10)	59.0 ± 12.57	8.47 ± 0.5	60.0 ± 6.85	8.62 ± 0.19	65.0 ± 8.84	8.67 ± 0.15
ImgNet(20)	73.5 ± 2.85	15.03 ± 0.6	71.5 ± 9.45	14.82 ± 0.51	75.5 ± 10.37	14.45 ± 0.49
MNIST-KMIST	95.01 ± 5.72	5.13 ± 0.09	94.5 ± 5.2	5.17 ± 0.22	93.5 ± 5.7	5.14 ± 0.19
MNIST-CIF10	98.4 ± 1.01	4.92 ± 0.16	97.88 ± 2.32	4.93 ± 0.11	98.0 ± 2.09	4.91 ± 0.09
CIF10-INV	98.0 ± 0.93	5.31 ± 0.19	94.88 ± 3.35	5.19 ± 0.24	94.38 ± 2.46	5.15 ± 0.2
CIF-ImgNet	68.38 ± 1.44	15.6 ± 0.65	64.62 ± 4.16	15.49 ± 0.35	67.5 ± 3.95	15.6 ± 0.73

Table 7. The average Masking measure with different autoencoders. The Strong autoencoder is trained for all epochs. The Weak autoencoders are each trained on a different subset of the data, then either 1 or all 5 are used.

Scenario	Strong	Weak (1)	Weak (5)
PMNIST	0.09 ± 0.01	0.12 ± 0.03	0.09 ± 0.01
SMNIST	0.08 ± 0.04	0.1 ± 0.05	0.09 ± 0.04
CIF10	0.12 ± 0.07	0.12 ± 0.05	0.12 ± 0.06
CIF100(10)	0.3 ± 0.05	0.29 ± 0.04	0.29 ± 0.03
CIF100(20)	0.19 ± 0.03	0.2 ± 0.02	0.2 ± 0.02
ImgNet(10)	0.37 ± 0.07	0.38 ± 0.03	0.39 ± 0.02
ImgNet(20)	0.28 ± 0.02	0.28 ± 0.01	0.29 ± 0.02
MNIST-KMIST	0.08 ± 0.02	0.09 ± 0.01	0.08 ± 0.01
MNIST-CIF10	0.02 ± 0.01	0.03 ± 0.01	0.03 ± 0.01
CIF10-INV	0.1 ± 0.01	0.1 ± 0.01	0.1 ± 0.01
CIF-ImgNet	0.23 ± 0.01	0.22 ± 0.01	0.22 ± 0.02

Table 8. The accuracy (Acc) and efficiency (Exp) of HGE for different values of $promotion\_path\_threshold$.

Threshold	0.9		0.95		0.98	
Scenario	Acc	Exp	Acc	Exp	Acc	Exp
PMNIST	99.25 ± 0.41	9.3 ± 0.73	99.39 ± 0.44	9.32 ± 0.8	99.76 ± 0.11	11.25 ± 1.02
SMNIST	96.76 ± 2.59	3.73 ± 0.22	98.26 ± 1.4	3.83 ± 0.21	98.26 ± 1.4	3.83 ± 0.21
CIF10	95.0 ± 5.66	4.08 ± 0.42	95.0 ± 5.66	4.17 ± 0.55	95.0 ± 5.66	4.17 ± 0.55
CIF100(10)	77.0 ± 1.9	8.95 ± 0.88	76.75 ± 1.9	9.33 ± 0.8	76.75 ± 1.9	9.49 ± 0.85
CIF100(20)	82.75 ± 7.52	16.55 ± 1.91	82.75 ± 7.52	17.55 ± 1.43	82.75 ± 7.52	17.55 ± 1.43
ImgNet(10)	61.5 ± 12.57	9.41 ± 0.28	61.5 ± 12.57	9.62 ± 0.38	61.0 ± 13.3	9.7 ± 0.42
ImgNet(20)	73.5 ± 5.76	18.7 ± 0.77	73.5 ± 5.76	19.02 ± 0.93	73.5 ± 5.76	19.02 ± 0.93
MNIST-KMIST	94.51 ± 5.34	6.07 ± 0.71	95.12 ± 5.83	6.23 ± 0.56	95.25 ± 5.94	6.42 ± 0.57
MNIST-CIF10	98.75 ± 0.77	5.23 ± 0.2	98.75 ± 0.77	5.23 ± 0.2	98.75 ± 0.77	5.29 ± 0.1
CIF10-INV	97.25 ± 1.3	6.04 ± 0.59	97.62 ± 1.2	6.25 ± 0.76	97.88 ± 0.71	6.62 ± 0.99
CIF-ImgNet	68.88 ± 1.2	17.63 ± 1.41	68.62 ± 1.2	18.63 ± 0.83	68.88 ± 1.49	19.06 ± 0.81

roach with $promotion\_path\_threshold = 0.9$. The large variance in the trees which can be produced allows the Upper approach to find a low cost tree with an accuracy barely above the cutoff (98% of the accuracy achieved by GE). On the other hand, the HGE results are less affected by $promotion\_path\_threshold$, thus showing that HGE is consistent in generating trees with close to optimal accuracy.

Table 9. The accuracy (Acc) and efficiency (Exp) of Upper for different values of *promotion_path_threshold*.

Threshold	0.9		0.95		0.98	
Scenario	Acc	Exp	Acc	Exp	Acc	Exp
PMNIST	98.19 ± 0.7	7.51 ± 0.3	99.37 ± 0.2	7.84 ± 0.16	99.7 ± 0.19	8.05 ± 0.13
SMNIST	98.0 ± 3.14	3.5 ± 0.1	99.75 ± 0.56	3.56 ± 0.09	99.75 ± 0.56	3.56 ± 0.09
CIF10	94.25 ± 5.27	3.64 ± 0.37	95.0 ± 5.66	3.76 ± 0.38	95.0 ± 5.66	3.85 ± 0.38
CIF100(10)	75.25 ± 3.11	6.82 ± 0.57	76.25 ± 2.34	7.43 ± 0.45	75.0 ± 4.59	8.02 ± 0.33
CIF100(20)	82.5 ± 8.66	11.73 ± 1.14	84.0 ± 8.59	12.84 ± 0.74	84.0 ± 8.59	12.84 ± 0.74
ImgNet(10)	60.0 ± 13.35	7.82 ± 0.73	60.5 ± 13.16	8.21 ± 0.59	59.0 ± 12.57	8.47 ± 0.5
ImgNet(20)	74.0 ± 5.48	14.46 ± 0.58	73.5 ± 2.85	15.03 ± 0.6	73.5 ± 2.85	15.03 ± 0.6
MNIST-KMIST	94.37 ± 6.31	5.04 ± 0.11	94.87 ± 6.19	5.06 ± 0.08	95.01 ± 5.72	5.13 ± 0.09
MNIST-CIF10	97.37 ± 0.8	4.9 ± 0.13	98.0 ± 0.91	4.91 ± 0.17	98.4 ± 1.01	4.92 ± 0.16
CIF10-INV	96.12 ± 1.28	5.02 ± 0.21	97.62 ± 1.03	5.19 ± 0.15	98.0 ± 0.93	5.31 ± 0.19
CIF-ImgNet	68.5 ± 0.56	13.17 ± 0.5	68.38 ± 1.3	14.75 ± 0.83	68.38 ± 1.44	15.6 ± 0.65

5 Conclusion

In this paper, we introduced the term Masking to describe the phenomenon where an expert is not evaluated due to hierarchical organisation. We proposed a Masking measure that is tree-independent and can be used to predict if a set of experts can be hierarchically organised effectively. We experimentally analysed the Masking measure and determined it to be highly correlated to the effectiveness of HGE. A closer analysis of the measure showed that it could explain the structure of the generated trees. The level of masking between experts from separate domains indicates whether the domains are easily separable, and thus whether the tree of experts will be clustered by domain.

Further, we proposed a rotating method by which an ensemble of autoencoders could be trained in a Continual Learning environment, thus reducing the variance of the autoencoding loss. The impact of this method on expert selection accuracy and hierarchical organisation was analysed and determined to be minimal. We hypothesise that whilst a lower variance can lead to more useful autoencoding losses, the proposed rotating method produces an ensemble of weaker autoencoders. It is possible that data augmentation or other methods could be used to produce an ensemble of strong autoencoders under the restrictions of the Continual Learning framework.

Finally, an ablation test on the *promotion_path_threshold* hyperparameter further demonstrated the tradeoff between expert selection accuracy and efficiency. It also showed that HGE is not reliant on a specific value of the hyperparameter.

Our approach to hierarchical organisation leaves several interesting issues open for future research. As we previously identified [22], one of these issues is in the changing relationships between experts in an Online Continual Learning setting. Whilst the HGE algorithm is able to effectively organise a set of experts, the tree is static and unable to account for the changing relationships as the experts continue to be trained. Further work is required to find a method by which the expert tree can be periodically updated to reflect changes in the experts. Another shortcoming in HGE is the poor efficiency when adding a new expert to the tree, as all descendants of siblings must be checked for Masking. It may be possible to exploit the relationships between existing experts to reduce the number of checks.

Disclosure of Interests. The authors have no competing interests to declare that are relevant to the content of this article.

A Appendix

Dataset Preprocessing. The images are preprocessed using the Torchvision Transforms library. The first step is to resize the images to ensure compatibility with the networks used. In the PMNIST, SMNIST and MNIST-KMNIST scenarios, the 28×28 images are flattened into a vector with 784 dimensions. In all other scenarios, the images are resized to 32×32.

Following this, the colours are preprocessed. In the MNIST-CIF10 scenario, the MNIST dataset is converted into a 3-channel grayscale image (r = g = b) to ensure compatibility with the Resnet-18 model. In the CIF10-INV scenario, the colour of each pixel is inverted to produce the Inverse CIFAR-10 dataset. Finally, in all scenarios the pixel values are re-scaled to [0,1].

Following the image preprocessing, the datasets are then split by class into separate tasks. Each experiment is repeated 5 times with a random split each time. In all 3 Tiny Imagenet scenarios, only 100 of the 200 available classes are used, and these are also randomly selected each experimental run.

Base Models. All models were implemented using PyTorch. We describe the architecture using the torch.nn API. In the PNIST, SMNIST and MNIST-KMNIST scenarios, the classification model for each expert is a 3-layer MLP. The layers in order are Linear(784,100), ReLU(), Linear(100,100), ReLU() and Linear(100,10). The outputs of the final layer are treated as logits and trained using CrossEntropyLoss(). In all other scenarios, the Resnet-18 [9] model is used for classification and similarly trained using CrossEntropyLoss().

A variational autoencoder is used for all scenarios. Each autoencoder consists of an encoder which outputs the mean and log-variance of the n-dimensional latent distribution, which is sampled using the reparameterisation trick. Let ϵ be an n-dimensional vector sampled from a Gaussian distribution with 0 mean and 1 variance. The latent sample is then $\mu + e^{(\sigma * 0.5)} * \epsilon$ where μ and σ are the mean and log-variance vectors outputted by the encoder. A decoder then reconstructs the original image from the latent sample. To train the autoencoder, the reconstruction error is computed using MSELoss(), then a KL-divergence loss is added. The KL-divergence loss $-0.5 * (1 + \sigma - \mu^2 - e^{\sigma})$ is computed from the mean and log-variance outputted by the encoder. To obtain a scalar, the loss is summed across the n-dimensions.

In the PNIST, SMNIST and MNIST-KMNIST scenarios, an MLP autoencoder with a 32-dimensional latent space is used. The encoder layers, in order, are Linear(784,512), ReLU(), then a separate Linear(512,32) for the mean and log-variance. The decoder layers in order are Linear(32,512), ReLU(), Linear(512, 784) and Sigmoid().

In all other scenarios, a convolutional autoencoder with 64-dimensional latent space is used. For reference, the arguments to Conv2d, in order, are input channels, output channels, kernel size, stride and padding. The encoder in order layers are Conv2d(3,32,3,1,1), BatchNorm2d(32), ReLU(), Conv2d(32, 64, 3, 1, 1), BatchNorm2d(64), ReLU(), Flatten(), Linear(65536, 128), and finally a separate Linear(128, 64) for the mean and log-variance. The decoder layers in order are Linear(64, 128), ReLU(), Linear(128, 65536), ReLU(), Unflatten(1, (64,32,32)), ConvTranspose2d(64, 32, 3, 1, 1), ReLU(), and ConvTranspose2d(32, 3, 3, 1, 1).

We tested regular autoencoders in place of variational autoencoders by simply using the encoder mean with no sampling, but found the results to be worse in all cases. We also experimented between SGD and Adam as the optimiser. In all scenarios, SGD with lr=0.01, momentum=0.9 and weight decay=0.0001 is used to train the classifier. In the CIF100, ImgNet and CIF-ImgNet scenarios, Adam with lr=0.001 and weight decay=0.0001 is used to train the autoencoder. In the remaining scenarios, SGD is used to train the autoencoder.

Hyperparameters. A batch size of 128 was used. The following hyperparameter values apply to all scenarios:

- Promotion_path_threshold = 0.98
- Expert replay buffer capacity = 10

The per-scenario hyperparameters are:

- PMNIST epochs = 40
- SMNIST epochs = 40
- CIF10 epochs = 200
- CIF100(10) epochs = 400
- CIF100(20) epochs = 400
- ImgNet(10) epochs = 400
- ImgNet(20) epochs = 400
- MNIST-KMNIST epochs = 100
- MNIST-CIF10 epochs = 200
- CIF10-INV epochs = 200
- CIF-ImgNet epochs = 400

In Sect. 4.3, the experts were trained using the above hyperparameters with the exception of SMNIST where 60 epochs were used instead. It was found that 40 epochs was not enough to complete training.

References

1. Aljundi, R., Chakravarty, P., Tuytelaars, T.: Expert gate: lifelong learning with a network of experts. In: 2017 IEEE Conference on Computer Vision and Pattern Recognition (CVPR), pp. 7120–7129 (2017). https://doi.org/10.1109/CVPR.2017.753
2. Bang, J., Kim, H., Yoo, Y., Ha, J.W., Choi, J.: Rainbow memory: continual learning with a memory of diverse samples. In: Proceedings of the IEEE/CVF Conference on Computer Vision and Pattern Recognition, pp. 8218–8227 (2021)

3. Buzzega, P., Boschini, M., Porrello, A., Abati, D., Calderara, S.: Dark experience for general continual learning: a strong, simple baseline. In: Proceedings of the 34th International Conference on Neural Information Processing Systems, NIPS 2020. Curran Associates Inc., Red Hook, NY, USA (2020)
4. Chaudhry, A., et al.: On tiny episodic memories in continual learning (2019). https://arxiv.org/abs/1902.10486
5. Clanuwat, T., Bober-Irizar, M., Kitamoto, A., Lamb, A., Yamamoto, K., Ha, D.: Deep learning for classical Japanese literature. CoRR abs/1812.01718 (2018). http://arxiv.org/abs/1812.01718
6. Dick, J., Nath, S., Peridis, C., Ben-Iwhiwhu, E., Kolouri, S., Soltoggio, A.: Statistical context detection for deep lifelong reinforcement learning. arXiv abs/2405.19047 (2024). https://api.semanticscholar.org/CorpusID:270095257
7. Goodfellow, I.J., Mirza, M., Xiao, D., Courville, A., Bengio, Y.: An empirical investigation of catastrophic forgetting in gradient-based neural networks (2013). https://doi.org/10.48550/ARXIV.1312.6211
8. Gunasekara, N., Pfahringer, B., Gomes, H.M., Bifet, A.: Survey on online streaming continual learning. In: Elkind, E. (ed.) Proceedings of the Thirty-Second International Joint Conference on Artificial Intelligence, IJCAI 2023, pp. 6628–6637. International Joint Conferences on Artificial Intelligence Organization (2023). https://doi.org/10.24963/ijcai.2023/743, survey Track
9. He, K., Zhang, X., Ren, S., Sun, J.: Deep residual learning for image recognition (2015). https://arxiv.org/abs/1512.03385
10. Hemati, H., Lomonaco, V., Bacciu, D., Borth, D.: Partial hypernetworks for continual learning (2023). https://arxiv.org/abs/2306.10724
11. Hihn, H., Braun, D.A.: Hierarchically structured task-agnostic continual learning. Mach. Learn. **112**(2), 655–686 (2023)
12. Kang, H., Mina, R.J.L., et al.: Forget-free continual learning with winning subnetworks. In: Proceedings of the 39th International Conference on Machine Learning, pp. 10734–10750. PMLR (2022). https://proceedings.mlr.press/v162/kang22b.html
13. Kirichenko, P., et al.: Task-agnostic continual learning with hybrid probabilistic models. CoRR abs/2106.12772 (2021). https://arxiv.org/abs/2106.12772
14. Kirkpatrick, J., Pascanu, R., et al.: Overcoming catastrophic forgetting in neural networks. Proc. Natl. Acad. Sci. **114**(13), 3521–3526 (2017). https://doi.org/10.1073/pnas.1611835114. https://www.pnas.org/doi/abs/10.1073/pnas.1611835114
15. Krizhevsky, A.: Learning multiple layers of features from tiny images. University of Toronto (2012)
16. Lecun, Y., Bottou, L., Bengio, Y., Haffner, P.: Gradient-based learning applied to document recognition. Proc. IEEE **86**(11), 2278–2324 (1998). https://doi.org/10.1109/5.726791
17. Lee, S., Ha, J., Zhang, D., Kim, G.: A neural Dirichlet process mixture model for task-free continual learning. CoRR abs/2001.00689 (2020). http://arxiv.org/abs/2001.00689
18. Lee, T.L., Storkey, A.: Chunking: continual learning is not just about distribution shift (2024). https://arxiv.org/abs/2310.02206
19. Li, Z., Hoiem, D.: Learning without forgetting (2017). https://arxiv.org/abs/1606.09282
20. Lomonaco, V., Maltoni, D.: Core50: a new dataset and benchmark for continuous object recognition. In: Levine, S., Vanhoucke, V., Goldberg, K. (eds.) Proceedings of the 1st Annual Conference on Robot Learning. Proceedings of Machine Learning Research, vol. 78, pp. 17–26. PMLR (2017). https://proceedings.mlr.press/v78/lomonaco17a.html
21. Lopez-Paz, D., Ranzato, M.: Gradient episodic memory for continuum learning. CoRR abs/1706.08840 (2017). http://arxiv.org/abs/1706.08840

22. Luong, K., Thielscher, M.: Hierarchically gated experts for efficient online continual learning. In: Proceedings of the 17th International Conference on Agents and Artificial Intelligence - Volume 2: ICAART, pp. 507–518. INSTICC, SciTePress (2025). https://doi.org/10.5220/0013190000003890
23. Parisi, G.I., Kemker, R., Part, J.L., Kanan, C., Wermter, S.: Continual lifelong learning with neural networks: a review. CoRR abs/1802.07569 (2018). http://arxiv.org/abs/1802.07569
24. Russakovsky, O., et al.: Imagenet large scale visual recognition challenge (2015). https://arxiv.org/abs/1409.0575
25. Shin, H., Lee, J.K., Kim, J., Kim, J.: Continual learning with deep generative replay (2017). https://arxiv.org/abs/1705.08690
26. Wang, L., Zhang, X., Su, H., Zhu, J.: A comprehensive survey of continual learning: theory, method and application (2024). https://arxiv.org/abs/2302.00487
27. Wortsman, M., et al.: Supermasks in superposition (2020). https://arxiv.org/abs/2006.14769
28. Xu, J., Zhu, Z.: Reinforced continual learning (2018). https://arxiv.org/abs/1805.12369
29. Yan, Q., Gong, D., Liu, Y., van den Hengel, A., Shi, J.Q.: Learning Bayesian sparse networks with full experience replay for continual learning. In: 2022 IEEE/CVF Conference on Computer Vision and Pattern Recognition (CVPR), pp. 109–118 (2022). https://doi.org/10.1109/CVPR52688.2022.00021
30. Yan, S., Xie, J., He, X.: DER: dynamically expandable representation for class incremental learning. In: 2021 IEEE/CVF Conference on Computer Vision and Pattern Recognition (CVPR), pp. 3013–3022. IEEE Computer Society, Los Alamitos, CA, USA (2021). https://doi.org/10.1109/CVPR46437.2021.00303. https://doi.ieeecomputersociety.org/10.1109/CVPR46437.2021.00303
31. Yoon, J., Yang, E., Lee, J., Hwang, S.J.: Lifelong learning with dynamically expandable networks. In: 6th International Conference on Learning Representations, ICLR 2018 (2018). https://openreview.net/forum?id=Sk7KsfW0
32. Zenke, F., Poole, B., Ganguli, S.: Continual learning through synaptic intelligence. In: Proceedings of the 34th International Conference on Machine Learning, ICML 2017, vol. 70, pp. 3987–3995. JMLR.org (2017)
33. Zeno, C., Golan, I., Hoffer, E., Soudry, D.: Task agnostic continual learning using online variational bayes. arXiv preprint arXiv:1803.10123 (2018)
34. Zhu, H., Majzoubi, M., Jain, A., Choromanska, A.: Tame: task agnostic continual learning using multiple experts (2022). https://arxiv.org/abs/2210.03869

A Unified Framework and Benchmark Study for Optimization of Diverse, Plausible, and Actionable Counterfactual Explanations

Jacob Sanderson(✉), Hua Mao, and Wai Lok Woo

School of Computer Science, Northumbria University, Newcastle NE1 8ST, UK
{jacob.sanderson,hua.mao,wailok.woo}@northumbria.ac.uk

Abstract. Counterfactual explanations offer intuitive, actionable insights into machine learning predictions by illustrating how minimal changes to an input can alter the output. High-quality counterfactuals must balance multiple properties–proximity, sparsity, plausibility, and diversity, while respecting domain constraints and decision complexity. In this paper, we present an extended study of DiPACE (Diverse, Plausible, Actionable Counterfactual Explanations), a gradient-based optimization framework designed to generate counterfactuals that jointly optimize all four key criteria. DiPACE introduces a perturbation-aware mechanism to escape local optima and a penalty-based refinement strategy to enforce user-defined quality thresholds during optimization. We evaluate DiPACE across binary and multi-class classification tasks using four real-world datasets from healthcare and finance. Extensive ablation studies demonstrate the necessity of each loss component, and comparisons with six baselines, including genetic, reinforcement learning, and generative approaches, show that DiPACE consistently achieves superior composite scores across all metrics. These results establish DiPACE as a flexible, interpretable, and high-performing method for generating robust counterfactuals in practical, high-stakes domains.

Keywords: Counterfactual Explanations · Explainable AI · Interpretable Machine Learning

1 Introduction

As artificial intelligence (AI) continues to shape decision-making across a wide range of domains–including healthcare [20,26], finance [1,27], cybersecurity [8], and climate resilience [19,25], the importance of explainable and trustworthy AI has become increasingly apparent. In such high-stakes contexts, understanding how and why AI systems arrive at particular decisions is essential for promoting transparency, ensuring fairness, and building user trust. Explainable AI (XAI) addresses this challenge by developing methods to make the behavior of complex machine learning (ML) models more interpretable and transparent to human users.

Among XAI techniques, counterfactual explanations (CFX) have gained significant traction due to their intuitive nature. A counterfactual explanation describes how an

H. J. van den Herik et al. (Eds.): ICAART 2025, LNAI 16517, pp. 642–659, 2026.
https://doi.org/10.1007/978-3-032-25032-2_31

input instance must change to receive a different prediction from a model, answering the question: "What minimal changes would lead to a different outcome?" [6,24]. This form of explanation is inherently actionable, providing users with potential paths to alter undesirable outcomes. For instance, a rejected loan applicant might learn what changes in income or employment status would have led to approval. This capacity to support recourse is especially important in decision-critical settings such as medicine, finance, and policy. However, generating high-quality counterfactuals is a non-trivial task, requiring the careful balancing of multiple desirable properties. Prior work has identified several key criteria for evaluating counterfactuals: proximity (the counterfactual should be close to the original instance), sparsity (it should change as few features as possible), plausibility (it should be realistic and lie within the data distribution), and diversity (it should provide a range of distinct alternatives) [4,10,21]. While these properties are widely acknowledged, most existing methods prioritize only a subset, often at the expense of others. Furthermore, many methods are restricted to binary classification settings, or offer limited support for domain-specific constraints [18].

To address these limitations, we previously introduced DiPACE (Diverse, Plausible, Actionable Counterfactual Explanations) [17], a flexible framework for generating counterfactuals that jointly optimize proximity, sparsity, plausibility, and diversity. DiPACE leverages gradient-based optimization combined with a perturbation mechanism to escape local optima, and allows user-defined constraints on feature mutability, ranges, and directional changes. In doing so, it offers a practical and adaptable approach for real-world deployment. Experimental results demonstrated that DiPACE achieved a more balanced trade-off across key counterfactual properties compared to baselines such as Wachter's method [24], DiCE [10], and CARE [14]. While promising, the original DiPACE study left several important research questions open. First, although DiPACE was designed to support practical decision making, its performance in multi-class settings remained underexplored. Additionally, comparisons with more recent and fundamentally different families of counterfactual generation methods, such as generative approaches (e.g., CounteRGAN [11]) and reinforcement learning-based methods (e.g., CFRL [16]) were not included in the original evaluation. These gaps limit the ability to generalize and contextualize DiPACE's performance in a rapidly evolving CFX landscape.

This paper addresses these gaps by presenting an extended evaluation of the DiPACE framework, including:

(i) Evaluation across binary and multi-class classification tasks, including datasets such as Heart Disease, Credit Approval, Obesity Levels, and Fetal Health, to test DiPACE's ability to generalize to more complex decision boundaries.
(ii) Comparison with a broader set of counterfactual generation baselines, encompassing six distinct optimization paradigms: gradient-based (Wachter), genetic (DiCE), GAN-based (CounteRGAN), reinforcement learning (CFRL), and latent-space optimization (QUCE). This provides a comprehensive benchmark of DiPACE's relative strengths and weaknesses.

Our results demonstrate that DiPACE maintains strong performance across all metrics and outperforms baselines on composite counterfactual quality scores in both binary and multi-class settings. The ablation study reveals which loss components are most critical to different counterfactual properties, offering guidance for practitioners aiming to adapt DiPACE to specific use cases. Notably, we find that the perturbation-based exploration mechanism significantly improves diversity without compromising plausibility or proximity.

2 Related Work

Counterfactual explanations have been studied extensively as a means to interpret model decisions, especially for structured (tabular) data. Prior literature has identified several key properties that high-quality counterfactuals should satisfy: they should be proximal to the original instance (entailing minimal overall change), sparse (altering as few features as possible), plausible (resembling realistic data points that satisfy domain constraints), and ideally diverse (offering multiple distinct alternatives) [2]. Proximity and sparsity make an explanation easier to achieve and understand by limiting changes to small, actionable modifications. Plausibility ensures the counterfactual lies on the data manifold and respects real-world feasibility (e.g., not suggesting an impossibly large income increase or an unrealistic age), and diversity, while not always addressed in early work, is beneficial in providing a range of options – increasing the chance that at least one explanation offers a usable and acceptable path for the individual user.

Many foundational approaches in this area optimize for a subset of these objectives. Proximity and sparsity were the focus of some of the earliest methods. Wachter et al. [24] introduced a seminal optimization-based approach that finds a counterfactual by minimizing a distance metric (typically L1 and/or L2) subject to the desired prediction change. This yields counterfactuals that are as close as possible to the original instance (high proximity), often resulting in relatively sparse modifications, but it does not guarantee that the suggestion is realistic or provide alternative options. Several others build on the idea of minimal changes. For example, Ustun et al. [22] formulate actionable recourse as an optimization problem for linear models, using integer programming to find the smallest-cost feature changes under user-defined feasibility constraints. This ensures any recommended action is not only small but also obeys domain rules (e.g. only increasing income, not changing immutable attributes), improving plausibility. Heuristic search methods like Growing Spheres [9] likewise seek the nearest decision-boundary point to achieve the desired outcome, effectively prioritizing proximity and minimal feature flips. These proximity-focused approaches, however, often operate in an unconstrained input space and can produce implausible results if not checked against the data distribution.

To address plausibility and actionability, another line of research integrates data-driven or knowledge-driven constraints. Poyiadzi et al. proposed FACE [13] (Feasible and Actionable Counterfactual Explanations), which finds counterfactuals via the shortest path over a graph of real instances. By walking through actual data points, FACE generates explanations that are "coherent with the underlying data distribution" and supported by feasible steps of change, ensuring realistic and achievable recourses. Other methods incorporate generative models or density estimators to keep suggestions on-manifold. For example, Van Looveren and Klaise [23], Pawelczyk et al. [12] and Duell et al. [5] leverage variational autoencoders to generate counterfactuals that stay close to training data distribution, adding latent-space or density-based penalties so that the result is a plausible data point.

Meanwhile, several works have recognized the importance of diversity in counterfactual explanations. Rather than returning a single solution, diversity-driven methods generate multiple counterfactuals that satisfy the desired outcome in qualitatively different ways. Mothilal et al. [10] introduced DiCE, which uses a determinantal point process-based objective to explicitly encourage diverse counterfactuals. By offering a selection of alternatives, DiCE gives end-users options – for example, one counterfactual might suggest improving credit score by increasing income, while another suggests reducing debt – which is valuable since certain suggestions may be impractical or undesirable for a given individual. Other approaches achieve diversity through clever search or optimization constraints. Russell [15] formulated the counterfactual search as a mixed-integer programming (MIP) problem and demonstrated how adding diversity constraints or finding multiple solutions of similar cost can yield a set of distinct explanations.

Only recently have researchers begun to aim for a more balanced, multi-objective approach. Some techniques combine objectives or use multi-step pipelines to cover more bases. Dandl et al. [3] proposed a genetic algorithm to approximate the Pareto-optimal set of counterfactuals trading off proximity, sparsity, and plausibility, while relying on the inherent stochasticity of genetic algorithms to support diversity. Rasouli and Yu [14] introduce CARE, a coherent actionable recourse method that uses a multi-objective genetic algorithm to simultaneously optimize for factors like distance, sparsity, and feasibility. CARE's evolutionary approach generates a population of candidate explanations and selects those that best balance multiple criteria. In a different vein, Guidotti [7] suggests an ensemble of counterfactual explainers to cover all desired properties. By combining "weak" explainers that each optimize a subset, the ensemble attempts to produce explanations satisfying minimality, plausibility, diversity, and other criteria together. These efforts indicate a recognition that no single existing method inherently excels across all four dimensions.

While the literature on tabular counterfactual explanations is rich, each family of methods tends to address some of the core objectives but not all. There is a clear gap in approaches that explicitly and simultaneously optimize proximity, sparsity, plausibility, and diversity in a unified framework. DiPACE fills this gap by introducing a structured and configurable approach that integrates all four criteria. Unlike prior methods that require a trade-off, or a manual choice between different explanation tools, our approach optimizes a single composite objective encompassing all four properties. It allows the relative emphasis on each aspect to be tuned to domain needs, ensuring that the generated counterfactuals are not only close and sparse, but also realistic for the individual's context and varied in their form. By addressing all major criteria together, our method provides more comprehensive and flexible explanations, representing a significant step toward more balanced counterfactual reasoning in tabular data settings.

3 Methodology

3.1 Overview

As in the original DiPACE, the aim is to generate diverse, plausible, sparse, and proximal counterfactuals. These qualities ensure that counterfactuals (CFs) are actionable, interpretable, and aligned with the underlying data distribution, while offering users a broad set of feasible alternatives. We adopt a gradient-based optimization strategy to efficiently minimize a weighted sum of loss terms, where each term corresponds to a desired CF quality. The optimization is conducted through direct manipulation of instance features while enforcing user-defined constraints, such as feature immutability, directionality of change, and acceptable value ranges.

To overcome the limitations of standard gradient descent–particularly its susceptibility to local optima in non-convex spaces–we introduce a perturbation-aware mechanism that activates when convergence stalls or fails to reach an acceptable loss. This mechanism injects controlled stochasticity to help escape poor minima and explore alternative solutions. Additionally, we implement a penalty-based refinement approach in DiPACE+, which dynamically adjusts the optimization pressure on specific loss components based on their deviation from user-defined thresholds. This allows practitioners to tailor the optimization process to specific domain requirements e.g., by enforcing stronger plausibility or higher sparsity when necessary, without manual tuning of loss weights during training. Pseudocode for the DiPACE and DiPACE+ algorithm is given in Algorithm 1.

3.2 Objective Function

Let $x^q \in \mathbb{R}^n$ denote the query instance and $C = c_1, \ldots, c_m$ be the set of m counterfactuals, each $c_i \in \mathbb{R}^n$. DiPACE optimizes the following total loss function:

$$\begin{aligned} L = L_{val}(f(C), y') + \lambda_{prox} L_{prox}(C, x^q) + \lambda_{spars} L_{spars}(C, x^q) + \\ \lambda_{plaus} L_{plaus}(C, X) + \lambda_{div}(1 - L_{div}(C)) + L_{cat}(C) \end{aligned} \tag{1}$$

Here, f is the predictive model, y' is the target class, X is the training data, and the λ weights control the contribution of each quality component. The final term L_{cat} regularizes categorical features.

3.3 Loss Components

Validity Loss. The fundamental requirement of any counterfactual explanation is that it results in a different predicted class than the original instance. Specifically, the generated counterfactuals must be classified with high confidence as the desired target class y'. To enforce this, we define a validity loss term that penalizes incorrect class predictions. For binary classification tasks, we apply the binary cross-entropy (BCE) loss. This loss function measures the discrepancy between the predicted probability p_i of the counterfactual x'_i belonging to the positive class and the desired label $y' \in \{0, 1\}$, averaged over a set of m counterfactual instances:

Input: Query Instance x^q, Model f, Hyperparameters θ
Parameters : Learning rate α, Weights λ, Thresholds τ, Scale Factors γ, Maximum Iterations μ, Maximum Perturbation Attempts δ
Output: Counterfactual Set C
Initialize $C \in \mathbb{R}^{m \times n}$ with $c_{ij} \sim \mathcal{N}(0,1)$
Let iteration count $t = 0$, perturbation count $p = 0$, previous loss $L_{prev} = \infty$
while $t < \mu$ ***and*** $|L - L_{prev}| \geq \tau_{ld}$ **do**
  Compute $L_{val}, L_{div}, L_{plaus}, L_{prox}, L_{spars}, L_{cat}$
  if *DiPACE+* **then**
    foreach $L_i \in \{L_{plaus}, L_{prox}, L_{spars}\}$ **do**
      if $L_i > \tau_i$ **then**
        $L_i \leftarrow L_i(1+\gamma_i)$
      end
    end
    if $L_{div} < \tau_{div}$ **then**
      $L_{div} \leftarrow L_{div}(1-\gamma_{div})$
    end
  end
  Compute total loss:
  $L \leftarrow L_{val} + \lambda_1(1 - L_{div}) + \lambda_2 L_{plaus} + \lambda_3 L_{prox} + \lambda_4 L_{spars} + L_{cat}$
  Compute gradients and update C via Adam optimizer
  Apply user constraints
  $L_{prev} \leftarrow L$
  $t \leftarrow t+1$
end
while $L > \tau_{pert}$ ***and*** $p < \delta$ **do**
  Perturb C by adding $\mathcal{N}(0, \gamma_{pert})$ to non-fixed features
  Re-run gradient-based optimization as above
  if $L \leq \tau_{pert}$ **then**
    return C
  end
  $p \leftarrow p+1$
end
return C *with lowest* L

Algorithm 1. DiPACE and DiPACE+ algorithms, adapted from [17].

$$L_{val}^{BCE} = -\frac{1}{m}\sum_{i=1}^{m}[y' \log(p_i) + (1-y')\log(1-p_i)] \tag{2}$$

For multi-class classification tasks, where the model outputs a probability distribution across cl classes, we use categorical cross-entropy (CE) loss. Let $y'ij \in \{0,1\}$ denote a one-hot encoding of the desired class for instance i, and pij be the predicted probability of class j. The CE loss is defined as:

$$L_{val}^{CE} = -\frac{1}{m}\sum_{i=1}^{m}\sum_{j=1}^{cl} y'ij \log(pij) \tag{3}$$

Proximity and Sparsity. To ensure counterfactuals remain both actionable and interpretable, we incorporate two complementary loss terms, proximity, and sparsity. Proximity encourages counterfactuals to remain close to the original query instance x^q, minimizing the magnitude of changes made to achieve the desired prediction. We compute the average absolute deviation of each counterfactual instance $c_i \in C$ from the query instance, normalized by the feature-wise median absolute deviation (MAD), which accounts for feature scale and improves robustness:

$$L_{prox} = \frac{1}{mn} \sum_{i=1}^{m} \sum_{j=1}^{n} \frac{|c_{ij} - x_j^q|}{MAD_j} \tag{4}$$

Here, m is the number of counterfactuals, n is the number of features, and MAD_j is the median absolute deviation of feature j across the dataset. Sparsity, on the other hand, aims to limit the number of features that are altered in each counterfactual. This improves user interpretability and feasibility by suggesting only minimal, targeted changes. We compute the proportion of features that differ from the original instance by more than a small threshold ϵ, averaged over the counterfactual set:

$$L_{spars} = \frac{1}{mn} \sum_{i=1}^{m} \sum_{j=1}^{n} \mathbb{1}(|c_{ij} - x_j^q| \geq \epsilon) \tag{5}$$

Here, $\mathbb{1}(\cdot)$ is an indicator function returning 1 if the change is significant and 0 otherwise. This loss penalizes excessive changes, favoring sparse counterfactuals that are more likely to be practical and comprehensible for end users.

Plausibility. To ensure counterfactuals are realistic and lie close to the data manifold, we include a plausibility term that penalizes instances which diverge from the observed data distribution. Inspired by Dandl et al. [3], we define plausibility as the normalized average distance between each counterfactual c_i and its k-nearest neighbors $x_j \in X$ from the training data.

$$L_{plaus} = \frac{1}{m} \sum_{i=1}^{m} \left(\frac{1}{k} \sum_{j=1}^{k} \frac{|c_i - x_j| - d_{min}}{d_{max} - d_{min} + \epsilon} \right) \tag{6}$$

Here, m is the number of counterfactuals, k is the number of nearest neighbors, $|c_i - x_j|$ denotes the distance (e.g., L1 norm) between the counterfactual c_i and observed instance x_j. d_{min} and d_{max} are the minimum and maximum distances among the k neighbors, used to normalize the loss to the $[0, 1]$ range, and ϵ is a small constant to prevent division by zero. By minimizing this term, we encourage the generation of counterfactuals that resemble real, previously seen examples, ensuring the returned explanations are not only theoretically valid but also practically plausible and trustworthy.

Diversity. Diversity ensures that the set of counterfactuals offers multiple distinct and actionable alternatives rather than near-identical solutions. To achieve this, we adopt the determinantal point process (DPP) approach introduced by Mothilal et al. [10], which encourages high pairwise dissimilarity within the counterfactual set. We construct a similarity kernel matrix K, where each entry reflects the inverse of the distance between counterfactual pairs c_i and c_j, and compute the determinant of this matrix to assess the diversity:

$$L_{div} = dpp\left(\frac{1}{1 + \sum_{l=1}^{n} |c_{il} - c_{jl}|}\right) \tag{7}$$

where $c_i, c_j \in C$ represents the set of m counterfactuals, and n is the number of features. The denominator ensures that higher distances (greater dissimilarity) result in lower similarity values. The DPP encourages a diverse set by assigning higher scores to configurations where the counterfactuals are more spread out in the feature space. In practice, since our optimization process minimizes the total loss, we subtract this term to cast the maximization of diversity into a minimization objective.

Categorical Regularization. When features include categorical variables encoded via one-hot encoding, counterfactuals must preserve valid encodings, i.e., each categorical variable must have exactly one active (non-zero) value among its components. Without regularization, gradient-based optimization may yield invalid encodings with non-binary values or multiple active categories.To enforce this structural constraint, we include a categorical regularization term:

$$L_{cat} = \sum_{v \in cat} \sum_{i=1}^{m} \left(\sum_{j=v_{start}}^{v_{end}} c_{ij} - 1 \right)^2 \tag{8}$$

Here, cat is the set of one-hot encoded categorical features, v_{start} and v_{end} define the index range for the one-hot group corresponding to categorical variable v, m is the number of counterfactuals c_i. The inner sum $\sum_{j=v_{start}}^{v_{end}} c_{ij}$ computes the total activation for the one-hot segment, and the squared deviation penalizes any deviation from a valid one-hot total of 1.

3.4 Optimization with Perturbation

We use the Adam optimizer to minimize the weighted sum of all loss components. Adam is well-suited for navigating complex, high-dimensional loss landscapes, offering adaptive learning rates and momentum-based updates that improve convergence speed and stability. However, gradient-based methods are susceptible to local optima, especially in non-convex spaces. To mitigate this, we introduce a perturbation-based escape mechanism. When the loss plateaus before reaching the desired threshold, we apply noise to the current counterfactuals C, selectively perturbing features that differ significantly from the original query instance x^q:

$$c_{ij} = c_{ij} + \gamma_{pert} \cdot \mathcal{N}(0, 1) \tag{9}$$

where γ_{pert} is a user-defined scale factor controlling the noise magnitude, $\mathcal{N}(0, 1)$ is a standard Gaussian distribution. This perturbation encourages exploration beyond local basins of attraction without compromising sparsity, since noise is only applied to changed features (i.e., $|c_{ij} - x_j^q| \geq \epsilon$).

The perturbation process is repeated until either the overall loss falls below a user-defined threshold, or a maximum number of perturbation attempts is reached. This strategy balances local refinement with global exploration, improving the robustness and completeness of the counterfactual search.

3.5 Penalty-Based Refinement

To further guide the optimization and ensure that generated counterfactuals satisfy minimum quality thresholds, we introduce a penalty mechanism that reinforces proximity, sparsity, plausibility, and diversity objectives when they fall outside user-defined tolerances. This mechanism supports more aggressive optimization by dynamically scaling the corresponding loss terms.

Let τ_{char} denote the threshold for a given characteristic (e.g., proximity, sparsity, plausibility), and γ_{char} be the penalty scale factor. For each characteristic loss $L_{char} \in L_{prox}, L_{spars}, L_{plaus}$, the penalized loss is computed as:

$$L_{char} = \begin{cases} L_{char}, & \text{if } L_{char} \leq \tau_{char} \\ L_{char} \cdot (1 + \gamma_{char}), & \text{otherwise} \end{cases} \tag{10}$$

In contrast, diversity is a maximization objective. Therefore, we apply a penalty when the diversity score L_{div} falls below a user-defined threshold τ_{div}:

$$L_{div} = \begin{cases} L_{div}, & \text{if } L_{div} \geq \tau_{div} \\ L_{div} \cdot (1 - \gamma_{div}), & \text{otherwise} \end{cases} \tag{11}$$

This penalty-based refinement enables the framework to prioritize improvement in underperforming aspects of the counterfactual set without requiring manual reweighting of loss components. It ensures that the final counterfactuals meet the desired standards for feasibility and informativeness, especially in high-stakes or constrained settings.

3.6 User Constraints

To ensure that counterfactual explanations remain actionable and domain-relevant, our framework supports several user-defined constraints that restrict the optimization space based on real-world feasibility. These constraints are applied during each optimization step, and include:

- Immutable features: Specify features that must remain fixed.
- Range bounds: Constrain values to acceptable intervals.
- Directional constraints: Allow only increase/decrease.

These constraints are implemented via masking and clipping during optimization, ensuring that the generated counterfactuals not only optimize the loss function but also comply with practical feasibility requirements.

3.7 Evaluation

Datasets. We perform evaluation across 4 datasets, described in Table 1. These datasets were chosen to reflect realistic application areas in healthcare and finance, and to test the method's ability to generalize across different levels of complexity and class cardinality.

Table 1. Description of the datasets evaluated in the study.

Dataset	Features	Instances	Classes
Heart Disease	13	303	2
Credit Approval	14	690	2
Obesity Levels	16	2111	7
Fetal Health	32	2126	3

Baselines. We compare DiPACE against several established counterfactual explanation methods, summarized in Table 2. Wachter et al.'s method is a foundational gradient-based approach that prioritizes minimal feature changes to achieve the desired prediction, but lacks mechanisms for encouraging diversity, sparsity, or plausibility. DiCE is a widely adopted framework that introduces diversity through a dedicated loss term and supports user-defined mutability constraints, although it does not consider sparsity or plausibility.

CFRL, CounteRGAN, and QUCE each incorporate plausibility implicitly via generative modeling. CFRL and QUCE operate in the latent space of a variational autoencoder (VAE), while CounteRGAN uses the discriminative loss of a generative adversarial network (GAN) to encourage realistic outputs. Among these, only CFRL supports the generation of multiple counterfactuals per instance, offering limited diversity, though without an explicit optimization term. Wachter, CounteRGAN, and QUCE each generate a single counterfactual per instance, precluding diverse recourse. In contrast, DiPACE directly optimizes for diversity, proximity, sparsity, and plausibility, making it a more holistic and configurable framework for generating actionable counterfactual explanations.

Evaluation Metrics. Our evaluation uses the same metrics optimized in the DiPACE loss function: proximity, sparsity, plausibility, and diversity. These are directly computed as described in the methodology section, but without the MAD weighting in the proximity computation. In addition to these, we introduce a confidence metric to assess how strongly each counterfactual is classified as the desired target class. This is defined as the model's predicted probability for the target class, averaged across the counterfactual set. Higher confidence indicates that the counterfactuals not only cross the decision boundary but do so decisively.

To support objective comparison across methods and datasets, we normalize all metrics to the [0,1] range. These normalized metrics are then aggregated into a composite

Table 2. Description of the counterfactual methods evaluated in the study.

Method	Proximity	Sparsity	Plausibility	Diversity	Multi-Class	Optimization
DiPACE [17]	✓	✓	✓	✓	✓	Gradient
Wachter [24]	✓	✗	✗	✗	✗	Gradient
DiCE [10]	✓	✗	✗	✓	✓	Genetic
CFRL [16]	✓	✗	✓[1]	✓	✓	RL[2]
CounteRGAN [11]	✗	✗	✓[1]	✗	✓	GAN
QUCE [5]	✓	✗	✓[1]	✗	✗	Gradient[2]

[1] Plausibility is encouraged through generative modeling rather than an explicit optimization objective.

[2] Optimization is performed in the latent space of a variational autoencoder.

score. For metrics where lower values are better (e.g., proximity, sparsity, plausibility), we invert the normalized scores so that higher values consistently indicate better performance, then compute the composite score as the mean of the five normalized metrics. This provides a holistic view of overall counterfactual quality and facilitates direct comparison across baselines.

4 Results

4.1 Ablation Study

We perform an ablation study by evaluating different combinations of our loss function terms, as well as DiPACE without the perturbation in the optimization, or the additional penalty for unsatisfactory loss values. Proximity is included in every combination, as it is fundamental to any CFX algorithm. We consider the following combinations:

1. Validity and Proximity
2. Validity, Proximity, and Sparsity
3. Validity, Proximity, and Plausibility
4. Validity, Proximity, and Diversity
5. Validity, Proximity, Sparsity, and Plausibility
6. Validity, Proximity, Sparsity, and Diversity
7. Validity, Proximity, Plausibility, and Diversity

as well as DiPACE, which is Proximity, Sparsity, Plausibility, and Diversity (Table 3).

Across all datasets, DiPACE consistently achieves the highest or near-highest composite score, confirming the effectiveness of optimizing for all four key qualities – sparsity, plausibility, proximity, and diversity – in tandem. When individual terms are removed or omitted, performance often degrades in at least one metric, illustrating the importance of a balanced multi-objective formulation.

In particular, omitting diversity (Combinations 1–3 and 5) leads to a noticeable drop in diversity scores, sometimes dramatically (e.g., 0.04 for Combination 1 on the Obesity dataset), and often reduces the overall composite score, suggesting that diversity contributes not only to option range but also indirectly improves confidence and

Table 3. Ablation Study of Loss Function Terms for Each Dataset.

		Loss Term Combinations								
Metric	DiPACE	1	2	3	4	5	6	7	W/o Pert.	W/o Pen.
Heart Disease Dataset										
Proximity ↓	0.18	0.19	0.18	0.32	0.15	0.43	0.47	0.43	0.49	0.44
Sparsity ↓	0.34	0.23	0.29	0.36	0.23	0.43	0.46	0.41	0.39	0.43
Plausibility ↓	0.48	0.84	0.81	0.22	0.67	0.26	0.97	0.20	0.63	0.58
Diversity ↑	0.84	0.61	0.70	0.88	0.87	0.91	0.92	0.89	0.82	0.78
Confidence ↑	0.91	0.67	0.64	0.84	0.75	0.87	0.57	0.84	0.83	0.83
Composite Score ↑	0.75	0.60	0.61	0.76	0.71	0.73	0.52	0.74	0.64	0.65
Credit Approval Dataset										
Proximity ↓	0.15	0.14	0.12	0.19	0.16	0.16	0.13	0.23	0.23	0.21
Sparsity ↓	0.22	0.19	0.16	0.21	0.20	0.20	0.17	0.25	0.27	0.24
Plausibility ↓	0.50	0.68	0.53	0.61	0.46	0.45	0.54	0.42	0.51	0.45
Diversity ↑	0.90	0.86	0.72	0.82	0.92	0.80	0.88	0.94	0.91	0.92
Confidence ↑	0.91	0.76	0.74	0.76	0.71	0.78	0.73	0.72	0.75	0.70
Composite Score ↑	0.79	0.76	0.73	0.71	0.76	0.75	0.75	0.75	0.73	0.74
Obesity Levels Dataset										
Proximity ↓	0.21	0.06	0.24	0.26	0.17	0.24	0.16	0.26	0.35	0.37
Sparsity ↓	0.23	0.25	0.25	0.32	0.29	0.25	0.36	0.20	0.35	0.40
Plausibility ↓	0.34	0.50	0.70	0.52	0.50	0.53	0.48	0.47	0.45	0.51
Diversity ↑	0.92	0.04	0.11	0.79	0.84	0.64	0.42	0.82	0.80	0.83
Confidence ↑	0.76	0.68	0.79	0.74	0.71	0.78	0.68	0.76	0.73	0.69
Composite Score ↑	0.78	0.58	0.54	0.69	0.72	0.68	0.62	0.73	0.68	0.65
Fetal Health Dataset										
Proximity ↓	0.34	0.29	0.33	0.47	0.46	0.35	0.29	0.46	0.40	0.45
Sparsity ↓	0.35	0.51	0.31	0.52	0.51	0.40	0.33	0.52	0.51	0.49
Plausibility ↓	0.42	0.56	0.51	0.42	0.49	0.48	0.63	0.45	0.54	0.47
Diversity ↑	0.96	0.82	0.86	0.89	0.90	0.91	0.83	0.95	0.94	0.93
Confidence ↑	0.79	0.78	0.79	0.74	0.72	0.78	0.73	0.74	0.71	0.72
Composite Score ↑	0.73	0.65	0.70	0.64	0.63	0.69	0.66	0.65	0.64	0.65

plausibility. On the other hand, removing plausibility (Combinations 1, 2, 4, and 6) often results in significantly worse plausibility scores (e.g., 0.84 on Heart Disease in Combination 1 vs. 0.48 in DiPACE), indicating that proximity and sparsity alone are insufficient to ensure realism. Combinations including only one or two additional terms beyond proximity (e.g., Combinations 1–4) tend to underperform compared to those that integrate three or more objectives. Notably, Combination 4, which includes diversity but not plausibility or sparsity, sometimes achieves relatively strong results (e.g., composite score of 0.76 on Heart Disease), demonstrating that diversity can compensate to some extent—but not fully—for missing other qualities.

Removing the perturbation mechanism or penalty scaling (last two columns) also leads to consistently worse results, especially in proximity and sparsity. This highlights the value of the perturbation strategy for escaping local minima and the penalties for enforcing thresholds when certain qualities fall below acceptable levels. Taken together, these findings support the central design philosophy of DiPACE: that counterfactual quality is inherently multi-dimensional, and optimizing for a single or partial subset of characteristics often leads to trade-offs. By combining all terms in a flexible, customizable loss function – and enhancing optimization with perturbation and penalties – DiPACE is able to provide superior, balanced counterfactuals across datasets.

4.2 Baseline Comparison

To evaluate the effectiveness of DiPACE, we compare it against a diverse set of baseline counterfactual explanation methods, including Wachter, DiCE, CFRL, CounteRGAN, and QUCE. Each baseline represents a different class of optimization strategy: gradient descent (Wachter), genetic algorithms (DiCE), reinforcement learning (CFRL), generative adversarial networks (CounteRGAN), and latent space optimization (QUCE). Results are shown across four datasets in Table 4 using five metrics: proximity, sparsity, plausibility, diversity, and confidence. A composite score summarizes overall performance, normalized such that higher values indicate better results.

Across all datasets, DiPACE consistently outperforms or matches the best-performing baselines in composite score. This highlights the advantage of explicitly balancing proximity, sparsity, plausibility, and diversity within a unified optimization framework. Notably, DiPACE achieves strong diversity scores without compromising on plausibility or proximity—qualities often sacrificed in other methods.

On the Heart Disease dataset, DiPACE delivers the highest composite score (0.75), outperforming DiCE and CFRL, which optimize only a subset of the qualities. DiCE shows strong performance on proximity and sparsity but performs poorly on plausibility and diversity, while CFRL yields moderate proximity and confidence but suffers in sparsity and diversity. CounteRGAN achieves high confidence, likely due to its generative nature, but fails in sparsity and diversity, producing less interpretable results. In the Credit Approval dataset, DiPACE again leads with a composite score of 0.81. DiCE performs well in confidence but offers limited diversity. QUCE, which optimizes in the latent space, achieves excellent proximity and confidence but at the cost of plausibility and diversity. This suggests that while latent space optimization can yield confident counterfactuals, it may not preserve interpretability or data realism without explicit constraints. For multi-class problems (Obesity Levels and Fetal Health), DiPACE remains competitive. It achieves the top composite score in both cases, outperforming DiCE and CFRL. CounteRGAN provides strong confidence scores but, as before, struggles with sparsity and diversity. The generative approach may produce plausible-looking counterfactuals, but they often lack actionable quality and variation.

The diversity metric clearly differentiates DiPACE from most baselines. While methods like DiCE and CFRL include limited diversity mechanisms, they rarely achieve the broad range of alternatives that DiPACE offers. In contrast, Wachter, QUCE, and

Table 4. Comparison with Baseline Methods.

Metric	DiPACE	Wachter	DiCE	CFRL	CounteRGAN	QUCE
Heart Disease Dataset						
Proximity ↓	0.18	0.02	0.14	0.29	0.32	0.12
Sparsity ↓	0.34	0.17	0.15	0.35	1.00	0.17
Plausibility ↓	0.48	0.83	0.59	0.68	0.39	0.72
Diversity ↑	0.84	0.00	0.44	0.12	0.00	0.00
Confidence ↑	0.91	0.75	0.64	0.80	0.81	0.96
Composite Score ↑	0.75	0.54	0.64	0.52	0.42	0.59
Credit Approval Dataset						
Proximity ↓	0.15	0.03	0.14	0.11	0.14	0.03
Sparsity ↓	0.18	0.10	0.13	0.16	1.00	0.07
Plausibility ↓	0.37	0.56	0.56	0.44	0.36	0.64
Diversity ↑	0.96	0.00	0.31	0.05	0.00	0.00
Confidence ↑	0.78	0.56	0.93	0.86	0.85	0.99
Composite Score ↑	0.81	0.64	0.68	0.64	0.63	0.65
Obesity Levels Dataset						
Proximity ↓	0.21	-	0.10	0.13	0.14	-
Sparsity ↓	0.23	-	0.10	0.29	1.00	-
Plausibility ↓	0.34	-	0.50	0.60	0.26	-
Diversity ↑	0.92	-	0.00	0.01	0.00	-
Confidence ↑	0.76	-	0.88	0.80	0.96	-
Composite Score ↑	0.78	-	0.64	0.56	0.51	-
Fetal Health Dataset						
Proximity ↓	0.34	-	0.06	0.07	0.16	-
Sparsity ↓	0.35	-	0.08	0.14	1.00	-
Plausibility ↓	0.42	-	0.69	0.50	0.26	-
Diversity ↑	0.96	-	0.20	0.02	0.00	-
Confidence ↑	0.79	-	0.67	0.76	0.99	-
Composite Score ↑	0.73	-	0.61	0.61	0.51	-

CounteRGAN return counterfactuals with little to no diversity, often repeating similar solutions. QUCE consistently achieves high prediction confidence, especially in the Heart Disease and Credit Approval datasets. However, this comes with limited diversity and modest plausibility scores, supporting the hypothesis that optimizing solely in latent space may produce high-certainty counterfactuals that are less representative or actionable in the original feature space.

Overall, these results demonstrate that DiPACE achieves a balanced trade-off across all key dimensions. Unlike most existing methods that specialize in a subset of objectives, DiPACE maintains a comprehensive optimization strategy that yields high-quality, feasible, and diverse counterfactuals suitable for real-world use cases.

5 Discussion

The results presented in the ablation study and baseline comparison provide strong empirical support for the design choices behind DiPACE. Our findings reinforce the importance of explicitly balancing multiple counterfactual explanation (CFX) objectives in a unified optimization framework.

The ablation study reveals that each component of the DiPACE loss function plays a distinct and complementary role. Proximity alone leads to counterfactuals that are close to the original instance but often lack plausibility, diversity, or predictive confidence. Adding sparsity improves actionability, but still fails to produce realistic or varied explanations. Including plausibility enhances realism, but without diversity, the counterfactual set offers limited insight into the model's decision boundary. Only when all four objectives are optimized together does the system consistently achieve high composite scores across datasets. Interestingly, combinations that exclude sparsity or diversity tend to produce less actionable or less informative results, respectively. In addition, removing the perturbation mechanism or penalty scaling leads to degraded performance, particularly on more complex datasets like Obesity Levels and Fetal Health. This highlights the value of DiPACE's adaptive optimization strategy in avoiding local minima and enforcing quality thresholds.

The baseline comparison further demonstrates that DiPACE provides more balanced and interpretable counterfactual explanations than existing state-of-the-art methods. While methods like DiCE and CFRL perform well on individual metrics, they typically underperform in one or more key dimensions. For example, DiCE achieves strong proximity and confidence, but suffers from low plausibility and diversity. CFRL produces moderate results across most metrics but fails to provide diverse solutions, limiting its utility in offering users a range of recourse options. Generative methods like CounteRGAN and QUCE perform well in terms of predictive confidence, but often produce implausible or redundant counterfactuals. This is particularly evident in the diversity and sparsity metrics, where both methods score poorly. The lack of diversity is concerning, especially in high-stakes domains where decision support tools should present a range of viable alternatives. QUCE's latent space optimization seems effective at pushing counterfactuals across the decision boundary with high confidence, but often at the expense of alignment with the observed data distribution. By contrast, DiPACE achieves the highest composite score on every dataset, demonstrating its generalizability across both binary and multi-class classification tasks. Its strong performance across proximity, sparsity, plausibility, and diversity confirms the value of a structured, multi-objective loss function combined with flexible constraint handling and adaptive optimization.

Beyond numerical performance, DiPACE excels in interpretability. The user-defined constraints for mutability, directionality, and feature ranges ensure that the generated counterfactuals are not only statistically valid but also contextually appropriate. Unlike black-box generative models or unconstrained search methods, DiPACE's design allows stakeholders to align explanation outputs with domain-specific feasibility constraints. Moreover, the perturbation mechanism and penalty scaling provide practical safeguards against suboptimal or low-quality solutions. These features act as built-in quality controls, enabling users to generate high-quality counterfactuals even when models exhibit irregular or flat loss landscapes.

Despite its strengths, DiPACE does have some limitations. First, the reliance on gradient-based optimization restricts its direct applicability to differentiable models. While this is mitigated in many real-world use cases through surrogate modeling, future work could extend DiPACE with hybrid optimization techniques or model-agnostic approximations. Second, while our plausibility term approximates alignment with the data distribution via k-nearest neighbors, it does not explicitly encode causal relationships. This could lead to plausible-looking counterfactuals that violate structural dependencies. Future extensions could incorporate causal constraints or domain knowledge into the loss function to further enhance realism. Lastly, runtime and scalability are not yet addressed in this study. Although DiPACE performs well on tabular datasets of moderate dimensionality, applying it to large-scale or high-dimensional data (e.g., images, time series) may require additional efficiency improvements or latent space adaptations.

6 Conclusion

In this work, we presented an enhanced and extended version of the DiPACE framework for generating counterfactual explanations (CFX) that balance proximity, sparsity, plausibility, and diversity in a unified, adaptable optimization pipeline. Building on the original DiPACE formulation, we introduced penalty-based refinement and perturbation-aware optimization to more effectively navigate the loss landscape and enforce user-defined thresholds for explanation quality. Through comprehensive ablation studies, we demonstrated that each component of the multi-objective loss function contributes uniquely to explanation quality, and that only their joint optimization yields consistently strong performance. Our results also highlight the importance of the perturbation mechanism and penalty scaling in overcoming local optima and refining explanations in complex domains. Comparison against widely used baselines–including gradient-based, genetic, reinforcement learning, and generative methods–showed that DiPACE consistently delivers more balanced and actionable explanations across multiple datasets. In particular, DiPACE outperformed existing methods on composite metrics by achieving strong proximity and sparsity without sacrificing plausibility or diversity. These findings establish DiPACE as a flexible, interpretable, and high-performing framework for counterfactual generation, suitable for deployment in sensitive real-world domains. By allowing users to control optimization weights, apply domain-specific constraints, and generate diverse yet realistic counterfactuals, DiPACE supports both transparency and user agency in AI-assisted decision-making.

In future work, we aim to extend DiPACE to explicitly incorporate causal reasoning, enabling the generation of counterfactuals that are not only statistically plausible but also causally valid. We also plan to explore scalability to structured and high-dimensional data, such as time series and spatial domains, and to investigate integration with generative priors or diffusion models for latent space optimization.

Disclosure of Interests. The authors have no competing interests to declare that are relevant to the content of this article.

References

1. Babaei, G., Giudici, P., Raffinetti, E.: Explainable fintech lending. J. Econ. Bus. **125**, 106126 (2023)
2. Brughmans, D., Melis, L., Martens, D.: Disagreement amongst counterfactual explanations: how transparency can be misleading. Top 1–34 (2024)
3. Dandl, S., Molnar, C., Binder, M., Bischl, B.: Multi-objective counterfactual explanations. In: Bäck, T., et al. (eds.) Proceedings of the International Conference on Parallel Problem Solving from Nature, pp. 448–469. Springer, Cham (2020). https://doi.org/10.1007/978-3-030-58112-1_31
4. Del Ser, J., Barredo-Arrieta, A., Díaz-Rodríguez, N., Herrera, F., Saranti, A., Holzinger, A.: On generating trustworthy counterfactual explanations. Inf. Sci. **655**, 119898 (2024)
5. Duell, J., Seisenberger, M., Fu, H., Fan, X.: Quce: The minimisation and quantification of path-based uncertainty for generative counterfactual explanations. arXiv preprint arXiv:2402.17516 (2024)
6. Guidotti, R.: Counterfactual explanations and how to find them: literature review and benchmarking. Data Min. Knowl. Discov. **36** (2022). https://doi.org/10.1007/s10618-022-00831-6
7. Guidotti, R., Ruggieri, S.: Ensemble of Counterfactual Explainers. In: Soares, C., Torgo, L. (eds.) DS 2021. LNCS (LNAI), vol. 12986, pp. 358–368. Springer, Cham (2021). https://doi.org/10.1007/978-3-030-88942-5_28
8. Kumar, P., Wazid, M., Singh, D., Singh, J., Das, A.K., Park, Y., Rodrigues, J.J.: Explainable artificial intelligence envisioned security mechanism for cyber threat hunting. Secur. Priv. **6**(6), e312 (2023)
9. Laugel, T., Lesot, M.J., Marsala, C., Renard, X., Detyniecki, M.: Inverse classification for comparison-based interpretability in machine learning. arXiv preprint arXiv:1712.08443 (2017)
10. Mothilal, R.K., Sharma, A., Tan, C.: Explaining machine learning classifiers through diverse counterfactual explanations. In: Proceedings of the 2020 Conference on Fairness, Accountability, and Transparency, pp. 607–617. ACM (2020). https://doi.org/10.1145/3351095.3372850
11. Nemirovsky, D., Thiebaut, N., Xu, Y., Gupta, A.: Countergan: generating counterfactuals for real-time recourse and interpretability using residual gans. In: Proceedings of the Thirty-Eighth Conference on Uncertainty in Artificial Intelligence. Proceedings of Machine Learning Research, vol. 180, pp. 1488–1497. PMLR (2022)
12. Pawelczyk, M., Broelemann, K., Kasneci, G.: Learning model-agnostic counterfactual explanations for tabular data. In: Proceedings of the web conference 2020, pp. 3126–3132 (2020)
13. Poyiadzi, R., Sokol, K., Santos-Rodriguez, R., De Bie, T., Flach, P.: Face: feasible and actionable counterfactual explanations. In: Proceedings of the AAAI/ACM Conference on AI, Ethics, and Society, pp. 344–350 (2020)
14. Rasouli, P., Chieh Yu, I.: Care: Coherent actionable recourse based on sound counterfactual explanations. Int. J. Data Sci. Anal. **17**(1), 13–38 (2024)
15. Russell, C.: Efficient search for diverse coherent explanations. In: Proceedings of the Conference on Fairness, Accountability, and Transparency, pp. 20–28. FAT* '19, Association for Computing Machinery, New York, NY, USA (2019). https://doi.org/10.1145/3287560.3287569

16. Samoilescu, R.F., Van Looveren, A., Klaise, J.: Model-agnostic and scalable counterfactual explanations via reinforcement learning. arXiv preprint arXiv:2106.02597 (2021)
17. Sanderson, J., Mao, H., Woo, W.L.: Dipace: Diverse, plausible and actionable counterfactual explanations. In: Proceedings of the 17th International Conference on Agents and Artificial Intelligence (2025)
18. Sanderson, J., Mao, H., Woo, W.L.: Gradcfa: A hybrid gradient-based counterfactual and feature attribution explanation algorithm for local interpretation of neural networks. IEEE Trans. Artif. Intell. (2025)
19. Sanderson, J., Tengtrairat, N., Woo, W.L., Mao, H., Al-Nima, R.R.: Xfimnet: an explainable deep learning architecture for versatile flood inundation mapping with synthetic aperture radar and multi-spectral optical images. Int. J. Remote Sens. **44**(24), 7755–7789 (2023)
20. Shin, H., et al.: Deep learning referral suggestion and tumour discrimination using explainable artificial intelligence applied to multiparametric mri. Eur. Radiol. **33**, 1–12 (2023)
21. Tsiourvas, A., Sun, W., Perakis, G.: Manifold-aligned counterfactual explanations for neural networks. In: International Conference on Artificial Intelligence and Statistics, pp. 3763–3771. PMLR (2024)
22. Ustun, B., Spangher, A., Liu, Y.: Actionable recourse in linear classification. In: Proceedings of the Conference on Fairness, Accountability, and Transparency, pp. 10–19 (2019)
23. Van Looveren, A., Klaise, J.: Interpretable counterfactual explanations guided by prototypes. In: Oliver, N., Pérez-Cruz, F., Kramer, S., Read, J., Lozano, J.A. (eds.) Joint European Conference on Machine Learning and Knowledge Discovery in Databases, pp. 650–665. Springer, Cham (2021). https://doi.org/10.1007/978-3-030-86520-7_40
24. Wachter, S., Mittelstadt, B., Russell, C.: Counterfactual explanations without opening the black box: Automated decisions and the gdpr. Harvard J. Law Technol. **31** (2018)
25. Wang, J., Sanderson, J., Iqbal, S., Woo, W.L.: Accelerated and interpretable flood susceptibility mapping through explainable deep learning with hydrological prior knowledge. Remote Sensing **17**(9), 1540 (2025)
26. Yagin, F.H., et al.: Explainable artificial intelligence model for identifying covid-19 gene biomarkers. Comput. Biol. Med. **154**, 106619 (2023)
27. Zhu, X., Chu, Q., Song, X., Hu, P., Peng, L.: Explainable prediction of loan default based on machine learning models. Data Sci. Manage. **6** (2023)

Graph-Transformer Multimodal Learning for Multi-agent Trajectory Forecasting Using MOPSO-Optimized Temporal Kolmogorov-Arnold Networks

Mohammad Reza Mohebbi[1,2(✉)], Elahe Kafash[3], and Mario Döller[1]

[1] Josef Ressel Center Vision2Move, University of Applied Sciences Kufstein Tirol, Kufstein, Austria
mario.doeller@fh-kufstein.ac.at

[2] Department of Computer Science and Mathematics, University of Passau, Passau, Germany
mohammadreza.mohebbi@fh-kufstein.ac.at

[3] Department of Computer Engineering, Imam Reza (AS) International University, Mashhad, Iran

Abstract. Precise forecasting of agent trajectories in complex urban environments has been recognized as a critical enabler for autonomous navigation, intelligent traffic control, and safety assurance in smart cities. In this work, a multimodal learning framework is proposed that fuses spatial and temporal reasoning for the prediction of future movements of heterogeneous agents. Spatial agent interactions are represented via a Graphormer architecture, whereas temporal dynamics are articulated via a Temporal Kolmogorov-Arnold Network (TKAN), which learns nonlinear temporal dependencies at multiple time steps. In order to be assured of optimal model configuration, in addition to hyperparameters, predictive accuracy, inference latency, and performance balance among agent types, a Multi-Objective Particle Swarm Optimization (MOPSO) algorithm is utilized to tune, simultaneously optimizing predictive accuracy, inference latency, and performance balance among agent types. Heterogeneous features such as agent category, velocity, acceleration, and traffic signal states are encoded to diversify input representations. Performance monitoring occurs through evaluation across large-scale, real-world datasets TUMDOT, inD, SIND, and pNEUMA, representing diverse urban scenes and agent distributions. High-quality performance is achieved in terms of Average Displacement Error (ADE) and Final Displacement Error (FDE), while, at the same time, incurring low inference times suitable for real-time applications. The proposed approach establishes a scalable and generalizable solution for multi-agent trajectory forecasting, contributing to the advancement of next-generation intelligent transportation systems.

Keywords: Multi-Agent Trajectory Forecasting · Graphormer · Temporal Kolmogorov-Arnold Network (TKAN) · Multi-Objective Particle Swarm Optimization (MOPSO) · Multimodal Learning · Autonomous Navigation · Spatiotemporal Modeling · Graph Neural Networks (GNNs) · Intelligent Transportation Systems (ITS)

H. J. van den Herik et al. (Eds.): ICAART 2025, LNAI 16517, pp. 660–686, 2026.
https://doi.org/10.1007/978-3-032-25032-2_32

1 Introduction

Urban traffic congestion remains one of the greatest challenges in modern cities, creating long trips, increased fuel usage, and additional air emissions, among other undesirable impacts on public health and sustainability impacts on cities [1,2]. The resulting economic impact, in terms of the stoppage of logistics, the decrease in productivity of the workforce, and the decrease in commercial performance, places severe limitations on the planning of infrastructure in cities. These problems are exacerbated by rapid urbanization rates, where growing populations consistently overwhelm transport networks well beyond the design capacities [3,4]. Congestion tends to start at crucial locations on roads where traffic volumes exceed threshold levels, creating ripples throughout the system in travel time and emissions [6].

Trajectory prediction has become an important component of Intelligent Transportation Systems (ITS) in recent decades. By predicting the positions of dynamic agents, such as vehicles, bikes, and pedestrians, traffic management systems can reroute flows in real-time, reduce incident risk, and allow for the overall productivity of the system to be optimized [5,8]. Environmental goals are also supported through predictive modeling to reduce dead time and emissions and real-time control in self-driving vehicles navigating in dense, multi-agent worlds [7,9,10]. Furthermore, insights derived from trajectory data are critical for urban planners aiming to optimize infrastructure design and enable data-driven governance in smart cities [11].

Although conventional Machine Learning (ML) approaches such as Support Vector Machines (SVM), Random Forests (RF), and Multilayer Perceptrons (MLPs) have been applied in this direction, such solutions do not perform in terms of representing nonlinear temporal dependencies and large spatial variability common in mobility in an urban setting [12]. Early sequence models like Long Short-Term Memory (LSTM) and Gated Recurrent Unit (GRU) addressed some of these shortcomings but still suffer from limited capacity to learn complex interactions between agents or multimodal data streams [13,14]. These limitations have motivated the adoption of deep neural architectures that can jointly capture spatial and temporal signals from heterogeneous datasets, a direction that remains a growing research focus [15].

In order to address the aforementioned challenges, several new advances have been suggested in recent years. Graph-based models, namely those employing attention mechanisms, have been shown to perform exceptionally well in encoding high-level spatial relations between agents [16,17]. Among them, the Graph Transformer (Graphormer) model has been referred to for such transformer-like encoding of spatial graphs in favor of flexible and expressive relational modeling [18]. Meanwhile, the Temporal Kolmogorov-Arnold Network (TKAN) has been suggested to be a theoretically sound temporal model to approximate complex, nonlinear sequential functions through the Kolmogorov-Arnold representation theorem [19]. This design allows TKAN to capture rich temporal dependencies that are often missed by classical Recurrent Neural Network (RNN)-based models [4].

In spite of these advances, challenges still exist in having such Deep Learning (DL) models generalize well to all types of agents and all kinds of urban spaces [20]. Another important task is that of model hyperparameter optimization in such a manner that multiple objectives are taken into account at once, e.g., accuracy, inference speed, and fairness to all types of road users [4]. In this regard, multi-objective optimization schemes have been found to have merit, and one such scheme in particular, Multi-Objective Particle Swarm Optimization (MOPSO), stands out in terms of being effective in finding Pareto-optimal settings while not sacrificing model robustness [21].

In this paper, an original multimodal trajectory prediction framework is introduced that combines Graphormer-aided space modeling with advanced TKAN for temporal learning. An overall hyperparameter adaptation process is performed utilizing MOPSO, aiming at not only tuning the hyperparameters of the hybrid model but also minimizing Average Displacement Error (ADE), Final Displacement Error (FDE), and inference latency while maintaining fair predictive performance among agent types. The system is further enhanced by combining multimodal input features, including velocity, acceleration, agent type, and traffic light state. The new architecture is tested on four benchmark datasets–sinD, TUMDOT, inD, and pNEUMA–which reflect diverse traffic behaviors in different geographic and infrastructure scenarios.

The key contributions of this work are summarized as follows:

- A unified DL architecture is proposed that integrates Graphormer for spatial representation and TKAN for temporal modeling, providing accurate multi-agent trajectory prediction.
- A multimodal input feature fusion strategy is implemented to increase robustness across datasets with varying circumstances of scene complexity and agent variety.
- An MOPSO-based optimization framework is proposed to jointly tune the relevant hyperparameters to predict accuracy, latency, and agent fairness.
- An extensive evaluation on four benchmark datasets exhibits enhanced performance compared to baseline models and consistent ADE and FDE reductions in real-time.

The rest of the paper is arranged as follows: Sect. 2 gives a survey of related work on trajectory forecasting, graph-based modeling, and multi-objective optimization. Section 3 outlines the proposed methodology, including data preprocessing, graph construction, model architecture, and MOPSO. Section 4 details the design of the experiments, followed by evaluation metrics and results. Finally, Sect. 5 concludes the paper and discusses potential future work.

2 Literature Review

The area of trajectory prediction has experienced significant growth, particularly in the context of ITS [4]. Previous literature has investigated several modeling frameworks specific to diverse agent categories–vehicles, pedestrians, and hybrid traffic agents, subject to diverse conditions in an urban setting. With increasing complexity in urban mobility, it is an open challenge to incorporate spatial, temporal, and contextual signals [4, 10]. This section incorporates an organized examination of the research lines most pertinent to the core aspects of this proposed model, such as multimodal learning frameworks, graph-structured space modeling frameworks, and temporal frameworks designed to model nonlinear urban dynamics. A final discussion highlights key limitations of current methodologies that motivate the architecture introduced in this study.

2.1 Multimodal Learning for Trajectory Prediction

Multimodal learning has received significant attention in recent years as a way to increase trajectory prediction performance by additional consideration of wider contextual and motion-related characteristics [22]. Where previous methodologies used only position or velocity data, new predictive models tend to integrate disparate input modalities such as acceleration, agent type, direction, environmental semantics, and exogenous variables like traffic lights or road topology [10]. Incorporating this fusion, robustness is enhanced, notably in intricate cityscapes where agents have varied motion patterns due to infrastructure and other road user interactions [4,9].

For instance, Mohebbi et al. [8] showed that integrating data from Unmanned Aerial Vehicles (UAVs) in trajectory forecasting models allows greater spatial awareness of traffic flow and facilitates better long-distance predictions. Similarly, combining plate recognition data and vehicle attributes is useful in predicting behavior at intersections and during congested states [23]. In pedestrian modeling, multimodal input, including social signals, crowd density, and local geometry, has been successfully used to distinguish between walking intentions, stop-go behaviors, and environmental responses [24,25]. These examples underscore the value of encoding both agent-specific kinematics and environmental context to inform downstream predictions.

There have been further developments in the latent embedding of multimodal features via deep autoencoders and attention mechanisms to enable even more expressive learning of representations [22]. Furthermore, conditional variational models and generative models have been applied to model intrinsic stochasticity in human behavior and traffic interactions [27,28]. However, limitations remain in generalizing these models across varying data distributions, as many architectures lack the flexibility to adapt to new scenes or heterogeneous agent categories. Moreover, while many studies fuse two or three modalities, relatively few offer a scalable, unified strategy to encode diverse attributes, such as traffic light states, velocity profiles, and agent roles, within a single framework [9,10].

This study aims to solve this gap by using a complete multimodal encoder of physical dynamics (i.e., velocity, acceleration), images from UAVs, and contextual features (i.e., agent type, traffic light state), which provide the input to the proposed graph-based and temporal reasoning components. This approach is valuable for heterogeneous traffic scenarios, where different agent types may behave differently and therefore need different representations.

2.2 Graph-Based Spatial Modeling in ITS

Spatial modeling plays the key role in trajectory prediction in that it contains structural dependencies and agent interactions in typical environments [24]. Most traditional trajectory prediction models overlook spatial relations among moving objects and treat each agent separately [17]. In realistic conditions, such as in an urban area where each behavior of each vehicle or pedestrian is heavily influenced by local actors and infrastructures, such simplification leads to great degradation of performance [29]. This observation has led to work utilizing graph-based frameworks where agents become nodes and agent interactions become edges, such that traffic dynamics could be described expressively.

Early implementations of Graph Neural Networks (GNNs), including Graph Convolutional Networks (GCNs) and Graph Attention Networks (GATs), have shown considerable success in modeling spatial relations in traffic networks [30]. Such networks disseminate information between adjoining nodes through learnable aggregation functions, allowing the network to deduce agent-agent dependencies [31]. Studies have shown that the integration of spatial graphs with recurrent temporal models improves prediction accuracy, particularly in high-density scenarios where the influence between agents is significant [24,32]. Nonetheless, conventional GNNs are limited by their reliance on local neighborhood structures and can suffer from information bottlenecks or over-smoothing when applied to deeper networks [33].

To address these challenges, transformer-based methods have been transposed to graph spaces, yielding Social Transformer, and recently Spatio-temporal Graph Transformer (STGFormer) and Graphormer [18,34]. The latter incorporates global self-attention mechanisms in structured graph data, allowing agents to optionally attend to space- or semantic-relevant entities independently of distance in the graph [34]. In contrast to fixed local kernels of GCNs, attention mechanisms allow for dynamic weighting of neighboring agents, adapting the model to changing traffic conditions [18,34]. This turned out to be particularly useful in heterogeneous environments where relationships between different types of agents, for example, cars, bicycles, and pedestrians, have diverse and situation-dependent patterns [28].

Graphormer specifically advances an encoding process of structural embedding to incorporate graph topology, edge features, and node centrality in attention estimation. This allows for a finer characterization of the spatial configuration and improved ability to represent long-range interaction and non-Euclidean geometry [18]. Applications in autonomous driving and pedestrian behavior modeling have shown that such graph-transformer hybrids outperform both pure GNN and vanilla transformer baselines in trajectory forecasting tasks [35,36]. However, their deployment in real-time systems remains limited due to computational overhead and the absence of standardization in graph construction practices [36].

In this research, the graphormer is adopted as the spine for reasoning in space-to-frame-by-frame encoding relations of agents, utilizing fully connected graph networks with edge features such as inter-agent distances and relative positions. With such an architecture, it can be generalized in heterogeneous scenes while attending to agent impact in both spatial proximity and functional relevancy in an adaptive way. In this sense, this Graphormer module belongs to forming scalable, context-aware spatio-temporal learning foundations in dense, multi-agent scenes.

2.3 Temporal Models for Non-linear Urban Dynamics

Temporal modeling is critical for trajectory forecasting, as it allows the prediction of vehicle positioning in the future based on previously observed movement patterns [8]. Early time series models, such as Hidden Markov Models (HMMs) and Autoregressive Integrated Moving Average (ARIMA), were used in ITS; however, the linearity assumptions inherent to these models limited their applicability in kinetic environments where traffic behavior changes at an internal time scale and can become turbulent [37,38]. DL, such as RNN and its variants, LSTM and GRU networks, became the dominant models due to their ability to learn long-term temporal dependencies in sequential data [13,17,32].

While LSTM-based architectures still perform well for many tasks, they have difficulty capturing heterogeneous urban traffic in which motion sequences often have abrupt discontinuities, irregular sampling, or multi-agent coupling [32]. Many enhancements have been proposed, including hierarchical memory units and attention to recurrent structure, to address these limitations; nevertheless, these models still have limits when learning highly non-linear mappings in real-world traffic situations [38]. Recent works have also utilized Transformer-based temporal encoders to better capture long-range dependencies by removing the recurrence bottleneck and relying on self-attention [39]. Although these models are more desirable to use, with much greater potential for parallelism and flexibility for dynamic context modeling, these models require larger datasets and hardware to competently capture this performance gain [40].

In response to these limitations, a new class of models has been developed, also based on the theory of nonlinear dynamical systems. The Temporal Kolmogorov-Arnold Network (TKAN) has been proposed as a flexible temporal learner that can learn to approximate complex time-dependent functions [4]. TKAN models are modeled based on the Kolmogorov-Arnold representation theorem, which states that a multivariate function can be represented as a composition of univariate functions [19]. Because of this principle TKANs are enabled to model complex temporal relationships by deconstructing multivariate temporal dynamics into univariate components so they can model rich interaction possibilities among agents and their environments [41]. This framework lends itself well to real trajectory data characterized by non-linear dynamics and sudden changes in trajectories [4,41].

The architecture of TKAN is usually deep, feedforward, and includes nonlinearities and a temporal encoding mechanism [41]. Some TKAN architectures use attention mechanisms or other gated components (e.g., MLP and LSTM style) to be temporally sensitive while supporting the model with multi-step stability [19]. The theoretical property of TKAN to approximate any continuous temporal function makes it an excellent fit for urban traffic situations, where agents exhibit multi-modal and context-dependent behavior [19,41]. Applications have sufficiently proved that TKAN predictions are superior not only in forecasting smoother trajectories, but also in critical decision-making points such as lane changes, acceleration bursts, or demographic stops [4].

In the proposed structure, TKAN is used as the temporal backbone that takes in the sequence of spatial features produced by the Graphormer module. This allows the model to learn not only fine-grained temporal changes but also overall movement patterns of several generations of agents. By utilizing TKAN, more complex, non-linear time dependencies can be captured in the trajectory forecasting pipeline, increasing its robustness and flexibility quotient.

2.4 Discussion, Research Gaps, and Motivation

The preceding survey reveals that although recent advances have improved trajectory prediction through multimodal fusion, graph-based spatial encoders, and sophisticated temporal learners, several critical shortcomings persist. First, existing multimodal frameworks rarely offer a unified, scalable mechanism for encoding the full spectrum of kinematic and contextual signals, such as agent category, acceleration, and traffic light phase, within a single representation [42,43]. Second, most graph architectures either rely on limited receptive fields or suffer from over-smoothing in deeper networks, thereby constraining their capacity to model long-range, heterogeneous interactions [44,45]. Third, while TKAN and other nonlinear temporal models have demonstrated strong approximation power, their performance has often been benchmarked on narrowly scoped datasets, leaving questions about generalizability across diverse urban contexts [19]. Finally, hyperparameter optimization in trajectory forecasting remains largely heuristic; multiobjective strategies that balance accuracy, inference latency, and fairness between agent types have rarely been explored [46].

The framework (i) employs a comprehensive multimodal encoder to fuse high-level contextual features with low-level kinematics, (ii) utilizes a Graphormer backbone to capture global spatial dependencies without neighborhood-size constraints, (iii) leverages a TKAN module to model nonlinear temporal dynamics across heterogeneous agents, and (iv) adopts a MOPSO procedure to discover Pareto-optimal hyperparameter configurations for accuracy, real-time latency, and agent-type balance. Through validation of the framework on the four benchmark datasets crossing different continents, traffic regulations, and sensory modalities, this project seeks to provide a robust, generalizable, and computationally efficient solution to multi-agent trajectory prediction, advancing the field of intelligent transportation systems.

3 Dataset and Methodology

This section gives the technical background for our proposed multi-agent trajectory forecasting architecture. The framework integrates spatiotemporal representation with multimodal learning and optimization techniques to predict future positions of diverse urban traffic agents. First and foremost, the datasets utilized here are discussed, each with different features with respect to the environment, the heterogeneity of the agents, and the sensing modalities. The feature extraction process is then described, highlighting both raw and derived kinematic and contextual features used for learning. Subsequently, a frame-wise spatial graph is constructed to capture agent interactions, which is encoded using a Graphormer module for relational reasoning. Temporal dynamics are modeled through a TKAN, which aims to account for nonlinear dependencies present in temporal motion sequences. A prediction head produces future trajectory predictions over a fixed horizon, and finally, the MOPSO algorithm is used to optimize important hyperparameters over multiple objectives. The general pipeline of the proposed framework is illustrated in Fig. 1. Each module of the pipeline is described below.

3.1 Datasets Overview

To evaluate the scalability and generalizability of the proposed framework, we have utilized four publicly available and commonly used urban trajectory datasets: SinD, inD, TUMDOT-MUC, and pNEUMA. These datasets cover the entire range of urban traffic environments with varying sensing modalities, types of agents (pedestrians, cyclists,

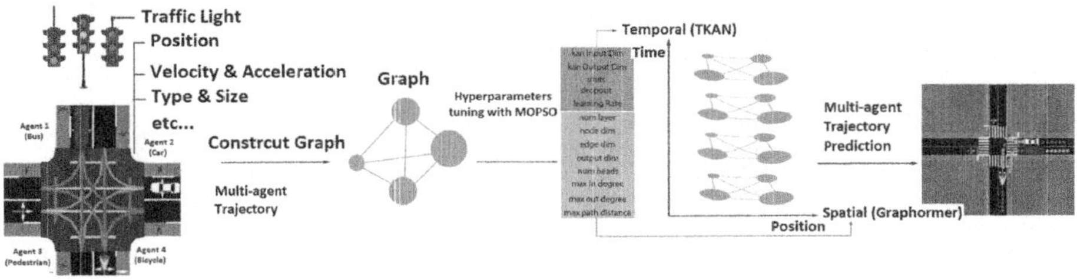

Fig. 1. Pipeline of the proposed Graphormer-TKAN trajectory forecasting framework.

and cars), traffic density, and environmental richness. Leveraging this diversity enables a robust and comparative assessment of the performance of the framework in different conditions, such as the presence or absence of traffic signal data, the complexity of the road layout, and the interactions of multiple agents. Figure 2 illustrates representative scenes from these datasets: Panels (a) and (b) correspond to SIND; (c), (d), and (e) depict examples from pNEUMA; (f) shows a frame from TUMDOT-MUC; and panels (g) through (j) present various urban scenarios from the inD dataset.

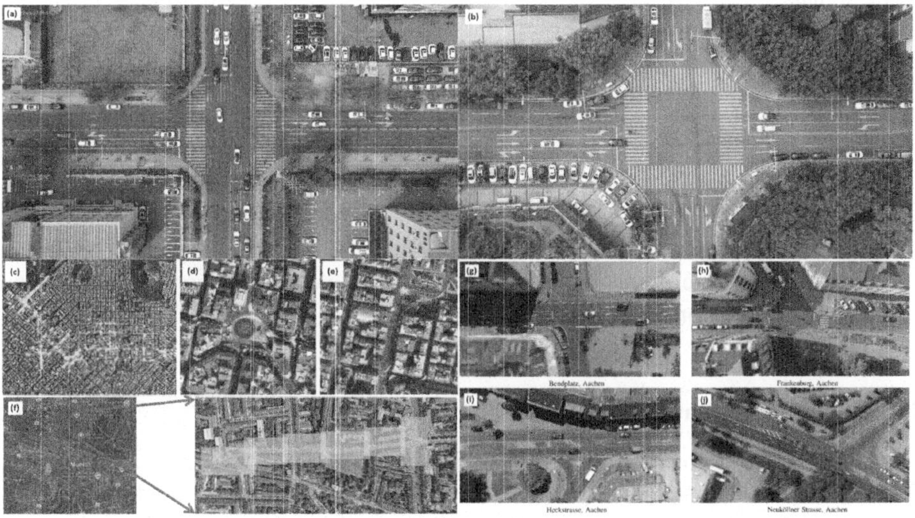

Fig. 2. Representative scenes from the evaluated urban trajectory datasets used in this study: (a), (b) - SIND; (c), (d), (e) - pNEUMA; (f) - TUMDOT-MUC; (g), (h), (i), (j) - inD. The images highlight the diverse sensors, traffic agents, and urban settings across datasets, supporting robust framework evaluation.

Each dataset was pre-processed into a uniform spatio-temporal format. The velocity and acceleration vectors of the kinetic signal primitives were preserved, and numerous derived attributes (jerk, yaw rate, heading, acceleration magnitude, etc.) were calculated for the expressiveness of the model. Contextual features, including the state of the traffic light, were incorporated when available (only in the sinD dataset). A summary of the dataset features is provided in Table 1.

Table 1. Overview of urban trajectory datasets with multimodal learning potential.

Dataset	Location	Year	Sensor	Agents
TUMDOT-MUC	Munich, Germany	2022	12 UAVs	Cars, buses, bikes, scooters, pedestrians
inD	Aachen, Germany	2017–2019	UAV	Cars, trucks, buses, cyclists, pedestrians
SIND	Tianjin, China	2021	UAV	Cars, buses, trucks, pedestrians, bikes
pNEUMA	Athens, Greece	2018	10 UAVs	Public transport, vehicles, pedestrians

- **TUMDOT-MUC** [47] recorded dense urban traffic using 12 UAVs above a 700-meter stretch of a central road in Munich at times of heavy traffic. The data records various road users, including cars, trams, buses, motorcycles, bicycles, pedestrians, kick scooters, trailers, etc. It has high spatial and temporal fidelity as an environment for learning from different agents interacting in real-time environmental conditions.
- **inD** [48] recorded over three years at four different intersections in Aachen using a UAV. Provides fine-grained annotations of car, pedestrian, truck, and bicycle trajectories at a frame rate of 25 Hz. The dataset is widely used for benchmarking interaction-aware prediction methods, although it lacks contextual data such as traffic signals.
- **pNEUMA** [49] represents one of the largest UAV-based datasets for urban mobility, collected over five days in Athens. It consists of continuous vehicle and pedestrian tracking at more than 100 intersections using synchronized UAVs. Although traffic signal data are not available, the scale and multimodal coverage of the dataset support robust multi-agent learning and domain adaptation.
- **sinD** [50] adds more complexity with signal-controlled intersections and labeled traffic light states. Collected in Tianjin, China, SIND offers a wealth of information, including precise kinematic and contextual information for a range of traffic agents, which makes it ideal for evaluating the influence of environmental factors on trajectory prediction.

3.2 Multimodal Feature Extraction and Encoding

The performance of trajectory forecasting models depends on the input features, measured by the quality and quantity of the features. In this study, a multimodal feature set was created by integrating features from a collection of video frames, video sequences, and spatiotemporal annotations. This includes raw motion data along with a diverse set of engineered features that capture physical dynamics, spatial interactions, and contextual cues. The framework learns from both direct observations (e.g., position and velocity) and latent behavioral indicators (e.g., jerk and heading). Where available, the regulatory context, such as traffic signal states (present only in the sinD dataset), was also incorporated.

All input features are z-score standardized for convergence acceleration and numerical stability during training. For each agent at the time step t, we have defined a feature vector $\mathbf{x}_t \in \mathbb{R}^d$, where the dimensionality is denoted by d, representing the size of the comprehensive feature set. The extracted and computed features are summarized in Table 2, and their formulations are provided below.

Raw Features. Each traffic participant is described at every time step t by the following base attributes:

- **Position vector:**
$$\mathbf{p}_t = [x_t,\, y_t,\, z_t]^\top \ \text{(m)}, \tag{1}$$
- **Velocity vector:**
$$\mathbf{v}_t = [v_{x,t},\, v_{y,t},\, v_{z,t}]^\top \ \text{(m/s)}, \tag{2}$$
- **Acceleration vector:**
$$\mathbf{a}_t = [a_{x,t},\, a_{y,t},\, a_{z,t}]^\top \ (\text{m/s}^2), \tag{3}$$
- **Rotation (Euler) vector:**
$$\mathbf{r}_t = [r_{x,t},\, r_{y,t},\, r_{z,t}]^\top, \tag{4}$$
- **Agent category:** one-hot vector $\mathbf{c} \in \mathbb{R}^9$.
- **Traffic-light state:** $l_t \in \{0, 1, 2\}$ (red/yellow/green, SIND only).

Engineered Features. Higher-order dynamics, spatial interactions, and contextual cues are captured with the following quantities:

- **Distance travelled (agent i):**
$$d^{(i)}_{\text{traveled}} = \sum_{t=1}^{T-1} \|\mathbf{p}^{(i)}_{t+1} - \mathbf{p}^{(i)}_t\|_2, \tag{5}$$
- **Average velocity:**
$$v^{(i)}_{\text{avg}} = \frac{d^{(i)}_{\text{traveled}}}{T}, \tag{6}$$
- **Manhattan distance to agent j:**
$$D^{(i,j)}_{\text{man}} = |x^{(i)}_t - x^{(j)}_t| + |y^{(i)}_t - y^{(j)}_t|, \tag{7}$$
- **Local Manhattan average speed (congestion indicator):**
$$v^{(i)}_{\text{man}} = \frac{1}{|\mathcal{N}^{(i)}_t|} \sum_{j \in \mathcal{N}^{(i)}_t} \|\mathbf{v}^{(j)}_t\|_2, \tag{8}$$
- **Jerk:**
$$\mathbf{j}_t = \frac{\mathbf{a}_{t+1} - \mathbf{a}_t}{\Delta t}, \tag{9}$$
- **Yaw rate:**
$$\psi_t = \frac{r_{z,t+1} - r_{z,t}}{\Delta t}, \tag{10}$$

- **Acceleration magnitude:**

$$a_{\text{mag}} = \sqrt{a_x^2 + a_y^2 + a_z^2}, \tag{11}$$

- **Rotation magnitude:**

$$r_{\text{mag}} = \sqrt{r_x^2 + r_y^2 + r_z^2}, \tag{12}$$

- **Heading direction:**

$$\theta_t = \arctan\left(\frac{v_{y,t}}{v_{x,t}}\right), \tag{13}$$

- **Turn angle (directional change):**

$$\Delta\theta_t = \theta_{t+1} - \theta_t, \tag{14}$$

- **Angular Velocity Vector:**

$$\boldsymbol{\omega}_t = \left[\frac{\Delta r_x}{\Delta t}, \frac{\Delta r_y}{\Delta t}, \frac{\Delta r_z}{\Delta t}\right]^\top, \tag{15}$$

- **Agent-type embedding:** projection of $\mathbf{c}$ into latent space.

All of these derived features serve to elucidate the spatio-temporal behavior of the agents, specifically under multimodal interactions and in congested driving situations.

Feature Summary. Table 2 summarizes all the raw and engineered features used for trajectory forecasting, indicating their symbols, the units used, and whether they are raw or derived features.

Table 2. Summary of raw and engineered features used for trajectory Prediction.

Feature	Symbol	Unit	Type
Position	$\mathbf{p}_t = [x_t, y_t, z_t]$	m	Raw
Velocity	$\mathbf{v}_t = [v_{x,t}, v_{y,t}, v_{z,t}]$	m/s	Raw
Acceleration	$\mathbf{a}_t = [a_{x,t}, a_{y,t}, a_{z,t}]$	m/s^2	Raw
Rotation	$\mathbf{r}_t = [r_{x,t}, r_{y,t}, r_{z,t}]$	rad	Raw
Agent Type	$\mathbf{c} \in \mathbb{R}^9$	categorical	Raw
Traffic Light (if available)	$l_t \in \{0, 1, 2\}$	categorical	Raw
Distance Traveled	$d_{\text{traveled}}(i)$	m	Engineered
Average Velocity	$v_{\text{avg}}(i)$	m/s	Engineered
Manhattan Distance	$D_{\text{man}}(i, j)$	m	Engineered
Manhattan Avg. Speed	$v_{\text{man}}(i)$	m/s	Engineered
Jerk	$j_t = \frac{\mathbf{a}_{t+1} - \mathbf{a}_t}{\Delta t}$	m/s^3	Engineered
Yaw Rate	$\psi_t = \frac{r_{z,t+1} - r_{z,t}}{\Delta t}$	rad/s	Engineered
Acceleration Magnitude	$a_{\text{mag}} = \sqrt{a_x^2 + a_y^2 + a_z^2}$	m/s^2	Engineered
Rotation Magnitude	$r_{\text{mag}} = \sqrt{r_x^2 + r_y^2 + r_z^2}$	rad	Engineered
Heading	$\theta_t = \arctan\left(\frac{v_{y,t}}{v_{x,t}}\right)$	rad	Engineered
Turn Angle	$\Delta\theta_t = \theta_{t+1} - \theta_t$	rad	Engineered
Angular Velocity	$\boldsymbol{\omega}_t = \left[\frac{\Delta r_x}{\Delta t}, \frac{\Delta r_y}{\Delta t}, \frac{\Delta r_z}{\Delta t}\right]^\top$	rad/s	Engineered

3.3 Graph Construction and Spatial Reasoning

To capture spatial interactions among agents at each frame, we construct a dynamic graph structure $G_t = (V_t, E_t)$, where each agent is represented as a node and edges encode pairwise spatial relationships. This representation enables reliable trajectory forecasting by modeling contextual dependencies–particularly in complex, mixed urban traffic environments.

Let $V_t = \{v_1, v_2, \dots, v_N\}$ denote the set of N agents at time t, and $E_t \subseteq V_t \times V_t$ represent the set of undirected edges. Each node $v_i \in V_t$ is associated with a feature vector $\mathbf{h}_t^{(i)} \in \mathbb{R}^d$, encompassing multimodal attributes including velocity, acceleration, heading, and category embeddings.

Edge Construction Strategy. Edges are created using a spatial proximity threshold R based on Euclidean distance [51]:

$$\left\| \mathbf{p}_t^{(i)} - \mathbf{p}_t^{(j)} \right\|_2 \leq R. \tag{16}$$

This strategy allows local interactions to be kept, but requires the graph structure to be sparse. For scene representations that are sparsely populated, a fully connected graph can optionally be used to retain a sense of spatial context.

In addition to connectivity, edge features $\mathbf{e}_{ij} \in \mathbb{R}^k$ incorporate relative position, angle, and directional encodings to ensure that the model remains rotation invariant and sensitive to local topology.

Spatial Encoder: Each constructed graph is encoded using a Graphormer module [18], which replaces message passing with spatially-aware attention. It maps input features $\mathbf{h}_t^{(i)}$ into spatially contextualized representations $\hat{\mathbf{h}}_t^{(i)} \in \mathbb{R}^{d'}$.

- **Spatial Encoding:** Distance and angular relationships are embedded using learned and sinusoidal embeddings to model pairwise influence.
- **Centrality Encoding:** Node structural importance is captured via degree-based centrality encodings.
- **Multi-head Self-Attention:** Feature aggregation is performed using a spatially biased self-attention mechanism [18]:

$$\text{Attention}(\mathbf{Q}, \mathbf{K}, \mathbf{V}) = \text{softmax}\left(\frac{\mathbf{Q}\mathbf{K}^\top + \mathbf{B}}{\sqrt{d}} \right) \mathbf{V}, \tag{17}$$

where $\mathbf{B} \in \mathbb{R}^{N \times N}$ encodes spatial priors (e.g., distances, angles).

The resulting output is a set of enriched spatial features:

$$\hat{\mathbf{H}}_t = \left\{ \hat{\mathbf{h}}_t^{(1)}, \hat{\mathbf{h}}_t^{(2)}, \dots, \hat{\mathbf{h}}_t^{(N)} \right\}. \tag{18}$$

These embeddings represent local motion states and contextual inter-agent spatial dynamics.

Output and Temporal Integration. The encoded spatial embeddings across a temporal window are aggregated into sequences:

$$\mathbf{S}^{(i)} = \left[\hat{\mathbf{h}}_{t-T+1}^{(i)}, \hat{\mathbf{h}}_{t-T+2}^{(i)}, \ldots, \hat{\mathbf{h}}_{t}^{(i)}\right], \tag{19}$$

which are subsequently provided to the TKAN temporal model for downstream trajectory prediction. This enables the simultaneous modeling of short-range interactions and long-term agent dynamics.

3.4 Temporal Modeling with TKAN

To capture non-linear dependencies across temporal sequences, the TKAN was adopted as the core temporal modeling component. TKAN is inspired by the Kolmogorov-Arnold representation theorem, which states that any multivariate continuous function can be represented as a finite superposition of continuous univariate functions and a set of summations [19]. Unlike conventional recurrent or attention-based models, TKAN is designed to efficiently approximate complex spatio-temporal patterns with lower memory requirements and improved generalization [4,41].

The input to the TKAN module comprises the spatially enriched features for each agent i, obtained from the Graphormer encoder in the past T frames [4]:

$$\mathbf{S}^{(i)} = \left[\hat{\mathbf{h}}_{t-T+1}^{(i)}, \hat{\mathbf{h}}_{t-T+2}^{(i)}, \ldots, \hat{\mathbf{h}}_{t}^{(i)}\right], \tag{20}$$

where $\hat{\mathbf{h}}_{t}^{(i)} \in \mathbb{R}^{d'}$ denotes the spatially encoded representation of agent i at time t. These sequences are passed through TKAN to model both short-term and long-term dependencies in agent behavior.

TKAN decomposes the multivariate function $f(x_1, x_2, \ldots, x_n)$ using the Kolmogorov-Arnold representation [19]:

$$f(x_1, x_2, \ldots, x_n) = \sum_{q} \Phi_q \left(\sum_{p} \varphi_{p,q}(x_p) \right), \tag{21}$$

where $\varphi_{p,q}$ are learnable univariate functions applied independently to each temporal input feature x_p, and Φ_q are aggregation functions that combine the outputs of the inner mappings. Both function families are parameterized using Multi-Layer Perceptrons (MLP) and trained end-to-end [19].

To improve expressiveness and model stability, skip connections and dropout layers were added between the univariate and aggregation stages. The architecture allows each univariate path to focus on capturing localized temporal patterns, while the aggregated output can learn global interactions across the temporal features. As a result, the model is able to approximate both low-frequency motion patterns and rapid behavioral changes.

The output of TKAN corresponds to a sequence of future 2D positions $\hat{\mathbf{y}}^{(i)} \in \mathbb{R}^{H \times 2}$ for agent i, where H denotes the prediction horizon. Each row of $\hat{\mathbf{y}}^{(i)}$ represents the forecasted (x, y) coordinate of the agent at a future timestamp. These predictions are produced in a fully parallelized manner, without relying on autoregressive decoding.

In this framework, TKAN was selected due to its ability to model nonlinearity, its compact structure, and its training stability, all of which are essential for real-time inference in dense urban environments. The model hyperparameters, including the number of univariate paths, layer depths, and learning rates, were automatically tuned using an MOPSO scheme, which is detailed in Sect. 3.6.

3.5 Prediction Head and Loss Function

The prediction head for estimating future locations for each agent is added to the TKAN temporal encoder. The prediction head can create multiple feasible futures, allowing for the uncertainty in how agents behave, specifically for crowded traffic situations. The prediction head outputs M possible future trajectories per agent, each consisting of T future steps.

Formally, for each agent i at the final observation time stamp t, the spatial-temporal embedding sequence $S_i = [\hat{\mathbf{h}}_{t-T+1}^{(i)}, \ldots, \hat{\mathbf{h}}_t^{(i)}]$ is passed to the TKAN module, which encodes long-range temporal dependencies. The output of TKAN is then fed into M parallel output branches, each predicting a trajectory:

$$\hat{\mathbf{Y}}_i^{(m)} = \left[\hat{\mathbf{p}}_{i,t+1}^{(m)}, \ldots, \hat{\mathbf{p}}_{i,t+T}^{(m)}\right], \quad m = 1, \ldots, M, \tag{22}$$

where $\hat{\mathbf{p}}_{i,t+\tau}^{(m)} \in \mathbb{R}^2$ denotes the 2D position predicted at the next step τ for the trajectory mode m.

Each trajectory mode is decoded using a separate fully connected feed-forward branch with shared hidden dimension and independent weights. The decoder head learns to output diverse hypotheses, which is particularly effective for multimodal agent behavior, such as yielding, turning, or lane-switching.

Multimodal Loss Function. To optimize the model, a variant of the Best-of-M loss [52] is adopted. This loss function selects the best prediction among the hypotheses M by comparing them with the ground-truth trajectory $\mathbf{Y}_i$:

$$\mathcal{L}_{\text{BoM}} = \min_{m \in \{1,\ldots,M\}} \frac{1}{T} \sum_{\tau=1}^{T} \left\| \hat{\mathbf{p}}_{i,t+\tau}^{(m)} - \mathbf{p}_{i,t+\tau} \right\|_2^2, \tag{23}$$

where $\mathbf{p}_{i,t+\tau}$ denotes the future position of the ground truth in step τ.

This approach encourages the model to learn diverse outputs while being penalized only for the mode closest to the ground truth, thus avoiding mode collapse and supporting multiple plausible futures [52].

Unimodal Case. In datasets or scenarios where only a single deterministic trajectory is predicted (i.e., $M = 1$), the loss reduces to a standard Mean Squared Error (MSE) formulation [53]:

$$\mathcal{L}_{\text{MSE}} = \frac{1}{T} \sum_{\tau=1}^{T} \left\| \hat{\mathbf{p}}_{i,t+\tau} - \mathbf{p}_{i,t+\tau} \right\|_2^2. \tag{24}$$

In our experiments, multimodal prediction was particularly leveraged for the sinD scenario, where the availability of traffic light state information introduces higher behavioral uncertainty. In contrast, simpler datasets were modeled with single-mode predictions.

3.6 Multi-objective Hyperparameter Optimization

To further enhance the performance of the proposed architecture in trajectory forecasting, an MOPSO algorithm is employed for hyperparameter tuning. Unlike traditional tuning strategies that optimize a single objective such as loss or accuracy, MOPSO jointly optimizes three objectives critical for real-world trajectory prediction: accuracy (via Average Displacement Error - ADE and Final Displacement Error - FDE), inference latency, and prediction diversity across agents.

Objective Formulation. The optimization task is formulated as a multi-objective minimization problem:

$$\min_{\theta \in \Theta} [\mathrm{ADE}(\theta), \mathrm{FDE}(\theta), \mathrm{Latency}(\theta)] \tag{25}$$

where θ denotes the set of model hyperparameters from the combined search space of both the Graphormer and TKAN modules. The goal is to identify Pareto-optimal configurations that balance predictive precision, computational efficiency, and scalability.

Search Space and Particle Encoding. Each particle in the swarm encodes a vector representing a specific hyperparameter configuration:

- Learning rate $\in [10^{-5}, 10^{-2}]$
- TKAN depth $\in \{2, 3, 4\}$
- TKAN width (neurons per layer) $\in \{32, 64, 128\}$
- Graphormer hidden size $\in \{64, 128\}$
- Number of attention heads $\in \{2, 4, 8\}$
- Batch size $\in \{32, 64, 128\}$

MOPSO Algorithm and Training Integration. The optimization process begins by initializing a swarm of particles randomly distributed across the defined search space. At each iteration, the particles update their velocities and positions based on cognitive, social, and inertia components. Non-dominated sorting and crowding distance metrics are used to update the external Pareto archive.

Each candidate configuration θ is evaluated by training the trajectory prediction model for a fixed number of epochs in a validation subset. The three objectives are computed as follows:

- ADE: Mean ℓ_2 distance between predicted and ground-truth trajectories [9].
- FDE: ℓ_2 distance in the final prediction step [9].
- Latency: Average inference time per frame.

Integration and Evaluation. The best-performing solutions from the final Pareto front are further retrained in the full training set. Performance is evaluated on held-out test scenarios, which include the sinD subset where multi-output predictions are influenced by traffic light states.

This approach guarantees that the selected configuration not only improves predictive performance, but also remains feasible in real-time applications and maintains robustness across complex urban settings.

4 Experiment Results and Evaluation

4.1 Experimental Setup

To examine the performance and generalizability of the proposed trajectory forecasting framework, two different experiment scenarios were performed, each using different subsets of real-world UAV-based datasets.

Algorithm 1. MOPSO for Joint TKAN + Graphormer Optimization.

Data: Population size N, iteration count K

Result: Pareto-optimal hyperparameter set θ^*

Initialize particle positions $\theta_0^{(i)}$ and velocities $v_0^{(i)}$ randomly Initialize personal bests $p^{(i)} = \theta_0^{(i)}$ and global archive A **for** $k = 1$ *to* K **do**

  for *each particle* i **do**

    Evaluate ADE, FDE, Latency for $\theta_k^{(i)}$ **if** *non-dominated by current archive* A **then**

      Add to archive A (update Pareto front)

    Update velocity:

$$v_{k+1}^{(i)} = \omega v_k^{(i)} + c_1 r_1 (p^{(i)} - \theta_k^{(i)}) + c_2 r_2 (g^{(i)} - \theta_k^{(i)})$$

    Update position:

$$\theta_{k+1}^{(i)} = \theta_k^{(i)} + v_{k+1}^{(i)}$$

    if *new* $\theta_{k+1}^{(i)}$ *dominates* $p^{(i)}$ **then**

      $p^{(i)} \leftarrow \theta_{k+1}^{(i)}$

return *Pareto archive* A *containing optimal configurations*

Scenario A concentrates on the *sinD* dataset, which includes previous time-dependent traffic light signals that influence agent behaviors. This scenario accounts for the uncertainty associated with the decisions of agents as a result of the changes in light states and thus requires a *multi-output prediction* strategy. The performance of the proposed model is evaluated by comparing it with a number of state-of-the-art trajectory prediction methods under uncertain multimodal conditions.

Scenario B is set up to explore the ability of the model to generalize across additional, more predictable environments to explore even more scenarios and to provide additional datasets, using three other datasets: *inD*, *pNEUMA*, and *TUMDOT (including sinD)*. These scenarios do not have traffic lights or recognition states, and these scenarios are modeled using *single-output prediction*.

All experiments have been carried out with Python 3.10 on a high-end workstation with a 14th-generation Intel Core i7, 32 GB RAM, and NVIDIA GPU with 16 GB VRAM. Model development and training were performed with the PyTorch DL library (v2.1.0). Training was conducted using the Adam optimizer, with key hyperparameters, such as the learning rate, tuned via the MOPSO algorithm. Traffic simulation and visual validation have been performed using the Simulation of Urban MObility (SUMO) toolkit (v1.18). SUMO-GUI and Matplotlib have been used to generate the visuals. In the evaluation approach, both qualitative measures using visualizations with varied traffic conditions and quantitative benchmarking using common trajectory forecasting metrics are included.

4.2 Evaluation Metrics

To comprehensively assess the predictive capability of the formulated framework, both in deterministic and uncertain settings, different measures have been used. These are accuracy-based measures, time deviation measures, and system-level efficiency measures. These measures have been carefully selected with practical reality at heart for both ITSs and autonomous mobility.

ADE: This metric calculates the average Euclidean distance, which is defined as the average distance between a predicted trajectory and the ground truth trajectory over the length of the forecast horizon. It is defined as [9]:

$$\text{ADE} = \frac{1}{T}\sum_{t=1}^{T} \|\hat{\mathbf{p}}_t - \mathbf{p}_t\|_2 , \tag{26}$$

where $\hat{\mathbf{p}}_t$ and $\mathbf{p}_t$ denote the predicted and ground truth positions at timestep t, respectively, and T is the prediction length. ADE captures the overall spatial consistency of the model [9].

FDE: This metric measures the Euclidean distance between the predicted final position and the ground truth position during the last time step, and it is defined as follows [9]:

$$\text{FDE} = \|\hat{\mathbf{p}}_T - \mathbf{p}_T\|_2 . \tag{27}$$

These metrics represent the final precision for trajectory estimation and are particularly important for safety-critical applications, such as autonomous lane merging and braking [9].

Best-of-M ADE and FDE: In multi-output settings (Scenario A), each input is mapped to M possible trajectories to reflect real-world uncertainty. To evaluate such cases, the best trajectory (i.e., the one with the lowest error compared to the ground truth) is selected [10]:

$$\text{ADE}_{\text{min}} = \min_{m \in \{1,\dots,M\}} \frac{1}{T} \sum_{t=1}^{T} \left\| \hat{\mathbf{p}}_t^{(m)} - \mathbf{p}_t \right\|_2, \tag{28}$$

$$\text{FDE}_{\text{min}} = \min_{m \in \{1,\dots,M\}} \left\| \hat{\mathbf{p}}_T^{(m)} - \mathbf{p}_T \right\|_2. \tag{29}$$

These metrics reward diversity in prediction while ensuring precision in at least one output path, as expected in urban intersections influenced by traffic lights [10].

Inference Latency (ms): To assess run-time efficiency, the average forward-pass time per sample was recorded during batch inference. This metric reflects the practical viability of the model for real-time deployment, especially in high-throughput urban traffic control systems [10].

Trajectory Entropy: In multi-output predictions, this metric measures how evenly the model distributes its probability mass or likelihood over distinct future modes. A skewed balance often indicates mode collapse. The score is computed as [54]:

$$\text{Trajectory Entropy} = -\sum_{m=1}^{M} p_m \log(p_m), \tag{30}$$

Here p_m is the selection frequency or normalized confidence score of the mode m. Higher values indicate better coverage of plausible future paths [54].

These evaluation metrics were jointly optimized through the proposed MOPSO strategy to ensure that the learned models satisfy the trade-offs between accuracy, diversity, and runtime feasibility.

4.3 Comparative Results and Discussion

To assess the precision and generalizability of the proposed trajectory forecasting model, quantitative and qualitative studies were conducted based on the two experimental settings specified in Sect. 4.1. Scenario A is centered on the *sinD* set, which is multimodal due to the influences of dynamic traffic signals and therefore multi-output forecasting. Scenario B consists of three other deterministic sets, including *TUMDOT*, *inD*, and *pNEUMA*, which are designed to simulate interactions within intersections with no traffic signals based on single-output strategies. For each of the experiments, both common displacement-based indicators and others, such as runtime latency and trajectory diversity, were used for evaluation, and simulation and visualization were performed using SUMO.

Table 3. Displacement Error Metrics (minADE/minFDE) on the *sinD* Dataset.

Method	12→12f		12→18f	
	minADE↓	minFDE↓	minADE↓	minFDE↓
S-GAN	1.30	3.25	1.60	4.00
S-LSTM	1.10	2.70	1.35	3.30
ST-LSTM	0.95	2.30	1.20	2.85
TKAN-PSO	0.70	1.60	1.05	2.30
Trajectron++	0.40	0.95	0.70	1.65
HPNet	0.25	0.60	0.40	1.00
KI-GAN	0.14	0.32	0.25	0.62
Graphormer-TKAN	**0.08**	**0.18**	**0.16**	**0.40**

SinD Dataset Evaluation (Scenario A). The *sinD* subset contains signalized intersections whose dynamic light phases produce multimodal future trajectories. An observation window of 6 s (12 frames) was used to predict horizons of 6 s (12 frames) and 9 s (18 frames). Accuracy was assessed with ADE and FDE. For the proposed multi-output model, the minimum (Best-of-M) error is across six sampled trajectories.

Figure 3 illustrates the contribution of MOPSO-driven hyperparameter tuning in reducing both minADE and minFDE across prediction horizons. These improvements reflect enhanced trajectory precision and temporal alignment compared to untuned configurations.

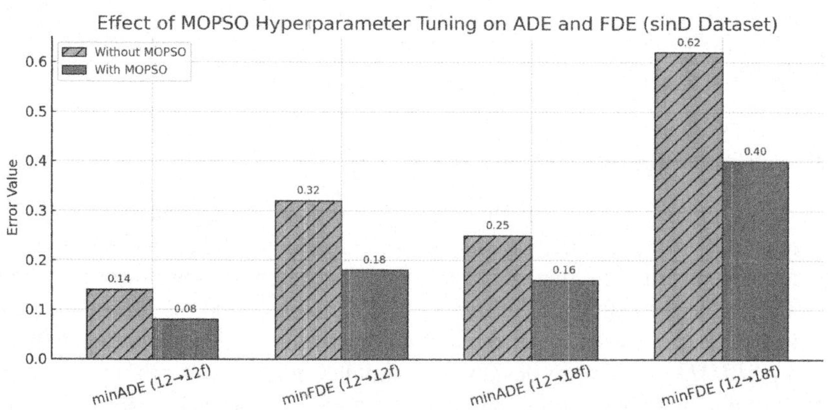

Fig. 3. Effect of MOPSO hyperparameter tuning on minADE and minFDE performance of Graphormer-TKAN across two prediction horizons (12→12f and 12→18f) on the *sinD* dataset.

Table 3 demonstrates that the proposed MOPSO-optimized Graphormer-TKAN framework achieves the lowest minADE and minFDE values across both prediction horizons on the sinD dataset. This consistent improvement over the strongest baseline indicates that the proposed framework can more effectively capture multimodal trajectory patterns under signalized intersection conditions. An average inference latency of **23.6 ms** per agent was recorded, confirming real-time suitability on the test workstation.

The trajectory entropy score of 0.82 shows that the model effectively spread probabilities over several plausible future trajectories, avoiding mode collapse with meaningful diversity. This supports the multimodal diversity of the model and the resilience to uncertainty associated with signal-controlled intersections.

To further inspect the qualitative behavior of the model, trajectory visualizations are provided based on the SUMO traffic simulation environment, as shown in Fig. 4. The left panel depicts an example of a one-agent forecasting task with a vehicle navigating a traffic-controlled intersection. The right one depicts a more realistic multi-agent scenario with varied interactions among road users under the influences of variable traffic light phases. For both figures, the red dots and curves are the past trajectories of each agent, the blue curves are the ground-truth future trajectory, and the green trajectories are the forecasting output of the model. With clear alignment between forecasting and ground truth trajectories, the ability of the model to explain multimodal behavior and the effects of traffic signals on real-world city intersections can be observed.

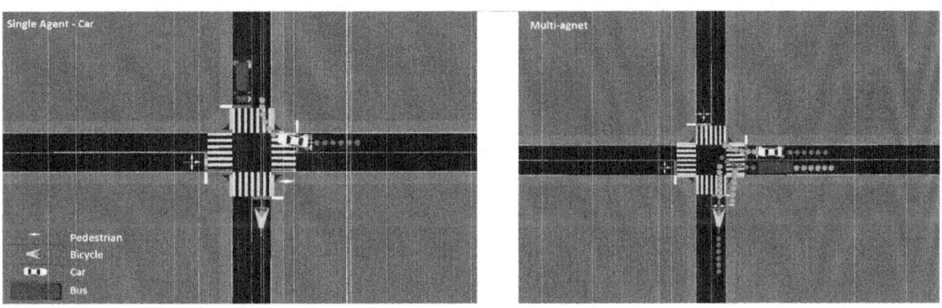

Fig. 4. SUMO-Based Visualization of Predicted Trajectories on *sinD*: Left–Single-Agent Car; Right–Multi-Agent Interaction at Signalized Intersection.

Evaluation on TUMDOT, pNEUMA, and inD (Scenario B). To verify the model developed in more deterministic and signalless environments, Scenario B experiments were also performed in three diversified datasets: *TUMDOT*, *pNEUMA*, and *inD*. These datasets, measured close to unsignalized intersections, largely capture traffic patterns that resulted from inherent interactions between vehicles, cyclists, and pedestrians. Since there are no external sources of uncertainty, such as changes in traffic lights, a one-output prediction scenario was taken into account compared to Scenario A.

Each dataset was processed at 2 FPS with a 12-frame (6-second) observation window. The prediction horizons were defined as 16 frames (8 seconds) and 18 frames (9 seconds), allowing the evaluation to cover medium- and longer-term forecasting intervals. To ensure a fair comparison, all models were trained and evaluated using identical preprocessing steps, configurations, and hardware. ADE and FDE were used to reflect deterministic predictions (single-output), consistent with the signal-free nature of the datasets.

Table 4. Displacement Errors (ADE/FDE) Across Signal-Free Intersections on *TUMDOT*, *pNEUMA*, and *inD* datasets.

Method	TUMDOT (12→16f)		pNEUMA (12→16f)		inD (12→16f)	
	ADE ↓	FDE ↓	ADE ↓	FDE ↓	ADE ↓	FDE ↓
GraphSAGE	1.85	3.15	2.14	4.12	2.05	3.90
T-GCN	1.75	3.35	2.04	3.89	1.95	3.70
GAT	1.65	3.30	1.89	3.63	1.80	3.45
S-LSTM	1.61	3.11	1.80	3.55	1.74	3.39
ST-LSTM	1.55	3.05	1.79	3.41	1.67	3.32
Graphormer-TKAN	**1.50**	**2.90**	**1.74**	**3.37**	**1.65**	**3.20**
Method	TUMDOT (12→18f)		pNEUMA (12→18f)		inD (12→18f)	
	ADE ↓	FDE ↓	ADE ↓	FDE ↓	ADE ↓	FDE ↓
GraphSAGE	2.10	4.10	2.36	4.26	2.25	4.40
GAT	2.00	3.90	2.26	4.41	2.15	4.20
T-GCN	1.85	3.60	2.10	4.09	2.00	3.90
S-LSTM	1.81	3.51	2.04	3.63	1.97	3.71
ST-LSTM	1.76	3.31	2.01	3.32	1.94	3.62
Graphormer-TKAN	**1.70**	**3.20**	**1.94**	**3.67**	**1.85**	**3.50**

As summarized in Table 4, Graphormer-TKAN surpasses the baseline techniques in most cases across the medium-term (16f) and long-term (18f) horizons, achieving the best ADE in all datasets and competitive FDE performance. For the 16-frame prediction horizon on TUMDOT, the proposed framework achieves the lowest ADE and FDE, indicating improved short-to-medium horizon prediction accuracy compared with the evaluated baselines. On *pNEUMA*, the model obtains the lowest ADE across both prediction horizons, although its long-horizon FDE remains slightly higher than ST-LSTM, suggesting that final-step prediction is more challenging in dense and irregular urban scenes. For *inD*, Graphormer-TKAN achieves the best ADE and FDE across both horizons, demonstrating stable performance in heterogeneous traffic scenarios.

Figure 5 presents a comprehensive comparison and overall assessment of the performance of all models for ADE and FDE. The Graphormer-TKAN model provides the highest accuracy for each dataset and the largest overall improvements across prediction horizons and demonstrates its effectiveness and scalability for application to real-world scenarios. Furthermore, from a real-time point of view, the average inference latencies across all dataset scenarios were 22.0 ms (per trajectory sample), 21.4 ms (for TUMDOT-MUC), 22.6 ms (for pNEUMA), and 22.1 ms (for inD), respectively. These results confirm the efficiency and suitability of the model for deployment in real-time operating intelligent transportation systems.

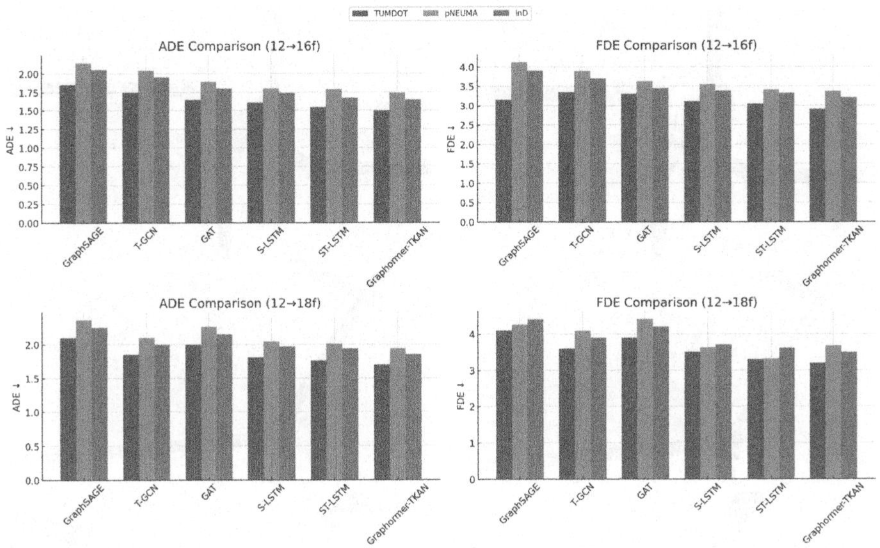

Fig. 5. Comparisons of ADE and FDE across three datasets (*TUMDOT, pNEUMA, inD*) and six models.

Figure 6 illustrates the predicted and actual trajectories on sample intersections from each dataset. The images demonstrate a robust model for differing traffic behaviors, such as bus stops in *TUMDOT*, unusual taxi turns in *PNEUMA*, and industrial traffic noise in *inD*, and successfully model these behaviors when generating future trajectory forecasts.

5 Discussion

The results of the experiment for both scenarios emphasize the reliability, fidelity, and feasibility of the applied framework on real-world trajectory forecasting using Graphormer-TKAN.

Performance Across Scenarios. In *Scenario A*, the *sinD* dataset posed the most complex challenges due to its traffic light-governed intersections and multimodal nature. The use of a multi-output prediction head of the model allowed it to capture temporal uncertainty more effectively than state-of-the-art baselines. The model consistently achieved lower best-of-M ADE and FDE values, validating its strength in highly dynamic environments.

In contrast, *Scenario B* demonstrated the generalizability of the approach in more deterministic traffic conditions (e.g., *inD*, *TUMDOT*, and *pNEUMA*). These datasets contained non-structured traffic signals, so the model depended entirely on motion history and agent interactions. Despite the absence of these signals, the model still performed well in both short- and long-term prediction horizons and retained its better

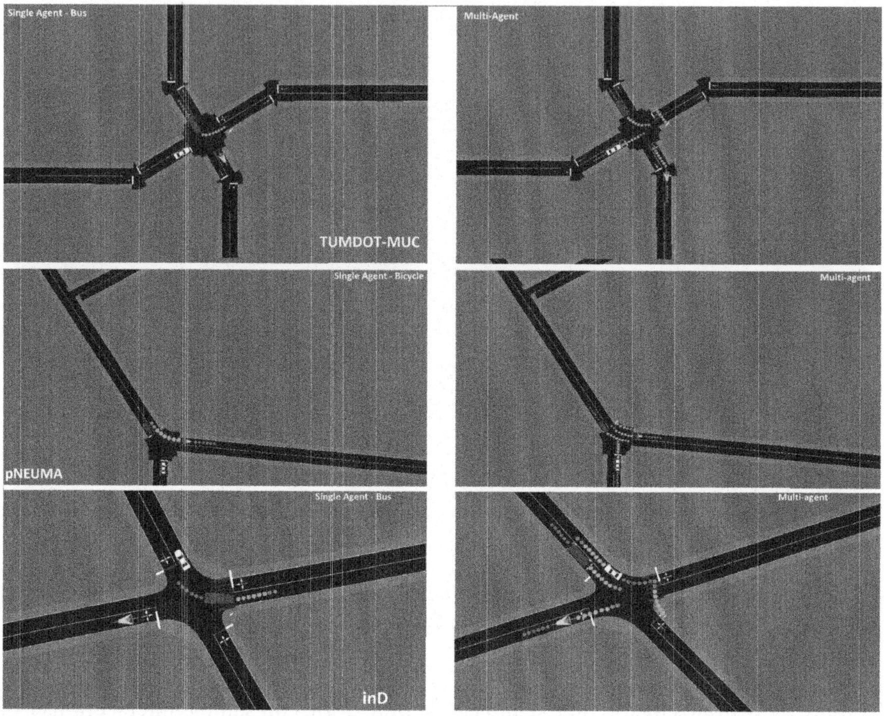

Fig. 6. Visual comparison of Predicted vs. Actual Trajectories in Scenario B (Red: Past, Blue: Ground Truth, Green: Prediction). (Color figure online)

performance when applied in different types of urban environments, even when complex and multimodal, as with *pNEUMA*.

Computational Efficiency and Real-Time Readiness. The average inference latency of 23.6 ms per sample demonstrates that the model is able to perform inference in real time. This performance is valuable for the company and the application of the method for UAV-supported traffic management systems that require real-time inference. The model also performed well on mode balance (0.82), which indicated that the predicted trajectories are diverse, not overly biased to often dominant modes, and minimize the chance of mode collapse.

Model Strengths and Limitations. Graphormer-TKAN benefited from the inherent spatial and temporal reasoning, especially when there are densely or asynchronously interacting agents. Its ability to encode categories of agents, heading, and acceleration allowed it to perform better with heterogeneity among vehicles, pedestrians, and cyclists. However, the model would suffer when there are long-term occlusions, histories of sparse motion, or sudden behavioral changes that were not experienced while training.

Practical Implications. The findings indicate that the model is a suitable candidate for application to UAV-based urban monitoring (e.g., at highly complex intersections or areas with high pedestrian traffic). Furthermore, the efficiency and ability of the model with consistently low prediction error in cities, traffic density, and sensor types highlight its applicability to generalize in geographies, which is an essential practice of smart transport systems.

6 Conclusion

This research developed an integrated trajectory prediction framework using Graphormer to capture spatial interaction and TKAN to learn temporal sequences, optimized simultaneously with MOPSO. The model effectively captures sophisticated inter-agent dynamics and context relations under various traffic settings using an extensive range of engineered features, like velocity, heading, acceleration, agent type, and relative spatial relations, within a graph-based model. To address both precision and practicality, MOPSO was used not only to adjust the hyperparameters but also to simultaneously optimize various competing goals, including ADE, FDE, latency of inference, and the trajectory entropy. Extensive experiments were carried out in two distinct scenarios: signalized intersections with multimodal uncertainty *(sinD)*, and more deterministic urban settings without traffic lights (*TUMDOT, inD, pNEUMA*). In both cases, the proposed method systematically outperformed state-of-the-art baselines over short- and long-term forecasting horizons, with better accuracy, scalability, and efficiency during inference. It should be noted that qualitative results on SUMO-based visualizations also validated the ability of the model to generate diverse and realistic future trajectories in different traffic settings. Adaptability within the framework to address both multi-output and single-output settings for trajectory forecasting and robustness within the datasets suggests the strong potential of extending the research towards implementation within real-time intelligent transportation and autonomous urban navigation settings.

Acknowledgment. The financial support of the Austrian Federal Ministry of Labor and Economy, the National Foundation for Research, Technology, and Development, and the Christian Doppler Research Association is gratefully acknowledged.

References

1. Mohebbi, M.R., Zada, M.J., Rostami-Shahrbabaki, M., Döller, M., Yamnenko, I.: Network traffic co-movement assessment via oriented basis signal processing and ensemble decision trees. In: 2024 IEEE 27th International Conference on Intelligent Transportation Systems (ITSC), Edmonton, AB, Canada, pp. 1948–1955. IEEE (2024). https://doi.org/10.1109/ITSC58415.2024.10919555

2. Mohebbi, M.R., Jaghargh, N.D., Döller, M., Zada, M.J.H., Yamnenko, I.: Network-Wide Traffic Prediction Via Bayesian State-Space Neural Networks and ARIMAX, In: 2025 IEEE 28th International Conference on Intelligent Transportation Systems (ITSC), Gold Coast, Australia, pp. 1459–1466, (2025). https://doi.org/10.1109/ITSC60802.2025.11423479
3. Mohebbi, M.R., Mohebbi Najm Abad, J., Kafash, E., Döller, M.: Towards Robust Urban Parking Violation Prediction Using Graph Kolmogorov–Arnold Networks and Liquid Neural Networks. In: Marcelloni, F., Madani, K., van Stein, N., Filipe, J. (eds) Computational Intelligence. IJCCI 2025. Communications in Computer and Information Science, vol. 2829. Springer, Cham (2026). https://doi.org/10.1007/978-3-032-15638-9_44
4. Mohebbi, M.R., Kafash, E., Döller, M.: Multi-agent trajectory prediction for urban environments with UAV data using enhanced temporal kolmogorov-arnold networks with particle swarm optimization. In: Proceedings of the 17th International Conference on Agents and Artificial Intelligence, vol. 2, pp. 586–597. SCITEPRESS (2025). https://doi.org/10.5220/0013243100003890
5. Mohebbi, M.R., Klinger, J., Abad, J.M.N., Döller, M., Tavasoli, M.: Advanced Driving Behavior Analysis Through Kolmogorov-Arnold Network and UAV Traffic Data. In: Huang, L., Greenhalgh, D. (eds) Proceedings of 17th International Conference on Machine Learning and Computing. ICMLC 2025. Lecture Notes in Networks and Systems, vol. 1475. Springer, Cham (2025). https://doi.org/10.1007/978-3-031-94892-3_23
6. Aittoniemi, E.: Evidence on impacts of automated vehicles on traffic flow efficiency and emissions: systematic review. IET Intel. Transp. Syst. **16**(10), 1306–1327 (2022)
7. Mohebbi, M.R., Kafash E., Döller, M.: Multimodal Graph-Based Reinforcement Learning for Multi-Agent Autonomous Navigation. In: 2025 IEEE 37th International Conference on Tools with Artificial Intelligence (ICTAI), Athens, Greece, pp. 299–304, (2025). https://doi.org/10.1109/ICTAI66417.2025.00046
8. Mohebbi, M.R., Tavasoli, M., Döller, M., Mohebbi Najm Abad, J., Hassan Zada, M.J., Yamnenko, I.: Vehicle trajectory prediction in congested urban traffic leveraging liquid neural network and UAV data. In: ACM International Conference on Machine Learning and Computing (ICMLC) (2025)
9. Wei, C., Wu, G., Barth, M.J., Abdelraouf, A., Gupta, R., Han, K.: KI-GAN: knowledge-informed generative adversarial networks for enhanced multi-vehicle trajectory forecasting at signalized intersections. In: Proceedings of the IEEE/CVF Conference on Computer Vision and Pattern Recognition (CVPR), pp. 7115–7124 (2024)
10. Yin, H., Xu, Y., Li, J., Zhang, H., Rigoll, G.: Knowledge-informed multi-agent trajectory prediction at signalized intersections for infrastructure-to-everything. arXiv preprint arXiv:2501.13461 (2025)
11. Klinger, J., Mohebbi, M.R., Döller, M.: Real transportation data benchmark: advancing efficiency through ML-based waiting time prediction. In: 2024 IEEE 27th International Conference on Intelligent Transportation Systems (ITSC), pp. 1166–1173. IEEE (2024)
12. Yang, B., Sun, S., Li, J., Lin, X., Tian, Y.: Traffic flow prediction using LSTM with feature enhancement. Neurocomputing **332**, 320–327 (2019)
13. Xie, G., Shangguan, A., Fei, R., Ji, W., Ma, W., Hei, X.: Motion trajectory prediction based on a CNN-LSTM sequential model. Sci. China Inf. Sci. **63**, 1–21 (2020)
14. Han, P., Wang, W., Shi, Q., Yue, J.: A combined online-learning model with K-means clustering and GRU neural networks for trajectory prediction. Ad Hoc Netw. **117**, 102476 (2021)
15. Tembhurne, J.V., Diwan, T.: Sentiment analysis in textual, visual and multimodal inputs using recurrent neural networks. Multimedia Tools Appl. **80**(5), 6871–6910 (2021)
16. Sun, C., Li, C., Lin, X., Zheng, T., Meng, F., Rui, X., Wang, Z.: Attention-based graph neural networks: a survey. Artif. Intell. Rev. **56**(Suppl 2), 2263–2310 (2023)

17. Li, J., Ma, H., Zhang, Z., Li, J., Tomizuka, M.: Spatio-temporal graph dual-attention network for multi-agent prediction and tracking. IEEE Trans. Intell. Transp. Syst. **23**(8), 10556–10569 (2021)
18. Ying, C., et al.: Do transformers really perform badly for graph representation? Adv. Neural. Inf. Process. Syst. **34**, 28877–28888 (2021)
19. Genet, R., Inzirillo, H.: TKAN: temporal Kolmogorov-Arnold networks. arXiv preprint arXiv:2405.07344 (2024)
20. Ma, Y., Zhu, X., Zhang, S., Yang, R., Wang, W., Manocha, D.: TrafficPredict: trajectory prediction for heterogeneous traffic-agents. In: Proceedings of the AAAI Conference on Artificial Intelligence, vol. 33, no. 1, pp. 6120–6127 (2019)
21. Habib, M., Aljarah, I., Faris, H., Mirjalili, S.: Multi-objective particle swarm optimization: theory, literature review, and application in feature selection for medical diagnosis. In: Evolutionary Machine Learning Techniques: Algorithms and Applications, pp. 175–201 (2020)
22. Cai, Y., et al.: Pedestrian motion trajectory prediction in intelligent driving from far shot first-person perspective video. IEEE Trans. Intell. Transp. Syst. **23**(6), 5298–5313 (2021)
23. Shan, X., Yu, W., Li, Z., Wang, C., Ren, Y., Zhang, J.: Vehicle trajectory-based traffic volume prediction on urban roads with fast-communication license plate recognition data. IEEE Trans. Intell. Transp. Syst. **25**(3), 2768–2778 (2023)
24. Wang, R., Song, X., Hu, Z., Cui, Y.: Spatio-temporal interaction aware and trajectory distribution aware graph convolution network for pedestrian multimodal trajectory prediction. IEEE Trans. Instrum. Meas. **72**, 1–1 (2022)
25. Zhang, E., Masoud, N., Bandegi, M., Lull, J., Malhan, R.K.: Step attention: sequential pedestrian trajectory prediction. IEEE Sens. J. **22**(8), 8071–8083 (2022)
26. Huang, F., Zhang, X., Li, C., Li, Z., He, Y., Zhao, Z.: Multimodal network embedding via attention based multi-view variational autoencoder. In: Proceedings of the 2018 ACM International Conference on Multimedia Retrieval, pp. 108–116 (2018)
27. Lv, K., Yuan, L., Ni, X.: Learning autoencoder diffusion models of pedestrian group relationships for multimodal trajectory prediction. IEEE Trans. Instrument. Meas. (2024)
28. Zhou, H., Yang, X., Ren, D., Huang, H., Fan, M.: CSIR: cascaded sliding CVAEs with iterative socially-aware rethinking for trajectory prediction. IEEE Trans. Intell. Transp. Syst. **24**(12), 14957–14969 (2023)
29. Li, Y., Jiang, Y., Xiong, Z., Wu, X.: Improving interaction-based vehicle trajectory prediction via handling sensing failures. IEEE Sens. J. (2024)
30. Vrahatis, A.G., Lazaros, K., Kotsiantis, S.: Graph attention networks: a comprehensive review of methods and applications. Future Internet **16**(9), 318 (2024)
31. Zhou, H., Ren, D., Xia, H., Fan, M., Yang, X., Huang, H.: AST-GNN: an attention-based spatio-temporal graph neural network for interaction-aware pedestrian trajectory prediction. Neurocomputing **445**, 298–308 (2021)
32. Singh, D., Srivastava, R.: Graph Neural Network with RNNs based trajectory prediction of dynamic agents for autonomous vehicle. Appl. Intell. **52**(11), 12801–12816 (2022)
33. Ju, W., et al.: A survey of graph neural networks in real world: imbalance, noise, privacy and OOD challenges. arXiv preprint arXiv:2403.04468 (2024)
34. Wang, H., et al.: STGformer: Efficient spatiotemporal graph transformer for traffic forecasting. arXiv preprint arXiv:2410.00385 (2024). https://doi.org/10.48550/arXiv.2410.00385
35. Vaswani, A., et al.: Attention is all you need. Adv. Neural Inf. Process. Syst. **30** (2017)
36. Singh, D., Srivastava, R.: Multi-scale graph-transformer network for trajectory prediction of the autonomous vehicles. Intel. Serv. Robot. **15**(3), 307–320 (2022)
37. Priambodo, B., Ahmad, A., Kadir, R.A.: Predicting traffic flow propagation based on congestion at neighbouring roads using hidden Markov model. IEEE Access **9**, 85933–85946 (2021)

38. Liu, T., Jiang, A., Miao, X., Tang, Y., Zhu, Y., Kwan, H.K.: Graph-based dynamic modeling and traffic prediction of urban road network. IEEE Sens. J. **21**(24), 28118–28130 (2021)
39. Peng, Z., Huang, X.: Spatial-temporal transformer network with self-supervised learning for traffic flow prediction. In: Proceedings of the STRL Workshop @ IJCAI (2022)
40. Hasan, F., Huang, H.: MALS-Net: a multi-head attention-based LSTM sequence-to-sequence network for socio-temporal interaction modelling and trajectory prediction. Sensors **23**(1), 530 (2023)
41. Xu, K., Chen, L., Wang, S.: Kolmogorov-Arnold networks for time series: bridging predictive power and interpretability. arXiv preprint arXiv:2406.02496 (2024)
42. Diraco, G., Rescio, G., Siciliano, P., Leone, A.: Review on human action recognition in smart living: sensing technology, multimodality, real-time processing, interoperability, and resource-constrained processing. Sensors **23**(11), 5281 (2023)
43. Zhu, Y., Wu, Y., Sebe, N., Yan, Y.: Vision+X: a survey on multimodal learning in the light of data. IEEE Trans. Pattern Anal. Mach. Intell. (2024)
44. Zheng, X., et al.: Graph neural networks for graphs with heterophily: a survey. arXiv preprint arXiv:2202.07082 (2022)
45. Rusch, T.K., Bronstein, M.M., Mishra, S.: A survey on oversmoothing in graph neural networks. arXiv preprint arXiv:2303.10993 (2023)
46. Hu, K., et al.: A review of research on reinforcement learning algorithms for multi-agents. Neurocomputing **2024**, 128068 (2024)
47. Kutsch, A., Margreiter, M., Bogenberger, K.: TUMDOT–MUC: data collection and processing of multimodal trajectories collected by aerial drones. Data Sci. Transp. **6**(2), 15 (2024)
48. Bock, J., Krajewski, R., Moers, T., Runde, S., Vater, L., Eckstein, L.: The inD dataset: a drone dataset of naturalistic road user trajectories at German intersections. In: 2020 IEEE Intelligent Vehicles Symposium (IV), pp. 1929–1934 (2020). https://doi.org/10.1109/IV47402.2020.9304839
49. Barmpounakis, E., Geroliminis, N.: On the new era of urban traffic monitoring with massive drone data: the pNEUMA large-scale field experiment. Transp. Res. Part C: Emerg. Technol. **111**, 50–71 (2020)
50. Xu, Y., et al.: SIND: a drone dataset at signalized intersection in China. In: 2022 IEEE 25th International Conference on Intelligent Transportation Systems (ITSC), pp. 2471–2478. IEEE (2022)
51. Gilbert, E.N.: Random plane networks. J. Soc. Ind. Appl. Math. **9**(4), 533–543 (1961)
52. Makansi, O., Ilg, E., Cicek, O., Brox, T.: Overcoming limitations of mixture density networks: a sampling and fitting framework for multimodal future prediction. In: Proceedings of the IEEE/CVF Conference on Computer Vision and Pattern Recognition (CVPR), pp. 7144–7153 (2019)
53. Madjid, N.A., et al.: Trajectory prediction for autonomous driving: progress, limitations, and future directions. arXiv preprint arXiv:2503.03262 (2025)
54. Zhang, Y., et al.: Trajectory entropy: modeling game state stability from multimodality trajectory prediction. arXiv preprint arXiv:2506.05810 (2025)

A Research Agenda for Usability and Generalisation in Reinforcement Learning

Dennis J. N. J. Soemers[1(✉)], Spyridon Samothrakis[2], Kurt Driessens[1], and Mark H. M. Winands[1]

[1] Department of Advanced Computing Sciences, Maastricht University, Maastricht, The Netherlands
{dennis.soemers,kurt.driessens, m.winands}@maastrichtuniversity.nl

[2] Institute for Analytics and Data Science, University of Essex, Colchester, UK
ssamot@essex.ac.uk

Abstract. It is common practice in reinforcement learning (RL) research to train and deploy agents in bespoke simulators, typically implemented by engineers directly in general-purpose programming languages or hardware acceleration frameworks such as CUDA or JAX. This means that programming and engineering expertise is not only required to develop RL algorithms, but is also required to use already developed algorithms for novel problems. The latter poses a problem in terms of the usability of RL, in particular for private individuals and small organisations without substantial engineering expertise. We also perceive this as a challenge for effective generalisation in RL, in the sense that is no standard, shared formalism in which different problems are represented. As we typically have no consistent representation through which to provide information about any novel problem to an agent, our agents also cannot instantly or rapidly generalise to novel problems. In this position paper, we advocate for a research agenda centred around the use of user-friendly description languages for describing problems, such that (i) users with little to no engineering expertise can formally describe the problems they would like to be tackled by RL algorithms, and (ii) algorithms can leverage problem descriptions to effectively generalise among all problems describable in the language of choice.

Keywords: Environment Descriptions · Generalisation · Reinforcement Learning

1 Introduction

Researchers in the field of reinforcement learning (RL) have largely converged on a small number of common APIs for the development of benchmark domains that are used to evaluate the performance of RL algorithms. New environments are customarily written in general-purpose programming languages such as `C++` or `Python`, and implement a Gym-based [22] API for learning algorithms to interface with environments. There are variants on this approach, such as PettingZoo [154] for multi-agent RL, but the general workflow remains similar.

H. J. van den Herik et al. (Eds.): ICAART 2025, LNAI 16517, pp. 687–713, 2026.
https://doi.org/10.1007/978-3-032-25032-2_33

At a high level, we may distinguish roughly two categories of RL research. On the one hand, there is research where the focus is on the development of new and improved (modifications of) training algorithms, typically not focused on any specific task. There may be a focus on certain categories of tasks (single-agent RL, multi-agent RL, RL for domains with vision-based inputs, RL for partially observable environments, RL for continuous action spaces, and so on), but existing and established frameworks with a suite of applicable domains are typically used for empirical evaluations. Researchers typically aim to demonstrate a high level of generality, by showing that an algorithm can effectively learn on a large collection of different environments within such a suite, as opposed to only a single environment. These environments are often games or other simulations, with arguably relatively limited direct real-world impact outside of their use as benchmarks for RL research. Examples of such suites of environments include the Arcade Learning Environment [13, 87], ProcGen [25], SMACv2 [37], and the DeepMind Control Suite [152]. On the other hand, there is research in which a single, concrete, high-impact "real-world" task is selected, and RL is used to improve performance on that one task. Substantial engineering effort is often dedicated towards implementing and optimising such a task for the purpose of this research. This engineering effort often requires highly specialised knowledge of, for example, programming for GPUs or other hardware accelerators, or of the inner workings of deep learning (DL) and RL algorithms, such that the task and its state and action representations can be implemented in such a way that the existing DL and RL techniques can be applied to their fullest potential. Examples include research focused on applications such as resource balancing for logistics [78], flight control for stratospheric balloons [12], compiler optimisations [27, 159], automated chip floorplanning [96], power grid management [167], alignment of large language models with human preferences [64, 110], and magnetic tokamak controllers [31].

While discussions on experimental methodologies and statistical analyses of empirical evaluations in RL have been on the rise within the research community [3, 53, 59, 60, 113], as well as discussions of how to select which environment(s) to use in experiments [113, 160], we see little to no discussion on *how* or *by whom* tasks (or environments) are described or implemented in the first place. In a recent position paper [146], we argued that the standard assumption that environments can be implemented (and heavily optimised) in general-purpose programming languages, by engineers familiar with machine learning, (i) poses a challenge to widespread adoption of RL for real-world use cases, and (ii) also leads the research community at large to miss out on interesting research directions with respect to generalisation and transfer in RL. While it may be acceptable to invest substantial engineering resources for the implementation of environments for large-scale projects with high potential impact, it impedes the application of RL by smaller organisations or private individuals. We posit that more widespread applications of RL will be greatly aided if the latter groups can express their tasks in user-friendly domain-specific languages (DSLs) [8, 95], or even in natural language.

Once we adopt a methodology in which environments are represented in explicit forms that can be provided as inputs to an agent (e.g., DSL or natural language snippets), we can also explore new forms of generalisation or transfer in RL, where effective

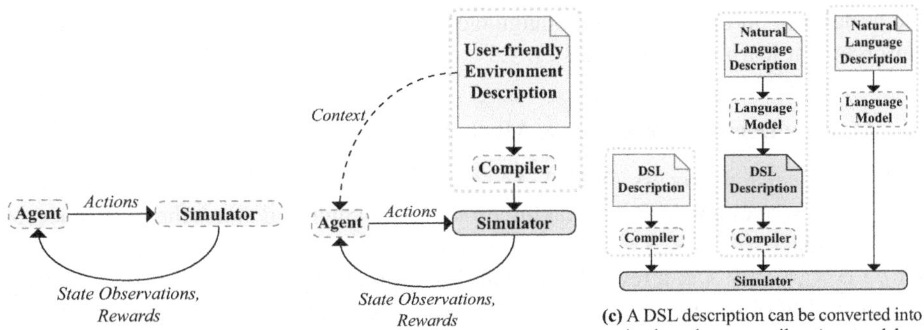

(a) A simulator of the environment is implemented in a general-purpose programming language. This is the most common setting in current research.

(b) The environment is described in a user-friendly language, and compiled into a simulator. The description may serve as additional input to the agent.

(c) A DSL description can be converted into a simulator by a compiler. A natural language description can first be translated into an intermediate DSL description by a language model, or can be translated directly with a language model serving as compiler.

Fig. 1. Orange boxes with dashed lines represent components that require substantial engineering or RL expertise. The green components can be provided by users with little to no engineering expertise. **(a)** A depiction of the customary setting in RL research. **(b)** The approach for which we posit that increased research attention is warranted (Sect. 3). **(c)** User-friendly environment descriptions may be written in a DSL, or in a natural language, where the latter approach may or may not generate an intermediate DSL description. Image source: [146]. (Color figure online)

generalisation or zero-shot transfer to unseen environments may become feasible given sufficient understanding of the task descriptions. Figure 1a depicts the setting where the environment is implemented directly in a general-purpose programming language, and Fig. 1b depicts the proposed settings, with Fig. 1c providing three examples of how the translation from a user-friendly environment description to a simulator may work. For tasks that take place in the physical world, such as non-simulated robotics tasks, a description of the reward function can suffice, as hardware and the real world with its laws of physics already dictate aspects such as the action space and transition dynamics. However, even in these cases, the ability to automatically generate a sufficiently accurate simulator from user-friendly descriptions would, in combination with sim-to-real transfer [170], still be highly beneficial [166].

This paper is an extension of a previous position paper [146]. The primary extensions consist of (i) a discussion of barriers to widespread adoption of RL other than the one that is our main focus (Sect. 5), and (ii) a detailed description of the research agenda we envision following from our position (Sect. 6). Furthermore, other sections throughout the paper have been updated to provide additional context, examples, and to reflect and relate our work to other recent developments in the field, such as the Ludax framework [158] and other related position papers [17,52,127].

2 Background

This section provides background information on (partially observable) Markov decision processes [55] and Markov games [161] (Subsect. 2.1)—two frequently used formalisations of sequential decision-making problems, which we argue users should be able to describe in more accessible languages than programming languages—and deep reinforcement learning (Subsect. 2.2).

2.1 Markov Decision Processes & Markov Games

A Markov decision process (MDP) $\mathcal{M} = \langle \mathcal{S}, \mathcal{A}, P, \rho \rangle$ is a formal description of a single-agent sequential decision-making problem, in which $\mathcal{S}$ denotes the state space, $\mathcal{A}$ the action space, $P : \mathcal{S} \times \mathcal{A} \times \mathcal{S} \mapsto [0, 1]$ a function that defines transition probabilities, and $\rho : \mathcal{S} \times \mathcal{A} \times \mathcal{S} \times \mathbb{R}$ a reward function. More precisely, $0 \leq P(s' \mid s, a) \leq 1$ gives the probability of observing a transition from a current state $s \in \mathcal{S}$ to a successor state $s' \in \mathcal{S}$ after executing an action $a \in \mathcal{A}$, and $\rho(r \mid s, a, s')$ denotes the probability of observing a real-valued reward $r \in \mathbb{R}$ after the same event. In some MDPs, it may be the case that only certain subsets of the full action space $\mathcal{A}$ are legal in certain states.

The behaviour of an agent may be described as a policy $\pi : \mathcal{S} \times \mathcal{A} \mapsto [0, 1]$, such that $0 \leq \pi(a \mid s) \leq 1$ denotes the probability with which the policy selects an action $a \in \mathcal{A}$ whenever the current state is $s \in \mathcal{S}$. At discrete time steps $t = 0, 1, \dots$, the agent observes the current state $S_t \in \mathcal{S}$, samples an action $A_t \sim \pi(\cdot \mid S_t)$ from its policy π, transitions into a successor state $S_{t+1} \sim P(\cdot \mid S_t, A_t)$, and receives a reward $R_t \sim \rho(S_t, A_t, S_{t+1})$. The most common objective is to select actions such that the returns G_0 are maximised, where $G_t = \sum_{k=0}^{\infty} \gamma^k R_{t+k+1}$ denotes sum of discounted rewards collected from time t onwards. Temporally distant rewards are discounted, relative to short-term rewards, by the discount factor $0 < \gamma \leq 1$.

The *state value function* $V^{\pi} : \mathcal{S} \mapsto \mathbb{R}$ gives the expected returns when action according to a policy π from any input state s onwards: $V^{\pi}(s) = \mathbb{E}_{\pi}[G_t \mid S_t = s]$. Similarly, the *state-action value function* $Q^{\pi} : \mathcal{S} \times \mathcal{A} \mapsto \mathbb{R}$ gives the expected returns of executing an input action a in an input state s, and sampling any subsequent actions from π: $Q^{\pi}(s, a) = \mathbb{E}_{\pi}[G_t \mid S_t = s, A_t = a]$.

Partially observable Markov decision processes (POMDPs) additionally feature an observation space $\mathcal{O}$, and a mapping $\phi : \mathcal{S} \mapsto \mathcal{O}$ from states to observations. In a POMDP, the agent cannot necessarily observe the current state S_t, but only an observation $O_t = \phi(S_t)$, where it is possible for multiple different states to map to the same observation.

The concept of Markov games may be viewed as a generalisation of (PO)MDPs for multi-agent settings [82]. In a Markov game, each of $k \geq 1$ players (or agents) has its own action space from which to select actions, and its own reward function. Transition probabilities between pairs of states are defined over the joint action space of all players. This paper uses the term *environment* to refer to problems that may be tackled by RL, regardless of whether they may be (PO)MDPs or Markov games.

2.2 Deep Reinforcement Learning

One of the main goals in reinforcement learning (RL) [151] research is the development of algorithms that can automatically learn strong policies from experience gathered within a (PO)MDP or Markov game. *Tabular* RL methods learn distinct state-action values or probabilities for every individual state-action pair in $\mathcal{S} \times \mathcal{A}$. This is only feasible in relatively small problems, and often wasteful in terms of data efficiency due to the lack of generalisation between related state-action pairs. RL methods with *function approximation* address these issues, by training function approximators that use features of states and/or actions, rather than enumerating the complete space. State-action pairs that are closely related to each other may be expected to have similar features, allowing for improved data efficiency through generalisation. One of the most popular and successful forms of RL with function approximation is deep RL, in which deep neural networks (DNNs) [74] are used as function approximators.

3 Description Languages for Environments

Subsection 3.1 describes the established practice where RL research is performed using environments that have been implemented, conforming to a standardised API such as the Gym API [22], in general-purpose programming languages or more specialised frameworks for hardware accelerators such as GPUs. It identifies potential issues that may arise when the entire research community focuses solely on such environments. As an initial step towards more user-friendly descriptions, Subsect. 3.2 discusses the use of DSLs for describing environments for use in RL research. Subsection 3.3 explores the possibility of using natural languages to define environments—arguably one of the most user-friendly language classes. Finally, Subsect. 3.4 presents the central position of this paper: a call for more (research attention for) benchmarks in which environments are described in DSLs or natural language.

3.1 Defining Environments in Programming Languages

Outside of cases where RL is applied directly in the physical world, such as some work in robotics [85], it is customary to implement the environments used for RL research in programming languages such as `C++` or `Python`. There is also a recent trend of using more advanced toolkits or libraries, such as CUDA or JAX [20], to enable the environments themselves—and not just DNN forward and backward passes—to make efficient use of hardware accelerators [15,18,28,41,42,51,69,71,89,118,130]. The latter approach can provide dramatic speed increases, but also imposes additional constraints on programming style and requires more specialised and advanced engineering skills.

Most developers of RL environments have converged to the API popularised by OpenAI Gym [22]. This API requires developers to implement:

- A definition of the *observation space*. For any state that an agent may ever reach in an environment, it will receive an observation from this space as input. The observation space may, for example, be a discrete set of integers, each of which uniquely identifies one element of the state space $\mathcal{S}$, or it may be subset of $\mathbb{R}^d$ for some dimensionality d, such that every state is described by a d-dimensional real-valued feature vector.
- A definition of the *action space* $\mathcal{A}$. It is typically assumed that agents must select any one element from this space as their action at each time step.
- A *reset* function, which resets the environment to an initial state.

- A *step* function, which takes an action from $\mathcal{A}$ as input, transitions from a current state $s \in \mathcal{S}$ to a successor state $s' \in \mathcal{S}$, and returns a real-valued reward r and an observation of s' (alongside several auxiliary variables). In this function, programmers essentially implement the transition and reward models P and ρ. This is typically done implicitly: the function usually implements a procedural algorithm that generates s' and r in a manner that ends up being consistent with the probabilities defined by P and ρ, without explicitly defining and sampling from the full distributions.

3.2 Domain-Specific Languages for Environments

A potential alternative to the standard practice of describing environments in general-purpose (or more advanced and complex hardware acceleration frameworks) is to use DSLs to describe sets of environments. This approach still requires significant engineering effort to develop a compiler that can translate valid descriptions from the DSL to a runnable simulator with an API for (learning) agents. However, once this compiler has been built, users with little to no programming experience may—depending on the complexity and user-friendliness of the DSL in question—use it to describe new environments that fit within the overarching domain supported by the DSL. Note that the requirement for a compiler to be implemented suggests that it would only ever be reasonable to use a DSL for sets of multiple environments, but never for a single environment. If there is only a single environment of interest, it would likely be easier to directly implement that environment itself in a programming language.

Numerous examples of DSLs for describing sequential decision-making problems already exist, though their adoption as benchmarks within the RL community is restricted compared to benchmarks such as the Arcade Learning Environment [13,87] or the DeepMind Control Suite [152], which are not based on DSLs. Examples include the Planning Domain Definition Language (PDDL) [93] for planning problems, and the Stanford Game Description Language [44,83], Ludi [24], Toss [63], the Video Game Description Language [134,136], Regular Boardgames [68], Ludii [115], Stratega [114], Griddly [9], MiniHack [133], and Ludax [158] for various ranges of games. PDDLGym [140] provides Gym environment wrappers around PDDL problems.

As an example, we provide a description of the game of Tic-Tac-Toe in the DSL of Ludii below. Note that some rules—such as players moving in turns, or the game ending in a draw when neither player can move—are not explicitly stated, because these are default settings and can therefore be omitted in this language. Games that deviate from these defaults can be described by explicitly including rules where appropriate.

Ludii Game Description Example

```
(game "Tic-Tac-Toe"
    (players 2)
    (equipment {
        (board (square 3))
        (piece "Disc" P1)
        (piece "Cross" P2)
    })
    (rules
        (play (move Add (to (sites Empty))))
        (end (if (is Line 3) (result Mover Win)))
    )
)
```

3.3 Describing Environments in Natural Language

While DSLs may already be considered a more user-friendly alternative to general-purpose programming languages [8, 95] for describing environments, natural language would be even more accessible to a wider userbase. Here, we provide an example of what a natural language description of the game of Tic-Tac-Toe might look like:

Natural Language Description Example

The game of Tic-Tac-Toe is played by two players on a grid of 3×3 square cells. Players take turns drawing their symbol—a circle for the first player, and a cross for the second—in an empty cell of their choice. The game ends in a win for a player if that player completes an orthogonal or diagonal line of three instances of their symbol. The game ends in a draw if the board is filled up with neither player achieving their win condition.

Although the state of the art of large language models (LLMs) is highly impressive [171], there are still concerns surrounding reliability and correctness [76]. In particular, we envision that ambiguities typically present in natural languages, as well as the tendency for humans to underspecify task descriptions (e.g., rules of games), will present substantial challenges that require further research. Recently, [2] demonstrated promising initial results for an LLM automatically generating executable environment code based on natural language descriptions, but it still requires an expert human in the loop who is able to interpret the generated code and provide feedback on potential mistakes. In the short term, it may be more realistically feasible to use a combination of natural language and DSLs, where an LLM first translates a natural language description to a DSL-based description [34, 109, 176], and a user can inspect the generated description and make corrections if necessary before it is compiled into a simulator. In the long term, if LLMs can be made sufficiently reliable, natural languages would likely be the most accessible modality for describing environments.

3.4 Research Focus on Description Languages for Environments

Before formally stating the central position of this paper, we make two core assumptions relating to the user-friendliness of DSLs and natural languages (Assumption 1), and the desirability of this user-friendliness (Assumption 2).

Assumption 1 *Defining environments, such as (PO)MDPs or Markov games, in domain-specific languages (DSLs) or natural languages can be more user-friendly than defining them in general-purpose programming languages.*

Increasing user-friendliness and lowering barriers to entry is a well-established potential motivation for the use of DSLs [8,95]. Note that there may also be other reasons for using DSLs, and there can be DSLs that do not substantially lower barriers to entry: this depends on the design of the DSL in question. For example, the logic-based Stanford Game Description Language [44,83] arguably still requires substantial technical expertise and writing games in it may be considered error-prone due to the large file size required for many interesting games. In contrast, allowing for clear and succinct descriptions that are easy to read and write was an explicit design goal for Ludii's description language [115]. Likely in no small part due to the language's level of accessibility, Ludii has amassed a library of over 1400 distinct official game descriptions,[1] including third-party contributions from game designers with little or no programming experience.[2]

In the case of natural languages, if any concerns around ambiguities and underspecification of environments can be adequately addressed, we see little reason to doubt that many users would indeed find them more accessible than programming languages. If procedures translating natural language descriptions directly into executable simulations cannot be made sufficiently reliable, a potential solution may be to use DSLs as an intermediate step. Users could first describe their tasks in natural languages, and they would ideally only have to verify or fix small issues in automatically generated descriptions in a user-friendly DSL afterwards.

Assumption 2 *Enabling environments to be defined in more user-friendly ways is desirable.*

First, we will acknowledge that lowering the barrier to entry for defining environments is not necessarily *always* of importance. For example, when RL is applied to an individual, specific domain with a high degree of scientific, societal, economic or other form of impact, it will often be worth investing substantial engineering effort into the environment definition. However, running such projects tends to be restricted to groups with direct access to RL experts.

A survey among AI engineers, AI designers, and RL engineers from AAA video game studios, independent developers, and industrial research labs—most of which do have direct access to a substantial amount of engineering expertise—revealed, among other concerns, an overreliance on engineering support, and difficulties in designing tasks for RL agents, as challenges for the adoption of RL and other AI techniques in

[1] https://ludii.games/library.php.

[2] https://ludii.games/forum/forumdisplay.php?fid=23.

video game development [58]. While not focused on RL (but, rather, AI in general) or environment descriptions, a recent study by [141] reveals a substantial disconnect between the technical know-how that AI designers expect users will have, and what they actually tend to have, as a core barrier to adoption of AI in practice. These studies point to the relevance of improving the user-friendliness of any aspect of the RL (or any AI) pipeline.

If we wish to democratise the use of AI [138] to the extent that users with little expertise in RL—or even programming—can apply it to their problems of interest, enabling environments to be defined in more user-friendly ways would be a requirement. Outside of RL, in the landscape of generative artificial intelligence (AI), substantial value is generated not necessarily just by the models themselves, but also by the release of user-friendly tools and interfaces to access the trained models. Famous examples include OpenAI's ChatGPT [108] and DALL·E 2 [120], Stability AI's models and interfaces for audio [147], image [117], and video [16] generation, Midjourney,[3] and Gradio apps [1]. We envision that a comparable workflow for RL would have a convenient interface for a user to describe their problem, after which a policy—ideally without requiring any further training (see Sect. 4)—would be able to start taking actions and solve the problem. In addition to easing the deployment of RL by non-engineers for their tasks of interest, domain experts of novel problems would also become able to create interesting new benchmark domains for RL researchers—similar to how [35] aimed to improve accessibility and facilitate further research for dynamic algorithm configuration. This leads to our position as follows:

Position

The RL research community should place greater focus on benchmarks with environments defined in user-friendly DSLs or natural languages.

Two clear lines of research that follow from Assumptions 1 and 2 would be the design of user-friendly DSLs for relevant application domains, as well as generating reliable translations from natural language to exectuable simulators. However, beyond these challenges related to getting simulators to run in the first place, we also argue that they should be used extensively as benchmarks in general RL research, and that existing benchmarks—with environments implemented directly in general-purpose programming languages—are not sufficient to evaluate how different algorithms and approaches might perform when later applied to environments defined in more user-friendly languages.

For example, consider the common assumption that the full action space $\mathcal{A}$ can be defined in advance, as described in Subsect. 3.1. While standardised APIs such as OpenAI Gym's [22] have undoubtedly aided and accelerated RL research, there is a risk that convergence of the community on such an API may have entrenched this assumption in the community. The ubiquity of this assumption may also be explained by its convenience in the context of deep learning research. There exists some early deep RL work [72, 124] where actions were treated as inputs of neural networks—hence requiring separate forward passes for every legal action to compute policies or state-action values.

[3] https://www.midjourney.com/.

However, it quickly became common practice—especially after the work on Deep Q-Networks by [99]—to treat actions as outputs. Requiring only a single DNN forward pass per state greatly improves computational efficiency, at the cost of requiring prior knowledge of the full action space.

In practice, the full action space (or a reasonably sized superset thereof) cannot always be automatically inferred from environment descriptions written in languages that prioritise aspects such as usability over support for robust automated inference. In the relatively verbose, logic-based S-GDL [44, 83], this is possible, and it is straightforward to build policy networks accordingly [49]. In contrast, in Ludii's DSL, which is substantially more succinct and arguably user-friendly [115], this does not appear to be feasible. The root of the issue is that succinct descriptions of, for example, game rules, are generally descriptions of procedures that may be used in any game state to generate the set of legal actions for that particular game state. Determining the full action space of the environment requires combinations of this information with an inference of what the entire state space may look like, and this is challenging if the semantics of the DSL are not readily available in a logic-based format. For example, the rule that legal moves consist of players placing one of their pieces on any empty cell in the game of *Hex* is formulated as `(play (move Add (to (sites Empty))))` in Ludii's DSL. In combination with knowledge of the size of the board (which is defined in a different rule), knowledge that there are no rules that can ever change the size of the board, and knowledge that there are no other rules for other types of moves, it is easy for humans to infer that the action space of this game must be equal to the number of cells on the board. However, without explicit, direct access to formal semantics of the many hundreds of keywords in Ludii's DSL [23], there is no clear way to make this inference in an automated and general manner that works for any game described in the language. Practical attempts at using deep learning with Ludii have therefore faced challenges such as *action aliasing*, where a single output node of a policy network may end up getting shared by multiple distinct legal actions [143]—an issue that is rarely considered possible in other deep RL research. [92] opted to forgo training a policy head altogether, sticking only to a state value function, for games written in another DSL. A similar problem surfaces in PDDLGym [140], which also requires careful treatment of action spaces due to a mismatch between PDDL and the customary assumptions about action spaces in RL.

These examples of multiple existing DSLs that conflict with the otherwise common assumption of prior knowledge of the full action space is merely one example of an important issue that is largely overlooked by current research. It cannot be ruled out that other types of issues, which are not adequately accounted for by the currently prevailing research methodologies, may surface as the community shifts focus to more benchmarks based on environments defined in DSLs or natural language.

4 Leveraging Environment Descriptions for Generalisation in RL

The previous section argues for the relevance of developing RL techniques that can operate on environments defined in DSLs or natural language, as opposed to general-purpose programming languages, the importance dedicating substantial research efforts on benchmarks following the same methodology, and potential issues that may surface and are underexplored in the current research landscape. However, in addition to potential issues, we also see opportunities. In particular, succinct—but complete—environment descriptions may serve as a powerful tool to improve (zero-shot) generalisation [66] across the set of all environments that may be described in the language of choice.

4.1 Generalisation in RL

The most straightforward setting in RL [151] is to have an agent interacting, collecting experience, and training in a single environment for some time, and to subsequently evaluate its performance in the same environment. This approach has a high risk of producing agents that overfit, in the sense that they may become overly reliant on spurious features, largely ignore state observations altogether and simply memorise trajectories of states or actions, or otherwise be incapable of handling even minor variations on the environment after training [87, 162, 168, 169].

A popular category of RL research with a higher degree of generalisation involves training agents on a subset of one or more closely-related environments, and evaluating them in the same set, or a different set of similar environments [19, 25, 26, 32, 38, 39, 62, 77, 94, 104, 149, 164]. Different environments in this case may be different levels of the same video game, or subtle variants of an environment with, for example, modified background or foreground colours or patterns, different values for the velocities of certain entities or other numeric parameters, or different reward functions. Particularly in the cases of meta RL [11, 40, 103, 119, 137, 175] and few-shot transfer learning [73, 102, 153, 174], at least a small amount of environment-specific fine-tuning prior to evaluation is also assumed. While prior research collectively covers variation along all dimensions of environments (variation in transition dynamics, variation in colours used in state observations, variation in goals or reward functions, etc.), the work described in each publication individually tends to be restricted to a smaller subset of these dimensions. Research on transfer learning in RL [73, 153, 174] is often similarly restricted in scope [43, 46, 47, 98, 129, 142, 155, 165]. [144] used DSL-based environment descriptions for (zero-shot) transfer learning between different board games, but only to a relatively small degree, where the transfer mechanism was not automatically learnt. [10, 70] automatically identified mappings or transferable features between games, but they used a low-level logic-based DSL, which is arguably lacking in terms of user-friendliness.

Sim-to-real transfer [170]—where policies are trained in simulation, but deployed on robots in the physical world—is another major category of generalisation in RL. However, in this case, the need for generalisation is an unfortunate reality due to inevitable differences between simulators and the real world. While some degree of variation is inevitable in this setting, it is typically intentionally kept as low as possible.

4.2 Leveraging Context for Generalisation

Theoretical work suggests that, in the worst case, strong assumptions on the similarity between different environments are required for efficient generalisation to be possible:

different environments must share an optimal policy [90]. One reason for the difficulty of generalisation to unseen environments, without strong restrictions on the degree of variation, is that epistemic uncertainty about relevant parameters of the current environment essentially turns the collection of all environments that the agent may face into a partially observable environment—even if the current state of each individual environment is fully observable [45].

The notion of such a collection of environments, each of which may be identified by certain parameters (a *context*), of which some may never be used for training and only appear at test time, may be formalised as a *contextual* [14,66] (PO)MDP or Markov game. In the formalism of [66], contexts may be as simple as just the value of a random seed that is used for procedural level generation, or take a more complex form such as a vector of parameters that describe important properties of the environment. Contexts may or may not be observable to the agent(s), although the ability to observe contexts—which should also carry sufficient information to enable disambiguation between environments—is required to resolve partial observability [45] induced by epistemic uncertainty.

Research on multi-task RL often involves providing contexts as inputs to agents, but these contexts tend to be far from full environment descriptions. For example, [32] provide a single or a handful of numeric values as context, which describe goal coordinates for robotic control tasks. It is common to provide short, language-based instructions or hints to guide the agent [6,50,65,79,84,88,97,107,139,163], but such instructions do not (fully) describe the environment. In cases where goals correspond to elements of the state space, universal value function approximators [135] can learn reusable skills and generalise by conditioning on goal states. [75,122,123] prompt agents with demonstrations of interactions by experts for disambiguation between environments and in-context learning, which is a form of context that is arguably more difficult to acquire than environment descriptions (requiring an environment-specific expert to have already been trained), whilst simultaneously carrying less information (it does not reveal information about any parts of the environment that are not explored in the demonstration). CARL [14] extends several well-established RL benchmarks with contexts, but these contexts take the form of dictionaries specifying values for only a handful of variables. [128] consider more elaborate task descriptions, but not necessarily ones that fully specify complete environments. [150] use a DSL to prescribe policies that an agent should execute, as opposed to describing the environment itself. [21] leverage text from strategy guides to guide search-based game playing agents, but these texts do not fully describe the environment, and were not used to improve generalisation to unseen environments. The textual descriptions provided to agents by [172] are perhaps closest to what we propose, although their descriptions are not sufficiently detailed to the extent that they could be compiled into a correct simulator, and are not meant to serve as a substitute for implementing the environment in a programming language.

4.3 Environment Descriptions as Context

If it is desirable to describe environments in succinct DSLs or in natural language, as posited in Sect. 3, then these descriptions may also be used to improve generalisation by serving as contexts. Crucially, leveraging such descriptions as context should not be viewed by peer reviewers as being a reduction in generality, or being restricted to a particular DSL, as the general workflow of providing environments in such a language is arguably more accessible and more general than using a programming language for many potential end users. An important property of such environment descriptions is that they come from a shared language, and it should be possible for humans as well as software to generate novel environment descriptions in the same language. We cannot only generate contexts from environments, but also generate environments (in the form of fully executable simulators) from contexts. From the researchers' point of view, this is valuable as it makes environments easily controllable and enables a wide variety of evaluation protocols [66]. From the learning agent's point of view, this property may also be valuable in that a program could actively learn about the description language that is used by procedurally generating new descriptions [24, 157], translating them into executable simulators, and learning in them—effectively forming their own curriculum of environments to learn from [33, 57, 111, 125, 132].

Furthermore, it could be argued that contexts that completely describe an environment—to the extent that they could be translated into executable simulators—are likely to be a prerequisite for unrestricted, zero-shot generalisation in RL [56]. Consider the generalisation abilities of humans. In some cases, humans can effectively generalise to unseen situations without relying on explicit task descriptions, but in others they cannot. For example, if a human plays a new video game for the first time, in which there is something that looks like fire, they can infer that they should likely avoid the fire—based on their related experience in the physical world and other video games. This relies on an implicit assumption that fire in this particular video game works similarly to how it works in other games, or in the real world, which may be incorrect. If a human is faced with a brand new board game, they cannot be expected to play it well if the rules of the game are not explained. Once the rules are explained, they may be able to play well immediately—based on their experience with related board games and ability to reason—without any direct experience with the game in question.

5 Other Barriers to Widespread Deployment of RL

While the focus of this paper is on the challenge posed to widespread adoption of RL by the customary use of programming languages for defining environments or tasks, this is not the only barrier. The choice to focus on environment descriptions and the languages in which they are described is due to our perception that this aspect of RL research and deployment is hardly if ever discussed, whereas other challenges are already more frequently acknowledged and discussed. However, we do not expect these different challenges, or solutions to them, to be completely orthogonal, and discuss how they may be related here.

5.1 Sample Efficiency and Computation Resource Requirements

Sample (in)efficiency and the requirement for substantial computation resources are frequently cited as pervasive issues in deep RL, both in terms of feasibility of deployment in the "real world" as well as research more generally [4, 101, 106]. This issue motivates the recent trend of implementing simulators to be entirely runnable on hardware accelerators via frameworks such as JAX, as discussed in Subsect. 3.1. When applicable, such an approach is highly effective at lowering the barrier to entry in terms of hardware requirements for RL research. However, this style of implementing environments is arguably even more demanding in terms of engineering expertise than using general-purpose programming languages, and is not directly helpful in terms of lowering the barrier to entry for deployment of RL by users without such engineering expertise.

In contrast, environments implemented in commonly-used DSLs [83, 115, 136] tend to have substantially lower simulation speeds than similar environments implemented directly in programming languages like `Java` or `C++`. This only exacerbates the need for computation resources—to make up for low simulation speeds—if RL is to be successful in these environments. We do not view this as an argument against using DSLs, but rather as an additional reason to focus even more on improving sample efficiency of RL. Only focusing on (methodologies for implementing) environments that permit running simulations at high speeds would be an inadvisable form of tunnel vision, not unlike how the *hardware lottery* [54] describes when certain algorithms receive more attention than others depending on their compatibility with current hardware. Alternatively, it may be possible to combine the high speed of hardware-accelerated programming with user-friendly domain specific languages. The Ludax framework [158] is a recent, and to our knowledge first, example of a system that compiles user-friendly game description languages (inspired by Ludii's language [115]) into native and hardware-accelerated simulation code via JAX. To what extent this can be effectively replicated with other languages, domains other than board games, or even simply a broader and more diverse set of board games than that currently supported by Ludax, remains to be seen in future research.

5.2 Complexity of Agent Design, RL Algorithm Selection, and Hyperparameter Tuning

Another challenge for the deployment of RL is lack of reliability (e.g., instability or high variance in performance levels over different random seeds), and the degree to which RL performance depends on selecting the right algorithms, optimisers, neural network architectures, hyperparameters, and other design decisions for each specific environment [7, 36, 105]. All of these are choices that tend to require a substantial amount of RL and engineering expertise, or the ability to run extensive experiments (e.g., grid searches for hyperparameters). However, advances in meta RL [11, 40, 103, 119, 137, 175] and AutoML (or AutoRL) [48, 100, 112] may help lower this barrier to entry [81]. It is plausible that the ability to provide succinct and information-rich environment descriptions as context, as discussed in Sect. 4, may also benefit these techniques.

6 Proposed Research Agenda

Building on the arguments and analyses from the previous sections, we propose a research agenda centred around the use of user-friendly languages to describe problems of interest (i.e., the environments in RL settings), with anticipated opportunities, new avenues for research, and challenges regarding aspects such as democratisation of the use of AI (specifically, RL), description language design, generalisation and transfer, sample efficiency, and AutoRL and meta RL.

While it is not necessarily an exhaustive list, and relative importance of each item may vary among different research and deployment contexts, we identify the following list of desiderata for environment description languages:

- *User-friendliness*: enabling end users with little programming or RL expertise to describe their optimisation problems of interest, such that RL can be applied to tackle them, is central to our proposed research agenda. This implies that any languages used to these environments ought to be user-friendly.
- *Complete and unambiguous environment specifications*: there is a substantial amount of work on providing *some* information about an environment as context to aid decision-making [6, 14, 50, 65, 79, 84, 88, 97, 107, 128, 139, 150, 163, 172], but unless descriptions are complete to the extent that they can be compiled into an executable simulator, they do not help alleviate the need for engineers with programming and RL expertise. A key exception is when training will be done in the real world (e.g., directly on physical robots), in which case only specifying goals, objectives, or reward functions would suffice.
- *Generality and expressiveness*: we remark that, as the orange boxes in Fig. 1b indicate, we still expect programming and RL expertise to be required in some parts of the proposed workflow. In particular, such expertise will still be required to build compilers for any designed language. Therefore, this workflow will only pay off, in terms of democratisation of the use of RL, if the same compiler can be re-used for multiple different (but presumably related) tasks, all describable without engineering expertise in the same user-friendly language. If there is only a single task of interest, a simulator for it might as well be implemented directly in code. This suggests that a sufficient degree of generality and expressiveness of the language is crucial: we ought to be able to describe a variety of different tasks in the same language. In practice, we expect that there may be tension between the desiderata of user-friendliness and generality. While we have no quantitative evidence at this point, our own practical experience, and conversations with others among the general game playing research community in particular, suggest that description languages that specifically target a restricted subset of domains such as video games [134, 136] or board games [115], using high-level keywords specific to that domain, tend to be easier to use than lower-level (e.g., logic-based) languages [44, 83].
- *Computational efficiency*: as discussed in Subsect. 5.1, high simulation speeds are desirable to speed up training, in particular due to the lack of sample efficiency in current RL techniques. Therefore, descriptions can ideally be compiled into computationally efficient simulators.
- *Facilitation of procedural generation*: especially in the case of highly expressive languages, it may be infeasible to manually write enough descriptions to provide sufficient coverage of the full space of all describable problems, which can in turn impair the ability to train policies that effectively generalise in a zero-shot manner across the space. For example, the t-SNE visualisation [86] in Fig. 2 depicts how even a relatively large set of 1059 different board games still leaves large uncovered

areas in the underlying space, which may be important to fill up with further example games for a model to effectively learn the precise semantics of the game description language, and implications on effective playing strategy. This may be addressed by procedurally generating new tasks to fill up uncovered parts of the space [157]. The design of the language and underlying problem representation can have a substantial impact on how easy or difficult it is for, e.g., evolutionary algorithms to navigate and construct suitable, novel elements of this space.

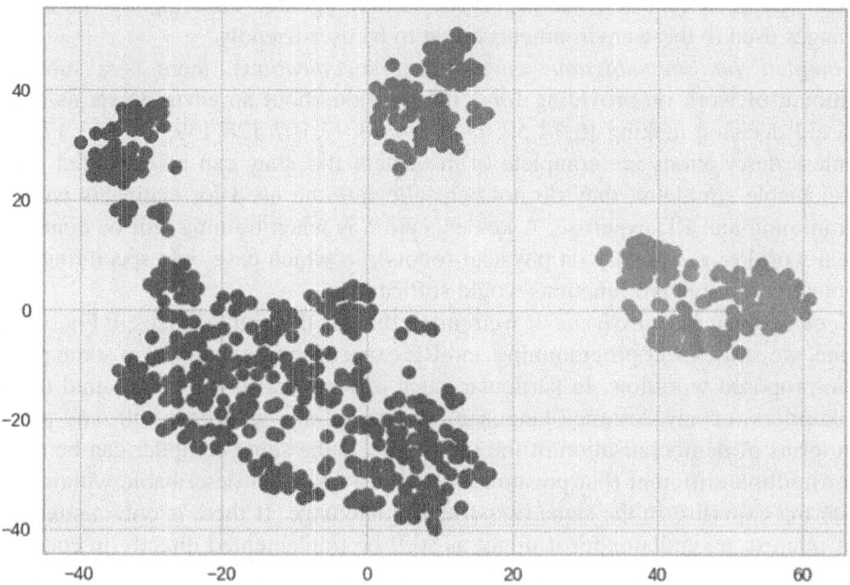

Fig. 2. A set of 1059 different board games, described in Ludii's game description language, reduced from a larger feature space [116] to two dimensions via a t-SNE embedding [86]. Image source: [148].

All of these desiderata should feature in evaluations of designed languages in our proposed research agenda. For some aspects, such as measuring computational efficiency of frameworks [67,158] and (theoretically) analysing the expressiveness of environment and goal description languages [68,80,131,145,156], this is already commonplace. Other aspects, such as ease of use for humans or suitability of representations for procedural content generation, are sometimes listed as design considerations [115], but lacking in terms of quantitative and objective evaluations in existing research (though there is some recent work in such directions [121]).

When we have a user-friendly description language in which end users can conveniently describe a variety of problems of interest, we still require an RL solution to tackling these problems. For the same end users to be able to also execute this step, we expect to require substantial advances in (i) generalisation, and/or (ii) AutoRL and meta RL. Advances in generalisation (discussed in more detail in Sect. 4) would enable us to pre-train an agent in a wide variety of environments described in the chosen language, and have it automatically generalise to novel problems described in the same language. In the case of successful zero-shot generalisation, this could even circumvent the need for training time and other resources (e.g., hardware) for the end user. Similarly, advances in AutoRL and meta RL (discussed in more detail in Subsect. 5.2) would circumvent the need for the end user to have the RL knowledge necessary to choose which algorithm(s) to use, but would not alleviate the need for training resources such as time and hardware.

7 Related Work

Mannor and Tamar [91] also caution against the excessive focus of the research community on algorithms in existing benchmarks, with little attention for deploying to novel problems, but they do not discuss ease of use, or user-friendly environment description languages as a potential solution. Zhu et al. [173] present Pearl as a framework meant to facilitate users applying RL to their real-world applications. However, this framework focuses on the design of agents, as opposed to environments, and does not alleviate the need for highly engineered environment implementations.

Rodriguez-Sanchez et al. [126] introduce RLang as a DSL that can be used to provide background or expert knowledge on any aspect of an MDP. However, they propose for such descriptions to be provided *in addition to* environment implementations in general-purpose programming languages, rather than as a replacement. Nevertheless, this could be an example of a DSL that could be used for our proposed research agenda. Jothimurugan et al. [61] describe a DSL that can be used to specify reward functions via, e.g., goals and constraints, but no other aspects of the environment. In the specific case of robotics in the physical world, natural language-based instructions for robots to follow [5] may suffice to provide widespread, easy access, as there is no need for a simulator, but this does not extend to many other (virtual) applications. Focusing specifically on the problem of representing goals (rather than full MDPs or RL problems), and not necessarily from the perspective of users who are not engineering or RL experts, Davidson et al. also consider goal representations [29] based on programs (essentially DSLs) [30] and natural languages, among other solutions.

While our position and proposed research agenda revolve around ideas such as user-friendliness and democratisation of the use of RL, we still view these issues largely from a technical angle by exploring how we may technically develop techniques to facilitate broader use of RL. Other recent position papers explore related ideas, such as the inherent value of application-driven AI research, recommended changes to peer review, hiring, and teaching policies in the machine learning community, and legal and ethical considerations when shifting research focus to real-world applications [52, 127]. In another recent position paper, Blili-Hamelin et al. [17] argue to shift away from an excessive focus on Artificial General Intelligence as a research goal, and rather be more specific and explicit about research goals and the exact meaning of notions such as "generality." Our proposed research agenda is in line with this, as we argue to focus on restricted subsets of problems, and build agents that can generalise specifically within the set of problems describable in any description language of choice.

8 Conclusion

The central position in this paper is to argue for a need for increased focus in the reinforcement learning (RL) research community on benchmarks in which environments are not implemented directly in general-purpose programming languages, but rather described in user-friendly domain-specific languages (DSLs) or even natural languages. The core reason for this is to empower end users with little to no programming or RL expertise to apply RL as a solution to their optimisation problems of interest: they only need to be able to describe their problems in the user-friendly language of choice. Furthermore, we see potential for advances in (zero-shot) generalisation and transfer within the set of problems describable in any such language, by using the environment descriptions as context on which to condition policies, value functions, and so on. We presented a complete outline of the research agenda we propose, accounting for desiderata and challenges such as user-friendliness, sample efficiency, and generalisation.

Disclosure of Interests. The authors have no competing interests to declare that are relevant to the content of this article.

References

1. Abid, A., Abdalla, A., Abid, A., Khan, D., Alfozan, A., Zou, J.: Gradio: hassle-free sharing and testing of ML models in the wild. In: 2019 ICML Workshop on Human in the Loop Learning (2019)
2. Afshar, A., Li, W.: DeLF: designing learning environments with foundation models. In: AAAI 2024 Workshop on Synergy of Reinforcement Learning and Large Language Models (2024)
3. Agarwal, R., Schwarzer, M., Castro, P.S., Courville, A., Bellemare, M.G.: Deep reinforcement learning at the edge of the statistical precipice. In: Ranzato, M., Beygelzimer, A., Dauphin, Y., Liang, P., Vaughan, J.W. (eds.) Advances in Neural Information Processing Systems, vol. 34, pp. 29304–29320. Curran Associates, Inc. (2021)
4. Agarwal, R., Schwarzer, M., Castro, P.S., Courville, A.C., Bellemare, M.: Reincarnating reinforcement learning: reusing prior computation to accelerate progress. In: Koyejo, S., Mohamed, S., Agarwal, A., Belgrave, D., Cho, K., Oh, A. (eds.) Advances in Neural Information Processing Systems, vol. 35, pp. 28955–28971. Curran Associates, Inc. (2022)
5. Ahn, M., et al.: AutoRT: embodied foundation models for large scale orchestration of robotic agents. In: IEEE ICRA 2024 Workshop on Vision-Language Models for Navigation and Manipulation (2024)
6. Andreas, J., Klein, D., Levine, S.: Modular multitask reinforcement learning with policy sketches. In: Proceedings of the 34th International Conference on Machine Learning, vol. 70, pp. 166–175. PMLR (2017)
7. Andrychowicz, M., et al.: What matters for on-policy deep actor-critic methods? A large-scale study. In: 2021 International Conference on Learning Representations (2021)
8. Aram, M., Neumann, G.: Multilayered analysis of co-development of business information systems. J. Internet Serv. Appl. **6**(13) (2015)
9. Bamford, C., Huang, S., Lucas, S.: Griddly: a platform for AI research in games. In: AAAI-21 Workshop on Reinforcement Learning in Games (2021)
10. Banerjee, B., Stone, P.: General game learning using knowledge transfer. In: The 20th International Joint Conference on Artificial Intelligence, pp. 672–677 (2007)

11. Beck, J., et al.: A survey of meta-reinforcement learning (2023). https://arxiv.org/abs/2301.08028
12. Bellemare, M.G., et al.: Autonomous navigation of stratospheric balloons using reinforcement learning. Nature **588**, 77–82 (2020)
13. Bellemare, M.G., Naddaf, Y., Veness, J., Bowling, M.: The arcade learning environment: an evaluation platform for general agents. J. Artif. Intell. Res. **47**(1), 253–279 (2013)
14. Benjamins, C., et al.: Contextualize me – the case for context in reinforcement learning. Trans. Mach. Learn. Res. (2023)
15. Bettini, M., Kortvelesy, R., Blumenkamp, J., Prorok, A.: VMAS: a vectorized multi-agent simulator for collective robot learning. In: Proceedings of the 16th International Symposium on Distributed Autonomous Robotic Systems, DARS 2022. Springer, Cham (2022)
16. Blattmann, A., et al.: Stable video diffusion: scaling latent video diffusion models to large datasets (2023). https://arxiv.org/abs/2311.15127
17. Blili-Hamelin, B., et al.: Position: stop treating 'AGI' as the north-star goal of AI research. In: Proceedings of the 42nd International Conference on Machine Learning (2025, to appear)
18. Bonnet, C., et al.: Jumanji: a diverse suite of scalable reinforcement learning environments in JAX. In: Proceedings of the International Conference on Learning Representations (2024)
19. Bou Ammar, H., Eaton, E., Ruvolo, P., Taylor, M.E.: Online multi-task learning for policy gradient methods. In: Xing, E.P., Jebara, T. (eds.) Proceedings of the 31st International Conference on Machine Learning. Proceedings of Machine Learning Research, vol. 32, pp. 1206–1214 (2014)
20. Bradbury, J., et al.: JAX: composable transformations of Python+NumPy programs (2018). http://github.com/google/jax
21. Branavan, S.R.K., Silver, D., Barzilay, R.: Learning to win by reading manuals in a Monte-Carlo framework. J. Artif. Intell. Res. **43**, 661–704 (2012)
22. Brockman, G., et al.: OpenAI gym (2016). https://arxiv.org/abs/1606.01540
23. Browne, C., Soemers, D.J.N.J., Piette, É., Stephenson, M., Crist, W.: Ludii language reference (2020). https://ludii.games/downloads/LudiiLanguageReference.pdf
24. Browne, C.B.: Automatic generation and evaluation of recombination games. Ph.D. thesis, Faculty of Information Technology, Queensland University of Technology, Queensland, Australia (2009)
25. Cobbe, K., Hesse, C., Hilton, J., Schulman, J.: Leveraging procedural generation to benchmark reinforcement learning. In: Daumé III, H., Singh, A. (eds.) Proceedings of the 37th International Conference on Machine Learning. Proceedings of Machine Learning Research, vol. 119, pp. 2048–2056 (2020)
26. Cobbe, K., Klimov, O., Hesse, C., Kim, T., Schulman, J.: Quantifying generalization in reinforcement learning. In: Chaudhuri, K., Salakhutdinov, R. (eds.) Proceedings of the 36th International Conference on Machine Learning. Proceedings of Machine Learning Research, vol. 97, pp. 1282–1289. PMLR (2019)
27. Cummins, C., et al.: Compilergym: robust, performant compiler optimization environments for AI research (2021). https://arxiv.org/abs/2109.08267
28. Dalton, S., Frosio, I.: Accelerating reinforcement learning through GPU Atari emulation. In: Larochelle, H., Ranzato, M., Hadsell, R., Balcan, M., Lin, H. (eds.) Advances in Neural Information Processing Systems, vol. 33, pp. 19773–19782. Curran Associates, Inc. (2020)
29. Davidson, G., Gureckis, T.M.: Toward complex and structured goals in reinforcement learning. In: Finding the Frame Workshop @ Reinforcement Learning Conference (2024)
30. Davidson, G., Todd, G., Togelius, J., Gureckis, T.M., Lake, B.M.: Goals as reward-producing programs (2024). https://arxiv.org/abs/2405.13242

31. Degrave, J., et al.: Magnetic control of tokamak plasmas through deep reinforcement learning. Nature **602**, 414–419 (2022)
32. Deisenroth, M.P., Englert, P., Peters, J., Fox, D.: Multi-task policy search for robotics. In: Proceedings of the 2014 IEEE International Conference on Robotics and Automation (ICRA), pp. 3876–3881 (2014)
33. Dennis, M., et al.: Emergent complexity and zero-shot transfer via unsupervised environment design. In: Advances in Neural Information Processing Systems, vol. 33, pp. 13049–13061 (2020)
34. Desai, A., et al.: Program synthesis using natural language. In: Proceedings of the 38th International Conference on Software Engineering, pp. 345–356. Association for Computing Machinery (2016)
35. Eimer, T., Biedenkapp, A., Reimer, M., Adriaensen, S., Hutter, F., Lindauer, M.: DACBench: a benchmark library for dynamic algorithm configuration. In: Proceedings of the Thirtieth International Joint Conference on Artificial Intelligence, pp. 1668–1674 (2021)
36. Eimer, T., Lindauer, M., Raileanu, R.: Hyperparameters in reinforcement learning and how to tune them. In: Krause, A., Brunskill, E., Cho, K., Engelhardt, B., Sabato, S., Scarlett, J. (eds.) Proceedings of the 40th International Conference on Machine Learning. Proceedings of Machine Learning Research, vol. 202, pp. 9104–9149. PMLR (2023)
37. Ellis, B., et al.: SMACv2: an improved benchmark for cooperative multi-agent reinforcement learning. In: Advances in Neural Information Processing Systems (2023, accepted)
38. Farebrother, J., Machado, M.C., Bowling, M.: Generalization and regularization in DQN (2018). https://arxiv.org/abs/1810.00123
39. Fernandéz, F., Veloso, M.: Learning domain structure through probabilistic policy reuse in reinforcement learning. Progress AI **2**(1), 13–27 (2013)
40. Finn, C., Abeel, P., Levine, S.: Model-agnostic meta-learning for fast adaptation of deep networks. In: Precup, D., Teh, Y.W. (eds.) Proceedings of the 34th International Conference on Machine Learning. Proceedings of Machine Learning Research, vol. 70, pp. 1126–1135 (2017)
41. Freeman, C.D., Frey, E., Raichuk, A., Girgin, S., Mordatch, I., Bachem, O.: Brax - a differentiable physics engine for large scale rigid body simulation (2021). http://github.com/google/brax
42. Frey, S., et al.: JAX-LOB: a GPU-accelerated limit order book simulator to unlock large scale reinforcement learning for trading. In: ICAIF 2023: Proceedings of the Fourth ACM International Conference on AI in Finance, pp. 583–591 (2023)
43. Gamrian, S., Goldberg, Y.: Transfer learning for related reinforcement learning tasks via image-to-image translation. In: Proceedings of the 36th International Conference on Machine Learning, pp. 2063–2072 (2019)
44. Genesereth, M., Thielscher, M.: General Game Playing. Synthesis Lectures on Artificial Intelligence and Machine Learning. Morgan & Claypool Publishers (2014)
45. Ghosh, D., Rahme, J., Kumar, A., Zhang, A., Adams, R.P., Levine, S.: Why generalization in RL is difficult: epistemic pomdps and implicit partial observability. In: Ranzato, M., Beygelzimer, A., Dauphin, Y., Liang, P., Vaughan, J.W. (eds.) Advances in Neural Information Processing Systems, vol. 34, pp. 25502–25515. Curran Associates, Inc. (2021)
46. Glatt, R., da Silva, F.L., Costa, A.H.R.: Towards knowledge transfer in deep reinforcement learning. In: Brazilian Conference on Intelligent Systems (BRACIS), pp. 91–96. IEEE (2016)
47. Glatt, R., Silva, F.L.D., da Costa Bianchi, R.A., Costa, A.H.R.: DECAF: deep case-based policy inference for knowledge transfer in reinforcement learning. Expert Syst. Appl. **156** (2020)

48. Goldie, A.D., Lu, C., Jackson, M.T., Whiteson, S., Foerster, J.N.: Can learned optimization make reinforcement learning less difficult? In: AutoRL Workshop @ ICML 2024 (2024)
49. Goldwaser, A., Thielscher, M.: Deep reinforcement learning for general game playing. In: The Thirty-Fourth AAAI Conference on Artificial Intelligence, pp. 1701–1708. AAAI Press (2020)
50. Goyal, P., Niekum, S., Mooney, R.J.: PixL2R: guiding reinforcement learning using natural language by mapping pixels to rewards. In: Proceedings of the 2020 Conference on Robot Learning. PMLR, vol. 155, pp. 485–497 (2021)
51. Gulino, C., et al.: Waymax: an accelerated, data-driven simulator for large-scale autonomous driving research. In: Proceedings of the Neural Information Processing Systems Track on Datasets and Benchmarks (2023)
52. Hartman, S., Ong, C.S., Powles, J., Kuhnert, P.: Position: we need responsible, application-driven (RAD) AI research. In: Proceedings of the 42nd International Conference on Machine Learning (2025, to appear)
53. Henderson, P., Islam, R., Bachman, P., Pineau, J., Precup, D., Meger, D.: Deep reinforcement learning that matters. In: Proceedings of the 32nd AAAI Conference on Artificial Intelligence, pp. 3207–3214. AAAI (2018)
54. Hooker, S.: The hardware lottery. Commun. ACM **64**(12), 58–65 (2021)
55. Howard, R.A.: Dynamic Programming and Markov Processes. The MIT Press, Cambridge (1960)
56. Irpan, A., Song, X.: The principle of unchanged optimality in reinforcement learning generalization. In: ICML 2019 Workshop on Understanding and Improving Generalization in Deep Learning (2019)
57. Jackson, M.T., et al.: Discovering general reinforcement learning algorithms with adversarial environment design. In: Advances in Neural Information Processing Systems, vol. 36, pp. 79980–79998 (2023)
58. Jacob, M., Devlin, S., Hofmann, K.: "It's unwieldy and it takes a lot of time"—challenges and opportunities for creating agents in commercial games. In: Proceedings of the Sixteenth AAAI Conference on Artificial Intelligence and Interactive Digital Entertainment, pp. 88–94 (2020)
59. Jordan, S.M., White, A., da Silva, B.C., White, M., Thomas, P.S.: Position: benchmarking is limited in reinforcement learning research. In: Salakhutdinov, R., et al. (eds.) Proceedings of the 41st International Conference on Machine Learning. Proceedings of Machine Learning Research, vol. 235, pp. 22551–22569. PMLR (2024)
60. Jordan, S.M.: Scientific experiments in reinforcement learning (2022). https://nips.cc/virtual/2022/63891, opinion talk contributed to the Deep Reinforcement Learning Workshop at NeurIPS 2022
61. Jothimurugan, K., Alur, R., Bastani, O.: A composable specification language for reinforcement learning tasks. In: Advances in Neural Information Processing Systems, vol. 32, pp. 13041–13051 (2019)
62. Justesen, N., Torrado, R.R., Bontrager, P., Khalifa, A., Togelius, J., Risi, S.: Illuminating generalization in deep reinforcement learning through procedural level generation. In: NeurIPS 2018 Workshop on Deep Reinforcement Learning (2018)
63. Kaiser, Ł., Stafiniak, Ł.: First-order logic with counting for general game playing. In: Proceedings of the AAAI Conference on Artificial Intelligence, vol. 25, pp. 791–796 (2011)
64. Kaufmann, T., Weng, P., Bengs, V., Hüllermeier, E.: A survey of reinforcement learning from human feedback. Trans. Mach. Learn. Res. (2025)
65. Kharyal, C., Krishna Gottipati, S., Kumar Sinha, T., Das, S., Taylor, M.E.: GLIDE-RL: grounded language instruction through DEmonstration in RL (2024). https://arxiv.org/abs/2401.02991

66. Kirk, R., Zhang, A., Grefenstette, E., Rocktäschel, T.: A survey of zero-shot generalisation in deep reinforcement learning. J. Artif. Intell. Res. **76**, 201–264 (2023)
67. Kowalksi, J., et al.: Efficient reasoning in regular boardgames. In: Proceedings of the 2020 IEEE Conference on Games, pp. 455–462. IEEE (2020)
68. Kowalski, J., Maksymilian, M., Sutowicz, J., Szykuła, M.: Regular boardgames. In: Proceedings of the 33rd AAAI Conference on Artificial Intelligence, vol. 33, pp. 1699–1706. AAAI Press (2019)
69. Koyamada, S., et al.: PGX: hardware-accelerated parallel game simulators for reinforcement learning. In: Advances in Neural Information Processing Systems (2023)
70. Kuhlmann, G., Stone, P.: Graph-based domain mapping for transfer learning in general games. In: Kok, J.N., Koronacki, J., Mantaras, R.L., Matwin, S., Mladenič, D., Skowron, A. (eds.) ECML 2007. LNCS (LNAI), vol. 4701, pp. 188–200. Springer, Heidelberg (2007). https://doi.org/10.1007/978-3-540-74958-5_20
71. Lange, R.T.: gymnax: a JAX-based reinforcement learning environment library (2022). http://github.com/RobertTLange/gymnax
72. Lange, S., Riedmiller, M.: Deep auto-encoder neural networks in reinforcement learning. In: Neural Networks. International Joint Conference (IJCNN 2010), pp. 1623–1630. IEEE (2010)
73. Lazaric, A.: Transfer in reinforcement learning: a framework and a survey. In: Wiering, M., van Otterlo, M. (eds.) Reinforcement Learning. Adaptation, Learning, and Optimization, vol. 12, pp. 143–173. Springer, Heidelberg (2012)
74. LeCun, Y., Bengio, Y., Hinton, G.: Deep learning. Nature **521**(7553), 436–444 (2015)
75. Lee, J.N., et al.: Supervised pretraining can learn in-context reinforcement learning (2023). https://arxiv.org/abs/2306.14892
76. Leivada, E., Marcus, G., Günther, F., Murphy, E.: A sentence is worth a thousand pictures: can large language models understand human language and the world behind words? (2024). https://arxiv.org/abs/2308.00109
77. Li, H., Liao, X., Carin, L.: Multi-task reinforcement learning in partially observable stochastic environments. J. Mach. Learn. Res. **10**(40), 1131–1186 (2009)
78. Li, X., Zhang, J., Bian, J., Tong, Y., Liu, T.Y.: A cooperative multi-agent reinforcement learning framework for resource balancing in complex logistics network. In: Agmon, N., Taylor, M.E., Veloso, E.E.M. (eds.) Proceedings of the 18th International Conference on Autonomous Agents and Multiagent Systems (AAMAS 2019), pp. 980–988 (2019)
79. Lifschitz, S., Paster, K., Chan, H., Ba, J., McIlraith, S.: Steve-1: a generative model for text-to-behavior in Minecraft (2023). https://arxiv.org/abs/2306.00937
80. Lin, S., Bercher, P.: On the expressive power of planning formalisms in conjunction with LTL. In: Proceedings of the International Conference on Automated Planning and Scheduling, vol. 32, pp. 231–240 (2022)
81. Lindauer, M., et al.: Position: a call to action for a human-centered AutoML paradigm. In: Proceedings of the 41st International Conference on Machine Learning. PMLR, vol. 235, pp. 30566–30584 (2024)
82. Littman, M.L.: Markov games as a framework for multi-agent reinforcement learning. In: Proceedings of the Eleventh International Conference on Machine Learning, pp. 157–163 (1994)
83. Love, N., Hinrichs, T., Haley, D., Schkufza, E., Genesereth, M.: General game playing: game description language specification. Technical report. LG-2006-01, Stanford Logic Group (2008)
84. Luketina, J., et al.: A survey of reinforcement learning informed by natural language. In: Proceedings of the Twenty-Eighth International Joint Conference on Artificial Intelligence, IJCAI 2019, pp. 6309–6317 (2019)

85. Luo, J., et al.: SERL: a software suite for sample-efficient robotic reinforcement learning. In: Towards Generalist Robots: Learning Paradigms for Scalable Skill Acquisition @ CoRL2023 (2023)
86. van der Maaten, L., Hinton, G.: Visualizing data using t-SNE. J. Mach. Learn. Res. **9**(86), 2579–2605 (2008)
87. Machado, M.C., Bellemare, M.G., Talvitie, E., Veness, J., Hausknecht, M., Bowling, M.: Revisiting the arcade learning environment: evaluation protocols and open problems for general agents. J. Artif. Intell. Res. **61**, 523–562 (2018)
88. Maclin, R., Shavlik, J.W.: Creating advice-taking reinforcement learners. Mach. Learn. **22**, 251–281 (1996)
89. Makoviychuk, V., et al.: Isaac gym: high performance GPU based physics simulation for robot learning. In: Vanschoren, J., Yeung, S. (eds.) Proceedings of the Neural Information Processing Systems Track on Datasets and Benchmarks, vol. 1. Curran (2021)
90. Malik, D., Li, Y., Ravikumar, P.: When is generalizable reinforcement learning tractable? In: Ranzato, M., Beygelzimer, A., Dauphin, Y., Liang, P., Vaughan, J.W. (eds.) Advances in Neural Information Processing Systems, vol. 34, pp. 8032–8045. Curran Associates, Inc. (2021)
91. Mannor, S., Tamar, A.: Towards deployable RL – what's broken with RL research and a potential fix (2023). https://arxiv.org/abs/2301.01320
92. Maras, M., Kępa, M., Kowalski, J., Szykuła, M.: Fast and knowledge-free deep learning for general game playing (student abstract). In: Proceedings of the AAAI Conference on Artificial Intelligence, vol. 38, pp. 23576–23578 (2024)
93. McDermott, D., et al.: PDDL—the planning domain definition language. Technical report. CVC TR98003/DCS TR1165, New Haven, CT: Yale Center for Computational Vision and Control (1998)
94. Mediratta, I., You, Q., Jiang, M., Raileanu, R.: A study of generalization in offline reinforcement learning. In: 2024 International Conference on Learning Representations (2024)
95. Mernik, M., Heering, J., Sloane, A.M.: When and how to develop domain-specific languages. ACM Comput. Surv. **37**(4), 316–344 (2005)
96. Mirhoseini, A., et al.: A graph placement methodology for fast chip design. Nature **594**, 207–212 (2021)
97. Misra, D., Langford, J., Artzi, Y.: Mapping instructions and visual observations to actions with reinforcement learning. In: Palmer, M., Hwa, R., Riedel, S. (eds.) Proceedings of the 2017 Conference on Empirical Methods in Natural Language Processing, pp. 1004–1015 (2017)
98. Mittel, A., Munukutla, P.S.: Visual transfer between Atari games using competitive reinforcement learning. In: 2019 IEEE/CVF Conference on Computer Vision and Pattern Recognition Workshops (CVPRW), pp. 499–501 (2019)
99. Mnih, V., et al.: Playing Atari with deep reinforcement learning (2013). https://arxiv.org/abs/1312.5602
100. Mohan, A., Benjamins, C., Wienecke, K., Dockhorn, A., Lindauer, M.: AutoRL hyperparameter landscapes. In: Faust, A., Garnett, R., White, C., Hutter, F., Gardner, J.R. (eds.) International Conference on Automated Machine Learning. Proceedings of Machine Learning Research, vol. 224. PMLR (2023)
101. Mohan, A., Zhang, A., Lindauer, M.: Structure in deep reinforcement learning: a survey and open problems. J. Artif. Intell. Res. **79**, 1167–1236 (2024)
102. Müller-Brockhausen, M., Preuss, M., Plaat, A.: Procedural content generation: better benchmarks for transfer reinforcement learning. In: Proceedings of the 2021 IEEE Conference on Games, pp. 924–931 (2021)

103. Nagabandi, A., et al.: Learning to adapt in dynamic, real-world environments through meta-reinforcement learning. In: Proceedings of the 2019 International Conference on Learning Representations (2019)
104. Nichol, A., Pfau, V., Hesse, C., Klimov, O., Schulman, J.: Gotta learn fast: a new benchmark for generalization in RL (2018). https://arxiv.org/abs/1804.03720
105. Obando-Ceron, J., Araú'jo, J.G.M., Courville, A., Castro, P.S.: On the consistency of hyper-parameter selection in value-based deep reinforcement learning. In: Reinforcement Learning Conference (2024, accepted)
106. Obando-Ceron, J.S., Castro, P.S.: Revisiting rainbow: promoting more insightful and inclusive deep reinforcement learning research. In: Meila, M., Zhang, T. (eds.) Proceedings of the 38th International Conference on Machine Learning, pp. 1373–1383. PMLR (2021)
107. Oh, J., Singh, S., Lee, H., Kohli, P.: Zero-shot task generalization with multi-task deep reinforcement learning. In: Proceedings of the 34th International Conference on Machine Learning, pp. 2661–2670. PMLR (2017)
108. OpenAI: Introducing ChatGPT (2022). https://openai.com/blog/chatgpt. Accessed 02 Jan 2024
109. Oswald, J., Srinivas, K., Kokel, H., Lee, J., Katz, M., Sohrabi, S.: Large language models as planning domain generators. In: Proceedings of the International Conference on Automated Planning and Scheduling, vol. 34, pp. 423–431 (2024)
110. Ouyang, L., et al.: Training language models to follow instructions with human feedback. In: Koyejo, S., Mohamed, S., Agarwal, A., Belgrave, D., Cho, K., Oh, A. (eds.) Advances in Neural Information Processing Systems, vol. 35, pp. 27730–27744. Curran Associates, Inc. (2022)
111. Parker-Holder, J., et al.: Evolving curricula with regret-based environment design. In: Proceedings of the 39th International Conference on Machine Learning. PMLR, vol. 162, pp. 17473–17498 (2022)
112. Parker-Holder, J., et al.: Automated reinforcement learning (autoRL): a survey and open problems. J. Artif. Intell. Res. **74**, 517–568 (2022)
113. Patterson, A., Neumann, S., White, M., White, A.: Empirical design in reinforcement learning (2023). https://arxiv.org/abs/2304.01315
114. Perez-Liebana, D., Dockhorn, A., Grueso, J.H., Jeurissen, D.: The design of "Stratega": a general strategy games framework. In: Osborn, J.C. (ed.) Joint Proceedings of the AIIDE 2020 Workshops co-located with 16th AAAI Conference on Artificial Intelligence and Interactive Digital Entertainment (AIIDE 2020). CEUR Workshop Proceedings (2020)
115. Piette, É., Soemers, D.J.N.J., Stephenson, M., Sironi, C.F., Winands, M.H.M., Browne, C.: Ludii – the ludemic general game system. In: Giacomo, G.D., et al. (eds.) Proceedings of the 24th European Conference on Artificial Intelligence (ECAI 2020). Frontiers in Artificial Intelligence and Applications, vol. 325, pp. 411–418. IOS Press (2020)
116. Piette, É., Stephenson, M., Soemers, D.J.N.J., Browne, C.: General board game concepts. In: Proceedings of the 2021 IEEE Conference on Games (CoG), pp. 932–939. IEEE (2021)
117. Podell, D., et al.: SDXL: improving latent diffusion models for high-resolution image synthesis (2023). https://arxiv.org/abs/2307.01952
118. Ponse, K., Kleuker, J.F., Moerland, T.M., Plaat, A.: Chargax: a JAX accelerated EV charging simulator. In: Reinforcement Learning Conference (2025, to appear)
119. Rakelly, K., Zhou, A., Quillen, D., Finn, C., Levine, S.: Efficient off-policy meta-reinforcement learning via probabilistic context variables. In: Chaudhuri, K., Salakhutdinov, R. (eds.) Proceedings of the 36th International Conference on Machine Learning. Proceedings of Machine Learning Research, vol. 97, pp. 5331–5340 (2019)
120. Ramesh, A., Dhariwal, P., Nichol, A., Chu, C., Chen, M.: Hierarchical text-conditional image generation with CLIP latents (2022). https://arxiv.org/abs/2204.06125

121. Rani, S., Booth, S., Sreedharan, S.: Goals vs. rewards: a comparative study of objective specification mechanisms. In: Reinforcement Learning Conference (2025, to appear)
122. Raparthy, S.C., Hambro, E., Kirk, R., Henaff, M., Raileanu, R.: Generalization to new sequential decision making tasks with in-context learning (2023). https://arxiv.org/abs/2312.03801
123. Reed, S., et al.: A generalist agent. Trans. Mach. Learn. Res. (2023)
124. Riedmiller, M.: Neural fitted Q iteration – first experiences with a data efficient neural reinforcement learning method. In: Gama, J., Camacho, R., Brazdil, P.B., Jorge, A.M., Torgo, L. (eds.) ECML 2005. LNCS (LNAI), vol. 3720, pp. 317–328. Springer, Heidelberg (2005). https://doi.org/10.1007/11564096_32
125. Rigter, M., Jiang, M., Posner, I.: Reward-free curricula for training robust world models. In: International Conference on Learning Representations (2024)
126. Rodriguez-Sanchez, R., Spiegel, B.A., Wang, J., Patel, R., Tellex, S., Konidaris, G.: RLang: a declarative language for describing partial world knowledge to reinforcement learning agents. In: Krause, A., Brunskill, E., Cho, K., Engelhardt, B., Sabato, S., Scarlett, J. (eds.) Proceedings of the 40th International Conference on Machine Learning. Proceedings of Machine Learning Research, vol. 202, pp. 29161–29178. PMLR (2023)
127. Rolnick, D., et al.: Position: application-driven innovation in machine learning. In: Proceedings of the 41st International Conference on Machine Learning. PMLR, vol. 235, pp. 42707–42718 (2024)
128. Rostami, M., Isele, D., Eaton, E.: Using task descriptions in lifelong machine learning for improved performance and zero-shot transfer. J. Artif. Intell. Res. **67**, 673–703 (2020)
129. Rusu, A.A., et al.: Progressive neural networks (2016). https://arxiv.org/abs/1606.04671
130. Rutherford, A., et al.: JaxMARL: multi-agent RL environments and algorithms in JAX. https://arxiv.org/abs/2311.10090 (2023)
131. Sakçak, B., Shell, D.A., O'Kane, J.M.: Limits of specifiability for sensor-based robotic planning tasks. In: Proceedings of IEEE International Conference on Robotics and Automation (ICRA) (2025, to appear)
132. Samvelyan, M., et al.: MAESTRO: open-ended environment design for multi-agent reinforcement learning. In: International Conference on Learning Representations (2023)
133. Samvelyan, M., et al.: Minihack the planet: a sandbox for open-ended reinforcement learning research. In: Advances in Neural Information Processing Systems (2021)
134. Schaul, T.: A video game description language for model-based or interactive learning. In: Proceedings of the IEEE Conference on Computational Intelligence in Games, pp. 193–200. IEEE (2013)
135. Schaul, T., Horgan, D., Gregor, K., Silver, D.: Universal value function approximators. In: Proceedings of the 32nd International Conference on Machine Learning. JLMR: W&CP, vol. 37, pp. 1312–1320 (2015)
136. Schaul, T.: An extensible description language for video games. IEEE Trans. Comput. Intell. AI Games **6**(4), 325–331 (2014). https://doi.org/10.1109/TCIAIG.2014.2352795
137. Schmidhuber, J.: On learning how to learn learning strategies. Technical report. FKI-198-94, Institut für Informatik, Technische Universität München (1994)
138. Seger, E., Ovadya, A., Siddarth, D., Garfinkel, B., Dafoe, A.: Democratising AI: multiple meanings, goals, and methods. In: Proceedings of the 2023 AAAI/ACM Conference on AI, Ethics, and Society, pp. 715–722 (2023)
139. Shu, T., Xiong, C., Socher, R.: Hierarchical and interpretable skill acquisition in multi-task reinforcement learning. In: International Conference on Learning Representations (2018)
140. Silver, T., Chitnis, R.: PDDLGym: gym environments from PDDL problems. In: ICAPS Workshop on Bridging the Gap Between AI Planning and Reinforcement Learning (PRL) (2020)

141. Simkute, A., Luger, E., Evans, M., Jones, R.: "It is there, and you need it, so why do you not use it?" Achieving better adoption of AI systems by domain experts, in the case study of natural science research (2024). https://arxiv.org/abs/2403.16895
142. Sobol, D., Wolf, L., Taigman, Y.: Visual analogies between atari games for studying transfer learning in RL (2018). https://arxiv.org/abs/1807.11074
143. Soemers, D.J.N.J., Mella, V., Browne, C., Teytaud, O.: Deep learning for general game playing with Ludii and Polygames. ICGA J. **43**(3), 146–161 (2022)
144. Soemers, D.J.N.J., Mella, V., Piette, É., Stephenson, M., Browne, C., Teytaud, O.: Towards a general transfer approach for policy-value networks. Trans. Mach. Learn. Res. (2023)
145. Soemers, D.J.N.J., Piette, É., Stephenson, M., Browne, C.: The Ludii game description language is universal. In: Proceedings of the 2024 IEEE Conference on Games, pp. 1–8 (2024)
146. Soemers, D.J.N.J., Samothrakis, S., Driessens, K., Winands, M.H.M.: Environment descriptions for usability and generalisation in reinforcement learning. In: Rocha, A.P., Steels, L., van den Herik, H.J. (eds.) Proceedings of the 17th International Conference on Agents and Artificial Intelligence, vol. 3, pp. 983–992 (2025)
147. Stability AI: Stable audio: Fast timing-conditioned latent audio diffusion (2023). https://stability.ai/research/stable-audio-efficient-timing-latent-diffusion. Accessed 4 Jan 2024
148. Stephenson, M., Soemers, D.J.N.J., Piette, É., Browne, C.: Measuring board game distance. In: Browne, C., Kishimoto, A., Schaeffer, J. (eds.) Computers and Games, CG 2022. LNCS, vol. 13865, pp. 121–130. Springer, Cham (2023)
149. Stone, A., Ramirez, O., Konolige, K., Jonschkowski, R.: The distracting control suite – a challenging benchmark for reinforcement learning from pixels (2021). https://arxiv.org/abs/2101.02722
150. Sun, S.H., Wu, T.L., Lim, J.J.: Program guided agent. In: International Conference on Learning Representations (2020)
151. Sutton, R.S., Barto, A.G.: Reinforcement Learning: An Introduction, 2nd edn. MIT Press, Cambridge (2018)
152. Tassa, Y., et al.: DeepMind control suite (2018)
153. Taylor, M.E., Stone, P.: Transfer learning for reinforcement learning domains: a survey. In: Mahadevan, S. (ed.) Journal of Machine Learning Research, vol. 10, pp. 1633–1685 (2009)
154. Terry, J.K., et al.: Pettingzoo: a standard API for multi-agent reinforcement learning. In: Advances in Neural Information Processing Systems, vol. 34, pp. 15032–15043. Curran Associates, Inc. (2021)
155. Tessler, C., Givony, S., Zahavy, T., Mankowitz, D., Mannor, S.: A deep hierarchical approach to lifelong learning in minecraft. In: Proceedings of the AAAI Conference on Artificial Intelligence, pp. 1553–1561. AAAI (2017)
156. Thielscher, M.: The general game playing description language is universal. In: Proceedings of the Twenty-second International Joint Conference on Artificial Intelligence, IJCAI-11, pp. 1107–1112 (2011)
157. Todd, G., Padula, A., Stephenson, M., Piette, É., Soemers, D.J.N.J., Togelius, J.: GAVEL: generating games via evolution and language models. In: Globerson, A., et al. (eds.) Advances in Neural Information Processing Systems, vol. 37, pp. 110723–110745. Curran Associates, Inc. (2024)
158. Todd, G., Padula, A.G., Soemers, D.J.N.J., Togelius, J.: Ludax: a GPU-accelerated domain specific language for board games (2025, under review)
159. Trofin, M., Qian, Y., Brevdo, E., Lin, Z., Choromanski, K., Li, D.: MLGO: a machine learning guided compiler optimizations framework (2021). https://arxiv.org/abs/2101.04808
160. Voelcker, C., Hussing, M., Eaton, E.: Can we hop in general? A discussion of benchmark selection and design using the Hopper environment. In: Finding the Frame workshop @ Reinforcement Learning Conference (2024)

161. van der Wal, J.: Stochastic Dynamic Programming, No. 139 in Mathematical Centre tracts, Morgan Kaufmann, Amsterdam (1981)
162. Whiteson, S., Tanner, B., Taylor, M.E., Stone, P.: Protecting against evaluation overfitting in empirical reinforcement learning. In: 2011 IEEE Symposium on Adaptive Dynamic Programming and Reinforcement Learning (ADPRL), pp. 120–127 (2011)
163. Williams, E.C., Gopalan, N., Rhee, M., Tellex, S.: Learning to parse natural language to gronuded reward functions with weak supervision. In: 2018 IEEE International Conference on Robotics and Automation, pp. 4430–4436 (2018)
164. Wilson, A., Fern, A., Ray, S., Tadepalli, P.: Multi-task reinforcement learning: a hierarchical Bayesian approach. In: Proceedings of the 24th International Conference on Machine Learning, pp. 1015–1022 (2007)
165. Yang, K.: Learn dynamic-aware state embedding for transfer learning (2021). https://arxiv.org/abs/2101.02230
166. Yang, M., et al.: Learning interactive real-world simulators. In: International Conference on Learning Representations (2024)
167. Yoon, D., Hong, S., Lee, B.J., Kim, K.E.: Winning the L2RPN challenge: power grid management via semi-Markov afterstate actor critic. In: Proceedings of the International Conference on Learning Representations (2021)
168. Zhang, A., Ballas, N., Pineau, J.: A dissection of overfitting and generalization in continuous reinforcement learning (2020). https://arxiv.org/abs/1806.07937
169. Zhang, C., Vinyals, O., Munos, R., Bengio, S.: A study on overfitting in deep reinforcement learning (2018). https://arxiv.org/abs/1804.06893
170. Zhao, W., Queralta, J.P., Westerlund, T.: Sim-to-real transfer in deep reinforcement learning for robotics: a survey. In: 2020 IEEE Symposium Series on Computational Intelligence (SSCI), pp. 737–744 (2020)
171. Zhao, W.X., et al.: A survey of large language models (2023). https://arxiv.org/abs/2303.18223. Accessed 25 Jan 2024
172. Zhong, V., Rocktäschel, T., Grefenstette, E.: RTFM: generalising to novel environment dynamics via reading. In: International Conference on Learning Representations (2020)
173. Zhu, Z., et al.: Pearl: a production-ready reinforcement learning agent (2023). https://arxiv.org/abs/2312.03814
174. Zhu, Z., Lin, K., Jain, A.K., Zhou, J.: Transfer learning in deep reinforcement learning: a survey. IEEE Trans. Pattern Anal. Mach. Intell. **45**(11), 13344–13362 (2023)
175. Zintgraf, L.: Fast adaptation via meta reinforcement learning. Ph.D. thesis, University of Oxford, Oxford, United Kingdom (2022)
176. Zuo, M., Velez, F.P., Li, X., Littman, M.L., Bach, S.H.: Planetarium: a rigorous benchmark for translating text to structured planning languages (2024). https://arxiv.org/abs/2407.03321

Author Index

H. J. van den Herik et al. (Eds.): ICAART 2025, LNAI 16517, pp. 715–716, 2026.
https://doi.org/10.1007/978-3-032-25032-2

The manufacturer's authorised representative in the EU is Springer Nature Customer Service Centre GmbH, Europaplatz 3, 69115 Heidelberg, Germany. If you have any concerns regarding our products, please contact ProductSafety@springernature.com

Printed and bound by CPI Group (UK) Ltd, Croydon, CR0 4YY
03/08/2026
02184503-0002